Unfair Dismissal

Employment Law Handbook

September 2015

Unfair Dismissal

Employment Law Handbook

Previous edition 2010

IDS
Floor 5
Friars House
160 Blackfriars Road
London SE1 8EZ
Email: ids.sales.support@thomsonreuters.com
Website: www.incomesdata.co.uk

ISBN 978 0 414 04986 4

IDS Employment Law Handbook, 'Unfair Dismissal', is published by Thomson Reuters (Professional) UK Limited trading as Incomes Data Services Limited (Registered in England & Wales, Company No. 16790446). Registered Office: 2nd Floor, 1 Mark Square, London, EC2A 4EG.

No natural forests were destroyed to make this product: only farmed timber was used and re-planted.

A CIP catalogue record for this book is available from the British Library.

Typeset by DC Graphic Design Ltd, Hextable, Kent BR8 7RG
Printed by St Austell Printing Co Ltd, St Austell Business Park, Cornwall PL25 4FD

Contents

Abbreviations

Courts

ECJ	European Court of Justice
ECHR	European Court of Human Rights
PC	Privy Council
SC	Supreme Court
HL	House of Lords
CA	Court of Appeal
Ct Sess	Court of Session
NICA	Northern Ireland Court of Appeal
QBD	Queen's Bench Division
Div Ct	(Queen's Bench) Divisional Court
KBD	King's Bench Division
ChD	Chancery Division
NIRC	National Industrial Relations Court
EAT	Employment Appeal Tribunal
ET	Employment Tribunal

Case references

AC	Law Reports, Appeal Cases
All ER	All England Law Reports
Ch	Law Reports, Chancery Division
CMLR	Common Market Law Reports
COET	Employment Tribunal folio number
EAT	Employment Appeal Tribunal unreported case number
ECR	European Case Reports
ET	Employment Tribunal unreported case number
EWCA	Court of Appeal unreported case number
ICR	Industrial Cases Reports
IRLR	Industrial Relations Law Reports
ITR	Industrial Tribunal Reports
KB	Law Reports, King's Bench Division
QB	Law Reports, Queen's Bench Division
SCOET	Scottish Employment Tribunal folio number
SLT	Scots Law Times
TLR	Times Law Reports
UKSC	Supreme Court unreported case number
WLR	Weekly Law Reports

Legislation

EA	Employment Act 2002
EqA	Equality Act 2010
ERA	Employment Rights Act 1996
ERelA 1999	Employment Relations Act 1999
ERelA 2004	Employment Relations Act 2004
ETA	Employment Tribunals Act 1996
TULR(C)A	Trade Union and Labour Relations (Consolidation) Act 1992

Statutory references, unless otherwise stated, are to the Employment Rights Act 1996 (ERA), except in Chapter 18 where references are to the 'Recoupment Regulations'.

Many cases in this Handbook were decided under legislation that preceded the ERA. Reference in made throughout to the corresponding provisions in the later consolidation statute and not to their antecedents in repealed legislation.

Introduction

In Addison v Babcock FATA Ltd 1987 ICR 805, CA, Sir John Donaldson, then Master of the Rolls, who had in 1972–74 been President of the National Industrial Relations Court when the right not to be unfairly dismissed was introduced, referred to a decision of that court and said that 'in those far-off days we fondly hoped and imagined that a few such decisions would finally settle the law and that the National Industrial Relations Court could then retire as an appellate court'.

Things have not worked out quite like that and although the National Industrial Relations Court was retired as an appellate court in 1974, it was replaced in due course by the Employment Appeal Tribunal. The flood of decisions on unfair dismissal law has continued unabated and there have been innumerable statutory amendments to the law as first set out in the Industrial Relations Act 1971.

The law, as amended, is now contained in the Employment Rights Act 1996 (ERA). This Act consolidated various statutes concerned with individual employment rights, such as the Employment Protection (Consolidation) Act 1978 and the Wages Act 1986, into a single statutory code. The law has not stood still, however, and the ERA itself has been amended many times over the years. Recent legislative developments include the repeal in 2011 of S.98(2)(ba), which listed 'retirement' as a potentially fair reason for dismissal. As a result, an employer wishing to fairly dismiss an older employee because of his or her advancing age needs to show that the reason for dismissal falls within one of the remaining potentially fair reasons for dismissal contained in S.98(1) and (2), and that the dismissal was reasonable in all the circumstances under S.98(4). In other words, the dismissal must be treated in the same way as any other dismissal – see further Chapter 8, 'Some other substantial reason', under 'Retirement dismissals'. Recent developments have also seen the introduction of a number of new categories of 'automatically' unfair dismissal, including automatically unfair dismissal of agency workers for asserting rights under the Agency Workers Regulations 2010 SI 2010/93. A full list of the categories of automatically unfair dismissal can be found in the Appendix to Chapter 9, 'Automatically unfair dismissal'.

Scope of Handbook

This Handbook aims to provide a clear and accurate statement of the law governing unfair dismissal. However, it does not cover every ground of unfair dismissal contained in the ERA. For example, unfair redundancy dismissals are dealt with in IDS Employment Law Handbook, 'Redundancy' (2011); dismissals relating to pregnancy, maternity, and family leave in IDS

Employment Law Handbook, 'Maternity and Parental Rights' (2014); working time dismissals in IDS Employment Law Handbook, 'Working Time' (2013); dismissals for reasons relating to the minimum wage in IDS Employment Law Handbook, 'Wages' (2011); dismissals made in connection with part-time workers' and fixed-term workers' rights in IDS Employment Law Handbook, 'Atypical and Flexible Working' (2014); and whistleblowing dismissals in IDS Employment Law Handbook, 'Whistleblowing at Work' (2013). Furthermore, dismissals made in connection with a transfer of an undertaking are covered in IDS Employment Law Handbook, 'Transfer of Undertakings' (2011), while industrial action and trade union dismissals are covered in IDS Employment Law Handbooks, 'Industrial Action' (2010) and 'Trade Unions' (2013) respectively.

Scheme of Handbook
The scheme of this Handbook is as follows:

- Chapter 1 covers the legal definition of dismissal

- Chapter 2 deals with the various exclusions from the right to claim that exist – e.g. where the claimant is not an employee or has insufficient qualifying service

- Chapter 3 tackles the central issue of unfairness in the statutory definition and explains how the reason for dismissal must be established and how tribunals approach the question of reasonableness

- Chapters 4 to 8 explain the application of the general principles discussed in Chapter 3 to the potentially fair reasons for dismissal that may be put forward – capability and qualifications, ill health, conduct, statutory ban and 'some other substantial reason'

- Chapters 9 to 11 are concerned with automatically unfair dismissals, discussing the special rules that apply to such dismissals before focusing on particular types of automatically unfair dismissal, including Sunday working dismissals, dismissals of occupational pension scheme trustees and employee representatives, dismissals relating to trade union blacklists, health and safety dismissals and dismissals for asserting a statutory right

- Chapters 12 to 17 consider the remedies available in unfair dismissal cases – reinstatement, re-engagement and compensation. Chapter 17 also covers interim relief orders

- Chapter 18 examines the mechanism for recoupment from compensation awards of social security benefits received by applicants

- Finally, Chapter 19 looks at the right of employees to receive a written statement of the reasons for dismissal.

It should be noted that many of the decisions cited in this Handbook are decisions of employment tribunals. These are intended to be illustrative only and are not binding on other tribunals, even if the facts and circumstances of the two cases appear to be identical.

The law is stated as at 1 August 2015. This Handbook completely replaces IDS Employment Law Handbook, 'Unfair Dismissal' (2010), which should now be discarded.

This publication aims to provide accurate, authoritative information and comment on the subjects it covers. It is offered to readers on the understanding that the publisher is not in business as a lawyer or consultant.

1 Dismissal

An employee who wishes to claim unfair dismissal must first show that he or **1.1** she has been dismissed within the meaning of S.95 of the Employment Rights Act 1996 (ERA). S.95 states that an employee will be treated as dismissed if:

- his or her contract of employment is terminated by the employer with or without notice – S.95(1)(a)

- he or she is employed under a limited-term contract and the contract expires by virtue of the limiting event without being renewed under the same terms – S.95(1)(b), or

- he or she has been constructively dismissed – S.95(1)(c). A constructive dismissal occurs when an employee resigns, with or without notice, because of a repudiatory breach of contract by the employer.

There is also a dismissal where an employee under notice of dismissal from the employer resigns on a date earlier than that on which the employer's notice is due to expire – S.95(2).

Note that if an employee is dismissed but that sanction is reduced on appeal **1.2** to, for example, demotion, the effect of the decision on appeal is to revive the contract of employment so as to treat the employee as if he or she had never been dismissed for the purposes of an unfair dismissal claim – Roberts v West Coast Trains Ltd 2005 ICR 254, CA. This general rule does not apply, however, where a contractual disciplinary policy provides that the sanction of demotion can only take effect with the employee's agreement and the employee does not accept the demotion – Piper v Maidstone and Tunbridge Wells NHS Trust EAT 359/12.

Dismissal on the ground of redundancy – which may give rise to an unfair dismissal claim – is defined separately in S.136(1) ERA in almost identical terms to those in S.95. However, there are two special cases where an employee is treated as not having been dismissed for the purposes of the statutory redundancy scheme:

- an employee who has been locked out by the employer and has resigned without notice cannot claim constructive dismissal on account of redundancy even though the employer's conduct might ordinarily have entitled him or her to do so – S.136(2). (For further details, see IDS Employment Law Handbook, 'Redundancy' (2011), Chapter 1, 'Dismissal', under 'Constructive dismissal – lock-outs')

- when an employee accepts a renewal of his or her contract or a re-engagement to take effect within four weeks of the old contract ending, there is no dismissal for redundancy purposes – S.138(1). The offer may be from the original employer or from an associated employer – S.146. (Note that S.138(1) applies only for the purposes of the statutory redundancy scheme and does not prevent an employee who has been re-employed from bringing an unfair dismissal claim – Jones v Governing Body of Burdett Coutts School 1999 ICR 38, CA.)

1.3 There are also two special cases where there is a dismissal under the ERA for the purposes of the statutory redundancy scheme only:

- certain events causing implied termination of the contract by operation of law (e.g. dissolution of partnership, death of an individual employer or appointment of a receiver by the court) – S.136(5)

- special cases of termination of 'employment' by statute (involving termination of membership of certain bodies covered by regulations – e.g. police forces and fire brigades). This applies even though the individuals concerned are not employees but statutory office holders – S.172.

Finally, it should be noted that the rules for giving counter-notice are stricter in relation to redundancy dismissals than in other cases. In an ordinary S.95 dismissal, an employee who is dismissed with notice and who then gives counter-notice to leave on a date before the expiry of the employer's notice is still treated as having been dismissed by the employer, and the reason for dismissal is taken to be the reason for which the employer's notice was given – S.95(2). In redundancy cases, however, the employee is treated as dismissed only if the counter-notice is given in writing within the 'obligatory period' of the employer's notice. This is the period, ending on the date of expiry of the employer's notice, which equates to the statutory notice period under S.86 or to the employee's contractual notice entitlement, whichever is the longer. If the employee gives notice before the obligatory period begins to run – where, for instance, the employer has been generous in giving a long notice period – he or she is not treated as having been dismissed for redundancy – S.136(3).

1.4 Redundancy dismissals are dealt with in IDS Employment Law Handbook, 'Redundancy' (2011), Chapter 1, 'Dismissal'. The remainder of this chapter contains a brief overview of the three categories of dismissal defined in S.95(1) – express dismissal by the employer, non-renewal of a limited-term contract and constructive dismissal – which apply in unfair dismissal cases. However, as a dismissal is in effect the termination of a contract of employment, these concepts are discussed in far greater depth in IDS Employment Law Handbook, 'Contracts of Employment' (2014), Chapter 11, 'Termination by dismissal'.

Note that the concepts discussed in this chapter apply to dismissals under both the ERA and the Trade Union and Labour Relations (Consolidation) Act 1992 (TULR(C)A), unless otherwise stated.

Non-dismissals

1.5

Before embarking on an explanation of what amounts to a dismissal, it is worth mentioning the other ways in which an employment contract can be terminated. These are:

- resignation of the employee
- termination by agreement between the employer and the employee
- termination by operation of law, including frustration of contract.

None of these count as a dismissal in law.

These 'non-dismissals' are considered briefly below. For a fuller treatment, see IDS Employment Law Handbook, 'Contracts of Employment' (2014), Chapter 12, 'Termination by resignation, agreement or performance', and Chapter 13, 'Termination by operation of law'.

Resignation. A resignation is the termination of a contract of employment by the employee. It need not be expressed in a formal way, and may be inferred from the employee's conduct and the surrounding circumstances – Johnson v Monty Smith Garages Ltd EAT 657/79.

1.6

Usually it is not difficult to recognise a resignation, but there are circumstances in which the situation may not be so clear. Examples are discussed in IDS Employment Law Handbook, 'Contracts of Employment' (2014), Chapter 12, 'Termination by resignation, agreement or performance', under 'Resignation'.

Note that situations where a contract comes to an end in ambiguous circumstances are considered in IDS Employment Law Handbook, 'Contracts of Employment' (2014), Chapter 11, 'Termination by dismissal', under 'Express dismissal'.

1.7

Termination by agreement. Parties to an employment contract are free to agree between themselves to terminate it. Both sides are then released from further performance of their obligations under the contract and the contract is discharged by mutual consent. When this happens there is no dismissal, the effect being similar to that of a resignation by the employee (although where there has been a resignation the employee may still potentially be able to claim constructive dismissal).

1.8

Since the effect of a termination by agreement is to deny the employee statutory employment protection rights, courts and tribunals are reluctant to make such a finding unless there is very clear evidence that an entirely voluntary agreement has been entered into. This is particularly so when the agreement is reached after notice of dismissal has already been given or provides that the contract will automatically terminate on the occurrence of a future event.

1.9 In general, courts and tribunals have been willing to hold that a voluntary redundancy will still be a dismissal if it is in response to a genuine redundancy situation. However, it would seem that early retirement is *not* a dismissal unless it is clearly involuntary. This appears to be the case even when circumstances are such that the employer would otherwise have had to make redundancies, although the position is not entirely clear, particularly in cases where the employee has already been issued with a notice of dismissal for redundancy and later takes early retirement instead.

For further details, see IDS Employment Law Handbook, 'Contracts of Employment' (2014), Chapter 12, 'Termination by resignation, agreement or performance', under 'Termination by agreement'.

1.10 **Termination by operation of law.** Contracts of employment may terminate at common law when certain supervening events take place or where the contract is frustrated. These are terminations by operation of law, not by dismissal or resignation. The effect at common law is that the contracts automatically come to an end and the obligations of the parties cease. However, in certain situations statute law intervenes to preserve employee rights that would otherwise vanish.

1.11 *Supervening events.* The general common law rule is that contracts of employment are automatically terminated on the occurrence of certain events, normally as a result of some act on the part of the employer. However, where there is a term in the contract, express or implied, which shows that the parties have agreed that certain events will not have the effect of ending the contract, the courts will give effect to that term.

The supervening events that will normally terminate a contract of employment automatically at common law are:

- death of the employer (where the contract is with an individual employer) or employee. (The death of either party might also be categorised as a frustrating event – see 'Frustration' below)

- dissolution or major reconstruction of a partnership

- appointment of a receiver by the court (but not the appointment of a receiver out of court by debenture holders)

- compulsory winding up by court order (but not a voluntary winding-up)

- permanent closure of the employee's workplace

4

- transfer of employer's business – at common law, the transfer of an employer's business to another person automatically terminates all existing contracts of employment. However, this rule has been superseded to a large extent by the Transfer of Undertakings (Protection of Employment) Regulations 2006 SI 2006/246.

Certain statutory provisions may also have the effect of automatically **1.12** terminating employment contracts. There is a general principle that when further performance of a contract becomes impossible because of legislation, e.g. when a particular office is abolished by statute, then the contract is discharged.

For details, see IDS Employment Law Handbook, 'Contracts of Employment' (2014), Chapter 13, 'Termination by operation of law', under 'Supervening events'.

Frustration. Frustration occurs when, through neither party's fault, some **1.13** reasonably unforeseeable event occurs which makes the contract impossible or unlawful to perform, or radically different from what the parties originally intended – Davis Contractors v Fareham Urban District Council 1956 AC 696, HL. When a contract is frustrated it comes to an end automatically by operation of law, without a dismissal on the part of the employer or a resignation on the part of the employee, and the parties are discharged from further obligations under it. Frustration is judged objectively and it is irrelevant that the parties believed or intended that the contract should continue – GF Sharp and Co Ltd v McMillan 1998 IRLR 632, EAT.

The most common events that can frustrate an employment contract are:

- employee's illness – an employee's prolonged or sudden serious illness or disability is capable of frustrating the employment contract

- imprisonment of employee – imprisonment of an employee is also capable of frustrating the employment contract – FC Shepherd and Co Ltd v Jerrom 1986 ICR 802, CA. Similarly, depending on the employee's ability to perform the contract and the surrounding circumstances, restrictive bail conditions or a remand in custody may also amount to a frustrating event

- exclusion from place of work by third party – the employee's exclusion from his or her place of work by a third party may also frustrate the employment contract.

However, frustration is not automatic and the tribunal will need to consider all **1.14** the surrounding circumstances. Where the frustrating event has been caused by the fault of either party, that party will not be entitled to rely on it to treat the contract as being at an end – FC Shepherd and Co Ltd v Jerrom (above). For further details see IDS Employment Law Handbook, 'Contracts of Employment' (2014), Chapter 13, 'Termination by operation of law', under 'Frustration'.

1.15 Express dismissal

A preliminary question that often arises, particularly in claims of unfair dismissal, is whether there has in fact been a dismissal at all. In these circumstances the burden of proof falls on the employee to show a dismissal. The standard of proof is that of the 'balance of probabilities' as normally applied in civil courts: the tribunal must consider whether it was more likely than not that the contract was terminated by dismissal rather than, for example, by resignation or by mutual agreement between employer and employee.

Doubt may arise as to whether a dismissal has taken place when the words or actions of the employer or employee give rise to ambiguity, either by their nature or because of the circumstances in which they took place. Furthermore, an apparent resignation may be treated as a dismissal if it was the result of an ultimatum along the lines of 'resign or you'll be fired', or if the resignation was induced by deceit or trickery on the part of the employer. These problems are discussed briefly below. For an in-depth analysis of the law, see IDS Employment Law Handbook, 'Contracts of Employment' (2014), Chapter 11, 'Termination by dismissal', under 'Express dismissal'.

1.16 Note that because a dismissal arises when the contract of employment is terminated, it is possible for there to be a dismissal even before the employee has actually started work pursuant to the contract. A person engaged under a contract of employment to start work at a future date can claim unfair dismissal if the contract was terminated by the employer for an inadmissible reason (for which no period of qualifying service is necessary) before that date – Sarker v South Tees Acute Hospitals NHS Trust 1997 ICR 673, EAT. Inadmissible reasons for dismissal are discussed in Chapter 9, 'Automatically unfair dismissals'.

1.17 Ambiguous words

Words that are capable of being interpreted as a resignation or a dismissal may not necessarily amount to such in the circumstances. When an employer tells an employee to 'get out' or says 'you are finished', the question arises as to whether this amounts to an express dismissal or a mere rebuke. (Note, however, that a rebuke may in some circumstances amount to a constructive dismissal – see 'Constructive dismissal' below.) Conversely, when an employee storms out of a meeting shouting 'I'm off', without stating whether this is a temporary or a permanent move, it may be unclear whether or not the employee has actually resigned.

Broadly speaking, the test as to whether ostensibly ambiguous words amount to a dismissal or a resignation is an objective one:

- all the surrounding circumstances (both preceding and following the incident) and the nature of the workplace in which the misunderstanding arose must be considered

- if the words are still ambiguous, the tribunal should ask itself how a reasonable employer or employee would have understood them in light of those circumstances.

The same objective test applies when the ambiguity occurs in correspondence **1.18** between employer and employee. Where an employee has received an ambiguous letter, the EAT has said that the interpretation 'should not be a technical one but should reflect what an ordinary, reasonable employee… would understand by the words used'. It added that 'the letter must be construed in the light of the facts known to the employee at the date he receives the letter' – see Chapman v Letheby and Christopher Ltd 1981 IRLR 440, EAT.

It is a well-established principle in the construction of commercial contracts that any ambiguity will be construed against the party seeking to rely on it. In Graham Group plc v Garratt EAT 161/97 the EAT held that this principle should also be applied to ambiguous words or acts in the context of a dismissal or resignation.

Unambiguous words   **1.19**
The general rule is that unambiguous words of dismissal or resignation may be taken at their face value without the need for any analysis of the surrounding circumstances – see Sothern v Franks Charlesly and Co 1981 IRLR 278, CA. There are, however, important qualifications to the general rule in the Sothern case that plain words are to be taken at their face value. Lord Justice Fox LJ thought that there might be an exception in the case of an immature employee, or a decision taken in the heat of the moment, or an employee being jostled into a decision by the employer. Dame Elizabeth Lane agreed, referring to exceptions in the case of 'idle words or words spoken under emotional stress which the employers knew or ought to have known were not meant to be taken seriously… [or] a case of employers anxious to be rid of an employee who seized upon her words and gave them a meaning which she did not intend'. In such cases it may be appropriate to investigate the context in which the words were spoken in order to ascertain what was really intended and understood.

What applies to an angry or emotional resignation may also apply – but more rarely – to an angry dismissal. In Martin v Yeomen Aggregates Ltd 1983 ICR 314, EAT, the employer angrily dismissed M but within five minutes realised it had been over-hasty and varied the penalty to one of two days' suspension. M, however, insisted that he had been dismissed and claimed unfair dismissal. The EAT held that, in the circumstances, there had been no dismissal. Mr Justice Kilner Brown said that it was desirable, as a matter of common sense and good industrial relations, that an employer (or employee) should – in special circumstances – have the opportunity of withdrawing words spoken in the heat of the moment. If words spoken in anger were immediately withdrawn, there was no dismissal.

1.20 The circumstances will need to be exceptional – as they were in the Martin case – to justify a finding of no dismissal. The general rule is that once notice to terminate a contract of employment has been given it cannot be withdrawn unilaterally but only by agreement between the parties – Harris and Russell Ltd v Slingsby 1973 ICR 454, NIRC.

This was reaffirmed by the Court of Appeal in CF Capital plc v Willoughby 2012 ICR 1038, CA. There, CFC plc had explored with W the possibility of her moving from an employment contract to a self-employed arrangement. After a meeting at which W expressed interest in the idea, subject to being given further details, CFC plc sent her a letter saying that she would be dismissed at the end of the month and engaged as a self-employed contractor. When W objected and pointed out that she had not agreed to this, CFC plc said that there had been a misunderstanding and that she could continue as an employee if she wished. However, W decided to take the dismissal letter at face value and lodged a claim of unfair dismissal. A tribunal rejected the claim, finding that there was no dismissal as CFC plc's genuine belief that W had agreed to become self-employed and subsequent attempt to withdraw the dismissal amounted to special circumstances. The EAT overturned that decision and the Court of Appeal rejected CFC plc's further appeal. The Court stressed that the 'special circumstances' exception is not strictly an exception to the rule that a notice of resignation or dismissal has effect according to the ordinary interpretation of its terms. Rather, it is a cautionary reminder to the recipient of the notice that, before accepting or otherwise acting upon it, he or she must satisfy him or herself that the giver of the notice did really intend to give a notice of resignation or dismissal. The need for such an exception will almost invariably arise in cases where the purported notice has been given orally in the heat of the moment by words that may quickly be regretted. In such cases, the recipient of the notice would be well advised to allow a 'cooling off' period before acting upon it, allowing the giver of the notice time to withdraw his or her words. However, the present case was not such a case, since CFC plc had plainly intended to dismiss W – it had conceded as much before the Court. The giving of notice may have been a mistake but, once given, it could not be unilaterally withdrawn.

1.21 Where it is alleged that an employee has agreed to the withdrawal of his or her dismissal, employment tribunals will generally look for an unequivocal statement from the employee to that effect. But sometimes agreement to a withdrawal can be inferred from the employee's conduct. In Brock v Minerva Dental Ltd 2007 ICR 917, EAT, for example, B was called to a disciplinary meeting on 28 September and dismissed with notice expiring on 16 December. That decision was confirmed by letter, which also informed B of his right of appeal. B appealed against the dismissal decision, contending that his dismissal was automatically unfair as a result of the employer's failure to follow the mandatory statutory dismissal procedures then in force. MD Ltd realised that it had not adhered to the correct procedure and consequently informed B that

8

'the letter of dismissal sent to you recently is therefore rescinded'. On 23 December B presented a tribunal claim for unfair dismissal, insisting that he had been dismissed on 16 December. The tribunal found that there had been no actual dismissal and struck out the claim. The EAT agreed, holding that, by appealing internally against his dismissal, B had sought and therefore effectively consented to his employer's withdrawal of the notice of dismissal. The notice had been withdrawn while B's appeal was live and there was no actual dismissal on which to found his claim.

It should be noted, however, that even if an employer's attempt to withdraw a dismissal is held to be ineffective, the employee may well be left with an empty remedy. This is because an offer to withdraw a dismissal is equivalent to an offer of reinstatement and the employee's refusal of reinstatement may well be treated as a failure to mitigate loss, disentitling him or her from a compensatory award – see further Chapter 16, 'Compensatory awards: adjustments', under 'Failure to mitigate losses'.

Ambiguous conduct 1.22

As noted above, the conduct of the parties is one of the surrounding circumstances to be taken into account when alleged words of dismissal or resignation are ambiguous. Occasionally, however, there are no direct words at all on either side but it is nonetheless argued that a dismissal (or resignation) can be inferred from the actions of the parties. If the employer's conduct is at issue, this will normally be a case of constructive dismissal (see 'Constructive dismissal' below) but sometimes it may be an express dismissal. In Kirklees Metropolitan Council v Radecki 2009 ICR 1244, CA, for example, the Court of Appeal held that removing an employee from the payroll while he was suspended and negotiating a compromise agreement was a sufficiently unequivocal statement of the employer's intention to terminate employment.

Conversely, an employee's conduct may sometimes lead to a finding that he or she has resigned. In Harrison v George Wimpey and Co Ltd 1972 ITR 188, NIRC, H became sick at Christmas and stayed away for four months without communicating with his employer, although he was in fact obtaining sick notes every two weeks. Sir John Donaldson said: 'Where an employee so conducts himself as to lead a reasonable employer to believe that the employee has terminated the contract of employment, the contract is then terminated.' The NIRC upheld a tribunal's finding of implied resignation by H, but also pointed out that the employer was under a duty to make enquiries and to warn the employee of its intentions.

In practice, however, it is only in exceptional circumstances that resignation 1.23 will be the proper inference to draw from an employee's conduct. It used to be open to an employer to argue that, if resignation could not be inferred, the employee's conduct nevertheless amounted to a fundamental breach of the

9

employment contract and had ended the contract automatically. This concept of 'constructive resignation', or 'self-dismissal', was firmly rejected by a majority of the Court of Appeal in London Transport Executive v Clarke 1981 ICR 355, CA, which held that a repudiatory breach by an employee – such as taking a seven-week holiday without permission – did not bring the contract to an end automatically. The contract would only end when the employer accepted the employee's breach – i.e. by dismissing the employee. If an employer refuses to have the employee back after an act of misconduct, the employer cannot claim that the employee has dismissed him or herself: this will be a dismissal by the employer. This also accords with the approach taken in Geys v Société Générale 2013 ICR 117, SC, in which the Supreme Court confirmed the application of the 'elective theory' to repudiatory breaches of an employment contract – i.e. that a repudiatory breach will only be effective to terminate the contract once the other party has elected to accept the breach.

1.24 Enforced resignation

It has long been established that if an employee is told that he or she has no future with an employer and is expressly invited to resign, then that employee is to be regarded as having been dismissed – see, for example, East Sussex County Council v Walker 1972 ITR 280, NIRC.

The principles to be considered in such circumstances were set out by the Court of Appeal in Martin v Glynwed Distribution Ltd 1983 ICR 511, CA. Sir John Donaldson MR said that: 'Whatever the respective actions of the employer and employee at the time when the contract of employment is terminated, at the end of the day the question always remains the same, "Who really terminated the contract of employment?". If the answer is the employer, there was a dismissal.' He went on to hold that this question was one of fact for the tribunal to decide in the circumstances of the particular case.

1.25 It is quite common for employees who are facing disciplinary proceedings to resign rather than suffer the ignominy of dismissal. In such circumstances it will usually be the employee who is held to have terminated the contract, provided it can be said that the resignation came about through his or her genuine choice. However, where an employee resigns before his or her internal appeal against dismissal is determined a tribunal may more readily find a dismissal.

What starts off as an enforced resignation – i.e. a dismissal – may become a voluntary one if the employee negotiates satisfactory financial terms and leaves because of them. For example, in Sheffield v Oxford Controls Co Ltd 1979 ICR 396, EAT, the director of a company was threatened with dismissal if he did not resign. Negotiations over a severance payment followed and an agreement was drawn up and initialled. The EAT held that there had been no dismissal. Satisfactory terms of resignation had emerged, so that the threat of dismissal was no longer the operative factor in the director's decision to resign.

However, not all negotiated termination payments will give rise to a finding of 1.26 mutually agreed termination. In Sandhu v Jan de Rijk Transport Ltd 2007 ICR 1137, CA, the Court of Appeal held that an employment tribunal had reached a perverse decision when finding that an employee had voluntarily resigned after agreeing severance terms at the same meeting at which the employer told him that he was being dismissed. The company had decided that S should be dismissed following allegations of misconduct and he was summoned to attend a meeting for this purpose, although he was not informed in advance about the allegations against him or the purpose of the meeting. The company's managing director opened the meeting by telling S that he was being dismissed. S then negotiated three months' extra salary and the short-term retention of his company car. Significantly, Lord Justice Wall noted that in no reported judgment had an employee legally resigned during the same meeting or interview at which the employer had first raised the possibility of dismissal.

Resignation induced by deception
1.27
A resignation obtained by dishonesty or deception will be a dismissal, since there is no genuine consent to the termination on the part of the employee. In Greens Motors (Bridport) Ltd v Makin, unreported 16.4.86, CA, for example, M, a sales manager, went to see his managing director with a medical certificate. He signed a note, typed by the managing director's wife, which he was told was a formality connected with sick pay and which he did not read because it was partly covered by other papers. This proved to be a note giving two months' notice of resignation and in due course the employer sent M his P45 with a letter thanking him for his loyal service. A tribunal found this to be a dismissal. The Court of Appeal held that on the facts found by the tribunal, M was expressly dismissed by the employer when he was sent his P45. The employer could not rely on a 'resignation' that had been obtained by fraudulent misrepresentation (nor could the employer have relied on one that had been obtained by an innocent misrepresentation).

Warning of future dismissal
1.28
A warning that dismissal is on the cards or is inevitable by a certain date will not amount to a dismissal and an employee who leaves his or her employment in such circumstances will be taken to have resigned. In Morton Sundour Fabrics Ltd v Shaw 1966 2 KIR 1, Div Ct, Mr Justice Widgery stated that an employer could not dismiss an employee by saying 'I intend to dispense with your services at some time in the coming months'. Notice to terminate a contract of employment must either state the date of termination or contain material from which the date can be positively ascertained. In that case S was warned of impending redundancy but no specific date was mentioned. He then got another job, gave in his notice and left. It was held that the employer had never given him notice to terminate, so he was not entitled to a redundancy

payment. Although a redundancy case, its principle is equally applicable to unfair dismissal law.

The same principles apply when an employee gives notice of an intention to resign but does not specify the date. In Ely v YKK Fasteners (UK) Ltd 1994 ICR 164, CA, E obtained a job in Australia and told his employer he would be resigning in due course. His employer went about arranging for his replacement, even though E at no stage gave formal notice indicating his final day of employment. The employer later told E that if he did not pinpoint a date his employment would be treated as terminated from 21 December. When the job in Australia fell through, E informed his employer (on 21 December) that he was no longer going to emigrate and wished to continue working. However, the employer chose to treat E as having resigned and would only consider re-employing him on different terms. The Court of Appeal upheld a tribunal decision that E had been (fairly) dismissed because he had merely given notice of his intention to resign at some time in the future. The employer had terminated the employment when choosing to treat it as coming to an end on 21 December.

1.29 Partial termination of employment

Terminating a divisible part of an employee's contract is not a dismissal if the employer gives reasonable notice. In Land and anor v West Yorkshire Metropolitan County Council 1981 ICR 334, CA, the employees were full-time firefighters who were also retained for additional duties in their spare time, for which they were paid extra. The employer, in conjunction with the Fire Brigades Union, decided to abolish part-time duties and gave the employees due notice of this. The employees continued to do their full-time jobs but complained that they had been unfairly dismissed from their part-time employment. The Court of Appeal held that there was only a single contract of employment: it could be divided into two parts which could be terminated separately. Since the employer had terminated the part of the contract covering part-time work with due notice, there was no breach of contract and there had been no dismissal because the single contract was still in existence (even if in an attenuated form).

The situation is different, however, if there are two (or more) separate contracts with the same employer. In such a case, termination of any one contract by the employer is a dismissal as far as *that* contract is concerned. The House of Lords in Lewis v Surrey County Council 1987 ICR 982, HL, held that separate contracts must be looked at separately. Their Lordships did, however, suggest (obiter) that there might be two exceptions:

• where the arrangements are simply a sham and the purported multiple contracts are in reality a single contract

- where, even though there were separate contracts, there was also a unifying collateral contract which could be described as an 'umbrella' contract – i.e. the reality was that there was a single contract, although there was no deliberate sham on the part of the employer.

Dismissal subject to appeal 1.30

Most disciplinary procedures provide a right of appeal against a decision to dismiss. If the appeal is successful and the employee is reinstated, then there is no dismissal – J Sainsbury Ltd v Savage 1981 ICR 1, CA. If an employee's appeal is unsuccessful, however, then the original dismissal is effective. The only question then is when that dismissal takes effect. The answer depends on the terms of the disciplinary procedure in question. If it provides that the contract continues until the appeal is determined, then the 'effective date of termination' (EDT) – as defined in S.97 ERA – is the date when the decision to dismiss is upheld. If, however, it states that dismissal takes effect subject to the employment being revived in the event of a successful appeal, then the EDT is the date of the initial decision to dismiss when that appeal is unsuccessful. The EDT, which is important as it determines the point at which the time limit for bringing an unfair dismissal claim begins to run, is discussed in depth in IDS Employment Law Handbook, 'Contracts of Employment' (2014), Chapter 14, 'Date of termination' (see in particular the section on 'Internal appeals against dismissal').

Non-renewal of limited-term contracts 1.31

Termination of a limited-term contract (LTC) without renewal is deemed to be a dismissal by virtue of S.95(1)(b) ERA. Employers who fail to renew LTCs are liable, therefore, to unfair dismissal claims in the same way as if they had actively ended the contracts. S.235(2A) ERA states that a contract of employment is a 'limited-term contract' if:

- the employment under the contract is not intended to be permanent, and

- provision is accordingly made in the contract for it to terminate by virtue of a limiting event.

Subsection (2B) goes on to define a 'limiting event' as:

- in the case of a contract for a fixed term, the expiry of the term

- in the case of a contract made in contemplation of the performance of a specific task, the performance of the task, and

- in the case of a contract which provides for its termination on the occurrence of an event (or the failure of an event to occur), the occurrence of the event (or the failure of the event to occur).

13

1.32 The expiry of a limited-term contract without renewal amounts to a dismissal even if the employee knew at the outset that it would not be renewed or that it was unlikely to be renewed – Nottinghamshire County Council v Lee 1980 ICR 635, CA.

Despite the fact that the wording of S.95(1)(b) appears to cover all non-renewals of limited-term contracts whether instigated by the employer, by the employee or by agreement, it seems that the non-renewal of a limited-term contract by mutual consent will not amount to a dismissal. In Manson and Johnston v (1) University of Strathclyde (2) Automated Microscopy Systems Ltd EAT 356/87, a case decided under the previous statutory regime relating to fixed-term contracts, M and J, two research fellows, agreed to the non-renewal of their fixed-term contracts with the university because they wanted to take up jobs with a company set up for the commercial exploitation of their research. On the particular facts of this case, the EAT was not prepared to view the non-renewal as a dismissal; rather, it was a termination by mutual agreement and the two were thus barred from claiming redundancy payments from the university. The EAT was swayed by the fact that there was no redundancy situation and that M and J could have stayed in the employ of the university if they had wished.

1.33 For further details see IDS Employment Law Handbook, 'Contracts of Employment' (2014), Chapter 11, 'Termination by dismissal', under 'Non-renewal of limited-term contracts'. For discussion of the rights of limited-term employees generally, see IDS Employment Law Handbook, 'Atypical and Flexible Working' (2014), Chapter 2, 'Fixed-term employees'.

1.34 Constructive dismissal

Section 95(1)(c) states that there is a dismissal when the employee terminates the contract, with or without notice, in circumstances such that he or she is entitled to terminate it without notice by reason of the employer's conduct. This form of dismissal is commonly referred to as 'constructive dismissal'.

In the leading case in this area, Western Excavating (ECC) Ltd v Sharp 1978 ICR 221, CA, the Court of Appeal ruled that for an employer's conduct to give rise to a constructive dismissal it must involve a *repudiatory breach of contract*. As Lord Denning MR put it: 'If the employer is guilty of conduct which is a significant breach going to the root of the contract of employment, or which shows that the employer no longer intends to be bound by one or more of the essential terms of the contract, then the employee is entitled to treat himself as discharged from any further performance. If he does so, then he terminates the contract by reason of the employer's conduct. He is constructively dismissed.'

In order to claim constructive dismissal, the employee must establish that:

- there was a fundamental breach of contract on the part of the employer

- the employer's breach caused the employee to resign

- the employee did not delay too long before resigning, thus affirming the contract and losing the right to claim constructive dismissal.

Note that a constructive dismissal is not necessarily an unfair one – Savoia v Chiltern Herb Farms Ltd 1982 IRLR 166, CA.

There is a large body of case law concerned with the concept of constructive dismissal. Here, we provide a basic outline of the elements necessary to found a successful claim: fundamental breach, resignation, causation and affirmation. For an in-depth discussion of the law in this area, see IDS Employment Law Handbook, 'Contracts of Employment' (2014), Chapter 11, 'Termination by dismissal', under 'Constructive dismissal'.

Fundamental breach 1.35

In order to identify a fundamental breach of contract on the part of the employer, it is first necessary to establish what the terms of the contract are. Individual actions by an employer that do not in themselves constitute fundamental breaches of any contractual term may have the cumulative effect of, for example, undermining the trust and confidence inherent in every contract of employment (see IDS Employment Law Handbook, 'Contracts of Employment' (2014), Chapter 4, 'Implied term of mutual trust and confidence', under 'Constructive dismissal'). A course of conduct can cumulatively amount to a fundamental breach of contract entitling an employee to resign and claim constructive dismissal following a 'last straw' incident even though the last straw by itself does not amount to a breach of contract – Lewis v Motorworld Garages Ltd 1986 ICR 157, CA.

Terms of the contract. Contractual terms may be either express or implied. 1.36 Express terms are those which have been specifically agreed between the parties, whether in writing or under an oral agreement. Implied terms are those that exist either because of the nature and circumstances of the contract itself, or because the law states that such a term is to be implied in the particular circumstances.

The grounds on which a term may be implied into a contract are very limited. It is not sufficient for the proposed term to be a reasonable one in all the circumstances. A term can only be implied if:

- it is necessary to give the contract 'business efficacy', or

- it represents the custom and practice in that employment and is 'reasonable, certain and notorious' – Devonald v Rosser and Sons 1906 2 KB 728, CA, or

15

- it is an inherent legal duty central to the relationship between employer and employee – for example, the duty to provide a safe system of work, or the duty not to undermine trust and confidence.

1.37 A term may also be implied from the conduct of the parties or because it is so obvious the parties are assumed to have intended it.

For a full treatment of express and implied terms in employment contracts, see IDS Employment Law Handbook, 'Contracts of Employment' (2014), Chapter 3, 'Contractual terms', and Chapter 4, 'Implied term of mutual trust and confidence'.

1.38 **Actual breach and anticipatory breach.** A fundamental breach of contract by the employer may be an actual or an anticipatory breach. An actual breach of contract arises when the employer refuses or fails to carry out an obligation imposed by the contract at a time when performance is due. An anticipatory breach arises when, before performance is due, the employer intimates to the employee, by words or conduct, that he does not intend to honour an essential term or terms of the contract when the time for performance arrives. For example, a reduction of 25 per cent without warning in an employee's monthly pay cheque is an actual breach, whereas a letter at the beginning of the month stating that 'with effect from the end of this month your salary will be reduced by 25 per cent' would be an anticipatory breach.

The danger faced by employees who resign in the light of an anticipatory breach is that they may be held to have acted too hastily. Vague or conditional proposals of a change in terms, conditions or working practices will not amount to an anticipatory breach and will not justify an employee resigning and claiming constructive dismissal. On the other hand, where the employer clearly indicates that an employee's contract is to be breached, the employee is not obliged to 'wait and see' whether the employer carries out the threat.

1.39 **Is breach fundamental?** Once a tribunal has established that the relevant contractual term exists and that a breach (actual or anticipatory) has occurred, it must then consider whether the breach is fundamental. This is essentially a question of fact and degree and the tribunal's decision will not be interfered with unless there is a misdirection in law or it is perverse. A key factor for the tribunal to take into account is the effect that the breach has on the employee concerned. Thus a £5 pay cut is clearly a more serious matter for an employee earning £100 per week than it is for an employee earning £500 and is therefore more likely to constitute a fundamental breach with regard to the former. Note, however, that where an employer breaches the implied term of trust and confidence, the breach is 'inevitably' fundamental – Morrow v Safeway Stores plc 2002 IRLR 9, EAT.

It makes no difference to the issue of whether or not there has been a fundamental breach that the employer did not intend to end the contract – Bliss v South East

Thames Regional Health Authority 1987 ICR 700, CA. Similarly, the circumstances that induced the employer to act in breach of contract are irrelevant to the issue of whether a fundamental breach has occurred – Wadham Stringer Commercials (London) Ltd v Brown 1983 IRLR 46, EAT.

In Tullett Prebon plc and ors v BGC Brokers LP and ors 2011 IRLR 420, CA, **1.40** the Court of Appeal appeared to depart from the long and well-established principle that the employer's subjective intentions are irrelevant when it suggested that an employer's intention, objectively assessed, was of paramount importance in assessing whether there had been a fundamental breach of contract. However, in Leeds Dental Team Ltd v Rose 2014 ICR 94, EAT, the Appeal Tribunal rejected the notion that the decision in Tullett Prebon had changed the law and confirmed that the test of whether there was a repudiatory breach of contract remains an objective one.

Reasonableness. In Western Excavating (ECC) Ltd v Sharp (above) the Court **1.41** of Appeal expressly rejected the argument that S.95(1)(c) ERA introduces a concept of reasonable behaviour by employers into contracts of employment. This means that an employee is not justified in leaving employment and claiming constructive dismissal merely because the employer has acted unreasonably. This was confirmed in Bournemouth University Higher Education Corporation v Buckland 2010 ICR 908, CA, where the Court upheld the decision of the EAT that the question of whether the employer's conduct fell within the range of reasonable responses is not relevant when determining whether there is a constructive dismissal.

Can breach be cured? In Bournemouth University Higher Education **1.42** Corporation v Buckland (above), the Court of Appeal rejected the notion that a repudiatory breach of contract can be cured unilaterally by the party in default, taking away the innocent party's option of acceptance (by resigning – see 'Resignation' below). However, while a fundamental breach of contract cannot be cured, there is nothing to prevent an employer trying to make amends in order to prevent such a breach occurring in the first place.

Resignation
1.43

Once it has been established that the employer has committed a repudiatory breach of contract, the employee must go on to show that he or she accepted the repudiation. This means that the employee must terminate the contract by resigning, either with or without notice. A contract will not actually come to an end until the employee has communicated to the employer, either by words or by conduct, the fact that he or she is terminating the employment – Edwards v Surrey Police 1999 IRLR 456, EAT. However, a resignation need not be expressed in a formal way. The fact of the employee's resignation may be inferred from his or her conduct and the surrounding circumstances – Johnson v Monty Smith Garages Ltd EAT 657/79. But simply presenting a claim for unfair dismissal to a tribunal will not be sufficient, even though the tribunal would have forwarded a copy of the complaint to the employer and the employer would have thus found out that the employee was not coming back – Rai v Somerfield Stores Ltd 2004 ICR 656, EAT.

Although an employee cannot submit a claim of unfair constructive dismissal before actually resigning, he or she may give notice and claim constructive dismissal before the notice expires – Presley v Llanelli Borough Council 1979 ICR 419, EAT. The date the notice expires then becomes the effective date of termination.

1.44 **Employee already in breach of contract.** One issue that remains unclear is whether an employee who is him or herself in fundamental breach can rely on the employer's repudiatory breach to resign and claim constructive dismissal. This question has arisen primarily in restrictive covenant cases but is of more general application and may be particularly relevant where the employee is taking industrial action. In RDF Media Group plc and anor v Clements 2008 IRLR 207, QBD, the High Court suggested that where an employee was him or herself in repudiatory breach of his or her contract of employment he or she could not accept the breach by the employer to bring the contract to an end. However, this proposition was doubted in another High Court case – Tullett Prebon plc and ors v BGC Brokers LP and ors 2010 IRLR 648, QBD – where Mr Justice Jack stated that: 'The ordinary position is that, if there is a breach of a contract by one party which entitles the other to terminate the contract but he does not do so, then the contract both remains in being and may be terminated by the first party if the second party has himself committed a repudiatory breach of the contract.' (Note that the High Court's decision to the effect that the brokers had no grounds for claiming constructive dismissal was subsequently upheld by the Court of Appeal – Tullett Prebon plc and ors v BGC Brokers LP and ors 2011 IRLR 420, CA. However, the Court of Appeal did not express a view as to the obiter comments made by Jack J.)

The position under Scots law, at least, appears to reconcile with Jack J's view. In Scotland, but not in England and Wales, the principle of mutuality of contract applies. This principle gives rise to the remedies of rescission and retention, which, in short, allow an innocent party to suspend the substantive obligations of the contract or withhold performance in response to a material breach of contract. The Court of Session held that these principles did not allow an employer to escape liability for constructive dismissal by relying on the fact that the employee had committed breaches of contract before he or she resigned. The Court held that, since the implied duty to maintain mutual trust and confidence is not one of the substantive obligations of the contract, it is not suspended as a result of a breach of contract. Although the Council might have been able to suspend its substantive obligations to provide pay and work in response to M's breaches, the implied term of mutual trust and confidence continued to bind it throughout.

A similar approach to that taken by Jack J was adopted in McNeill v Aberdeen **1.45** City Council (No.2) 2015 ICR 27, Ct Sess (Inner House), and Atkinson v Community Gateway Association 2015 ICR 1, EAT. However, in the later case the EAT emphasised that, in the context of an unfair constructive dismissal claim, an employee's antecedent breach would be relevant to compensation.

It seems that it will ultimately fall to the Court of Appeal to give a definitive ruling on what effect, if any, an employee's breach of contract has on his or her ability to claim constructive dismissal.

Causation
1.46

An employee will be regarded as having accepted the employer's repudiation only if his or her resignation has been caused by the breach of contract in issue. This means that if there is an underlying (or ulterior) reason for the employee's resignation, such that he or she would have left anyway irrespective of the employer's conduct, then there has not been a constructive dismissal. In Walker v Josiah Wedgwood and Sons Ltd 1978 ICR 744, EAT, W was subjected to a number of slights by his employer and handed in his resignation. When asked why he was leaving he replied that he had got a better job. He also said that what the employer was doing was right for the company but that he would have no part in it. The EAT said that this indicated no more than that W had a better job to go to and did not like the employer's management style: there was no indication that he was leaving because of any breach of contract on the part of the employer.

Sometimes there is more than one reason why an employee leaves a job. For instance, he or she may feel some dissatisfaction with the present job and have received an offer of something that promises to be better. Where there are mixed motives, a tribunal must determine whether the employer's repudiatory breach was an effective cause of the resignation. However, the breach need not be 'the' effective cause – Wright v North Ayrshire Council 2014 ICR 77, EAT. As Mr Justice Elias, then President of the EAT, stated in Abbycars (West Horndon) Ltd v Ford EAT 0472/07, 'the crucial question is whether the repudiatory breach played a part in the dismissal', and even if the employee leaves for 'a whole host of reasons', he or she can claim constructive dismissal 'if the repudiatory breach is one of the factors relied upon'.

Note that a delay in resigning following a repudiatory breach may (as discussed **1.47** under 'Affirmation of contract' below) indicate that the claimant has affirmed the contract. It may alternatively indicate that the repudiatory breach is not the effective cause of the resignation.

19

1.48 **Demonstrating causation.** In Weathersfield Ltd t/a Van and Truck Rentals v Sargent 1999 ICR 425, CA, the Court of Appeal held that it was not necessary for an employee, in order to prove that a resignation was caused by a breach of contract, to inform the employer immediately of the reasons for his or her resignation. It was for the tribunal in each case to determine, as a matter of fact, whether or not the employee resigned in response to the employer's breach rather than for some other reason.

Thus, it seems that an employee need not expressly inform the employer of his or her reasons for resigning in order to show that he or she resigned because of the employer's breach. However, there must clearly be sufficient evidence from which a tribunal can infer the reason or reasons for the employee's resignation.

1.49 ## Affirmation of contract

We have already dealt with the situation where an employee's premature resignation defeats a claim of constructive dismissal (see 'Fundamental breach – actual breach and anticipatory breach' above). If, on the other hand, the employee waits too long after the employer's breach of contract before resigning, he or she may be taken to have affirmed the contract with the same result – loss of the right to claim constructive dismissal. In the words of Lord Denning MR in Western Excavating (ECC) Ltd v Sharp 1978 ICR 221, CA, the employee 'must make up his mind soon after the conduct of which he complains: for, if he continues for any length of time without leaving, he will lose his right to treat himself as discharged'. This was emphasised again more recently by the Court of Appeal in Bournemouth University Higher Education Corporation v Buckland 2010 ICR 908, CA, although Lord Justice Jacob did point out that, given the pressure on the employee in these circumstances, the law looks very carefully at the facts before deciding whether there has really been an affirmation.

An employee may continue to perform the employment contract under protest for a period without necessarily being taken to have affirmed the contract. There comes a point, however, when delay will indicate affirmation. In WE Cox Toner (International) Ltd v Crook 1981 ICR 823, EAT, for example, C, a company director, was accused of gross dereliction of duty on insubstantial grounds by his fellow directors and was threatened with dismissal. Six months of angry correspondence, largely conducted through solicitors, followed before the employer finally refused to withdraw the accusation and threats. A month later, C tendered his resignation and claimed that he had been unfairly constructively dismissed. A tribunal considered that C could not be said to have affirmed the contract because he had never accepted the position but instead had protested vigorously. When it finally became clear that the company would not withdraw the allegations, it was not unreasonable for C to take time to look around for another job before he resigned. C had been unfairly dismissed and his claim was not ruled out by the seven-month delay. The EAT held that the tribunal had misdirected itself. Mere delay by itself did not constitute an

20

affirmation of the contract, but if the delay went on for too long it could be very persuasive evidence of an affirmation. The tribunal should have taken account of the fact that throughout the seven-month period C had continued to work and be paid under the contract. Even if it were arguable that he was working under protest for six months, the delay for a further month after the company had finally made its intentions clear was fatal to C's claim that he had not affirmed the contract.

If the employee is able to point to special circumstances, this may justify a delay **1.50** in resigning. In Post Office v Roberts 1980 IRLR 347, EAT, for example, where an employee continued working while her union representative was attempting to investigate the true position with her employer, a delay of six weeks was acceptable. The EAT held that the 'real point of time' at which the employee had to make a decision did not arrive until the full facts became clear and attempts to solve the problem had failed.

Special circumstances also arise when an employer imposes new terms on an employee at short or no notice. The employee is not obliged to make up his or her mind at once as to whether or not to accept the change and a reasonable trial period is permitted so that the employee can try working under the new terms before deciding what course to take. This common law trial period is often confused with the statutory trial period which applies when a redundant employee is offered alternative work. The two are, however, quite separate. The statutory trial period is for a maximum of four weeks. The common law trial period, on the other hand, has no fixed duration. It may, depending on the circumstances, be more than four weeks, or it may be less.

An employee's absence from work during the time he or she was alleged to have **1.51** affirmed the contract may be a pointer against a genuine affirmation. That said, affirmation can be implied by prolonged delay and/or if the innocent party calls on the guilty party for further performance of the contract by, for example, claiming sick pay.

Resignation with notice. At common law, an employee wishing to claim **1.52** wrongful constructive dismissal must resign without notice. However, the situation as regards unfair constructive dismissal is different because S.95(1)(c) ERA provides that a dismissal will take place where an employee resigns with or without notice 'in circumstances in which he is entitled to terminate without notice by reason of the employer's conduct'.

Thus, in an unfair constructive dismissal claim, the act of giving notice cannot by itself constitute affirmation. However, where an employee resigns with notice but, despite doing so, acts in a way that is consistent with affirmation, he or she may be taken to have affirmed the contract. In Cockram v Air Products plc 2014 ICR 1065, EAT, C resigned following his unsuccessful grievance, giving seven months' notice rather than the three months required by his

21

contract. An employment judge struck out his unfair constructive dismissal claim as having no reasonable prospect of success: he considered that C had given longer notice 'for his own ends rather than any altruistic reason' and had therefore affirmed the contract. This decision was upheld on appeal by the EAT, which held that S.95(1)(c) must be considered as a whole, taking account both of the fact that an employee is entitled to resign with notice and the words 'in circumstances in which he is entitled to terminate it without notice by reason of the employer's conduct'.

1.53 **Continuing breaches.** An employee can exercise his or her right to rely upon the breach at any time while it is continuing. In Reid v Camphill Engravers 1990 ICR 435, EAT, R claimed that over a period of three years his employer had paid him a lower salary than the statutory (and therefore contractual) minimum set by a Wages Council. The tribunal held that because R did not resign when he discovered that he was being underpaid, he had affirmed the contract and could no longer use the breach as a basis for his claim. The EAT overturned this decision. The employer had been in continuing breach of contract. Even if R had not reacted to the first breach, it was open to him to rely on it when his employer committed further breaches.

1.54 **'Last straw' cases.** A course of conduct can cumulatively amount to a fundamental breach of contract entitling an employee to resign and claim constructive dismissal following a 'last straw' incident, even though the last straw by itself does not amount to a breach of contract – see Lewis v Motorworld Garages Ltd 1986 ICR 157, CA. The Court of Appeal in that case stressed that it is immaterial that one of the events in the course of conduct was serious enough in itself to amount to a repudiatory breach and that the employee did not treat the breach as such by resigning.

In Omilaju v Waltham Forest London Borough Council 2005 ICR 481, CA, the Court of Appeal explained that the act constituting the last straw does not have to be of the same character as the earlier acts, nor must it constitute unreasonable or blameworthy conduct, although in most cases it will do so. But the last straw must contribute, however slightly, to the breach of the implied term of trust and confidence. An entirely innocuous act on the part of the employer cannot be a final straw, even if the employee genuinely, but mistakenly, interprets the act as hurtful and destructive of his or her trust and confidence in the employer. The test of whether the employee's trust and confidence has been undermined is objective. And while it is not a prerequisite of a last straw case that the employer's act should be unreasonable, it will be an unusual case where conduct which is perfectly reasonable and justifiable satisfies the last straw test.

1.55 Moving on to the issue of affirmation of contract in cases where the employee resigns as a result of a last straw incident, one question that arises is whether, by continuing to work after each incident, the employee has waived the breach and affirmed the contract. The EAT offered guidance to tribunals on this question in JV Strong and Co Ltd v Hamill EAT 1179/99, where it stated that where there is a series of unpleasant incidents about which the employer does nothing, it could not see how the breach of contract by the employer could be permanently waived simply by the employee continuing to work. The EAT acknowledged that such behaviour is normally an example of waiver, but in cases where there has been a course of conduct the tribunal must consider whether the last straw incident is a sufficient trigger to revive the earlier ones. In doing so, it must take account of the nature of the incidents, the overall time span, the length of time between the incidents, and any factor that may have amounted to a waiver of any earlier breaches. The EAT added that the tribunal must also consider the nature of the alleged waiver. It is not enough that the facts give rise to either an express or an implied waiver. The tribunal must also consider whether it was a 'once and for all' waiver or one that was conditional on there being no repetition of the same conduct.

Support for this approach can be found in Logan v Commissioners of Customs and Excise 2004 ICR 1, CA, where the Court of Appeal held that where an employee is complaining about an employer's course of conduct culminating with an act alleged to constitute the last straw, there is no need for there to be 'proximity in time or in nature' between the last straw and the previous act of the employer. And in Lochuack v London Borough of Sutton EAT 0197/14 Mr Justice Langstaff, then President of the EAT, noted that an employee may well prefer to remain in his or her job notwithstanding a breach of contract by the employer and may therefore take no action for some time following that breach. In his view, a failure to elect to treat the contract as repudiated does not waive the breaches, it 'merely declines to make the choice'. If a subsequent event takes place that adds to the previous breach or breaches, this may effectively 'resuscitate' the past. In these circumstances, the tribunal will need to have regard to everything that has happened in order to assess whether: (a) there is or has been a repudiatory breach which the employee is now entitled to accept; and (b) the employee has resigned at least partly in response to such breach.

2 Exclusions from right to claim

Employees only

Continuous service threshold

Special categories of worker

Settlements and contracting out

Time limits

There are various circumstances in which an individual may be precluded from **2.1** bringing a claim of unfair dismissal under the Employment Rights Act 1996 (ERA). For example, there are a number of statutory restrictions on the right to claim:

- the right only applies to 'employees' (with the exception of 'employee shareholders') – see 'Employees only' below

- employees must have at least two years' continuous employment to qualify for the right (unless the dismissal is for an automatically unfair reason) – see 'Continuous service threshold' below

- various categories of worker, such as police officers and certain mariners, are excluded under specific provisions of the ERA – see 'Special categories of worker' below.

In addition, some exclusions arise under general law: **2.2**

- *illegality in the employment contract* – the general rule is that an illegal contract is unenforceable and no statutory employment rights can be enforced under it. However, depending on the type of illegality, the knowledge and intent of the parties may be significant. For a full discussion, see IDS Employment Law Handbook, 'Contracts of Employment' (2014), Chapter 7, 'Void terms and illegality', under 'Illegality'

- *diplomatic or state immunity* – it is a general rule of international law that foreign states are entitled to immunity in civil actions unless they are engaging in purely commercial transactions or they elect to waive immunity. However, the State Immunity Act 1978 removes that immunity in respect of proceedings relating to certain contracts of employment. For further details, see IDS Employment Law Handbook, 'Employment Tribunal Practice and Procedure' (2014), Chapter 2, 'Tribunals' jurisdiction', under 'State and diplomatic immunity'

25

- *claims that lie outside the territorial reach of the ERA* – the ERA itself is silent as to its territorial reach. However, case law has restricted its scope to employment in Great Britain unless exceptional circumstances arise that extend its reach to individuals working abroad. For extensive discussion on this subject, see IDS Employment Law Handbook, 'Employment Tribunal Practice and Procedure' (2014), Chapter 2, 'Tribunals' jurisdiction', in the section 'Territorial limitations', under 'Territorial reach – unfair dismissal and other ERA rights'.

2.3 The ERA also allows the parties to exclude the jurisdiction of a tribunal by agreement in the following circumstances (which are discussed under 'Settlements and contracting out' below):

- where there is a settlement under the auspices of an Acas conciliator
- where there is a settlement under the auspices of the tribunal itself
- where there is a 'settlement agreement'
- where there has been collective contracting out through a dismissal procedures agreement.

Finally, the tribunal's jurisdiction may also be challenged on the ground that the claim was presented out of time – see 'Time limits' below.

Unfair dismissal claims are frequently challenged at the outset on the ground that one or more of the above exclusions operate to deprive the tribunal of jurisdiction to hear the claim.

2.4 **Industrial action dismissals.** Special rules apply to industrial action dismissals that have the effect of depriving employees dismissed for taking part in a strike or other industrial action of the right to claim unfair dismissal except in very limited circumstances. These rules, which are contained in the Trade Union and Labour Relations (Consolidation) Act 1992 (TULR(C)A), are discussed at length in IDS Employment Handbook, 'Industrial Action' (2010), Chapter 8, 'Industrial action dismissals', under 'Dismissal during unofficial action', 'Dismissal during "protected" official action' and 'Dismissal during "non-protected" official action'. Briefly, the relevant provisions provide that:

- an employee has no right to complain of unfair dismissal if at the time of dismissal he or she was taking part in unofficial industrial action unless the reason for the dismissal was one of certain protected reasons such as health and safety – S.237 TULR(C)A
- an employee who is dismissed for taking part in protected industrial action (i.e. lawfully organised official action) will be treated as having been automatically unfairly dismissed if the dismissal took place during the protected period, or after the end of that period where certain specified conditions are met – S.238A

- an employee who is selectively dismissed when taking part in official industrial action or locked out by his or her employer in circumstances where S.238A does not apply is entitled to claim unfair dismissal – S.238.

National security. Section 10(1) of the Employment Tribunals Act 1996 **2.5** provides that an employment tribunal 'shall dismiss' an unfair dismissal complaint if 'it is shown that the action complained of [in other words, the dismissal] was taken for the purpose of safeguarding national security'. This used generally to be taken to mean that dismissal for the purpose of safeguarding national security was *automatically fair*. However, in B v BAA plc 2005 ICR 1530, EAT, the EAT held that an employment tribunal should not reject an employee's unfair dismissal claim simply on the basis that the dismissal was carried out for the purpose of safeguarding national security. The tribunal should go on to consider whether dismissal was within the range of reasonable responses available to the employer. This case is dealt with in more detail in Chapter 3, 'Unfairness', under 'Automatically fair and unfair dismissals'.

Bankruptcy. It is worth noting that bankruptcy – which deprives a person of **2.6** the right to bring or pursue legal proceedings to recover money or property in which his or her creditors will have an interest – does *not* prevent an employee from pursuing a claim for unfair dismissal. This is because unfair dismissal is a cause of action personal to the employee. In Grady v HM Prison Service 2003 ICR 753, CA, the Court of Appeal held that unlike a claim of wrongful dismissal, which is a monetary claim and therefore vests in the trustee in bankruptcy, a claim of unfair dismissal is primarily directed at the restoration of a contractual relationship in which the claimant's skill and labour are the essential commodity. Under the ERA an employment tribunal must first consider the reinstatement or re-engagement of an employee who is found to have been unfairly dismissed before turning to the question of compensation. A claim for reinstatement or re-engagement, and indeed a significant element of the compensation that can be awarded in lieu of these, does not form part of a bankrupt's estate, even though the eventual fund (if an award is made) may. It is a claim of a unique kind that provides for the restoration of something that can only be done by the claimant. For more on remedies for unfair dismissal, see Chapter 12, 'Remedies'.

Employees only   **2.7**

Only employees can claim unfair dismissal rights. An employee is defined in S.230(1) ERA as 'an individual who has entered into or works under (or, where the employment has ceased, worked under) a contract of employment'. 'Contract of employment' is in turn defined as a 'contract of service or apprenticeship, whether express or implied, and (if it is express) whether oral or in writing' – S.230(2). This raises the question of when it can be said that someone is employed under a 'contract of *service*', as opposed to a contract for *services*, as in the latter case he or she would be self-employed, i.e. an 'independent contractor', not an employee.

There is no precise and uniformly applied legal definition of a contract of employment. As Lord Justice Denning put it in Stevenson Jordan and Harrison Ltd v Macdonald and Evans 1952 1 TLR 101, CA: '[I]t is almost impossible to give a precise definition… It is often easy to recognise a contract of service when you see it, but difficult to say wherein the difference lies.' In practice, it is obvious enough in the great majority of cases whether a worker is an employee or an independent contractor, but there is a grey area between the two and borderline cases have generated a large body of case law. Over the years the courts have developed a number of tests of employment status and have viewed a variety of factors as relevant in particular cases. The tendency in recent years has been to take a broad and flexible approach to the question of who is an employee and the courts and tribunals have adopted what has become known as the *multiple* or *mixed* test. This involves the proposition that no single test is conclusive and that what the tribunal or court must do is weigh up all the relevant factors and decide whether, on balance, the relationship between the parties is governed by a contract of employment. The test seems originally to have been formulated by Mr Justice MacKenna in Ready Mixed Concrete (South East) Ltd v Minister of Pensions and National Insurance 1968 2 QB 497, QBD, but has been developed in a number of subsequent cases. Following the decisions in Carmichael and anor v National Power plc 1999 ICR 1226, HL; Express and Echo Publications Ltd v Tanton 1999 ICR 693, CA; and Hewlett Packard Ltd v O'Murphy 2002 IRLR 4, EAT, it is clear that four essential elements *must* be fulfilled for a contract of employment to exist. There must be:

- a contract (between the worker and the alleged employer)
- an obligation on the worker to provide work personally
- mutuality of obligation
- an element of control over the work by the employer.

2.8 This area of law is dealt with in considerable detail in IDS Employment Law Handbook, 'Contracts of Employment' (2014), Chapter 2, 'Employment status', under 'Tests of employment status' and 'Multiple test'. Here we simply provide a brief outline of the relevant factors.

2.9 **Requirement of a contract.** In order for an individual to have 'employee' status, there must be a contract in existence and it must be between the party doing the work and the party for whom the work is done. This can be a problem in cases where a third party, such as an agency, is involved, as often no express agreement will exist between the individual (the agency worker) and the party for whom that individual is carrying out the work (the client). However, the courts have acknowledged that a contractual relationship may be implied between the client and agency worker in certain limited circumstances – see Dacas v Brook Street Bureau (UK) Ltd 2004 ICR 1437, CA, and James v Greenwich Borough Council 2008 ICR 545, CA.

A prerequisite for a contract is an *intention to create legal relations*. For example, in Roberts v Major Read on behalf of the Salvation Army and anor ET Case No.1304316/08 a tribunal found that a religious officer of the Salvation Army was not an employee for the purpose of an unfair dismissal claim, as he had entered into an agreement which expressly excluded legal relations. The agreement was valid as its purpose was not to avoid obligations imposed by employment legislation but to give effect to the spiritual nature of the working arrangement.

2.10 For full details of the prerequisites of a contractual relationship, see IDS Employment Law Handbook, 'Contracts of Employment' (2014), Chapter 1, 'Formation of contract'.

2.11 **Personal performance.** It is the essence of a contract of service that an individual undertakes to supply his or her services personally – Express and Echo Publications Ltd v Tanton (above). However, a limited or occasional power of delegation may not be fatal to the existence of a contract of service – see MacFarlane and anor v Glasgow City Council 2001 IRLR 7, EAT, and Byrne Bros (Formwork) Ltd v Baird and ors 2002 ICR 667, EAT.

For further details, see IDS Employment Law Handbook, 'Contracts of Employment' (2014), Chapter 2, 'Employment status', under 'Multiple test – personal performance'.

2.12 **Mutuality of obligation.** The requirement that there be mutuality of obligation is usually expressed as an obligation on the employer to provide work and a corresponding obligation on the employee to accept and perform any work offered. So, an unpaid volunteer who worked for a Citizens Advice Bureau for one or two days a week was not an employee for the purpose of bringing a claim of unfair dismissal. There could be no contract of employment where the volunteer was not obliged to attend work and received no remuneration. Travelling expenses and free training were not sufficient to amount to remuneration – Melhuish v Redbridge Citizens Advice Bureau 2005 IRLR 419, EAT. Other relevant considerations include whether there are any notice requirements or whether a worker is free to leave at any time.

Whether there is sufficient mutuality of obligation is most often at issue in cases where an individual has carried out work on a casual, irregular or sporadic basis over a period of time. The question then is whether mutuality of obligation subsists during those periods when the individual is not working, so as to give rise to a continuous 'global' contract of employment spanning the separate engagements. The required obligation generally consists of an exchange of

29

mutual promises of future performance. Where there has been a regular pattern of work over a period of time, a court or tribunal is more likely to infer the existence of a continuing overriding arrangement.

2.13 In the absence of a global contract it may still be possible to establish that a contract of employment exists in relation to each individual assignment, with the result that the individual is regarded as an employee in respect of each individual engagement (although in these circumstances the employee may find it difficult to establish the necessary two years' continuous service for bringing an unfair dismissal claim – see 'Continuous service threshold' below.) In Little v BMI Chiltern Hospital EAT 0021/09 L accepted that there was no overriding global contract of employment and that between engagements there was no mutuality of obligation. However, he contended instead that each separate period of work for BMI represented a separate contract of employment during which the necessary mutuality of obligations existed. The EAT held that he was not an employee because there was no obligation to provide him with work – nor indeed to pay him – for the whole of any assignment. There was no mutuality of obligation even on the basis of a succession of individual assignments. While there was a contract in place when L worked, it was in fact and law a contract for freelance services and not one of employment.

Mutuality of obligation is discussed at length in IDS Employment Law Handbook, 'Contracts of Employment' (2014), Chapter 2, 'Employment status', under 'Multiple test – mutuality of obligation'. It is also considered in the context of casual working arrangements in IDS Employment Law Handbook, 'Atypical and Flexible Working' (2014), Chapter 5, 'Zero-hours and other "atypical" contracts', under 'Casual and seasonal workers – are casual staff employees?'.

2.14 **Control.** While it is uncertain exactly how much control by the alleged employer over the worker is necessary in order for there to be a contract of service, it is clear from the case law that the work does not have to be carried out under the employer's actual supervision or control. However, indirect control in the form of the employer's right to terminate the contract if the individual fails to meet the required standards is not by itself sufficient. Some element of direct control over what the individual does is required. The requirement of control is often a problem in the context of agency work. For further detail, see IDS Employment Law Handbook, 'Contracts of Employment' (2014), Chapter 2, 'Employment status', under 'Multiple test – control'.

2.15 **Surrounding circumstances.** If all of these elements (a contract, personal service, mutuality of obligation and control) are present, the contract may be one of employment. The next step is to consider the surrounding circumstances of the case. While it is impossible to draw up a complete list of the factors that should be weighed in the balance, as every case will depend upon its own facts, the kinds of detail which may be relevant include:

- whether the person doing the work provides his or her own equipment
- whether he or she hires staff
- the degree of financial risk taken by the individual doing the work
- whether he or she has responsibility for investment and management
- whether the work done by the individual is an integral part of the employer's business
- the intentions of the parties.

As a general rule, the greater the degree of personal responsibility an individual takes in any of the matters set out above, the more likely it is that he or she will be an independent contractor rather than an employee.

Miscellaneous factors that may indicate the existence of a contract of employment include: **2.16**

- any prohibition on working for other companies or individuals
- control by a disciplinary code laid down by the employer
- remuneration by way of payment of wages or salary
- payment during absence for illness
- paid holidays
- membership of a company pension scheme.

As indicated above, it is often atypical workers such as casual workers and homeworkers who are most likely to have difficulty in establishing employee status. These and other special categories of worker are discussed in IDS Employment Law Handbook, 'Contracts of Employment' (2014), Chapter 2, 'Employment status', under 'Specific categories of worker', and in IDS Employment Law Handbook, 'Atypical and Flexible Working' (2014), Chapter 5, 'Zero-hours and other "atypical" contracts', under 'Zero-hours contracts – employment rights under zero-hours contracts' and 'Casual and seasonal workers – are casual staff employees?'.

Finally, note that the issue of employment status was categorised by the Privy **2.17** Council in Lee Ting Sang v Chung Chi-Keung and anor 1990 ICR 409, PC, as a mixed question of fact and law. The tribunal's interpretation of a set of circumstances is a question of fact and is not open to appeal unless it involves an error of law or is perverse. However, if an individual's employment status turns upon the interpretation of a contractual document, that is a question of law and is open to appeal. In Clark v Oxfordshire Health Authority 1998 IRLR 125, CA, the Court of Appeal pointed out that only in exceptional cases will the question of employment status turn solely upon the construction of written documents. In the majority of cases, held the Court, the question will also involve the tribunal in an investigation and evaluation of the factual circumstances in which the work is performed. This approach appears, broadly speaking, to have been affirmed by the House of Lords in Carmichael and anor v National Power plc 1999 ICR 1226, HL. For further detail, see IDS Employment Law Handbook, 'Contracts of Employment' (2014), Chapter 2, 'Employment status', under 'Question of law or fact?'.

2.18 Employee shareholders

The Growth and Infrastructure Act 2013 introduced a new category of excluded worker – the 'employee shareholder' – with effect from 1 September 2013. S.31 of that Act inserted S.205A into the ERA, creating 'employee shareholder' status. This is a new breed of worker who, in return for a minimum of £2,000 of shares in the employer's business, forgoes some of the employment protection rights to which an 'employee', as defined by the ERA, would otherwise be entitled. One such right is the right to claim 'ordinary' unfair dismissal under S.94 – see S.205A(2)(c) ERA.

In response to widespread concern that the new employee shareholder regime could give rise to abuse, the Government imposed conditions and procedural requirements on the establishment of employee shareholder status. Among other things, whenever an employer proposes hiring an individual on an employee shareholder basis, the employer must provide the individual with a statement setting out the employment protection rights affected and giving details of the entitlements and restrictions that attach to the shares – S.205A(1) and (5). Furthermore, the individual must receive independent advice on the terms and effects of the proposed employee shareholder agreement (S.205A(6)) and the employer must pay the individual's reasonable costs in obtaining that advice (S.205A(7)).

2.19 There are also certain protections for current employees who are offered (or forced to accept) employee shareholder status. S.47G ERA makes it unlawful for an employer to subject an employee to a detriment on the ground that the employee refused an offer to become an employee shareholder and S.104G makes it automatically unfair to dismiss an employee for the reason (or the principal reason) that the employee refused an offer to become an employee shareholder.

For fuller details on the statutory scheme, see IDS Employment Law Handbook, 'Atypical and Flexible Working' (2014), Chapter 7, 'Employee shareholders'.

2.20 Continuous service threshold

To qualify for the right to claim unfair dismissal, employees must generally show that they have been continuously employed for at least two years – S.108(1) ERA. (Note that this qualifying period only applies to England, Wales and Scotland. The ERA does not apply to Northern Ireland, with the equivalent rights being found in the Employment Rights (Northern Ireland) Order 1996 SI 1996/1919, which imposes a 12-month qualifying period.)

There are a number of exceptions to the rule that in order to bring an unfair dismissal claim an employee must have been continuously employed for a minimum period of time – see 'Exceptions to continuous service threshold' below. However, for the great majority of unfair dismissal cases the qualifying period of two years' continuous employment applies. 'Year' means a year of 12 calendar months and 'month' means a calendar month – S.210(2) ERA. In Pacitti Jones v O'Brien 2005 IRLR 888, Ct Sess (Inner House), the Court of Session held that the date on which an employee started work is included when computing his or her period of continuous employment for unfair dismissal purposes. Thus an employee who worked from 8 April 2002 until 7 April 2003 had the one year's continuous service then necessary to bring a claim.

Clearly, there are two essential dates for the purposes of computing an **2.21** employee's period of continuous employment. These are the date employment began (see below) and the effective date of termination (EDT). The EDT is discussed in IDS Employment Law Handbook, 'Contracts of Employment' (2014), Chapter 14, 'Date of termination'.

A period of continuous employment *begins* with the day on which an employee starts work – S.211(1)(a); Pacitti Jones v O'Brien (above). In General of the Salvation Army v Dewsbury 1984 ICR 498, EAT, the EAT held that this refers to the beginning of the employee's employment under the relevant contract of employment and not to when the employee first turns up physically to start work. In that case D, a teacher, accepted a post expressed as starting on 1 May, which was a Saturday. However, because of the weekend and the May Day Bank Holiday, she did not actually start her duties until 4 May, the following Tuesday. The EAT held that she must be treated as having 'started work' on 1 May, with the result that she just qualified to bring an unfair dismissal claim.

There are two cases in which an artificial adjustment is made retrospectively to **2.22** the start date which may affect the qualifying period of continuous service in unfair dismissal cases – S.211(3):

- if an employee is absent from work because he or she has been taking part in a strike or because of a lock-out by the employer, the start of employment is deemed to have been postponed by the number of days (not working days) between the last working day before the strike or lock-out and the day on which work is resumed – S.216(2)

- there is a similar postponement of the start date if an employee is absent because of military service – S.217(2).

2.23 'Continuous employment' is a technical term. It means a period of continuous employment computed in accordance with the rules set out in Ss.210–219 ERA, which provide a complete definition of what is meant by 'continuously employed' – Wood v York City Council 1978 ICR 840, CA. These rules deal with three main issues:

- when a week worked under a contract of employment does and does not count as a week of continuous employment

- breaks in employment and when these count as periods of continuous employment even though there is no employment contract in existence

- when continuity is preserved after a change of employer (for example, in Da Silva v Composite Mouldings and Design Ltd 2009 ICR 416, EAT, an employee who was dismissed on the voluntary liquidation of one company and employed by another retained his continuity of service under S.218, since both companies had the same owner who had retained control throughout the relevant period).

These issues are considered in detail in IDS Employment Law Handbook, 'Continuity of Employment' (2012), to which reference should be made regarding all aspects of continuous employment.

2.24 Exceptions to continuous service threshold

There are a number of exceptions to the normal rule that two years' continuous service must be shown in order to claim unfair dismissal.

2.25 Automatically unfair dismissals. Most importantly, *no* period of qualifying service is required to bring a claim of automatically unfair dismissal for one of the 'inadmissible' reasons (with two exceptions noted below) – see S.108 ERA, Ss.154 and 239(1) TULR(C)A, para 164 of Schedule A1 to the TULR(C)A, S.12(4) of the Employment Relations Act 1999 and Reg 18(4) of the Employee Study and Training (Procedural Requirements) Regulations 2010 SI 2010/155. These inadmissible reasons are listed in the Appendix to Chapter 9, 'Automatically unfair dismissals'. Therefore, in cases where an employee has less than two years' service, it is crucial to determine at the outset whether or not his or her dismissal was for one of the inadmissible reasons.

As noted above, there are two grounds of automatically unfair dismissal where the qualifying limit in S.108(1) *does* apply:

- dismissals because of a spent conviction, and

- dismissals where there is a transfer of an undertaking.

2.26 Redundancy. The qualifying limit does not apply to dismissals for redundancy where selection for redundancy was for one of the inadmissible reasons – see S.108(3)(h) ERA, S.154 TULR(C)A, and para 164, Sch A1 TULR(C)A.

Note, though, that there are a few automatically unfair reasons for dismissal for which no provision is made in respect of selection for redundancy – see Chapter 9, 'Automatically unfair dismissals', under 'Automatically unfair reasons – redundancy dismissals'.

Political opinion dismissal. Section 108(1) does not apply where 'the reason **2.27** (or, if more than one, the principal reason) for the dismissal is, or relates to, the employee's political opinions or affiliation' – S.108(4). In other words, an employee who is dismissed on the ground of his or her political opinions or affiliation does not need to show any minimum period of qualifying service in order to bring an unfair dismissal claim.

Section 108(4) was introduced in June 2013 following criticism by the European Court of Human Rights (ECtHR) in Redfearn v United Kingdom 2013 IRLR 51, ECtHR, over the lack of an exception to the qualifying service rule in respect of dismissals on the ground of political opinion. According to the Court, this failure meant that the UK was in breach of Article 11 of the European Convention on Human Rights, which protects freedom of assembly and association. The case arose on a complaint by R, a minibus driver employed by a private sector company to transport disabled people, the majority of whom were Asian. He was dismissed after being elected as a local councillor for the British National Party. As he did not have sufficient continuity of service to bring an unfair dismissal claim under the ERA, he instead sought to rely on the Race Relations Act 1976 (RRA) (since repealed and re-enacted in the Equality Act 2010 (EqA)), arguing that his dismissal was 'on racial grounds' and so unlawful. The Court of Appeal overturned the EAT and upheld the tribunal's original decision that the dismissal was not discriminatory on the ground of race. After he was refused leave to appeal to the House of Lords, R brought a challenge in the ECtHR, asserting that the lack of a remedy amounted to a breach of his Article 11 rights.

The ECtHR noted that an unfair dismissal claim would be an appropriate **2.28** domestic remedy for a person who claimed to have been dismissed on the ground of his or her political beliefs or affiliations and that the tribunal hearing the claim would have to take Article 11 into account when deciding whether the dismissal was for a potentially fair reason and was reasonable. It held that the RRA did not provide R with adequate protection and so the qualifying period under the ERA (then one year) caused him a detriment, in that it deprived him of the only means by which he could have effectively challenged his dismissal at the domestic level on the ground that it breached his Article 11 rights. The Court accepted that, in principle, it was reasonable and appropriate for the UK to limit the right to claim unfair dismissal to those who have been continuously employed for at least a year. However, it noted that a number of exceptions to the continuous service threshold had been created to offer additional protection to employees dismissed on certain prohibited grounds, such as race, sex and religion, but no additional protection was afforded to employees who were dismissed on account of their political opinion or affiliation. The Court stated that it was incumbent on states to take 'reasonable and appropriate' measures to protect employees from dismissal on the ground of political opinion or affiliation, either through the creation of a further exception to the qualifying period for unfair dismissal or through a free-standing claim for unlawful discrimination on the ground of political opinion or affiliation. The UK statutory scheme was therefore deficient in this respect.

The Court's decision appears to be based – at least in part – on a misunderstanding of UK unfair dismissal law, in that it is not the case that exceptions to the qualifying period are made for dismissals on the ground of race, sex or religion. An employee dismissed on any of these grounds may bring a claim of discriminatory dismissal under the EqA regardless of his or her length of service, but that is a separate cause of action to a claim of unfair dismissal under the ERA. As explained above, there are a number of automatically unfair dismissal provisions in the ERA in respect of which the normal qualifying period for unfair dismissal does not apply. However, there is no specific exception in the case of 'race, sex or religion', or indeed most of the other characteristics protected under the EqA.

2.29 **Other exceptions.** There are some further limited exceptions to the general rule that an employee must show two years' continuous employment in order to claim unfair dismissal:

- the qualifying period is *one month* where the employee is dismissed in circumstances in which he or she would qualify for paid suspension on medical grounds – S.108(2) ERA. The medical suspension provisions, which are rarely used, are set out in Ss.64–65 ERA and cover a limited range of occupations – basically those involving lead, certain dangerous chemicals and radiation

- the qualifying limit does *not* apply in relation to the dismissal of office holders who have fair dismissal rights under Reg 33 of the Ecclesiastical Offices (Terms of Service) Regulations 2009 SI 2009/2108 – Reg 33(3) of those Regulations

- the qualifying limit does not apply 'if the reason (or, if more than one, the principal reason) for the dismissal is, or is connected with, the employee's membership of a reserve force' – S.108(5) ERA. (A 'reserve force', as defined in S.374 of the Armed Forces Act 2006, includes the Territorial Army, the Royal Navy Reserve, the Royal Marines Reserve and the Royal Auxiliary Air Force.) It is worth noting that it is also a criminal offence to dismiss reservists solely or mainly because they are called out or are likely to be called out – S.17 Reserve Forces (Safeguard of Employment) Act 1985.

Lawfulness of continuous service threshold 2.30

The right to claim unfair dismissal is a domestic right: that is, it does not originate from European Union law. Nevertheless, there has been some suggestion that the requirement for an employee to pass a continuous service threshold in order to claim unfair dismissal is incompatible with Article 30 of the Charter of Fundamental Rights of the European Union, which states that 'every worker has the right to protection against unjustified dismissal, in accordance with Community law and national laws and practices'. However, the European Court of Justice (ECJ) refused to hear a similar argument raised in Poclava v Toledano C-117/14, ECJ, where a Spanish court asked the ECJ whether it violated EU law or was incompatible with Article 30 for particular employment contracts to be made subject to a one-year probationary period during which the employee could freely be dismissed (similar in effect to having a one-year service threshold for claiming unfair dismissal). The ECJ observed that the provisions of the Charter were applicable to Member States only when they were implementing EU law. Given that the contracts in the case were not fixed term but of indefinite duration, the EU Fixed-term Work Directive (No.99/70) did not apply and there were no other specific obligations under EU law with respect to probationary periods. Thus, the situation did not fall within the scope of EU law and the ECJ concluded that it had no jurisdiction to consider the questions referred to it. It seems unlikely, therefore, that the continuous service threshold on unfair dismissal claims in the UK could successfully be challenged on the ground of incompatibility with EU law, particularly given that the UK has a limited opt-out from the Charter.

Special categories of worker 2.31

There are a number of provisions in the ERA that deal with unfair dismissal rights in relation to specific categories of worker such as crown employees, the police and mariners.

Crown employees 2.32

The question of whether Crown employees work under contracts of employment is dealt with in IDS Employment Law Handbook, 'Contracts of Employment' (2014), Chapter 2, 'Employment status', under 'Specific categories of worker – crown servants'. In practice, the issue is irrelevant in the context of unfair dismissal, because S.191(1) expressly applies the unfair dismissal provisions to 'persons in Crown employment' in the same way as to other employees – with the exception of S.101, which makes it automatically unfair to dismiss certain shop workers and betting workers who refuse to work on Sundays (a provision unlikely to apply to many Crown employees in any event).

Members of armed forces. Service in the armed forces is regarded as 'Crown 2.33 employment'. At first glance, the rights of members of the armed forces are set out in S.192. This applies the provisions dealing with Crown employment to members of the armed forces, but with certain exceptions. However, S.192 has yet to be brought into force. Instead, the 'transitory provisions' set out in para 16 of Schedule 2 to the Act continue to apply. These provide (through the substitution of modified text) that unless and until S.192 is brought into effect, it should be read as if the provisions in S.191 – which apply the unfair dismissal provisions to persons in Crown employment – do *not* apply to service as a member of the armed forces. Thus members of the armed forces are currently excluded from the right to claim unfair dismissal. (Note that in McQuade v Secretary of State for Defence, unreported 7/10/03, Ct Sess (Outer House), the Court of Session held that the exclusion of members of the armed forces from the unfair dismissal scheme did not breach their rights under the European Convention on Human Rights.)

However, para 16(1) of Schedule 2 makes it clear that S.191 *does* apply to employment by territorial, auxiliary and volunteer reserve associations (known since 1999 as Reserve Forces' and Cadets' Associations (RFCA)), which deliver support services to the reserve forces and their cadets. In other words, RFCA staff can claim unfair dismissal. Furthermore, members of the reserve forces themselves retain the right not to be unfairly dismissed from their 'day jobs'.

2.34 **National security.** It used to be the case that, subject to a limited number of exceptions relating to automatically unfair dismissals, unfair dismissal rights were generally excluded in the case of Crown employees in respect of whom a Minister had issued a certificate to certify that employment of a particular description or the employment of a particular person should be excluded from protection for the purpose of safeguarding national security. That exception no longer exists (although there remains a question over whether members of the security services are excluded from the protection conferred by S.103A ERA against being unfairly dismissed on the ground of making a protected disclosure – see IDS Employment Law Handbook, 'Whistleblowing at Work' (2013), Chapter 2, 'Who is protected?', under 'National security – specific exclusion of protected disclosure rights').

2.35 **House of Commons and House of Lords staff**
Sections 194 and 195 provide that unfair dismissal rights apply to relevant members of the House of Lords staff and the House of Commons staff as they apply in relation to other employment, subject to two exceptions:

- S.101 – automatically unfair dismissal for Sunday working (see Chapter 9, 'Automatically unfair dismissals', under 'Dismissal for refusing to work on Sunday')

- S.102 – automatically unfair dismissal of an occupational pension scheme trustee in connection with his or her duties in that capacity (see Chapter 9,

'Automatically unfair dismissals', under 'Dismissal in connection with occupational pensions').

'Relevant member of the House of Lords staff' means any person who is employed under a contract of employment with the Corporate Officer of the House of Lords – S.194(6). 'Relevant member of the House of Commons staff' means any person who was appointed by the House of Commons Commission or is employed in the refreshment department or who is a member of the Speaker's personal staff – S.195(5).

Police   2.36

People employed in the police service are generally excluded from unfair dismissal rights – S.200(1). 'Police service' means service as a member of a constabulary maintained by virtue of an enactment, or service in any other capacity by virtue of which a person has 'the powers or privileges of a constable' – S.200(2). This definition has been held to be wide enough to cover constables with limited powers, such as park constables – see Redbridge London Borough Council v Dhinsa and anor 2014 ICR 834, CA. However, note that in London Borough of Wandsworth v Vining and ors EAT 0234/13 the EAT has allowed some park constables to pursue an appeal arguing that the exclusion of their claims gave rise to a lack of an effective domestic remedy in the light of their rights under the European Convention on Human Rights and under EU law. So far as we are aware, this appeal has yet to be heard.

Prison staff are not covered by S.200 and may therefore bring unfair dismissal claims – S.126 Criminal Justice and Public Order Act 1994. So, too, may civilian police employees working in supporting roles: for example, Jenner v North Yorkshire Police Authority ET Case No.2500930/10 concerned an unfair dismissal claim by a crime recording assistant who worked for the police force recording and handling sensitive information relating to victims of crime, suspects, offenders and incidents.

There are two important exceptions to the general rule that persons employed **2.37** in the police service are excluded from bringing unfair dismissal claims. These relate to:

- health and safety dismissals under S.100 ERA (see Chapter 10, 'Health and safety dismissals'), and

- dismissals for making a protected disclosure under S.103A ERA (see IDS Employment Law Handbook, 'Whistleblowing at Work' (2013), Chapter 2, 'Who is protected?', under 'Police') – S.200(1).

Where either of these exceptions applies, a person who holds the office of constable or an appointment as a police cadet will be treated as employed by the relevant officer (as defined) under a contract of employment – Ss.43KA and 134A.

2.38 Share fishermen and women

The master and crew of a fishing vessel who are remunerated only by a share in the profits or gross earnings of the vessel on which they are employed are excluded from unfair dismissal rights – S.199(2). In Goodeve v Gilson's 1985 ICR 401, CA, the Court of Appeal considered the case of a fisherman who had been remunerated by a share in the profits of the whole fleet of vessels operated by his employer. It held that the singular could not be read as including the plural in the words 'the vessel', so that S.199(2) did not apply. The employee was not a share fisherman as defined and he was not, therefore, excluded from the right to claim unfair dismissal.

2.39 Mariners

Persons employed on board a ship registered in the UK under S.8 of the Merchant Shipping Act 1995 can only bring a claim of unfair dismissal if:

● the ship is registered as belonging to a port in Great Britain

● under his or her contract of employment, the person employed does not work *wholly* outside Great Britain, and

● he or she is ordinarily resident in Great Britain – S.199(7) and (8).

(Great Britain means England, Scotland and Wales; the UK means Great Britain and Northern Ireland. Neither expression includes the Channel Islands or the Isle of Man.)

2.40 The rules governing the right of mariners to bring unfair dismissal claims used to be contained in S.196(5), which was repealed by the Employment Relations Act 1999. However, very similar wording is used in S.199, which was inserted by the same Act, with the result that the case law interpreting S.196(5) is likely to be relevant to the interpretation of S.199. Much of the case law concerned with S.196(5) centred on the phrases 'wholly outside Great Britain' and 'ordinarily resident in Great Britain'. In Royle v Globtik Management Ltd 1977 ICR 552, EAT, the employer managed three tankers, two of which were registered in London and one in the Bahamas. R, who was resident in Great Britain, worked only on the London-registered ships. However, he worked only on voyages between the Persian Gulf and the Far East, although he had been on a three-day course in Liverpool during his employment. The EAT held that he was not entitled to bring an unfair dismissal claim on two grounds:

● he worked wholly outside Great Britain (the three days in Liverpool being too trivial to count)

● he could not be said to have been employed to work on a UK-registered ship because he could at any time have been transferred to the Bahamas-registered ship (which seemed to involve reading the word 'exclusively' into S.196(5)).

40

In Wood v Cunard Line Ltd 1991 ICR 13, CA, W worked exclusively on a UK- **2.41** registered ship based in Puerto Rico. He had been recruited at, and was paid by, the head office in Southampton and his standard form contract stated that each voyage terminated in Great Britain. In practice, however, the ship never entered UK waters. The Court held that employment was wholly outside Great Britain even though the employee travelled to the ship from Great Britain and was paid the appropriate rate of pay during the trip. Employment is wholly outside Great Britain if the *work on board the ship* is performed wholly outside Great Britain – even if the employment technically begins when the employee is in Great Britain.

In Huggins v Geest Transportation Group COET 818/200 H worked exclusively on a UK-registered ship and his employment was not wholly outside Great Britain. However, he was not ordinarily resident in Great Britain because his home was in the West Indies. It followed that he was disqualified from presenting an unfair dismissal claim.

Foreign-registered ships. Section 199(7) and (8) applies only to those who are **2.42** employed on ships registered under S.8 of the Merchant Shipping Act 1995, i.e. on UK-registered ships. Mariners employed on foreign-registered ships are covered by the more general principles governing territorial jurisdiction under the ERA – Diggins v Condor Marine Crewing Services Ltd 2010 ICR 213, CA (see IDS Employment Law Handbook, 'Employment Tribunal Practice and Procedure' (2014), Chapter 2, 'Tribunals' jurisdiction', in the section 'Territorial limitations', under 'Territorial reach – unfair dismissal and other ERA rights').

In the Diggins case, D was employed by CMCS Ltd as chief officer on a ship which, although registered in the Bahamas, operated between the Channel Islands and Portsmouth. D was required to stay on board throughout his fortnightly rosters, but otherwise his home was in Lowestoft. In April 2007 he was dismissed and his subsequent unfair dismissal claim was rejected by the employment tribunal as D did not meet the conditions set down in S.199(7). The EAT allowed D's appeal, holding that the tribunal did have jurisdiction notwithstanding his failure to meet the criteria in S.199(7), as D was a 'peripatetic employee' based in Great Britain (and therefore covered by the ERA in accordance with the guidance laid down by the House of Lords in Lawson v Serco Ltd and two other cases 2006 ICR 250, HL). CMCS Ltd appealed to the Court of Appeal, arguing that S.199(7) alone determines the right of those who work on ships to claim unfair dismissal. The Court disagreed. That subsection only applies to those who are employed on ships registered under S.8 of the Merchant Shipping Act 1995. If they are employed on ships not registered under that Act, a tribunal might still have jurisdiction under the case law relating to territorial reach generally. The Court then went on to consider whether, on the facts, the employment tribunal had jurisdiction to hear D's case. It held that CMCS Ltd may have been based in Guernsey but D

41

'had no real connection with that place and he had even less so with the Bahamas, where the ship was registered'. It supported the EAT's conclusion that his tours of duty started and finished in Portsmouth. Therefore he was a peripatetic employee based in Great Britain and accordingly CMCS Ltd's appeal was dismissed.

2.43 Settlements and contracting out

The general rule is that nobody can contract out of unfair dismissal rights and obligations: any purported agreement to this effect will be void, whether or not it is contained in a contract of employment – S.203(1). Statute, however, expressly provides for a number of exceptions to this general rule. These are: settlements reached under the auspices of an Acas conciliator, settlement agreements, and collective contracting out under a dismissal procedures agreement. In addition, a settlement recorded by the tribunal may effectively bar a claim.

2.44 Tribunal settlements
Where a settlement has been incorporated into a tribunal decision dismissing the application upon withdrawal by the claimant, the claimant will be prevented or 'estopped' from bringing another claim in respect of the same facts or issues – unless the decision to dismiss is successfully reviewed or appealed. This is because the doctrine of 'res judicata' – which bars the reopening of a legal issue or cause of action that has already been decided – is not restricted to cases where a tribunal has given a reasoned decision on the substantive issues in the case. A tribunal's order dismissing a claim upon the claimant's withdrawal is also a judicial decision and not a mere administrative act – Barber v Staffordshire County Council 1996 ICR 379, CA.

For more detail on the effect of estoppel and res judicata in the context of tribunal settlements, see IDS Employment Law Handbook, 'Employment Tribunal Practice and Procedure' (2014), Chapter 2, 'Tribunals' jurisdiction', in the section 'Relitigation: res judicata and abuse of process', under 'What is a decision? – withdrawal'.

2.45 Acas settlements
There is an exception to the general rule against contracting out where an Acas conciliator has taken action and an agreement has been reached that the employee will refrain from instituting or continuing with a complaint – S.203(2)(e). The agreement will be binding if the conciliator has 'taken action' under S.18A, S.18B or S.18C of the Employment Tribunals Act 1996. These sections refer to Acas's powers and duties to attempt to conciliate employment disputes, including under the 'early conciliation' scheme introduced in April 2014.

'Taking action' is not defined and so should be given its ordinary meaning so as to cover any action taken by an Acas officer in relation to the claim – Allma

Construction Ltd v Bonner EATS 0060/09. The case law suggests that a conciliator's involvement in an individual case need not be particularly extensive for a binding settlement to be reached. In Slack v Greenham (Plant Hire) Ltd and anor 1983 ICR 617, EAT, for example, the EAT said that a conciliator is under no obligation to explain unfair dismissal (or other) rights to an employee, particularly where the employee is keen on a quick settlement and does not have it in mind to complain of unfair dismissal. Furthermore, in Moore v Duport Furniture Products Ltd 1982 ICR 84, HL, the House of Lords held that simply recording a settlement's terms on a COT3 form (the standard form used for this purpose) constituted taking action under S.18 (now Ss.18A–18C) and barred any unfair dismissal complaint by the employee. This was so even though the conciliator took no part in arriving at the settlement because it was agreed by the parties in his absence. (Note, however, that there has since been a policy shift on Acas's part and it now seems unlikely that a conciliator would simply rubber-stamp a settlement to which the parties to an employment dispute have already agreed.) In Allma Construction Ltd v Bonner (above) the Scottish EAT held that an Acas officer had 'taken action' under S.18 (now S.18C) where the extent of his involvement had been to leave a message on the employer's answering machine that the claimant had accepted the employer's offer to settle his unfair dismissal claim for £1,000. The EAT noted that 'taking action' does not require an Acas officer to broker a settlement or record it: his or her statutory duty is simply to 'endeavour to promote a settlement of the proceedings'.

However, there do appear to be some limits to the application of Ss.18A–18C. **2.46** In Slack v Greenham (Plant Hire) Ltd (above), for example, the EAT expressed the opinion that a conciliated settlement could be set aside if a conciliator acted in bad faith, adopted unfair methods or was not impartial. And in O'Rourke v Airport Catering Services ET Case No.31930/83 a tribunal set aside a settlement on the ground that it was based on a mutual mistake of the parties, who both erroneously believed that the employee's pension was worth a good deal more than was actually the case. Futhermore, in Trafford Carpets Ltd v Barker EAT 206/90 the EAT held that a conciliated agreement was a sham and did not deprive the tribunal of jurisdiction where its terms wrongly indicated that no payment in lieu of notice had been made and did so with a view to misleading a Government Department about the employee's eligibility for an Enterprise Allowance.

Conciliated settlements are usually recorded on COT3 forms, but there is no requirement that they be in writing. Provided there is clear evidence of an oral agreement between the parties in which a conciliator has been an intermediary, this will constitute a binding settlement which will bar the employee from bringing an unfair dismissal claim – Gilbert v Kembridge Fibres Ltd 1984 ICR 188, EAT. However, although an agreement to settle a claim does not have to be in writing, the parties must have entered into a contractually binding agreement.

Acas settlements are discussed in detail in IDS Employment Law Handbook, 'Employment Tribunal Practice and Procedure' (2014), Chapter 2, 'Tribunals' jurisdiction', under 'Acas-conciliated (COT 3) agreements'.

2.47 Settlement agreements

Settlement agreements represent another exception to the general rule in S.203(1) that individuals cannot contract out of unfair dismissal rights. By virtue of S.203(2)(f), S.203(1) does not apply where a settlement agreement is entered into, thereby making it possible for parties to settle an employment dispute between themselves without the intervention of an Acas conciliator. (Note that 'settlement agreement' is the name for what used to be called a 'compromise agreement' until a change of terminology came into effect on 29 July 2013 by virtue of S.23 of the Enterprise and Regulatory Reform Act 2013.)

In order to be binding a settlement agreement must:

- be in writing

- relate to the particular proceedings

- only be made where the employee has received advice from a relevant (and fully insured) independent adviser as to the terms and effect of the proposed agreement and in particular its effect on his or her ability to pursue his or her rights before a tribunal

- identify the adviser, and

- state that the conditions regulating settlement agreements have been satisfied – S.203(3).

2.48 A person is a relevant independent adviser if he or she:

- is a qualified lawyer (i.e. in England and Wales, a person authorised to exercise a right of audience or to conduct litigation within the meaning of the Legal Services Act 2007; in Scotland, an advocate or a solicitor who holds a practising certificate – S.203(4))

- is an officer, official, employee or member of an independent trade union who has been certified in writing by the trade union as competent to give advice and as authorised to do so on behalf of the trade union

- works at an advice centre (whether as an employee or as a volunteer) and has been certified in writing by the centre as competent to give advice and as authorised to do so on behalf of the centre, or

- is a person of a description specified in an order made by the Secretary of State – S.203(3A). (Note that the Settlement Agreements (Description of Person) Order 2004 SI 2004/754 extends the type of person who can give legal advice in relation to settlement agreements to Fellows of the Institute of Legal Executives practising in a solicitors' practice, although many such Fellows are in fact authorised to conduct litigation or have rights of audience and will count as qualified lawyers within the meaning of S.203(4).)

Section 203(3B) adds that a person is *not* a relevant independent adviser in relation to the employee (or worker) if he or she is:

- employed by or is acting in the matter for the employer or an associated employer

- a trade union or advice centre adviser and the trade union or advice centre is the employer or an associated employer

- an advice centre adviser and the employee (or worker) makes a payment for the advice received

- a person specified in an order made by the Secretary of State under S.203(3A) and any condition specified in the order in relation to the giving of advice by persons of that description is not satisfied.

2.49 The terms of S.203(3) will be strictly enforced by tribunals and a failure to comply with any of the above requirements is likely to render the agreement void. There is, however, some uncertainty as to what is needed in order for the agreement to 'relate to the particular proceedings'. In Hinton v University of East London 2005 ICR 1260, CA, the Court of Appeal ruled that the parties needed to identify expressly the particular proceedings to which the compromise agreement relates, either by a generic description (e.g. 'unfair dismissal') or by referring to the section of the relevant statute (e.g. S.98 ERA – general right to complain of unfair dismissal). It was not enough to use a rolled-up expression such as 'all statutory rights', or to refer merely to the title of a statute – e.g. 'the Employment Rights Act 1996' – and assume that such a reference would effectively settle all and any claims under that Act.

Having dealt with the statutory requirements, the Appeal Court went on to make some observations on an obiter basis about good practice when drafting compromise agreements, suggesting that employers should not use standard form agreements that seek to compromise every conceivable employment right irrespective of whether it is relevant to the particular circumstances.

2.50 There is also some uncertainty as to whether the agreement has to *identify the adviser* in the body of the agreement in order for it to be valid. In Lambert v Croydon College ET Case No.35472/96 the agreement failed to state the name of the legal adviser. Although it was clear from the surrounding correspondence who that adviser was, the tribunal held that the agreement had failed to satisfy the requirements of S.203(3). In Sankyo Pharma (UK) Ltd v Bartlett EAT 687/99, on the other hand, there was no reference to the employee's adviser, a solicitor, in the body of the compromise agreement, although a covering letter with the agreement did identify the adviser. The tribunal found that the

45

conditions regulating compromise agreements had not been complied with. However, in the course of allowing the appeal and remitting the case to a freshly constituted tribunal, the EAT commented that it was not aware of there being an EAT authority suggesting that a solicitor's signature must be on the document containing the agreement itself.

Once a valid settlement agreement has been reached, the employee is barred from bringing a claim of unfair dismissal, even if the terms of the agreement are subsequently breached by the employer. However, a tribunal may be able to hear the employee's claim for breach of the agreement by virtue of its contractual jurisdiction under the Employment Tribunals Extension of Jurisdiction (England and Wales) Order 1994 SI 1994/1623. Note, however, that tribunals have jurisdiction in contractual matters only in respect of a claim that 'arises or is outstanding on the termination of the employee's employment'. A tribunal was able to hear a claim for breach of a compromise agreement in Rock-It Cargo Ltd v Green 1997 IRLR 581, EAT, since the agreement in that case was concerned with the terms upon which the employee's employment was to be brought to an end. Most settlement agreements, however, are likely to be made some time after termination when a tribunal hearing of the unfair dismissal complaint is pending. Such agreements, if broken, will have to be enforced in the ordinary courts – see, for example, Miller Bros and FP Butler Ltd v Johnston 2002 ICR 744, EAT.

2.51 For further discussion of settlement agreements, see IDS Employment Law Handbook, 'Employment Tribunal Practice and Procedure' (2014), Chapter 3, 'Conciliation, settlements and ADR', under 'Settlement agreements'.

2.52 Dismissal procedures agreements
Section 110 ERA states that the right to claim unfair dismissal will be excluded where there is a valid dismissal procedures agreement between the parties that has been approved by the Secretary of State. Where S.110 applies, rights under the agreement are substituted for statutory unfair dismissal rights. Various criteria must be met before an agreement can be approved – e.g. the remedies provided for unfair dismissal must be on the whole as beneficial as those provided by the ERA and the procedures must include a right to arbitration or, at the very least, the right to arbitration on a point of law – S.110(3).

2.53 Time limits

Employees who have the right to claim unfair dismissal will generally lose that right if they fail to present their claim to a tribunal before the end of three months beginning with the effective date of termination – S.111(2)(a) ERA. (For discussion of the effective date of termination (EDT), see IDS Employment Law Handbook, 'Contracts of Employment' (2014), Chapter 14, 'Date of termination'.) Tribunals have a discretion to extend the time limit if the claimant can show that it was not reasonably practicable to put the claim in on time *and* that the claim has been submitted within a reasonable time of its becoming practicable to present the complaint – S.111(2)(b) (or, in the case of 'blacklisting' dismissals under S.104F, where the tribunal considers it to be 'just and equitable' to do so – S.111(5).) The time limit may also be extended to allow for early conciliation or cross-border mediation – Ss.111(2A), 207A and 207B.

Effect of internal appeals. In general, the fact that a claimant is pursuing an internal appeal against dismissal does not mean that he or she will be given extra time within which to present an unfair dismissal claim. In Palmer and anor v Southend-on-Sea Borough Council 1984 ICR 372, CA, the Court of Appeal held that the existence of an internal appeal cannot by itself justify extending the time limit. However, the existence of an internal appeal may be one of a number of factors a tribunal takes into account in determining whether it was reasonably practicable for an employee to submit his or her claim within the three-month time limit. In John Lewis Partnership v Charman EAT 0079/11, for example, the EAT upheld an employment judge's decision that it was not reasonably practicable for a claimant to present his unfair dismissal claim because he was awaiting the outcome of an internal appeal in circumstances in which he was reasonably ignorant of the existence of a time limit. **2.54**

Retrospective claims. It would seem that the fact that an employee was unaware of having a legal right to bring an unfair dismissal claim is not a ground for the tribunal to exercise its discretion under S.111(2)(b). This issue was particularly significant in the light of European-led changes, which have removed, or threaten to remove, previous restrictions on the right to bring a claim. Most important of these was the abolition of the minimum hours threshold that had previously prevented many part-time employees from claiming unfair dismissal. The removal of the hours threshold created problems for employees who were dismissed prior to its abolition and had been unable to claim unfair dismissal as a result. Can employees in these circumstances bring proceedings retrospectively under the new law, or are such claims out of time? **2.55**

This question arose in Biggs v Somerset County Council 1996 ICR 364, CA, where B presented a claim for unfair dismissal 18 years after her dismissal from her part-time post, but within three months of the House of Lords' decision in R v Secretary of State for Employment ex parte Equal Opportunities Commission and anor 1994 ICR 317, HL, which held that the hours threshold was unlawful. The Court of Appeal, taking a highly restrictive approach, dismissed her claim on the ground that it was 'reasonably practicable' within the meaning of S.111(2)(b) ERA for B to have presented her claim within three months of her dismissal. The Court's reasoning was that the decision in the EOC case, rather than changing the law, was declaratory of what the law had always been, since the primacy of European law had been established by the European Communities

47

Act 1972. The words 'reasonably practicable' are directed to difficulties faced by an individual claimant – for example, illness. There was no legal impediment in 1976 to prevent someone who claimed to be unfairly dismissed from presenting a claim and arguing that the restriction on claims by part-time workers was indirectly discriminatory. In addition, B could not rely upon Article 157 of the Treaty on the Functioning of the European Union (then Article 119 of the EC Treaty) – which enshrines the principle of equal pay in EU law – to claim unfair dismissal and disapply UK time limits, since Article 157 did not confer a separate right to compensation for unfair dismissal.

2.56 The rules governing the time limits for bringing an unfair dismissal claim are discussed in full in IDS Employment Law Handbook, 'Employment Tribunal Practice and Procedure' (2014), Chapter 5, 'Time limits'.

3 Unfairness

Reason for dismissal

Reasonableness of dismissal

Fairness of internal procedure

Automatically fair and unfair dismissals

When a claim for unfair dismissal is being heard by a tribunal, there are **3.1** various matters that need to be established. As the previous two chapters have explained, the employee will have to show that he or she was employed under a contract of employment and that he or she was, indeed, dismissed. The tribunal will also have to ascertain whether there is anything, such as the lack of two years' continuous service, that excludes the employee from bringing a claim. In this chapter we consider the central issue – the fairness or unfairness of the dismissal.

Section 98 of the Employment Rights Act 1996 (ERA) indicates how a tribunal should approach the question of whether a dismissal is fair. There are normally two stages:

- first, the employer must show the reason for the dismissal and that it is one of the potentially fair reasons set out in S.98(1) and (2)

- if the employer is successful at the first stage, the tribunal must then determine whether the dismissal was fair or unfair under S.98(3A) and (4). This requires the tribunal to consider whether the employer acted reasonably in dismissing the employee for the reason given.

Note, however, that there are a number of reasons for dismissal which can be **3.2** described as automatically fair or unfair, meaning that the question of reasonableness does not arise.

In this chapter we:

- deal with the general considerations that apply to showing the reason for dismissal: who has to show what; what happens if the employer puts forward the wrong reason; what happens if there is more than one reason for dismissal; and what happens if information comes to the attention of the employer after the decision to dismiss has been made

- consider the general approach taken by tribunals to the question of reasonableness

49

- look at the question of procedural unfairness – i.e. did the employer act unreasonably in failing to follow a fair procedure when dismissing the employee; and

- briefly discuss the automatically fair and unfair reasons for dismissal contained in the ERA (automatically unfair dismissals are discussed in greater depth in Chapter 9, 'Automatically unfair dismissals').

Note that this chapter is concerned with unfairness generally. Later chapters deal with the specific reasons for dismissal provided for in S.98(1) and (2) and consider fairness in those contexts.

3.3 Reason for dismissal

There are five potentially fair reasons for dismissal set out in S.98(2). These are:

- a reason related to the capability or qualifications of the employee for performing work of the kind which he or she was employed by the employer to do (see Chapter 4, 'Capability and qualifications', and Chapter 5, 'Ill health')

- a reason related to the conduct of the employee (see Chapter 6, 'Conduct')

- that the employee was redundant (see IDS Employment Law Handbook, 'Redundancy' (2011), Chapter 8, 'Unfair redundancy')

- that the employee could not continue to work in the position he or she held without contravening (either on the employee's part or on that of the employer) a duty or restriction imposed by or under an enactment (see Chapter 7, 'Statutory ban')

- 'some other substantial reason' ('SOSR') of a kind such as to justify the dismissal of an employee holding the position which that employee held (see Chapter 8, 'Some other substantial reason').

Note that 'retirement' has been removed from the list of potentially fair reasons for dismissal found in S.98(2). The implications of this are discussed under 'Retirement' below.

3.4 Employer must prove its reason for dismissal

It is up to the employer to show the reason for dismissal and that it was a potentially fair one – i.e. one that fell within the scope of S.98(1) and (2) and was capable of justifying the dismissal of the employee. A 'reason for dismissal' has been described as: 'a set of facts known to the employer, or it may be of beliefs held by him, which cause him to dismiss the employee' – Abernethy v Mott, Hay and Anderson 1974 ICR 323, CA.

The burden of proof on employers at this stage is not a heavy one. The employer does not have to prove that the reason actually did justify the dismissal because that is a matter for the tribunal to assess when considering the question of reasonableness. As Lord Justice Griffiths put it in Gilham and ors v Kent County Council (No.2) 1985 ICR 233, CA: 'The hurdle over which the employer has to jump at this stage of an inquiry into an unfair dismissal complaint is designed to deter employers from dismissing employees for some trivial or unworthy reason. If he does so, the dismissal is deemed unfair without the need to look further into its merits. But if on the face of it the reason could justify the dismissal, then it passes as a substantial reason, and the inquiry moves on to [S.98(4)], and the question of reasonableness.'

In cases of dismissal for capability or conduct, where the statute only refers to **3.5** a reason which 'relates to' either of these grounds, it is sufficient that the employer genuinely believed on reasonable grounds that the employee was incompetent or guilty of misconduct. The employer does not have to prove the offence or inadequacy – Alidair Ltd v Taylor 1978 ICR 445, CA. Furthermore, an honest belief held on reasonable grounds will be enough, even if it is wrong.

If, on the other hand, the dismissal is asserted to be for redundancy or because of a statutory ban on continued employment, the employer must show that what is being asserted is true – i.e. that the employee was in fact redundant as defined by statute or that an enactment did in fact prohibit continued employment. However, a genuine belief that redundancy or a statutory ban applies may, in certain circumstances, amount to SOSR justifying the dismissal of the employee – see, for example, Hounslow London Borough Council v Klusova 2008 ICR 396, CA.

Note that the reason for dismissal may be determined by reference to the mind of **3.6** a third party to whom the disciplinary procedure or investigation has been delegated. In GM Packaging (UK) Ltd v Haslem EAT 0259/13 the managing director and owner of the business, M, appointed a firm of HR consultants to investigate allegations against H. The consultant who investigated the matter recommended dismissal, which M sanctioned. H appealed and the appeal hearing was held by a different consultant, who recommended that the appeal be rejected. M agreed and H's dismissal was upheld. The EAT held that, in these circumstances, the set of facts constituting the reason for dismissal were those known to the consultants, who recommended dismissal, rather than to M, who merely sanctioned the decision. The tribunal had found that the process undertaken by the consultants was a genuine and proper procedure for this small business to follow. Since M had accepted their recommendations, it was inconsistent of the tribunal to ascribe to M a different reason for dismissal (based upon his own knowledge of the facts) simply because he had the last word.

Where the employer fails to show a potentially fair reason for dismissal, tribunals are not obliged to ascertain the real reason for dismissal if there is insufficient evidence to do so – Hertz (UK) Ltd v Ferrao EAT 0570/05. In these circumstances the dismissal will be unfair.

3.7 Identification of 'real' reason for dismissal

Employers sometimes incorrectly identify their reason for dismissal. This may be due to a genuine mistake about the law or may amount to a deliberate attempt to conceal the true reason. They may, for instance, be acting out of kindness, as where an employer dismisses for 'redundancy' when the real reason is incompetence or, less kindly, when the real reason relates to, for example, anti-union attitudes. A distinction needs to be drawn here between the facts (or beliefs) that caused the dismissal, which are crucial to ascertaining the reason for dismissal, and the label that the employer has used, which is not normally determinative.

The general approach taken by tribunals is to discover the real reason behind the dismissal by examining all the facts (and beliefs) that caused it. They do not have to accept the employer's stated reason where supporting evidence is poor or where they suspect that there was an ulterior motive. Some examples:

- **Associated Society of Locomotive Engineers and Firemen v Brady** 2006 IRLR 576, EAT: B, the General Secretary of the respondent trade union, was dismissed after a fracas at a workplace barbecue. The union argued that the dismissal was for misconduct. However, the EAT held that the tribunal had been entitled to find on the facts that the real reason for the dismissal was the employer's political antipathy towards B, irrespective of the fact that his misconduct might well have justified dismissal

- **St James Management Services Ltd v Power** EAT 0562/10: P worked for a small business. She and the managing director of the business had had a sexual relationship. She was later made redundant on the basis that the business had to cut costs. The tribunal found that the managing director had arbitrarily decided to dismiss P because of his embarrassment about his relationship with her. The EAT upheld the tribunal's finding of unfair dismissal. The tribunal's finding went to the heart of the employer's decision to dismiss

- **Dawes v Samworth Brothers Distribution Ltd** ET Case No.1900254/11: D was employed by SBD Ltd as a lorry driver. It was a condition of working in the food industry that work was done until the job was finished and in order to satisfy this condition, D's contract required him to comply with requests to work reasonable amounts of overtime. He applied for a day's holiday on Boxing Day but his request was refused due to the needs of the business. He arrived for work that day at 8.00 am only to discover that he would be required to stay until 10.00 or 11.00 pm in order to complete the job. He told SBD Ltd that he did not wish to work overtime that day but had found others who were willing to complete the planned route. (His wife had recently undergone tests for cancer and he wanted to spend as much time with her as possible, although he did not tell his employer this.) He was dismissed for refusing to obey a reasonable management instruction.

The employment tribunal held that the real reason for dismissal was the employer's concern that no penalty other than dismissal could be imposed for fear of opening the floodgates or setting a precedent for other drivers to refuse to carry out part of their planned routes. SBD Ltd was setting an example by dismissing D, not taking a decision based on individual circumstances. That was not the action of a reasonable employer and D's dismissal was therefore unfair.

3.8 It is important to bear in mind that where the employer fails to show a potentially fair reason for dismissal, tribunals are not obliged to ascertain the real reason for dismissal if there is insufficient evidence to do so – Hertz (UK) Ltd v Ferrao EAT 0570/05. In these circumstances the dismissal will be unfair.

If an employee wishes to cast doubt on an employer's seemingly fair reason for dismissal, he or she must adduce some evidence in this regard. In London Borough of Brent v Finch EAT 0418/11 the employer had dismissed F for gross misconduct after she failed to follow a number of financial control procedures at the school where she worked. An employment tribunal found that the real reason for dismissal was not the procedural failings but the school's view that F was being dishonest with school funds. Overturning that decision on appeal, the EAT stressed that while cases such as Associated Society of Locomotive Engineers and Firemen v Brady (above) established that a tribunal does not have to accept the reason put forward by the employer, a decision that there was an alternative reason had to be based on an assertion by the employee and supporting evidence. While it was clear from Brady that there is a low evidential burden of proof on an employee seeking to cast doubt on the employer's reason for dismissal, there had to be *some* evidence in this regard. In the instant case, F had not alleged that her dismissal was actually by reason of dishonesty, either during the disciplinary process or at any stage of the tribunal proceedings. Instead, the tribunal had substituted a reason for dismissal that was based on an 'ongoing innuendo' by one of the employer's witnesses. This was an error of law.

3.9 In Governing Body of John Loughborough School and anor v Alexis EAT 0583/10 the EAT emphasised that the fact that the employer has a prior reason for wishing to dismiss an employee – i.e. a 'predisposition' to do so – does not by itself mean that if the employee subsequently does something which constitutes a different ground for dismissal, that later conduct is not the reason, or principal reason, for a dismissal. Whether it is or not is a question of fact for the tribunal to decide. In that case, A was a teacher, whom the school's governing body had decided was not up to the job and whom it had resolved to dismiss. However, before the school commenced formal capability proceedings, there was a demonstration at the school in support of the claimant, organised by parents and members of the church associated with the school. While A knew that the demonstration was planned, it was not suggested that she had initiated or encouraged it. However, the school took the view that she had failed to conduct a proper assessment of the risks posed by a demonstration on school premises and summarily dismissed her for gross misconduct. An employment tribunal found that the school's concern over A's capability was the effective principal reason for dismissal, even though her misconduct could have founded a fair conduct dismissal. Since A had ostensibly been dismissed for misconduct, this meant her dismissal was unfair. The EAT upheld the tribunal's decision upon appeal. It summarised the dismissing panel's mindset as being that 'they went into the process determined – because of their "predisposition" – to use it in order to achieve the claimant's dismissal if that were possible, but acknowledging that if they were advised that dismissal was not within the range of reasonable options on the facts as proved they would have to go the long way round after all'. The EAT considered that, on this basis, the tribunal was entitled to find that the true principal reason for dismissal was the school's concern over A's capability.

Where an employment tribunal finds that the employer has attached the wrong label to a dismissal, it should consider the possible impact on the parties of finding a different reason to that cited by the employer. As Mr Justice Waite put it in Hotson v Wisbech Conservative Club 1984 ICR 859, EAT, 'even in those cases where... no more than a change of label is involved... great care must always be taken to ensure that the employee is not placed, as a result of the change in the label... at a procedural or evidential disadvantage'. The same is true in respect of a change in label that puts the employer at such a disadvantage.

3.10 **Wrong label – same facts/beliefs.** Where the employer has made a genuine mistake and where the facts (or beliefs) that led it to dismiss were known to the employee at the time of the dismissal and those facts (or beliefs) were fully aired in the tribunal proceedings, the tribunal may ignore the wrong label. The leading case is Abernethy v Mott, Hay and Anderson 1974 ICR 323, CA, where A, a civil engineer, refused to work away from head office and was dismissed on the ground of 'redundancy'. When he brought an unfair dismissal claim, the employer stated that the reason for dismissal was redundancy and/or incapability. The tribunal held that A was not redundant and that there was no redundancy situation, but that he had been fairly dismissed on the ground of incapability. On appeal, A argued that the employer, having ostensibly dismissed him for redundancy, should not have been allowed to rely on a different reason before the tribunal. The Court of Appeal held that the employer was entitled to rely on the set of facts which led to A's dismissal. Since these facts were made clear to A at the time of dismissal, it did not matter that the employer attached the wrong legal label to them.

This point was emphasised again by the Court of Appeal in Brito-Babapulle v Ealing Hospital NHS Trust 2014 EWCA Civ 1626, CA. There, B, a consultant haematologist, had seen private patients during paid sick leave despite having been told not to do so by the Trust's medical director as it could be construed as fraud. Following an investigation and disciplinary hearing, the Trust dismissed B, the dismissal letter stating that 'the allegation constituted fraud which could be considered as gross misconduct'. An employment tribunal dismissed B's unfair dismissal claim, holding that the Trust was entitled to find that B's actions amounted to gross misconduct. Before the Court of Appeal, B argued that the reason for her dismissal identified in the dismissal letter was fraudulent conduct and that the tribunal had erred because it had failed to identify whether her conduct amounted to fraud and, if it did, to say why it did so. Dismissing the appeal, the Court observed that it was an elementary rule of natural justice and disciplinary proceedings that a party should know the case that he or she has to meet and whether the allegation is one of dishonesty. However, there had never been any doubt about the allegations against B and her misconduct had been clearly identified. While there were dangers in using an emotive word, such as fraud, as a label rather than as a description of alleged conduct, the nature of the charge and a full account of the evidence had been made clear to B before the disciplinary hearing. Having found that B had been told that seeing private patients during paid sick leave was impermissible, the Trust had been entitled to conclude that her behaviour amounted to gross misconduct. Whether the label of fraud or dishonesty was attached as well was immaterial.

Three further examples where the tribunal was entitled to ignore the **3.11** employer's label:

- **Jocic v London Borough of Hammersmith and Fulham and ors** EAT 0194/07: the tribunal introduced a different reason for the dismissal (SOSR instead of redundancy). The EAT held that this substitution was no more than the attachment of a different label to precisely the same set of facts and had not caused any prejudice to J. It therefore upheld the tribunal's conclusion that the dismissal was fair on the basis of SOSR. The EAT stated that if the difference between the reason relied upon by the employer and the reason found by the tribunal goes to facts and substance and might have made some substantial or significant difference to the way in which the hearing was conducted or in the material that would have been put before the tribunal, then the tribunal's substitution will be an error of law. Otherwise, the difference should be seen as one of relabelling, which is perfectly acceptable at law

- **Hannan v TNT-IPEC (UK) Ltd** 1986 IRLR 165, EAT: H was dismissed from his post as a regional sales manager and his employer contended that the dismissal was by reason of redundancy. An industrial tribunal found that the reason for the dismissal was a reorganisation constituting SOSR, and not redundancy, even though this was not pleaded by the employer or canvassed before the tribunal. It went on to find that dismissal for SOSR was fair. H appealed to the EAT, arguing that he had been unfairly deprived of the opportunity of developing his case. The EAT dismissed his appeal, holding that the difference was simply and genuinely one of labels; that all the facts and issues had been fully canvassed at the tribunal hearing; and, most importantly, that the complainant would not have conducted his case differently in any significant way if he had known the course that the tribunal was going to take. No injustice had been suffered and the EAT refused to interfere with the tribunal's decision

- **Screene v Seatwave Ltd** EAT 0020/11: S was dismissed by a letter which referred to 'gross misconduct'. However, when he lodged an unfair dismissal claim, S Ltd's response characterised the dismissal as being for capability. The tribunal found S's dismissal fair for misconduct. He appealed, arguing that such a finding was not open to the tribunal given the label S Ltd had placed on the dismissal in its response. He asserted that the facts as found by the tribunal would have been insufficient to support a capability dismissal, which entails different procedural and evidential requirements to a conduct dismissal. The EAT dismissed the appeal. It was clear that the true reason for dismissal was misconduct and the tribunal hearing had clearly proceeded on that basis. Despite the different label in S Ltd's response, there was no prejudice to S in the hearing being conducted in this way, since he was in no doubt about the reason for his dismissal and the facts on which it was based.

3.12 **Wrong label – different facts/beliefs.** Where the employee has not been confronted with the full and true nature of the allegations against him or her, nor had an adequate opportunity to consider and answer those allegations, the dismissal is likely to be unfair. Two examples:

- **Hotson v Wisbech Conservative Club** 1984 ICR 859, EAT: the stated reason for the dismissal of a club barmaid was gross inefficiency in handling bar takings (which related to her capability to perform her job). During the tribunal hearing of her unfair dismissal complaint the tribunal chairman (now called judge) suggested, and the employer's representative agreed, that the employer was really alleging dishonesty rather than inefficiency (in other words, misconduct). The tribunal proceeded to find the dismissal fair on the ground of suspected dishonesty. The EAT held that the difference between inefficiency and dishonesty was more than a mere change of label. The charge of dishonesty should have been stated at the outset or not stated at all: at the very least the employee should have had the fullest opportunity to consider the implications of the charge and to answer it. Here, therefore, the change of reason went to the very substance of the allegations leading to dismissal. It was not simply a matter of changing the label from capability to conduct since there was also a fundamental shift in the facts/beliefs leading to dismissal

- **Murphy v Epsom College** 1985 ICR 80, CA: M was dismissed on the ground of redundancy. A tribunal found that this was a fair dismissal either for redundancy or for SOSR, without specifying what that reason was and despite the fact that the employer had never argued the latter as a ground for dismissal before the tribunal. The EAT agreed that this was a fair dismissal for redundancy, but said that the tribunal should not have found SOSR as this had been neither pleaded nor expressly raised at the tribunal: natural justice required that no party should have a case decided against them on a ground on which they have not had an opportunity to be heard. The Court of Appeal upheld the EAT's decision.

Change of label affecting fairness. Although the label assigned to a particular **3.13** set of facts will not normally be crucial, there will be situations in which it can affect the tribunal's assessment of fairness, in some instances to the detriment of the employee, in others to the detriment of the employer. It might, for example, make a significant difference to the way in which the hearing is conducted or to the material that is put before the tribunal – see Jocic v London Borough of Hammersmith and Fulham and ors (above). In London Borough of Hackney v Benn 1996 EWCA Civ 561, CA, the employer had, in accordance with a detailed disciplinary code, classified B's manifest failure to do her job properly as gross misconduct and dismissed her without warning. The tribunal found that B was actually dismissed for incapacity and that she should therefore have been given a warning about the standard of her work. The Court of Appeal held that the tribunal had substituted its own view for that of a reasonable employer. In a case where such a detailed disciplinary code was followed so carefully, a tribunal should be slow to find that the employer had misdescribed the reason for dismissal. While the label to be attached to a particular set of facts leading to dismissal was not normally crucial, in this case it had impeded the tribunal in considering what the range of reasonable responses to that particular set of facts was. The Court commented that where an employer has an established disciplinary procedure and follows that procedure both in the classification of the matters to be investigated and the method of investigation, an employment tribunal has to be very careful before it makes a reclassification. A finding of fair dismissal was substituted.

Two contrasting examples:

- **Wilson v Post Office** 2000 IRLR 834, CA: W was dismissed for unacceptable levels of short-term absence. In its response to W's tribunal claim for unfair dismissal, the Post Office cited 'incapability by reason of unsatisfactory attendance record' as the reason for dismissal. The tribunal found that the reason for dismissal was incapability on the ground of ill health and that the dismissal was unfair. The Court of Appeal remitted the case, ruling that the real reason for dismissal had not been capability but W's failure to comply with the Post Office's attendance procedure, which fell within SOSR. Therefore, different factors needed to be taken into account when judging the reasonableness of the dismissal, with W's future health prospects carrying less weight than they would in a capability dismissal

- **Williams v Cheshire Fire and Rescue Service** EAT 0621/07: W was dismissed because of his poor absence record and the EAT held that the tribunal was entitled to find that the reason for dismissal was conduct. The fact that the Rescue Service had submitted that the dismissal was for capability or SOSR did not oblige the tribunal to accept that analysis. Once it had identified the reason, the tribunal had considered the totality of the circumstances in deciding whether the dismissal was within the band of reasonable responses (and concluding that it was). This, said the EAT, was 'markedly different' to the situation in Wilson (above), where the tribunal had concentrated on the state of the claimant's health when looking at the question of reasonableness.

3.14 **Reason expressly rejected by employer at time of dismissal.** Tribunals are not entitled to find a dismissal fair for a reason that the employer could have relied on but expressly decided against. In Devonshire v Trico-Folberth Ltd 1989 ICR 747, CA, D had a very bad record of sickness absences, had received formal verbal and written warnings and, after a final absence of seven weeks, was dismissed because of her attendance record. At an internal appeal the employer rescinded the dismissal and instead decided to terminate D's employment on medical grounds. A tribunal said that dismissal because of D's attendance record would have been perfectly fair: the employer had taken the appropriate procedural steps and could not be expected to tolerate D's attendance record any longer. But the employer had deliberately chosen not to dismiss D on that ground. Instead she had been dismissed on medical grounds and this was wholly unfair because there had been no medical investigation of D's condition and no consultation with her. It was immaterial that the employer could have dismissed D fairly for another reason because the employer had made it plain that she was not going to be dismissed for that other reason. Both the EAT and the Court of Appeal upheld the tribunal's decision.

Similarly, in Nejjary v Aramark Ltd EAT 0054/12 the EAT held that, in finding that an employee's misconduct dismissal was fair, an employment tribunal had erred by taking into account the employee's disciplinary record, on which the employer had expressly not relied when it made the decision to dismiss. N was dismissed for failing to check the booking sheet for an event, leading to a customer complaint, which brought the company into disrepute. This was deemed to be an act of gross misconduct on its own and sufficient to justify summary dismissal. An employment tribunal found that while no reasonable employer would have dismissed an employee for the one incident in question, N's dismissal was nevertheless reasonable in accordance with S.98(4) ERA. It noted that, although A Ltd 'distanced itself' from N's record, the tribunal was obliged to take account of all the circumstances. It therefore had regard to the fact that N had a live warning, and a second warning against which an appeal was pending, for the same issues.

The EAT held that the tribunal had acted contrary to the principle approved **3.15** by the Court of Appeal in Foley v Post Office 2000 ICR 1283, CA. In that case, the Court said that the tribunal's proper function is to determine only whether the decision made by the employer fell within the range of reasonable responses. The tribunal should not put itself into the position of the employer and decide what it would have done in the circumstances (see further 'Reasonableness of dismissal – the "band (or range) of reasonable responses" test' below). Here, A Ltd had based its decision to dismiss entirely upon one single act of misconduct. The past matters that the tribunal had taken into account were not referred to in its dismissal letter, the letter rejecting N's appeal or its response to the claim. In fact, A Ltd had explicitly stated during the disciplinary process that it had not taken account of N's previous record. In accordance with the correct application of S.98(4), the tribunal should have restricted its considerations to whether the specific reason for which N was dismissed – namely, the single failure to check the booking sheet – was sufficient for his dismissal to fall within the range of reasonable responses. As the tribunal had clearly found that no reasonable employer would have dismissed N for that single act, this ground of appeal would be allowed and N's claim of unfair dismissal had to succeed.

Change of reason by employer on appeal to EAT. An employer will not **3.16** generally be allowed to change its pleaded reason for dismissal on appeal from a tribunal decision. The leading case is Nelson v BBC (No.1) 1977 ICR 649, CA, where N, a BBC radio producer, was dismissed on the ground of redundancy. A tribunal found this to be a fair dismissal for redundancy but on appeal the EAT thought that there was probably no redundancy but instead found a fair dismissal for SOSR, saying that the difference in labels was 'only a very technical point'. N appealed further. The Court of Appeal held that N was not redundant as argued by the BBC. Redundancy had been the only defence pleaded before the tribunal and there had been no application to amend the defence. The BBC should not have been allowed to raise a quite different ground for dismissal on appeal and this was not merely a technical point. The EAT had erred in applying the tribunal's findings of fact, made in the context of a redundancy dismissal, as if they had been found in relation to a dismissal for SOSR, which was a completely different defence. The BBC had not established its pleaded reason for dismissal, so N's dismissal was unfair.

In fact, in the Nelson case the employer's argument rested on a very narrow and legally mistaken interpretation of N's contract: the conduct of the case on both sides would have been quite different if the employer had argued SOSR as the reason for dismissal or indeed if the tribunal of its own accord had decided that the dismissal was for SOSR, as happened in Hannan v TNT-IPEC (UK) Ltd (above). In that case, the EAT held that the difference was simply and genuinely one of labels; that all the facts and issues had been fully canvassed at the tribunal hearing; and, most importantly, that the complainant would not have

59

conducted his case differently in any significant way if he had known the course that the tribunal was going to take. No injustice had been suffered and the EAT refused to interfere with the tribunal's decision.

3.17 In summary, employers should be careful to plead the right reason for dismissal. If in doubt, they should plead in the alternative – e.g. 'dismissal was because of redundancy or, alternatively, for some other substantial reason resulting from the reorganisation of the business'. Tribunals may find dismissal to have been for an unpleaded reason, i.e. they may correct the employer's label, but only if all the issues have been ventilated at the hearing and there has been no prejudice to the complainant. Moreover, as Nelson v BBC (No.1) (above) shows, if the tribunal fails to correct the label, the employer will generally be unable to introduce a new label upon appeal.

3.18 Multiple reasons for dismissal

Employers may have more than one reason for dismissal: indeed, in the case of a particularly unsatisfactory employee, they may have several. The ERA, however, requires them to show the reason or, if there was more than one, the principal reason for the dismissal – S.98(1)(a).

This provision is aimed at preventing employers from putting forward multiple reasons under different headings in the hope that one or two might be accepted by the tribunal, a tactic used in Smith v Glasgow City District Council 1987 ICR 796, HL. In that case S was a senior deputy director in the Council's Works Department who was dismissed after an internal investigation by a special committee. In a letter to S from the committee, four reasons for dismissal were set out, all relating to conduct or capability. A tribunal found that the employer had not established the second charge against S (which was agreed to have been a particularly serious one); it also indicated that it viewed the fourth charge as less serious than the others. Nevertheless, the tribunal held that dismissal was fair in all the circumstances and the EAT agreed. The House of Lords, upholding the Court of Session, held that the tribunal had found that one serious charge against S was neither established in fact nor believed to be true on reasonable grounds. The Council had failed to show what the principal reason for dismissal was and, in any case, it was not shown that the charge which was not established was neither the principal reason for dismissal nor formed part of the principal reason. Since what was at least an important part of the reason for dismissal was not made out at all, the tribunal should have found that the Council had failed to show a reason and that S's dismissal was consequently unfair.

3.19 The decision in the above case will apply where the employer has a number of different complaints against the employee, each of which form part of its reason to dismiss. In such a case, the tribunal must examine all those complaints because together they comprise the reason for dismissal. The tribunal must then go on to assess fairness under S.98(4) on the basis of that composite reason. In Robinson v Combat Stress EAT 0310/14 an employment tribunal identified three separate complaints, including one of sexual assault, which together formed the employer's reason for dismissal ('the composite reason'). The tribunal found that the investigation into the allegation of sexual assault was 'deeply flawed', since no reasonable employer would have carried it out in the way CS had. It nevertheless concluded that dismissal based upon the remaining two complaints was fair. The EAT held that the tribunal had erred in sidelining the complaint of sexual assault (which was arguably the most serious) and looking separately at the other two complaints without appreciating that they were only part of the employer's reason for dismissal. The tribunal's reasoning – that CS could have come to a perfectly fair decision to dismiss if it had eliminated from its consideration the allegation of sexual assault – was undermined by the fact that CS *had* taken that allegation into account. The tribunal should have considered not what it would have been reasonable and fair for an employer to have thought, but what CS actually thought and whether, having regard to the totality of its reasons, dismissal was reasonable.

If, however, the employer is alleging different grounds for dismissal and that each ground justified dismissal independently of the others, it will be sufficient if at least one of the grounds is established (provided the tribunal agrees that it was the principal reason for dismissal and that it would justify dismissal independently of the other grounds) – Carlin v St Cuthbert's Co-operative Association Ltd 1974 IRLR 188, NIRC. In Tayeh v Barchester Healthcare Ltd 2013 ICR D23, CA, the EAT held that where an employee faced disciplinary proceedings relating to more than one charge, a tribunal has to consider whether the employer regarded the charges as being cumulative or standing alone. If the charges were cumulative, in the sense that all of them together formed the principal reason for dismissal, it would be fatal to the fairness of the dismissal if any significant charge were found to have been taken into account without reasonable grounds. If, however, each charge stood on its own – for example, independent acts of gross misconduct each meriting dismissal – then they would require separate consideration in determining whether it was reasonable to dismiss. It might be reasonable to dismiss for one of the charges even if it were not reasonable to dismiss for the other (if, for example, one had been properly investigated but the other had not). The Court of Appeal upheld the EAT's decision and dismissed the appeal.

3.20 It will be different if the employer simply categorises the same matters in two different ways as reasons for dismissal. In Shakespeare and anor v National Coal Board, unreported 30.3.88, CA, two miners were dismissed for aggressive and threatening behaviour towards colleagues who had worked during the miners' strike. The NCB gave as reasons for dismissal contraventions of S.90 of the Mines and Quarries Act 1954 and Reg 9 of the General Duties and Conduct Regulations 1956. It was later conceded that S.90 was not a proper ground for dismissal and had been cited in error. It was argued that since it was unknown whether or not S.90 formed the principal reason for dismissal, the NCB had failed to show a valid reason for dismissal. The Court of Appeal rejected this argument, saying that it was perfectly clear what the reason for dismissal was – the alleged conduct of the two miners. The fact that the NCB had tried to pin two different labels on it was immaterial. Therefore, the Court of Appeal upheld the tribunal's decision that the dismissals were fair.

3.21 Constructive dismissal

Constructive dismissals can pose problems for employers when explaining their reasons for dismissal. When an employee claims that he or she has been unfairly constructively dismissed, there has not in fact been any 'dismissal' at all by the employer. The employee has resigned as a result of the employer's fundamental breach of contract and a kind of legal fiction converts this into a dismissal. However, despite the fact that the employer has not expressly dismissed the employee it must still show the reason for dismissal.

In this situation, the reason for dismissal is the reason for which the employer breached the contract of employment – see Lord Justice Browne-Wilkinson in Berriman v Delabole Slate Ltd 1985 ICR 546, CA. Typically, the employer's reason for dismissal will be SOSR – see Chapter 8, 'Some other substantial reason'. For example, in Genower v Ealing, Hammersmith and Hounslow Area Health Authority 1980 IRLR 297, EAT, the employer moved G to a different job in breach of contract. The reason for doing so was SOSR – the fact that the employer was carrying out a reorganisation of the business. Since the tribunal had found that the employer had good reason for moving staff around and that it had adopted a fair procedure, the EAT upheld the tribunal's decision that the dismissal was fair.

3.22 If an employer does not attempt to show a potentially fair reason at all in a constructive dismissal case but instead simply relies on the argument that there was no dismissal, a tribunal will be under no obligation to investigate the reason for dismissal (or its reasonableness) for itself – Derby City Council v Marshall 1979 ICR 731, EAT. This essentially means that the dismissal, if shown, will be automatically unfair because no reason for dismissal has been given.

Therefore, it will always be the safest course for employers to plead a reason for dismissal even if they are denying that the employee was ever dismissed – i.e. denying that they were in fundamental breach of contract. When setting out its grounds of resistance in the response form (ET3), the employer should start by denying that the employee was dismissed, setting out the grounds for so doing. It should then put forward an alternative ground of resistance, i.e. on the basis that the employee was dismissed, using some form of words such as: 'Alternatively, if, which is denied, the claimant was dismissed, the dismissal was for some other substantial reason justifying dismissal and was not unfair in all the circumstances.' Tribunals often do find constructive dismissals to be fair, but only if the employer has shown the reason for dismissal and is found to have acted reasonably.

Reason must apply at time of dismissal   3.23
In determining the reason for a dismissal, the tribunal may only take account of those facts (or beliefs) that were known to the employer at the time of the dismissal. This means that no account will be taken of matters coming to light or occurring after the dismissal has taken place – W Devis and Sons Ltd v Atkins 1977 ICR 662, HL. Thus, if an employee is dismissed on the employer's whim for no reason at all, the dismissal will not be made retrospectively fair if the employer later finds that the employee had been engaged in long-standing and large-scale embezzlement from the company that would have amply justified the dismissal if it had been discovered earlier. But such matters will be very relevant in assessing compensation – see Chapter 16, 'Compensatory awards: adjustments', under '"Just and equitable" reductions – misconduct not known to employer at date of dismissal'.

That said, where an employee is dismissed with notice the dismissal does not take place until the notice expires, so a tribunal may take account of events which occurred during the notice period, as well as the reason stated in the notice, in order to establish the real reason for dismissal – Parkinson v March Consulting Ltd 1998 ICR 276, CA. In Williamson v Alcan (UK) Ltd 1978 ICR 104, EAT, the employee was dismissed because of his chronic ill health, but there was medical evidence from a specialist that he had made a spontaneous recovery during the notice period. The case was remitted to a different tribunal to reconsider in light of the new evidence. In doing so, the EAT stated that if – after the date notice of dismissal was given and before the contract had actually come to an end – the employer acquired information which would indicate that it ought not to have dismissed the employee, that dismissal could well become unfair if it did not withdraw the notice.

That case was followed in Stacey v Babcock Power Ltd 1986 ICR 221, EAT,   3.24
where the employee was fairly dismissed for redundancy with three months' notice. During the notice period the employer obtained a new contract for which a number of new workers were recruited. However, the dismissed employee was not offered a job. The EAT held that the events during the notice period turned what was initially a fair dismissal into an unfair one. Similarly, in South Tyneside Council v Ward EAT 0358/10 the EAT held that the tribunal had erred in treating the unfairness of W's dismissal as standing or falling at the date when notice was given in October 2007. In doing so, it had 'exclude[d] the possibility of a dismissal, which was potentially unfair when the clock of notice was activated, becoming nevertheless fair by the time the clock stop[ped]'.

Evidence of events after dismissal may, exceptionally, serve as corroboration of an employer's reason for dismissal. In W Devis and Sons Ltd v Atkins 1976 ICR 196, QBD, Mr Justice Phillips gave the example of an employee dismissed for drunkenness at work and thought that subsequent evidence of habitual insobriety would be relevant in corroborating evidence of earlier drunkenness.

3.25 An employer cannot use information obtained during an internal appeal hearing against dismissal to substitute a different reason for dismissal – Monie v Coral Racing Ltd 1981 ICR 109, CA. However, the House of Lords held in West Midlands Co-operative Society Ltd v Tipton 1986 ICR 192, HL, that information revealed in the course of an internal appeal that relates to the original reason for dismissal should be taken into account when considering the fairness of that dismissal, irrespective of whether the internal appeal takes place before or after the dismissal has been effected. This case is discussed further under 'Reasonableness of dismissal – reasonableness test applies at the time of dismissal' and 'Fairness of internal procedure – internal appeals' below. (For more information on internal appeals, see Chapter 6, 'Conduct' under 'Disciplinary proceedings – right of appeal'.)

3.26 Retirement

Following legislative changes in 2011, 'retirement' is no longer a potentially fair reason for dismissal under S.98(2) ERA. Thus, an employer wishing to fairly dismiss an employee as a result of his or her advancing age will need to show that the reason for dismissal falls within one of the remaining five potentially fair reasons for dismissal contained in S.98(1) and (2) (see 'Reason for dismissal' above), and that the dismissal was reasonable in all the circumstances under S.98(4). In other words, the dismissal is treated in the same way as any other dismissal.

It is likely that in the majority of retirement dismissal cases employers will put forward either capability or SOSR as the reason for dismissal. The former would apply where, for example, the employer considers that due to advancing age the employee is no longer capable of performing to the required standard. It must be stressed, however, that an employer's assertion that an employee is no longer sufficiently capable is likely to be subjected to a high degree of scrutiny and an employer who dismisses an employee without undertaking an assessment of his or her capabilities is surely heading for a finding of unfair dismissal. A full consideration of capability dismissals can be found in Chapter 4, 'Capability and qualifications'. In addition, if the employee's performance is affected by an age-related illness, the employer should have regard to the matters considered in Chapter 5, 'Ill health'. An employer is likely to rely on SOSR as the reason for dismissal where dismissal is in accordance with a compulsory retirement policy. This is discussed in Chapter 8, 'Some other substantial reason', under 'Retirement dismissals'.

Industrial pressure to dismiss 3.27

An employer can be faced with a situation in which the workforce demands, for whatever reason, that a certain employee be dismissed, and backs up this demand by taking, or threatening to take, industrial action. S.107 ERA states that in such a case an employer who responds by dismissing the employee in question will not be able to rely on the industrial pressure as the reason for the dismissal if the employee subsequently brings a claim before a tribunal. Questions as to the main reason for dismissal, and whether it was reasonable to dismiss for that reason, will be decided as if no such pressure had been exerted.

Section 107, therefore, creates a legal fiction whereby the real reason for dismissal has to be ignored. So, if the only reason for the dismissal the employer can show is pressure from industrial action, the tribunal is bound to find the dismissal unfair because the employer has failed to establish a potentially fair reason as required by S.98(1) ERA. Thus, in Hazells Offset Ltd v Luckett 1977 IRLR 430, EAT, a studio manager was dismissed because union representatives indicated to the employer that they would not work with him. The EAT agreed with the tribunal that the real reason for the dismissal was union pressure accompanied by threats of industrial action. But S.107 prevented the employer from saying so and prevented the tribunal from taking account of the real reason for dismissal. Since the real reason could not be put forward, the employer was unable to show any reason at all and the dismissal was therefore unfair.

If, however, the employer had another reason for dismissal – even if it was not **3.28** the principal reason – the tribunal will ignore the industrial pressure and determine the fairness of the dismissal on the merits of the subsidiary reason. But the very fact that it was a subsidiary reason may mean that it is unlikely to have had sufficient bearing on the decision to dismiss to make the decision for the subsidiary reason fair.

For further information on industrial pressure to dismiss, see IDS Employment Law Handbook, 'Industrial Action' (2010), Chapter 10, 'Industrial pressure to dismiss'.

Written reasons for dismissal 3.29

Dismissed employees with two years' continuous service have the right to ask their employers for a written statement giving particulars of the reasons for their dismissal – S.92 ERA. These statements are admissible in tribunal proceedings as evidence of the employer's reasons for dismissal. Employees dismissed while they are pregnant or during ordinary or additional maternity or adoption leave are entitled to such a statement without having to request it and regardless of their length of service – see Chapter 19, 'Written reasons for dismissal', for further details.

3.30 ## Reasonableness of dismissal

Once an employer has shown a potentially fair reason for dismissal, the tribunal must go on to decide whether the dismissal for that reason was fair or unfair. This involves deciding whether the employer acted reasonably or unreasonably in dismissing for the reason given in accordance with S.98(4). That provision states: 'the determination of the question whether the dismissal is fair or unfair (having regard to the reason shown by the employer) – (a) depends on whether in the circumstances (including the size and administrative resources of the employer's undertaking) the employer acted reasonably or unreasonably in treating it as a sufficient reason for dismissing the employee, and (b) shall be determined in accordance with equity and the substantial merits of the case'.

It is for the *tribunal* to determine whether an employer acted reasonably under S.98(4) and not for a party to concede or agree – Adama v Partnerships in Care Ltd EAT 0047/14. There, A, a nurse at a care home, was dismissed for gross misconduct after his employer, PIC Ltd, found that he had used excessive force against one of the patients. During cross-examination at the tribunal hearing, A conceded that dismissal was appropriate if the allegations against him were proved. The tribunal dismissed A's claim but, in light of his concession, did not address the question of the fairness of his dismissal in its judgment. The EAT held that its failure to do so was a fundamental error. The assessment of reasonableness under S.98(4) was a mandatory determination for the tribunal to make and not for a party to concede or agree. The EAT remitted the case to a differently constituted tribunal to consider the issue.

3.31 As S.98(4) makes clear, it is not enough that the employer has a reason that is capable of justifying dismissal. The tribunal must be satisfied that, in all the circumstances, the employer was actually justified in dismissing for that reason. In this regard, there is no burden of proof on either party and the issue of whether the dismissal was reasonable is a neutral one for the tribunal to decide – Boys and Girls Welfare Society v Macdonald 1997 ICR 693, EAT. Thus in Makro Self Service Wholesalers Ltd v Rees EAT 0559/07, where R was dismissed for sexual harassment at work, the EAT held that a tribunal had erred in law by finding that the employer had failed to establish that there were reasonable grounds for believing that R was guilty of the alleged misconduct, since this wrongly placed the burden of proof on the employer.

Where an employment tribunal considers the S.98(4) question of fairness in respect of a reason different to that found to have been behind the dismissal, this will amount to a misdirection and the EAT will usually remit the case (to the same or a different tribunal). This happened in Secretary of State for Justice v Norridge and anor EAT 0443/13 where, following a disciplinary investigation into allegations that she had attended a rugby match and been socialising during her sickness absence, N was dismissed for gross misconduct. In subsequent proceedings for unfair dismissal, an employment tribunal found that the real reason for N's dismissal was her conduct during the disciplinary investigation itself, as opposed to the original disciplinary charges against her. However, it proceeded to consider the question of fairness under S.98(4) by reference to the original charges, finding that N's dismissal was unfair because no reasonable employer could have concluded that the allegations against N were proven without obtaining specific medical evidence as to the nature of her condition. On appeal the EAT held that the tribunal had erred in law by failing to apply the test of fairness to the reason it had found for dismissal. However, it could not conclude that a finding of unfair dismissal would inevitably follow: whether or not dismissal was fair would depend on an analysis of the circumstances surrounding N's conduct during the disciplinary process. The case was therefore remitted to the tribunal to decide this point anew.

3.32 Whether or not an employer has acted reasonably is not a question of law. The wording of S.98(4) has the effect of giving tribunals a wide discretion to base their decisions on the facts of the case before them and in the light of good industrial relations practice – Union of Construction, Allied Trades and Technicians v Brain 1981 ICR 542, CA. But while the question is essentially one of fact, the appellate courts have nevertheless developed certain general principles, some of which have crystallised into principles of law. Chapters 4 to 8 deal with the different potentially fair grounds for dismissal whose fairness is determined under S.98(4) and the principles that are applied in those particular contexts, i.e. capability and qualifications, ill health, conduct, statutory ban and SOSR.

Focus on employer, not employee
3.33

An important point to note about the reasonableness test is that it is the employer's conduct which the tribunal has to assess, not the unfairness or injustice to the employee. Two examples:

- **Chubb Fire Security Ltd v Harper** 1983 IRLR 311, EAT: H was dismissed for refusing to accept a considerable drop in income on the reorganisation of his employer's business. A tribunal decided that the employer had acted unreasonably. The EAT held that the tribunal had applied S.98(4) incorrectly. It had made no finding as to the advantages to the employer of the reorganisation and the reasonableness of its implementation and appeared to have concentrated its approach on the reasonableness of H's belief that the change to his terms and conditions would be disadvantageous to him. It had erred in not asking the right question — did the employer act reasonably in dismissing H for his refusal to accept the new term? In answering that question the tribunal should have considered whether the employer was acting reasonably in deciding that the advantages to the company of implementing the proposed reorganisation outweighed any disadvantage which H might suffer. The mere fact that an employee is reasonable in refusing disadvantageous changes does not, therefore, mean that an employer is unreasonable in dismissing for that refusal

- **Garside and Laycock Ltd v Booth** 2011 IRLR 735, EAT: G and L Ltd was undergoing trading difficulties and asked its employees to accept a 5 per cent reduction in pay. B was one of only two employees, of more than 80 in total, who refused and he was dismissed. The tribunal decided that G and L Ltd had established SOSR as the ground for B's dismissal but that, under S.98(4), it had been unreasonable to dismiss him. Among other things, it found that it was reasonable for B to seek to maintain terms and conditions which he had enjoyed for many years and, in particular, not to agree to a significant reduction in pay in favour of an uncertain bonus scheme. The EAT held that this finding amounted to an error of law. The tribunal had assessed the reasonableness of the decision by asking what it was reasonable for the employee to do. That was the reverse of the statutory question that ought to be asked under S.98(4), i.e. whether the *employer* had acted reasonably or unreasonably in treating the reason as a sufficient reason for dismissing the employee. The focus of the tribunal's attention must be on the reasoning and reasonableness of the employer and not on what it is reasonable or unreasonable for the employee to do. It may well be – and indeed was generally to be hoped and expected – that the decision of an employer, in order to be reasonable, will take account of whether the employee him or herself regards it as reasonable or unreasonable; but that is very different from saying that the decision depends upon what the employee thinks is reasonable or unreasonable.

3.34 As the Harper case (above) demonstrates, injustice to the employee is not completely ignored and will be balanced against the benefits gained by the employer when considering whether the employer acted reasonably. However, in another case on similar facts – Richmond Precision Engineering Ltd v Pearce 1985 IRLR 179, EAT – the EAT stated that the task of weighing the advantages to the employer against the disadvantages to the employee is merely one factor which tribunals have to take into account when asking whether the employer acted reasonably. In that case, the tribunal should also have considered whether the offer to P of less favourable terms was one which a reasonable employer could have made in the circumstances faced by RPE Ltd and whether RPE Ltd had acted unreasonably in treating P's refusal of the offer as a reason for dismissing him.

It is important to note that the *potential* consequences to the employer can be taken into account when deciding whether dismissal was fair. In Wincanton plc v Atkinson and anor EAT 0040/11 the two claimants were employed as lorry drivers by W plc. A routine check revealed that they had been driving with lapsed HGV licences for the previous one month and five months respectively. They were dismissed because of the potential adverse consequences to W plc, which included criminal prosecution, loss of insurance coverage, loss of operator's licence and damage to business, although no such adverse consequences had actually occurred. The tribunal noted that the consequences of driving a lorry loaded with dangerous goods without insurance were 'horrific to contemplate'. However, it concluded that no reasonable management weighing the character of the misconduct against the actual risk and consequences could have reached the decision to dismiss. It accordingly found the dismissal unfair but reduced the claimants' compensation by 60 per cent for contributory fault.

Allowing W plc's appeal, the EAT held that the tribunal had erred in not **3.35** attaching sufficient importance to the seriousness of the damage that W plc could have suffered as a result of the claimants' failure to renew their licences and by focusing instead on the lack of actual damage. The tribunal's approach would mean that a driver could never be fairly dismissed for driving after negligently consuming excess alcohol, as long as the journey was safely completed. Given the seriousness of the potential consequences of the claimants' conduct in the instant case, it had to be concluded that dismissal fell well within the range of reasonable responses.

Tribunals must not substitute their own views **3.36**
The test of whether or not the employer acted reasonably is usually expressed as an objective one – i.e. tribunals must use their own collective wisdom as industrial juries to determine 'the way in which a reasonable employer in those circumstances, in that line of business, would have behaved' – NC Watling and Co Ltd v Richardson 1978 ICR 1049, EAT. Nonetheless, there is also a subjective element involved inasmuch as tribunals must also take account of the honest beliefs of the employer at the time of the dismissal.

What tribunals must not do is put themselves in the position of the employer and consider what they themselves would have done in the circumstances. They must not usurp a function which is properly that of management. What a tribunal must decide is not what it would have done if it had been management, but whether the employer acted reasonably – Grundy (Teddington) Ltd v Willis 1976 ICR 323, QBD. As the Court of Appeal explained in Foley v Post Office; HSBC Bank plc (formerly Midland Bank plc) v Madden 2000 ICR 1283, CA, although members of the tribunal can substitute their decision for that of the employer, that decision must not be reached by a process of substituting themselves for the employer and forming an opinion of what they would have done had they been the employer.

In London Ambulance Service NHS Trust v Small 2009 IRLR 563, CA, the **3.37** Court of Appeal held that a tribunal had slipped into the 'substitution mindset' and wrongly substituted its own view for that of the employer regarding the reasonableness of S's dismissal for misconduct. When determining the issue of

69

liability, the tribunal should have confined its consideration of the facts to those found by the Trust at the time of dismissal. Instead, it had referred to its own findings of fact about S's conduct, including facts that had been disputed at the disciplinary hearing. Although the tribunal was bound to come to its own view for the purpose of deciding the extent to which S contributed to his dismissal, that was a different issue. The decision on contributory fault was one for the tribunal to make if it decided that the dismissal was unfair. However, the decision to dismiss was for the Trust to make. Lord Justice Mummery suggested that, as a general rule, it might be better practice for the tribunal to keep its findings of facts relevant to the employer's decision to dismiss separate from its findings of facts that are only relevant to other issues such as contributory fault.

Two further cases where the tribunal adopted the wrong approach:

* **Enable Care and Home Support Ltd v Pearson** EAT 0366/09: an employment tribunal examined how 'a reasonable employer' would have regarded the charges against P that led to her dismissal. In doing so, the EAT held that it had wrongly substituted its own view of the seriousness of the charges for that of the employer. The question was not whether the diluted reason as found by the tribunal was sufficient for dismissal, but whether the employer's reason was sufficient

* **CRO Ports London Ltd v Wiltshire** EAT 0344/14: the EAT held that the tribunal had wrongly reached its finding of unfair dismissal based on the evidence available to it instead of the facts available to the employer at the time of dismissal. Its conclusion that further investigation by the employer would have uncovered factors that placed the employee's conduct in a different context had derived from the evidence before the tribunal, not that before the employer. The tribunal had failed to see the significance of the employee's admissions of fault from the employer's perspective at the time. Given that the employee, who held a supervisory role, had admitted he knew that a dangerous procedure was used and had done nothing about it, it was hard to see why the employer's decision to limit the scope of its investigation did not fall within the range of reasonable responses. The matter was remitted to a differently constituted tribunal for fresh consideration.

3.38 By way of contrast, in Bowater v Northwest London Hospitals NHS Trust 2011 IRLR 331, CA, the Court of Appeal overturned an EAT decision that the tribunal had wrongly substituted its view for that of the employer. The Court of Appeal held that the tribunal had not impermissibly substituted its own view by having regard to how 'a large proportion of the population' would view a lewd comment, on which the dismissal was based. B, a staff nurse, was dismissed for gross misconduct following a comment she made while straddling the naked genitals of a patient who was suffering from a fit, the comment being: 'It's been a few months since I have been in this position with a man underneath me.' Six weeks later she was dismissed for gross misconduct, despite her unblemished disciplinary record and the fact that no member of the public, or the patient, was aware of the comment. The tribunal held that B was unfairly dismissed, finding that, at worst, the comment could have been described as lewd and that a 'large proportion of the population' would have considered it to be merely humorous. The EAT allowed the employer's appeal, holding that the tribunal had taken into account an irrelevant factor with its 'large proportion of the population' test. Instead, it should have considered how a reasonable NHS Trust would have treated that comment. B appealed. The Court of Appeal held that it was evident that the tribunal had in fact applied the correct 'band of reasonable responses' test, rather than imposed its own view of what it would have been appropriate for the employer to do in the circumstances. It was common ground that the remark was intended to be humorous. The EAT had been overcritical and the Court of Appeal agreed with the majority of the tribunal that summary dismissal in the circumstances was wholly unreasonable. It noted that it is important in such cases that the EAT pay 'proper respect' to the decision of the tribunal, to which Parliament has entrusted the responsibility of making difficult and borderline decisions in relation to the fairness of a dismissal. The Court of Appeal also noted that the EAT must not, under the guise of perversity, substitute its own judgment for that of the tribunal.

Similar concerns were expressed by Lord Justice Mummery in Brent London Borough Council v Fuller 2011 ICR 806, CA. In restoring the decision of an employment tribunal that F had been unfairly dismissed, Mummery LJ cautioned that an appellate body, be it the EAT or the Court of Appeal, must be on its guard against making the very same legal error as the tribunal in that case stood accused of making: namely, substituting its own subjective view of the dismissal. Mummery LJ further observed that while a tribunal's judgment should be 'read carefully to see if it has in fact correctly applied the law which it said was applicable', the scrutiny must not be 'so fussy that it produces pernickety critiques'. The EAT in the instant case had placed too much emphasis on the language of the tribunal's decision and had consequently overlooked the fact that it had correctly directed itself that it must not substitute its subjective view for that of the employer.

3.39 The guidance given by Mummery LJ in the Fuller case was reiterated in Newbound v Thames Water Utilities Ltd 2015 EWCA Civ 677, CA. In that case, N was responsible for inspecting certain types of equipment in the sewers. At one such inspection, he entered a sewer without breathing apparatus in contravention of a new provision in TWU Ltd's health and safety policy. Despite his 34 years' service with a clean disciplinary record, N was dismissed for gross misconduct. The tribunal found his dismissal to be unfair but the EAT substituted a finding that it had been fair. The Court of Appeal noted that the issue on appeal was not whether the EAT's decision was correct but whether the tribunal had made an error of law. The Court held that the tribunal had been entitled to find that no reasonable employer would have dismissed in the circumstances.

Key findings of fact made by the tribunal included that the change to TWU Ltd's health and safety policy was a comparatively new one and employees had not been trained in its significance. Furthermore, N had previously exercised his discretion as to whether to use breathing apparatus and these decisions had not resulted in disciplinary action as TWU Ltd had been prepared to rely on his experience. The Court emphasised that it was important not to overlook the requirement in S.98(4) that tribunals must decide whether an employer has acted reasonably or unreasonably in deciding to dismiss 'in accordance with equity and the substantial merits of the case'. In the Court's view, this indicated that Parliament did not intend a tribunal's consideration of a case like this to be a matter of procedural box-ticking. TWU Ltd was attempting to stretch the band of reasonable responses to an infinite width.

Tribunals should be careful not to substitute their own judgment where an employee is dismissed for breach of an employer's policy, such as a substance abuse policy. They should not attempt to determine whether the employee was actually in breach. Instead they should assess whether the employer's interpretation and application of the policy was reasonable in the circumstances – BP Chemicals v Fitzpatrick EAT 67/05.

3.40 **'Band (or range) of reasonable responses' test**
Employers often have at their disposal a range of reasonable responses to matters such as the misconduct or incapability of an employee, which may span summary dismissal down to an informal warning. It is inevitable that different employers will choose different options. In recognition of this fact, and in order to provide a 'standard' of reasonableness that tribunals can apply, the 'band of reasonable responses' approach was formulated. This requires tribunals to ask: did the employer's action fall within the band (or range) of reasonable responses open to an employer?

This approach was approved by the Court of Appeal in British Leyland (UK) Ltd v Swift 1981 IRLR 91, CA, where Lord Denning MR stated: 'The correct test is: Was it reasonable for the employers to dismiss him? If no reasonable employer would have dismissed him, then the dismissal was unfair. But if a reasonable employer might reasonably have dismissed him, then the dismissal was fair. It must be remembered that in all these cases there is a band of reasonableness, within which one employer might reasonably take one view: another quite reasonably take a different view.'

3.41 The test was applied in Iceland Frozen Foods Ltd v Jones 1983 ICR 17, EAT, where a tribunal had phrased its finding of unfair dismissal as follows: '*in our view* neither of the applicant's faults, either singly or taken together, came anywhere near being sufficiently serious to make it reasonable to dismiss him applying the provisions of [S.98(4)]' (our stress). The EAT held that the tribunal had misdirected itself by substituting its own opinion for the objective test of the band of reasonable responses. Mr Justice Browne-Wilkinson summarised the law concisely and his summary is frequently quoted and applied by tribunals:

'We consider that the authorities establish that in law the correct approach for the... tribunal to adopt in answering the question posed by [S.98(4)] is as follows:

(1) the starting point should always be the words of [S.98(4)] themselves;

(2) in applying the section [a] tribunal must consider the reasonableness of the employer's conduct, not simply whether they (the members of the... tribunal) consider the dismissal to be fair;

(3) in judging the reasonableness of the employer's conduct [a] tribunal must not substitute its decision as to what was the right course to adopt for that of the employer;

(4) in many (though not all) cases there is a band of reasonable responses to the employee's conduct within which one employer might reasonably take one view, another quite reasonably take another;

(5) the function of the... tribunal, as an industrial jury, is to determine whether in the particular circumstances of each case the decision to dismiss the employee fell within the band of reasonable responses which a reasonable employer might have adopted. If the dismissal falls within the band the dismissal is fair: if the dismissal falls outside the band it is unfair.'

3.42 Following a number of cases that challenged the primacy of the 'band of reasonable responses' test, it was emphatically reaffirmed by the Court of Appeal in Foley v Post Office; HSBC Bank plc (formerly Midland Bank plc) v Madden 2000 ICR 1283, CA, where Lord Justice Mummery confirmed that the test as expounded in Iceland Frozen Foods remained binding on employment tribunals. He explained further that cases involving extreme facts did not render the 'range of reasonable responses' test perverse or unhelpful. It is simply that the approach will not be required in every case. He said: 'There will be cases in which there is no band or range to consider. If, for example, an employee, without good cause, deliberately sets fire to his employer's factory and it is burnt to the ground, dismissal is the only reasonable response. If an employee is dismissed for politely saying "good morning" to his line manager, that would be an unreasonable response. But in between these extreme cases there will be cases where there is room for reasonable disagreement among reasonable employers as to whether dismissal for the particular misconduct is a reasonable or an unreasonable response. In those cases it is helpful for the tribunal to consider "the range of reasonable responses".'

More recently, the EAT in Enable Care & Home Support Ltd v Pearson EAT 0366/09 explained the test thus (in the context of a misconduct dismissal): 'if across the spectrum of reasonable employers' sanctions some would dismiss and some would impose a sanction short of dismissal, then dismissal falls within the band and is fair. The dismissal will only be unfair if dismissal is a sanction outside that spectrum; that no reasonable employer would have dismissed the employee for the employer's reason.'

3.43 Dismissal does not have to be the last resort before it can fall within the range of reasonable responses. In Quadrant Catering Ltd v Smith EAT 0362/10 the tribunal directed itself that an employer should view dismissal as a last rather than a first resort and that it will only be in serious cases of misconduct supported by no doubt as to the facts that a dismissal will be justified. In other circumstances, a warning would be the appropriate sanction. The EAT overturned the tribunal's finding of unfair dismissal (and remitted the matter to a fresh tribunal for reconsideration), holding that it had erred in directing itself that dismissal was a last resort and that had materially influenced its conclusion that dismissal fell outside the range of reasonable responses.

A case where dismissal fell just inside the range of reasonable responses:

- **Rawley v National Car Parks ET Case** No.2205017/06: R and some of her colleagues were invited to a drinks party by Westminster City Council, which was in negotiations for a contract with NCP. A colleague had concerns about R's behaviour during the party and rang her manager, who texted R's mobile phone saying she needed to go home and he would speak to her the next day. She replied that she would go when she wished. When he advised her strongly to go home, she sent a text saying, 'sack me I don't care'. She was called to a disciplinary hearing, where she admitted to being 'happily drunk and the life and soul of the party'. She was summarily dismissed for acting in a discourteous manner to a client and bringing NCP into disrepute. The tribunal considered that the decision to dismiss was somewhat severe and that it would have imposed a written warning. However, it reminded itself that it could not substitute its view for that of the employer. It held that the decision to dismiss was close to the boundary of the range of reasonable responses, but was just within it.

3.44 In Royal Bank of Scotland Group plc v Wilson EAT 0363/08 the EAT cautioned against the use of emotive language by tribunals when considering the reasonableness of dismissal. W, a personal mortgage adviser, had arranged a mortgage with a customer on behalf of her son and daughter-in-law. Without seeing the couple or obtaining their signed consent, W submitted an electronic mortgage application to the bank's mortgage department with instructions that, contrary to its normal practice, it was not to withdraw the application fee from the prospective mortgagors' account. However, the department did withdraw the fee from the account. The couple decided not to proceed with the application and complained that the fee had been withdrawn without their consent. W was subsequently dismissed for gross misconduct. The tribunal held that this fell 'well outside' the range of reasonable responses, being a 'gross over-reaction' to a technical error, which had no serious consequences. The tribunal had 'little sympathy' for the bank, considering that it only had itself to blame for any embarrassment which arose.

In the EAT's judgment, the tribunal's reasoning demonstrated that, while endorsing the 'range of reasonable responses' test, in reality it had substituted its own decision for that of the employer. The tribunal's conclusion that W's was 'an error of a technical nature' and that he did no more than 'cut a bureaucratic corner' was plainly not how the bank viewed the matter. The question for the tribunal was whether it was reasonable for the bank to take the view that it was a serious and not a technical matter, and this depended, at least in part, on whether the bank had brought home to W by its training and procedures what his role was and why the bank placed importance on the training and procedures it had implemented. The EAT noted the 'unusually robust' language used by the tribunal and observed that a tribunal is always wise to look with particular care at its reasoning and findings of fact before it expresses criticism in emotive language. Expressions of indignation were not a substitute for, and were often inimical to, careful findings of fact and application of the law.

As these cases show, the application of the range of reasonable responses test is **3.45** not an exact science and, certainly in borderline cases, there is scope for different tribunals to apply the test differently. Therefore the decisions they reach will be difficult to challenge unless the tribunal has, while purporting to apply the test, clearly substituted its own judgment – see further 'Appeals to EAT' below.

Note that the 'range of reasonable responses' test applies not only to the decision to dismiss but also to the procedure by which that decision is reached – J Sainsbury plc v Hitt 2003 ICR 111, CA; Whitbread plc (t/a Whitbread Medway Inns) v Hall 2001 ICR 699, CA (see the section on 'Fairness of internal procedure' below, under 'Procedural fairness integral to reasonableness test – range of reasonable responses test applies' below for further details). It may also apply to lesser sanctions where these amount to a fundamental breach of contract entitling the employee to resign and claim unfair dismissal. In Blanchard v B&Q plc ET Case No.1200935/11, for example, B was employed by B&Q plc as a customer services adviser and forklift truck driver in its Watford store. He had an accident in the store while driving a forklift truck near customer entrance gates. The gates open automatically to allow customers into the store. Due to a malfunction, they also opened automatically when approached from within the store, although they were not meant to do so. This was well known to B and the other forklift truck drivers. Despite this knowledge, B nevertheless drove near the gates in such a way that they swung open and hit the rear of his truck. He had been trying to drive his truck in such a way that the doors would not open but had misjudged the angle at which to do so. B was dismissed for gross misconduct; namely, a serious breach of health and safety

75

and forklift truck procedures. Following an appeal B was reinstated subject to the imposition of a final warning, immediate and indefinite removal of his forklift truck licence and transfer to a different location. B regarded these conditions as excessively harsh and he resigned. The tribunal upheld his claim for unfair constructive dismissal. It was clear from the CCTV footage that classifying the accident as serious misconduct meriting summary dismissal was outside the band of reasonable responses. B's driving could not be described as reckless and nor had he wilfully disobeyed any instructions. Although the decision to dismiss was reversed on appeal, the unjustified imposition of the final written warning was itself capable of amounting to a repudiatory breach of contract. This was further compounded by the unjustified indefinite removal of B's licence and by transferring him to another location that B&Q plc knew would involve a longer and more inconvenient journey. The disciplinary sanctions were not ones that a reasonable manager would have imposed.

3.46 Dismissal for gross misconduct not inevitably fair. Although dismissal for gross misconduct will often fall within the range of reasonable responses, this is not invariably so. This was made clear by the EAT in Brito-Babapulle v Ealing Hospital NHS Trust 2013 IRLR 854, EAT, which overturned an employment tribunal's decision because it was based upon that false premise. The EAT noted that the tribunal's approach gave no scope for consideration of whether mitigating factors rendered the dismissal unfair, notwithstanding the gross misconduct. Such factors might include the employee's long service, the consequences of dismissal and any previous unblemished record. The tribunal was suggesting that the existence of gross misconduct – which is often a contractual issue – is determinative of whether a dismissal is unfair, whereas the test for unfair dismissal depends on the separate consideration called for under S.98 ERA.

The decision in Brito-Babapulle is reflected in the Acas guide, 'Discipline and grievances at work', which states that, when deciding whether a disciplinary penalty is appropriate and what form it should take, consideration should be given to, among other things, the employee's disciplinary record (including current warnings), general work record, work experience, position and length of service; any special circumstances that might make it appropriate to adjust the severity of the penalty; and whether the proposed penalty is reasonable in view of all the circumstances.

3.47 Facts or beliefs known to employer

In determining the reasonableness of a dismissal, the tribunal can only take account of those facts (or beliefs) that were known to those who took the actual decision to dismiss (after reasonable investigation). In this regard, the Court of Appeal in Orr v Milton Keynes Council 2011 ICR 704, CA, held (by a majority) that an employer cannot know everything known to its employees. It therefore upheld the EAT's decision that an employee was not unfairly dismissed when information that would have mitigated his misconduct was

76

known to his line manager but not to the manager who decided on dismissal. O was dismissed following a disciplinary hearing, which he did not attend, to consider an incident where he was rude to his manager. The investigating officer, C, found that the rudeness amounted to gross misconduct and O was dismissed. C did not know that the argument at the centre of the incident had been caused by O's manager's underhand attempt to change O's working hours and that he had made a racially derogatory comment to O.

The Court of Appeal, by a majority, decided that there could still be a fair dismissal in these circumstances. It rejected O's 'novel' argument that his manager's knowledge of the mitigating circumstances could be attributed to the Council as the employer. When assessing the fairness of a dismissal under S.98, the Court's majority view was that it is the person deputed to carry out the employer's functions whose knowledge or state of mind counts as the employer's knowledge or state of mind – in this case, C. Reasonableness must therefore be considered in the light of that person's investigation and knowledge. To impute C with knowledge of behaviour that he could not reasonably acquire through the appropriate disciplinary procedure would impose a more onerous duty than that set out in S.98. In the majority's view, if the investigation is as thorough as could reasonably be expected, it will support a reasonable belief in the findings, whether or not some information has not been uncovered.

A similar line of argument was advanced by the claimant in Mitchell v St Joseph's **3.48** School EAT 0506/12 and also rejected. M, a school bursar, was dismissed when the board of governors discovered that he had failed to inform it of the school's precarious financial situation. It was an express term of M's contract of employment that he should keep books of account, monitor the school's budget and report the state of the school's financial affairs to the board. The EAT held that dismissal was fair in the circumstances. In particular, it rejected M's argument that, as he had informed two members of the board of some of the issues that were the subject of the gross misconduct charge, the board could not have genuinely believed in his guilt. Under the terms of his contract, M was under a personal duty to report to the board of governors and he had failed to do so. Nor could it be said that disclosure to two members of the board meant that the board as a whole had knowledge of the school's finances. In the Orr case (above) the Court of Appeal had made it clear that knowledge of the circumstances that gave rise to the charge of gross misconduct could not be attributed to the dismissing officer in the course of the investigation. The EAT considered that the same principle applied to the attribution of knowledge at a stage earlier than an investigation into the employee's alleged gross misconduct.

Reasonableness test applies at time of dismissal
3.49

The reasonableness test is based on the facts or beliefs known to the employer *at the time of the dismissal*. (The same applies when determining the actual reason for dismissal – see 'Reason for dismissal – reason must apply at time of dismissal'

77

above.) A dismissal will not be made reasonable by events which occur after the dismissal has taken place – W Devis and Sons Ltd v Atkins 1977 ICR 662, HL.

It is therefore important to establish 'the time of the dismissal'. In Alboni v Ind Coope Retail Ltd 1998 IRLR 131, CA, the Court of Appeal said that the legislation made it plain that a dismissal means the actual termination of employment, not the giving of notice. Thus, when determining the reasonableness of a dismissal, a tribunal must have regard to what occurred between the date the employee was given notice and the date on which dismissal took effect and not simply to the facts known to the employer when notice was given.

3.50 There may be occasions where an employee is summarily dismissed but has a right to an internal appeal. If the appeal is successful, then the employee is retrospectively reinstated as if there were no dismissal, whereas if the appeal is unsuccessful then the dismissal stands. The question of how to treat information gained during an internal appeal was dealt with in West Midlands Co-operative Society Ltd v Tipton 1986 ICR 192, HL. In that case the House of Lords said, in relation to contracts of employment providing an appeals procedure, that both the original and the appellate decision by an employer to dismiss are necessary elements in the overall process of dismissal. To separate them and to consider only one half of the process in determining whether the employer acted reasonably in dismissing an employee is artificial. Therefore, although it would be wrong for an employer to dismiss an employee for a reason that only surfaced during the appeals process, a tribunal should consider facts that came to light during the appeal in considering whether the employer's decision to dismiss was reasonable.

3.51 Size and administrative resources of employer's undertaking
In determining whether the employer acted reasonably in the circumstances, the tribunal must have regard to the 'size and administrative resources of the employer's undertaking' – S.98(4)(a) ERA. There are two situations in which these factors are particularly significant in determining reasonableness:

- when assessing what kind of disciplinary procedure and, particularly, internal appeals machinery is practicable for the employer

- when there is a question as to whether suitable alternative work should have been provided for the employee, for example in redundancy cases or in cases where the employee is no longer capable of doing his or her current job but could perform less onerous tasks.

3.52 Some examples:

- **Royal Naval School v Hughes** 1979 IRLR 383, EAT: a tribunal had criticised a girls' boarding-school for not providing a mechanism to appeal beyond the board of governors who took the decision to dismiss. The EAT thought this criticism unfounded and pointed out that it could be impossible to provide an apparatus for higher appeals in a small organisation

- **Appleyard v FM Smith (Hull) Ltd** 1972 IRLR 19, ET: it was fair to dismiss a maintenance fitter/driver who lost his driving licence in a small firm with only three fitters – although it might not have been in a large firm

- **MacKellar v Bolton** 1979 IRLR 59, EAT: the dismissal of a doctor's receptionist was held to be fair. The EAT pointed out that a GP 'is not armed with an elaborate personnel department and a number of subsidiary commanders between him and [his receptionist]'. Nor, when patients complain, is it reasonable to expect him to arrange a formal disciplinary hearing with witnesses

- **Bevan Harris Ltd (t/a The Clyde Leather Co) v Gair** 1981 IRLR 520, EAT: the dismissal of a foreman on the ground of capability was found to be fair. The EAT held that it was unreasonable, in view of the small size of the business, to expect the employer to demote instead of dismissing, even if an alternative job was available

- **Pickard v Wm Morrison Supermarkets plc** ET Case No.1800162/10: in finding that a freezer operative's dismissal for misconduct was unfair, the tribunal was largely influenced by WMS plc's size and administrative resources.

Size and administrative resources will not, however, excuse a total absence of **3.53** proper procedural steps. In De Grasse v Stockwell Tools Ltd 1992 IRLR 269, EAT, a small firm dismissed a machinist for redundancy with no warning, consultation or consideration of alternative employment. The EAT held that the fact that an employer is a small undertaking may affect the nature or formality of the consultation process – i.e. it may be informal – but it cannot excuse a total lack of consultation.

In GM Packaging (UK) Ltd v Haslem EAT 0259/13 an employment tribunal endorsed a small employer's use of an external HR consultancy to investigate alleged misconduct. The owner of GMP Ltd, M, called in the consultancy because he was involved as a witness in the matters under investigation. The consultant who conducted the investigation recommended dismissal, which M sanctioned. When the employee appealed, a different consultant heard the appeal and recommended rejecting it, M agreed, and the dismissal was upheld. The tribunal considered that this was a reasonable procedure for a small business to follow and rejected the argument that M had, in effect, both decided on dismissal and rejected the appeal himself. The EAT did not interfere with the tribunal's conclusion on appeal.

Equity   3.54
Section 98(4)(b) requires tribunals to determine the reasonableness of a dismissal 'in accordance with equity and the substantial merits of the case'. Equity, in this context, is equivalent to 'fair play'. It is invoked particularly in misconduct cases when a dismissed employee complains that his or her employer

has dealt more leniently with other employees in similar circumstances, although its application is not confined to this scenario.

3.55 **Inconsistent treatment.** Inconsistency of punishment for misconduct may give rise to a finding of unfair dismissal, as the Court of Appeal recognised in Post Office v Fennell 1981 IRLR 221, CA. In that case F had been dismissed for striking a colleague during a quarrel in the canteen. A tribunal found the dismissal unfair, pointing out that the Post Office had acted differently in comparable cases, and ordered re-engagement. In the Court of Appeal Lord Justice Brandon cited the words 'having regard to equity and the substantial merits of the case' (contained in the precursor to S.98(4) ERA) and said: 'It seems to me that the expression "equity" as there used comprehends the concept that employees who misbehave in much the same way should have meted out to them much the same punishment, and it seems to me that [a] tribunal is entitled to say that, where that is not done, and one man is penalised much more heavily than others who have committed similar offences in the past, the employer has not acted reasonably in treating whatever the offence is as a sufficient reason for dismissal.'

Brandon LJ made two further observations. First, it is for the tribunal to decide whether, on the facts, there was sufficient evidence of inconsistent treatment. As he pointed out, the tribunal would have less detailed information regarding other cases allegedly dealt with more leniently by the employer than the information in the case before it. His second point stressed that while a degree of consistency was necessary, there must also be considerable latitude in the way in which an individual employer deals with particular cases.

3.56 Another leading case in this area – Hadjioannou v Coral Casinos Ltd 1981 IRLR 352, EAT – was decided by the EAT within two months of the Court of Appeal's decision in Fennell. The EAT also recognised the importance of consistency of treatment but placed more emphasis on the employer's ability to be flexible in such matters. On the facts of that particular case it was found that there had been no evidence of inconsistent treatment. Nevertheless, and without reference to the Fennell case, the EAT stated that a complaint of unreasonableness by an employee based on inconsistency of treatment would only be relevant in limited circumstances:

- where employees have been led by an employer to believe that certain conduct will not lead to dismissal (see 'Creating "false sense of security"' below)

- where evidence of other cases being dealt with more leniently supports a complaint that the reason stated for dismissal by the employer was not the real reason

- where decisions made by an employer in truly parallel circumstances indicate that it was not reasonable for the employer to dismiss.

The third of these circumstances appears slightly more restrictive than that envisioned in Post Office v Fennell (above), particularly since the EAT added the comment that, in its view, there would not be many cases where the evidence would show truly similar circumstances. The EAT also stressed the danger inherent in attaching too much weight to consistency of treatment when the proper emphasis when applying S.98(4) is on the 'particular circumstances of the individual employee's case'. Moreover, the EAT deprecated the idea of a 'tariff' approach to misconduct cases.

3.57 The EAT's decision in Hadjioannou was subsequently endorsed by the Court of Appeal in Paul v East Surrey District Health Authority 1995 IRLR 305, CA, in a judgment that did not refer to the decision in Post Office v Fennell (above). Nor was Fennell referred to in Securicor Ltd v Smith 1989 IRLR 356, CA, where the Court of Appeal held that where two employees, C and S, were dismissed for the same incident and C was successful on appeal but S was not, the question to be asked was whether the appeal panel's decision was so irrational that no employer could reasonably have accepted it. The Court of Appeal held S's dismissal to be fair on the ground that there was a clear and rational basis for distinguishing between the cases of C and S; namely, that S was more to blame for the incident than C.

The Securicor decision was relied upon by the EAT in London Borough of Harrow v Cunningham 1996 IRLR 256, EAT, a case in which two employees, S and W, undertook a private job for personal gain in breach of the employer's disciplinary code. S was dismissed for gross misconduct whereas W was not. The employer – taking into account W's seven years of service, together with his satisfactory work performance and disciplinary record – felt able to stop short of dismissal and instead issued a final written warning. C, on the other hand, was already subject to a final written warning relating to his conduct. The EAT overturned the tribunal's finding that C's dismissal was unfair because he had been treated differently to W: the tribunal had failed to ask whether the distinction made between the two employees was irrational and had instead substituted its own view for that of the employer.

3.58 The Court of Appeal's decision in Newbound v Thames Water Utilities Ltd 2015 EWCA Civ 677, CA, is an example of a case where there was an unjustified difference in treatment by an employer of two employees involved in the same incident, albeit they were performing different roles. In that case N was responsible for inspecting certain types of equipment in the sewers. At one such inspection, he and a contractor entered a sewer without breathing apparatus contrary to TWU Ltd's health and safety policy. A was the manager in charge of the site who had checked gas readings and not objected to N and the contractor entering the sewer. Following disciplinary hearings, N was dismissed for gross misconduct while A received a written warning. TWU Ltd justified the difference in treatment on the basis that A was relatively inexperienced and had

81

felt pressured to complete the task by more experienced team members, including N, who had 34 years' service. The Court of Appeal held that the employment tribunal had been entitled to find that this was not an appropriate case for disparity in treatment and that N's dismissal was unfair. The Court noted the tribunal's key findings: A was in overall charge of the site; he allowed N and the contractor to enter the sewer twice without breathing apparatus; A was charged with misconduct rather than gross misconduct; A was interviewed as part of the investigation before the disciplinary hearings but N was not; and A received a written warning while N was dismissed. Lord Justice Bean observed that he had 'rarely seen such an obvious case of unjustified disparity'.

Although Post Office v Fennell (above) was not referred to in any of these subsequent cases, they do not contradict it but merely put a different emphasis on the same rule. Employers, while retaining flexibility of response to employee behaviour, have to act reasonably in the sanctions they choose to apply. Any change of punishment policy without warning, any dismissal for faults previously condoned or any unjustified difference in treatment of employees in similar positions will contribute towards making the dismissal unfair.

3.59 Three examples of how the rule has been applied:

- **East Riding of Yorkshire Council v Cowton** EAT 0432/08: C worked as a care worker at a home for adults with severe learning difficulties. In 2006 a complaint was made about her standard of care and she was taken through the employer's capability procedure, by the end of which her capability issues were resolved. However, she was warned that any further issues would be dealt with under the employer's disciplinary procedure. In June 2007 she was invited to a disciplinary meeting to face an allegation that she had given a resident mashed, instead of puréed, potato contrary to what was specified in the resident's care plan, causing her to choke and putting her at risk of further complications. Two other workers had fed mashed food to the same resident and other residents had also wrongly been fed mashed food. The employer dismissed C but did not discipline or dismiss any other worker who had served mashed food. The tribunal held that the dismissal of C was unfair because she had been treated differently to the other workers. The EAT held that the tribunal had wrongly substituted its own view and that it should have asked whether it was reasonable for the employer to have reached the view that C's position was different. Plainly it was, because unlike the other care workers, C had gone through a capability procedure and been expressly warned that any further issues would be dealt with under a disciplinary procedure

- **Epstein v Royal Borough of Windsor and Maidenhead** EAT 0250/07: E and B were lifeguards at a swimming pool. They were both on duty when a swimmer suffered an epileptic fit and nearly drowned. E had assumed from the movement of the swimmer's hands and feet that he was playing a breath-holding game and so took no action. B did not notice the swimmer at all. Luckily one of the swimmer's friends eventually raised the alarm, which caused E to enter the water and assist. E was dismissed for a gross error of judgement whereas B was not even disciplined. The EAT held that it was reasonable for the employer to conclude that B had not been in a position to see the swimmer and therefore was not at fault. Furthermore, even if there had been some failure of omission by B, that would not excuse E's offence of commission and would not render E's dismissal unfair

● **Mist v TK Maxx** ET Case No.1802500/06: M was summarily dismissed for selling counterfeit goods on the employer's premises after being seen placing DVDs in staff pigeon holes and admitting that he had copied DVDs for colleagues. M pointed out that some of his customers were managers – including his own line manager – and others were in responsible posts including the loss prevention team. Moreover, he said that he had been pressured by some staff, including managers, to provide the DVDs. The employer's rules, however, made it clear that employees were responsible for their own actions, and any illegal or wrongful act could not be justified on the basis that it was ordered by a superior. The tribunal held that M could reasonably have been expected to conclude that his actions had been condoned. Regardless of the statement in the employer's rules, it was not in accordance with equity for an employee to be dismissed for conduct in which his own line manager and 16 other managers were actively colluding.

As is clear from the cases above, where several employees are involved in the **3.60** misconduct, employers should weigh up their respective culpability, their individual circumstances and any mitigating/aggravating factors when deciding whether it is reasonable to differentiate between them. For example, acknowledgement of wrongdoing by one employee may justify treating that employee more leniently than another involved in the same incident – Paul v East Surrey District Health Authority 1995 IRLR 305, CA (recently cited by the Court of Appeal in Newbound v Thames Water Utilities Ltd 2015 EWCA Civ 677, CA). This weighing-up exercise should take place before deciding on the penalty to be imposed, otherwise dismissal of only one of the employees is likely to fall outside the range of reasonable responses – see, for example, Jones v Wrekin Housing Trust Ltd ET Case No.2900634/06.

Individual circumstances justifying inconsistent treatment were found to exist in General Mills (Berwick) Ltd v Glowacki EAT 0139/11. There, G was dismissed for a serious breach of health and safety procedures. The previous year another employee, S, had not been dismissed for a breach of procedure so serious that it caused him a debilitating injury. The tribunal concluded that the inconsistent treatment rendered G's dismissal unfair but the EAT overturned that decision on appeal. The tribunal had failed to have proper regard to GM Ltd's unchallenged evidence that, were it not for S's serious injury and

83

consequent absence, he too would have been disciplined and dismissed for gross misconduct. He was, in fact, later dismissed for incapacity. The EAT held that since the difference in circumstances fully explained the difference in treatment and GM Ltd's approach was reasonable in both cases, the only possible conclusion was that G's dismissal was fair.

3.61 Employers can also fall foul of S.98(4) if they attempt to treat employees in a consistent manner but without regard to the circumstances of each individual employee. For example, in Merseyside Passenger Transport Executive v Millington EAT 232/89 M worked on a passenger ferry. During one of his shifts he went to a pub to have lunch. He was joined by two other employees, H and W. The employer had a strict rule that employees should not enter licensed premises while working. A member of management went to the pub and immediately suspended all three employees. There was no suggestion that M was drunk – he had merely gone to the most convenient place to obtain food – but H and W acted in a way consistent with their being drunk. On the following day, all three were summarily dismissed. Management believed that it risked an unfair dismissal claim if it did not treat all three alike for breaching the same rule. However, the tribunal took the view that there were enough differences between M's conduct and that of H and W, coupled with mitigating factors on M's behalf, to make a reasonable employer distinguish between them and treat M more leniently. The EAT agreed. It added that to treat all employees the same as a matter of course, without considering the particular circumstances of each individual, simply could not be done.

In considering disparity of treatment, employment tribunals must be careful not to substitute their own view for that of the employer. In Kier Islington Ltd v Pelzman EAT 0266/10 P had been employed as a loader of building site rubble. He was dismissed for gross misconduct following an incident of 'bombing', the practice of throwing materials from upper floor properties instead of carrying them downstairs. He had thrown a door which hit and injured an elderly resident's foot and damaged the door of her flat. Some four years previously, three other employees had received written warnings for bombing. One of them had acted as a lookout and no one had been hurt. That incident followed a memo warning employees that bombing was unacceptable. The memo had not been circulated to P and P had not been aware of the earlier incident, although his manager had told him not to practise bombing. KI Ltd took the view that P's conduct was more serious than the earlier incident because he had caused injury to a resident, damage to property and damage to the company's reputation, and had not used a lookout. The tribunal found that the dismissal fell outside the range of reasonable responses, first because of the disparity of treatment between the earlier incident and the instant one, and secondly because no written instruction had been issued to staff indicating the seriousness of bombing following the earlier incident. It held that the earlier incident would rationally be regarded as more serious by any reasonable employer because the employees involved had been aware of the memo. It also observed that the absence of injury to anyone had not been a factor in the earlier disciplinary penalty.

Overturning the tribunal's decision, the EAT observed that the memo issued **3.62** before the earlier bombing incident had done no more than inform employees that bombing was unacceptable, which P had known. It had not warned employees of the penalty for disregarding it. The tribunal had observed that the absence of injury to anyone in the earlier incident had not been a factor in that disciplinary penalty. However, the fact that P had caused injury and secondary damage had been taken into account by KI Ltd. The tribunal did not in terms find that to be an irrational distinction and it plainly was not. Furthermore, the absence of the precaution of a lookout in the instant case had been a rational distinction to make and the tribunal had not dealt with the perceived damage to KI Ltd's reputation. It had erred in undertaking its own assessment of comparability of the two incidents. If it had considered the proper question of whether KI Ltd's reasoning had been irrational – applying the test set out in Securicor Ltd v Smith (above) – the answer would have been that it plainly had not been. The EAT therefore upheld KI Ltd's appeal, reversed the finding of the employment tribunal and declared that P's dismissal was fair.

Creating 'false sense of security'. The concept of equity will come into play **3.63** where the employer had led the employee to believe that he or she would not be dismissed for certain conduct – Hadjioannou v Coral Casinos Ltd (above). Some examples:

- **Sarkar v West London Mental Health NHS Trust** 2010 IRLR 508, CA: the Court of Appeal upheld a tribunal's decision that the Trust had unfairly dismissed S for gross misconduct under its formal disciplinary procedure, when it had initially taken the view that the misconduct could be dealt with under its 'Fair Blame Policy' (FBP) – a dispute resolution procedure designed to deal with less serious matters. The tribunal was entitled to regard the initial use of the FBP as an indication of the Trust's view that the misconduct was relatively minor and that it was prepared to deal with it under a procedure that could not result in S's dismissal. The tribunal did not err in law in concluding that it was inconsistent of the Trust to then charge S with gross misconduct based on the same matters

- **Ryan v Helpline Group plc** ET Case No.3302226/07: R, who delivered and collected cars for HG plc, caused damage to two cars on 3 March 2007. The employer took no immediate action. However, in May one of the employer's clients complained that R had damaged a wall when delivering a car and R was called to a disciplinary hearing on 28 June in relation to both incidents. The employer decided not to take any further action regarding the incident in May but dismissed him for the incident in March on the basis that this constituted gross misconduct. The tribunal, by a majority, held that the employer's failure to take action after the March incident gave a clear indication to R that he was not going to be disciplined and it was contrary to equity to dismiss him after such a lapse of time

- **Wilson v Security Plus Ltd** ET Case No.1902594/08: W worked as a member of a cash and valuable transit crew. On 4 September 2008 he entered a building society wearing his safety helmet, as he was required to do, but shortly after entering the premises he removed the helmet to wipe his forehead. He was subsequently summarily dismissed for gross misconduct. He had taken his helmet off some four weeks earlier when he went to the toilet, and had been told by the employer that failing to wear his helmet at all times was regarded as gross misconduct and could result in his dismissal. He was given no disciplinary sanction on that occasion. The tribunal held that dismissal was outside the range of reasonable responses. The incidents in August and September were materially similar, yet on the first occasion he was not even given a warning. This gave W a 'false sense of security'. The employer's handbook and training procedures stressed the importance of wearing the helmet at all times but had not made it clear that failure to wear the helmet for whatever reason would lead to dismissal

- **JJ Food Service Ltd v Kefil** 2013 IRLR 850, EAT: K had been employed by JJFS Ltd for 14 years, latterly as stock control manager. He received an informal warning highlighting deficiencies in his management style. Several months later, following an investigation into a complaint by a number of employees, JJFS Ltd dismissed K on the basis that he had abused his position by threatening employees' job security, which had created an intimidating environment. The employment tribunal found that it was outside the range of reasonable responses to dismiss K in respect of his management style, without giving him a formal warning that he might be dismissed if this did not change, especially since he had not been given any management training after the previous informal warning. The EAT refused to interfere with the tribunal's decision. While it accepted that there was 'no special magic' about a written warning, the issue was whether the employee had been told or should have realised that his behaviour would or could lead to his dismissal. The significant point on which the tribunal focused was not the absence of a warning but the fact that K had been given no indication that a potential consequence of further misconduct would be dismissal. The EAT commented that 'the over-authoritarian manager is not unknown in industry… and it would be unfortunate if such managers were not warned, if the circumstances were such that they might not clearly have understood, that repeat of that conduct might lead to dismissal.'

3.64 These cases can be contrasted with Kier Islington Ltd v Pelzman (above), where the EAT held that while in an ideal world KI Ltd would have sent a memo to all staff emphasising the seriousness of 'bombing' and the possible disciplinary consequences if it continued, the absence of a formal written instruction did not render P's dismissal for bombing unfair. The fact that bombing was a clear and serious breach of health and safety was the crucial determining factor. The EAT observed that P had 30 years' service and knew that bombing was prohibited. It must have been 'blindingly obvious' to him that throwing material from an upper floor balcony, particularly without a lookout, gave rise to a risk of injury to persons below. Although a formal written instruction to that effect would have been a 'counsel of perfection', the EAT was not persuaded that on the particular facts of the case its absence rendered the dismissal unfair, particularly when P had not been misled by the earlier written warnings for bombing, of which he was unaware. In addition, KI Ltd's disciplinary procedures gave examples of gross misconduct, which included gross negligence, bringing the company into disrepute and conduct which jeopardised health and safety.

In Christou and anor v London Borough of Haringey 2013 ICR 1007, CA, the claimants prayed in aid the doctrine of res judicata in contending that their dismissals following the instigation of a second set of disciplinary proceedings for the same misconduct were unfair. C and W were initially disciplined under the Council's 'simplified' disciplinary procedure – which was usually invoked for relatively minor misconduct – and given a written warning for the way in which they had dealt with the case of Baby P, a child under the Council's supervision who had died as a result of parental neglect and abuse. Following the trial of Baby P's abusers, the Secretary of State appointed a new Director of Children's Services for the Council, who concluded that the previous disciplinary procedures against the claimants were 'blatantly unsafe, unsound and inadequate'. Fresh disciplinary proceedings resulted in their summary dismissal for gross misconduct and they brought unfair dismissal claims on the basis that it was unfair to reopen the earlier determinations. A majority of the tribunal rejected the claims, deciding that the misconduct justified dismissal and that the new management was entitled to take a different view of the material facts and instigate a second set of disciplinary proceedings. These facts therefore distinguished the case from Sarkar v West London Mental Health NHS Trust (above). This decision was upheld by the EAT.

3.65 Before the Court of Appeal, the claimants argued, among other things, that the doctrine of 'res judicata' applied to the simplified procedure to estop the Council from reopening the disciplinary process and that this meant that their dismissals were necessarily unfair. This judicial doctrine applies to prevent a party from relitigating an issue that has already come before a court or tribunal and been decided. The Court of Appeal rejected the claimants' argument, holding that the doctrine applies to adjudication procedures which involve establishing the existence of a legal right or 'determining a dispute'. The purpose of employment disciplinary procedures is not to allow a body independent of the parties to determine a dispute between them but to enable the employer to determine whether the employee has acted in breach of contract. The fact that procedures may be contractual or provide safeguards that typically apply to adjudicative bodies does not alter their basic function or purpose. Even if res judicata did apply, the Court continued, a dismissal in breach of the doctrine would not necessarily be unfair – S.98 ERA would still require a consideration of whether the employer had acted reasonably in all the circumstances.

The Court also rejected the claimants' related argument that the second disciplinary procedure was an abuse of process, holding that this doctrine, too, only applies to adjudications. In any event, tribunals considering whether a dismissal in circumstances such as those in the instant case is fair must ask whether it was fair to institute the second proceedings at all. That is essentially the same question as whether it is an abuse of process to reopen the matter. Having rejected the claimants' grounds of appeal, the Court concluded that the majority of the tribunal had been entitled to find that, since the allegations of misconduct against the claimants were very serious and involved risk to the public, the Council's new management had been justified in taking a different view of the gravity of the conduct. The unfair dismissal claims therefore failed.

3.66 The Court's conclusion could leave employees feeling concerned that a disciplinary decision taken against them might not be as final as they thought. However, they should take comfort from the fact that the circumstances of the case were unusually grave and that a tribunal considering the fairness of a dismissal will scrutinise very carefully an employer's reasons for dismissing an employee for conduct which previously appeared to warrant a lesser sanction.

3.67 **Fair dealing with workforce.** In Garside and Laycock Ltd v Booth 2011 IRLR 735, EAT, the EAT allowed an appeal against a tribunal's decision that an employee was unfairly dismissed for refusing to accept a pay cut that the employer had proposed as an alternative to compulsory redundancies (which amounted to 'some other substantial reason' for dismissal). The tribunal had erred by considering the reasonableness of the employee's refusal, rather than the reasonableness of the employer's decision to dismiss. Remitting the case, the EAT gave guidance for the tribunal in assessing reasonableness and drew its attention to the consideration of equity mandated by S.98(4)(b). It noted that, on the present facts, equity could involve consideration of whether management was to be subject to the proposed pay cut as well as the workforce, and whether the implied equitable concept of fair dealing was observed in the manner in which the pay cut was negotiated.

3.68 **Contractual rights and duties**

Contractual obligations are, of course, of great significance in many unfair dismissal cases but they are not necessarily decisive. The test remains the overall test of reasonableness and employers may well be acting reasonably even if they are in breach of contract. Equally, they may be acting unreasonably if they adhere to the letter of their contractual rights.

Thus, a wrongful dismissal – e.g. a dismissal without notice in a case not involving gross misconduct – will not be unfair if the employer would otherwise be reasonable in dismissing – Treganowan v Robert Knee and Co Ltd 1975 ICR 405, QBD. As the High Court observed, statutory unfair dismissal protection has in no way altered the scope to claim wrongful dismissal. An employer defending a wrongful dismissal claim must be able to show that the employee's act of gross misconduct constituted a repudiatory breach of contract justifying summary dismissal. The reasonableness or otherwise of the employer's actions is irrelevant. Where, however the employer is defending an unfair dismissal claim, the tribunal must consider the reasonableness of the employer's actions in treating the conduct as a sufficient reason for dismissal.

In Roberts and ors v Mid-Glamorgan County Council EAT 193/76 the EAT **3.69** pointed out that 'the whole of the legislation from [the Industrial Relations Act 1971] onwards on fair and unfair dismissal is designed to apply *irrespective of the law of contract*' (our stress) and the EAT has emphasised again and again since then that employment tribunals must not conflate the common law test of wrongful dismissal with the statutory test for unfair dismissal. Three examples:

- **Brito-Babapulle v Ealing Hospital NHS Trust** 2013 IRLR 854, EAT (discussed under '"Band (or range) of reasonable responses" test' above): the EAT held that the tribunal had erred by suggesting that the existence of gross misconduct, which is often a contractual issue, is determinative of whether a dismissal is unfair: the test for unfair dismissal depends on the separate consideration called for under S.98 ERA

- **Weston Recovery Services v Fisher** EAT 0062/10: the EAT held that the employment tribunal had erred by taking the view that because the conduct in question did not amount to gross misconduct, the dismissal was statutorily unfair. S.98 ERA was concerned with the sufficiency of the conduct reason for dismissal. It was not concerned with the common law concept of gross misconduct, i.e. conduct by the employee amounting to a repudiatory breach of the contract of employment entitling the employer to terminate the contract without notice or pay in lieu of notice

- **CRO Ports London Ltd v Wiltshire** EAT 0344/14 (discussed further under 'Tribunals must not substitute their own views' above): the EAT held that the tribunal had not separated the findings relevant to wrongful dismissal from those relevant to unfair dismissal. While that might not have been fatal, it made it difficult to be sure that the tribunal had clearly kept in mind the very different tests to be applied in reaching its conclusions on the two types of dismissal.

The distinction between wrongful and unfair dismissal was usefully explained **3.70** by the EAT in BSC Sports and Social Club v Morgan 1987 IRLR 391, EAT. In that case M was dismissed without notice when, after repeated warnings, he

89

failed in his capacity as club steward to maintain an adequate standard of hygiene and cleanliness. A tribunal found that, while the employer was fully justified in dismissing him for misconduct, the fact that his dismissal was summary (i.e. without notice) rendered it unfair. The EAT, following Treganowan v Robert Knee and Co Ltd (above), allowed the employer's appeal, stating that 'the factor of summary dismissal can only be considered in the context of whether or not it was reasonable to dismiss at all. In other words a summary dismissal may be evidence of a failure to show that the dismissal itself was a reasonable response. No doubt there have been many occasions when Industrial Tribunals have relied on a summary dismissal as a material consideration when assessing the reasonableness of the act of dismissal. If this Industrial Tribunal had approached the case in that way we should not have been able to interfere. However... it was an error in point of law to say that it was reasonable to terminate the employment and that the fact of instant dismissal made it unfair dismissal. Once a decision to dismiss has been reached on reasonable grounds, it is for the employer to decide whether or not to dismiss with notice or summarily. If he does so without notice the employer may be open to an action for wrongful dismissal. It seems to us that in preserving the remedy of wrongful dismissal the legislature recognises that there are cases in which instant dismissal, though not unfair, is nevertheless wrongful.'

A wrongful dismissal was found to be fair in MPI Ltd v Woodland EAT 0548/06, where W was summarily dismissed for various performance failures and for taking unauthorised leave, which the tribunal found to be a dismissal related to capability. The tribunal went on to hold that instant dismissal of W was not within the band of reasonable responses: although a need to improve his performance had been brought to W's attention, no formal warning had been given. However, dismissal on notice would have been a reasonable response. The EAT overturned the tribunal's decision on the basis that it had expressly found that dismissal on notice would have been reasonable. Having reached the conclusion that it was reasonable and fair to dismiss, the tribunal ought in law to have found the dismissal to have been fair irrespective of the fact that it believed that the dismissal should have been on notice.

3.71 Impact of Human Rights Act

Section 6 of the Human Rights Act 1998 (HRA) makes it unlawful for a *public* authority to act in a way that is incompatible with the rights laid down in the European Convention on Human Rights (ECHR). Although it is not directly unlawful for a *private* employer to act in a manner incompatible with the ECHR, S.3 HRA requires that courts and tribunals must, so far as possible, read and give effect to UK legislation in a way compatible with Convention rights. This interpretative obligation applies to all domestic legislation, including the ERA, and draws no distinction between legislation governing public authorities and that governing private individuals. Furthermore, as noted by the Court of Appeal in X v Y 2004 ICR 1634, CA, an employment tribunal is a 'public authority' within the meaning of S.6(3) HRA. The effect of this, said the Court, is to reinforce the tribunal's 'extremely strong interpretative obligation' imposed by S.3 when dealing with a case involving a private employer.

In X v Y the Court of Appeal commented that as tribunals have to take account of fairness, the reasonable response of the reasonable employer, equity and the substantial merits of the case in the normal course of deciding an unfair dismissal claim under S.98, it would be reasonable to expect that a decision in favour of the employer would not involve a breach of an employee's Convention rights in any event. However, the Court acknowledged the possibility that this might not always be the case and went on to suggest a framework of questions for tribunals dealing with unfair dismissal claims involving *private* employers in which HRA issues arise:

- do the circumstances of the dismissal fall within the ambit of one or more of the Articles of the ECHR? If they do not, the Convention is not engaged and need not be considered

- if they do, does the state have a positive obligation to secure enjoyment of the relevant Convention right between private persons? If it does not, the Convention right is unlikely to affect the outcome of an unfair dismissal claim against a private employer. (Note that both Article 8 – the right to privacy and family life – and Article 14, which requires the state to secure to individuals the enjoyment of their rights under the Convention without discrimination, do impose such an obligation on the state but were found not to be engaged on the facts of X v Y – see below)

- if it does, is the interference with the employee's Convention right by dismissal justified?

- if it is not, was there a permissible reason for the dismissal under the ERA that does not involve unjustified interference with a Convention right? If there was not, the dismissal will be unfair for the absence of a permissible reason to justify it

- if there was, is the dismissal fair, tested by the provisions of S.98 ERA, reading and giving effect to them under S.3 HRA so as to be compatible with the Convention right?

3.72 Where public employers are involved, the questions for the tribunal will be similar, although step two can be bypassed. As noted above, S.6 HRA makes it unlawful for a public authority to act in a way which is incompatible with ECHR rights. However, in X v Y, the Court of Appeal noted that an employment tribunal does not have jurisdiction to hear a claim under S.6. Therefore, if an employee dismissed by a public authority wishes to argue that his or her dismissal was unfair under S.98 ERA because one of his or her Convention rights has been breached, he or she will need to rely on S.3 HRA, rather than S.6, to claim that S.98 should be read in a way which is compatible with the Convention right in question. S.6 may not, however, be completely irrelevant to unfair dismissal claims: tribunals are likely to take their interpretative duties under S.3 even more seriously when public authorities are involved. In Pay v Lancashire Probation Service 2004 ICR 187, EAT, the EAT, exercising its interpretative obligations under S.3 HRA, accepted that a public authority employer will not act reasonably under S.98 if it violates employees' Convention rights. The EAT thought that, at least as far as public authority employers were concerned, the words 'reasonably or unreasonably' in S.98(4) should be interpreted as including the phrase 'having regard to the applicant's Convention rights'. In this context, a public authority employer would not have acted 'reasonably' under S.98(4) where it was found to have unjustifiably breached an employee's Convention rights.

The analysis undertaken by Lord Justice Mummery in X v Y was considered – and given wholehearted approval – by the Court of Appeal in Turner v East Midlands Trains Ltd 2013 ICR 525, CA. The employee, T, had been dismissed by her private sector employer on what she asserted was very slight evidence of fraud. Her unfair dismissal claim failed in both the employment tribunal and the EAT. On appeal to the Court of Appeal, she argued that the dismissal potentially breached her Article 8 right to a private life, in so far as it harmed her reputation, and that the long-established 'range of reasonable responses' test under S.98(4) ERA did not do justice to Article 8 requirements. Accordingly, she contended, the tribunal was in error in applying that test alone and not considering Article 8 specifically. The Court rejected this argument. Lord Justice Elias stated that, like Mummery LJ, he found it difficult to see how a procedure which could be considered objectively fair if adopted by a reasonable employer could nonetheless be properly described as an unfair procedure within the meaning of Article 8. Although it is the case that, where Article 8 interests are engaged, matters bearing on the culpability of the employee must be investigated with a full appreciation of the potentially adverse consequences, the band of reasonable responses test allows for a heightened standard to be adopted where those consequences are particularly grave. In Elias LJ's view, the band of reasonable responses test provided a sufficiently robust, flexible and objective analysis of all aspects of the decision to dismiss to ensure compliance with Article 8. Sir Stephen Sedley gave a concurring judgment, noting that the 'band of reasonable responses is itself catholic enough to accommodate whatever standard of due process Article 8 calls for in a particular case'.

3.73 A slightly different approach was taken by the EAT in Hill v Governing Body of Great Tey Primary School 2013 ICR 691, EAT, in relation to dismissal by a *public* body. H was a school dinner assistant who was dismissed for speaking to a child's parents and the press about an incident involving children in the school playground. An employment tribunal found that her dismissal was procedurally unfair but that she could have been fairly dismissed two months later had a fair procedure been followed and limited her compensation accordingly. The EAT allowed her appeal on compensation, holding that the tribunal had failed to take human rights considerations properly into account when assessing the possibility of the school dismissing fairly. The EAT noted that while an employment tribunal has no jurisdiction to consider a claim under the HRA, any potential breach of a Convention right is nonetheless relevant in considering the fairness of a dismissal. So, if H's dismissal penalised her for exercising her right to freedom of expression, to which she was entitled under Article 10, the fact that the school was a public authority with a duty to ensure that freedom would be relevant in assessing the fairness of dismissal. The right to freedom of expression is a qualified right that can be restricted for a number of reasons set out in Article 10(2). The tribunal was required to consider whether such restriction could be justified. However, in this case it had erred by paraphrasing those qualifications when it should have applied the actual legislative wording. The case was therefore remitted for fresh consideration of this point.

In the Hill case the EAT was prepared to accept that a separate consideration of the ECHR right (there, the right to freedom of expression under Article 10) was required, over and above the established principles governing unfair dismissal. This can be contrasted with Turner v East Midlands Trains Ltd (above), where the Court of Appeal held that the 'range of reasonable responses' test is already flexible enough to afford whatever protection Article 8 requires. Turner involved a private sector employer and so the claimant was restricted to arguing that the tribunal, in determining her claim, was under a duty to ensure that her human rights were not infringed. The approach in Hill was slightly different in that, as a public authority employee, the claimant could assert that her employer's own duty not to infringe her human rights fettered its power to dismiss. This therefore reinforces the general assumption that human rights arguments are more likely to be effective in cases involving public sector employers than in those involving private ones.

Interestingly, in none of the above cases was a Convention right found to have **3.74** been breached on the facts. In X v Y (above) the employee had been dismissed after his employer discovered that the police had cautioned him for engaging in sexual activity with another man in a public toilet. Upholding the tribunal's decision that the dismissal was fair, the Court of Appeal concluded that since the activity that led to the dismissal did not take place in private, the employee's Article 8 right to respect for his private life, and thus his right under Article 14 not to suffer discrimination in relation to his Convention rights, had not been engaged. It followed that the tribunal's duty under S.3 HRA to interpret S.98(4) ERA in a way compatible with Convention rights had not been triggered. The fact that the employee wished to keep the matter private did not make it part of his private life or deprive it of its public aspect.

Similarly, in Pay v Lancashire Probation Service (above) – where P, a probation officer specialising in the treatment of sex offenders, was dismissed following his employer's discovery that he was director of a business involved in sadomasochistic activities and that he performed acts of domination over women at a private members' club – the EAT agreed with the tribunal that P's activities were in the public domain (since photographs had been published on the internet) and therefore could not be described as part of his private life. It followed that Article 8 was not relevant to the claim. The EAT also endorsed the tribunal's view that Article 10 (which protects freedom of expression) had not been infringed: the employer's action had been justified under Article 10(2) (which places limitations on the right to freedom of expression) in view of the risk of damage to the reputation of the probation service that P's activities posed.

3.75 P subsequently took his case to the European Court of Human Rights (see Pay v United Kingdom 2009 IRLR 139, ECtHR), which was prepared to proceed on the assumption that P's activities were not in the public domain and that, therefore, Article 8 was applicable. This was because P's activities took place in a nightclub that was likely to be frequented only by like-minded people and the photographs of him published on the internet had been anonymised. However, in light of the sensitive nature of P's work, the interference with P's right to privacy was justified in accordance with Article 8(2) since his activities, if they became widely known, would compromise his work with sex offenders and damage the reputation of the Service. For the same reason the interference with his Article 10 right was justified under Article 10(2).

Note that the Court of Appeal has held that Article 6 of the ECHR, which provides that an individual has the right to a fair hearing, may in certain circumstances provide employees with the right to legal representation at disciplinary hearings – Kulkarni v Milton Keynes Hospital NHS Foundation Trust and anor 2010 ICR 101, CA. However, the Supreme Court's decision in R (on the application of G) v Governors of X School 2011 ICR 1033, SC, suggests that these circumstances will be fairly rare. These cases, which did not involve unfair dismissal claims, are discussed further in Chapter 6, 'Conduct', under 'Disciplinary proceedings – right to be accompanied'. A discussion of the HRA in the particular context of misconduct dismissals can be found in Chapter 6 under 'General considerations – impact of Human Rights Act'.

3.76 Pre-termination negotiations

An employment tribunal dealing with a claim of unfair dismissal is largely unhindered in the matters it may take into consideration when determining the reasonableness of a dismissal. This is subject to one caveat: S.111A(1) ERA prevents tribunals taking into account any offer made, or discussions held, with a view to an employee's employment terminating on agreed terms – commonly referred to as 'protected conversations'. S.111A(1) does not apply, however, to claims of automatically unfair dismissal – S.111A(3). Furthermore, tribunals have a degree of discretion to include consideration of 'anything said or done which in the tribunal's opinion was improper, or was connected with improper behaviour' – S.111A(4).

Acas has produced a statutory Code of Practice on Settlement Agreements to help employers and employees understand the implications of S.111A. While the Code is not binding, it may be relied on by tribunals when considering relevant cases. Further guidance on the confidentiality of pre-termination settlement negotiations can be found in the non-statutory 'Guide on Settlement Agreements', also produced by Acas.

Protected conversations are fully discussed in IDS Employment Law Handbook, 'Employment Tribunal Practice and Procedure' (2014), Chapter 13, 'Evidence', under 'Evidence of settlement negotiations – pre-termination negotiations'.

Appeals to EAT 3.77

Tribunal decisions on reasonableness are essentially findings of fact and an appeal to the EAT or a higher appellate court will lie only on a question of law. Appeals will therefore succeed only in the following circumstances:

- where the tribunal misdirected itself as to the law

- where the tribunal misdirected itself on the undisputed facts or ignored important factual considerations which it should have taken into account, or

- where the decision was perverse in the sense that it was one that no reasonable tribunal could have reached on the evidence before it.

Tribunal misdirected itself as to law. The most common instance of this is 3.78 where the tribunal has substituted its own view of what an employer should have done, instead of asking whether what the employer did fell within the range of reasonable responses open to him – for examples, see 'Tribunals must not substitute their own views' above. In Brent London Borough Council v Fuller 2011 ICR 806, CA, Lord Justice Mummery cautioned that an appellate body, be it the EAT or the Court of Appeal, must be on its guard against making the very same legal error as the tribunal stood accused of making: namely, substituting its own subjective view of the dismissal. He further observed that while a tribunal's judgment should be 'read carefully to see if it has in fact correctly applied the law which it said was applicable', the scrutiny must not be 'so fussy that it produces pernickety critiques'. He identified three appellate weaknesses in particular: over-analysis of the reasoning process; being hypercritical of the way in which the decision is written; and focusing too much on particular passages or turns of phrase to the neglect of the decision read in the round. Turning to the tribunal's decision in the instant case, Mummery LJ

95

agreed with the employer and the EAT that some passages in the judgment invited criticism – particularly its use of the expression 'we felt'. Taken as a whole, however, he did not consider that the flaws in the wording justified setting aside the tribunal's decision. On reading the decision in the round, Mummery LJ considered that the tribunal had correctly directed itself as to the law by asking whether a hypothetical reasonable employer would have dismissed F. That question had been answered in the negative when the tribunal stated that 'no reasonable employer would have dismissed her for a one-off incident' and 'any reasonable employer would have imposed a lesser penalty'.

Similarly, in JJ Food Service Ltd v Kefil 2013 IRLR 850, EAT, the EAT commented that, 'a substitution mindset is all too easy to allege. There is a great danger which is readily apparent to those of us who sit day by day in this tribunal that employers who do not like the result which a tribunal has reached, but cannot go so far as to say it is necessarily perverse, seek to argue that the very fact of the result in the circumstances must indicate a substitution. That is not, in our view, a proper approach... In order to see if a tribunal has stepped beyond the permissible and gone outside the scope of its duty as set out in S.98(4), it is necessary to have regard to a tribunal's decision as a whole, but what one is looking for is some indication that the tribunal has, in dealing with a complaint of unfair dismissal, asked not whether what the employer did was fair but asked instead what it would have done in the light of the basic and underlying facts.' (A discussion of the substantive point at issue in this case can be found under 'Equity – creating "false sense of security"' above.)

3.79 It is also a misdirection in law to misapply the onus of proof: it is not for the employer to prove that a dismissal was reasonable – that is a matter for the tribunal to decide. Also, the standard of proof in unfair dismissal proceedings is the civil one of the 'balance of probabilities' – i.e. 'was it more likely than not that...?' The criminal law standard of proof – 'beyond reasonable doubt' – has no place in unfair dismissal cases.

3.80 **Tribunal misdirected itself on facts**. An appeal will be successful where the tribunal misdirected itself on the undisputed facts or ignored important factual considerations which it should have taken into account. In British Leyland (UK) Ltd v Swift 1981 IRLR 91, CA, S was dismissed after a company road fund licence was found on his own vehicle and he pleaded guilty to its fraudulent use in a magistrate's court. Despite abundant evidence of gross misconduct a tribunal found the dismissal unfair. However, in giving its decision the tribunal took no account of the fact that S had persistently lied both to the police and to his employer: neglect of this highly significant consideration was one reason for setting aside the decision.

3.81 **Tribunal decision perverse.** A tribunal decision will be perverse if it was one that no reasonable tribunal could have reached on the evidence before it. In Williams and ors v Whitbread Beer Co Ltd, unreported 19.6.96, CA, the Court of Appeal stated that a tribunal decision should only be set aside on the ground that it is perverse if the decision was not a permissible option on the facts found. For example, in London Transport Executive v Clarke 1981 ICR 355, CA, C asked for six weeks' leave to go to Jamaica in 1979. The employer refused: C had had long periods of absence in the previous three years and had taken leave in Jamaica in 1977. C defied the employer by going to Jamaica for seven weeks anyway. The employer dismissed him while he was away and a tribunal held that the dismissal was unfair on the ground that the employer should have waited to discuss matters on his return. The majority of the Court of Appeal held this finding to be perverse as it 'outrages common sense'.

Note, however, that in Bowater v Northwest London Hospitals NHS Trust 2011 IRLR 331, CA (discussed under 'Tribunals must not substitute their own views' above), the Court of Appeal warned against the EAT, under the guise of perversity, substituting its own judgment for that of the tribunal. This was echoed by the EAT in JJ Food Service Ltd v Kefil 2013 IRLR 850, EAT, where it stated: 'It is rare for an Appeal Tribunal to interfere with the decision of an employment tribunal where perversity is alleged; that is because of the height of the hurdle which the Appellant must overcome. He must show that the decision reached is wholly impermissible. Various phrases have been used in different cases to describe the same result, from "flying in the face of reason" to "provoking astonished gasps from the amazed observer".'

Fairness of internal procedure   3.82

The interpretation given to the wording of S.98(4) by the courts has had the effect of introducing the concept of a procedurally unfair dismissal – i.e. a dismissal that is unfair because the employer has failed to follow a fair procedure. The concept, which does not appear in the legislation, was developed in the early 1970s and approved by the House of Lords in W Devis and Sons Ltd v Atkins 1977 ICR 662, HL. It became a dominant feature of employment relations in that decade but waned in the early 1980s following the widespread application of the 'no difference rule' – first formulated in British Labour Pump Co Ltd v Byrne 1979 ICR 347, EAT. This rule basically meant that where there was a proven procedural irregularity in an otherwise fair dismissal – e.g. a failure to consult over redundancy – but it could be shown that carrying out the proper procedure would have made no difference, then the dismissal would be fair.

The House of Lords resoundingly rejected this approach in Polkey v AE Dayton Services Ltd 1988 ICR 142, HL. In that case P was summarily dismissed for redundancy with no warning or consultation and the tribunal hearing his unfair dismissal claim said that: 'There could be no more heartless disregard of the provisions of the code of practice than that.' It was referring to the (now repealed) 1972 Industrial Relations Code of Practice, para 46 of which said: 'If

97

redundancy becomes necessary, management in consultation, as appropriate, with employees or their representatives, should: (i) give as much warning as practicable to the employees concerned.' The tribunal, however, went on to hold that if the employer had acted in accordance with the Code of Practice, the result would not have been any different. The House of Lords unanimously condemned this approach on the grounds that it was contrary to the decision in W Devis and Sons Ltd v Atkins (above) and contrary to the plain wording of S.98(4). That section simply directs tribunals to consider whether the employer acted reasonably when dismissing. Their Lordships reasoned, therefore, that the employer's actions in dispensing with a fair procedure were highly relevant to the question of whether a dismissal is fair. With this landmark decision, the pendulum swung back in favour of a proper procedure.

3.83 The position changed again with the enactment of the Employment Act 2002, which introduced the (now-repealed) statutory dispute resolution procedures (SDRPs) in 2004 and inserted a new S.98A into the ERA, which partially reversed Polkey and reinstated the 'no difference' rule, albeit only in circumstances where the minimum obligations of the SDRPs had been observed. However, S.98A was repealed by the Employment Act 2008, with the result that the law has returned to the Polkey position, and employers can no longer invoke the 'no difference' rule when defending a failure to adopt a fair procedure, except in exceptional cases (see 'Exception to Polkey' below). The SDRPs were also repealed by the 2008 Act but, despite what many commentators have said, their abolition has not simply meant a return to the pre-2004 regime since parties are now expected to comply with a revised Acas Code of Practice on Disciplinary and Grievance Procedures. A failure to comply with the Code will be taken into account by tribunals when assessing liability. However, unlike the SDRPs, it will not automatically render a dismissal unfair. The Code is considered in more detail under 'Acas Code of Practice' below.

3.84 **Procedural fairness integral to reasonableness test**
The House of Lord's decision in Polkey v AE Dayton Services Ltd (above) firmly establishes procedural fairness as an integral part of the reasonableness test under S.98(4). As stated by Lord Bridge in that case, where an employer fails to take the appropriate procedural steps, the one question a tribunal is not permitted to ask in applying the reasonableness test is whether it would have made any difference if the right procedure had been followed. That question is simply irrelevant to the issue of reasonableness (although very relevant to the issue of compensation). Thus, if there is a failure to adopt a fair procedure at the time of the dismissal, whether set out in the Acas Code of Practice or otherwise – for example, in the employer's disciplinary rules – the dismissal will not be rendered fair simply because the unfairness did not affect the end result. However, any compensation will be substantially reduced – see Chapter 16, 'Compensatory awards: adjustments', under '"Polkey reductions"'.

While a failure to comply with procedural safeguards will not *automatically* render a dismissal unfair, Lord Bridge itemised the procedural steps that will be necessary in the great majority of cases if an employer is to be considered to have acted reasonably in dismissing:

- in a case of incapacity, giving an employee fair warning and a chance to improve

- in a case of misconduct, investigating fully and fairly and hearing what the employee wants to say in explanation or mitigation

- in a case of redundancy, warning and consulting affected employees, adopting a fair basis for selection and taking reasonable steps to redeploy affected employees.

In addition, when determining the question of reasonableness, the tribunal should have regard to the procedures set out in the Acas Code of Practice, which is discussed under 'Acas Code of Practice' below. **3.85**

But it should be stressed that while the procedural steps outlined above should generally be followed, not every procedural defect will render a dismissal unfair. In London Central Bus Company Ltd v Manning EAT 0103/13, for example, the EAT held that a procedural defect in the appeal process could only render a dismissal unfair if it denied the employee the opportunity of showing that the employer's reason for dismissal could not reasonably be treated as sufficient (see further 'Internal appeals' below).

It is important to bear in mind that S.98(4) ERA poses one unitary question: whether the dismissal was fair or unfair, having regard to the reason shown by the employer – USDAW v Burns EAT 0557/12. According to the EAT in that case, this means that the tribunal must not treat the reasonableness of the decision to dismiss and the reasonableness of the procedure as if they are two separate questions, each of which must be answered in the employer's favour before the dismissal can be considered fair. It is not, however, an error of law for a tribunal to deal with the substantive and procedural elements of the decision to dismiss separately, provided that its approach leads to an overall determination as to the fairness or unfairness of the dismissal. The Burns case is discussed further under 'Range of reasonable responses test applies' below. **3.86**

Relevance of employer's reason for dismissal. In Westminster City Council v Cabaj 1996 ICR 960, CA, the Court of Appeal stated that although employers should follow the agreed procedures, a failure to do so would not necessarily mean that a dismissal is unfair. The question a tribunal must decide in cases of unfair dismissal is not whether in all the circumstances the employer acted reasonably, but the narrower question under S.98(4) of whether the employer acted reasonably in treating the reason shown as a sufficient reason for dismissing the employee. In remitting the case, the Court of Appeal said that **3.87**

the tribunal should first ask whether the failure to convene a properly constituted appeal panel impeded the employee in demonstrating that the real reason for his dismissal was not sufficient. It should also consider the employer's reason (if any) for deciding to dismiss C without observing the requirements of the disciplinary code.

The Cabaj judgment makes clear the importance of a proper procedure in helping to ensure that the employer's decision to dismiss is reasonable for the reason given. For example, in many misconduct cases it will be difficult for the employer to establish that its belief in the employee's guilt – and therefore any subsequent dismissal – is reasonable without having first held an investigation. However, if an employee is caught red-handed in the course of serious misconduct, an investigation may not be as crucial. This was confirmed in Taylor v OCS Group Ltd 2006 ICR 1602, CA, where the Court of Appeal stressed that the tribunal's task under S.98(4) is not only to assess the fairness of the disciplinary process as a whole but also to consider the employer's reason for the dismissal as the two impact upon each other. It stated that where an employee is dismissed for serious misconduct, a tribunal might well decide that, notwithstanding some procedural imperfections, the employer acted reasonably in treating the reason as sufficient to dismiss the employee. Conversely, the Court considered that where the misconduct is of a less serious nature, so that the decision to dismiss is nearer the borderline, the tribunal might well conclude that a procedural deficiency had such impact that the employer did not act reasonably in dismissing the employee.

3.88 It is important to remember that S.98(4) requires an employment tribunal to focus on the employer's reason for dismissing rather than its own perception of that reason. In Uniqwin UK Ltd v Weston EAT 0454/13 an employment tribunal decided that a shopping centre manager had been unfairly dismissed for gross misconduct when he allegedly appropriated a cash payment without authority and failed to account for tax and national insurance on it. The decision was overturned on appeal. Among other things, the EAT agreed with the employer that a reasonable investigation must relate to the belief which the employer has formed of the conduct, Here, the judge had failed to consider whether the employer had carried out a reasonable investigation in light of *its* belief in the alleged misconduct and instead had erroneously applied a general concept of what constitutes a reasonable investigation.

3.89 **Range of reasonable responses test applies.** When assessing whether the employer adopted a reasonable procedure, tribunals should use the range of reasonable responses test that applies to substantive unfair dismissal claims (see 'Reasonableness of dismissal – "band (or range) of reasonable responses" test' above) – J Sainsbury plc v Hitt 2003 ICR 111, CA; Whitbread plc (t/a Whitbread Medway Inns) v Hall 2001 ICR 699, CA. In McAlney v E.on UK plc ET Case No.2406839/08, for example, M was employed by E UK plc as a customer services representative. He also worked as a private taxi driver and the employer was fully aware of this. M was dismissed following an allegation by a fellow employee, G, that he had picked up a fare in his taxi while he was on sick leave. The tribunal held that the way the employer carried out the subsequent investigation and disciplinary procedure fell outside the range of reasonable responses in that the employer had interviewed M without giving him full details of G's allegations, depriving M of the opportunity to put forward a substantive and meaningful response; did not allow external witnesses to give evidence; and refused to consider any evidence that might exculpate M – for example, a written statement that had been produced by a member of the public. Although satisfied that the employer had an honest belief in M's guilt, the tribunal concluded that this belief had been formed hastily without the appropriate enquiries being made, without relevant evidence being taken into account, and without proper consideration being given to the evidence that was before it. This meant the decision to dismiss fell outside the range of reasonable responses and was unfair.

Note, however, that when applying the range of reasonable responses test a tribunal must not treat the reasonableness of the dismissal and the reasonableness of the procedure as two separate questions, each of which has to be answered in favour of the employer before the dismissal can be considered fair. In USDAW v Burns EAT 0557/12 an employment tribunal held that USDAW's decision to dismiss B on the grounds of some other substantial reason fell within the range of reasonable responses, in that the respondent had acted reasonably in treating this as a reason for dismissing B. However, the tribunal went on to find that, in relation to the procedure USDAW had followed, its failure to look for suitable alternative employment for B rendered the dismissal unfair. On appeal, USDAW argued that the tribunal had impermissibly split its decision into two parts, treating substance and procedure as if they were separate questions. The EAT noted that S.98(4) ERA poses one unitary question: whether the dismissal was fair or unfair, having regard to the reason shown by the employer. In J Sainsbury plc v Hitt (above) Lord Justice Mummery had observed that the need to apply the objective standards of the reasonable employer applies as much to the question of whether the investigation into the suspected misconduct was reasonable in all the circumstances as it does to the reasonableness of the decision to dismiss for the conduct reason. The EAT commented that he therefore plainly saw the two strands of 'substance' and 'procedure' as both requiring the adoption of the reasonableness test, but both feeding into one overall assessment which falls to be made by the tribunal. In the EAT's view, the tribunal had not fallen into the trap of asking, and answering, two separate questions relating to substance and procedure. Reading the judgment as a whole, it was clear that the tribunal was answering the questions that were posed to it in two strands, and that it had drawn those strands together in one overall assessment when finding that the case for unfair dismissal was made out.

3.90 In Amazon.co.uk Ltd v Hurdus EAT 0377/10 the EAT held that an employment tribunal had substituted its own view of what a proper redundancy selection procedure ought to entail for the 'real question' of whether the employer had adopted and applied a system that fell within the range of reasonable responses open to it. H was employed as a grade 6 senior recruiter in A Ltd's corporate recruiting section. In 2008, another employee, M, transferred over as a grade 5 recruiter from the operations recruiting section. Eight months later, M was promoted to the same grade as H and performed the same function. Following a decrease in the volume of work a decision was made that only one recruiter was required. H and M were entered into a redundancy selection process based on the last two years' performance. For one criterion, 'leadership principles and values', H scored 11 points whereas M scored 13. On that basis M was chosen to remain in the post. The tribunal held that H had been unfairly dismissed because the assessment of M against H had not been a like-for-like comparison as M had been in a lower grade role for much of the previous two years. Allowing A Ltd's appeal, the EAT held that the tribunal had expressed its own view of how the redundancy model adopted by A Ltd might be improved, rather than asking whether that model fell within the range of reasonable responses. It was for the employer to adopt a selection process, not the employment tribunal.

3.91 Exception to Polkey

In Polkey v AE Dayton Services Ltd (above) it was stated that if an employer could reasonably have concluded that a proper procedure would be 'utterly useless' or 'futile', it might well be acting reasonably in not putting one in place. This was a matter for the tribunal to consider in the light of the circumstances known to the employer at the time of the dismissal. Lord Bridge expressed the view that such cases would be 'exceptional' and, because of this, the appellate courts have been cautious about finding dismissals fair where the proper procedure has been ignored on the ground that to follow it would have been futile. Nonetheless, there have been cases where the EAT has held that the circumstances were exceptional enough to 'excuse' the employer from following the proper disciplinary procedure. Two examples:

- **MacLeod v Murray Quality Foods Ltd** EAT 290/90: M worked in MQF Ltd's factory, which was struggling financially. The factory received a large order from a new customer and it was a matter of some urgency that the order be executed on time. Tea breaks were cancelled until the order was completed. M ignored this instruction and, after being warned that he would be dismissed if he did not return to work, was dismissed. The tribunal found that the circumstances were sufficiently urgent to justify the employer issuing the instruction, even though tea breaks were provided for in M's contract. It found the dismissal fair. The EAT accepted that the procedure was flawed in that no investigation had been carried out. Nonetheless, it agreed with the tribunal's finding on the basis that M knew why he was being dismissed and he had the opportunity to make representations to the managing director. Referring to Polkey, the EAT said that the circumstances of the case were 'exceptional'

- **Ellis v Hammond and anor t/a Hammond and Sons** EAT 1257/95: E had received several warnings, including three formal written warnings, about her conduct and her work. Matters came to a head when she was asked to work harder and, in response, swore at her supervisor and started throwing things at another employee. After a further warning, she swore at everybody and left. She did not report for work the following week and was dismissed without the benefit of a final disciplinary hearing. The EAT upheld a tribunal's decision that E had been fairly dismissed, even though the employer had decided to dispense with a final disciplinary hearing. The EAT stressed that the correct question for the tribunal to ask was whether the decision not to hold a final disciplinary hearing was justified at the time of the dismissal, not in the light of being wise after the event.

The test for tribunals to use is an objective test. They must ask whether an employer, acting reasonably, could have made the decision that it would have been futile to follow proper procedures – Duffy v Yeomans and Partners Ltd 1995 ICR 1, CA.

Acas Code of Practice   3.92
The latest version of the Acas Code of Practice on Disciplinary and Grievance Procedures ('the Acas Code'), issued under S.199 of the Trade Union and Labour Relations (Consolidation) Act 1992 (TULR(C)A), came into effect on 11 March 2015. This version reflects the EAT's decision in Toal and anor v GB Oils Ltd 2013 IRLR 696, EAT, in relation to the role of the companion in disciplinary or grievance hearings – see Chapter 6, 'Conduct', under 'Right to be accompanied'. The Code contains a section on handling disciplinary issues and sets out six steps employers should normally follow, namely:

- establish the facts of each case (paras 5–8)

- inform the employee of the problem (paras 9–10)

- hold a meeting with the employee to discuss the problem (paras 11–12)

- allow the employee to be accompanied at the meeting (paras 13–16)

- decide on appropriate action (paras 17–24)

- provide employees with an opportunity to appeal (paras 25–28).

The introduction to the Acas Code also states that it is important to 'deal with issues fairly' whenever a disciplinary process is being followed. This includes dealing with issues promptly and without unreasonable delay; acting

103

consistently; carrying out any necessary investigations; and giving employees the opportunity to put their case before any decisions are made (see para 4).

3.93 **Relevance of Acas Code to liability.** A failure to follow the Acas Code is relevant to the question of liability and will be taken into account by a tribunal when determining the reasonableness of a dismissal in accordance with S.98(4) – S.207 TULR(C)A. However, it will not render the dismissal automatically unfair and the tribunal will take all the circumstances into account. Para 3 of the Code makes it clear that 'tribunals will take the size and resources of an employer into account when deciding on relevant cases and it may sometimes not be practicable for all employers to take all of the steps set out in this Code'. However, there is a risk in departing from the Acas Code since employers will be banking on an employment tribunal agreeing that such departure was reasonable.

Two contrasting examples:

- **Singh v Borgers Ltd** ET Case No.1312543/09: S was dismissed after admitting that he was responsible for supplying defective parts to the employer's major customer. A tribunal held that the dismissal was procedurally unfair. The employer had failed to comply with the Acas Code in a number of ways: the investigation and hearing were carried out by the same person; S was not notified of the hearing in writing, or provided with reasonable time to prepare his case before the hearing, or advised of his right to be accompanied at the meeting; and, finally, the appeal was not 'heard' as envisaged by para 25 of the Code – the employer had simply carried out a desk exercise and informed S that his appeal was not upheld. Furthermore, and irrespective of the Acas Code, the disciplinary procedure operated by the employer contravened both natural justice and well-established good industrial relations practice in that, for example, it did not allow S a proper opportunity to prepare his case in advance of the disciplinary hearing and failed to provide S with an effective appeal process

- **Buzolli v Food Partners Ltd** EAT 0317/12: FP Ltd failed to inform B in a final written warning that further misconduct might result in dismissal, or to warn him prior to a disciplinary hearing (in relation to a separate incident six months later) that his behaviour amounted to misconduct that might result in his dismissal. Both are procedural steps recommended in the Acas Code. Nevertheless, the EAT upheld the tribunal's decision that, despite the procedural flaws, dismissal was reasonable in the circumstances. The misconduct in question – a preventable collision resulting in significant damage to a company vehicle – was one of the examples of gross misconduct given in FP Ltd's disciplinary policy, and common sense dictated that any misconduct committed by him, while he was already subject to a final written warning, could result in his dismissal.

The Acas Code states that 'a fair disciplinary process should always be followed **3.94** before dismissing for gross misconduct' (para 22). Thus, unless the misconduct is so heinous as to require instant dismissal – e.g. where there is a danger to life or immediate severe harm to the business – even serious conduct cases should be dealt with in the normal way. However, where immediate dismissal is deemed necessary, it is arguable that the lack of a fair procedure would not render it unfair as the exception in Polkey v AE Dayton Services Ltd 1988 ICR 142, HL, would apply – see 'Exception to Polkey' above. In addition, cases such as Taylor v OCS Group Ltd 2006 ICR 1602, CA (discussed under 'Relevance of employer's reason for dismissal' above and 'Internal appeals' below), suggest that the more serious the misconduct alleged, the more likely it is that a dismissal tainted by procedural irregularities would nonetheless be fair. This ties in with what was discussed under 'Procedural fairness integral to reasonableness test' above; namely, that S.98(4) ERA poses one unitary question: whether the dismissal was fair or unfair, having regard to the reason shown by the employer – i.e. the reasonableness of the procedure must not be treated as a separate issue from the reasonableness of the dismissal. Taking this holistic approach to the question of fairness, an employment tribunal can perhaps more easily 'forgive' procedural irregularities where it was clear from the outset that the employee was guilty of serious misconduct.

Relevance of Acas Code to compensation. A failure to follow the Acas Code **3.95** is not only relevant to the question of liability, but also to assessment of compensation. Assuming the dismissal is found to be unfair, compliance with the Code by both employer and employee will be taken into account when determining whether there should be an adjustment to any award – S.207A TULR(C)A. This section applies to most tribunal claims, including unfair dismissal, and provides that the tribunal can increase an award of compensation by up to 25 per cent if it finds that the employer has unreasonably failed to follow the Code, or decrease it by up to 25 per cent if the employee has unreasonably failed to follow the Code, if it considers it just and equitable in all the circumstances to do so. Adjustments for breach of the Acas Code are discussed in Chapter 16, 'Compensatory awards: adjustments', under 'Adjustments for breach of Acas Code of Practice'.

Ambit of Acas Code. The Acas Code expressly covers disciplinary issues **3.96** relating to 'misconduct' and 'poor performance', both of which are potentially fair reasons for dismissal under the ERA: the former on grounds of 'conduct' under S.98(2)(b); the latter on grounds of 'capability or qualifications' under S.98(2)(a). Although the Code sets out one disciplinary procedure to deal with both conduct and performance issues, many employers are likely to have a separate capability procedure in place to deal with the latter. This is recognised in the introduction to the Code, which provides that 'if employers have a separate capability procedure they may prefer to address performance issues under this procedure' – para 1. However, it goes on to emphasise that 'the basic

105

principles of fairness set out in this Code should still be followed, albeit that they may need to be adapted'.

Not all dismissals fall within the Code's ambit, however: redundancy dismissals and the non-renewal of fixed-term contracts are specifically excluded. Moreover, there are a number of types of dismissal that do not sit easily within the Code's reach. For example, the category 'capability or qualifications' in S.98(2)(a) ERA encompasses more than simply poor performance and it is unclear how the Code applies to the broader issues of incapability on grounds of sickness absence or lack of qualification that are embraced by it. Arguably the Code does not apply, since in most such cases there is an absence of 'fault' on the part of the employee, taking them outside the 'disciplinary' area. The same applies to dismissals by reason of statutory ban or for SOSR – although at least one employment tribunal has taken the view that SOSR dismissals are covered by the Acas Code on the ground that they are not expressly excluded (see Cummings v Siemens Communications Ltd ET Case No.3500013/10). Furthermore, in Jefferson (Commercial) LLP v Westgate EAT 0128/12 the EAT did not discount the possibility that the Code may, in certain circumstances, apply to SOSR dismissals, noting that para 1 of the Code states that disciplinary situations '*include* misconduct and/or poor performance' (our stress). However, while it conceded that 'the word "include"… might suggest that misconduct and poor performance is not a conclusive list', it did not consider that the Code was relevant to the instant case, where the SOSR amounted to an irretrievable breakdown of mutual trust and confidence.

3.97 In Lund v St Edmund's School, Canterbury 2013 ICR D26, EAT, the EAT stated that it is not the outcome of the process which determines whether the Acas Code applies, but its initiation. In its view, the Code applies where disciplinary proceedings are – or ought to be – invoked against an employee. In that case, a school teacher was dismissed for SOSR as a result of a breakdown in relationships with colleagues caused by his own conduct. In the EAT's view, once the school had called L's conduct into question and thought that it might lead to his dismissal, it should have invoked the disciplinary procedure. That was the case even if it ultimately decided to dismiss him for a non-disciplinary reason.

It should also be noted that Appendix 4 of the non-statutory Acas Guide, 'Discipline and grievances at work' ('the Acas Guide'), which accompanies the Acas Code, envisages that the Code will apply in cases of ill health, although it recommends a 'more sympathetic and considerate approach', particularly if the employee is disabled and where reasonable adjustments at the workplace might enable them to return to work.

3.98 But even if the Acas Code does not apply, an employer cannot simply dispense with procedural fairness. Polkey v AE Dayton Services Ltd (above) and related case law will still be relevant and tribunals will need to be satisfied that the employer has followed a fair and appropriate procedure in the circumstances.

For example, in a redundancy case the employer should warn and consult affected employees, adopt a fair basis for selection and take reasonable steps to redeploy affected employees. Moreover, in many cases the reasons for dismissal may overlap and employers should be wary of abandoning the Acas Code altogether. Indeed, the Code sets out general standards of good practice that may be relevant in circumstances not specifically covered by it: S.207 TULR(C)A is widely drafted and obliges tribunals to take into account a provision of the Code whenever they consider it to be relevant.

For further information on the Acas Code of Practice on Disciplinary and Grievance Procedures, reference should be made to IDS Employment Law Supplement, 'Disciplinary and Grievance Procedures' (2009).

Internal policies and procedures

3.99

In considering the fairness of a dismissal the tribunal will also consider whether an employer has complied with its own internal policies and procedures. In Sinclair v Wandsworth Council EAT 0145/07, for example, S was found to be unfit for work because of drink and was suspended. Following disciplinary action, he was dismissed. The tribunal was satisfied that the Council had conducted a full and reasonable investigation into the events and that, in view of an earlier written warning given to S, and of the limited steps he had taken to address his alcohol problem, dismissal was within the range of reasonable responses available to the employer. Nevertheless, the majority of the tribunal (comprising the two lay members) found that S's dismissal was procedurally unfair under S.98(4) ERA because of two material defaults on the Council's part in the application of its alcohol policy. First, the policy had not been provided to S or his supervisors until immediately before the disciplinary hearing that resulted in his dismissal. Secondly, the Council had failed to spell out precisely what S would need to do in order to stop the disciplinary action and had not made it clear that if he did not seek treatment the action would continue.

The employment judge disagreed with the majority. In his view, the message of the alcohol policy – if not the policy itself – had been made plain to S, in that he was sufficiently informed that disciplinary action could be put on hold if he underwent treatment. In any event, the employment judge felt that any unfairness prior to the disciplinary hearing was cured on appeal. Nevertheless, owing to the views of the majority, the tribunal concluded that S had been unfairly dismissed. The EAT held that the tribunal was entitled to find that the employer's failure to implement its alcohol policy when disciplining an employee with an alcohol problem rendered the dismissal unfair. While conceding that it was possible for an appeal hearing to cure earlier deficiencies in an employer's procedure, the EAT decided that the majority had been entitled to find that the deficiencies identified had not been cured. Accordingly, it declined to disturb the tribunal's decision that S had been unfairly dismissed.

3.100 An employer's failure to follow the correct internal procedure before dismissing an employee – the principal oboist in an orchestra – was held to be unfair by the Court of Appeal in Welsh National Opera Ltd v Johnston 2012 EWCA Civ 1046, CA. In the Court's view, the tribunal was wrong to conclude that concerns about the employee's ensemble playing could not be dealt with under the audition procedure for 'poor artistic performance' set out in the applicable collective agreement. By subjecting the employee instead to a modified version of the ordinary disciplinary procedure reserved for non-artistic capability issues, the employer had acted outside the range of reasonable responses, rendering the dismissal unfair.

3.101 Internal appeals

The Acas Code recommends that employees be provided with an opportunity to appeal against any disciplinary action taken against them, such as dismissal. As this recommendation is part of the Code, an unreasonable failure to provide an appeal risks incurring liability and/or an adjustment to any compensation award in related tribunal proceedings.

However, there may be circumstances in which an opportunity to appeal is not necessary and where the lack of any further meeting or appeal may not render the dismissal unfair. In Jefferson (Commercial) LLP v Westgate EAT 0128/12, for example, the EAT held that the lack of any further meeting or appeal following an initial meeting at which it was confirmed that trust and confidence had been lost on both sides did not render the dismissal unfair. In its view, having a further meeting which, on the tribunal's findings of facts, would simply have restated the position, would have been a 'meaningless charade'.

3.102 In terms of general fairness, the courts have established that defects in the original disciplinary hearing and pre-dismissal procedures can be remedied on appeal. In a case that was subsequently followed on a number of occasions – Whitbread and Co plc v Mills 1988 ICR 776, EAT – the EAT suggested that in order for this to happen the appeal must be in the nature of a full rehearing of the case rather than a mere review of the original decision. However, in Taylor v OCS Group Ltd 2006 ICR 1602, CA, the Court of Appeal held that the EAT in Whitbread had not established a rule of law that only a rehearing – as opposed to a review – was capable of curing earlier defects. Such a rule would fetter a tribunal's discretion when considering the fairness of the dismissal under S.98(4). It was evident, said the Court, that Whitbread had not always been properly understood and that tribunals had been tempted to categorise appeal hearings either as rehearings or reviews. In view of the confusion surrounding Whitbread, the Court suggested that it would be advisable not to cite it in future cases. The tribunal's task under S.98(4), the Court stressed, is to assess the fairness of the disciplinary process as a whole. Where procedural deficiencies occur at an early stage, the tribunal should examine the subsequent appeal hearing, particularly its procedural fairness and thoroughness, and the open-mindedness of the decision-maker.

An appeal may, therefore, cure earlier defects. Conversely, the way in which an appeal is carried out may make an otherwise fair dismissal unfair, particularly if the employee has a contractual right of appeal. In West Midlands Co-operative Society Ltd v Tipton 1986 ICR 192, HL, the House of Lords held that a dismissal may be unfair where the employer has refused to entertain an appeal to which the employee was contractually entitled on the basis that the employee was thereby denied the opportunity of showing that the employer's reason for dismissing him or her could not reasonably be treated as sufficient. Tipton was applied by the employment tribunal in Evans v Wolverhampton City Council ET Case No.1307237/07, where E, who was dismissed because of his absence record, had a contractual right of appeal. The tribunal was satisfied that the employer had carried out a reasonable investigation and that dismissal was within the range of reasonable responses. However, bearing in mind Tipton – which held that, where an employment contract provided an appeals procedure, both the employer's original and appellate decisions to dismiss are necessary elements in the overall process of dismissal – the tribunal found that E's dismissal was unfair because of the way in which the appeal hearing was conducted. For example, a number of new matters were raised on appeal but the employer provided no documentary evidence as to why the appeal was rejected. The employer's 'considerable and largely unexplained delay' in determining the appeal – over four months after the decision to dismiss was made – added to the tribunal's concerns regarding the conduct and outcome of the appeal process.

3.103 However, the mere fact that there was a procedural failing in the appeal process will not of itself be sufficient to displace the fairness of the original dismissal. In London Central Bus Company Ltd v Manning EAT 0103/13 M, a bus driver, was dismissed on ill-health grounds. An employment tribunal found the dismissal unfair solely on the basis that the employer had failed to show M a list of unsuitable vacancies at the appeal hearing. The EAT overturned the decision on appeal, holding that a procedural defect in the appeal process, while relevant, could only render a dismissal unfair if, as stated in the Tipton case (above), it denied the employee the opportunity of demonstrating that the reason for his or her dismissal was not sufficient for the purpose of S.98(4). In the instant case, M had not been deprived of that opportunity, as showing him a list of jobs that he was not medically fit to perform would have been an utterly futile exercise. The EAT accordingly substituted a finding that he was fairly dismissed.

An employer who departs from the decision of an appeal panel will not necessarily be acting outside the band of reasonable responses. This was made abundantly clear by the EAT in Kisoka v Ratnpinyotip (trading as Rydevale

Day Nursery) 2014 ICR D17, EAT. There, K was dismissed from her job at a nursery for gross misconduct following a disciplinary hearing. When she appealed she was told that her appeal would be heard by an independent body whose decision would be final and that she would have no further right of appeal. Although the appeal panel allowed the appeal, the employer decided not to implement its decision and K was dismissed. An employment judge dismissed her claim of unfair dismissal, finding that on the evidence before the employer it had had reasonable grounds for finding K guilty of misconduct and that its decision to confirm the dismissal, made after investigating further information and giving consideration to the appeal panel's decision, had been reasonable in all the circumstances. Upon appeal, the EAT rejected K's argument that the employer could only reasonably have departed from the appeal panel decision had there been exceptional circumstances. This would be to put a gloss on the statutory language of S.98(4). It should be left to the good sense of employment tribunals to reach their judgments applying the statutory test to the individual facts of the case before them. In the instant case, the judge was perfectly entitled to take the view that the overall procedure followed was not unfair and that the decision of the employer was not unreasonable.

3.104 For a more detailed consideration of what amounts to a fair procedure in a given set of circumstances see Chapters 4 to 8, which consider each of the potentially fair reasons for dismissal. In particular, Chapter 6, 'Conduct', deals with disciplinary proceedings and the conduct of internal appeals.

3.105 Overlapping grievance and disciplinary issues

It is common for grievance and disciplinary matters to overlap but this can cause problems for employers deciding how to proceed. It is likely to prove difficult to resolve a grievance at the same time as pursuing disciplinary proceedings. If the employee is dismissed while the grievance procedure is ongoing, he or she may argue that the way the grievance was handled rendered the dismissal procedurally unfair. However, the employer may not wish to postpone disciplinary action indefinitely until the employee is satisfied that the grievance has been dealt with, particularly if the grievance is protracted. The Acas Code of Practice provides little guidance. It gives the example of an employee who raises a grievance during a disciplinary process, stating that the disciplinary process 'may be temporarily suspended' to deal with the grievance. It then goes on to state that where the disciplinary and grievance issues are related, it may be appropriate to deal with them 'concurrently' (para 46).

The Acas Guide provides examples of where it may be appropriate to consider suspending the disciplinary procedure to deal with a grievance, namely:

- where the grievance relates to a conflict of interest that the manager holding the disciplinary hearing is alleged to have

- where bias is alleged in the conduct of the disciplinary meeting

- where management has been selective with the evidence it has supplied to the manager holding the meeting

- where there is possible discrimination.

There is no guidance (either in the Code or its Guide) as to how long it might be appropriate to suspend proceedings for.

The case of Samuel Smith Old Brewery (Tadcaster) v Marshall and anor EAT **3.106** 0488/09 provides some useful guidance for employers dealing with concurrent disciplinary and grievance issues. M and his wife managed a pub for the employer. The employer informed them that staffing hours had to be reduced for financial reasons. The couple refused to implement the proposed reduction and raised a grievance. Following a grievance hearing the employer revised its proposed reduction of hours. It provided an opportunity to appeal the decision but stated that in the meantime the employees were required to implement the change, failing which disciplinary action might be taken. However, the two employees refused to comply and appealed against the grievance hearing decision. The employer instigated disciplinary proceedings but the employees refused to attend any disciplinary hearings until the grievance procedure had been exhausted. The employer proceeded with a hearing in their absence, following which it dismissed M and his wife for gross misconduct; namely, a 'deliberate refusal to carry out lawful instructions'. The employment tribunal concluded that the dismissal was within the range of reasonable responses but found that as the employees had been deprived of their right to pursue the grievance appeal, they had been unfairly dismissed.

The EAT overturned the tribunal's decision, holding that there was no authority for the proposition that it was necessary to complete the entire grievance procedure before a disciplinary hearing could take place. Furthermore, it was only in the rarest of cases that it would be outside the range of reasonable responses for an employer to proceed with a disciplinary process before hearing a grievance appeal, at least in the absence of clear evidence of unfairness or prejudice to the employee. The decision that no reasonable employer would have arranged for the grievance appeal to be heard until after the disciplinary hearing where there had been a repeated and ill-advised refusal to comply with a reasonable instruction was wrong in law and amounted to a substitution of the tribunal's views for those of the employer. The tribunal reached its decision with the benefit of hindsight, i.e. knowing that M and his wife would have complied with the instruction if their grievance was unsuccessful.

This decision will come as some relief to employers. However, it does not mean **3.107** that they can rush headlong to dismissal when grievance issues are outstanding. They will generally need to be sensitive to the issues raised in the grievance and to have gone some way towards dealing with it. For example, in the above case the grievance procedure was well under way before disciplinary action was

111

taken and the EAT acknowledged that the fact that the employer had already held a grievance hearing made its case stronger. Moreover, the employees' grievance had been quite protracted and they had continued to ignore the employer's instruction (which was found to be lawful) for about three months, at some significant cost to the employer. The EAT also noted that neither the management agreement nor the employer's disciplinary procedure contained a 'standstill' provision, providing that where a grievance had been raised in relation to a change in the status quo, the status quo was to be preserved until the determination of the grievance.

The Appeal Tribunal in the Marshall case did suggest that an employer might be expected to complete a grievance procedure before starting or continuing disciplinary proceedings where not to do so would cause clear prejudice to the employee. This might be the case where the grievance relates to discrimination or bullying or where bias is alleged in the conduct of the disciplinary or grievance hearing, or indeed in any other of the instances set out in the Acas Guide (see above). In Idris v London Borough of Redbridge ET Case No.3203259/10, for example, I was dismissed because he had been on sick leave for over a year. The employer had followed its capability procedure, holding several meetings with I and exploring ways that he could be enabled to return to work. However, the tribunal held that I's dismissal was unfair on the basis that I had lodged a legitimate grievance about the employer's treatment of him, which had not been completed. I had made it clear to the employer that he did not feel he could return to work until his grievance was resolved and occupational health had stated that the grievance issue needed to be resolved quickly to enable him to return to work. In those circumstances it was outside the band of reasonable responses to dismiss I before completing the grievance procedure. The tribunal did however reduce I's compensation by 70 per cent on the basis that it was more likely than not that I would not have returned to work, even had the grievance been completed.

3.108 Where grievance and disciplinary procedures are being run concurrently, the issues should generally be dealt with separately to prevent one from influencing or overshadowing the other. In Tweedle v Mid-Yorkshire Hospitals NHS Trust ET Case No.1801749/05, for example, T raised a grievance about a number of work-related issues, including bullying and an unmanageable workload. However, the subsequent investigation and grievance hearing focused on T's performance and capability, rather than on her complaints. T resigned, complaining about the manner in which her grievance had been dealt with, in particular that the employer had failed to take it seriously. A tribunal subsequently upheld her claim for constructive unfair dismissal, concluding that T was entitled to take the view that her complaints were being side-stepped. It noted that the investigatory report concentrated on her performance and capability and gave no explanation as to how this related to her complaints of bullying and harassment, etc.

Automatically fair and unfair dismissals 3.109

In the section headed 'Reason for dismissal' above, we listed the potentially fair reasons for dismissal set out in the ERA: if the employer establishes one of these reasons, the tribunal must then go on to consider whether it acted reasonably in dismissing for that reason. There are, however, certain reasons for dismissal which can be described as automatically fair or unfair in the sense that if one of these reasons is established the tribunal *must* find the dismissal fair or unfair (as the case may be) and the question of reasonableness does not arise.

Automatically fair dismissals. There are two situations where dismissal may 3.110 be described as automatically fair:

- where the employee was taking part in unofficial industrial action – S.237 TULR(C)A (see IDS Employment Law Handbook, 'Industrial Action' (2010), Chapter 8, 'Industrial action dismissals'). In these circumstances, employees do not have the right to complain of unfair dismissal at all. However, S.237 does not apply where the reason for dismissal (or selection for redundancy) is shown to be one of the following automatically unfair reasons – jury service; maternity and family leave; health and safety; employee representatives; protected disclosures; flexible working; pension scheme membership; assertion of the statutory right to time off to care for dependants; or time off for study or training – S.237(1A)

- where the employer was conducting a lock-out or the employee was taking part in official industrial action and the employer dismisses all relevant employees and does not re-employ any of them within three months – S.238 TULR(C)A (again, see IDS Employment Law Handbook, 'Industrial Action' (2010), Chapter 8, 'Industrial action dismissals'). In these circumstances tribunals will be prohibited from considering whether the dismissals were fair or unfair. However, S.238 does not apply where S.238A renders a dismissal automatically unfair (i.e. where an employee is dismissed because he or she took lawful industrial action in certain circumstances). Nor does it apply where the reason for dismissal (or selection for redundancy) is shown to be one of the following automatically unfair reasons – jury service; pregnancy and family leave; health and safety; employee representatives; flexible working; pension scheme membership; assertion of the statutory right to time off to care for dependants; or time off for study or training – S.238(2A).

Until fairly recently, it was generally accepted that dismissal for the purpose of safeguarding national security was also automatically fair. S.10(1) of the Employment Tribunals Act 1996 (ETA) provides that an employment tribunal 'shall dismiss' an unfair dismissal complaint if 'it is shown that the action complained of was taken for the purpose of safeguarding national security'. However, in B v BAA plc 2005 ICR 1530, EAT, the EAT held that an

113

employment tribunal should not reject an employee's unfair dismissal claim simply on the basis that the dismissal was carried out for the purpose of safeguarding national security. The tribunal should go on to consider whether dismissal was within the range of reasonable responses available to the employer. Mr Justice Burton, giving the EAT's judgment, stated that, in order to invoke S.10(1), an employer must prove, first, its reason for an employee's dismissal and, secondly, that dismissal for such reason was for the purpose of – and not necessarily that it had the effect of – safeguarding national security. In doing so, the employer is not required to prove the underlying facts and show that a threat to national security existed. The EAT went on to conclude, however, that a proper construction of S.10(1) requires a tribunal, notwithstanding a national security reason for dismissal, to consider whether the employer's decision to dismiss, as opposed to taking some other action such as redeployment, was reasonable. In the EAT's view, imposing such a reasonableness test upon national security dismissals would accord with a tribunal's obligation under the Human Rights Act 1998 to read S.10(1) in a way which gives effect to an individual's right to a fair trial under Article 6 of the European Convention on Human Rights.

3.111 The EAT's decision to import the 'reasonableness' test in S.98(4) ERA into S.10(1) ETA seems a touch contrived, notwithstanding the argument that S.10(1) might otherwise offend Article 6 of the European Convention. Up to now, it has been generally accepted that S.10(1) exists specifically to ensure that questions of reasonableness do not arise when dismissals are shown to be for the purpose of safeguarding national security. Arguably, therefore, the EAT's interpretation of S.10(1) ascribes a meaning to the provision which is diametrically opposed to its intended purpose.

In the circumstances, it is perhaps unsurprising that parts of the EAT's reasoning are somewhat unclear. In the last paragraph of the judgment, Mr Justice Burton seems to suggest that if a tribunal concludes that a national security dismissal is unreasonable, it should go on to consider whether the action complained of – i.e. the unfair dismissal – was itself for the purpose of safeguarding national security. Yet surely this is a question that the tribunal will already have answered in the affirmative at a much earlier stage of the proceedings when trying to establish whether S.10(1) is relevant to the case. Furthermore, Burton P does not make it clear what the effect of an unreasonable national security dismissal would be. One of the EAT's concerns was that, in the above circumstances, justice required the tribunal to consider whether the employer should have redeployed the employee as an alternative to dismissal. Rather than requiring the reasonableness test, however, this issue arguably turns on the original question of whether the employer's reason for dismissing the employee – as opposed to removing her from her post – was for the purpose of safeguarding national security, or for some other reason.

Automatically unfair dismissals

3.112

There are now numerous categories of automatically unfair dismissal (subject to various qualifications and exceptions). These are discussed in Chapter 9, 'Automatically unfair dismissals'.

4 Capability and qualifications

Definitions

Establishing lack of capability

Reasonableness

Procedural factors

Section 98(1)(b) and (2) of the Employment Rights Act 1996 (ERA) sets out the **4.1** potentially fair reasons for dismissing an employee. One such reason is where the dismissal 'relates to the capability or qualifications of the employee for performing work of the kind which he was employed... to do' – S.98(2)(a).

In this chapter we look first at the definitions of the two key words in the statutory provision – 'capability' and 'qualifications'. We then consider what an employer has to do to establish lack of capability or qualifications as a reason for dismissal. Finally, we deal with assessing the reasonableness of a dismissal on the ground of incapability and with the procedural factors involved.

Definitions
4.2

Section 98(2)(a) focuses on two key concepts: capability and qualifications, which, if lacking, can amount to potentially fair reasons for dismissal.

Capability
4.3
Capability is defined in S.98(3)(a) ERA as 'capability assessed by reference to skill, aptitude, health or any other physical or mental quality'. Examples of employees who have been held to be lacking in capability include:

- an inflexible and unadaptable worker – Abernethy v Mott, Hay and Anderson 1974 ICR 323, CA

- an employee who failed to reach the employer's standards, even if those standards were higher than those of similar employers – Fletcher v St Leonard's School EAT 25/87

- workers who could not meet management's raised standards – Gozdzik and Scopigno v Chlidema Carpet Co Ltd EAT 598/78

- an employee who, although efficient, was difficult and abrasive and so affected the quality of the staff's work generally – Bristow v Inner London Education Authority EAT 602/79.

In addition to these examples there are many cases in which incapability has stemmed from sickness or disability. These are dealt with separately in Chapter 5, 'Ill health'.

4.4 **Work of kind employee was employed to do.** The employee's alleged incapability must relate to the 'work of the kind which [the employee] was employed by the employer to do' – S.98(2)(a) ERA. Whether an employee is capable of doing the work which he or she was employed to do must be determined in accordance with the employee's current contractual obligations. This is particularly relevant where there has been a variation of the original employment contract, either by oral or written agreement, or by conduct. An example:

- **Plessey Military Communications Ltd v Brough** EAT 518/84: B was taken on as a miller. Shortly after starting work, he developed dermatitis and was taken off 'wet work' and put on 'dry work' as a vibro miller. Six months later he returned to wet work but suffered from dermatitis again, so the employer transferred him back to dry work, where he remained for some 18 months until he was dismissed. The employer argued that B was contractually employed to do wet work, which he was incapable of doing. On the facts, the employment tribunal found that the employer had transferred B permanently to dry work. On appeal, the EAT said that this showed that the terms of B's contract, and therefore his contractual position, had changed and that his capacity had to be assessed in accordance with that change.

However, a dismissal for incapacity may be fair even though the employee can still perform some of his or her contractual duties. In Shook v Ealing London Borough Council 1986 ICR 314, EAT, the claimant was employed as a social worker. Her appointment letter gave the employer the right to vary the duties and designation of the post. Back troubles prevented the claimant from continuing her social work and she was dismissed when the employer was unable to find alternative work for her. The EAT rejected the claimant's argument that the test for incapacity was to look not only at what she was actually doing at the time, but also at what she might potentially be called upon to do within the terms of the contract. The EAT said that the employer did not have to show that the claimant was incapable of performing every activity that she might be called upon to do – the reason for dismissal had to 'relate' to an employee's capability. However widely the claimant's contract was construed, her disabilities related to the performance of her duties, even though they may well not have affected all of them.

4.5 **Intransigent, inflexible or difficult employees.** Such employees are covered by the 'aptitude' or 'mental quality' part of the statutory definition, in so far as these shortcomings affect performance or relations with colleagues or customers. Where, however, an employee's personality leads to defiant clashes

118

with management or supervisors, or affects fellow employees' morale, the reason for dismissal may shade into conduct, or the resultant disharmony may be classed as 'some other substantial reason' justifying dismissal. In practice, employers get over these labelling problems by making a 'plea in the alternative' and citing alternative reasons on the ET3 (Response to Employment Tribunal Claim) form.

Where mental qualities clearly affect performance and efficiency or relations with clients and customers, the reason for dismissal is most appropriately categorised as lack of capability. In AJ Dunning and Sons (Shopfitters) Ltd v Jacomb 1973 ICR 448, NIRC, the claimant was regarded as 'competent, experienced, [with] a detailed knowledge of building law and was loyal, conscientious and meticulous'. But his uncooperative and unbending nature meant that he got on badly with clients. Indeed, several contractors refused to have him on their sites. As he clearly lacked the necessary aptitude and mental quality for the job of contracts manager, he was fairly dismissed for incapability.

Physical qualities or characteristics. Any physical quality may constitute a **4.6** potentially fair reason for dismissal if it means that someone is incapable of doing the job he or she was employed to do. In Bradley v Business Press International Ltd ET Case No.20265/83 the claimant started work in a photographic processing laboratory. Shortly afterwards an eye test revealed that he was colour-blind, which meant that he was physically unsuited to the work. His dismissal was therefore fair. And in Raymond v Dorset County Council ET Case No.426/79 the claimant was a fireman who wore spectacles. Health and Safety Regulations were introduced that prohibited firemen with spectacles wearing breathing apparatus. As the claimant's vision was well below the minimum recommended by the Home Office, he was fairly dismissed for lack of capability.

Note that care must be taken when dealing with disabled workers, since the Equality Act 2010 makes it unlawful to discriminate against disabled people and imposes a duty on employers to take reasonable steps to make certain types of adjustment to accommodate disabled workers. In Dyer v London Ambulance NHS Trust EAT 0500/13 the EAT observed that, although it will be rare for there to be circumstances in which no reasonable adjustment can be made, the facts of that case – where the claimant suffered a severe, life-threatening reaction to aerosols and perfume and so could not work in an office where such products were used – were an example of such exceptional circumstances. However, the EAT warned tribunals to think 'long and hard' before reaching a similar conclusion, or before concluding that a dismissal for reasons of capability was fair where there were adjustments that could have been made. For further information, see IDS Employment Law Handbook, 'Discrimination at Work' (2012), Chapter 6, 'Disability'; Chapter 20, 'Discrimination arising from disability'; and Chapter 21, 'Failure to make reasonable adjustments'.

4.7 **Overlap with misconduct.** Some cases of incapability may really be cases of misconduct. This was recognised by the EAT in Sutton and Gates (Luton) Ltd v Boxall 1979 ICR 67, EAT, when it said that 'capability' should be treated as applying to those cases in which the incapability is due to inherent incapacity. Where someone fails to come up to standard through his or her own carelessness, negligence or idleness, this is not incapability but misconduct. The main significance of the distinction is in respect of assessment of the employee's contribution to the dismissal, but it is also relevant in determining the steps that a reasonable employer ought to take before dismissing the employee – see 'Procedural factors' below.

In some cases conduct and capability can overlap as reasons for dismissal and it may prove difficult to distinguish between the two. In UPS Ltd v Harrison EAT 0038/11 for example, H, a driver, was dismissed after he had three avoidable accidents within a 12-month period. The employer's rules categorised this as incapability, which could result in dismissal on notice. H's first two accidents took place in January. At a disciplinary hearing in February, H admitted that they had been avoidable. He received a written warning in respect of the first accident and, simultaneously, a final written warning in respect of the second. The final written warning stated that a further accident within 12 months might result in dismissal. The third accident took place in December and H contended that it had not been avoidable, but the employer disagreed and dismissed H, citing misconduct as the reason. An employment tribunal found that the real reason for dismissal was capability, not conduct, and that the dismissal was unfair because H had been driving carefully at the time of the third accident and the employer had applied its 'three strikes' rule too prescriptively. The EAT, however, overturned the tribunal's decision, holding that when identifying whether the reason for dismissal related to conduct or capability, a tribunal should first make findings as to the employer's own reasons for dismissal, and then assess how those reasons should be characterised in terms of S.98. A tribunal is not bound by the label the employer puts on its reasons, but it is seeking to characterise the employer's reasons rather than to make findings of its own about the employee's conduct or capability. In this case, the tribunal had erred in starting from its own finding that H had been driving carefully at the time of the third accident, rather than from the employer's finding that each of H's three accidents had been avoidable. The case was therefore remitted to a different tribunal for rehearing.

4.8 Determining how best to categorise the reasons for dismissal can be especially difficult for employers filling in their ET3 response forms. If the reasons for dismissal do overlap, all that is required of employers is that they identify which in their own mind was the principal reason for dismissal – Hart v Sussex Group Training Association EAT 239/78. Failure to state accurately the precise statutory reason will not be fatal where the facts reveal a substantial reason under the ERA. An example:

120

- **Wood v Agnew Stores (Holdings) Ltd** EAT 582/85: an off-licence manager was dismissed for 'misconduct' because of large stock deficits. The employment tribunal preferred to regard this as a reason relating to capability but found that any mistake in nomenclature did not make the dismissal unfair. The EAT agreed that this was 'simply a matter of label' and that there was an evidential basis for the dismissal either way.

It will not necessarily matter, therefore, that the true reason for dismissal is found to be different from the one proffered by the employer, provided there is no change in the facts relied on and the employee is not disadvantaged in meeting the employer's case – see Chapter 3, 'Unfairness', under 'Reason for dismissal – identification of reason', for further details. Nevertheless, as discussed in Chapter 3, in some cases a failure to attach the correct label may be fatal for the employer. For example, in Home Charm Retail Ltd v Smith EAT 137/82 a store manager was dismissed for 'gross incompetence', even though he had made the store extremely profitable. The EAT upheld a finding of unfair dismissal because it could not see how the employee could have been incapable. The employer's concern centred on the manager's failure to follow strict paperwork procedures, and the EAT acknowledged that if the problem had been treated as one of misconduct then the employer might have escaped unfair dismissal liability. However, the employer did not present evidence which would have supported such a ruling.

Similarly, in Cobb v Governing Body of Tadcaster Grammar School ET Case **4.9** No.1803914/06 a tribunal held that the school had unfairly dismissed C, the head of science, for gross misconduct when the real reason was a fairly minor issue of capability. Each February, C voluntarily took the school sixth form on a skiing trip. In 2006, C stayed in separate accommodation. The trip passed without incident, but the school believed that his staying in separate accommodation amounted to a serious failure in his duty of care as party leader and dismissed him for gross misconduct. The tribunal held that C's failing was a matter of capability not misconduct, but that it did not affect his ability to carry out his role of head of science. An appropriate course of action would have been to suspend C from leading school trips until he had completed retraining in this area.

If an employee reacts badly to capability issues raised by his or her employer, this reaction can itself become a misconduct issue. This happened in Lewis v Blue Arrow Ltd ET Case No.2901344/06 after L was called to a capability meeting to discuss his reluctance to work in aircraft tanks, as required by his employer, because he suffered from claustrophobia. The next day his partner phoned the employer to say that L was ill. When L's manager called to find out the nature of his illness, L became very angry and was abusive towards him. A tribunal upheld the employer's decision to dismiss L for gross misconduct.

121

4.10 **Purported redundancy dismissals.** Employers are often tempted to make dismissals by reason of an employee's incapability more palatable by asserting 'redundancy' as the reason for dismissal. However, such good intentions can backfire. If challenged in the employment tribunal, an employer who has put forward redundancy as the sole reason for dismissal will be expected to show that the dismissal meets the statutory definition of redundancy in S.139(1) ERA. If it transpires that there has been no cessation of the business or cessation or diminution in the requirements of the business for employees to carry out work of a particular kind, then the dismissal cannot be for redundancy and may well be unfair on the basis that the employer has not made out the true reason for dismissal. An example of such a case is Enticknap v Musgrave Generators Ltd ET Case No.1902453/09. There, a home-working employee's ability to perform his sales role declined when he moved to live in France in 2005, as the distance meant that he was often unable to attend face-to-face client meetings, which were important for maintaining client relationships. He was dismissed in 2009, purportedly for redundancy, after he turned down the offer of an alternative sales role on terms that would have required him to move back to the UK. An employment tribunal expressed surprise that the employer – whose business was entirely UK-based – had ever agreed to keep the employee on after his move to France. However, the tribunal took a clear view that there was no redundancy situation in this case: there had been no diminution in the employer's need for employees to carry out UK sales work. Accordingly, the dismissal was found to be unfair (although the tribunal accepted that the employee could have been dismissed fairly on the ground of capability following an appropriate procedure).

That said, an employer who has implemented capability procedures in dealing with an underperforming employee may escape a finding of unfair dismissal if the only error it commits is labelling the reason for dismissal 'redundancy' rather than 'capability'. In Barbeary v John Laing Services Ltd ET Case No.2204621/97, for example, B was an Operations Director for JLS Ltd, with overall responsibility for a number of contracts, including a substantial one with AW. Serious problems arose with that contract, as a result of which AW informed B that it was imposing a time penalty. Two months later, AW suspended the contract on safety grounds, and shortly afterwards terminated it, alleging fundamental breach of contract by JLS Ltd. B was told that the loss of the contract made his continued employment untenable, and he was dismissed – ostensibly by reason of redundancy – and paid six months' salary in lieu of notice. A tribunal dismissed B's claim for unfair dismissal, holding that the reason for dismissal was lack of capability rather than redundancy. In the circumstances, and in view of B's seniority, the employer was entitled to hold him responsible for the loss of the contract. The economic loss this caused, the safety implications and the fact that B had been put on notice about the various problems during the progress of the contract, brought dismissal within the range of reasonable responses.

Some other substantial reason? As noted in Chapter 8, 'Some other substantial **4.11** reason', SOSR is a catch-all category that can be used by employers to justify dismissal. However, given the general nature of this category, it is not surprising that tribunals have sometimes found that a purported dismissal for SOSR was, in fact, for a more specific reason, such as capability. Two examples:

- **Lauffer v Barking, Havering and Redbridge University Hospitals NHS Trust** 2009 EWHC 2360, QBD: L, who had been employed by the Trust since 1998 as a consultant general surgeon, was involved in a number of operations that resulted in injury to the patients and, on a few occasions, in their death. L was suspended from practice and, following a meeting on 25 June 2009, was dismissed on the basis that the Trust had lost trust and confidence in him. The Trust stressed that the dismissal was not for misconduct or capability. L contended that the Trust should have followed its capability procedure, which provided for a detailed pre-hearing procedure, including retraining, counselling and performance review. L applied to the High Court for an interim injunction to restore him to the position he was in prior to the June meeting to enable him to engage in the capability pre-hearing process. The Trust argued that L had been dismissed for SOSR and that the contractual capability procedure was therefore not engaged. In granting L's injunction the Court noted that a loss of trust and confidence could fall under the category of 'some other substantial reason' (see Chapter 8, 'Some other substantial reason', under 'Miscellaneous reasons', for further details). However, in this case, the evidence indicated that it was L's lack of judgement and insight that gave rise to the Trust's concern. It was strongly arguable, said the Court, that this lack went to L's capability to perform his role as a surgeon and that what was relied upon as the cause for the loss of trust and confidence was actually an adverse view of L's capability. The Court therefore granted L's interim injunction and restored him to the position he was in prior to the meeting on 25 June when, as contended by L, the pre-hearing process under the Trust's capability procedure would be contractually available to him

- **Logan v Siemens Medical Solutions** ET Case No.1804973/06: the employer summarily dismissed L following a number of concerns raised by customers. In its response to L's unfair dismissal claim, the employer contended that the dismissal was fair for SOSR. The tribunal noted that third-party pressure to dismiss could amount to 'some other substantial reason' (see Chapter 8, 'Some other substantial reason', under 'Third-party pressure to dismiss', for further details). However, no such pressure had been exerted in this case. The tribunal considered that the reason could be more appropriately categorized as capability (as it involved L's performance and

123

attitude). Therefore, the information received from the customers should either have been investigated to see if specific problems could be identified, or dealt with as a capability issue with a view to seeing if L's performance could be improved. It certainly did not justify the employer dismissing L without notice.

4.12 Qualifications

'Qualifications' for the purposes of S.98(2)(a) ERA are defined as 'any degree, diploma or other academic, technical or professional qualification relevant to the position which [the employee] held' – S.98(3)(b). In Blue Star Ship Management Ltd v Williams 1978 ICR 770, EAT, the EAT held that 'qualifications', as defined, are concerned with 'matters relating to aptitude and ability' and that a 'mere licence, permit or authorisation' is not a qualification unless it is substantially concerned with the aptitude or ability of the employee to do the job. Thus, holding a driving licence is a qualification, because it relates to aptitude or ability to do a job which necessitates driving. But simply being registered as a seafarer or holding a union card would not be a qualification as defined.

The statutory definition of qualifications not only covers certificates of qualification that can be taken from one employer to another as evidence of an employee's authoritatively recognised ability to do a particular job, but also includes in-house aptitude tests devised by an employer, provided they are relevant to the particular job – Blackman v Post Office 1974 ICR 151, NIRC.

4.13 Qualification requirements need not necessarily be expressly stated in the contract of employment. They may be inferred from the job advertisement or implied from the nature of the job itself. Thus, in Tayside Regional Council v McIntosh 1982 IRLR 272, EAT, M was recruited as a motor mechanic. The job advertisement stated that possession of a clean current driving licence was essential, but M's contract made no mention of this. The EAT held that possession of a driving licence was clearly an essential and continuing condition of M's employment; he was therefore fairly dismissed when he was disqualified from driving.

Qualification dismissals usually arise where an employee is engaged on the understanding that he or she will acquire a particular qualification but then fails to do so. In Blackman v Post Office (above), for instance, B was employed as an unestablished post and telegraph officer who had to take an aptitude test after satisfactorily completing a trial period. He was allowed three attempts but failed each time (although only narrowly on the last occasion). Although there were no complaints about his practical work, his dismissal for lack of qualifications was held to be fair.

4.14 **Change in employer's requirements.** Qualification requirements that applied at the outset of the employment relationship are not to be regarded as fixed and

124

unchanging. In a fast-developing world qualifications can easily become outmoded as a result of new techniques or reorganisation, or the company's changing pattern of work. In Rooney v Davic Engineering Ltd ET Case No.14518/79, for example, the claimant had passed the company's trade test and successfully completed a three-month probationary period. When one side of the business declined, a particular customer began to represent 90–95 per cent of the company's business. This customer insisted that only those welders who had obtained a particular qualification be allowed to work on components intended for him. The claimant, who had been warned of the consequences of failure, took the test three times and failed each time. When the customer refused to waive the regulations and give the claimant another chance, the company dismissed him as it did not have enough work to keep him fully occupied. The employment tribunal found the dismissal fair.

Similarly, in Owen v Rhymney Valley District Council ET Case No.10316/87 the claimant's contract of employment did not originally require swimming-pool attendants to renew their life-saving qualification periodically. However, the tribunal held that the employer acted reasonably in varying the claimant's contract to include this requirement and so his dismissal for failing to renew his qualification was fair.

4.15 Although employers may change their policy regarding staff qualifications, they must act reasonably towards those serving employees who do not meet the new criteria. In Evans v Bury Football Club Co Ltd EAT 185/81 E was a professional footballer on a fixed-term contract when injury brought his playing career to an end. He was offered and accepted a job with the same club as assistant physiotherapist. A new manager was then appointed who required a qualified physiotherapist and did not consider E suitable because of his lack of experience and qualifications. E was given a week's notice of non-renewal before the expiry of his contract. A tribunal found his dismissal fair. The EAT upheld E's appeal, holding that, although the employer had changed its policy for good reason, it was not reasonable to dismiss the employee when contrary expectations had been raised in his mind.

4.16 **Lapse or loss of qualifications.** If an employee loses qualifications that are needed for his or her job, then dismissal is likely to be fair if no alternative employment is available. Loss of qualifications arises most frequently in relation to driving licences, as in Tayside Regional Council v McIntosh (above), where holding a licence was an 'essential and continuing condition' of M's employment and so his dismissal for disqualification from driving was fair. A similar conclusion was reached in respect of an otherwise exemplary employee employed as a sales representative who lost his driving licence after failing a breathalyser test while driving outside of work duties – Anderson v Safety Kleen UK Ltd EAT 306/90. In that case, the matter was not treated as a disciplinary offence but as the loss of an essential qualification for the job which the employee was employed to do. (See also Chapter 7, 'Statutory ban', under 'Driving bans'.) Likewise, in Devon and Cornwall Police and Crime Commissioner v Weavin EAT 0215/14 the employee lost his qualification as an Accredited Financial Investigator (AFI) after his employer raised concerns about his performance with the independent accreditation body. The employer applied its capability procedure in an attempt to address the employee's performance failings but was not satisfied that he had improved and, in any event, could not allow him to continue working as an AFI without accreditation. The EAT overturned a tribunal's finding of unfair dismissal. Although the tribunal had identified procedural failings in the capability process, the loss of accreditation formed part of the employer's reason for dismissal and was, in itself, sufficient to ground a fair dismissal for lack of capability.

Even if an employee subsequently regains the relevant qualification, this will not automatically render him or her capable of performing his or her duties. In Mathews v DHL Air Ltd EAT 0089/05 M, a pilot, had his Civil Aviation Authority (CAA) medical licence revoked because he was suffering from an anxiety-related disorder. Such a licence is a prerequisite for all working pilots. The employer subsequently decided that it had no option but to dismiss M given there was no assurance that he would regain his licence and he had refused an offer of alternative employment involving ground duties. By the time M's internal appeal against dismissal was heard, the CAA had restored his medical licence. M argued that this meant he had regained the capability to perform flying duties. However, the employer considered that M would not be operationally fit to fly until he had successfully completed a period of ground duties. Since M refused to undertake ground duties, his appeal against dismissal failed. A tribunal dismissed M's unfair dismissal claim, holding that the employer had a right to insist upon M performing ground duties as a means of rehabilitation. The EAT upheld the tribunal's decision, noting that while M had regained the necessary qualification for flying, the tribunal was entitled to find that he had not yet regained the necessary capability.

4.17 *Ill health.* If the employee loses his or her qualification due to ill health, the reason for dismissal will be capability (i.e. loss of the relevant qualification) rather than sickness. This may have implications for the steps an employer should follow prior to dismissal. Two contrasting examples:

- **Sayers v Loganair Ltd** EATS 0084/04: S had worked as a pilot on the basis that he was the sole aircrew. He became ill after being splashed by a disinfectant. Following a medical examination, a limitation was placed on his pilot's licence by the CAA, such that it was only valid if he was accompanied by a co-pilot. It was initially envisaged that the limitation would remain in place for approximately six months, but it was subsequently extended following a further medical examination. S was then dismissed on the basis that the restriction on his licence had not been lifted. He was advised by the employer that no alternative employment, such as a position on a multi-crew aircraft, was available. An employment tribunal held that S had been dismissed for a potentially fair reason; namely, the fact that he had ceased to hold the necessary licence to do the job for which he had been employed. However, it went on to conclude that S's dismissal was unfair because the employer should have obtained an up-to-date assessment of his state of health before deciding to dismiss him. The EAT held that this conclusion was flawed: a further medical examination would have made no difference to the restriction on S's licence since the employer's doctor had no power to alter the restriction. Furthermore, the employer had not been presented with any medical evidence or advice by or on behalf of the employee that his medical condition was likely to improve in the near future to the extent that the restriction would be lifted. Had the tribunal found dismissal to be on the ground of ill health, an up-to-date medical examination by the employer might have been required prior to dismissal. However, that was not the case here

- **NHS Fife Health Board v Stockman** EATS 0048/13: S, a doctor, was convicted for driving under the influence of alcohol and his medical registration was suspended by the General Medical Council on an interim basis, for a period of up to 18 months. S was dismissed on capability grounds six weeks into the suspension, shortly after beginning an addiction treatment programme. The employer's approach to loss of medical registration was to jump straight to the final stage of its capability procedure, meaning that an employee who lost his or her registration would not receive the investigation and support that applied at the earlier stages. The EAT upheld a tribunal's finding of unfair dismissal, on the basis that a reasonable employer would have obtained up-to-date medical evidence to identify how S was responding to the treatment programme and would have considered how long the suspension was likely to last in practice. In so holding, the EAT considered that the tribunal had been entitled to take into account evidence that treatment programmes of the kind S had embarked on had good success rates, and that the GMC often lifted interim suspensions after six or nine months where medical evidence confirmed a doctor's recovery. The decision was also influenced by the fact that, had S simply been off sick, he would have had a contractual entitlement to sick pay for up to 12 months.

Establishing lack of capability   4.18

Where an employer seeks to rely on incapability or lack of qualifications as the ground for dismissal, the onus is on it to show that this was the actual reason or principal reason for dismissal. But this should not be mistaken as meaning that an employer must objectively establish that a dismissed employee lacked capability. As Lord Denning MR put it in Alidair Ltd v Taylor 1978 ICR 445,

127

CA: 'Whenever a man is dismissed for incapacity or incompetence it is sufficient that the employer honestly believes on reasonable grounds that the man is incapable or incompetent. It is not necessary for the employer to prove that he is in fact incapable or incompetent.'

Put another way by Lord Justice Geoffrey Lane in the same case, the Court of Appeal's test of a fair capability dismissal (aside from procedure) has two elements:

- does the employer honestly believe this employee is incompetent or unsuitable for the job?

- are the grounds for that belief reasonable?

4.19 The Alidair case was decided in 1978. At that time, the onus was still on the employer to demonstrate both its belief in the employee's incapability, *and* the reasonableness of that belief. Shortly thereafter, however, S.6 of the Employment Act 1980 removed the onus on the employer in so far as the requirement to show reasonableness was concerned. As a result, the burden of proof in respect of the reasonableness of the employer's belief, and whether the employer has conducted a reasonable investigation to verify its belief, is neutral.

What the tribunal has to decide is whether there was material in front of the employer that satisfied the employer of the employee's inadequacy or unsuitability and on which it was reasonable to dismiss. An example of a case in which a tribunal did not consider there to be sufficient material on which the employer could establish capability as its reason for dismissal is Secretary of State for Justice v Baverstock EAT 0363/14. There, the employer relied on the fact that the employee had been unable to complete her full range of duties for her full hours in the 12 months leading up to her dismissal. Upholding a finding of unfair dismissal, the EAT stated that the tribunal had been entitled to find that the real reason for dismissal was the employee's disability and that the evidence presented by the employer 'was "not sufficiently strong" material to support a contention that the true reason for dismissal was capability'.

4.20 It is for the employer to set the standards asked of employees; tribunals cannot substitute their own view of an employee's competence. Employers can insist on levels of performance that are higher than those at comparable institutions. In Fletcher v St Leonard's School EAT 25/87, for example, the EAT said that an independent school was entitled to set its own standards of teaching, even if they were higher than those in a local state school, and so its dismissal of a teacher who failed to meet those higher standards was fair.

4.21 **Satisfying test**

The test set down in Alidair Ltd v Taylor 1978 ICR 445, CA, means that an employer has to produce evidence of poor performance and show that this was its real reason for dismissing the employee. In Kent County Council v Maidment

EAT 3/87 a teacher was dismissed following complaints about his competence by the school's headmistress. The teacher was given no reason for his dismissal and when he claimed unfair dismissal the Council produced no evidence from the members of the disciplinary subcommittee that took the decision to dismiss. The EAT upheld a tribunal finding that the employer had failed to prove the reason or principal reason for dismissal and that the dismissal was therefore unfair. It noted that the evidence tendered suggested that the reason for dismissal was 'a clash of personalities' and held that the tribunal was correct to find that there was insufficient evidence to establish the true reason for dismissal.

The availability of evidence of an employee's incapability will vary from job to job. In Fletcher v St Leonard's School EAT 25/87, for example, the employer could point to evidence that pupils' grades had fallen below the school's normal levels. Similarly, the incompetence of sales people can be shown by their failure to reach targets set by the employer. The incompetence of a pieceworker can be measured in the same way. However, failure to meet such targets does not always justify dismissal. The tribunal will take into account all the surrounding circumstances: whether the target was realistic; the reasons for the employee not attaining the target; how other sales staff fared and the employee's length of service. Two contrasting examples:

- **Sibun v Modern Telephones Ltd** 1976 IRLR 81, ET: S had been selling satisfactorily for 20 years. However, over a period of 15 months, his sales missed targets by 25 per cent. After several warnings, S was dismissed. A tribunal held that it was unreasonable to judge him on results over the last 15–18 months after his long period of satisfactory service. In the circumstances, a three-year period should have been allowed before it would have been fair to dismiss

- **R & M Gaskarth v Campbell** EAT 0008/12: the EAT overturned a tribunal's finding that the dismissal of a pub landlord for failing to meet takings targets over a period of 18 months was unfair. Although initial poor results could be attributed to the closure of local businesses, which deprived the pub of some of its customer base, it was not unreasonable for the employer to attribute responsibility for the pub's falling takings over the remainder of the period to the landlord. In addition, the employer was entitled to be concerned about the landlord's negative attitude and his apparent inability to act as a welcoming host. The case was remitted for rehearing by a fresh tribunal.

4.22 The incompetence of managers is often more difficult to measure and prove. In Cook v Thomas Linnell and Sons Ltd 1977 ICR 770, EAT, the EAT said that if an employer has genuinely come to believe over a period of time that a manager is incompetent, that in itself is evidence of incapability. However, it will be necessary to see whether there is supporting evidence. This may include evidence of a fall-off in trade or complaints from customers or colleagues. In Queensway

Discount Warehouses Ltd v McNeall EAT 569/85 the employer established incapability as the reason for dismissal based on a genuine belief that the manager was unable to motivate staff or deal with customers' orders and that his store presented a poor image. The tribunal's finding of fair dismissal was upheld by the EAT. Even where a senior employee's technical competence cannot be criticised, a lack of essential leadership skills can justify an employer's decision to dismiss for lack of capability. This was the case in Masson v Meggitt Avionics Ltd EAT 0183/13, in which the EAT commented that evidence as to leadership skills is 'always difficult to tie down in a concrete manner'. Where the employer's witness had satisfied the tribunal that the employee did not meet the necessary standards and there had been genuine but unsuccessful attempts by the employer to secure improvements in the employee's performance, the tribunal had been entitled to find that the dismissal was fair.

4.23 **Single acts of negligence or incompetence.** Incapability is usually established over a period of time, during which the employee's incompetence or inability to meet reasonable standards becomes apparent. However, in rare cases, a one-off act can sometimes be relied upon by employers to establish incapability, particularly if the act so undermines confidence in the employee that the employer is justified in dismissing for it. In Alidair Ltd v Taylor (above), for example, a pilot put the lives of many passengers at risk when he landed his aircraft negligently. This amounted to a sufficient reason for dismissal in view of his gross incompetence and the potentially calamitous consequences of his actions. And in Clark v Airflow Streamlines plc ET Case No.29621/83 an experienced car mechanic negligently left an old oil seal in place during a presale service. As a result, the purchaser of the car drove only 11 miles before the engine seized up and the rear wheels locked. The majority of the tribunal, while sympathising with the mechanic, found the dismissal fair in view of the potential danger and the damage to the employer's reputation.

In general, however, tribunals are unlikely to be sympathetic to an employer who dismisses an employee – particularly a long-serving employee – on account of a single error of judgement in circumstances where that error, although perhaps costly, is not potentially calamitous. In Day v Diemer and Reynolds Ltd 1975 IRLR 298, ET, a tribunal held the dismissal of a print machine operator to be unfair where he was dismissed because he had failed to follow a procedure designed to ensure that the gathering of various sections of a book was done properly and in the right order. Although his error led to a print run of more than 7,000 faulty books, the tribunal ruled that the sanction of dismissal was out of all proportion to the employee's mistake. A similar conclusion was reached by the tribunal in Jones v London Co-Operative Society 1975 IRLR 110, ET, where a till operator was dismissed for ringing up the wrong amount on the till and failing to give the customer a receipt. Although such errors were identified as grounds for summary dismissal in the Staff Code, the tribunal held that the employer had not acted reasonably in dismissing the employee for a one-off mistake, honestly made, in circumstances where she had an unblemished record and had been operating under considerable pressure on the day of the incident.

The fact that a serious incident has occurred on a particular employee's watch **4.24** is not necessarily evidence of incapability and all the circumstances need to be taken into account. For example, in Mezey v South West London and St George's Mental Health NHS Trust 2010 IRLR 512, CA, M, a consultant psychiatrist since 1991, allowed B, a patient suffering from a persistent delusional disorder, one hour's unsupervised leave in the hospital grounds. B absconded during this time and the next day attacked and killed a stranger. An investigating panel was convened to look into M's care and management of B. The panel's report found that it was not appropriate for M to have granted B unescorted ground leave before she had personally assessed him. Nevertheless, it concluded that this did not amount to serious professional incompetence. The Trust proposed to convene a capability hearing to consider the report's findings but M sought an injunction from the High Court to prevent the Trust from holding the hearing, contending that it would be in breach of contract. She submitted that the purpose of the contractual capability procedure was to improve future performance but the report had found that there was no issue of lack of capability in her case. The Court agreed and granted the injunction, holding that it was not open to the Trust to impose any capability sanction under the Department of Health (DoH) capability procedure on the basis of the report.

The Court of Appeal dismissed the Trust's appeal. Although the investigating panel had found that M had failed to deliver an adequate standard of care, a capability issue would only arise under the DoH capability procedure if that failure was caused by 'lack of knowledge, ability or consistently poor performance' and M's capability to practice had thereby been called into question. The findings of the report precluded such a judgment being made, having concluded that M's decision to grant unescorted leave, while inappropriate, was not likely to put other patients or the public at risk in the future and might well have been made by other competent practitioners. The report also emphasised that M was an obviously conscientious and competent consultant psychiatrist. Therefore, far from being called into question, her capability to practice had been vindicated. In the light of those findings, the threshold for invoking the capability procedure had not been crossed and the High Court had been right to conclude that to hold a capability hearing was a breach of contract which could be restrained by injunction.

Small but persistent errors. A number of small incidents, by themselves **4.25** relatively unimportant, may add up over a period of time to a sufficient reason for dismissal. Miller v Executors of John C Graham 1978 IRLR 309, EAT, concerned a farm manager whose technical qualifications and abilities were not questioned by his employer. However, following a number of small incidents the employer concluded that he was not capable of performing his managerial duties. He was warned about this but, after some initial improvements, matters deteriorated again. The EAT upheld the tribunal's finding that the dismissal was fair.

4.26 Systems of assessment. An employee's unsatisfactory results in periodic appraisals or performance management reviews often form the basis for initiating capability procedures that may eventually lead to dismissal. However, before accepting that it was reasonable to dismiss by reason of incapability, tribunals will often expect to see other evidence of incompetence in addition to the view of the manager responsible for conducting the employee's appraisal.

Sometimes, the introduction of a new appraisal system reveals a lack of capability in employees whose performance had not hitherto been called into serious question. In Gozdzik and Scopigno v Chlidema Carpet Co Ltd EAT 598/78, for example, the inefficiency of two employees was not fully revealed until a new bonus system was introduced. Their dismissal was held to be fair even though the employer had previously tolerated their lack of productivity.

4.27 Inconsistent evidence. An employer's case that an employee is (or has become) incapable of doing his or her job, or has failed to reach the requisite standards, can be undermined by evidence to the contrary. For example, the employee may seek to rebut the employer's claim by citing his or her track record in recent performance reviews or appraisals or by showing that he or she has been in receipt of discretionary benefits (such as bonuses) as evidence that the employer's contention is not valid. In White v British Telecommunications plc ET Case No.2700114/11 W had been placed under a performance management procedure and was dismissed when the employer decided he had failed to make sufficient improvements. However, shortly before his dismissal, W was allocated more staff to manage and awarded a large bonus, which was based in part on the achievement of personal performance goals. An employment tribunal held that this was inconsistent with the employer's case that W's performance was not of a sufficient standard, and therefore found the dismissal unfair.

Employers should, therefore, be careful to ensure that any dismissal is for a genuine capability reason and is not motivated by age discrimination. In Hetherington v London Borough of Brent and ors ET Case No.3303672/11 H, aged over 60, resigned after the school at which she worked subjected her to intensive observation and undue criticism of her performance. This was found to be part of a deliberate campaign to get rid of her because – given her age and experience – she cost more to employ than a young junior teacher. The written reports of H's observed lessons showed that she was, in general, meeting applicable standards, and there was evidence that the oldest teacher at the

132

school had also resigned after receiving similar treatment. An employment tribunal held that H had been unfairly constructively dismissed and subjected to age discrimination.

Reasonableness

Once the reason for dismissal has been established, the question of whether the dismissal was fair or unfair in the particular circumstances of the case will be judged according to the 'reasonableness' test set out in S.98(4) ERA, which is discussed in detail in Chapter 3, 'Unfairness', under 'Reasonableness of dismissal'. Under that test, the tribunal will consider not only what steps a reasonable employer would have taken when faced with an employee who does not come up to scratch, but also what steps the employer should have taken at the very start to minimise the risk of poor performance and to create the conditions that allow an employee to carry out his or her duties satisfactorily.

Proper training, supervision and encouragement are essential, especially where the employee has been promoted to a new job. If the employer fails to provide instruction and support at the outset, or sets unrealistic standards for an employee, then a subsequent dismissal for incompetence may be unfair. Three examples:

- **Fowler v Hertfordshire County Council** ET Case No.1501047/06: F, a teacher, was invited to a meeting to discuss some concerns the head teacher had about her. At the outset of the meeting the head announced that it was an informal capability meeting and gave F a letter listing 13 concerns, none of which was about F's teaching ability. The nature of the meeting and the number of concerns came as a complete surprise to F. The head had prepared a list of targets, including that one of F's lessons be observed each week for a four-week period. Two days later, when the head informed F that she would observe a lesson the following Monday, F resigned. The tribunal, by a majority, found that F had been unfairly constructively dismissed, holding that it was difficult to see how an employee could have any trust and confidence in an employer who initiated a capability procedure, even an informal one, when there were no grounds for doing so; set onerous targets for which there was no justification; and invited an employee to attend one meeting but then without warning turned it into something different and more serious

- **Mansfield Hosiery Mills Ltd v Bromley** 1977 IRLR 301, EAT: B was first employed as a boiler service fitter. The employer's advertisement for the job stated that he would receive training but in fact he received none. He did his job well at first and was promoted to plant maintenance supervisor. However, a number of complaints were made about his lack of enthusiasm (rather than technical competence). The EAT upheld the tribunal's finding

133

that the employer's failure to supervise, train and encourage a new or newly promoted employee or to warn the employee of likely dismissal are circumstances to be taken into account when considering reasonableness and may outweigh the employee's shortcomings

- **Steelprint Ltd v Haynes** EAT 467/95: S Ltd introduced a new computer system and, as a result, H's workload changed from proofreading to inputting orders onto the computer system. She failed to meet the speed and accuracy targets for inputting information and was dismissed. The EAT agreed with the tribunal's finding of unfair dismissal. H had not received any training to raise her typing performance and S Ltd had shown no flexibility in allowing her to do other tasks at which she may have excelled.

4.29 By contrast, in Queensway Discount Warehouses Ltd v McNeall EAT 569/85 a salesman was promoted to a managerial position, only to be dismissed after two disastrous trial periods. The employee claimed that the dismissal was unfair because he had not been put through the company's management training programme and so the employer had not fulfilled the company's responsibilities to someone newly promoted. The tribunal rejected this argument on the grounds that the employee was an experienced assistant manager and his failings were not due to lack of training.

4.30 Alternative employment

Despite adequate training and support, some employees still fail to make the grade. In such cases there is no obligation upon the employer to offer employment in a subsidiary position. Even where the employee has reached his or her position through promotion, that employee has no automatic right to return to his or her old job (unless there is provision to that effect in the contract). The employer's duty to consider redeploying the employee will depend on the circumstances of each particular case, although the size and administrative resources of the business will be especially important – see Bevan Harris Ltd (t/a The Clyde Leather Co) v Gair 1981 IRLR 520, EAT, a case which involved a small family business where redeployment was impracticable.

However, even a multinational company may not necessarily be acting unreasonably if it fails to offer a long-serving employee alternative work. In Tyndall v Burmah Oil Trading Ltd EAT 655/83 an employee with a good work record became incompetent and was retired early. He claimed unfair dismissal on the ground that the company should have found a niche for him. The EAT, however, thought early retirement was a reasonable response as there was a recession and the employee was nearing retirement age. And in Sonvadi v Superdrug Stores plc ET Case No.57554/94 the claimant was dismissed in July 1994 from his post as manager of one of the employer's stores by reason of incapability. The main grounds were his lack of communication with his staff and his failure to motivate them. He had joined the company as a trainee manager, been promoted to assistant manager, and then promoted to the post of manager in April 1993. His principal ground of complaint was that, in so far as he was perceived to be incapable, dismissal was not a reasonable response. At most, he should have been demoted in line with a provision in the company handbook that demotion could be used as an alternative to dismissal. In rejecting his claim of unfair dismissal the tribunal held that there is no rule of law that demotion should automatically be considered in capability dismissals. The employer was entitled in the circumstances of the instant case to come to the view that the claimant's appointment as an assistant manager would not work. Furthermore, in Bevan Harris Ltd (t/a The Clyde Leather Co) v Gair (above), the EAT emphasised that the correct test is whether the dismissal fell within the range of options open to a reasonable employer in the circumstances and held that a tribunal had therefore applied the wrong test in deciding that the dismissal was unfair because a reasonable employer would have considered demotion rather than dismissal.

Employers will never be expected to create a post for an employee artificially **4.31** but, in borderline cases, if a job is available and the employer has not offered it, the scales may be tipped in favour of the employee. There is a limit, however, to how far an employer will be expected to accommodate an employee who is incapable of mastering the skills of the particular job that he or she is employed to do. In Watson v Commissioners of Inland Revenue ET Case No.2105124/03 the question arose as to whether an employer had failed to act reasonably when declining to move W into a job that did not require the specific skills in respect of which the employee was especially weak. W accepted that the employer had reasonably reached a view that he was incapable of carrying out his duties to a satisfactory standard and conceded that the procedure leading to his dismissal had been fair. However, he contended that his dismissal was nonetheless unfair in that, given the large number of duties that someone in his grade could be called upon to undertake, he should have been moved sideways into a post that did not require him to perform the duties that he was incapable of carrying out satisfactorily. The tribunal rejected this argument and held that W had not been unfairly dismissed. There was no duty on the employer to move the employee sideways: were it otherwise, the employer might never be able to dismiss an employee such as the claimant fairly for lack of capability, since the employer would have to exhaust every potential post first.

By contrast, the tribunal in Johnson v British Telecommunications plc ET Case No.1200125/09 reached the opposite conclusion. J had 24 years' service, only the last three of which had been in the sort of project management role in which his performance was found to be wanting. The tribunal considered that BT had acted reasonably in rejecting the possibility of moving J to a more junior project management role, since the skills required were the same as in his current, senior role. However, J had worked in many different roles for BT over the years and the tribunal held that a reasonable employer (of BT's size and

135

resources) would have considered redeploying J to a different type of role, in which he may well have been able to perform to a sufficient standard. The dismissal was therefore unfair.

4.32 Procedural factors

It has long been recognized that employers should follow a fair procedure before dismissing an employee for incapability. In Lewis Shops Group v Wiggins 1973 ICR 335, NIRC – approved by the EAT in Littlewoods Organisation Ltd v Egenti 1976 ICR 516, EAT – the NIRC commented that 'the general concept of fair play inherent in the disciplinary procedures should also guide management in considering a dismissal for inefficiency'. This means that, in general, an employer should be slow to dismiss an employee for incapability 'without first telling the employee of the respects in which he is failing to do his job adequately, warning him of the possibility or likelihood of dismissal on this ground, and giving him an opportunity of improving his performance' – James v Waltham Holy Cross UDC 1973 ICR 398, NIRC. This can be broken down into the following basic steps:

- proper investigation/appraisal of the employee's performance and identification of the problem
- warning of the consequences of failing to improve
- a reasonable chance to improve.

In Burns v Turboflex Ltd EAT 377/96 the EAT emphasised the fact that employers should allow employees to answer allegations of poor performance. In that case the claimant was dismissed while he was out of the country. The EAT held that it was contrary to the rules of natural justice to deny him the chance to respond to the allegations made against him.

4.33 Having frank conversations about an employee's performance can be unpleasant, but employers should resist the temptation to do away with a proper procedure out of a sense of kindness or a wish to spare the employee an ordeal, since doing so could result in a finding of unfair dismissal. Indeed, whatever the employer's motivation, if an employer fails to follow the correct procedural steps it is very likely that a tribunal will rule that it acted unreasonably and unfairly. And where the Acas Code of Practice on Disciplinary and Grievance Procedures applies, the tribunal may well increase the compensation it awards by up to 25 per cent (see 'Acas Code of Practice' below).

It is also important that the employer follow the correct procedure that is appropriate to the circumstances. This is illustrated by the case of Welsh National Opera Ltd v Johnston 2012 EWCA Civ 1046, CA. The Court of Appeal held that the tribunal was wrong to conclude that concerns about an orchestral oboist's ensemble playing could not be dealt with under the audition procedure for 'poor artistic performance', as set out in the applicable collective agreement. By subjecting the oboist instead to a modified version of the ordinary disciplinary procedure reserved for non-artistic capability issues, the employer had acted outside the range of reasonable responses, rendering his subsequent dismissal unfair.

Settlement agreements as alternative. Given the requirement to issue warnings **4.34** and to allow a reasonable time for improvement at each stage, a proper capability procedure may take several months to conclude. In addition, such a procedure requires considerable input from the employer in terms of management and HR time and resources. It can also be a stressful experience for the employee, who will be concerned about exactly what he or she must do in order to retain his or her job. It can therefore be tempting for the employer to attempt to bypass a potentially lengthy and resource-intensive capability procedure by offering the employee the option of a quick, negotiated exit, formalised with a settlement agreement in which the employee waives his or her right to bring any claims against the employer.

However, the employer may be reluctant to enter into settlement negotiations for fear that, if they do not end in agreement, anything said during negotiations may be disclosed by the employee in subsequent legal proceedings. The employee might, for example, treat the employer's approach as a breach of the implied term of trust and confidence and resign, claiming unfair constructive dismissal and breach of contract. Alternatively, if the employee rejects settlement in favour of proceeding with a capability procedure and is then dismissed after failing to make the required improvements, he or she might claim unfair dismissal, and seek to refer to the offer of a settlement agreement as evidence that the capability procedure was a sham.

There are two provisions which are potentially relevant in these circumstances **4.35** and which may ensure that unsuccessful settlement negotiations will remain confidential between the employer and the employee. The first is the 'without prejudice' rule, which prevents written or oral statements made in a genuine attempt to settle an existing workplace dispute from being relied on in any subsequent legal proceedings. The second is S.111A ERA, which came into force on 29 July 2013 and provides that any offer made or discussions held with a view to an employment relationship being terminated on agreed terms is inadmissible in unfair dismissal proceedings. The without prejudice rule and S.111A are discussed in detail in IDS Employment Law Handbook, 'Employment Tribunal Practice and Procedure' (2014), Chapter 13, 'Evidence', in the section 'Evidence of settlement negotiations', under '"Without prejudice" negotiations' and 'Pre-termination negotiations' respectively.

137

4.36 Acas Code of Practice

As explained in Chapter 3, 'Unfairness', under 'Fairness of internal procedure – Acas Code of Practice', the revised Acas Code of Practice on Disciplinary and Grievance Procedures ('the Acas Code') sets out principles for handling disciplinary and grievance procedures in the workplace with which employers and employees are expected to comply. The Code is relevant to the question of liability and will be taken into account by a tribunal when determining the reasonableness of a dismissal in accordance with S.98(4) – S.207 Trade Union and Labour Relations (Consolidation) Act 1992 (TULR(C)A). If the dismissal is found to be unfair, the tribunal can increase (or indeed decrease) an award of compensation by up to 25 per cent for an unreasonable failure to follow the Code if it considers it just and equitable to do so – S.207A TULR(C)A.

The Acas Code contains a section on handling disciplinary issues (pages 5–9), which sets out the steps employers must normally follow, namely:

- establish the facts of each case

- inform the employee of the problem

- hold a meeting with the employee to discuss the problem

- allow the employee to be accompanied at the meeting

- decide on appropriate action

- provide the employee with an opportunity to appeal.

4.37

Scope of Acas Code. The Introduction to the Acas Code states that it is designed to help employers and employees deal with disciplinary and grievance situations in the workplace and confirms that 'disciplinary situations' include 'poor performance'. This clearly embraces many of the situations considered above; for example, where the employee is inflexible and un-adaptable or has simply failed to meet the employer's targets. However, it does not appear to cover 'qualification' cases, since in most of these there is an absence of 'fault' on the part of the employee. Nevertheless, an employer will still need to follow a fair and appropriate procedure in such cases and the Code establishes general standards of good practice that may prove helpful.

The Acas Code sets out one disciplinary procedure to deal with both 'conduct' and 'poor performance'. This is somewhat surprising given that such issues have traditionally been viewed as best dealt with under separate procedures – disciplinary (for misconduct) and capability (for poor performance). In Littlewoods Organisation Ltd v Egenti (above), for example, the EAT stated that 'the same fairly strict requirement of various steps of procedure, which exists in cases of dismissal for misconduct, where it is a disciplinary measure, is or may be different from a situation in which the dismissal is on the ground of lack of competence or lack of capability'. Indeed, a tribunal could find that an employer has acted unfairly if a performance issue is treated in exactly the same way as a conduct issue. For example, the employer may need to be more sensitive to the needs of an employee with a performance issue, since he or she may be trying his or her best but may simply not be up to the job. Furthermore, giving an employee the opportunity to improve is likely to be more important in performance cases.

Many employers do have a separate capability procedure in place. This is **4.38** recognised in the introduction to the Acas Code, which provides that, 'if employers have a separate capability procedure they may prefer to address performance issues under this procedure'. It goes on to state that 'the basic principles of fairness set out in this Code should still be followed, albeit that they may need to be adapted'.

The Acas Code implies that where an employer does have a separate capability procedure, the employer may choose which to follow. Employers should be cautious in doing so as tribunals may find dismissal to be unfair if there are capability procedures in place that were not adhered to. Nevertheless, a failure to follow either procedure to the letter will not necessarily render a dismissal unfair. In UPS Ltd v Harrison EAT 0038/11, for example, the employer had both a disciplinary procedure and a capability procedure. On the facts, it was difficult to identify whether the employee's actions – having three avoidable road accidents in a company vehicle within 12 months – constituted misconduct or incapability. The employer's policies categorised this as incapability, but the employer dealt with the employee primarily, though not entirely, in accordance with its disciplinary procedure. The EAT held that 'the question was not whether UPS failed to follow its own policy, but whether the procedure it followed was reasonable. No policy or procedure can possibly cover every circumstance; and a dismissal is not necessarily unfair by reason of a breach of a policy or procedure.'

However, switching from one procedure to the other without good reason may **4.39** be unwise. In Bennett v Cornwall County Council and ors ET Case No.1701815/06, for example, the tribunal held that a switch by the employer from a capability to a disciplinary procedure without any reason or explanation was unfair. It meant that the 'whole push' of the procedure was radically different, although the subject matter was substantially the same. It was not reasonable to expect B to properly meet the concerns presented in a different framework and with a different intention.

Investigation/appraisal   4.40
The introduction to the Acas Code states that 'employers should carry out any necessary investigations, to establish the facts of the case'. As mentioned in the section 'Establishing lack of capability' above, the onus is on the employer to show a potentially fair reason for dismissal. This may be difficult to do in

139

relation to capability dismissals if the employer has not carried out a proper investigation of the employee's failings in performance. Investigation may highlight the reason for the employee's poor performance and may bring to light management's own failings. This in turn may determine what a reasonable response by management should be. Since complaints about an employee's incapability must relate to 'work of the kind which he was employed by the employer to do' (S.98(2)(a) ERA), investigation and appraisal must obviously take place in the context of the job the employee was employed to do. Furthermore, if the employer's complaint is that the employee lacks a relevant qualification, this should be investigated to ensure, for example, that the qualification is really necessary for the employee to carry out his or her duties.

If the employer fails to investigate, dismissal may be unfair in two ways: first, because no potentially fair grounds were shown; and, secondly, because the dismissal was not handled properly. The employer must ensure that the employee is aware of the charges being levelled and allow him or her the opportunity to state his or her case. In British Midland Airways Ltd v Gilmore EAT 173/81 a pilot was only made aware of the charges against him at his disciplinary hearing and he was not aware that the company had any intention of dismissing him. In addition, the findings of the hearing were never communicated to him. Instead he was merely told that he was dismissed. The EAT held that the dismissal was unfair because of these breaches of natural justice. It said that procedural requirements could not be waived merely because the employee was involved in a job where incompetence could result in death. (Note that the dismissal of an airline pilot for a single act of incompetence is likely to be fair in principle – see Alidair Ltd v Taylor 1978 ICR 445, CA. However, in that case the employee was given a full opportunity to hear what was said against him and to state his case.) In SMT Sales and Service Co Ltd v Irwin EAT 485/79 the performance results of a branch manager with 27 years' service fell below targeted levels. The branch manager was dismissed instantly when he refused to resign. There was no investigation into the reason for his poor performance and his dismissal was therefore held to be unfair.

4.41 **More than one suspect.** Where one of two employees is suspected of being responsible for acts or omissions meriting dismissal and the employer, despite reasonable investigation, cannot discover which of them is to blame, it may be fair to dismiss both of them. This rule is not confined to dismissals for misconduct and can apply equally to dismissals for incapability – Guberman v Augustus Barnett (Scotland) Ltd EAT 152/85. However, this rule is not applied lightly. In another EAT decision, it was made clear that suspicion must have been narrowed to the point of certainty that it must have been one of two employees who was guilty of the act complained of – Leyland Vehicles Ltd v Wright EAT 712/81.

Probationers. Employees on probation are a special case because tribunals and **4.42** courts consider it particularly important that reasonable steps are taken to maintain appraisal of probationers throughout the probationary period. This was stressed by the EAT in Post Office v Mughal 1977 ICR 763, EAT, where it said that: 'The question for the... tribunal is: have the employers shown that they took reasonable steps to maintain appraisal of the probationer throughout the period of probation, giving guidance by advice or warning when such was likely to be useful or fair; and that an appropriate officer made an honest effort to determine whether the probationer came up to the required standard, having informed himself of the appraisals made by supervising officers and any other facts recorded about the probationer? If this procedure is followed, it is only if the officer responsible for deciding upon selection of probationers then arrives at a decision which no reasonable assessment could dictate, that [a] tribunal should hold the dismissal to be unfair.'

In White v London Transport Executive 1981 IRLR 261, EAT, it was argued, on the basis of the principle laid down in Mughal, that there is an implied term in every probationary contract of employment that the employer is bound to support, assist, offer guidance to and train the probationary employee. The EAT rejected this argument, but said that 'the right term to imply is... an obligation on the employer to take reasonable steps to maintain an appraisal of a probationer during a trial period, giving guidance by advice or warning where necessary'. A failure to guide and train may render an otherwise fair dismissal unfair – ILEA v Lloyd 1981 IRLR 394, CA.

It is likely to be rare in practice that a probationer will able to claim that his or **4.43** her dismissal for lack of capability is unfair. This is because probationary periods are typically limited to the first six (sometimes 12) months of the employee's employment, whereas S.108 ERA restricts the right to claim ordinary unfair dismissal to employees who have two or more years' continuous service. However, there are some employers who use longer probationary periods, and some who apply probationary periods to promotions for existing employees.

Hearing
4.44
The Acas Code requires a 'disciplinary hearing' to be held for the employee to answer any allegations of poor performance. However, many employers may prefer to have a capability hearing for performance issues, reserving disciplinary hearings for conduct issues. As noted above, the Code allows employers to use their own capability procedures to address performance issues, provided the 'basic principles of fairness' set out in the Code are still followed. An example:

- **Buckley v Barker and Stonehouse Ltd** ET Case No.2500923/05: on 16 November 2004 B, an assistant store manager at Darlington, was invited by the Managing Director's secretary to attend a meeting on 18 November. Having no idea what the meeting was to be about, B asked the Company

141

Director for clarification but he said that she would find out on the day. The meeting took place with the two directors and B (who was unrepresented). She was informed that they had several fundamental concerns about her performance which they wanted to discuss with her; for example, her lack of commercial awareness. B was given two options: to move from Darlington to Middlesbrough as an assistant manager for a period of retraining; or to stay and face a disciplinary/capability hearing. B asked for two or three days to think about the situation but was told that the company would like to get a decision that day. B telephoned the Company Director later that day to tell him she was going to resign. The tribunal upheld B's claim for unfair constructive dismissal. It held that although the employer was within its rights to have a meeting to discuss B's perceived shortcomings, the way it had gone about it was unfair. It had called her to a meeting without giving her any details or advising her of her right to be accompanied. Although retraining in Middlesbrough might have been an option further down the line, the employer should first have clearly informed B of the improvements required in her performance and given her a period in which to comply.

This case indicates that what an employer sees as an 'informal chat' may in fact be a disciplinary/capability hearing with the added procedural requirements that entails, such as the right to be accompanied (see 'Right to be accompanied' below). It also highlights the fact that if an employer does not follow the correct procedure, not only is there a risk of a finding of unfair dismissal at a later date, but, more immediately, an employee may be entitled to resign and claim constructive dismissal.

4.45 It is not uncommon for employees facing criticism of their performance to go off sick shortly before a hearing is due to take place. An employer does not need to postpone the hearing indefinitely in these circumstances, but proceeding too quickly in the employee's absence may lead to a finding of unfairness. In Bridgeman v Family Mosaic Housing Association ET Case No.2201804/11, for example, the employee was already on a final written warning for poor performance, and the hearing at which that warning was issued had been delayed twice, at the employee's request. When the employee's performance did not improve, the employer scheduled a further capability hearing. The employee went off sick, and the employer decided to go ahead with the hearing in her absence. A tribunal found the dismissal procedurally unfair, holding that it was premature for the employer to proceed in the employee's absence on the first occasion that she was unable to attend. The right to have a hearing and put one's case is 'the bedrock of a fair dismissal process'. However, the tribunal accepted that the employee would have been fairly dismissed for incapability after a hearing and her compensation was limited accordingly.

4.46 **Right to be accompanied.** Under S.10 of the Employment Relations Act 1999 (ERelA), where a worker 'reasonably requests' to be accompanied at a

142

'disciplinary hearing', the employer must permit the worker to be accompanied by a 'companion'. The companion – chosen by the worker – may be a trade union representative or a fellow worker – S.10(2A).

A disciplinary hearing is defined in the ERelA as a hearing that could result in:

- the administration of a formal warning – S.13(4)(a)

- the taking of some other action – S.13(4)(b)

- the confirmation of a warning issued or some other action taken – S.13(4)(c) (this applies to appeal hearings).

Therefore, even if the employer is holding what it terms a 'capability' hearing **4.47** to discuss performance issues, the statutory right to be accompanied would still apply if it is likely to result in a formal warning or some other action.

For further information on the right to be accompanied, and in particular what is meant by the term 'reasonably requests' in S.10 ERelA, see Chapter 6, 'Conduct', under 'Disciplinary proceedings – right to be accompanied'.

Right to legal representation. It is generally accepted that neither the ERelA **4.48** nor the Acas Code confers an entitlement to have a legal representative present at a capability hearing. However, the Court of Appeal has held that Article 6 of the European Convention on Human Rights, which provides that an individual has the right to a fair hearing, may provide employees with the right to legal representation in circumstances where the hearing may determine the employee's right to practise his or her profession – Kulkarni v Milton Keynes Hospital NHS Foundation Trust and anor 2010 ICR 101, CA. However, the judgments of the Supreme Court in R (on the application of G) v Governors of X School 2011 ICR 1033, SC, and the Court of Appeal in Mattu v University Hospitals of Coventry and Warwickshire NHS Trust 2013 ICR 270, CA, suggest that these circumstances will be rare. These cases, which did not involve unfair dismissal claims, are discussed further in Chapter 6, 'Conduct', under 'Disciplinary proceedings – right to legal representation'.

Right to call witnesses. Paragraph 12 of the Acas Code states that both **4.49** employees and employers should be able to call relevant witnesses. This has raised some eyebrows, not least because case law is somewhat ambiguous on this point. However, the rules of natural justice, in so far as they apply to disciplinary hearings, require that an employee know precisely what the accusations against him or her are and have a full opportunity of stating his or her case. It seems appropriate, therefore, that the question of whether or not it is reasonable to allow a witness to be called in a particular case should be decided in light of these principles. The right to call witnesses is discussed in greater detail in Chapter 6, 'Conduct', under 'Disciplinary proceedings – disciplinary hearings'.

4.50 **Warnings**

In Polkey v AE Dayton Services Ltd 1988 ICR 142, HL, Lord Bridge observed that in the great majority of cases employers will not be considered to have acted reasonably in dismissing for incapability unless they have given the employee fair warning and a chance to improve. In practice, most employers will have already incorporated a system of warnings into their procedures. Even before Polkey, warnings were considered a necessary procedural requirement, particularly in cases of misconduct, and this requirement was applied to dismissals for capability as early as 1973 – Winterhalter Gastronom Ltd v Webb 1973 ICR 245, NIRC.

The Acas Code confirms the importance of warnings as part of the disciplinary or capability process, stating at para 19: 'Where misconduct is confirmed or the employee is found to be performing unsatisfactorily it is usual to give the employee a written warning. A further act of misconduct or failure to improve performance within a set period would normally result in a final written warning.'

4.51 In the context of incapability, warnings are most appropriate where it is in the employee's power to improve his or her performance. Warnings give incompetent employees the opportunity to improve their performance and management a chance to pinpoint the reason for poor performance, be it insufficient training, weak support from colleagues, personality problems, lack of effort or a genuine inability to perform the job competently. However, there is no hard-and-fast rule that a dismissal will necessarily be unfair if no formal warning is given. The Acas Code itself merely states that it is 'usual' to give a written warning, implying that there are some cases where a warning will not be needed. The important question is whether the employee was aware of the employer's dissatisfaction with his or her work – Laycock v Jones Buckie Shipyard Ltd EAT 395/81. Clearly, though, such an awareness will usually be brought home by a formal warning and, in practice, warnings of some kind should be given in most cases (but see further below). This is particularly so in light of the fact that employers risk any award of compensation for unfair dismissal being increased by up to 25 per cent if the tribunal considers that they unreasonably failed to comply with the Code (see Chapter 16, 'Compensatory awards: adjustments', under 'Adjustments for breach of Acas Code of Practice').

Employers should make it clear to employees that they are warning them and the consequences of a failure to improve performance should be set out in clear terms – for instance, that it 'may result in dismissal or some other contractual penalty such as demotion or loss of seniority' (para 21 of the Code). An example:

- **British Sulphur Corporation v Lawrie** EAT 159/86: L, a researcher, acquitted herself well in most aspects of her job but her written work for the company journal was substandard. She told her departmental head that she did not want to write any more articles and shortly afterwards she was dismissed. The EAT (by a majority) upheld a tribunal decision that the dismissal was unfair. The company had given L no warning about the consequences of a failure to improve and had allowed an insufficient period of time for any improvement to be assessed. If L had been formally warned that failure to improve would mean dismissal she might have agreed to continue to write articles and, with instruction, might have improved.

4.52 After a warning has been given, the employer should abide by its terms. For example, having given an employee a warning of possible demotion, it may be unfair for the employer then to dismiss for incompetence demonstrated during the period of the warning – Marks and Spencer plc v Williams EAT 528/81.

An employer wishing to dismiss an employee for not performing his or her duties properly following an earlier warning should ensure that the warning is relevant to the current problem; otherwise, dismissal may be unfair. For example, in Eccles v Ribble Motor Services Ltd EAT 609/90 the EAT held that an employer who dismissed an employee for fundamental incompetence was not entitled to take into account a prior warning for carelessness. Similarly, when someone is promoted, a warning to the effect that he or she will not be able to step back down to the previous role if unable to perform the new role to a satisfactory standard will not generally be sufficient if it later becomes necessary to dismiss the employee for incompetence in the new role, unless the employee had been expressly put on probation – Eddels v Anna French Ltd EAT 848/93.

4.53 According to the Court of Appeal in Davies v Sandwell Metropolitan Borough Council 2013 IRLR 374, CA, there are rare circumstances – such as where a prior warning was 'manifestly inappropriate' – in which it may be legitimate for a tribunal to 'go behind' a final written warning given before dismissal. In General Dynamics Information Technology Ltd v Carranza 2015 IRLR 43, EAT, the EAT considered that the guidance given in the Davies case limits the possibility of reopening an earlier warning to circumstances where the warning was allegedly issued in bad faith, manifestly improper or issued without any prima facie grounds. For further discussion of when a tribunal should reopen an earlier warning, see Chapter 6, 'Conduct', in the section 'Disciplinary proceedings', under 'The decision – prior disciplinary record'.

In some circumstances a warning can be implied. In Judge International Ltd v Moss 1973 IRLR 208, NIRC, for example, the failure to review an employee's salary was held to be sufficient to put him on his guard. Similarly, a warning could be implied from the deterioration of a close working relationship, such as that which pertains between a managing director and his personal secretary – Brown v Hall Advertising Ltd 1978 IRLR 246, EAT. However, given the importance attached to warnings in the Acas Guide (a non-statutory and non-binding document which accompanies and expands upon the Acas Code), such cases are likely to be few and far between.

145

4.54 The Lord Chancellor in Polkey v AE Dayton Services Ltd 1988 ICR 142, HL, emphasised that there would be some occasions where the failure to warn employees about their shortcomings would not render a dismissal unfair. Furthermore, the Acas Code states that 'if an employee's first misconduct or unsatisfactory performance is sufficiently serious, it may be appropriate to move directly to a final written warning. This might occur where the employee's actions have had, or are liable to have, a serious or harmful impact on the organisation' (para 20). This implies that a warning should only be dispensed with altogether in exceptional circumstances and it must be stressed that there is no hard-and-fast rule as to when warnings are unnecessary – each case must be considered on its own facts. The following are the main categories of capability dismissal where warnings have successfully been dispensed with.

4.55 **Gross incompetence or unsuitability.** It may be fair to dismiss without warning where the employee's continued employment is against the interests of the business, either because of gross inadequacy or where the employee would not have changed his or her ways in any case – James v Waltham Holy Cross UDC 1973 ICR 398, NIRC. As Sir John Donaldson said, 'cases can arise in which the inadequacy of performance is so extreme that there must be an irredeemable incapability. In such circumstances, exceptional though they no doubt are, a warning and opportunity for improvement are of no benefit to the employee and may constitute an unfair burden on the business.'

The EAT applied this principle in Littlewoods Organisation Ltd v Egenti 1976 ICR 516, EAT. A costs clerk responsible for the company's audits was dismissed without being given an explicit warning that he would be treated this way if his performance did not improve, although his work had been unfavourably assessed more than once. A tribunal found the dismissal to be unfair. On appeal the EAT remitted the case, reminding the tribunal that there may be cases in which a person may be so incompetent that warnings are not necessary, and a person in the clerk's position must, in all the circumstances, have been aware that dismissal was on the cards.

4.56 It may also be unnecessary to warn an employee who refuses to admit that his or her performance is not up to scratch: a tribunal may infer that a warning would have been to no avail.

4.57 **Intransigent or inflexible attitudes.** It may, in some circumstances, also be pointless warning an employee whose attitude towards his or her work or workplace is intransigent or inflexible. This is particularly true where it is clear that the employee is constitutionally incapable of changing or is simply unwilling to do so. In AJ Dunning and Sons (Shopfitters) Ltd v Jacomb 1973 ICR 448, NIRC, the NIRC allowed an appeal from a tribunal finding of unfair dismissal based on the lack of a specific warning of dismissal. What the tribunal should have done, the NIRC said, was to ask whether the nature of the employee's incapacity – in this case, his unbending and uncooperative nature and inability to get on with clients – was such that, had he received a warning, he might have been able or likely to improve.

Single acts of gross incompetence/negligence. The potentially disastrous **4.58** consequences of one mistake may excuse an employer for dismissing without a prior warning where those consequences are so serious that the employer cannot be expected to suffer the risk of the employee's continuing employment (although this does not negate the need to investigate the matter and give the employee an opportunity to state his or her case). In Alidair Ltd v Taylor 1978 ICR 445, CA, the Court of Appeal approved the following statement made by the EAT: 'In our judgement there are activities in which the degree of professional skill which must be required is so high, and the potential consequences of the smallest departure [from] that high standard are so serious, that one failure to perform in accordance with those standards is enough to justify dismissal. The passenger-carrying airline pilot, the scientist operating the nuclear reactor, the chemist in charge of research into the possible effects of, for example, thalidomide, the driver of the Manchester to London express, the driver of an articulated lorry full of sulphuric acid, are all in the situation in which one failure to maintain the proper standard of professional skill can bring about a major disaster.'

But just because, in some job contexts, the consequences of making a single mistake can be potentially calamitous does not mean that a rare mistake by an experienced employee carrying out such a job will always justify dismissal. In Boxall v Surrey and Sussex Healthcare NHS Trust ET Case No.3101155/99, for example, B had 30 years' experience in midwifery. During that time, she had been disciplined only once as a result of a cot death following a home delivery. Part of the disciplinary sanction applied on that occasion comprised six months' supervised practice in the community. The incident that resulted in B's dismissal concerned the birth of a stillborn child to a patient in her care. The Trust concluded that B had been negligent in that she had not read a CTG trace properly and had failed to follow up the patient's complaints about a particular pain. It accepted that her negligence was due to a lack of skill rather than a reckless disregard of duty, but decided that retraining would not be recommended in view of the fact that B had recently undergone a period of supervised practice and because she failed to acknowledge her incompetence. In holding that B's dismissal was outside the band of reasonable options open to the employer, the tribunal concluded that the Trust had attached disproportionate weight to the fact that B had undergone supervised practice in the community. This was not relevant to the issue of retraining in a hospital labour ward where the stillbirth had taken place. Furthermore, B's perceived inability to recognise her own failings was something that could have been addressed by training.

Employees in senior positions. There is apparently conflicting case law on **4.59** whether senior employees and managers need to be warned that they are failing to achieve the standards of performance required of them. By the very nature of

147

their jobs, said the NIRC in James v Waltham Holy Cross UDC (above), such employees may be aware of what is required of them and fully capable of judging for themselves whether they are achieving that requirement. However, three years later the EAT in McPhail v Gibson 1977 ICR 42, EAT, took a contrary view and suggested that an explicit warning for senior employees is particularly important. Whether an express warning is required will depend on the circumstances of the individual case. In all cases, however, the important question is whether the manager, as with all grades of employee, was aware that his or her job was in jeopardy. In Laycock v Jones Buckie Shipyard Ltd EAT 395/81 the EAT acknowledged that, although such an awareness will usually be brought home by a formal warning, 'as a matter of common sense, the higher someone is in the managerial scale the more likely it is that he will be conscious of the satisfaction or lack of satisfaction that his performance is giving'.

The relationship between status and capability was considered by the EAT in Burns v Turboflex Ltd EAT 377/96. In that case B, a managing director, was dismissed for having failed to take adequate steps to devise and implement a business plan following the takeover of the company for which he worked. By a majority, a tribunal found his dismissal to be fair, notwithstanding that B had been out of the country when he was dismissed and had never received anything in writing regarding the employer's concerns over his progress in developing the business plan. The majority thought that, as a senior executive, B should have been aware that his failure to make sufficient progress with the business objectives put his job at risk. On appeal, the EAT held that the tribunal's decision was fundamentally flawed in that it failed to distinguish between the need to provide a warning of dismissal and the need to give the employee an opportunity to meet the criticisms of his or her capability. The failure by the employer to accord B such an opportunity vitiated the tribunal's decision that B's dismissal was fair.

4.60 In its judgment the EAT made the following observations regarding the necessity of issuing warnings in capability dismissal cases: 'We do not consider that it is possible to lay down as a proposition of law any general rule that is dependent upon the status or the nature of the job. A van driver employed at a modest salary does not need to be warned that he should not drink before he drives; the personnel director of a large company does not need to be told that he should not make racist or sexist comments about or to members of his staff; a pilot does not need to be warned that he should not crash the plane. There can in our view be no absolute rule as to when warnings are or are not inappropriate. All must depend upon the facts of the case.'

4.61 Reasonable opportunity to improve
Providing the employee with an opportunity to improve was identified by Lord Bridge in Polkey v AE Dayton Services Ltd 1988 ICR 142, HL, as being necessary in the great majority of cases if the employer is to act reasonably.

148

Para 21 of the Acas Code states that a warning should set out what improvement in performance is required, together with a timescale. Obviously, if an employer warns an employee that his or her job is in danger but fails to provide that employee with a reasonable opportunity to improve, or allow itself the opportunity to assess whether improvement has taken place, a dismissal may be found to be unfair.

In Steelprint Ltd v Haynes EAT 467/95 the EAT upheld an employment tribunal's finding of unfair dismissal in respect of an employee, H, who had been denied training as a means of helping her to improve defects in her performance. H had originally been employed as a proofreader but, following the introduction of computer technology, she was required to undertake computer inputting tasks for which she had to learn to touch-type. She failed to master this new skill and, having initiated a period of monitoring, the employer issued a series of warnings over a three-month period, which culminated in H's dismissal. A tribunal held the dismissal to be unfair, primarily on account of the lack of any offer of training by the employer or any consideration of moving H onto other tasks at which she was more adept. In upholding that finding, the EAT observed: 'The tribunal came to the conclusion that to expect someone to take on what is effectively a new job without considering the full training was outside the range of responses that a reasonable employer would contemplate before going on to dismiss. We cannot see anything in that conclusion [that could] remotely [be] said to be unfounded on the evidence.'

4.62 Employment tribunals' definitions of a reasonable improvement period will differ greatly and depend on the circumstances of each case. In Evans v George Galloway and Co Ltd 1974 IRLR 167, ET, a man with six years' service was thought to deserve six months, rather than five weeks, while in Winterhalter Gastronom Ltd v Webb 1973 ICR 245, NIRC, three months was thought suitable for a sales director with two years' service. And in Clark v Johnson EAT 484/78 the EAT extended a long-serving butcher's improvement period from one to nine months.

In Sibun v Modern Telephones Ltd 1976 IRLR 81, ET, the tribunal thought that important factors in determining a reasonable period were length of service, performance during that service and the extent to which the employee's results were falling below the expected. An additional factor might be how long the employee had known of the employer's dissatisfaction before a formal warning was given – Leighton v British Industrial Fastenings Ltd COET 1161/202.

4.63 Longer periods to improve are often appropriate in situations where the employee has been asked to do new kinds of work. In British Sulphur Corporation v Lawrie EAT 159/86 (see 'Warnings' above) the EAT's faith in the employee improving as a writer was partly fuelled by the fact that she had very recently been switched from pure research work to writing for the company journal. She was given insufficient instruction and an insufficient period of time over which her journalism could be assessed. And in Playle v Turmeric Ltd COET 813/215 the employee inherited a long-standing accounting system which was harshly criticised by auditors. Dismissal was unfair because the employee should have been given more time to remedy the system.

Employers should not set unrealistic targets during the improvement period, particularly if they have waited for some time before acting and kept their doubts about the employee to themselves. However, an employee cannot complain if he or she has freely agreed to the target – Bach-Price v International Equipment and Services Exhibition Organisation Ltd EAT 453/79.

4.64 Where two incidents of incompetence occur in quick succession, an employer may wish to deal with both at a single hearing. In UPS Ltd v Harrison EAT 0038/11 the employee had two avoidable road accidents in less than a month. Following a disciplinary hearing, the employer issued a first written warning in respect of the first accident and, simultaneously, a final written warning in respect of the second accident. The final written warning stipulated that a third avoidable accident within 12 months could result in dismissal. The issue of two warnings at once was not contemplated in the employer's policies. When the employee had another accident 11 months later, he was dismissed. A tribunal found that the issue of two warnings simultaneously made the employee's subsequent dismissal unfair, because it deprived him of the chance to improve between the two warnings. The EAT disagreed, stating that the question that must be considered is not whether the employer has followed its own policies, but whether the procedure that an employer has followed overall is reasonable.

4.65 **Providing support and measuring improvement.** It is important that an employer is not seen as merely going through the motions when presenting an employee with an opportunity to improve his or her performance. In this regard, the employer may come unstuck if the evidence at a tribunal shows that the capability procedure put in place lacks any objective basis by which improvement could be measured or that the employer has neglected to provide any support to the employee in his or her efforts to improve. Three examples:

- **Williams v Pembrokeshire County Council** ET Case No.1602049/03: W began working for the Council in 1974 and in 1997 was promoted to the post of home manager of a residential home. From 1999 onwards concerns were expressed about her managerial capability, which led to the Council's capability procedure being invoked. As part of that procedure she was transferred in 2002 to a different residential home, but still in the capacity of home manager. W's line manager retained an office at the home and had responsibility for her in relation to the capability procedure. In March 2003 W was called to a hearing under the procedure and told that as she had shown no improvement she was to be dismissed. A tribunal held the dismissal to be unfair. It found that there had been a 'self-fulfilling prophecy' that W would fail from the time of her transfer in 2002. The Council had failed to take proper account of her length of service and had failed to give her a correspondingly lengthy and supported period for consolidation and improvement. In supervising W during the improvement period, the line manager had adopted a remote, backseat role. The action plan did not contain any fair or objective measurement by which any improvement could be judged. Instead, the manager had merely relied on hearsay and speculative reports from other staff

- **Davis v Sainsbury's Supermarkets Ltd** ET Case No.2702104/10: D worked as a personnel and training manager at one of the employer's stores. A new store manager, with a somewhat chaotic management style, was appointed in February 2009. In March 2010, D was called to a disciplinary hearing to discuss her capability. She made it clear in the hearing that she blamed the new store manager for many of the failings identified. She was given a final written warning, to remain on her file for 12 months. The following day, D was informed that she was being transferred to another store. She was told, 'You are going to Oxford, and be under no illusion, my girl, there are challenges there, it's not an easy store.' D resigned not because of the final written warning but because she felt that she had received no support or understanding from the employer and would not receive it in the future. A tribunal upheld D's unfair constructive dismissal claim, taking the view that she could not tolerate being sent to another store to carry out the same role without any support mechanisms being put in place, and the comment made to her about Oxford was a clear demonstration that her future was on the line and she could not look to the employer for support

- **White v British Telecommunications plc** ET Case No.2700114/11: W had worked for BT for 21 years, 16 of those in a managerial role. In mid-2009 concerns were raised about his performance. He was off work suffering from stress and depression for two months shortly afterwards and was referred to occupational health ('OH'). At the end of October, W was put on a formal performance management programme and in November BT received a report from OH stating that he remained quite vulnerable and it might take him longer to fully recover and get back to his normal working routine. W was notified in January 2010 that he had failed to make sufficient improvements and was given a final warning. He was dismissed on performance grounds in July. A tribunal found W's dismissal unfair. BT was aware that W's wife had been seriously ill in late 2008 and early 2009, and this would have had an understandable impact on his performance. A reasonable employer would have given him time to restore his performance without putting him under intense management pressure. Furthermore, in view of the OH report, a reasonable employer would have delayed the implementation of a formal performance management programme and given support to W to improve his performance in a less pressured environment. The tribunal did

151

not accept BT's argument that the performance management programme was intended to provide support; it expressly contemplated dismissal as a possible outcome and therefore imposed significant pressure on W. Had W been given the appropriate support in a welfare context, he would not necessarily have had to be taken through the performance management programme that led to his dismissal.

4.66 **Lapsed warnings.** The Acas Code explicitly provides that employees should be told how long a warning will remain current – para 21. However, it cannot be assumed that warnings automatically lapse at the end of an improvement period. Whether it can be inferred that the warning has lapsed will depend on the circumstances. This was made clear in Kraft Foods Ltd v Fox 1978 ICR 311, EAT, where the EAT said: 'There is sometimes a tendency for a warning to be regarded as having lapsed if a period of time has gone by. In certain circumstances, of course, that may be true. Here, however, the company were dealing with a man who, in the end, was not capable of doing the job; he fell short of the requirements. It seems to us that it is wrong to say that, where a man has been given six months in which to improve, if the employer gives him a further period of time beyond the six months, the employer is to be criticised thereafter for saying that the employee did not act in accordance with the warning at the end of the period of time. It may well be that the employer is being over-generous; but being over-generous is not the same thing as being unreasonable.'

Furthermore, the Court of Appeal has further held – albeit in the context of a misconduct dismissal – that it is not necessarily unfair for an employer to take into account an 'expired' warning – Airbus UK Ltd v Webb 2008 ICR 561, CA (discussed further in Chapter 6, 'Conduct', in the section 'Disciplinary proceedings', under 'The decision – expired warnings'). All will depend on the circumstances and if, for example, an employee has been led to believe that his or her performance is no longer being monitored at the end of an improvement period, it may then be unfair to dismiss him or her for poor performance, at least without a further warning.

4.67 **Monitoring progress.** The employer should monitor the employee's progress during the improvement period. The fact that an employee has shown at least some capacity to improve may be taken into account by a tribunal when determining whether the dismissal for failing to make sufficient improvement falls within the band of reasonable responses. An example:

• **Tufail v Scottish Life Assurance Co** ET Case No.28133/95: T began working for the employer in 1987 and had a satisfactory record until 1993, when she was transferred to a new department. Her annual appraisal for 1994 graded her work as unsatisfactory, as a result of which she was given a written warning. Two months after that, her Divisional Manager reported that her standard of work had improved to the extent that he was now satisfied with her performance. At her next appraisal, her work was again graded

152

as unsatisfactory and she was given another warning – this time described as a 'first and final warning'. Her performance was then monitored weekly. The employer's assessment was that, while T's performance had improved, the degree of improvement was not sufficient to bring her up to the required standard and she was dismissed. In holding her dismissal to be unfair, the tribunal observed that the fact that T had shown the requisite improvement a year earlier proved that she had it within her ability to improve to an acceptable standard. A reasonable employer would have considered her previous good service and her demonstrated ability to improve, and would have allowed her more time.

Some employees may not appreciate having their performance monitored by the employer and may consider the degree of supervision imposed to be oppressive. In National Society for the Prevention of Cruelty to Children v Dear EAT 0553/08 the employee was disciplined for failing to make proper records of calls he received on the employer's helpline – such records being essential to the employer's work in the protection of children. The employee's performance was then monitored and he was required to have his call log books signed off by a manager each day. The employee resigned and claimed unfair constructive dismissal. His claim was upheld by an employment tribunal but this verdict was reversed by the EAT. In the EAT's view, 'where there has been a failure to follow proper procedures it is normal for an employer to require monitoring to secure compliance with those procedures. That monitoring is not regarded as a punishment or as a sanction but as a legitimate management instruction'. The employer's actions were therefore not calculated or likely to destroy mutual trust and confidence.

'No difference' rule

4.68

In Polkey v AE Dayton Services Ltd 1988 ICR 142, HL, the House of Lords ruled that employers could not argue that a procedurally improper dismissal was nevertheless fair because it would have made no difference if the employer had followed a fair procedure. Their Lordships held that an employer's actions in dispensing with a fair procedure were highly relevant to the question of whether an employer acted reasonably in dismissing, and that tribunals were not entitled to take into account, when determining the fairness or otherwise of a dismissal, whether a proper procedure would have made any difference to the employer's decision to dismiss. Only in wholly exceptional cases where it could be shown that carrying out a proper procedure would have been 'utterly useless' or 'futile' would procedural failures be overlooked when considering reasonableness for the purposes of S.98(4) ERA. Lord Bridge in Polkey itemised the procedural steps which will be necessary in the great majority of cases if an employer is to be considered to have acted reasonably. Speaking of capability dismissals in particular, he mentioned that giving an employee fair warning and

153

a chance to improve would generally be expected. Polkey and the so-called 'no difference' rule are discussed further in Chapter 3, 'Unfairness', under 'Fairness of internal procedure'.

4.69 Right of appeal

Denying an employee a right of appeal against the decision to dismiss on the ground of capability or lack of qualifications is likely to lead to the conclusion that the dismissal is unfair, particularly if the right of appeal was contractual – see West Midlands Co-operative Society Ltd v Tipton 1986 ICR 192, HL. Indeed, the Acas Code recommends that employees be provided with an opportunity to appeal and an unreasonable failure to provide an appeal therefore risks an uplift to any compensation awarded – para 26 (see Chapter 16, 'Compensatory awards: adjustments', under 'Adjustments for breach of Acas Code of Practice').

As stated at para 27 of the Acas Code, an appeal should be dealt with impartially and, wherever possible, by a manager who has not previously been involved in the case. Ideally, the appeal should be heard by a higher level of management than that which made the decision to dismiss. However, as was recognised by the EAT in Royal Naval School v Hughes 1979 IRLR 383, EAT, in smaller organisations this may not always be practicable.

4.70 Furthermore, dismissal is likely to be unfair on procedural grounds if the rules of natural justice are not observed in any appeals process. In a capability context, this means that the employer must inform the employee of his or her shortcomings, give him or her a chance to be heard, and act honestly. In Campion v Hamworthy Engineering Ltd 1987 ICR 966, CA, C was dismissed for poor workmanship following a disciplinary hearing held by the works manager. C appealed to the company's welfare officer, who listened to arguments from both sides and then adjourned. Following a private discussion with the works manager in another room, the welfare officer announced that the dismissal was upheld. The Court of Appeal restored an employment tribunal's finding of unfair dismissal and agreed that there had been a serious breach of natural justice when the welfare officer retired with the works manager to deliberate over C's case.

For more on the conduct of internal appeal hearings, see Chapter 6, 'Conduct', under 'Disciplinary proceedings – right of appeal'.

5 Ill health

General considerations

Long-term ill health

Persistent short-term absences

Alternative employment

Ill-health benefits

Factors affecting reasonableness

Particular types of sickness

Ill health is a potentially fair reason for dismissal as it relates to the employee's **5.1** capability of performing the work he or she was employed to do – S.98(2)(a) Employment Rights Act 1996 (ERA). As stated in Chapter 4, 'Capability and qualifications', under 'Definitions – capability', capability is assessed by reference to skill, aptitude, *health or any other physical or mental quality* – S.98(3)(a) ERA. However, different considerations apply to *ill health*-related capability dismissals to those that apply to *performance*-related capability dismissals (discussed in Chapter 4).

It is not normally difficult to show that the reason for dismissal was ill health as this tends to result in either long-term absence, as in the case of a serious illness or injury, or in frequent short absences over a long period. However, absenteeism per se will not be sufficient to show incapability due to ill-health and, if dismissing for capability on this ground, the employer will also need to establish that there is an underlying medical condition. This is almost always the case where long-term absence is concerned and may well be the case where there are frequent short-term absences. However, short-term absences may also be caused by a number of different and unconnected minor illnesses, in which case different considerations apply and the reason for dismissal may not fall within the category of capability at all. This is dealt with under 'Persistent short-term absences' below.

Employees with underlying health problems may struggle into work rather **5.2** than take sick leave. This could well affect their performance or behaviour at work and should be taken into account by an employer when deciding what action to take. In such circumstances, whether the matter is treated as relating to performance/conduct or ill health will depend on a number of factors, including the employer's awareness of the health problem, the extent to which it is actually causing the employee's poor performance/misconduct and the nature of the poor performance/misconduct in question. This issue is most

155

likely to arise where the employee suffers from mental health problems and is discussed further under 'Particular types of sickness – mental illness' below. (Note that if the employee's performance is *not* affected by his or her ill health but the employer nonetheless seeks to dismiss in order to protect the employee's health from the consequences of carrying on working, this will not amount to a capability dismissal. In Jagroop v Autogrill Retail UK Ltd ET Case No.2704520/09, for example, J suffered from lupus, which involved recurrent extreme fatigue. She asked if she could work compressed hours, working four rather than five days a week, in order to minimise travelling. The employer refused but considered that she could not continue with her current working pattern and dismissed her on the ground of capability. A tribunal found that there was no evidence of any issue as to J's capability and the only recent medical advice was that she was functionally fit to work her contracted hours. The dismissal was for some other substantial reason ('SOSR') and was unfair.)

If an employee's ill health causes him or her to lose a qualification required to perform his or her job, the reason for dismissal is likely to be loss of the relevant qualification, rather than ill health. While still a capability issue, different considerations may apply – Sayers v Loganair Ltd EATS 0084/04. If the employer is uncertain as to which reason to rely on, it is probably sensible to deal with the matter, at least initially, as a potential ill-health dismissal, as such dismissals require employers to follow more rigorous procedural steps. (Capability issues arising out of poor performance and lack of qualifications are dealt with in Chapter 4, 'Capability and qualifications'.)

5.3 Once it is established that the reason for the employee's dismissal was ill health, the second limb of the fairness test under S.98(4) comes into play: did the employer act reasonably in treating ill health as a sufficient ground for dismissal? Much will depend on the procedure the employer followed as consultation with the employee and expert medical advice are often crucial to the question of reasonableness. Procedural factors are dealt with under 'Long-term ill health' and 'Persistent short-term absences' below.

If the employer has followed a fair procedure, whether or not its decision to dismiss is fair will depend on a number of factors – considered under 'Factors affecting reasonableness' below. Certain types of sickness or disability – in particular, pregnancy- and maternity-related illnesses, drink- and drugs-related illnesses, mental illnesses and HIV/AIDS – need to be handled with especial care and are considered in more detail under 'Particular types of sickness' below.

5.4 As discussed in Chapter 3, 'Unfairness', under 'Reasonableness of dismissal – "band (or range) of reasonable responses" test', and under 'Fairness of internal procedure – procedural fairness integral to reasonableness test', the 'range of reasonable responses' test of fairness will apply to both the decision to dismiss and the procedure that was followed in reaching that decision. In this regard, see Pinnington v City and County of Swansea and anor EAT 0561/03, where the EAT stated that the test should apply to the way employers inform themselves of the true medical position, applying the Court of Appeal's decision in J Sainsbury plc v Hitt 2003 ICR 111, CA. (Note that the Pinnington case was appealed to the Court of Appeal but not on this point – see Pinnington v Swansea City and County Council and anor 2005 ICR 685, CA.) As the EAT found in Yorkshire Bus Group Ltd v Kahut EAT 344/96, a tribunal will err in law if it finds 'something completely outside the band of reasonableness, when demonstrably it is not'. In that case, K had been absent for more than 12 months with back pain. There was medical evidence that K was unfit for work, he had been regularly consulted, and K himself had told his employer he had no intention of coming back to work. The EAT found that it was perverse of a tribunal to hold that dismissal of K in these circumstances did not fall within the band of reasonable responses.

General considerations 5.5

Dismissal for ill health is not a neatly self-contained area of law. As indicated above, it is not always clear whether the dismissal of an employee suffering ill health is for capability or for some other potentially fair reason such as conduct or SOSR. Due to these blurred boundaries, employers may be uncertain what procedure to apply in dealing with the issue, and in particular whether or not to follow the Acas Code of Practice on Disciplinary and Grievance Procedures before dismissing.

Furthermore, a number of additional considerations can arise in an ill-health context, beyond simply the law on unfair dismissal. The most obvious of these is disability discrimination: as many of the cases discussed in this chapter indicate, ill health that is significant enough to lead to dismissal is often significant enough to amount to a disability under the Equality Act 2010 (EqA). In such cases, in addition to acting reasonably in dismissing under the ERA, employers will have to consider their duty to make reasonable adjustments and to avoid unlawful disability discrimination. And in the case of older employees, employers will need to be alive to the possibility of age discrimination – given that there is now no 'default retirement age', some employees will continue working well into their seventies and eighties. Finally, on a more basic level, if an employee is entirely unable to carry out his or her contractual duties because of illness, it might be argued that there is no dismissal at all, because the contract is frustrated.

Before turning to specific aspects of dismissal on the ground of ill health, we briefly note the general impact of these tangential issues.

Acas Code of Practice on Disciplinary and Grievance Procedures 5.6
It is not entirely clear whether the revised Acas Code of Practice on Disciplinary and Grievance Procedures ('the Code') applies to ill-health dismissals. While the

Code does not specifically refer to sickness absence, the accompanying non-statutory Acas Guide, 'Discipline and grievances at work' ('the Guide'), devotes a considerable amount of space to the issue (see Appendix 4: 'Dealing with absence'). The Guide makes a distinction between persistent short-term absences – suggesting that in some circumstances these may be dealt with as a disciplinary matter, in which case the Code would apply – and longer-term absence where 'employers need to take a more sympathetic and considerate approach'.

In practice, application of the Code may depend on whether an employee is being dismissed for a poor attendance record, in which case there is likely to be uncertainty as to whether or not the Code should be followed, or for ill health, in which case it will be a capability issue and the Code will not apply. In Mathews v British Telecommunications plc ET Case No.2205791/10, for example, a tribunal considered that the Code was not applicable in a case where the employee had been off work for some time suffering from stress. However, as we make clear under 'Persistent short-term absences – label for dismissal' below, it can be a difficult distinction to make and employers should carry out the necessary investigations, including obtaining medical evidence where appropriate, before any action is taken. Since the purpose of an investigation is to establish the facts, this is the equivalent of the first step recommended in the Code. A properly conducted investigation should then establish the next appropriate step to be taken.

For further discussion of this issue, see the introduction to Chapter 8, 'Some other substantial reason', under 'Acas Code of Practice'.

5.7 Disability discrimination

Liability for disability discrimination and for unfair dismissal must be considered separately. If the underlying illness amounts to a disability under S.6 EqA a dismissal may amount to unlawful discrimination even if it is found to be fair under the ERA: a disability-related dismissal that cannot be justified under the EqA will not be automatically unfair under the ERA as separate considerations of reasonableness apply under S.98(4) ERA – HJ Heinz Co Ltd v Kenrick 2000 ICR 491, EAT. However, the Court of Appeal has acknowledged that the approach to justification under the EqA is similar, though not identical, to that taken to determination of whether or not an employer has acted reasonably in treating the reason for dismissal as a sufficient reason to dismiss for the purposes of an unfair dismissal claim – Post Office v Jones 2001 ICR 805, CA.

The relationship between unfair dismissal and disability discrimination is considered further under 'Long-term ill health – relevance of Equality Act 2010', and in the section 'Persistent short-term absences' under 'Unconnected minor ailments – disability-related absences' below. For a detailed discussion of disability discrimination more generally, see IDS Employment Law Handbook, 'Discrimination at Work' (2012).

158

Age discrimination

5.8

The 'default retirement age' and the statutory retirement procedure were repealed on 6 April 2011 and in consequence 'retirement' ceased to be a potentially fair reason for dismissal under S.98 ERA. Thus, an employer wishing to fairly dismiss an older employee because of his or her advancing age needs to show that the reason for dismissal falls within one of the potentially fair reasons for dismissal contained in S.98(1) and (2) ERA, and that the dismissal was reasonable in all the circumstances under S.98(4). In other words, the dismissal is treated in the same way as any other dismissal.

Where an employee's health or performance deteriorates, the employer is likely to seek to rely on capability/ill health as a potentially fair reason for dismissal. For example, an employee may be dismissed because his or her productivity levels have declined due to diminished mental performance or physical health problems such as arthritis or poor eyesight; or because he or she has to take frequent time off work because of age-related health problems. (If the dismissal is in accordance with a compulsory retirement policy the employer is likely to rely on SOSR as the reason for dismissal – this is discussed in Chapter 8, 'Some other substantial reason', under 'Retirement dismissals'.)

Employers seeking to dismiss for such reasons will need to ensure not only that **5.9** they have complied with the law on unfair dismissal, but also that they have considered whether dismissal may amount to unlawful discrimination on the ground of age under the EqA. This is likely to be the case if the employer has simply made assumptions about an older employee's capabilities without undertaking a proper assessment.

The relationship between unfair dismissal and age discrimination is touched on under 'Long-term ill health – relevance of Equality Act 2010' below. For a more detailed discussion of the law governing age discrimination, see IDS Employment Law Handbook, 'Discrimination at Work' (2012).

Frustration

5.10

In theory, an employee's prolonged or sudden serious injury or disability is capable of frustrating the employment contract. Frustration of a contract occurs where, through no fault of either party, some reasonably unforeseeable event takes place which makes future performance of the contract either impossible or something radically different from what was initially contemplated. The effect of frustration is that the contract, together with all the rights and obligations of the parties under it, terminates automatically without a dismissal.

Tribunals are generally reluctant, however, to find that an employment contract has been frustrated as this means that the employee loses all employment rights, including the right to claim unfair dismissal. Employers should therefore be cautious in invoking the doctrine of frustration. The best view would seem to be that employers should only rely on frustration where the unforeseen event

159

renders all further employment permanently impossible. Even then, they should also plead an alternative defence – that if there was a dismissal (i.e. the contract was not frustrated) it was a fair dismissal on the ground of the employee's prolonged incapability through sickness. But before doing this, they need to make sure that they have followed the correct procedures for sickness dismissals and have complied with any obligations imposed by the EqA.

The doctrine of frustration is discussed at some length in IDS Employment Law Handbook, 'Contracts of Employment' (2014), Chapter 13, 'Termination by operation of law', under 'Frustration'.

5.11 Long-term ill health

There are two key aspects to a fair dismissal for long-term illness or injury involving long-term absence from work. First, where an employee has been absent from work for some time, it is essential to consider *whether the employer can be expected to wait longer for the employee to return* – Spencer v Paragon Wallpapers Ltd 1977 ICR 301, EAT. According to the Court of Session in S v Dundee City Council 2014 IRLR 131, Ct Sess (Inner House), the tribunal must expressly address this question, balancing the relevant factors in all the circumstances of the individual case. Such factors include whether other staff are available to carry out the absent employee's work; the nature of the employee's illness; the likely length of his or her absence; the cost of continuing to employ the employee; the size of the employing organisation; and, balanced against those considerations, the 'unsatisfactory situation of having an employee on very lengthy sick leave'. These factors are essentially the same as those affecting the reasonableness of ill health dismissals in general, and are discussed under 'Factors affecting reasonableness' below.

Secondly, a *fair procedure* is essential. This requires, in particular:

- consultation with the employee

- a thorough medical investigation (to establish the nature of the illness or injury and its prognosis), and

- consideration of other options; in particular, alternative employment within the employer's business.

5.12 An employee's entitlement, if any, to enhanced ill-health benefit will also be highly relevant – see 'Ill-health benefits' below. A booklet produced by Acas, 'Managing attendance and employee turnover', states that employees on long-term sick leave can be dismissed 'only as a last resort once all other options have been considered'.

The revised Acas Code of Practice on Disciplinary and Grievance Procedures (and its accompanying Guide, 'Discipline and grievances at work') may provide

160

some useful guidance when it comes to the procedure an employer should adopt prior to dismissal, although as discussed under 'General considerations – Acas Code of Practice on Disciplinary and Grievance Procedures' above, it is not certain that the Code applies to sickness absence situations, particularly long-term absence.

Employers will also need to consider their additional obligations under the **5.13** equalities legislation since, where long-term ill health is concerned, it is highly likely that the underlying illness will amount to a disability under the EqA. In its Guide to the Acas Code, Acas recommends that employers 'take a more sympathetic and considerate approach, particularly if the employee is disabled and where reasonable adjustments at the workplace might enable them to return to work' (see Appendix 4). Furthermore, where ill health is linked to advancing age, it may be necessary to consider the possibility of age discrimination. The impact of the EqA on unfair dismissal law is considered under 'Relevance of Equality Act 2010' below.

Impact on work performance. Note that while in the majority of cases **5.14** involving long-term ill health the employee will be absent from work, there are cases in which an employee's condition does not result in absence, but does affect his or her work performance. Dismissal in such circumstances may still be for capability, and the principles discussed in this chapter with regard to consultation, medical investigation and so on will still apply. However, the dismissal may nonetheless be unfair if it can be shown that the employer could reasonably have made adjustments to enable the employee to continue or if the employee's illness did not affect his or her performance of essential duties. In Jones v Techflow Marine Ltd ET Case No.2509159/10, for example, J suffered from osteoarthritis, making it difficult for him to sit in one position for a long time. When he made it clear that he was not prepared to make long-haul flights unless he was given a guarantee that he would not have to sit in standard economy class he was called to a medical review hearing and dismissed. A tribunal decided that his dismissal was unfair because J was fully competent to carry out his duties on site and in the office. The only difficulty related to his unwillingness to fly standard economy on long-haul flights but, as he was prepared to fly in 'economy comfort' seating, the circumstances in which he would have refused to fly were unlikely. The employer offered no evidence that it was so concerned about J's unwillingness to perform an essential part of his duties that it had taken immediate steps to replace him.

Consultation with employee
5.15

In the context of long-term sickness absence, consultation has a number of purposes, which include: establishing the true medical position, keeping the employer abreast of the employee's progress and keeping the employee up to date with the employer's position, which is particularly important if the employer is considering dismissal. Since warnings are not normally considered

161

to be appropriate in cases of long-term sickness, given a total absence of fault on the employee's part, consultation assumes greater importance. As Lord McDonald stated in Taylorplan Catering (Scotland) Ltd v McInally 1980 IRLR 53, EAT: 'It would be absurd to apply a procedure of formal warnings to cases of genuine ill health.' This reinforces the view that the Acas Code of Practice, with its in-built warnings, does not apply to long-term ill-health dismissals – see 'General considerations – Acas Code of Practice on Disciplinary and Grievance Procedures' above.

The EAT stressed the importance of consultation and discovering the true medical position in the leading case of East Lindsey District Council v Daubney 1977 ICR 566, EAT, where Mr Justice Phillips stated: 'Unless there are wholly exceptional circumstances, before an employee is dismissed on the ground of ill health it is necessary that he should be consulted and the matter discussed with him, and that in one way or another steps should be taken by the employer to discover the true medical position. We do not propose to lay down detailed principles to be applied in such cases, for what will be necessary in one case may not be appropriate in another. But if in every case employers take such steps as are sensible according to the circumstances to consult the employee and to discuss the matter with him, and to inform themselves upon the true medical position, it will be found in practice that all that is necessary has been done. Discussions and consultation will often bring to light facts and circumstances of which the employers were unaware, and which will throw new light on the problem. Or the employee may wish to seek medical advice on his own account, which, brought to the notice of the employers' medical advisers, will cause them to change their opinion. There are many possibilities. Only one thing is certain, and that is that if the employee is not consulted, and given an opportunity to state his case, an injustice may be done.' In Taylorplan Catering (Scotland) Ltd v McInally (above) the EAT added that consultation is also necessary to balance the employer's need for the work to be done against the employee's need for time to recover.

5.16 Proper consultation with the employee should include:

- discussions at the start of the illness and periodically throughout its duration and informing the employee if the stage when dismissal may be considered is approaching
- personal contact with the employee
- consideration of the medical evidence – see 'Medical investigation' below
- consideration of the employee's opinion on his or her condition
- consideration of what can be done to get the employee back to work
- consideration of offering alternative employment, if any, in the employer's business – see 'Alternative employment' below

162

- consideration of an employee's entitlement to enhanced ill-health benefits, if available – see 'Ill-health benefits' below.

There have been a number of cases where a failure to consult the employee has resulted in a finding of unfair dismissal. East Lindsey District Council v Daubney (above) is a good example. D was dismissed on the ground of ill health. The Council had acted upon a report prepared by its physician, which was based on an examination carried out by another doctor and merely stated that D was 'unfit to carry out the duties of his post and should be retired on the grounds of permanent ill health'. The dismissal was found by a tribunal to be unfair because D had not had an opportunity to state his case or to obtain an independent medical opinion. The EAT noted that the physician's report was 'verging on the inadequate' because it was lacking in detail. However, it held that the Council would have been entitled to act upon the report, 'brief as it was', if it had consulted D and discussed the matter with him.

There was a complete lack of consultation in Chambers v Franco's ET Case **5.17** No.1502408/10 where C, who suffered from Crohn's disease, was employed as an assistant chef. His condition deteriorated and he had to make more frequent visits to the toilet. His employer became angry and threw a plate at him, which made C feel stressed and caused his condition to flare up. He telephoned in sick the next morning and received a text dismissing him. A tribunal found that C was unfairly dismissed: he was not warned that his job was at risk, and there was no discussion with him about his illness, its likely prognosis, or the steps that could be taken to help him manage his condition at work.

Discussions. Discussions should be held periodically throughout the absence **5.18** – from the onset of the illness up to and including the decision to dismiss. The Acas Guide recommends that where an employee is on long-term sick leave, the employee and the employer should keep in regular contact and the employee should be kept fully informed if there is any risk to his or her employment (see page 73). Even if an employer has obtained medical evidence, it is important to consult the employee before any decision to dismiss is taken in order to keep the employee informed and to ensure that the medical report has not been misinterpreted. Some examples:

- **WM Computer Services Ltd v Passmore** EAT 721/86: P suffered from severe depression and took a number of months' sick leave. During his absence his employer kept in close contact with him, refused to accept his resignation on one occasion, and extended his sickness benefit. However, when the decision to dismiss was taken, the employer failed to consult P, relying only on a medical report prepared by the company medical adviser. Both the tribunal and the EAT held the dismissal to be unfair. Even though the procedure had been perfectly adequate at earlier stages, when the decision to dismiss was made the employer had failed to consult P personally. The EAT emphasised that while the medical evidence 'loomed large' in the case, the decision whether or not to dismiss P was an employment one, not a medical one. In addition, the EAT criticised the employer for failing to seek clarification from the medical adviser and upheld the tribunal's finding that the employer had misconstrued the medical report, wrongly concluding that it recommended that P should not return to work

- **Prospects for People with Learning Difficulties v Harris** EAT 0612/11: PPLD provided supported living services for people with disabilities and employed H as a support worker caring for severely disabled clients. H was herself disabled, suffering from a rare congenital musculoskeletal condition which meant she could not perform certain manual tasks, including cardio-pulmonary resuscitation. This did not initially prevent H from being granted the requisite first aid certificate but when the requirements changed and she failed to obtain renewal of her certificate, she was suspended from work. After obtaining an occupational health report, PPLD transferred H from the night shift to the day shift but she was suspended again on the ground of her own safety following a risk assessment. In the light of another occupational health report stating that any increased risk to her own safety was minimal, H was told that she could return to work and was invited to a meeting to 'review her situation' but was not told that her job was at risk. At this meeting on 4 November 2010, PPLD told H that a provisional decision to dismiss her had already been taken. Subsequently, H was dismissed and her internal appeal failed. An employment tribunal found that H's dismissal was procedurally unfair as there had been no consultation on the underlying medical condition or evidence as contemplated in East Lindsey District Council v Daubney (above). Upholding the tribunal's decision, the EAT rejected PPLD's argument that the November meeting was merely an introductory meeting. If an employer is considering the dismissal of a disabled employee on the ground of capability, it should consult the employee in good time so that the employee knows the seriousness of the position and can consider his or her response. That had not happened here and the lack of consultation could not be rectified subsequently. The time for consultation to begin was before the start of the formal dismissal process

- **Harris v Monmouthshire County Council** ET Case No.1603912/13: H was a senior education welfare officer who suffered from depression, sinusitis, asthma and an underactive thyroid. She was allowed to work from home on a regular basis but in 2010 a new line manager discouraged this. Their relationship deteriorated and she took sickness absence. The employer met and corresponded with H about her concerns with her line management, the possibility of ill-health retirement and alternative jobs, and ultimately she was invited to a meeting to discuss her employment. At that meeting, the employer stated that it was considering termination of employment on the ground of capability and informed H that she had a right of appeal against any decision to dismiss. H was subsequently dismissed and a tribunal found the dismissal unfair on the ground that she had not been adequately warned of the possibility of her dismissal in advance. Letters sent by the employer did not spell out the possibility of dismissal in clear terms until after two consultation meetings. In the tribunal's view, where dismissal is contemplated 'it is not sufficient for correspondence to hint at the possibility; this leaves room for confusion, particularly in circumstances where the claimant was unwell'. By the time of the second consultation meeting H was under the impression that she would depart by way of ill-health retirement and thus did not have an opportunity to make informed representations against dismissal.

Personal contact. When employees are on long-term sick leave, a certain **5.19** amount of written correspondence will be inevitable. However, employers should try to ensure regular personal contact with the employee to avoid any argument that there was no proper consultation prior to dismissal. In Post Office v Stones EAT 390/80, for example, the EAT upheld a tribunal's decision that the employer's 'paper consideration' of S's attendance record prior to dismissing her was not enough. Had the employer carried out a fuller analysis, based on closer personal contact with S, it would have reached a different decision.

Furthermore, one-to-one conversations can ensure that any misunderstandings based on written correspondence are dealt with. In Higgins v Secretary of State for Work and Pensions (Jobcentre Plus) ET Case No.2105983/10 H had been absent from work for over a year with a heart condition when he was asked to produce a phased return to work plan. He prepared a plan that envisaged a phased return over 26 weeks but the employer responded by letter offering a phased return over 13 weeks. H indicated to a manager that he would not accept this and he was dismissed. A tribunal decided that the dismissal was unfair. The employer had concluded that H had rejected its terms without checking with H directly. Moreover, the tribunal found that the letter had misrepresented the terms on which it was proposed that H would return. Had these been clarified with H directly, he might have realised that there would be an ongoing review throughout the 13-week period and that it might be extended.

At the same time, an employer should be sensitive to the employee's need for **5.20** space to convalesce and should consider the employee's right to privacy under Article 8(1) of the European Convention on Human Rights – see Chapter 3, 'Unfairness', under 'Reasonableness of dismissal – impact of Human Rights Act', for further details. Where the employee's condition makes him or her effectively house-bound, an employer wishing to meet for the purposes of consultation will need to visit him or her at home. An employer should ideally gain the employee's consent, explaining the reason for the visit and who will be attending. An employer should also consider less intrusive options, such as contact by Skype, telephone or even e-mail, since face-to-face meetings will not always be necessary. Much will depend on the circumstances of the particular

165

employee and an employer would be well advised to establish the employee's preferred form of communication in the initial stages of consultation. An employer should certainly not pressure an employee to attend meetings or respond to communications before he or she is ready to do so. In Crease v Lloyds TSB Bank plc ET Case No.2340796/09 C was signed off work suffering from an adjustment disorder. She did not want any contact with her line manager or team members as this would cause her distress, but she submitted a medical disclosure form and contacted the employer each time she met her consultant. Nevertheless, her line manager sent her a letter and the employer started to phone her every fortnight. Her employment was eventually terminated and a tribunal found that she had been unfairly dismissed. Among other things, the employer had exacerbated C's condition by constantly pressuring her, contrary to the medical advice and C's own wishes.

5.21 **Employee's opinion.** The employee's opinion as to his or her likely date of return and what work he or she will be capable of performing should be considered. In S v Dundee City Council 2014 IRLR 131, Ct Sess (Inner House), the Court of Session emphasised the need to consult the employee and take his or her views into account, but observed that this factor could operate for or against dismissal. If the employee states that he or she is anxious to return to work as soon as possible and hopes to be able to do so in the near future, this will operate in his or her favour. On the other hand, if the employee states that he or she is no better and does not know when he or she will be able to return to work, this will be a significant factor operating against him or her.

In that case S was interviewed by police in connection with a serious allegation made against him by a woman with whom he had had an affair. This resulted in difficulties in his marriage, and he and his wife separated. He was signed off work for 'nervous debility' and subsequently for depression and anxiety. At a meeting where S was warned that consideration would be given to terminating his employment if he could not return to work very soon, S indicated that he was still receiving treatment but had not been making progress, despite attempts to return to work. However, a medical report indicated that S's health was improving, that he was not permanently incapacitated, and that he might be able to return in one to three months. S was dismissed and a tribunal held that the dismissal was unfair as no reasonable employer would have dismissed S without further investigation of his medical state, given the views expressed in the medical report. The Court of Session, however, considered that the tribunal should have weighed S's evidence – which did not suggest that he was in a position to return to work in the immediate future – against the medical report. It therefore remitted the case to allow the tribunal to reconsider the matter.

5.22 Two further examples:

- **Bennett v Safeway Stores Ltd** ET Case No.2101807/04: B went on sick leave on 11 November 2003, suffering from carpal tunnel syndrome. On 2 March

2004 her employer, SS Ltd, received a medical report stating that she had undergone an operation six weeks previously and that recovery was likely to take six to eight weeks, after which a return to work on light duties was recommended for two to three weeks. However, on 5 April B was signed off work for a further six weeks due to post-operative problems and B confirmed on 19 April that there was no change in her condition. At this stage SS Ltd suggested possible alternative vacancies but B made it clear that she would not be able to undertake any of them. On 28 April, SS Ltd dismissed her, since it was difficult to continue to cover her absence by getting other staff to work additional hours and the difficulty would only be exacerbated with the approach of summer. A tribunal dismissed her claim for unfair dismissal. SS Ltd had fully considered the possibility of B returning to her own position (with any adjustments) and the possibility of alternative work. It had reasonably concluded that there was no possibility of any of these options working in the foreseeable future and B appeared to be in agreement with this at the time. Although an employer would normally be expected to obtain an up-to-date medical report before deciding to dismiss, it was reasonable for SS Ltd to conclude that a further medical report would provide no fresh information, given B's own belief (consistent with the medical certificates still being issued) that she would not be fit to return in the foreseeable future. In addition, it had a pressing business need to appoint someone permanently to her post

- **Portman v Bromley Hospitals NHS Trust** EAT 1300/96: P, a hospital ward manager, was off sick for a long time with Hodgkin's disease. When she returned, her work was poor and she had intermittent relapses. P insisted that her work was not affected by her illness. The hospital went on to invoke a capability procedure, eventually giving P the choice between demotion or dismissal for incompetence. P then requested early retirement on ill-health grounds (although this was subsequently rejected). The doctor who examined her for retirement purposes reported that she had severe depression and would never again be fit for work. P was dismissed solely on the ground of incompetence. The appeal panel upheld this decision, although it found that ill health was a contributory factor. The EAT upheld the tribunal's finding of fair dismissal on the basis that the hospital had reasonably concluded that P did not meet the required standards of competence and P had consistently denied – until just prior to her dismissal – that her health had affected her performance.

However, an employer should not place too much reliance on an employee's **5.23** opinion. This is particularly true where the employee is suffering from mental illness but it also applies in the case of physical ill health, as the following case illustrates:

- **Nikola-Erotokritou v Hertfordshire County Council** ET Case No.3302508/10: N-E was a chef manager in a school. She developed

167

tendinitis in her hands and had to take a number of sickness absences. In August 2009 a consultant reported that she should be able to return to work as long as she had help with heavy lifting. The employer decided not to make adjustments to help N-E with lifting because N-E had said that she would have difficulty with a number of aspects of her work, not just heavy lifting. She was dismissed on capability grounds. A tribunal upheld her unfair dismissal claim, finding that given the medical evidence, the employer had placed too much reliance on N-E's pessimistic view of her own capabilities.

5.24 **Fit notes.** Where an employee is off work for any length of time he or she will need to obtain a 'statement of fitness for work' (colloquially known as a 'fit note') from the doctor. The fit note scheme is discussed in more detail under 'Medical investigation – GP's opinion/fit notes' below. For present purposes it is sufficient to mention that the intention behind the scheme is to promote discussion at an early stage in an employee's illness as to what can be done to get the employee back to work as soon as possible. If the fit note states that the employee may be fit for work, the employer should discuss with the employee whether there are any changes that could help him or her return to work, taking into account any advice given in the fit note. But given that GPs and other doctors do not necessarily understand the type of workplace or job involved, employers should be wary of following any advice without discussing the practical implications with the employee first – and also, as appropriate, with the employee's line manager, HR adviser, trade union and/or occupational health specialist.

Thus, while the fit note scheme does not have any direct impact on the question of whether a dismissal for capability on the ground of ill health is reasonable, it is likely to encourage employers to consider – and to discuss with the employee – potential alternatives to dismissal.

5.25 **Right to be accompanied.** Under S.10 of the Employment Relations Act 1999 (ERelA), where a worker 'reasonably requests' to be accompanied at a 'disciplinary hearing', the employer must permit the worker to be accompanied by a 'companion'. The companion – chosen by the worker – may be a trade union representative or a fellow worker – S.10(2A).

A disciplinary hearing is defined in the ERelA as a hearing that could result in:

- the administration of a formal warning – S.13(4)(a)

- the taking of some other action – S.13(4)(b)

- the confirmation of a warning issued or some other action taken – S.13(4)(c) (this applies to appeal hearings).

5.26 Therefore, even if the employer is holding what it terms a 'capability' meeting to discuss the employee's ill health, the statutory right to be accompanied would still apply if it is likely to result in dismissal. The statutory right to be accompanied is discussed in Chapter 6, 'Conduct', under 'Disciplinary proceedings – right to be accompanied'.

Circumstances in which consultation is not required. The EAT in East **5.27** Lindsey District Council v Daubney 1977 ICR 566, EAT, envisaged that consultation could only be dispensed with if there were 'wholly exceptional circumstances'. Not surprisingly, the number of cases where a failure to consult properly has not resulted in a finding of unfair dismissal is small.

However, in the following case special circumstances were held to exist which excused the employer's failure to consult:

- **Eclipse Blinds Ltd v Wright** 1992 IRLR 133, Ct Sess (Inner House): W, a registered disabled person with a heart complaint, was a full-time receptionist. After nine years' employment her health had deteriorated to the point where she had to work part time and she then went off sick for a further 13 weeks. She told the company that she thought her health was improving and gave it permission to contact her GP, who wrote to say that W's health was not good and that there was no possibility of her returning to work in the near future. It therefore appeared that W did not realise the seriousness of her illness. The employer had to replace W but, concerned that she was unaware of the true medical position, decided simply to write a letter rather than consult her personally over her dismissal in case it inadvertently slipped out. The Court of Session held that the employer had a genuine concern to avoid giving W information about her health and in these special circumstances had not acted unreasonably.

Taking this decision to its logical conclusion, an employer may be acting **5.28** reasonably in not consulting an employee where this might result in disclosure of information contained in a medical report that would be likely to cause serious harm to the employee's physical or mental health. (Note that S.7 of the Access to Medical Reports Act 1988 provides an exemption from the employee's right to access a medical report concerning him or her in such circumstances – see 'Medical investigation – access to medical reports' below.) An employer may also be acting reasonably in not consulting where the employee is suffering from mental ill health that renders him or her delusional – Wright v Commissioners of Inland Revenue EAT 385/79.

There also appears to be an exception to the obligation to consult where the employment is of a special nature which requires, for example, a higher than usual level of attendance or that employees be of robust health, particularly where there is a contractual term to that effect. Two examples:

- **Leonard v Fergus and Haynes Civil Engineering Ltd** 1979 IRLR 235, Ct Sess (Inner House): L was a steel fixer on a North Sea oil platform working to a fixed deadline in severe conditions. His contract contained

169

a term, agreed with his union, that anyone absent for two shifts in a 14-day period would be classed as unsuitable for North Sea work. The Court held that dismissal in reliance on this term was fair because the relationship between the employer and the employee was of an 'exceptional and special nature'. It said that L had not been dismissed merely on the ground of ill health but for failing to meet an essential requirement of his contract that he must not be frequently absent on medical grounds. The Daubney guidelines had 'no relevance whatever' given the exceptional and special nature of the employment in this case. (The Court here appears to be suggesting that there was some other substantial reason (SOSR) for the dismissal, meaning that the more prolonged procedural requirements for ill-health dismissals did not apply. SOSR is dealt with in Chapter 8, 'Some other substantial reason')

- **Taylorplan Catering (Scotland) Ltd v McInally** 1980 IRLR 53, EAT: M was a barman at a workman's camp in the Shetlands, a job that was 'arduous' and involved 'unusual working conditions'. He became depressed and was advised by his doctor that he was unsuited to the working conditions in such an isolated environment. He was not consulted before being dismissed. The EAT, overturning a tribunal's finding of unfair dismissal, agreed that in normal cases a measure of consultation was needed before dismissing an employee for ill-health reasons. It noted, however, that in some cases employers will have an express clause, such as the one in Leonard (above), to the effect that after a specified number of absences an employee will be deemed unsuitable for the work and his or her employment will be terminated. Although there was no such express clause in this case, the employer's need for employees of robust health was 'patent' and it was 'clearly established' that M was medically unsuited to the work. Furthermore, M knew that this was the medical view before he was dismissed. Consultation would have served no useful purpose since its dual aims – of balancing an employer's and an employee's needs and establishing the true medical position – had already been met.

5.29 It could be argued that in the Taylorplan case, as in the Leonard case, the unusual working conditions could have amounted to SOSR for dismissal. However, the EAT treated it as an ill-health dismissal and relied on the decision in British Labour Pump Co Ltd v Byrne 1979 ICR 347, EAT. This laid down a rule that where there was a proven procedural irregularity in an otherwise fair dismissal but it could be shown that carrying out the proper procedure would have made no difference, then the dismissal would be fair. However, the Byrne case was subsequently overturned by the House of Lords in Polkey v AE Dayton Services Ltd 1988 ICR 142, HL, and for this reason, the Taylorplan decision should be treated with some caution. Under Polkey, only if an employer could reasonably conclude that a proper procedure would be 'utterly useless' or 'futile' might it be acting reasonably in ignoring it. It will be rare for a tribunal to find that consultation prior to an ill-health dismissal would be futile, particularly as consultation is recognised as being an integral part of such dismissals (effectively taking the place of warnings). Even if there is little prospect of the employee returning to work, the general requirement for employers to take a sympathetic and considerate approach would normally dictate that some manner of consultation should take place. Polkey and its implications are discussed in detail in Chapter 3, 'Unfairness', under 'Fairness of internal procedure'.

Medical investigation

5.30

Mr Justice Phillips in East Lindsey District Council v Daubney 1977 ICR 566, EAT, stated that 'in one way or another steps should be taken by the employer to discover the true medical position' prior to any dismissal. In most cases this will involve consultation with doctors. A failure to seek proper medical advice (where this is appropriate) is likely to result in a finding of unfair dismissal. Some examples:

- **Parsons and Co Ltd v Kidney** EAT 788/87: after K had been absent for several weeks her doctor informed the employer that she was suffering either from back strain or a slipped disc. Recovery from the former would take about six weeks and from the latter about 12. The employer arbitrarily chose to accept the more serious of the two diagnoses and dismissed K instead of attempting to clarify the complaint. The EAT found the dismissal unfair. Not only had there been a failure to consult with K, there had also been a failure to establish clearly the nature of her disability and the likely length of her absence

- **Fry v Russell Williams Textiles Ltd** ET Case No.28250/94: F's employer gave her time off for an operation, believing that it was for medical reasons. After the operation, the company found out that it was for cosmetic surgery, which it did not consider to be a medical reason at all. F was dismissed for conduct on the basis that she had deceived the company that her operation was for medical reasons. A tribunal found that the company had failed to establish conduct as a proper reason to dismiss. F had had the operation on the advice of a physician to remove an overlarge stomach. It was clear from F's evidence that over the years this had had a psychological as well as a physiological effect on her: psychological because it caused her stress and physiological because her job was made difficult by her inability to bend down. In the tribunal's view, these reasons came under the general banner of 'medical'. The tribunal held that the employer was not acting within a range of reasonable responses when concluding that cosmetic surgery was not medical. Medical advice should have been obtained

- **Millington v Wandsworth Council** ET Case No.2302863/06: M went on long-term sick leave on 31 October 2005 suffering from stress. She wrote to the Council on 16 January 2006 saying she had been given a fit

171

to return to work certificate by her GP and that she was planning to return on 6 February. On 26 January she was called to a sickness review meeting and was told that a possible outcome might be dismissal. At the end of the meeting she was dismissed, the Council having concluded that M had said nothing to convince it that her attendance would improve upon her return to work. A tribunal held that in the absence of medical evidence to support its view, the Council had no reasonable grounds for its belief that her attendance would not improve in the future

• **Herold v Secretary of State for Justice** ET Case No.2302144/12: H, a prison officer, became depressed in July 2009 and took 33 days off work. In February 2010 he stopped taking his medication because he felt better, but in December that year he suffered a breakdown after he was assaulted by a prisoner and took several months off work. He undertook a phased return but had a relapse in July 2011. Shortly after his return at the end of August he was invited to a capability hearing and dismissed. A tribunal found that his dismissal was unfair because the employer had no up-to-date medical evidence. At the time of the capability hearing H had returned to full working hours, suggesting that the most recent occupational health report dated 1 August 2011 was inaccurate and needed to be refreshed. The tribunal also considered it relevant that no face-to-face consultation had taken place between H and occupational health since May; that the employer ignored the fact that H was about to undergo therapy; and that the employer failed to implement a phased return or make a further referral as the medical report on which it did rely had recommended. Dismissal in such circumstances was 'precipitate, ill considered and unreasonable'.

5.31 Note that, while East Lindsey District Council v Daubney (above) is considered the leading authority on medical investigation in the context of a fair capability dismissal, the sufficiency of the employer's belief in the grounds for dismissal is still governed by British Home Stores Ltd v Burchell 1980 ICR 303, EAT. Although that case was decided in the context of a conduct dismissal, it set down general principles of reasonableness with wider application – namely, that the employer must genuinely believe in its stated reason for dismissal, having conducted a reasonable investigation, which yields reasonable grounds for the employer's conclusion. The EAT in DB Schenker Rail (UK) Ltd v Doolan EATS 0053/09 emphasised that, while Daubney requires an employer to establish the 'true medical position' before deciding to dismiss, that should not be read as requiring a higher standard of enquiry than required for a misconduct dismissal. The Burchell approach, requiring that a reasonable investigation into the matter be carried out, still applies.

The Court of Session in S v Dundee City Council 2014 IRLR 131, Ct Sess (Inner House), emphasised this point, observing that while employers must take steps to discover the employee's medical condition and his or her likely prognosis, this merely requires the obtaining of proper medical advice. East Lindsey District Council v Daubney (above) only requires employers to take 'such steps as are sensible according to the circumstances'; not to pursue detailed medical examination. In the Court of Session's view, the tribunal had attached too much importance, in the circumstances of the case, to the need to obtain a further medical opinion as to the claimant's state of health. Given that an occupational health consultant had reported that the claimant's health was improving and that he was likely to be able to return to work within one to three months, the Court considered that it was 'difficult to see how further medical advice could clarify matters'. The employer had a medical opinion, and it had to balance that against the claimant's view, which was that he was not improving. The question was not whether further medical advice was needed but whether a reasonable employer, in view of the occupational health report, the continuing sick note from the claimant's GP, and the claimant's own views, would have waited longer, or whether the decision to dismiss was within the range of reasonable responses open to such an employer.

That said, in circumstances where the medical advice might have changed, the **5.32** employer may be acting unreasonably if it fails to get an up-to-date medical report before dismissing. Two examples:

- **Hampson v Cheshire East Community Health** ET Case No.1301717/10: H suffered from chronic migraine attacks, which meant that she had to take sickness absence from time to time. In May 2009 she suffered a recurrence of health problems and took sick leave. In October occupational health reported that she would be off work for at least three to six months but that the long-term outlook was good. The employer decided to terminate her employment on the ground of capability. A tribunal decided that her dismissal was procedurally unfair in that the employer had failed to make the reasonable adjustment of postponing the final appeal decision because new evidence had come to light from H's medical practitioners. The employer should have gone back to them seeking more exacting evidence on her prognosis, in particular with regard to her return to work date

- **Mehmood v British Telecommunications plc** ET Case No.2302775/12: M developed an eye condition in 2007 that manifested itself by bleeds in his eye. This was a recurring condition, and each time it occurred it could result in a significant period of absence. After a long pattern of recurring absence, M was dismissed in February 2012 under the absence management procedure. A tribunal found that the employer had in general acted entirely fairly. However, given that it was on notice at the dismissal hearing and particularly at the appeal stage that M had had an operation on his eye in January 2012 that could possibly have changed this pattern, the employer should reasonably have made further enquiries regarding M's prognosis. Instead it relied on a medical report that was almost a year old.

173

5.33 In all cases, it is important to remember that the decision to dismiss remains a matter for the employer, not a medical matter, and the employer needs to assess the medical advice critically before deciding what steps to take. See 'Acting in accordance with medical advice' below.

5.34 **GP's opinion/fit notes.** The first medical opinion sought should normally be that of the employee's own GP. In any case in which an employee is absent due to ill health beyond the period that can be self-certified, he or she is likely to have obtained – and provided to the employer – a 'statement of fitness for work' (colloquially known as a 'fit note') from the doctor who is responsible for his or her care (see the Social Security (Medical Evidence) and Statutory Sick Pay (Medical Evidence) (Amendment) Regulations 2010 SI 2010/137). This note will indicate the nature of the illness, the period of absence that is initially expected, and what the employee might be capable of doing on his or her return. However, the employer should not approach the GP directly without the employee's consent, because of the doctor's duty of confidentiality to the patient. Furthermore, the employer will need to comply with its obligations under the Access to Medical Reports Act 1988 when requesting information (see 'Access to medical reports' below).

The fit note gives the doctor the option of declaring the patient either 'not fit for work' or 'may be fit for work taking account of the following advice'. The form then gives a list of four typical examples of modifications that could be appropriate, which the doctor can tick – namely, a phased return, amended duties, altered hours and/or workplace adaptations – and a space in which he or she can add comments and/or more detailed advice. The Department for Work and Pensions' guidance for employers and line managers, 'Getting the most out of the fit note' (January 2015), stresses that the advice given in the fit note is about the employee's fitness for work in general, and not specifically aimed at his or her current job. The guidance suggests that possible changes might include:

- changing job or location
- changes to work equipment
- reduced or flexible hours
- adjustments to work premises
- a phased return to work
- giving some of the employee's tasks to someone else
- providing training or additional supervision
- providing a reader or interpreter
- working from home
- voice-activated software

174

- arranging a mentor or work buddy
- working in a team instead of by themselves (or vice versa)
- arranging for an occupational health assessment.

Where a fit note states that the employee may be fit for work, the employer may **5.35** need to seek clarification, either from the GP or from a specialist, as well as discussing the situation with the employee (see 'Consultation with employee – fit notes' above). Simply ignoring the suggestions in the guidance, or failing properly to consider them, could render any subsequent dismissal unfair, as consultation with the employee and consideration of alternative employment are usually key factors in a fair dismissal for capability (see 'Consultation with employee' above, and 'Alternative employment' below). Recommendations in a fit note may also amount to reasonable adjustments for the purposes of the EqA. Furthermore, if the employer fails to implement advice in a fit note on the employee's return to work and his or her condition deteriorates, the fit note might be put forward as evidence that this was foreseeable for the purposes of any personal injury claim against the employer.

On the other hand, where a fit note states that the employee is 'not fit for work' in circumstances where he or she has been off sick for some time, an employer may be able to rely on the note as evidence that it could not make any changes that would have allowed the employee to return to work. However, the employer may be expected to get another medical opinion in these circumstances. If the employee is off sick for four weeks, or the GP thinks that he or she is likely to be off for that long, then the employee can be referred to the 'Fit for Work' scheme. Under this scheme, the employee receives an assessment that provides advice on interventions and commences a 'return to work plan'. If the employee consents, this plan will be shared with the GP and the employer.

Examination by specialists. A decision to dismiss on medical grounds will not **5.36** be reasonable unless the employer has all the relevant facts which are either known or could reasonably be discovered at the time the decision is made. Where there is any doubt, a specialist's report may be necessary and any decision to dismiss without one may be unfair, especially if a specialist report is pending or has been recommended. Two examples:

- **Edwards v Curtis of Burnham Ltd** ET Case No.17694/95: E had been off work for a long time with RSI. At the company's request her GP sent it a report stating that he was unable to say when E would be able to work and that he would recommend that she seek the advice of a consultant. The employer invited E to come in to work to discuss matters. During the meeting, E explained that she had an appointment to see a consultant in two days' time. She was nonetheless dismissed. The dismissal was held to be unfair: the employer should have waited for the consultant's opinion before dismissing

175

- **Airbus UK Ltd v Wilson** EAT 0061/06: W suffered a serious accident at work in February 2003 in which he injured his back. The employer, AUK Ltd, was provided with a medical report in June 2004 which stated that W had a phobic anxiety about returning to the one place that would allow the process of rehabilitation to begin. The report also suggested obtaining a specialist's opinion but was pessimistic that W would ever be fit to return to work. Subsequently W was assessed by a clinical psychologist. However, the employer dismissed W without waiting for the psychologist's report because it had experienced a significant upturn in business but had strict rules about headcount, meaning that W could not be replaced, even on a temporary basis, while he was still on the books. The EAT upheld a tribunal's finding that W was unfairly dismissed because of AUK Ltd's failure to seek further information about the assessment carried out by the psychologist. The employer had been selective in its interpretation of the first medical report, choosing to ignore the 'less palatable' part recommending a specialist opinion, which 'did not fit in with the requirements of the business'.

5.37 **Acting in accordance with medical advice.** Provided an employer consults the employee and allows the employee to state his or her case, it will not normally be criticised for dismissing in accordance with proper medical advice. Employers are not under a duty to evaluate medical advice unless it is plainly inaccurate or based on inadequate examination – Liverpool Area Health Authority (Teaching) Central and Southern District v Edwards 1977 IRLR 471, EAT. The test is whether the employer knew the advice was flawed in this way, or ought reasonably to have known it, and that no reasonable employer would have been entitled to rely upon the report – First Manchester Ltd v Kennedy EAT 0818/04.

In East Lindsey District Council v Daubney 1977 ICR 566, EAT, D's employer asked the district community physician whether D should be retired early on ill-health grounds. The doctor's response was in the affirmative and so D was dismissed without the employer obtaining a full medical report or an independent medical opinion and without personally consulting him. The EAT found the dismissal unfair because of the lack of consultation, but also gave some sound advice regarding medical enquiries. It is not the function of employers, the EAT said, to turn themselves into some sort of medical appeal tribunal to review the opinions and advice of their medical advisers. Employers should not set themselves up as medical experts – the decision to dismiss is not a medical question but an employment question to be answered by the employer in the light of available medical advice.

5.38 The advice sought in each case will depend on the individual circumstances. In Daubney, the EAT criticised the employer for being too restrictive in the advice it sought, which explained why the medical opinion stated only that the employee was 'unfit to carry out the duties of his post and should be retired on the grounds of permanent ill health'. This, said the EAT, was 'verging on the

176

inadequate' because 'the employer may well need more detailed information before being able to make a rational and informed decision whether to dismiss'. However, it considered on balance that the employer would have been entitled to act on the opinion, brief as it was, had it consulted D.

Inadequate medical advice was also at issue in Gildersleve v Department for Work and Pensions ET Case No.1602559/11, where G suffered from post-traumatic stress disorder, which affected his concentration levels. However, an occupational health report did not suggest that this rendered him incapable of doing his job. G continued to fail to meet his targets on a regular basis and a further occupational health report advised that he had a good prognosis, but did not address the extent to which his condition might affect his productivity. He was dismissed. A tribunal decided that his dismissal was unfair. The DWP had expected occupational health to make management decisions, when if it had thoughtfully assessed the occupational health advice it would have taken into account G's variable productivity, recognised the shortcomings in the advice given, and sought further information. Had the DWP made the reasonable adjustment of reducing the targets slightly, and measured his performance over a week rather than on an hourly basis to take account of G's variable concentration levels, he would have met those targets.

5.39 Employers should, so far as possible, ensure that they remain neutral when requesting information to avoid appearing to favour a particular outcome. Furthermore, employers should be careful not to 'pick and choose' which parts of the advice to rely upon, especially if ignoring advice that is more favourable to the employee – Airbus UK Ltd v Wilson EAT 0061/06. Finally, employers should, if requested, give employees reasonable opportunity to counter the medical evidence with a further report – Liverpool Area Health Authority (Teaching) Central and Southern District v Edwards (above).

5.40 **Prognosis.** When deciding whether or not to dismiss an employee for lack of capability, an employer must take into account not only the employee's current level of fitness but also his or her likely future level of fitness.

If there is evidence that an employee's condition will worsen should he or she return to work, that may make dismissal fair, even if the employee is currently fit to do the job. In House v Greene King Services Ltd ET Case No.1500987/07, for example, H sustained a knee injury in 1991, before he began working for GKS Ltd. In April 2006 he had to undergo emergency surgery on his knee and was signed off work. A medical report produced in December 2006 said that his work as a drayman for GKS Ltd had accelerated the wear and tear on his knee, but the knee had responded well to surgery and H's consultant fully supported his return to work as a drayman. The employer was concerned that H's work could contribute to a recurrence of his knee problem and wrote to the consultant for further information but received no reply. It then obtained a further occupational health opinion which stated that H's work would have a negative impact on his knee and bring forward the time when he would require a knee replacement operation. While H was fit to return to work, the report said that ideally he should be provided with a role without significant lifting. Since GKS Ltd had no alternative work to offer, H was dismissed on capability grounds. A tribunal held that although H was fit for work at the time of his dismissal, his employer had genuine concerns, based on medical evidence, that if H returned to work he would suffer further damage to his knee. The likelihood of further injury was sufficiently serious and substantial to make dismissal a reasonable response.

5.41 On the other hand, if an employer ignores a favourable prognosis, a dismissal may be unfair. In Mehmood v British Telecommunications plc ET Case No.2302775/12 M developed an eye condition in 2007 that manifested itself by bleeds in his eye. This was a recurring condition and each time it occurred it could result in a significant period of absence. After a long pattern of recurring absence, M was dismissed in February 2012 under the absence management procedure. A tribunal found that the employer had in general acted entirely fairly. However, given that it was on notice at both the dismissal hearing and at the appeal stage that M had had an operation on his eye in January 2012 that could possibly have changed this pattern, the employer should reasonably have made further enquiries regarding M's prognosis. Instead it relied on a medical report that was almost a year old.

5.42 **Conflicting medical reports.** If two medical reports conflict, the failure to investigate further (perhaps by way of a third opinion) could render dismissal unfair, particularly where there is a substantial difference of opinion. In Fearnley v Initial Healthcare Services ET Case No.21959/95, for example, F, who suffered from a mild form of epilepsy, had epileptic seizures on three occasions in 1994. She lost consciousness on two occasions for a few seconds and then carried on normally. Her GP stated that her epilepsy was stable but the doctor instructed by the employer stated that her epileptic seizures represented a significant risk to herself and others. The employer tried, to no avail, to find alternative work for F. In the meantime, she produced a letter from a neurological registrar at the University of Wales that contradicted the opinion of the employer's doctor. The employer considered investigating the discrepancy between the reports but did not do so. A tribunal found her subsequent dismissal unfair on the basis that had the employer investigated further, it was 'almost certain' that F would not have been dismissed. This was underlined by the fact that, following her dismissal, she was examined by another doctor, who confirmed the opinion of the neurological registrar. However, it was not a question of 'being wise after the event'. The employer had recognised that there was a substantial difference of opinion which put it on notice that further investigation was required.

178

In Liverpool Area Health Authority (Teaching) Central and Southern District v Edwards (above) the EAT suggested that where there were conflicting medical reports, the matter should be remitted to the doctor who issued the first report, who may or may not be persuaded of the other doctor's view on a further examination. It also suggested that where a second (or indeed third) medical opinion is being sought, that doctor should have sight of the previous medical report(s) to ensure consistency and that all relevant issues are covered.

5.43 If an employer relies on one medical opinion in preference to another that is more favourable to the employee, it should have good reason for doing so. In Evers v Doncaster Monk Bridge Ltd ET Case No.26661/78 a tribunal thought it reasonable for the employer to rely on the company doctor's report instead of that of E's doctor, as the company doctor was aware of the dangers inherent in E's working environment, whereas E's doctor was not. But if the report of the employer's own doctor suggests that the only way to reconcile conflicting diagnoses or prognoses is to obtain a report from an independent consultant, failure to do so will almost certainly be unfair – British Gas plc v Breeze EAT 503/87. And in In Brammel v North West Regional Railways Ltd ET Case No.70014/95 a tribunal found that where the employer's doctor thought B – who had contracted viral meningitis and been off work for almost a year – was fit to work and his GP disagreed, an independent report should have been commissioned from the hospital consultant.

5.44 **Employee's refusal to cooperate.** Any attempt by an employer to compel an employee to undergo a medical examination may entitle the employee to resign and claim unfair constructive dismissal unless the contract of employment expressly provides for such power. In Bliss v South East Thames Regional Health Authority 1987 ICR 700, CA, B, a consultant at an NHS hospital, was involved in an acrimonious and protracted dispute with a colleague. As a result, the regional medical officer asked him to undergo a medical examination by a psychiatric consultant. B refused and resigned, suing for damages for breach of contract. It was common ground before the Court of Appeal that there was an implied term in B's contract of employment that the employer was entitled to require him to undergo a medical examination if it had reasonable grounds for believing that he might be suffering from a physical or mental disability that might cause harm to patients. However, since the committee whose duty it was to investigate such cases did not find any mental or pathological illness, the employer had no reasonable grounds for requiring the examination and was in breach of trust and confidence when it unreasonably insisted upon it.

However, if an employee refuses to cooperate in providing medical evidence the employer is entitled to base its decision on the relevant facts available, even if those facts are insufficient to give the full medical position. The Acas Guide recommends that, in such circumstances, the employee should be informed in writing that a decision will be taken on the basis of the information available

179

and that it could result in dismissal (page 74). Dismissal may then be fair. In Tahir v Sainsbury's Supermarkets Ltd ET Case No.1801002/07, for example, T injured his back on 31 May and went off work sick. He provided sick notes from his GP but withheld his consent to the release of his GP records to SS Ltd's occupational health service. SS Ltd dismissed him on 3 November believing, on the basis of its consultation, that he was unlikely to be fit to return to work in the near future. His unfair dismissal claim was rejected by a tribunal, which held that SS Ltd could not safely allow T to return to work in the face of a medical certificate saying he was unfit for work and given the employer's own observations of T's physical state. The employer had to make a decision on whether it was appropriate to dismiss on the limited information it had, having made reasonable attempts to obtain further information. Given the duration of T's sickness absence, it was entitled to dismiss when it did.

5.45 However, dismissal may be unfair if the employer has not made reasonable attempts to obtain the necessary medical evidence by alternative means. In Mathews v British Telecommunications plc ET Case No.2205791/10 a tribunal considered that in circumstances where M was declining to engage with an occupational health assessment a reasonable employer would have been wise to depart from its normal procedure and seek a report from his GP. M may well have declined to give permission for this but BT plc simply did not ask. By failing to do this, and then deciding to dismiss in the absence of any meaningful medical evidence, BT plc had acted unreasonably.

5.46 **Access to medical reports.** The Access to Medical Reports Act 1988 gives individuals certain rights in respect of reports relating to their health that have been prepared by a medical practitioner 'who is or has been responsible for the clinical care of the individual'. Under the Act:

- an employer who wishes to contact an employee's doctor must notify the employee in writing and must secure his or her written consent before doing so

- in giving such notification, the employer must inform the employee of his or her right to withhold consent, to have access to the report and to then withhold consent for it to be supplied, and to request amendments to the report

- if the employee states that he or she wishes to have access to the report, the employer must tell the doctor when making the application and at the same time let the employee know that the report has been requested

- the employee must contact the doctor within 21 days of the date of the application to make arrangements to see the report

- if the employee considers the report to be incorrect or misleading, he or she can make a written request to have it amended

- if the doctor refuses to amend the report, the employee has the right to ask him or her to attach a statement to the report reflecting the employee's view on any matters of disagreement

- the employee has the right to withhold consent to the report being supplied to the employer.

There is an exemption from the rights to access under the 1988 Act where **5.47** 'disclosure would in the opinion of the practitioner be likely to cause serious harm to the physical or mental health of the individual or others or would indicate the intentions of the practitioner in respect of the individual' – S.7. Failure by an employer to consult with the employee in such circumstances may fall into the range of reasonable responses – see 'Consultation with employee – exceptions' above.

Note that the 1988 Act only covers reports prepared by a medical practitioner responsible for the worker's care. If a report is requested by an occupational health consultant instructed by the employer, for example, the individual's rights to access will be limited to those provided by the Data Protection Act 1998.

Data protection. When dealing with employees' health records, employers **5.48** should pay heed to the Data Protection Act 1998, as medical information will constitute 'sensitive personal data' under that Act. Employers should refer to Part 4 of the Employment Practices Code, issued by the Information Commissioner, which covers information about workers' health.

Exceptions. In East Lindsey District Council v Daubney 1977 ICR 566, EAT, **5.49** the EAT appeared to envisage that only in 'wholly exceptional circumstances' would an employer not be required to take steps to discover the true medical position. This might possibly apply where the employment is of a special nature, requiring, for example, a higher than usual level of attendance – Leonard v Fergus and Haynes Civil Engineering Ltd 1979 IRLR 235, Ct Sess (Inner House). There, the employer's failure to inquire into the nature of L's incapacity did not make his dismissal unfair – see 'Consultation with employee – exceptions' above for further details.

Note that the 'Polkey exception' – whereby an employer might exceptionally be entitled to dispense with a proper procedure if it could reasonably have concluded that this would have been 'utterly useless' or 'futile' – may be even less likely to apply in the case of medical investigation. In Millington v Wandsworth Council ET Case No.2302863/06, for example, the tribunal found that without an up-to-date medical report as at the time of M's dismissal, it was unable to carry out the investigation required under Polkey to establish whether M would have been dismissed in any event. To do so would be to 'embark on a sea of speculation based on the very failure to obtain a medical report and investigate [the] true medical position which we find to be one of the reasons for the unfairness of [M's] dismissal'.

5.50 Relevance of Equality Act 2010

The medical investigation may reveal or confirm that the employee's illness amounts to a disability under the EqA. If this is the case, the employer will need to tread particularly carefully since dismissal could amount to unlawful discrimination even if it is found to be fair under the ERA. Liability for disability discrimination under the EqA must be considered separately from liability for unfair dismissal under the ERA. For example, a dismissal may amount to discrimination 'arising from disability' under S.15 EqA unless it can be justified. However, a dismissal that cannot be justified does not automatically fail the reasonableness test under S.98(4) ERA – HJ Heinz Co Ltd v Kenrick 2000 ICR 491, EAT. Conversely, there may be situations where a dismissal is unfair under the ERA (for example, because there is some procedural defect) but nonetheless justified under the disability discrimination legislation. The EAT confirmed in Royal Liverpool Children's NHS Trust v Dunsby 2006 IRLR 351, EAT (discussed under 'Persistent short-term absences – unconnected minor ailments' below), that the equalities legislation does not impose an absolute obligation on an employer to refrain from dismissing an employee who is absent wholly or in part on the ground of ill health due to disability – it simply requires such a dismissal to be justified.

The EqA also imposes on employers a separate duty to make reasonable adjustments for disabled workers, giving rise to a stand-alone discrimination claim. If an employer fails to make a reasonable adjustment that would have avoided the need to dismiss an employee, the dismissal may well fall foul of the reasonableness test set out in S.98(4) ERA. This was certainly the view of the employment tribunal in Nikola-Erotokritou v Hertfordshire County Council ET Case No.3302508/10. In that case N-E developed tendinitis in her hands and had to take a number of sickness absences. In August 2009 a consultant reported that she should be able to return to work as long as she had help with heavy lifting. The employer made no adjustments and dismissed her on capability grounds. The tribunal found that the employer had failed to make reasonable adjustments and that the dismissal was unfair. It stated: 'It seems to us illogical and perverse to hold that the dismissal can be fair and yet at the point of dismissal the respondent failed to make reasonable adjustments... if and so long as it would be reasonable for the respondent to make reasonable adjustments, it must follow that dismissal cannot lie within the range of reasonable responses. That position would only prevail once the reasonable adjustments which it was the respondent's duty to seek to apply had been tried and found to have failed.' Two further examples:

- **Douglas v Bournemouth Borough Council** ET Case No.3103140/09: D suffered from depression, anxiety and panic attacks, and an obsessive compulsive disorder. Her health deteriorated and she was signed off work. After D had been absent for five months, a report from occupational health indicated that redeployment might well be beneficial to D and could facilitate

182

an earlier return to work, but that it was unlikely she could return within four or five months. However, the employer terminated her employment and a tribunal upheld her claims of a failure to comply with the duty to make reasonable adjustments and unfair dismissal. It would have been a reasonable adjustment for the employer to have extended D's employment to allow for reasonable consideration of redeployment. Its failure to do so, combined with other procedural failings, also rendered D's dismissal unfair

- **Coldicott v Vale of Mowbray Ltd** ET Case No.2501923/11: C worked as a factory operative making pork pies. She suffered from a number of health conditions, including a deformed big toe, a prolapsed disc in her back, and arthritis. She had significant periods of absence that eventually led to her dismissal. A tribunal decided that VM Ltd had failed to make a reasonable adjustment of adapting equipment to enable C to use it without suffering pain and that dismissal in the absence of investigating the provision of the adjustment rendered her dismissal unfair.

A failure to make a reasonable adjustment may also amount to an unfair **5.51** constructive dismissal, as the following cases demonstrate:

- **Meikle v Nottinghamshire County Council** 2005 ICR 1, CA: the Court of Appeal held that failing to implement certain reasonable adjustments to the working conditions of a disabled worker amounted to a constructive dismissal. M suffered from an eye condition and the Court held that the employer's persistent and long-term failure either to enlarge her written materials or to amend her timetable breached the implied term of trust and confidence and rendered her dismissal unfair

- **Perry Motor Sales Ltd v Evans** EAT 0275/14: the EAT upheld a tribunal's decision that a motor technician with hand/arm vibration syndrome had been unfairly constructively dismissed when his employer had failed properly to implement reasonable adjustments whereby E should not have been required to undertake work using power or air tools, or working 'blind'. The EAT concluded that the employer's discriminatory conduct was one of a series of acts giving rise to a breach of the implied term of trust and confidence.

By contrast, in Bryant v London Borough of Havering ET Case No.3204452/09 **5.52** a tribunal decided that despite the fact that B's employer had failed to comply with the duty to make reasonable adjustments, this did not render his dismissal unfair. B suffered from kidney disease and visual impairment. His employer was concerned that he was not doing enough work and began discussions with him about expanding his role. In March 2008 B went on sick leave, concerned that if he returned he would again be pressured to take on more work than he considered he could manage. He was dismissed in May 2009 on the ground of incapability due to absence. A tribunal decided that the employer had failed to

183

make reasonable adjustments in that it should have allowed him to start work early to avoid traffic, but that dismissal was within the range of reasonable responses. The employer had offered some reasonable adjustments; had invited B to explore alternative roles (to which he had not responded); and had followed its processes consistently.

Finally, it should be noted that a dismissal for certain long-term conditions, such as dementia, arthritis, or age-related macular degeneration, may amount to unlawful indirect *age* discrimination. While dismissal in such circumstances may be objectively justifiable – particularly where the condition in question is progressive and/or terminal – the discrimination question under the EqA should be considered separately from the fairness question under the ERA. Consultation, medical assessment, and consideration of reasonable adjustments will all play a vital role in such cases, both in justifying any potential discrimination and in ensuring that any dismissal is fair.

5.53 Persistent short-term absences

Employers dealing with persistent short-term absenteeism should first establish the reasons for the absences. There are a number of possible reasons for such absences – for example, they could be caused by a series of minor unconnected ailments, such as colds and stomach upsets; by recurrent conditions such as back problems or asthma; or by family, personal or childcare problems. In addition to absence for genuine reasons, there is also the possibility of employees 'skiving' by, for example, taking advantage of the self-certification scheme or abusing agreed time-off arrangements.

Where the sickness absences are genuine they may be due to a series of unconnected, minor ailments or, even if seemingly unconnected, be caused by an underlying medical condition (which could also amount to a disability under the EqA). Determining the cause will make a crucial difference to the procedure that must be followed.

5.54 Unconnected minor ailments

Employers wishing to dismiss for persistent short-term absenteeism will not generally be expected to follow the procedure required in cases of long-term illnesses (see 'Long-term ill health' above). As stated by the EAT in International Sports Co Ltd v Thomson 1980 IRLR 340, EAT, where an employer is concerned with an employee's unacceptable level of intermittent absences due to unconnected minor ailments, it would be placing too heavy a burden on the employer to require it to carry out a formal medical investigation. The EAT went on to say that, in any event, such an investigation would 'rarely be fruitful because of the transient nature of the employee's symptoms and complaints'. In such cases there comes a time when a reasonable employer is entitled to say 'enough is enough' and, so long as warnings have been given, treating the frequent absences as a sufficient reason for dismissing is likely to fall within the band of reasonable responses – Post Office v Jones 1977 IRLR 422, EAT.

In Rolls-Royce Ltd v Walpole 1980 IRLR 343, EAT, for example, W's absenteeism record averaged over 40 per cent for the last three years of his employment. Most of the absences were certified by a doctor, being the result of, for example, injuries sustained while playing rugby. The employer gave him warnings that the absences – which followed no particular pattern – were getting out of hand and followed company procedure meticulously. Since there seemed no reason to anticipate any improvement, W was eventually dismissed for capability. A tribunal found the dismissal unfair but the EAT, by a majority, allowed the employer's appeal in light of the fact that W's poor attendance extended over a period of three years and there was no suggestion that he was suffering from any underlying condition that rendered him more susceptible to illness than his fellow employees. In the circumstances, a medical examination, for example, by the employer's own doctor would have been of no assistance.

5.55 In International Sports Co Ltd v Thomson (above) the EAT stated that in cases of persistent intermittent absenteeism an employer should:

- carry out a fair review of the attendance record and the reasons for absence

- give the employee an opportunity to make representations, and

- give appropriate warnings of dismissal if things do not improve.

If there is no adequate improvement in the attendance record, then, said the EAT, dismissal will be justifiable. This will be so regardless of whether or not the reasons for the absences are genuine. An example:

- **Davis v Tibbett and Britten Group plc** EAT 460/99: D was dismissed following persistent short-term absences that were all caused by genuine though unconnected medical reasons, such as a broken ankle, food poisoning, a sleep disorder and a muscle injury. D appealed against a tribunal's finding that he had not been unfairly dismissed, submitting that the employer's belief that the absences were not genuine played a part in his dismissal. The EAT, however, dismissed the appeal, holding that there was no evidence that the employer had questioned the authenticity of D's ill-health reasons. It was, said the EAT, possible for absences to be unreasonable, even if genuine. The EAT held that it was well established that persistent absenteeism may be an admissible reason for dismissal and in those circumstances whether or not the employee is at fault is immaterial. The employer in this case was entitled to look at the whole history and decide whether or not it was prepared to continue to shoulder the burden of an employee who had been absent on so many occasions. This was not a case where it would have been helpful to seek medical evidence since there had been a large number of unconnected ailments. The EAT cited with

185

approval the comments made in the International Sports case where the absences were also for genuine but unconnected illnesses.

5.56 **'Enough is enough'.** It is impossible to say with absolute precision at what point an employee's absenteeism will reach the level where 'enough is enough'. In International Sports Co Ltd v Thomson (above) T's absence had reached a level of about 25 per cent in the last 18 months of her employment, while in Davis v Tibbett and Britten Group plc (above) D had taken a total of 217 days' sick leave in the three years prior to his dismissal.

Much will depend on the particular circumstances of the case. For example, in some industries absences may be particularly damaging and employers may not be expected to tolerate high levels of absenteeism. In Patval v London Borough of Camden ET Case No.2203464/07, for example, the tribunal accepted that there were often ongoing issues affecting the users of IT services for which there needed to be a flexible and reliable response from IT support. Any absences in IT support, therefore, caused the employer severe disruption. Similarly, in Davis v Tibbett and Britten Group plc (above) the regular attendance of employees such as D was an important factor in the employer's transport business, given the stringent demands placed on it by its principal customer.

5.57 If the employer has a sickness absence policy in place (with triggers and warnings), this will alert employees to what the employer considers an unacceptable level of absence. Provided the policy is consistently applied, it will generally be reasonable for the employer to rely on this.

5.58 **Opportunity to make representations.** An employee should always be given a chance to explain his or her absences. Ideally, an employer should ensure that someone speaks to an employee after every absence. This will give the employee a chance to discuss any problems he or she may be having either domestically or with the job. It could also reveal the existence of an underlying medical condition (see 'Underlying medical condition' below). At the very least, an employee should be consulted at the point when his or her record is causing concern so that he or she has an opportunity to explain the absences. In Backhouse v Coleman's of Stamford ET Case No.19865/95, for example, B was dismissed for absenteeism after being absent for 38 days in 11 months. She had received five verbal warnings and had been given a written warning six months before her dismissal. Following an absence of three weeks, the employer dismissed B without holding a disciplinary meeting or giving her any opportunity to state her case. The tribunal found that B's dismissal was unfair.

It is important that an employer does not make assumptions about an employee's absences, since treating genuine sickness absence as misconduct can lead to a finding of unfair dismissal. In Leeson v Makita Manufacturing Europe Ltd EAT 0911/00 L had been signed off work for a week and prescribed antibiotics. He went to play golf on the fifth day of his sick leave to get some fresh air and exercise after being confined indoors all week. The EAT held that the fact that L was well enough to do some recreational activity did not justify the employer's conclusion that he was fit enough to work.

Warnings. Although 'warnings' or 'cautions' may seem inappropriate in cases **5.59** of absence caused by genuine illness, they are a necessary step given that such absences can lead to dismissal. Formal warnings were certainly viewed as factors going to the reasonableness, and hence fairness, of the dismissals in International Sports Co Ltd v Thomson (above) and Rolls-Royce Ltd v Walpole (above). Furthermore, the Acas Guide advises that in all cases of persistent short-term absence the employee should be told what improvement in attendance is expected and warned of the likely consequences if this does not happen. This adds weight to the argument that the Acas Code applies to cases of short-term absenteeism, at least in cases where the ailments are minor and unrelated (see 'General considerations – Acas Code of Practice on Disciplinary and Grievance Procedures' above). It is therefore instructive to summarise the recommendations made in the Acas Guide (at pages 71–72):

- unexpected absences should be investigated promptly and the employee asked for an explanation at a return-to-work interview

- if there are no acceptable reasons then the employer may wish to treat the matter as a conduct issue and deal with it under the disciplinary procedure – see Chapter 6, 'Conduct', under 'Disciplinary proceedings'

- where there is no medical certificate to support frequent short-term, self-certified absences, then the employee should be asked to see a doctor to establish whether treatment is necessary and whether the underlying reason for the absence is work-related. If no medical support is forthcoming, the employer should consider whether to take action under the disciplinary procedure

- if the absence could be disability-related the employer should consider what reasonable adjustments could be made in the workplace to help the employee

- if the absence is because of temporary problems relating to dependants, the employee may be entitled to have time off under the provisions of the ERA relating to time off for dependants

- if the absence is because the employee has difficulty managing both work and home responsibilities then the employer should give serious consideration to more flexible ways of working

- in all cases the employee should be told what improvement in attendance is expected and warned of the likely consequences if this does not happen

- if there is no improvement, the employee's length of service, performance, the likelihood of a change in attendance, the availability of suitable alternative

187

work where appropriate and the effect of past and future absences on the organisation should all be taken into account in deciding appropriate action.

5.60 The Guide also advises employers to keep absence records so that absence can be monitored and any problems addressed at an early stage, and to deal with persistent absence promptly, firmly and consistently in order to show both the employee concerned and other employees that absence is regarded as a serious matter. However, employers should avoid reaching decisions that are primarily intended to communicate a message to the rest of the workforce: in Leeson v Makita Manufacturing Europe Ltd EAT 0911/00 a tribunal held that the reason for L's dismissal was the employer's desire to 'be seen to be tackling the absenteeism problem'. The EAT held that this was not a fair reason for dismissal because it had more to do with the employer's wish to make an example of the employee to deter others than with dealing with his genuine sickness absence.

The language used in warnings for absenteeism should be appropriate to the circumstances. Two examples:

- **Lynock v Cereal Packaging Ltd** 1988 ICR 670, EAT: the EAT emphasised that where there was genuine illness it should not be treated as a disciplinary matter and that employers had to treat each case individually with 'sympathy, understanding and compassion'. However, it said, the purpose of a 'warnings' system was to give a 'caution' that the stage had been reached where, with the best will in the world, continued employment would become impossible

- **Davis v Tibbett and Britten Group plc** (above): the EAT criticised the warnings that had been issued on the basis that they were couched in language appropriate for disciplinary matters, rather than persistent absenteeism on account of genuine ill health. Even so, it did not consider that the use of inappropriate language in itself tainted the employer's procedure with unfairness.

5.61 If the employer does issue a warning, it must abide by its terms. In Scott v Birmingham City Council ET Case No.1303486/04 S had taken an exceptional amount of sick leave. His employer made it clear that any further period of sustained sickness absence within the following six months would trigger a capability hearing to consider his future employment. Following a further period of absence S was invited to attend the capability hearing. At that stage the employer made the decision to dismiss S. However, following the meeting it sent a letter to S stating that he had six months in which to improve his attendance. Some two months after sending that letter, the employer dismissed S following another capability hearing. The tribunal held that had the employer dismissed S following the first capability meeting, that dismissal would have been fair. However, by sending the letter giving him six months to improve, the employer had effectively invoked the absence procedure again, confusing the position and misleading C. Therefore, C's dismissal was unfair.

Furthermore, a warning in respect of persistent absences should not be combined with a warning for other matters to justify dismissal. In Adan v Asda Stores Ltd ET Case No.1202390/08 A had an exemplary attendance record for the first two years of his employment. However, on a number of occasions after November 2006 he was spoken to and counselled about his absences and lateness. On 20 November 2007 he was given a verbal warning for taking an unauthorised break. On 19 March 2008 he was given a final written warning for refusing to obey a reasonable management instruction. The next month he was off work on certificated sickness absence for two weeks, which triggered the employer's absence procedure. He was called to an investigatory meeting and then a disciplinary hearing, following which he was issued with a verbal warning. However, the employer's disciplinary procedure provided that an employee who has a live final written warning and commits a further offence would be dismissed. Therefore, the employer felt compelled to dismiss A. His unfair dismissal claim was upheld by a tribunal on the basis that no reasonable employer would 'tot up' a final written warning for misconduct with a verbal warning issued for breach of an absence policy when the absence was by reason of genuine certified sickness absence.

Triggers. Many absence policies specify certain procedures, such as oral and written warnings, that will be triggered when the number of absences reaches a particular level. Employers should ensure that any absence procedure is applied consistently and that the consequences of failing to comply with the procedure are properly communicated to employees. Two examples: **5.62**

- **Connorton v British Steel plc** ET Case No.2502634/99: C had the worst attendance record at the plant in which he worked. Although he had been given two written warnings, one in November 1995 and one in July 1997, his absences had in general been treated leniently. After absences from work on 23 and 24 April 1999 C was called to a meeting at which he disclosed, for the first time, that he had an alcohol problem, that this was the reason for his absences, and that he had now resumed counselling. However, the employer decided that C's claim to have an alcohol problem could not be accepted as a way of avoiding disciplinary action and dismissed him. The tribunal held that the dismissal was unfair. C had never been given a final warning and had no reason to believe that his employer would not continue to treat him with the same leniency it had shown in the past. When he went to the meeting he had no idea that it might result in his dismissal

- **Hayes v London Borough of Croydon** ET Case No.2301152/10: H had a history of depression. She took occasional days off work due to minor illness but in April/May 2008 her marriage broke down and she faced repossession of her house and this led to a serious episode of depression and a 49-day absence from work. At the time she was informed that this would not be taken into account for the purpose of triggering the sickness management

189

policy. However, in April 2009 she was absent for three days suffering from sickness and diarrhoea and she was dismissed. A tribunal found that H had been unfairly dismissed as she had been led to expect that the 49 days would not be taken into account; she was treated inconsistently compared to a colleague whose absence due to stress related to his child's serious illness was discounted; and the general improvement in her attendance and the good standard of her work were not considered.

5.63 As the Hayes case illustrates, employers should not adhere too rigidly to absence procedures where this would result in unfairness to the employee. Other factors may also be relevant. In Cowans v Royal Mail Group Ltd ET Case No.2300604/11, for example, a tribunal considered that an employer had acted unreasonably in failing to note that C's absences that led to the triggering of the various stages of the attendance procedure were on account of depression initiated by the death of his friend. He was well on his way to recovery and there was nothing to suggest that his performance would not return to its previous acceptable level. His dismissal was therefore unfair.

5.64 **Disability-related absences.** Employers may need to be flexible about the way schemes designed to improve attendance are operated in respect of employees who have a disability. The fact that some of the absences are related to a disability does not necessarily mean, however, that dismissal for persistent absence will be unfair (or indeed discriminatory).

5.65 In Royal Liverpool Children's NHS Trust v Dunsby 2006 IRLR 351, EAT, repeated sickness absence ultimately led to D's dismissal after the Trust's four-stage sickness absence procedure had been exhausted. At the 'stage four' hearing, D contended for the first time that two of her absences had been due not merely to headaches, as previously recorded, but to migraines caused by gynaecological problems, which would not recur since her medication had been changed. At a subsequent tribunal hearing it was assumed that D's gynaecological problems amounted to a disability under the Disability Discrimination Act 1995 (DDA) (since repealed and superseded by the EqA). In the tribunal's view, if the disability-related absences had been disregarded, the 'stage two' review would not have taken place and the review in June 2004 would therefore have been stage three rather than stage four, meaning that D would not have been at risk of dismissal. The tribunal consequently allowed the unfair dismissal claim, finding that it had not been reasonable for the Trust to treat disability-related absences as part of the 'totting-up' review process. The tribunal also held that the dismissal was not justified under the DDA because D would not have been at risk of dismissal in June 2004 had it not been for the disability-related absences. The EAT overturned the tribunal's decision, holding that there was no absolute rule that an employer acts unreasonably if it treats disability-related absences as part of a 'totting-up' review process or as part of a reason for dismissal on the ground of repeated short-term absence. If, however, the tribunal considered that it was unreasonable to do so in this case, it should have explained why. D's assertion for the first time at the fourth stage of the sickness absence procedure that just two absences nearly a year before should be left out of account did not necessarily make it unreasonable for the Trust, looking at the whole pattern, to dismiss. There was no rule that an employer, in operating a sickness absence procedure, must discount disability-related absences.

The EAT also held that the DDA does not impose an absolute obligation on an **5.66** employer to refrain from dismissing an employee who is absent wholly or in part on the ground of ill health due to disability – it simply requires such a dismissal to be justified. Accordingly, a tribunal cannot conclude that a dismissal is not justified merely because the employee was absent on the ground of disability. The EAT allowed the appeal and remitted the case to a fresh tribunal for rehearing. However, in doing so it noted the apparent strength of the employer's case, based on D's 'appalling' absence record and the fact that periodic and repeated absence caused the Trust severe operational difficulties.

The EAT in Dunsby did not consider the question of whether D's disability-related absences should have been discounted as a reasonable adjustment under the DDA. Nevertheless, the tone of the EAT's judgment suggests that it is not automatically the case that failure to discount such absences will amount to a failure to make reasonable adjustments. The fact that only a small proportion of D's absences were disability-related appears crucial to the EAT's decision. Where the vast majority of short-term absences are caused by a disability, there would be an underlying medical condition and the employer should implement its long-term sickness procedure with a view (once all other options have been explored) to dismissing by reason of ill health rather than for persistent absenteeism – see 'Underlying medical condition' below.

Factors to be taken into account if no improvement. The Acas Guide states **5.67** that if there is no improvement in the employee's absence record, the following factors should 'all be taken into account in deciding appropriate action':

- the employee's length of service
- performance
- the likelihood of a change in attendance
- the availability of suitable alternative work where appropriate, and
- the effect of past and future absences on the organisation (page 72).

In addition, the employer should consider: 'the nature of the illness; the likelihood of it recurring or some other illness arising; the length of the various absences and the spaces of good health between them; the need of the employer for the work done by the particular employee; the impact of the absences on

191

others who work with the employee; the adoption and the carrying out of the policy; the important emphasis on a personal assessment in the ultimate decision and of course, the extent to which the difficulty of the situation and the position of the employer has been made clear to the employee so that the employee realises that the point of no return, the moment when the decision was ultimately being made may be approaching' – Lynock v Cereal Packaging Ltd 1988 ICR 670, EAT.

5.68 Both the Acas Guide and the Lynock case suggest that the likelihood of future illnesses/absences is a factor to be taken into account and in Davis v Tibbett and Britten Group plc EAT 460/99 the EAT endorsed the tribunal's finding that it was reasonable for the employer to conclude, given D's past absenteeism, that he was unlikely to meet an acceptable standard of attendance in the future. However, the Lynock case also makes it clear that if the employer has justifiably reached the point where 'enough is enough' (due to the sheer number of absences) it will not then need to investigate the likelihood of a change in attendance: the EAT said 'it seems to us to be impossible to give a reasonable prognosis or projection of the possibility of what will happen in the future. Whilst an employer may make enquiries… it is in no way… an obligation on the employer so to do because the results may produce nothing of assistance to him.' For that very reason, the EAT held that the employer was not required to seek further medical advice. Nor will the fact that the employee happens to be fit and working at that point make any difference. As stated by the EAT, 'there is no principle that the mere fact that an employee is fit at the time of dismissal makes his dismissal unfair; one has to look at the whole history and the whole picture'.

Although length of service may be a relevant factor, it is not determinative. In Regan v Magneti Marelli UK Ltd EAT 577/99 the EAT upheld a tribunal's decision that R had been fairly dismissed for persistent absenteeism, despite his having been employed there for almost 30 years. The employer had given a number of warnings and essentially reached the point where 'enough was enough'.

5.69 Underlying medical condition

If it becomes clear that there is an underlying medical condition that has been the cause of a significant number of an employee's short-term absences, the employer would be well advised to seek a medical opinion in order to determine the extent and likely duration of the medical condition, and whether, and if so how soon, treatment will bring the absenteeism down to an acceptable level. Particular thought should be given to whether the underlying condition amounts to a disability under the EqA since the employer would then have a duty to consider whether there are any reasonable adjustments that could be made to help the employee. The employer should also be aware that any dismissal might amount to disability discrimination.

192

If an underlying condition does come to light, the employer may need to treat past absences more leniently and, especially if there is unlikely to be any improvement, should regard the case as one of long-term illness rather than short-term absenteeism (see 'Long-term ill health' above). After all, it might be considered unfair to treat an employee who takes persistent short-term absences for an underlying medical condition differently to an employee who takes long-term absence for an underlying medical condition.

Some examples: 5.70

- **Asafu-Adjaye v London Borough of Camden** ET Case No.2201504/07: over the course of about two years A took a considerable amount of sick leave. It transpired that this was because he suffered from chronic back pain. The employer's own occupational health advisers made it clear on a number of occasions that A's good health could be restored following physiotherapy but the employer eventually dismissed A for capability, contending that it had done everything that could reasonably be expected. A tribunal accepted that the employer had 'conscientiously' followed the correct procedure for long-term illness over a 'sympathetically extensive period of time'. Furthermore, the employer had sought medical advice, adjusted A's duties and looked at redeployment. Nevertheless, the tribunal held that A's dismissal for ill-health reasons was unfair. In fairness to A's 22 years of service, any reasonable employer would have awaited the outcome of the medically recommended though 'much overdue' physiotherapy (either through the NHS or at the employer's expense) – provided that the treatment took place in the reasonably near future and A agreed to participate fully

- **Jones v Interserve Project Services Ltd** ET Case No.3302615/09: J took time off work suffering from irritable bowel syndrome and depression and was given a stage one warning for attendance. In February 2009 he was absent from work for two days, with his company mobile phone switched off, and only notified IPS Ltd of the reason for his absence on the third day. He was dismissed for misconduct. A tribunal upheld his unfair dismissal claim, observing that the true reason for dismissal was capability. Given that J was clearly suffering from depression, IPS Ltd should have obtained a medical report on his condition before dismissing

- **Wilford v Secretary of State for Justice** ET Case No.1502341/11: W had multiple sclerosis, which caused her to take a number of absences. Various adjustments were made that enabled her to continue working but in June 2010 she was transferred to a new department without consultation. She went off sick again and in August was dismissed at a capability hearing. A tribunal upheld her unfair dismissal claim, noting that she was dismissed under the 'unsatisfactory attendance' procedure, despite the fact that her illness qualified as a serious underlying medical condition and should not

193

have been processed under that procedure. Moreover, the decision to dismiss was made without reference to the up-to-date medical reports and without properly consulting W.

5.71 Label for dismissal

In cases of persistent absences due to ill health, there are at least two potential reasons for dismissal: the ill health itself (where there is an underlying medical condition) or the resultant absenteeism (where this has reached the point where 'enough is enough', provided the illnesses are minor and unconnected). The cases demonstrate that the distinction is crucial when it comes to the procedure that should be followed. It is less obvious, however, what statutory label should be attached to the dismissal when it comes to tribunal proceedings. As noted in Chapter 3, 'Unfairness', under 'Reason for dismissal', there are five potentially fair reasons for dismissal set out in S.98. The three most relevant for our purposes are capability, 'some other substantial reason' (SOSR) and conduct.

It is clear that where an employee is being dismissed on the ground of ill health, the correct label will be *capability*. The courts and tribunals have, however, been less certain about what category absenteeism falls into: in International Sports Co Ltd v Thomson 1980 IRLR 340, EAT, the EAT was of the view that absenteeism amounted to 'conduct' but could also be SOSR; in Davis v Tibbett and Britten Group plc EAT 460/99 it was described as 'incapacity'; in Williams v Cheshire Fire and Rescue Service EAT 0621/07 it was considered to be 'conduct'; and in Lynock v Cereal Packaging Ltd 1988 ICR 670, EAT, it was held to be 'capability', but the EAT felt it 'might possibly have been a question of conduct'. The Appeal Tribunal admitted that 'neither word is entirely apposite to the situation'.

5.72 The Court of Appeal provided some clarification on the issue in Wilson v Post Office 2000 IRLR 834, CA. In that case W was dismissed for unacceptable levels of short-term absence. In its response to W's tribunal claim for unfair dismissal, the Post Office cited 'incapability by reason of unsatisfactory attendance record' as the reason for dismissal. The tribunal went on to find that the reason for dismissal was incapability on the ground of ill health and that the dismissal was unfair. The Court of Appeal remitted the case, having found that the real reason for dismissal had not been capability but W's failure to comply with the Post Office's attendance procedure, which fell within SOSR. Therefore, different factors needed to be taken into account when judging the reasonableness of the dismissal, with W's future health prospects carrying less weight than they would in a capability dismissal.

It seems clear from this that an employer who dismisses an employee for persistent absenteeism will be dismissing for SOSR, rather than capability. This appears logical since the employer is less concerned with the employee's capability to do the job per se than with his or her past absenteeism. Furthermore,

194

'conduct' does not seem an appropriate label given the EAT's emphasis in cases such as Lynock v Cereal Packaging Ltd (above) that absenteeism should not be treated as a disciplinary matter.

In Ridge v HM Land Registry EAT 0485/12 the EAT observed that it can be a **5.73** difficult question whether to classify a dismissal following repeated periods of absence as a capability dismissal or one for SOSR. It advised that if considerations of the employee's capability assessed by reference to skill, aptitude, health or another physical or mental quality are at the forefront of the employer's mind when dismissing, then the reason for dismissal will relate to the capability of the employee to perform work of the kind that he or she was employed to do within the meaning of S.98(2)(a). If, however, the recurring absences themselves are the reason for dismissal, particularly in cases of repeated short-term absence for a variety of reasons, then the better label may be SOSR under S.98(1)(b).

For example, in Tagro v Royal Mail Group 2013 NICA 30, NICA, T, a postal worker, was absent several times, triggering all three stages of his employer's attendance procedure. An occupational health provider assessed T and concluded that he had a skin complaint which at times affected his heels and ankles but that he was fit for full work duties. After receiving a stage two warning under the procedure, he sustained a shoulder injury at work. Although his absences continued, he did not proceed to stage three as the attendance procedure did not apply to work injuries. However, after receiving physiotherapy his absences continued, as he was suffering stress and depression. Ultimately he was dismissed after a final stage three hearing for breaching the attendance procedure. The employer stated that the reason for dismissal was 'conduct'. However, the Northern Ireland Court of Appeal upheld a tribunal's decision that the breach in fact constituted SOSR and that T's dismissal was fair.

As noted in Chapter 3, 'Unfairness', under 'Reason for dismissal – identification **5.74** of "real" reason for dismissal', the label assigned to dismissal is not normally crucial *unless* it affects the fairness of dismissal. If an employer makes it clear that the reason for dismissal is persistent absenteeism, dismissal will not be rendered unfair merely because the dismissal letter states it is 'on the ground of capability'. However, if an employer, perhaps for compassionate reasons, leads the employee to believe that the reason for his or her dismissal is capability, rather than persistent absenteeism, it will not then be able to rely on SOSR at tribunal. Dismissal will then be unfair if the employer did not investigate the medical position, as required for capability dismissals. This was made clear in Devonshire v Trico-Folberth Ltd 1989 ICR 747, CA, where D had a number of sickness-related absences from work. After several warnings she was dismissed for her 'unacceptable attendance record'. An internal appeal panel decided, on compassionate grounds, that her employment ought to be terminated because she was medically unfit to do the job, not for poor attendance. A tribunal found that, had D been dismissed for the original reason – poor attendance – the dismissal would have been fair, but once the reason became medical unfitness 'the whole picture changed'. It held that the dismissal was unfair because the employer had carried out insufficient investigation into D's medical condition and insufficient consultation with the employee and her GP to warrant dismissal for ill health. The employer appealed, arguing that the tribunal should not have awarded D any compensation given that the employer could have dismissed her fairly on the ground of poor attendance. She had, therefore, suffered no loss as the result of her dismissal. However, both the EAT and the Court of Appeal affirmed the tribunal's decision regarding compensation. The Court of Appeal held that there was no evidence that had the employer known of the legal consequences of its compassionate approach, it would instead have dismissed D for poor attendance.

Of course, if an employer dismisses an employee for absenteeism (i.e. SOSR) when it clearly should have been treated as an ill-health capability dismissal, that will also be unfair. However, there may well be circumstances where the dividing line between SOSR and capability is unclear. For example, the employee may have an appalling absence record, some of which is due to an underlying medical condition and some of which is due to minor and unconnected ailments. In these circumstances, it is a matter of judgement whether the dismissal is for SOSR or capability, depending perhaps on what proportion of the absences are unconnected and what proportion are based on an underlying condition. This difficulty was highlighted in Millington v Wandsworth Council ET Case No.2302863/06, where M had what was described by the tribunal as an 'appalling' absence record, all due to certified illness. Some of those illnesses were caused by anxiety and depression but some were completely unrelated. The tribunal noted that throughout the history of the case there had been confusion as to whether M was being dismissed on the ground of her past attendance record (SOSR) or on the ground of her medical capability for future employment. On balance, the tribunal held that the principal reason for dismissal was related to her capability. Accordingly M's dismissal was unfair since the employer had failed to follow the guidelines for capability/ill health dismissals in East Lindsey District Council v Daubney 1977 ICR 566, EAT (see 'Long-term ill health' above), notably in failing to obtain an up-to-date medical report relevant to M's most recent absence.

5.75 If an employer is in any doubt about whether it is dealing with a capability or absenteeism issue, it should initially deal with the matter as one of capability since this involves the application of a longer and more detailed procedure. However, where the employer believes that the employee is taking sick leave dishonestly or, perhaps, as the tribunal suggested in Millington, that the employee has deliberately or negligently put him or herself at risk of injury or ill health, the employer could treat it as a conduct issue. This requires more detailed investigation than is generally necessary for a dismissal for SOSR – for example, evidence will be needed to substantiate the employer's belief that the employee was not sick or that he or she was negligent. However, the employer would not need to show that the employee's absenteeism had reached such a level that it was entitled to say 'enough is enough'.

Given the myriad circumstances that can arise, and given that there is still some legal uncertainty over the appropriate label – for example, in Williams v Cheshire Fire and Rescue Service EAT 0621/07 the EAT held that, notwithstanding the Court of Appeal's decision in Wilson v Post Office (above), a tribunal was correct to categorise the employee's poor attendance record as 'conduct' – it is probably sensible to plead in the alternative, i.e. 'dismissal was because of some other substantial reason or, alternatively, for capability or alternatively for conduct'. However, employers should make it clear, both at the time of dismissal and in their response, that the actual reason for dismissal was, for example, persistent absenteeism.

Conduct dismissals are discussed in detail in Chapter 6, 'Conduct', while dismissals for SOSR are considered in Chapter 8, 'Some other substantial reason'.

Alternative employment   5.76

Employers have a duty to consider redeploying employees who are not able to carry out some or all of their former duties due to ill health where alternative work exists that the employee may be able to do. There is no onus on employers to create a special job where none exists – Merseyside and North Wales Electricity Board v Taylor 1975 ICR 185, QBD – although such a duty may, exceptionally, arise in a claim for reasonable adjustments under the EqA – Southampton City College v Randall 2006 IRLR 18, EAT. Unless the medical evidence indicates that there is no possibility of an employee being fit to return to work in *any* capacity, a failure on an employer's part to consider the question of alternative employment may be sufficient to render a dismissal unfair. In Dick v Boots the Chemist Ltd EAT 68/91, for example, D, a store detective, was severely assaulted by a shoplifter she had apprehended. She was absent from work 'indefinitely'. Almost three years later a doctor reported that it was unlikely that she would ever be fit for her job again. The tribunal was satisfied that there had been sufficient consultation – with the employee, her medical advisers and the company's welfare services manager – and was prepared to excuse the employer's failure to consider alternative employment on the ground that, on the basis of the doctor's report, this would have been futile. The EAT disagreed and said the tribunal had erred. The company's procedure had been seriously flawed by the complete failure to consider the question of alternative employment.

But while employers are not obliged to create jobs, they must be prepared to be somewhat flexible. Two examples:

197

- **Garricks (Caterers) Ltd v Nolan** 1980 IRLR 259, EAT: a maintenance fitter was dismissed when heart trouble meant he could no longer work shifts, only days. The EAT upheld the tribunal's decision of unfair dismissal. Fairness, it said, does not require the employer to go to unreasonable lengths to accommodate an employee who is not able to carry out his or her job to the full extent. However, there is a duty to investigate existing possibilities and establish whether arrangements could be made to accommodate the employee in the jobs available (in this case, providing some assistance with lifting)

- **Silver v Royal Borough of Windsor and Maidenhead** ET Case No.2536/88: the employer was criticised for not having discussed the possibility of alternative employment fully with the employee. The employer had failed to offer her alternative employment as a telephonist/receptionist, even on a trial basis, and had failed to discuss the possibility of alternative employment with her. This was not excused by the employer's belief that S had an unsuitable temperament for such work.

5.77 Where the ill health arises because of the nature of the work itself, employers may be acting unreasonably if they do not take reasonable steps to remove the cause. Three examples:

- **Jagdeo v Smiths Industries Ltd** 1982 ICR 47, EAT: J became ill when moved to a new factory department that required her to do more soldering than before and she became allergic to solder fumes. Unsuccessful attempts were made to alleviate the problem by the use of three different types of mask. No alternative work was available for her. However, an officer of the Health and Safety Executive had suggested that the problem had been successfully eliminated at other factories by the use of an extractor fan. The EAT held that in the absence of any explanation from the company as to what steps, if any, had been taken to install extractor fans, it was impossible for the tribunal to decide whether the employer had acted reasonably. The case was remitted to be heard on that point

- **Thanet District Council v Websper** EAT 1090/01: the EAT upheld a tribunal's decision that, in refusing to transfer W to an alternative role to alleviate work stress, the Council had breached an implied term that it should provide a safe place to work, leading to a finding of unfair constructive dismissal, based on W's resignation in response

- **Rubery Owen-Rockwell Ltd v Goode** EAT 112/80: G, a machine operator, was allergic to a particular coolant used by the machine which he operated, resulting in his suffering considerable sinus problems. On the basis of a medical report he was dismissed. The EAT found the dismissal unfair as there were other machines he could have operated that either used other coolants

198

or used no coolant at all. These alternatives should have been explored even if they would have involved demotion, lower pay or lower status.

A 'suitable vacancy' may, therefore, involve a demotion, lower pay or lower **5.78** status. In British Gas Services Ltd v McCaull 2001 IRLR 60, EAT, the EAT held that a tribunal had erred in finding a dismissal unfair on the ground that an offer of alternative employment involved a reduction in pay of between 23 and 30 per cent. The job was the only suitable alternative employment available and was offered at the going rate. This could not be said to be outside the range of reasonable responses open to the reasonable employer.

As the fairness of a dismissal is assessed at the time of dismissal, alternative employment that arises during the notice period should be considered. In Portals Ltd v Gates EAT 202/80 G was certified unfit for work by the company's doctor after being absent for over a year and he was given nine months' notice. His dismissal duly took effect nine months later. However, during that time a suitable vacancy had arisen but was not offered to G. The EAT found the dismissal unfair as events happening between the giving of notice and the effective date of termination must be considered (see Chapter 3, 'Unfairness', under 'Reasonableness of dismissal – reasonableness test applies at time of dismissal', for further details).

The possibility of future redeployment should also be explored. In Douglas v **5.79** Bournemouth Borough Council ET Case No.3103140/09 D suffered from depression, anxiety and panic attacks, and an obsessive compulsive disorder. Her health deteriorated and she was signed off work. After D had been absent for five months, a report from occupational health indicated that redeployment might well be beneficial to D and could facilitate an earlier return to work, but that it was unlikely she could return within four or five months. The employer terminated her employment and a tribunal upheld her unfair dismissal claim on the basis that by dismissing when it did, the employer effectively shut the door on reasonable consideration of redeployment. In the tribunal's view, a reasonable employer with the same level of resources would have extended D's employment with a view to her being redeployed.

An employer's duty to assist employees by offering alternative employment is reinforced by the duty to make reasonable adjustments in respect of disabled employees under the EqA (discussed in IDS Employment Law Handbook, 'Discrimination at Work' (2012), Chapter 21, 'Failure to make reasonable adjustments'). For example, in Ferguson v London Borough of Barnet ET Case No.3300322/05 a tribunal held that the employer's failure to consider F for alternative employment amounted to a failure to make a reasonable adjustment under the DDA (since repealed and superseded by the EqA), which was 'inextricably linked' with the decision to dismiss her. The failure to take account of its duties under the DDA meant F had been unfairly dismissed.

199

5.80 If as a reasonable adjustment an employee is transferred to a new job, he or she should be given time to adjust. This could involve a trial period, allowing the employee to work from home, a gradual build-up to full-time hours or additional training. These factors, which are relevant to the reasonableness of an adjustment, may well be taken into account by a tribunal when assessing the reasonableness of an employer's decision to dismiss.

5.81 ## Ill-health benefits

The purpose of enhanced ill-health retirement benefits, permanent health insurance (PHI) or other contractual sickness and disability schemes would be defeated if an employer could end or deny entitlements under such a scheme by dismissing employees when they become unfit for work. As a result, case law has established that there is an implied *contractual term* that an employee will not be dismissed without good cause if the effect or intention is to deny his or her rights under a PHI or similar scheme – see, for example, Aspden v Webbs Poultry and Meat Group (Holdings) Ltd 1996 IRLR 521, QBD, and Villella v MFI Furniture Centres Ltd 1999 IRLR 468, QBD. (For further details, see IDS Employment Law Handbook, 'Contracts of Employment' (2014), Chapter 3, 'Contractual terms', in the section 'Principal implied terms', under 'Employer's implied obligations – health insurance, sick pay and redundancy schemes'.)

This principle was extended to unfair dismissal law in First West Yorkshire Ltd t/a First Leeds v Haigh 2008 IRLR 182, EAT, where the EAT held that it was unreasonable, and thus unfair, for an employer to dismiss an employee by reason of long-term ill health without first considering whether he or she was contractually entitled to be medically 'retired' and granted an ill-health pension. Given this, the tribunal had been fully entitled to find that the employer should have waited for a medical specialist to report back on whether or not H was likely to be permanently incapacitated before dismissing him for incapacity. That case was subsequently followed in Burton v East North East Homes Ltd ET Case No.1810624/09, where the tribunal held that the employer had acted unreasonably in failing to obtain a consultant's report on B's long-term prognosis before dismissing him for capability. By dismissing B, the employer was substantially hindering his application for ill-health retirement under the pension scheme. As the available medical evidence did not give a prognosis, the employer should have at least attempted to obtain a consultant's report in order to assess B's eligibility under the scheme before dismissing him.

5.82 In CFS Management Services Ltd v Thomas EAT 0511/11 CFS Ltd accepted that its income protection scheme would be available to T, who had taken substantial periods of sick leave, if he was found to be medically unfit for work. However, contrary to the views of his GP and consultant endocrinologist, the company's occupational health adviser decided that T was fit for work and therefore not eligible for the scheme. CFS Ltd accepted this conclusion but, having regard to the other medical evidence as well as its own assessment of T's health problems, decided that he was unlikely to return to work and dismissed him for incapacity. It was not disputed that T would have remained employed if he had fallen within the terms of the income protection scheme. The EAT upheld T's unfair dismissal claim, holding that CFS Ltd's decision to dismiss him by reason of long-term ill health fell outside the range of responses open to a reasonable employer. CFS Ltd knew that the occupational health adviser's report, which contradicted its own conclusions as to the likelihood of T's return to work, was flawed. In these circumstances, it was not reasonable for it to rely on the report so as to deprive T of the benefits of the income protection scheme and, consequently, continued employment with the company.

Clearly, an employer who dismisses an employee for ill-health reasons merely by virtue of the fact that he or she has applied for a permanent ill-health pension, or any other ill-health benefit scheme for that matter, will be acting unfairly. In Langley-Ingress v Governing Body, The Grove School ET Case No.2901908/06, for example, the employer maintained that since L had applied for a permanent ill-health pension, she had thereby self-declared herself as unfit for further work. The tribunal held that equating an application for ill-health retirement with de facto incapacity was very unfair indeed. It stated that employees must be allowed to sound out the possibility of ill-health retirement without fear of being estopped from asserting their capability for work thereafter if their application for ill-health retirement did not succeed. The tribunal also criticised the employer for relying on medical reports prepared in the context of L applying for ill-health retirement, remarking that there was 'little wonder' that they were pessimistic about her prospects of returning to work. A fair process demanded provision of more up-to-date medical reports, and a proper examination of the employee at a time when she was no longer motivated by a desire to obtain ill-health retirement benefits.

However, the employer cannot be held responsible where an insurer considers **5.83** an employee ineligible for ill-health benefits. Two examples:

- **Garman v Bell Microproducts Ltd** ET Case No.2407124/09: a tribunal found that where an insurance company had refused a claim for PHI benefits and the company's internal appeal procedures had been exhausted, a dismissal which had the effect of preventing the claimant from qualifying for PHI benefits was not thereby rendered unfair

- **Harris v Monmouthshire County Council** ET Case No.1603912/13: a tribunal considered that an employer had not failed to support H's application for ill-health retirement. A medical report was sought by an independent occupational health adviser, whose opinion was that H did not qualify. The employer facilitated H's appeal against this decision and in the circumstances there was nothing further it could have done.

201

If it transpires that an employee is entitled to an ill-health pension and he or she freely elects to take it, there will be no dismissal as termination will be by mutual agreement. The employer should, however, be careful not to pressure the employee into choosing between ill-health early retirement and dismissal since a tribunal might find that there was no genuine mutual agreement in these circumstances and conclude that the employee was actually dismissed – see Chapter 1, 'Dismissal', under 'Express dismissal – enforced resignation'.

5.84 Factors affecting reasonableness

For a decision to dismiss to be fair, it must be balanced and informed in the light of the particular facts relating to the employee concerned. As noted above, where an employee is suffering from an underlying medical condition (leading to either long-term absence or persistent short-term absences), the procedure used will be paramount to the question of fairness. If a full and fair procedure is not followed (in particular, consultation, medical investigation and the consideration of other options, such as alternative employment) dismissal is likely to be unfair. However, procedure is not the only consideration and there are a number of other factors that are commonly taken into account by tribunals when assessing the fairness of a dismissal.

5.85 Nature, length and effect of illness

As discussed in Chapter 4, 'Capability and qualifications', under 'Definitions – capability', the employee's alleged incapability must relate to 'work of the kind which [the employee] was employed by the employer to do' – S.98(2)(a) ERA. This is determined in accordance with the employee's current contractual obligations – see, for example, Plessey Military Communications Ltd v Brough EAT 518/84. Employers do not have to prove that an employee's illness renders him or her incapable of performing all the duties under the contract. They only have to show that the ill health relates to the employee's capability and that it was a sufficient reason to dismiss – Shook v Ealing London Borough Council 1986 ICR 314, EAT. Nevertheless, the proportion of work an employee is still able to carry out at the time of dismissal will be relevant to the issue of reasonableness.

If the employer concludes, following consultation with the employee and a medical investigation, that the condition is unlikely to improve and there is no prospect of a return to work in the foreseeable future even if adjustments are made, dismissal may be fair. For example, in Smith v Post Office ET Case No.7707/95 a tribunal took account of the fact that the chances of a clinically depressed employee on three types of medication achieving satisfactory attendance in the future were remote, when considering the fairness of his dismissal for persistent short-term absences.

202

Full consideration must, however, be given to any recent improvement in the **5.86** employee's condition and/or attendance record. In Scott v Secretary of State for Scotland EAT 196/88 S, who had taken a significant amount of sick leave (largely due to a neck injury) in the past, was only absent for six out of the last 185 days. The EAT thought that this factor, along with the lack of consultation and medical investigation, made her dismissal unfair. Similarly, in Post Office v Stones EAT 390/80 (see 'Long-term ill health – consultation with employee' above) there was evidence that the employee's marital difficulties, the cause of much of her ill-health absence, were behind her when she was dismissed. The EAT upheld a tribunal's finding that any reasonable employer would have concluded that there had been a distinct improvement in the employee's attendance record and that there were good prospects for the future.

If an employer reasonably reaches the conclusion (following consultation and medical advice) that the employee will not be fit for work for a prolonged period of time, the fact that, following his or her dismissal, he or she recovers more quickly than anticipated will not render the dismissal unfair – Arriva Scotland v Weir EATS 0068/05. That said, where an employee is dismissed with notice the dismissal does not actually take place until the notice expires, so a tribunal may take account of any changes that occur during the notice period. In Williamson v Alcan (UK) Ltd 1978 ICR 104, EAT, the employee was dismissed because of his chronic ill health, but there was medical evidence from a specialist that he had made a spontaneous recovery during the notice period. The case was remitted to a different tribunal to reconsider in light of the new evidence. In remitting, the EAT stated that if – after the date notice of dismissal was given and before the contract had actually come to an end – the employer acquired information which would indicate that it ought not to have dismissed the employee, that dismissal could well become unfair if it did not withdraw the notice.

Furthermore, the House of Lords held in West Midlands Co-operative Society **5.87** Ltd v Tipton 1986 ICR 192, HL, that information revealed in the course of an internal appeal that relates to the original reason for dismissal should be taken into account when considering the fairness of that dismissal, irrespective of whether the internal appeal takes place before or after the dismissal has been effected.

Illness caused by employer   5.88
If the employer was in any way responsible for the employee's illness that led to the dismissal, this may be a factor that is taken into account by a tribunal when deciding on the fairness of the dismissal – Royal Bank of Scotland v McAdie 2008 ICR 1087, CA. In reaching this decision the Court of Appeal endorsed the decisions in Edwards v Governors of Hanson School 2001 IRLR 733, EAT, and Frewin v Consignia plc EAT 0981/02 and overruled the decision in London Fire and Civil Defence Authority v Betty 1994 IRLR 384, EAT, in so far as it

203

held that the employer's responsibility for the incapacity was irrelevant to the issue of whether the dismissal was fair. The Court accepted that it may be necessary to 'go the extra mile' in such circumstances; for example, being more proactive in finding alternative employment for the employee or putting up with a longer period of sickness absence.

The Court also emphasised, however, that the fact that an employer is at fault for causing the incapacity does not *necessarily* mean that a resulting dismissal will be unfair. Indeed, in the case before it it upheld the EAT's decision (overruling the tribunal) that M – whose stress-related illness had been caused by the Bank – had not been unfairly dismissed. The Court approved the EAT's view that there was in truth no alternative to dismissal. The medical evidence was unequivocal, both that M was unfit for work and that there was no prospect of recovery. Moreover, M had expressly stated that she would never be able to return to work. This was not, therefore, a case where there was something more that the Bank, having caused the illness, could and should have done to try to save M's employment.

5.89 Neither the EAT nor the Court of Appeal felt it necessary to consider what the effect of an employer maliciously causing an employee's ill health would be in cases of unfair dismissal. The EAT did, however, have some difficulty with the implication in Edwards v Governors of Hanson School (above) that in such a case there could never be a fair dismissal.

5.90 **Employee's length of service**
Several first instance decisions have suggested that in ill-health cases, as in conduct cases, more tolerance should be shown towards a hardworking, long-serving employee, particularly where his or her period of absence is comparatively short. In Ginns v Leon Motor Services Ltd ET Case No.27872/78, for example, a tribunal thought that the ill-health absence of a long-serving employee should be treated in a different manner to that of a short-term employee. An employee with only one or two years' service may not, it said, expect the same beneficial treatment as might an employee with ten years' service. This meant that G, an employee with a total of 29 years' service, was entitled to expect more consideration and better treatment.

Three further examples:

* **Clarke v Pickering Kenyon** ET Case No.47091/93: a tribunal held that an absence of three and a half months because of illness did not give rise to a reasonable cause for dismissal where the employee had 18 and a half years' service. The tribunal noted that her job could have been filled by temporary staff without difficulty and at no extra expense as C was not being paid her salary during that period

204 ────────────────────────────────

- **Alexander v Downland Retirement Management Ltd** ET Case No.3103380/03 (considered under 'Ill-health benefits' above): the tribunal noted that the decision to dismiss A appeared to have ignored her good record and 17 years' service, which the tribunal considered should have been a significant factor to weigh in the balance

- **Mathews v British Telecommunications plc** ET Case No.2205791/10: the tribunal considered that as M was a very long-standing employee (of 30 years' service) with no significant prior record of sickness absence, BT plc should have 'gone the extra mile' to obtain medical evidence and to consider moving M to alternative work.

However, these cases should be treated with some caution following the decision **5.91** of the Court of Session in S v Dundee City Council 2014 IRLR 131, Ct Sess (Inner House). In that case, the Court of Session considered that the tribunal had adopted an incorrect approach in treating the employee's 35 years of service as a factor that was *automatically* relevant to a decision to dismiss for ill health. The Court observed that in an appropriate case long service may show that the employee is 'a good and willing worker with a good attendance record, someone who would do his utmost to get back to work as soon as he could' (by analogy with conduct cases, where evidence that an employee has worked for a long time without misconduct may be a strong indication that either he or she is unlikely to have done anything seriously wrong or what he or she has done can be treated as a temporary aberration). The critical question is whether, on the circumstances of each case, the length of the employee's service, and the manner in which he or she worked during that period, yields inferences that indicate that the employee is likely to return to work as soon as he or she can.

The Dundee City Council case was subsequently followed in Harris v Monmouthshire County Council ET Case No.1603912/13. There the tribunal noted that there was no record that MCC had taken into account H's lengthy service (20 years) at the meeting where the decision was made to dismiss her and that it would have expected this factor to have been mentioned. However, in the light of the Dundee City Council case and the medical evidence available at the time – that H was unfit for any work and the prognosis was uncertain – it did not consider that MCC's failure to consider length of service affected the overall fairness of the dismissal.

In any event, long service can sometimes count against an employee. In Mathews **5.92** v British Telecommunications plc (above) the tribunal considered that M's length of service and seniority made his lack of engagement with BT plc less excusable. He knew very well what BT plc's procedures and expectations were with regard to sickness absence, yet 'signally failed' to observe these procedures.

205

5.93 Availability of temporary cover

In S v Dundee City Council 2014 IRLR 131, Ct Sess (Inner House), the Court of Session listed a number of factors that were relevant to the question of whether an employer could be expected to wait longer before dismissing an employee who has been on long-term absence due to ill health. Among these was the availability of temporary cover: on the facts of the case, the employer had a temporary labour agreement under which it could call on temporary staff to fill posts where required and they were available to perform tasks that would otherwise be performed by the absent employee.

Of course, the nature of the job may make it impracticable to use a temporary replacement; or, if the employee is taking frequent short-term absences, this may not be feasible. In Patval v London Borough of Camden ET Case No.2203464/07 the importance of P's position in IT support to the employer's operation was taken into account when deciding that his dismissal for a number of both short- and long-term absences was fair. IT support was critical to the employer's operation generally and was vital for all departments and service users.

5.94 Effect on other employees

The effect of continued absence or illness on other employees may also be relevant to the question of fairness. Two examples:

- **Ali v Tillotsons Containers Ltd** 1975 IRLR 272, ET: A was a member of a production team whose bonuses depended on its output. As a consequence of A's absences through ill health and the employer's inability to find an adequate replacement for him, the other members of the team lost money. A tribunal found this a relevant consideration in the decision to dismiss A

- **Patval v London Borough of Camden** ET Case No.2203464/07: to avoid delay in a fast-moving industry, P's work in IT support had to be done by one of his colleagues. This meant they had less time for their own duties, which further impacted on service users. The tribunal found that it was reasonable to expect an employee who had started a task to complete it to prevent repetition. Furthermore, some tasks could not be simply handed over part-way though without incurring a substantial amount of work. After a number of both short- and long-term absences, the employer was entitled to say 'enough is enough' and dismiss.

5.95 Effect on output or sales

The general effect on output or sales may also be considered, especially in smaller concerns where there may be no possibility of arranging cover. Moreover, if the industry in which the employee works is particularly fast-moving, absence could cause the employer serious disruption – see, for example, Patval v London Borough of Camden (discussed under 'Effect on other employees' above).

Size of employer

5.96

Section 98(4) ERA states that tribunals should take account of the 'size and administrative resources of the employer's undertaking' in assessing reasonableness. Thus, for example, a large company may be expected to have greater resources to cover absences for a longer period and to help employees get back to work than a small family firm. Two examples:

- **S v Dundee City Council** 2014 IRLR 131, Ct Sess (Inner House): the employer was a large organisation. It was obvious that such an organisation could absorb costs better than an employer with fewer employees and this was therefore a factor to be taken into account in assessing whether the employer could have been expected to wait longer before dismissing

- **Ferguson v London Borough of Barnet** ET Case No.3300322/05: the tribunal noted that the employer was a comparatively large undertaking with a human resources department and a legal department. This made the employer's failure to make reasonable adjustments under the DDA all the more inexcusable and dismissal was unfair.

Nature of employment

5.97

Where employment is of a special nature that requires a higher than usual level of attendance, or that employees be of robust health, dismissal for absenteeism may be fair, particularly if there is an express or implied term in the contract covering the situation. Two examples:

- **Leonard v Fergus and Haynes Civil Engineering Ltd** 1979 IRLR 235, Ct Sess (Inner House): L was a steel fixer on a North Sea oil platform working to a fixed deadline in severe conditions. His contract contained a term, agreed with his union, that anyone absent for two shifts in a 14-day period would be classed as unsuitable for North Sea work. The Court of Session held that dismissal in reliance on this term was fair because the relationship between employer and employee was of an 'exceptional and special nature'. It said that L had not been dismissed merely on the ground of ill health but for failing to meet an essential requirement of his contract

- **Taylorplan Catering (Scotland) Ltd v McInally** 1980 IRLR 53, EAT: the employee was a barman in a workmen's camp at Sullom Voe, Shetland, a job that was 'arduous' and involved 'unusual working conditions'. After several months T developed behavioural problems and depression, apparently caused by the stress of working in these conditions. The EAT found his dismissal fair because the employer's need for employees of robust health was 'patent' and it was 'clearly established' that M was medically unsuited to this sort of work.

However, it should be noted that the working conditions in both these cases were extreme. If a term similar to that in the Leonard case was inserted into the

207

contract of an employee working in a more normal environment, a dismissal in reliance on it without more would in all likelihood be unfair, as unfair dismissal is a question of 'reasonableness', not 'breach of contract'. (These cases are also discussed in the section 'Long-term ill health' above, under 'Consultation with employee – circumstances in which consultation is not required'.)

5.98 There are also other, less extreme, circumstances where the effect of an employee's absence can be particularly damaging and may be a persuasive factor when assessing a dismissal's fairness. Some examples:

- **Betteridge v St Helens Council** ET Case No.2102835/04: B worked in one of the Council's schools, which was made subject to 'special measures' during 2003. B suffered from chronic back pain and depression and in October 2003 she went on sick leave suffering from depression. By March 2004 the Council's consultant occupational physician reported that he doubted whether B would be able to cope with the pressures occasioned by the school being on special measures and that, although he was confident she would improve greatly in the future, in practical terms it looked as if she might not return to work. The Council wanted to make a decision about B's continued employment before the date of the next medical review in order to be able to make arrangements for the following academic year and it arranged for the physician to see B again after five weeks. He reported that he did not think she would return to work in the foreseeable future and she was dismissed in May. A tribunal rejected B's unfair dismissal claim, noting that she had effectively been absent for an academic year and the school was in the degrading position of being subject to special measures – a 'devastating blow' for which strong action was urgently needed. It held that the Council was entitled to take the view that effective and swift action was called for in order to provide pupils with certainty and continuity in the following year and to save the reputation of the school and ensure its continuance

- **Patval v London Borough of Camden** ET Case No.2203464/07: P was employed in IT support. The tribunal accepted that there were often ongoing issues affecting the users of IT services for which there needed to be a flexible and reliable response from IT support. Any absences in IT support, therefore, caused the employer severe disruption

- **Davis v Tibbett and Britten Group plc** EAT 460/99: the regular attendance of employees such as D was an important factor in the employer's transport business, given the stringent demands placed on them by its principal customer.

5.99 **Health and safety**

A dismissal may be fair if the employee's continued employment poses a health or safety risk to the employee or to third parties. For example, in Harper v National Coal Board 1980 IRLR 260, EAT, H, an epileptic, attacked and displayed violence towards some of his fellow employees during occasional fits. The EAT acknowledged the employer's duty to exercise reasonable care for the safety of other employees and reluctantly found the dismissal fair. And in Singh-Deu v Chloride Metals Ltd 1976 IRLR 56, ET, S's job in a lead smelting factory was not particularly skilled but demanded that he constantly had his wits about him, since it involved filtering toxic dust and fumes. There was a difference of medical opinion as to whether it would be safe to let him return to work after he had been diagnosed as having schizophrenia. However, the tribunal was satisfied that to allow S to return to work was a risk nobody could take in this 'highly dangerous industry'.

Arguably, the real reason for dismissal in the cases above was not capability on the ground of the employee's ill health, but SOSR, on the ground of the risk posed to other employees – see Chapter 8, 'Some other substantial reason'. Note, too, that an employer considering dismissal on similar facts today would need to avoid discriminating against the employee under the EqA on the ground of his or her disabilities.

Sick pay
5.100

The fact that sick pay is provided or has ceased to be payable is a factor to be taken into account in deciding whether an employer could be expected to wait longer before dismissing an employee on long-term sick leave, and in considering the reasonableness of any ill health-related dismissal. However, it is merely one of the factors to be considered and is not conclusive: dismissal effected during the currency of sick pay arrangements will not necessarily be unfair and nor will it necessarily be fair to dismiss once sick pay entitlements have been exhausted. Indeed, in S v Dundee City Council 2014 IRLR 131, Ct Sess (Inner House), the Court of Session considered that the fact that an employee had exhausted his sick pay entitlement and was no longer receiving salary was a factor suggesting that the employer could be expected to wait longer before dismissing. Although the employer would still have incurred administrative costs and the costs of occupational health service referrals, it was 'inherently improbable' that these would have been very large.

In Hardwick v Leeds Area Health Authority 1975 IRLR 319, ET, a tribunal held it unfair to dismiss H as soon as her sick pay entitlement had been exhausted in accordance with an established Health Service rule, particularly as she had indicated that she would be returning to work just one week later. The employer acted unreasonably in following an established but outmoded rule irrespective of the circumstances. In Coulson v Felixstowe Dock and Railway Co 1975 IRLR 11, ET, on the other hand, the tribunal held that the dismissal of an employee before his sick pay entitlement had run out was fair since his absence had caused a good deal of inconvenience. The sick pay scheme, it said, was only a financial arrangement and did not indicate the amount of sickness absence to which the employee was entitled.

209

5.101 An employer should not assume that just because an employee is receiving sick pay there is no need to consider alternative employment. In Konczak v BAE Systems (Operations) Ltd ET Case No.2405642/06, a disability discrimination claim, a tribunal held that the employer should have investigated K's ill-health absence before she had exhausted her entitlement to sick pay (almost one year after her sick leave began). Had the employer addressed the issue sooner there was a possibility, said the tribunal, that it would have been able to find suitable alternative employment for her. Certainly, it would have had longer in which to do so.

Employers should note, however, that it may be unfair to dismiss an employee by reason of long-term ill health without first considering whether he or she was contractually entitled to be medically 'retired' and granted an ill-health pension – First West Yorkshire Ltd t/a First Leeds v Haigh 2008 IRLR 182, EAT (see 'Ill-health benefits' above). Furthermore, a failure to pay sick pay may amount to a breach of contract sufficient to found a constructive dismissal. For example, in Summer Bridge Doors Ltd v Pickering EAT 1088/02 the EAT found that a failure to pay even statutory sick pay to a disabled woman amounted to a fundamental breach of contract.

5.102 Fit notes

As explained under 'Long-term ill health – medical investigation' above, employees absent beyond the self-certification period will obtain a 'statement of fitness for work' (colloquially known as a 'fit note'), which gives the doctor the option of declaring the patient either 'not fit for work' or 'may be fit for work taking account of the following advice'. If a doctor declares that the employee is not fit for work, this may justifiably lead an employer to conclude that there is no alternative but to consider dismissing the employee. However, the employer should certainly not dismiss an employee purely on this basis and should investigate the medical position further. Nor, of course, should it simply ignore any suggestions made in a fit note.

5.103 Particular types of sickness

There are many types of illness or disability that can cause problems at work. In this section we consider briefly some of the more common ones that arise.

5.104 Pregnancy and maternity dismissals

It is automatically unfair to dismiss an employee for reasons related to 'pregnancy, childbirth or maternity' or maternity leave – S.99 ERA and Reg 20 of the Maternity and Parental Leave etc Regulations 1999 SI 1999/3312 (MPL Regulations). In an ill-health context, the most relevant reason is usually one related to the pregnancy of an employee, given that women may have to take time off work because of pregnancy-related illness.

Pregnancy-related dismissals are discussed in depth in IDS Employment Law Handbook, 'Maternity and Parental Rights' (2015), Chapter 12, 'Detriment and unfair dismissal', in the section 'Automatically unfair dismissal', under 'Pregnancy, childbirth and maternity – pregnancy-related dismissals'.

Drink and drugs

5.105

Long-term alcoholism and, to a lesser extent, dependence on illegal drugs are now generally treated as serious illnesses, with many employers adopting special policies allowing time off for medical treatment and counselling. Bodies such as the Chartered Institute of Personnel and Development (CIPD) and Alcohol Concern recommend that employees with a drink or drug dependency should be regarded as sick and that employers should therefore focus on rehabilitation rather than dismissal. This is backed up by the Acas Guide, which states that employers should consider whether it is appropriate to treat the problem as a medical rather than a disciplinary matter (page 75). However, there will be times when the employer feels it has no option but to dismiss an employee who has been drinking or taking drugs (either on or off duty). The employer will then need to decide whether to approach the issue as one of capability or misconduct.

Capability or misconduct? Generally speaking, an employer should treat **5.106** alcohol or drug dependency as a capability issue. This could be evidenced by diminished performance coupled with long bouts of certified sickness. Conduct, on the other hand, is usually relied on when the employee has committed an isolated act related to drink or drugs. Occasional absence or occasional on-duty drinking suggests irregular drinking and is therefore likely to be a conduct issue.

When the drink/drug problem first comes to the employer's attention, it will need to decide whether to deal with the problem as a capability or conduct issue, since the procedural requirements are different for each. If the employer chooses the wrong label at this stage, it could result in a finding of unfair dismissal. In Mather v Tayside Regional Council SCOET S/1842/78, for example, M's poor attendance was because of alcoholism. Attempts were made to have him retired on medical grounds but he was certified fit. Following a warning, M was dismissed for uncertified absenteeism. The dismissal was unfair. In the tribunal's view the employer should not have treated it as a disciplinary issue but as a sickness problem and should have obtained medical advice on the prospects of treatment and recovery.

In this chapter we concentrate on alcoholism and drug addiction as illnesses **5.107** and, therefore, as capability issues. Conduct issues arising from drinking and taking drugs are dealt with in Chapter 6, 'Conduct', under 'Drinking, drugs and smoking'.

211

5.108 **Alcoholism.** Alcoholism can be a free-standing condition or may stem from a separate underlying illness. In either case, it should normally be treated as a capability issue and even where it is a free-standing condition, or one that exacerbates other medical problems, employers should seek appropriate medical advice. In Critchlow v Independent Safeguarding Authority ET Case No.2500175/10 C had a number of medical problems caused by excessive alcohol consumption. Occupational health reported that she was fit to return to work on restricted duties, avoiding duties where there was a significant risk of organisational harm or reputational embarrassment if she performed inefficiently or transgressed the ISA's alcohol policy. The ISA decided that it could not continue to employ C under such restrictions and terminated her employment. A tribunal decided that she had been unfairly dismissed, in that the ISA had failed to undertake reasonable enquiries. C and her GP had maintained that her alcohol consumption was under control and, in failing to commission a report from an expert on her alcohol consumption and dependency, the ISA did not have reasonable grounds for C's dismissal. However, her award of compensation was reduced to reflect her culpability in that her excessive alcohol intake exacerbated her other illnesses and she had been less than open with the ISA about her drinking problem.

Where there is an underlying illness, employers may be expected to show more tolerance. In Strathclyde Regional Council v Syme EAT 233/79 S was a school janitor for ten years. During the last two there were complaints that he drank and at a disciplinary interview he promised to resign if found drunk again. Later he had hospital treatment but after another incident he was held to that promise and he resigned. The tribunal found this to be a dismissal. The EAT, upholding the tribunal's finding of unfairness, considered that S's problem should have been treated as medical, not disciplinary, and independent medical evidence should have been obtained since there was evidence before the tribunal to show that he suffered from bipolar disorder and that this was the cause of his drinking. So while dismissal might have been fair in a straight case of alcoholism (bearing in mind the employer's duties to pupils and other staff), in the circumstances it was unfair.

5.109 Once an employer has established, on the basis of medical evidence, that an employee's drinking is associated with an underlying medical condition, it should follow the guidelines set down in East Lindsey District Council v Daubney 1977 ICR 566, EAT – see 'Long-term ill health' above. Misdemeanours such as lateness, erratic behaviour or poor performance may well be symptoms of that medical problem and should be treated accordingly. The employer should also seek to ascertain whether the underlying illness amounts to a disability for the purposes of the EqA, or whether the alcoholism itself has given rise to another illness that amounts to a disability. However, alcoholism itself does not amount to a disability for the purposes of the Act – Reg 3 Equality Act 2010 (Disability) Regulations 2010 SI 2010/2128 (see IDS

Employment Law Handbook, 'Discrimination at Work' (2012), Chapter 6, 'Disability', under 'Physical or mental impairment – excluded disabilities'.

In some cases, the danger of relapse and the nature of the employee's job may make dismissal a reasonable response. For example, employers in the drink trade could argue that dismissal of an alcoholic employee falls within the range of reasonable responses because he or she should not be allowed easy access to alcohol. Two further examples:

- **Singh v NEI International Combustion Ltd** ET Case No.5288/80: S, who had received treatment for alcoholism, was passed fit for work but with the proviso that he would need constant supervision. This was impracticable because he was an overhead crane-driver. His dismissal for capability was fair because there was no alternative work available

- **Strathclyde Regional Council v Syme** (above): the EAT suggested that had the school janitor been suffering purely from alcoholism (and not from the underlying bipolar disorder), dismissal might have been fair, in view of the employer's duties to pupils and other staff.

5.110 As these cases illustrate, tribunals take a strict view where health and safety is involved. This is hardly surprising, since employers have obligations under common law and various statutes, notably the Health and Safety at Work etc Act 1974, to keep their employees (and others) safe. Employers are obliged to take reasonable steps to ensure that employees are not acting under the influence of alcohol or drugs if this is likely to risk the health and safety of others. Furthermore, there may be an absolute prohibition on the possession of alcohol (and drugs) where safety considerations are paramount; for example, on ships and oil rigs. Dismissal for alcoholism is therefore more likely to be fair in these circumstances.

Despite the tendency to regard alcoholism as an illness, there will still be occasions where it will be reasonable to treat it as a conduct issue. For example, if an employee fails to undergo treatment, dismissal for misconduct may be a reasonable response. In Carter v Plevshire Ltd ET Case No.21893/81 C was warned that he would be dismissed if he made no effort to overcome his drink problem. His refusal to attend Alcoholics Anonymous or to seek medical help finally made the employer realise that it would be impossible to continue to employ him. In the circumstances the dismissal was fair, even though C was medically certified as suffering from 'nervous debility' at the time. Misconduct, i.e. failure to give up the drinking and to be reliable and come to work, was the reason for his dismissal, not his illness.

5.111 Furthermore, manifestations of the illness in the form of gross misconduct are usually viewed as such. In Evans v Bass North Ltd EAT 715/86, for example, E, an alcoholic, had been employed as a chef for 11 years. His employer had always taken a sympathetic view of his problem, but he was dismissed on

213

Christmas Eve for gross misconduct after breaking a prohibition against drinking in the kitchen and for later threatening the manager. The EAT found the dismissal fair for misconduct, even though it acknowledged that E was suffering from a disease.

The Acas Guide indicates that serious incapability at work brought on by alcohol or illegal drugs may also amount to gross misconduct (at page 32).

5.112 **Drug dependency.** Drug addiction, like alcoholism, should in theory be treated as an illness. However, tribunals have almost invariably regarded drug-related dismissals as a conduct issue – see Chapter 6, 'Conduct', under 'Drinking, drugs and smoking – drugs'. One reason for this could be the fact that most incidents of drug abuse at work involve cannabis. While 'hard' drugs like heroin are known to be addictive, there is a school of thought that holds that 'softer' drugs like cannabis do not form a clinical dependency. An argument based on ill health for the use of cannabis might, therefore, be difficult to sustain, although there is always the possibility that an employee takes cannabis because of an underlying medical condition, such as Parkinson's disease, or for pain relief.

Another, more obvious, factor explaining the different approach taken to drug-related dismissals is that the use of non-prescription drugs amounts to a criminal offence. Furthermore, employers themselves can commit an offence under the Misuse of Drugs Act 1971 if they know that illegal drugs are being used or distributed on their premises. Despite this, the Acas Guide has bracketed drink and drug abuse together, encouraging employers to treat both matters in the same way (pages 74–75). It remains to be seen whether tribunals will similarly equate the two issues. Two contrasting cases:

- **Walton v TAC Construction Materials Ltd** EAT 526/80: W was dismissed when his employer discovered that he was a registered drug addict, despite the fact that he was being successfully treated for his heroin addiction. The EAT held that dismissal in pursuance of a company policy against employing drug addicts was within the range of reasonable responses open to an employer

- **Davis v British Airways Board** EAT 139/80: D was dismissed after receiving a conditional discharge for forging prescriptions for amphetamines, which he used to counteract fatigue. A major reason for dismissal was the employer's view that the drugs rendered him incapable of working. The EAT upheld a tribunal's decision that dismissal was unfair because the employer should have properly investigated the effect of the drugs on D's capability.

5.113 As noted above, there is a distinction to be drawn between the use of drugs proscribed by the criminal law and other drugs. The Acas Guide cites serious incapability brought on by the use of *illegal* drugs as an example of misconduct (page 32), suggesting that the abuse of legal drugs should be treated differently.

214

In Chappell v SYP Ltd ET Case No.2800461/02 C took an overdose of paracetamol while at work. She was dismissed for misuse of drugs. In finding her dismissal unfair, the tribunal commented that it was unreasonable of the employer to accuse her of 'misusing drugs' as the phrase invariably connotes the use of drugs such as ecstasy and cannabis.

Where illegal drug use has led to a separate and distinct medical condition, the issue becomes one of ill-health capability, particularly if there is no evidence that the employee is continuing to take drugs – see, for example, McDonald v Cape Contracts Ltd SCOET S/2085/84 (discussed under 'Mental illness' below). Furthermore, although drug addiction itself is not a disability for the purposes of the EqA, it may, like alcoholism, be a *symptom* of an underlying disability that is protected.

Alcohol and drug policies. Some employers have alcohol and drug policies in place that are more comprehensive than the minimum procedure required by statute. Generally, the more detailed the policy, the more effective it will be in dealing with the problem. When determining the fairness of a dismissal the tribunal will consider any relevant internal policy and the extent to which it has been adhered to. **5.114**

In Angus Council v Edgley EAT 289/99 the employer had a policy on alcohol abuse whereby employees with drinking problems would be given the opportunity to seek diagnosis and specialist help. The EAT upheld a tribunal's decision that the failure to implement that policy in respect of an employee who had been found drinking in a pub during working hours led to the employee's dismissal being unfair. Since it was clear from the disciplinary history of the employee that he had an alcohol problem, it was unreasonable of the employer to treat the pub incident as a one-off that could be dealt with under its normal disciplinary procedures.

By contrast, the employer in NHS Fife Health Board v Stockman EATS 0048/13 acted unfairly in adhering too rigorously to its capability policy in dealing with a doctor whose registration with the General Medical Council was suspended on an interim basis after he was convicted of driving while under the influence of alcohol. The employer's capability policy was such that loss of registration meant that the employer could jump straight to the final stage, depriving the employee of the benefit of the investigation and support process provided by stages one and two. In these circumstances it was essential that any decision to dismiss was taken only after consideration of all the circumstances, which should have included up-to-date information about the employee's medical treatment and progress and the likely duration of the suspension. However, by adhering strictly to the capability policy, the employer had failed to consider this vital information and had applied its policy in such a way as to make its decision to dismiss inevitable. **5.115**

215

5.116 **Mental illness**

Mental illness covers a variety of conditions ranging from stress, depression, anxiety and eating and obsessive compulsive disorders, to (more rarely) bipolar disorder, schizophrenia and psychosis. Guidance produced jointly by the CIPD and the mental health charity Mind, 'Managing and supporting mental health at work: disclosure tools for managers' (December 2011), stresses that mental ill health does not automatically equate to poor performance and many people with mental health problems perform highly at work (page 8). In addition, many employees will suffer from stress and anxiety from time to time, while being in good mental health generally (see the Acas booklet, 'Promoting positive mental health at work' (September 2014) (page 4)). However, mental health issues can impact on employees' performance and productivity and can sometimes lead to long or frequent periods of absence, or erratic or irrational behaviour.

Dismissal may therefore have to be considered in some cases. A decision to dismiss on the ground of mental ill health is, like a dismissal on the ground of other ill health, an employment decision and not a medical one, but should be taken in the light of medical advice – WM Computer Services Ltd v Passmore EAT 721/86. However, as Lord McDonald pointed out in Thompson v Strathclyde Regional Council EAT 628/83, incapacity on this ground is 'an exceptionally delicate and sensitive field'. Therefore, cases involving mental ill health should be approached in a similar manner to other types of illness but handled perhaps with greater tolerance and support. Employers should also be aware that mental illness may constitute a disability for the purposes of the EqA.

5.117 **Fair procedure.** Consultation with the employee, medical investigation and consideration of alternative employment are just as important where the employee suffers from a mental illness as where he or she suffers from a physical illness. Employers must do their utmost to discover what the true medical position is.

However, given the nature of mental illness, greater reliance may have to be placed on medical advice than on consultation (although it may be difficult, if not impossible, for doctors to predict the duration of the symptoms and when the employee may be fit to resume work). Indeed, in some cases, consultation may give a very misleading impression, especially where, for example, the employee is suffering from paranoia or where a depressive illness is attributed by the employee to the stresses and strains of the working environment itself.

5.118 There have been many instances where a dismissal on the ground of mental illness has been held to be unfair through lack of, or inadequate, medical investigation or consultation. Two examples:

- **WM Computer Services Ltd v Passmore** EAT 721/86: P was dismissed after prolonged absences associated with depression. He returned to work after being certified fit by his own psychiatrist. He was asked to see the

216 ───────────────────────────────────

company doctor, who reported more pessimistically on P's fitness although he did not certify P unfit. The employer decided to dismiss P on the basis of the company doctor's report and only sought the doctor's further advice on how best to terminate the employment. P's absence had been substantial, his work poor, his conduct unstable and he might have made a second suicide attempt. Nevertheless, the EAT upheld a tribunal's finding of unfair dismissal since the employer had misconstrued its doctor's report – written without knowledge of the employer's intention to dismiss – as recommending that P should not return to work. In addition, there had been a failure to consult P and no real consideration of possible redeployment

- **Peacock v Vi-Seal Tapes Ltd** ET Case No.20821/80: P was under warning for absenteeism and lateness. His depression and drinking were known to the company. His dismissal for a week's absence without sending in a medical certificate was unfair. The employer had been informed that he was suffering another bout of depression and should have investigated further.

Performance and behavioural problems. If an employer recruits someone **5.119** suffering from a mental illness, the employee's performance should be judged by standards which make appropriate allowances for the condition. Should performance drop below that standard, then a dismissal is potentially fair. If the illness first manifests itself during employment, employers will still be expected to show tolerance and take the illness into account when judging an employee's performance and conduct. It may also need to change tack and treat it as an ill-health capability issue. Two examples:

- **McDonald v Cape Contracts Ltd** SCOET S/2085/84: McD, an apprentice engineer, was involved in a violent incident at work which resulted in his being hospitalised for schizophrenia. Seven months later he submitted a medical certificate to his employer declaring that he was fully fit to return to work. His employer subsequently wrote to his GP for his medical history. Her reply, which set out a positive prognosis, mentioned that his illness was drug-induced. The employer subsequently dismissed McD for gross misconduct. A tribunal found the dismissal unfair. The employer had ignored the fact that McD had been suffering from a very acute psychotic illness and had concentrated instead on the conduct itself and the fact that it was drug-induced. Having regard to the medical advice available at the time, it was not within the range of reasonable responses for the employer to treat the matter as one of misconduct for which McD should be held responsible. Instead it should have treated it as a capability matter relating to his health. Therefore, it should have been concerned not with the incident some nine months earlier, disturbing as it was, but with the question of whether McD was fit to resume his apprenticeship

- **Dolan v Chief Constable of Avon and Somerset Constabulary** ET Case No.1402819/06: D joined the Constabulary as a police officer in 1975 and

217

by May 2003 had been promoted to the post of Detective Inspector in the Criminal Investigation Department (CID). However, in March 2004 he began to suffer stress relating to matters outside work and in September he went on sick leave until the following January. The deterioration in his mental health coincided with concerns about his performance at work and in February he was moved from the CID to a uniformed duty inspector role. The Constabulary put in place measures to improve D's performance but in August 2005 it commenced a formal procedure in respect of unsatisfactory performance and eventually D resigned in October 2006. A tribunal upheld his claim for unfair constructive dismissal and disability discrimination. The employer never questioned whether the sudden deterioration in D's performance might be due to the fact that he was still suffering from mental illness. It should have deferred its unsatisfactory performance procedure until it was established that the problems did not arise from his medical condition. In failing to do so, and subjecting M to comments about his performance, the employer had not only failed to make reasonable adjustments but had also engaged in conduct likely or calculated to destroy trust and confidence.

5.120 As the Dolan case demonstrates, if the illness amounts to a disability, the employer will also be required to make reasonable adjustments under the EqA. However, even where the illness does not amount to a disability, any adjustments made by the employer in an attempt to avoid dismissal will be taken into account by a tribunal when assessing whether or not it was fair.

Mental illness may render an employee unsuitable for continued employment when it results in unacceptable behaviour or an inability to perform adequately. In some cases behaviour may be violent, in other cases unreliable, and erratic behaviour could be hazardous. In all these situations, once investigation and consultation has taken place, the reasonableness of a decision to dismiss will ultimately depend on the facts. Some examples:

- **Wright v Commissioners of Inland Revenue** EAT 385/79: the Inland Revenue knew that W was a schizophrenic when he was appointed to his job. After two years he started suffering delusions, claiming that he was under surveillance by MI5 agents, with whom his doctor was in league, all of which disrupted work in the office. W refused medication and was reluctant to go into hospital. After lengthy interviews and medical investigations, he was dismissed on the ground that his condition rendered him incapable of carrying out his duties. The EAT affirmed the tribunal's finding of fair dismissal

- **Halton Borough Council v Hollett** EAT 559/87: during the course of his employment, it came to light that H suffered from a psychotic illness for which he was taking medication. His behaviour at work became increasingly rash and the employer received a complaint. During a disciplinary hearing H admitted that he had reduced his medication because his GP had said that

218

he could do so if he felt fit enough. The employer did not investigate this further but issued a final written warning, saying it was up to H to take the full medication as recommended. Shortly before the written warning was due to lapse, the employer received another complaint about H's behaviour. As the written warning was still current, H was dismissed. On appeal a consultant psychiatrist's report was produced stating that H's eccentric behaviour was perhaps due to too low a dosage and recommending that it be increased. The EAT upheld a tribunal's finding of unfair dismissal, holding that some sort of medical investigation should have taken place. H was 'trying his best' and his mental illness should have been taken into account. The tribunal had before it clear evidence to suggest that the employer had used a relatively trivial complaint about H as an excuse for dismissing him

- **Singh-Deu v Chloride Metals Ltd** 1976 IRLR 56, ET: S was employed at a lead smelting factory. His job was not particularly skilled but demanded that he constantly had his wits about him, since it involved filtering toxic dust and fumes. The effect of a mistake could be disastrous, not only for the rest of the workforce but for the whole neighbourhood. S was diagnosed by his own doctor and by the company doctor as having paranoid schizophrenia. His subsequent dismissal was fair even though there was a difference of medical opinion as to whether it would be safe to let him return to work. The tribunal was satisfied that to allow S to return to work was a risk nobody could take in this 'highly dangerous industry.'

Capability or conduct? If an employee relies on a mental illness to explain or excuse misconduct, the employer should investigate the matter further before dismissing (or confirming the decision to dismiss). It may then need to treat the issue as one of capability, rather than conduct. Some examples: **5.121**

- **City of Edinburgh Council v Dickson** EATS 0038/09: the EAT held that the dismissal of an employee for watching pornography on a school computer was unfair. His employer had rejected his claim that his uncharacteristic behaviour was the result of a hypoglycaemic episode caused by his diabetes without investigating or understanding his medical condition

- **Broomfield v National Car Parks Ltd** ET Case No.1402076/10 a tribunal found that while it had been reasonable for an employer to dismiss B for misconduct where he was absent from work without explanation and failed to respond to any communications, it was outside the range of reasonable responses for the employer not to make further investigations once B's father explained that B had been sectioned and was in a psychiatric hospital

- **Cooper v HBOS plc** ET Case No.2800220/11: C was a telephony mortgage consultant who was given a final warning for call avoidance, and then dismissed after he had provided advice, which was outside his role. When questioned, C said that he had 'not been fully himself', might have a memory problem, and 'the mind plays funny tricks'. During his disciplinary hearing he said he was stressed and his concentration had gone. On appeal, he said he was receiving treatment for a work-related psychological disorder and that his health problems might have impacted on his performance. A tribunal upheld his unfair dismissal claim, finding that no reasonable employer would have persisted in treating his behaviour as a misconduct issue to the exclusion of considering whether it could have been a result of his mental health issues.

5.122 Interestingly, in City of Edinburgh Council v Dickson (above) the EAT concluded that once the tribunal had found that D was not responsible for his conduct, its 'heinousness' then became irrelevant for misconduct purposes. This was not a case, said the EAT, where the employee's actions, although involuntary, were so extreme that it was unreasonable for him to return to his previous post, and nor did the Council argue that the inappropriate behaviour might recur. Had that been the case, the Council might have been entitled to dismiss D for capability, rather than conduct, provided a fair procedure was followed.

Where the conduct is serious the employer may be entitled to dismiss for misconduct even though the conduct was linked to some extent to the employee's mental health. In Frost v West Midlands Police Authority ET Case No.1303344/06 F was involved in a road traffic accident in 1997 which resulted in him suffering pain and discomfort from that time on. He maintained that the pain caused him to become agitated or irritable from time to time. In October 2005 he was alleged to have behaved inappropriately by making homophobic comments to a representative of the employer's Lesbian, Gay, Bisexual and Transgender Forum. At the subsequent disciplinary hearing he said that he was suffering discomfort and he could only put his behaviour down to his 'head being bad'. He was dismissed as he was already on a final written warning for inappropriate sexual behaviour. His doctor produced a report for his appeal stating that his physical condition and associated pain might lead to irritability and agitation, resulting in him making comments that might seem inappropriate, and asking the employer to look at his case in a sympathetic light. Although a tribunal held that it was unfair to dismiss F for the conduct in question, it accepted in principle that the employer was entitled to treat it as a conduct issue and concluded that F had contributed to his dismissal by 20 per cent. The medical evidence indicated that, despite his physical and mental impairments, he should be regarded as responsible for his actions.

5.123 Even where the employee's mental condition is such that his or her actions were involuntary, dismissal for misconduct may not be unreasonable. In North Lancashire Teaching Primary Care NHS Trust v Howorth EAT 0294/13 H suffered a number of catastrophic events in her personal life over a short period, including the death of her brother-in-law, her husband leaving home, receiving a diagnosis of breast cancer, and the death of a friend to the same disease. On 2 July 2008 she left a supermarket without paying, forced her way out of the store and drove away after trapping one person who attempted to restrain her with her car door and with a shopper on her car bonnet. She had no recollection of these incidents and the medical evidence supported a diagnosis of automatism. However, she pleaded guilty to theft, battery and dangerous driving, and was dismissed from her employment. The EAT upheld a tribunal's decision that the employer had acted within the range of reasonable responses in that H had been found guilty of serious criminal offences, which were relevant to her role as a health visitor in that she was banned from driving for 12 months, and it considered that there was a risk of recurrence. The employer had considered redeployment and ways in which it might mitigate the impact of the disciplinary process, but felt that it had no option but to dismiss.

In general, when deciding whether dismissal should be for conduct or capability, much will depend on the seriousness of the conduct and the severity of the employee's condition. In Scott v South Thames Corporation EAT 157/96 the EAT made the point that there is no legal rule or principle which lays down mutually exclusive procedures for dealing with health problems and with problems arising out of an employee's conduct. In each case, the question of whether the employer acted reasonably will depend on the circumstances.

Refusal to undergo examination or treatment. An employer cannot dismiss 5.124 an employee simply for refusing to undergo a psychiatric or medical examination, especially where it does not have the contractual power to insist that the employee does so – Bliss v South East Thames Regional Health Authority 1987 ICR 700, CA (see 'Long-term ill health – medical investigation' above). However, where an employee exhibits performance- or behaviour-related problems at work and refuses to undergo an examination, the employer is entitled to base its decisions on the information available. In Petch v DHSS EAT 851/86 P was dismissed after the Civil Service Medical Advisory Service certified him incapable of working properly due to his depression. His own doctor had certified him fit shortly before but P withheld permission for consultation between the doctors. His unfair dismissal claim failed on the ground that he himself had prevented a full medical investigation and that the decision had to be made on the available evidence.

Similarly, an employee's refusal to take medication may justify dismissal if this causes his or her condition to worsen (or there is a risk that it will do so). In Gillies v Scottish Equitable Life Assurance Society EAT 295/88, for example, G, an actuary, had a history of paranoid schizophrenia. In a conversation with his employer he stated that he believed he was being drugged or poisoned through the office ventilation system. The employer was aware of the employee's earlier mental illness and sought medical advice. Medical reports suggested that his health was deteriorating owing to his refusal to take

221

medication and that no reliance should be placed on his work until he had been treated. However, he absolutely refused treatment and the employer, concerned about the safety risk posed by his continued employment, eventually dismissed him, following a period of suspension. The EAT held that his dismissal was fair despite the fact that the quality of G's work up until his suspension was high. On the evidence before it, it was reasonable for the Society to consider G unfit for work, given the risk of a continuing deterioration in his condition and his disruptive behaviour.

5.125 **Illness caused by stress at work.** Where the mental illness has been caused by stress at work, it may be necessary for the employer to 'go the extra mile' by, for example, being more proactive in finding alternative employment for the employee or putting up with a longer period of sickness absence – see Royal Bank of Scotland v McAdie 2008 ICR 1087, CA (discussed under 'Factors affecting reasonableness – illness caused by employer' above).

5.126 **Alternative work.** The possibility of alternative work should be discussed with an employee who would otherwise be dismissed, although there is no obligation to create a new job (see 'Alternative employment' above).

Employers should not simply assume that an employee suffering from a mental illness can no longer cope with the pressures of the job; consultation is still necessary. Two examples:

- **Ginns v Leon Motor Services Ltd** ET Case No.27872/78: G had worked well for the employer for 29 years, latterly as a foreman, before suffering a nervous breakdown. His employer wrote to him after he had been absent for four weeks saying that it would be unfair to subject him to the same pressure so he would be relieved of his foreman's duties. The employer did not mention either his new duties or whether his pay would be affected and failed to answer his letters. G successfully claimed unfair constructive dismissal, the tribunal holding it had rarely seen such a clear case of repudiatory conduct by an employer. It also criticised the complete lack of consultation, which was an 'elementary requirement of fairness and good practice' when an employer is contemplating ill-health dismissal

- **Marriott v Rolle Medical Partnership** ET Case No.1700920/06: M worked for her employer for almost 16 years, latterly as office manager. She went on sick leave in October 2005, suffering from stress resulting from her obsessive compulsive disorder (OCD). Her GP reported in March 2006 that she was making good progress and that a structured, graded return to work would enable her to return to being a useful and productive member of staff. The employer, however, considered that M's OCD meant that she was not able to return to her old role as office manager given that the work was inherently pressured. It therefore offered her the role of secretary on less pay but M accepted voluntary redundancy rather than take up the new post.

222

A tribunal held that M had been forced into taking voluntary redundancy when her role was not redundant. This meant redundancy could not be a potentially fair reason for dismissal and she had therefore been unfairly dismissed. The employer had effectively made an assumption that because of her condition M should be denied the opportunity to return to her previous level of responsibility and in so doing had gone against the advice of M's GP.

Dementia. Following the removal of retirement as a potentially fair reason for dismissal in 2011, many employees are now more likely to work well into their old age. As a result, the incidence of dementia developing during employees' working lives will almost certainly increase. As dementia is a syndrome associated with the ongoing decline of the brain and its abilities, a diagnosis will in many cases mean that the employee's ability to function in the working environment rapidly diminishes, making termination of employment inevitable. **5.127**

However, the NHS advises that some types of dementia may be treatable and reversible; for example, where the underlying cause is a brain tumour, anxiety or depression, vitamin deficiency, or the side effects of medication. Furthermore, in the majority of cases where the condition is neurodegenerative and irreversible, an early diagnosis can nevertheless ensure that sufferers get treatment to slow down its development and enable to them to maintain mental function. For these reasons, employers should be cautious about moving to dismissal as soon as an employee informs them that he or she has been diagnosed with dementia. As with any long-term condition, employers must ensure that they conduct appropriate medical investigations; consult the employee; discuss options to support the employee to stay in work if he or she wishes and is able to do so (such as part-time or other flexible working, and/or a decreased workload); and provide information and guidance about finishing work as the condition advances or if the employee does not wish to continue working (see the Alzheimer's Society position statement on employment and dementia, available on its website).

HIV/AIDS

5.128

Dismissal of an employee simply because he or she is HIV positive is likely to be unfair unless it is a rare case where the job involves a real danger of infecting fellow employees or the public, such as certain healthcare jobs. Even in these circumstances the employer would almost certainly be expected to have considered alternative employment before dismissing. Employers should also bear in mind that any dismissal may well amount to disability discrimination under the EqA if not handled properly, as individuals who suffer from HIV are deemed to have a disability from the point of diagnosis without having to show that they have an impairment that has (or is likely to have) a substantial adverse long-term effect on their ability to carry out day-to-day activities.

Employers need to be alive to the possibility of bullying of employees with HIV, given the stigma and ignorance that still exists. If measures are not put in

223

place to combat this, an employer runs the risk of unfair constructive dismissal claims under the ERA, as well as claims of disability discrimination or sexual orientation discrimination under the EqA. Furthermore, an HIV-positive employee who is stigmatised or discriminated against at work may well suffer from stress and depression, which may lay the employer open to personal injury claims.

5.129 In certain fields, such as health care work, an HIV-positive employee could pose a health risk to others. The employer's duty to make reasonable adjustments under the EqA means that measures must be put in place to negate those risks to enable the employee to continue working (either in his or her normal job with modifications or in an alternative job where there is less risk involved). However, if an employer has done all it reasonably can and the employee still poses a significant risk, the employer may be entitled to dismiss him or her fairly for health and safety reasons. This may amount to SOSR for dismissal under S.98(1)(b) – see Chapter 8, 'Some other substantial reason'. Conversely, if the employee either wilfully or carelessly neglects the health and safety measures put in place by the employer, it may then be fair to dismiss him or her for misconduct – see Chapter 6, 'Conduct', under 'Disobedience'.

5.130 **Capability dismissals.** Dismissal of an employee who is suffering from an illness associated with AIDS is potentially fair when the reason relates to the employee's ability to do the job. However, the fact that someone has become ill as a result of being infected with the HIV virus does not mean that he or she should be treated differently from any other employee with a non-contagious life-threatening illness. Accordingly, where an infected employee is absent from work for long or short periods of time, the employer must follow the normal sickness procedure: investigation, consultation and consideration of alternative employment.

A person who has developed full-blown AIDS may not be fit enough to work again and in that situation a dismissal for capability might be fair. It is also possible that the contract has been frustrated – see IDS Employment Law Handbook, 'Contracts of Employment' (2014), Chapter 13, 'Termination by operation of law', under 'Frustration'.

5.131 **Dismissals due to third-party pressure.** Employers are sometimes faced with strong pressure from members of the workforce or customers to dismiss or transfer an employee who is, or is believed to be, HIV positive. The pressure may originate from a fear of being infected themselves or from personal prejudices. However, apart from a few identifiable risk areas such as healthcare work, an HIV-infected person poses no risk to others through normal work or social contact. Most of the potential areas of conflict can therefore be resolved through education and consultation.

224

In so far as other employees are concerned, employers have an implied contractual duty to render reasonable support to an employee who is being harassed by colleagues – Wigan Borough Council v Davies 1979 ICR 411, EAT. Failure to do so may entitle the employee to resign and claim constructive dismissal, depending on the seriousness of the breach. It is the responsibility of employers to take appropriate action to remedy the situation. They should allay the fears of employees who are concerned about the transmission of HIV, primarily through informing and educating them. If these measures have no effect, an employer may have to consider transferring one or more of them to a different location. In certain circumstances the employer may also need to consider disciplining or dismissing employees who harass a colleague. In Philpott v North Lambeth Law Centre ET Case No.11212/86, for example, the tribunal held that the dismissal of two solicitors who refused to work with H, a newly engaged solicitor who had worked for Gay Switchboard, on the ground that he would introduce AIDS into the law centre, was fair. They were dismissed for a number of reasons, including the malicious manner in which they had brought the issue of AIDS to the attention of their fellow employees and members of the public.

However, it may not be practicable for an employer to dismiss employees for **5.132** refusing to work with an infected person as this could lead to widespread disruption of the workforce. In this situation the employer may be left with no option but to transfer or dismiss the employee who has, or is suspected of having, HIV or AIDS. Such a dismissal is likely to be for SOSR but employers should be aware that they cannot justify such a dismissal by reference to any pressure involving the calling or organising of a strike or other industrial action – S.107 ERA (see Chapter 8, 'Some other substantial reason', under 'Third-party pressure to dismiss – threat of industrial action'). But if the pressure takes other forms, whether the dismissal is fair will depend on all the circumstances, although tribunals will not expect employers to crumble too easily under pressure, particularly if it is from a relatively small group of employees. It will be of fundamental importance that the employer did everything possible to resolve the situation, distanced itself from the views and actions of the employees and explained the situation fully to the HIV-infected employee before taking action. In Buck v The Letchworth Palace Ltd ET Case No.36488/86 B, a homosexual cinema projectionist, was dismissed without notice after he was convicted of an indecency offence in a public toilet and his colleagues refused to work with him, fearing that they might catch AIDS, even though B did not himself have AIDS. Although a tribunal found the dismissal fair, this was because the reason for dismissal was B's off-duty criminal conduct rather than the pressure imposed by his colleagues and their 'unreasonable prejudices'. The tribunal was critical of the employer's handling of the matter and its complete failure to consult with B.

Disclosure and confidentiality. Confidentiality is of particular concern to **5.133** many employees who are HIV positive or have AIDS. The National AIDS Trust

225

(NAT) has produced a resource pack, 'HIV at Work', which states that while disclosure may be beneficial, there is no justification for asking an employee to disclose HIV-related information unless their infection is affecting their ability to perform their job or there is an occupational risk of transmission. It recommends selective disclosure to HR, occupational health or whoever it is felt is most appropriate to be entrusted with the information.

If the employer breaches confidentiality without good reason, this may found a claim for unfair constructive dismissal. Two contrasting cases:

• **Dos Santos v Fitch Ratings Ltd** ET Case No.2203907/08: following a few periods of sick leave DS discovered that he was HIV positive. He informed his line managers, M and G, but emphasised how important it was to him that the information should be kept confidential. M and G felt genuine concern for DS and sought to provide support. They persuaded him to inform HR but he stressed the importance that the information should not be divulged any further. However, a few days later M passed the information on to her line manager, P, as she felt he needed to understand the seriousness of the condition underlying DS's frequent absences. P then called DS into a meeting to express his support. DS was extremely upset to discover that his confidence had been broken and felt so betrayed that he resigned in response. A tribunal upheld DS's claim for unfair constructive dismissal. It considered that M's disclosure involved a breach of the implied term of trust and confidence: although it was not calculated to destroy that relationship, the tribunal considered it was *likely* to do so. DS disclosed highly personal information under strict terms of confidence, which was breached. The tribunal also upheld DS's claim for unlawful harassment under what is now the EqA

• **Tucker v Burgess (trading as Ferndown Fruit Market)** ET Case No.3103296/06: T began working for B, a sole trader, as a shop assistant in 2003, having been diagnosed as being HIV positive some seven years earlier. In 2006, T told B of her condition and subsequently gave B a letter from the hospital saying that she had been prescribed new medication that could cause unpleasant side effects within the first four weeks. B showed the letter to an employee who was in charge of the shop when he was not there, so she could keep an eye on T. When T discovered that B had shown the letter to her colleague, she was shocked and upset by the 'breach of trust and confidentiality' and resigned. However, a tribunal rejected her claim for unfair constructive dismissal on this ground, holding that disclosure of the hospital letter was a proper management decision and not a breach of confidentiality.

5.134 Failing to respect an employee's confidentiality may also amount to a breach of his or her right to privacy under Article 8(1) of the European Convention on Human Rights, which can be taken into account by a tribunal under S.98(4)

226

ERA when assessing the fairness of dismissal – see Chapter 3, 'Unfairness', under 'Reasonableness of dismissal – impact of Human Rights Act' for further details. Furthermore, employers have a legal duty to safeguard the confidentiality of an employee's personal and medical information under the Data Protection Act 1998.

HIV testing. Sometimes employers wish to introduce HIV testing of their **5.135** employees. However, they should be aware that, in the absence of an express term governing HIV screening, an order by the employer that members of the workforce submit to an HIV test against their will could amount to a fundamental breach of the implied term of trust and confidence, entitling the employees to resign and claim unfair constructive dismissal.

A right to test employees might be implied where the employee has life-and-death responsibilities for others; for example, a train driver. This is because, in some cases, people with the AIDS virus develop dementia. Another situation might be where the job involves travel to countries where restrictions on entry are imposed. Similarly, where the nature of the employee's job entails a greater risk of transmission – for example, health-care work – there may be a right to test. The NAT resource pack states that mandatory HIV testing of healthcare workers involved in surgical procedures may be justified. However, in the vast majority of cases the employer will need to obtain the individual's express consent to testing and any dismissal for refusal to give consent is likely to be unfair.

Even where there is a contractual term governing HIV screening, this will not **5.136** entitle the employer to carry out tests in all circumstances. Nor can an employer necessarily dismiss an employee for refusing to take a test, even if technically he or she is in breach of contract. The employer would need to have a valid reason for requiring the test and should explain to the employee what the consequences of persistent refusal to take the test might be. Some of the issues relevant to drug and alcohol testing are likely to be relevant here – see Chapter 6, 'Conduct', under 'Drinking, drugs and smoking'.

Age-related macular degeneration

5.137

Age-related macular degeneration (AMD) is the primary cause of visual impairment in the UK. As age is the main risk factor in this condition, more cases of AMD are likely to emerge as the working population ages. In the majority of cases, dismissal should not be considered for an employee with AMD: as with any other kind of incurable visual impairment, adjustments should be made to enable the employee to continue in work. These might include magnifying lenses for reading, large print publications, intensive reading lights, or screen-reading software. Advice and assistance is available from the Government's Access to Work scheme, and from organisations such as Action for Blind People and the Royal National Institute of Blind People.

227

Dismissing without pursuing such adjustments is likely to be unfair, and constitute disability discrimination under the EqA.

If the nature of the employee's work is such that it requires unaffected vision, dismissal on grounds of capability may need to be considered as AMD is irreversible (although it does not result in total blindness). In such cases, the same approach should be adopted as with any other long-term health condition (see 'Long-term ill health' above).

6 Conduct

General considerations

Absenteeism and lateness

Sleeping on duty

Personal appearance

Attitude problems and abusive language

Disobedience

Disloyalty

Unauthorised use of computers

Drinking, drugs and smoking

Theft, dishonesty and fraudulent conduct

Violence and fighting

Criminal offences at work

Criminal offences outside of employment

Disciplinary proceedings

Misconduct is a potentially fair reason for dismissal under S.98(2)(b) of the **6.1** Employment Rights Act 1996 (ERA). In this chapter, we look at some of the more general considerations applicable to all conduct dismissals – such as establishing conduct as the reason for dismissal and the requirements of the reasonableness test – before moving on to the main categories of misconduct into which most cases fall. We then look at certain specific issues that can arise where the misconduct in question constitutes a criminal offence. Finally, we set out the procedural steps that employers should ordinarily follow during disciplinary proceedings when dealing with employee misconduct.

General considerations   6.2

An employer faced with the possibility of dismissing an employee by reason of misconduct will have to consider a number of issues in order to ensure that any resulting dismissal is not unfair. Clearly, specific forms of misconduct will raise their own particular issues. But before examining these, it is appropriate to discuss the general considerations that apply to all cases irrespective of the nature of the misconduct in question. These include:

229

- establishing conduct as a potentially fair reason for dismissal under S.98(2)(b)

- relevant considerations affecting the 'reasonableness' of dismissing for misconduct under S.98(4) ERA

- the concept of 'gross misconduct', which, if made out, entitles the employer to dismiss an employee summarily (i.e. without notice)

- how the Human Rights Act 1998 may affect the fairness or unfairness of dismissals for certain types of misconduct.

6.3 Establishing reason for dismissal

It is the employer who must show that misconduct was the reason for dismissal. According to the EAT in British Home Stores Ltd v Burchell 1980 ICR 303, EAT, a three-fold test applies. The employer must show that:

- it believed the employee guilty of misconduct

- it had in mind reasonable grounds upon which to sustain that belief, and

- at the stage at which that belief was formed on those grounds, it had carried out as much investigation into the matter as was reasonable in the circumstances.

This means that the employer need not have conclusive direct proof of the employee's misconduct – only a genuine and reasonable belief, reasonably tested.

6.4 The Burchell test was subsequently approved by the Court of Appeal in W Weddel and Co Ltd v Tepper 1980 ICR 286, CA, and more recently in Panama v London Borough of Hackney 2003 IRLR 278, CA. However, while the test remains a useful guide, the case itself was decided at a time when the burden of proof was on the employer to show not just the reason for dismissal, but also that it acted reasonably in treating that reason as sufficient grounds to dismiss the employee. But the onus on the employer to show reasonableness was removed by S.6 of the Employment Act 1980 and the EAT has therefore cautioned that the application of the Burchell test without reference to this change may lead tribunals into error in respect of the burden of proof – see Boys and Girls Welfare Society v Macdonald 1997 ICR 693, EAT, and, more recently, Singh v DHL Services Ltd EAT 0462/12. Indeed, His Honour Judge McMullen QC, giving the judgment of the EAT in Singh, indicated that it is only the first of the three aspects of the Burchell test identified above that the employer must prove. The burden of proof in respect of the other two elements of the test is neutral. HHJ McMullen QC lamented the fact that tribunals commonly misdirect themselves on the burden of proof where Burchell is involved, commenting that 'it is with great dismay that we have yet again to repeat to Employment Tribunals that the law changed 33 years ago and they should get with it'.

Although the Burchell case was concerned with a suspicion of dishonesty, the principles laid down by the EAT in that case have become the established test for determining the sufficiency of the reason for dismissal in other types of conduct case where the employer has no direct proof of the employee's misconduct, but only a strong suspicion. However, the test is clearly not appropriate to all misconduct cases: take 'appearance' cases, for example. Here it is usually easy to tell whether the employee is breaking a dress rule or not. In such cases the focus is more on whether the decision to dismiss falls within the range of reasonable responses under S.98(4), not whether the employer has shown a statutorily acceptable reason for the dismissal under S.98(2).

Employer's 'knowledge'. In Orr v Milton Keynes Council 2011 ICR 704, CA, **6.5** the Court of Appeal rejected the argument that information known to one manager could be imputed to another manager carrying out the investigation. There, O was dismissed following a disciplinary hearing, which O did not attend, to consider an incident where he was rude to his manager. The investigating officer, C, found that the rudeness amounted to gross misconduct and O was dismissed. C did not know that the argument at the centre of the incident had been caused by O's manager's underhand attempt to change O's working hours, and that he had made a racially derogatory comment to O. The Court of Appeal, by a majority, decided that there could still be a fair dismissal in these circumstances. It rejected O's 'novel' argument that his manager's knowledge of the mitigating circumstances could be attributed to the Council as the employer. The Court's majority view was that it is the person deputed to carry out the employer's functions whose knowledge or state of mind is intended to count as the employer's knowledge or state of mind – in this case, C. Reasonableness must therefore be considered in the light of that person's investigation and knowledge. If the investigation is as thorough as could reasonably be expected, it will support a reasonable belief in the findings, whether or not some information has been missed.

A similar argument was advanced by the claimant in Mitchell v St Joseph's School EAT 0506/12. There, M, a school bursar, was dismissed when the board of governors discovered that he had failed to inform it of the school's precarious financial situation. It was an express term of M's contract of employment that he should keep books of account, monitor the school's budget and report the state of the school's financial affairs to the board. The EAT held that dismissal was fair in the circumstances. In particular, it rejected M's argument that, as he had informed two members of the board of some of the issues that were the subject of the gross misconduct charge, the board could not have genuinely believed in his guilt. Under the terms of his contract, M was under a personal duty to report to the board of governors and he had failed to do so. Nor could it be said that disclosure to two members of the board meant that the board as a whole had knowledge of the school's finances. In Orr v Milton Keynes Council (above) the Court of Appeal had made it clear that knowledge of the

231

circumstances that gave rise to the charge of gross misconduct could not be attributed to the dismissing officer in the course of his investigation. The EAT considered that the same principle applied to the attribution of knowledge at a stage earlier than an investigation into the employee's alleged gross misconduct.

6.6 **Employee's own assessment of behaviour generally irrelevant.** Provided the employer had a reasonable belief that the employee was guilty of misconduct, it is generally irrelevant that the employee did not consider the behaviour inappropriate him or herself. In Cunliffe v Primagraphics Ltd ET Case No.1500499/06 the employee put forward the – in the tribunal's view – 'novel and ambitious' argument that, since he did not personally regard the e-mail he had sent round the office to be offensive and inflammatory, the employer did not have grounds for the belief that he had breached the company's e-mail and internet policy. As the tribunal said: 'If pushed to its logical conclusion, this would amount to a submission that an employee could distribute material which was plainly and objectively offensive and which had caused great offence to its recipients but that this would not constitute the commission of a disciplinary offence if the employee personally did not find it offensive.' Such an interpretation had to be rejected. Here, there was no doubt that the e-mail – calling for immigrants who were 'complaining [about] our way of life' to leave the country – was objectively offensive and the employee should reasonably have been aware that it was such; indeed, he acknowledged as much in cross-examination when he said that the e-mail 'would not offend a white, British patriot'. The dismissal was fair.

Note, however, that the employee's assessment of his or her conduct may be of some relevance in cases where the alleged misconduct involves dishonesty. This was recognised by the EAT in Gondalia v Tesco Stores Ltd EAT 0320/14 – see further 'Theft, dishonesty and fraudulent conduct – dishonesty' below.

6.7 **Two or more suspects.** Where more than one employee is suspected of misconduct, the Burchell requirements of 'genuine belief on reasonable grounds after reasonable investigation' do not apply. This rule was laid down by the Court of Appeal in Monie v Coral Racing Ltd 1981 ICR 109, CA – a case of suspected theft where more than one employee was under suspicion but the culprit was unidentifiable. The Court held that where two employees are suspected of misconduct and the employer, despite investigation, cannot discover which of them is to blame, it may be fair to dismiss both on reasonable suspicion short of actual belief. It is not clear, however, just what degree of suspicion of one or the other's guilt is necessary. Sir David Cairns referred to 'virtual certainty', Lord Justice Dunn to 'a reasonable suspicion' and Lord Justice Stephenson to 'reasonable belief'.

The Monie case has since been followed in a range of other circumstances; for example, where one of two employees was to blame for fighting – British Aerospace v Mafe EAT 565/80, and where damage was due to faulty servicing by one of two workers – McPhie and anor v Wimpey Waste Management Ltd 1981 IRLR 316, EAT. It was distinguished, however, in Leyland Vehicles Ltd v Wright EAT 712/81, where the EAT held that there was 'no reasonable conclusive proof' that one of the two dismissed employees must have been guilty of theft.

The Monie principle is also capable of being applied to cases where three or **6.8** more employees are under suspicion. In Parr v Whitbread and Co plc 1990 ICR 427, EAT, the EAT set out five guidelines to be considered by tribunals in cases of 'group' or 'blanket' dismissals for both misconduct and incapability. If a tribunal is able to find on the evidence before it that:

- an act had been committed which if committed by an individual would justify dismissal

- the employer had made a reasonable – i.e. a sufficiently thorough – investigation into the matter and with appropriate procedures

- as a result of that investigation the employer reasonably believed that more than one person could have committed the act

- the employer had acted reasonably in identifying the group of employees who could have committed the act and that each member of the group was individually capable of so doing

- as between the members of the group the employer could not reasonably identify the individual perpetrator

then, provided that the beliefs are held on solid and sensible grounds at the date of dismissal, the employer is entitled to dismiss each member of the group.

Where any one of a group of employees could have committed a particular offence, the fact that one or more members of that group are not dismissed does not render dismissal of the others unfair provided that the employer is able to show solid and sensible grounds (which do not have to be related to the relevant offence) for differentiating between members of the suspected group. There is no 'all or none' principle applying to group dismissals – Frames Snooker Centre v Boyce 1992 IRLR 472, EAT.

Where conduct admitted. The Burchell guidelines are clearly most appropriate **6.9** where misconduct is suspected. Little purpose would be served by an investigation where the misconduct is admitted – Royal Society for the Protection of Birds v Croucher 1984 ICR 604, EAT. Indeed, the Court of Appeal has said that where an employee has either pleaded guilty to, or been convicted of, a criminal offence, it would be 'ridiculous' to conclude that the employer did not have reasonable grounds for believing that the offence had been committed – P v Nottinghamshire County Council 1992 ICR 706, CA. However, the reasonableness test contained in S.98(4) (see 'Reasonableness of

233

a conduct dismissal' below) must still be applied and the employer must consider whether that particular conduct warranted dismissal. There may also be special circumstances in which the reasonable employer would still be expected to carry out its own investigation – e.g. where new matters came to light. These last two points were stressed by the EAT in Secretary of State for Scotland v Campbell 1992 IRLR 263, EAT.

The EAT in Scottish and Southern Energy plc v Innes EATS 0043/10 confirmed the limited relevance of investigation under the third limb of the Burchell test to cases of admitted misconduct. It overturned an employment tribunal's finding of procedural unfairness where the employer had not investigated whether the employee's ill health (depression) explained his admitted misconduct – which took the form of excessive use of the internet at work despite a previous warning. The EAT thought that while failure to investigate the employee's state of health may be highly relevant in the case of a capability dismissal under S.98(2)(a) ERA, the issue would not normally arise in the case of a misconduct dismissal. The employer was entitled to base its decision on the facts as admitted by the employee at the time, which did not indicate any causal link between his depression and the misconduct.

6.10 That said, it may not always be reasonable for the employer to fail to investigate whether an employee's misconduct is a result of his or her ill health. In Cooper v HBOS plc ET Case No. 2800220/11, for example, C worked as a telephone mortgage consultant. He had an unblemished disciplinary record until, in August 2010, he was given a final warning for alleged call avoidance. The employer then discovered that C had on one occasion given advice about likely changes to interest rates, which was outside his remit. When asked about this, C said that he had 'not been fully himself', that he might have a memory problem, and that 'the mind plays funny tricks'. Following a disciplinary hearing at which C said he was stressed and that his concentration had gone, C was dismissed for gross misconduct. In his internal appeal, C stated that he was receiving treatment for a work-related psychological disorder and asserted that his health problems might have impacted on his performance. His appeal was dismissed. C successfully claimed unfair dismissal. The tribunal considered that, in view of C's proven ability and his assertions as to his health, no reasonable employer would have persisted in treating C's behaviour as wilful misconduct without at least investigating whether it could have been a result of mental health problems.

Similarly, in CRO Ports London Ltd v Wiltshire EAT 0344/14 the claimant had admitted that he bore full responsibility for an accident involving a heavy lift, which had come about because of his breach of health and safety rules. However, at a disciplinary hearing he pointed out that the employer had effectively condoned the practice as a means of dealing with time pressures. Despite this, he was summarily dismissed. An employment tribunal found the dismissal unfair, because the employer had not carried out a reasonable investigation into the employee's explanation for his misconduct. Upholding an appeal against that decision, the EAT stressed that where the grounds relied upon by the employer to justify dismissal include the employee's admission of his or her misconduct, the question becomes whether the employer acted within the range of reasonable responses of the reasonable employer in limiting the scope of its investigation in the light of those admissions – this being the effect of the earlier decision in Royal Society for the Protection of Birds v Croucher (above).

Nature of conduct and relevance of time frame. Conduct does not have to be 6.11 blameworthy to fall within the ambit of S.98(2), although blameworthiness could be relevant when considering the dismissal's fairness. Nor will mere lapse of time necessarily prevent the misconduct from being a prescribed reason for dismissal where there is a clear causal link between the two. Both these aspects were stressed by the EAT in Jury v ECC Quarries Ltd EAT 241/80, which rejected J's arguments that behaviour could not be 'conduct' unless it was reprehensible; and that the lapse of time (he was dismissed five months after his refusal to retrain as a Class 2 HGV driver when all Class 3 vehicles went out of service) prevented his refusal from being the reason for the dismissal. That said, the EAT in Kilduff v Mind in Bradford EAT 0568/04 made it clear that an honest or reasonable mistake was a relevant factor when considering the question of what conduct took place and how criticisable that conduct was.

Third-party allegations. The extent to which an employer can rely on 6.12 allegations made by a third party when reaching a decision on whether to dismiss was considered in Henderson v Granville Tours Ltd 1982 IRLR 494, EAT, where the EAT found it unreasonable to dismiss on customers' complaints alone, no matter how truthful and reliable the complainants might be. Further investigation is needed, even by small firms, before a reasonable belief in the misconduct can be established. This point was made again more recently in Sneddon v Carr-Gomm Scotland Ltd 2012 IRLR 820, Ct Sess (Inner House), a case concerning allegations that an employee had shouted at and bullied a vulnerable care user. The allegations were based on a brief note of the evidence of a single third party witness given in a short phone call, with no other corroborating evidence, and was strongly contested by the employee. The Court held that, in these circumstances, a reasonable employer would have gone back to the third party witness to obtain a clearer and more detailed account.

More than one potentially fair reason. It is generally accepted that more than 6.13 one potentially fair reason under S.98 ERA can apply to an employee's dismissal. For example, in Perkin v St George's Healthcare NHS Trust 2006 ICR 617, CA, the employee's style of management seriously undermined the proper running of the Trust at a most senior level and adversely reflected on the Trust

235

both internally and externally. The Court of Appeal said that his dismissal could have been for the potentially fair reasons of 'conduct', 'capability' or 'some other substantial reason'. Consequently, it is not necessarily incumbent on the employer to restrict itself to just one potentially fair reason before the tribunal. However, categorisation will certainly affect the steps that the employer will need to take prior to dismissal in order to ensure fairness. For this reason, an employer would be well advised to settle on a single category of potentially fair reason to ensure that it follows the correct procedure prior to taking any disciplinary action.

6.14 Reasonableness of a conduct dismissal

Establishing that the reason for dismissal relates to the employee's conduct under S.98(2)(b) ERA is simply the first stage in the process. While the Burchell test is relevant to establishing the employer's belief in the employee's guilt – and, therefore, to establishing the reason for dismissal – it applies equally to the question of whether it was reasonable for the employer to treat that reason as a sufficient reason to dismiss in the circumstances under S.98(4) ERA – see Foley v Post Office; HSBC Bank plc (formerly Midland Bank plc) v Madden 2000 ICR 1283, CA. However, as noted above, the burden of proof is neutral when it comes to reasonableness.

When assessing whether the Burchell test has been met, the tribunal must ask itself whether what occurred fell within the 'range of reasonable responses' of a reasonable employer. The Court of Appeal has held that the 'range of reasonable responses' test applies in a conduct case both to the decision to dismiss and to the procedure by which that decision was reached. In J Sainsbury plc v Hitt 2003 ICR 111, CA, the Court found that a tribunal had substituted its own decision as to whether or not an investigation into alleged misconduct was reasonable. This, it said, was an error of law. The relevant question was whether it was an investigation that fell within the range of reasonable responses that a reasonable employer might have adopted. In Whitbread plc (t/a Whitbread Medway Inns) v Hall 2001 ICR 699, CA, a similar result was reached in relation to admitted misconduct. (Note, however, that in certain circumstances there will be no 'range' of reasonable responses. For example, if an employee deliberately sets fire to his or her employer's factory, dismissal is the only reasonable response. Conversely, if an employee is dismissed for politely saying 'good morning', this would be unreasonable – see Foley v Post Office; HSBC Bank plc (formerly Midland Bank plc) v Madden (above).)

6.15 The procedural steps usually required of an employer in conduct cases are discussed at the end of this chapter under 'Disciplinary proceedings'. However, it is important to note at this stage that the procedural steps required of employers have undergone a fair amount of change in recent years. In October 2004 the Government introduced the statutory dispute resolution procedures, with the primary aim of encouraging parties to seek early resolution of disputes in the workplace. They also set out minimum procedural steps – contained in the statutory dismissal and disciplinary procedures (DDPs) – that employers were required to follow prior to contemplating taking any disciplinary action. Failure to follow the DDPs meant that any dismissal was automatically unfair under S.98A(1) ERA. However, failure to follow a procedure other than one required by the statutory DDPs would not be regarded as by itself making the employer's action unreasonable if the employer could show that it would have decided to dismiss the employee if it had followed the procedure – S.98A(2).

The compulsory DDPs no longer apply, following the repeal of the statutory dispute resolution procedures and S.98A ERA in 2009. Instead, employers are expected to have regard to the principles for handling disciplinary and grievance procedures in the workplace set out in the revised Acas Code of Practice on Disciplinary and Grievance Procedures ('the Acas Code'). The Code is relevant to the question of liability and will be taken into account by a tribunal when determining the reasonableness of a dismissal in accordance with S.98(4) – S.207 Trade Union and Labour Relations (Consolidation) Act 1992 (TULR(C)A). Furthermore, if the dismissal is found to be unfair, the tribunal can increase (or indeed decrease) an award of compensation by up to 25 per cent for an unreasonable failure of either party to follow the Code if it considers it just and equitable to do so – S.207A TULR(C)A.

The effect of the repeal of the statutory DDPs and, in particular, S.98A(2) ERA, **6.16** is that, in determining the reasonableness of a dismissal, tribunals are once again forbidden from asking whether procedural failings would have made any difference to the decision to dismiss. In other words, an employer is unable to argue in its defence that even if it had followed a fair procedure, it still would have dismissed the employee. This was the position that was first established by the House of Lords in Polkey v AE Dayton Services Ltd 1988 ICR 142, HL, although their Lordships also made it clear that the issue of whether a failure to follow a proper procedure made any difference to the decision to dismiss could be taken into account when calculating the compensatory award at the remedies stage. A tribunal may reduce such an award proportionately to the chance that the employee would have been fairly dismissed in any event had a proper procedure been complied with. These so-called 'Polkey reductions' to compensation are considered in detail in Chapter 16, 'Compensatory awards: adjustments', under "Polkey reductions"'.

Gross misconduct   6.17

Whether an employee's behaviour amounts to misconduct or gross misconduct can have important consequences. Gross misconduct may result in summary dismissal, thus relieving the employer of the obligation to pay any notice pay. Exactly what type of behaviour amounts to gross misconduct is difficult to pinpoint and will depend on the facts of the individual case. However, it is

237

generally accepted that it must be an act which fundamentally undermines the employment contract (i.e. it must be repudiatory conduct by the employee going to the root of the contract) – Wilson v Racher 1974 ICR 428, CA. Moreover, the conduct must be a deliberate and wilful contradiction of the contractual terms or amount to gross negligence – Laws v London Chronicle (Indicator Newspapers Ltd) 1959 1 WLR 698, CA, and Sandwell and anor v Westwood EAT 0032/09.

Even if an employee has admitted to committing the acts of which he or she is accused, it may not always be the case that he or she acted wilfully or in a way that was grossly negligent. In Burdett v Aviva Employment Services Ltd EAT 0439/13 B, who suffered from paranoid schizophrenia, stopped taking his medication without the benefit of medical advice. He consequently suffered a relapse and sexually assaulted four women, including two colleagues. B admitted committing the sexual assaults and was dismissed for gross misconduct. The EAT overturned a tribunal's finding that the dismissal was fair. The evidence was that B had only committed the assaults because of his mental impairment and he had not admitted wilful misconduct. The tribunal had failed to properly evaluate whether there were reasonable grounds for the employer to conclude that B's conduct amounted to culpable gross misconduct. Although it was not strictly necessary for it to address the point, the EAT went on to consider the question of sanction. Assuming that there were reasonable grounds for a finding of gross misconduct, the tribunal should have assessed whether it was within the range of reasonable responses for the employer to dismiss B for that gross misconduct. It cannot simply be assumed that a finding of gross misconduct will always justify dismissal. Evidence of mitigation was very relevant in this case and the tribunal had erred in failing to consider its impact on the reasonableness of the sanction imposed.

6.18 The Acas Code states that the employer's disciplinary rules should give examples of what the employer regards as gross misconduct, i.e. conduct that it considers serious enough to justify summary dismissal (see para 24). The Code suggests this might include theft or fraud, physical violence, gross negligence or serious insubordination. Although there are some types of misconduct that may be universally seen as gross misconduct, such as theft or violence, others may vary according to the nature of the organisation and what it does. In workplaces with significant health and safety risks, for example, any breach of a health and safety procedure may be viewed as gross misconduct justifying dismissal, whereas a similar breach in a workplace where workers are not exposed to the same level of risk may warrant only a warning. If an employer views certain behaviour as very serious and capable of amounting to gross misconduct because of the nature of the business but that behaviour might not be viewed in the same way elsewhere, it is particularly important to include it in the disciplinary rules so that employees are aware of that fact.

The non-statutory Acas Guide, 'Discipline and grievances at work' ('the Acas Guide'), which accompanies the Acas Code, gives the following examples of gross misconduct that might be included:

- theft or fraud
- physical violence or bullying
- deliberate and serious damage to property
- serious misuse of an organisation's property or name
- deliberately accessing internet sites containing pornographic, offensive or obscene material
- serious insubordination
- unlawful discrimination or harassment
- bringing the organisation into serious disrepute
- serious incapability at work brought on by alcohol or illegal drugs
- causing loss, damage or injury though serious negligence
- a serious breach of health and safety rules
- a serious breach of confidence (page 31).

A failure to list certain types of behaviour as gross misconduct may mean that **6.19** the employer cannot rely on them to dismiss summarily. In Basildon Academies v Amadi EAT 0343/14, for example, A, a part-time tutor, was summarily dismissed for gross misconduct after he failed to disclose to his employer the fact that he had been accused of sexual impropriety in another employment. Upholding his claim of unfair dismissal, an employment tribunal found that A's contract with the Academy included an obligation to inform his employer of any criminal convictions or cautions, and to report any impropriety committed by himself or colleagues during the course of their employment, but it did not require him to report *accusations* of impropriety. This decision was upheld on appeal by the EAT, which also rejected the notion that there was any implied contractual duty to disclose the allegations. The EAT commented that, in the absence of a contractual obligation to disclose, it was hard to characterise A's failure to do so as misconduct, let alone gross misconduct.

In determining the reasonableness of a summary dismissal, the tribunal must have regard to whether the employer had reasonable grounds for its belief that the employee was guilty of gross misconduct. In Eastland Homes Partnership Ltd v Cunningham EAT 0272/13 the EAT held that the employment tribunal had fallen into error when it failed to consider whether it was reasonable for the employer to characterise the employee's conduct as gross misconduct. C, a caretaker on a housing estate, was dismissed after failing to disclose to his employer that his wife was named as a beneficiary in the will of one of the estate's tenants. The tribunal found that, given his long service, exemplary disciplinary record and the support he received from the tenants on the estate, no reasonable employer would have dismissed him. The EAT overturned the decision on appeal, holding that the tribunal never asked itself whether it was reasonable for the employer to regard C's conduct as gross misconduct. If the employer's view that the misconduct is serious enough to be characterised as gross misconduct is objectively justifiable, that should be considered as one of the circumstances against which to judge whether it was reasonable for the employer to have treated the conduct as a sufficient reason to dismiss under S.98(4) ERA.

6.20 Even where gross misconduct may justify summary dismissal, an employer suspecting an employee of such conduct should still follow a fair procedure, including a full investigation of the facts. If an employer does establish a reasonable belief that the employee is guilty of the misconduct in question, it must still hold a meeting and hear the employee's case, including any mitigating circumstances that might lead to a lesser sanction. Accordingly, even if the employee has committed an act of gross misconduct, the fairness or otherwise of any subsequent dismissal remains to be determined in accordance with the statutory test.

6.21 Impact of Human Rights Act

Since the implementation of the Human Rights Act 1998 (HRA), courts and tribunals in the United Kingdom have had to have regard to the European Convention on Human Rights (ECHR) when reaching a decision. S.3 HRA provides that courts and tribunals must interpret Acts of Parliament and statutory instruments in a way that is compatible with the Convention rights, so far as it is possible to do so. This paves the way for claimants to argue before a tribunal that, where the circumstances of their dismissal fall within the ambit of a Convention right, the tribunal must consider, in determining the question of fairness under S.98(4) ERA, whether the employer unjustifiably interfered with the right in question.

Note that while employees working in the private sector can assert that domestic rights, such as the right not to be unfairly dismissed, should be interpreted in a manner consistent with the ECHR, they cannot bring direct claims based on Convention rights. Public sector employees, on the other hand, can bring a direct claim against their employer under S.7 HRA for any breach of Convention rights.

6.22 The way in which the courts and tribunals have dealt with human rights arguments in unfair dismissal cases generally is discussed in detail in Chapter 3, 'Unfairness', under 'Impact of Human Rights Act'. In relation to misconduct, the Convention rights most frequently relied on by employees are Article 8 (right to respect for private and family life) and Article 10 (right to freedom of expression). Such rights may be particularly relevant in the following types of case:

- drug or alcohol cases: where the employer wishes to impose drug or alcohol testing in the workplace, an employee may argue that the testing process interferes with his or her Article 8 rights. It is therefore important for employers to ensure that their behaviour in the context of such testing is proportionate to the seriousness of the allegations against the employee. See further the section 'Drinking, drugs and smoking' below, under 'Drug and alcohol testing – human rights issues'

- offensive e-mails: it is relatively common for employers to monitor their employees' use of company e-mail. Where such monitoring uncovers evidence that an employee has sent or received inappropriate material, the employer may take disciplinary action. However, employees may argue that such monitoring breaches their Article 8 rights and that dismissing them for sending or receiving the relevant content constitutes a breach of their right to freedom of expression under Article 10. These issues are discussed in the section 'Unauthorised use of computers' below, under 'Sending offensive images or jokes – human rights issues'

- social media and blogging: similarly, employees who are dismissed for making inappropriate or offensive comments on social media may argue that the employer's action in checking up on their online profiles interferes with their right to privacy under Article 8. There are also cases in which employees have sought to rely on their Article 10 rights to establish that dismissal on the basis of their comments on social media is unfair. See further the section 'Unauthorised use of computers' below, under 'Social media and blogging – human rights issues'.

6.23 Human rights arguments may also come into play in relation to the disciplinary process. Where an employer uses covert surveillance to gather evidence of an employee's misconduct, for example, Article 8 issues could well be raised. This is discussed in the section 'Disciplinary proceedings' below, under 'Investigation – gathering evidence'.

In addition, the Court of Appeal has held that Article 6 ECHR, which provides that an individual has the right to a fair hearing, may in certain circumstances provide employees with the right to legal representation at disciplinary hearings – Kulkarni v Milton Keynes Hospital NHS Foundation Trust and anor 2010 ICR 101, CA. However, judgments of the Supreme Court in R (on the application of G) v Governors of X School 2011 ICR 1033, SC, and the Court of Appeal in Mattu v University Hospitals of Coventry and Warwickshire NHS

241

Trust 2013 ICR 270, CA, suggest that these circumstances will be rare. These cases, which did not involve unfair dismissal claims, are discussed further under 'Disciplinary proceedings – right to legal representation' below.

6.24 Absenteeism and lateness

In general, absenteeism and lateness will not merit dismissal for a first offence. In such cases the recalcitrant employee should be warned of the consequences of further absences and be given the chance to explain before dismissal. However, there may be cases where the consequences of a first absence or a first episode of lateness is serious enough to justify dismissal without warning. This was so in Galloway v K Miller (Contractors) ET Case No.S/2430/81, where the employer lost a valuable contract because of G's absence from work. His dismissal, despite his previous good record, was fair in the circumstances, said the tribunal. So too in Ward v Coincheck Electronics Ltd ET Case No.1805368/03, where W was dismissed for one day's absence. The employer was a small company and W's role was key to a busy production process. It was clearly stated in W's contract that unauthorised absence constituted gross misconduct.

6.25 Lateness

Where a warning has been given about lateness but the employee continues to be tardy, the employer should ask for an explanation and check the reasons before dismissing. In one employee's case, dismissal for being late seven days out of 77, after being warned to improve his timekeeping, was unfair – because on three of these days he was held up by a railway dispute. But his colleague who had been late 12 times out of 88 was fairly dismissed – Hallett and anor v MAT Transport Ltd 1976 IRLR 5, ET.

6.26 Absenteeism

The 2010 Acas Advisory Booklet, 'Managing attendance and employee turnover', provides useful guidance to employers on how to handle persistent short-term absenteeism. It states, among other things, that:

- unexpected absences should be investigated promptly and the employee asked for an explanation at a return-to-work interview

- if there are no acceptable reasons then the matter should be treated as a conduct issue and dealt with under the disciplinary procedure

- where there is no medical certificate to support frequent short-term self-certified absences, then the employee should be asked to see a doctor to establish whether treatment is necessary and whether the underlying reason for absence is work-related. If no medical evidence in support of the absences

242

is forthcoming, the employer should consider whether to take action under the disciplinary procedure

- if the absence could be disability-related, the employer should consider what reasonable adjustments could be made in the workplace to help the employee (see IDS Employment Law Handbook, 'Discrimination at Work' (2012), Chapter 21, 'Failure to make reasonable adjustments')

- if the absence is because of temporary problems relating to dependants, the employee may be entitled to time off under the provisions of the ERA relating to time off for dependants (see IDS Employment Law Handbook, 'Maternity and Parental Rights' (2015), Chapter 11, 'Time off for dependants')

- if the absence is as a result of the employee's pregnancy, the employer should record this separately. Employers should tread carefully in cases of absenteeism occasioned by pregnancy because the employee has the right to take time off for ante-natal and other pregnancy-related care and enjoys special protection against detrimental treatment (see IDS Employment Law Handbook, 'Maternity and Parental Rights' (2015), Chapter 1, 'Time off for ante-natal care', and Chapter 12, 'Detriment and unfair dismissal')

- if the absence is because the employee has difficulty managing both work and home responsibilities, then the employer should give serious consideration to more flexible ways of working. All employees who have completed 26 weeks' continuous service with their employer have the right to request flexible working arrangements – including job-sharing, part-time working, flexi-time, working from home/teleworking and school-time contracts – and employers must have a good business reason for rejecting any application (see IDS Employment Law Handbook, 'Atypical and Flexible Working' (2014), Chapter 4, 'Flexible working')

- in all cases the employee should be told what improvement in attendance is expected and warned of the likely consequences if this does not happen

- if there is no improvement, the employee's length of service, performance, the likelihood of a change in attendance, the availability of suitable alternative work, and the effect of past and future absences on the organisation should all be taken into account in deciding on appropriate action.

The Advisory Booklet goes on to state that it is very important to deal with **6.27** persistent absence promptly, firmly and consistently in order to show both the employee concerned and other employees that absence is regarded as a serious matter and may result in dismissal. An examination of records will identify those employees who are regularly absent and may disclose an absence pattern. In such cases employers should make sufficient enquiries to determine whether the absence is because of genuine illness or for other reasons. If the absence is because of a genuine illness, it should not be dealt with under the disciplinary

243

procedure – Davis v Tibbett and Britten Group plc EAT 460/99. It is therefore important that an employer does not make assumptions about an employee's absences, since treating genuine sickness absence as misconduct can lead to a finding of unfair dismissal – see, for example, Millington v Wandsworth Council ET Case No.2302863/06, where the tribunal did not consider that certified absences could be treated as a 'conduct' issue save in circumstances where the employee had deliberately or negligently put him or herself at risk of injury or ill health.

Absenteeism will generally fall under the 'conduct' label where the employee is away from work without authorisation or where he or she is not genuinely off work sick. Ill health absence – both long- and short-term – is considered in detail in Chapter 5, 'Ill health'. Note that dismissal for absence because of imprisonment is not considered to be a 'conduct' dismissal but dismissal for 'some other substantial reason' – Kingston v British Railways Board 1984 ICR 781, CA (see Chapter 8, 'Some other substantial reason').

6.28 **Unauthorised absence.** Where an employee stays away from work without the employer's permission, this is likely to found a fair dismissal, especially where he or she has been warned of the consequences. In Nestle (UK) Ltd v Thacker EAT 279/98 an employee who took a holiday despite having been refused permission and warned of possible dismissal if she went was fairly dismissed on her return despite her length of service and previous unblemished record. However, even when an employee has had prior warning that taking a holiday without permission will result in dismissal, the employer should still hold a disciplinary hearing to discuss the matter. In Heskey v Adwest Rearsby Ltd EAT 158/97 H's request to take an extended holiday was refused and he was told that he would be dismissed if he went on the holiday regardless. He did so, and was dismissed. AR Ltd dispensed with the disciplinary and appeal hearings as, owing to his absence, H was unable to attend and any hearing would therefore have been useless. The EAT held that AR Ltd should have waited until H returned before holding a disciplinary hearing. The case was remitted for a rehearing before a different tribunal.

The fairness of a dismissal for unauthorised absence may depend on a number of factors, including the seniority of the employee concerned, how recently any requirement to work on particular dates was introduced, whether the employee has been warned of the consequences of unauthorised absence and the employer's normal practice in such situations. In Stott v Next Retail Ltd ET Case No.2100960/11, for example, S worked as a sales assistant for eight contractual hours per week, plus four hours' overtime. At the end of November, a poster was put up in the store where she worked stating that all staff would be required to work on Christmas Eve, 27 and 28 December. S sent her manager a note saying that she could not work on Christmas Eve because she had already paid a deposit to attend her husband's work Christmas function on that date, but expressing a willingness to work on other dates over the Christmas period. Her manager told her that this was not acceptable and that she might face disciplinary action if she was not at work on Christmas Eve. S did not attend work on Christmas Eve but did work on 27 and 28 December as required. She was called to a disciplinary hearing on 4 January and was summarily dismissed. The tribunal noted that S was not management level and only worked eight hours per week; the requirement to work on Christmas Eve had only been imposed the previous year due to the employer's decision to bring forward the commencement of its sale to Boxing Day; while S had been told that she might face disciplinary action, she was not warned that her absence might result in her dismissal; and it was uncommon for the employer to dismiss its store staff for single instances of unauthorised absence. In the circumstances, therefore, the tribunal found the dismissal unfair.

6.29 Employers should take care when framing disciplinary rules governing the taking of holiday and the need for prior approval. In George Ellison Ltd v Brown EAT 338/03 B was dismissed for going on holiday despite the express refusal of his managing director, who also wished to take holiday on the same dates. While finding that B's dismissal was unfair because the MD was the 'judge in his own cause', the EAT also noted that B was not acting in an unauthorised manner because the rules – which were contractual – stated that those employees who had not got approval for their holiday would be allocated the two weeks following 22 July. This was the period during which B was absent. The EAT dismissed the argument that the rule applied only to those who had not sought approval at all rather than to all employees who had not got approval, including those for whom approval had been refused.

Dismissal for unauthorised absences for religious purposes may also be fair, although in such circumstances an employer would normally be expected to warn the employee about the consequences of his or her continued absences before taking action and, where possible, do its best to find a more suitable alternative job – see, for example, Hill v BXL Plastics Ltd ET Case No.23340/81. However, employers should be careful to ensure that their treatment of employees who are absent for religious reasons does not amount to direct or indirect discrimination contrary to the Equality Act 2010 (EqA) – see IDS Employment Law Handbook, 'Discrimination at Work' (2012), at Chapter 11, 'Religion or belief', and Chapter 14, 'Prohibited conduct: general principles'.

6.30 Even where an employee has obtained prior permission for taking a period of annual leave, overstaying that leave may found a fair dismissal if the employment contract provides that such conduct would be likely to result in dismissal. In Ali v Joseph Dawson Ltd EAT 43/89 the employer employed a considerable number of people from Pakistan and India who often wanted to take extended leave to go home. In order to control the exercise of these long periods of leave, the company introduced a scheme that, if operated successfully, would benefit both

245

the employees and the employer. However, it had to be strictly operated and failure to adhere to the arrangement would be likely to result in dismissal. The claimant took extended leave and was dismissed for overstaying his leave by one week. He had been delayed because of his failure to ensure that he had the necessary entry documents. He was dismissed after a five-minute hearing and the EAT upheld the tribunal's finding of fair dismissal. Another overstay case in which the employee's dismissal was held to be fair is Bhopal v Virgin Media Ltd ET Case No.3201800/10. There, B had his employer's approval for a two-week holiday to India, with an agreed return date of 6 April. However, B's ticket had a fixed return date of 30 April. On the date he was due to return to work, B phoned his manager to say that he was still in India and was unable to get a ticket home. B eventually returned to work on 26 April. At the subsequent disciplinary hearing, B claimed that his father had booked the ticket on his behalf and that the travel agency had told him he could change the return date once he arrived in India. However, the tribunal found that B had only attempted to change his return date at the end of his agreed period of holiday, once his manager had made clear to him on the telephone that unauthorised absence was a serious matter. The tribunal considered that the employer's decision to dismiss B for gross misconduct fell within the range of reasonable responses.

6.31 **'Phoney' sickness absences.** Obviously, 'phoney' sickness absences tend to justify tougher action by employers than absences occasioned by a recurrent illness – which might be better dealt with in the same way as long-term sickness absences – or absences caused by unrelated, minor ailments.

Four examples:

- **Nkengfack v London Borough of Southwark** 2002 EWCA Civ 711, CA: the Court of Appeal upheld a tribunal's decision that the dismissal of a teacher in a small school who was seen working in her own hair salon while purporting to be off sick with back pain was fair. The dishonesty inherent in her conduct was an important factor

- **Shail v Swindon Pressings Ltd** EAT 0771/04: the EAT held that the employer fairly dismissed an employee who was observed carrying out building work at a residential property while off sick

- **Gill v SAS Ground Services Ltd** ET Case No.2705021/09: an employment tribunal found that the dismissal of an employee who attended London Fashion Week while signed off sick following an operation was fair. G claimed that her attendance at the event was 'essentially social', but her Facebook page referred to her auditioning models and choreographing a fashion show, and linked to a YouTube video showing her walking along a catwalk and presenting flowers to a designer. The tribunal accepted that the employer's view that G had 'crossed the line' by performing other work while off sick was within the range of reasonable responses. The fact that

246

the employer had obtained its evidence from G's Facebook page did not make the disciplinary process unfair

- **Evans v Universal Trade Frames Ltd** ET Case No.1303200/11: a tribunal found the dismissal of an employee who had staged a fall at work and taken two weeks' sick leave to be fair. The employer had carefully analysed its CCTV footage of the incident and its belief that the fall was staged was reasonable in the circumstances.

However, an employer should avoid acting on a mere suspicion that the **6.32** employee is not genuinely ill, thereby risking a finding of unfair dismissal in the absence of reasonable grounds for believing the employee guilty of misconduct. Instead, it should conduct a reasonable investigation to try to ascertain the true situation. In Leeson v Makita Manufacturing Europe Ltd EAT 0911/00 L had been signed off work for a week and prescribed antibiotics. He went to play golf on the fifth day of his sick leave to give himself the benefit of some fresh air and exercise after being confined indoors all week. The EAT held that the fact that L was well enough for some recreational activity did not justify the employer's conclusion that he was fit enough to work.

Where the employer has conducted a reasonable investigation and does have reasonable grounds for believing that the employee has been guilty of misconduct, dismissal in cases of 'phoney' sickness absence will usually be fair, but the employer must still consider any mitigating circumstances that might mean dismissal is not reasonable in a particular case. In Brito-Babapulle v Ealing Hospital NHS Trust 2014 EWCA Civ 1626, CA – a case concerning a consultant haematologist who was dismissed when her employer discovered that she had been seeing private patients during a period of sick leave from her NHS role – the Court of Appeal approved a comment made by the EAT on this point. According to the EAT, 'the lay members of this tribunal would emphasise that in the employment world claiming sick pay whilst working elsewhere is in general regarded very seriously by employers. In their experience any substantiated case almost inevitably will lead to dismissal, not least because if it did not, the employer might find it difficult to distinguish on any proper basis between the cases of other employees doing the same. That is not, however, to say that it is an inevitable conclusion.'

Sleeping on duty

6.33

By itself, sleeping on duty, although misconduct, is usually insufficient to ground a fair dismissal, although it may attract a very severe warning – McDonagh v Johnson and Nephew (Manchester) Ltd EAT 140/78. Additional factors are taken into account by tribunals. These include whether the employer has a clear rule on the matter known to all those affected – see, for example, Ayub v Vauxhall Motors Ltd 1978 IRLR 428, ET, although the absence of such

247

a rule will not necessarily render the dismissal unfair: all the circumstances must be considered. The following are all relevant factors in considering the reasonableness of a decision to dismiss for this type of misconduct.

6.34 **Consistency in applying rule or practice.** In Olender and ors v IMI Yorkshire Imperial Ltd ET Case No.25296/80 a tribunal found it unfair to dismiss senior and otherwise satisfactory employees for sleeping on duty where another employee with less service had been treated differently.

6.35 **Employee's work record.** In Singh v British Railways Engineering Ltd ET Case No.7200/80 it was not unfair to dismiss the employee for sleeping away from his workplace while on duty, particularly in view of his poor employment record. Conversely, the employer's failure to take into account the employee's satisfactory record was an important consideration in the Olender case (above), where the dismissal was found to be unfair.

Note that sleeping on duty is sometimes the 'last straw' that, added to an indifferent record, puts an end to the employer's patience (see the Singh case above). However, previous disciplinary warnings will not necessarily have this cumulative effect. In Lonrho Textiles Ltd v Cryan EAT 737/78 a serious warning for dangerous skylarking which could, on its own, have justified dismissal, was not sufficient background for such a sanction when the same employee was caught sleeping on duty. His compensation was, however, cut by 50 per cent to reflect his contributory conduct. (For a more detailed discussion of the relevance of previous warnings to the fairness of dismissal, see 'Disciplinary proceedings' below, under 'The decision – prior disciplinary record').

6.36 **Length of service.** An employee's long and unblemished service should always be considered by the employer before taking the decision to dismiss. In Vargich v Newage International Ltd ET Case No.1900763/03 the dismissal of the claimant was unfair given his 18 years of unblemished service, a recent bereavement and the fact that no harm was caused. Similarly, in Newton and anor v Ryder plc ET Case No.2801633/06 the employer failed to take into account the claimants' length of service (17 years) and clean disciplinary record. However, the fact that an employee has long service and a clean work record may not render a dismissal for sleeping on duty unfair where serious damage is caused or safety is prejudiced – see, for example, Crosby v United Molasses Co Ltd ET Case No.23761/81.

6.37 **Health and safety.** Employers should be wary of treating sleeping while on duty as automatically warranting dismissal without looking into all the circumstances. In particular, the nature of the work and the employee's working hours may alert the employer that there are underlying health and safety issues that need to be addressed before any such decision can be taken. This is especially important where the employee in question is working at night. An example:

- **Newton and anor v Ryder plc** ET Case No.2801633/06: N and M, who worked as mechanics, were dismissed for sleeping while on duty – an offence identified in the employee handbook as gross misconduct. They admitted that they would occasionally nod off during the night, but maintained that they had not deliberately set out to sleep: when they stopped doing manual work and sat down to do paperwork, they would occasionally drop off for a few minutes or occasionally for up to 20 minutes. The tribunal found the dismissals unfair. A reasonable employer would have made a distinction between a premeditated plan to go to sleep – e.g. making up a bed or going off to a quiet corner – and simply dropping off while working. Moreover, N had previously raised with R plc the difficulty of working nights and the need to review arrangements for breaks. A reasonable employer would have tackled the issue primarily as a health and safety matter.

Conversely, where safety is prejudiced or serious damage caused as a result of an employee falling asleep, the employee's dismissal is likely to be fair. So, for example, in Crosby v United Molasses Co Ltd ET Case No.23761/81 a tribunal found that it was fair to dismiss a good and willing employee with long service for falling asleep on duty when this caused some £10,000 worth of damage.

Deliberate or repeated conduct. As noted in the Newton case (above), **6.38** employers should generally make a distinction between a situation where an employee simply drops off unintentionally and one where there is a deliberate plan to sleep while on duty. In MacPherson v NFT Distribution Operations Ltd ET Case No.1200350/11 M was one of a small number of workers who held a key to the employer's first aid room. During one shift, the employer noticed that M was missing from his workstation. He was discovered locked in the first aid room in a state of partial undress. The employer conducted a disciplinary investigation, which uncovered evidence to the effect that M had deliberately shut himself in the first aid room in order to take a nap, and that he had done this on previous occasions and had bragged about it to a colleague. An employment tribunal held that where sleeping on duty was repeated and deliberate, rather than accidental, this demonstrated an abuse of trust by the employee and the dismissal was therefore fair.

Personal appearance **6.39**

Employers are entitled to a large measure of discretion in controlling their company's image, including the appearance of staff, especially when their duties bring them into contact with the public or where their mode of dress affects hygiene or safety standards. Even if no rules are laid down about this, there is likely to be an implied term that employees wear suitable and acceptable clothes at work and refrain from wearing ornaments or articles of jewellery that endanger them or their fellow-workers or offend against commonly accepted standards.

A balance must be struck between the interests of the business and the reasonable freedom of the employee, said the EAT in Boychuk v HJ Symons Holdings Ltd 1977 IRLR 395, EAT. When striking that balance, tribunals will take into account factors such as:

- the employer's reasons for the requirements
- whether the requirements are spelled out in the contract
- the employee's reason for objecting
- the way the employer sets about enforcing the standard it insists on.

6.40 In every case, the tribunal will examine the facts to see whether the needs of the business justify the appearance rule. Tribunals have been quite bold in asserting their own view of what is reasonable – and in some cases have put the employer's view down to mere prejudice or excessive fussiness. However, what they cannot do is dictate the standards they would have allowed had they been in the employer's shoes.

6.41 **Fitting business image.** This is an area of commercial judgement and there will be a range of views a reasonable employer might take. In Eales v Halfords Ltd ET Case No.25468/80 E was told at his interview that there were strict dress rules – he must wear sensible black or brown shoes, dark trousers of conservative cut, collar and tie. He committed occasional minor transgressions by wearing light trousers or shoes, but the last straw came when he dyed his hair yellow. The tribunal thought the employer had rather overestimated the smartness required to serve in a bicycle shop in Mansfield and found E's dismissal unfair. In Higham v International Stores COET 589/50, on the other hand, H wore sandals, no socks and no tie to work. After warnings, he was dismissed on the ground that his standard of dress in a middle-class store was likely to alienate customers.

6.42 **Uniform rules.** Tribunals are likely to accept that in service or retail industries a uniform is reasonably necessary – either to ensure that the employee can be readily identified by the customer (e.g. flight attendants, hotel door-keepers, etc) or simply to project the image of the company. Refusal to wear the appropriate uniform may result in dismissal. In Mayor v Merseyside Passenger Transport Executive ET Case No.30017/86 M, a bus driver required to wear an authorised uniform, was given a final written warning for wearing a Father Christmas outfit at Christmas time. He was subsequently dismissed for wearing a non-regulation shirt with no collar and very short sleeves. The tribunal found the dismissal fair, holding that the employer was entitled to take into account M's pattern of disobedience. However, exceptions may need to be made for individual employees. For example, in Malik v British Home Stores ET Case No.29014/79, a race discrimination case, an employment tribunal held that a department store should have permitted a Muslim woman to wear trousers instead of a skirt under the uniform overall.

Offending other employees or customers. In Lengthorn v RA Bird and Co **6.43** Ltd ET Case No.11522/83 the claimant was fairly dismissed after his employer received complaints from shop customers about prominent love-bites on his neck. Despite warnings and suggestions that he wear a roll-neck sweater the employee refused to treat the matter seriously, leaving his employer with little alternative but to sack him.

Similarly, in Boychuk v HJ Symons Holdings Ltd (above), the employee was dismissed after warnings and discussions for persisting in wearing lesbian badges. The EAT held that it was within the employer's discretion to forbid badges that could be offensive to fellow employees and customers. But, it continued, 'that does not mean that an employer, by a foolish or unreasonable judgement of what could be expected to be offensive, can impose some unreasonable restriction. It does mean that a reasonable employer, who after all is ultimately responsible for the interests of the business, can be allowed to decide what, upon reflection and mature consideration, could be offensive.' The employer can act on its judgement without waiting to see whether in fact offence is taken.

Safety and hygiene. Tribunals are sympathetic to employers seeking to impose **6.44** safety rules. However, employers must first investigate any complaints the employee might have and, if possible, remedy such grievances before resorting to discipline – British Aircraft Corporation Ltd v Austin 1978 IRLR 332, EAT (where the employee complained about the safety glasses provided and refused to wear them). In Kirkcaldy District Council v Baxter EAT 540/78 the EAT held that it was unreasonable to expect a dustman to continue working in driving rain for which inadequate protective clothing was provided: his demands for a fresh set were reasonable and his dismissal was unfair.

The standard of personal hygiene required of an employee may be influenced by a number of factors including the nature of the job; the product, if any; the process of production itself; and the reasonable demands of fellow employees. In Singh v RHM Bakeries (Southern) Ltd EAT 818/77 the EAT upheld a tribunal's decision that the employee, whose job involved handling food, was fairly dismissed for breaking a clear company rule against wearing beards imposed in the interests of hygiene. And in O'Boyle v British Telecommunications ET Case No.35813/81 the employee was fairly dismissed after failing to heed warnings to improve his personal hygiene. Other employees had made numerous complaints that they could no longer work with or alongside him because of his body odour, so something had to be done.

Employee's objections. In Catharell v Glyn Nuttall Ltd ET Case No.7935/81 **6.45** the employer's dismissal of an apprentice electrician for refusing to have his

251

long hair cut was held to be unfair. The tribunal said that 'as long as his hair length was not detrimental to the [employer's] business or his performance of his duties, [he] was entitled to determine for himself the personal question'. In general, the employee's objections have to be balanced against the employer's reasons for the rule in question and some objections weigh more heavily than others. Objections based on religious dress conventions, for instance, are taken very seriously indeed and may outweigh an employer's interest in uniformity. Any physical discomfort may also be a good reason for refusing to comply – Kirkcaldy District Council v Baxter (above).

6.46 Handling appearance problems

Employees' appearance at work can be a sensitive issue (particularly as it is not merely restricted to clothing but may also cover, for example, styles and length of hair, piercings, make-up and tattoos). Employers must therefore tread carefully when the issue arises and should follow a fair procedure.

6.47 **Make position clear.** Except in obvious cases, employees cannot be expected to realise that their appearance is unsuitable unless they are told what the company's policy is. An employee who refuses to comply should be told of the employer's reasons, otherwise he or she may reasonably believe there is no good reason for the rules. In Catharell v Glyn Nuttall Ltd ET Case No.7935/81 (discussed under 'Employee's objections' above) the employer had conveyed the impression that its objection to long hair was on 'purely aesthetic grounds'.

6.48 **Interpret rules reasonably.** In Kirkcaldy District Council v Baxter EAT 540/78 the employer could not rely on a rule that dustmen would work in inclement weather if appropriate clothing was provided, because the protective clothing provided was in fact letting in water and had ceased to be 'appropriate'.

6.49 **Consult on new rules.** In Teagle v Whelton Sinclair COET 947/47 new rules were introduced only after the claimant had worked in the office for two years. That this was done by means of a notice, unheralded by any discussions, was a major factor leading to the finding of unfairness. Similarly, in Leaper and anor v Delta Hotels Ltd t/a Sheraton Inn ET Case No.S/3799/76 a new uniform (which the employees thought hideous) was produced as a fait accompli after the employees had been promised they would not have to wear anything they disliked. Dismissal was held to be unfair.

6.50 **Investigate alleged breaches.** In Eales v Halfords Ltd ET Case No.25468/80 the district superintendent authorised dismissal for 'yellow' dyed hair without going to see the employee for himself. The tribunal called this lapse 'unforgivable'. If he had interviewed the employee, the district superintendent would have discovered that the employee had permission to dye his hair blonde and that he was prepared to re-dye it darker.

Warn and discuss before dismissing. It will be very rare for a clothing offence **6.51**
to amount to gross misconduct such that dismissal for a single offence is
justified. On the other hand, a settled determination to disobey a reasonable
rule is likely to justify dismissal in the absence of very good reasons for objecting.
So this is an area where procedure makes all the difference. Two examples:

- **Rowntree v Lakeside Country Club Ltd** ET Case No.16409/78: R had
  been employed as a barmaid (with no dress restrictions) for nearly a year
  before she was told to change out of her jeans, which she did. A few weeks
  later she wore them again and was dismissed. The tribunal said the order
  not to wear jeans was not within the terms of R's contract, but anyway she
  should not have been dismissed for a single offence

- **Gavin v Paul Dean (Football and Turf Accountant) Ltd** ET Case
  No.2406940/97: G was dismissed for not complying with the dress code,
  which she said was too expensive. The dismissal was unfair because the
  employer did not take full account of G's personal circumstances or consider
  making a financial contribution as it had with other employees. It also failed
  to warn G of the risk of dismissal and ignored a possible compromise she
  put forward.

Note that dress rules that discriminate, either directly or indirectly, on grounds
of sex, race, disability, religion or belief, sexual orientation, gender reassignment
or age may fall foul of anti-discrimination legislation – see IDS Employment
Law Handbook, 'Discrimination at Work' (2012), Chapter 25, 'Discrimination
during employment', under 'Dress codes and appearance'.

Attitude problems and abusive language   6.52

The general rule – as stated in the Acas Code of Practice – is that, except in
cases of gross misconduct, employees should never be dismissed for a first
disciplinary offence. The House of Lords made it clear in Polkey v AE Dayton
Services Ltd 1988 ICR 142, HL, that an exception will only be permitted when
the employer has formed a considered and reasonable view that a warning
would be 'utterly useless' or 'futile'.

Thus, where employees adopt an intransigent or bloody-minded attitude
towards their employer, behave rudely or use abusive language, it will only be
fair to dismiss without warning or a chance to explain where the attitude or
rudeness demonstrates a clear intention to act in that way and is not merely the
result of a passing emotion. In such cases, said the NIRC in James v Waltham
Holy Cross UDC 1973 ICR 398, NIRC, 'there can be no point in giving [the
employee] an opportunity of restating a view the expression of which led to the
decision to dismiss'. But the NIRC warned that employers 'should be slow to

253

conclude that an opportunity to reflect and a subsequent opportunity to explain could in no circumstances produce a changed situation in which dismissal would be unnecessary'.

6.53 Persistent attitude problems

Where an employee has persistently displayed a negative attitude, the giving of a formal warning may well focus the mind and lead to the adoption of a more positive attitude and a willingness to change on the part of the employee. As the EAT commented in Foster v Somerset County Council EAT 0355/03, attitude is 'something which was potentially capable of change, however unlikely it may have appeared to be'.

But sometimes warnings will have no effect whatsoever. In Mintoft v Armstrong Massey Ltd t/a UAC Motors of Scarborough EAT 516/80, for example, an experienced sales manager, M, persistently refused to comply with his employer's paperwork procedures (detailed recording of faults and repairs in second-hand cars), introduced so that the garage could give warranties with some degree of confidence. In August and November 1979 he was sent letters requiring him to follow these procedures. In late March 1980 he received another letter stating that there had been no improvement and warning of dismissal if there was another occurrence. He went off sick a few days later and when he returned was met with criticism about the state of the used cars. In the presence of the managing director M was abusive to his own branch manager, restated his dislike of the system and said in clear terms that he was not prepared to operate it. He was then dismissed. The tribunal found that M's attitude was such that he was never going to change his view about the system. The EAT upheld the tribunal's finding of fair dismissal. It rejected the argument that it was unfair not to give M an opportunity to change his ways in compliance with the March warning. This was because M had made it plain he was not going to operate the procedure: 'It is really upon that attitude at that meeting and previously that the company decided to dismiss. It seems to us, in the light of the status of these two men in the depot, that the... tribunal was perfectly entitled to conclude that a further period would not have achieved any result.'

6.54 Nor will the employer necessarily act unreasonably by not giving the employee a chance to improve. In Perkin v St George's Healthcare NHS Trust 2006 ICR 617, CA, the employee's style of management seriously undermined the proper running of the healthcare trust at a most senior level and adversely reflected on the trust both internally and externally. A tribunal found – and the EAT and the Court of Appeal both subsequently agreed – that he was unlikely to change his behaviour. In the circumstances, dismissal was a reasonable response. (Note that the tribunal went on to find the dismissal procedurally unfair but, given that there was a 100 per cent chance that the employee would have been dismissed even if a fair procedure had been followed and that he was entirely to blame for his dismissal, his compensation was reduced to nil.) However, that case can be contrasted with JJ Food Service Ltd v Kefil 2013 IRLR 850, EAT, where the EAT upheld the decision of an employment tribunal that an employer's decision to dismiss K for his authoritarian style of management was unfair. K had previously received an informal warning for this type of behaviour, but the warning had not made it clear that he might be dismissed if he did not change his ways and nor had the employer provided him with any management training.

An interesting point made in Perkin v St George's Healthcare NHS Trust (above) is that 'personality' is not a potentially fair reason for dismissal under S.98, although the person's personality can manifest itself in a way that can bring it within the 'conduct' category.

Reason for intransigence or inflexibility. Tribunals should have regard to the 6.55 cause of the employee's intransigent attitude when deciding whether it was fair to dismiss him or her for adopting it. In Mock v Glamorgan Aluminium Co Ltd EAT 493/80 it was the managing director's initial fundamental breach of contract (assault on M) that triggered M's unyielding attitude; it was this that destroyed the trust and good faith essential in employment contracts, not M's attitude, so the dismissal was unfair. In such cases, however, the employee's non-conciliatory attitude might be a factor justifying a reduction in compensation.

Abusive language   6.56
The fairness of a dismissal for bad language must obviously depend on the individual circumstances of each case – see Burnett v City of Glasgow District Council EAT 491/76, for example, where it was fair to dismiss an employee who used foul and abusive language to his manager when refusing to obey a legitimate order. Most cases are not so clear-cut, however, and it is almost always a question of context and degree, as the following two wrongful dismissal cases demonstrate:

- **Pepper v Webb** 1969 1 WLR 514, CA: a gardener's refusal, using four-letter words, to carry out an order amounted to a repudiatory breach of contract when seen in the light of his previous insolence and inefficiency. The gardener's wrongful dismissal claim therefore failed

- **Wilson v Racher** 1974 ICR 428, CA: obscene phrases used by a gardener in exasperation at the employer's persistent and largely unfounded criticisms were not repudiatory. Lord Justice Edmund Davies suggested the test was whether in the circumstances 'the... use of this extremely bad language... made impossible the continuance of the master and servant relationship, and showed that the plaintiff was indeed resolved to follow a line of conduct which made the continuation of that relationship impossible'.

The problem of swearing and abuse usually arises in one of two ways: either as a history of foul-mouthed conduct (in which case warnings would be

255

appropriate) or as a single serious outburst. In either case the real problem is probably a breakdown of the working relationship – of which bad language is a symptom, not a cause. Thus the tribunal should consider the abusive words in light of all the circumstances. Note that although most cases involve verbal outbursts, there are also cases where the abusive or obscene language is written down. Below, we set out the main factors to be taken into account by tribunals assessing the fairness of any dismissal for bad language.

6.57 **Effect on discipline within company.** This is especially relevant where allowing the employee's language to go unchecked may impact on the authority of superiors. Dismissal for swearing at a superior can be fair if it constitutes a serious threat to management authority and undermines the employer/employee relationship. In MacIsaac v James Ferries and Co Ltd EAT 1442/96, for example, M was very abusive towards his superior, calling him 'a thief, a liar and a cheat' and 'the worst… disaster ever to join the company'. The EAT relied on Wilson v Racher (above) and held that as M's behaviour had caused an irreparable breach in the working relationship between him and his superior, a continuation of that relationship was quite impossible.

Insubordinate behaviour is something that tribunals and courts will not typically condone. In Bate v Samworth Brothers Ltd t/a Samworth Distribution ET Case No.1301113/06, for example, B was fairly dismissed when he subjected his superior to a barrage of verbal abuse because he was unhappy with an instruction he had been given. His superior had asked him three times to stop swearing at him. The employer has a duty to create a working environment in which managers and supervisors are able to issue instructions to the workforce with confidence. B's refusal to carry out a reasonable instruction was an aggravating feature. However, it is recognised that situations often develop where both parties are to blame and the dismissal of an employee provoked by the employer may be unfair (see Wilson v Racher (above)).

6.58 **Status of employee.** The status of the employee concerned can be relevant where, for instance, the employee using bad language is a member of management and the objects of his or her disfavour are his or her superiors. In Morris v Sperry Corporation EAT 51/81 M was fairly dismissed for reacting to a business reorganisation in terms which the tribunal could only describe as 'florid in the extreme'. He described his superiors as liars, used profanities, and was overheard 'ranting and raving'. The EAT said his conduct was so much out of keeping with his position as a senior executive that he could no longer be employed.

6.59 **Workplace environment.** Words that are acceptable on a construction site may be unacceptable in an office. Tribunals judge the offence complained of in the light of the commonly accepted standards of the particular work environment in which the language was used. Thus in Crewe v Dominion Garage Ltd COET 1164/158 the tribunal accepted that bad language is pervasive in a garage or workshop. However, where the employee's job brings him or her into contact with the public, customers or suppliers, the use of bad language could adversely affect the employer's business reputation and so justify dismissal – Sketchley v Kissoon EAT 514/79. In Guyers v Ashworth Hospital Authority ET Case No.2103665/01, for example, a nurse was fairly dismissed for using profane language when describing a patient in a note to a colleague. (Rudeness to or in front of customers is discussed further under 'Behaviour towards customers' below.)

Provocation. An employer's duty to act reasonably before dismissing someone **6.60** means that it should investigate the events leading up to the use of bad language, as well as the incident itself. Provocation may excuse an employee's outburst and justify the reaction it caused. The context may well be an important factor here – in Little v Greenhams Ltd ET Case No.1700135/02 a tribunal put weight on the fact that L swore in order to speed up evacuation during a fire drill for which he was responsible. It therefore found his subsequent dismissal unfair.

Heat-of-the-moment outbursts should also be treated with particular caution. The seriousness of the offence needs to be weighed against the likelihood of recurrence and the degree of provocation suffered – Charles Letts and Co Ltd v Howard 1976 IRLR 248, EAT.

Quite often bad language is a symptom of a personality clash. In these **6.61** circumstances, the reason for dismissal might be 'some other substantial reason', not 'conduct' – Lasharie v Brass and Alloy Pressings (Deritend) Ltd EAT 35/81 (see further Chapter 8, 'Some other substantial reason').

Chance to apologise. The EAT said in Charles Letts and Co Ltd v Howard **6.62** (above) that an opportunity to apologise for using abusive language is important, especially where the outburst was a sudden explosion of temper by an employee under the influence of drink. The person deciding whether to dismiss should allow a cooling-off period and give the employee an opportunity to apologise before it is too late.

Mitigating circumstances. In Croucher v Royal Mail Group plc ET Case **6.63** No.3301206/07 C, a postman, was summarily dismissed for calling a colleague a 'sneaky cunt' when he pressed him for parcels for delivery before they were meant to be ready. The tribunal found that the dismissal was unfair because the employer failed to take account of a number of mitigating factors. For instance, C had been provoked; he had apologised and offered to attend mediation; the day of the incident was the first anniversary of his father's death; and he had experienced ongoing difficulties with his mother over the past year. The employer maintained that it operated a policy of zero tolerance of bad language, but there was no evidence of this being communicated to the workforce. However, C's blameworthy conduct was assessed at 25 per cent and his compensation reduced accordingly.

257

Similarly, in Amps v Truro Marquees and Catering Ltd ET Case No.1702692/09 A had been attacked with a paintball gun by a colleague while at work and had sustained minor injuries. He drove in his paint-spattered van back to the depot, where he swore at, and had a heated altercation with, his manager, who felt threatened and dismissed him there and then. The tribunal held that while A's behaviour amounted to misconduct, it was perfectly understandable in the circumstances and instant dismissal was outside the range of reasonable responses. The employer owed a duty of care to A to protect him from the colleague (who was known to have violent tendencies and was subsequently convicted of assault and jailed for seven months). In the tribunal's view, a reasonable employer would have allowed a cooling-off period and then had a meeting with A at which an appropriate sanction could have been imposed.

6.64 **Actual words used.** In Hunt v Royal Mail Group Ltd ET Case No.2702308/07 H, who took part in industrial action, used 'particularly unpleasant obscene language' against a colleague who was crossing the picket line. While the wording used was similar to that in Croucher v Royal Mail Group plc (above), it seems that the context distinguished this case, with the effect that H's dismissal was fair. He had deliberately used the words with the clear purpose of causing offence. The context in which the abusive language is used is therefore important.

6.65 **Non-cooperation between employees**

Employers faced with the problem of employees who refuse to cooperate with each other should take reasonable steps to try to improve the relationship and satisfy themselves that the situation is irredeemable before deciding that dismissal is the only answer – Turner v Vestric Ltd 1980 ICR 528, EAT.

Where employers' attempts to conciliate fail, dismissal is likely to be fair, especially where the conflict manifests itself in an act of gross misconduct. Thus in Greaves v London Borough of Newham EAT 673/82 G's dismissal for sending her employer a list of serious and unsubstantiated allegations about her boss was fair, even though she was not totally to blame for the differences that had arisen between them.

6.66 Allegations of bullying, harassment or discriminatory conduct against an employee may lead to a fair dismissal on conduct grounds. Much will depend on the circumstances. In Vaux Breweries Ltd v McNaughton EAT 937/98 M was dismissed when he admitted to certain allegations of sexual harassment, such as saying 'squeeze me' to female members of staff who walked by and talking of 'thrashing' staff members if they did something wrong. The EAT held that it was within the range of reasonable responses for an employer, faced with such admissions in a case involving young female members of staff who left employment complaining of sexual harassment by a manager of a unit employing only women, to impose the sanction of dismissal. The fact that another employer might reasonably have issued a warning was beside the point.

Even one-off or relatively minor incidents of racist language may be grounds for a fair dismissal. In Price v Uxbridge College ET Case No.3318423/06 P was accused of using the expression 'monkey boy' three times when referring to an Asian colleague. She denied this, but the employer decided to dismiss, taking into account the fact that P had a propensity to use nicknames, the existence of discrepancies in her evidence, and her conduct generally. P maintained that the dismissal was unfair and pointed to the fact that a colleague who had placed racially offensive words on the employer's intranet was not dismissed. The tribunal found the dismissal fair: the employer had reasonable grounds for concluding that P was guilty of making the offending remark; it had followed a fair procedure; and, against a background of racial tolerance and equality of opportunity which was the mainstay of the employer as an educational institution, it had acted reasonably in treating the words used as racist and as amounting to gross misconduct. Moreover, the employer had significant reasons for treating P differently from the way the other employee had been treated. That employee had not directed offensive remarks against a specific individual and had recognised the impropriety of her conduct, made a remorseful admission and apologised. By contrast, P equivocated between denial and attempts at justification.

Similarly, in Look Ahead Housing and Care Ltd v Rudder EAT 0163/10 the **6.67** EAT held that a housing charity had acted fairly in dismissing R, a tenancy support officer, for a one-off racist comment made in front of a service user. R had been due to have a one-to-one meeting with the service user, but was prevented from entering the meeting room as it was being used by a colleague for prayer. R was alleged to have commented, in a loud voice, 'This is not a place for prayer. If people need to do so, they should go to the church.' The service user reminded R that the colleague in question was Muslim so could not go to a church to pray and complained to the charity about R's comment. Overturning a tribunal's finding of unfair dismissal, the EAT held that having regard to the nature of the organisation – a charity serving disadvantaged clients from all racial and religious backgrounds, for whom equality of treatment was imperative – and the fact that it had a zero tolerance policy towards any discriminatory conduct, dismissal fell within the range of reasonable responses.

Where threatening or abusive language or behaviour between employees exacerbates an already sensitive situation it is likely to justify dismissal even though, under normal circumstances, such a drastic move might be considered unreasonable. In Shakespeare and anor v National Coal Board, unreported 30.3.88, CA, for instance, two employees returning to work after the 1984/85 miners' strike were dismissed for threatening and insulting three miners who

259

had returned to work earlier. Their dismissal was held to be fair despite the fact that such behaviour would not ordinarily have warranted such harsh measures.

6.68 While an employee's unacceptable behaviour, in clear breach of workplace policies, may justify a decision to dismiss, an employer's failure to take account of mitigating factors is likely to take the employer's decision outside the range of reasonable responses open to it. So, in Heaney v Lloyds TSB Bank plc ET Case No.2402140/06 the tribunal found that the employer had unfairly dismissed H after four – out of a total of 11 – allegations of harassment against him were found proven. H had 31 years' unblemished service and the last matter complained of had taken place a year earlier and there had been no further blameworthy conduct since. However, his compensation was reduced by 30 per cent to take account of H's contributory conduct.

Employers should note that all employees are entitled to the same protection against abuse from other employees. In Morris v Network South Central EAT 8/97 an employee was dismissed for verbally abusing his ex-wife, who also worked on the company's premises. The EAT could find no fault with the tribunal's decision that all employees were entitled to equal protection and that the dismissal was therefore fair.

6.69 Behaviour towards customers
Employers will be particularly concerned to ensure that customer-facing staff conduct themselves politely and properly at all times. Dismissal for rudeness to or in front of a client or customer, or for adopting a negative attitude with clients, may well be fair but this will depend on the nature of the employee's behaviour and the surrounding circumstances, as the following cases demonstrate:

• **Kennedy v E.On Energy Solution** ET Case No.1901086/13: K, a call-centre employee, was fairly dismissed for regularly hanging up on customers and telling one customer to 'bugger off'. K was aware that calls were routinely recorded and the employer was entitled to rely on the recording of the 'bugger off' call at K's disciplinary hearing

• **Drydale v Vennskap Ltd** ET Case No.1201766/12: D was unfairly dismissed for telling a customer to 'shut up' during a heated discussion when the customer sought to collect winnings from a gaming machine at the bar in which D worked. The tribunal held that the employer should have taken into account the surrounding circumstances, including the fact that D was in considerable pain as she had accidentally squirted beer into her eye from a keg and that it had not been established that D had actually sworn at the customer – a fellow employee had witnessed the incident and corroborated D's account that the actual swear words she had used were not specifically directed at the customer

260

- **Marote v Psycare Ltd** ET Case No.3302912/12: M was unfairly dismissed for using the word 'fanny' in front of the resident of a care home. The resident's niece only complained about her aunt's care six months after the incident in question and the employer's investigation was extremely informal and far too slow. The employer's reason for dismissal – abuse of a resident – was not made out. M had a poor grasp of English and a 13-year record of exemplary service. Use of the word 'fanny' was inappropriate, but even an employee fluent in English would have been entitled to a warning for the use of such a word

- **AJ Dunning and Sons (Shopfitters) Ltd v Jacomb** 1973 ICR 448, NIRC: a contracts manager fell out with a number of the company's major clients. A tribunal found the dismissal unfair for lack of warning. The NIRC disagreed on appeal. The evidence showed that the manager knew his conduct was putting his job in jeopardy and that he was incapable of changing.

Disobedience 6.70

Implied into every employment contract is an obligation on the employee to obey the employer's lawful (i.e. contractual) and reasonable orders. Refusal to do so is a potentially fair reason to dismiss for misconduct.

However, the mere fact that an employee has disobeyed an instruction – even if he or she is in breach of contract – does not guarantee that a tribunal will find the dismissal fair. The question of whether the employee was in breach of contract in disobeying the order is a relevant, but not conclusive, factor. This stems from the fact that the fairness of a dismissal under S.98(4) ERA is based on the question of reasonableness. Accordingly, an employer may give an order that is perfectly legitimate under the contract only to find that the dismissal of an employee who disobeys it is unfair. On the other hand, an instruction may not fall within the terms of the contract but dismissal for failure to obey it may nonetheless be fair – provided the employer acted reasonably.

Tribunals faced with disobedience dismissals usually concentrate on three **6.71** main issues:

- whether the order given was legitimate

- whether the order was reasonable

- the reasonableness of the employee's refusal.

Was order legitimate? The answer to the question of whether an order was **6.72** legitimate will normally depend on whether it was one that the employer could give under the terms of the contract. If it was, then by disobeying that order the employee will usually be committing an act of misconduct; if it was not, then the employer's insistence on compliance will almost certainly be in breach of

261

contract. In Skelton v Biddles (Bookbinders) Ltd EAT 332/86 S's contract said that he was entitled to use of a company car 'for personal transport' but his employer forbade him to use the car for any holiday. He wanted to leave it at a friend's house near Luton Airport and was dismissed when he refused to obey the employer's order not to do so. The EAT held the dismissal to be unfair because the contract gave S exclusive use of the car – he was entitled to use it as his own personal property. In such circumstances, S was entitled to disregard his employer's contrary order.

To ascertain whether an employee is contractually bound to obey an instruction, tribunals will consider sources such as the contract of employment itself and any particulars of employment issued under S.1 ERA. These will identify express terms such as the nature of the job, the employee's workplace(s), hours, holiday entitlement, etc. Other relevant sources include such things as collective agreements and work rules. Terms will also be implied by common law, e.g. that employees will obey all legitimate and reasonable instructions and cooperate with the company in performing their jobs. Finally, other terms may derive from unwritten custom and practice operating in a particular trade or area.

6.73 Note that an employee's contractual obligation is sometimes wider than the ambit of the duties he or she usually performs. In Glitz v Watford Electric Co Ltd 1979 IRLR 89, EAT, the claimant was engaged as a copy typist/general clerical duties clerk. At the time of her engagement it was not contemplated that she would operate a duplicating machine, nor was she asked to do so during the following three years. However, the EAT held that in the context of a small clerical team working for a small employer, she was contractually obliged to operate the duplicator since it fell within the ambit of 'general clerical duties'.

Employers should be cautious of placing too much emphasis on the contractual position, however. In Redbridge London Borough Council v Fishman 1978 ICR 569, EAT, Mr Justice Phillips stated that 'many dismissals are unfair although the employer is contractually entitled to dismiss the employee. Contrariwise, some dismissals are not unfair although the employer was not contractually entitled to dismiss the employee.' This warning was heeded in Farrant v Woodroffe School 1998 ICR 184, EAT, where the employee was held to have been fairly dismissed for refusing to accept a change in his duties, even though it transpired that his employer had no right under the contract to insist on the change. The EAT said that where an employer relies upon a refusal to obey an instruction as the reason for the dismissal, the lawfulness of the instruction will be relevant to, but not determinative of, the fairness of the dismissal.

6.74 **Was order reasonable?** Employees are not bound to obey all lawful instructions. While the contractual obligations are important, it is the reasonableness of the instruction (and whether the employer acted within the band of reasonable responses in dismissing) that is crucial in an unfair dismissal claim. As at common law, employees are able to refuse lawful instructions that are dangerous or unreasonable. Two examples:

- **Davies v Jack Troth t/a Richards Transport** EAT 81/87: D, an HGV driver, arrived at work and was told to collect a trailer from Sheffield and take it to Grimsby. After he collected the trailer a fault developed and it became clear that D would not get to Grimsby that day without breaking hours regulations. D rang his employer telling him that he had neither the clothes nor the money to stay overnight and so he wanted to return to the depot. His employer was incensed and dismissed him. The EAT found the dismissal unfair. It accepted that the employer could contractually require D to make for Grimsby and stay overnight but concluded that asking him to do so when he had no money or change of clothes was an unreasonable instruction

- **Whymark v Louis Reece Ltd** ET Case No.47043/95: LR Ltd was finding business difficult and decided to ask the staff to complete a questionnaire designed to test their awareness of the profit and turnover needed to survive. W thought the test a waste of time and refused to complete it. His dismissal for gross insubordination was held to be unfair. Although the tribunal understood the employer's concerns, it thought that the questionnaire was nothing short of juvenile.

6.75 Just as an employer may act unreasonably in giving a lawful instruction, dismissal of an employee for refusing to comply with an order which has no contractual basis may be fair. In Coward v John Menzies (Holdings) Ltd 1977 IRLR 428, EAT, for example, C, a branch manager at Letchworth, was considered not to be up to that post. As a result the employer offered him a transfer to Swansea (with no financial loss) for retraining as an assistant manager. He refused and was dismissed. The EAT held that, even if there were no contractual right to require C to transfer, the employer had acted reasonably in the interests of the business.

6.76 **Reasonableness of employee's refusal.** In cases where an employee complains of being dismissed for refusing to comply with an order, it is not only the nature of the employer's order which is relevant under S.98(4) but also the reasonableness of the employee's refusal to carry it out – Union of Construction, Allied Trades and Technicians v Brain 1981 ICR 542, CA. In that case, the editor of the union's newspaper refused to sign an undertaking which effectively meant that he would be liable for any libels against a construction industry journal that were printed in the paper even though he had no way of controlling the content of articles written by senior officers. He was dismissed – unfairly, held the Court of Appeal. Lord Justice Donaldson said that when dismissal is for refusal to obey an instruction, 'the primary factor which falls to be considered by the reasonable employer deciding whether or not to dismiss his recalcitrant employee is the question, "Is the employee acting reasonably or

263

could he be acting reasonably in refusing to obey my instruction?"' According to the Court, even if the employer had been acting reasonably in ordering the employee to sign the undertaking (which it doubted), the employee's refusal to sign was reasonable and so the dismissal was unfair.

6.77 The importance of the employee's reasons for disobeying is illustrated in the following examples:

- **Osborn Transport Services v Chrissanthou** EAT 412/77: the EAT declined to overturn a tribunal's conclusion that it was unfair to dismiss C for refusing to pick up a load from a specific customer. This was because C had previously had a bad experience with the customer and had been given an undertaking that he would not have to go there again. Factors like these outweighed the urgency of his employer sending a driver and the fact that no others were readily available

- **Intercity East Coast Ltd v McGregor** EAT 473/96: M stayed behind after work one evening to talk to the local union representative. His supervisor told him that he was trespassing on railway premises and that he should go home. The following day the train on which M was scheduled to work was running late, with the result that M would have been obliged to remain on railway premises beyond his scheduled hours. He refused to work his shift on the basis of his supervisor's comments the previous evening. He was dismissed. The EAT upheld the tribunal's finding of unfair dismissal, subject to an element of contributory fault

- **Eastland v TNT UK Ltd** ET Case No.3301528/11: E was unfairly dismissed for refusing to carry out his manager's instruction to empty a lorry that had arrived at the depot where he worked. The incident was investigated by S, the manager whose instruction E had refused to obey. E raised a grievance alleging that the reason he had refused to carry out S's instruction was that S had sworn at him and that a colleague, J, had witnessed the incident and would be able to back this up. The employer failed to investigate E's grievance or interview J and E was dismissed following a disciplinary hearing. At the tribunal hearing of E's unfair dismissal claim, the disciplinary decision-maker admitted that if there had been evidence that S had sworn at E, he would not have dismissed E for his disobedience

- **Chappel v Hoist Hire Services Ltd** ET Case No.1402131/12: a mechanic was dismissed after he refused to attend a breakdown which would have resulted in him working overtime. Under his contract, he could be required to work overtime but he had an informal verbal agreement with his manager that he would not be forced to do so. The employer's instruction was given in such a way that the employee thought it was a request and that he was entitled to refuse it. A tribunal found the dismissal fair; the fact that an instruction is given politely does not entitle an employee to refuse it.

264

Tribunals will expect an employer to have investigated an employee's refusal **6.78** and perhaps then to have reconsidered its own requirements. However, there is no absolute requirement on an employer to enquire further into reasons given by the employee, as long as the employee is given the opportunity to speak in his or her defence – Aitken v Weatherford UK Ltd 2005 1 SC 360, Ct Sess (Inner House).

We discuss some common scenarios in which employees may refuse to obey their employer's instructions below.

Refusal to work overtime **6.79**

If an employee has been dismissed for refusing to work overtime, the tribunal will look initially at the contract to determine whether or not overtime was a contractual requirement. As noted above, the contractual position is not conclusive to the fairness of the dismissal, but it is certainly a key starting point in many cases.

Even if there is no contractual term, dismissal of an employee for refusal to work overtime may be reasonable on the ground of business necessity. For example, in Horrigan v Lewisham London Borough Council 1978 ICR 15, EAT, a driver transporting disabled people for the social services department ended his hours at 4.30 pm and did voluntary overtime after that. Often his rounds did not end until 6 pm. After giving notice that he would not do the overtime on a daily basis he was dismissed. The EAT held that the dismissal was fair. Although the overtime was non-contractual, the Council could not be expected to tolerate a situation of not knowing from one day to the next whether the employee would be available to work the overtime necessary to finish his rounds.

This contrasts with Steels v Goldsmith Garage Ltd EAT 467/87 where the **6.80** claimant, who had 20 years' service, suddenly refused to work on Saturday mornings, although he had done so for the past three years. This was due to a misunderstanding about safety factors. The employer dismissed him but the employee backtracked on realising that he had been dismissed. The tribunal found the dismissal fair because the employee was in breach of a contractual obligation. However, the EAT overruled this, saying that it was unfair to dismiss a man with 20 years' service who had never previously refused to work overtime and had indicated that he would work the shifts on learning that the alternative was dismissal.

Changing working hours **6.81**

Problems often occur when an employer seeks to introduce contractual overtime, or to alter working hours in some other way. A unilateral change in working hours will almost inevitably be a breach of contract. If the employer imposes the change and the employee resigns, the employee can then argue that

265

he or she has been constructively dismissed. In some circumstances, however, the employer may simply dismiss an employee who refuses to accept the change. In Davies v East Midland Motor Services Ltd t/a Stagecoach ET Case No.2801401/11, for example, D was dismissed when he refused to change his working hours from a regular 6 am to 2 pm shift to a rota pattern. D's contractual hours were not specified in writing, but a tribunal found that his regular shifts had become contractual by way of custom and practice. The employer's unilateral imposition of the rota pattern was in breach of contract and was unreasonable and its dismissal of D for his refusal to change his hours was therefore unfair.

But the fact that the employer is in the wrong contractually does not mean that the dismissal will necessarily be unfair. The tribunal will look to see whether the employer had sound business reasons for the change in hours and will consider whether the employer had adequately consulted the employee to see whether his or her objections to the change could be allayed. In many cases, dismissals in these circumstances may be fair for 'some other substantial reason' – see Chapter 8, 'Some other substantial reason'.

6.82 Refusal to retrain

If an employee refuses to retrain – when retraining is necessary to meet business contingencies or to improve the employee's performance – an employer may have no option but to dismiss.

Provided the retraining instruction is reasonable, dismissal may be fair even if there is no explicit warning of the consequences of non-compliance. In Jury v ECC Quarries Ltd EAT 241/80 the employee was dismissed when his employer's last HGV Class 3 vehicle went out of service. He had twice previously refused to train for Class 2 driving. The EAT held that the employee had refused to put himself in a position to drive other vehicles and although the offers of retraining were five and 12 months prior to dismissal the employee must have been aware he was putting his job at risk. Although he was not explicitly warned of dismissal, he ought to have understood that his job was in jeopardy as a result of his refusal. Similarly, in Minter v Wellingborough Foundries (BL Cars Ltd) EAT 105/80 it was fair for the employer to ask a professional employee – a nurse – to retrain, particularly as there were doubts about her capability, and it was fair to dismiss her when she refused without adequate reason.

6.83 Refusal to transfer

Dismissal for refusal to move to a different workplace frequently occurs where the employee's contract contains an express mobility clause that the employer is seeking to enforce. For instance, in Waton v Balfour Kilpatrick Ltd ET Case No.S/1172/90 W, an electrician, had an express mobility clause in his contract which said that he could be 'transferred to work on any job or site on which the company operates'. For 14 years W had worked in his native Scotland but he was dismissed when he refused to transfer to a job in England. Dismissal was fair, said a tribunal, because the mobility clause gave the employer a clear contractual right to move W. The tribunal thought that the employer was reasonable to enforce the clause because of the nature of the construction industry, the need for flexibility among staff and the common practice among builders of transferring their employees to different sites according to their needs.

However, because it is the reasonableness of the order that is important, dismissal of an employee can be unfair – even if the employer has a clear contractual right to transfer the employee. In Wilson v IDR Construction Ltd 1975 IRLR 260, ET, W refused to go to a new construction site on the following day, although the employer had a contractual right to order him to do so, and he was promptly dismissed. If the employer had investigated properly, it would have become clear that W was only refusing to move on that one day and that he had genuine reasons – his wife was ill and his car was being repaired. But W was not given a chance to explain and his dismissal was held to be unfair.

Thus, even when equipped with an unambiguous mobility clause, employers **6.84** should investigate the reasons underpinning an employee's refusal to transfer. They should also consider whether there are alternatives to relocating the employee. In Holman v Forestry Commission ET Case No.19474/86 a civil servant based in Cardiff was offered relocation to Edinburgh when his unit was closed down, but he had strong domestic reasons for wanting to stay in South Wales. He was dismissed for being in breach of a contractual mobility obligation after refusing to relocate. The tribunal found that the claimant was a loyal, efficient employee who had been doing some useful temporary work. It also noted that 13 posts at his grade had become available in South Wales. It thought that the employer had acted unreasonably in not waiting another six months; had this been done, there was a 50 per cent chance that a post could have been found for the employee.

Implied terms. Note that tribunals will imply reasonable terms even into **6.85** unambiguous express mobility clauses – United Bank Ltd v Akhtar 1989 IRLR 507, EAT. In that case A, a bank employee, worked in Leeds on a low salary. His contract contained a mobility clause which stated that he could be transferred to any of the bank's workplaces in the UK. A was told to move to the bank's Birmingham branch without notice. He was offered no relocation expenses and he refused on both financial and personal grounds (his wife had just suffered a miscarriage). He resigned and claimed unfair constructive dismissal. Before the tribunal, the bank argued that it could not have been in fundamental breach of A's contract and have constructively dismissed him because it had an absolute contractual right to transfer A and any payment of relocation expenses was purely discretionary. Mr Justice Knox, however, upheld

267

the tribunal's finding of unfair dismissal. He said that the operation of a contractual mobility clause was subject to three overriding implied terms:

- reasonable notice must be given before exercising the power to transfer an employee

- a mobility clause must be operated in such a way as to make it feasible. An employee should not be required to do something which was, in practice, impossible

- a mobility clause is subject to the general duty not to behave in a way likely to destroy mutual trust and confidence between employer and employee.

The EAT confirmed that it was impossible for A to move at short notice without relocation money and that the trust and confidence integral to the contract had been destroyed by the employer. The bank was in breach of the three overriding implied terms and A had thus been unfairly constructively dismissed. (If A had been expressly dismissed, it would have been the reasonableness of the employer's order that would have been crucial, not the contractual mobility clause, and it seems likely that the employer would have been held to have acted unreasonably in enforcing the clause.)

6.86 Refusing change in duties

Where an employee refuses to do a specific part of his or her job, or objects to a change in duties, the employer may be left with little alternative. In Hood v Scotsman Publications Ltd EAT 113/90, for example, H, a very senior journalist, had been working for The Scotsman for nearly 30 years. He was an assistant editor who primarily edited the letters page but was also a chief leader writer. When a new editor, L, arrived, he decided that the paper should feature obituaries and insisted that H edit the new service. H persistently refused – even though he had been relieved of most of his other duties so that he could devote his energies to the obituaries service. H believed that he was being sidelined into a dead-end job and he regarded it as a demotion. This dispute continued and L did make some concessions, but he eventually dismissed H for refusing to take on the obituaries service. The tribunal held that dismissal was a reasonable response: before L became editor it was reasonably common for employees to be moved into different areas and throughout his career H himself had done various jobs on the paper. The tribunal said that there was no evidence that he had been demoted and the right of the editor to implement editorial policy had to be recognised. The EAT upheld the tribunal's finding.

But contrast the following two cases:

- **Wiggins Teape Fine Papers Ltd v Murchison** EAT 322/89: M was dismissed for refusing to carry out stocktaking that he was contractually required to do. The EAT upheld the tribunal's finding of unfair dismissal. The tribunal took the view that dismissal was not a penalty open to the employer under the disciplinary procedure for M's offence. Furthermore, dismissal was excessive and unreasonable given the length of M's service, although he had contributed to his dismissal by 50 per cent

- **London Probation Board v Lee** EAT 0493/08: the employee was dismissed for refusing to carry out new duties following a transfer. He was asked to provide training for people but refused because he believed that they would then take over his own job. As a disciplinary sanction, he was moved to a different job at a different location. The employee objected to the transfer and, when he refused to perform his new duties, was dismissed. The tribunal found the dismissal unfair and the EAT agreed. Although his contract of employment contained a mobility clause, it did not permit the compulsory transfer to other duties. In any event, the use of any power to transfer as a disciplinary sanction was unlawful. The tribunal summarised the situation as follows: '[The employee] was given an unreasonable and unlawful order to move location and jobs and was then disciplined and dismissed for not having complied with that original unlawful order. No reasonable employer would act in such a manner.'

Short-term emergencies   6.87

Tribunals recognise that in times of emergency employers may have to ask employees to do work which they would not normally do. In Grigg v Daylay Eggs Ltd EAT 426/79 the EAT held that it was reasonable for the employer to expect a senior employee to help out in an emergency by working away from home for a fortnight, albeit in difficult conditions, and fair to dismiss him for refusing.

Similarly, in Tennent Caledonian Breweries Ltd v McKiddie EAT 674/86 M was a licensee of a pub that was owned by TCB Ltd. Following several disorderly incidents and allegations of widespread drug use on the premises, the Licensing Board called a hearing to decide whether M or the company could continue to hold a licence. M had not been present at the pub when some of the incidents occurred and the employer instructed him to stay on the premises seven days a week until the Licensing Board had made its decision. When the employer found out that he was not present as instructed, he was dismissed. The EAT overturned a tribunal decision that the dismissal was unfair and held that dismissal was within the range of reasonable responses. It said that the loss of the licence was a very serious matter and M had disobeyed a clear instruction given in a crisis situation.

Flouting specific instructions   6.88

As stated earlier (see 'Disobedience' above), tribunals will first consider whether the employer's instruction was legitimate and reasonable. In Payne v Spook Erection Ltd 1984 IRLR 219, EAT, an employee was unfairly dismissed for refusing to operate a system designed to keep tabs on the workforce. The EAT

269

held that the scheme was 'obviously and intolerably unfair' and 'wholly unacceptable as a matter of good industrial relations practice' and the employee could not reasonably be expected to implement it.

Furthermore, an employer cannot reasonably ask an employee to do a dishonest or illegal act, even though it ostensibly falls within the scope of the employer's powers. Thus in Morrish v Henlys (Folkestone) Ltd 1973 ICR 482, NIRC, an employee's dismissal for refusing to connive at falsification of company records was unfair. However, the fact that the employee doubts the legality of the employer's instruction will not necessarily mean that dismissal for refusal to comply with it will be unfair. In Barton v Royal Borough of Greenwich EAT 0041/14 B informed the Information Commissioner's Office (ICO) of a suspected data security breach by a member of his employer's management and only reported the issue to his line manager after contacting the ICO. The employer informed B that it would investigate the issue and instructed him not to contact the ICO again while its investigation was ongoing unless he had his manager's permission. B was dismissed after he called the ICO to question whether the employer was entitled to issue such an instruction. The EAT upheld a tribunal decision to reject B's unfair dismissal and whistleblowing claims. B's communications with the ICO did not amount to protected disclosures and, in any event, the reason for dismissal was B's misconduct in flouting the employer's specific instruction. On appeal, B sought to argue that the employer's instruction was unlawful and this meant that dismissal for refusal to comply with it was unfair. The EAT refused to consider this argument as it had not been raised before the tribunal, but commented that it would have found that the instruction was not unlawful in any event. It was a temporary and conditional limitation on B's contact with the ICO that the tribunal had considered reasonable for the employer to impose. Furthermore, the EAT commented, whether or not an instruction was lawful is a relevant, but not a decisive, consideration when assessing the reasonableness of dismissal.

6.89 Tribunals will look at the way an employer has handled wilful or persistent disobedience of specific orders in deciding whether a dismissal was fair. As the EAT said in Kaye v Blackwell (Contracts) Ltd EAT 765/78, 'there may be circumstances where, there having been several requests followed by a repeated and settled refusal to do the work, it is right and proper for the employer to dismiss albeit there has been no previous written or oral warning'.

Wilful disobedience will not always merit dismissal, however. In Bluemink Ltd t/a Caledonia Crane Hire v Thomson EAT 291/85 the employee was unfairly dismissed for refusing to come to work one morning because of a hangover. The EAT held that such misconduct was only one of the material considerations the tribunal had to consider. Others included the employee's previous good conduct.

Flouting company rules/working practices   6.90

In Ladbroke Racing Ltd v Arnott and ors 1983 IRLR 154, Ct Sess (Inner House), the Court of Session stated that dismissal for breach of a company rule is not necessarily fair – it still has to be decided whether dismissal was a reasonable response to the particular breach. Similarly, an 'automatic' dismissal for breaching company rules was held to be unfair in Marks and Spencer plc v O'Connell EAT 230/95. In that case the employer failed to consider the circumstances surrounding an employee's breach of the smoking regulations.

One issue that may be relevant to the question of fairness is whether or not the employee was aware of the rule in question. In Donachie v Allied Suppliers Ltd EAT 46/80 the EAT held that it was unreasonable to dismiss an employee for failure to comply with a material term of the contract of which he was unaware and of which he could not reasonably have been aware. In Amachree v Wandsworth Borough Council ET Case No.2328606/09 A was dismissed for discussing issues of religious belief during an interview with a service user – which prompted the service user to complain – and then disclosing confidential information about the service user to the press in breach of the employer's instruction to keep the matter confidential. The tribunal found the dismissal fair in the round, noting that A had been well aware of the employer's rules concerning confidentiality. However, it commented that if A's sole offence had been the discussion of religion, this might not have founded a fair dismissal because there were no set guidelines and A was not aware of the employer having a rule dealing with such matters.

Minor, one-off or first breaches of company rules. In Lock v Cardiff Railway   6.91
Company Ltd 1998 IRLR 358, EAT, the claimant was dismissed for asking a teenage passenger on his train to leave because he did not have a ticket or the money to pay the fare. The boy was left in a strange area with no means of getting home. The dismissal was found to be unfair because it was a one-off act of misjudgement and the employee had never been warned that dismissal could result.

However, there may be circumstances where single breaches of the rules may found a fair dismissal. This was the case in AAH Pharmaceuticals v Carmichael EAT 0325/03, where the employee was found to have been fairly dismissed for breaching company rules on leaving drugs in his delivery van overnight. The EAT commented: 'In any particular case, exceptions can be imagined where, for example, the penalty of dismissal might not be imposed, but equally, in our judgment, when a breach of a necessarily strict rule has been properly proved, exceptional service, previous long service and/or previous good conduct may properly not be considered sufficient to reduce a penalty of dismissal.' Similarly, in Noor v Metroline Travel Ltd EAT 0059/14 N was fairly dismissed for a first offence of covering up the CCTV camera on the bus he was driving. The employer's policy on the importance of CCTV was well-publicised and made it

271

clear that covering the camera would be viewed as gross misconduct. N's grief at the news of his brother's recent death did not explain his actions and the employer was entitled to treat the incident seriously. The EAT took the view that dismissal may have been a harsh response, but the tribunal had been entitled to find that it fell within the range of reasonable responses.

6.92 In Bryant v Sage Care Homes Ltd EAT 0453/11 B, an experienced nurse, was dismissed after she failed to report, and record, a drug error in breach of Nursing and Midwifery Council (NMC) guidelines and to appreciate the seriousness of her omission. The EAT held that the dismissal was fair and rejected her submission that the decision by the NMC's Conduct and Competence Committee not to proceed with 'fitness to practice' proceedings against her affected the reasonableness of the employer's decision to dismiss. The NMC discharged a very different function from that of the employer: the former considered whether, in the light of the drug error and the whole of her 44-year career, she remained fit to practise as a nurse, whereas the latter looked at whether it should dismiss her from her employment for misconduct committed by breaching professional guidelines. In any event, the employer could not be expected to delay a decision on the employee's future until the professional body had reached its own conclusion – which, in this case, was not until 16 months after B's dismissal.

6.93 **Repeated refusals to comply with company rules/working practices.** Tribunals are increasingly being asked to rule on cases where employees refuse to perform a particular aspect of their overall duties, often for religious reasons. For instance, there was the well-publicised case of the Christian registrar – Islington London Borough Council v Ladele 2010 ICR 532, CA – who was subjected to disciplinary proceedings when she refused to conduct civil partnerships. She complained that the Council's treatment of her constituted unlawful discrimination on the ground of her religion or belief. Although this argument initially succeeded before the tribunal, both the EAT and the Court of Appeal held that she had not been discriminated against and that, accordingly, her various claims failed.

Although unfair dismissal law played no role in the Ladele case (in which the claimant remained a Council employee), it is worth noting that this type of case could throw up questions of whether the employer can fairly dismiss the employee – either expressly or constructively – in these circumstances. In McFarlane v Relate Avon Ltd 2010 ICR 507, EAT, for example, the employee's discrimination claim was accompanied by a claim for unfair constructive dismissal. In that case, McF objected, on religious grounds, to providing sex therapy to same-sex couples. With regard to the unfair dismissal claim, RA Ltd argued that it had been reasonable to dismiss McF on the basis that he had given an assurance that he would work with same-sex clients, and thus comply with RA Ltd's equal opportunity and ethical practice policies, when in fact he had no intention of doing so. This argument failed before the tribunal because it found that McF had never actually given such an assurance. As a result, the employer had no reasonable belief that gross misconduct had been committed. However, RA Ltd succeeded with the alternative argument that this was a dismissal for 'some other substantial reason' (SOSR) and that it was reasonable for it to dismiss an employee who was, to put it no higher, equivocal about his willingness to conduct himself in accordance with principles which – legitimately, as the tribunal had held – RA Ltd regarded as of fundamental importance. This finding was upheld by the EAT on appeal.

Although the employee's dismissal was found to have been fair for SOSR, it **6.94** seems that similar considerations would have applied if the employer had been entitled to proceed with the 'conduct' ground for dismissal – i.e. on the basis that the employee had given an unequivocal assurance that he would abide by the employer's equal opportunity and ethical practice policies. In other words, that dismissal in these circumstances would, subject to any mitigating factors, have been a reasonable response to the employee's refusal to act in accordance with his assurance.

Disobedience for health and safety reasons **6.95**

Employees sometimes refuse to carry out instructions because of health and safety fears. It is automatically unfair for an employer to dismiss an employee for an 'inadmissible reason' relating to health and safety under S.100 ERA (see Chapter 10, 'Health and safety dismissals'). In other words, the question of reasonableness does not arise. However, dismissals for health and safety reasons that fall outside the scope of S.100 are governed by the ordinary rules contained in S.98. In particular, the tribunal has to decide whether or not the employer acted reasonably in dismissing. It is an implied term in contracts of employment that the employer will provide employees with a safe system of work and take reasonable care for their safety. As part of this duty, employers must investigate 'promptly and sensibly' all bona fide complaints about safety drawn to their attention by employees – British Aircraft Corporation Ltd v Austin 1978 IRLR 332, EAT. Failure to do so may entitle an employee to terminate his or her contract and claim unfair constructive dismissal.

In addition, employers are subject to numerous statutory health and safety regulations. However, because the crucial factor in unfair dismissal cases is the reasonableness of the employer's actions, its contractual and statutory health and safety obligations, although relevant, are not conclusive. In most cases tribunals will not need to make a finding on whether these statutory obligations have been contravened. Instead they will need to consider whether adequate precautions have been taken to ensure employees' safety and, if not, whether it was practicable to take such precautions. As a result, an employer could be in breach of a statutory duty regarding health and safety, but dismissal for an employee's refusal to work may still be fair.

273

6.96 This point is well illustrated by Lindsay v Dunlop Ltd 1980 IRLR 93, EAT, where L was employed in the tyres curing section, where hot rubber tyres gave off fumes thought to be toxic. The employer was aware that there was no efficient local ventilation and so asked the employees to wear masks as a temporary measure pending a report from the Health and Safety Commission. Most employees accepted this but L did not and, when he persisted in refusing to work in the area until the fumes were dispersed, he was dismissed. A tribunal held that the dismissal was fair but L appealed on the grounds that the employer was in breach of the statutory duty under S.63 of the Factories Act 1961 and also the common law duty to provide a safe system of work. The EAT rejected L's appeal, holding that, although a tribunal may consider the employer's legal obligations when deciding whether the dismissal was reasonable, it was unnecessary to make findings on whether or not such obligations had been complied with. The EAT found that, although L had a genuine fear of injury from the fumes, the employer did not act unreasonably in requiring him to wear a mask while further advice was sought – especially since his fellow employees had agreed to work under those conditions.

The Lindsay case should be contrasted with Smith Anderson and Co Ltd v MacGregor EAT 369/89, where M worked for 12-hour shifts on machinery that generated great heat and gave him throat infections. M complained about the conditions and the lack of ventilation in the workroom. The employees were not meant to leave the room during working hours and M was dismissed when he was seen outside the workroom four times during a shift. The EAT upheld the tribunal's finding that the employer had acted unreasonably. The instruction that M should not go outside the room during the shift was not reasonable in view of the conditions in the room and the need for the employees to get occasional breaths of fresh air.

6.97 **Investigating complaints.** If an employee objects to his or her working conditions, the employer should investigate the matter promptly and communicate its findings to the employee. If an employer jumps the gun and dismisses an employee for refusing to work when there are unresolved health and safety complaints, dismissal is likely to be unfair. This was the situation in Heaps, Collis and Harrison Ltd t/a Air Power Centre v Burt EAT 173/99, where the employee raised concerns about the levels of radioactivity on a barge on which he was working. His grievance had not been finally disposed of at the time of his suspension and summary dismissal. The EAT upheld the tribunal's finding of unfair dismissal on the ground that the employer had been unduly precipitate.

6.98 ## Disloyalty

Every employment contract contains an implied term of fidelity and good faith, which means that the employee must not act in a manner contrary to the interests of the employer. Apart from underlining the element of personal commitment to the employer essential in an employment context, the term may also apply outside strict working hours. It exists for so long as the employment subsists, whether or not the employee is actually turning up to work, and may continue after employment has been terminated.

Dismissal 6.99
Breach of the implied duty of fidelity and good faith will normally entitle the employer to dismiss the employee summarily for gross misconduct at common law – Boston Deep Sea Fishing and Ice Co v Ansell 1888 39 ChD 339, CA. A single act of misconduct will suffice where it is 'serious, wilful and obvious' and strikes at the root of the contract of employment – Bishop v Graham Group plc EAT 800/98. However, a breach of this term (or, indeed, an express 'loyalty' clause) will not necessarily render the dismissal fair under the ERA. The test that tribunals apply is not whether the employee was in breach of contract, but whether the employer acted reasonably in all the circumstances in dismissing the employee for being in breach.

A tribunal will consider whether the employer had a genuine and reasonable belief, based on reasonable investigation, that the employee was in breach of the duty of fidelity. Dismissal on the ground of suspicion alone will only be justifiable where that suspicion is great and the anticipated loss to the company large – but in such cases the dismissal would be for 'some other substantial reason', not conduct, said the EAT in S and U Stores Ltd v Bessant EAT 8/82 (see further Chapter 8, 'Some other substantial reason'). However, in the vast majority of cases there must be sufficient evidence to sustain a reasonable belief in the employee's guilt. If this is established, the tribunal must go on to consider whether the employer acted reasonably in dismissing. Different considerations will apply depending on the nature of the breach.

Dismissal for breach of the implied term of fidelity normally arises where 6.100 the employee:

- discloses confidential information

- competes, or prepares to compete, with the employer, or

- 'moonlights' outside of working hours.

Disclosure of confidential information 6.101
Where employees have access to confidential information and trade secrets, there is an implied duty not to use that information except for the purposes authorised by the employer. In Monk v Vine Products EAT 248/79 the employee, a personnel and training manager, disclosed to shop stewards some figures for proposed wage increases, forcing the company to conclude a productivity deal different from that which it had intended. When the company was again disadvantaged by similar incidents, the managing director lost confidence in the

275

employee and dismissed him. The EAT upheld the tribunal's decision that it was fair to do so.

Dismissal for the misuse or leaking of confidential information will usually fall within the range of reasonable responses – provided the employer has carried out a reasonable investigation and taken account of any mitigating factors. The importance of the information involved may be relevant to the tribunal's considerations. For example, trivial information leaked accidentally, or without gain in mind, may not give grounds for a fair dismissal – see, for example, Sullivan v Associated Heat Services Ltd ET Case No.5985/80. Indeed, the leaking of quite important and sensitive information may not justify dismissal if the employee did so unintentionally. In Steadman v Department for Work and Pensions ET Case No.1102513/10 S, a compliance officer at a Job Centre, was found to have been unfairly dismissed following a complaint that a customer's personal information had been produced in a court case. The employer's investigation revealed that S had accessed and printed the customer's records at the relevant time but could not explain how the documents came into the possession of a third party. S maintained that she had the documents on her desk and that they must have been taken while she was distracted. The tribunal held that S had breached the employer's rules on confidentiality and its clear desk policy but it was not possible to establish that S had done so deliberately, as opposed to merely recklessly. The employer's procedure categorised recklessness as 'misconduct' rather than 'gross misconduct' and, in view of S's 29 years of good service and the fact that the employer had allowed her to continue working for several months after the incident in question (indicating that it had not, in fact, lost trust and confidence in her), dismissal was outside the range of reasonable responses.

6.102 The purpose for which the information is used may also be taken into account. In Williams v Wrexham Maelor Hospital NHS Trust ET Case No.26079/96, for example, W was dismissed for obtaining the name and address of a patient from hospital records to enable her to pursue a claim for industrial injury with the Department of Social Security (now part of the Department for Work and Pensions). The tribunal found that dismissal was outside the range of reasonable responses because of W's clean disciplinary record and long service, and the employer's failure to take account of the purpose for which W had acquired the information.

6.103 **Public interest.** It is arguable that an employee dismissed for disclosing confidential information may be able to challenge the fairness of his or her dismissal on the basis that the disclosure was in the public interest. In Veitch v Broadgate Farm Cooperative Ltd ET Case No.2505366/01, for example, a care worker was dismissed for breaching her duty of confidentiality to someone in her care. The employee told a colleague that a volunteer worker she was allowing to use machinery was suffering from a depressive illness, had declined to take his medication and was prone to impulsive behaviour. The tribunal acknowledged her duty of confidentiality but said that serious consequences could follow when professionals fail to share information with those who 'need to know'. The dismissal was therefore unfair.

However, tribunals are not always so sympathetic to employees who claim to have acted in the public interest. In Byford v Film Finances Ltd EAT 804/86 the employee suspected that the directors of the company were carrying out illegal activities in connection with share transfers. She leaked confidential information to the minority shareholders of the company, who commenced legal action as a result. The EAT upheld the tribunal's decision that the employer had no option but to dismiss an employee who had gone behind her employer's back and been deceitful.

6.104 Note that certain disclosures are protected by law under S.103A ERA, which states that an employee who is dismissed for making a protected disclosure will be treated as automatically unfairly dismissed – for details see IDS Employment Law Handbook, 'Whistleblowing at Work' (2013), Chapter 6, 'Dismissal'.

6.105 **Risk of disclosure of confidential information.** Dismissal of an employee who has a close relative or associate working for a competitor may be fair for SOSR if there is a conflict of interest or a real risk of trade secrets or confidential information being disclosed (even accidentally) as a result (see Chapter 8, 'Some other substantial reason'). Every case turns on its facts and much will depend on the position of both individuals, the level of access they have to confidential information and the importance of that information – Skyrail Oceanic Ltd v Coleman 1980 ICR 596, EAT.

6.106 **Competing and preparing to compete**
Employees who actively compete with their employers will be in breach of the implied duty of fidelity. The general rule here is that an employer is entitled to defend itself against unfair competition and to take whatever reasonable steps are necessary in order to achieve that end – RS Components Ltd v Irwin 1973 ICR 535, NIRC. The breach of trust does not have to result in severe damage for dismissal to be fair. What is important is the actual breach itself and not the extent of loss. In Mansard Precision Engineering Co Ltd v Taylor and anor 1978 ICR 44, EAT, the EAT held that two senior employees concerned in establishing a business in competition with their employer were fairly dismissed for breach of trust, even though the damage caused was slight. 'Once it is recognised,' the EAT said, 'as it must be, that there has to be mutual confidence and trust, the mere fact that it is breached at all seems to us to be a perfectly justifiable, reasonable and sufficient reason for the employer to say, "I no longer have trust in you, I no longer have confidence in you. You must go".'

Conversely, a mere desire on the part of the employee to 'go it alone', absent any concrete steps in that direction having been taken, is unlikely to adversely

277

affect the employer's trust in the employee so as to justify the drastic sanction of dismissal. In Crowther v David Hayton Ltd ET Case No.2513952/10 C told his employer he wished to set up in business on his own, but said that it could be weeks or even months before he did so. The employer asked C to think about resigning, as it considered there to be a conflict of interest. When C said he had decided not to resign, he was dismissed for gross misconduct and a conflict of interest. C successfully claimed unfair dismissal. The tribunal held that there was no evidence that C had taken customer information for his own purposes, or taken any other steps that crossed a line and amounted to a breach of trust and confidence.

6.107 It will be apparent from the above that a mere *intention* to set up in competition is not in itself a breach of the implied contractual duty of loyalty and fidelity justifying dismissal – to breach the duty the employee's acts must go beyond this. In Laughton and anor v Bapp Industrial Supplies Ltd 1986 ICR 634, EAT, the EAT took the view that, in the absence of an express term that is not in restraint of trade, there must be some evidence that the employee had done or was about to do some wrongful act – for example, misuse confidential information. There, two employees of a nuts and bolts manufacturer were summarily dismissed when their employer discovered that in their spare time they had written to ten of their employer's suppliers informing them of their intention to start up their own business and asking for lists of the suppliers' products and prices. The EAT held that the dismissals were unfair. It pointed out that the employees had not misused confidential information or otherwise abused their position. Their contact with the suppliers amounted to a mere enquiry. Moreover, the employees were still devoting their working time and talents to their employer's business.

The Laughton case should not be seen as a green light to employees to pursue their competitive plans while still employed. The case turned very much on its own facts and a different tribunal might have construed the approach made by the employees to the suppliers as solicitation of the employee's suppliers, which would have been a breach of the implied duty of fidelity – see 'Soliciting customers or suppliers' below. Nevertheless, the case does establish the principle that it is not in itself gross misconduct for an employee to make preparations for a future business to be conducted after his or her employment with the current employer has terminated.

6.108 This point was made by the EAT in Khan and anor v Landsker Child Care Ltd EAT 0036/12, in which it held that the employer's discovery of a business plan for a new business that would be in competition with its own did not automatically reveal gross misconduct. In that case, two colleagues had written a business plan to attract investment to set up residential care homes that would be in competition with those of their employer. When the employer discovered the plan, it dismissed them for gross misconduct on the basis that they were planning to set up in business in competition, using the employer's resources to assist them. The employment tribunal dismissed the employees' unfair dismissal claims, rejecting their argument that the plan was 'just an idea' and did not signal a serious intention to set up their own business. On appeal, the EAT held that the tribunal had failed to address – following Laughton and anor v Bapp Industrial Supplies Ltd (above) – the question of whether the employees' future intention to compete in itself constituted gross misconduct. It had also failed to provide evidence of, or to analyse, what resources had been used, and whether the information contained therein could properly be described as confidential, or was simply the kind of knowledge and expertise that a person in the claimants' position would have accumulated over the number of years that he or she had been employed. The case was remitted to the tribunal to consider these matters.

Two examples where the employees' preparatory activities *did* go beyond a mere intention to compete and thus justified dismissal: **6.109**

- **Marshall v Industrial Systems and Control Ltd** 1992 IRLR 294, EAT: M, the managing director of ISC Ltd, formed a business plan with another manager to commence business in competition with ISC Ltd and, in particular, to obtain distribution rights from ISC Ltd's major client. They approached a third senior employee and invited him to join them. The EAT held that M's summary dismissal for gross misconduct was fair. This was not simply a matter of forming an intention to compete in the future, as was the position in Laughton and anor v Bapp Industrial Supplies Ltd (above), since M had formed a concrete plan to obtain business from his employer's best client and had taken steps towards fulfilling that objective

- **Adamson v B and L Cleaning Services Ltd** 1995 IRLR 193, EAT: A was a foreman for a contract cleaning company. When the contract on which he was working came up for renewal, he informed his employer that he had asked for himself to be put on the tender list. The employer dismissed him when he refused to withdraw his tender. The EAT held that the dismissal was fair. The employee had not merely been testing the market with a view to competing with the employer; he had approached a customer with the intention of taking work and revenue away from his employer.

In general, the more concrete the preparatory steps taken, the more likely it is that the employee will have breached his or her duty of fidelity. However, whatever the circumstances, the employer should always investigate the matter and give the employee the opportunity to put his or her case before resorting to dismissal. Employees might change their minds if faced with the prospect of being dismissed before they are ready to start out on their own. It is always a question of fact whether or not an opportunity to cancel plans would have made a difference, and a warning should always be given if the employee's preparations are far from maturity – Ladbroke Racing Ltd v Mason and anor 1978 ICR 49, EAT.

279

6.110 Where an employer is aware that employees are aiding competitors, then it is important not to ignore such behaviour. In Thorn (UK) Ltd v Little EAT 455/95 L was employed as a service engineer. It was common practice for the service engineers to hand out the business cards of competitors when the customers' machines were not covered by a warranty. T (UK) Ltd was aware of this practice but had done nothing to stop it. L was dismissed after a customer complained about receiving one of the business cards. The EAT upheld the tribunal's finding of unfair dismissal on the ground, inter alia, that the employer had failed to take any steps to stamp out what was a very old practice. Possible steps could involve surveillance, although employers should use a degree of caution before resorting to such tactics. However, in Haynes and anor v Daimler Chrysler (UK) Ltd t/a Mercedes Benz and ors ET Case No.2302821/02 the tribunal rejected an argument that in instructing private detectives to keep employees' homes under surveillance, the employer had in any way breached their human rights. The employer suspected that the employees might be working in competition by servicing and repairing cars for their own benefit and the surveillance revealed details of deliveries of motor parts and evidence of an employee test-driving customers' cars, which was strictly forbidden under company rules. The resulting dismissals were fair.

Note that simply seeking work with a competitor, or giving notice to work for one, is not generally an admissible reason for dismissal – unless there are grounds for believing that the employee was intending to abuse his or her confidential position and information – Harris and Russell Ltd v Slingsby 1973 ICR 454, NIRC.

6.111 **Soliciting customers or suppliers.** It is well established that soliciting an employer's customers for the employee's own benefit, or for the benefit of a third party, will merit dismissal. Nonetheless, employers must not act without having carried out a proper investigation and given the employee a chance to explain. In Baxter v Wreyfield EAT 9/82, for example, the employer dismissed B without investigating further a customer's complaint that she had been approached about transferring her custom to a new business to be started by B and her husband. The EAT found that in light of the facts known to the employer at the time, dismissal was unfair. However, since the evidence disclosed that the employee was in fact guilty of misconduct that would justify dismissal, no compensation was awarded.

6.112 **Poaching staff/offering work to other employees.** There are differing views on whether an employee who invites or persuades other employees to join him or her in a competing business is in breach of the implied duty of fidelity. In Marshall v Industrial Systems and Control Ltd (above) M had drafted a business plan with another senior manager and together they had approached a third senior employee and invited him to join them. The EAT held that M had breached the duty of fidelity and that his subsequent summary dismissal was fair. By contrast, in Tithebarn Ltd v Hubbard EAT 532/89 H, a senior sales trainer, told P, another employee, that he intended to leave T Ltd and set up his own competing business and invited P to join him. The EAT held that H's actions did not amount to a breach of his implied duty of fidelity and his dismissal was therefore unfair. H had merely carried out preparatory acts and had simply invited P to work for him in due course.

'Moonlighting' 6.113

Taking a job outside working hours is not in itself a breach of the implied duty of fidelity, even where that job involves working for a competitor. The general rule at common law is that, in the absence of an express term, employees are free to do what they want during their off-duty hours provided that these activities do not interfere with or harm the employer's legitimate business interests – Hivac Ltd v Park Royal Scientific Instruments Ltd 1946 1 Ch 169, CA. In determining whether the damage to the employer is such as to breach the employee's implied obligation of fidelity, regard will be had to the type of work involved, the position of the employee within the employer's organisation, the employee's hours of work, and the risk and extent of potential commercial harm to the employer.

Similar factors are taken into consideration when a tribunal considers the fairness of a dismissal for moonlighting. If spare-time working is directly damaging to the employer's interests, or creates a risk of serious harm, it may rank as straightforward gross misconduct and justify dismissal. Thus, employees who possess valuable commercial skills or have access to trade secrets will obviously have to be careful. So too will employees whose work is such that it cannot be properly performed if they engage in extra-mural activities. For example, it would be improper for a solicitor's trainee to work for another solicitor in his or her spare time. There might be a real risk of embarrassment to the main employer if the trainee were asked to act for a client in his or her spare time who was the opposing party in a case in which the main employer was engaged. In this situation there would be a genuine conflict of interest and a dismissal would probably be fair, provided the appropriate procedures had been followed.

As not all spare-time work, even for a competitor, will breach the implied term 6.114 of fidelity, employers should tread cautiously before dismissing employees for engaging in spare-time work which does not harm their business interests. Two examples:

- **Nova Plastics Ltd v Froggatt** 1982 IRLR 146, EAT: F, an odd-job man, did spare-time work for a rival company which did not greatly affect his employer. The EAT thought the tribunal was entitled to conclude that he was not in breach of trust simply because he happened to work for a competitor in his spare time. The nature of F's work was such that it could not possibly

281

amount to any serious aid to the rival as a competitor. His dismissal was therefore unfair

- **EETPU v Parnham and anor** EAT 378/78: Mr and Mrs P worked as kitchen assistant and cook at a trade union conference centre. Mrs P obtained a weekend job at a café and the couple were promptly dismissed for disloyalty. The EAT upheld a tribunal's finding that dismissal of the husband and wife was unfair. Mrs P's spare-time job had done nothing to harm the employer's interests. In addition, the employer had failed to warn them or give them a chance to explain, or even to provide an adequate grievance procedure.

Employers who dismiss on the ground that spare-time work is damaging their business interests must be sure of their ground. This means that they must carry out a reasonable investigation in order to satisfy themselves that an employee's outside activities pose a threat to or undermine their business interests – EETPU v Parnham and anor (above). In Scottish Daily Record and Sunday Mail (1986) Ltd v Laird 1996 IRLR 665, Ct Sess (Inner House), L was the editor of a newspaper whose employment contract expressly prohibited him from having any interest in any competing business. He was dismissed when his employer discovered that he was involved in the publication of two free regional newspapers. A tribunal held that the dismissal was unfair, pointing out that the employer had made no enquiries into the circulation of the two free newspapers, the area which the papers covered or their advertising rates. Had the employer done so, it would have become clear that the employee's outside interests were of a relatively minor nature which could cause only minimal harm to his employer. The Court of Session agreed that no reasonable employer would have dismissed without making proper enquiries as to the extent and circumstances of L's involvement with the other newspapers.

6.115   In certain circumstances spare-time work may not harm the employer's business interests, but a dismissal may be rendered fair because of other aspects of the employee's conduct. In Casson v John Lewis and Co Ltd EAT 266/77, for example, a manager failed to inform the employer of her own outside business activities as required by the rules, and then lied about it. Her dismissal was fair even though her extra-curricular activities did the employer no harm and were quite unconnected with the business.

Similarly, in Enterprise Liverpool plc v Bauress and anor EAT 0645/05 B and E were discovered using their employer's van and materials to moonlight during working hours while they should have been carrying out work for one of the employer's clients. The tribunal found that their subsequent dismissals were unfair: another employee, who was also found to have been moonlighting during working hours, had not been dismissed. On appeal, however, the EAT overturned the tribunal's decision, holding that the employer had fairly dismissed in this case. It accepted that, in the absence of an established policy for dealing with this particular type of misconduct, the employer's decision not to dismiss an employee created a benchmark or point of reference against which the standards of a reasonable employer could thereafter be tested. Where the employer subsequently imposed a more serious disciplinary sanction in any case of sufficiently similar misconduct, the tribunal must ask itself whether the employer had good reason for departing from the set benchmark. With this in mind, the EAT held that there were good reasons for treating B and E differently from the other employee, who had been issued with a final written warning for the same offence. First, B and E had maintained, throughout the disciplinary process, that they had prior permission from their supervisor to be where they were, which was not true; the other employee, on the other hand, had immediately admitted his guilt. Secondly, the other employee had 30 years' good service, whereas B and E had just finished their apprenticeships. The EAT held that it fell within the band of reasonable responses to regard these as sufficient reasons to depart from the benchmark.

Express 'loyalty' terms

6.116

Employers may enlarge and extend the basic duty of fidelity by including an express provision in the employment contract restricting breach of confidentiality, competition or even simply other work without written permission. On the whole, decisions in cases where such terms exist tend to go against the employee who flouts them. For example, in Winder v Commissioners of Inland Revenue ET Case No.1101770/97 W was dismissed for writing to a political organisation offering to reveal sensitive information. The employer's rules prohibited misuse of information acquired in the course of employment. Although no disclosure had taken place, the tribunal found that the employer was entitled to conclude that the offer was a breach of the duty to maintain confidence contained in the standing rules.

However, the existence of express terms is by no means decisive. Broad general clauses prohibiting any other engagement are probably too vague and sweeping to justify dismissal for participating in a completely different occupation outside working hours. In Barratt v Co-operative Insurance Society Ltd ET Case No.9436/82, for example, B was an insurance agent whose contract prohibited him from engaging 'in any other occupation'. He inherited a life interest in a run-down pub from his mother and gave his wife some help in sorting out the business. The employer dismissed him after hearing about this. A tribunal found that the dismissal was unfair. The contractual term was vague, there had been no adequate investigation and B's interest in the pub was probably not an 'occupation' anyway.

Refusal to agree to restrictive covenants

6.117

Employers often try to protect their business interests by means of a restrictive covenant in their employees' contracts of employment, or in separate 'non-competition' or 'non-disclosure' agreements. Where an employee refuses to

283

accept such a covenant, dismissal for that refusal may potentially be fair for 'some other substantial reason'. This is discussed in Chapter 8, 'Some other substantial reason', under 'Protecting employers' interests'.

6.118 Unauthorised use of computers

Given the widespread use of the internet and e-mail at work, employers would be well advised to put in place rules regarding their use. This is particularly important as e-mails sent from work accounts can expose the company to liability for discrimination and/or defamation. As is the case with all disciplinary rules, it is important that employees are made aware of them and told that dismissal can result from breach.

Acas has produced an advice leaflet, 'Internet and e-mail policies', which gives guidance on how to draw up an effective computer-use policy. It stresses the importance of tailoring the policy to the needs and the culture of the individual workplace, clearly setting out the permitted uses of IT equipment at work as well as outlining the consequences of breach. The policy should also expressly identify any monitoring or interception that might be lawfully undertaken and the reasons for such monitoring so as to ensure compliance with the employer's obligations under the Data Protection Act 1998 (DPA). The DPA does not prohibit monitoring but, as explained at Part 3 of the Information Commissioner's Employment Practices Code, 'any adverse impact of monitoring on individuals must be justified by the benefits to the employer and others'. This is also an area where human rights law may come into play, notably Article 8 (the right to respect for private and family life) and Article 10 (the right to freedom of expression) of the European Convention on Human Rights. These provisions are discussed briefly under 'Sending offensive images or jokes' and 'Social networking and blogging' below. A more general discussion of the relevance of human rights law to the fairness of dismissals is included in Chapter 3, 'Unfairness', under 'Impact of Human Rights Act'.

Below, we discuss the most common types of unauthorised use of computers in – or connected to – the workplace that may, after a reasonable investigation, result in a fair dismissal.

6.119 Accessing pornographic material
Unless it is of an obscene nature, the mere downloading of 'ordinary' pornography by an employee at work will not necessarily be regarded by an employment tribunal as amounting to gross misconduct justifying summary dismissal. However, if employees have been informed as part of a computer-use policy that downloading, viewing or circulating pornography at work will be regarded as a dismissible offence, it is likely to be fair – subject to proper investigation and disciplinary procedures – to dismiss an employee, even for a first offence. Contrast the following two cases:

- **London Borough of Hillingdon v Thomas** EAT 1317/01: the EAT overturned the tribunal's finding that the summary dismissal of T for accessing pornography using the employer's facilities and during work time was unfair. The categorisation of the offence as gross misconduct was within the range of reasonable responses. Although the employer had no IT policy in place and the disciplinary procedure generally characterised this type of conduct as misconduct and not gross misconduct, the disciplinary procedure went on to state that it may be viewed as gross misconduct 'according to the circumstances or the position which the employee held'

- **Royal Bank of Scotland v Goudie** EAT 0693/03: G was disciplined and dismissed for breaching the employer's IT security policy by sending via external e-mail certain images that the employer considered pornographic. The bank used an internal matrix to categorise images it considered offensive. Categories in the mid-range could be considered as either gross misconduct or misconduct. The matrix also set out certain mitigating factors that might be taken into account. However, the matrix was not disclosed to G and she did not have the opportunity to test the application of the criteria to the circumstances of her case during the disciplinary process. The EAT upheld the finding of a tribunal that her dismissal was unfair. The matrix had a direct impact on the outcome of the disciplinary process and it was clearly important for the employee to be aware of how the employer graded the material and the sanctions it applied, and the possible mitigating factors.

6.120 Even where there is evidence that the employee has accessed pornographic material on a work computer in clear breach of the computer-use policy, an employer who fails to conduct a reasonable investigation into the incident will struggle to defend an unfair dismissal claim. In particular, the employer should not be distracted by the 'conduct' label into thinking that no medical evidence needs to be considered where the employee relies on a medical condition to explain or excuse his or her misconduct. In City of Edinburgh Council v Dickson EATS 0038/09 the employee, who was employed as a community learning and development worker, was found in the school's community computer suite watching pornographic images. A disciplinary investigation revealed that on the same morning he had visited a magazine website containing inappropriate sexual imagery. The employee said that he had no recollection of either incident but, if they had occurred, his behaviour must have been the result of a hypoglycaemic episode caused by his diabetes. At the disciplinary hearing, the employee's explanation for his behaviour was rejected and he was summarily dismissed. An employment tribunal found that the employee had been unfairly dismissed and the EAT agreed. The employer had rejected his explanation without investigating or understanding his medical condition (he had type 1 diabetes, which was poorly controlled). Furthermore, it had taken into account the uninformed opinion of a third party – namely, the HR adviser's pharmacist wife – and dismissed the informed opinion of the employer's

285

occupational health doctor. By rejecting evidence that was capable of explaining the employee's behaviour and memory loss, the employer had come to a decision that no reasonable employer could have reached.

Furthermore, where managers adopt an attitude that appears to conflict with the employer's otherwise clear computer-use policy, the fairness of a dismissal for breach of that policy may be called into question. In Caller v Newham University Hospital ET Case No.2301242/10, for example, C was dismissed when it was discovered that his computer files contained several obscene images and a sexually explicit video clip and that C had viewed this material at work. The employer's computer-use policy permitted personal use of work computers but prohibited obscene material. However, there was evidence that C's managers, P and M, had effectively condoned the viewing of such material as they had allowed an inappropriate image – showing P's head superimposed on the body of a scantily clad young woman – to be displayed on the office wall for several months, and it had been P who had forwarded the most offensive video clip to C, whereas C had not forwarded the clip to anyone. An employment tribunal considered that the managers' attitude 'muddied' the employer's computer-use policy and the dismissal was therefore unfair. The tribunal was also influenced by the disparity of treatment between C and P: P had only received a six-month written warning despite having lied about her involvement in forwarding the video clip.

6.121 Sending offensive images or jokes

An employer should always be concerned about its employees' behaviour where such behaviour has the potential to cause upset either to a fellow employee or a client or customer, as it may be vicariously liable for any harassment caused. An employer's computer-use policy should therefore clearly set out that, for example, the sending of images or jokes that could be considered offensive by the recipient will not be condoned. However, where there is evidence that the policy has not been applied stringently, it is unlikely to be of much assistance to an employer in defending an unfair dismissal claim. In Robinson v Network IT Recruitment Ltd ET Case No.2901763/04, for example, the employee produced evidence that 'jokey' e-mails, some of which the tribunal found 'disgusting and offensive', were frequently circulated within the office without reprimand. Nor were there proper IT systems (including firewalls) in place to prevent adult images and jokes proliferating. In these circumstances, the tribunal found that a reasonable employer would not have regarded the sending of an image that depicted a young baby being held up in front of a mirror with a superimposed penis as a strict liability gross misconduct offence: the employee had sent it to two female colleagues with whom he was on good terms and the particular image related to a running joke between them. Furthermore, the tribunal found that the employer had used this incident to justify getting rid of a troublesome employee. However, the tribunal reduced the employee's compensation by 15 per cent by reason of contributory conduct.

It is worth pointing out that it would not be open to an employee accused of sending offensive material contrary to the employer's internet and e-mail policy to argue that he or she knew that the recipient would not regard it as obscene. The employer is entitled to take an objective approach, applying a 'man-on-the-Clapham-omnibus' test, to determine whether any particular image or text breaches the company's standards of e-mail use, provided the test is applied fairly and in a non-discriminatory way and the standards are well known and enforced through the company's policy.

Even conduct that takes place away from the workplace can in certain **6.122** circumstances amount to misconduct justifying dismissal. In Gosden v Lifeline Project Ltd ET Case No.2802731/09 G forwarded a racist and sexist chain e-mail, outside working hours, from his home computer to the home computer of a former colleague, Y, who worked for HMPS, one of LP Ltd's clients. Y in turn forwarded the e-mail on, which caused it to enter HMPS's computer system. LP Ltd investigated the incident and, following a disciplinary hearing, dismissed G for carrying out an act that might damage its reputation and for breaching its equal opportunities policy. An employment tribunal rejected G's claim that the dismissal was unfair. LP Ltd had been entitled to take the view that sending an offensive e-mail to an employee of one of its biggest clients might damage its reputation and integrity. The tribunal had regard to G's right to privacy but considered that the fact that the e-mail was clearly intended to be disseminated – it stated, in capital letters, 'It is your duty to pass this on!' – took it outside the realm of purely private correspondence.

The reasonableness of a dismissal for sending offensive images or jokes may depend in part on the employee's attitude to his or her conduct, i.e. whether the employee recognises that he or she has acted inappropriately and the employer can trust him or her not to repeat that conduct. The employee in Henderson v London Borough of Hackney 2011 EWCA Civ 1518, CA, was an inclusion manager at a school, whose role involved mentoring extremely vulnerable pupils, some of whom had been victims of sexual abuse. She was summarily dismissed for viewing sexually explicit images and videos at work – including one of a man and woman having sex in a car park and one of a kangaroo masturbating – and forwarding them to colleagues using her work e-mail account, during school hours and from her office computer. The Court of Appeal upheld an employment tribunal's finding that the dismissal was fair. The school's evidence before the tribunal was that, had H recognised her error of judgment, she would probably have received a final written warning. However, H's attitude throughout was that she had been entitled to do as she did as there was no policy expressly prohibiting such conduct, and she only agreed not to repeat her conduct because she had been told to. The Court of

287

Appeal took the view that spelling out that the conduct in question was gross misconduct should not have been necessary for a person in H's position. It was entirely appropriate for the internal disciplinary panel and the tribunal to have regard to the vulnerability of the pupils and to the importance of the school having trust and confidence in a senior employee to whom it had entrusted their care. The Court also rejected H's argument that the dismissal was unfair as it amounted to an unjustified infringement of her right to freedom of expression under Article 10 of the European Convention on Human Rights (EHRC) – see 'Human rights issues' immediately below.

6.123 **Human rights issues.** Where an employer relies on ostensibly private electronic correspondence as evidence of misconduct justifying dismissal, the employee is likely to raise arguments based on rights under the ECHR (annexed to the Human Rights Act 1998) in support of his or her unfair dismissal claim. In particular, he or she may argue that the employer has breached the right to respect for private life (Article 8) and the right to freedom of expression (Article 10).

It is worth noting at the outset that an employee will only be able to bring Article 8 into play where he or she has a reasonable expectation of privacy in respect of the relevant correspondence. In Atkinson v Community Gateway Association 2015 ICR 1, EAT, the EAT emphasised that whether an employee has an expectation of privacy in e-mails sent using the employer's systems will depend on the facts of the particular case. A was employed by CGA, a housing association, as director of resources from 2005 until his resignation in March 2011, at a time when he was under investigation for misconduct. During the course of the investigation, CGA accessed A's work e-mails and discovered that he had been sending overtly sexual messages, often during working hours, to a woman with whom he was having a relationship. The disciplinary investigation was expanded to include this issue but A resigned before the disciplinary proceedings were completed and claimed that he had been unfairly constructively dismissed because of the way in which the investigation had been conducted. He also claimed that CGA had interfered with his right to respect for his private life under Article 8 by accessing his personal e-mails. On this point, the EAT held that the tribunal had been entitled to find that A had no reasonable expectation of privacy in relation to the personal e-mails he sent from his work computer and that Article 8 was therefore not engaged. Whether or not there is a reasonable expectation of privacy depends on the facts of the particular case. Here, the tribunal had correctly taken into account, among other things, the clear terms of the e-mail policy that A had himself written, the fact that none of the e-mails concerned had been marked 'personal' or 'private' as required by the policy, and the fact that A had used the 'wingdings' font in an attempt to conceal the sexual nature of the messages, which indicated that he knew that they might one day be read.

Article 10 was relied on by the employee in Henderson v London Borough of **6.124** Hackney (above), where H was summarily dismissed for viewing and forwarding sexually explicit images and videos using her work e-mail account, during school hours and from her office computer. On appeal, the Court of Appeal noted that where there is an interference with the right to freedom of expression, whether such interference is justified must be considered in the context of the nature of the restriction the employer seeks to place upon the right. Commenting on the facts of that case, Lord Justice Pill stated: 'This cannot be said to be the most profound interference with the right of freedom of expression. All that is sought to be subject to the sanction is the use by the applicant of a computer at her place of work and it is restricted only to the extent that she, in the employer's view, should not have placed pornographic material upon it and received it and transmitted it to a fellow employee.' The Court had no difficulty in concluding that any interference with H's right to freedom of expression in this case was justified and proportionate for the protection of 'health or morals', in accordance with Article 10(2).

For a discussion of the general approach a tribunal should take where an employee raises a human rights argument in support of an unfair dismissal claim, see Chapter 3, 'Unfairness', under 'Impact of Human Rights Act'.

Accessing confidential information

6.125

If an employee deliberately uses an unauthorised password to access confidential information to which he or she is not entitled, that will amount to gross misconduct and will usually justify summary dismissal. The question of whether the employer had substantial grounds for dismissal in such a case does not depend upon the employee's motive for gaining access to the information – Denco Ltd v Joinson 1991 ICR 172, EAT. Mr Justice Wood, in giving the judgment of the EAT, stressed the desirability of making it abundantly clear to employees that unauthorised interference with computers will carry severe penalties.

Excessive personal use

6.126

Most employers condone occasional, limited and appropriate personal use of the computer while at work. However, where the employee spends an excessive amount of time surfing the web, he or she may have difficulty persuading a tribunal that any resulting dismissal was unfair. In McKinley v Secretary of State for Defence ET Case No.2302411/04, for example, the tribunal found that the employee was fairly dismissed when it was discovered that he spent between 10 and 15 per cent of daily working time on non-work-related internet use – although it thought that this conduct fell within the 'outer reaches of the definition of gross misconduct'. In reaching this conclusion, it took into account that McK was employed in a senior position (he was the chief financial officer), that he was in charge of the company's IT policy and that, in an organisation

289

without access to broadband internet, his extensive and persistent misuse of the internet had serious resource and cost implications for the employer.

The terms of the employer's computer usage policy and how it is generally enforced in practice will be of central relevance to the fairness of a dismissal for what the employer alleges is excessive personal use, as the following cases demonstrate:

- **Scarlett and anor v Gloucester City Council** ET Case No.1401395/12: the employees were held to have been unfairly dismissed because the employer had failed adequately to investigate their assertion that personal use of the internet outside of core hours was tolerated by management, and because the employer's disciplinary policy did not identify personal use of the internet at work as an example of gross misconduct

- **Meadows v East Riding of Yorkshire Council** ET Case No.1805363/12: the employee was fairly dismissed for having conducted personal spread-betting transactions using his professional log-in for the Bloomberg trading platform. The employer's policy clearly forbade the use of work facilities for conducting personal research and trading.

6.127 Social networking and blogging

The popularity of social networking sites, such as Facebook, Twitter and Instagram, and the practice of blogging – keeping a form of publicly available on-line diary – has given rise to its own particular set of problems for employers. Some employers block access to social networking sites altogether, whereas others condone occasional use while at work. In any event, employers should always specifically address this issue in their IT policies, decide what is appropriate in their workplace and ensure that the policy is applied consistently. Discipline and dismissal will not necessarily be unreasonable in the absence of such a policy, but having a clear policy and procedures in place reduces the risk of unfairness in such proceedings. A prudent employer will also inform its employees that posting on social media or personal blogs, even in their spare time, may give grounds for disciplinary action, including dismissal, in certain circumstances.

A word of caution, however: even where dismissal may be a reasonable response in the circumstances, employers would be well advised to refrain from hastily making a decision to dismiss without considering the consequences. For example, the employer may want to consider issuing a warning to an employee who occasionally moans about his or her workplace in a personal blog that is not read by many people. By contrast, taking a heavy-handed approach and dismissing the employee, even if this is fair under S.98(4) ERA, may generate more bad publicity for the employer than the employee's blog posts ever did.

6.128 It should be clear that any offensive, defamatory or discriminatory comments on any social network or blog could result in disciplinary action that may lead to dismissal. If an employee publishes in a public forum comments that are defamatory of his or her employer, libel proceedings may be taken by the employer in the same way as if the defamatory comments had been published anywhere else. If the comments damage the employer's reputation or are intended or likely to destroy the relationship of trust and confidence between employer and employee, discipline and dismissal will be legitimate courses of action. It is unlikely that employees will be able to hide behind pseudonyms to evade such action, as employers will generally be able to obtain an order for disclosure of the identity of the person who posted the libellous material from the host website – see Totalise plc v The Motley Fool Ltd and anor 2001 EWCA Civ 1897, CA.

By contrast, inoffensive comments on a social networking site used for personal, not work, purposes will not generally justify disciplinary action, even if they have the potential to upset people who hold deeply felt opposite views. This was emphasised by the High Court in Smith v Trafford Housing Trust 2013 IRLR 86, ChD, a breach of contract (not unfair dismissal) case. There, the Trust demoted S to a non-managerial position, with a 40 per cent reduction in pay, for posting comments on his Facebook page indicating his disapproval of gay marriage in church. Unusually, S continued to work for the Trust in his new job and brought proceedings in the High Court, claiming that his demotion and pay cut amounted to a breach of contract. The Court upheld the claim, accepting that S's behaviour did not amount to misconduct and so there was no contractual basis for the demotion. While it was true that S's Facebook page identified him as a Trust employee, the Court rejected the Trust's argument that the comments had the potential to damage its reputation. It could not see how S's moderately expressed views on gay marriage in church, on his personal Facebook page and out of working hours, could sensibly lead any reasonable reader to think worse of the Trust for having employed S in a managerial role. Nor had he, given the social context, illegitimately promoted his religious and political views or failed to treat his colleagues with respect and dignity.

6.129 The question of misuse of social media in the context of an unfair dismissal claim came before the EAT for the first time in Game Retail Ltd v Laws EAT 0188/14. L, a risk and loss prevention investigator for GR Ltd, had a personal Twitter account that he used to follow 100 of GR Ltd's stores. 65 of those stores followed his account in return. L was dismissed for gross misconduct for posting offensive material on his Twitter account. An employment judge found that dismissal was not within the range of reasonable responses but the EAT held that he had erred by substituting his own view for that of a reasonable employer and by drawing conclusions that were perverse. For instance, he had concluded that there was 'no evidence that any member of staff in fact had access to [the offensive material] let alone raised a complaint about it or was offended'. However, L's tweets could be seen by the 65 stores that followed his account and at least one member of staff – the store manager who had reported the offensive material – had accessed L's tweets and felt sufficiently strongly about their content to inform GR Ltd. The EAT remitted the case to a fresh tribunal to decide the issue of reasonableness. It declined, however, to provide any guidance for future unfair dismissal cases involving misuse of social media. Such cases are fact-sensitive and to lay down a list of criteria by way of guidance would run the risk of encouraging a tick-box mentality which is inappropriate in unfair dismissal cases.

Open access to online networks and discussion forums – whether at work or from home – also raises the issue of potential breaches of confidentiality. Quite apart from any express restrictions, employees owe implied contractual duties of fidelity and confidentiality to their employer (see 'Disloyalty – disclosure of confidential information' above) and any information that an employee posts on a public forum about the employer's business has the potential to give rise to breach of those duties. For example, if a disgruntled employee reveals his or her employer's trade secrets in a blog or Facebook post, this will amount to a disciplinary issue capable of leading to dismissal. Furthermore, the employer could seek an injunction ordering that the material be removed, and may be able to recover damages for any consequent loss based on the employee's breach of contract.

6.130 However, a distinction should be drawn between material that either defames the employer or breaches confidence on the one hand, and comments or opinions tending to disparage the employer or fellow employees or which the employer simply does not care for on the other hand. If the material is not actually damaging to the employer, then it is unlikely that the relationship of trust and confidence will be so seriously undermined as to permit the employer to dismiss. In the wrongful dismissal case of Mason v Huddersfield Giants Ltd 2013 EWHC 2869, QBD, for example, a rugby player was summarily dismissed by his club for gross misconduct after his girlfriend posted a photo on M's Twitter feed without his knowledge. The photo was of his teammate's anus and had been taken by the teammate on M's phone without his knowledge during an end-of-season drinking session. M's contract included a clause that required him to uphold the reputation of the club at all times. However, the High Court held that M – who had deleted the Tweet after he sobered up and realised the inappropriateness of the picture – had not committed a fundamental breach. The Court took the view that if the club was seriously concerned that its reputation might be tarnished by the offending tweet, it would have issued an apology to its supporters, or indicated to them that it was taking disciplinary action against M. Furthermore, taking into account the fact that the club had condoned the drinking session in question, as well as a public 'naked run' undertaken by players who had not scored a try during the season, the Court considered that the central requirements of M's contract were concerned with his performance as a player on the pitch rather than as a family role model off the pitch. His wrongful dismissal claim was therefore successful.

Nonetheless, employers may be entitled to treat posts that bring the business into disrepute as misconduct, in which case disciplinary action may be appropriate. Whether dismissal will be fair will very much depend on the circumstances, including the nature of the employee's work, his or her position within the company, the nature of the comments made, whether such behaviour is covered by the employer's disciplinary and/or computer-use policy and the damage, if any, caused to the employer as a result of the comments. In Young v Argos Ltd ET Case No.1200382/11 A Ltd had put in place a social networking policy that informed employees of the conduct it expected of them when they undertook social networking. A Ltd also had an anti-harassment and bullying policy that contained examples of unacceptable behaviour, which included offensive personal comments in texts, tweets, posts or e-mails and acts that deliberately isolated or excluded a colleague. The policies also made clear that comments amounting to harassment and bullying could constitute gross misconduct and result in summary dismissal. When a former employee posted a comment on Facebook about Y's manager, saying that she was as much use as a chocolate teapot, Y indicated that she liked the comment by clicking the 'like' function on the page. She also replied that this had been the worst year in her 15 years with A Ltd and she was so happy that her former colleague had escaped. Y was called to a disciplinary hearing where she apologised, promised to do nothing similar in the future and stressed that she had apologised to the manager. Nevertheless, A Ltd decided to dismiss her. An employment tribunal found the dismissal to be unfair. No reasonable employer could have concluded that Y's comments amounted to gross misconduct: they were not serious enough to amount to bullying and harassment in breach of the social networking policy, being no more than 'workplace gossip or routine criticism of an employer'.

Social media posts as evidence of other misconduct. Given the propensity of 6.131 individuals to post about their day-to-day activities on social media, it is unsurprising that employers occasionally discover – via social media – that an employee has been engaged in some form of misconduct unrelated to his or her social media usage. In Gill v SAS Ground Services UK Ltd ET Case No.2705021/09, for example, the employer discovered that G had taken part in an event at London Fashion Week while she was on sick leave. At a disciplinary hearing, G stated that her attendance at London Fashion Week was 'essentially social', but this was not accepted by her employer as her Facebook page referred to her auditioning 300 models and choreographing a fashion show. An employment tribunal found that G's dismissal for gross misconduct – specifically, carrying out alternative work while on sick leave – was fair.

The claimant in Gill does not appear to have argued that it was unreasonable for her employer to rely on information from her Facebook page as evidence of her misconduct. However, an employee might conceivably seek to make such an argument on the basis that, in accessing and relying on such information,

293

the employer has infringed the employee's right to respect for his or her private life under Article 8 ECHR (see 'Human rights issues' below).

6.132 The employee might also argue that in monitoring his or her social media pages the employer is in breach of the Data Protection Act 1998. In its social media guidance for employers, Acas notes that employees should be warned if an employer intends to monitor their social media pages and states: 'An employer should try to find alternatives to checking staff use of social media, if it can. It needs to justify the use of monitoring, showing that the benefits outweigh any possible adverse impact.' And the Supplementary Guidance to the Information Commissioner's Employment Practices Code states that: 'If monitoring is to be justified on the basis that it is necessary to enforce the organisation's rules and standards, these rules and standards must be known and understood by workers' (para 3.1.3). The Guidance recommends setting out any applicable rules in a policy that is clearly communicated to employees. It continues: 'Either in this policy or separately, the employer should go on to set out the circumstances in which monitoring may take place, the nature of the monitoring, how information obtained through monitoring will be used, and the safeguards that are in place for the workers who are subject to the monitoring.'

Of course, these issues will be of less relevance where an employee's social media posts showing that the employee has engaged in misconduct have come to the employer's attention not through its own monitoring of the employee's social media activity, but through disclosure by another employee. However, the employer will still need to conduct a reasonable investigation if it is to be able to dismiss fairly on the basis of such information.

6.133 **Human rights issues.** Use of social media is another area (see also 'Sending offensive images and jokes' above) where human rights, in particular the right to respect for private life (Article 8) and the right to freedom of expression (Article 10) under the ECHR, may come into play. Briefly, employers who check up on a prospective or current employee's online profile could be interfering with that individual's Article 8 right to respect for his or her private life. It is questionable, however, whether information that an individual makes freely available on an openly accessible website could reasonably be considered part of his or her private life and whether Article 8 will be engaged in these circumstances – see Pay v United Kingdom 2009 IRLR 139, ECtHR.

Whether an employee has a reasonable expectation of privacy in respect of his or her posts on social media so as to be able to rely on Article 8 was considered by an employment tribunal in Crisp v Apple Retail Ltd ET Case No.1500258/11. C worked at AR Ltd's Norwich store. As part of his induction, he was told that he should be careful about how he presented himself in public, on online social networks and on blogs; that activities outside work that affected AR Ltd's business interests were covered by company policy and guidelines regardless of whether he identified himself as employed by AR Ltd; and that there could be

294

disciplinary consequences arising from online postings. In addition, AR Ltd had e-mail and electronic communication guidelines stating that employees should not display commentary about its products, services or initiatives on personal websites and that violation could result in disciplinary action, including dismissal. A colleague alerted C's manager to a number of posts on C's Facebook page, which included complaints about his work and about Apple applications not working. AR Ltd investigated and C was summarily dismissed. Although the employment tribunal acknowledged that dismissal might appear harsh in the circumstances, it rejected C's unfair dismissal claim. Given the importance of protecting its company image – which was made clear in policies and training – AR Ltd was entitled to view C's comments as gross misconduct. On the Article 8 point, the tribunal noted that although C had set up his Facebook account to be visible only to his 'friends', he was well aware that Facebook posts can easily be passed on by those who have access to them. Indeed, details of C's comments were provided to AR Ltd by one of his Facebook 'friends'. In these circumstances, C did not have a reasonable expectation of privacy in respect of his Facebook posts and Article 8 was therefore not engaged.

Similarly, in Teggart v TeleTech UK Ltd NIIT 007904/11 the Northern Ireland **6.134** industrial tribunal held that the dismissal of an employee for making vulgar comments about the promiscuity of a female colleague on his Facebook page was reasonable in the circumstances and was therefore fair. Although the comments did not bring the employer's reputation into serious disrepute, the harassment of a colleague was sufficiently serious on its own to justify the dismissal of the employee for gross misconduct. Furthermore, having made his comments public, the employee had no reasonable expectation of privacy for the purposes of Article 8 of the European Convention on Human Rights.

Where disciplinary action leads to dismissal, the question of whether dismissal was fair in accordance with S.98(4) ERA may have to be considered in the light of the employee's Article 10 rights. This arguably includes the right to moan publicly about one's working conditions and/or colleagues, so long as it does not involve damaging or libellous statements. However, even where a Convention right has been interfered with, the employer's actions may be justified – for example, because of the risk of damage to the employer's reputation. Two contrasting examples:

- **Crisp v Apple Retail Ltd** (above): C was found to have been fairly dismissed for making negative comments about his work at AR Ltd and about Apple products on his Facebook page. The tribunal held that, given the importance of protecting its company image – which was made clear in policies and training – AR Ltd was entitled to view C's comments as gross misconduct. In relation to Article 10, the tribunal held that the right to freedom of expression was engaged, but that AR Ltd's conduct in limiting C's exercise of this right was justified under Article 10(2) for the

295

protection of its reputation. The tribunal commented that the particular form of expression in this case was not as important as other forms of expression (such as political opinion), whereas it was clearly damaging to AR Ltd's reputation

• **Smith v Trafford Housing Trust** 2013 IRLR 86, ChD: the Trust demoted S to a non-managerial position, with a 40 per cent reduction in pay, for posting comments on his Facebook page indicating his disapproval of gay marriage in church. The High Court upheld S's claim that his demotion and pay cut amounted to a breach of contract, on the basis that S's behaviour did not amount to misconduct and so there was no contractual basis for the demotion. In relation to S's right to freedom of expression under Article 10, the Court commented that an employer may legitimately restrict or prohibit an employee from promoting his or her religious or political beliefs at work, or in a work-related context, but it would be surprising to find that an employer had, by the incorporation of a code of conduct into the employee's contract, extended that prohibition to his or her personal or social life. It would not be reasonable to construe the employer's Equal Opportunities Policy as applying to every situation outside work where an employee comes into contact with one or more colleagues as that would impose too great a fetter on the employee's freedom of speech.

For a more general discussion on the impact of human rights law in the context of unfair dismissal, see Chapter 3, 'Unfairness', under 'Impact of Human Rights Act'.

6.135 ## Drinking, drugs and smoking

Employees whose performance or behaviour at work is affected by alcohol or drugs leave themselves open to fair dismissal on the ground of either capability or conduct. However, there is an increasing trend towards treating long-term alcoholism and, to a lesser extent, drug dependency as serious illnesses, with many employers having specific policies allowing time off for medical treatment and counselling. Chronic abuse resulting in diminished performance and long bouts of absence from work is clearly a 'sickness' problem and employers should take reasonable steps to investigate the true medical position and the prospects of rehabilitation before deciding whether the individual's employment can be continued (see Chapter 5, 'Ill health', under 'Particular types of sickness – drink and drugs'). A problem with alcohol or drugs may also be a symptom of a disability, in which case the employee may be protected under the Equality Act 2010 (although addiction to drugs or alcohol as a free-standing condition is excluded from the definition of 'disability' contained in that Act). But, at the other end of the spectrum, there are straightforward cases of drink and drug misconduct where the employee recklessly or even deliberately disregards company rules or acceptable standards of conduct. Here, employers may be justified in adopting a less tolerant approach – especially where there is a company rule identifying drunkenness and drug use at work as meriting dismissal.

A simple example of a fair dismissal for being drunk at work is Weir v Stephen Alans Jewellers EAT 550/97, where the employee was the manager of a jeweller's shop who had gone to watch a football match in a nearby pub one afternoon. He had drunk three or four pints at the pub and failed to lock up the shop properly at the end of the day. He was dismissed for gross misconduct. The EAT could find no fault in the tribunal's finding of fair dismissal.

Drinking on or off duty   6.136
Disciplinary breaches such as drunkenness or possessing drink at work normally point to 'conduct' as the reason for dismissal and are generally assumed to be a serious matter. In Adamson v Mitchells & Butlers Retail Ltd ET Case No.1502919/09, for example, CCTV footage showed A, a pub manager, being pushed around the pub car-park in a wheelie bin by one of his colleagues. The bin fell over, causing injury to A and leaving broken glass on the ground by the pub door. Having initially lied to the employer about the cause of his injuries, A admitted at a disciplinary hearing that he had been drunk and could provide no explanation for his behaviour. A tribunal found that A's dismissal for gross misconduct was fair. However, even in cases where the employer has conducted a reasonable investigation and can demonstrate that it has a genuine belief that the employee was guilty of the misconduct in question, Acas advises that consideration should be given to whether it would be appropriate to treat the problem as a medical rather than a disciplinary matter (see the Acas Advisory Booklet, 'Health, work and wellbeing').

The need for investigation and medical advice is well illustrated by Martin v British Railways Board EAT 362/91. M was dismissed when his manager thought he was drunk at work – his eyes looked glazed and his speech was slurred. At his internal appeal, M told the employer that he had not been drunk but suffered from hypertension, the symptoms of which resembled drunkenness. His appeal was dismissed and the EAT in Scotland confirmed the tribunal's finding of unfair dismissal. The employer should have made further investigations to discover whether H's apparently drunken state was in fact the result of a medical condition.

Problems arise where it is not immediately clear whether a drinking (or drug)   6.137
problem falls within the 'sickness' category or the 'misconduct' category. Choosing the wrong label will not be fatal in itself. However, the confusion could lead to wrong steps being taken or right ones not being taken when they should be. Two examples:

• **Strathclyde Regional Council v Syme** EAT 233/79: S was a school janitor for ten years. During the last two there were complaints that he drank and at a disciplinary interview he promised to resign if found drunk again. Later he had hospital treatment but after another incident he was held to his promise and resigned. The tribunal found this to be a dismissal. The EAT, upholding the tribunal's finding of unfairness, considered that S's problem should have been treated as medical, not disciplinary, and independent medical evidence should have been obtained since there was evidence before the tribunal to show that S suffered from bipolar disorder and that this was the cause of his drinking. So while dismissal might have been fair in a straightforward case of alcoholism (bearing in mind the employer's duties to pupils and other staff), in the circumstances it was unfair

- **Preston v MBDA (UK) Ltd** ET Case No.2405916/02: the employer had known for some time that P had a serious drink problem. After an incident when he was believed to be smelling of alcohol, he admitted having been drinking at lunchtime and allegedly admitted to having had a drink on the premises. A disciplinary hearing was called and P was summarily dismissed for gross misconduct. The tribunal found the dismissal to be unfair since, although the employer had accepted that P was suffering from an illness, it had dealt with it purely as a misconduct issue. However, P's compensatory award was limited because, had the employer correctly approached the matter on a capability basis, it would have made no difference to the decision to dismiss.

Where an employee's drinking is associated with a medical condition, misdemeanours such as lateness, erratic behaviour or poor performance will often be part of that medical problem. However, manifestations of the illness in the form of gross misconduct may still be treated as such, and tribunals recognise that employers can reach the point where they are entitled to say 'enough is enough'. In Evans v Bass North Ltd EAT 715/86, for example, the employee, an alcoholic, had been employed as a chef for 11 years. His employer had always taken a sympathetic view of his problem, but he was dismissed on Christmas Eve after breaking a prohibition against drinking in the kitchen and for threatening the manager. The EAT found the dismissal fair for misconduct, even though it acknowledged that the employee was suffering from a disease.

6.138 **Alcohol rule/policy.** Employers who have disciplinary rules against drinking at work are at an advantage when it comes to justifying dismissals. The existence of a rule increases the likelihood of a tribunal finding that a dismissal for an isolated incident, without warnings, was fair – the rule itself operating as a warning. But if a rule is to have that effect, the consequences of breach must also be clear.

In Dairy Produce Packers Ltd v Beverstock 1981 IRLR 265, EAT, an employee was dismissed for drinking in a public house when he should have been working. He claimed that others who had been drinking during working hours had been subjected to less severe penalties. The company argued that it was reasonable to distinguish between the employee's case and the others as in the other instances the drinking had taken place on the premises. The EAT decided that if employers wished to impose different penalties in such circumstances, they had to make this clear in either their rules or the contract of employment. That had not been done in this case and the dismissal was therefore unfair.

Any 'drinking' rule must be applied in a reasonable and not a rigid or inflexible **6.139** way. In Charlery v Glendale Grounds Management ET Case No.6002920/98 the employer had a rule stating that employees under the influence of alcohol might be summarily dismissed. This rule was applied unwisely to an employee who was seen walking along a road outside the park at which he was an attendant, holding a can of beer. His dismissal was found to be unfair on the basis that drinking half a can of beer during a lunch break where there had been no specific warning against doing so was not sufficient misconduct to justify dismissal. And in Scottish Grain Distillers Ltd v McNee and anor EAT 34/82 the employer had an inflexible rule that unauthorised possession of alcohol led to summary dismissal. In a locker search, jars with a small amount of liquid containing on analysis 1 per cent or less of ethyl alcohol were found in the two claimants' lockers. Both were dismissed. The EAT, upholding the tribunal's finding of unfair dismissal, considered that even if the liquid could fairly be described as alcohol, the breach was trivial.

Employers need to be clear about what it is they wish to prohibit. In Liberty Living plc v Reid EAT 0039/10 the EAT agreed with the majority decision of a tribunal that an employee summarily dismissed for drinking a pint of lager shandy off work premises during working hours had been unfairly dismissed. There were various inconsistencies between the relevant provisions in LL plc's alcohol policy and its disciplinary policy. The disciplinary policy stated that 'being under the influence of alcohol... during working hours' could be categorised as gross misconduct that could lead to summary dismissal. Meanwhile, the alcohol policy provided that consuming alcohol 'while performing company business or in the workplace' was prohibited, but did not state that this amounted to gross misconduct, only that breach of the prohibition could result in disciplinary action 'up to and including discharge'. The EAT noted that the consumption of a single alcoholic drink outside the workplace during working hours was not, in itself, prohibited by the policy, and the fact that the policies distinguished between drinking alcohol and being under the influence meant that the employer could not treat the former as proving the latter. Moreover, the alcohol policy was only drawn to R's attention after he had been dismissed.

Similarly, in McElroy v Cambridgeshire Community Services NHS Trust ET **6.140** 3400622/14 McE was employed as a healthcare assistant by the Trust. On 21 August 2013, a colleague told McE's line manager that he smelt of alcohol. She interviewed him and took the same view, although McE explained that he had drunk a couple of beers the night before. McE was suspended pending an investigation under the Trust's disciplinary policy, which gave being unfit for duty through the effect of drink as an example of gross misconduct. This was defined in the substance-misuse policy to mean the employee being incapable of functioning effectively at work. The substance-misuse policy did not ban drinking alcohol shortly before coming to work but recommended that employees avoid doing so. During the investigation, McE denied coming to work drunk although the investigation report noted a number of previous occasions when managers had expressed concern at smelling alcohol on McE. However, there had been no concerns about his behaviour. Following a disciplinary hearing, McE was dismissed for attending work under the influence of alcohol, thereby putting himself, colleagues and patients at risk. His appeal was rejected and he claimed unfair dismissal. The employment judge held that Mr McElroy had been unfairly dismissed. The judge took into account the fact that, as a public body with statutory responsibility for providing proper care for patients, some of whom would be vulnerable, the Trust would want to be vigilant in maintaining proper standards. However, a reasonable employer would not, given the absence of evidence that he had been incapable of functioning effectively at work, have concluded that McE was unfit for duty as defined by the Trust's policies. The reasonable employer would not, without evidence of some accompanying impairment of performance, treat smelling of alcohol as amounting to gross misconduct or conduct justifying dismissal.

Just as the existence of clear disciplinary rules may help an employer defend a claim of unfair dismissal, the existence of an alcohol policy that states that an employee 'will' be given the opportunity to seek diagnosis and specialist help may affect how a reasonable employer should deal with an employee with alcohol dependency. In Sinclair v Wandsworth Council EAT 0145/07 the EAT upheld a tribunal's finding that the dismissal of S was unfair because, despite having such a policy, the employer did not apply it. Any reasonable employer would have informed the employee of the alcohol policy – S had only been provided with a copy immediately before the disciplinary hearing that resulted in his dismissal – and that disciplinary action could only be suspended if he actively sought to address his alcohol problem. S had not been given the opportunity of accepting treatment as an alternative to disciplinary action.

6.141 **Change in rules.** Any change in the rules must be brought to the employees' attention and a failure to do so may result in a finding of unfair dismissal. In Claypotts Construction Ltd v McCallum EAT 699/81 the employee overstayed his lunch break in a pub by an hour and was dismissed. His written particulars of employment stated that such offences would be dealt with by a recorded warning but more recently employees had been orally informed that such conduct would not be tolerated. The EAT, upholding the tribunal's finding of unfair dismissal, said that the employer was not entitled to dismiss summarily, because any alteration in the rules had not been adequately drawn to the employee's attention. (Note that where the new rules are brought in by formal agreement with the union the employer is generally entitled to assume that members are aware of them – Gray Dunn and Co Ltd v Edwards 1980 IRLR 23, EAT (although see W Brooks and Son v Skinner below).)

If rules are introduced as a temporary measure – say, to prevent loss of production at Christmas – employers should tread carefully, especially if excesses have been condoned in the past. In W Brooks and Son v Skinner 1984 IRLR 379, EAT, an employee was dismissed under the provisions of a new rule for failing to report to work after over-indulging at the Christmas party. Although the rule had been agreed with the union, individual employees were not informed and an employee would not reasonably have expected dismissal to be the sanction given the employer's previous leniency in such matters.

Give employee opportunity to explain. Giving an employee a chance to respond fully and thoughtfully to the allegations may mean taking him or her off work and not holding an interview until he or she sobers up. The importance of this goes beyond simply establishing whether the employee was drinking: it is to allow the employee to put forward any explanation he or she may have. **6.142**

Failure to give the employee an opportunity to apologise is particularly important in the case of a sudden loss of temper under the influence of drink. In Charles Letts and Co Ltd v Howard 1976 IRLR 248, EAT, a case where underlying tensions erupted into a row with the manager when the employee was drunk, the EAT said: 'In our view, particularly in a case of what appears to have been a sudden explosion and loss of temper by a man who was under the influence of drink, it must be important for an officer, weighing the pros and cons of dismissal or of lenience, to send for the man concerned and to give him every opportunity and encouragement to climb off his high horse and to apologise, so that matters can be put right before it is too late.'

The employee's explanation may also reveal that there are work-related reasons for his or her alcohol abuse. For example, the employee may explain that he or she has started drinking heavily as a result of feeling unable to cope with his or her workload. The employer should further investigate any such claims and ensure that any problems at work are adequately addressed and that the employee receives the appropriate support. Failing this, a tribunal may find that dismissing the employee in these circumstances was unfair. **6.143**

Mitigating circumstances. Even if a rule has been breached, there may be mitigating circumstances that make a dismissal unfair. In Weetabix Ltd v Criggie and anor EAT 344/89 two employees contravened a clear company rule when they were caught drinking on an evening shift. However, their dismissals were held to be unfair as there were mitigating factors. The employees had not bought the alcohol to drink at work – one of them intended it for his fishing trip after the shift; they had finished their allotted work; neither was drunk; and **6.144**

one of them was suffering from a domestic upset, which they were discussing over the drink.

In Hepworth Pipe Co Ltd v Chahal EAT 611/80 the claimant had worked well as a crane driver for nine years. He was known by his employer to be a diabetic. One morning he arrived for work apparently drunk and was dismissed after admitting drinking the evening before. On appeal, he claimed his condition was aggravated by lack of insulin. The EAT, upholding the tribunal's finding of unfair dismissal, held that the tribunal had adopted the correct approach in finding the dismissal unfair on the ground that the employer ought to have investigated any possible circumstances mitigating the employee's apparently drunken state.

6.145 **Drinking previously condoned.** Where drinking has previously been condoned, summary dismissal will in most cases be unfair. In such cases, a clear warning that an employee's job is in danger if such conduct is repeated is necessary. In Sandon and Co Ltd v Lundin EAT 421/76 a managing director had formed the habit of leaving work at 11.30 am to visit the pub, often returning as late as 3 pm, smelling of drink though not drunk. His chairman hinted that he should resign because of poor trading results but he refused to do so and was then dismissed by the board for misconduct. The EAT agreed with the tribunal that the dismissal was unfair. There should have been a plain warning – instead of which the employee had been allowed to go on like this for two years.

6.146 **Health and safety.** Tribunals take a very strict view where health and safety is involved. This is hardly surprising, since employers have obligations under common law and various statutes, notably the Health and Safety at Work etc Act 1974, to keep their employees safe.

Employers are obliged to take reasonable steps to ensure that their employees are not acting under the influence of alcohol or drugs if this is likely to risk the health and safety of others. In Connor v George Wimpey ME and C Ltd EAT 387/82 it was held to be fair to dismiss an oil-rig scaffolder for being drunk when returning to work – work where safety on platforms and during transport thereto was heavily stressed. There were stringent rules in C's contract that provided for possible dismissal in these circumstances but, even if there had been no specific reference to drinking and possible dismissal in the contract, the EAT would have found it well within the discretion of a prudent employer instantly to dismiss an employee found to be so much under the influence of alcohol as to be considered unsafe to be let on board the transport plane. The safety requirements of North Sea platforms and transport needed no emphasis – particularly the strict control of alcohol. And in Douglas v Britannia Airways Ltd ET Case No.6956/87 an air stewardess was fairly dismissed for drinking on several flights. The tribunal stressed that the safety of the passengers, especially in an emergency situation, was central to her job and that in her condition she put lives in jeopardy.

Indeed, employees themselves have a duty under the Health and Safety at Work **6.147** etc Act 1974 to look after their colleagues. In Akerman v London Central Bus Company Ltd ET Case No.1100546/07 A, a manager in a bus company, was dismissed for failing to report that he had spotted one of the company's engineers in a pub, drinking a pint of what appeared to be alcohol when he was about to go on duty. Instead A – who knew that the company treated failure to observe rules affecting safety or the consumption of alcohol while on duty or during any break in duty, or reporting for work under the influence of alcohol, as gross misconduct – told the engineer that drinking could have cost him his job and took him off driving duties for a month. The tribunal found that A had been fairly dismissed for gross negligence for his failure to enforce the alcohol policy. He had put his desire to help a colleague above his duty as a manager to protect safety, which in a bus company is the single most important part of the job. Had another manager not caught the engineer drinking at a later date, he could still be undertaking work on buses while under the influence of alcohol. The tribunal held that dismissal was not outside the range of reasonable responses, despite the fact that A had 12 years' service.

If dismissals for potential danger are fair, dismissals for drunken negligence are even more likely to be so. In Richardson v Teesside Farmers Oils Ltd COET 335/116 R was drunk at a Christmas party and let a woman colleague, who had no driving licence, drive his loaded oil tanker. She hit a wall, causing minor damage. The tribunal found the dismissal to be fair, despite R's eight years' service and some procedural lapses by the employer. He was breaking the law and putting at risk fellow employees and the employer's operating licence.

Even where there is only evidence of off-duty drinking, a dismissal may still be **6.148** fair. In McLean v McLane Ltd EAT 682/96 the claimant, a fork-lift truck driver, was dismissed after his employer read in a newspaper that he had been convicted of being drunk and disorderly and in possession of cannabis. Although there was no evidence of his ever having come to work under the influence of alcohol or drugs, his employer was concerned that it could happen and worried about the consequences if it did. The EAT held that the dismissal was fair.

Note that S.27 of the Transport and Works Act 1992 creates a number of criminal offences aimed at certain categories of railway worker who go to work under the influence of alcohol. Operators who fail to exercise all due diligence to prevent the commission of any such offence by those who work for them will also be guilty of an offence – S.28. Breath tests may be carried out by a constable who has reasonable cause to suspect that a railway worker has been drinking – S.29. It is also a criminal offence to drive a motor vehicle if under the influence of drink – see the Road Traffic Act 1988. Furthermore, if the employee concerned is disqualified from driving, this may have repercussions for his or her employment – see Chapter 7, 'Statutory ban', under 'Driving bans'.

303

6.149 **Employer's reputation.** One reason sometimes advanced by employers to justify dismissal for drinking is that their public reputation has been, or will be, damaged by the employee's actions. Such an argument was accepted in HB Raylor v McArdle EAT 573/84 where the employee had been seen 'legless' on a building site. His dismissal was held to be fair, even though at the time he was off-duty, as the employer was acting reasonably in considering that his presence in such a state would undermine the confidence of the employer's site agents. The tribunal in Thornalley v Linkage Community Trust ET Case No.2600377/11 took a similar approach. The Trust was a charity that cared for people with learning difficulties. T's duties included establishing relationships with possible partner organisations as well as interacting with the service users for whom the Trust provided care. During a two-day trip to visit ten potential partner organisations, T and a colleague, B, got drunk in their hotel bar and then continued drinking in T's hotel room until 1 am, only stopping when the hotel's security staff asked them to quieten down. On check-out, neither apologised to the hotel staff or made any mention of damage they had caused to hotel property by spilling red wine on surfaces in T's room. Following a complaint by the hotel, the Trust investigated and discovered that T and B had not visited all of the organisations they had intended to, most likely because B was feeling hungover on the second day of the trip. B and T were both summarily dismissed. Rejecting T's unfair dismissal claim, the tribunal accepted the Trust's view that, while B was the primary perpetrator, T had not acted to stop the behaviour: if she could not be trusted to keep a colleague out of trouble on a night away, how could she be trusted to be responsible for the vulnerable service users she worked with? The tribunal also accepted the Trust's evidence that charities are extremely vulnerable to adverse publicity and the press would have had a field day if news of B and T's behaviour had been reported.

6.150 **Dismissal for other people's drinking.** In some circumstances, employees may be dismissed as a result of other people's drinking. The most obvious instances involve schoolteachers. In West Sussex County Council v Bell EAT 60/86 the EAT considered that the claimant's dismissal was fair because he had, among other things, bought an under-age pupil a drink at a pub and allowed such pupils to drink whisky at his house, one of whom became intoxicated. Similarly, if a senior manager allows employees to drink on the premises in breach of company rules, his or her dismissal may be fair – see Williams v Ciba-Geigy Plastics and Additives Co EAT 87/81. (See also 'Health and safety' above.)

6.151 **Drugs**
Drug addiction, like alcoholism, should in theory be treated as an illness. However, tribunals have almost invariably regarded drug-related dismissals as a misconduct issue. Perhaps the reason for the different approach is that the use of drugs, unlike alcohol, can amount to a criminal offence. Furthermore,

304

employers themselves can commit an offence under the Misuse of Drugs Act 1971 if they know that illegal drugs are being used or distributed on their premises.

Note also that S.27 of the Transport and Works Act 1992 creates a number of criminal offences aimed at certain categories of railway worker who go to work under the influence of drugs. And operators who fail to exercise all due diligence to prevent the commission of any such offence by those who work for them will also be guilty of an offence – S.28. It is also a criminal offence to drive a motor vehicle if under the influence of drugs – see the Road Traffic Act 1988.

Drugs policy. Rules expressly prohibiting the use of drugs at work are not **6.152** particularly common, except in jobs that are involved in some way with the dispensing or manufacture of drugs such as work in pharmacies or hospitals. However, company rule or not, dismissal will usually be a reasonable response to drug use at work. In Anderson and anor v Oak Motor Works Ltd ET Case No.21967/81, for example, two employees were caught smoking cannabis in the workshop where they were rebuilding engines. The tribunal decided that the employer's fears about health and safety were justified and the dismissals fair. But employers must still investigate properly. In Templeman v Freight and Repair Service (Taunton) Ltd ET Case No.21126/85 a tribunal found that the employer's grounds for supposing that T's erratic behaviour at work was due to smoking cannabis on duty were too vague.

Even if an employee is simply caught in possession of cannabis on company premises, dismissal may be a reasonable response. In Asda Stores Ltd v Coughlan EAT 0453/10 the EAT overturned a tribunal's finding that C's dismissal was unfair. C had purchased cannabis in the car park of the store where he worked from a colleague who was well known for supplying it. He placed the cannabis in his locker, intending to take it home at the end of his shift, but the smell attracted attention and the locker was searched. AS Ltd's disciplinary policy treated unlawful possession of drugs as gross misconduct, and C was accordingly dismissed. The tribunal considered the dismissal unfair because AS Ltd had failed to apply its drugs and alcohol policy, in which it committed to supporting employees with substance abuse problems. The EAT noted that C did not have a drug addiction – he had admitted to AS Ltd that cannabis was new to him. The support available under the drugs and alcohol policy was therefore not applicable and AS Ltd had acted reasonably in treating his cannabis possession as gross misconduct in accordance with its disciplinary policy.

There is a distinction between the taking of drugs proscribed by the criminal **6.153** law and other drugs. In Chappell v SYP Ltd ET Case No.2800461/02 the claimant took an overdose of paracetamol while at work. She was dismissed for misuse of drugs. In finding her dismissal unfair, the tribunal commented

305

that it was unreasonable of the employer to accuse her of 'misusing drugs' as that phrase invariably connotes the use of drugs such as ecstasy and cannabis.

In deciding whether dismissal was within the range of reasonable responses, a tribunal will take into account a number of different factors, including:

- whether the conduct was on or off duty
- whether the employer's confidence in the employee has been irredeemably undermined
- safety at work
- contact with children or young people
- the effect on the employer's reputation and business
- the illegality of the employee's actions
- any mitigating factors.

These are discussed in turn below.

6.154 **Off-duty drug use.** Employees' conduct outside the workplace is not usually a sufficient ground for dismissal. The general attitude of tribunals to off-duty drug use – usually made known to the employer by a criminal charge or conviction – is that it merits dismissal only if it adversely affects relationships with other employees or business contacts, or threatens the employer's reputation and thus the business. This was the view of the EAT in Norfolk County Council v Bernard 1979 IRLR 220, EAT, upholding a tribunal's decision that dismissal of a teacher after his conviction for possession of cannabis was unfair. The employee was a drama specialist who spent most of his time instructing teachers, although he would sometimes teach teenagers in demonstration classes and was involved with church and other youth groups. He was convicted on guilty pleas and fined for possession and cultivation of cannabis after a few leaves were found in his car, following which he was dismissed. The tribunal accepted his evidence that he had been given them a few months before, smoked two or three cigarettes made from them, and had then forgotten about them. They also accepted evidence that he was highly competent and very well liked, had a high moral character and disapproved of drug use. Since the conviction arose from a single incident, the result of foolishness not vice, the tribunal felt that dismissal was excessive. The EAT agreed.

That case can be contrasted with McLean v McLane Ltd EAT 682/96, in which the claimant, a fork-lift truck driver, was dismissed after his employer read in a newspaper that he had been convicted of being drunk and disorderly and in possession of cannabis. Although there was no evidence of his ever having come to work under the influence of alcohol or drugs, his employer was concerned that, with two previous convictions for possession of cannabis, it could happen, and worried about the consequences if it did. The EAT held that the dismissal was fair.

Interview and prompt investigation are necessary even if there has been a **6.155** conviction. A conviction is only proof that the employee is 'guilty as charged', but in the context of unfair dismissal there may still be explanations, mitigating factors or arguments that the employee wants to put forward in response to the employer's proposed sanction. For instance, despite a conviction, the employee may not actually smoke cannabis, as in Tabor v Mid Glamorgan County Council ET Case No.8353/81, where the employee knew that the plant was being grown in his garden but did not use it himself – although in that case the dismissal was found to be fair in view of other circumstances (see 'Contact with children or young people' below). Or there may have been only one isolated incident, as in Norfolk County Council v Bernard (above).

If criminal proceedings are pending, an employer does not necessarily have to await the outcome before deciding to dismiss provided it has acted reasonably in reaching that decision and has conducted a proper investigation (see 'Criminal offences at work – criminal trial pending' below).

Trust and confidence. If an employer's trust and confidence in an employee is **6.156** irredeemably undermined by an employee's drug use, a resulting dismissal could be fair. In Mathewson v RB Wilson Dental Laboratory Ltd 1989 IRLR 512, EAT, M was arrested and charged during his lunch break for being in possession of a small quantity of cannabis bought for personal use. After returning to work an hour late, he owned up to the offence and was promptly dismissed. Before the tribunal, the employer successfully argued that M had breached a company rule and, in any event, it was not possible to continue to employ someone who was 'involved in drugs'. The employer stressed that M was a skilled employee and expressed fears about the adverse impact an admitted drug user might have on young impressionable employees. While this decision seems harsh – M had not been convicted, there were procedural defects and the employer had an obvious moral revulsion to drugs – the confidence integral to the employment relationship had clearly vanished after M's arrest.

Safety factors. Although tribunals do accept a proven safety risk as a good **6.157** reason to dismiss, it does not relieve employers of their duty to investigate. In Davis v British Airways Board ET Case No.31890/79 the claimant had given eight years' satisfactory service as an airline steward before his employer found out that he had been using amphetamines and dismissed him for taking drugs which could incapacitate him for work and endanger the company's reputation. It was held that the employer was unreasonable in not inquiring further into the medical effects of the drug. But where further investigation will not provide any additional information an employer may be justified in dismissing based on the evidence it has available – Kuehne and Nagel Ltd v Cosgrove EAT 0165/13. In that case C – a warehouse operative in a safety-critical role – was dismissed when she tested positive for cannabis. C admitted having smoked cannabis the previous weekend (and it was agreed before the tribunal that this historic use could produce a positive test result). The tribunal found that the employer had dismissed because of the positive result. However, it held that the dismissal was unfair – in part because the employer had not conducted further investigations to establish whether the positive test result was because C was in fact under the influence or was simply due to her historic use of the drug. Overturning the tribunal's decision, the EAT held that the employer could not be criticised for failing to conduct further tests when – as the tribunal had accepted – the relevant tests were not capable of assessing current intoxication. Furthermore, the tribunal had erred in ignoring the fact that the employer's policies – introduced because of the safety-critical environment in the warehouse – provided that a positive drug test result in itself constituted gross misconduct. The case was remitted to a fresh tribunal for rehearing.

6.158 **Contact with children or young people.** Where the employee's work means that he or she regularly comes into contact with children or young people, this is seen as an important factor in drug abuse cases, especially where the employee is in a position to influence them, such as a teacher. In Norfolk County Council v Bernard (above) – a case in which dismissal was found to be unfair – stress was placed on the fact that the employee was not normally in contact with children, and that he took a strict moral attitude towards drug-taking and felt he would not be embarrassed in dealing with drug problems among pupils. In Tabor v Mid Glamorgan County Council (above), by contrast, the employee taught teenage pupils daily and his replies to the local authority committee showed that he did not agree with the law's approach to cannabis. Although he did not use the drug himself and had been fined only £10 by the magistrates for allowing others to grow it in his garden, the committee felt that it could not leave him in charge of children. The tribunal found the dismissal to be fair.

6.159 **Damage to company's reputation.** The public's attitude to someone involved with drugs is often a potent factor in a tribunal's decision. Frequently, it comes down to a question of local publicity, although the attitude of tribunals tends to vary with the case. In Gunn v British Waterways Board EAT 138/81 a lock-keeper was demoted after a record of unreliability and cannabis convictions and then dismissed after he was convicted of stealing money and drugs and his employer's name was mentioned in the papers. The EAT held that this was a fair dismissal even though performance of the employee's duties, which were menial, would not be affected. The Board's reputation as a responsible employer was at stake. Similarly, in Morgan v Railtrack plc ET Case No.2305231/02 a signalman's dismissal for refusing to submit to a drug test following a signalling error that resulted in a train being sent along the wrong track was found to be fair. The Eurostar train involved in the incident was carrying a number of tabloid journalists and, owing to the potential for adverse publicity, it had made sense for the employer to require the employee to take a drug test in order to protect the company's reputation.

Illegality. The fact that an employee has committed an illegal act will in itself **6.160** often be a factor in the charge of misconduct. In Anderson and anor v Oak Motor Works Ltd (above), where the two employees had been caught smoking cannabis at work, the employment tribunal observed that the illegality was a consideration and that most employers would share this view. And in Tabor v Mid Glamorgan County Council (above) the tribunal shared the employer's concern that a teacher should not show disrespect for the law – the employee in that case had told a committee that he did not agree with the outlawing of cannabis.

Mitigating factors. In Davis v British Airways Board (above) the claimant had **6.161** begun to take amphetamines because of fatigue and depression caused partly by the strain of long-haul flights. His resulting dismissal was held to be unfair since his employer had failed to investigate adequately the true medical effects of such drugs. And in Burns v Dart Pleasure Craft Ltd ET Case No.2095/80 the employee claimed that he had smoked cannabis because of matrimonial difficulties. The tribunal suggested that a reasonable employer would not have dismissed but would have given an ultimatum and waited to see if the employee gave up, especially as the boats he worked on were laid up for the winter and the only work to be done was on-shore. However, in Asda Stores Ltd v Coughlan (above) the EAT held that C's dismissal for purchasing cannabis on the employer's premises and possession of cannabis at work plainly fell within the range of reasonable responses, notwithstanding the fact that C had 21 years' service and a clean disciplinary record, and was suffering from stress at the time due to his own and his partner's illnesses.

As with alcohol abuse, the employer should proceed carefully where the employee asserts that his or her drug-taking is a direct result of problems at work, such as a heavy workload. The employer may be well advised to investigate and, if appropriate, provide support before making a decision whether to dismiss.

Finally, if an employer finds out about a previous drug offence and dismisses **6.162** the employee for failing to disclose it, the dismissal may be unfair under S.4(3)(b) of the Rehabilitation of Offenders Act 1974. If a conviction becomes 'spent' under that Act, dismissal for failing to disclose it is automatically unfair – see 'Criminal offences at work – previous convictions' below.

Drug and alcohol testing
6.163

Employers have obligations under the common law and various statutes, most notably the Health and Safety at Work etc Act 1974, to keep their employees safe. For this reason, an employer's drug and alcohol policy may include provision for testing to ensure that employees are not acting under the influence

309

of alcohol or drugs if this is likely to give rise to a risk to the health and safety of others. However, the extent to which employers have the right to require employees to undertake drug or alcohol testing is limited. Moreover, given the intrusiveness of the testing procedure, employers must tread carefully – the necessity of drug or alcohol testing must be balanced against employees' right to respect for privacy: the employer must not investigate drug or alcohol use (which, if it does take place, will usually occur away from work) unless there is real concern that, without such testing, safety or security at work may be compromised. Unreasonable requests to submit to a test may also leave the employer open to claims of unfair constructive dismissal on the ground that the employer's conduct has destroyed or seriously damaged the relationship of mutual trust and confidence between the employer and the employee. In addition, employers must not forget the need to comply with the provisions of the Data Protection Act 1998 when processing employees' health information.

Some employers reserve a right to test staff in contracts of employment. If an employee has accepted this and then refuses a test, he or she will be in breach of contract. Nevertheless, the employer should have regard to all the circumstances, including any mitigating factors, before dismissing the employee. In the absence of a contractual term, employers cannot require employees to take an alcohol or drug test unless there are legitimate safety concerns. And even where testing is justified employers must get the employee's consent to obtain a sample each time a test is carried out. Otherwise testing would constitute assault under the common law.

6.164 Testing for drug misuse or alcohol abuse in the workplace usually takes one of two forms: 'with cause' testing, where employers have a reasonable suspicion that an employee's performance is impaired through the use of alcohol or drugs and that impairment gives rise to safety risks, or random testing – i.e. randomly testing a number of employees at regular intervals.

6.165 **'With cause' testing.** Where an employer has a reasonable suspicion that an employee has taken drugs or is intoxicated and that this impacts on safety at work, it may ask the employee to take a test. What amounts to 'reasonable suspicion' will obviously depend on the circumstances, but it is likely that there must be some signs to alert the employer that there may be substance abuse, e.g. lack of concentration, unusual irritability or aggression, a deterioration in relationships with colleagues, customers or management, increased short-term absenteeism, poor time-keeping or impaired job performance.

Even if the employer has evidence of alcohol or drug use, it should not make a hasty decision to dismiss where such use does not impact on work performance. Two examples of the importance of a reasonable investigation in these circumstances:

310

- **Nichols v Network Rail Infrastructure Ltd** ET Case No.2802555/06: N, who started work at 8 am, was asked to take a breath test when a colleague noticed that his breath smelled of alcohol. In fact, N had drunk alcohol the previous evening. The test showed an alcohol level of 25mg per 100ml of blood, which was below the maximum permissible level of 29mg. Despite this, N was then asked to provide a urine sample. He agreed and was suspended pending the result. The urine sample was found to contain a level of alcohol in excess of the limit (55 mg). He was called to a hearing and dismissed. An employment tribunal found that his dismissal was unfair. It noted that N's job was safety critical but found that there were mitigating factors – such as N's 'wholly worthy record of service' spanning 30 years – and that the employer failed to conduct a sufficient investigation. On the day in question, N's conduct had not given any grounds for concern that he might be unfit for work and he had readily cooperated. Furthermore, the employer's rules provided that an alcohol level of 30–79mg may result in dismissal, whereas a level of 80mg or above would automatically result in dismissal. Thus, the employer was under an obligation to consider exercising discretion, but it had failed to do so. It made no enquiry as to mitigating factors. It also failed to disclose to N the grounds the company had for believing that the disparity in the levels indicated by the breathalyser and the urine sample was not unusual. There was also a question as to whether the employer had the right to require a urine sample when the breath test was negative. All of these matters should have given the employer pause for thought

- **Bailes v First Bristol Ltd** ET Case No. 1401728/12: a tribunal held that B, a bus driver who tested positive for cocaine following a passenger complaint that he appeared to be under the influence of cannabis, was dismissed unfairly as the employer had failed to conduct a reasonable investigation. When confronted with the positive result, B claimed that this was due to his having eaten his sandwiches ten minutes before taking the saliva test, just after he had handled hundreds of pounds' worth of banknotes as he was cashing up from his shift. The employer was aware of the risk that bank notes may be contaminated with cocaine, but did nothing to investigate the possibility that this could explain B's positive result. B commissioned a hair strand test at his own expense but the employer initially refused to adjourn the disciplinary hearing to wait for the result of this test. The tribunal held that this particular procedural failure had been cured on appeal, as the appeal manager had waited for the hair strand test result – which was negative – and had consulted an expert as to its significance. However, the misconduct with which B was charged was not 'having taken cocaine' but 'having failed the drug test'. If there was a possibility of sample contamination and/or an innocent explanation for B's positive result, then dismissal was not within the range of reasonable responses. (Interestingly, the employer appealed

311

to the EAT – not against the finding of unfair dismissal but against the tribunal's refusal to make a Polkey deduction – see First Bristol Ltd v Bailes EAT 0526/13. The employer relied on an expert report it had commissioned which suggested that B's test result would not have been due to B having handled contaminated bank notes alone and it therefore could have fairly dismissed B following a reasonable investigation. The EAT found that the tribunal had overlooked this report and remitted the case on that point.)

6.166 These cases can be contrasted with McFarlane and ors v Alcoa Europe Flat Rolled Products ET Case No.1304583/05. There, the employer's drugs and alcohol policy, which was incorporated into employees' terms and conditions of employment, deemed impairment through drugs or alcohol to exist when employees were found to have consumed drugs or alcohol in an unsanctioned or unreported way (as determined by an appropriate test). Owing to this wording, the claimants, who tested positive for cannabis, were unable to argue that they were not impaired by drugs while at work. The tribunal found that, on the employer's definition of 'impairment', the company was entitled to conclude that the claimants were impaired. Since they worked in a safety-critical environment, dismissal was within the band of reasonable responses.

This type of testing is also often carried out where there has been a workplace accident or incident that has caused, or could have caused, a danger to health or safety at work and there is evidence that the employee's conduct has had some bearing on the incident. For example, in Morgan v Railtrack plc (above) the tribunal found that M's dismissal for refusing to submit to a drug test following a signalling error was fair.

6.167 **Random testing.** Testing employees at random, usually for drugs, is particularly prevalent in safety-critical industries, such as transport or manufacturing. Even in industries where safety is paramount, however, employers must refrain from adopting a 'one-size-fits-all' approach to workplace testing. There is unlikely to be justification for testing the whole workforce where different employees pose different safety risks depending on the type of work they carry out. The Supplementary Guidance to the Information Commissioner's Employment Practices Code, intended to help employers comply with their obligations under the Data Protection Act 1998, advises that: 'a train driver or signal engineer whose actions are impaired through exposure to alcohol or drugs would generally pose a significantly greater safety risk than would a ticket inspector or rail enquiries clerk. This difference in risk should be reflected in carrying out an impact assessment. Information about ticket inspectors or rail enquiries clerks should not be obtained through testing simply on the basis that "fairness" somehow requires that if drivers or signal engineers are tested, they should be tested as well' (para 4.4.4).

The Guidance also notes that, as a general rule, testing should be designed to ensure safety at work. However, in exceptional circumstances, employers may be justified in testing to detect illegal use where such use would 'breach the worker's contract of employment, conditions of employment or disciplinary rules, and cause serious damage to the employer's business, e.g. by substantially undermining public confidence in the integrity of a law enforcement agency' (para 4.4.5). This may be relevant to some very senior employees, whose drug or alcohol use, if made public, would have serious implications for the employer's reputation or public standing.

An example of a straightforward fair dismissal for testing positive after a **6.168** random drug test is Roberts v British Railways Board EAT 648/96. There, the employer operated an alcohol and drugs policy which involved random testing of its staff – a policy which, the tribunal found, was 'of great importance so far as safety in the railway network is concerned'. The policy stipulated that a positive test would result in the employee's dismissal. When the employee tested positive for cannabis in a random test, he was summarily dismissed. The tribunal ruled that the dismissal was fair and the EAT upheld that finding. Similarly, in Sutherland v Sonat Offshore (UK) Inc EAT 186/93 an employee who worked on an offshore rig was dismissed as a result of a positive drug screening without a formal disciplinary hearing. The EAT said that this was a case in which the employer was entitled to take the view that, from the time the urine sample was confirmed as positive, to hold a formal hearing would serve no useful purpose.

But where the facts are not so straightforward the employer will need to investigate the matter. In Gayle v Works 4 Ltd ET Case No.2300786/07 G, who was black and of Afro-Caribbean descent, was required to periodically submit to random drug tests. The result of one such test was negative, but the information supplied to W4 Ltd indicated that there were trace elements of cannabis and cocaine. Even though the information supplied by the testing company made it clear that this did not equate to a positive test, W4 Ltd took the view that it indicated drug use and required G to attend another test. The night before the second test, G was admitted to hospital and signed off work for two weeks. On his return, he was called to a disciplinary meeting for having failed to attend the second test. In a break from usual practice, R, W4 Ltd's managing director, dealt with the disciplinary hearing. Despite G producing an e-mail from the testing company confirming that the results of the first test were negative, a sickness certificate and a letter from his GP explaining the condition that had caused his visit to hospital, R stated that he believed G was trying to avoid having the test because he had drugs in his system and that G would have to be dismissed. R presented no evidence to back up his assertion, other than saying he had heard it through 'word of mouth'. Nor did he respond to the suggestion that his actions were influenced by G's race. The letter of dismissal G eventually received not only referred to the missed test, but relied on the traces found in the original drug test. The dismissal was found to be unfair (as well as discriminatory).

313

6.169 If an employer has not previously operated random drug testing and wishes to introduce it, it must ensure that the workforce is properly consulted. Otherwise, a dismissal for failure to comply with the new testing requirements is likely to be unfair. In Bedford v H Young Holdings plc t/a Animal ET Case No.3102295/09, for example, the employer exercised a zero tolerance policy in respect of using, consuming, or being under the influence of, alcohol or illegal drugs at work. The policy did not refer to employees' use of illegal drugs or alcohol outside the working environment. Concerned that employees were working in breach of the policy, the employer introduced a new policy providing for random alcohol and drug testing and stating that positive tests would result in disciplinary action and could lead to dismissal. Failure to submit to a test or attempts to evade a test would be treated in the same way as a positive result. B informed his employer that he smoked cannabis in the evenings to relieve stress, but had stopped smoking it in response to the introduction of drug testing. Less than a week later, B was required to undergo a test but he refused as he believed he would test positive and because he disputed the employer's right to impose testing. He was called to a disciplinary hearing and was summarily dismissed for refusing to be tested. The tribunal held that B was unfairly dismissed. The employer failed to consult properly with the workforce on the introduction of drug testing – it amounted to a fundamental change in policy, which it was unreasonable to introduce without meaningful consultation. B was compliant with the policy as it stood prior to the introduction of the testing; he did not use or buy drugs at work and there was no evidence that he was under the influence of drugs at work. B had raised concerns as to the legality of being required to undergo testing and about his position were he to be tested, yet the employer failed to address those concerns.

6.170 **Human rights issues.** Employers should be wary of invading the privacy of their employees unnecessarily as it can leave them open to legal challenges. The testing procedure itself is highly invasive. The obtaining of samples can be intrinsically degrading because employees will need to remove their outer clothing and urinate in secure rooms or lavatories in which the water supply has been turned off. Another person may have to be present at the test to ensure there is no specimen-tampering. Laboratory procedures can also entail invasions of personal privacy. Urinalysis reveals not only the presence of illegal drugs, but also the existence of many other physical and medical conditions, including genetic predisposition to disease, the use of prescription drugs and pregnancy.

As mentioned previously under 'General considerations – impact of Human Rights Act', since the introduction of the Human Rights Act 1998 (HRA), courts and tribunals have been required, so far as possible, to interpret domestic legislation in a way that is compatible with the fundamental rights laid down in the European Convention on Human Rights (ECHR). This paves the way for claimants to argue that, in determining the fairness of a dismissal under S.98(4) ERA, tribunals must consider whether the employer unjustifiably interfered with a Convention right. In the context of testing for alcohol or drugs at work, the Convention right most likely to be relied upon is the right to respect for private and family life found in Article 8 ECHR. A tribunal might well have to consider whether the testing process undertaken by an employer interfered with the employee's right to respect for his or her private life under Article 8(1) and, if so, whether that interference was nevertheless justified by virtue of Article 8(2) in that it was necessary in a democratic society as being, for example, in the interests of public safety.

Thus, employers should ensure that their behaviour in the context of alcohol **6.171** and drug testing is proportionate to the seriousness of the allegations against the employee, as any interference with the employee's private life will be permissible only if it is necessary to achieve a legitimate aim. In Whitefield v General Medical Council 2003 IRLR 39, PC, the GMC had good reason to be concerned about a general practitioner's fitness to practice and accordingly required him to refrain from drinking any alcohol whatsoever and to submit to random blood and urine testing as a condition of being permitted to continue practising as a GP. This, he argued, infringed his right under Article 8 to respect for his private life, particularly in that it restricted his right to drink even in a social context. However, the Privy Council considered that the requirement to refrain from drinking and to submit to random testing was not an interference under Article 8(1), as his right as a GP to an unrestricted social life had to give way to the wider public interest in ensuring that he did not present a risk to the public. Alternatively, even if the GMC's conditions did infringe the claimant's Article 8(1) rights, the Privy Council reasoned that, on the facts of the case, the infringement was a proportionate means of achieving a legitimate aim – namely, the protection of health, or the protection of the rights and freedoms of others – for the purposes of Article 8(2).

The impact of the HRA was also considered, albeit obiter, by the EAT in O'Flynn v Airlinks the Airport Coach Co Ltd EAT 0269/01. In that case, the claimant was a customer care assistant working in the private sector who was dismissed when she tested positive for cannabis following a random drug test – the employer operated a zero tolerance policy with respect to drugs. The EAT held that the employee's claim of unfair dismissal was not affected by the HRA because the act she complained of took place before the HRA came into force. Nevertheless, the EAT went on to express its conclusions on what impact the HRA would have had if it had been in force and applicable to the case. In particular, the EAT thought that the policy only infringed the employee's right to respect for her private life to the extent that it required her to provide a urine sample as part of an established and unopposed random screening process, and also to the extent that the practical effects of the testing process meant that no drugs with persistent detectable characteristics could be taken by employees in their private time without jeopardising their employment. However, when considering whether those infringements were 'proportionate'

315

within the terms of Article 8(2), the EAT took the view that it was permissible for an employer to interfere with an employee's private life to a degree that is in accordance with the law and necessary in a democratic society in the interests of, among other things, public safety. Where an employee has responsibility for public safety in the course of his or her employment, there can be no suggestion that drug or alcohol testing or a zero tolerance policy for safety reasons would be disproportionate.

6.172 Being obiter, the EAT's comments above are not binding on tribunals, although they are helpful in demonstrating the way in which Article 8 issues may well interplay with the consideration of unfair dismissal in the context of drug and alcohol misconduct. As a general rule, employers should ensure that they do not use random drug testing as a means of policing private behaviour that is likely to have no discernible impact on job performance. Such testing may well amount to an interference with Article 8(1) that is not capable of justification under Article 8(2).

For a general discussion of the impact of human rights law on unfair dismissal claims, see Chapter 3, 'Unfairness', under 'Impact of Human Rights Act'.

6.173 Smoking

Subject to some limited exemptions, smoking in enclosed or substantially enclosed workplaces is illegal in the UK – see the Health Act 2006 and accompanying regulations. In addition to premises, the smoking ban applies to work vehicles that are used by more than one person and vehicles used by members of the public.

The Health Act 2006 created two key offences, which incur criminal liability and are punishable by a fine. The first is committed by anyone who smokes in a smoke-free environment. The second is committed by employers who fail to prevent smoking in a smoke-free place, although there are possible defences available.

6.174 Given that employers are under a statutory obligation to prevent smoking in enclosed or substantially enclosed workplaces, employees who flout a smoking ban are likely to face disciplinary action. However, whether smoking in a smoke-free place of work justifies dismissal remains open to question. Dismissal in these circumstances must still be within the range of reasonable responses of a reasonable employer. A number of questions are important in this context. First, is there a workplace smoking policy? If there is, does the policy, and/or the employees' contracts, make it clear that smoking in a smoke-free area can amount to gross misconduct? And have the policy and its consequences been adequately explained to employees? If any of these questions is answered in the negative, an employer may have difficulty persuading a tribunal that a single instance of smoking warranted dismissal without notice. Giving a final written

316

warning for a first offence, and dismissing if it is repeated, may be a more sensible course of action.

The following two cases pre-date the introduction of the smoking ban but nonetheless provide useful examples of the factors tribunals will take into account when determining whether dismissal fell within the band of reasonable responses:

- **Marks and Spencer plc v O'Connell** EAT 230/95: an employee's summary dismissal for a single instance of smoking in front of a store, in contravention of staff regulations, was held to be unfair because the employer had not considered the individual circumstances of the case. This was so notwithstanding that the regulations provided for automatic dismissal for any employee found smoking in a prohibited area. Both the tribunal and the EAT dismissed the argument that the policy would be unworkable if exceptions were allowed and held that, in circumstances where the employee was working a 12-hour night shift, the employer's response was unreasonable

- **Singh v Walkers Snack Foods Ltd** EAT 412/97: an employee was fairly dismissed for smoking in a place where smoking was banned despite the fact that he had worked there for 18 years, had an unblemished record, had just heard news of his two brothers' ill health and was supported by a petition signed by 75 per cent of the workforce. The EAT said that although its sympathy lay with the employee, the employer had taken all these mitigating factors into account and dismissal was within the range of reasonable responses – even if it was on the harsh side.

6.175 Following the introduction in 2007 of the ban on smoking in enclosed or substantially enclosed spaces, one might have expected tribunals to become more sympathetic to employers who wish to take a strict approach towards employees found smoking in a smoke-free workplace. However, the surrounding circumstances, including any mitigating factors, must still be taken into account, as the following two cases – which post-date the introduction of the ban – demonstrate:

- **Allen v WM Morrisons Supermarkets plc** ET Case No.2318024/07: an employee was found to have been fairly dismissed for smoking part of a cigarette during a night shift, contrary to the employer's new policy, which had been introduced in response to the national smoking ban. The policy had been properly disseminated to the workforce and was understood by the employee. The employee had initially denied smoking and had then laughed about it when challenged. He was in a managerial role, so was obliged to set a good example for other staff. Dismissal was therefore within the range of reasonable responses

- **McDonough v Bagnall UK Ltd** ET Case No.2104773/09: the employer had operated a smoke-free workplace since the smoking ban came into force.

317

In June 2009, a colleague reported having seen M smoking in his company vehicle and M was dismissed for gross misconduct. A tribunal found the dismissal unfair, accepting M's case that smoking in company vehicles was widespread and that he had not previously been sanctioned in any way for smoking in his vehicle. In view of the employer's previous tolerance of smoking, moving straight to summary dismissal for this particular incident was unfair.

6.176 **Health and safety.** There are two specific situations in which a dismissal for smoking in a smoke-free area will almost inevitably be held to be fair – these are where smoking is banned for health and safety or for hygiene reasons. Some examples:

- **O'Hara v Avana Bakeries** ET Case No.711/86 (a case pre-dating the smoking ban): a bakery worker was dismissed after being caught smoking in contravention of a 'no smoking' rule. An employment tribunal found the dismissal to be fair, stressing that in a company manufacturing fresh foods it was a matter of great importance that foreign bodies such as cigarette ends did not find their way into the food. There were signs prominently displayed that prohibited smoking everywhere but in the canteen and notices had been issued stating that employees caught smoking would be instantly dismissed. Although the policy had been flouted in the past, the company had since moved to a strict observance of the ban; something, the tribunal said, that the employer should have made clear to employees. However, at the time of his misbehaviour, the employee had been well aware of the implications of illicit smoking and the dismissal was therefore fair

- **Newton v R Manners and Sons** ET Case No.2504125/06 (again, this case pre-dates the smoking ban): RM operated a very strict policy about smoking on company premises and in company vehicles, and the disciplinary procedures stated that breach of the no-smoking policy constituted gross misconduct. One afternoon, N was seen smoking a cigarette in a company vehicle. Following an investigation, N was called to a disciplinary hearing and summarily dismissed for breach of the no-smoking policy, even though he insisted that it was the first and only time he had smoked in a vehicle. An employment tribunal found that N was fairly dismissed. Although this was undoubtedly a harsh policy, it seemed that any employee who took a single puff on a cigarette in a company vehicle would be liable for dismissal. As the company was a food-handling business, dismissal did not fall outside the range of reasonable responses

- **Smith v Michelin Tyre plc** ET Case No.100726/07 (this case post-dates the smoking ban): the employer's decision to dismiss a long-serving employee for a one-off breach of a workplace smoking policy was fair. The employer had always prohibited smoking, except in authorised areas, because of the use of flammable products in its production process. Weighing the employee's personal circumstances against the importance of the policy in preserving the employer's business, its property and the lives of the other staff, dismissal was a reasonable response.

Constructive dismissal. Prior to the introduction of the national smoking ban **6.177** it was not uncommon for employees to argue that since they had been allowed to smoke for a considerable amount of time, they had an implied term in their contracts of employment allowing them to smoke. This issue was considered by the EAT in Dryden v Greater Glasgow Health Board 1992 IRLR 469, EAT. There, it held that there was no implied term in the employee's contract entitling her to facilities enabling her to smoke at work and that a total ban on smoking on the employer's premises was a 'works rule' within the scope of the employment contract, rather than a unilateral variation of that contract. Moreover, the EAT held that 'where a rule is introduced for a legitimate purpose, the fact that it bears hardly on a particular employee does not, in our view, justify an inference that the employer has acted in such a way as to repudiate the contract'.

The upshot of Dryden is that an employee who smokes will struggle to show that the introduction of a smoking ban (outside the employer's premises, for example) amounts to his or her employer conducting itself in a manner calculated or likely to erode the trust and confidence between employee and employer. A constructive dismissal claim founded on the introduction of a smoking ban would be much more likely to succeed if it focused on an employer's method of implementation rather than on the ban itself. Even a total ban on smoking can be said to have a legitimate purpose, but if it is introduced without consultation or advance warning, and no provision is made for employees to adapt, the employer's conduct could be viewed as repudiatory.

While the contract of employment offers little relief to employees struggling to **6.178** cope with a total smoking ban, it does offer assistance to non-smokers. There is a well-established implied term in every contract of employment that an employer must provide a safe working environment. Extending this theme, the EAT in Waltons and Morse v Dorrington 1997 IRLR 488, EAT, has held that an implied term exists to the effect that an employer must provide a working environment that is reasonably tolerable – including the quality of the air – for the performance of its employees' duties. Given that the dangers of passive smoking are substantial, an employee who is exposed to smoke in the workplace and whose employer does not respond to his or her concerns could rely on this implied term to found a constructive dismissal claim. In the Dorrington case, which pre-dated the national smoking ban, D was a secretary who worked in offices where members of staff were allowed to smoke. She had informed her employer that she was not comfortable working in a smoky environment and adjustments were made whereby the secretaries were only allowed to smoke in a designated room, and other staff only in their offices, but the location of the

319

designated room meant that the changes did not reduce D's exposure to smoke. D resigned and claimed unfair constructive dismissal. Upholding her claim, the tribunal and the EAT both accepted that the employer's failure to remedy her situation had amounted to a repudiatory breach of its contractual obligations, and that D, having given the new arrangements a chance to work, had resigned in response to that breach.

While the factual circumstances of D's case are unlikely to reoccur following the introduction of the smoking ban, the case is likely to be of relevance to claims made by employees who either find themselves exposed to smoke which is entering their workplace from outdoors, or who perform their duties outdoors in a smoke-filled environment. As a result, employers need to think carefully about where to permit smoking in parts of the workplace that are not enclosed or substantially enclosed – for example, a designated smoking area that sits immediately below an open window could expose staff working near that window to a large amount of smoke.

6.179 **Incapacity.** Damage to health through smoking could result in an employee becoming unfit for work, thus providing grounds for dismissal for incapacity (see Chapter 5, 'Ill health'). Even where a dismissal for incapacity is found to be unfair, a tribunal may reduce the compensation on account of the employee's contributory fault in having brought the illness upon him or herself – see, for example, Parrott v Yorkshire Electricity Board 1972 IRLR 75, ET.

6.180 **E-cigarettes.** In recent years, many new products have become available that mimic tobacco cigarettes and are increasingly being used by smokers seeking to quit, and even by individuals who have previously been non-smokers. These products are mostly battery operated and produce a vapour, rather than a smoke. They may or may not use nicotine and some are flavoured with, for example, fruit or menthol. The types of product available include e-cigarettes, personal vaporizers (PVs), and electronic nicotine delivery systems (ENDS).

Since the operation of these products does not involve the burning of any substance, they are not covered by the Health Act 2006 smoking ban. Employers must therefore decide whether or not to allow employees to use e-cigarettes and similar products in the workplace and, if so, whether such use should be subject to restrictions (e.g. implementing a policy that confines their use to certain designated areas and/or specified break times).

6.181 Acas has produced some guidance, 'E-cigarettes in the workplace', aimed at assisting employers when deciding what approach to take. It identifies the following factors for employers to consider:

- individuals often use e-cigarettes as part of a plan to stop smoking – something employers may wish to support

- however, other employees may find the vapour from e-cigarettes irritating. In addition, the long term risks of e-cigarettes are unknown and the vapour could potentially create a health risk for others through passive consumption. Although the risks here are thought to be lower than for real cigarettes, the World Health Organisation has reported that the vapour emitted by e-cigarettes is not merely 'water vapour' as frequently claimed, but a vapour that may contain nicotine and other toxic particles

- given the visual similarity between some e-cigarette products and real cigarettes, employees or customers may think that real cigarettes are being smoked in the workplace. Acas therefore recommends that such use should be subject to prior line management approval

- if e-cigarettes are permitted, some employees might try to argue that real cigarettes should be allowed too (subject to the limitations imposed by the Health Act 2006).

As far as we are aware, the first tribunal case to consider the use of e-cigarettes **6.182** in the workplace was Insley v Accent Catering ET Case No.3200687/14. There, I, a catering assistant who worked at a school, was suspended by her employer after the school complained that she had been seen smoking on school premises in full view of the pupils. I had in fact been using an e-cigarette. The school's policy forbade smoking cigarettes but did not deal expressly with e-cigarettes. Shortly before a disciplinary hearing was due to take place, I resigned, claiming unfair constructive dismissal. A tribunal dismissed I's claim, holding that the employer had acted reasonably and appropriately in suspending I in response to the school's complaint and conducting the disciplinary investigation and had not committed a repudiatory breach of contract. However, the tribunal commented that had I gone through the disciplinary procedure and been dismissed by the employer, her dismissal might have been unfair because the use of e-cigarettes was not expressly prohibited in the school's smoking policy.

The Insley case demonstrates the importance for employers of having a clear policy on e-cigarettes in place. As with the introduction of any new policy, it is best practice for employers to consult with employees in advance of the policy coming into effect and to ensure that any policy is properly communicated to employees.

Theft, dishonesty and fraudulent conduct   6.183

It is generally accepted that theft and fraud amount to serious misconduct justifying summary dismissal at common law. Such conduct may also amount to criminal behaviour and could lead to a separate and parallel investigation by the police and possibly to criminal charges. Where this happens, an array of additional considerations comes into play. These are considered under 'Criminal offences at work' below. In this section, we focus on the issues that

321

are specifically relevant to ensuring that dismissal for theft and similar misconduct is fair.

6.184 **Theft offences.** Not all dismissals for theft will necessarily be fair. It depends on the circumstances. In one case, an employee with 15 years' blameless service was seen wearing the supervisor's watch, which had gone missing some six months previously. His dismissal was held to be unfair partly because of his record, but also because a distinction was drawn between theft from the employer, which breaches the confidence between employer and employee, and other theft – for example, from a fellow employee – which will not always call for such drastic action – Johnson Matthey Metals Ltd v Harding 1978 IRLR 248, EAT.

By contrast, in McCafferty v Royal Mail Group Ltd EATS 0002/12 an employee's long service was held not to be sufficient mitigation to outweigh the seriousness of his conduct. M, a postman, had been allowed to travel to work by taxi and to charge this to the employer's taxi account whenever he was asked to work on his days off. However, unknown to the employer, he continued to use the account on his normal working days. He made no mention of this to his manager, even when he was late for work after the account was closed. The employer discovered that M had charged a total of £2,422.80 to the taxi account and, despite his 19 years with the company, dismissed him for theft. In its view, M knew that he did not have permission to use the account and he had tried to conceal the fact that he was using it. His job demanded absolute trust and integrity, which had been compromised by his actions. A majority of the employment tribunal found that dismissal was fair in the circumstances and the EAT upheld that decision.

6.185 Although some dismissals for minor thefts will be unfair, there are circumstances where an employer would be justified in dismissing an employee for even the most petty of crimes. In Gamestec Leisure Ltd v Magee EAT 0419/02 the employer supplied fruit machines to the licensed retail trade. It was a cash-based business requiring the highest possible standards from employees who, like the claimant, had unsupervised access to the money in the machines. The employer was informed by two licensees that there was a cash discrepancy at two sites, of £8 and £3 respectively. The claimant was the service engineer responsible for both sites. He admitted taking £3 from one machine but claimed he put it back. He explained the £8 discrepancy on the presence of children who were fiddling with his tool box. On this basis, the employer disregarded the £8 discrepancy but considered that the £3 discrepancy amounted to either theft or gross negligence. M was therefore dismissed. The EAT overturned the decision of the tribunal and found that dismissal was within the range of reasonable responses.

6.186 **Dishonesty.** Dishonest conduct may be less clear-cut than theft. In John Lewis plc v Coyne 2001 IRLR 139, EAT, the employee was dismissed for making personal calls without permission, which the employer characterised as dishonesty in resulting disciplinary proceedings. The employer's rules indicated that unauthorised personal calls would be treated very seriously. The EAT stated that the best working test for dishonesty is that propounded by the Court of Appeal in the criminal law case of R v Ghosh 1982 QB 1053, CA. According to that test, there are two aspects to dishonesty: one objective, one subjective. First, one must decide whether according to the ordinary standards of reasonable and honest people what was done was dishonest. Secondly, one must consider whether the person concerned must have realised that what he or she was doing was by those standards dishonest. In many cases, it will be obvious. However, it was not necessarily obvious that using the employer's phone for personal reasons was dishonest. Much would depend on the circumstances of the case, which the employer did not investigate in any way. Thus the dismissal was unfair.

However, while it may be helpful for an employment tribunal to have regard to the Ghosh test in misconduct cases involving dishonesty, it is not an error of law if it fails to do so. This was the view of the EAT in Gondalia v Tesco Stores Ltd EAT 0320/14, a case concerning the dismissal of a store employee for claiming a refund under the employer's 'double the difference' policy – which was applicable to goods that had been labelled with the incorrect price – when she knew that the items were wrongly labelled. The employer took the view that this amounted to dishonesty, whereas the employee did not appear to recognise that she had done anything wrong. The EAT emphasised that the question to be asked under S.98(4) is whether in all the circumstances the employer acted reasonably or unreasonably in treating the dishonesty as a sufficient reason for dismissing the employee. The EAT went on to cast some doubt on whether the Ghosh test was appropriate at all in the field of employment law. In obiter (i.e. non-binding) comments, it stated that it may in future be necessary to consider the extent to which it is helpful or sensible to have opened a gateway into employment law from criminal jurisprudence. It had some sympathy for the view that it may be too complicated to import a further consideration into the steps to be taken in deciding whether a dismissal was fair or unfair under S.98(4) ERA. The EAT did accept, however, that the subjective state of mind of an employee accused of misconduct is a relevant consideration, as is an objective view of that conduct.

Fraudulent conduct. Almost all disciplinary procedures stipulate that 'clocking' **6.187** offences will be treated as gross misconduct likely to result in summary dismissal. In Rotherham Engineering Services Ltd v Harrison EAT 735/77 H, a charge-hand, left work one and a half hours early, even though he was well aware that his employer regarded such an offence as serious. He had arranged with his gang for them to clock him out at the proper time. The EAT held his dismissal fair, saying it was obliged to approach the case on the basis that

323

'clocking offences must be regarded by any employer and indeed by any tribunal as serious offences'.

But not all dismissals for fraudulent conduct will necessarily be fair. Dishonesty at the 'lower end of the spectrum' might, in the light of surrounding circumstances, merit a warning instead. Tribunals must look at the equity of the case and at the individual facts involved before deciding what lies within the band of reasonable responses – Schering Chemicals Ltd v Maginn EAT 180/83. Despite this, tribunals must be careful not to fall into the trap of substituting their own decision for that of the reasonable employer. In Anglian Home Improvements Ltd v Kelly 2005 ICR 242, CA, the Court of Appeal held that the tribunal had erred in this way and overturned its decision. The tribunal had been wrong to hold that K's conduct in massaging financial records in order to meet his targets was not serious enough to merit dismissal, despite the fact that the employer's rules held that deliberate falsification of records was gross misconduct.

6.188 Even where the employee does not gain from his or her ostensibly fraudulent conduct, it may so undermine the employer's confidence that dismissal will be fair – AEI Cables Ltd v McLay 1980 IRLR 84, Ct Sess (Inner House). This is particularly true in those occupations where stringent rules regarding the use and control of monies are essential and relations between management and staff require trust and good faith. In Mecca Leisure Ltd v Haggerty and ors EAT 324–6/83, for example, it was fair to dismiss a bingo hall manager for transferring cash to another branch to cover a colleague's float shortage until it could be replaced after the weekend. He was a senior employee entrusted with considerable amounts of money and had breached his employer's trust and confidence. Where, however, the employee is unaware that what he or she is doing is dishonest it may be unreasonable to dismiss without a warning, although again much depends on the circumstances of the case – Rees v Borough of Afan EAT 461/82.

Employees often seem to treat fiddling expenses as a perk rather than gross misconduct. However, even if the employee genuinely believes he or she is entitled to the sums wrongly claimed, dismissal is often fair – especially if the employee is in a position of trust. In Uniqwin UK Ltd v Weston EAT 0454/13 the employer dismissed the manager of a shopping mall whose responsibilities included the collection of rent from outdoor market stall-holders on bank holiday Mondays when it discovered that he had been keeping back £200 of the rent for himself and £50 for each of the market cleaners. The manager claimed that he was entitled to act in this way, as the previous owners of the shopping mall had expressly authorised him to do so, but the employer did not accept this explanation. The employer took the view that the manager's conduct was fraudulent, and was particularly concerned that the manager was not declaring his additional income for tax and national insurance purposes.

324

Overturning an employment tribunal's finding of unfair dismissal, the EAT held that in circumstances where the manager had failed to disclose his actions to the employer, and the income could not have been declared for tax purposes, it was clearly within the range of reasonable responses for the employer to view the manager's actions as gross misconduct justifying summary dismissal.

The distinction between dishonest behaviour and fraudulent behaviour is not **6.189** always easy to draw. However, the label attached to the employee's conduct is not crucial provided that he or she was aware that his or her behaviour was unacceptable and amounted to misconduct. In Brito-Babapulle v Ealing Hospital NHS Trust 2014 EWCA Civ 1626, CA, B, a consultant haematologist, had seen private patients during paid sick leave despite having been told not to do so by the Trust's medical director as it could be construed as fraud. Following an investigation and disciplinary hearing, the Trust dismissed B, the dismissal letter stating that the behaviour 'constituted fraud which could be considered as gross misconduct'. An employment tribunal dismissed B's unfair dismissal claim. Before the Court of Appeal, B argued that the reason for her dismissal identified in the dismissal letter was fraudulent conduct and that the tribunal had erred because it had failed to identify whether the Trust had a genuine belief that her conduct amounted to fraud and, if it did, to say whether it had reasonable grounds for that belief having conducted a reasonable investigation. Dismissing the appeal, the Court observed that it was an elementary rule of natural justice that a party should know the case that he or she has to meet and whether the allegation is one of dishonesty. However, there had never been any doubt about the allegations against B and her misconduct had been clearly identified. While there were dangers in using an emotive word, such as fraud, as a label rather than as a description of alleged conduct, the nature of the charge and a full account of the evidence had been made clear to B before the disciplinary hearing. Having found that B had been told that seeing private patients during paid sick leave was impermissible, the Trust had been entitled to conclude that her behaviour amounted to gross misconduct. Whether the label of fraud or dishonesty was attached as well was immaterial.

Violence and fighting
6.190

When considering the fairness of a dismissal for violence, tribunals should apply the test set out in British Home Stores Ltd v Burchell 1980 ICR 303, EAT, of genuine belief on reasonable grounds after reasonable investigation that the employee was guilty of misconduct – Ducal Ltd v McPherson EAT 466/80. However, tribunals should bear in mind that the burden of proof is on the employer in respect of the 'genuine belief' element of the test only: the burden in respect of the other two elements is neutral (see 'General considerations – establishing reason for dismissal' above).

6.191 Investigation

What is reasonable by way of investigation will vary depending on the circumstances – Malik v National Plastics Ltd EAT 682/78. A failure to investigate or interview the participants in a fight will not always be unfair – if they fight in the office in front of a manager, for example, as in Reid v Giltspur Bullens Transport Services Ltd EAT 549/78. Neither does reasonableness demand that everyone in the vicinity of the fight should be questioned – particularly where large numbers are involved – Harkins v Scottish Region, British Gas Corporation EAT 593/80. However, if only a few employees are present, an employer who fails, without good reason, to question them all will not usually be held to have acted reasonably, particularly where there are conflicting accounts of what actually happened. One good reason for not questioning all those present may be the fear of prejudicing the employees' trial – Malik v National Plastics Ltd (above). (For a fuller discussion on investigations pending trial, see 'Criminal offences at work' below.)

Where, after reasonable investigation, it remains uncertain who started the fight, employers may sack all the participants fairly, unless there are circumstances that make this unreasonable. In British Aerospace v Mafe EAT 565/80 the EAT stated that, in so far as spontaneous violence is concerned, 'fighting is frequently regarded as justification for the dismissal of the participants without the employer being required to draw fine distinctions between the relative guilt of those involved'. However, in Spur Way Foods Ltd v Zafar EAT 0180/14 the EAT cautioned that while 'it can sometimes be extraordinarily difficult to identify what action has been taken by which participant in a struggle or melee which lasts for only a brief period of time… each employee is an individual, with an individual case, entitled to individual consideration and therefore, separately, to the individual consideration of the employer's thought processes leading to his dismissal of that employee'.

6.192 Reasonableness of decision to dismiss

Fighting at work is generally regarded as gross misconduct justifying dismissal without prior warning. In serious cases this is so even though there is no disciplinary rule specifically forbidding it. In CA Parsons and Co Ltd v McLoughlin 1978 IRLR 65, EAT, the EAT said that 'in these days it ought not to be necessary for anybody… to have in black-and-white in the form of a rule that a fight is something which is going to be regarded very gravely by management'. However, employers should note that not all fighting is to be regarded as equally serious and not all fights will justify dismissal without prior warning.

Clear rules known to all employees, warning them of what they can expect, will be an important factor and a failure to provide such rules may tip the balance against an employer. In Meyer Dunmore International Ltd v Rogers 1978 IRLR 167, EAT, for instance, the employee was dismissed for fighting after a minor dispute which he did not start. The EAT upheld the tribunal's finding that the dismissal was unfair on the grounds that there was no clear rule about fighting, the employer's investigation was unsatisfactory, and, though there was some machinery about, there was no evidence that the fighting was particularly dangerous.

But even where there is an express disciplinary rule, employers cannot assume **6.193** that dismissal for breach of it will necessarily be fair. Such dismissals must still be reasonable in all the circumstances under S.98(4) ERA. This is illustrated by the EAT's decision in Taylor v Parsons Peebles NEI Bruce Peebles Ltd 1981 IRLR 119, EAT, where a tribunal was held to have erred in law in finding that the employer acted reasonably in dismissing an employee with long service and good conduct for striking a fellow worker – simply because the company's disciplinary rules laid down that such an offence would lead to dismissal. 'The proper test,' said the EAT, 'is not what the policy of the... employers was but what the reaction of a reasonable employer would have been in the circumstances. That reaction would have taken into account the long period of service and good conduct which the appellant was in a position to claim.'

Below, we discuss some of the factors tribunals take into account when determining the question of reasonableness.

Proper procedure. The form and adequacy of a disciplinary inquiry depends **6.194** on the circumstances of the case – see further 'Disciplinary proceedings' below.

Consistency of punishment. Employers who, without warning, act out of line **6.195** with responses adopted in comparable cases of violence or fighting in the past may be held to have acted unreasonably. In Post Office v Fennell 1981 IRLR 221, CA, F was summarily dismissed for assaulting a fellow employee in the canteen. When he complained of unfair dismissal he alleged that a number of employees had been treated differently in the past for similar offences. The tribunal found his dismissal unfair, partly because it felt that the Post Office had exaggerated the offence and partly because of the Post Office's inconsistent behaviour. Both the EAT and the Court of Appeal agreed with the tribunal's finding of inconsistency. The Court of Appeal held that there was evidence before the tribunal that the Post Office had departed from a previous course of conduct without warning and this was sufficient material to support the tribunal's conclusion that the dismissal was unfair.

Similarly, inconsistency of treatment between employees accused of the same offence is a factor tribunals will take into account, although the respective roles each employee played in the incident, their past records and their level of contrition may justify the different treatment. The guiding principle is whether the distinction made by the employer was within the band of reasonable responses open to it – Walpole v Vauxhall Motors Ltd 1998 EWCA Civ 706, CA. In UK Coal Mining v Raby EAT 1124/02 the EAT held that R had been

327

unfairly dismissed, where he and another employee were equally culpable in respect of a fight that took place in a mine, but the other employee received only a written warning. Although R had struck the first blow, this had been light and in response to serious provocation by the other employee. The fact that R had an expired written warning on his file, whereas the other employee had a clean disciplinary record, was also not a rational basis for distinguishing between the two of them. However, the EAT commented that it would have found R's dismissal fair had the other employee also been dismissed.

6.196 **Health and safety.** Even modest incidents of fighting or violence, where close to machinery or where dangerous implements are to hand, will be treated extremely seriously by tribunals because of the potential consequences. In Greenwood v HJ Heinz and Co Ltd EAT 199/77 the EAT said: 'It seems to us that it is quite wrong to say that a management faced with fighting, even of a very modest nature, in a workplace where there is a large amount of machinery would be perverse in deciding that whoever started the fight must be dismissed. The potential for danger which any degree of violence involves in close proximity to machinery is blindingly obvious. It is difficult enough sometimes to keep people who have to operate machines safe from hurting themselves in the machinery, even in the absence of any violence at all. Add some violence, and the risk of serious injury to other people, let alone severe interference with the work, is clearly great. While circumstances must of course vary infinitely, in our judgment it certainly does not go without saying that to dismiss by reason of one blow, or even by reason of the threat of a blow, is by itself plainly wrong. It may be in some circumstances wrong. It may well be a perfectly proper thing for management to do.'

6.197 **Status of parties involved.** Attacks on supervisors or managers by subordinates will normally result in a fair dismissal but not inevitably so. Again, all the circumstances must be considered – Capps v Baxter and Down Ltd EAT 793/78. In London Borough of Ealing v Goodwin EAT 121/79 a disabled road-sweeper had been at odds with his supervisor for some time when matters came to a head. Following an argument, the employee struck the supervisor. The EAT held the dismissal unfair. Although the actual assault was quite a minor one, the EAT said it is never trivial for an employee to strike a superior. However, there were exceptional circumstances in this case – namely, that the employee was disabled and had 23 years' unblemished service.

Attacks by supervisors on subordinate employees are no less serious and may justify dismissal. And even minor assaults may so destroy the relationship of trust and good faith between employer and employee as to entitle the employee to treat the contract as at an end and claim unfair constructive dismissal – Mock v Glamorgan Aluminium Co Ltd EAT 493/80.

6.198 **Mitigating circumstances.** Matters such as provocation, long service and good conduct should always be taken into account. So too should the employee's attitude in the aftermath of the incident – whether he or she expresses remorse and/or offers an apology, for example. Tribunals will look at the severity of the provocation and whether the employee's response to it was proportionate. In Capps v Baxter and Down Ltd (above), for example, the EAT recognised that the claimant, whose wife's fidelity had been called into question by a foreman, was acting under severe provocation when he struck the latter. In these circumstances, the EAT did not agree with the employer that dismissal was the inevitable consequence of the claimant's action. And in Stanton and Staveley Ltd v Ellis EAT 48/84 the employer acted unreasonably in dismissing an employee for assaulting a colleague who had racially abused him. The employer had taken the decision to dismiss in line with company policy without looking into the nature and degree of provocation involved.

Long service and good conduct may also be important mitigating factors. In Taylor v Parsons Peebles NEI Bruce Peebles Ltd (above), for example, the employee's dismissal in accordance with the company's disciplinary rules was unfair. The employer should have taken account of the employee's long service and good conduct before coming to a decision. It might be more reasonable in such circumstances to allow the employee a chance to calm down, apologise and give an undertaking to behave in the future – Taylor Woodrow Construction Ltd v Veale EAT 544/76.

Threats of violence. When considering dismissal for threats of violence, one of **6.199** the factors employers should take into account is the atmosphere of fear and intimidation caused by the threat – British Communications Corporation Ltd t/a Racal BCC Ltd v Smart EAT 227/79. The employee's attitude afterwards and any apology he or she offers should also be taken into consideration – see Taylor v Tibbett and Britten UK ET Case No.2400283/00, where the employee, who had worked for the employer for 14 years and had an exemplary record, briefly lost his temper and threatened another employee. He later apologised and offered to do whatever was necessary to make amends. The tribunal held that the decision to dismiss in these circumstances was one which no reasonable employer would have taken.

Off-duty fighting and violence
6.200

The important factor here is the link between the off-duty conduct and the workplace. In Malik v National Plastics Ltd EAT 682/78 the claimant and others were dismissed for engaging in serious fighting outside the workplace and after hours. It resulted in substantial injury to participants and 'discord, fear and even perhaps terror' throughout the workplace. The EAT held the dismissal fair. The incident had occurred sufficiently close to the works and sufficiently close to working hours as plainly to have an effect upon the industrial life of the factory. In another case, Eggleton v Kerry Foods Ltd EAT 938/95, the claimant had been warned about his behaviour towards another employee with whom there was some problem over a woman. He got into a

329

fight with the other employee and was dismissed. The dismissal was held to be fair even though the fight took place off-site because it affected working arrangements. Contrast Lanarkshire Health Board v McLeish EAT 22/91, however, where an employer attempted to establish an adverse connection between the employee's work as an auxiliary nurse and her assault upon a fellow employee outside working hours. The EAT concluded that in this case the assault was unrelated to the workplace and did not indicate that the employee was prone to violent behaviour or that she would, as a consequence, be a danger to her patients.

6.201 Criminal offences at work

Dismissal is an employment and not a criminal matter. In a case where the employee is believed to have committed misconduct in relation to his or her employment that also constitutes a criminal offence (e.g. theft, drug-taking, physical assault or business fraud), an employer is not required to be sure 'beyond reasonable doubt' that the employee has actually committed the offence before dismissing. When deciding the sufficiency of the employer's reason for dismissal in such cases, employment tribunals will usually take into account the guidelines established in British Home Stores Ltd v Burchell 1980 ICR 303, EAT (see 'General considerations – establishing reason for dismissal' above). Under those guidelines, employers need only have a genuine belief on reasonable grounds after reasonable investigation that the employee committed the offence in question. Moreover, as we have seen, tribunals must not substitute their own view of whether dismissal was reasonable but should ask whether it fell within the range of reasonable responses open to the reasonable employer – British Leyland (UK) Ltd v Swift 1981 IRLR 91, CA.

When an employee is suspected of misconduct capable of amounting to a criminal offence, one of the considerations for the employer will be whether to refer the matter to the police. Employers faced with this situation should bear in mind the obiter comments made by the Court of Appeal in Crawford and anor v Suffolk Mental Health Partnership NHS Trust 2012 IRLR 402, CA. There, two nurses were alleged to have used an unauthorised form of restraint on an elderly dementia patient. They appealed against a decision of the EAT overturning a tribunal's finding of unfair dismissal. Allowing the appeal in part, Lord Justice Elias commented that he found it 'little short of astonishing' that the police had been involved. While it was important, in his view, that hospitals in this situation must be seen to be acting transparently and not concealing wrongdoing, they also owed duties to their long-serving staff. In the words of Elias LJ: 'Being under the cloud of possible criminal proceedings is a very heavy burden for an employee to face. Employers should not subject employees to that burden without the most careful consideration and a genuine and reasonable belief that the case, if established, might justify the epithet "criminal" being applied to the employee's conduct.' In this case, there was obvious justification for restraining the patient, even if the appropriate procedures for doing so had not been employed.

If police involvement is deemed appropriate and the employee is subsequently **6.202** charged with a criminal offence, this can have an important bearing on the nature of the employer's internal investigations and the timing of any ensuing dismissal – see 'Criminal trial pending' below.

More than one suspect

6.203

As we saw in the section 'General considerations' above, under 'Establishing reason for dismissal – two or more suspects', where two or more employees are suspected of dishonesty and the employer, despite investigation, cannot discover who is to blame, it may be fair to dismiss all the suspects on reasonable suspicion short of actual belief. In Monie v Coral Racing Ltd 1981 ICR 109, CA, money was stolen from the employer's safe in circumstances where only the manager or assistant manager could have taken it. Both were dismissed on the ground that at least one of them must be guilty of theft and there was no way of telling which. In such circumstances the Court of Appeal held the dismissal to be fair.

In the Monie case the employer's suspicion had been narrowed down to the point of certainty that a serious theft had been committed by one or both of two men, although it was impossible to tell which. Where, however, the employer has no 'reasonable conclusive proof' that one of those dismissed was guilty, the principle in Monie will not apply and actual belief must be shown – Leyland Vehicles Ltd v Wright EAT 712/81.

Criminal trial pending

6.204

The mere fact that an employee has been charged with a criminal offence is not sufficient on its own for the employer to conclude that the offence has been committed. In Scottish Special Housing Association v Cooke and ors 1979 IRLR 264, EAT, the EAT considered this to be a 'very dangerous doctrine'. It held that 'the mere fact of a charge of theft being preferred, standing by itself and without any further information available to the employer, is not sufficient to constitute reasonable grounds'.

While employers need not wait until the outcome of the criminal trial before dismissing an employee, they must obtain sufficient material to justify their decision to dismiss. The fact that a criminal court later acquits the employee will not affect the fairness or otherwise of the employer's decision made at the time of the dismissal – Harris (Ipswich) Ltd v Harrison 1978 ICR 1256, EAT.

Criminal proceedings and police involvement in a case can have an important **6.205** bearing on the timing of dismissal and the kind of investigation an employer can properly carry out. On the one hand, the employer must make its own enquiries into alleged criminal acts. On the other, the fact that criminal charges

331

have been brought may limit what it can do. Only minimal investigation is likely to be necessary where the employee is caught red-handed or makes a confession to the police. Thus in Scottish Special Housing Association v Linnen 1979 IRLR 265, EAT, the claimant was fairly dismissed when copper belonging to his employer was found by the police in his garden. And in Parker v Clifford Dunn Ltd 1979 ICR 463, EAT, the EAT found it reasonable to rely on the employee's confession of theft to the police. In such cases, the EAT said, it is 'entirely reasonable for the company to depend upon what the police... put forward as the result of that investigation, rather than themselves intervening by way of independent inquiries'. (Such a dismissal must nonetheless be carried out fairly. Any procedural defect may otherwise render it unfair – Rumbelows Ltd v Ellis EAT 664/87.) Where the evidence is not so clear-cut, however, further investigation will be necessary and employers 'ought to take reasonable steps to obtain the proper material' on which to decide whether or not to dismiss – Chard and Hodge v Strand Hotels EAT 305/77.

Whether the employer puts its own internal investigation on hold while the police investigation is under way is essentially a matter for the employer to decide. In Secretary of State for Justice v Mansfield EAT 0539/09 the claimant, a prison officer, was unhappy about the employer's decision to suspend the disciplinary proceedings while the police investigation into his alleged misconduct was ongoing. He argued that the suspension resulted in unreasonable delay. The EAT rejected this argument, holding that the employer's decision to postpone the disciplinary hearing while the police were still gathering evidence and while a Crown Court prosecution was under way was entirely proper and could not be said to be unreasonable.

6.206 **Police charges can inhibit employer's enquiries.** In Carr v Alexander Russell Ltd 1979 ICR 469, Ct Sess (Outer House), the Court of Session went so far as to say that it would be improper for employers to carry out any form of internal investigation into alleged dishonesty, or to question the employee, when a criminal prosecution is pending because of the risk of prejudicing the subsequent criminal trial. This appears to remain the approach of Scottish tribunals. However, in Harris (Ipswich) Ltd v Harrison (above) the EAT in England expressly refrained from following the Carr case. It thought that the employer should discuss the matter with the employee, not only to give the employee a chance to put his or her side but also to discuss the action which the employer proposed to take.

Difficulties can arise where the employee stays silent in order to protect him or herself. An employee's refusal to take part in the employer's investigation – perhaps because of legal advice that participation may prejudice the criminal proceedings – does not mean that dismissal before the outcome of the criminal proceedings is known will necessarily be unfair. In such a case 'the employer is entitled to consider whether the material which he has is strong enough to justify... dismissal without waiting. If there are doubts, then no doubt it would be fair to wait. On the other hand, if the evidence produced is, in the absence of an explanation, sufficiently indicative of guilt, then the employer may be entitled to act' – Harris and anor v Courage (Eastern) Ltd 1981 ICR 496, EAT (upheld by the Court of Appeal – 1982 ICR 530, CA).

In the Courage case H and S were charged with the theft of beer from their **6.207** employer. They had been told to take a company lorry from the depot to a garage. A similar lorry was later seen being loaded up with kegs of beer at a depot close to the garage. H was recognised, and a description of another man was consistent with his being S. The lorry was driven off at speed, grazing the depot gates as it went. Shortly afterwards, the vehicle was found by the police with H and S in it. The lorry had paint on it from the depot gate and had almost exactly the same registration number as given by one of the witnesses at the depot. The company set the disciplinary procedure in motion but the employees, on the advice of their lawyers, declined to take part. They were dismissed, but were subsequently acquitted in the crown court. The Court of Appeal upheld the EAT's conclusion that the dismissals were fair. The Court considered that, in the absence of an explanation from H and S, the employer reasonably believed them to be involved in the theft.

No protestations of innocence. The decision in the Courage case shows that **6.208** one of the reasons for offering employees the chance to put their side is to strengthen the employer's case if they refuse to participate in the disciplinary process. In Carr v Alexander Russell Ltd (above) Lord McDonald thought it significant that the employee had made no protestations of innocence and no attempt to use the grievance procedure, although he knew of it. His Lordship did not think the employer was under a duty to demand an explanation before deciding to dismiss: the employee should have proclaimed his innocence unbidden.

Confessions retracted. An employee may retract a confession given to the **6.209** employer once he or she realises that criminal proceedings are to be commenced. However, this will not prevent the employer being able to rely on that original confession if it is reasonable, in the circumstances, to do so – University College at Buckingham v Phillips 1982 ICR 318, EAT. In that case the EAT said, 'we think that, in the majority of cases, a later retraction will not substantially remove the force of the original confession. But it is not a matter on which we can lay down any general rule: it is a matter for the... tribunal to decide in each case.'

Injunction to prevent dismissal. As a general rule, the courts are unwilling to **6.210** grant an injunction stopping an employer from dismissing employees. However, in R v British Broadcasting Corporation ex p Lavelle 1983 ICR 99, QBD, the High Court said that an employee could seek an injunction to stop a dismissal taking effect where this was necessary to prevent a real danger of miscarriage of

333

justice in a criminal case. In that case the employee had sought an injunction to stop her employer proceeding with her internal appeal (against her dismissal for theft) because she thought her explanation to her employer might prejudice her criminal trial for the same offence. However, the High Court judge decided that, on the facts of the case, there would be no miscarriage of justice if the employer continued hearing her appeal and the injunction was therefore refused.

6.211 After criminal trial

Where an employer leads the employee to believe that it will be bound by the outcome of the criminal trial, it runs the risk of acting unfairly if it dismisses the employee after an acquittal. And since many acquittals are obtained on very technical grounds, employers may wish to reserve their position on whether or not to dismiss until all the evidence has come to light during the trial. If an employer does make such a reservation, it should make its position crystal clear to the employee.

There is another reason why employers may wish to wait before making a decision on whether to dismiss. Further evidence, though not sufficient to secure a criminal conviction, may still reveal a serious breach of duty or discipline justifying dismissal. For example, a cashier charged with theft from a till, guilty or not, is often undoubtedly in breach of company rules in respect of the way in which the till has been operated. And an employee who removes goods from the premises, whether criminally guilty or not, is often in breach of company rules by acting in this way – Harris (Ipswich) Ltd v Harrison 1978 ICR 1256, EAT. Where the employer decides that the evidence that has come to light at the trial gives it reasonable grounds to dismiss for a breach of company rules, it should make this clear to the employee concerned. In Greater Manchester Passenger Transport Executive v Sheikh unreported 28.6.76, EAT, a bus driver was suspended and later charged with theft. He was acquitted but the company decided to dismiss for breaches confirmed by the trial. The EAT upheld the finding of unfairness. In the EAT's view, where employers suspend and await the outcome of a trial, 'they need to make it very clear... that they are dismissing the employee, not for the offence which has been found not to be proved, but for the underlying failure to follow the procedure which had also given rise to the charge being made'.

6.212 Where an employee has been convicted of a dishonest act, this may well constitute reasonable grounds for the employer's belief in the employee's guilt, but it is still necessary for the employer to carry out such investigations as are reasonable in the circumstances – Secretary of State for Scotland v Campbell 1992 IRLR 263, EAT. In that case the claimant was convicted of embezzling club funds. He maintained that the way the club was run made it difficult for him to control the finances. He was only one member of a large committee involved in managing the club. The tribunal found that a reasonable employer would have conducted a detailed investigation into how the finances had got into such a state before dismissing and the EAT upheld the finding of unfair dismissal.

Employers do not have to await a criminal appeal and subsequent appeals will not affect the fairness of a dismissal: once the outcome of the trial is known, a guilty verdict might well suffice to form an adequate basis for dismissal. In Kingston v British Railways Board 1984 ICR 781, CA, the employee was found guilty of assault. The facts had been fully investigated at the crown court and it was reasonable for the employer to rely on the verdict without conducting independent investigations before dismissing (since the employee was in prison serving his sentence). This was so notwithstanding the fact that the conviction was subsequently quashed by the Court of Appeal.

6.213 An employment tribunal should be wary of relying too heavily upon the pronouncements of the criminal trial judge when deciding whether or not an employee's subsequent dismissal falls within the band of reasonable responses. In Hensman v Ministry of Defence EAT 0067/14 H was found guilty of public indecency, having covertly photographed and videoed a fellow employee in various stages of undress. In sentencing him to three years' community service, the trial judge commented that due to a mental disorder H was not to blame for his actions. The EAT held that the tribunal was wrong to rely solely on the sentencing remarks of the trial judge when deciding that H's subsequent dismissal was unfair. It should also have considered the MoD's particular concerns, notably its concerns about breach of trust and covert conduct. The matter was a remitted to a fresh tribunal to decide the issue.

Where an employer has dealt with an employee's misconduct before any criminal proceedings are concluded, it is not then entitled to change its mind in light of a subsequent criminal conviction unless new evidence has come to light. In Central Nottinghamshire Area Health Authority v Shine EAT 562/82 the employee was given a written warning for neglecting her patients and misusing their money. Subsequently she was convicted of receiving stolen goods (i.e. goods bought with that money) and she was summarily dismissed. The EAT held that the dismissal was unfair because the employer had imposed a double penalty for the same offence. No new evidence had emerged to justify the employer's change of mind.

When to dismiss

6.214 Delay in investigation may make the dismissal unfair. In Marley Homecare Ltd v Dutton 1981 IRLR 380, EAT, for instance, the dismissal of a cashier was found to be unfair because of too long a delay (one week) between test purchases and confronting the employee. She could neither remember the incident nor put forward an explanation. However, lengthy inquiry may sometimes be needed to confirm a suspicion. In Refund Rentals Ltd v McDermott 1977 IRLR 59, EAT, the EAT held that 14 weeks' delay for investigation of a suspected theft

335

could not be said to make dismissal unfair when the investigation provided reasonable grounds for the employer's suspicions – even though the employee might have been lulled into a belief that the incident was closed. The moral may be that, to avoid a finding of unfair dismissal, employers should be open about their suspicions from the start, make it plain what it is they are investigating, and suspend with pay (unless the contract allows for suspension without pay) while they look into things.

Where there is insufficient evidence to sustain a reasonable belief in an employee's guilt, it will generally be unfair to dismiss prior to a trial settling the matter. But if it is inappropriate to allow the employee to remain in his or her old post in the meantime, there are two possibilities open to the employer: suspension or temporary transfer.

6.215 **Suspension.** Suspension pending the outcome of a criminal trial (and/or the conclusion of the employer's internal investigations) will often be an appropriate course of action. However, employers should bear in mind the obiter comments made by the Court of Appeal in Crawford and anor v Suffolk Mental Health Partnership NHS Trust 2012 IRLR 402, CA. There, two nurses were alleged to have used an unauthorised form of restraint on an elderly dementia patient. They appealed against a decision of the EAT overturning a tribunal's finding of unfair dismissal. Allowing the appeal in part, Lord Justice Elias commented: 'It appears to be the almost automatic response of many employers to allegations of this kind to suspend the employees concerned, and to forbid them from contacting anyone, as soon as a complaint is made, and quite irrespective of the likelihood of the complaint being established… I appreciate that suspension is often said to be in the employee's best interests; but many employees would question that, and in my view they would often be right to do so. They will frequently feel belittled and demoralised by the total exclusion from work and the enforced removal from their work colleagues, many of whom will be friends. This can be psychologically very damaging. Even if they are subsequently cleared of the charges, the suspicions are likely to linger, not least I suspect because the suspension appears to add credence to them.' (For discussion of the circumstances in which suspension can amount to a breach of the implied duty of trust and confidence, see IDS Employment Law Handbook, 'Contracts of Employment' (2014), Chapter 4, 'Implied term of mutual trust and confidence', under 'Breach by employer – disciplinary matters'.)

The employer must make it quite clear that an employee is being suspended pending the outcome of the trial and that only after this will a final decision about his or her future (including dismissal) be made. It may, however, be months before the trial. Unless the employer has a contractual right to suspend without pay, the employee must receive full wages for the entire period. If he or she is not paid, the employee may be entitled to bring a claim in the employment tribunal for unlawful deduction from wages, or even constructive dismissal. But any tribunal claim by the employee should be brought as soon as possible, as awaiting the outcome of the trial is likely to be an inadequate excuse for a late application – Trevelyans (Birmingham) Ltd v Norton 1991 ICR 488, EAT (see further Chapter 2, 'Exclusions from right to claim', under 'Time limits'). Even if there is a contractual right to suspend without pay, the tribunal may imply a term to the effect that such suspension will only last for a reasonable period unless the contract expressly states the length of time employees can be suspended.

If the employer suspends an employee but undertakes to wait until after the criminal charge has been disposed of before making a final decision, dismissal in breach of that undertaking may be unfair unless the employee is told of the change in the employer's attitude and given a chance to make representations. In Harris (Ipswich) Ltd v Harrison 1978 ICR 1256, EAT, the claimant was charged with theft from his employer and was suspended on pay until the charge could be dealt with. However, when it was learnt that he had elected for a trial by jury that was not likely to take place for some time, he was dismissed. The EAT considered that it was the employer's duty 'before deciding to change their mind and to dismiss him without awaiting the result of the trial in the crown court, first to make some enquiry of him… [T]o dismiss him in those circumstances, without any enquiry at all, was unfair… [T]here was no reason… why they should not have communicated with his solicitors… [H]ad they sought to discuss the matter… no doubt the matter could have been thrashed out, and it would have been difficult to say… that they had acted unfairly.' Similarly, in Z v A 2014 IRLR 244, EAT, A was employed by Z as a school caretaker. Outside work, an allegation was made to the police that he had once sexually abused a child. A was suspended while a police investigation took place. After the investigation had been going on for almost a year, A was dismissed on the basis that trust and confidence had broken down. An employment tribunal's finding that the dismissal was unfair was upheld by the EAT. An important factor was that the allegation had been given no additional force by the endorsement of the police or any other authoritative body. The fact that the employer's duty was first and foremost to its children did not remove its responsibility to its employees. Part of the weakness in the employer's case was that, having waited for more than a year while the police investigation was conducted, it dismissed A just when the investigation was drawing to a conclusion on the basis that – whatever the outcome – the employment could not continue. If that were indeed the position, then it would have been more consistent of the employer to have dismissed much sooner.

Temporary transfer. As with suspension, temporary transfer is only permissible **6.216** where the employer has the contractual right to impose such a change. However, where it is made clear that the transfer is only a temporary measure until the trial and there is no loss of pay, then, even if the employee claims constructive dismissal, the employer may be able to persuade the tribunal that such dismissal

337

was nonetheless fair. Indeed, it may even be arguable that a temporary job transfer with no loss of pay does not amount to a fundamental breach of contract entitling an employee to claim constructive dismissal in the first place, in which case he or she will be taken not to have been dismissed – rather, he or she will be taken to have resigned – and the question of unfair dismissal will not arise – Scott v Aveling Barford Ltd 1978 ICR 214, EAT.

6.217 Employee on remand

An employee may be remanded in custody or on bail pending trial. Where an employee is remanded in custody, it should be remembered that he or she has not been convicted of any offence. Unless, therefore, the employer has carried out a reasonable investigation, and dismissal can be said to be a reasonable response in the circumstances, it would be unwise for the employer to dismiss for conduct reasons. It might, however, be reasonable to dismiss at an early stage for 'some other substantial reason' ('SOSR') if the organisation cannot manage without a replacement and the prospects of a quick release are bleak – see Chapter 8, 'Some other substantial reason'.

Alternatively, the contract of employment may come to end by operation of law through the employee's inability to perform it while on remand – or where bail conditions substantially interfere with normal working – in which case there is no dismissal. Whether or not bail conditions or remand 'frustrate' the contract in this way will depend on the facts of each case, although, as a general rule, tribunals are reluctant to find that there has been a frustration. For further details, see IDS Employment Law Handbook, 'Contracts of Employment' (2014), Chapter 13, 'Termination by operation of law', under 'Frustration'.

6.218 Custodial sentences

If, at the end of criminal proceedings, an employee is sentenced to long-term imprisonment, the employer may decide to dismiss. It is likely to be a fair dismissal for conduct if the employee's offence was related to his or her work. It may also be a fair dismissal for SOSR if the circumstances of the imprisonment are such as to reflect adversely on the employer's image or to destroy trust and confidence in the employee – see Chapter 8, 'Some other substantial reason'. A custodial sentence may also 'frustrate' the contract – see IDS Employment Law Handbook, 'Contracts of Employment' (2014), Chapter 13, 'Termination by operation of law', under 'Frustration'.

6.219 Previous convictions

An employer, particularly one that is operating in a sector where honesty and integrity are seen as paramount, such as the financial services sector, may wish to know whether an employee has any past criminal convictions for dishonesty. The circumstances in which the employer is entitled to this type of information will largely depend on the nature of the work carried out.

Spent convictions under Rehabilitation of Offenders Act. An employee is **6.220** under no obligation to disclose to any employer a conviction that is 'spent' under the Rehabilitation of Offenders Act 1974 (ROA). A conviction is 'spent' after a period varying in length depending on the gravity of the original sentence. Once a conviction is spent, the person is treated as having committed no offence at all and any questions about his or her past convictions or conduct (e.g. on an application form) are taken as not referring to a spent conviction – S.4(2) ROA. Moreover, a spent conviction, or a failure to disclose one, is not a proper ground for dismissing an employee or prejudicing him or her in any way in the job – S.4(3)(b) ROA.

Until March 2014, the ROA applied only to minor offences; namely, those attracting a sentence of no more than 30 months' imprisonment. However, under reforms introduced by S.139 of the Legal Aid, Sentencing and Punishment Act 2012, the scheme was extended to cover convictions resulting in a sentence of up to four years in prison. The reforms also reduced the period that must elapse before a conviction becomes 'spent'. For example, whereas previously a conviction resulting in a sentence of between 6–30 months' imprisonment would become spent ten years after the date of conviction, now such a conviction becomes spent after a period of four years plus the length of the original sentence.

Certain professions (doctors, dentists, solicitors and barristers, for example) **6.221** and office holders (applicants for judicial or law enforcement posts) are not protected by the ROA; nor are holders of certain posts with local authorities, like teachers and social workers. Similarly, the ROA does not apply to certain regulated occupations, including managers of abortion clinics, registered firearms dealers and anyone applying to work in an occupation regulated by the Gaming Board – see the Rehabilitation of Offenders Act 1974 (Exceptions) Order 1975 SI 1975/1023 ('the ROA Exceptions Order').

Dismissal for having, or failing to disclose, a spent conviction is not one of the automatically unfair reasons for dismissal listed in the ERA (see Chapter 9, 'Automatically unfair dismissals', for a full list). But it seems that the effect of S.4(3)(b) ROA, read with S.4(2), is such that a tribunal need not consider general questions of fairness under S.98(4) ERA where a spent conviction, or failure to disclose it, has been relied on in the decision to dismiss.

This interpretation garners some support from case law. In Property Guards **6.222** Ltd v Taylor and anor 1982 IRLR 175, EAT, the EAT upheld a tribunal's finding that two security guards were unfairly dismissed when their employer learnt that they both had minor spent convictions for dishonesty which they had failed to disclose. It is not clear, however, whether the EAT believed that it followed from S.4(3) ROA that the decision to dismiss on the basis of the spent conviction was not a proper ground for dismissal under S.98(1) or (2) ERA and was therefore necessarily unfair, or whether there was a justifiable reason for

339

dismissal but that by virtue of S.4(3) the employer did not act reasonably in treating it as a sufficient reason for dismissing the employees.

In Hendry and anor v Scottish Liberal Club 1977 IRLR 5, ET, a tribunal justified a finding of unfair dismissal on the basis of both these approaches. However, we would suggest that the correct view is that if the employer's reason for dismissal is that the employee has, or has concealed, a spent conviction, the employer has not shown a justifiable reason for dismissal so as to satisfy S.98(1) or (2) ERA and the dismissal is therefore automatically unfair. Moreover, the spent conviction does not need to be the principal reason for dismissal for the ex-offender's claim to succeed: it will be sufficient for the spent conviction to play a material part in the decision to dismiss.

6.223 **Unspent convictions.** Where an employee conceals convictions for dishonesty that are not spent, he or she forfeits the employer's trust on discovery of this deception and may be fairly dismissed despite satisfactory service. In Torr v British Railways Board 1977 ICR 785, EAT, the EAT rejected the argument that the ROA was part of a wider public policy that made it unfair to dismiss a person because he or she has a previous conviction irrespective of other circumstances. 'It is of the utmost importance,' said the EAT, 'that an employer seeking an employee to hold a position of responsibility and trust should be able to select for employment a candidate in whom he can have confidence. It is fundamental to that confidence that the employee should truthfully disclose his history so far as it is sought by the intending employer.' In that case the employee's deliberate lie regarding his conviction had destroyed 'the foundation on which the requisite confidence of master and servant has to be built'. Therefore, although the employee had been working satisfactorily as a guard for 16 months, the dismissal was fair.

6.224 **Criminal record checks.** Under Part V of the Police Act 1997, organisations that are recruiting for posts exempted from the scope of the ROA may obtain information on employees' criminal records from the Disclosure and Barring Service (DBS), which replaced the Criminal Records Bureau (CRB) with effect from December 2012. For example, an employer may ask an individual applying for a position in the care sector to apply for an enhanced DBS check, which will not only provide details of any convictions or cautions but could include any information that the chief officer of the relevant police force reasonably believes to be relevant. Any information thus disclosed, even if it amounts to unproven allegations, may be relied on by an employer in deciding whether or not to dismiss. However, in R (on the application of John Pinnington) v Chief Constable of Thames Valley Police 2008 EWHC 1870 (Admin), QBD, the High Court warned against employers applying a blanket policy of dismissing any individual who is unable to provide a 'clean' certificate.

In B v A EAT S/0029/06 B was dismissed from his post as a full-time support worker with a charity that provided care to extremely vulnerable young people.

The dismissal followed the charity's receipt of an 'enhanced disclosure' letter from the Chief Constable, which disclosed an allegation that B had, in 1993, committed a serious sexual offence. B contended that someone else had eventually been convicted of the offence, but his dismissal was upheld after an appeal. B had not been able to persuade the police to retract the disclosure and the charity had not assisted B by asking the police to verify his contention. B brought an unfair dismissal claim against the charity. His claim was upheld on the basis that the charity's failure to assist B was outside the band of reasonable responses. On appeal, the EAT overturned that decision. Although the tribunal had regarded the charity's failure to ask the police to verify B's assertion as unreasonable, it had made no findings as to whether B had actually requested such assistance or as to what would have happened if the charity had in fact asked. Furthermore, the tribunal had not made a finding that dismissal itself was outside the band of reasonable responses. In fact, the tribunal had stated that upon receipt of the disclosure from the Chief Constable, the charity had no choice but to dismiss. In light of this, the EAT was of the opinion that the tribunal's decision had been 'plainly wrong', and that 'the only conclusion that a reasonable tribunal could have arrived at... is that it was reasonable for the respondents not to have approached the police... and that, in the whole circumstances, the decision was a fair one'.

6.225 It should be noted that in the B v A case, rather than remitting the matter for reconsideration by the tribunal, the EAT substituted a finding that the dismissal was fair. While that was an outcome decided on the particular facts of the case, it is difficult to conceive of a situation where the result might be different: the upshot of the decision is that it is not for the employer but for the individual employee to challenge the police about the non-conviction information supplied.

Another case involving a challenge to a criminal record disclosure was Washington v First West Yorkshire Ltd ET Case No.1810239/09. When W had applied for his job as a bus driver for vulnerable passengers, he had signed a statement confirming that he had no convictions and indicating his understanding that if the employer were to discover that he did, in fact, have any convictions, this could lead to dismissal. The employer subsequently required W to obtain a criminal record check, the results of which indicated a conviction against someone with W's name and W was therefore asked to provide fingerprints in order to verify whether or not it was the same person. The result of the fingerprint analysis was positive but W disputed it. The employer told W to follow the CRB complaints procedure to challenge the result and W said that his lawyer, M, was pursuing his complaint. The employer became concerned at how long the process was taking and attempted to contact W's lawyer. However, it could not find his details on the solicitors' roll or on the website of the law firm W had said he was using. Eventually, the employer managed to speak to M by phone and M admitted he had not made any application to the CRB. The

341

employer concluded that W had persuaded M to impersonate a solicitor in an attempt to conceal his conviction and W was dismissed for gross misconduct. The tribunal found the dismissal fair. W's conduct by seeking to mislead the employer about something as important as a CRB check had destroyed all trust and confidence that the employer could have in him.

6.226 In early 2013, the Court of Appeal, hearing three applications for judicial review in R (on the application of T) v Chief Constable of Greater Manchester and ors and other cases 2013 EWCA Civ 25, CA, made a declaration that the statutory criminal record checking scheme was incompatible with the right to respect for private and family life under Article 8 of the European Convention on Human Rights. The Court held that, while the scheme pursued the legitimate aims of protecting employers and vulnerable persons, and enabling employers to make an assessment as to whether an individual was suitable for a particular kind of work, requiring the disclosure of all recorded convictions and cautions, without taking account of factors such as the seriousness of the crime and the age of the offender at the time, was disproportionate. It therefore found a breach of Article 8 and left it to Parliament to revise the scheme. The Court also held that the obligation on a job applicant under the ROA Exceptions Order (see 'Spent convictions under Rehabilitation of Offenders Act' above) to disclose all convictions and cautions to a prospective employer was in breach of Article 8. The Government appealed against this decision but the Supreme Court upheld the Court of Appeal's decision that the criminal records checking scheme was in breach of Article 8. However, it overturned the Court of Appeal's declaration that the ROA Exceptions Order was ultra vires (i.e. that the Government had exceeded its powers when making the Order) because the implication of such a declaration was that the operation of the Order *always* violated Article 8, whereas in some cases – perhaps many – the circumstances of a conviction or caution would mean that its disclosure *would* be proportionate to the legitimate objective behind the Order – see R (on the application of T) v Chief Constable of Greater Manchester and ors and other cases 2014 UKSC 35, SC.

Subsequent to the Court of Appeal's decision in the above case, new filtering rules for criminal records checks, removing many of the spent convictions and cautions that were previously disclosable, came into effect on 29 May 2013. Under the new rules, an adult conviction that did not result in a custodial sentence and that dates back 11 years or more will be removed from a DBS certificate if it is the individual's only offence. An adult caution will be removed after six years have elapsed since the date of the caution. Similar rules apply to those who were under the age of 18 at the time of the offence. However, certain offences, such as sexual and violent offences, will remain disclosable. The relevant changes to the ROA Exceptions Order were made by the Rehabilitation of Offenders Act 1974 (Exceptions) Order 1975 (Amendment) (England and Wales) Order 2013 SI 2013/1198.

Criminal offences outside of employment 6.227

The scope of 'conduct' as a potentially fair reason for dismissal under S.98(2)(b) ERA is not limited to conduct in the course, or within the scope, of employment. It also covers conduct outside of employment 'so long as in some respect or other it affects the employee, or could be thought to be likely to affect the employee, when he is doing his work' – Singh v London Country Bus Services Ltd 1976 IRLR 176, EAT.

Adverse connection between offence and employment. When dismissal is 6.228
contemplated by the employer on the basis of a criminal offence committed outside employment, the tribunal will place particular emphasis on whether there is an adverse connection between the offence and the employment. The Acas Code of Practice on Disciplinary and Grievance Procedures states that consideration needs to be given to what effect the charge or conviction of a criminal offence has on the employee's suitability to do the job and his or her relationship with the employer, work colleagues and customers (see para 31).

An employer's failings in this regard were considered by the Court of Session in CJD v Royal Bank of Scotland 2014 IRLR 25, Ct Sess (Inner House). There, RBS dismissed CJD after he had a domestic altercation with his girlfriend, another RBS employee, which resulted in him being charged with assault and breach of the peace. The dismissing officer accepted that CJD acted in self defence – he pushed his girlfriend onto a sofa after she had scratched his face. Nevertheless, he took the view that CJD should be dismissed because, as a result of the assault, he presented a risk to the employer, its employees and its property. The employment tribunal, upholding CJD's unfair dismissal claim, found that RBS failed to show a potentially fair reason for dismissal. The Court of Session agreed. In the Court's view, the EAT had made it clear in Thomson v Alloa Motor Company Ltd 1983 IRLR 403, EAT, that 'conduct' within the meaning of S.98(2)(b) ERA means 'actings of such a nature, whether done in the course of employment or outwith it, that reflect in some way upon the employer-employee relationship'. According to the Court, it was difficult to see how the action of an employee, acting in self defence, pushing another person onto a sofa in a domestic situation could be such as to reflect upon the relationship between that employee and his employer. The tribunal's finding of unfair dismissal was accordingly upheld.

Nature of employee's job. The types of criminal offence that most commonly 6.229
affect the employment relationship are those involving sexual conduct, violence or dishonesty. The factors that persuade tribunals that there is an adverse connection between conduct and employment will obviously vary from case to case. A tribunal will pay attention to all the circumstances – including the employee's length of service, status, relations with fellow workers, influence over vulnerable groups and the effect on the business. In Lloyds Bank plc v

343

Bardin EAT 38/89 a part-time cleaner was dismissed after she pleaded guilty to three charges of obtaining money by deception. The EAT decided that the issue was not whether the employee was actually a security risk but whether the bank acted reasonably in all the circumstances in treating her as one. On this basis, the EAT found an adequate link between the offence and the employee's type of work to warrant dismissal.

The nature of the employee's job was considered crucial by the EAT in Moore v C and A Modes 1981 IRLR 71, EAT. There, the claimant, a section leader in one of the employer's stores, was dismissed after 20 years' service for shoplifting at another store. The dismissal was held to be fair. On appeal, the EAT commented: 'It seems to us to be quite unreal to expect any employer in the retail trade not to dismiss someone who has, for 20 years, been a trusted employee, who is reasonably believed to have been stealing just down the road although not from the employers themselves, because nobody should be more alive than such an employee to the damage which is caused by what is commonly called shoplifting.'

6.230 Potential damage to an employer's reputation is also considered to be an important factor in these cases. This is particularly pertinent where public service employees are concerned. In Gunn v British Waterways Board EAT 138/81, for instance, the employee was dismissed after breaking into a surgery to steal some drugs. The EAT rejected a plea that his job was unaffected and pointed to the effect on the employer's reputation and the adverse reaction of the workforce.

However, the EAT has also held that the impact on an employee of allegations of serious criminal misbehaviour with regard to the loss of his or her job and the effect on his or her reputation and future employment prospects is relevant to whether a dismissal is fair. In A v B 2003 IRLR 405, EAT, a residential social worker was suspended pending an investigation into allegations that he had had an inappropriate relationship with a 14-year-old in his care. The EAT said that such allegations must always be the subject of the most careful investigation, given the potential effect that they could have on the employee.

6.231 **Criminal charge itself amounts to misconduct.** Some criminal charges relating to an employee's conduct outside of work may be considered so serious that the employer can fairly dismiss the employee on the basis of the charge alone, regardless of whether the employee has actually committed the offence in question. In Kearney v Royal Mail Group Ltd ET Case No. 3100476/10 the employee was dismissed because he had been charged with murder. The section of the employer's code of conduct dealing with criminal offences outside of work required the employer to consider whether 'the offence is one that makes the individual unsuitable for his/her type of work or unacceptable to other employees or the business'. The employer took its decision before the outcome of the criminal trial was known, but the internal appeal was postponed until after the trial had concluded (and the employee had been convicted and sentenced to life imprisonment). The employee's unfair dismissal claim was presented to an employment tribunal by his daughter because the employee – being in prison – could not attend in person. The tribunal held that murder was such a serious offence that dismissal on the basis of the charge itself was fair. In so holding, the tribunal took into account the significant amount of press coverage of the case and the consequent impact on the employer's reputation, as well as the fact that one of the employee's bail conditions was that he could not talk to witnesses in the case, two of whom were colleagues, and that another colleague had refused to work with the employee after he was charged. The tribunal commented that it would have been wrong for the employer to conduct its own investigation into whether the employee was actually guilty of murder. The employer had followed as fair a procedure as it could, given the difficult circumstances.

Disciplinary proceedings 6.232

As explained in Chapter 3, 'Unfairness', a conduct dismissal will not normally be treated as fair unless certain procedural steps have been followed. Without following such steps, it will not in general be possible for an employer to show that it acted reasonably in treating the conduct reason as a sufficient reason to dismiss. In Polkey v AE Dayton Services Ltd 1988 ICR 142, HL, Lord Bridge itemised the procedural steps as follows:

- a full investigation of the conduct, and

- a fair hearing to hear what the employee wants to say in explanation or mitigation.

When assessing whether the employer adopted a reasonable procedure, tribunals will use the range of reasonable responses test that applies to substantive unfair dismissal claims. As Lord Justice Mummery said in J Sainsbury plc v Hitt 2003 ICR 111, CA: 'The range of reasonable responses test (or, to put it another way, the need to apply the objective standards of the reasonable employer) applies as much to the question whether the investigation into the suspected misconduct was reasonable in all the circumstances as it does to the reasonableness of the decision to dismiss for the conduct reason.'

In Taylor v OCS Group Ltd 2006 ICR 1602, CA, the Court of Appeal further 6.233 stressed that a tribunal's task under S.98(4) ERA is not simply to assess the fairness of the disciplinary process as a whole but also to consider the employer's reason for the dismissal as the two impact upon each other. It stated that where an employee is dismissed for serious misconduct, a tribunal might well decide that, notwithstanding some procedural imperfections, the employer acted reasonably in treating the reason as sufficient to dismiss the employee. Conversely, the Court considered that where the misconduct is of a less serious nature, so that the decision to dismiss is nearer the borderline, the tribunal

345

might well conclude that a procedural deficiency had such impact that the employer did not act reasonably in dismissing the employee.

Until April 2009, employers were required to follow, at a minimum, the procedural steps set out in the statutory dismissal and disciplinary procedures (DDPs). Failure to comply with the DDPs meant that a subsequent dismissal was automatically unfair by virtue of S.98A(1) ERA. The DDPs, and with them S.98A(1), were repealed with effect from 6 April 2009. In their place, employers are expected to have regard to the matters set out in the revised Acas Code of Practice on Discipline and Grievance Procedures ('the Acas Code') when contemplating taking disciplinary action. The Acas Code is relevant to the question of liability and will be taken into account by a tribunal when determining the reasonableness of a dismissal in accordance with S.98(4) – S.207 Trade Union and Labour Relations (Consolidation) Act 1992 (TULR(C)A). Furthermore, if the dismissal is found to be unfair, the tribunal can increase (or indeed decrease) an award of compensation by up to 25 per cent for an unreasonable failure to follow the Code if it considers it just and equitable to do so – S.207A TULR(C)A (for further details, see Chapter 16, 'Compensatory awards: adjustments', under 'Adjustments for breach of Acas Code of Practice').

6.234 Where the tribunal finds that the employer failed to adopt a fair procedure at the time of the dismissal, whether as set out in the Acas Code or elsewhere (for example, in the employer's disciplinary rules), then save in wholly exceptional cases the dismissal will not be rendered fair simply because the unfairness did not affect the end result. That, as the House of Lords established in Polkey v AE Dayton Services Ltd (above), is an issue that is only relevant in determining the level of compensation – see '"No difference" rule' below, and Chapter 16, 'Compensatory awards: adjustments', under '"Polkey reductions"'.

Note that where an employer's disciplinary procedure is contractual, an employee could seek an injunction to prevent the employer from continuing with a disciplinary process in breach of the requirements of that procedure – see IDS Employment Law Handbook, 'Contracts of Employment' (2014), Chapter 3, 'Breach of contract', under 'Equitable remedies – injunctions'.

6.235 **Acas Code of Practice**
The Acas Code of Practice on Disciplinary and Grievance Procedures ('the Acas Code') sets out basic requirements for fairness that will be applicable in most conduct cases. It is intended to provide the standard of reasonable behaviour in most instances and, although not in itself legally binding, it is admissible as evidence before a tribunal. In particular, a tribunal must take its provisions into account where they are relevant to the case in question and a failure to follow the Code can result in an adjustment in compensation of up to 25 per cent in a subsequent employment tribunal claim – Ss.207 and 207A TULR(C)A.

346

The Acas Code's section on handling disciplinary issues (paras 5–31) sets out the steps employers must normally follow, namely:

- carry out an investigation to establish the facts of each case
- inform the employee of the problem
- hold a meeting with the employee to discuss the problem
- allow the employee to be accompanied at the meeting
- decide on appropriate action
- provide employees with an opportunity to appeal.

We examine these basic steps in detail below.

The Code does acknowledge that it may sometimes not be practicable for **6.236** employers to take all of the steps set out therein and dismissal in such cases may still be reasonable. Conversely, even if all the steps have been followed to the letter, dismissal may nevertheless be unfair.

In order to expand on and explain these basic steps, a non-statutory and non-binding Acas Guide, 'Discipline and grievances at work', accompanies the Acas Code ('the Acas Guide'). It provides detailed practical advice on the formulation and operation of disciplinary procedures. By way of general advice, the guide states that procedures should:

- be in writing
- be non-discriminatory
- provide for matters to be dealt with speedily
- allow for information to be kept confidential
- tell employees what disciplinary action might be taken
- say what levels of management have the authority to take the various forms of disciplinary action
- require employees to be informed of the complaints against them and supporting evidence, before a disciplinary meeting
- give employees a chance to have their say before management reaches a decision
- provide employees with the right to be accompanied
- provide that no employee is dismissed for a first breach of discipline, except in cases of gross misconduct
- require management to investigate fully before any disciplinary action is taken

347

- ensure that employees are given an explanation for any sanction

- allow employees to appeal against a decision

- apply to all employees, irrespective of their length of service, status or number of hours worked

- ensure that any investigatory period of suspension is with pay and specify how pay is to be calculated during such period. If, exceptionally, suspension is to be without pay, this must be provided for in the contract of employment

- ensure that any suspension is brief and is never used as a sanction against the employee prior to a disciplinary meeting and decision. Keep the employee informed of progress

- ensure that the employee will be heard in good faith and that there is no pre-judgement of the issue

- ensure that, where the facts are in dispute, no disciplinary penalty is imposed until the case has been carefully investigated and there is a reasonably held belief that the employee committed the act in question (see page 13).

6.237 Obviously, it is not possible to devise a procedure that is fully applicable in all circumstances. In this regard, it is recognised both in S.98(4) ERA and in the Acas Code that allowances must be made for the particular circumstances of each case and for the size and administrative resources of the employer's undertaking. Furthermore, while application of the principle in Polkey v AE Dayton Services Ltd (above) puts great emphasis on the importance of a fair procedure, the House of Lords in that case also stressed that a failure to comply with procedural safeguards would not automatically render a dismissal unfair as there would be cases where a proper disciplinary procedure would be 'utterly useless' or 'futile', in which case the employer might well be acting reasonably in ignoring it. However, Lord Bridge expressed the view that such cases would be 'exceptional' (see '"No difference" rule' below).

6.238 Investigation

An employer should carry out a full investigation before deciding whether dismissal is a reasonable response in the circumstances. There are unlikely to be many cases in which an employer could successfully argue that investigation would have made no difference to the decision to dismiss. Applying the test in British Home Stores Ltd v Burchell 1980 ICR 303, EAT (as amended by the Employment Act 1980 in respect of the burden of proof – see 'General considerations – establishing reason for dismissal' above), the employer should not act on the basis of mere suspicion: it must have a genuine belief that the employee is guilty, based on reasonable grounds, after having carried out as much investigation into the matter as was reasonable in all the circumstances. The employer's task is to gather all the available evidence. Once in full possession of the facts, the employer will be in a position to make a reasonable decision about what action to take. It is also important that the employer puts itself into a position of being able to make specific rather than general allegations against the employee.

An employer who fails to establish all the facts risks a finding that a resulting dismissal was unfair both in respect of a failure to carry out a reasonable investigation and a failure to comply with the Acas Code, which carries an attendant risk that any compensation payable will be increased by up to 25 per cent (see Chapter 16, 'Compensatory award: adjustments', under 'Adjustments for breach of Acas Code of Practice').

Gross misconduct. The Acas Code states that 'a fair disciplinary process **6.239** should always be followed before dismissing for gross misconduct' (para 23). Thus, unless the misconduct is so heinous as to require instant dismissal – e.g. where there is a danger to life or a risk of immediate severe harm to the business – even serious conduct cases should be dealt with in the normal way. (Where immediate dismissal is deemed necessary, it is arguable that the lack of a fair procedure would not render it unfair as the exception in Polkey v AE Dayton Services Ltd (above) would apply – see '"No difference" rule' below. But even if the dismissal was found to be unfair, a tribunal might find that the failure to comply with the Code was reasonable in the circumstances and that it would not be just and equitable to make an uplift to any award of compensation.)

What is a 'reasonable' investigation? The extent of the investigation and the **6.240** form that it takes will vary according to the particular circumstances. In some cases, as the Code explains, the investigation stage will only involve the employer collating evidence; in others, an investigatory meeting with the employee will be required (para 5). If the employer decides to hold an investigatory meeting, it is important that it should not result in disciplinary action (para 7). If it becomes clear during the course of such a meeting that disciplinary action is needed, the meeting should be adjourned and the employee given notice of a separate disciplinary hearing and told of his or her right to be accompanied. (Note that an employee's statutory right to be accompanied only applies to a disciplinary hearing, not an investigatory meeting, unless the employer's own procedure extends the right to investigatory meetings – see 'Right to be accompanied' below.)

There is no hard-and-fast rule as to the level of inquiry the employer should conduct into the employee's (suspected) misconduct in order to satisfy the Burchell test. This will very much depend on the particular circumstances, including the nature and gravity of the case, the state of the evidence and the potential consequences of an adverse finding to the employee. In ILEA v Gravett 1988 IRLR 497, EAT, Mr Justice Wood (then President of the EAT) offered the following advice: 'at one extreme there will be cases where the employee is virtually caught in the act and at the other there will be situations where the issue is one of pure inference. As the scale moves towards the latter end, so the

349

amount of inquiry and investigation which may be required, including questioning of the employee, is likely to increase.'

6.241 In Miller v William Hill Organisation Ltd EAT 0336/12 the EAT acknowledged that there is a limit to the steps an employer should be expected to take to investigate an employee's alleged misconduct. How far an employer should go will depend on the circumstances of the case, including the amount of time involved, the expense and the consequences for the employee of being dismissed. In this case, the EAT considered that it would not have been too onerous for the employer to watch five hours of CCTV footage which would have supported M's version of events and not involved any additional expense. Therefore, the tribunal's finding that the employer had been justified in not viewing the whole of the footage was unsound. In the EAT's view, the only conclusion the tribunal could have reached was that the investigation which had been carried out prior to the decision to dismiss M for theft was not as thorough as the circumstances warranted. It therefore substituted a finding that M had been unfairly dismissed.

By contrast, in Shrestha v Genesis Housing Association Ltd 2015 IRLR 399, CA, the Court of Appeal upheld an employment tribunal's finding that it was not necessary for an employer to investigate every incident and explanation in respect of an employee who was dismissed for claiming mileage that was in excess of the recommended journey times. The employer's investigation had revealed that the mileage claimed was almost twice that recommended by the AA and RAC and exceeded that claimed for the same journeys in the previous year, and the disciplinary hearing had given consideration to all of the defences put forward by the employee. The Court considered that the employer's assessment that the explanations did not provide a plausible reason why every single journey had a higher mileage was reasonable in the circumstances and no further inquiry was necessary.

6.242 The Acas Guide emphasises that the more serious the allegations against the employee, the more thorough the investigation conducted by the employer ought to be (page 17). In A v B 2003 IRLR 405, EAT, the EAT stated that the gravity of the charges and the potential effect on the employee will be relevant when considering what is expected of a reasonable investigation. In its view, an investigation leading to a warning need not be as rigorous as one likely to lead to dismissal. In that case the fact that the employee, if dismissed, would never again be able to work in his chosen field was by no means as irrelevant as the tribunal appeared to think. Serious criminal allegations must always be carefully investigated and the investigator should put as much focus on evidence that may point towards innocence as on that which points towards guilt. This is particularly so where the employee has been suspended and cannot communicate with witnesses. But having said this, the EAT accepted that the standard of reasonableness will always be high where dismissal is a likely consequence, so the serious effect on future employment and the fact that criminal charges are involved may not in practice alter that standard. Such factors merely reinforce the need for a careful and conscientious inquiry.

The Court of Appeal picked up on this point in Salford Royal NHS Foundation Trust v Roldan 2010 ICR 1457, CA (perhaps unsurprisingly, since Lord Justice Elias, sitting in the Court of Appeal, had given judgment in A v B when he was President of the EAT). In Roldan, the employee, a nurse who was dismissed for gross misconduct, not only faced criminal charges but also the risk of deportation. The Court considered that the threat of deportation, which might have resulted from a dismissal, was equally as deserving of careful investigation as the potential criminal charges the employee faced. Accordingly, the potentially serious adverse consequences that dismissal would have had on the employee reinforced the tribunal's finding that procedural errors meant that the dismissal was unfair.

6.243 Thus it seems that if a dismissal could blight an employee's career in some significant way, tribunals will be required to scrutinise the employer's procedures all the more carefully.

6.244 **Facts in dispute?** An investigation should be carried out whenever there is a factual issue to be determined. In Scottish Daily Record and Sunday Mail (1986) Ltd v Laird 1996 IRLR 665, Ct Sess (Inner House), the claimant was dismissed for failing to inform his employer of some outside professional interests. Although there was no dispute that he should have informed his employer of those other interests and had not done so, the Court stated that an investigation should nonetheless have taken place because there was a dispute as to whether there was a conflict between the employer's business on the one hand and the employee's outside professional interests on the other.

Conversely, where an employee admits an act of gross misconduct and the facts are not in dispute, it may not be necessary to carry out a full investigation. In Boys and Girls Welfare Society v Macdonald 1997 ICR 693, EAT, the claimant was employed as a residential social worker in a children's home. During an altercation, he spat at one of the children. He admitted doing so at the disciplinary hearing and was dismissed. The EAT said that it was not always necessary to apply the test in British Home Stores Ltd v Burchell (above) where there was no real conflict on the facts. Therefore it was not necessary for the employer to interview the boy with whom the employee had the altercation or to consider the extreme provocation under which the employee was placed. Similarly, in Community Integrated Care Ltd v Smith EAT 0015/08 the EAT in Scotland held that it was reasonable for the employer to treat the employee's comment 'I'm not saying I didn't say it', when confronted with a complaint that she verbally abused a patient, as an admission of her guilt. In these circumstances, the employer did not have to conduct any further investigation into the matter as there was no real dispute about the fundamental facts.

351

6.245 The EAT in Scotland has also emphasised the limited relevance of investigation when it comes to the consideration of mitigating factors in cases of admitted misconduct. In Scottish and Southern Energy plc v Innes EATS 0043/10 it overturned an employment tribunal's finding of procedural unfairness where the employer had not investigated whether the employee's ill health (depression) explained his admitted misconduct. The employer was entitled to base its decision on the facts as admitted by the employee at the time, which did not indicate any causal link between his depression and the misconduct.

6.246 **Delay.** The investigation should be carried out without unreasonable delay. The Acas Code emphasises the importance of establishing the facts and putting allegations to the employee promptly before recollections fade. So, in RSPCA v Cruden 1986 ICR 205, EAT, for example, an unjustifiable delay of seven months before disciplinary proceedings were commenced against an RSPCA inspector made an otherwise fair dismissal unfair, even though the employee suffered no prejudice.

That case can be contrasted with Christou and anor v London Borough of Haringey 2012 IRLR 622, EAT, where the EAT upheld an employment tribunal's decision that the claimants' dismissals for misconduct were fair, despite an 18-month delay between the alleged misconduct and (a second set of) disciplinary proceedings being instigated against them. The facts of this case were somewhat unusual, however, as they arose out of Haringey Council's failure to prevent the death of an abused baby and the subsequent public outcry. Ordinarily such a delay is unlikely to fall within the band of reasonable responses. The Christou case is discussed further in Chapter 3, 'Unfairness', under 'Reasonableness of dismissal – equity'. (Note that the EAT's decision was subsequently upheld on different grounds by the Court of Appeal, which did not revisit the issue of delay – Christou and anor v London Borough of Haringey 2013 ICR 1007, CA.)

6.247 **Intervening police investigation.** The employer's investigation may be hampered where the alleged misconduct is also the subject of a police inquiry. However, tribunals will not necessarily regard this as a valid excuse for a delay in completing the disciplinary procedure. Much will depend on the individual circumstances of the case. In A v B 2003 IRLR 405, EAT, the employee was suspended in mid-1997 and a disciplinary hearing did not take place until December 1999. Even taking account of the fact that police investigations took place between October 1997 and October 1998, such delays were held by the EAT to be 'grossly improper'. However, in another case where an allegation against an employee became part of a wide-ranging police investigation into allegations of ill-treatment of inmates at a prison, a delay of two years did not render the dismissal of the prison worker unfair where full written evidence had been taken at an early stage – Newman v HM Prison Service ET Case No.3104586/02.

352

Impartiality. The Acas Guide stresses that employers should keep an open **6.248** mind when carrying out an investigation: their task is to look for evidence that supports as well as weakens the employee's case. If disciplinary action results in dismissal and there is an indication that the employer has pre-judged the outcome, that can be enough to make the dismissal unfair – see, for example, Sovereign Business Integration plc v Trybus EAT 0107/07.

Paragraph 6 of the Acas Code states that 'where practicable, different people should carry out the investigation and disciplinary hearing'. Such a division of functions is recognised by the courts as an important indicator of impartiality. For example, in Warren James Jewellers Ltd v Christy EAT 1041/02 C was dismissed on suspicion of theft when the bank paying-in slip for a day when she was left in charge of the shop was short by £1,000. In holding that her dismissal was unfair, the employment tribunal found that there had been no reasonable investigation, pointing to the fact that, among other things, the area manager who acted as the investigating officer was also responsible for disciplining and dismissing C.

The same principle of impartiality extends to those acting as witnesses in an **6.249** investigation. In **Moyes v Hylton Castle Working Men's Social Club and Institute Ltd** 1986 IRLR 482, EAT, M was dismissed from his job as club steward after two incidents in which he allegedly sexually harassed a barmaid, the second of which was observed by the chairman and the assistant secretary of the club. The investigation was carried out by a sub-committee of five, which included the two club officials who were witnesses. A subsequent meeting of the full committee, which again included the chairman and assistant secretary, made the decision to dismiss. Overturning the employment tribunal's decision that the involvement of the two officials in the capacity of both witness and judge did not make the dismissal unfair, the EAT held that this was a breach of natural justice and any reasonable observer would conclude that justice did not appear to have been done and had not been done. The EAT acknowledged that there could be cases where a witness to an incident would have to make the decision to dismiss but in the present case found that it was entirely unnecessary for the two officials to act in both roles.

However, as the EAT accepted in the Moyes case, it is not always possible in small organisations for functions to be separated in this way. In Barlow v Clifford and Co (Sidcup) Ltd EAT 0910/04 the EAT made it clear that where there are a limited number of people available it is not necessarily unfair for the same people to be involved in the early stages of the disciplinary process and in the final decision to dismiss.

At the end of the day, it is for the tribunal to determine, on the facts of the **6.250** particular case and after having regard to the nature of the allegations made, the manner of the investigation, the size and capacity of the employer's undertaking, and all other relevant circumstances, whether it was unfair for the

353

investigator to also chair the disciplinary meeting and be the dismissal decision-taker – Premier International Foods Ltd v Dolan and anor EAT 0641/04.

Where a disciplinary investigation is conducted by a manager against whom the employee has previously raised a grievance, this will not necessarily make the process unfair – Jinadu v Docklands Buses Ltd and ors EAT 0434/14. However, an important feature in that case was the fact that the disciplinary hearing itself was conducted – and the decision to dismiss taken – by an independent manager who had no connection to the employee's grievance. Similarly, the fact that one of the witnesses to the employee's alleged misconduct was present in the investigatory interviews with other witnesses will not necessarily be fatal. In Monji v Boots Management Services Ltd EAT 0292/13 the EAT held that, although the tribunal had taken the view that it was inappropriate for the witness to be present, it had been entitled to find that he could not have influenced the evidence and there was no suggestion that any of the evidence had been contaminated by his presence.

6.251 **Gathering evidence.** In conducting the investigation, an employer should interview witnesses, although there is no need to interview every available witness once a fact has been clearly established. However, the investigation may be flawed if an obvious witness is overlooked. For example, where the employer relied on a second-hand account of a fight between two employees instead of interviewing the only eye-witness, the investigation was found to be flawed – Baxters (Butchers) Ltd v Hart EAT 934/83.

Similarly, failing to reinterview a vital witness as more information comes to light may be fatal. In Sneddon v Carr-Gomm Scotland Ltd 2012 IRLR 820, Ct Sess (Inner House), S, a care-worker, was dismissed by CGS Ltd following allegations that he had shouted at and bullied a vulnerable care user during an overnight stay. The allegations were made by the care user's neighbour to her friend, who also worked for CGS Ltd and who duly reported back what the neighbour had told her. CGS Ltd began an investigation, which included a short conversation between the investigating manager, F, and the neighbour, of which F made brief notes. It was primarily this evidence on which CGS Ltd relied when deciding to dismiss S. However, the investigation had also involved F questioning S's colleagues, none of whom identified any concerns about his conduct or his treatment of the care user concerned; there had been no complaint by the care user; and S strongly contested the allegations. In the circumstances, therefore, the Court of Session held that an employment tribunal had been entitled to find that a reasonable employer would have gone back to the neighbour to explore matters more fully and double check on the detail, the reliability and the credibility of her account, rather than relying on her initial conversation with F, which took place at a preliminary stage in the investigation. The dismissal was therefore unfair.

But, as always, what amounts to a fair investigation will depend on the **6.252** particular facts of the case. In Stuart v London City Airport 2013 EWCA Civ 973, CA, S was dismissed for dishonesty and breach of trust after he walked out of the duty-free shop at the airport where he worked without paying for the goods he held in his hands. S did not dispute the essential fact of the allegation but asserted that (i) he had not realised that he had stepped outside the boundary of the shop, and (ii) he had only stepped outside to talk to a friend, not with any dishonest intent. The dismissing officer relied on a witness statement from a shop cashier saying that she saw S conceal items under his jacket as evidence of dishonesty. However, the cashier did not give oral evidence during the disciplinary proceedings and the dismissing officer refused to look at CCTV footage of the shop. A tribunal found that this was nonetheless a reasonable investigation and the Court of Appeal upheld that decision on appeal. After inspecting the shop layout for himself, the dismissing officer decided that it was impossible for S to believe that he had never left the area of the duty-free shop. Having therefore formed a view as to S's credibility on this point, it was reasonable for the dismissing officer not to carry out further investigations in relation to the alleged concealment of the goods.

A similar conclusion was reached in Shrestha v Genesis Housing Association Ltd 2015 IRLR 399, CA. There, an employee was dismissed for making claims for mileage that was significantly higher than that recommended by the AA and RAC. The Court of Appeal upheld the employment tribunal's decision that it was not necessary in the circumstances for the employer to carry out a detailed investigation into the employee's explanation that he had been forced to take longer journeys due to roadworks, one-way systems and parking difficulties. It was clear to the employer that these reasons could not fully explain the discrepancy in mileage. The employer was not required to act on the employee's request, for example, to contact the local authority to confirm whether there was a lack of parking spaces.

Human rights issues. Employers sometimes resort to using covert surveillance **6.253** to gather evidence of an employee's misconduct. However, it is arguable that the use of such methods amounts to a breach of the employee's right to respect for private and family life under Article 8 of the European Convention on Human Rights. As mentioned under 'General considerations – impact of Human Rights Act' above, S.3 of the Human Rights Act 1998 provides that courts and tribunals must interpret domestic legislation in a way that is compatible with Convention rights, in so far as it is possible to do so. This paves the way for claimants to argue before a tribunal that, where the circumstances of their dismissal fall within the ambit of a Convention right, the tribunal must consider, in determining the question of fairness under S.98(4) ERA, whether the employer unjustifiably interfered with the right in question.

355

The relationship between covert surveillance and human rights arose for consideration in McGowan v Scottish Water 2005 IRLR 167, EAT. There, a public sector employee had been dismissed after his employer obtained evidence through covert surveillance of his home that he was falsifying time sheets. The employee claimed that he had been unfairly dismissed because his right to respect for his private and family life under Article 8 had been breached. Article 8 was found to be engaged in the circumstances, as the EAT accepted that covert surveillance which involved tracking the movements of all of the inhabitants of a home 'raises... a strong presumption that the right to have one's private life respected is being infringed'. However, in rejecting the employee's claim, it held that the employer's action was justified as it was protecting its assets and was investigating what was effectively a criminal activity.

6.254 The EAT also rejected a claim of unfair dismissal in City and County of Swansea v Gayle EAT 0501/12. There, G had twice been observed by a senior employee playing squash in a sports centre near the office while he was still clocked in at work. The employer hired a private investigator, who covertly filmed G leaving the sports centre on several occasions. After the employer dismissed him for fraud, G claimed unfair dismissal. The tribunal found that the investigation was unreasonable in that it involved an unjustified interference with G's Article 8(1) right. In its view, once G had been seen at the sports centre for a second time, the employer had all the evidence it needed to establish its reasonable belief in his guilt and it was therefore disproportionate to initiate covert surveillance. The EAT overturned this decision on appeal. It held that there was no breach of Article 8, bearing in mind that G was filmed in a public place, but even if there had been, it would have been justified under Article 8(2) in pursuance of the legitimate aims of preventing crime and protecting the rights of others. The EAT also pointed out that the tribunal's competence to consider Article 8 is limited to the Article's interaction with the employment rights within the tribunal's jurisdiction, and it is only where a breach of that Article is relevant to the dismissal that it is likely to be held unreasonable. Thus, the tribunal's finding that the employer's behaviour was disproportionate could have no impact on the employer's reasonableness in forming a view, upon the material available, that G was guilty. It is unlikely that an investigation will ever be held unreasonable because it is too thorough.

6.255 **Information supplied by third parties.** It may be acceptable for the employer to rely on witness statements and related information provided to it from other sources, notably the police. The extent to which this may permissibly limit the employer's own investigation into the matter will invariably depend on the particular circumstances. The following two cases provide useful examples of the extent to which employers may be able to rely on evidence gathered by the police.

356

In Harding v Hampshire County Council EAT 0672/04 allegations of serious misconduct were made against H, who worked for the Council as a youth project worker. The police investigated the allegations (which were that H had committed sexual offences against three young boys and accessed child pornography on his computer), but eventually decided that there was not enough evidence to proceed to criminal charges. In due course, the Council began its own investigation, which relied to a large extent on the material assembled during the police inquiry. The Council, after a lengthy review of the information compiled by the police, decided that there was sufficient evidence to conclude that H had committed acts of gross misconduct and, following a disciplinary hearing, he was summarily dismissed. An employment tribunal found the dismissal fair, specifically rejecting H's submission that the employer had not conducted a reasonable investigation because it had to a large extent relied on the police inquiry and not made further enquiries of its own.

On appeal, the EAT could find no fault with the tribunal's conclusion. It noted **6.256** that there is no general rule or principle of law as to whether it is sufficient in an individual case for an employer, where there has been a police investigation into alleged misconduct, to rely upon the product of that investigation and to make no further investigation of its own. Whether it is reasonable for the employer to conduct further investigation will depend on the facts of the individual case. In H's case, the police investigation had been 'manifestly detailed'. The material provided to the employer included numerous witness statements, the records of the interviews of the relevant children, reports from the police computer expert and H's computer expert, and three interviews the police had conducted with H himself. Absent any suggestion that any of the witness statements were no longer accurate, there was no obligation on the employer to reinterview the witnesses. Moreover, the employer had tried to conduct a further interview with H, but he had refused to participate. Bearing in mind that the correct test is not whether there could have been further investigation but whether the investigation that was carried out was reasonable in all the circumstances, it was clear that, in this case, there were no further enquiries that the employer should have made.

In Rhondda Cynon Taf County Borough Council v Close 2008 IRLR 868, EAT, the employee, a care worker, sought to distinguish her situation from that of the claimant in the Harding case by arguing that the allegation that formed the basis of the police investigation against her differed from the allegations that were the subject of the employer's disciplinary investigation: the police had investigated a possible manslaughter charge following the death of a patient, whereas the employer had dismissed her for sleeping on duty and swearing in front of patients. The EAT was not convinced, however. It held that it was not outside the band of reasonableness for an employer to choose not to carry out its own independent questioning of witnesses in a disciplinary procedure but instead to rely on police witness statements, even

357

though those statements had been made to the police in relation to a different investigation. Furthermore, where certain matters are raised and dealt with in witness statements on the ground that the evidence may be relevant to a subsequent trial, and these statements are confirmed, it is irrelevant that the focus of the criminal investigation was different. Another consideration in this case was that the police witness statements had been made close to the time of the alleged misconduct, which meant that there was every reason to suppose that they would have been more reliable than statements taken by the employer as part of a disciplinary investigation almost three years later. The EAT therefore concluded that: 'The council obtained evidence based on the witness statements; they confirmed that the witnesses still stood by those statements; they allowed cross-examination of two of those witnesses; and they assessed the evidence of the witnesses they heard, and concluded that they were more reliable than the claimant. That is essentially what the employers have to do in circumstances of this kind.'

6.257 Both the above decisions are helpful to employers: they say that investigations need not be started again from scratch where the police have already looked into the matter. Nonetheless, employers should make sure that they carefully evaluate the information received from the police and consider whether any parts of that information need to be revisited and/or require additional investigation.

Occasionally, evidence of the employee's misconduct emerges from more unusual sources. In Banks v Inland Revenue Liverpool ET Case No.2102391/04 B brought discrimination claims against IR, which were dismissed by the tribunal. The tribunal was scathing in its criticism of B: it concluded that she was a bully who was given to manipulative conduct in order to get her own way, and that her claims had been made with malicious intent. On the basis of the tribunal's judgment, IR took disciplinary action against B and dismissed her for serious and gross misconduct. B complained of unfair dismissal, alleging that her dismissal was procedurally unfair because IR failed to conduct its own inquiry into her alleged misconduct and impermissibly relied on the tribunal's judgment. The tribunal hearing her unfair dismissal claim rejected this allegation. In its view, IR was entitled to rely on the tribunal's findings of fact, which had been 'damning in respect of the way the claimant had conducted herself both within the actual proceedings and during her employment with the respondent'. In these circumstances, there was no need for the employer to carry out an internal investigation. It could instead rely upon the judgment of the tribunal, which had considered ten days of evidence before reaching its decision. However, the tribunal noted the 'unusual facts of this case' and stressed that its decision was 'not a green light for respondents to use judgments of the tribunal as justification for dismissing those employees who have been unsuccessful in… litigation' against their employer. It is worth noting that the employee in this case did not seek to bring a victimisation claim (i.e. alleging that she had been dismissed because she had previously brought proceedings against her employer). However, an employer who chose to dismiss on the basis of a tribunal judgment could well be faced with such a claim in another case.

Criminal proceedings pending. Where criminal proceedings are pending, **6.258** matters can become complicated. For example, internal inquiries will often be hampered by the employee's reluctance to discuss the incident. Nevertheless, an employer should do its best to satisfy itself of the employee's guilt. If it carried out a reasonable investigation, and can show that it believed that the employee was guilty of misconduct meriting dismissal, then a subsequent acquittal on a criminal charge arising out of the same events would not of itself make the dismissal unfair. In Ali v Sovereign Buses (London) Ltd EAT 0274/06 the EAT reviewed the authorities on the issue and concluded that there is no hard-and-fast rule as to what an employer should do when deciding whether to press ahead with disciplinary proceedings when there is a criminal trial pending. It will depend on the circumstances of the case, although the employer should not dismiss too easily.

For a more general discussion on the impact of criminal proceedings on dismissal, see 'Criminal offences at work' above.

Suspension. In some circumstances, an employer may feel it necessary to **6.259** suspend the employee while the investigation is being carried out – notably, in gross misconduct cases. However, the Acas Code recommends that, if a suspension with pay is considered necessary, it should be as brief as possible and kept under review and it should be made clear to the employee that the suspension does not amount to disciplinary action (para 8). Furthermore, the Court of Appeal commented in Crawford and anor v Suffolk Mental Health Partnership NHS Trust 2012 IRLR 402, CA, that even where there is evidence supporting the employer's investigation, suspension 'should not be a knee-jerk reaction, and it will be a breach of the duty of trust and confidence towards the employee if it is'. Suspension without pay will be in breach of contract unless there is a clear contractual term allowing it.

Providing details of charges and possible consequences   6.260

If, once the investigation has been completed, disciplinary action is considered necessary, the Acas Code states that the employer should inform the employee in writing of the charge(s) against him or her and the possible consequences of the disciplinary action (para 9). This communication should contain enough information to enable the employee to prepare an answer to the case and should give details of the time and venue for the disciplinary hearing (para 10). It would normally be appropriate to provide copies of any written evidence, including witness statements.

However, a failure to inform an employee in writing that dismissal is a possible consequence of disciplinary action will not inevitably render a dismissal unfair. In Buzolli v Food Partners Ltd EAT 0317/12, for example, the EAT held that,

359

as a matter of common sense, it should have been clear to the employee who was already subject to a final written warning that further misconduct could result in his dismissal. Furthermore, the misconduct in question – a preventable collision resulting in significant damage to a company vehicle – was one of the examples of gross misconduct given in the employer's disciplinary policy. The EAT therefore upheld the tribunal's decision that, despite some procedural flaws, dismissal was reasonable in the circumstances.

6.261 It is important that the employee knows the full allegations against him or her. The Court of Appeal has stated that disciplinary charges should be precisely framed and evidence limited to those particulars – Strouthos v London Underground Ltd 2004 IRLR 636, CA. It is not only fundamental that employees should know the case against them, but where there is evidence against them they should also know what that evidence is. However, there is no general rule that a failure to make the evidence available to an employee either before, or at the outset of, the hearing will always amount to a breach of natural justice. Statements should be disclosed where the essence of the case against the employee is contained therein and where he or she has not otherwise been informed of the nature of that case. However, where the employee is fully aware of that case and has a full opportunity to respond to the allegations and the obtained statements are peripheral to the decision reached, the failure to disclose will not render a dismissal unfair – Hussain v Elonex plc 1999 IRLR 420, CA.

6.262 There are many cases in which a failure to inform an employee of the full allegations against him or her or to disclose the relevant evidence has led to a finding of unfair dismissal. Four examples:

- **Hotson v Wisbech Conservative Club** 1984 ICR 859, EAT: the stated reason for the dismissal of a club barmaid was gross inefficiency in handling bar takings. During the tribunal hearing of her unfair dismissal complaint the chairman suggested, and the employer's representative agreed, that the employer was really alleging dishonesty. The tribunal proceeded to find the dismissal fair on the ground of suspected dishonesty. The EAT held that the difference between inefficiency and dishonesty was more than a mere change of label. The charge of dishonesty should have been stated at the outset or not stated at all: at the very least the employee should have had the fullest opportunity to consider the implications of the charge and to answer it

- **A v B** 2003 IRLR 405, EAT: A, a residential social worker, was dismissed after the employer decided, after a disciplinary hearing, that allegations that he had had an inappropriate relationship with a 14-year-old in his care were well founded. The EAT held that the dismissal was unfair. It acknowledged that it will often be enough if an employee knows the gist of the evidence against him. Additionally, if an employer reasonably forms a view that certain evidence is immaterial and cannot assist the employee, then it need

360

not necessarily be disclosed. However, in this case, the young girl's evidence was not entirely consistent – she had made allegations against a number of other people and others had given evidence which conflicted with hers. It was therefore important that all the documentation was made available

- **Old v Palace Fields Primary Academy** EAT 0085/14: O, a teacher, was dismissed for gross misconduct as a result of the way she handled an incident of bullying in her class. Witness statements from two of the pupils who were present at the time could have been helpful to O's defence, but they were not shown to the disciplinary panel or to O. The EAT accepted that the panel had been reasonably entitled to assume that it had before it all relevant material. However, the case was remitted for rehearing on the basis that the tribunal judge should have considered whether the procedural irregularity of not providing to O material that could have helped her case rendered the dismissal procedurally unfair

- **South West London and St George's Mental Health NHS Trust v Pooloo and anor** EAT 0513/12: the claimants were nurses on a mental health ward who had been dismissed for gross misconduct. In deciding to dismiss, the employer had relied in large part on evidence given by the ward's service users. The service users had been medically assessed to check their capacity and reliability to serve as witnesses, with the result that two of them were identified as unlikely to be reliable witnesses due to their medical conditions. The EAT held that the employer should have disclosed this information to the claimants during the disciplinary process and that its failure to do so was one of the factors that rendered the claimants' dismissals procedurally unfair.

Right to be accompanied

6.263

When informing the employee of the time and venue for the disciplinary meeting, the employer should advise the employee of his or her right to be accompanied (para 10). Under S.10 of the Employment Relations Act 1999 (ERelA), where a worker 'reasonably requests' to be accompanied at a 'disciplinary hearing', the employer must permit the worker to be accompanied by a 'companion'. The companion – chosen by the worker – may be a trade union representative or a fellow worker – S.10(2A) and (3). (The circumstances in which an employee might have a right to be accompanied by a legal representative are discussed under 'Right to legal representation' below).

A disciplinary hearing is defined in the ERelA as a hearing that could result in:

- the administration of a formal warning – S.13(4)(a)

- the taking of some other action – S.13(4)(b)

- the confirmation of a warning issued or some other action taken – S.13(4)(c) (this applies to appeal hearings).

361

6.264 The chosen companion may address the hearing in order to put the worker's case, sum up that case and respond on the worker's behalf to any view expressed at the hearing – S.10(2B) ERelA. He or she may also confer with the worker. However, the companion may not answer questions on behalf of the worker, address the hearing if the worker does not wish it, prevent the employer from making its case or prevent any other person from making a contribution – S.10(2C). An employee has a statutory right to ask for a meeting to be rescheduled if necessary in order for his or her chosen companion to attend as long as the alternative date suggested is within five working days of that proposed by the employer – S.10(4) and (5).

Although S.10 ERelA provides that a worker is only entitled to be accompanied if he or she 'reasonably requests' it, the reasonableness criterion does not extend to the identity of the companion. So long as the companion meets one of the definitions in S.10(3), the employer must agree to that companion. This is now stated in the Acas Code of Practice, which was revised with effect from 11 March 2015 to reflect the EAT's decision in Toal and anor v GB Oils Ltd 2013 IRLR 696, EAT. There, the EAT held that the suggestion in the previous Code that an employer could veto a worker's choice of companion – if, for example, he or she worked in a remote geographical location – was not permissible. However, the revised Code suggests that as a matter of good practice, workers should 'bear in mind the practicalities of the arrangements' (para 14). The revised Code also specifies that a worker may alter his or her choice of companion.

6.265 What amounts to a 'reasonable' request is not specified. The revised Code states that a request does not have to be made in writing or within a certain time frame. However, it suggests that a worker 'should provide enough time for the employer to deal with the companion's attendance at the meeting' and that this may include giving the name of the companion in advance of the meeting and identifying whether he or she is a fellow worker or trade union official or representative. In Shone v Oxford and Cherwell Valley College ET Case No.2701364/13 the employee was a teacher who faced allegations that he had failed to cover topics on which his students were shortly due to be examined. The employer scheduled a hearing for the last day of the school term and refused the employee's request for a postponement – made the day before the hearing – because it was concerned to hold the disciplinary hearing before the school holidays began. The employee then made a request to be accompanied just 11 minutes before the disciplinary hearing was due to start. The employee did not have a companion available to attend the hearing at that time and was therefore effectively asking for a last-minute postponement. The tribunal held that, in the circumstances, the request was unreasonable and the employer did not breach S.10 ERelA by proceeding with the disciplinary hearing in the employee's absence.

Right to legal representation

It is generally accepted that neither the ERelA nor the Acas Code confers an entitlement to have a legal representative present at a disciplinary meeting. However, it has been suggested that in certain circumstances Article 6 of the European Convention on Human Rights – which provides that an individual has the right to a fair hearing in the determination of his or her civil rights or of any criminal charge – may do so. The argument is that, where an employer's internal disciplinary proceedings have the potential to seriously affect the employee's future employment – such as in the case of allegations of serious misconduct against a medical professional – the employee in effect faces a determination of his or her civil right to practise his or her profession. (Of course, this argument only applies directly in the public sector, where employers are required by the Human Rights Act 1998 (HRA) to observe Convention obligations. In the private sector the onus is on tribunals to interpret domestic legislation in a way that is compatible with Convention rights in so far as it is possible to do so.)

The Supreme Court has rather taken the wind out of the sails of this argument, however. In R (on the application of G) v Governors of X School 2011 ICR 1033, SC, G, a teaching assistant, was subject to a disciplinary investigation into allegations that he had formed an inappropriate relationship with a 15-year-old boy. He was permitted representation at the hearing by either a trade union representative or a colleague, but not by a solicitor. Following the hearing, G was summarily dismissed and the school reported his dismissal to the Independent Safeguarding Authority (ISA) (now replaced by the Disclosure and Barring Service) for it to determine whether G should be placed on a 'barred list' preventing him from working with children in future. He appealed against the decision to dismiss and requested legal representation at the appeal. This request was also refused. The High Court granted G's application for judicial review, holding that Article 6 entitled him to legal representation at the disciplinary and appeal hearings. The Court of Appeal rejected the school's appeal against that decision, holding that the disciplinary proceedings were determinative of G's civil right to practise his profession and so attracted Article 6 protection. Although Article 6 does not necessarily entail a right to legal representation in civil proceedings (unlike criminal proceedings), the level of protection depends on the gravity of the issue at stake. Given that G's right to practise his profession was at risk, he should have been afforded the opportunity of legal representation in the disciplinary proceedings.

The Supreme Court by a majority (Lord Kerr dissenting) allowed the school's appeal. There was no dispute that the ISA barring procedure would determine G's right to practise his profession. However, the majority of the Court was not persuaded that the school's disciplinary proceedings were so intimately connected with the ISA procedure that Article 6 should apply at both stages. Lord Dyson, giving the leading judgment, agreed with Lord Justice Laws' formulation in the Court of Appeal that the proceedings would be so connected if it could be said that the disciplinary proceedings would have a 'substantial influence or effect' on the ISA proceedings, but did not accept that that standard was met here. Lord Dyson was satisfied that the ISA would exercise its own independent judgement in finding facts and making an assessment of their gravity and significance. Although the ISA would not be obliged to conduct an oral hearing with cross-examination, His Lordship did not think this detracted from its ability to reach a fair and independent conclusion, since it is rare that a conflict of evidence must be resolved solely or even primarily by reference to a witness's demeanour. He also rejected G's assertion that the ISA would be significantly influenced by the school governors' view of the facts as found. (Lord Kerr's reason for dissenting was that the decision-making in the barring procedure would inevitably be influenced by the school governors' report of their findings to the ISA, such that Article 6 required legal representation at the disciplinary stage.)

Prior to the Supreme Court's decision in the X School case, case law appeared to be moving towards establishing a 'right' to legal representation in disciplinary hearings. The Court of Appeal's decision in Kulkarni v Milton Keynes Hospital NHS Foundation Trust and anor 2010 ICR 101, CA, is a case in point. There, K, a junior doctor accused of misconduct involving inappropriate touching of a patient, successfully argued that he had a contractual right to legal representation. This meant that his alternative argument, based on Article 6, did not require determination, but Lady Justice Smith indicated that she would have accepted it. She noted that case law of the European Court of Human Rights indicates that Article 6 does not apply where all that is at stake is the loss of a specific job. However, where the outcome of the proceedings is potentially more serious, such as the loss of the right to practise a particular profession, Article 6 would then be engaged. In the instant case, K was facing an accusation of serious sexual misconduct and, if found guilty, would effectively be barred from employment in the NHS.

6.268 It is noteworthy that Lord Dyson in the X School case did not disagree with Lady Justice Smith's analysis of Article 6's application to the facts of Kulkarni. Lord Dyson noted that Kulkarni was an example of a situation where the employer's disciplinary proceedings were, as a matter of fact, dispositive of the employee's right to work in his chosen field. Thus, although the X School case appears to reduce the scope for applying Article 6 to workplace disciplinary proceedings, it does not detract from the general principle that Article 6 may apply if the employer's procedure effectively determines the employee's right to practise his or her profession.

That said, the general principle has limited application in any event since, outside the medical profession, it is difficult to imagine closely analogous circumstances to those of Kulkarni. Even within the medical profession such cases will be few and far between. In R (on the application of Puri) v Bradford Teaching Hospitals NHS Foundation Trust 2011 EWHC 970 (Admin), QBD, the High Court held that a disciplinary hearing that resulted in an NHS surgeon's dismissal did not deprive him of his right to practise his profession and so was not required to be Article 6 compliant. Although it would be difficult for him to find a post within the NHS or elsewhere of the same seniority and speciality as that of the post from which he had been dismissed, it would not be impossible. He remained a practising doctor, albeit that he no longer had the opportunity to carry out the high-level surgery in which he had specialised when working for the Trust.

A narrow interpretation of the circumstances in which disciplinary proceedings **6.269** could be said to be determinative of an employee's right to practise his or her profession was also adopted in Mattu v University Hospitals of Coventry and Warwickshire NHS Trust 2013 ICR 270, CA. In that case the Court of Appeal unanimously held that Article 6 did not apply to the disciplinary hearings provided for in M's contract of employment, nor to the Trust's ultimate decision to dismiss. The Court did not accept that M's dismissal would have the practical effect of preventing him from practising as a doctor. That was sufficient to resolve the matter on appeal, but a majority of the Court – Lords Justice Stanley Burnton and Elias – went on to express obiter (i.e. non-binding) views that cast doubt on Smith LJ's statement (also obiter) in Kulkarni v Milton Keynes Hospital NHS Foundation Trust and anor (above) that 'Article 6 is engaged where an NHS doctor faces charges which are of such gravity that, in the event they are found proved, he will be effectively barred from employment in the NHS'. Stanley Burnton and Elias LJJ considered that if Smith LJ's statement were taken to its logical conclusion, private and public sector employers would be held to different standards and, given the fact that the Kulkarni analysis depends on the consequences of disciplinary action, it would be difficult to know in advance whether Article 6 applied or not.

None of these cases was initiated in an employment tribunal or indeed involved a claim of unfair dismissal. However, employment tribunals are likely to interpret the requirement for reasonableness under S.98(4) ERA in accordance with Article 6, bearing in mind their obligation under S.3 HRA to interpret UK legislation (including the ERA) compatibly with Convention rights. Therefore, failure – at least by public sector employers – to allow for legal representation in the very limited circumstances in which it is appropriate to do so could render a dismissal procedurally unfair. This might apply even to *private* employers, given the framework of questions for tribunals dealing with unfair dismissal claims in which human rights issues arise that is set out by the Court of Appeal in X v Y 2004 ICR 1634, CA – see Chapter 3, 'Unfairness', under 'Reasonableness of dismissal – impact of Human Rights Act' for details. Furthermore, in Kulkarni v Milton Keynes Hospital NHS Foundation Trust

365

and anor (above), Smith LJ stated that the issue could be framed in terms of natural justice under domestic law, as well as breach of Article 6.

6.270 It is important to note, however, that even if Article 6 does apply, that does not inevitably mean that any breach will render a resulting conduct dismissal unfair. In Ministry of Justice v Parry EAT 0068/12 the EAT overturned a tribunal's decision that Article 6 applied to internal disciplinary proceedings on the ground that that decision had been inadequately reasoned. The EAT went on to accept (on an obiter basis) the MoJ's contention that, even if Article 6 did apply – and the employee was denied the legal representation it prescribes – that would not necessarily mean that the dismissal was unfair for the purposes of the ERA. Although the principle of effectiveness suggests that it will be a rare case in which a violation of Article 6 in the processes leading to dismissal does not render the dismissal unfair, there may be exceptional cases in which, given their particular circumstances, it may be otherwise – whether because of particular features of the substantive merits of the case or because the additional advantage conferred by honouring Article 6 is so minimal as not to detract from overall fairness. Accordingly, even if the tribunal on remission were to find that Article 6 did apply, it would still have to consider whether the dismissal procedure was, overall, fair.

6.271 **The disciplinary hearing**

The purpose of the disciplinary hearing is twofold: it allows the employer to find out whether or not the misconduct has been committed and it allows the employee to explain the conduct and any mitigating circumstances. The Acas Code states that the disciplinary hearing should be held 'without unreasonable delay whilst allowing the employee reasonable time to prepare their case' (para 11). Employers and employees (and their companions) should make every effort to attend (para 12).

The Acas Guide recommends that employers arrange for someone who is not involved in the case to attend to take a note and act as a witness to what was said (page 19). If the employee needs an interpreter or facilitator because of a language barrier or understanding difficulties, the Guide suggests that the employer consider providing one. The attendance of an individual in this role may be in addition to the employee's companion. Although the Guide says that 'ideally one person should carry out both roles', this will not necessarily be practical and employers should always remember that the overriding test in a case of unfair dismissal is one of reasonableness in the circumstances. Note that if the employee has a disability and needs an interpreter or other assistant at the hearing in order to remove any disadvantage he or she faces as a result of that disability, an employer's refusal to allow one may be a breach of its duty to make reasonable adjustments under the Equality Act 2010 – see IDS Employment Law Handbook, 'Discrimination at Work' (2012), Chapter 21, 'Failure to make reasonable adjustments'.

Conduct of hearing. The Acas Code sets out the following requirements: **6.272**

- the employer should explain the complaint against the employee and go through the evidence that has been gathered

- the employee should be allowed to set out his or her case and answer any allegations that have been made

- the employee should be given a reasonable opportunity to ask questions, present evidence and call witnesses

- the employee should be given an opportunity to raise points about any information provided by witnesses

- where an employer or employee intends to call relevant witnesses they should give advance notice that they intend to do this (para 12).

The Acas Guide points out that the purpose of the hearing is to establish the facts rather than to catch people out, and suggests that it contain the following five elements:

- a statement of the complaint by the employer outlining the complaint and the evidence

- the employee's reply answering any allegations that have been made

- general questioning and discussion, which should be a two-way process

- summing up

- adjournment before a decision (pages 20–22).

Even if misconduct is admitted, the employee should at least be given an **6.273** opportunity to explain. If, however, the employee declines to offer any explanation, the employer will not be prevented from proceeding further and, if it is reasonable, dismissing the individual – W Weddel and Co Ltd v Tepper 1980 ICR 286, CA. However, the employer should be careful to make the employee fully aware of what is happening and of the possible consequences of a refusal to speak at the hearing.

A failure to ensure that the employee is given a fair chance to refute any allegations of misconduct against him or her may lead a tribunal to conclude that the decision to dismiss was a foregone conclusion. In Sands v Duke Contractors Ltd ET Case No.1100153/07, for example, S went off sick in July 2006 with a broken ankle and produced medical certificates to that effect during the ensuing months. In November, DC Ltd summarily dismissed him for gross misconduct; among other things, it questioned his inability to return to work. An employment tribunal upheld S's unfair dismissal claim, finding that DC Ltd had failed to conduct a fair disciplinary hearing: it did not present the allegations against S clearly; withheld witness statements that were allegedly in its possession; adopted an accusatory manner during the hearing, which put S

367

in the position of having to defend himself; asked him closed questions, which inhibited his capacity to respond fully and openly; and failed to take S's responses into account.

6.274 **Absence of bias.** It is a cardinal principle of natural justice that the person conducting the proceedings should not be a 'judge in his own cause'. In other words, the decision-maker should not have a direct interest in the outcome of the proceedings and should not give any appearance of bias or partiality. Commonly cited evidence of bias is where a supervisor or manager involved in the disciplinary proceedings was also involved at an earlier stage in the case and so may already have formed an opinion. In order to minimise the possibility of bias, the disciplinary procedure should separate the processes of investigation, decision-making and appeal wherever possible. In Whitbread plc (t/a Whitbread Medway Inns) v Hall 2001 ICR 699, CA, the claimant's dismissal was found to be unfair despite his admission of guilt because the manager holding the disciplinary meeting had initiated the investigation and was biased against him, as she had already made up her mind to dismiss. Similarly, in Perkin v St George's Healthcare NHS Trust 2006 ICR 617, CA, the person who had talked of wanting an 'exit strategy' for a difficult employee was the wrong person to chair his disciplinary hearing.

The issue of bias was further considered – in the context of an appeal from a grievance decision – by the EAT in Watson v University of Strathcylde 2011 IRLR 458, EAT. W was concerned about the behaviour of her colleague, T, the director of the University's marketing and communications office. She felt that he was violent and aggressive, and it also transpired that T had been convicted of a breach of the peace. T's offer to resign was declined on the basis of the version of the incident that T gave to Dr W, the Secretary to the University. Dr W then publicly pledged the University's support for T. W filed a grievance against T, which was rejected, and she appealed. She objected to Dr W's presence on the appeal panel. He was a powerful figure in the University, had been a member of the committee that appointed T and had spoken out in support of T at the time of his conviction. When her objection and appeal were rejected, W resigned and claimed unfair constructive dismissal, citing victimisation by T, Dr W's public support of him, and Dr W's appointment to the appeal panel despite a clear conflict of interest. A tribunal rejected her claim, finding that it would have been 'the norm' for Dr W to be included on the appeal panel.

6.275 On appeal, the EAT overturned the tribunal's decision. It held that, when W had objected to Dr W's inclusion on the appeal panel, the question for the University had not only been whether there would be actual bias on his part, but also whether there was apparent bias. The EAT referred to the test in Porter v Magill 2002 AC 357, HL, where the House of Lords said that the key question was whether a fair-minded and informed observer, having considered the facts, would conclude that there was a real possibility that a tribunal, or any member of it, was biased. The EAT said that 'we are not suggesting that an employer setting up a grievance appeal panel is routinely required to consider specifically whether or not there is "apparent bias" in the panel, expressly applying the Porter v Magill test in doing so, but what is, in our view, clear, is that any reasonable employer requires to have regard to the need to afford an employee a fair hearing of her grievance throughout, including at the appeal stage'. The EAT went on to conclude that any reasonable employer could only have decided that it was unfair to include Dr W on the appeal panel. Accordingly, it substituted a finding of unfair dismissal.

Although absence of bias is important, it has also been recognised that the requirement that there should be no possibility of bias cannot be applied in absolute terms in the employment field. It may be unreasonable – particularly in smaller businesses – to expect the different stages of investigation and adjudication to be conducted by different individuals, or to expect those individuals to be unaffected by daily contact with each other. As the EAT has said: 'In the end the only thing that matters is whether the disciplinary tribunal acted fairly and justly' – Haddow and ors v Inner London Education Authority 1979 ICR 202, EAT. Similarly, the fact that a disciplinary decision is taken by the employee's line manager – who will frequently have pre-formed views about the qualifications and competencies of the employee – will not necessarily render the dismissal unfair, particularly where the employer's normal disciplinary procedure provides for the line manager to undertake the decision-making role – Norland Managed Services Ltd v Hastick EAT 0005/12.

6.276 In GM Packaging (UK) Ltd v Haslem EAT 0259/13 an employment tribunal endorsed a small employer's use of an external HR consultancy to investigate alleged misconduct. M, the owner of GMP Ltd, called in the consultancy because he was involved in the matters under investigation as a witness. The consultant who conducted the investigation recommended dismissal, which M sanctioned. When the employee appealed, a different consultant heard the appeal and recommended rejecting it. M agreed and the dismissal was upheld. The tribunal considered that this was a reasonable procedure and rejected the argument that M had, in effect, both decided on dismissal and rejected the appeal himself. The EAT did not interfere with the tribunal's conclusion on appeal.

6.277 **Non-attendance of employee.** Paragraph 25 of the Acas Code states that 'where an employee is persistently unable or unwilling to attend a disciplinary meeting without good cause the employer should make a decision on the evidence available'. In Bashir and anor v Sheffield Teaching Hospital NHS Foundation Trust EAT 0448/09, for example, the EAT upheld the decision of an employment tribunal that two married employees had not been unfairly dismissed (or subjected to race discrimination). Given the claimants' unreasonable and obstructive behaviour, the employer had been justified in holding grievance and disciplinary hearings in their absence and this procedural irregularity did not affect the overall fairness of the decision to dismiss.

There are obvious areas for dispute here over the definitions of 'persistently' and 'without good cause' and employers should exercise caution before proceeding with a disciplinary hearing in an employee's absence.

6.278 Before making a decision on how to proceed when an employee is repeatedly unable or unwilling to attend a meeting, the Acas Guide suggests that the employer take into account the following considerations:

- any rules the organisation has for dealing with failure to attend disciplinary meetings
- the seriousness of the disciplinary issue under consideration
- the employee's disciplinary record (including current warnings), general work record, work experience, position and length of service
- medical opinion on whether the employee is fit to attend the meeting
- how similar cases in the past have been dealt with (page 20).

In William Hicks and Partners (A Firm) v Nadal EAT 0164/05 the employer acted unfairly by jumping to conclusions about an employee's fitness to attend a meeting. N was suspended over a number of allegations including bullying and intimidation of staff. A couple of days later, N's doctor wrote to the employer to say that N was suffering from stress and was not fit to attend any hearing in the foreseeable future. The employer nonetheless arranged a disciplinary hearing, but it was postponed on a couple of occasions following the receipt of further sick notes. Eventually, however, the hearing took place in N's absence after the employer discovered that she had been in negotiations with a new employer. The EAT upheld the tribunal's finding of unfair dismissal on the ground that N's employer should not have ignored medical advice it had commissioned without 'compelling evidence' that N was 'pulling the wool over her own doctor's eyes' or 'authoritative contrary medical evidence' about her fitness, neither of which it had. The EAT pointed out that the opportunity for an employee to put his or her side of matters had long been established as an essential part of a reasonable investigation. It accepted that there may be cases where an employer had made proper enquiries, including sufficient medical enquiries, to establish that the employee was fit to attend a hearing but had unreasonably declined to do so without just cause. However, it said that this must be an exception to the general rule that disciplinary hearings should always involve the presence of the employee.

6.279 **Composition of disciplinary panel.** The person who is selected to take charge of the disciplinary hearing should be competent to do so. In Thomson v Imperial

College Healthcare NHS Trust EAT 0218/14 the EAT upheld an employment tribunal's conclusion that it was unreasonable to assign P to chair the disciplinary panel which dismissed T. Although P held a sufficiently senior role within the Trust, he had not undergone any training and had no experience of disciplinary hearings. The decision to appoint P, and his subsequent misapplication of the Trust's disciplinary procedures, took the dismissal outside the range of reasonable responses.

Where an employee's case is heard by a disciplinary panel, a change in the composition of the panel between the hearing date and the decision to dismiss may give rise to allegations of procedural unfairness. This issue arose for consideration in Union of Construction Allied Trades and Technicians v Dooley EAT 0088/12, where the hearing panel consisted of nine members, only seven of whom were involved in the subsequent decision to dismiss D for gross misconduct. The employment tribunal concluded that the absence of the two members from the decision-making process was a fundamental procedural flaw, rendering D's dismissal unfair. The EAT upheld the tribunal's decision. In doing so, it stated that an employee facing a hearing before a disciplinary panel has a legitimate expectation that, other things being equal, the composition of the panel will remain the same from start to finish. However, it also stated that there may nevertheless be circumstances where it is fair to proceed with reduced numbers. Where the expectation that the whole panel will be involved throughout is disappointed, that may justify a finding of serious procedural unfairness sufficient to vitiate the fairness of the dismissal. In deciding whether or not that is the case, it will be relevant to consider both the reason why one or more panel members have dropped out and the real or reasonably perceived prejudice to the employee.

In the instant case, one of the panel members had experienced travel difficulties **6.280** and the other, G, was on holiday. While the tribunal did not expressly consider whether it would have been possible for the decision to be postponed for a reasonable period so that both members could attend, the EAT considered that it was implicit from the tribunal's judgment that – given that only a month had passed since the hearing – this was far from impossible. In the EAT's view, G's absence in particular was fundamental to D's case since his evidence indicated that he would have argued strongly against dismissal. Strictly speaking, the EAT said, that fact by itself was probably of little significance – the fairness of the decision to press ahead in G's absence had to be judged on what was known at the time and it was not clear to what extent G had already shown his hand at the earlier hearing. However, even in G's absence, the EAT noted that there were divided views about how to proceed and this was not seen as an open-and-shut case. On balance, therefore, the EAT concluded that the tribunal had been entitled to find that it was unfair of the panel to proceed to a decision in the absence of two of its members.

371

6.281 **Witnesses.** Often employers will be faced with diametrically conflicting accounts of an alleged incident with no, or very little, additional evidence to provide corroboration one way or the other. In these circumstances, said the Court of Appeal in Salford Royal NHS Foundation Trust v Roldan 2010 ICR 1457, CA, although it is incumbent on employers to form a genuine belief on reasonable grounds that the misconduct has occurred, they are not obliged to believe one employee over another. Lord Justice Elias, giving the judgment of the Court, explained that sometimes it may be proper for employers to say that they cannot resolve the conflict and therefore do not find the case proved against the accused employee, without coming down in favour of one side or the other.

Where witness evidence exists that could be helpful to an employee's defence, that evidence should be made available to the employee – see 'Providing details of charges and possible consequences' above. If a witness wishes to remain anonymous, the Acas Guide advises employers to take written statements, seek corroborative evidence, and check that the person's motives are genuine (page 19).

6.282 **Cross-examination of witnesses.** As mentioned under 'Conduct of hearing' above, the Acas Code recommends that the employee should be given an opportunity to call witnesses (para 12). However, this suggestion has raised some eyebrows, not least because case law is more ambiguous on this point. In Santamera v Express Cargo Forwarding t/a IEC Ltd 2003 IRLR 273, EAT, the EAT stated that cross-examination will be an exception in employment disciplinary proceedings. On the facts, the allegations involved bullying and the witness felt intimidated by the claimant. The employer reasonably believed that the allegations were true. In these circumstances, the dismissal was not rendered unfair by the refusal to allow the employee to cross-examine the witness. However, although the rules on fairness contained in S.98(4) ERA do not require an employer to carry out 'a forensic or quasi-judicial investigation', it did not follow that an employer will never be obliged to allow an employee to cross-examine his or her accusers during disciplinary proceedings. The EAT emphasised that in each case a tribunal must decide with reference to the facts before it whether the employer's procedure had been fair and reasonable.

Admittedly, the Acas Code does not specifically state that employees have the right to cross-examine witnesses, merely to call them. However, there would be little point in calling a witness to attend a hearing if questions could not be put to him or her and it has to be assumed that the intention behind the Code is to allow witnesses to be questioned.

6.283 The Santamera decision leaves open the question of when it would be reasonable for an employer to allow cross-examination of witnesses. The rules of natural justice, in so far as they apply to disciplinary hearings, require that an employee know precisely what the accusations against him or her are and have a full opportunity of stating his or her case. It seems appropriate, therefore, that the question of whether or not it is reasonable to allow a witness to be called in a particular case should be decided in light of these principles. In Rhondda Cynon Taf County Borough Council v Close 2008 IRLR 868, EAT, the EAT rejected the employee's argument that her dismissal was rendered unfair by the employer's failure to make all the witnesses available for cross-examination. She had been able to challenge the evidence against her and to cross-examine two witnesses who gave oral evidence at the disciplinary hearing. In the end, however, the employer had assessed the evidence of the witnesses and concluded that they were more reliable than her.

If an allegation has been made by, or evidence obtained from, an individual who is not employed by the employer (e.g. a customer), it may not be practicable or desirable for him or her to attend a disciplinary hearing. In such cases, the Acas Guide recommends that the employer try to get a written statement from that person (page 19). If the witness wishes to remain anonymous, the Guide advises employers to take written statements, seek corroborative evidence, and check that the person's motives are genuine.

6.284 There may be a right to cross-examine witnesses – or at least a prohibition on admitting hearsay evidence in the absence of the opportunity to cross-examine witnesses – if the right to a fair trial under Article 6 of the European Convention on Human Rights applies to the proceedings. In R (on the application of Bonheoffer) v General Medical Council 2012 IRLR 37, QBD, a doctor successfully challenged a decision of the GMC's 'fitness to practise' panel (FTPP) to admit hearsay evidence against him. The FTPP hearing was concerned with allegations of serious sexual misconduct while B was working in a foreign country, in respect of which the majority of the evidence came from a single witness in that country. The witness was prepared to travel to the United Kingdom and give evidence to the FTPP but the GMC considered that that would expose him to a significantly increased risk of harm. Accordingly, the GMC proposed to rely on transcripts of video-taped interviews, transcripts of a conversation between the witness and a third party, and hearsay accounts given by others as to what they were told by him. The High Court, undertaking a judicial review of that decision, rejected the GMC's argument that the serious nature of the allegations, coupled with the public interest, meant that they ought to be investigated, even if that meant admitting evidence that would not have been admissible in criminal proceedings without appropriate safeguards. In the Court's view, the case law on Article 6 indicates that the more serious the allegations against a person, the greater the importance of ensuring proper procedural safeguards.

The Bonhoeffer case is only of direct relevance to public sector employers, who are bound by the Human Rights Act 1998 to respect Convention rights. Even then, employers' disciplinary proceedings will only rarely engage the protections of Article 6. While there is authority to suggest that Article 6 may be engaged if an employer's disciplinary proceedings have the potential to determine an employee's civil right to practise his or her profession, the decisions of the Supreme Court in R (on the application of G) v Governors of X School and anor 2011 ICR 1033, SC, and the Court of Appeal in Mattu v University Hospitals of Coventry and Warwickshire NHS Trust 2013 ICR 270, CA, indicate that such circumstances are likely to arise very rarely – see further 'Right to legal representation' above.

6.285 **Protecting identity of informants.** Where an employer receives evidence from an informant who wishes to remain anonymous, the employee is potentially disadvantaged by not being able to challenge that person's evidence. The Acas Guide advises that in these circumstances, employers should take written statements, seek corroborative evidence, and check that the person's motives are genuine (page 19).

The EAT set out guidelines for employers to follow in Linfood Cash and Carry Ltd v Thomson and anor 1989 ICR 518, EAT, with the express purpose of trying to maintain a balance of interest between protecting the anonymity of the informant and providing a fair hearing for the employee. The EAT made the following suggestions:

- informants' statements should be reduced to writing (although they might need to be edited later to preserve anonymity)

- in taking statements it is important to note the date, time and place of each observation or incident; the informant's opportunity to observe clearly and accurately; circumstantial evidence, such as knowledge of a system, the reason for the informant's presence or any memorable small details; and whether the informant had any reason to fabricate evidence

- further investigation should then take place, corroboration being clearly desirable

- tactful enquiries into the character and background of the informant would be advisable

- a decision must then be taken whether to hold a disciplinary hearing, particularly when the employer is satisfied that the informant's fear is genuine

- if the disciplinary process is to continue, the responsible member of management at each stage of the procedure should personally interview the informant and decide what weight is to be given to his or her evidence

- the informant's written statement – if necessary with omissions to avoid identification – should be made available to the employee and his or her representative

374

- if the employee or his or her representative raises an issue that should be put to the informant, it may be desirable to adjourn the disciplinary proceedings so that the chairman can question the informant

- it is particularly important that full and careful notes should be taken at disciplinary hearings when informants are involved

- if evidence from an investigating officer is to be taken at a hearing it should be prepared in writing where possible. (Note that this final point is not limited to cases where an investigation has been started because of statements made by an informant.)

However, as the EAT itself noted: 'Every case must depend upon its own facts, **6.286** and circumstances may vary widely.' In Ramsey and ors v Walkers Snack Foods Ltd and anor 2004 IRLR 754, EAT, the Linford guidelines were not followed to the letter. In particular, full statements were not taken from informants at the outset and the statements that were taken were heavily edited. In addition, the informants were only interviewed by one manager, who was not involved in the disciplinary process. However, the EAT noted that the case involved multiple informants who were terrified of being identified because they worked in a factory with a close-knit community. They were thus unwilling to sign statements unless they had been sufficiently edited so as to remove any risk of identification. Nor did they wish to be exposed to further questioning that might risk their identities becoming known. In the circumstances, the risk of reprisals was real. The EAT stated that, when considering whether or not the approach taken was fair, the focus should be on the reasons for granting anonymity in the first place. On this basis, as the tribunal had made a clear finding that the offer of anonymity was reasonable and the employer genuinely believed that no information would be provided unless it was entirely confidential, the approach taken was fair, notwithstanding non-compliance with the Linford guidelines in some respects.

The same approach was followed in Surrey County Council v Henderson EAT 0326/05, where the employer had given anonymity to five complainants who accused the employee of having threatened them and their families with violence. The employee was not provided with copies of their statements. The tribunal found that his dismissal was unfair but the EAT overturned that decision and remitted the case to be reconsidered by a different tribunal. In its view, the tribunal had failed to consider whether, having regard to the reasons why the complainants insisted on anonymity, the procedure adopted by the employer in the particular circumstances of this case fell within or outside the band of reasonable responses. That band may include some reasonable employers who would have disclosed the witness statements taken from the five complainants, either in full or in redacted form, or in some other summary form, and others who would not, given the promises of confidentiality made by

375

the employer to those complainants based on their fears and concerns for themselves and their families.

6.287 There is generally no breach of natural justice in relying on the evidence of an anonymous informant at a disciplinary hearing. It is well established that the rules of natural justice, in so far as they apply to disciplinary hearings, only require that an employee should know precisely what the accusations against him or her are and have a full opportunity to state his or her case. There is no prescriptive right to be allowed to cross-examine witnesses (see 'Cross-examination of witnesses' above). In any case, witnesses other than anonymous informants – e.g. employees of other companies or members of the general public – may be unwilling to appear at internal disciplinary hearings and cannot be compelled to do so. The EAT's guidelines in Linfood Cash and Carry Ltd v Thomson and anor (above), appropriately amended, could be useful in all cases where a witness is reluctant to appear in person.

An employer will not always be able to guarantee the anonymity of an informant. In P v T Ltd 1997 ICR 887, ChD, P's reputation in the industry in which he worked was destroyed when accusations were made against him by an anonymous informant. His employer, despite having lost a claim of unfair dismissal, refused to disclose either the nature of the allegations against P or the identity of the informant. As P was not in a position to counter the allegations, he was unable to repair his reputation and was therefore unable to find a new job. The High Court granted his application for an order requiring T Ltd to reveal both the nature of the allegations and the identity of his accuser. The Court decided that it had discretion to order the disclosure of an informant's identity where this was necessary to enable an employee to know whether he or she had a civil action for defamation or malicious falsehood against the informant whose information had led to the employee's dismissal. It was intolerable, the Court said, that an individual could be stained by serious allegations, the nature of which he or she had no means of discovering, and be left in a position where he or she could not even invoke the law to defend his or her reputation.

6.288 **Grievance raised during disciplinary procedure.** The Acas Code states that where an employee raises a grievance during a disciplinary process the disciplinary process may need to be temporarily suspended in order to deal with the matter (para 46). However, where the grievance and disciplinary cases are related, it may be appropriate to deal with both issues concurrently. The Code clearly intends employers to have a discretion to deal with the situation appropriately that was not available to them under the (now-repealed) statutory disciplinary procedures. The accompanying Acas Guide suggests that a suspension of the disciplinary procedure may be appropriate where:

- the grievance relates to a conflict of interest that the manager holding the disciplinary meeting is alleged to have

- bias is alleged in the conduct of the disciplinary meeting

- management has been selective in the evidence it has supplied to the manager holding the meeting

- there is possible discrimination (page 22).

In Jinadu v Docklands Buses EAT 0434/14 J, a bus driver, was dismissed for gross misconduct after she repeatedly refused to participate in further training and assessments following complaints about her poor driving. During the disciplinary process, J raised a grievance about some of the managers involved, but her employer continued with the disciplinary process and ultimately decided to dismiss her. Appealing against an employment tribunal's finding that her dismissal was fair, J argued that the employer ought to have put the disciplinary process on hold in order to deal with her complaint against the managers. The EAT gave this argument extremely short shrift, rejecting it in a single sentence: 'In particular, I reject Mr Ogilvy's submission that the respondents were obliged to put the disciplinary investigation on hold until they had dealt with the appellant's grievances.' This decision appears to give some support to the view that it will not necessarily be unfair for an employer to press on with disciplinary proceedings where an employee raises a grievance while those proceedings are ongoing. However, the brevity with which the EAT dealt with the point means that there is still no real practical guidance for employers – beyond that set out in the Acas Guide – as to the circumstances in which fairness may, in fact, require them to place disciplinary proceedings on hold to deal with a grievance.

The decision   6.289

It is good practice for the employer to adjourn the disciplinary hearing in order to consider the case before coming to a decision. The Acas Code states that 'after the meeting' the employer should decide whether or not disciplinary or any other action is justified and inform the employee accordingly in writing (para 18).

In deciding whether disciplinary action is appropriate and, if so, what form it should take, the Acas Guide suggests that employers consider:

- whether the rules of the organisation indicate what the likely penalty will be as a result of the particular misconduct

- the penalty imposed in similar cases in the past

- whether standards of other employees are acceptable, and whether this employee is not being unfairly singled out

- the employee's disciplinary record (including current warnings), general work record, work experience, position and length of service

377

- any special circumstances which might make it appropriate to adjust the severity of the penalty

- whether the proposed penalty is reasonable in all the circumstances

- whether any training, additional support or adjustments to the work are necessary (pages 27–28).

6.290 **Length of service.** The employee's length of service is relevant when deciding the appropriate sanction. In Strouthos v London Underground Ltd 2004 IRLR 636, CA, the Court held that the fact that S had been employed for 20 years with no relevant previous warnings was material. While acknowledging that there can be conduct so serious that dismissal is appropriate irrespective of length of service, the EAT had been wrong to say that length of service was not relevant.

However, an employee's long service can also count against him or her. In Somers v Metropolitan Police Authority ET Case No. 2318747/10, where the employee (who worked for the police) gave false details when arrested, the tribunal stated that 'the difficulty with the claimant's length of service was whilst on the one hand it was rightly argued that she had a long and untarnished career, on the other hand it was concluded that with her long years of service she really ought to know and indeed did know what was her duty'.

6.291 **Prior disciplinary record.** Rarely will previous warnings be irrelevant when an employer is considering dismissal – see, for example, Cunliffe v Primagraphics Ltd ET Case No.1500499/06 (where the employer decided that the appropriate penalty was dismissal in circumstances where the employee, who was already subject to a final written warning for insulting and intimidating a colleague, sent an offensive e-mail around the office). In deciding the fairness of such a dismissal, tribunals will take into account the previous warnings issued, even if such warnings related to different kinds of conduct from that for which the employee is ultimately dismissed – Auguste Noel Ltd v Curtis 1990 ICR 604, EAT. However, where a final warning was clearly unreasonable, and where that final warning contributes to a later dismissal, the dismissal may be unfair – Co-operative Retail Services Ltd v Lucas EAT 145/93. The EAT in Lucas noted that, as a general rule, it is not for the tribunal to sit in judgment on whether a final warning was reasonably given, but it is entitled to satisfy itself that the warning was issued in good faith and that there were prima facie grounds for it. In particular, if there is anything to suggest that the warning was issued for an oblique motive or if it was manifestly inappropriate, the tribunal could take that into account in determining the fairness of a later dismissal in reliance on that warning.

This was confirmed by the Court of Appeal in Davies v Sandwell Metropolitan Borough Council 2013 IRLR 374, CA, although Lord Justice Mummery entered a few caveats. First, the starting point should always be S.98(4) ERA, the question

378

being whether it was reasonable for the employer to treat the conduct reason, taken together with the circumstances of the final written warning, as sufficient to dismiss the claimant. Secondly, it is not for the tribunal to reopen the final warning and consider whether it was legally valid or a nullity. And thirdly, the questions of whether the warning was issued in good faith, whether there were prima facie grounds for imposing it and whether it was 'manifestly inappropriate' are all relevant to the question of whether dismissal was reasonable, having regard, among other things, to the circumstances of the warning. Lord Justice Beatson confirmed that only rarely would it be legitimate for a tribunal to 'go behind' a final written warning given before dismissal. Where there has been no appeal against a final warning, or where an appeal has been launched but not pursued, there would need to be exceptional circumstances for a tribunal to, in effect, reopen the earlier disciplinary process.

The Sandwell case was relied on in General Dynamics Information Technology **6.292** Ltd v Carranza 2015 ICR 169, EAT, where the EAT commented that the guidance in that case showed that an employer was not required to reopen a final written warning save in limited circumstances. According to the EAT, 'if an issue of the kind set out in Sandwell is raised (i.e. if the earlier warning was allegedly issued in bad faith, manifestly improper or issued without any prima facie grounds) an earlier stage of a process may require revisiting; but otherwise an employer is entitled to proceed on the basis of what has already been decided'.

If, however, a tribunal has cause on the facts to consider whether a prior warning was manifestly inappropriate, it should do so – Simmonds v Milford Club 2013 ICR D14, EAT. According to the EAT, if a prior sanction applied by an employer was not in accordance with the terms of the employer's own disciplinary policy, this could give rise to a concern that the sanction was manifestly inappropriate. However, the term 'manifestly inappropriate' indicated a higher threshold than the test of reasonableness of a dismissal and manifest inappropriateness would accordingly not be easily established.

These cases raise a related question – to what extent may an employer rely on a **6.293** final warning that the employee is challenging by way of appeal? The Acas Code makes it clear that the imposition of any disciplinary sanction, not just dismissal, should come with the possibility of an appeal (para 26). However, case law indicates that if an appeal against a warning is outstanding when the employer comes to decide on the appropriate sanction for further misconduct, the employer does not need to ignore the warning entirely. According to the Court of Appeal in Tower Hamlets Health Authority v Anthony 1989 ICR 656, CA, the employer may still take the warning into account, but must also have regard to the fact that it is subject to an undetermined appeal. Where an appeal has been launched but not pursued, both Lord Justice Lewison and Lord Justice Beatson in Davies v Sandwell Metropolitan Borough Council (above) suggested (obiter) that it would be reasonable for an employer to take into account the fact that an appeal against an earlier disciplinary sanction has been withdrawn or abandoned when considering whether to rely on that sanction in later proceedings.

A final warning might need to be disregarded if it has been unlawfully imposed, but only if that unlawfulness has been established. In Gayle v Sandwell and Birmingham Hospitals NHS Trust 2011 ICR D3, CA, G was employed as a nurse for the Trust. When she became a representative for UNISON, the Trust asked her to agree with P (a manager) the principles that would govern her time off for union business. G and P had not reached an agreement by the time that G wanted time off to attend a union meeting in June 2006, so she obtained permission from her line manager instead. She was given a final written warning for attending the meeting without having agreed the parameters for so doing with P. G later faced disciplinary action for an unrelated act of misconduct, which was found proved, and she was dismissed. G brought proceedings in the employment tribunal claiming, among other things, that the final written warning constituted an unlawful detriment related to her trade union activities, contrary to S.146 of the Trade Union and Labour Relations (Consolidation) Act 1992, and that her dismissal was unfair. The tribunal dismissed the claims. Crucially, it found that the warning was imposed for G's failure to comply with a management instruction, and not for the purpose of penalising her trade union activities. It referred to Tower Hamlets Health Authority v Anthony (above) and Stein v Associated Dairies Ltd 1982 IRLR 447, EAT, taking these cases as authority for the proposition that it could only go behind the decision to impose the final written warning if it had been made in 'bad faith' with no prima facie grounds. Both the EAT and Court of Appeal subsequently approved the tribunal's approach. The Court of Appeal endorsed the general principle of law established by the Anthony and Stein cases and, applying that principle, it held that the Trust had properly taken account of the final written warning in its decision to dismiss.

6.294 Where it is alleged that a warning was given in bad faith, the tribunal must hear evidence on the point. In Way v Spectrum Property Care Ltd 2015 EWCA Civ 381, CA, an employment tribunal excluded evidence to the effect that a final written warning – which was later relied upon to dismiss W – was given in bad faith. It went on to hold that the dismissal was fair. The EAT concluded that, while the tribunal had been wrong to exclude the evidence of bad faith, it would have made no difference to the tribunal's decision, even had it been admitted. The Court of Appeal held that this was an error of law: the EAT had, in effect, proceeded upon the basis that a warning given in bad faith may be relied upon to justify a dismissal which, absent the warning, would not have occurred. This was contrary to the decisions in Davies v Sandwell Metropolitan Borough Council (above) and Wincanton Group plc v Stone 2013 ICR D6, EAT (discussed immediately below).

380

In Wincanton Group plc v Stone (above) Mr Justice Langstaff, President of the EAT, usefully summarised the general principles to be applied by tribunals as to the relevance of earlier warnings when determining the fairness of a dismissal:

- the tribunal should take into account earlier warnings issued in good faith

- if the tribunal considers that a warning was issued in bad faith, it will not be valid and cannot be relied upon by the employer to justify any subsequent dismissal

- where a warning was issued in good faith, the tribunal should take account of any relevant proceedings, such as internal appeals, that may affect the validity of the warning, and give them such weight as it considers appropriate

- the tribunal may not 'go behind' a valid warning to hold that it should not have been issued or that a 'lesser category' of warning should have been issued

- the tribunal will not be going behind the warning where it takes into account the factual circumstances giving rise to it. There may be a considerable difference between the circumstances giving rise to the first warning and those considered later. Just as a degree of similarity will tend in favour of a more severe penalty, so a degree of dissimilarity may, in appropriate circumstances, tend the other way

- the tribunal may also take account of the employer's treatment of other employees since the warning was issued. This may show that an employer has subsequently been more or less lenient in similar circumstances

- the tribunal must remember that a final written warning always implies, subject only to any contractual terms to the contrary, that any subsequent misconduct of whatever nature will usually be met with dismissal, and only exceptionally will dismissal not occur.

In Sweeney v Strathclyde Fire Board EATS 0029/13 the issue before the EAT **6.295** was whether it was reasonable for an employer to take into account a 'live' final written warning that was issued *after* the misconduct which was the subject of the disciplinary proceedings was committed. Although the facts are rather unusual, the case gives some guidance on when such a warning may be taken into account. S had over 20 years' good service with SFB as a retained fireman and had reached the rank of watch commander. In July 2010 he was charged with an offence of domestic assault on his wife. In August he received a final written warning for unauthorised absence from work as he had gone to work overseas between March and June 2010 without seeking prior authorisation from SFB. In March 2011, at his criminal trial, S pleaded guilty to domestic assault and was sentenced to 180 hours' community service. Subsequently, SFB carried out an investigation into the behaviour that had led to S's criminal conviction and dismissed him for conduct not befitting a watch commander. S claimed unfair dismissal. The employment tribunal found that

SFB would have issued S with a final written warning had there not been a 'live' final written warning on his file. However, the tribunal concluded that SFB's decision to dismiss fell within the band of reasonable responses. S appealed, arguing that, as a matter of law, a final written warning could not be relevant to conduct that pre-dated it.

Dismissing the appeal, the EAT held that SFB was entitled to take into account everything that was on S's file, including the final written warning for unauthorised absence. It rejected S's contention that the final written warning could only be construed as referring to misconduct taking place after the date of the warning. An unexpired written warning – final or otherwise – is a fact which a reasonable employer is entitled to have in mind when deciding whether or not to dismiss. The EAT stated that while it is correct that a warning is an admonition that tells the employee that future misconduct will have certain consequences, it is also a recording of the commission of misconduct in the mind of both employer and employee. The Appeal Tribunal agreed with SFB's submission that 'a warning is "Janus like" in that it looks both ways'. SFB had been entitled to proceed as it had and, in all the circumstances of the case, had not acted unreasonably.

6.296 Note that where an employer is justified in dismissing an employee for the present misconduct alone, the validity or otherwise of a prior warning will not in practice impact upon the fairness of the dismissal – Adegbola v Marks and Spencer plc 2013 EWCA Civ 1808, CA. In that case, A had a live final written warning on her file. She had brought an appeal against that warning but the employer had declined to hear it because it was brought out of time. A was then investigated for her attitude towards her manager and alleged misuse of her staff discount card. She was ultimately dismissed for both offences and claimed that the dismissal was unfair, in part because the employer had had regard to the prior warning, the validity of which she disputed. The Court of Appeal upheld a tribunal's decision that A's dismissal was fair. During the disciplinary proceedings, A had admitted buying products for resale using her staff discount card. The tribunal had found – and the Court of Appeal agreed – that this misconduct alone was sufficiently serious to justify dismissal. Accordingly, the fact that the tribunal had wrongly stated that it did not have jurisdiction to consider the validity or otherwise of the existing warning did not affect the result.

6.297 **Expired warnings.** It is usual for expired warnings to be disregarded by employers when deciding whether disciplinary action is appropriate. In Diosynth Ltd v Thomson 2006 IRLR 284, Ct Sess (Inner House), the Court of Session said that an employee was entitled to assume that a warning, which would cease to have effect after 12 months, meant exactly what it said. Accordingly, the employer acted unreasonably in taking the expired warning into account when deciding to dismiss the employee by reason of misconduct.

The dismissal, which would not have been carried out had the warning not been on his file, was thus unfair.

That said, the Court of Appeal in Airbus UK Ltd v Webb 2008 ICR 561, CA, distinguished the Diosynth decision, commenting that that case was not authority for a broad proposition that an expired warning must be ignored for all purposes. In the Airbus case, the claimant was the only one of four employees caught watching television outside the normal break time to be dismissed. The other three, who were given a final written warning, had no prior disciplinary record, whereas the claimant had previously been given a final written warning that had expired three weeks previously. The Court held that the employer had been entitled to take the claimant's expired warning into account when deciding whether it was reasonable to dismiss.

Although these decisions may initially appear difficult to reconcile, on closer **6.298** reading they are not in fact entirely contradictory. As the Court of Appeal explained in the Airbus case, once the warning ceased to have effect as a penalty, it could not be relied on as the reason for dismissal. But this did not mean that the misconduct in respect of which the penalty was imposed could not be relevant to the consideration of the reasonableness of the employer's later action in dismissing the employee for similar misconduct. In the words of Lord Justice Mummery: 'The language of S.98(4) is wide enough to cover the employee's earlier misconduct as a relevant circumstance of the employer's later decision to dismiss the employee, whose later misconduct is shown by the employer to the employment tribunal to be the reason or principal reason for the dismissal.'

In Diosynth Ltd v Thomson (above) the employer had not been entitled to dismiss the employee by reason of the expired warning on his file in circumstances where his misconduct was not sufficient, on its own, to justify dismissal. In other words, the expired warning was not capable of 'tipping the balance' in favour of dismissal. By contrast, in Airbus UK Ltd v Webb (above) the employee was dismissed by reason of his misconduct, not because he had an expired final written warning on his file. The employer, having considered that the conduct of all four employees (including the claimant) was sufficiently serious to result in dismissal, had been entitled to take into account, when considering any mitigating circumstances, that the claimant had a previous expired warning for misconduct whereas the other three had clean disciplinary records. In these circumstances, the employer's decision to dismiss only the claimant had been reasonably open to it.

It follows from this that the Airbus case does not give employers a free hand to **6.299** treat expired warnings as still being in effect. Rather, it establishes that, once a warning for misconduct has expired, an employer does not artificially have to pretend that the previous misconduct never took place when dealing with further acts of misconduct on the part of the same employee. It still remains good practice to 'wipe the slate clean' after a warning has expired, but the Court's decision emphasises that just because something is contrary to notions of good practice does not invariably mean that it will be unreasonable. The question for tribunals is, as ever, whether the degree of reliance on the previous misconduct and/or the expired warning was reasonable in the circumstances.

Expired warnings are discussed further under 'Penalties – time limits for warnings' below.

6.300 **Consistency of treatment.** As the Acas Guide points out, fairness does not mean that similar offences will always call for the same disciplinary action (page 28). Each case must be looked at in the context of its particular circumstances, which may include health or domestic problems, provocation, or justifiable ignorance of the rule or standard involved. The Acas Guide gives two scenarios based on an example involving disciplinary action taken against an employee who has made a series of mistakes concerning delivery dates, with the result that a customer has threatened to take its business elsewhere. In the first scenario, the employee had received relevant training and her team leader and section manager had stressed to her the importance of agreeing delivery dates. In the second, she had received no training or guidance from her supervisor or manager. In the first scenario, a final written warning was deemed appropriate, whereas no disciplinary action was warranted in the second.

In Paul v East Surrey District Health Authority 1995 IRLR 305, CA, the Court of Appeal held that an employer is entitled to take into account not only the nature of the conduct and the surrounding facts but also any personal circumstances affecting the employee. That case concerned a nurse who was dismissed for drinking on duty. He argued that his dismissal was unfair since colleagues who had also been drinking on duty had not been dismissed. The Court found that the attitude of the employee to his or her conduct may be a relevant factor in deciding whether a repetition of it is likely and commented: 'Thus an employee who admits that the conduct proved is unacceptable and accepts advice and help to avoid a repetition may be regarded differently from one who refuses to accept responsibility for his actions, argues with management or makes unfounded suggestions that his fellow employees have conspired to accuse him falsely.'

6.301 The employer must consider the circumstances of each individual employee. Three examples:

*   **Merseyside Passenger Transport Executive v Millington** EAT 232/89: M worked on a passenger ferry. During one of his shifts he went to a pub to have lunch. He was joined by two other employees, H and W. The employer had a strict rule that employees should not enter licensed premises while working. A member of management went to the pub and immediately suspended all three employees. There was no suggestion that M was drunk

– he had merely gone to the most convenient place to obtain food – but H and W acted in a way consistent with their being drunk. On the following day, all three were summarily dismissed. Management believed that it risked an unfair dismissal claim if it did not treat all three alike for breaching the same rule. However, an employment tribunal took the view that there were enough differences between M's conduct and that of H and W, coupled with mitigating factors on M's behalf, to make a reasonable employer distinguish between them and treat M more leniently. The EAT agreed. It added that to treat all employees the same as a matter of course, without considering each individual's particular circumstances, simply could not be done

- **Levenes Solicitors v Dalley** 2008 EWCA Civ 69, CA: the Court of Appeal found that the employer had not acted unreasonably in dismissing D for failing to issue a claim in time when another solicitor who had failed to serve proceedings in time on three occasions had not been dismissed. The fact that D was also facing a charge of being absent from work for no good reason justified the difference in treatment

- **Newbound v Thames Water Utilities Ltd** 2015 EWCA Civ 776, CA: N was part of a team responsible for sewer maintenance. His work took place underground, often in hazardous conditions. Prior to being sent on a job, N had agreed with management that he would wear full breathing apparatus when inside the sewer and he signed a risk assessment form confirming this. However, on the day – with the agreement of A, the manager in charge of that particular job – N entered the sewer without breathing apparatus. When the employer became aware of this, it initiated a disciplinary investigation. The end result was that N was dismissed for gross misconduct, whereas A was given a written warning. Overturning the EAT, the Court of Appeal held that the employment tribunal had been entitled to find that this was not an appropriate case for disparity in treatment and that N's dismissal was unfair. The Court noted the tribunal's key findings: A was in overall charge of the site; he allowed N and the contractor to enter the sewer twice without breathing apparatus; A was charged with misconduct rather than gross misconduct; A was interviewed as part of the investigation before the disciplinary hearings but N was not; and A received a written warning while N was dismissed. Lord Justice Bean observed that he had 'rarely seen such an obvious case of unjustified disparity'.

Penalties. Where an employee has been found to have committed misconduct, **6.302** the employer will need to determine the penalty to be imposed. Employers have a number of penalties at their disposal, ranging from a first warning to summary dismissal. However, they should be guided by their disciplinary policy and must ensure that any penalty imposed is commensurate to the misconduct committed by the employee – otherwise they risk a finding of unfair dismissal or, in the case of a warning or suspension, being in fundamental breach of the duty of trust and confidence (leading to an unfair constructive dismissal). In Macaulay v Saga Publishing Ltd ET Case No.1103038/06, for example, M was given a final written warning after playing a practical joke on a colleague. An employment tribunal found that the employer's penalty was too harsh, as it meant that M would not get a pay increase and bonus, and he had been entitled to treat himself as constructively dismissed. The maximum penalty for M's conduct should have been a verbal warning.

6.303 *First written warning.* The Acas Code states that where misconduct is confirmed it is usual to give the employee a written warning (para 19). The employee should also be given sufficient time in which to improve. However, it may not be necessary to give the employee an opportunity to improve where there is evidence that he or she is unlikely to change his or her behaviour in future – Perkin v St George's Healthcare NHS Trust 2006 ICR 617, CA.

Employers may have as many stages in their procedures as they consider appropriate. For example, some procedures may include an 'informal' stage applicable to minor first offences (although note that if such action results in a written record, it may not be viewed as informal for the purpose of the right to be accompanied – see 'Right to be accompanied' above) and/or more than one formal warning stage before a final written warning is given. What is important is that parties are aware of which stage has been reached and its consequences. In Sarkar v West London Mental Health NHS Trust 2010 IRLR 508, CA, the Court of Appeal upheld an employment tribunal's decision that the Trust had unfairly dismissed S for gross misconduct through its formal disciplinary procedure, when it had initially taken the view that the misconduct could be dealt with under its 'Fair Blame Policy' (FBP) – a dispute resolution procedure designed to deal with less serious matters. The tribunal was entitled to regard the initial use of the FBP as an indication of the Trust's view that the misconduct alleged against S was relatively minor and that it was prepared to deal with it under a procedure that could not result in his dismissal. The tribunal did not err in law in concluding that it was inconsistent of the Trust to then charge S with gross misconduct based on the same matters.

6.304 A written warning, whether first or final, should set out the nature of the misconduct and the change to behaviour required, with a timescale (para 21 of the Acas Code). The employee should be told how long the warning will remain current and informed of the consequences of further misconduct within the set period – for instance, in the case of a final warning, that it may result in dismissal or some other contractual penalty such as demotion or loss of seniority. A failure by the employer to comply with any of these requirements may make it unreasonable to rely on the warning in any future disciplinary action.

A record of the warning should be kept, but it should be disregarded for disciplinary purposes after a specified period (e.g. six months). The Acas Guide

386

also suggests that the warning should inform the employee of his or her right to appeal and the timescale within which an appeal must be made (page 34).

6.305 *Final written warning.* A further act of misconduct within a set period would normally result in a final written warning (para 19 of the Code). However, where an employee's first misconduct is sufficiently serious – for example, it has had or may have had a serious harmful impact on the organisation – it may be appropriate to move directly to a final written warning (para 20).

A final written warning may also be used where misconduct is sufficiently serious to amount to gross misconduct justifying summary dismissal but the circumstances are such that dismissal is not deemed appropriate, as illustrated by the following example taken from the Acas Guide:

> A long-serving employee returns from a celebratory lunch having consumed too much alcohol. He is very apologetic and promises that it will not happen again. Although being unfit for work because of excessive alcohol is listed in the company rules as gross misconduct, taking into account his ten years' service and exemplary record, the employer decides not to dismiss but to give him a final written warning (page 31).

6.306 *Time limits for warnings.* There is no set time limit for a written warning: the Acas Code only requires that a timescale be included (para 21) and the example of six months given in the Acas Guide is purely that. The Guide recommends that, 'except in agreed special circumstances, any disciplinary action taken should be disregarded for disciplinary purposes after a specified period of satisfactory conduct' (page 33). It states that normal practice is for different types of warning to remain in force for different periods; for example, six months for a first written warning and 12 months for a final written warning (or more in exceptional circumstances). It suggests that the established period should be set out in the disciplinary procedure and that warnings should cease to be 'live' when that period has expired. However, the Guide does provide for exceptions. First, where there is a pattern of an employee's conduct improving during the period of a warning and lapsing shortly afterwards, it suggests that his or her previous record can be taken into account when deciding how long a future warning should last. Secondly, although stating that a decision to dismiss should not be based on an expired warning, the Guide accepts that the fact that there is an expired warning may explain an employer's decision not to substitute a lesser penalty.

Since an employee's prior disciplinary record is often a factor in deciding whether dismissal is an appropriate sanction, both parties will benefit from knowing whether a previous warning has expired. (For further discussion of expired warnings, see 'Expired warnings' above.)

6.307 *Dismissal.* The Acas Code makes it clear that a decision to dismiss should only be taken by a manager who has the authority to do so and that the employee

387

should be informed as soon as possible of the reasons for the dismissal, the date on which the employment contract will end, the appropriate period of notice and the right of appeal (para 22).

An employee with at least two years' service at the effective date of termination has a statutory right under S.92 ERA to receive a written statement of the reasons for his or her dismissal if he or she requests one. If such a request is made, the employer must provide the statement within 14 days. An employee who is pregnant or who is on maternity or adoption leave which is brought to an end by the dismissal is entitled to written reasons for dismissal without having to make a request and regardless of length of service. A failure to provide written reasons will result in an award of two weeks' pay to the employee – S.93 ERA (see Chapter 19, 'Written reasons for dismissal').

6.308 *Other sanctions.* Sanctions other than dismissal, such as transfer, demotion or suspension without pay, should only be imposed if they are provided for in the employee's contract, or with the employee's agreement – see the Acas Guide (page 29).

The question of alternative employment is normally considered relevant to an employer's reasonableness in dismissing where there has been little or no contributory behaviour on the part of the employee dismissed – for example, in situations of incapacity and redundancy. However, the Court of Appeal's decision in P v Nottinghamshire County Council 1992 ICR 706, CA, appears to have extended this duty to consider redeployment to certain misconduct cases. In that case the employee was dismissed from his position as an assistant groundsman at a girls' school run by Nottinghamshire County Council. He had pleaded guilty to a charge of indecent assault against his daughter and asked for two further offences of indecent conduct with two older daughters to be taken into account. At the time of his dismissal he was informed that an attempt would be made by the Council to redeploy him in the Highways Department. However, he was not accepted there on account of his sickness record. His complaint of unfair dismissal was upheld by a tribunal in a majority decision. When the matter reached the Court of Appeal, it stated that in an appropriate case, and where the size and administrative resources of the employer's undertaking permit, it may be unfair to dismiss an employee without first considering whether he or she could be redeployed in an alternative job, notwithstanding that it is clear that the employee could not be allowed to continue in his or her original job.

6.309 Unfortunately, the Court of Appeal provided no real guidance as to what might constitute an 'appropriate case' when it comes to dismissals for misconduct. It may well be that in such cases alternative employment need only be investigated where the dismissal would not have been regarded as necessary in the first place if the employee had been employed in a different post.

The EAT in Barcelos v London Borough of Hammersmith and Fulham EAT 0331/03 distinguished the Nottinghamshire County Council case, holding that an employer's failure to consider the possibility of redeployment would not invariably render a dismissal unfair. In that case, the employee's failure to follow the employer's reasonable instructions had a bearing on the trust and confidence required for a continuing employment relationship. Consequently, the tribunal had been entitled to conclude that the employer had been reasonable to reject the option of alternative employment.

'No difference' rule

6.310

In Polkey v AE Dayton Services Ltd 1988 ICR 142, HL, the House of Lords ruled that employers could not argue that a procedurally improper dismissal was nevertheless fair because it would have made no difference if the employer had followed a fair procedure. Their Lordships held that an employer's actions in dispensing with a fair procedure were highly relevant to the question of whether an employer acted reasonably in dismissing, and that tribunals were not entitled to take into account, when determining the fairness or otherwise of a dismissal, whether a proper procedure would have made any difference to the employer's decision to dismiss. Only in wholly exceptional cases where it could be shown that carrying out a proper procedure would have been 'utterly useless' or 'futile' would procedural failures be overlooked when considering reasonableness for the purposes of S.98(4) ERA. Polkey and the so-called 'no difference' rule are discussed further in Chapter 3, 'Unfairness', under 'Fairness of internal procedure'.

Right of appeal

6.311

The Acas Code states that: 'Where an employee feels that disciplinary action taken against them is wrong or unjust they should appeal against the decision. Appeals should be heard without unreasonable delay and ideally at an agreed time and place. Employees should let employers know the grounds for their appeal in writing' (para 26). This makes it clear that the right to appeal applies to all disciplinary hearings that end in disciplinary action being taken, not just those resulting in dismissal, with the result that a refusal to allow an employee to appeal at any stage of the procedure could lead to an uplift in any compensation award under S.207A of the Trade Union and Labour Relations (Consolidation) Act 1992 if the employee subsequently brings a successful tribunal claim. It also imposes an obligation on the employee to appeal in writing, with the result that any failure to do so may be taken into account by an employment tribunal when determining any related claim and any resulting compensation may be reduced accordingly under S.207A – see Chapter 16, 'Compensatory awards: adjustments', under 'Adjustments for breach of Acas Code of Practice'. Delay by either party also has the potential to lead to an adjustment – either an uplift or a reduction – in the compensation awarded. The employee has a statutory right

389

to be accompanied at an appeal hearing – Ss.10(1), (2) and 13(4)(c) ERelA 1999 (see further 'Right to be accompanied' above).

The Acas Guide states that the opportunity to appeal against a disciplinary decision is essential to natural justice and that an appeal may be raised on any number of grounds such as new evidence, undue severity or inconsistency of the penalty (page 34). It also says that an appeal can be either a review of the disciplinary sanction or a rehearing, which reflects the Court of Appeal's judgment in Taylor v OCS Group Ltd 2006 ICR 1602, CA. In that case the Court held that the task for an employment tribunal when considering whether the employer acted reasonably in dismissing is to assess the fairness of the disciplinary process as a whole. Where procedural deficiencies occur at an early stage, the tribunal should examine the subsequent appeal hearing, particularly its procedural fairness and thoroughness, and the open-mindedness of the decision-maker.

6.312 The Guide warns against using an appeal to punish the employee for appealing and recommends that it should not result in any increase in the penalty as this may deter individuals from appealing (page 34). The Court of Appeal's decision in McMillan v Airedale NHS Foundation Trust 2014 IRLR 803, CA, supports this view. There, the employee had appealed unsuccessfully against a final written warning. The employer indicated to the employee that it considered trust and confidence between them to have broken down and that it would reconvene the disciplinary panel to consider the appropriate sanction. Upholding a decision of the High Court to grant an injunction preventing such action by the employer, the Court of Appeal referred to the Acas Guide and noted that the right of appeal is intended to benefit the employee, not the employer. To allow an increase in the disciplinary sanction on appeal would effectively be to enable the employer to usurp the employee's right in this regard. As Lord Justice Underhill stated: 'If an employer wishes to have the right under its disciplinary procedures to increase the sanction on appeal it must be expressly provided for.'

Once a decision has been made, employees should be informed in writing of the results of the appeal hearing 'as soon as possible' (Acas Code, para 29).

6.313 Internal appeals part of dismissal process. Section 98(4) ERA requires employment tribunals to consider whether or not the employer acted reasonably in treating the reason for dismissal as a sufficient reason. It was argued before the House of Lords in West Midlands Co-operative Society Ltd v Tipton 1986 ICR 192, HL, that tribunals should only consider the employer's actions in relation to matters known before and at the time of the dismissal. However, their Lordships rejected this argument on the ground that injustice could result if an employer acts reasonably on the facts known at the time of the dismissal but quite unreasonably in maintaining that decision in the light of new facts established in the course of the appeal procedure. Accordingly, they held that the employer's actions at the appeal stage are relevant to the reasonableness of the whole dismissal process.

A failure to carry out a reasonable and proper procedure at each stage of the dismissal process, including the appeal stage, will be taken very seriously. In Stoker v Lancashire County Council 1992 IRLR 75, CA, S was dismissed for misconduct. The decision was then subject to two appeal hearings by different subcommittees of LCC. The first subcommittee confined its activities to reviewing the 'penalty' only, not the reason for the decision, despite the fact that S's contract clearly entitled him to full hearings before both subcommittees. The Court of Appeal held that a reasonable employer can be expected to comply with the full requirements of an appeal procedure set out in its own disciplinary code and any failure to do so is a matter that must be taken into consideration when judging the reasonableness of the employer's action. Since neither the employment tribunal nor the EAT had considered the employer's failure to comply with the requirements of the contractual appeal procedure, the case was remitted to a differently constituted tribunal for reconsideration.

In Westminster City Council v Cabaj 1996 ICR 960, CA, the claimant was **6.314** dismissed for irregular timekeeping. Although the disciplinary code stated that he was entitled to an appeal against his dismissal in front of a panel of three Council members, only two members heard his appeal. The Court of Appeal ruled that, although employers should follow the agreed procedure, not every plain and significant breach of agreed disciplinary procedures will inevitably render a dismissal unfair. The question that an employment tribunal must decide is not whether in all the circumstances the employer acted reasonably, but the narrower question under S.98(4) ERA of whether the employer acted reasonably in treating the reason shown as a sufficient reason for dismissing the employee. The relevance of an employer's failure to follow an agreed disciplinary procedure therefore lies in whether that failure denied the employee the opportunity of demonstrating that the reason for his or her dismissal was not sufficient. This is a question for the tribunal to decide on the facts. In the instant case the tribunal should have first decided whether the failure to have a full appeal panel was such that the claimant was denied the opportunity of demonstrating that the real reason for his dismissal was insufficient, and then considered the employer's reasons for the failure to observe the disciplinary code. Since it could not be said that the tribunal's answers to those questions would inevitably lead it to a conclusion that the dismissal was unfair, the case was remitted to a differently constituted tribunal to consider the matter afresh.

The Cabaj case is therefore authority for the proposition that not every procedural defect at the appeal stage will have the effect of rendering a dismissal unfair. A similar conclusion was reached in Sartor v P and O European Ferries (Felixstowe) Ltd 1992 IRLR 271, CA. There, the employee's appeal was defective in that the two members of staff who heard the appeal had also been

391

involved in the original investigation of the misconduct and could not be said to be independent. The Court of Appeal declined to overturn the tribunal's finding of fair dismissal as the employment tribunal had not erred in law in reaching its conclusion. However, a majority of the Court of Appeal said that they would have reached a different conclusion on the facts and employers are well advised to adhere carefully to their disciplinary procedures.

6.315 It is clear from these cases that what will affect fairness is the existence of a defect that renders the appeal process defective in the sense that that process should or could have found a flaw in the original decision to dismiss. Conversely, defects in the original disciplinary procedures may be remedied on appeal. For this purpose, it is irrelevant whether the appeal hearing takes the form of a rehearing or a review as long as the appeal is sufficiently thorough to cure the earlier procedural shortcomings. This was established by the Court of Appeal in Taylor v OCS Group Ltd 2006 ICR 1602, CA, which finally laid to rest the notion, derived from the EAT's decision in Whitbread and Co plc v Mills 1988 ICR 776, EAT, that only a full rehearing of the case (rather than a mere review of the original decision) was capable of curing an earlier defect. After careful analysis of the decision in Whitbread, the Court in the Taylor case said that the Appeal Tribunal had used the words 'rehearing' and 'review' as mere illustrations of the kind of hearings that would be thorough enough to cure an earlier defect in the disciplinary process. It had not propounded a rule of law that only a rehearing – as opposed to a review – was capable of curing these defects. Such a rule would fetter a tribunal's discretion when considering the fairness of the dismissal under S.98(4). It was evident from other reported cases that Whitbread had not always been properly understood and that tribunals have been tempted to categorise appeal hearings either as rehearings or reviews. In view of the confusion surrounding Whitbread, the Court suggested that it would be advisable for it not to be cited in future cases.

In Adeshina v St George's University Hospitals NHS Foundation Trust and ors EAT 0293/14 the tribunal held that the flaws at the first stage of the disciplinary process were remedied on appeal, notwithstanding the fact that the appeal itself did not fully comply with the Acas Code, in that the panel included one member who had had previous dealings with the claimant and another who was more junior than the manager who took the final decision to dismiss. The EAT refused to interfere. The tribunal had considered the composition of the appeal panel in the round, including the fact that it contained an independent member, and found that there had been no bias.

6.316 If the appeal hearing is itself fundamentally flawed, however, it cannot remedy earlier defects, as was made clear in Byrne v BOC Ltd 1992 IRLR 505, EAT. There, B was dismissed for falsifying overtime claims. The tribunal was satisfied that the procedural defects leading up to dismissal were sufficient to render the dismissal unfair – the initial hearing was convened with undue haste, only 30 minutes after B's return from holiday, and B was not told in advance that she was charged with an offence involving dishonesty. It found, however, that the appeal hearing had remedied the earlier inadequacies. The EAT agreed that the appeal had remedied the defects but found that the appeal itself was unfair in that the person hearing it was 'judge in his own cause'. Since the appeal was unfair, it was incapable of curing earlier defects.

The conduct of the appeal hearing is therefore very important. The principles of natural justice should be observed so far as possible (see 'The disciplinary hearing' above). However, there is one principle of natural justice that is, in the EAT's view, often too impracticable in the commercial context to be insisted on rigidly: that is the rule that there should be different people handling every stage of the disciplinary process and that they should avoid having contact with each other during that process – see Rowe v Radio Rentals Ltd 1982 IRLR 177, EAT. There the EAT recognised that it was inevitable that those involved in the original decision to dismiss would be in daily contact with their superiors in line-management and that total disconnection cannot be achieved. From the decided cases, what appears to be relevant is the degree of involvement by the same person at the different stages. Two contrasting examples:

- **Rowe v Radio Rentals Ltd** (above): R was dismissed for trading for personal gain when employed as a TV engineer. His immediate superior, L, made the decision to dismiss him. L reported this decision to W, the Regional Controller. R appealed against the dismissal and the appeal was heard by W. The appeal was dismissed and R complained to a tribunal that the dismissal was unfair. The EAT upheld the employment tribunal's decision that the dismissal was not unfair on the ground that W's earlier involvement in the dismissal process was simply to be informed of the decision to dismiss. W could not properly be regarded, when hearing the appeal, as being a 'judge in his own cause' and justice had therefore been done

- **Byrne v BOC Ltd** 1992 IRLR 505, EAT: B's manager, P, had been involved in the investigation of B's overtime claims. He made the decision to bring charges and had consulted the personnel department to find out what the appropriate procedure and penalty would be. He also conducted the appeal hearing. These factors led the EAT to the 'inescapable conclusion' that P, when hearing the appeal, was a 'judge in his own cause'. Thus the appeal hearing was unfair.

6.317 While it is recognised that the person who investigated the offence might need to be present at the appeal hearing to give factual information, a tribunal is likely to take a dim view of that person remaining behind after the hearing to discuss matters with the ultimate decision-maker. Such a practice smacks of bias and may be sufficient to render a dismissal unfair. In Lawton v Park Cake Bakeries EAT 90/88, for example, L, a charge-hand, was dismissed for assaulting another employee. The investigation was carried out by J, who also conducted

393

the hearing at which L was dismissed. J attended the appeal hearing, which was conducted by B, and remained behind while B reached his decision. The EAT held that there was no breach of natural justice in J being involved in the appeal hearing, but it was 'highly undesirable' that J should have stayed behind afterwards. However, the employment tribunal had accepted the evidence of witnesses who said that the decision was B's and B's alone and this fact had not been challenged by L. The EAT upheld the tribunal's finding of fair dismissal but with the warning that, without such evidence, the dismissal might well have been unfair on procedural grounds.

For further discussion on the general principles of bias, whether at the disciplinary hearing or the appeal stage, see 'The disciplinary hearing – absence of bias' above.

6.318 The Acas Guide states that, wherever possible, an appeal should be heard by someone senior to the person who took the original disciplinary decision – although it recognises that this may not always be feasible, particularly in smaller organisations (page 34). Pipecoil Technology Ltd v Heathcote EAT 0432/11 is an example of a case where the employer failed to comply with this recommendation and the dismissal was therefore found to be unfair. There, the original disciplinary decision had been taken by the company's managing director, who was found by an employment tribunal to have approached the hearing with a closed mind, having already decided to dismiss the employee. The employee's appeal was then heard by another director, who upheld the decision to dismiss. This was contrary to the employer's own disciplinary procedure, which stated that appeals should be heard by the managing director. The EAT held that, in these circumstances, the employment tribunal had been entitled to conclude that there was a concern over whether the director hearing the appeal would feel able to overturn the original decision of the managing director. As a result, the appeal did not cure the earlier defects in the procedure and the dismissal as a whole was unfair.

Although the appeal is an important part of the dismissal procedure, an employer who dismisses an employee against the recommendation of an appeal panel will not necessarily contravene S.98(4). The test remains whether the employer's conduct was reasonable in all the circumstances. In Kisoka v Ratnpinyotip (t/a Rydevale Day Nursery) 2014 ICR D17, EAT, K was dismissed for gross misconduct based on evidence which, in the employer's view, established that she had tried to start a fire at the children's nursery where she worked. K appealed to an independent appeal panel which, taking into account further information produced by her, decided to overturn the employer's decision to dismiss. The employer then investigated the assertions made by K to the appeal panel but, finding them unsubstantiated, concluded that there remained a number of reasons why K should be considered responsible for starting the fire. It therefore decided not to implement the appeal panel's decision. K complained of unfair dismissal but an employment tribunal rejected her claim and the EAT upheld the decision. According to the EAT, the tribunal was entitled to find that the employer's procedure was fair and that its decision to dismiss was reasonable. As the tribunal had rightly taken into account, the employer was responsible for the welfare of children and was concerned not to re-employ a member of staff where there remained reasonable grounds for believing that she had tried to start a fire. The EAT specifically rejected K's submission that a reasonable employer could only depart from the decision of an appeal panel in 'exceptional circumstances'. This would put an unnecessary and unhelpful gloss on the statutory language of S.98(4), which was designed to be applied in a practical fashion by employment tribunals to the individual facts of the case.

Changing reason for dismissal on appeal. Nothing in principle prevents an **6.319** employer's appeal panel upholding a decision to dismiss on a different basis from that on which the original decision was made. This might happen if facts that emerge during the appeal process throw a different light on the original circumstances of the dismissal. For the dismissal to be fair, though, the employer must ensure that whatever grounds remain still justify dismissal. In Perry v Imperial College Healthcare NHS Trust EAT 0473/10 P worked for the Trust as a mobile midwife and for a different employer as a family planning nurse in a clinic. P's second job did not overlap with her work for the Trust and was carried out during different hours. She went on sick leave from her job at the Trust as a result of a knee injury, but continued to work in her other, more sedentary, role during this time. When the Trust discovered that P was working while on sick leave it dismissed her for fraudulently or dishonestly claiming sick pay. P appealed, seeking to rely on medical evidence showing that, while her injury prevented her doing mobile work, there was nothing preventing her fulfilling her clinic-based role. The appeal panel, when it came to appreciate the true factual position, nonetheless upheld the decision to dismiss. It relied instead on a clause in P's contract requiring her to obtain the permission of her line manager if she wished to work while on sick leave, which she had not done as she did not think that the clause applied to her. The panel noted that P's failure to disclose her ability to work in a non-mobile role deprived the Trust of the opportunity of redeploying her to other duties.

The EAT held that the appeal panel's decision to confirm the dismissal was unfair. By the time of the appeal, it should have been clear that the ground for the initial decision was no longer established. The panel was still entitled to conclude that P was in breach of contract by failing to notify her superiors of her continued employment elsewhere, and that she had thereby acted in bad faith. However, it was not entitled to conclude that that failure interfered with any scheme or arrangement for redeploying P to alternative work, as there was no evidence that this was the Trust's practice in such circumstances. Thus, the grounds for a finding of misconduct had by this stage narrowed to a minor

395

deception at most and it was unreasonable of the appeal panel to conclude that dismissal was an appropriate sanction.

6.320 In Jinadu v Docklands Buses EAT 0434/14 the employee was initially dismissed for refusing to attend corrective training following a customer complaint about her driving. She then agreed to attend the relevant training and her internal appeal was adjourned to allow her to do so. However, she went on to fail the assessment at the end of the training course. Her appeal against dismissal was rejected at a reconvened hearing. An employment tribunal found the employee's dismissal – for repeated refusal to undertake necessary training – to be fair. However, the EAT overturned this decision and remitted the case for rehearing. Following the internal appeal, it was not clear whether the employer was still relying on the employee's original misconduct, or whether it was instead dismissing on the basis of a lack of capability. The tribunal had thus erred in failing to identify the reason for dismissal of the internal appeal and whether dismissal for that reason was fair.

6.321 **Effective date of termination.** If the employee is unsuccessful on appeal, then the effective date of termination of the employment contract will ordinarily be the date of the original dismissal – see further IDS Employment Law Handbook, 'Contracts of Employment' (2014), Chapter 14, 'Date of termination', under 'Internal appeals against dismissal'. If successful, then the employee will be treated as having been suspended pending the outcome of the appeal and will obviously be entitled to receive full back pay for the period of the suspension – West Midlands Co-operative Society Ltd v Tipton 1986 ICR 192, HL. This means also that an employee will not have been dismissed for the purposes of an unfair dismissal claim – Roberts v West Coast Trains Ltd 2005 ICR 254, CA.

7 Statutory ban

> **Establishing the reason**
>
> **Reasonableness**
>
> **Driving bans**
>
> **Work permits**

'Statutory ban' is a convenient shorthand expression for the potentially fair **7.1** reason for dismissal set out in S.98(2)(d) of the Employment Rights Act 1996 (ERA). This covers the situation where the employee cannot continue to work in the position which he or she holds without contravention (either on the employee's part or on that of the employer) of a duty or restriction imposed by or under an enactment.

It is for the employer to show that there is a statutory prohibition which makes it impossible for the employee to carry on in the same job. If successful, the employer will have established a potentially fair reason for dismissal, but that alone will not be conclusive of the issue of fairness. The tribunal will still have to consider whether the employer acted reasonably in dismissing under S.98(4): if the employer could, for example, easily have changed the employee's job so that he or she could do it legally, dismissal is likely to be unfair.

In this chapter we deal first with establishing the reason for dismissal and then **7.2** go on to consider the general approach of tribunals to the issue of reasonableness in this context. Finally, we look at two common categories of statutory ban dismissals: cases involving loss of a driving licence and cases involving work permits.

Establishing the reason
7.3

The employer must show that continued employment of the employee does in fact contravene a statutory enactment. It is not enough to show – as it would be in the case of a conduct or capability dismissal – a genuine belief on reasonable grounds and after reasonable investigation that there would be such a contravention. This is because S.98(2)(a) and (b) refers to a reason which *relates to* capability or qualifications and conduct and this is wide enough to cover the employer's genuine and reasonable belief. But S.98(2)(d) does not contain the words 'relates to' and the employer must prove the actual existence of the statutory ban – Bouchaala v Trusthouse Forte Hotels Ltd 1980 ICR 721, EAT.

397

Failure to establish the existence of a statutory ban will not necessarily be fatal, however, as the employer may be able to establish a different reason for dismissal – see 'Overlapping reasons for dismissal' below. But if the employer relies solely on a statutory ban that does not in fact apply it will fail to show a reason for dismissal at all – thus in effect making the dismissal automatically unfair. An illustration:

- **City of Birmingham District Council v Elson** EAT 609/78: the Schools Regulations 1959 SI 1959/364 provided that 'a person who is not a qualified teacher may be employed... if no qualified teacher is available to give the instruction'. E was an unqualified teacher and she was dismissed when a qualified teacher became available, the only reason for dismissal being the employer's belief that it would be illegal to retain her services. The EAT held that the employer's interpretation of the Regulations was wrong. In the context, 'employed' must mean 'taken on' or 'appointed'. The Regulations did not require an existing employee to be dismissed: they only meant that there should be no new appointment of an unqualified teacher if a qualified teacher was available. The employer could not rely on S.98(2)(d) and E's dismissal was therefore unfair.

7.4 If there is a statutory ban in place, tribunals and courts have no business considering whether the ban and the policy underlying it are reasonable: they are only concerned with whether the employer has established the existence of a statutory prohibition and that it applies to the employee's job. Whether or not the employer has applied the statutory ban reasonably affects the reasonableness of dismissal, but it cannot affect the reason for dismissal – Woodcock v University of Cambridge EAT 332/79.

Section 98(2)(d) applies in respect of any duty or restriction 'imposed by or under an enactment'. 'Enactment' for these purposes includes not only statutes but delegated legislation (statutory instruments) and regulations made under statutory instrument. In the Woodcock case the enactment at issue was a university statute made by the University Commissioners under the Universities of Oxford and Cambridge Act 1923. The EAT stressed that the wording in S.98(2)(d) is 'restriction imposed by or under an enactment' so that the university statute was covered.

7.5 Overlapping reasons for dismissal

A genuine belief, reached on reasonable grounds and after reasonable investigation, that an employee's continued employment would be illegal is not enough to establish a valid reason for dismissal under S.98(2)(b) if that belief is erroneous. But it may amount to 'some other substantial reason' (SOSR) for dismissal under S.98(1)(b) and the dismissal may be fair – Bouchaala v Trusthouse Forte Hotels Ltd 1980 ICR 721, EAT. In that case the company was told by the Department of Employment that it could no longer legally employ

B (a Tunisian) because of work permit rules, so he was dismissed. In fact, B had been given indefinite leave to remain in the UK and did not need a work permit. The EAT held that a genuine belief that continued employment would be illegal could amount to SOSR and that the dismissal was fair in the circumstances.

The moral is that employers should always plead SOSR as an alternative reason for dismissal. The employer did so in the Bouchaala case and (unnecessarily as it turned out) in Woodcock v University of Cambridge (above). But in City of Birmingham District Council v Elson (above) the employer relied exclusively on a mistaken interpretation of statutory regulations and lost. The EAT noted that no question of reasonableness or reliance on legal advice had been argued before the tribunal.

7.6 In some cases there may well be more than one alternative ground for dismissal. For example, in Bryan v Kennerty Farm Dairies Ltd EAT 584/87 a distribution manager lost his driving licence and the employer pleaded capability (not statutory ban) as the reason for dismissal. A tribunal thought that the real reason for dismissal was one relating to conduct, but found the dismissal fair. The EAT upheld the decision, but thought that the tribunal could equally well have found SOSR to be the reason for dismissal. In that case the factual reason for dismissal was fully ventilated and argued by both sides before the tribunal so that the employee was not put at a disadvantage as a result of the employer using the wrong label – see further Chapter 3, 'Unfairness', under 'Reason for dismissal – identification of "real" reason for dismissal'. For more discussion on driving ban cases see 'Driving bans' below.

Automatic termination by statute

7.7 Certain statutory provisions may have the effect of automatically terminating employment contracts. There is a general principle that when further performance of a contract becomes impossible because of legislation – e.g. when a particular office is abolished by statute – then the contract is discharged – Reilly v The King 1934 AC 176, Privy Council (Canada). In Tarnesby v Kensington and Chelsea and Westminster Area Health Authority (Teaching) 1981 ICR 615, HL, the House of Lords held that the suspension of T's doctor's registration for disciplinary reasons automatically terminated his employment as a hospital consultant. This was because S.28(1) of the Medical Act 1956 provided that no unregistered doctor should hold an appointment as a hospital medical officer. And while suspension no longer has this effect, the argument would still apply if a doctor's name was permanently removed from the register.

However, in Shrewsbury and Telford Hospital NHS Trust v Lairikyengbam 2010 ICR 66, EAT, an NHS Trust that had employed a locum consultant on a series of fixed-term contracts spanning almost four years had acted beyond its powers since it had not sought the committee approval required by the relevant Regulations. Consequently, the consultant's formal contract of employment

399

was void. Nevertheless, the EAT held that the continued performance of his duties meant that he was still an 'employee' within the meaning of the ERA and thus entitled to pursue an unfair dismissal claim. The case was remitted to a new tribunal to decide whether the reason for his ultimate dismissal was the statutory ban on his employment.

7.8 Reasonableness

If the employer has made out the reason for dismissal – the existence of a statutory ban on the employee's continued employment in the job – a tribunal must then decide whether it was reasonable to dismiss for this reason. This will involve consideration of such matters as:

- the likely duration of the ban
- whether it affects the whole or only part of the employee's work
- whether the employee can readily be redeployed.

Four cases illustrating how these factors are taken into account:

- **Madan v St Helens and Knowsley Community NHS Trust** ET Case No.2100813/01: M worked for the NHS Trust as a clinical medical officer. She also ran a slimming clinic separately from her work for the Trust. The Trust became aware that the General Medical Council (GMC) had referred complaints against her work at the slimming clinic to its Professional Conduct Committee. It agreed that she could continue to work, provided her work was monitored, pending the outcome of the GMC investigation. A few weeks later the GMC suspended M from practice and the Trust immediately terminated her employment because it would be illegal for her to continue working. She claimed unfair dismissal. The tribunal held that M was dismissed because of a statutory ban but that the dismissal was unfair because there was no consultation and no opportunity for her to explore alternatives

- **Yarrow v QIS Ltd** ET Case No.32972/76: Y was a radiographer whose employment was subject to the Ionisation Radiation (Sealed Sources) Regulations 1969, which made it unlawful to employ as a radiographer anybody who contracted one of a number of specified diseases. Y contracted psoriasis – a specified disease – and was dismissed. The tribunal found that the employer had considered suspension, but psoriasis was a recurrent condition with no known cure and Y had to be regarded as permanently unfit to work as a radiographer. There was no alternative work available and his dismissal was held to be fair

- **Balogun v Lucas Batteries Ltd** ET Case No.1270/79: B, a machine operator working on processes involving lead, began to suffer from hypertension. The Control of Lead at Work Regulations in force at the time made it an offence knowingly to employ a person with hypertension in lead processing. The employer went to a good deal of trouble to try to find an alternative job but none was available and B was dismissed. The tribunal held that the dismissal was a fair dismissal for statutory ban

- **Ascroft v Lancashire Magistrates' Courts Committee** ET Case No.35867/80: A's duties were partly those of a magistrates' court clerk and partly administrative. New regulations – the Justices' Clerks (Qualification of Assistants) Rules 1979 SI 1979/570 – were issued in draft form in 1976 and A became aware that from October 1980 he would have to hold a valid training certificate, which involved passing some exams. In 1976 he failed the exams; in 1977 he did not resit because of a muddle about dates; in 1978 he refused to resit; in 1979 he failed again; and in 1980 he refused to resit. Since he had ceased to be qualified to sit as a court clerk he was dismissed. The tribunal held that there were no alternative vacancies and A could not be kept solely on administrative duties, and so his dismissal was fair.

7.9 In cases like Ascroft, where the statutory ban comes into operation when an employee fails to acquire the necessary qualifications, the employer's failure to assist the employee to qualify may be a factor making dismissal unfair. In Sandhu v Department of Education and Science and anor 1978 IRLR 208, EAT, S was a trainee teacher who was prohibited from teaching under the Schools Regulations 1959 SI 1959/364 when the DES declared him unsuitable as a teacher. A tribunal found his ensuing dismissal automatically fair because the employer had no option but to dismiss. The EAT held that this ignored S's case, which was that the DES decision was largely based on reports from S's employer and that the employer had discriminated against him and had treated him unreasonably during his probationary period. The EAT remitted the case to a new tribunal to look at the events leading up to S's dismissal and consider whether the employer had acted reasonably towards S.

7.10 **Precipitate dismissal may also be unfair.** If there is a possibility of obtaining an extension of time to allow an employee a further opportunity to gain a qualification, it may be unreasonable to dismiss before it is known whether an extension will be granted. In Sutcliffe and Eaton Ltd v Pinney 1977 IRLR 349, EAT, the Hearing Aid Council Act 1968 prohibited the employment of hearing aid dispensers for more than five years unless they passed certain exams. P was a trainee hearing aid dispenser who failed the exams three times, the last time being just before the end of the five-year period. His name was removed from the register of hearing aid dispensers and it would have been a criminal offence, punishable by a fine of up to £100 a day, for the employer to continue to employ him. P was therefore dismissed, but he then successfully applied for an extension to sit the exam again. The EAT held that the fact that to continue to employ somebody could be a breach of statute was not conclusive of the reasonableness of his or her dismissal. In this case it was very unlikely that any

401

proceedings would have been taken against the employer if P had been kept on and an extension of the training period had been applied for. The tribunal had been entitled to find that the employer had acted unreasonably and that P's dismissal was unfair.

This case should be treated with some caution, however, as the decision seems to be a particularly harsh one for the employer, who was faced with either dismissing the employee or committing a criminal offence. It was also decided before the 'range of reasonable responses' test was fully developed. It is certainly arguable that a different tribunal, faced with similar facts, might find dismissal in these circumstances to be fair. But having said that, a not dissimilar approach was taken by the EAT in Kelly v University of Southampton 2008 ICR 357, EAT, where K, an American citizen who was employed as a lecturer by the university, had her employment summarily terminated when her visa expired. She had applied for indefinite leave to remain in the UK and this was granted two weeks later. The EAT considered that even if the seriousness of an alleged contravention made it reasonable for an employer to dismiss speedily, there is no reason why provision should not be made for an appeal – particularly where the illegal state of affairs is disputed, or technical, or arises from an oversight which can be remedied by the time an appeal would have been heard.

7.11 Driving bans

Driving bans are the main cause of statutory ban dismissals. When an employee has lost his or her driving licence, tribunals will normally expect the employer to consider the following matters before deciding on dismissal:

- whether driving is an essential part of the job or whether the employee can satisfactorily carry on his or her duties without a driving licence

- whether retaining the employee will mean dislocation and inconvenience

- whether there is another job to which the employee could be redeployed

- whether the employee has been given an opportunity to express his or her views and whether any suggestions made have been reasonably considered.

Some examples:

- **Toase v Milk Marketing Board** ET Case No.24778/76: T was a mechanic fitter (who held an HGV licence) and his work involved driving an average of 139 miles a month on road tests, etc. When he lost his licence his foreman said that his six colleagues could cover for his driving duties, even though one of the other mechanic fitters did not hold a driving licence. However, T was dismissed. The tribunal held that the statutory ban was made out as the reason for dismissal, but that the employer acted unreasonably in dismissing because T could have continued his employment without driving

- **Riley v ADT Fire and Security plc** ET Case No.2403497/05: R, who had worked for the company for 22 years as an installation engineer – a job that required him to drive – was banned from driving for two years for a drink-driving offence. The company was initially able to team him up with an apprentice who could drive, but after about ten months the apprentice was no longer available. He was offered two alternative posts which he turned down, and his employment was terminated on notice. His claim for unfair dismissal was rejected. Some employers might have been prepared to wait for a further year for R to regain his driving licence, but the company was entitled to decide that it could not wait for the remaining period of the driving ban to expire. Dismissal was within the band of reasonable responses

- **Roberts v Toyota (GB) Ltd** EAT 614/80: it was an implied term in R's contract as an area sales manager that he should hold a driving licence. He received a 12-month driving ban for a drink-driving offence and was dismissed. Prior to his conviction he told the national sales manager that if he lost his licence he would be prepared to purchase a company car and provide a driver to drive him in the course of his work. This was put to the board of directors, which considered that it was impracticable. The EAT held that the tribunal was fully entitled to hold that the dismissal was fair in these circumstances.

7.12 The employee's conduct may be a factor in assessing the reasonableness of the dismissal. For instance, in Handforth v Olaf Olsen (Newmillerdam) Ltd ET Case No.9012/79 H was a sales secretary who needed to drive. She held an Australian licence and obtained a provisional licence from the DVLC (now the DVLA), but did not tell the employer that she was not qualified to drive on her own in the UK. This came to light when her company vehicle was damaged in a minor accident and an insurance claim was repudiated. The tribunal held that H's dismissal because of a statutory ban was fair since she had misled her employer.

In a similar case, Morris v Haven Industrial Services Ltd ET Case No.04281/81, M, a foreman installation fitter, used a company vehicle. When his employer decided to check on driving qualifications M lied and said he had mislaid his licence. However, enquiries to the police showed that he had no licence at all. The tribunal held that he was fairly dismissed for gross misconduct, rather than for statutory ban.

7.13 By way of contrast, the EAT upheld the tribunal's decision in Arbuckle Smith and Co Ltd v Holmes EAT 178/87 that H's dismissal was unfair where he had been dismissed for misconduct after being charged by the police with driving an HGV without the appropriate licence. A proper investigation would have revealed that the management knew all along that H was only in possession of a provisional licence. There had been no deliberate deception on H's part

403

and he could have been given other duties on a temporary basis until he obtained a full licence.

Employers will be expected to follow a fair procedure before dismissing an employee who has been disqualified from driving. This will include consultation with the employee to see if any alternative arrangements can be made during the period of the driving ban and possibly allowing a trial period to see if those arrangements are practical. In Ager v Inforex (UK) Ltd ET Case No.23962/79, for example, A's contract expressly stated that dismissal would follow the loss of his driving licence. The employer rejected out of hand a suggestion that A's wife could do the necessary driving. A tribunal found the dismissal unfair because the employer should at least have given this arrangement a trial run (although it awarded only four weeks' pay in compensation to reflect the likelihood that the arrangement would not have worked). And in Mathieson v WJ Noble and Son Ltd 1972 IRLR 76, ET, a salesman who was disqualified from driving engaged a private chauffeur to drive him during the disqualification period and made arrangements to pay additional insurance premiums on his company car, with the agreement of the company chairman. The company, however, dismissed him before these arrangements could be put into operation. A tribunal did not think that M was contractually obliged to drive in any event, so that no statutory ban applied to his continued employment. It would, however, also have found the dismissal unfair under S.98(4) because of the employer's unreasonableness.

7.14 But in Ashton Paper Mills Ltd v Haines EAT 361/79 a tribunal found dismissal of a timber inspector, for whom mobility was essential, unfair because the employer did not give serious consideration to his proposal to provide a driver. The EAT, however, thought that the tribunal should have given some consideration to the practicability of the scheme put forward (about which the EAT was clearly sceptical) and remitted the case for it to do so.

Employers should also adopt a consistent approach when deciding whether to dismiss. In Buckley v Alpha Catering Services Ltd ET Case No.3104588/99, for example, B was disqualified from driving for three years. It was his second driving ban. Agreement could not be reached on alternative duties and he was dismissed. The tribunal accepted the employer's argument that B was required to hold a licence and that the situation was not of the employer's making but arose from B's serious misbehaviour. However, the dismissal was unfair because another employee who could reasonably be required to drive from time to time was neither dismissed nor transferred when she was disqualified from driving. The employer did not carry out a sufficiently detailed investigation into the way other employees had been treated.

7.15 Premature action by the employer may make dismissal unfair. This may happen if the employer dismisses before it is certain that the employee will lose his or her licence or before it is known how long the driving ban will be. Some illustrations:

- **Greenhalgh v Nixdorf Computer** ET Case No.15839/82: G was dismissed after a positive breath analysis. The tribunal held that his dismissal was unfair because it was premature to dismiss before the outcome of the court hearing was known. But G was awarded only net pay to the date of the court hearing, since the tribunal found 100 per cent contributory conduct

- **Somerville v Ofrex Ltd** ET Case No.14908/82: S, a service engineer, was dismissed when it was found that his (New Zealand) driving licence was invalid in the UK. In fact, he obtained a valid licence five weeks later. The tribunal found that his dismissal was unfair because the employer had acted with unnecessary haste and should have investigated more thoroughly

- **Meehan v Chelmsford Star Co-operative Society Ltd** ET Case No.35769/81: M, a field TV engineer, was a diabetic but was certified fit to drive by his doctor. However, the DVLC (now the DVLA) revoked his licence subject to a right of appeal. His licence was in fact restored after about ten weeks, but the employer had dismissed him promptly as soon as he lost it. The tribunal held that his dismissal was unfair because the employer should have awaited the outcome of M's appeal.

Even when tribunals do find a dismissal unfair they are likely to find a substantial degree of contributory conduct if the ban was because of drink-driving or traffic offences. Thus, in Toase v Milk Marketing Board (above), for example, contribution was assessed at 50 per cent.

In Nairne v Highland and Islands Fire Brigade 1989 IRLR 366, Ct Sess, N was **7.16** dismissed after a second drink-driving ban. A tribunal found the dismissal unfair on procedural grounds and concluded that N had contributed to it by 25 per cent. The EAT held that this was perverse and substituted a finding of 75 per cent contribution: N had been warned, it was his second offence in two years, he was a senior officer required to set an example, and he was required to hold a valid driving licence. The Court of Session upheld the EAT's judgment on appeal.

Where, however, the employee was not at fault, as in Meehan v Chelmsford Star Co-operative Society Ltd (above), where diabetes was the cause of the driving ban, there will obviously be no contributory fault.

Work permits 7.17

Under S.15 of the Immigration, Asylum and Nationality Act 2006 employers are liable to pay a civil penalty of up to £20,000 per employee if they employ a person who is subject to immigration control and who is not legally entitled to work in the UK (if an employer *knowingly* employs an illegal immigrant the

405

possible fine is unlimited and the employer can face a jail sentence of up to two years – S.21). The question of whether a person has a right to remain in the UK is separate to that of whether they have a right to work here, and until 2001, decisions on these matters were in the hands of two different government departments. This led to considerable confusion and it was not uncommon for the different departments to give differing advice. For example, in Bouchaala v Trusthouse Forte Hotels Ltd 1980 ICR 721, EAT, the company was told by the Department of Employment (now part of the Department for Work and Pensions, which no longer deals with issues of immigration in employment) that it could no longer legally employ B (a Tunisian) because of work permit rules and he was dismissed. In fact, B had been given indefinite leave to remain in the UK by the Home Office and did not need a work permit.

7.18 Two more cases showing the potential pitfalls:

- **Kelly v University of Southampton** 2008 ICR 357, EAT: K, an American citizen, was offered a job as a lecturer by the university, subject to her completing the necessary immigration processes. While she received permission from one government department to work for 60 months, the Home Office issued her with a visa granting her leave to remain in the UK for only 48 months. Concerned that it would be committing a criminal offence by continuing to employ her after the expiration of her visa, the university terminated her employment by letter backdated to the last day of her leave to remain. K was given no right of appeal as the university believed that her employment had terminated by operation of law. K obtained indefinite leave to remain in the UK two weeks later. The EAT held that the university would not have committed an offence by continuing to employ her, since she had lawful permission to work and S.98(2)(d) did not therefore apply. But even if the statutory ban had been established, dismissal would nevertheless have been unreasonable. Even if the seriousness of an alleged contravention makes it reasonable for an employer to dismiss speedily, there is no reason why provision should not be made for an appeal – particularly where the illegal state of affairs is disputed, or technical, or arises from an oversight which can be remedied by the time an appeal would have been heard

- **Hounslow London Borough Council v Klusova** 2008 ICR 396, CA: K, a Russian national, was employed by the Council from 2000. She had leave to remain in the UK until May 2004. Before her leave expired she made various attempts to extend it and no final decision had been made even by the time her unfair dismissal claim reached the Court of Appeal. In March 2005 K was briefly detained by the immigration authorities, who released her subject to various conditions stated in an immigration officer's letter, one of which was that she could not work. In fact, K had a letter from the Home Office which indicated that she was entitled to work pending the determination of her application to remain. The Council asked her for proof that she was entitled to work and her solicitors responded by asking for clarification of the Council's grounds for thinking she did not have such entitlement. Not having received the proof it had asked for, the Council dismissed her summarily. When K claimed unfair dismissal, the Council sought to rely on the statutory ban. The Court of Appeal held that K had official leave to remain and work in the UK from the Home Office at the time of her dismissal, and this could not be altered by an immigration officer's letter. A person lawfully in the UK under a limited right to remain and to undertake employment who makes a valid application to extend his or her leave to remain before it expires is permitted, by virtue of S.3C of the Immigration Act 1971, to continue in employment when the right to remain expires pending the determination of his or her application. In consequence, there was no statutory ban on K working and the Council could not rely on this ground.

These cases illustrate the importance of an employer arguing SOSR as an **7.19** alternative to statutory ban, especially where immigration status is concerned. (SOSR was in fact argued in both cases but at the time the statutory dismissal and disciplinary procedures were in place and, because neither employer had followed those procedures, the dismissals were automatically unfair. The statutory procedures, which were abolished by the Employment Act 2008, did not apply to statutory ban cases but did apply to SOSR dismissals.)

8 Some other substantial reason

Business reorganisations

Protecting employers' interests

Third-party pressure to dismiss

Breakdown in working relations

Expiry of limited-term contracts

Transfer of undertakings

Retirement dismissals

Miscellaneous reasons

In the preceding chapters we have considered three of the potentially fair **8.1** reasons for dismissal specified in S.98(2) of the Employment Rights Act 1996 (ERA): capability or qualifications, conduct, and statutory ban. Another potentially fair reason listed in S.98(2) – redundancy – is discussed in IDS Employment Law Handbook, 'Redundancy' (2011), Chapter 8, 'Unfair redundancy'. In this chapter we focus on S.98(1)(b), which provides a final potentially fair reason for dismissal – 'some other substantial reason' ('SOSR').

Section 98(1)(b) is a catch-all category covering dismissal for 'some other substantial reason of a kind such as to justify the dismissal of an employee holding the position which the employee held'. Sir John Brightman – in RS Components Ltd v Irwin 1973 ICR 535, NIRC – stated that 'Parliament may well have intended to set out in [S.98(2)] the common reasons for a dismissal, but can hardly have hoped to produce an exhaustive catalogue of all the circumstances in which an employer would be justified in terminating the services of an employee'. S.98(1)(b) provides a residual potentially fair reason for dismissal that employers may be able to use if the reason for dismissal does not fall within the four specific categories in S.98(2).

Note that SOSR under S.98(1)(b) must be of a kind such as to justify the **8.2** dismissal of *an employee holding the job in question*. In Cobley v Forward Technology Industries plc 2003 ICR 1050, CA, the Court of Appeal considered whether the dismissal of a chief executive following a successful company takeover could amount to SOSR. It held that although in most circumstances a change in the ownership of a company's shares will *not* affect the employment relationships between the company and its staff, different considerations apply to the dismissal of a chief executive than to that of a secretary or storeman. The employer was entitled in the circumstances to rely on SOSR.

409

As long as it is not a S.98(2) reason, any reason for dismissal, however obscure, can be pleaded on grounds of SOSR – with the proviso that it must be a *substantial* reason and thus not frivolous or trivial; and must not be based on an inadmissible reason such as race or sex – Willow Oak Developments Ltd t/a Windsor Recruitment v Silverwood and ors 2006 ICR 1552, CA. However, while the reason for dismissal needs to be substantial, it need not be sophisticated – merely *genuine*. For example, in Harper v National Coal Board 1980 IRLR 260, EAT, H was dismissed because he sometimes attacked fellow employees during his epileptic seizures. The employer held inaccurate beliefs concerning epileptics in general. The tribunal found dismissal to be fair either on the ground of capability or for SOSR. The EAT said that an employer cannot claim that a reason for dismissal is substantial if it is a whimsical or capricious reason which no ordinary person would entertain. It stated that where, however, the belief is 'one which is genuinely held, and particularly is one which most employers would be expected to adopt, it may be a substantial reason even where modern sophisticated opinion can be adduced to suggest that it has no scientific foundation'. The EAT therefore upheld the tribunal's decision. (Note, though, that if these facts arose today, the disability discrimination provisions of the Equality Act 2010 would apply – see IDS Employment Law Handbook, 'Discrimination at Work' (2012), Chapter 26, 'Dismissal', under 'Dismissal "because of" protected characteristic – disability'.)

8.3 The employer is required to show only that the substantial reason for dismissal was a potentially fair one. Once the reason has been established, it is then up to the tribunal to decide whether the employer acted reasonably under S.98(4) in dismissing for that reason. As in all unfair dismissal claims, a tribunal will decide the fairness of the dismissal by asking whether the decision to dismiss fell within the range of reasonable responses that a reasonable employer might adopt. Depending on the circumstances, this may involve consideration of matters such as whether the employee was consulted, warned and given a hearing, and/or whether the employer searched for suitable alternative employment.

In other words, to amount to a substantial reason to dismiss, there must be a finding that the reason *could* – but not necessarily does – justify dismissal – Mercia Rubber Mouldings Ltd v Lingwood 1974 ICR 256, NIRC. Indeed, tribunals that confuse the employer's burden of establishing SOSR as the reason for dismissal with the tribunal's overall assessment of the reasonableness of the dismissal under S.98(4) may find themselves overruled on appeal. In Gilham and ors v Kent County Council (No.2) 1985 ICR 233, CA, the County Council had to reduce expenditure in line with Government policy or face serious financial penalties. Consequently, G was offered a contract which meant less pay. She turned it down and complained that she had been unfairly dismissed. The tribunal held that the Council had not made out a substantial reason for dismissal because it did not consider the reason put forward as one that reasonably justified dismissal in the circumstances. However, the Court of

Appeal held – obiter – that the tribunal had fallen into error in law by confusing the test for establishing a reason for dismissal with the test of reasonableness under S.98(4). The Court said that it was impossible to argue that the stated reason for dismissal – the Council's need to reduce its expenditure – was not SOSR that could potentially justify dismissal. And in Cobley v Forward Technology Industries plc (above) the Court of Appeal confirmed that identification of a substantial reason for dismissal does not require consideration of fairness, which falls to be considered at a later stage.

SOSR is most often invoked where: **8.4**

- the employer is trying to reorganise the business and/or change the terms and conditions of employment in some way

- the employer is trying to protect its interests either by preventing employees from setting up in competition, or by taking steps to avert a potential leakage of confidential information or damage being caused to its reputation

- there has been third-party pressure to dismiss the employee

- the trust and confidence necessary for the employment relationship to function has broken down irremediably

- a limited-term contract has expired

- dismissal for 'economic, technical or organisational' reasons, that falls short of redundancy, has followed a transfer of an undertaking; or

- the employee is dismissed upon reaching the employer's compulsory retirement age.

This chapter deals with each of these scenarios in turn and also examines various miscellaneous reasons for dismissal that can be classified as SOSR.

SOSR or conduct/capability? By its very nature, SOSR is not to be construed **8.5** as meaning a reason that is of the same kind as one of those set out in S.98(2) – RS Components Ltd v Irwin (above). However, SOSR can include reasons containing elements of conduct or capability. If it is unclear which reason applies, employers can plead SOSR in the alternative and attempt to prove both. In Huggins v Micrel Semiconductor (UK) Ltd EATS 0009/04 the EAT upheld a finding that a dismissal was for SOSR when it was caused by a breakdown in trust and confidence related to the employee's conduct. And in Wilson v Post Office 2000 IRLR 834, CA, the Court of Appeal held that an employer had dismissed an employee for SOSR because his attendance record did not meet the requirements of the agreed procedure. Even though the employee's absences had been caused by ill health, the Court held that the tribunal had erred when it characterised this as a capability dismissal – see further 'Miscellaneous reasons – persistent absences' below.

411

Note, however, that in Perkin v St George's Healthcare NHS Trust 2006 ICR 617, CA, a tribunal held that the dismissal of a senior executive whose manner and attitude towards colleagues had led to a breakdown in the employer's confidence in him and rendered it impossible for the senior executives to work together as a team was for 'conduct [or] some other substantial reason', adding that both were potentially fair reasons within the meaning of S.98(1). On appeal, the Court of Appeal held that the tribunal had not erred even though, in the Court's view, it would have been preferable if the tribunal had analysed the dismissal as being for SOSR rather than for conduct. However, the tribunal's failure to characterise the reason for dismissal as SOSR was not fatal to its reasoning or to the safety of its decision.

8.6 **Acas Code of Practice.** The reasonableness of an employer's dismissal procedure will normally be assessed by reference to the Acas Code of Practice on Disciplinary and Grievance Procedures. Although the Code is non-binding, an unreasonable failure to follow its recommendations may result in an adjustment of compensation of up to 25 per cent following a successful tribunal claim.

There is some doubt over whether the Code is intended to apply to SOSR dismissals. The Code specifically does not apply to dismissal on the non-renewal of a fixed term contract, which may amount to SOSR (see 'Expiry of limited-term contracts' below) – para 1 of the Code. However, the EAT in Jefferson (Commercial) LLP v Westgate EAT 0128/12 did not discount the possibility that the Code might apply to other kinds of SOSR dismissals, noting that para 1 states that disciplinary situations '*include* misconduct and/or poor performance' (our stress). While the EAT conceded that 'the word "include"… might suggest that misconduct and poor performance is not a conclusive list', it did not consider the Code relevant to the instant case, where the SOSR amounted to an irretrievable breakdown of mutual trust and confidence. And in Lund v St Edmund's School, Canterbury 2013 ICR D26, EAT, the EAT concluded that the Code applied to a dismissal which was not based on the employee's conduct per se but on the effect of his conduct on others, which amounted to SOSR. In the EAT's view, the Code applies not only in circumstances where disciplinary proceedings are invoked against an employee, but also in circumstances where they should have been, as it is not the outcome of the process which determines whether the Code applies but its initiation. In that case, a school teacher was dismissed for SOSR as a result of a breakdown in relationships with colleagues caused by his own conduct. In the EAT's view, once the school had called L's conduct into question and thought that it might lead to his dismissal, it should have invoked the disciplinary procedure. That was the case even if it ultimately decided to dismiss him for a non-disciplinary reason.

8.7 At least one tribunal has taken the view that the Code does apply to SOSR dismissals, on the ground that it does not expressly exclude them – see Cummings v Siemens Communications Ltd ET Case No.3500013/10. However, in Murray v Hillingdon Credit Union Ltd ET Case No.3302682/11 the tribunal took the opposite view, reasoning that because the Acas Code does not apply to redundancy dismissals, it could not apply to the kind of 'reorganisation dismissal' before it, which was 'analogous to redundancy'.

For detailed consideration of the Acas Code, see Chapter 3, 'Unfairness', under 'Fairness of internal procedure – Acas Code of Practice'.

Contributory fault. Most dismissals for SOSR do not involve any fault on the part of the employee. It follows that when a dismissal for SOSR is found to be unfair, it is rare for contributory conduct to be an issue in assessing compensation. Where contributory fault is found, it is most likely to be in cases involving a breakdown in trust and confidence for which the employee was at least partially to blame – see, for example, Perkin v St George's Healthcare NHS Trust (above), Butcher v Salvage Association EAT 988/01 and Huggins v Micrel Semiconductor (UK) Ltd (above). **8.8**

Business reorganisations **8.9**

Tribunals have long recognised the right of employers to dismiss employees who refuse to go along with a business reorganisation. As Lord Denning MR put it in Lesney Products and Co Ltd v Nolan and ors 1977 ICR 235, CA: '[I]t is important that nothing should be done to impair the ability of employers to reorganise their workforce and their terms and conditions of work so as to improve efficiency.' Employees may, therefore, be dismissed either for refusing to agree to changes arising out of a business reorganisation or because their services are no longer required owing, for example, to the introduction of new technology.

Where an employee is dismissed for refusing to agree to a change in working conditions that the employer is entitled to impose under the contract, the dismissal may be for misconduct. However, dismissals of employees who refuse to accept a business reorganisation are often pleaded under SOSR.

Of course, a dismissal in the context of a reorganisation may in fact be for redundancy, not SOSR, if the statutory definition of redundancy is satisfied – see IDS Employment Law Handbook, 'Redundancy' (2011), Chapter 2, 'Redundancy', under 'Definition of "redundancy"'. Occasionally, the distinction may be unclear. However, an employer should be wary of trying to disguise a genuine redundancy situation as a business reorganisation because, for example, it wants to avoid making redundancy payments. In Moore v Midas Precision Metalwork Ltd ET Case No.1200536/09, for example, a sheet metal worker claimed unfair dismissal when he refused to accept a change to his terms and conditions that meant that he would have been put on a three-day week. The employer had suffered badly as a result of a downturn in orders and feared that it would be unable to afford redundancy payments. It claimed that M's dismissal **8.10**

413

was not for redundancy, but for SOSR as a result of a business reorganisation. However, the tribunal found that M's dismissal was mainly attributable to the fact that the requirements of the business for employees to carry out sheet metalworking had diminished. M was therefore dismissed principally because he was redundant.

8.11 Establishing SOSR as reason for dismissal

To establish SOSR as the reason for dismissal where there has been a business reorganisation, the employer does not have to show that a reorganisation or rearrangement of working patterns was essential. In Hollister v National Farmers' Union 1979 ICR 542, CA, the Court of Appeal said that a 'sound, good business reason' for reorganisation was sufficient to establish SOSR for dismissing an employee who refused to accept a change in his or her terms and conditions. This reason is not one the tribunal considers sound, but one 'which management thinks on reasonable grounds is sound' – Scott and Co v Richardson EAT 0074/04.

It is not for the tribunal to make its own assessment of the advantages of the employer's business decision to reorganise or to change employees' working patterns. In fact, the employer need only show that there were 'clear advantages' in introducing a particular change, to pass the low hurdle of showing SOSR for dismissal. The employer does not need to show any particular 'quantum of improvement' achieved — Kerry Foods Ltd v Lynch 2005 IRLR 680, EAT. In that case, the advantage to the employer in introducing a new rota for managers was sufficient to show SOSR for dismissing a manager following his refusal to accept new terms and conditions that included a move to a six-day week and a reduction in his holiday entitlement (see below).

8.12 Some examples of cases in which the employer demonstrated dismissal for SOSR on the basis of a business reorganisation:

- **Scott and Co v Richardson** (above): the EAT held that the tribunal had erred not only by substituting its own opinion of whether the employer's business decision to change to a shift system of work gave the employer a discernible advantage, but also in ruling that the advantage to the employer had to be so substantial that it mitigated the consequences of the dismissal. Having found that the employer had introduced the shift system to ensure that work done in the evenings would be done at normal rates of pay and not at overtime rates, thereby making the business more profitable, the tribunal should have concluded that the profit motive was a sound commercial reason for carrying out the reorganisation and that S's dismissal for refusing the change was for SOSR

- **Tasneem v Dudley Group of Hospitals NHS Trust** EAT 0232/10: the level of concerns expressed by GPs about the quality of service provided by the NHS Trust led to fears that the Trust would lose its teaching status and that there would be a further deterioration in reputation. To help address this, the Trust decided to appoint two new substantive consultants and reduce the number of locum consultants accordingly. T, who was working as a locum, applied for but was not appointed to one of the new roles and subsequently lost his existing position. The EAT upheld a tribunal's decision that his dismissal was for SOSR and was fair. In making the changes the Trust had been motivated by legitimate concerns to improve the quality of its service

- **Murray v Hillingdon Credit Union Ltd** ET Case No.3302682/11: HCU Ltd was staffed by two part-time employees: a manager, M, and an administration officer, A. Due to concerns about excessive workloads, increasing cases of default and falling profitability, HCU Ltd decided to restructure the posts, replacing them with three new part-time posts of credit controller, senior administration officer and a special projects administration officer. M and A had to undergo an intensive interview process for the new roles, as a result of which A was appointed to the senior administration officer post but M's application for the credit controller post failed and she was dismissed on the ground of redundancy. The tribunal decided that the dismissal was not for redundancy – as HCU Ltd still required employees to do the kind of work M had been doing – but was for SOSR, as M had been dismissed because the existing duties and workloads had been reorganised and expanded into three posts. However, her dismissal was unfair.

8.13 Employers must do more than simply assert that there were 'good business reasons' for a reorganisation involving dismissals. A tribunal must be satisfied that changes in terms and conditions were not imposed for arbitrary reasons – Catamaran Cruisers Ltd v Williams and ors 1994 IRLR 386, EAT. Employers will also be expected to prove the reason for dismissal and, as a result, to submit evidence showing just what the business reasons were and that they were substantial. Some examples:

- **Banerjee v City and East London Area Health Authority** 1979 IRLR 147, EAT: the Health Authority had a policy of amalgamating part-time consultancies into full-time posts. When the part-time employee with whom B shared duties left, the Health Authority scrapped both part-time posts and replaced them with a full-time post to which B was not appointed. He complained of unfair dismissal. The Health Authority produced no evidence of the advantages of the policy or the importance attached to it. The EAT held that in these circumstances no tribunal could conclude that there was a substantial reason for dismissal

- **Mukherjee v Kensington, Chelsea and Westminster Area Health Authority (Teaching)** EAT 284/80: the Health Authority carried out a merger of consultancy posts, with one of the consultants, M, losing her job as a result. The Health Authority submitted full evidence about its need to

415

reorganise and about its genuine efforts to find alternative employment for M. M's dismissal was found to be fair for SOSR

- **Kerry Foods Ltd v Lynch** (above): the employer adduced a number of reasons for introducing a six-day week and a reduction in holiday entitlement for L, a manager. First, it did not want to operate a two-tier system with managers at different depots working different rotas; secondly, it wanted to rectify an historical situation whereby Saturday was not perceived as being a normal working day because there was no management presence; thirdly, the depots with managers working the same rota as their team showed an improvement in their Saturday trading performance; and finally, there was a need to improve the quality of the supervisory cover. It did not need to provide evidence of either the adverse impact or the quantum of improvement to satisfy the definition of SOSR.

8.14 Imposing contractual changes

The fact that an employee is contractually entitled to resist the change does not mean that his or her dismissal will be unfair – Bowater Containers Ltd v McCormack 1980 IRLR 50, EAT. Although, as a basic principle of contract law, variations to a contract of employment must be agreed by both parties in order to take effect, an employer can fairly dismiss an employee for refusing to accept detrimental changes to his or her terms and conditions where there is a sound business reason to do so. And, as the EAT pointed out in Catamaran Cruisers Ltd v Williams and ors (above), 'sound business reasons' are not restricted to situations where the survival of the business is at stake.

Since any dismissal for refusal to carry out duties that *are* countenanced by the contract is likely to be for misconduct, employers will need to be clear as to whether the duties being imposed fall within the scope of the employment contract, or require a variation of that contract. If the latter is the case, a dismissal for misconduct for refusing to comply is likely to be unfair and may involve a breach of contract, whereas a dismissal with notice under the existing contract, coupled with an offer of employment on the varied terms, will be potentially fair for SOSR, assuming there is a legitimate business reason for the variation. In Rumani v Thyssenkrupp Materials (UK) Ltd ET Case No.1305900/06, for example, a tribunal found that R had been unfairly dismissed for misconduct for refusing to carry out accountancy work for a separate company that was not within the terms of his contract. It noted that had the employer analysed the matter properly, it could have required R to accept a variation 'in the circumstances of their poor trading position and the fact that [R] had the ability and time to carry out the duties'. The employer could have given R notice and offered employment on the varied terms, and if R refused, he would have been dismissed with notice for SOSR.

416

The fact that an employer with a sound business reason for imposing changes **8.15** in fundamental breach of contract can dismiss fairly for SOSR led one claimant to argue that 'a contract of employment is not worth the paper it is written on' – Baker v Securicor Omega Express Ltd EAT 91/98. However, as the lay members of the EAT in Catamaran Cruisers Ltd v Williams and ors (above) were at pains to point out, 'the fact that the authorities show that an employer is not restricted, when offering less attractive terms and conditions of employment, to a situation where the survival of his business is at stake, does not provide an open door to change'. This fact is illustrated in UB (Ross Youngs) Ltd v Elsworthy EAT 264/91, where an employer attempted, as part of a reorganisation, to rearrange the shift pattern of an employee in such a way as to make it impossible for her to meet her obligations under her contract of employment. The employer had thus breached the implied term of trust and confidence between employer and employee and the EAT was unconvinced that there was SOSR for dismissal.

Another approach would be to argue that SOSR can be established so long as the employer has a sound business reason for imposing changes in fundamental breach of contract – but that tribunals should, in assessing unfairness under S.98(4) ERA, consider both whether the employer acted reasonably and whether the dismissal was equitable. In Garside and Laycock Ltd v Booth 2011 IRLR 735, EAT, the EAT accepted that SOSR was established when an employee was dismissed for refusing to accept a pay cut that the employer had proposed as an alternative to compulsory redundancies. However, when remitting the case to the tribunal to consider reasonableness, the EAT emphasised that the tribunal should consider the equity of a dismissal for this reason, in accordance with S.98(4)(b). The EAT indicated that equitable considerations might include whether management was to be subject to the proposed pay cut as well as the workforce, and whether the implied equitable concept of fair dealing was observed in the manner in which the pay cut was negotiated. See 'Reasonableness of change' below and, more generally, Chapter 3, 'Unfairness', under 'Reasonableness of dismissal'.

Some examples of cases where the dismissal was found to be for SOSR: **8.16**

- **Roberts v Acumed Ltd** EAT 0466/09: for historical reasons one of A Ltd's area sales managers, R, was remunerated on a more advantageous basis than its other four area sales managers. His commission was based on total sales, whereas theirs was based on annual increase in sales. Sales had been increasing year on year and as a result R's remuneration had grown out of all proportion to his contribution, In addition, A Ltd wanted to establish parity between the area managers. After attempts to renegotiate R's terms failed, A Ltd terminated his employment contract and offered him a new one on terms commensurate with the other area sales managers. R claimed unfair dismissal but the tribunal decided that A Ltd had shown that his dismissal was for SOSR. On appeal, the EAT upheld the tribunal's decision

- **Lawford v B&Q plc** ET Case No.1102144/08: L worked as a kitchen sales design consultant. He claimed unfair dismissal after refusing to accept changes in his terms and conditions which would, among other things, have reduced his basic salary by over £4,000 per annum. He had been employed by B&Q for over 20 years and had exemplary discipline, attendance and performance records. However, a tribunal found that his dismissal was for SOSR and was fair. There had been no consistency in the remuneration of B&Q plc's 600 design consultants, which had been fixed by local managers. B&Q plc had a valid and substantial business reason to reorganise the design consultants' remuneration package, to drive profitable sales and provide consistency and transparency between branches and pay bands. The process was carefully thought out and implemented over a period of nearly two years

- **Blain v Augustus Martin Ltd** ET Case No.3204980/09: AM Ltd was an advertising printer. It suffered huge losses during the recession and made staff cut-backs. However, by the middle of 2009 it had reduced its workforce as far as it could while still retaining sufficient staff to satisfy customer orders and so asked its employees to accept a temporary 10 per cent wage reduction. B was the only employee to object during consultation. AM Ltd terminated his contract on notice and offered him a new contract on the reduced salary. The tribunal found that B was dismissed for SOSR. AM Ltd clearly had sound business reasons to reduce employees' wages given its substantial losses and the need to make savings of £2 million. The reduction was intended to be temporary until it returned to profitability

- **Hill v Holmes-Naden Estates Ltd** ET Case No.2402092/11: H worked in lettings for HNE Ltd, an estate agent. She worked part-time hours to allow her to drop her children off at school in the morning and to collect them in the afternoon. The lettings business grew and HNE Ltd decided that there was a need for additional staff resources. Considering that it would be very difficult to find another employee to job-share with H, HNE Ltd asked her to change to a full-time role. H explained that she was unable to do so because of her childcare commitments but she put forward some alternative suggestions. These were not pursued and ultimately H was dismissed. The tribunal found that HNE Ltd had a sound business reason for seeking to vary H's hours – in that it needed additional staff resources in the letting department – and that it had accordingly established SOSR for dismissing her. However, the dismissal was unfair under S.98(4) as it fell outside the range of reasonable responses.

Reasonableness of change   8.17

If there are good business reasons for the change in terms and conditions or working practices, the employer will invariably establish SOSR as the potentially fair reason for dismissal under S.98(1)(b) of an employee who refuses to accept the change. This is only part of the fairness test, however. Under S.98(4) the tribunal must also consider the reasonableness of the change and of the dismissal. This involves considering whether, in all the circumstances, including the employer's size and administrative resources, the employer acted reasonably in treating the business reason as a sufficient reason to dismiss. A tribunal will err in law if it substitutes its own view of whether or not the employer acted reasonably in the circumstances rather than asking whether the decision to dismiss for SOSR fell within the range of reasonable responses that a reasonable employer might adopt – William Cook Sheffield Ltd v Bramhall and ors EAT 0899/03.

If there is a sound business reason for a reorganisation, the reasonableness of the employer's conduct must be judged in that context – St John of God (Care Services) Ltd v Brooks and ors 1992 ICR 715, EAT. For example, in Roberts v Acumed Ltd EAT 0466/09 the EAT held that a tribunal had not erred in finding that an employee's dismissal was fair within the meaning of S.98(4) (although it subsequently held that the dismissal was rendered unfair because of the employer's failure to follow the now-repealed statutory dismissal procedure). Due to an anomaly in his terms and conditions, R was earning vastly more commission than his colleagues and would soon be earning more than his managing director. Given that A Ltd had conducted 'protracted and detailed' negotiations with R for some nine months; had considered all of R's arguments; had put its own case for harmonisation carefully to him; and had taken steps to adjust his earnings in order to ameliorate the effect of the adjustment it proposed, its ultimate decision to dismiss R after he indicated that he was not prepared to accept a variation in terms was clearly 'within the range of reasonable responses to be expected of an employer faced with the same problem'.

Balancing needs of employer and employee. Tribunals must focus on the   8.18
statutory test under s.98(4) and resist the urge to promote one factor above all others as a crucial indicator of fairness. This is especially the case where the proposed new terms are worse than existing terms. In this situation, tribunals have fallen into error in focusing solely on the reasonableness of the employer in seeking to introduce the changes, or, alternatively, on the reasonableness of the employee in refusing them. The following cases illustrate the correct approach:

• **Richmond Precision Engineering Ltd v Pearce** 1985 IRLR 179, EAT: the new owner of the company proposed changes to terms and conditions of employment in order to harmonise them with those of its existing workforce. For P, the changes involved a reduction in his hourly pay rate, an

419

increase in hours, a reduction in his holiday entitlement and loss of certain benefits. Despite extensive negotiations, during which the employer made some concessions, P refused to accept the changes and was dismissed. In considering the fairness of the dismissal for SOSR, the EAT held that the tribunal had wrongly considered the sole question of whether the employer had acted reasonably in deciding that the advantages to the company of implementing the proposed reorganisation outweighed any disadvantage the employee might suffer. This, said the EAT, was merely one factor to be considered in the circumstances. It did not follow that just because there were disadvantages to the employee, the employer had acted unreasonably in treating his refusal to accept the terms as sufficient reason to dismiss

- **St John of God (Care Services) Ltd v Brooks and ors** 1992 ICR 715, EAT: a hospital faced with a severe cash crisis offered new, inferior terms to the workforce. 140 out of 170 employees accepted the new terms. Employees who did not accept the new terms were dismissed. The tribunal found the dismissals unfair on the ground that the terms and conditions offered were not terms that a reasonable employer would have offered in the circumstances. The EAT rejected the tribunal's approach, stressing that the reasonableness of a dismissal must be looked at in the full context of a business reorganisation: no one factor should be concentrated on to the exclusion of others. The reasonableness of the new terms on offer was not the crucial or sole test of fairness. Such an approach lent undue importance to the reasonableness of the employee's refusal and failed to acknowledge that both employer and employee may be acting reasonably according to their own legitimate interests, which may be irreconcilable

- **Catamaran Cruisers Ltd v Williams and ors** 1994 IRLR 386, EAT: following the purchase of a company, the new owners proposed new terms and conditions of employment to improve safety and efficiency. Although most employees accepted the changes, a few did not and they were dismissed for their refusal to accept the new contracts. In remitting the case to a tribunal to decide on the fairness of the dismissal, the EAT directed the tribunal to carry out a 'balancing process', considering the position from both the employees' and the employer's point of view. It approved comments made by the EAT in Chubb Fire Security Ltd v Harper 1983 IRLR 311, EAT, to the effect that even if it was reasonable for an employee to refuse to accept the new terms, it did not necessarily follow that it was unreasonable for the employer to dismiss

- **Copsey v WWB Devon Clays Ltd** 2005 ICR 1789, CA: C, a Christian, was dismissed following his refusal to work a seven-day shift pattern which might sometimes have required him to work on a Sunday. C brought a claim of unfair dismissal, contending that he had been dismissed on account of his religious beliefs. The tribunal found that C had been fairly dismissed for SOSR. It found that the employer had a sound business reason for requiring the change in C's working pattern – namely, significant increases in production requirements. Moreover, it had done everything it could to avoid dismissing C, including offering him other job opportunities within the company. The Court of Appeal held that the tribunal's failure to consider C's right to 'manifest his religion' under Article 9 of the European Convention on Human Rights did not affect the outcome of the case, since the same decision would have been reached if the tribunal had held that Article 9 applied. The change in shift patterns was an economic necessity for the employer, which had done all it could to avoid dismissing the employee and to accommodate his desire not to work on Sundays. (Note that the facts of this case took place before the Employment Equality (Religion or Belief) Regulations 2003 SI 2003/1660 came into force. Under those Regulations (now subsumed into the Equality Act 2010), the employer's requirement that the employee work on Sundays would probably amount to an act of indirect discrimination – see IDS Employment Law Handbook, 'Discrimination at Work' (2012), Chapter 11, 'Religion or belief', under 'Manifestation of religion or belief – is a right to manifest protected by S.10 EqA?', and Chapter 16, 'Indirect discrimination: proving disadvantage', under 'Indirect discrimination in context – indirect religion or belief discrimination'.)

Other factors. A range of other factors may also be relevant to the question of reasonableness under S.98(4). These include: **8.19**

- whether or not proposed new terms have been agreed with a recognised trade union. In Catamaran Cruisers Ltd v Williams and ors (above), the employer had agreed the new contracts with the recognised trade union. The EAT directed that this was relevant to the question of reasonableness. Similarly, in Sandford and anor v Newcastle upon Tyne Hospitals NHS Foundation Trust EAT 0324/12 the EAT considered it relevant that the trade union did not oppose a proposed re-banding of the employees' posts under the Agenda for Change process

- consultation with both the trade union (where appropriate) and individual employees. In Trebor Bassett Ltd v Saxby and anor EAT 658/91 the employer failed to explain to S and B how the proposed changes to their contracts would affect them. The EAT upheld the tribunal's decision that, by not consulting the employees about the effect of the changes, the employer had not acted reasonably and the dismissals were therefore unfair. (Interestingly, the proposed changes concerned the arrangements for overtime – to which there was no contractual entitlement. The EAT held that as the employees worked overtime on a very regular basis, such that it had become 'institutionalised', TB Ltd should have consulted about changes to the arrangements.) In Murray v Dewramet Ltd EAT 319/98 the EAT found that the degree of consultation required will vary with the circumstances,

421

particularly in relation to rationalisation exercises. What is important is that employees have an opportunity to be involved in a meaningful way. However, note that in Sandford and anor v Newcastle upon Tyne Hospitals NHS Foundation Trust (above), the EAT confirmed that the employees' dismissals and re-engagement on less advantageous terms were fair overall despite the fact that there was a failure to consult either with the trade union or with the individual employees. The breaches of procedure occurred well before the disciplinary process leading to the dismissals

- the number of employees who ultimately agree to accept the changes to terms and conditions. In St John of God (Care Services) Ltd v Brooks and ors (above), 140 out of 170 employees accepted the changes and the EAT held that this was relevant to fairness. The relevance of this factor was also expressly approved by the EAT in Catamaran Cruisers Ltd v Williams and ors (above). In Sandford and anor v Newcastle upon Tyne Hospitals NHS Foundation Trust (above), the tribunal took into account the fact that 91 per cent of affected employees accepted the new terms in deciding that the claimants had been fairly dismissed; and in Blain v Augustus Martin Ltd ET Case No.3204980/09 the tribunal noted the relevance of the fact that all of the workforce save the claimant agreed to a temporary reduction in wages

- whether the employer had reasonably explored all alternatives to dismissal. In Copsey v WWB Devon Clays Ltd (above) and Sandford and anor v Newcastle upon Tyne Hospitals NHS Foundation Trust (above) the fact that the employer had done this was considered to be relevant to the question of reasonableness. By way of contrast, in Hill v Holmes-Naden Estates Ltd ET Case No.2402092/11 the claimant had put forward a number of alternatives to a proposed variation in her working hours, including cross-training of sales staff, internal or external recruitment, job-share to cover the extended hours, and assistance with childcare costs. The fact that the employer failed to seriously consider any of these and took no steps to explore alternatives was a factor that rendered her dismissal for SOSR unfair.

8.20 In Docherty and anor v SW Global Resourcing Ltd 2013 IRLR 874, Ct Sess (Inner House), the Court of Session held that where an employer takes action against an employee which amounts to a dismissal without having considered the legal consequences, or on a mistaken view of what those consequences would be, the dismissal may still be fair. In that case, the employees claimed constructive dismissal when the employer attempted to move them onto zero-hours contracts without realising that this would change their employment status and cause them to lose their accrued statutory rights, such as the right to a redundancy payment. The Court held that, in determining whether the dismissals were fair, it was for the tribunal to assess whether the employer's ignorance of the law was excusable and, if it was, whether that was a decisive consideration or one that was outweighed by other factors. The case was remitted to the tribunal to reconsider the fairness question.

Constructive dismissal

8.21

On the reorganisation of a business some employees may feel dissatisfied with their new terms and conditions or duties. Where a change in terms or working conditions is unilaterally imposed by the employer and the change amounts to a fundamental breach of contract, the employee is entitled to resign and claim unfair constructive dismissal. Where this happens, the employer will usually plead SOSR as the reason for dismissal. In this somewhat artificial situation, a tribunal must establish the principal reason for the fundamental breach of contract that led to the constructive dismissal – Genower v Ealing, Hammersmith and Hounslow Area Health Authority 1980 IRLR 297, EAT. SOSR will be made out if, applying the test laid down in Hollister v National Farmers' Union 1979 ICR 542, CA (discussed under 'Establishing SOSR as reason for dismissal' above), the imposed terms are part of a reorganisation for which the employer has a sound business reason.

Two contrasting examples in which SOSR was pleaded in response to a constructive dismissal claim:

- **UB (Ross Youngs) Ltd v Elsworthy** EAT 264/91: as part of a reorganisation the employer attempted to rearrange E's shift pattern in such a way as to make it impossible for her to meet her obligations under her contract of employment. (To have carried out her obligations would have meant that she and her husband, who also worked shifts, would never be at home at the same time.) The employee resigned and claimed unfair constructive dismissal. The employer was found to have breached the implied term of trust and confidence between employer and employee and the EAT was unconvinced that there was SOSR for dismissal

- **Lee v Total Convenience Stores UK Ltd** ET Case No.1201712/06: L was employed at a petrol station to check stock, make orders and count money. In February 2006 the employer discovered a shortfall of £1,000 in its takings. Following an investigation L was completely exonerated. However, the employer noted that the site had failed to follow company policy and procedures. As a consequence, it decided that L would not be required to count cash from the main safe, as best practice specified that safe access should be limited to one person. L considered this a diminution in his role and he stopped attending work and claimed unfair constructive dismissal. The tribunal found that in altering L's duties, the employer had fundamentally breached L's contract and he was entitled to resign. However, it concluded that the employer took the action it did for sound commercial business reasons and that L's dismissal was potentially fair for SOSR.

423

8.22 Once a tribunal has found a potentially fair reason for dismissal – i.e. SOSR – it must go on to consider the question of reasonableness under S.98(4). A constructive dismissal is not automatically unfair – Savoia v Chiltern Herb Farms Ltd 1982 IRLR 166, CA. The principles governing reasonableness under S.98(4) apply to both express and constructive dismissals and are discussed under 'Reasonableness of change' above. Two constructive dismissal examples:

- **Baker v Securicor Omega Express Ltd** EAT 91/98: SOE Ltd imposed a change from weekly to monthly pay. B objected and resigned, claiming that he had been unfairly constructively dismissed. It was accepted both that the company had acted in fundamental breach of contract in imposing the change and that it had a good business reason for doing so. At issue was the fairness of the dismissal. The EAT upheld the decision of the tribunal that the constructive dismissal was fair. The tribunal had taken into account all relevant factors, including the degree of consultation that took place between the employer and both the trade union and B individually, the transitional arrangements offered (including an interest-free loan), the fact that over 8,000 employees finally accepted the change, and the fact that there was no reduction in earnings, merely a change to the method of payment. The tribunal had also rightly balanced the employer's need for uniformity with the disadvantage suffered by B, who was in debt and had to meet a number of weekly repayments to creditors

- **Avery Label Systems Ltd v Toal** EAT 243/91: ALS Ltd reorganised its business with the result that T was demoted from manager to 'team leader'. In this new role T's managerial salary was red-circled but he did not receive additional shift payments to compensate him for an enforced return to shift-working. The EAT held that in all the circumstances the tribunal was entitled to take the view that T was unfairly constructively dismissed.

8.23 Protecting employers' interests

Employers are entitled to protect their commercial interests against threats posed by their employees' actions and to take the necessary steps to achieve that end. If dismissal is the step taken, then assuming there has been no misconduct, SOSR will generally be relied on. There are three main motivations behind such dismissals: first, the employer is seeking to protect its confidential information; secondly, the employer wishes to restrict competition; and thirdly, the employer is seeking to protect its reputation against a risk posed by an employee's activities. We consider these in turn below (although in many cases they will overlap).

8.24 Protecting confidential information
If a breach of confidence has already occurred, that is a matter of conduct – see Chapter 6, 'Conduct', under 'Disloyalty – disclosure of confidential information'.

424

But dismissal of an employee because of a suspicion that he or she may leak or use confidential information in the future is usually described as being for SOSR. Frequently such a suspicion arises where the employee has a close relative or associate working for a competitor.

In order for employers to establish a substantial reason for dismissal in such circumstances, they must show that a genuine commercial risk would be posed by continuing to employ the employee. In Abey v R and E Holdings (Yorkshire) Ltd t/a Quick Pass School of Motoring ET Case No.14985/82, for example, a driving school receptionist had a long-standing relationship with one of the instructors. When he left to set up in competition, it had a substantial effect on the employer's business. The tribunal held A's dismissal to be fair. However, in Weal v Insulpak Ltd ET Case No.1116/63 W was a quality controller whose father – the works director – moved to a competitor. A tribunal found her dismissal unfair, pointing out that she did not have much access to confidential information and that the relationship between a father and a grown-up daughter living at home was quite different from that of a husband and wife.

In Simmons v SD Graphics Ltd EAT 548/79 the EAT said that there is no rule **8.25** of law or general principle governing the situation where two employees with a close personal relationship both hold confidential information and work for competing companies. Whether or not dismissal in these circumstances is fair is a question of fact for the tribunal. In that case S was a telephonist/filing clerk with access to confidential information. She lived with a senior sales manager who moved to work for an aggressive competitor. S was dismissed. The EAT upheld the tribunal's finding that she had been fairly dismissed for SOSR. By contrast, in Skyrail Oceanic Ltd (t/a Goodmos Tours) v Coleman 1980 ICR 596, EAT, C was dismissed from her job with a travel agent when she married a man employed by a rival travel agent and the EAT upheld the tribunal finding that this dismissal was unfair. The tribunal had rightly held that the dismissal was for SOSR, taking account of the level of access to confidential information by the two people, the importance of that information, and the positions they held. It was well known that industrial espionage was a particular problem with travel agents and C had access to most of the confidential information held by her employer. However, she had given an undertaking not to divulge confidential information and there was no evidence that she had leaked any. In these circumstances, fairness dictated that she be given sufficient warning to allow her to seek other employment. (Note that the EAT's decision on the question of sex discrimination was reversed by the Court of Appeal – Skyrail Oceanic Ltd (t/a Goodmos Tours) v Coleman 1981 ICR 864, CA.)

Note that in cases where an employee is dismissed because of his or her relationship with a competitor's employee, he or she may also be in a position to bring a claim of direct discrimination on the ground of marital or civil partnership status under S.13 of the Equality Act 2010. However, such a claim will fail

425

unless the employee can demonstrate that he or she was dismissed as a result of his or her marital or civil partnership status, and that an employee in a different but equally close relationship would not have been dismissed. See further IDS Employment Law Handbook, 'Discrimination at Work' (2012), Chapter 8, 'Marriage and civil partnership', under 'Protection under the Equality Act'.

8.26 Restricting competition

In RS Components Ltd v Irwin 1973 ICR 535, NIRC, the employer, which manufactured electrical components, found that employees were leaving, setting up in competition and soliciting former customers, which was very damaging to the business. The employer imposed a restrictive covenant on all sales staff to prevent them from soliciting customers for up to 12 months after leaving employment. I refused to agree to the new terms and was dismissed. The NIRC held that the dismissal was for SOSR and was reasonable. It added that it would also be reasonable for employers, when developing new technical processes, to require employees to agree to a restriction on the use of the knowledge they acquired of the new techniques and to dismiss them if they refused.

Even if the restriction an employer seeks to impose is unreasonably wide and therefore likely to be unenforceable, the dismissal of an employee for a refusal to agree to it may well be *potentially* fair for SOSR. In Willow Oak Developments Ltd t/a Windsor Recruitment v Silverwood and ors 2006 ICR 1552, CA, W Ltd was experiencing loss of staff and confidential information to competitors. It sought to address this by asking a number of its employees to sign new employment contracts containing wide restraint clauses. These prohibited employees, first, from poaching W Ltd's employees and ex-employees for a period of 12 months after the termination of employment and, secondly, from working for a wholly or partly competing business for six months after termination. The employees were given little opportunity to consider the restraint clauses or to seek professional advice, and were not warned that they would be dismissed if they rejected the new terms. When they refused to sign, they were dismissed. They subsequently brought claims of unfair dismissal. The tribunal decided that W Ltd's reason for the dismissals – i.e. the employees' refusal to accept the new terms – could not amount to SOSR because at least one of the restrictions was unreasonably wide. However, the Court of Appeal held that this was wrong. The question asked by S.98(1) is whether the employer's reason is 'of a kind' to justify the dismissal. The Court said that this means that the reason should fall into a category that is not excluded by law as a ground for dismissal. Accordingly, if the reason is whimsical or capricious or dishonest or discriminatory, it will be excluded by S.98(1). But if the reason falls into a category that can legally form a ground for dismissal, then it can be potentially fair as SOSR under S.98(1). An employee's refusal to accept covenants proposed by the employer for the protection of its legitimate interests can legally be a ground for dismissal.

426

However, this does not give employers carte blanche to impose new restrictive **8.27** covenants on existing employees. The reasonableness or otherwise of a proposed restriction will be one of the factors to be considered when the tribunal proceeds to the next stage of determining whether the employer acted reasonably in treating the employee's refusal as a sufficient reason to dismiss him or her. On the facts of the Willow Oak case, the reasonableness of the proposed covenants proved not to be relevant, since the manner in which the employer tried to force the employees to agree to the covenants made a finding of unfair dismissal inevitable. In other cases of this sort, however, the question of whether the covenants are legally enforceable may well be relevant to determining the fairness of the dismissal. Where this is so, the guidance given by Mr Justice Burton when the case was before the EAT may be useful. He suggested that, if the proposed covenant appears to be plainly unreasonable, or its excessively wide terms are not severable, that may make it easier for the tribunal to conclude that there was unfairness. If the proposed contract or covenant is arguably unenforceable, there will be a greater need to consider the approach of the employer, in particular the amount of time given to the employees to consider the proposals and whether they had the opportunity to obtain legal advice. If the covenant is plainly reasonable, then the fairness of the procedure will need to be considered, but the tribunal may well be satisfied that the dismissal was fair.

Note that the Court's decision in Willow Oak effectively (though not explicitly) overrules the EAT's decision in Forshaw and ors v Archcraft Ltd 2006 ICR 70, EAT, which held (on similar facts) that an employee's refusal to agree to an unreasonably wide restrictive covenant could not constitute SOSR for dismissal. However, the correct approach appears to have been adopted (in this respect) in Teknek Electronics Ltd v Munro EAT 1291/97, where the employer sought to impose an extremely onerous covenant upon M. When M refused to accept, he was dismissed. The employer told him he could have his job back if he agreed to the condition. The tribunal found that the reason for dismissal was SOSR in that it was legitimate for the employer to seek to protect the company's interests by imposing the covenant. However, dismissal was not reasonable in the circumstances. The EAT upheld this decision, commenting that the claimant was not contractually obliged to accept the covenant and the employer had essentially resorted to blackmail in attempting to impose a covenant that was so onerous it was probably unenforceable.

Preventing damage to reputation **8.28**
An employer that dismisses an employee after receiving information that the employee has been engaged in activities that could seriously damage the employer's business or reputation may be able to show SOSR for the dismissal. This is so even if the employee's conduct is unproven, or not directly relevant to his or her working responsibilities. (Note that if it can be shown that the

427

employee's activities have brought the employer into disrepute, a dismissal is more likely to be for gross misconduct – see Chapter 6, 'Conduct', under 'General considerations – gross misconduct'.)

In Leach v Office of Communications 2012 ICR 1269, CA, L was employed in a senior position by Ofcom, a public authority. His job did not involve working with children or with issues specifically related to children, but child protection was one of Ofcom's responsibilities. In November 2007 the Metropolitan Police Child Abuse Investigation Command contacted Ofcom and made a number of allegations against L, including that he had indecently assaulted a child and had visited brothels known to supply children. Ofcom took the view that the allegations carried a 'significant risk of reputational damage'. L was asked to a disciplinary meeting and, although he denied the allegations, Ofcom concluded that it had to accept the police advice that L was a risk to children. It considered this to be a breach of the trust and confidence at the heart of the employment contract and dismissed L with immediate effect. A tribunal held that L had been fairly dismissed for SOSR. Given the nature of Ofcom's work, the allegations and L's role, dismissal was within the range of reasonable responses and there were no reasonable alternatives available.

8.29 The EAT refused to interfere with that decision on appeal and, on L's further appeal, the Court of Appeal wholeheartedly endorsed the EAT's analysis. The EAT had taken the view that, when an employer receives information under an official disclosure regime that an employee poses a risk to children, it must in principle be entitled to treat that information as reliable. An employer cannot be expected to carry out its own independent investigation to test the reliability of the information since it will typically have neither the expertise nor the resources to do so. That said, an employer will not be acting reasonably if it takes an uncritical view of the information disclosed and if it is in a position to question the reliability of the information it ought to do so. Applying those principles to the instant case, the tribunal's finding that Ofcom adopted an appropriately critical approach in questioning the police about the reliability of their sources was unimpeachable. As for Ofcom's reference to 'breakdown in trust and confidence' as the reason for dismissal, the EAT thought that it was necessary to identify more particularly why the disclosure was said to have made it impossible for Ofcom to continue to employ L. Nonetheless, it was clear what the tribunal had in mind when finding that this was a sufficient reason for dismissal. Ofcom was at risk of serious reputational damage, which would be exacerbated if it emerged that it had been warned by the responsible authorities about L's activities but had taken no action. The tribunal was entitled to regard the dismissal as justified on that basis. Both the Court of Appeal and the EAT acknowledged the injustice to L of Ofcom acting on untested allegations. However, any injustice caused to L was not caused by Ofcom but by those who had accused him and the police who had given credence to the allegations.

428

By contrast, the EAT in Z v A 2014 IRLR 244, EAT, upheld an employment tribunal's decision that a school caretaker's dismissal, after allegations were made against him of historical sex abuse, was not for SOSR, and nor was it fair – demonstrating the truth of Lord Justice Mummery's observation in Leach v Office of Communications (above) that whether the reason for dismissal is 'substantial' will depend on all the relevant circumstances, which differ from case to case. The police reported to a school that an allegation had been made of historical sex abuse by the school caretaker, A. The head teacher, X, suspended A from duty despite her initial concern that the accusation was malicious. After about a year, she decided to recommend dismissal to the school governors on the ground that the trust and confidence she had in him had broken down to the point where it was irreparable 'due to the very serious nature of the allegations'. The governors dismissed A, despite indications that the police were hoping to conclude their investigations within two weeks and the fact that none of the witness statements taken supported the claim. The governors concluded that the allegation created a serious safeguarding issue for the school and that even if A were to be completely exonerated, the trust and confidence in him had been eroded.

A claimed unfair dismissal and the tribunal concluded that the reason for **8.30** dismissal – that there had been an accusation of historical child abuse against A – was not a substantial reason justifying the dismissal of a person holding the position that A held. A bare accusation by itself could not amount to a substantial reason justifying dismissal, otherwise the mere fact of an allegation by a pupil or parent against a teacher, however wild or frivolous, would be sufficient to dismiss. The tribunal recognised that it was necessary to strike a balance and to weigh the school's responsibilities against A's interests, but said that 'to condemn on the basis of accusation alone is a standard that a reasonable employer would not have adopted'. The accusation led to no more than a suspicion that A was a risk to children, unsupported by any authoritative evidence or opinion. The tribunal also found that, in any event, no reasonable employer would have treated this as a sufficient reason to dismiss. The school had failed to act within the band of reasonable responses in relation to the procedure it adopted by relying on notes without disclosing them to A; by failing to make further enquiries when A informed the governors that the matter would be concluded imminently; and by waiting 14 months to dismiss him, having decided to do so irrespective of the outcome of police investigations.

On appeal, the EAT upheld the tribunal's decision. Mr Justice Langstaff, President of the EAT, acknowledged the difficulty of balancing the issues that arise in cases of unsubstantiated allegations of sexual abuse, but observed that Leach v Office of Communications (above) had established a clear line of authority to guide employers and tribunals when carrying out such a task.

429

Although the duty of an employer concerned with serving children was first and foremost to safeguard those children, that did not remove its responsibility to its employees.

8.31 In Pritchard v Partnerships in Care Ltd ET Case No.1605036/11 an employment tribunal found that P, a head chef working in a secure mental hospital, was unfairly dismissed after serving a prison sentence for offences under the Public Order Act 1986. When he was convicted, and throughout his sentence, PIC Ltd repeatedly assured P that it wanted to retain him. However, after P returned to work PIC Ltd received an anonymous letter threatening adverse publicity for PIC Ltd if P continued in employment. PIC Ltd felt that there could be serious repercussions for the hospital and so dismissed P 'on the grounds of the nature of your criminal conviction and the impact that would have upon working in an environment with vulnerable adults'. The tribunal found that the reason for dismissal was SOSR; namely, the risk of damage to PIC Ltd's reputation by adverse publicity. However, the dismissal was unfair. PIC Ltd took no steps to identify the writer of the letter, and nor did it disclose it to P. Before receiving the letter, PIC Ltd considered that P's convictions had no impact on his suitability to perform his job and was of the opinion that he could return without any alteration to his role and without the need to conduct a risk assessment. In deciding to dismiss purely in response to the anonymous letter PIC Ltd was acting outside the range of reasonable responses of a reasonable employer.

In one somewhat unusual case, the problem was not what the employee had done but what he was not doing that led to his dismissal for SOSR due, in part, to the risk of public criticism. In Anderson v Chesterfield High School EAT 0206/14 A had been employed at a school but once he was elected leader of a city council he ceased to work there. He and the council that employed him at the school agreed that he should continue as an employee but on the basis that he would be paid the maximum allowed as paid leave to enable employees to hold public office under S.10 of the Local Government and Housing Act 1989. His post was held open and the council also continued to pay pension contributions. A subsequently became an elected city mayor, receiving an annual allowance of almost £80,000. The school became an academy and A's employment transferred under TUPE to CHS. CHS then terminated the arrangement with A. The EAT upheld a tribunal's decision that A had been dismissed for SOSR. CHS had acted reasonably in taking the view that the continuation of an arrangement whereby A was paid about £4,500 per annum by a publicly funded school without having to provide any services for an indefinite period was of no value to pupils, caused instability within the school, and might lead to significant criticism. The EAT commented that CHS's desire to end the arrangement with A, which could have been a 'public relations disaster', was a 'clear example' of SOSR for dismissal.

430

Third-party pressure to dismiss

8.32

In some circumstances an employer may feel compelled to dismiss an employee because of pressure from a third party. The pressure may come from a valued customer who threatens to withdraw his or her custom unless an employee is dismissed, or from a third party who wields influence over the employer. In such circumstances SOSR is often relied on as the reason for dismissal.

In Dobie v Burns International Security Services (UK) Ltd 1984 ICR 812, CA, a County Council had a contractual right to approve or disapprove the employment or continued employment of security staff provided by the employer at Liverpool Airport. Friction developed between a senior local authority employee and D, who was dismissed as a result. D brought a claim of unfair dismissal. The tribunal ruled that third-party pressure to dismiss can amount to SOSR and the Court of Appeal upheld this decision. (Note that the ratio in Dobie was doubted by the Court of Appeal in Jafri v Lincoln College 2014 ICR 920, CA, in relation to a separate procedural matter.)

The employer does not have to establish the truth of any allegations made 8.33 against the employee or agree with the request to dismiss in order to rely on third-party pressure as the reason for dismissal. This may seem harsh, but, as the EAT pointed out in Henderson v Connect South Tyneside Ltd 2010 IRLR 466, EAT, it would be 'equally harsh for an employer to have to bear the consequences of the client's behaviour; and Parliament has not chosen to create any kind of mechanism for imposing vicarious liability or third party responsibility for unfair dismissal'. In Edwards v Curtis t/a Arkive Computing EAT 845/95 E was dismissed at the insistence of C's only customer, who had complained about the standard of his work. E argued that he had been dismissed for lack of capability and sought to argue that he was capable of doing his job. The tribunal, rejecting E's suggestion, held that the dismissal had resulted from the pressure applied by the customer and was therefore fair. The EAT upheld the tribunal's decision.

However, although an employer does not need to establish the truth of any allegations made by a third party against an employee, an employer cannot simply hide behind the decision of the client and must do everything that it reasonably can to avoid or mitigate any injustice to the employee – Henderson v Connect South Tyneside Ltd (above). This point is discussed under 'Reasonableness' below.

Tribunals will accept customer pressure as SOSR if the evidence points to an 8.34 ultimatum having been served on the employer, such as in Edwards v Curtis t/a Arkive Computing (above). But there does not have to be a direct instruction to dismiss, if the effect of the pressure amounts to the same thing. Sometimes a customer may simply demand a higher standard of work without naming

431

anyone, but if the employer knows where the fault lies, and warnings are not heeded, there may be a good reason for dismissal.

However, the employer must show that *some* pressure was exerted by the customer. In Grootcon (UK) Ltd v Keld 1984 IRLR 302, EAT, K was dismissed because his employer – a firm of contractors on a North Sea oil rig belonging to BP – said that BP would not have him back on the rig because he was unfit. The only direct evidence was a telex from BP saying that K would have to be cleared by its medical department. The EAT held that to rely on third-party pressure as a cause of dismissal, the employer must adduce proper evidence of this.

8.35 In Securicor Guarding Ltd v R 1994 IRLR 633, EAT, the EAT held that it was unfair of SG Ltd to dismiss R on the ground that R's pending prosecution for sexual offences against children would offend the sensibilities of the customer for whom R carried out his duties. SG Ltd should at least have asked that customer whether there was any objection to the continued employment of R. Similarly, in Gray v Visual Statement EAT 171/95 VS was concerned about the number of hours that G was working. VS's funding came partly from Urban Aid, which had specified that only one person was to work full time. In an attempt to reduce the number of hours that G worked, VS took action that resulted in G's dismissal. The EAT said that although there was a suggestion that the Urban Aid funding might have been at risk, there did not appear to have been any attempt made to investigate what Urban Aid's response to the situation would have been. Therefore, there could have been no pressing necessity for VS to end G's employment.

It may not be sufficient for the employer simply to point to a decision taken by a third party as the reason for dismissal. In Pillinger v Manchester Area Health Authority 1979 IRLR 430, EAT, a research biochemist was dismissed because an outside organisation – a medical research body – withdrew funds from his research project. The EAT said that as the employer had not shown any reason for the third-party decision to withdraw funds, no substantial reason for dismissal had been established. It was not sufficient merely to say that the funds had been withdrawn, making it impossible to continue to employ P.

8.36 If the pressure put on the employer is improper, the employer may fail to establish a reason for dismissal. In Lavelle v Alloa Brewery Co Ltd EAT 655/85, for example, L, a barman, was arrested in the bar where he worked and told that he would be charged with obstructing the police. No charges were preferred but the police intimated to the pub that its licence would be at risk if L were not dismissed. The pub bent to this pressure. The employer argued that such pressure constituted SOSR but the EAT disagreed, holding that improper police pressure to dismiss an employee could not be SOSR and that therefore the employer had established no reason for dismissal. However, in Davenport v Taptonholme for Elderly People EAT 559/98 the EAT recognised that Lavelle was an exceptional and highly unusual case that laid down no general principle.

432

In that case, the employer ran a registered care home for the local authority. The authority was therefore in a position to dictate to the employer in respect of those persons who should not be employed at the home. After allegations of abuse were made against D, the authority conducted an investigation and recommended that D no longer be employed at the home. As a result, D was dismissed. Although the tribunal considered that the authority had treated D unjustly, this could not prevent the employer from relying on SOSR. If the authority's decision had been ignored, the home could have been closed. In contrast to the Lavelle case, the EAT found no evidence of improper pressure being brought to bear upon the employer.

In one unusual case – Parker v Stephens and Scown Solicitors ET Case No.1701281/98 – the employee was employed by a firm of solicitors as a caretaker. He became involved in a dispute with a client of the firm, who complained that P had access to his files and could use information to further the dispute. P was dismissed and the tribunal held that there was SOSR for the dismissal. In so doing, it noted that solicitors are in a unique position and their clients give them confidential information in trust. In view of the terms of a robust letter sent by P to the client, the client's concerns justified dismissal.

Reasonableness   8.37

Employers must act reasonably when dismissing as a result of third-party pressure. It is not enough for an employer simply to show that there was third-party pressure to dismiss an employee, thereby establishing SOSR as the reason for dismissal. The tribunal will also need to consider whether it was reasonable to dismiss the employee because of that pressure – S.98(4) ERA.

Two contrasting examples:

- **Rigblast Energy Services Ltd v Hogarth** EAT 665/93: H was employed on an oil rig by R Ltd, which, in turn, was engaged by T, the operator of the rig. The contract between R Ltd and T required R Ltd to remove any employee whom T considered unsuitable. Following an injury sustained by H and his ensuing absence from work, T, without giving any reason, refused to allow H to return to work. R Ltd had no other positions available for H and he was dismissed. The EAT upheld the tribunal's finding of unfair dismissal. H had never been warned that T had the contractual entitlement to stop any employee working on the rig and, more importantly, R Ltd had not taken sufficient steps to find out why T did not want H to return to work on the rig

- **SK v NOL** ET Case No.1401180/07: when SK applied to NOL for a job he disclosed the fact that he was an ex-offender and was on the sex offenders register. He was subsequently employed as a support worker assisting the police and probation service to monitor serious offenders, including sex offenders. However, a police officer recognised SK and the police decided they would not work with him, even though NOL made it clear that there

433

were proper precautions and risk management arrangements in place. NOL offered SK an alternative job, which would not have involved him working with the police, but he did not accept it and he was dismissed. The tribunal found that the decision by the police not to work with SK amounted to SOSR justifying his dismissal. NOL made all reasonable efforts to persuade the police to change their view and its decision not to proceed with a joint meeting with the police was reasonable in all the circumstances.

8.38 In Dobie v Burns International Security Services (UK) Ltd 1984 ICR 812, CA, the Court of Appeal said that, in considering reasonableness, tribunals should look at the conduct of the employer and, crucially, whether dismissal is an injustice to the employee. However, the Court also pointed out that an argument based on injustice is less likely to be sustainable if the employee's own contract warned that a third party could intervene to have him or her removed. Furthermore, a reasonable employer would be expected at least to consider whether the employee could be redeployed to a post in which there is no contact with the third party concerned – Norwest Construction Co Ltd v Higham EAT 278/82. In KCA Drilling Ltd v Breeds EATS 130/00, another oil rig case, the employee's contract of employment stated that the employer was required to comply with any request from the employer's client – the oil company that owned the oil rig on which it was contracted to work – to remove the employee from the rig. In this situation – and where the employee had refused offers of redeployment – the resulting dismissal was fair.

An employer must do everything that it reasonably can to avoid or mitigate the injustice brought about by the stance of the third party – Henderson v Connect South Tyneside Ltd (above). And in a case of 'patent injustice' the employer may have to 'pull out all the stops'. In that case the EAT gave the example of an employer trying to change the third party's mind or, if that is impossible, trying to find the employee alternative work. Provided that an employer has attempted this, any eventual dismissal is likely to be fair. On the facts, the EAT held that H, a school minibus driver, had been fairly dismissed after his employer's client refused him work in the light of untested allegations of sexual abuse. H's employer had acted reasonably in trying to persuade the client to change its mind and in trying to find H alternative work. H had sought to argue before the EAT that, since the only available alternative employment required the possession of a Public Carry Vehicle Licence, the employer should have funded him through a course to obtain the licence (the employer had in fact already funded him twice to take this course in the past, but the employee had both times failed the test). It would be interesting to have known the EAT's views on whether such a course of action represented the kind of 'stop' which an employer needs to pull out to prevent injustice to the employee, but the EAT refused to consider the point because it had not been raised before the tribunal.

In Bancroft v Interserve (Facilities Management) Ltd EAT 0329/12 the EAT **8.39** held that a tribunal had not properly applied the principles in Henderson. B, a chef employed by IFM Ltd, was dismissed after the manager of the bail hostel where he worked asked the Home Office to exercise a contractual right to prevent B working in the hostel. The EAT held that the tribunal was wrong to find that IFM Ltd had done everything it could to mitigate the injustice caused by the Home Office's request. The tribunal had not made necessary findings of fact as to why the employer did not investigate the poor working relationship between B and the hostel manager in the period between the manager contacting the Home Office and B's dismissal. Although the issue did not specifically arise in the present case, the EAT went on to note that the question of whether an employer has taken adequate steps to mitigate injustice as a result of a third party's request for the removal of an employee may require consideration of whether the employer should have taken steps earlier to try to remedy a problem before it became an insuperable problem leading to dismissal.

Two further examples:

- **Osanyinibi v Executive Group Ltd** ET Case No.6000556/00: O was dismissed from his job as a station cleaner following a call from the hygiene manager at the station to his employer. The employer was anxious to retain the contract for cleaning at the station and dismissed O after failing to persuade the station to change its mind. The tribunal found that as a result of real commercial pressure there was SOSR for dismissal. However, there was no evidence that the employer had taken any account of the injustice to O and the dismissal was therefore unfair

- **Greenwood v Whiteghyll Plastics Ltd** EAT 0219/07: WP Ltd employed G to carry out shop fittings at various stores. For some time, G worked at stores owned by M, one of WP Ltd's major customers. However, in July 2006 M made complaints about G's standard of work and subsequently told WP Ltd that G was barred from working in its stores. Unable to find G alternative work owing to 'no spare capacity', WP Ltd dismissed him. The tribunal concluded that WP Ltd had dismissed G for SOSR and had acted reasonably in doing so. However, the EAT upheld G's appeal. There was no evidence before the tribunal to show that WP Ltd had considered the nature and extent of any injustice to G and the tribunal had also fallen into error in failing to consider this matter. It may well have been the case that had the tribunal considered any injustice to G, it would have decided that it made no difference to the decision to dismiss. On the other hand, the injustice may have been so severe – and on this point the EAT thought it noteworthy that the tribunal made no finding criticising G's work or his capability – that the employer should have reorganised its business, enabling G to take another job within the company.

435

8.40 Difficulties with other employees

Third-party pressure to dismiss can often come from other employees who are in dispute with, or disapprove of, a colleague in some way. Disruption among employees is obviously harmful to an employer's business interests and, if it reaches a substantial level, such disruption may justify dismissal of the employee in question for SOSR. In Treganowan v Robert Knee and Co Ltd 1975 ICR 405, QBD, for example, there was a severe personality clash between T and the other women in her office over the merits of a 'permissive society' and the atmosphere soured considerably when T boasted about a sexual liaison she had had with someone half her age. T was dismissed and the High Court affirmed that the employer had shown SOSR and the dismissal was fair.

The employer should, however, take steps to try to alleviate the situation and should not dismiss the employee until it can reasonably conclude that the breakdown in relationships is irremediable. Failure to take reasonable steps to improve relationships will make the dismissal unfair – Turner v Vestric Ltd 1980 ICR 528, EAT. In deciding on the ultimate reasonableness of such a dismissal, the tribunal will consider whether the relationships can be patched up and also whether the objections of the fellow employees are reasonable or motivated by blind prejudice. For example, in Bown v Bristol City Council ET Case No.1402472/10 a tribunal found that B's dismissal was unfair where the option of mediation was raised at various stages prior to the disciplinary hearing but was not pursued before BCC concluded that the working relationship between B and his line manager had irretrievably broken down. Following its own policy, BCC was required to ensure that all reasonable efforts had been taken to avert a dismissal. Having regard to the fact that B had had an unblemished disciplinary record for over 20 years and that exceptional circumstances had led or contributed to the discord in the working relationship, it could not reasonably be concluded that there was an irretrievable breakdown in relationships until mediation had at least been attempted.

Note that personality clashes and breakdowns in working relationships are also considered under 'Breakdown in working relations' below.

8.41 Threat of industrial action

If the pressure coming from other employees, whether via their union or not, is in the form of industrial action, or the threat of industrial action, then special considerations apply. Under S.107 ERA employers are not allowed to invoke shop-floor pressure as a reason for dismissal, so SOSR cannot be argued in such circumstances. For example, in Simpson v Moore Paragon UK Ltd ET Case No.25097/85 S, a printer, was sent to prison for incest. His employer said that his job would be kept open for him but, when he returned, the workforce refused to work with him. S was dismissed. Before the tribunal, the employer denied that the workforce had actually threatened to take industrial action and pleaded SOSR as the reason for dismissal. However, the tribunal found that the whole workforce had informed their supervisors that they refused to work with S and that such pressure was sufficient to come within S.107. Thus the employer had not established a potentially fair reason for dismissal.

Breakdown in working relations 8.42

A commonly-cited SOSR for dismissal is 'loss of trust and confidence' between the parties. In Hutchinson v Calvert EAT 0205/06 H, who suffered from muscular dystrophy and was seriously disabled, employed C as a carer. The nature of this employment relationship was necessarily very intimate and, as the EAT put it, had to be 'based on complete trust and confidence'. The relationship was satisfactory for more than two and a half years but then became frayed. The tribunal found that in May 2004 C mentioned to H that she needed to discuss with his mother details of holiday due and sick pay, and to satisfy herself as to whether her employer was H or his mother. A couple of days later they had another conversation, during which H became agitated and upset. He subsequently dismissed C as he did not want her to continue caring for him, on the basis that the relationship between them had broken down. C claimed unfair dismissal and a tribunal found that SOSR had not been made out and that the dismissal was procedurally unfair. On appeal, however, the EAT held that the tribunal had applied the wrong test in ascertaining the reason for dismissal. It noted that – following Harper v National Coal Board 1980 IRLR 260, EAT – so long as an employer can show a genuinely held belief that it had a fair reason for dismissal, that reason may be a substantial reason provided it is not whimsical or capricious, even where modern sophisticated opinion can be produced to suggest that it has no scientific foundation. The tribunal had failed to consider whether H genuinely believed that the relationship between himself and C had broken down and could not be retrieved. In addition, in determining whether the dismissal was fair under S.98(4), the tribunal had failed to take into account the very special circumstances of the case. The EAT remitted the case to be determined by a fresh tribunal.

While there is some authority to suggest that for a breakdown of trust and confidence to occur there must be some action on the part of one of the parties, this should not be relied upon as a point of general principle. In Wadley v Eager Electrical Ltd 1986 IRLR 93, EAT, W was employed servicing and repairing domestic appliances principally in customers' homes. His wife worked as a shop assistant for the same business. She was suspected of misappropriating monies and convicted and sentenced for offences relating to 137 matters over a 22-year period, the total sum amounting to nearly £2,200. She was then dismissed and the employer, convinced of W's complicity, dismissed him too, without informing him of any specific matters for which he was under suspicion. A tribunal found that the trust and confidence between employer and employee had completely broken down and that W's dismissal was for SOSR and not

437

unfair. The EAT, however, overturned the tribunal's decision, holding that it had not been the act of the employee that had caused any breakdown of trust and confidence and it was impossible to accept that the behaviour of W's wife could lead to a breach of confidence in the trust residing in W.

8.43 However, in Leach v Office of Communications 2010 IRLR 844, EAT (a decision wholeheartedly approved by the Court of Appeal in Leach v Office of Communications 2012 ICR 1269, CA), the EAT dismissed L's submission that where a breakdown in trust and confidence arose as a result of a disclosure by the Metropolitan Police Child Abuse Investigation Command to his employer as to the risk L posed to children, that breakdown was not a reason for dismissal in itself if it was not linked to acts of misconduct on his part. The EAT held that in the particular circumstances of the case, the employer was entitled to rely on the disclosure and the concerns that the disclosure raised: it was not necessary for the employer to prove that that breakdown was as a result of misconduct on L's part.

In Governing Body of Tubbenden Primary School v Sylvester 2012 ICR D29, EAT, the Appeal Tribunal rejected the argument that, when considering a SOSR dismissal for loss of confidence, an employment tribunal was not entitled to have regard to the circumstances leading up to that loss. There, a deputy head teacher, S, was friendly with a fellow teacher, who was arrested and suspended for possessing indecent images of children (who were not pupils at the school). She maintained the friendship and 18 months later, with little prior warning, she was suspended and disciplinary proceedings were initiated. An internal appeal panel found that her actions had not brought the school into disrepute, nor did they pose a safeguarding risk to children at the school, but nonetheless the head teacher had lost confidence in her such that her continued employment was untenable and her dismissal was confirmed. The school maintained that this was SOSR. The tribunal accepted this, but found the dismissal unfair in the circumstances, especially since the employer had not only failed to warn S of the risk to her employment but had appeared to condone her conduct in maintaining the friendship. The school appealed to the EAT, arguing that the tribunal was not entitled to have regard to the absence of a warning or the causes of the loss of confidence but should be restricted to the fact of that loss. This argument was rejected on the basis that S.98(4) ERA entitled the tribunal to take a broader view. The context was analogous to a dismissal for misconduct, where a warning or its absence would be highly relevant to any consideration of fairness.

8.44 Despite the fact that 'loss of trust and confidence' has been relied upon to found SOSR for dismissal in many cases, employers (and tribunals) should be cautious when using this terminology, which originally arose in the context of constructive dismissal. In McFarlane v Relate Avon Ltd 2010 ICR 507, EAT, a relationship counsellor was dismissed for objecting to having to provide sex therapy to same-sex couples and he claimed religion and belief discrimination and unfair dismissal. With regard to the unfair dismissal claim, the tribunal accepted RA Ltd's argument that it had lost trust and confidence in McF because he was equivocal about his willingness to conduct himself in accordance with RA Ltd's equal opportunity and ethical practice policies, which it regarded as of fundamental importance. The EAT upheld this finding on appeal, but Lord Justice Underhill, then President of the EAT, commented that referring to trust and confidence in this context was 'unhelpful' as in almost all cases where an employee is dismissed for something he or she has done, the employer will have lost trust and confidence in him or her. It was more helpful to focus on the employee's specific conduct rather than use such general terminology. Nevertheless, on the facts of the case the tribunal had been entitled to find that the dismissal was for SOSR and that the employer had acted fairly and reasonably in treating the employee's equivocation over something the employer regarded as an important aspect of the job as sufficient reason to dismiss.

In similar vein, the EAT in Leach v Office of Communications 2012 ICR 1269, CA (discussed under 'Protecting employers' interests – preventing damage to reputation' above), the EAT admonished the tendency of parties to assume that 'loss of trust and confidence' automatically brings obligations under an employment contract to an end, which it does not. The EAT emphasised the importance of identifying why the employer considered it impossible to continue to employ the employee – in that case, the employer's need to avert damage to its reputation. The Court of Appeal concurred. Lord Justice Mummery noted that 'breakdown in trust and confidence' is not a convenient label to stick on any situation in which the employer feels let down by an employee or which the employer can use as a valid reason for dismissal whenever a conduct reason is unavailable or inappropriate.

8.45 An example of a case in which the employer relied inappropriately on the 'loss of trust and confidence' mantra is Handshake Ltd v Summers EAT 0216/12, where the EAT held that an employment tribunal was entitled on the facts of the case to find that a disagreement about salary and bonus did not result in a breakdown of trust and confidence so as to amount to SOSR. S was employed in a small company in the senior management team, which consisted of three people. There was disagreement between the parties as to S's entitlement to part of the share capital of H Ltd. Attempts were made to resolve this but without success, until S's solicitors finally wrote to H Ltd asserting that their client was 'losing all trust and confidence in respect of his employment'. Finally, H Ltd invited S to a meeting at which H Ltd stated that it believed that the relationship had 'completely broken down' and become unworkable. S was subsequently dismissed. However, the tribunal concluded that the real reason for the dismissal in the mind of the decision-maker was not a loss of trust and confidence but a power struggle over the terms of S's contract, bonus and shares. It found that if S had signed up to new terms then he would probably

439

not have been dismissed. On appeal, the EAT upheld the tribunal's decision, observing that it could not be right that an employee, even a senior one, who opens up a debate leading to a dispute over a term of his employment was by that alone acting in breach of the duty to maintain trust and confidence. It acknowledged that the manner in which such a dispute is conducted could amount to a breach of trust and confidence. But here the tribunal did not find anything repudiatory in the way in which the debate was conducted to indicate that trust and confidence had evaporated. Although the relationship was said to be souring, on the evidence life was in fact going on much as before: the parties were able to continue their work and were simply disputing how much money S was entitled to.

In some circumstances, employers may attempt to rely on SOSR for dismissal in order to avoid having to dismiss an employee for misconduct. However, if conduct was the genuine reason for the employee's dismissal, the employer may risk a finding of unfair dismissal if it neglected to follow an applicable disciplinary procedure. Nevertheless, every case must be examined on its facts. In Ezsias v North Glamorgan NHS Trust 2011 IRLR 550, EAT, the EAT held that an employment tribunal had *not* erred in finding that an employer's dismissal of an employee following the breakdown of the working relationship between him and his colleagues was for SOSR rather than conduct. The EAT observed that while tribunals should be on the lookout in such cases to see whether an employer is using the rubric of SOSR as a pretext to conceal the real reason for the employee's dismissal, in Ezsias the tribunal was alive to the refined but important distinction between dismissing the claimant for his conduct in causing the breakdown of his relationships and dismissing him for the fact that those relationships had broken down. The tribunal was entitled to find that it was the fact of the breakdown which was the reason for the claimant's dismissal and that his responsibility for that breakdown was incidental. In the circumstances, the employer's failure to follow the contractual disciplinary procedure did not render the dismissal unfair because that procedure did not apply to dismissals for SOSR.

8.46 By contrast, in Bown v Bristol City Council ET Case No.1402472/10 a tribunal, while recognising that SOSR is apt to include circumstances where there has been a fundamental breakdown in working relationships such that it is no longer practicable for the employment to continue, considered that a city council should have followed its disciplinary procedure rather than its SOSR policy where the breakdown in working relationships was caused by an employee's conduct. B, an arboricultural officer, made a decision not to impose tree preservation orders on a group of trees on a public highway. This decision was extremely controversial and attracted public criticism and BCC subsequently reversed it. B challenged BCC's decision in the Administrative Court, but his claim was dismissed on the basis that he lacked standing to bring the proceedings. BCC brought a disciplinary charge against B that he had brought BCC into disrepute and an investigation concluded that there had been a breakdown in trust and confidence in consequence of B's actions and his decision to bring proceedings. A hearing was convened under BCC's SOSR policy and B was ultimately dismissed because his 'inappropriate and ill-advised' action had resulted in 'an irretrievable breakdown of relationships' with management. The tribunal concluded that given that the breakdown resulted from B's conduct, BCC should have treated it as a conduct issue. Consequently, the manner in which BCC pursued the matter rendered the dismissal unfair.

Personality clashes

8.47

In Perkin v St George's Healthcare NHS Trust 2006 ICR 617, CA, P worked for an NHS trust as its finance director. His responsibilities included managing a team of employees, liaising with senior colleagues and establishing working relationships with people outside the Trust. When members of staff raised concerns about his personality and management style, the Trust's chief executive asked him to resign. P refused. At a subsequent disciplinary hearing, the Trust's chairman concluded that P's management style had led to a breakdown of confidence in his ability to fulfil his role among the executive team. He had also failed to establish the necessary relationships with stakeholders and external advisers to advance the Trust's interests. Moreover, his 'personal attacks' on colleagues, 'extending on occasions to abuse', had made it impossible for him to resume his previous role and re-establish an effective working relationship with them. As a result, P was summarily dismissed and he brought a claim for unfair dismissal. The tribunal found that the reasons for dismissal were 'conduct [and] some other substantial reason' and held that the Trust's action had been a reasonable response, but that the dismissal was procedurally unfair.

P appealed to the EAT, which upheld the tribunal's findings. On appeal to the Court of Appeal, P challenged the tribunal's decision on several grounds, including that he had effectively been dismissed on the ground of his personality. The Court agreed that personality, of itself, cannot be a ground for dismissal. For there to be a potentially fair reason for dismissal, an employee's personality must manifest itself in such a way as to bring the actions of the employer within S.98. In this case, the tribunal had concluded that P's unacceptable behaviour and the breakdown in confidence between him and the Trust, for which he was responsible and which had the potential of damaging the Trust's operations, amounted to the potentially fair reasons of conduct and SOSR. The Court acknowledged that the tribunal seemed to treat the case mainly as one of conduct, and although the Court itself would have properly classified it as falling within the category of SOSR, the tribunal's failure to do so was not fatal to its reasoning and did not affect the safety of its decision.

As the Perkin case suggests, there is a fine line between SOSR and conduct **8.48** when it comes to cases involving personality clashes. In Huggins v Micrel Semiconductor (UK) Ltd EATS 0009/04 the relationship between H and management deteriorated to the point that a disciplinary meeting was arranged to discuss H's attitude. In the course of that meeting it became clear that the issue was more complex and that H had problems with his health. Management sought to investigate this further but H refused to disclose a medical report obtained from his GP. When H wrote an intemperate letter undermining the management of the company – while still refusing to disclose the report – he was dismissed. The EAT found no error of law when the tribunal characterised this dismissal as being for SOSR, in that H's conduct had caused or contributed to a breakdown in trust and confidence. The dismissal was fair in the circumstances, although no recognised orthodox procedure had been followed. The EAT noted that the employer's business was very small and that H had chosen not to help resolve the issues by refusing to disclose the medical report.

However, while an irreconcilable personality clash can in some circumstances constitute SOSR for dismissal, if an employer could have easily organised its business in such a way that the conflict situation could have been avoided then it may not in fact give rise to a substantial reason justifying dismissal. In SA Brain and Co Ltd v Philippart EAT 0571/06 P was employed as a pub manager by SAB Co Ltd, a brewery. His relationship with his line manager deteriorated and he went on sick leave and lodged a grievance. SAB Co Ltd changed P's line manager and he returned to work. There were no further problems until a major management reorganisation, which resulted in P's original line manager being reappointed. P acted inappropriately and was dismissed for misconduct, but as an alternative SAB Co Ltd also relied on SOSR because of a loss of trust and confidence. The EAT agreed with the tribunal that its finding that SAB Co Ltd could have reorganised its business in a way that avoided P being managed by his former line manager meant that SOSR could not apply.

8.49 Refusal to work with particular employee/manager

Dismissing an employee because his or her refusal to work with a particular employee has created an impasse may be for SOSR. In Rowe v West Sussex County Council and anor ET Case No.3101926/11, for example, R, a teaching assistant, had an affair with S, a teacher, which they conducted away from school. The relationship ended when R discovered that S had, during the course of that time, engaged in a close personal relationship with another teaching assistant. R took sick leave. The school made efforts to implement a plan for her to return to work in a way that would minimise contact with S, but she refused to return while S remained employed there. However, the school concluded that it had no grounds to dismiss S and no power to transfer him to another school. Accordingly, the school dismissed R and the tribunal concluded that it was entitled to do so for SOSR due to the impasse in the working situation.

Similarly, in Driskel v Peninsula Business Services Ltd and ors 2000 IRLR 151, EAT, D was sexually harassed by her manager. Her internal complaint was rejected but she refused to return to her job unless the manager was moved elsewhere. The manager refused to move. An employment tribunal found that the employer had been manoeuvred into an impasse in which it had to dismiss either D or her manager. It chose to dismiss D and this decision was for SOSR. The EAT overturned the tribunal's decision that D had not been sexually harassed but upheld its decision that she had been fairly dismissed. It emphasised that the employer had made a genuine investigation of D's complaints; had genuinely tried to accommodate D with acceptable employment, even involving promotion; and had genuinely sought to persuade both parties to moderate their position. Even if the tribunal had correctly found sex discrimination, this would not have meant that the manager's position was so weakened that an impasse – soluble only by dismissal of one or the other of them – would not have arisen. In these circumstances, the tribunal was entitled to hold that D's dismissal was fair. (Note, however, that this case is likely to be confined to its very particular facts and that, in the vast majority of cases involving the dismissal of a victim of sexual harassment, the dismissal will be held to be unfair.)

Expiry of limited-term contracts 8.50

As discussed in Chapter 1, 'Dismissal', under 'Non-renewal of limited-term contracts', when a limited-term contract expires and is not renewed, the employee is effectively dismissed – S.95(1)(b) ERA. This applies to contracts that are stated to be for a fixed term and to those that are limited by the completion of a task or by a particular event (or the non-occurrence of a particular event) – S.235(2B). However, the expiry of a limited-term contract is not itself a potentially fair reason for dismissal. The employer must still establish that the expiry falls within one of the potentially fair reasons set out in S.98(1) and (2): the most commonly adduced in such circumstances being SOSR and redundancy. In Tansell v Henley College Coventry 2013 IRLR 174, EAT, an employment tribunal dismissed T's claim for unfair dismissal, holding that the reason for his dismissal was the expiry of the fixed term and that the process by which the contract came to an end was entirely legitimate and fair. Allowing T's appeal, the EAT noted that the non-renewal of a fixed-term contract was a dismissal by virtue of S.95(1)(b). In other words, the expiry of T's contract was the dismissal itself, not the reason for it. The tribunal had erred by eliding the mode of dismissal with the reason for dismissal. The reason must be one of those listed in S.98(2) or SOSR, and the tribunal must decide whether the reason relied on by the employer is among those listed.

Where redundancy is not applicable, the expiry of a limited-term contract can be SOSR for dismissal but this is not automatically the case – Terry v East Sussex County Council 1976 ICR 536, EAT. In that case the EAT said that the expiry of a fixed-term contract could be SOSR for dismissal but it was still up to the employer to show what the reason was and establish that it was

443

substantial. If the expiry of a limited-term contract was automatically SOSR for dismissal, employers could hide behind pleas of SOSR simply by calling a contract limited-term when the real reason for termination was something else altogether. (Note, however, that there are certain limited circumstances set out in S.106(1) ERA where the termination of a limited-term contract will be treated as being for SOSR – see 'Temporary cover' below.)

8.51 Employers are expected to show clear evidence of a substantial reason for dismissal due to the expiry of a limited-term contract, as the following cases demonstrate:

- **Primary Fluid Power Ltd v Brislen** EAT 0611/04: the EAT upheld a tribunal's decision that the dismissal of an apprentice three months after the conclusion of his fixed-term apprenticeship was unfair. On 3 July 2000 B started a three-year apprenticeship with PFP Ltd and this required him to work at PFP Ltd's premises as well as studying at college. By the time of the end of his apprenticeship in July 2003 he was still engaged on a City and Guilds course and had also started an NVQ Level 3 course. B's statement of terms and conditions of employment was varied on 21 July 2003 and signed by a senior manager to indicate that 'a successful probation/induction has been served'. B was subsequently dismissed on 25 November 2003 because there was no permanent position for him and he claimed unfair dismissal. PFP Ltd argued that B's employment had terminated at the end of his fixed-term apprenticeship and this had been prolonged until the end of November when it had learned that the City and Guilds course was completed and B had started on the NVQ Level 3. It argued that the dismissal was therefore for SOSR. The tribunal held that the contract made it clear that the apprenticeship came to an end in July 2003. There was no evidence to suggest that there was a consensual extension of the apprenticeship to November to take account of the courses B was undertaking. PFP Ltd tried to argue that it had a genuine and reasonable belief, albeit a mistaken one, that the fixed-term apprenticeship ended in November. But the EAT noted that PFP Ltd had in its possession all the relevant contractual documents and it could have clarified the position in July but did not do so. The dismissal was unfair

- **West Midlands Regional Health Authority v Guirguis** EAT 567/77: G's fixed-term contract as a locum consultant radiologist was not renewed because the regional health officer thought it an undesirable policy to employ locums. The evidence showed, however, that locums were often employed for a longer period than G had been employed for. The employer had therefore failed to show that it had any policy, let alone a policy which amounted to a substantial reason for G's dismissal. Thus it failed to establish a potentially fair reason for dismissal.

444

In Fay v North Yorkshire County Council 1986 ICR 133, CA, the Court of **8.52** Appeal clarified the circumstances in which the expiry of a limited-term contract can amount to SOSR: it must be shown that the contract was adopted for a genuine purpose, which was known to the employee, and that that purpose had ceased to be applicable. F, a teacher, was employed under four successive fixed-term contracts and when her last contract was not renewed she brought an unfair dismissal claim. The tribunal ruled that her dismissal was for SOSR and reasonable. The Court of Appeal upheld this decision. The tribunal had been entitled to conclude that the short-term contracts under which F had been successively employed were the ordinary kind of fixed-term contract and were for the genuine purpose of covering a period of temporary absence. The purpose of the contract had been brought to F's attention and, when that purpose came to an end and the post was filled by someone else, the short-term contract was not renewed.

Reasonableness

8.53

Once the employer has established a potentially fair reason for dismissing a limited term employee, the tribunal must decide whether the dismissal was fair or unfair. Communicating the purpose of the contract to the employee is likely to be an important factor in such cases. In Adams v Coventry University ET Case No.1303464/07, for example, A was initially employed by the University on a temporary contract. At the end of September 2005 she was offered a permanent job by the local Council, at which point the University offered her improved conditions in order to retain her services. A was left with the impression that she was to become a permanent employee, although on 10 October she accepted a fixed-term contract for one year. The contract was further extended, but A was dismissed after the person whose job she had been covering returned to work from maternity leave. The tribunal upheld A's claim for unfair dismissal. She had not been told that she was being employed only to cover an absent employee and the temporary contract she was offered did not mirror the maternity absence. She was offered the contract because the University wanted to persuade her to stay at a time when she had been offered a permanent job elsewhere. There were further extensions to her contract without any reference to the extensions covering maternity absence. The University should also have done more to look for suitable alternative employment.

The failure to look for suitable alternative employment was also a consideration in Rochdale Metropolitan Borough Council v Jentas EAT 494/01 where J, a temporary employee, was repeatedly re-engaged on a series of one-month contracts for a period of 20 months. When her final temporary contract came to an end her employment terminated. A tribunal found that there was SOSR for the decision not to renew her contract but that the dismissal was unfair because the employer had not considered whether suitable temporary work was available in another department. J had a substantial period of service, had

445

moved from position to position, and had sought to obtain a permanent position with the employer. The EAT upheld this decision, but commented that it was a 'one-off case on particular facts'.

8.54 Where a permanent position is created to replace a temporary post, the employer may be expected to help the temporary incumbent apply for the permanent post. Two examples:

- **Gavin v Home Office Immigration and Nationality Directorate** ET Case No.1802566/01: G was unsuccessful in his application for the permanent post, which was filled by an external candidate. Although a Council order providing that permanent posts could only be filled by open competition established SOSR for the non-renewal of G's fixed-term contract, the tribunal held that the employer should have done more than simply tell G of the vacancy in a casual phone call. He should have been pointed in the right direction and told of the application procedure

- **Darbyshire v The Governing Body of All Saints CE Primary School** ET Case No.2405746/05: D was employed as a teacher on a temporary fixed-term contract from 1 September 2004 to 31 August 2005 or the return of the post holder from maternity leave, whichever was the sooner. There were no problems over her abilities during the year and she made it clear to the head teacher on a number of occasions that she would like to remain at the school should the teacher on maternity leave decide not to return. Early in July 2005 a teaching assistant in the school told the head teacher that she would like to apply for the post if the teacher did not return. The head teacher approached the governing body, who agreed the appointment. D was informed of the appointment on 12 July and her employment terminated on 31 August. A tribunal found that D had been unfairly dismissed. It was unreasonable for the school not to have given D the opportunity to be considered for the post or to take any steps to consult her before giving the post to another person. Had the governing body been made aware of D's wish to remain at the school it would have given serious consideration to her superior qualifications.

8.55 Note that the Fixed-term Employees (Prevention of Less Favourable Treatment) Regulations 2002 SI 2002/2034 give employees on limited-term contracts the right to be informed by their employer of all available vacancies within the establishment in which they work – Reg 3(6). It is likely that a failure by the employer to comply with this duty will be a factor in the consideration of the fairness of any dismissal. Furthermore, an employee on a limited-term contract that has previously been renewed, or who has been re-engaged on a limited-term contract before the start of the current contract, will be treated as a permanent employee if he or she has amassed four years' continuous service – Reg 8. The only exception is where employment for a limited term can be justified on objective grounds. Needless to say, termination of such a contract on the basis that it has expired would not be considered a substantial reason to dismiss, and nor would it be fair.

For further discussion of the unfair dismissal rights of limited-term employees, see IDS Employment Law Handbook, 'Atypical and Flexible Working' (2014), Chapter 2, 'Fixed-term employees', under 'Unfair dismissal rights'.

Temporary cover   8.56

The non-renewal of a temporary contract to cover for an absent employee – for example, one who is suffering long-term illness – does not fall within the definition of redundancy. If the absent employee later decides not to return, thus creating a job vacancy, and the temporary employee is not offered the post, dismissal is still not for redundancy but may be for SOSR – Whaite v Dumfries and Galloway Regional Council EAT 223/92. Similarly, where the limited-term contract is to replace an employee who is away on secondment, the return of the seconded employee will be the reason for dismissal, not redundancy – Greater Glasgow Health Board v Lamont EATS 0019/12. In that case, it was accepted that the job in question was only ever a 'single employee job', so that there was no question of any diminution in the employer's requirement for employees to carry out work of a particular kind within the definition of redundancy in S.139 ERA. However, SOSR could be relied upon in such circumstances.

Indeed, there are a number of circumstances where the ERA specifically provides that the dismissal of a temporary replacement employee will be potentially fair for a substantial reason. S.106 provides that a dismissal will be for SOSR where the replacement employee is dismissed to make way for the return of the original employee who has been absent for one of the following reasons:

- pregnancy or childbirth
- adoption leave
- shared parental leave
- medical or maternity suspension.

However, S.106 only applies if, when the temporary employee is engaged, the **8.57** employer informs him or her in writing that the employment would be terminated on the return of the original employee – S.106(2) and (3). Furthermore, even if the dismissal of a temporary replacement employee is deemed to be potentially fair for SOSR under S.106, tribunals must still consider the reasonableness of such a dismissal under S.98(4) – S.106(4). If, for example, there are other positions that the temporary replacement employee could fill, it is likely that the employer will have acted unreasonably in dismissing, thereby rendering the dismissal unfair.

447

Section 106 is discussed in detail in IDS Employment Law Handbook, 'Maternity and Parental Rights' (2015), Chapter 14, 'Replacement employees', under 'Dismissal of replacement'.

8.58 Transfer of undertakings

SOSR is often cited as the reason for dismissal in cases where there has been a transfer of an undertaking. The Transfer of Undertakings (Protection of Employment) Regulations 2006 SI 2006/246 (TUPE) protect employees' employment in these circumstances, primarily by providing an effective remedy for those who are dismissed because of the transfer. Here, we provide an overview of the transfer regime to demonstrate the relevance of SOSR in this context. For a more detailed examination of unfair dismissal in the context of TUPE, see IDS Employment Law Handbook, 'Transfer of Undertakings' (2011), Chapter 4, 'Unfair dismissal'.

Regulation 7 TUPE provides that a dismissal is *automatically unfair* if 'the sole or principal reason for the dismissal is the transfer' – Reg 7(1). This applies to dismissals of employees of either the transferor or the transferee, whether carried out before or after the transfer and irrespective of whether or not the employee in question is assigned to the organised grouping of resources or employees that is, or will be, transferred – Reg 7(1) and (4). (For more on automatically unfair dismissals generally, see Chapter 9, 'Automatically unfair dismissals'.)

8.59 (Before TUPE was amended with effect from 31 January 2014, Reg 7(1) used to state that a reason *connected with* the transfer that was not an economic, technical or organisational reason ('an ETO reason') entailing changes in the workforce would also be automatically unfair. Although this is no longer explicitly mentioned, it appears to be the Government's intention that dismissal for a reason connected with the transfer remains covered by the new test – see the guidance issued by the Department of Business, Innovation and Skills, 'Employment Rights on the Transfer of an Undertaking: A guide to the 2006 TUPE Regulations (as amended by the Collective Redundancies and Transfer of Undertakings (Protection of Employment) (Amendment) Regulations 2014) for employees, employers and representatives' (January 2014) ('the BIS guidance').)

However, Reg 7(1) does *not* apply where the sole or principal reason for a dismissal is an ETO reason entailing changes in the workforce of either the transferor or the transferee before or after a relevant transfer – Reg 7(2) and (3). Such dismissals are potentially fair. If the sole or principal reason for such a dismissal is wholly unconnected with the transfer, then whether or not this reason is potentially fair falls to be assessed in the normal way under S.98(1) and (2). However, if the reason is the transfer or a reason connected with it, Reg 7(3)(b) provides that the reason for dismissal will be taken to be SOSR under S.98(1)(b) ERA, unless the reason is redundancy, in which case redundancy will be taken to be the reason for dismissal under S.98(2)(c). Most cases in which an ETO defence has been available to an employer have involved either a reduction in workforce numbers or dismissals due to significant changes to job functions. Many of these are likely to meet the statutory definition of redundancy contained in S.139 ERA, in that the requirements of the business for employees to carry out work of a particular kind will have ceased or diminished – see IDS Employment Law Handbook, 'Redundancy' (2011), Chapter 2, 'Redundancy', under 'Definition of "redundancy"'. However, as discussed below, SOSR may be applicable in some situations.

Reasonableness. Note that having determined whether the ETO reason **8.60** entailing changes in the workforce amounts to redundancy or SOSR, the tribunal then needs to assess the employer's reasonableness in treating that reason as justifying the employee's dismissal under S.98(4) in the normal way – see Chapter 3, 'Unfairness'.

Economic, technical, or organisational reasons...   8.61

TUPE does not contain a definition of an ETO reason. The BIS guidance suggests that ETO reasons are likely to include:

- a reason relating to the profitability or market performance of the transferee's business (i.e. an economic reason)

- a reason relating to the nature of the equipment or production processes which the transferee operates (i.e. a technical reason); or

- a reason relating to the management or organisational structure of the transferee's business (i.e. an organisational reason).

Tribunals have generally sought to give the ETO exception in Reg 7 a narrow meaning. In Wheeler v Patel and anor 1987 ICR 631, EAT, the EAT said that an economic reason for dismissal entailing a change in the workforce must relate to the conduct of the business concerned: broader economic reasons did not fall within the scope of the clause. Therefore, the transferor's desire to obtain an enhanced price for the business or to achieve a sale by capitulating to the transferee's demands to dismiss the workforce did not constitute an ETO reason. This approach was endorsed by the Court of Appeal in Whitehouse v Charles A Blatchford and Sons Ltd 2000 ICR 542, CA, which said that 'the words "economic, technical or organisational reason entailing changes in the workforce" clearly support the conclusion that the reason must be connected with the future conduct of the business as a going concern'.

Note, however, that the dismissal of an employee by the transferor prior to the **8.62** transfer, for reasons that relate solely to the future conduct of the business by the transferee after the transfer, is not capable of being for an ETO reason – Hynd v Armstrong and ors 2007 IRLR 338, Ct Sess (Inner House).

_____ **449**

For a full discussion of ETO reasons, see IDS Employment Law Handbook, 'Transfer of Undertakings' (2011), Chapter 4, 'Unfair dismissal', under 'Dismissals potentially fair for an "ETO reason" – economic, technical or organisational reason'.

8.63 ... entailing changes in the workforce

An ETO reason must involve 'changes in the workforce' if it is to be a potentially fair reason for dismissal. This may mean a change in the workplace – Reg 7(3A). Otherwise, the Court of Appeal has held that this must amount to a reduction in the numbers or a change in the functions of the workforce. It is not sufficient merely that there has been a change in the identity of some of the staff, where, for instance, dismissals were followed by the engagement of new staff to replace the old – Berriman v Delabole Slate Ltd 1985 ICR 546, CA.

In the Berriman case, the Court of Appeal also held that the transferor or transferee must show that the changes in the workforce were *necessary*. It is not enough simply to show an ETO reason for dismissal that incidentally involved changes in the workforce. The Court of Appeal construed the words 'economic, technical or organisational' to mean that the employer must show some sort of imperative behind the dismissal – i.e. that it was necessary and not merely desirable in the commercial interests of the business. According to Lord Justice Browne-Wilkinson, 'the phrase "economic, technical or organisational reason entailing changes in the workforce"... requires that the change in the workforce is part of the economic, technical or organisational reason. The employers' plan must be to achieve changes in the workforce. It must be an objective of the plan, not just a possible consequence of it.'

8.64 However, the ETO reason need not entail changes in the whole of the workforce. In Nationwide Building Society v Benn and ors 2010 IRLR 922, EAT, the EAT held that the ETO argument was available even though the changes at issue affected only transferred employees, and not the entirety of the workforce.

For full details, see IDS Employment Law Handbook, 'Transfer of Undertakings' (2011), Chapter 4, 'Unfair dismissal', under 'Dismissals potentially fair for an "ETO reason" – entailing changes in the workforce'.

8.65 Constructive dismissal

An employee's common law right, upon the employer's fundamental breach of contract, to resign and treat him or herself as dismissed is preserved in the context of a TUPE transfer by Reg 4(11). Constructive dismissal claims depend on the employee being able to establish that the employer committed a repudiatory breach of a fundamental term of the employment contract, and that he or she resigned because of that breach – see Chapter 1, 'Dismissal', under 'Constructive dismissal'. Although a constructive dismissal is not necessarily unfair (as discussed under 'Business reorganisations – constructive dismissal' above), any fundamental breach of contract that is a result of the transfer – for example, unilateral changes to transferring employees' terms and conditions to align them with the transferee's existing workforce – will render a constructive dismissal automatically unfair.

Employers who impose changes in the job functions of employees may have a defence to a claim of automatically unfair constructive dismissal if they can show an ETO reason entailing a change in the workforce. As mentioned above, the Court of Appeal in Berriman v Delabole Slate Ltd 1985 ICR 546, CA, construed the phrase 'entailing changes in the workforce' narrowly to mean changes in the overall numbers or functions of the employees looked at as a whole. A fundamental change in job functions may be sufficient to constitute a 'change in the workforce' for the purposes of Reg 7(2), so that, for example, a constructive dismissal brought about by a transferee's insistence that an acquired employee change his or her job function might be potentially fair for SOSR.

For further discussion, see IDS Employment Law Handbook, 'Transfer of Undertakings' (2011), Chapter 4, 'Unfair dismissal', under 'Constructive dismissals'.

Material detriment dismissal

8.66

Regulation 4(9) provides a remedy for an employee who envisages being materially worse off as a result of a transfer, but not to such an extent that he or she can claim constructive dismissal. The employee does not have to show that there was a breach of contract, let alone a fundamental one. Reg 4(9) provides that where a transfer involves or would involve 'a substantial change in working conditions to the material detriment' of the employee, he or she can treat the contract as terminated by dismissal. There is nothing in TUPE to suggest that the rules in Reg 7(1) and (2) on the unfairness of TUPE-connected dismissals do not apply to a 'material detriment' dismissal just as much as they apply to other express and constructive dismissals. So, such a dismissal is liable to be automatically unfair unless either it is found to be entirely unconnected to the transfer, or it is for an ETO reason entailing changes in the workforce, in which case it will be potentially fair for SOSR (or redundancy).

For a detailed discussion, see IDS Employment Law Handbook, 'Transfer of Undertakings' (2011), Chapter 4, 'Unfair dismissal', under 'Material detriment dismissals'.

Employee objection to transfer

8.67

Employees have the right to object to a transfer, in which case they will not automatically transfer – Reg 4(7). Where this happens, the transfer operates to terminate the contract of employment with the transferor without the objecting employee being treated for any purposes as dismissed – Reg 4(8). There is an

451

exception where the transfer involves or would involve a substantial change in the employee's working conditions to his or her material detriment under Reg 4(9) (see 'Material detriment dismissals' above) or where the employee resigns and claims constructive dismissal under Reg 4(11) in response to a repudiatory breach of contract by the employer. However, the latter situation is complex: see IDS Employment Law Handbook, 'Transfer of Undertakings' (2011), Chapter 4, 'Unfair dismissal', under 'Constructive dismissals – resignation in anticipation of a breach by the transferee'.

For more detail on objecting to the transfer, see IDS Employment Law Handbook, 'Transfer of Undertakings' (2011), Chapter 2, 'Who transfers?', under 'Objecting to the transfer', and Chapter 4, 'Unfair dismissal', under 'Material detriment dismissals – interrelationship with the right to object'.

8.68 Retirement dismissals

Until the introduction of the Employment Equality (Age) Regulations 2006 SI 2006/1031 ('the Age Regulations'), employees at or over their 'normal retiring age' (or, in the absence of a normal retiring age, the default retirement age (DRA) of 65) were, with some exceptions, precluded from claiming unfair dismissal by S.109 ERA. The Age Regulations repealed this provision from 1 October 2006. Since then, there has been no 'upper age limit' on the right to claim unfair dismissal.

To counterbalance the repeal of the upper age limit, S.98(2)(ba) ERA, which was inserted by the Age Regulations on the same day, introduced 'retirement' as a potentially fair reason for dismissal. This meant that if employers followed certain procedural requirements set out in S.98ZG ERA and Schedule 6 to the Age Regulations they could fairly dismiss by reason of retirement any employee who had reached the age of 65 – or any specified 'normal retirement age' of or over 65 – without having to show that the decision to dismiss was reasonable under S.98(4). Where an employee had a normal retirement age of below 65, his or her dismissal would not be potentially fair on the ground of retirement unless the employer could objectively justify the normal retirement age as being a proportionate means of achieving a legitimate aim, under what is now S.13(2) of the Equality Act 2010 (EqA). (When the EqA came into force on 1 October 2010, it revoked most of the Age Regulations but Schedule 6 was retained, meaning that the statutory retirement regime remained the same for the purpose of assessing the fairness of retirement dismissals.)

8.69 However, following a review, the Government decided to abolish both the DRA of 65 and the statutory retirement procedure. The Employment Equality (Repeal of Retirement Age Provisions) Regulations 2011 SI 2011/1069 repealed the relevant aspects of the ERA and the Age Regulations, subject to transitional provisions, from 6 April 2011. This means that as the law now stands, 'retirement' is *not* a potentially fair reason for dismissal under S.98 ERA. Thus, an employer wishing to fairly dismiss an older employee because of his or her advancing age needs to show that the reason for dismissal falls within one of the potentially fair reasons for dismissal contained in S.98(1) and (2) ERA, and that the dismissal was reasonable in all the circumstances under S.98(4). In other words, the dismissal is treated in the same way as any other dismissal.

Of course, dismissing an employee on the ground that he or she has reached a particular age is prima facie direct age discrimination under the EqA. However, unlike the other characteristics protected by the EqA (e.g. sex and race), it is possible for employers to justify direct age discrimination under S.13(2) EqA. Thus, despite the fact that there is no longer any statutory DRA, an employer can still seek to impose its own compulsory retirement age and avoid claims of direct age discrimination if it can objectively justify its actions – see 'Objectively justifying compulsory retirement' below. And it is likely that an employer dismissing an employee because he or she has reached such an objectively justified retirement age would seek to rely on SOSR as a potentially fair reason for dismissal in any unfair dismissal claim – see 'SOSR as potentially fair reason for compulsory retirement'.

Dismissal for age-related performance and health issues. Regardless of his or **8.70** her age, an employee may be dismissed for a potentially fair reason which is genuinely not age-related. Where, for example, an 80-year-old employee is dismissed for redundancy or misconduct, the categorisation of his or her dismissal will be the same as if he or she were 28. The situation may be more complicated, however, where an employer wishes to dismiss an employee because of a deterioration in his or her performance, or because of ill health, that is age-related or perceived as such.

Where an employee's performance deteriorates, the employer is likely to seek to rely on capability as a potentially fair reason for dismissal. It must be stressed, however, that an employer's assertion that an employee is no longer sufficiently capable is likely to be subjected to a high degree of scrutiny and an employer who dismisses an employee without undertaking an assessment of his or her capabilities is likely to be heading for a finding of unfair dismissal. This is discussed in Chapter 4, 'Capability and qualifications', under 'Establishing lack of capability'.

Where an employee is suffering ill health, the employer may seek to rely on **8.71** either capability or SOSR as the reason for dismissal where the dismissal is, in the circumstances, not directly because of the employee's health but because of his or her persistent absences. Dismissal in such circumstances is discussed in Chapter 5, 'Ill health', under 'General considerations' and 'Persistent short-term absences'.

453

8.72 SOSR as potentially fair reason for compulsory retirement

An employer is likely to rely on SOSR as the reason for dismissal where the dismissal is in accordance with a compulsory retirement policy. As a first step, the employer would need to show that the compulsory retirement age is objectively justified as a proportionate means of achieving a legitimate aim – see 'Objectively justifying compulsory retirement' below. Clearly, this must be established to ensure that the dismissal does not fall foul of the EqA. However, it is also arguable that only a non-discriminatory reason for dismissal is capable of amounting to SOSR 'of a kind such as to justify the dismissal' under S.98(1)(b) ERA. In Willow Oak Developments Ltd t/a Windsor Recruitment v Silverwood and ors 2006 ICR 1552, CA (a case concerning dismissal for SOSR for refusing to accept fresh restrictive covenants – see 'Protecting employers' interests – restricting competition' above), the Court of Appeal was of the view that for a reason to be 'of a kind' to justify dismissal within the meaning of S.98(1)(b), it should fall into a category that is 'not excluded by law as a ground for dismissal... Accordingly, if the reason is whimsical or capricious or dishonest... or is based on *an inadmissible ground such as race or sex*' (our stress) it will be excluded by S.98(1). This would seem to imply that if the reason for an employee's dismissal is the application of a compulsory retirement policy that is discriminatory on the ground of age because it is not objectively justified, that reason is incapable of amounting to SOSR for the purposes of defending an unfair dismissal claim.

Even if an employer's compulsory retirement policy *is* objectively justified, tribunals are unlikely to accept as SOSR the simple fact that a dismissal was in accordance with that policy. In Leach v Office of Communications 2012 ICR 1269, CA (discussed under 'Protecting employers' interests – preventing damage to reputation' above), the Court of Appeal concurred with the EAT's emphasis on the importance of identifying *why* the employer considered it impossible to continue to employ the employee, rather than simply seeking to rely on a convenient label for dismissal. While Leach concerned a dismissal citing a breakdown in trust and confidence, it is likely that tribunals will similarly seek to examine the precise aims of an employer's retirement policy to determine if these are capable of amounting to SOSR.

8.73 In this regard, some of the 'legitimate aims' accepted by the courts as potentially justifying the age discrimination inherent in forced retirements may be of relevance. For example, in Seldon v Clarkson Wright and Jakes 2012 ICR 716, SC, the Supreme Court accepted that staff retention, workforce planning and limiting the need to expel individuals by way of performance management were all legitimate aims capable of justifying the application of a retirement age to partners in a law firm. Furthermore, the aim of giving younger employees the chance of promotion and facilitating workforce planning is endorsed in the Acas guidance booklet, 'Working without the DRA' (2011). It is entirely feasible that these kinds of reason could be accepted by a tribunal as substantial enough to justify the dismissal of an employee on reaching the employer's retirement age. In so far as the aims identified in the case law and the Acas guidance contribute to the long-term success of a business – by promoting staff retention and creating progression prospects to attract talented new recruits – they can be seen as 'good business reasons' for dismissing employees at the end of their careers.

On the other hand, SOSR can only be relied on where it justifies the dismissal of 'an employee holding the position which the employee held' – S.98(1)(b) ERA. Any retirement policy would therefore need to be tailored to the factors affecting specific jobs. For example, in customer service and support roles, where there tends to be a high staff turnover rate, there would be a less pressing need to create vacancies by dismissing older employees. This is in contrast to professional and managerial roles where 'job blocking' might well be a legitimate concern, as it was in the Seldon case. Thus, even within the same organisation, the business case for enforcing a retirement age may vary between job types and so a blanket policy may not stand up to scrutiny as a potentially fair reason for dismissal.

Reasonableness. Establishing that a retirement dismissal is for legitimate aims **8.74** that can be categorised as SOSR is only the first step in establishing a fair dismissal, however. Once the reason has been established, the tribunal must decide whether the employer acted reasonably under S.98(4) in dismissing for that reason by considering whether the decision to dismiss fell within the range of reasonable responses that a reasonable employer might adopt. In retirement situations, this is likely to involve consideration of matters such as whether the employee was consulted and given plenty of notice; whether thought was given to whether a later retirement age would be appropriate; and whether retirement could be avoided altogether by adopting some other strategy. For example, even if dismissal from the employee's particular position was for a substantial reason, did the employer search for suitable alternative employment in respect of which retirement at that age was not required? Assessing reasonableness is likely to involve some of the considerations that are relevant to assessing proportionality in the context of objectively justifying discrimination (see 'Objectively justifying compulsory retirement – proportionate means' below) but tribunals must take care to apply the two tests separately. Age discrimination and unfair dismissal are fundamentally different jurisdictions, and the question of justification is distinct from that of reasonableness. It is by no means a foregone conclusion that a tribunal would accept that, since the employer's retirement age policy was justified, a dismissal for SOSR was fair.

It is worth noting that even if we are incorrect in our view that a retirement dismissal in reliance on a discriminatory policy cannot be potentially fair for SOSR (see discussion of Willow Oak Developments Ltd t/a Windsor Recruitment v Silverwood and ors (above)), a dismissal in accordance with a discriminatory

455

policy is in any event unlikely to be fair under S.98(4). However, a tribunal will err in law if it fails to address the question of fairness separately – HJ Heinz Co Ltd v Kenrick 2000 ICR 491, EAT.

8.75 Objectively justifying compulsory retirement

The justification of direct age discrimination is discussed in detail in IDS Employment Law Handbook, 'Discrimination at Work' (2012), Chapter 15, 'Direct discrimination', under 'Justifying direct age discrimination', and – with specific reference to retirement dismissals – in Chapter 26, 'Dismissal', under 'Retirement'. Here we simply provide an overview of the relevant statutory provisions and case law.

A dismissal on the ground that an employee has reached a particular age is prima facie direct age discrimination under S.13(1) EqA. This provides that an employer directly discriminates against a person if:

- it treats that person less favourably than it treats or would treat others; and

- the difference in treatment is because of a protected characteristic (in this case, age).

Nevertheless, direct age discrimination – such as the application of a retirement age – may be justified (i.e. made lawful) under S.13(2) if it can be demonstrated that it is a 'proportionate means of achieving a legitimate aim'. Thus, despite the fact that there is no statutory default retirement age, employers may nevertheless impose their own compulsory retirement age if they can justify doing so.

8.76 **Legitimate aims.** The first consideration in determining whether an employer's compulsory retirement age is justified is whether it is applied in pursuit of a legitimate aim. Essentially, this means that the employer must provide a 'reason why' it wants to enforce a particular retirement age. The Supreme Court in Seldon v Clarkson Wright and Jakes (a partnership) 2012 ICR 716, SC, established that in the context of justifying direct discrimination – as opposed to indirect discrimination, where a less stringent test applies – legitimate aims capable of justifying discrimination must have a social policy objective and not be purely individual reasons particular to the employer's situation, such as cost reduction or improving competitiveness. The Court noted that the ECJ had identified two broad categories of legitimate social policy objective: 'inter-generational fairness' and 'dignity'.

Having established an aim falling within one of these categories, the employer must then go on to show that it is legitimate in the particular circumstances of the employment concerned. Baroness Hale in Seldon gave the following two examples:

- the aim of improving the recruitment of young people in order to achieve a balanced and diverse workforce. 'This is in principle a legitimate aim. But if there is in fact no problem in recruiting the young and the problem is in retaining the older and more experienced workers then it may not be a legitimate aim for the business concerned'

- the aim of avoiding the need for performance management. This may be a legitimate aim, but if in fact the business already has sophisticated performance management measures in place, it may not be legitimate to avoid them for only one section of the workforce.

Proportionate means. If a legitimate aim has been established, the tribunal **8.77** must then consider whether the means deployed to achieve that aim were proportionate, i.e. that the retirement age was a proportionate means of achieving the aim. This is a balancing exercise, which weighs the legitimate aim against the discriminatory effect the retirement policy has on employees who reach the retirement age. Among the issues for consideration are why the employer has chosen the particular retirement age; the alternatives (be they a higher retirement age or a completely different approach); and how the retirement age has been applied in practice. Where a retirement age is deployed as a means of guarding against an age-related drop in performance, tribunals are likely to demand clear evidence that the age set by the employer correlates with such a decline.

In Seldon v Clarkson Wright and Jakes (a partnership) (above) Baroness Hale stressed that to be proportionate, a measure must be both an appropriate means of achieving the legitimate aim and (reasonably) necessary in order to do so. She also warned that 'businesses will now have to give careful consideration to what, if any, mandatory retirement rules can be justified'.

Miscellaneous reasons 8.78

The open-ended nature of SOSR has meant that a wide variety of reasons have been held to be capable of falling within its ambit. Below are just some examples.

Reviewing pay structures to ensure equal pay compliance. In Wolstenholme **8.79** v Scout Association ET Case No.3201875/11 W was to be made redundant in 2008 but instead was offered a post two grades below her previous post with pay protection 'in perpetuity'. By 2010 SA became concerned that there was a risk that historic individual pay scales might breach the principle of equal pay and it engaged external consultants to carry out a pay and benefits review with the purpose of establishing a non-discriminatory, fair and transparent pay structure. W was one of 12 employees who were identified as receiving pay in excess of the value of the job. She refused a new contract on a lower salary and was ultimately dismissed. The tribunal considered that she was dismissed fairly for SOSR stemming from SA's reasonable belief that it was under a legal obligation to ensure compliance with equal pay legislation by harmonising the pay structure, and that to do so would further good employment relations. Its process for re-evaluating pay structures was meticulous in that it considered principles set out by the Equality and Human Rights Commission, took legal advice and implemented the recommendations of an independent consultancy. It also undertook full consultation.

8.80 **Persistent absences.** In Wilson v Post Office 2000 IRLR 834, CA, the Court of Appeal held that the dismissal of an employee for his persistent absences was for SOSR. Although ill health had caused the absences, the employer's reason for dismissal was that W's attendance record did not meet the requirements of the agreed attendance procedure. The tribunal had erred in characterising the reason for dismissal as capability and assessing fairness accordingly.

In Ridge v HM Land Registry EAT 0485/12 the EAT observed that it can be a difficult question whether to classify a dismissal following repeated periods of absence as a capability dismissal or one for SOSR. It advised that if considerations of the employee's capability assessed by reference to skill, aptitude, health or another physical or mental quality are at the forefront of the employer's mind when dismissing the employee, then the reason for dismissal will relate to the capability of the employee for performing work of the kind which he or she was employed to do. If, however, the recurring absences themselves are the reason for dismissal, having triggered the operation of an attendance policy, then the better label may be SOSR, particularly in cases of repeated short-term absence for a variety of reasons.

8.81 For example, in Tagro v Royal Mail Group 2013 NICA 30, Court of Appeal (Northern Ireland), T, a postal worker, was absent several times, triggering all three stages of his employer's attendance procedure. An occupational health provider assessed T and concluded that he had a skin complaint which at times affected his heels and ankles but that he was fit for full work duties. After receiving a stage two warning under the procedure, he sustained a shoulder injury at work. Although his absences continued, he did not proceed to stage three as the attendance procedure did not apply to work injuries. However, after receiving physiotherapy his absences continued, as he was suffering stress and depression. Ultimately he was dismissed after a final stage three hearing, for breaching the attendance procedure. The employer stated that the reason for dismissal was 'conduct' but the Northern Ireland Court of Appeal upheld a tribunal's decision that the breach in fact amounted to SOSR for dismissal and that the dismissal was fair.

Employers should be aware that although dismissals for short but persistent periods of absence may be fair for SOSR, issues may arise under the EqA where the underlying reason for the absences amounts to a disability – see IDS Employment Law Handbook, 'Discrimination at Work' (2012), Chapter 26, 'Dismissal', under 'Dismissal "because of" protected characteristic – disability'.

458

For further discussion of the approach to dismissal for persistent absences, see Chapter 5, 'Ill health', under 'Persistent short-term absences'.

Inappropriate conduct in private capacity. In Abiaefo v Enfield Community **8.82** Care NHS Trust EAT 152/96 the EAT upheld a tribunal's finding that a health visitor was fairly dismissed for SOSR when it was discovered that she had hit her small son with a stick.

Similarly, the fact that an employee has been charged with criminal offences may amount to SOSR. In A v City of Bradford Metropolitan District Council ET Case No.1800011/99 A was suspended after he was investigated and then charged by the police with sexual abuse of children. The Council then dismissed A rather than waste public money on continuing his suspension until the case came to trial. It did not investigate the allegations on the express instructions of the police. A tribunal found A's dismissal fair for SOSR. The decision to dismiss was within the band of reasonable responses; especially given the fact that A's job had brought him into contact with children. And in Pay v Lancashire Probation Service 2004 ICR 187, EAT, the EAT upheld a tribunal's decision that the dismissal of a probation officer responsible for treating sex offenders because of his links to a business involved in sadomasochistic activities was for SOSR under S.98(1) and also fair under S.98(4).

In the above cases the employees' conduct, though carried out in a private **8.83** capacity, was inappropriate, particularly with regard to the areas in which they respectively worked. However, private conduct can amount to SOSR even in circumstances where the nature of the conduct is not necessarily in direct conflict with the employee's working responsibilities, but poses a risk of serious damage to the employer's business or reputation – see 'Protecting employers' interests – preventing reputational damage' above. It is worth noting in this regard that when Pay v Lancashire Probation Service (above) was referred to the European Court of Human Rights, it was held that his dismissal did not breach his right to respect for his private life under Article 8 of the European Convention on Human Rights because his dismissal was justified in view of the sensitive nature of his work with sex offenders – Pay v United Kingdom 2009 IRLR 139, ECtHR.

Genuine but mistaken belief that continued employment would contravene **8.84** **law.** In Hounslow London Borough Council v Klusova 2008 ICR 396, CA, the Court of Appeal held that an employer's genuine but mistaken belief in the unlawfulness of a Russian national's continued employment under immigration rules was SOSR for dismissal. The employer's failure to consult the employee over its concerns as to the lawfulness of her employment or to consider Home Office guidance on immigration checks was not so serious as to evidence a lack of genuine belief in the unlawfulness of her continued employment.

Note that dismissal under S.98(1)(b) because of a genuine but mistaken belief in the lawfulness of continued employment should be distinguished from dismissal under S.98(2)(d) because of the existence of a statutory prohibition that prevents the employee from carrying on in the same job. To rely on a so-called 'statutory ban' as a potentially fair reason for dismissal an employer must show that continued employment of the employee *does in fact* contravene a statutory enactment; genuine belief that this is so is not enough. See further Chapter 7, 'Statutory ban', under 'Establishing the reason'.

8.85 **Imprisonment of employee.** A long prison sentence may amount to a frustrating event that brings the contract to an end automatically – see IDS Employment Law Handbook, 'Contracts of Employment' (2014), Chapter 13, 'Termination by operation of law', under 'Frustration'. However, if a sentence is too short to frustrate the contract, and the employee is dismissed, SOSR can be invoked as the reason for dismissal – Kingston v British Railways Board 1984 ICR 781, CA. The nature of the offence, as well as the length of service, are relevant to the question of whether the dismissal was fair.

In Rangwani v Birmingham Heartlands and Solihull NHS Trust (Teaching) ET Case No.1302910/98 R, a GP, was charged with conspiring to murder his mistress. He was remanded in custody for two months and then released on bail pending his trial. Although R's contract was not frustrated – given his length of service and the employer's failure to investigate how long he was likely to be unavailable for work – a tribunal found that he had been dismissed for SOSR when the employer failed to renew his latest fixed-term contract. It held that patients would be very concerned that the doctor treating them was facing serious criminal charges, allegedly involving the misuse of drugs.

8.86 **Employed couples.** Where a couple are employed together and one partner has been dismissed or has left the employment, the fairness of the dismissal of the remaining partner often depends on the extent to which the job was dependent on the partner who has left. In Kelman v GJ Oram 1983 IRLR 432, EAT, Mr K managed a pub with his wife as assistant. When Mr K was dismissed for stock deficiencies, Mrs K was also dismissed. The EAT agreed with the tribunal's finding that Mr K's dismissal was unfair, but that his wife's dismissal was fair. Her husband's dismissal meant that it was impracticable for her employment to continue and so dismissal was fair for SOSR.

Where a joint contract provides that the dismissal of one partner will automatically result in the dismissal of the other, the employer is under a duty to both partners to investigate any allegations of misconduct. In Scottish and Newcastle Retail Ltd v Stanton and ors EAT 1126/96 the employer failed to investigate Mr S's alleged misconduct and as a result both his dismissal and the dismissal of his wife were unfair. Her dismissal was inexorably linked to her husband's dismissal and the employer was therefore under a duty to Mrs S to investigate the allegation against her husband.

460

In Great Mountain and Tumble Rugby Football Club v Howlett EAT 173/88 **8.87**
Mr and Mrs H were employed as a 'steward and wife to assist' and the contract
stipulated that if one left, the other's contract would also be terminated. The
marriage broke up and, after his wife left, Mr H was dismissed. The tribunal
pointed out that Mrs H's duties were minimal and that her absence would
make little difference to the running of the club. The reason for dismissal – Mrs
H's departure – was not a sufficient reason.

Note that a finding that such a dismissal is fair will not in itself prevent a
tribunal from finding that it nevertheless amounted to sex discrimination or
discrimination on the ground of marital or civil partnership status under the
EqA – see IDS Employment Law Handbook, 'Discrimination at Work' (2012),
Chapter 8, 'Marriage and civil partnership'.

Dismissal to make room for relative in small family business. In Priddle v **8.88**
Dibble 1978 ICR 149, EAT, P, a farm labourer, was dismissed when the
employer wanted his own son to take over. The tribunal found the dismissal
fair for SOSR. It said that P had known from the start of his employment that
the employer's son would eventually work on the farm and that it was natural
and in accordance with farming tradition for D to employ his son with a view
to handing the farm over to him.

Misrepresenting facts affecting employment. If an employee conceals facts or **8.89**
lies about qualifications in order to get a job, this may be SOSR for dismissal.
In Taylor-Pearce v Gwent Health Authority ET Case No.7281/86 T-P obtained
a post as a senior registrar in geriatric medicine after exaggerating his
qualifications. When this was discovered he was dismissed in spite of his claims
that the mistake was made by the typist who typed his curriculum vitae. The
tribunal found dismissal for SOSR and held that it was reasonable to dismiss
having found that T-P had knowingly misstated details about his career.

Similarly, in WH Smith Ltd v Kite EAT 562/95 the EAT held that an employee
could be fairly dismissed for SOSR after he had failed to disclose that he had a
previous conviction. Despite the fact that the company had not asked K whether
he had previous convictions, when it eventually found out, there was a
breakdown in trust and confidence, which, the EAT held, could be a fair reason
for dismissal. See also 'Breakdown in trust and confidence' above.

Erroneous belief that employee has resigned. In Ely v YKK Fasteners (UK) **8.90**
Ltd 1994 ICR 164, CA, the employee informed his employer that he intended
to resign but never in fact did so. A few months later he changed his mind and
said that he would not be leaving after all. The employer, however, insisted that
he had resigned and that his change of heart did not alter this position. The
tribunal held that E had not resigned but had merely given notice of his intention
to resign at some future date. Thus, in informing E that his employment was at
an end, the employer had dismissed him. However, the dismissal was for SOSR

461

and was fair in the circumstances. This decision was upheld on appeal by both the EAT and the Court of Appeal.

A similar argument failed, however, in Harris v Cray Valley Ltd ET Case No.1804985/06. H became engaged over the Christmas break in 2005. She lived in Grimsby and her fiancé lived in Liverpool and it was her intention to sell her house and move to Liverpool. However, she would only move if she was able to sell her house: if she could not sell it, her fiancé might move to Grimsby. Relying on H's stated intention to leave, her employer carried out a reorganisation and her primary duties were reassigned within the company. On 5 June, her employer wrote to her asking her to formalise the details of her leaving date. She was upset by the letter and made it clear that she had not given notice to leave, and did not wish to do so. However, her employer insisted that she leave. A tribunal upheld her claim of unfair dismissal. The tribunal noted that it is possible for a dismissal based on an incorrect assumption that someone had resigned to be a fair dismissal for SOSR, but in this case H had made it clear that she had not resigned before her employer took action to terminate her contract.

8.91 **Dismissal of chief executive following takeover.** In Cobley v Forward Technology Industries plc 2003 ICR 1050, CA, C, the chief executive of FTI plc, was removed from the board of directors following a successful takeover. His position as chief executive was conditional on his remaining a director of the company and he was dismissed accordingly. The Court of Appeal found that his dismissal was for SOSR. The dismissal was fair given C's position and the commercial realities of the situation, of which he had been well aware.

Cobley was followed by the EAT in Mountain Spring Water Co Ltd v Colesby EAT 0855/04. In that case a director of M Ltd, B, was wrongfully excluded from its management and shareholding for long periods of time, during which C effectively ran the company. After court proceedings B was restored to his position as a major shareholder and he then brought a resolution, which was passed, for C to be removed from the office of director of the company. Under the company articles of association, C's employment as an executive director was automatically terminated at the same time as she was removed from the office of director. However, the EAT noted that this did not resolve the issue of whether or not her dismissal was unfair, which depended not on contract law but on S.98 ERA. It concluded that the breakdown in trust and confidence between the company, following the re-establishment of B's shareholding, and C, who had run the company in his absence and been party to the opposition to his court proceedings, was capable of being SOSR and remitted the issue of unfair dismissal for reconsideration by the same tribunal. (See also 'Breakdown in working relations' above.)

8.92 **Refusal to accept stop-and-search policy.** In Trotter v Grattan plc EAT 0179/03 G plc, a large mail order company, introduced a random stop-and-search policy after consultation with the workforce and trade unions. The policy was brought in because the company was worried about theft and about staff storing customer information on mobile phones. T resigned and brought a claim of unfair constructive dismissal because he objected to searches of the body and mobile phones. The tribunal found that the introduction of the policy had been a unilateral variation of T's contract of employment and that there had been a breach of the implied term of trust and confidence entitling him to resign, but held that the (constructive) dismissal was fair. The EAT upheld the tribunal's decision. The 'dismissal', which had been carried out for SOSR, had been reasonable in the circumstances. The policy had been introduced to deter employees from stealing and such policies were common throughout industry. Accordingly, the introduction of the policy had fallen within the band of reasonable responses open to the employer.

Inability to agree rescheduled working hours. In Taylor and ors (partners in **8.93** the Cornerstone Practice) v Crockford EAT 0370/13 the EAT held that a tribunal had not erred in finding that the dismissal of an employee for refusing to agree to a rescheduling of her working hours was a dismissal for SOSR. C worked as a receptionist for a general practice 30 hours a week at agreed times. The partners asked her if she would work another afternoon session but she refused. The partners implemented the new rota anyway as they considered they had a right to do so under her contract. When C did not comply she was dismissed for failing to obey a lawful instruction. A tribunal found that C was dismissed because she and the partners could not agree on the rescheduling of her hours. The EAT upheld its conclusion that given this finding, C's dismissal was for SOSR, not misconduct.

9 Automatically unfair dismissals

Categories of automatically unfair reasons

Different rules applicable to automatically unfair dismissals

Dismissal in connection with jury service

Dismissal for refusing to work on Sunday

Dismissal of employee representatives

Dismissal in connection with right to be accompanied

Dismissal in connection with pensions

Dismissal in connection with tax credits

Dismissal relating to study and training

Appendix – list of automatically unfair reasons for dismissal

Certain reasons for dismissal can be described as 'automatically unfair' in the **9.1** sense that, if one of these reasons is established, the employment tribunal *must* find the dismissal unfair. Claims of ordinary unfair dismissal (i.e. those not based on automatically unfair reasons) require a tribunal to consider: (i) whether the employer's reason for dismissal is one of the potentially fair reasons set out in S.98(1) and (2) of the Employment Rights Act 1996 (ERA); and, if the reason is potentially fair, (ii) whether, in the circumstances of the case, the employer acted reasonably or unreasonably in treating that reason as a sufficient reason for dismissing the employee – S.98(4). However, consideration of the reasonableness of the decision to dismiss is entirely irrelevant when it comes to claims based on any of the statutory provisions that render a dismissal automatically unfair. In such cases, the focus of the tribunal's inquiry will be on establishing, on the evidence, whether the prohibited reason was the reason or principal reason for dismissal. If it was, then there is no option but for the tribunal to find the dismissal unfair.

This chapter starts by considering the categories of automatically unfair reasons for dismissal, a full list of which can be found in the Appendix to this chapter. We then outline the different rules that apply to automatically (as opposed to ordinary) unfair dismissals so far as qualifying for the right to claim, burden of proof and remedies are concerned. Finally, we examine in greater detail those categories of automatically unfair reasons for dismissal that are not dealt with elsewhere in IDS Employment Law Handbooks.

465

9.2 **Categories of automatically unfair reasons**

There are numerous categories of automatically unfair dismissal (subject to various qualifications and exceptions) that emanate from a number of different statutory sources. A full list can be found in the Appendix to this chapter but include:

- dismissal for making a *protected disclosure* – S.103A ERA (see IDS Employment Law Handbook, 'Whistleblowing at Work' (2013), Chapter 6, 'Dismissal', under 'Unfair dismissal')

- dismissal for *asserting a statutory right* – S.104 ERA (see Chapter 11, 'Dismissal for asserting a statutory right')

- dismissal in connection with the entitlement to *paid annual leave and other rights* under the Working Time Regulations 1998 SI 1998/1833 – S.101A ERA (see IDS Employment Law Handbook, 'Working Time' (2013), Chapter 7, 'Enforcement and remedies', under 'Complaints to tribunals – automatically unfair dismissal')

- dismissal in connection with *trade union membership, activities or use of union services* – S.152 Trade Union and Labour Relations (Consolidation) Act 1992 (TULR(C)A) (see IDS Employment Law Handbook, 'Trade Unions' (2013), Chapter 12, 'Unfair dismissal')

- dismissal where there is a *transfer of an undertaking* and the transfer is the reason or principal reason for the dismissal – Reg 7(1) Transfer of Undertakings (Protection of Employment) Regulations 2006 SI 2006/246 (TUPE). Note, however, that if the employer can establish that there is an 'economic, technical or organisational reason entailing changes in the work force' ('an ETO reason') under Reg 7(2), dismissal will not be automatically unfair and the fairness of dismissal will fall to be judged by reference to S.98 ERA (see IDS Employment Law Handbook, 'Transfer of Undertakings' (2011), Chapter 4, 'Unfair dismissal').

9.3 The vast majority of automatically unfair reasons for dismissal are dealt with elsewhere in IDS Employment Law Handbooks. The following categories (which are not dealt with elsewhere) are discussed later in this chapter:

- dismissal in connection with *jury service* – S.98B ERA

- dismissal for *refusing to work on Sunday* – S.101 ERA

- dismissal of an *employee representative or candidate* for the purpose of collective redundancies or a transfer of an undertaking – S.103 ERA

- dismissal in connection with *the right to be accompanied* at disciplinary or grievance hearings – S.12(3) Employment Relations Act 1999

- dismissal of an *occupational pension scheme trustee* in connection with his or her duties in that capacity – S.102 ERA

- dismissal in connection with the information and consultation rights of *occupational or personal pension scheme members* under the Occupational and Personal Pension Schemes (Consultation by Employers and Miscellaneous Amendment) Regulations 2006 SI 2006/349 – para 5, Sch 1 to those Regulations

- dismissal in connection with an employee's *right to be automatically enrolled* in a workplace pension scheme – S.104D ERA

- dismissal in connection with *working tax credits* to which the employee may be entitled – S.104B ERA

- dismissal in connection with the *right to request study and training* – S.104E ERA.

Note that dismissal for an employee's political opinions or affiliation is *not* an **9.4** automatically unfair dismissal, although – unlike most ordinary unfair dismissals – employees dismissed for this reason are not required to show two years' continuous service before they can submit a claim – S.108(4) (see Chapter 2, 'Exclusions from right to claim', in the section 'Continuous service threshold', under 'Exceptions to continuous service threshold – political opinion dismissals').

Future extension of reasons
9.5
The list of automatically unfair reasons for a dismissal has grown substantially in recent years, as most new employment rights are accompanied by a right not to be unfairly dismissed for exercising that right. At the time of writing there is one additional automatically unfair reason for dismissal that has been inserted into the ERA by an Act of Parliament but has not yet been brought into force by a commencement order:

- dismissal of an employee under the age of 18 for exercising, or seeking to exercise, rights to participate in education or training under Ss.27–28 of the Education and Skills Act 2008 – S.101B ERA.

Redundancy dismissals
9.6
In the context of redundancy dismissals, an employee who is dismissed by reason of redundancy will be regarded as having been automatically unfairly dismissed where: (i) the circumstances constituting the redundancy are shown to have applied equally to one or more other employees in the same undertaking who held positions similar to that held by the employee and who have not been dismissed by the employer; and (ii) the reason or principal reason for which the employee was selected for redundancy is one of the reasons set out in S.105(2A)–(7N) – S.105(1) ERA. By virtue of S.153 and para 162 of

467

Schedule A1 TULR(C)A, the same applies to redundancy dismissals in connection with trade union membership; activities or use of union services; trade union recognition; or the securing of bargaining arrangements. The automatically unfair reasons for selection for redundancy set out in the ERA and TULR(C)A are virtually identical to the automatically unfair reasons for dismissal listed in the Appendix, with the exception of:

- the right to be accompanied at a disciplinary or grievance hearing under S.10 of the Employment Relations Act 1999

- a 'spent' conviction within the terms of the Rehabilitation of Offenders Act 1974. (It is arguable, however, that even if the principal reason for dismissal is redundancy, the employee may still be able to claim automatically unfair dismissal. This is because S.4(3)(b) of the 1974 Act provides that 'a conviction which has become spent... shall not be a proper ground for dismissing... a person... *or for prejudicing him in any way* in any occupation or employment' (our stress). If an employer selects an employee for redundancy because of a spent conviction, this is clearly prejudicial and could therefore fall within Reg 4(3)(b))

- a refusal to become an employee shareholder under S.205A ERA

- the right to be accompanied to a meeting to discuss a request to undertake study or training under Reg 16 of the Employee Study and Training (Procedural Requirements) Regulations 2010 SI 2010/155, or

- the transfer of an undertaking (where there is no ETO reason). Note that redundancy, in any event, is likely to amount to an ETO reason under Reg 7(2), meaning that the fairness of dismissal must be judged by reference to S.98 ERA.

9.7 Where selection for redundancy is for any of these reasons, dismissal is not automatically unfair and the ordinary unfair dismissal rules apply (i.e. was the selection reasonable in all the circumstances?). However, if the employee can show that the principal reason for dismissal was not redundancy but one of the five reasons listed directly above, then he or she will be able to claim automatically unfair dismissal.

9.8 Different rules applicable to automatically unfair dismissals

The rationale behind making some reasons for dismissal automatically unfair is a public policy one: there is a sufficient public interest in protecting employees who are dismissed for such reasons. This public policy is also reflected in modifications made to the normal rules that apply to qualifying for the right to claim unfair dismissal, to the availability of interim relief and to the level of compensation that can be recovered, in respect of some (though not all) automatically unfair reasons (see further below).

Note, however, that in all other respects, the normal rules apply. Thus, in Audere Medical Services Ltd v Sanderson EAT 0409/12 the EAT confirmed that as matter of principle there was no reason why a 'Polkey' reduction or a reduction for contributory fault could not be made in cases of automatically unfair dismissal, provided the circumstances warrant it. Polkey reductions and reductions for contributory fault are considered in Chapter 16, 'Compensatory awards: adjustments', under '"Polkey reductions"' and 'Contributory conduct'.

Qualifying service   9.9

Where an employee is dismissed (or selected for redundancy) for an automatically unfair reason, the two-year service requirement for the right to claim unfair dismissal does not apply – S.108 ERA; Ss.154 and 239 TULR(C)A; para 164, Sch A1 TULR(C)A; S.12(4) Employment Relations Act 1999. The two exceptions to this are:

- dismissals because of a spent conviction, and
- dismissals where there is a transfer of an undertaking.

For further discussion, see Chapter 2, 'Exclusions from right to claim', under 'Continuous service threshold – exceptions to continuous service threshold').

Burden of proof   9.10

It is sometimes asserted that, in claims of automatically unfair dismissal, it is for the claimant to prove that the dismissal was for a prohibited reason. But this is not strictly accurate. As with ordinary unfair dismissal, the burden is technically on the employer to show the reason for dismissal. Usually, the employer seeks to discharge this by showing that, where dismissal is admitted, the reason for it was one of the potentially fair reasons under S.98(1) and (2) ERA. It will therefore normally be the employee who argues that the real reason for dismissal was an automatically unfair reason. In these circumstances, the employee acquires an evidential burden to show – without having to prove – that there is an issue which warrants investigation and which is capable of establishing the competing automatically unfair reason that he or she is advancing. However, once the employee satisfies the tribunal that there is such an issue, the burden reverts to the employer, who must prove, on the balance of probabilities, which one of the competing reasons was the principal reason for dismissal – Maund v Penwith District Council 1984 ICR 143, CA.

The Maund case was considered by the Court of Appeal in Kuzel v Roche Products Ltd 2008 ICR 799, CA, where the employee contended that, having rejected the employer's reason for dismissal, the tribunal was compelled to find that the real reason for dismissal was that put forward by the employee, in this

469

case a reason falling within S.103A ERA (protected disclosure). The Court, however, disagreed. If an employer does not show to the satisfaction of a tribunal that the reason for dismissal was the one put forward by the employer, it is open to the tribunal to find that the real reason was that asserted by the employee. But it does not follow, as a matter of either law or logic, that the tribunal *must* find that, if the reason was not that put forward by the employer, then it must have been that asserted by the employee. It may be open to the tribunal to find that, on a consideration of all the evidence in the particular case, the true reason for dismissal was not advanced by either side.

9.11 The Kuzel case was followed in Marshall v Game Retail Ltd EAT 0276/13, where the claimant was dismissed as redundant days before the company in which he was employed was transferred. He argued that he had in fact been automatically unfairly dismissed for a reason connected with the transfer but his claim was rejected by the employment tribunal. On appeal, the EAT held that the employment judge had failed to apply the principle in Kuzel, which had the effect that, once the claimant had produced some evidence in support of his or her case, the burden lay on the employer to establish that the reason for the dismissal was not the automatically unfair reason. The judge had imposed a higher burden on the claimant and had rejected his case on the basis that he had not discharged the evidential burden. The case was therefore remitted to the same tribunal to reconsider.

In Nunn v Royal Mail Group Ltd 2011 ICR 162, EAT, the EAT observed that 'in discrimination claims, there is clearly a necessity to exercise a degree of care in relation to the establishment of primary facts. In order to set up the shifting burden of proof, the court is urged to look carefully in relation to what inferences can be drawn from those facts, particularly as the basic information will often be in the hands of the employer rather than the employee.' However, in automatically unfair dismissal claims (as with ordinary unfair dismissal claims), 'the burden is on the employer, there being no need for the employee to set up sufficient facts for that burden to exist. Obviously, a tribunal, in assessing what reasons the employer is putting forward, will have in mind what the employee is saying about the reason, and will need to test the employer's witnesses in relation to those matters that point to a reason other than that that the employee is putting forward. But, at the end of the day, it is a matter for the tribunal to come to a view as to whether, on the balance of probabilities, the employer has satisfied them as to the reason.'

9.12 There is one important qualification to the above. Where the employee lacks the requisite continuous service to claim ordinary unfair dismissal (i.e. two years), he or she will acquire the burden of proving, on the balance of probabilities, that the reason for dismissal was an automatically unfair reason – Smith v Hayle Town Council 1978 ICR 996, CA, and Ross v Eddie Stobart Ltd EAT 0068/13.

Interim relief

Interim relief is an emergency interlocutory procedure designed to ensure the preservation of the status quo – i.e. the employee's employment – pending the hearing of the unfair dismissal complaint. It is governed by Ss.128–132 ERA and is available in respect of the following categories of automatically unfair dismissal:

- dismissal related to the carrying out of designated health and safety activities (S.100(1)(a) ERA)

- dismissal in connection with the performance of functions as a health and safety representative or member of a safety committee (S.100(1)(b) ERA)

- dismissal in connection with the performance of functions or activities as a working time representative or as a candidate for such a role (S.101A(d) ERA)

- dismissal in connection with the performance of functions as a trustee of a relevant occupational pension scheme (S.102(1) ERA)

- dismissal in connection with candidature or performance of functions or activities as an employee representative for the purposes of consultation on collective redundancies or proposed transfer of an undertaking (S.103 ERA)

- dismissal related to the making of a protected disclosure (S.103A ERA)

- dismissal related to trade union blacklists (S.104F ERA)

- dismissal in connection with the statutory right to be accompanied at a disciplinary or grievance hearing – S.12(5) Employment Relations Act 1999

- dismissal in connection with an employee's right to be accompanied at a meeting to consider a request to enter into study or training – Reg 18(5) Employee Study and Training (Procedural Requirements) Regulations 2010 SI 2010/155

- dismissal related to trade union membership, activities or use of union services – S.161(1) TULR(C)A

- dismissal for an impermissible reason connected with the statutory trade union recognition procedures (para 161(2), Sch A1 TULR(C)A).

It should be noted that interim relief is not available in cases of *selection for* **9.14** *redundancy* for any of the above reasons. This is because the availability of interim relief hinges on the *reason* for dismissal. In a case where an employee claims to have been selected for redundancy due to an automatically unfair reason, the reason for dismissal remains redundancy – see McConnell and anor v Bombardier Aerospace/Short Brothers plc (No.2) 2009 IRLR 201, NICA.

Full details of the interim relief procedure are provided in Chapter 17, 'Additional awards and interim relief', under 'Interim relief'.

9.15 Compensation for automatically unfair dismissals
Special rules governing the basic and compensatory awards apply to some automatically unfair dismissals.

9.16 Basic award. In certain cases of automatically unfair dismissal, a minimum basic award applies – S.120 ERA. There are three different levels of minimum basic award depending on the reason for dismissal.

In respect of dismissals (or selection for redundancy) relating to:

- the carrying out of designated health and safety activities (S.100(1)(a))
- the performance of functions as a health and safety representative or member of a safety committee (S.100(1)(b))
- the performance of functions as an employee representative under the Working Time Regulations 1998 or as a candidate for such a role (S.101A(d))
- the performance of the functions of an occupational pension trustee (S.102(1))
- the performance of the functions of an employee representative (or candidate) for the purposes of consultation on collective redundancies or proposed transfer of an undertaking (S.103)

there is a minimum basic award of £5,807 (as from 6 April 2015) – S.120(1).

In respect of dismissals relating to trade union blacklists under S.104F there is a minimum basic award of £5,000 (as from 2 March 2010) – S.120(1C). For further details, see Chapter 13, 'Basic awards', under 'Calculation of basic award'.

9.17 Compensatory award. Section 124(1) ERA imposes a statutory cap on compensatory awards for unfair dismissal of £78,335 (as of 6 April 2015) or a year's pay, whichever is the lower. However, S.124(1) does not apply where the reason for the dismissal was that the employee:

- carried out or proposed to carry out activities in connection with preventing or reducing risks to health and safety at work, having been designated by the employer to do so (S.100 ERA)
- performed or proposed to perform the functions of a health and safety representative, or member of a safety committee, either in accordance with arrangements established by statute or after being recognised as such by the employer (S.100(1)(b))
- made a protected disclosure (S.103A), or
- was selected for redundancy and the reason for selection was one of the above reasons (S.105(3) and (6A)) – S.124(1A).

Where S.124(1A) applies, there is no limit on the amount of compensatory award that can be awarded. For further details, see Chapter 14, 'Compensatory awards: types of loss', under 'Nature and maximum amount of award – exceptions to statutory limit'.

The general rules relating to calculation of the compensatory award are **9.18** discussed in Chapter 14, 'Compensatory awards: types of loss'; Chapter 15, 'Compensatory awards: pension loss'; and Chapter 16, 'Compensatory awards: adjustments'.

Dismissal in connection with jury service
9.19

Section 98B(1) ERA provides that an employee will be regarded as unfairly dismissed if the reason (or, if more than one, the principal reason) for the dismissal is that he or she has been summoned to attend for jury service under the Juries Act 1974, Part 1 of the Coroners and Justice Act 2009, the Court of Session Act 1988 or the Criminal Procedure (Scotland) Act 1995, or has been absent from work because he or she attended court in pursuance of being so summoned.

The employee will, however, lose the protection of S.98B(1) if the employer shows that: (a) the circumstances were such that the employee's absence in pursuance of being so summoned was likely to cause substantial injury to the employer's undertaking; (b) the employer brought those circumstances to the attention of the employee; (c) the employee refused or failed to apply to the appropriate officer for excusal from, or a deferral of, the obligation to attend court; and (d) the refusal or failure was not reasonable – S.98B(2). The 'appropriate officer' for these purposes is defined in S.98B(3), although in practice the officer will usually be identified in the letter accompanying the summons for jury service.

Two contrasting examples of claims brought under S.98B: **9.20**

- **Sullivan v Vitamatic Ltd** ET Case No.3203494/09: S began employment with V Ltd in May. In July she informed the company that she was going to require six to eight weeks' sick leave to recover from planned major surgery and at least two weeks off in December to attend jury service. When asked whether she would be able to defer the jury service, she replied that she had already done so and did not think she could again. V Ltd told her that while it could cope with her absence on sick leave, her time off for jury service would be problematic because another member of staff would be on holiday at the same time. The following week she was dismissed because of poor performance and the company's inability to cover her sickness absence. The tribunal upheld S's claim for automatically unfair dismissal under S.98B. It was satisfied that S's performance was not the reason for her dismissal.

473

Rather it was the combination of her absence from work for her operation, together with her absence in December at a crucial time when another member of staff was going to be away. The tribunal found that without the absence in December, S would not have been dismissed. Therefore, the fact that she had been summoned for jury service was the principal reason for her dismissal. The tribunal was entirely satisfied that V Ltd was aware that this was not a permissible reason for dismissal. That was why it was careful not to mention it in the dismissal letter and why it was careful to put forward a number of other reasons for its decision to dismiss

- **Bell v Annis t/a A-Line Coaches** ET Case No.2505599/08: in January B received a summons to serve on a jury from 25 February, which stated that the penalty for failing to attend could be a fine of £1,000. The summons also stated that an application could be made to be excused from jury service or for it to be postponed. B's employer told him that it might not be able to release him from duty in February due to staff shortages. In addition, it had released him for jury service only the year before. It prepared a letter for B requesting that he be excused from jury service, which he signed and posted on his way home from work. Two days later he resigned, saying that he had signed the letter under duress, knowing that he risked a fine and/or a prison sentence. An employment tribunal dismissed his claim for automatically unfair constructive dismissal. B's employer was entitled to ask him to apply not to undertake jury service in February. There were legitimate business reasons for this, which had been made known to B. Any pressure applied was not unreasonable or inappropriate. B knew, or ought to have known, that he was not at risk of being fined or imprisoned. And if his application to defer jury service was not accepted, there was no evidence that his employment would have been terminated.

9.21 Dismissal for refusing to work on Sunday

The provisions relating to Sunday trading that were previously contained in the Sunday Trading Act 1994 and the Betting, Gaming and Lotteries Act 1963 (as amended by Schedule 8 to the Deregulation and Contracting Out Act 1994) are now contained in the ERA. Initially these provisions applied only to England and Wales. However, they were extended to Scotland from 6 April 2004 by the Sunday Working (Scotland) Act 2003.

The purpose of the Sunday trading provisions is to safeguard the employment rights of shop and betting workers who object to working on Sunday. To that end, the ERA provides that shop or betting workers who enjoy 'protected' or 'opted-out' status have the right to refuse to do Sunday work and any agreement or provision of an employment contract is unenforceable in so far as it requires the employee to work on a Sunday – Ss.37 and 43. The employee also has the right not to suffer any detriment as a result of refusing to work on a Sunday – S.45. Furthermore, any dismissal for a refusal or threatened refusal to do Sunday work is deemed to be automatically unfair – S.101.

9.22 Under S.101 ERA, an employee is deemed to have been unfairly dismissed, regardless of his or her length of service, if:

- the employee is a shop worker or a betting worker

- he or she enjoys 'protected' or 'opted-out' status

- the reason or principal reason for the dismissal is that the employee refused, or was threatening to refuse, to work on Sundays or on a particular Sunday. (So far as 'opted-out' workers are concerned, this only applies in respect of Sundays falling three months after service of the opting-out notice.)

These requirements are considered in turn below.

Note that additional unfair dismissal protection is provided for a shop worker or betting worker who has given, or proposes to give, his or her employer an opting-out notice. Such an employee can claim automatically unfair dismissal under S.103(3) if this is the principal reason for dismissal. This is discussed further under 'Reason for dismissal' below.

'Shop' and 'betting' workers
9.23 In order to benefit from the protection of S.101, an employee must be either a 'shop worker' or a 'betting worker' as defined by Ss.232 and 233 ERA. Other workers are not covered.

9.24 **Shop workers.** A 'shop worker' is an employee who, under his or her contract of employment, is or may be required to do shop work – S.232(1). 'Shop work' is defined in S.232(2) as 'work in or about a shop... on a day on which the shop is open for the serving of customers'. S.232(3) states that a 'shop' includes any premises where any retail trade or business is carried on. 'Retail trade or business' includes the business of a barber or hairdresser, the business of hiring goods other than for use in the course of a trade or business, and retail sales by auction. However, it does not include catering businesses – i.e. the sale of meals, refreshments or intoxicating liquor for consumption on the premises on which they are sold, or the sale of meals or refreshments prepared to order for immediate consumption off the premises – or the sale of programmes, catalogues and similar items at theatres or other places of amusement – S.232(6) and (7).

It is clear from the wording of the statutory provisions that the definition of 'shop worker' extends beyond workers who are directly involved in serving customers (such as sales assistants and checkout operators). During the committee stage of the Sunday Trading Bill, the Minister (Mr Peter Lloyd) said that the definition of shop work and, consequently, shop workers, would include 'cleaners, storemen, shelf-fillers and trolley supervisors... The definition would also include clerical workers at the back or above the shop or doing

475

work related to the shop. Staff of the shop and staff cafeterias and managers on or about the premises would also be covered... van drivers based at the store, who deliver goods to customers, would also be included. In fact, all those whose work is connected with and for a shop that decides to open on a Sunday will be covered' (Hansard, 9 February 1994, vol.237, cols.297–298).

9.25 The Minister's statement suggests that, while the definition of 'shop worker' should be construed broadly, it is necessary for the employee who claims to be a shop worker actually to be based at the store in question or to do a substantial amount of work at the store when it is open for serving customers. It is clear that a delivery driver taking goods from the store to customers may be a shop worker, but what of the delivery driver who brings goods to the store from a warehouse? In Williams v Asda Stores Ltd EAT 306/96 the claimant was employed by Asda as an HGV driver. He worked from a regional distribution centre. His HGV was loaded by warehouse staff at the distribution centre and he then drove to various Asda stores to make deliveries. The claimant was involved in unloading the goods at the stores and occasionally in transporting goods from one Asda store to another. He claimed that his work amounted to work 'in or about a shop' within the meaning of S.232(2). The employment tribunal looked to the statements of the Minister set out above, but also noted that the Minister had stated that he did not think that the definition of shop work covered drivers working for another company who deliver goods to a store but who do not work at or around the store. The tribunal could not see how the definition could exclude those working for a third party delivering to a store but include those working for the employer delivering to the store. On that basis, the tribunal found that the claimant was not a shop worker. The EAT, in effect, upheld that conclusion following an appeal by the claimant against the tribunal's subsequent decision that he had not been dismissed for asserting a statutory right. In dismissing the appeal, the EAT held that the claimant did not have statutory protection in respect of refusing to undertake Sunday working because he was not a shop worker as defined.

As noted above, S.232(3) provides that a 'shop' includes any premises where any retail trade or business is carried on. The term is not restricted to traditional high street type stores and can include, for example, car repairers – see Rafiq v National Tyres Ltd ET Case No.5200977/99. In Horler and ors v Makro Self Service Wholesalers Ltd ET Case No.42131/95 a tribunal had to decide whether a wholesale cash-and-carry business fell within that definition. The employer pointed out that there were restrictions on who could buy goods at the company's premises. Transactions could only be carried out on production of a 'Makro Tradecard' and individuals had to be registered under a business name and produce identification in order to obtain such a card. Invoices were issued in the name of the business and payment had to be made either by the person named on the card or by company cheque. However, the tribunal noted that in practice a large proportion of the public were able to obtain cards. Any of the cardholders – of whom there were some 200,000 – could make a purchase and any of their friends could come in as guests and arrange for purchases to be made for them by the cardholder. Many of the goods offered for sale were particularly suitable for customers' own personal use or consumption and the store turned a blind eye to the purposes for which the goods were bought. In those circumstances, it was impossible to regard the store as anything other than an operation that included a significant proportion of retail sales. The tribunal concluded that the Sunday trading provisions applied.

However, the opposite conclusion was reached in Markall v Automobile **9.26** Association ET Case No.2404839/99, where the claimant was employed by the AA to answer telephone calls from members about membership services. The tribunal rejected her claim that she was a shop worker because, although she was clearly involved in selling and had sales targets to meet, that was not a sufficient basis for concluding that she worked in a shop. The ordinary and everyday meaning of 'shop' did not extend to the premises in which the claimant worked and AA members would not for a moment consider that they were telephoning a shop when they rang to make enquiries about their membership.

Specific statutory provision is made in respect of premises that are used mainly for purposes other than those of retail trade or business and would not (apart from S.232(3)) be regarded as a shop. In these circumstances, only that part of the premises which is used wholly or mainly for the purposes of retail trade or business, or wholly or mainly for the purposes of both retail trade or business and wholesale trade, is to be regarded as a shop – S.232(4). 'Wholesale trade' means the sale of goods for use or resale in the course of a business or the hire of goods for use in the course of a business – S.232(5). This provision precludes the possibility that the whole of a church or museum, for example, might be defined as a shop merely because there is a gift shop on the premises.

Betting workers. Betting workers as defined in S.233 ERA are also covered by **9.27** the Sunday trading provisions. A 'betting worker' is an employee who, under his or her contract of employment, is or may be required to do betting work – S.233(1). 'Betting work' is defined as work at a track for a bookmaker on a day on which the bookmaker acts as such at the track, being work which consists of or includes dealing with betting transactions, and work in a licensed betting office on a day on which the office is open for use for the effecting of betting transactions – S.233(2). 'Betting transactions' includes the collection or payment of winnings – S.233(3).

Sunday work must involve shop work or betting work. Under S.101(1), the **9.28** dismissal must be caused by the employee's refusal to do 'shop work' or 'betting work' on Sunday. As noted above, 'shop work' is defined in S.232(2) as 'work in or about a shop… on a day on which the shop is open for the serving of customers'. It follows that an employee will not be protected against dismissal, even though he or she is employed as a shop worker throughout the week, if

477

the work that he or she is asked to do on a Sunday takes place when the shop is closed to customers. This would cover work such as shelf-stacking, stocktaking or other activities that take place when the shop is not open to the public. In Sands v Donlan ET Case No.3226/95 S was employed in the greetings cards section of a shop. She was asked to work on a Sunday in preparation for Christmas sales. The shop was not going to be open for the serving of customers on that day. S refused and was dismissed. A tribunal found that the principal reason for her dismissal was her refusal to work on the Sunday in question. However, the work that S was being asked to do on that Sunday was not 'shop work', as the shop would not be open to the public. Consequently, S had not been dismissed because of a refusal to do shop work on a Sunday and her dismissal was not automatically unfair.

9.29 **Protected and opted-out status**
Only 'protected' or 'opted-out' shop and betting workers are covered by the unfair dismissal provisions in S.101. Essentially, a protected worker is a worker who was already employed as a shop or betting worker (but not solely to work on Sunday) when the Sunday trading provisions came into force, or a worker who cannot be contractually required to work on Sundays. An opted-out worker is a worker who has given his or her employer a written notice opting out of Sunday work.

9.30 **Protected status.** Under S.36(3) ERA any shop or betting worker will be a 'protected' worker if, under the terms of his or her contract, he or she is not and cannot be required to work on Sundays, and could not be required to do so even if Part IV of the ERA (which deals with Sunday working) were disregarded. This provision applies regardless of whether the employee was in employment at the 'relevant commencement date' (as to which see below). An employer's right to require an employee to work on Sunday is a question of construction of the relevant contract of employment.

Alternatively, a shop or betting worker in England and Wales (but not Scotland) will have protected status if he or she meets the following criteria (which in effect apply only to long-serving employees):

- the worker must have been in employment as a shop/betting worker on the day before the 'relevant commencement date' – S.36(2)(a). (The relevant commencement date is 26 August 1994 for shop workers and 3 January 1995 for betting workers – i.e. the respective dates on which the Sunday Trading Act 1994 and Schedule 8 to the Deregulation and Contracting Out Act 1994 came into force)

- on that day, he or she must not have been employed to work only on Sunday – S.36(2)(a)

478

- the worker must have been continuously employed during the period beginning with the day before the relevant commencement date and ending with the 'appropriate date' – S.36(2)(b). (The appropriate date means the effective date of termination for the purposes of S.101–101(4))

- he or she must have been a shop/betting worker throughout that period of continuous employment, or throughout every part of it during which his or her relations with the employer were governed by a contract of employment – S.36(2)(c).

Scotland is expressly excluded from the scope of S.36(2) by S.244(2) ERA.

Section 36(4), which again only applies to England and Wales, deems an **9.31** employee to be a protected worker for the purposes of S.36(2)(a), despite the fact that the employment relationship had ceased by the day before the relevant commencement date, if:

- the employee's continuity of employment was preserved at the commencement date by virtue of S.212(3) or S.219 ERA (absence by reason of sickness, temporary cessation of work or arrangement or custom, or absence pending the reinstatement/re-engagement of a dismissed employee), and

- when the employment relationship ceased, that employee was a shop worker or betting worker and was not employed to work only on Sunday.

Opted-out status. Section 40 ERA provides that an 'opted-out' shop or betting **9.32** worker is an employee who:

- under his or her contract of employment, is or may be required to work on Sunday (whether or not as a result of previously giving an opting-in notice – see 'Loss of protected or opted-out status – opting in' below), but who is not employed to work only on Sunday; and

- who has given his or her employer a signed and dated notice stating in writing that he or she objects to Sunday working (an 'opting-out notice').

To satisfy the statutory requirements, the worker must have been in continuous employment as a shop or betting worker during the period beginning with the day on which the opting-out notice was given and ending with the effective date of termination of the contract – Ss.41(1) and 101(4). Opted-out shop or betting workers do not obtain the unfair dismissal protection afforded by S.101 (for refusing to work on Sunday) in respect of any Sunday falling within the three-month period after the opting-out notice was served – Ss.41(3) and 101(2). Note, however, that this three-month 'waiting period' does not apply to the unfair dismissal protection afforded by S.101(3) (i.e. unfair dismissal for giving, or proposing to give, an opting-out notice). Therefore, an employee who refuses to work Sundays, serves an opting-out notice and is dismissed two months later can claim automatically unfair dismissal contrary to S.101(3), but

479

not S.101(1), unless he or she is dismissed for *proposing* to refuse to work on Sundays or a particular Sunday once the three months have expired.

9.33 An employer has a duty under S.42 to provide any shop or betting worker who is or may be required under his or her contract of employment to work on Sunday (whether or not as a result of previously giving an opting-in notice – see 'Loss of protected or opted-out status – opting in' below), but who is not employed to work only on Sunday, with a statement in the prescribed statutory form explaining the employee's right to opt out of Sunday work and the consequences of such action, including the right not to be dismissed as a result of opting out – see S.42(4). The statement must be provided within two months of the worker becoming a shop or betting worker to whom this section applies. Failure to comply with this requirement has the effect, where the employee has given an opting-out notice, of reducing the three-month notice period specified in S.41(3), during which the worker cannot claim the protection of S.101 against unfair dismissal, to one month – S.42(2). However, an employer will not be treated as having failed to comply if the employee serves the opting-out notice within two months of becoming entitled to receive the statutory statement – S.42(3).

9.34 **Loss of protected or opted-out status – opting in.** A shop or betting worker will lose protected status if he or she gives the employer an 'opting-in notice' and, after giving that notice, makes an 'express agreement' with the employer to do shop or betting work on Sunday or on a particular Sunday – S.36(5). Similarly, under S.41(2) an opted-out shop or betting worker loses that status if he or she gives the employer an 'opting-in notice' after previously giving an opting-out notice, and then expressly agrees to do shop work or betting work on Sunday or a particular Sunday.

An opting-in notice for the above purposes is a written notice, signed and dated by the worker, in which he or she expressly states that he or she wishes to work on Sunday or does not object to Sunday working – S.36(6). An 'express agreement' is not defined, however. It would seem to encompass verbal as well as written agreements: an employee who voluntarily turns up for work on a particular Sunday pursuant to a request made by the employer might, therefore, be regarded as having given 'express agreement'. This is in contrast to the prior opting-in notice, which must always be in writing.

9.35 Once a worker becomes opted in, he or she will lose the specific protection of S.101 and will only reacquire it if he or she serves a further opting-out notice and waits three months.

9.36 ## Reason for dismissal

The circumstances in which shop and betting workers are protected against dismissal for refusing to work on a Sunday are listed in S.101. This provides that dismissal will be automatically unfair where:

480

- the employee is a protected shop worker or betting worker, or an opted-out shop or betting worker, and the reason for the dismissal (or, if more than one, the principal reason) is that the employee refused or proposed to refuse to do shop or betting work on Sunday or on a particular Sunday – S.101(1), or

- the employee is a shop worker or a betting worker and the reason or principal reason for dismissal is that he or she gave, or proposed to give, an opting-out notice to the employer – S.101(3).

Selection for redundancy. The dismissal of an employee who is selected for **9.37** redundancy on either of the above grounds is also automatically unfair if the principal reason for the dismissal is that the employee was redundant but the redundancy situation applied equally to one or more other employees who held similar positions in the same undertaking and who were not dismissed – S.105(1) and (4).

Principal reason for dismissal – showing causation. An employee who claims **9.38** that he or she has been dismissed either for refusing (or proposing to refuse) to do shop/betting work on a Sunday, or because he or she gave (or proposed to give) an opting-out notice, will need to show that the refusal or giving of notice was actually the reason or, if there was more than one, the principal reason for dismissal. A 'principal reason' is the reason that operated in the employer's mind at the time of dismissal – per Lord Denning MR in Abernethy v Mott, Hay and Anderson 1974 ICR 323, CA. If, on the evidence, a tribunal concludes that the objection to Sunday working or the serving of an opt-out notice was not the main reason for dismissal, the dismissal will not be automatically unfair. In these circumstances, if the employee has sufficient continuous service to claim ordinary unfair dismissal, the tribunal may go on to consider whether the dismissal was, in any event, unfair under S.98 ERA.

Two contrasting examples:

- **Thompson v Benny Dee (Wood Green) Ltd** EAT 637/98: T, who worked in a shop, voluntarily agreed to work some Sundays if required. When she asked for a Saturday off, the employer acceded to her request but placed her on the rota to work on the Sunday. When she asked if she could have that day off as well, she was told that it would be difficult but was not given a final answer. Her name remained on the rota for the Sunday but, without checking the rota again, she left work on the Friday and returned on the Monday morning. A disciplinary meeting was held at which T would only say that the employer had known she was not coming in on the Sunday. At the end of the meeting, she handed an envelope to the employer containing an opt-out notice and verbally stated that she was a Christian and did not want to work on Sundays. T was advised to return the following day, having given further thought to her absence on the Sunday. She arrived 20 minutes late, only to make it clear that she had nothing to add to what she had already said. She was then dismissed. On her claim for unfair dismissal, the employment tribunal found that the service of the opting-out notice was intended as a tactic to put pressure on the employer, but that she had not been dismissed by reason of serving the notice. Rather, her dismissal was because of her non-attendance on a Sunday when she was rostered to work. As she lacked the necessary qualifying service to claim ordinary unfair dismissal under S.98, her claim was dismissed. On appeal, the EAT upheld the tribunal's reasoning, confirming that T had not been dismissed for serving a notice opting out of Sunday working

- **Gregory v Park Garden Centre t/a Almondsbury Garden Centre** ET Case No.1402255/03: G began working for the employer as a trainee assistant manager in July 2002. He was appraised in September 2002 and told that the employer was impressed with his work. No issues were raised as to his capability. He generally worked from Friday to Tuesday, having Wednesday and Thursday off. However, his wife worked from Monday to Friday, and their working patterns put a strain on their relationship. On 25 May 2003 G wrote to the employer saying that he had decided to exercise his right to object to working on Sundays, but by way of compromise offered to work every second Sunday. The employer did not reply formally to his letter, but on 29 June he was summoned to a meeting where he was summarily dismissed but given a month's pay in lieu of notice. The employer claimed that G had never shown competence in his job and he was dismissed summarily to avoid his accruing the right to claim unfair dismissal. On his claim for automatically unfair dismissal, a tribunal held that G was dismissed because he had exercised his right to opt out of Sunday working. The dismissal was therefore automatically unfair.

9.39 **Refusal to work on Sunday.** It would appear that the reference in S.101(1) to an employee's 'refusal' to work on a Sunday should be construed fairly broadly. In Gasking v The Sweater Shop plc ET Case No.65065/94, for example, G was employed as a supervisor in a shop. She qualified as a protected shop worker because she had been in employment on the day before the Sunday Trading Act 1994 came into force. Initially, G's employer required her to work every third Sunday. She was subsequently asked to work every Sunday but, after a few months working under the new arrangement, she expressed a wish to work on alternate Sundays instead. After receiving no response to her request, G said that she would prefer to be demoted to sales assistant rather than continue to work every Sunday. Shortly afterwards, she was dismissed. The tribunal had to decide whether the dismissal came about because G 'refused (or proposed to refuse) to do shop work… on Sunday or on a particular Sunday'. In the tribunal's view, it was necessary to adopt a broad construction of the verb 'to refuse'. 'To refuse' meant 'to deny, to decline, to reject'. On that basis, the tribunal decided that a willingness to be demoted rather than to work every Sunday could amount to a refusal to work on Sunday.

482

The tribunal went on to find on the facts that it was G's refusal to work on a Sunday that was the reason or principal reason for her dismissal. It rejected the employer's argument that the real reason for the dismissal was that G was unsuitable for the post of supervisor and that there was no other position available for her in the store. In particular, the tribunal noted that G had received no warnings about her performance; she had been dismissed shortly after making the request for demotion; and the employer had given a number of evasive responses when G's mother enquired as to the reason for the dismissal.

Religious discrimination. It should be noted that a provision, criterion or **9.40** practice that staff must work on a Sunday could, in the absence of objective justification, amount to indirect discrimination on the grounds of religion or belief – see further IDS Employment Law Handbook, 'Atypical and Flexible Working' (2014), Chapter 4, 'Flexible working', under 'Discrimination claims – religious employees'.

Dismissal of employee representatives 9.41

Section 103 ERA provides that an employee will be regarded as unfairly dismissed if the reason (or, if more than one, the principal reason) for the dismissal is that the employee, being an employee representative for the purposes of collective consultation on redundancies or transfers of undertakings, or a candidate in an election for such representatives, performed or proposed to perform any functions or activities as such an employee representative or candidate.

It is also automatically unfair to select an employee representative (or candidate) for redundancy on these grounds where the reason (or principal reason) for the dismissal was redundancy but the redundancy situation applied equally to one or more other employees in the same undertaking who held positions similar to the employee and who were not dismissed – S.105(1) and (6).

Identifying employee representatives. Section 103 applies to persons who **9.42** are 'employee representatives' for the purposes of Chapter II of Part IV TULR(C)A (in the case of redundancy consultation) and for the purposes of Regs 9, 13 and 14 of the Transfer of Undertakings (Protection of Employment) Regulations 2006 SI 2006/246 (TUPE) (in the case of transfers of undertakings). So far as redundancy consultation is concerned, S.196 TULR(C)A provides that persons are 'employee representatives' if:

- they have been elected by employees for the specific purpose of being consulted by their employer about dismissals it has proposed, or

- having been elected or appointed by employees (whether before or after dismissals have been proposed by their employer) otherwise than for that specific purpose, *it is appropriate*, having regard to the purposes for which

483

they were elected, for the employer to consult them about the proposed dismissals. (It is interesting to note that different wording to that highlighted in italics has been adopted in the TUPE consultation provisions – compare with the italicised wording below.)

In either case, they must be employed by the employer when they are elected (or appointed). The collective redundancy consultation provisions are contained in Ss.188–198 TULR(C)A and are discussed in detail in IDS Employment Law Handbook, 'Redundancy' (2011), Chapter 12, 'Collective redundancies'.

9.43 So far as consultation under the TUPE Regulations is concerned, the meaning of 'employee representatives' is similar, but not identical. Under Reg 13 (which concerns the duty to inform and consult upon the transfer of an undertaking), 'employee representatives' are whichever of the following employee representatives the employer chooses:

- employee representatives appointed or elected by the affected employees otherwise than for the purposes of Reg 13, who (having regard to the purposes for, and the method by which they were appointed or elected) *have authority from those employees* (compare with the italicised wording in the redundancy consultation provisions set out above) to receive information and to be consulted about the transfer on their behalf – Reg 13(2)(b).

- employee representatives elected by any affected employees, for the purposes of this Regulation, in an election satisfying the requirements of Reg 14(1).

The provisions relating to consultation on the transfer of an undertaking, contained in Regs 13 and 14 TUPE Regulations, are discussed in IDS Employment Law Handbook, 'Transfer of Undertakings' (2011), Chapter 8, 'Information and consultation'.

9.44 The concept of 'employee representative' is also relevant for the purposes of Reg 9 of the TUPE Regulations, which permits employees' terms and conditions of employment to be varied where the transferor is subject to certain insolvency proceedings. The permitted variations must be agreed between the transferor, transferee and 'appropriate representatives'. In essence, these are union representatives if there is a recognised independent trade union or, if there is no recognised trade union, employee representatives who have been elected either specifically for the purposes of Reg 9 or for other purposes provided they have authority to agree changes to contracts of employment on behalf of employees (Reg 9(2) and (3)) – see further IDS Employment Law Handbook, 'Transfer of Undertakings' (2011), Chapter 6, 'Transfer of insolvent companies', under 'Relevant insolvency proceedings – changing terms and conditions'.

9.45 **Trade union representatives not covered.** It is worth bearing in mind that under the relevant provisions employers *must consult with union representatives* about collective redundancies/transfers of undertakings if there is a recognised trade union. Only if there is no recognised union are they required to consult with employee representatives, as defined above. Trade union representatives involved in redundancy/TUPE consultations do not fall within S.103/105 ERA. They will however, be covered by Ss.152 and 153 TULR(C)A, which provide protection from automatically unfair dismissal/redundancy for, among other things, taking part in trade union activities – see IDS Employment Law Handbook, 'Trade Unions' (2013), Chapter 12, 'Unfair dismissal'.

Minimum basic award and interim relief. The dismissal of an employee **9.46** representative is one of the dismissals to which the minimum basic award provided for in S.120(1) ERA (currently £5,807) applies – see 'Different rules applicable to automatically unfair dismissals – compensation for automatically unfair dismissals' above. Such dismissals also allow the claimant to apply for interim relief – see 'Different rules applicable to automatically unfair dismissals – interim relief' above.

Dismissal in connection with right to be accompanied

9.47

Section 10 of the Employment Relations Act 1999 affords a worker the right to be accompanied by a colleague or trade union official to any disciplinary or grievance hearing. The worker's companion is not restricted to merely taking notes: for instance, he or she can put the worker's case to the panel and respond on the worker's behalf to any view expressed at the hearing – S.10(2B). For further details, see Chapter 4, 'Capability and qualifications', under 'Procedural factors – hearing', and Chapter 6, 'Conduct', under 'Disciplinary proceedings – right to be accompanied'.

To ensure that workers are not dissuaded from exercising their rights under S.10 for fear of reprisals from their employer, S.12(3) provides that an employee will be treated as having been automatically unfairly dismissed if the reason (or, if more than one, the principal reason) for the dismissal was that:

- he or she exercised or sought to exercise the right to be accompanied under S.10, or

- he or she accompanied or sought to accompany another worker (whether of the same employer or not) pursuant to a request under that section.

However, selection for redundancy on the above grounds will not be **9.48** automatically unfair – see 'Categories of automatically unfair reasons – redundancy dismissals' above.

Interim relief is available for claimants pursuing a claim of automatically unfair dismissal under S.12(3) – see 'Different rules applicable to automatically unfair dismissals – interim relief' above.

485

9.49 Although the right to be accompanied has now been in place for over a decade, there has been very little litigation under S.12(3). However, in Evans v Open Sight ET Case No.3100599/11 an employment tribunal found that an employee who was dismissed at a three-month probationary review meeting shortly after representing a colleague at a disciplinary hearing and at a time when she was making preparations to represent two more colleagues at similar hearings, had been automatically unfairly dismissed under S.12(3). In reaching this conclusion, the tribunal relied in part on the fact that the employer had engaged in correspondence with an HR adviser prior to dismissing the claimant. The tribunal considered it inconceivable that this correspondence would have taken place if, as the employer contended, the reason for dismissal was capability or conduct – the claimant's lack of qualifying service meant the employer could dismiss for those reasons with impunity. The tribunal also noted that the employer appeared to be under the mistaken belief that an employee required its permission before accompanying colleagues: no such permission is required under S.10 of the 1999 Act.

9.50 Dismissal in connection with pensions

In this section we consider the three forms of automatically unfair dismissal linked to pensions:

- dismissal of occupational pension scheme trustees

- dismissal in relation to employees' information and consultation rights in respect of occupational and personal pensions, and

- dismissal in connection with an employee's right to be automatically enrolled into a workplace pension scheme.

9.51 Dismissal of occupational pension scheme trustees

Section 102 ERA provides that an employee will be regarded as unfairly dismissed if the reason (or, if more than one, the principal reason) for the dismissal is that the employee performed, or proposed to perform, any of his or her functions as a trustee of a relevant occupational pension scheme. The same protection extends to any director of a company who is a trustee of a relevant occupational pension scheme (i.e. a director of a corporate trustee) – S.102(1A).

It is also automatically unfair to select a trustee for redundancy on the same ground where the reason (or principal reason) for the dismissal was redundancy but the redundancy situation applied equally to one or more other employees in the same undertaking who held positions similar to the employee and who were not dismissed – S.105(1) and (5).

9.52 'Relevant occupational pension scheme' for the purposes of S.102 means an occupational pension scheme as defined in S.1 of the Pension Schemes Act 1993

486

and which is established under a trust – S.102(2). Broadly, such a scheme aims to provide benefits to, or in respect of, people in a particular employment or employments, and is established by (or by persons who include) the employer, a relevant employee, or an interested body. The administration of the scheme must either fall within the UK or within another country outside the European Economic Area. Where a pension scheme fails to meet this description – as will be the case in respect of a personal pension scheme and, probably, a group personal pension scheme – the scheme trustees will not fall within the protection of S.102.

An employee-trustee who presents a complaint of unfair dismissal under S.102(1) is entitled to apply for interim relief – see 'Different rules applicable to automatically unfair dismissals – interim relief' above. Dismissal of an employee-trustee also attracts a minimum basic award under S.120(1) (currently £5,807) – see 'Different rules applicable to automatically unfair dismissals – compensation for automatically unfair dismissals' above.

Pension consultation dismissals   9.53
The Occupational and Personal Pension Schemes (Consultation by Employers and Miscellaneous Amendment) Regulations 2006 SI 2006/349 require employers to engage in an information and consultation process with employee representatives when seeking to make changes to occupational or personal pension schemes. A provision similar to S.103 ERA (see 'Dismissal of employee representatives' above) governing unfair dismissal in this context is found in para 5 of Schedule 1 to the Regulations.

Paragraphs 5(1)–5(3) provide that an employee who is either a consulted representative or a candidate to be such a representative shall be regarded as unfairly dismissed if the reason (or, if more than one, the principal reason) for dismissal is that:

- the employee performed or proposed to perform the functions of a representative under the Regulations

- the employee exercised or proposed to exercise the right to paid time off under paras 2 or 3 of the Schedule, or

- the employee (or a person acting on his or her behalf) made or proposed to make a request to exercise such a right.

In addition, paras 5(1) and 5(4) provide that any employee who is an active or 9.54
prospective member of an occupational or personal pension scheme, irrespective of whether or not he or she is a representative or candidate, shall be regarded as unfairly dismissed if the reason (or, if more than one, the principal reason) for dismissal is one specified in para 5(5). The reasons specified in para 5(5) are that the employee:

487

- made, or proposed to make, a complaint to an employment tribunal to enforce a right or secure an entitlement under Schedule 1 to the Regulations. It is immaterial whether the employee actually had the right or entitlement, or whether it was infringed, provided the claim to the right and (if applicable) the claim that it had been infringed were made in good faith – para 5(6). (For discussion of the concept of 'good faith' see Chapter 11, 'Dismissal for asserting a statutory right', under 'Requirement of good faith')

- complained, or proposed to complain, to the Pensions Regulator about a failure to consult over changes in accordance with the Regulations

- stood as a candidate in an election for employee representatives

- attempted to influence by lawful means the voting in elections for representatives

- voted in such an election

- expressed doubts about whether such an election was properly conducted.

9.55 In respect of the last four of these reasons, para 5(5)(h) specifies that it will also be an automatically unfair reason for dismissal if the employee is dismissed for proposing to do, failing to do, or proposing to decline to do any of these things.

It is also automatically unfair to select an employee for redundancy on any of the grounds set out above where the reason (or principal reason) for the dismissal was redundancy but the redundancy situation applied equally to one or more other employees in the same undertaking who held positions similar to the employee and who were not dismissed – S.105(1) and (7I).

9.56 Pension auto-enrolment dismissals

The Pensions Act 2008 introduced radical reforms to workplace pensions with the introduction of the automatic enrolment scheme. The main provisions of the Act were brought into force on 30 June 2012 by the Pensions Act 2008 (Commencement No.13) Order 2012 SI 2012/1682. The employer's duties, which are being staggered over a period of time, are set out in Chapter 1 of Part 1 of the Act.

Under the new scheme, employers are required to automatically enrol eligible 'jobholders' (a wide category that includes employees, workers and agency workers) into a workplace pension scheme and make contributions of at least 3 per cent of 'qualifying earnings', as defined by S.13 of the Act. They are also subject to a number of information and consultation obligations. To prevent abuse of the system a number of new offences have been created, including wilful failure by an employer to comply with the Act's automatic enrolment provisions, an offence punishable by up to two years' imprisonment and/or a fine – S.45. (Further details on auto-enrolment are available on the Pensions Regulator's website.)

It is important to note that while the main provisions of the Pensions Act 2008 **9.57** came into force on 30 June 2012, employers were not obliged to implement auto-enrolment at that date. This is because commencement of the employer's duties is being staggered over a period of time under the Employers' Duties (Implementation) Regulations 2010 SI 2010/4. Very large employers, i.e. those with 120,000 or more members in their PAYE schemes, were covered from 1 October 2012, while employers with 50,000 or more PAYE members were covered from 1 November 2012. The scheme is gradually being extended to smaller employers over the following five years, with all employers to be covered by April 2017.

A new head of automatic unfair dismissal has been added to the ERA to protect employees who are dismissed for a reason relating to their rights under the Pensions Act 2008. S.104D(1) ERA provides that an employee will be regarded as unfairly dismissed if the reason (or, if more than one, the principal reason) for the dismissal is that:

- any action was taken, or was proposed to be taken, with a view to enforcing in favour of the employee a requirement imposed on the employer by or under the 2008 Act

- the employer was prosecuted for an offence under S.45 of the Act as a result of action taken for the purpose of enforcing such a requirement in favour of the employee, or

- any of the relevant provisions of the Act apply to the employee, or will or might apply. (This extends to employees of smaller employers who are not yet subject to the Act's requirements but will be by the time the scheme is fully implemented in April 2017.)

It is immaterial for the purposes of the first two reasons whether or not the **9.58** requirement applies in favour of the employee, or whether or not it has been contravened, provided the claim that the requirement applies, and (if applicable) the claim that it has been contravened were made in good faith – S.104D(2). (For discussion of the concept of 'good faith' see Chapter 11, 'Dismissal for asserting a statutory right', under 'Requirement of good faith'.)

It is also automatically unfair to select an employee for redundancy on any of the above grounds where the reason (or principal reason) for the dismissal was redundancy but the redundancy situation applied equally to one or more other employees in the same undertaking who held positions similar to the employee and who were not dismissed – S.105(1) and (7JA).

Dismissal in connection with tax credits   9.59

Working tax credits were introduced by the Tax Credits Act 2002 and are payments designed to top up the earnings of working people (employed and self-employed) on low incomes, including those who do not have children.

489

They comprise a number of elements depending on the circumstances of the worker concerned, including elements to support the costs of approved or registered childcare and to help working households in which someone has a disability. Payment of tax credits is made via the employer through normal pay except in respect of the childcare element, which is paid directly to the main carer.

Schedule 1 to the Tax Credits Act 2002 amended the ERA to introduce protection for employees against dismissal for claiming entitlement to working tax credits. S.104B(1) ERA provides that an employee will be regarded as unfairly dismissed if the reason (or, if more than one, the principal reason) for the dismissal is that:

- the employee is entitled, or will or may be entitled, to a working tax credit

- the employee (or someone on his or her behalf) took or proposed to take action with a view to securing the benefit of, or enforcing a right to, a working tax credit, or

- as a result of action taken by or on behalf of the employee to secure the benefit of, or enforce the right to, a working tax credit, the employer was fined or had proceedings brought against it pursuant to the 2002 Act.

9.60 Section 104B(2) makes it clear that, in respect of the second and third reasons listed above, it is irrelevant whether the employee actually has the right to a working tax credit or whether that right has been infringed. However, for either of those two reasons to apply, the employee's claim to the right and (if applicable) the claim that it has been infringed must have been made in good faith. (For discussion of the concept of 'good faith' see Chapter 11, 'Dismissal for asserting a statutory right', under 'Requirement of good faith'.)

It is also automatically unfair to select an employee for redundancy on any of the grounds specified in S.104B(1) where the reason (or principal reason) for the dismissal is that the employee was redundant and the redundancy situation applied equally to one or more other employees who held similar positions in the same undertaking and who were not dismissed – S.105(1) and (7B).

9.61 Dismissal relating to study and training

On 6 April 2010, the Government introduced a new right for employees to request to undertake study and training. The rules governing the operation of this right are found in Ss.63D–63K ERA; the Employee Study and Training (Eligibility, Complaints and Remedies) Regulations 2010 SI 2010/156 ('the Eligibility, Complaints and Remedies Regulations'); the Employee Study and Training (Procedural Requirements) Regulations 2010 SI 2010/155 ('the

Procedural Requirements Regulations'); and the Employee Study and Training (Qualifying Period of Employment) Regulations 2010 SI 2010/800 ('the Qualifying Period of Employment Regulations').

A detailed discussion of the new right falls outside the scope of this Handbook, but a basic understanding of the process is necessary to put the unfair dismissal provisions into context. However, first it is important to note that the Government initially intended to stagger the introduction of the study and training provisions. When it was introduced, the right to request study and training applied only to employees of companies employing at least 250 people. From 6 April 2011, it was going to be extended to all employees (provided they fulfilled the basic qualifying conditions discussed below). However, in an announcement made to coincide with the Budget speech on 23 March 2011, the Government indicated that the April 2011 extension would no longer go ahead. The right therefore remains available only to those employed in undertakings with 250 or more employees.

Right to request

9.62

As the name implies, the right to request study and training is fairly limited in scope. An employee is not entitled to have his or her request granted, but merely to have it considered seriously and for rejections to be made on legitimate grounds. The right is very similar to the right to request flexible working – see IDS Employment Law Handbook, 'Atypical and Flexible Working' (2014), Chapter 4, 'Flexible working'.

The right to request study and training applies to employees aged 18 or over who have 26 weeks or more continuous employment – S.63D(6) ERA and Reg 2(1) Qualifying Period of Employment Regulations. To begin the right to request process, the employee must make a written and dated application to his or her employer, which states that it is an application under S.63D – S.63D(5) and Reg 4 Eligibility, Complaints and Remedies Regulations. The application must be for the purpose of enabling the employee to undertake study or training (or both) in order to improve:

- the employee's effectiveness in the employer's business, and

- the performance of the employer's business – S.63D(3) and (4).

Once an employer has received an application, and assuming that it does not immediately agree to the terms of the request, it should convene a meeting with the employee within 28 days to discuss the application – S.63F(4) and Reg 4 Procedural Requirements Regulations. The employee is entitled to be accompanied to this meeting by a colleague of his or her choosing – Reg 16 Procedural Requirements Regulations.

9.63

Following the meeting, the employer has 14 days in which to inform the employee of its decision – Reg 5 Procedural Requirements Regulations. If the

491

decision is to grant the request (in part or in full), then the employer should provide details of the agreed training; its location and provider; what qualification it will lead to; whether the time spent training will be paid; any changes to working hours; and how the tuition costs will be met – Reg 6(2) Procedural Requirements Regulations. If the employer refuses the application, it must state which of the grounds for refusal listed in S.63F(7) it is relying on, explain why that reason (or reasons) applies and offer the chance of an appeal (setting out the procedure for doing so) – Reg 6(3) Procedural Requirements Regulations. The grounds for refusal (in part or in full) are:

- that the training would not improve the employee's effectiveness or the performance of the business

- the burden of additional costs

- detrimental effect on ability to meet customer demand

- inability to reorganise work among existing staff

- inability to recruit additional staff

- detrimental impact on quality

- detrimental impact on performance

- insufficiency of work during the periods the employee proposes to work, and

- planned structural changes – S.63F(7).

9.64 Reason for dismissal

There are two provisions dealing with automatically unfair dismissal in relation to a request to undertake study and training: S.104E ERA and Reg 18 Procedural Requirements Regulations.

9.65 Section 104E ERA. Section 104E states that a dismissal will be regarded as unfair if the reason for dismissal is that the employee:

- made, or proposed to make, an application under S.63D

- exercised, or proposed to exercise, a right conferred by S.63F

- brought proceedings against the employer under S.63I, or

- alleged the existence of any circumstance which would constitute a ground for bringing such proceedings.

It is also automatically unfair to select an employee for redundancy on any of the above grounds where the reason (or principal reason) for the dismissal is that the employee was redundant and the redundancy situation applied equally to one or more other employees who held similar positions in the same undertaking and who were not dismissed – S.105(1) and (7BB).

The 'proceedings under S.63I' referred to above are a claim that the employer **9.66** has not complied with the provisions of the Procedural Requirements Regulations, a claim that the employer's reason for refusing the request is not one of those specified in S.63F(7), or a claim that the employer's refusal was based on incorrect facts.

To state that S.104E is clumsily drafted would be putting it mildly. The provision rendering dismissal automatically unfair where the employee has exercised a right conferred by S.63F appears to make little sense because S.63F is entitled 'Employer's duties in relation to application' and does not confer any positive rights on employees. However, the Procedural Regulations were made in accordance with S.63F, so we can assume that the tribunals and courts will adopt a purposive interpretation of S.104E and treat the rights conferred by S.63F as being those contained in the Procedural Requirements Regulations.

Regulation 18 of Procedural Regulations. In addition to S.104E, there is a **9.67** provision dealing with automatically unfair dismissal in the Procedural Requirements Regulations. Reg 18 relates exclusively to the right to be accompanied at a meeting (including an appeal meeting) to discuss the employee's S.63D application and states that an employee will be regarded as unfairly dismissed if the reason (or, if more than one, the principal reason) for dismissal is that the employee:

- exercised or sought to exercise his or her right to be accompanied under Reg 16, or

- having been asked by a colleague to accompany him or her to a meeting under Reg 16, accompanied or sought to accompany him or her to that meeting.

There is, however, no corresponding provision rendering selection for redundancy automatically unfair on these grounds.

Interim relief is available for claimants pursuing a claim of automatically unfair dismissal under Reg 18 – Reg 18(5).

9.68 ## Appendix – list of automatically unfair reasons for dismissal

There are numerous categories of automatically unfair dismissal (subject to various qualifications and exceptions), which emanate from a number of different statutory sources. They are:

- dismissal for a reason relating to jury service – S.98B ERA (see 'Dismissal in connection with jury service' above)

- dismissal in connection with the right to time off for dependants under S.57A ERA; time off to accompany a pregnant woman to an ante-natal appointment under S.57ZE ERA; or time off to attend adoption appointments under Ss.57ZJ and 57ZL ERA – S.99(3) ERA; Reg 20(3)(e)(iii) Maternity and Parental Leave etc Regulations 1999 SI 1999/3312 ('the MPL Regulations'); Reg 29(3) Paternity and Adoption Leave Regulations 2002 SI 2002/2788 ('the PAL Regulations') (see IDS Employment Law Handbook, 'Maternity and Parental Rights' (2015), Chapter 12, 'Detriment and unfair dismissal', under 'Automatically unfair dismissal')

- dismissal for a reason relating to pregnancy, childbirth or family leave (i.e. maternity, adoption, shared parental, unpaid parental or paternity leave) under Part VIII ERA – S.99(3) ERA; Reg 20 MPL Regulations; Reg 29 PAL Regulations; Reg 43 Shared Parental Leave Regulations 2014 SI 2014/3050 (see IDS Employment Law Handbook, 'Maternity and Parental Rights' (2015), Chapter 12, 'Detriment and unfair dismissal', under 'Automatically unfair dismissal')

- dismissal for a health and safety reason – S.100 ERA (see Chapter 10, 'Health and safety dismissals')

- Sunday working dismissals – S.101 ERA (see 'Dismissal for refusing to work on Sunday' above)

- dismissal in connection with the entitlement to paid annual leave and other rights under the Working Time Regulations 1998 SI 1998/1833; the Merchant Shipping (Working Time: Inland Waterways) Regulations 2003 SI 2003/3049; the Fishing Vessels (Working Time: Sea-fishermen) Regulations 2004 SI 2004/1713; the Cross-border Railway Services (Working Time) Regulations 2008 SI 2008/1660; or the Merchant Shipping (Hours of Work) Regulations 2002 SI 2002/2125 – S.101A ERA (see IDS Employment Law Handbook, 'Working Time' (2013))

- dismissal of an occupational pension scheme trustee in connection with his or her duties in that capacity – S.102 ERA (see 'Dismissal in connection with pensions – dismissal of occupational pension scheme trustees' above)

494

- dismissal of an employee representative or candidate for the purpose of collective redundancies or a transfer of an undertaking – S.103 ERA (see 'Dismissal of employee representatives' above)

- dismissal for making a protected disclosure – S.103A ERA (see IDS Employment Law Handbook, 'Whistleblowing at Work' (2013), Chapter 6, 'Dismissal')

- dismissal for asserting a statutory right – S.104 ERA (see Chapter 11, 'Dismissal for asserting a statutory right')

- dismissal in connection with the entitlement to the national minimum wage – S.104A ERA (see IDS Employment Law Handbook, 'Wages' (2011), Chapter 5, 'The national minimum wage')

- dismissal in connection with working tax credits to which the employee may be entitled – S.104B ERA (see 'Dismissal in connection with tax credits' above)

- dismissal in connection with the right to request flexible working – S.104C ERA (see IDS Employment Law Handbook, 'Atypical and Flexible Working' (2014), Chapter 4, 'Flexible working')

- dismissal in connection with an employee's right to be automatically enrolled into a workplace pension scheme – S.104D ERA (see 'Dismissal in connection with pensions – pension auto-enrolment dismissals' above)

- dismissal in connection with the right to request study and training (subject to an exemption for employers with fewer than 250 employees) – S.104E ERA and Reg 18(3) Employee Study and Training (Procedural Requirements) Regulations 2010 SI 2010/155 (see 'Dismissal relating to study and training' above)

- dismissal for a reason relating to a trade union blacklist prohibited under the Employment Relations Act 1999 (Blacklists) Regulations 2010 SI 2010/493 – S.104F ERA (see IDS Employment Law Handbook, 'Trade Unions' (2013), Chapter 12, 'Unfair dismissal', under 'Trade union blacklists')

- dismissal for refusing an employer's offer to become an employee shareholder – S.104G ERA (see IDS Employment Law Handbook, 'Atypical and Flexible Working' (2014), Chapter 7, 'Employee shareholders')

- dismissal because of a 'spent' conviction within the terms of the Rehabilitation of Offenders Act 1974 (ROA), unless the employee falls into a category excluded from the provisions of that Act by a statutory order – S.4(3)(b) ROA – see Chapter 6, 'Conduct', under 'Criminal offences at work – previous convictions')

- dismissal in connection with trade union membership, activities or use of union services – S.152 Trade Union and Labour Relations (Consolidation)

Act 1992 (TULR(C)A) (see IDS Employment Law Handbook, 'Trade Unions' (2013), Chapter 12, 'Unfair dismissal')

- dismissal in connection with an application or campaign for trade union recognition or the securing of bargaining arrangements – para 161, Sch A1 TULR(C)A (see IDS Employment Law Handbook, 'Trade Unions' (2013), Chapter 6, 'Statutory recognition', under 'Detriment and dismissal')

- dismissal for taking official industrial action in certain circumstances – S.238A TULR(C)A (see IDS Employment Law Handbook, 'Industrial Action' (2010), Chapter 8, 'Industrial action dismissals')

- dismissal in connection with the right to be accompanied at disciplinary and grievance hearings under S.10 of the Employment Relations Act 1999 (ERelA) – S.12(3) ERelA (see 'Dismissal in connection with right to be accompanied' above)

- dismissal where there is a transfer of an undertaking and the transfer is the reason or principal reason for the dismissal – Reg 7(1) Transfer of Undertakings (Protection of Employment) Regulations 2006 SI 2006/246 (TUPE) (see IDS Employment Law Handbook, 'Transfer of Undertakings' (2011), Chapter 4, 'Unfair dismissal')

- dismissal relating to the performance of the functions of, or activities as, a member or representative (or candidate for election as a member or representative) of a European Works Council or in relation to a request made for time off in order to perform such functions/activities – Reg 28 Transnational Information and Consultation of Employees Regulations 1999 SI 1999/3323

- dismissal in connection with the rights of part-time workers under the Part-time Workers (Prevention of Less Favourable Treatment) Regulations 2000 SI 2000/1551 – Reg 7 (see IDS Employment Law Handbook, 'Atypical and Flexible Working' (2014), Chapter 3, 'Part-time workers')

- dismissal in connection with the rights of fixed-term employees under the Fixed-term Employees (Prevention of Less Favourable Treatment) Regulations 2002 SI 2002/2034 – Reg 6 (see IDS Employment Law Handbook, 'Atypical and Flexible Working' (2014), Chapter 2, 'Fixed-term employees')

- dismissal in connection with information and consultation rights under the Information and Consultation of Employees Regulations 2004 SI 2004/3426 – Reg 30

- dismissal in connection with the information and consultation rights of occupational or personal pension scheme members under the Occupational and Personal Pension Schemes (Consultation by Employers and Miscellaneous

Amendment) Regulations 2006 SI 2006/349 – para 5, Sch 1 (see 'Dismissal in connection with pensions – pension consultation dismissals' above)

- dismissal in connection with the information, consultation and negotiation rights of employees regarding the establishment and operation of European cooperative societies under the European Cooperative Society (Involvement of Employees) Regulations 2006 SI 2006/2059 – Reg 31

- dismissal in connection with the information, consultation and negotiation rights of employees involved in cross-border mergers under the Companies (Cross-Border Mergers) Regulations 2007 SI 2007/2974 – Regs 46 and 47

- dismissal in connection with the information, consultation and negotiation rights of employees regarding the establishment and operation of European public limited liability companies under the European Public Limited-Liability Company (Employee Involvement) (Great Britain) Regulations 2004 SI 2004/2326 – Reg 29 European Public Limited-Liability Company (Employee Involvement) (Great Britain) Regulations 2009 SI 2009/2401

- dismissal of an agency worker who has the status of 'employee' for alleging a breach of – or asserting rights, bringing proceedings, giving evidence or doing anything under – the Agency Workers Regulations 2010 SI 2010/93 – Reg 17 (see IDS Employment Law Handbook, 'Atypical and Flexible Working' (2014), Chapter 1, 'Agency workers').

10 Health and safety dismissals

Employees have the right not to be dismissed if they complain about, or refuse **10.1** to work in, unsafe conditions – S.100 Employment Rights Act 1996 (ERA). This right has its origins in, and must be interpreted in the light of, EU Directive No.89/391 on the introduction of measures to encourage improvements in the safety and health of workers at work ('the Directive').

Section 100 provides that where an employer dismisses an employee for a prohibited health and safety reason, the dismissal is automatically unfair. This means that the reasonableness of the employer's action in dismissing is not a matter which is taken into consideration by the tribunal.

A number of special rules appertaining to S.100 dismissals should be borne **10.2** in mind:

- the right contained in S.100 applies to all employees regardless of their length of service – S.108(3)(c)

- any health and safety representative or safety committee member who presents a complaint under S.100(1)(a) or (b) (see 'Scope of protection' below) is entitled to interim relief – S.128(1) (see Chapter 17, 'Additional awards and interim relief', under 'Interim relief')

- dismissal of a health and safety representative or safety committee member under S.100(1)(a) or (b) is a category of dismissal that attracts a minimum basic award (£5,807 as from 6 April 2015) – S.120(1) (see Chapter 13, 'Basic awards', under 'Calculation of basic award')

- there is no upper limit on the compensatory award for a dismissal that is automatically unfair for any of the reasons contained in S.100 – S.124(1A) (see Chapter 14, 'Compensatory awards: types of loss', in the section 'Nature and maximum amount of award', under 'Amount of week's pay and statutory cap – exceptions to statutory limit')

- unlike in cases of ordinary unfair dismissal, individuals employed in the police service are not excluded from bringing claims of automatic unfair dismissal under S.100 – S.200(1).

499

10.3 Scope of protection

Section 100 provides that an employee is automatically unfairly dismissed if the reason, or principal reason, for dismissal is that he or she:

- carried out, or proposed to carry out, activities in connection with preventing or reducing risks to health and safety at work, having been designated by the employer to do so – S.100(1)(a)

- performed, or proposed to perform, any functions of a health and safety representative, or member of a safety committee, either in accordance with arrangements established by statute or after being acknowledged as such by the employer – S.100(1)(b)

- took part, or proposed to take part, in consultation with the employer pursuant to the Health and Safety (Consultation with Employees) Regulations 1996 SI 1996/1513 or in an election of safety representatives within the meaning of those Regulations, whether as a candidate or otherwise – S.100(1)(ba)

- brought to the employer's attention, by reasonable means, circumstances connected with his or her work which he or she reasonably believed were harmful or potentially harmful to health or safety – S.100(1)(c). (This only applies where there is either no health and safety representative or safety committee or it was not reasonably practicable for the employee to raise the matter by those means)

- in circumstances of danger which he or she reasonably believed to be serious and imminent and which he or she could not reasonably be expected to avert, left, proposed to leave or (while the danger persisted) refused to return to his or her place of work or any dangerous part of his or her place of work – S.100(1)(d)

- in circumstances of danger took, or proposed to take, appropriate steps to protect him or herself or other persons from danger which he or she reasonably believed to be serious and imminent – S.100(1)(e).

10.4 Whether an employee has taken, or proposed to take, appropriate steps for the purposes of this final ground is to be judged by reference to all the circumstances, including his or her knowledge and the facilities and advice available to him or her at the time – S.100(2). If, however, an employer shows that it was, or would have been, so negligent of the employee to take the steps that he or she took, or proposed to take, that a reasonable employer might have dismissed him or her, then the employee's dismissal will not be regarded as automatically unfair – S.100(3). In such cases the fairness of the dismissal will be determined according to the usual test under S.98(4).

500

Redundancy selection

Section 105 provides that an employee selected for redundancy on one of the grounds specified in S.100(1) will be treated as automatically unfairly dismissed where the reason (or principal reason) for the dismissal was redundancy but the redundancy situation applied equally to one or more other employees in the same undertaking who held positions similar to that of the employee and who were not dismissed. The special rules listed in the introduction to this chapter apply equally to selection for redundancy on health and safety grounds, save that interim relief is not available.

Comparators. The requirement for comparators who have not been dismissed **10.6** is not merely cosmetic. In O'Dea v ISC Chemicals Ltd 1996 ICR 222, CA, the Court of Appeal dealt with similar provisions on selection for redundancy on trade union grounds under S.153 of the Trade Union and Labour Relations (Consolidation) Act 1992 (TULR(C)A). In rejecting the claimant's appeal, the Court emphasised that there must be other employees holding a similar position who were similarly at risk of redundancy but not dismissed. If no such comparators exist, the claim must fail. However, in identifying whether there were others who held similar positions to the claimant, the Court ruled that time spent working as a shop steward would not by itself distinguish a person from other employees for this purpose.

Selection criteria. While the fact that an employee has acted as a health and **10.7** safety representative or has taken some action in respect of a health and safety matter cannot be a fair reason for selecting that individual for redundancy, neither can it be a factor allowed to operate in the employee's favour in a selection exercise. As in cases of employees who have been engaged in trade union activities, an employer must take a neutral stance in relation to the skills and knowledge that a health and safety representative has acquired when drawing up redundancy selection criteria.

In Smiths Industries Aerospace and Defence Systems v Rawlings 1996 IRLR 656, EAT, a health and safety representative was selected for redundancy on the basis of a points system relating to performance at work. He argued that he had been automatically unfairly dismissed because the points system did not recognise the skills that he had developed in his role as health and safety representative. The EAT rejected that argument. In the Appeal Tribunal's view, there was no evidence suggesting that his health and safety duties led to bias against him. Nor had his dismissal been unfair on ordinary principles under what is now S.98(4). Health and safety representatives were not entitled to receive more favourable treatment than their fellow employees in the pool for redundancy selection. Acting as a safety representative did not amount to a 'second job' and health and safety duties did not therefore form part of the duties performed under the contract of employment. Taking a representative's

501

performance of health and safety duties into account when conducting a redundancy exercise would result in discrimination in that employee's favour.

10.8 This principle applies regardless of whether the employee is a trade union-appointed safety representative under S.100(1)(b), or a person designated by the employer to carry out activities in connection with health and safety at work under S.100(1)(a). In Shipham and Co Ltd v Skinner EAT 840/00 the EAT found that although there were factual distinctions between the two roles – in particular, that the employee's role as a designated health and safety adviser could be described as a 'second job' for which he received additional payment – this did not merit a difference in approach when considering the fairness of selection for redundancy under ordinary unfair dismissal principles.

10.9 Who is protected?

Sections 100 and 105 ERA apply to employees only – see Chapter 2, 'Exclusions from right to claim'. There is no specific power under the ERA to extend the right to non-employees (although under S.209 the Secretary of State has the power to extend the right not to suffer a detriment on health and safety grounds contained in S.44). There is a general power in S.23 of the Employment Relations Act 1999 allowing the Government to extend to non-employees the protection of any right contained in the ERA but no such order has yet been made under that provision. However, unless or until the right to claim unfair dismissal on health and safety grounds is extended to at least some categories of non-employee, there may be some conflict with the Directive, which aims to protect 'workers'. Although the Directive defines a 'worker' using the language of employment, it also uses the phrase 'employment relationship', which can be interpreted in a wider manner than a contract of employment in the UK.

In Costain Building and Civil Engineering Ltd v Smith and anor 2000 ICR 215, EAT, the EAT considered the position of S, an agency worker working at a building site, who was purportedly appointed by a trade union as a safety representative on the site. His contract was later cancelled at the behest of the client. When considering his complaint of automatic unfair dismissal under S.100(1)(b), the tribunal found that S was an employee of the client, ignoring several factors that weighed against such a finding. Overturning this decision, the EAT found that S was not an employee of the client as there was no contract between them. It noted that under the Safety Representatives and Safety Committees Regulations 1977 SI 1977/500, a person appointed by a trade union to be a safety representative must be an employee. As such, the purported appointment by the trade union was ineffective in law. The EAT stated that appointment as a safety representative did not automatically mean that S was an employee, nor that he was thereby elevated to that status.

Health and safety of third parties 10.10

In Von Goetz v St George's Healthcare NHS Trust EAT 1395/97 the EAT saw no reason to limit the ambit of S.100 (and, in particular, subsections 1(c) and 1(e)) to harm, or the possibility of harm, to fellow employees, or to any employees, and could extend to the health and safety of third parties such as, for example, hospital patients. To this extent, the EAT had no problem in accepting that the domestic legislation went further than required by the Directive, the terms of which are expressly limited to the health and safety of workers.

Reason for dismissal – burden of proof 10.11

As noted above, S.100 provides that an employee is to be regarded as having been automatically unfairly dismissed if the reason or principal reason for dismissal was one of the health and safety grounds listed in S.100(1). S.105 extends protection to those who are selected for redundancy on one of those grounds. In many cases where these provisions are relied on there will be a dispute between the employer and the employee as to the real reason for the dismissal.

In these circumstances, if the employee has sufficient qualifying service to bring an ordinary unfair dismissal claim (i.e. has at least two years' continuous service), the burden of proof is on the employer to prove the reason for the dismissal on the balance of probabilities. This was established by the Court of Appeal in Maund v Penwith District Council 1984 ICR 143, CA, in relation to a claim for automatically unfair dismissal on trade union grounds under S.152 TULR(C)A. The Court went on to hold that once the employer has shown a reason for dismissal, there is an evidential burden on the employee to produce some evidence to show that there is a real issue as to whether or not the reason given is true. Once this is done, the onus remains on the employer to prove the real reason for dismissal.

Where, however, an employee does not have enough qualifying service to bring 10.12 an ordinary unfair dismissal claim, the burden of proof is on the employee to show an automatically unfair reason for dismissal for which no qualifying service is required. This was decided by the Court of Appeal (by a majority) in Smith v Hayle Town Council 1978 ICR 996, CA, again in relation to a claim under S.152 TULR(C)A, and was applied in relation to what is now S.100 in Tedeschi v Hosiden Besson Ltd EAT 959/95 and Parks v Lansdowne Club EAT 310/95. In the latter case the employee claimed that he had been dismissed for raising concerns about fire extinguishers at the premises where he worked while the employer said that he was dismissed for gross misconduct. The employee's claim failed as he had not discharged the burden of showing that his dismissal was for a health and safety reason. The EAT upheld this finding.

503

10.13 ## Reason for dismissal – causation

In seeking to establish the reason, or principal reason, for dismissal it is necessary to ask why the employer acted as it did. In Balfour Kilpatrick Ltd v Acheson and ors 2003 IRLR 683, EAT, a group of employees were dismissed for failing to attend work. The men left the site on which they worked and refused to return until the company had dealt with their health and safety concerns. The company argued that it had dismissed the men not on health and safety grounds but because of their absence. If they had been absent for other reasons, they would still have been dismissed. Although the EAT ultimately found that the facts did not fall within any of the S.100 reasons, it nonetheless considered whether – if they had – the S.100 reason could be said to be the principal reason for dismissal. By analogy with Chief Constable of West Yorkshire Police v Khan 2001 ICR 1065, HL, a House of Lords case on victimisation under the Race Relations Act 1976, the EAT found that it was necessary to ask why a person acted as he or she did. If the employer had no knowledge of the protected act (or S.100 reason) or dismissed for an independent reason, the dismissal will not be automatically unfair. A 'but for' test is inappropriate. On the facts, however, the company was aware of the reason for the employees' absence and dismissed them for that reason even though it was unconcerned about it. It was irrelevant that it would have dismissed them for absences for a host of other reasons. The fact that the company was dismissing because of the failure to return to work and was indifferent to the reason why the men were not at work was immaterial. It knew what the employees were asserting the reason to be. Although it did not decide the point, the EAT commented that it was likely that an employer would equally be liable if it had the opportunity to find out the reason for the absence but chose not to take it.

In Namoale v Balfour Beatty Engineering Services Ltd EAT 0126/12 an employment tribunal struck out N's claim of automatic unfair dismissal on the basis that he was unable to establish the necessary causal link between his raising health and safety concerns and the subsequent disciplinary action that was taken against him that led to his dismissal. In so deciding, the employment judge considered the fact that three other people had faced disciplinary action, one of whom was also dismissed, and that none of them had raised health and safety concerns. However, the EAT held that it was wrong to categorise N as being in the same position as those others. Of the four who were disciplined, only N asserted that he had raised health and safety issues that brought him within the remit of S.100. N's case was that, when he objected to breaches of the health and safety regime by the others, he was put into the same boat as them and disciplined. The EAT therefore remitted the matter to the tribunal to be heard in full.

504

Automatically unfair dismissal and industrial action   10.14

Where the principal reason for dismissal (or selection for redundancy) is one that falls within the scope of S.100, the employee is to be regarded as having been unfairly dismissed. But what if the actions of the employee amount to industrial action? S.237(1) TULR(C)A provides that an employee has no right to complain of unfair dismissal if at the time of dismissal he or she was taking part in an unofficial strike or other unofficial industrial action. S.238A protects employees taking part in official industrial action in certain specified circumstances but where this section does not apply, employees cannot complain of unfair dismissal if they were taking part in official industrial action unless the employer has selectively dismissed or re-engaged within three months of the date of the complainant's dismissal – S.238(2). However, Ss.237(1A) and 238(2A) state that the provisions barring individuals from the right to complain of unfair dismissal where they were taking part in industrial action at the time of dismissal do not apply where the reason for the dismissal is a health and safety reason under S.100. It is therefore no defence for the employer to argue that an employee's refusal to work in circumstances of danger amounted to industrial action.

However, industrial action may have a bearing on whether one of the automatically unfair reasons can be made out. This was highlighted in Balfour Kilpatrick Ltd v Acheson and ors 2003 IRLR 683, EAT, where employees took unofficial action because of widespread concerns about the adverse effects of the weather on working conditions. They sought to argue that their actions fell within S.100(1)(c) or (d). However, in the course of its decision, the EAT held that industrial action was not a reasonable means of bringing health and safety concerns to the attention of the employer for the purposes of S.100(1)(c). Although it would have been reasonable for the purposes of S.100(1)(d), any serious and imminent danger had ceased by the time the employer dismissed the employees and therefore S.100(1)(d) did not come into play. As no S.100 reason could be established, the men lost any right to compensation. They could not bring a claim for ordinary unfair dismissal because they were involved in unofficial industrial action at the time of their dismissal.

Constructive dismissal claims   10.15

Section 95(1) states that, for the purposes of Part X ERA (which includes S.100), an employee is dismissed by his or her employer 'if... the employee terminates the contract under which he is employed (with or without notice) in circumstances in which he is entitled to terminate it without notice by reason of the employer's conduct'. It is clear, therefore, that S.100 covers constructive dismissal claims.

It is well established that the type of conduct which gives rise to a constructive dismissal under the ordinary unfair dismissal rules must involve a fundamental breach of contract by the employer – Western Excavating (ECC) Ltd v Sharp

505

1978 ICR 221, CA. And it is clear that by punishing an employee in some way for his or her health and safety activities, an employer may be guilty of a fundamental breach, most usually of the implied duty of trust and confidence. What is less clear, however, is whether any breach of S.100 would entitle an employee to resign and claim that he or she has been constructively dismissed. To put it another way, did the legislators intend any breach of the health and safety provisions to be treated as a fundamental breach or is it a question of fact and degree in each case?

10.16 The answer to this question remains unclear, with conflicting decisions at tribunal level and no appellate authority on point. In Baddeley v Mehta t/a Supascoop ET Case No.46041/94 the tribunal held that the right to claim under what is now S.100 arises only where the employer dismisses the employee or fundamentally breaches the employee's contract as a punishment for the employee's health and safety activity. However, in Teasdale v Walker t/a Blaydon Packaging ET Case No.2505103/98 an employee raised a concern with his employer over the condition of ropes used to secure pallets to his lorry. The employer took no steps to deal with this complaint and required the employee to continue using the ropes. The employee treated himself as constructively dismissed, with the tribunal identifying a breach of the implied term to ensure the health and safety of the employee. In the tribunal's view, this breach was fundamental because the employer had failed to comply with S.100(1)(c) ERA.

It may be that this issue is largely academic anyway. In many cases that fall within S.100, tribunals have found breaches of the implied duty of trust and confidence or of the implied duty on employers to take reasonable care to ensure the health and safety of their employees. Furthermore, if an employee raises a health and safety concern as a grievance, he or she may be able to show a breach of trust and confidence if the employer fails to deal with the grievance adequately or at all. Moreover, in WA Goold (Pearmak) Ltd v McConnell and anor 1995 IRLR 516, EAT, it was held that an employer's failure to provide employees with a proper procedure for dealing with work-related grievances (in this case, about a drop in pay) was a breach of the implied term in their contracts of employment that the employer would reasonably and promptly afford a reasonable opportunity to the employees to obtain redress of any grievance they might have. The employees were therefore entitled to resign and claim that they had been constructively dismissed. Applying this approach, an employee can surely argue that if the employer ignores his or her grievance about a health and safety matter, the employer's actions would amount to a breach of contract sufficient to entitle the employee to resign and claim constructive dismissal.

10.17 Three cases involving claims of unfair constructive dismissal under S.100:

- **Skelton v Artel Services Ltd** ET Case No.3104190/99: S, who had raised a number of health and safety complaints with his employer over the years, was

506

instructed to drive a truck with no near-side wing mirror. When S refused, his manager shouted at him and told S that he would have to stand in the yard all day as there was no other work for him to do. S walked out and did not return. A tribunal held that he had been constructively dismissed. Telling S to stand in the yard was demeaning and humiliating and in fundamental breach of the implied duty of trust and confidence. The dismissal was unfair as it fell within the scope of S.100(1)(c) – S had brought to his employer's attention matters that he reasonably believed were potentially harmful to health and safety

- **Bragg v Gilbert Foods** ET Case No.43924/96: B complained repeatedly to his employer about the company's failure to provide him with protective gloves. His job involved removing frozen meat from a vat full of ice-cold water. Without gloves, his hands became numb and B eventually contracted pneumonia. When he returned to work he made a further request for gloves and resigned when none were forthcoming. A tribunal found that the employer was in fundamental breach of the implied duty to provide and maintain a safe workplace and a safe system of work. The dismissal was unfair because it fell within S.100(1)(c) – B had brought the potentially harmful issue of the absence of gloves to his employer's attention and the employer had refused to provide them

- **Castell v Ian Williams Ltd** ET Case No.1701885/08: C, an electrician, attended a site where he assessed that he was going to have to work dangerously by handling live wires, or illegally by isolating the power without authority from the power company. Despite this his supervisor instructed him to carry out the work and when he refused he was sent to another of IW Ltd's sites. The work was subsequently carried out by another electrician, who isolated the power illegally. Over the next two days there were other instances relating to health and safety that caused C concern and he decided to resign as he believed there was a culture of dishonesty and undertaking shortcuts and that if he stayed he would be forced to carry out tasks that would present a serious risk to health and safety. Dismissing C's claim that he was dismissed for health and safety reasons, the tribunal concluded that, although his concerns about his employer's attitude to health and safety were justified, the circumstances giving rise to those concerns were not of such serious and imminent danger that he could not reasonably have been expected to avert them. The company did not exert significant pressure on him to work in circumstances of risk; when he refused to undertake work no action was taken against him; and he was not criticised for the stand he took in relation to health and safety. Having resigned before taking steps to raise his concerns at a senior level, C had acted 'precipitately'.

10.18 Employee's own medical condition

Where employees are dismissed because of a medical condition – because either their own health or that of others might be put at risk by their continued employment – the matter does not fall within the scope of the health and safety provisions of S.100. The fairness of the decision to dismiss will be dealt with under the normal unfair dismissal provisions or, if relevant, the disability discrimination provisions of the Equality Act 2010 (EqA) – see Chapter 5, 'Ill health', and IDS Employment Law Handbook, 'Discrimination at Work' (2012), Chapter 26, 'Dismissal', under 'Dismissal "because of" protected characteristic – disability'. Three examples:

- **Lane Group plc and anor v Farmiloe** EAT 0352/03: F, a warehouseman, suffered from psoriasis, a skin condition that made it impossible for him to wear the protective footwear provided by the employer. The employer investigated the possibility of finding alternative footwear but this was found to be medically unacceptable. A health and safety officer with the local council confirmed that the wearing of protective footwear was obligatory under health and safety regulations. F was dismissed. The EAT found that the employer was not in breach of the Disability Discrimination Act 1995 (now subsumed within the EqA) and remitted the case to the tribunal for a decision on whether the dismissal was unfair under normal unfair dismissal provisions, while suggesting that the employee's case had been seriously undermined by its findings that the requirement for protective footwear was absolute

- **Dixon v Gatwick Parking Service Ltd** ET Case No.37420/94: D, a part-time public service vehicle driver, was absent for six weeks suffering from angina. The employer was concerned about the safety of passengers having a driver with a heart condition and spoke to a number of agencies, including the Health and Safety Executive and the DVLC (now DVLA). It became clear from the insurance brokers, however, that if an accident did occur the insurance would not cover the claim. D was therefore dismissed. A tribunal held that the dismissal was fair within the terms of S.98(4)

- **Walker v Unijet Group plc** ET Case No.57825/94: W, a reservation agent whose work required him to use a keyboard, was absent from work suffering from RSI. He was asked to return on administrative duties but was unable to do so because even to hold a pen or piece of paper could have damaged him: he needed complete rest. W was dismissed on medical grounds and he claimed that the dismissal was in breach of S.100(1)(c) and (d). The tribunal held that, while it would have been dangerous for W to work at all, the danger related to W subjectively and the statutory test is an objective one. W was unfit for work and had been dismissed for that reason. However, the tribunal had no jurisdiction to hear W's unfair dismissal complaint under S.98 as he did not have the requisite length of service.

508

Health and safety representatives

Section 100(1)(a) and S.100(1)(b) protect only those employees who are designated health and safety representatives. Their health and safety activities may well put them in conflict with the employer and the provisions are designed to offer some protection against being penalised for carrying out their proper functions. As discussed in Chapter 9, 'Automatically unfair dismissals', under 'Employee representatives', trade union representatives and employee representatives enjoy a similar protection from dismissal to that found in S.100(1)(a) and (b), with the result that case law decided under one provision can prove highly relevant in a claim brought under another.

The manner in which a health and safety representative carries out his or her designated functions may be relevant to a claim under S.100(1)(a). In Goodwin v Cabletel UK Ltd 1998 ICR 112, EAT, G, a construction manager, was responsible for ensuring that the employer's subcontractors complied with relevant statutory health and safety requirements. G complained of safety breaches by one particular subcontractor, recommending that it should not be given any further work. The employer did not approve of G's approach, which it found confrontational, and took the view that it was G's job to help the subcontractors improve their safety standards. Subsequent safety breaches led to further friction between the subcontractor and G and this prompted the employer to demote G to a position where he would not be in direct contact with the subcontractor. G resigned and claimed constructive dismissal under S.100(1)(a). The tribunal rejected G's claim on the ground that S.100(1)(a) does not protect a safety representative in the event of dismissal for the way in which he or she carries out health and safety duties. The employer had never sought to suppress or limit G's health and safety duties; G had merely been advised and admonished as to his method of discharging those duties.

The EAT held that the tribunal had erred in finding that S.100(1)(a) did not apply if the dismissal was due to the manner in which a safety representative carried out his or her duties. Applying a similar approach to that adopted by the Court of Appeal in Bass Taverns Ltd v Burgess 1995 IRLR 596, CA – a case involving dismissal for trade union activities – the EAT made it clear that the protection afforded to the manner in which a designated employee carries out health and safety activities should not be diluted by too easily finding acts done for that purpose to be a justification for dismissal. On the other hand, not every act, however malicious or irrelevant to the task in hand, must necessarily be treated as a protected act in circumstances where dismissal would be justified on legitimate grounds. In the instant case, the question that the tribunal should have asked was whether the manner in which the employee approached the health and safety problems took him outside the scope of the protected health and safety activities. The EAT remitted the case to a different

509

tribunal for it to consider the matter afresh, although it commented that a finding adverse to G would be 'surprising' given that the tribunal had found G to be a man of competence and integrity who had acted in the best interests of the firm.

The case of Shillito v Van Leer (UK) Ltd 1997 IRLR 495, EAT, illustrates how difficult it can be to determine whether the acts of a health and safety representative fall within the scope of S.100(1)(a) and (b) in situations where he or she may have had mixed motives. In that case S was a senior shop steward and a health and safety representative for one particular area. A number of employees in a different area expressed concern about an odour given off by a solvent. S went to management and insisted that the affected employees receive medical attention. He was subsequently disciplined for not following the agreed procedures in the employer's safety manual. S claimed that this amounted to an unlawful detriment within the terms of S.44 ERA, which prohibits action short of dismissal for a health and safety reason.

10.21 A tribunal found that S had acted outside his duties as the safety representative for his designated area and had confused his role as shop steward with that of a safety representative. In its view, he had acted as a shop steward in trying to embarrass the employer over health and safety matters. On appeal, S argued that the tribunal had misdirected itself by considering his motives and whether he had acted reasonably, pointing out that the legislation did not require health and safety representatives to act reasonably in order for the statutory protection to apply. The EAT agreed that, if S had been disciplined for performing the functions of a health and safety representative, the reasonableness of his behaviour would have been irrelevant, even if his purpose was to embarrass the employer. However, it was clear that S had not been disciplined in connection with his duties as a safety representative because he was not the representative for that area. S's intention was not, therefore, to pursue a health and safety matter but to pursue a personal agenda to embarrass the company. Since his actions fell outside the scope of his duties as a safety representative and he acted in bad faith, he was not able to rely on the statutory protection.

Note that although the above case was decided under S.44, the decision is relevant to a claim brought under S.100. This is because the circumstances giving rise to a complaint under both sections are the same. Thus, any interpretation of the acts protected by S.44 will apply to the same acts protected by S.100 and vice versa.

10.22 Some further examples:

- **Ratcliffe v Green Corns Ltd** ET Case No. 2401758/06: R, GC Ltd's health and safety manager, prepared a report in which he expressed concerns about the level of assaults on staff. The report was not well received by management; it was thought to be over-critical and patronising, and in some respects stated the obvious. The chief executive said the report placed R 'in contempt of his colleagues', while the HR director told R that there was no way back for him after the report. A few days later he offered R a 'dignified' exit by way of redundancy and proposed a compromise agreement involving payment of £6,000 tax-free in lieu of notice. R refused to accept the compromise agreement, but his 'redundancy' was still put into effect. The tribunal found that there was no doubt that the report was central to R's dismissal and that the production of the report – which raised genuine concerns – was part of his normal duties as health and safety manager. The reason for dismissal thus fell within S.100(1)(a)

- **South West Trains Ltd v McDonnell** EAT 0052/03 (a case concerned with similar provisions covering dismissals for trade union activities): a shop steward, McD, was seeking to speak to a colleague, E, about strike action and membership of a trade union. This was found to be within his trade union activities. However, E subsequently complained that in speaking to him McD had subjected him to intimidation and harassment. Such behaviour fell outside the bounds of legitimate activity. A tribunal found that regardless of what had actually happened between the two, the employer had believed that McD was guilty of harassment and intimidation. The principal reason for dismissal was therefore misconduct. The EAT held that it was open to the tribunal to reach this conclusion on the evidence

- **Sears v RS Cockerill (Farms) Ltd** ET Case No.1803943/98: S was appointed as a health and safety representative and continually raised health and safety concerns with the employer. He was dismissed for constantly pestering the employer. However, as the pestering was done in good faith in order to improve working conditions, the tribunal held that S was dismissed for performing his health and safety functions

- **Nicholls v St Helier NHS Trust** ET Case No.2305780/97: N was a designated health and safety representative accused by a colleague of harassment. N had supplied her with protective trousers that were too big and some bicycle clips with which to hold them up. He had also given her protective safety goggles with eyelashes painted on them. N was dismissed for harassing his colleague although he claimed that he had merely used unusual methods to encourage his colleague to take appropriate safety measures. The tribunal found that the real reason for dismissal was the employer's belief that N was guilty of harassment. In reaching this conclusion the tribunal made it clear that it had a duty in S.100 cases to look behind the employer's stated reason for dismissal in order to ascertain if the real reason was connected with health and safety.

511

10.23 Employees who are not health and safety representatives

Section 100(1)(ba), S.100(1)(c), S.100(1)(d) and S.100(1)(e) all protect individual employees who are not health and safety representatives. Each subsection will apply in different circumstances and has its own restrictions or limitations. For this reason, they need to be dealt with separately. However, there may be a degree of overlap. The fact that a matter falls within one subsection does not preclude its being protected by another – Balfour Kilpatrick Ltd v Acheson and ors 2003 IRLR 683, EAT.

10.24 Section 100(1)(ba)

This subsection protects employees who take part (or propose to take part) in consultations with employers under the Health and Safety (Consultation with Employees) Regulations 1996 S1 1996/1513 or in elections of safety representatives within the meaning of those Regulations (whether as a candidate or not). The 1996 Regulations, which came into force on 1 October 1996, require, inter alia, that employers inform and consult employees or safety representatives on matters relating to health and safety at work. As far as we are aware, there have been no decided cases under this subsection.

10.25 Section 100(1)(c)

This subsection provides that an employee will be regarded as automatically unfairly dismissed if the reason (or principal reason) for dismissal was that the employee brought to the employer's attention, by reasonable means, circumstances connected with his or her work that the employee reasonably believed were harmful or potentially harmful to health or safety. It only applies if there was no safety representative or safety committee at the employee's place of work or, if there was such a representative or committee, it was not reasonably practicable for the employee to raise the matter by those means.

In Balfour Kilpatrick Ltd v Acheson and ors 2003 IRLR 683, EAT, the EAT identified three requirements that need to be satisfied for a claim under S.100(1)(c) to be made out. It must be established that:

- it was not reasonably practicable for the employee to raise the health and safety matters through the safety representative or safety committee

- the employee must have brought to the employer's attention by reasonable means the circumstances that he or she reasonably believes are harmful or potentially harmful to health or safety, and

- the reason, or principal reason, for the dismissal must be the fact that the employee was exercising his or her rights.

A distinction must be drawn between S.100(1)(c) – which protects the raising **10.26** of a safety issue – and S.100(1)(d) and S.100(1)(e), which protect the safety of the employee. In ABC News Intercontinental Inc v Gizbert EAT 0160/06 G, a news reporter, had indicated to his employer an unwillingness to travel to war zones in Iraq and Afghanistan. When he was made redundant following budget cuts, G contended that the dismissal was automatically unfair under S.100(1)(c). An employment tribunal concurred, concluding that the principal reason for selecting G for redundancy was his refusal to travel to war zones. Allowing ABC's appeal, the EAT held that such a reason cannot fall within the purview of S.100(1)(c) because it does not relate to the employee bringing a health and safety matter to the employer's attention. On the tribunal's findings, the reason for G's dismissal was that he would not go to war zones, and ABC needed reporters who would. That reason was more closely related to S.100(1)(d) and (e), but G's dismissal could not be automatically unfair under either of those provisions because he had not been in imminent danger (see 'Section 100(1)(d) – serious and imminent danger' below).

Appropriate channels. Section 100(1)(c) covers any employee who, by **10.27** reasonable means, brings a health and safety matter to the employer's attention. On the face of it, however, the employee must go through a safety committee or representative wherever possible. Several employees have lost tribunal claims because they did not go through the appropriate channels, preferring instead to take the matter into their own hands. However, in Balfour Kilpatrick Ltd v Acheson and ors (above), the EAT took a robust approach to its interpretation of this requirement. In that case, adverse weather conditions led to protective clothing and footwear becoming very wet in heavy rain. There was no means of drying it quickly. There were also large areas of standing water on the building site in question, increasing the dangers of working with electricity and the risk of disease. Employees chose to raise their concerns with union representatives rather than the appointed safety representatives. When the employer refused to resolve the situation, the men went home. They were dismissed when, a few days later, they still refused to return to work.

The EAT accepted that it would have been reasonably practicable for the men to approach the safety representatives but held that it was 'highly artificial' for employees to concern themselves with the appropriate route of communicating a matter of serious and imminent concern to the employer. The important thing is that the message is communicated quickly and succinctly. The EAT noted that Article 13(2)(d) of EU Directive No.89/391 on the introduction of measures to encourage improvements in the safety and health of workers at work obliges employees to 'immediately inform the employer and/or the workers with specific responsibility for the safety and health of workers of any work situation they have reasonable grounds for considering represents a serious and immediate danger to safety and health and of any shortcomings in the protection arrangements'. In order to ensure that S.100 was compatible with the Directive,

513

the EAT inserted a phrase into subsection (e) so that it read: 'in circumstances of danger which the employee reasonably believed to be serious and imminent, he took (or proposed to take) appropriate steps to protect himself or other persons from the danger or to communicate these circumstances by any appropriate means to the employer'. According to the EAT, this would in turn restrict the scope of S.100(1)(c), although it commented that 'there might be better ways of achieving the same result'. In any event, the EAT was clear that an employee performing his or her obligations under the Directive in immediately informing the employer of a serious danger could not be lawfully dismissed on that ground under English law. Therefore, the employees were entitled to raise their concerns with the trade union representatives.

10.28　On behalf of the employer it was then argued that although on the day the men walked out there was a serious and imminent danger to health, this was no longer the case a few days later when the men had still not returned to work and were dismissed accordingly. By this time, it was argued, the men should have sought to resolve the matter with the safety representatives. The EAT was unconvinced. Where the employer had continued without protest to discuss matters directly with the union representatives, the EAT held that those representatives should be treated as representatives of workers on matters of health and safety 'by reason of being acknowledged as such by the employer'. The employer's argument bore 'no relation to reality'.

The impact of this case on the scope of S.100(1)(c) is not entirely clear. The EAT appears to be saying that the facts actually fell within S.100(1)(e) as construed in light of the Directive. If this is correct, then it may be that the requirement to use appropriate channels remains in cases that do not involve serious and imminent danger and therefore still fall within S.100(1)(c). However, in such cases, where the employer deals with trade union representatives rather than safety representatives without complaint, the trade union representatives may be treated as such for the purposes of the section. Alternatively, on the facts of this case at least, the EAT could be saying that in order to ensure compatibility with the Directive, the requirement for a tribunal to assess the reasonable practicability of communicating with safety representatives is effectively disapplied. In any event, the important message is that by virtue of the Directive, the courts and tribunals will take a robust approach to the interpretation of S.100 and employers will not be allowed to resort to technical legal arguments in order to circumvent the protection afforded by it.

10.29　**Means of bringing concerns to employer's attention.** In Balfour Kilpatrick Ltd v Acheson and ors (above), the employer also argued that taking industrial action could not be considered a reasonable means of bringing the men's health and safety concerns to the employer's attention. Here the EAT agreed, commenting that neither could it be said to amount to 'informing' the employer under Article 13 of the Directive. Although in some exceptional circumstances employees could communicate concerns to their employer by action rather than words (where, for example, an employee points out a hazard to an employer who is some distance away), this did not extend to the taking of industrial action.

Two further examples of means that were not considered reasonable:

- **Tate v Salvesen Logistics Ltd** EAT 226/97: T raised health and safety concerns in a casual conversation initiated by a director of an associated company of the employer. Although T asked for the conversation to be treated in confidence, the director refused and passed on details to the employer. T was dismissed. The EAT upheld a tribunal's decision that it was not reasonable for T to raise his concerns in this manner. He should have raised them with his line manager

- **Stephens v NFT Distribution Ltd** ET Case No.1201794/98: S persistently raised health and safety concerns in letters which his employer found to be offensive, continuing to do so even after he was instructed to desist. S was dismissed. A tribunal found that S had not used reasonable means to communicate his concerns. His letters were offensive, patronising, flippant and entirely lacking in respect. No employer could be expected to tolerate them.

Reasonable grounds for belief. The question of what amounts to reasonable **10.30** grounds for believing that there were circumstances harmful to health and safety was considered in Kerr v Nathan's Wastesavers Ltd EAT 91/95. In that case K was dismissed because he refused to drive a vehicle that, in his opinion, might have become overloaded by the end of the working day. The tribunal dismissed his unfair dismissal claim because, although K's belief was genuine, it was not based on reasonable grounds. The employer had a procedure whereby employees could either return to the depot or telephone in to arrange for a second vehicle to meet them somewhere so that they could swap vehicles. K had not taken advantage of this practice and therefore did not have reasonable grounds for thinking that the request to drive the vehicle was potentially harmful to safety.

The EAT upheld the tribunal's decision and gave some guidance on the correct approach to take when deciding whether an employee has the reasonable belief required by S.100(1)(c). The EAT emphasised that not too onerous a duty of enquiry should be placed on the employee in this regard. The purpose of the legislation is to protect employees who raise matters of health and safety; the fact that concern might be allayed by further enquiry need not mean that the employee's concern is not reasonable. On a different point, the EAT also stated that it was irrelevant whether or not the employer had acted unreasonably when considering a claim under the subsection.

10.31 In Joao v Jurys Hotel Management Ltd EAT 0210/11 the EAT held that the fact that working arrangements proposed by the employer are not unlawful does not mean that an employee cannot reasonably believe that they were. In that case JHM Ltd proposed that J work nine consecutive night shifts. After J raised concerns about health and safety and the law, JHM Ltd dismissed him. A tribunal, hearing his complaint of automatically unfair dismissal under S.100(1)(c), found that the proposed arrangement was not in breach of the Working Time Regulations 1998 SI 1998/1833. That being so, it could not see how J could reasonably think that there had been a health and safety risk, particularly when Parliament had stated that such an approach was perfectly lawful. The EAT allowed J's appeal against that decision. It held that there was a disconnect between the tribunal's finding that the arrangement was lawful and its finding that J could not reasonably have believed otherwise – the second finding did not follow from the first. The claim was remitted to a different tribunal.

That said, vague, generalised assumptions by the employee about the risks involved are unlikely to amount to a reasonable belief without more. In Hindmarch v Chemrock Cryogenics UK Ltd ET Case No.2500983/06, for example, H was a highly skilled employee in a niche area of work – lining petrochemical tanks – who could be required by CC Ltd to work anywhere in the world. In August 2005 he refused to go to Qatar, insisting that because of the state of alert relating to terrorist attacks, he would not work in any Muslim country. He claimed that his subsequent dismissal was automatically unfair by virtue of S.100(1)(c). The tribunal held that H had made a generalised assumption about the safety of UK nationals working in Muslim countries. Although he believed there was a higher risk, that belief, having been reached without any reference to the safety and security measures CC Ltd would have put in place, was not based on reasonable grounds.

10.32 **Potentially harmful to third parties.** Section 100(1)(c) protects employees who bring to their employer's attention by reasonable means circumstances connected with their work which they reasonably believed were harmful or potentially harmful. In Brendon v BNFL Flurochemicals Ltd EAT 766/95 the question arose as to whether S.100 is confined to health and safety in the workplace, or whether it protects employees who express concern about potential damage to third parties outside the workplace, such as consumers of a company's products or the general public. The question arose when B, a sales executive for a company selling a variety of chemicals, was dismissed for his poor sales performance but alleged that the real reason was his concern over a health and safety matter. One of the chemicals produced by the company was used in many countries in the course of eye operations. The chemical was prohibited in the United States, however, because it was thought to cause blindness. B suspected that a customer who had ordered a quantity of the chemical intended to export it illegally to the United States and he was concerned

516

about the risk the chemical posed for American eye patients. B devoted a lot of time to investigating the potential side-effects of the chemical and it was around this time that his sales began to fall. When his employer dismissed him he claimed that his dismissal was automatically unfair. The tribunal dismissed B's claim and he appealed.

The EAT accepted that it was arguable that S.100 might stretch beyond hazards in the workplace and that an employee might legitimately be concerned about something which happened elsewhere. However, it did not decide the point. Instead, it upheld the tribunal's decision that B had been dismissed on account of his poor sales record and that health and safety matters played no part. The EAT pointed out that S.100(1)(c) refers to an employee raising health and safety matters with the employer 'by reasonable means'. It was unlikely that the provision entitled B to devote so much time to his health and safety concerns that his work suffered and his sales fell.

10.33 A tribunal took the view that S.100(1)(c) did cover complaints about hazards to third parties in Lines v Johnson t/a County Coaches ET Case No.2500359/96. In that case L was dismissed because he refused to drive a 29-seater bus to transport 33 passengers. A tribunal found the dismissal unfair under S.100(1)(c). The employer had required L to use the bus in contravention of the Public Service Vehicles (Carrying Capacity) Regulations 1984 SI 1984/1406, the purpose of which is to ensure the safety of passengers. Similarly, in Barton v Wandsworth Council ET Case No.11268/94 a tribunal held that an ambulance driver's concerns for the safety of patients following a reduction in the quality of the escort service provided to assist patients in ambulances was a concern that could be protected by the health and safety provisions of the ERA.

It seems unlikely that the legislation was not intended to protect employees bringing to their employer's attention matters that affect the health or safety of others outside the workplace. The point which the EAT made clear in Brendon v BNFL Flurochemicals Ltd (above), however, is that while S.100(1)(c) probably does protect an employee who brings the matter to the employer's attention, it may not protect acts which go beyond that. Once an employee has informed the employer of the potential risk, it is unlikely that he or she will be protected under this subsection for pursuing the matter further. However, S.100(1)(d) and (e) are more wide-ranging than S.100(1)(c) in that they protect an employee who walks off the job or actually does something to avert danger or protect others – so long as the danger is 'serious and imminent' and the steps taken are not inappropriate or negligent (see 'Section 100(1)(d)' and 'Section 100(1)(e)' below).

10.34 Even if S.100(1)(c) were restricted to matters of health and safety in the workplace, an employee bringing concerns about health and safety outside the workplace to the employer's attention would very likely be covered by the automatically unfair dismissal provision in S.103 ERA, which governs

517

'protected disclosures' – see 'Section 100(1)(e) – protected disclosures' below, and IDS Employment Law Handbook, 'Whistleblowing at Work' (2013).

10.35 Some cases brought under S.100(1)(c):

- **Jahanqir v Sim Felt Ltd and ors** ET Case No.1804301/12: J made a number of health and safety complaints to his employer about the safety of machinery and the fact that toilet facilities were unavailable to staff. When his employer took no action he sought advice from the Citizens Advice Bureau (CAB), which contacted his employer. However, still no action was taken and the CAB, acting on J's behalf, then wrote to the Health and Safety Executive (HSE). J was dismissed for complaining to the HSE and his dismissal was automatically unfair under S.100(1)(c)

- **Stephanou v Teaching Personnel Ltd** ET Case No.1200183/97: the office premises at which S worked were devastated by fire. When S had finished helping his employer clear up he tried to go back to his telephone sales duties. However, because there was no heating and all the windows were open to disperse the smoke and fumes, S asked to leave early because he was so cold. Although it was clear that H, the director to whom he spoke, was not pleased about the request, he granted permission. However, later that evening H called to dismiss S. The tribunal found that S was dismissed for protesting about having to stay at work in conditions that posed a risk to health and safety. There was no nominated safety representative and his protest therefore fell within S.100(1)(c)

- **Hobell v J Todd t/a Todd Opticians** ET Case No.61769/94: H was dismissed after one week's employment as an optical receptionist. She had made it clear to her employer that she was dissatisfied with arrangements for lunch times. There were no settled breaks – she was expected to eat her lunch while working – and she could go out only if this was convenient to others. The employer's response was to the effect that if she did not like the job she did not have to stay. H then wrote to the employer setting out her belief that the Shops Act 1950 and health and safety legislation entitled her to a fixed lunch-hour. The employer dismissed her on receiving the letter. The tribunal held that the dismissal was automatically unfair. H had clearly been dismissed because of the letter in which she had quite reasonably brought to her employer's attention her belief that the lunch-time arrangement was harmful or potentially harmful to her health and safety

- **Akinbobola v Swirl Court Services** ET Case No.28720/96: a representative of the workforce attended a meeting with the employer at which the provision of protective equipment was discussed. The employees' understanding was that an agreement had been reached whereby they were not required to carry out work for which protective equipment was necessary but not available. On one occasion, A was sent home without pay when he refused to work with chemicals from a container which contained no explanatory label without goggles and gloves. On another occasion, he refused to pick up litter from an underground railway tunnel unless he was provided with a torchlight and litter picker. They were not provided and he was dismissed for 'his failure to work on many occasions'. The tribunal held that his dismissal was unfair under S.100(1)(c).

Section 100(1)(d)

10.36

This subsection protects employees who left, proposed to leave, or refused to return to their place of work in circumstances of danger which they reasonably believed to be serious and imminent and which they could not reasonably have been expected to avert.

Reasonable belief. In Begum v Sunlight Services Group Ltd ET Case No.2304046/97 a tribunal had to consider the reasonableness of an employee's belief that her working conditions fell within the scope of S.100(1)(d). B worked in the 'clean' room of her employer's laundry business. Her job was to pack laundered surgical gowns. The 'clean' room was a controlled environment and its air conditioning system was unable to cope with extremes of temperature. B and her colleagues had to stand to work and were expected to stay until the workload for the day had been processed. During a period of very hot weather, B and her colleagues asked whether they could be allowed to open their protective gowns or open the door to the clean room because the heat and humidity was making them feel unwell and they had been allowed to do so in a previous year during intense heat. A supervisor refused and passed on the request to a manager, C. B did not speak good English. Through her colleagues she explained to C that the heat was intolerable and that unless something was done they would go home before the end of the shift. C told them that if they went home they would be doing so for good. She took no steps to investigate the complaint and did not check the temperature. B and others did not fully understand the extent of C's ultimatum and left because they considered conditions unsafe. They were dismissed.

10.37

After they had left, the temperature was found to be 74°F, equal to or just below the employer's recommended maximum temperature. There was no thermometer in the room. The tribunal found that B had a reasonable belief that the heat and humidity constituted a serious and imminent danger: because she had no means of objectively checking the temperature and her manager had refused to do so, her only way of judging the temperature was by her own assessment and she felt it was too hot to work and it was making her feel ill.

Similarly, in Stevenson v The Original London Sightseeing Tour Ltd ET Case No.2328201/09 – a detriment case brought under S.44(1)(e) ERA, which protects workers from being subjected to a detriment in the same circumstances as S.100(1)(e) – S refused to drive a bus that had a crack in the windscreen

10.38

519

which, despite being drilled a number of times (to stop it spreading), was getting worse. However, his employer's workshop supervisor believed that the bus was roadworthy as the crack did not affect the driver's view. S explained that he believed that the crack was illegal and if he was pulled over by the Vehicle and Operator Services Agency they would deem the vehicle unfit. He wanted clarification of what was legal and safe to drive. The employment tribunal accepted that S's fears that the bus was dangerous to drive were genuine and reasonable based on his substantial experience as a driver as well as what he had been told by the assistant traffic manager. His concerns about the safety of the bus were not addressed and he was unaware that his employer planned to replace the screen imminently.

By contrast, in Akintola v Capita Symonds Ltd 2010 EWCA Civ 405, CA, the Court of Appeal held that an employment tribunal had been entitled to find that A did not have a reasonable belief that he was in circumstances of serious and imminent danger for the purposes of a claim under S.100(1)(d). A was employed by CS Ltd as a senior structural engineer. He was instructed to go to Marble Arch underground station to provide structural advice. However, on arrival at the site A found that he was expected to enter a confined space in a tunnel through a manhole. He refused to do so for safety reasons and later resigned. He presented a claim for, among other things, constructive dismissal on the basis that the principal reason for his resignation was the imminent danger created by the incident at Marble Arch. The employment tribunal held that A was unable to prove that there was a serious or imminent danger, noting that there was in existence a method statement and that Westminster Council (which owned the tunnel) had sent in a specialist team to undertake all the necessary monitoring before anyone else was allowed in.

10.39 In Edwards and ors v Secretary of State for Justice EAT 0123/14 – another detriment case brought under S.44(1)(d) – the claimants had refused to be driven to work at HMP Dartmoor on a road that had been closed due to heavy snowfall. An employment judge held that since some of the claimants' colleagues had been successfully ferried to work in four-wheel drive vehicles, it followed that none of the claimants could have held a reasonable belief that there were circumstances of danger which were both serious and imminent and which they could not reasonably be expected to avert. On appeal the EAT held that the employment judge had not addressed the pivotal question of whether the claimants had been told that the police had given approval for the road to be traversed. Furthermore, the judge had erred by failing to consider the reasonable belief of each individual claimant and by regarding the fact that no accident had happened as conclusive evidence of an absence of serious and imminent danger. The matter was remitted to a different employment judge for a rehearing.

10.40 **Serious and imminent danger.** Claims brought under S.100(1)(d) will fail if the employee concerned is unable to show that he or she acted in circumstances of danger which he or she reasonably believed to be serious and imminent. What amounts to a serious and imminent danger is a question of fact and will vary from case to case.

In Harvest Press Ltd v McCaffrey 1999 IRLR 778, EAT, M complained about the behaviour of H, a colleague with whom he shared the night shift. Upon finding out about M's complaint, H became very abusive. M, concerned for his safety, went home, telephoned his manager and refused to return to work unless H was removed or dismissed. The following day, the employer spoke to H about the incident and telephoned M to inform him that by walking out in the middle of a shift he was taken to have resigned. A tribunal subsequently found that M had been dismissed in circumstances that fell within S.100(1)(d). In upholding this decision, the EAT commented that S.100(1)(d) was intended to be wide, the word 'danger' being used without limitation. There was no reason to restrict circumstances of danger to those generated by the workplace itself. The EAT gave a number of examples involving the presence or absence of other employees that could fall within S.100(1)(d), in addition to that provided by the facts of the case itself:

- premises becoming unsafe as a result of an unskilled and untrained employee working on dangerous processes in the workplace, where the danger of a mistake extends to those working with him or her

- the absence of a person with specific safety responsibilities where dangerous processes were being carried out

- a foolhardy employee determined to indulge in horseplay persistently adopting dangerous practices in the workplace.

10.41 The EAT concluded that S.100(1)(d) covered any danger, however originating. A sensible employer would have spoken to M to form a view as to whether his concerns were genuine and acted accordingly.

In Begum v Sunlight Services Group Ltd, discussed under 'Reasonable belief' above, the tribunal applied the Oxford dictionary definition of 'danger', which reads: 'liability or exposure to harm or injury; risk, peril'. In the tribunal's opinion, there was therefore no need for the danger to be life-threatening. Because there was no way for the danger in that case to be objectively assessed, the employees' subjective feelings were enough to establish reasonable belief that the danger was serious and imminent.

10.42 It is important to realise that circumstances of danger may change over a period of time. In Balfour Kilpatrick Ltd v Acheson and ors 2003 IRLR 683, EAT, a tribunal found that there had been circumstances of danger that the employees reasonably believed to be serious and imminent sufficient to justify a mass walk-out on the day those circumstances arose. The employees were engaged in electrical work on a building site. The site was on marshy ground susceptible

521

to flooding and the Portakabins in which working clothes were kept were inadequately heated. Heavy rain led to wide areas of standing water, increasing the risk of exposure to Weil's disease carried by rats on the site. There were also concerns about the dangers of working with electricity in the wet conditions. Moreover, protective clothing and boots were soaking wet. The men were justified in walking out and refusing to work in these circumstances. However, four days later the men were still refusing to work and it was this refusal that led to their dismissal. The tribunal found that the weather had improved and the clothing and boots had largely dried. The men were no longer reasonable in their belief that danger was still serious and imminent. There was no challenge to this finding before the EAT.

10.43 The following cases, some of which were decided under the similar wording contained in S.100(1)(e) (see 'Section 100(1)(e)' below), give useful examples of 'serious and imminent' danger:

- **Bush v AP Construction (Geddington) Ltd** ET Case No.1201929/10: B was sent home from work one day and not paid because he refused to travel in a lorry driven by a colleague who was smoking. The colleague had previously agreed not to smoke in the lorry but on that day had said that he intended to do so. B was then put onto another job but when he made further complaints to APC(G) Ltd he was dismissed. The employment tribunal was not convinced that being exposed to passive smoking amounted to a serious and imminent danger

- **Hoyle v Nottingham Ambulance Service NHS Trust** ET Case No.2601392/98: H, an ambulance driver in the patient transport service, raised a number of concerns with his employer in a series of confrontational letters. He claimed he faced a danger in loading stretchered patients into ambulances without ramps and in following a schedule that he believed encouraged drivers to break the speed limit. The employer acknowledged there was a problem and was taking steps to deal with it. In the meantime, H was instructed to raise any further concerns with the safety representative. Instead, H made complaints to the Health and Safety Executive and to the police. A tribunal found that H did not believe the risk was serious and imminent. The risk of harm was avoidable by H taking care and seeking assistance where necessary. The transfer schedules were only a guide and were not an encouragement to break the speed limit

- **Dent v Greater Reading Omnibus Co Ltd** ET Case No.2700330/97: D was a bus driver. When his indicators failed, D stopped the bus to report the failure and refused to drive it any further. D was dismissed, either expressly or constructively. A tribunal found that the condition of the bus gave rise to a circumstance of danger and that D reasonably believed that danger to be serious and imminent

522

- **Dodd v Blue Star Engineering Ltd** ET Case No.31942/94: D worked in the electronics department but because of a shortfall of work she was transferred to work on a machine known as a grinding master. D refused to operate the machine because it was a dusty and dirty job and the position in which she had to stand was dangerous because of the continual passing of men carrying aluminium strips. D was sent home to think over her decision. The following day D still refused and her employment was terminated. The tribunal noted that D had not complained to the safety representative and decided that D's only real complaint was that the machine was dirty. The tribunal held that this did not constitute circumstances of danger within S.100

- **Ballard v Rushlake Services Ltd** ET Case No.1101336/98: B worked for a small company engaged in the removal of asbestos from premises. On one particular job, he became concerned that P, the employer's managing director, was setting up the work in a way different to the method statement that had been submitted to the Health and Safety Executive (HSE). P instructed the employees to work in a way that reduced costs and he disregarded the HSE guidelines as impractical when B drew his attention to them. B felt he was unable to work safely and called in the HSE. He was dismissed. A tribunal found that B had a reasonable belief that he was working in circumstances of serious and imminent danger. It heard evidence to that effect from the HSE officer called to the job site.

Section 100(1)(e)

10.44

This subsection protects employees who, in circumstances of danger that they reasonably believed to be serious and imminent, took (or proposed to take) appropriate steps to protect themselves or other persons from the danger. The cases discussed above under S.100(1)(d) on the question of 'serious and imminent' danger apply equally to this subsection. In Masiak v City Restaurants (UK) Ltd 1999 IRLR 780, EAT, the Appeal Tribunal held that 'other persons' can include members of the public and is not restricted to other employees or workers of the employer. Therefore it was open to M, who walked out of his employer's restaurant having refused to cook food that he considered to be a potential health hazard, to bring a claim for automatic unfair dismissal under S.100(1)(e).

Whether an employee has taken, or proposed to take, appropriate steps for the purposes of this subsection is to be judged by reference to all the circumstances, including his or her knowledge and the facilities and advice available to him or her at the time – S.100(2). A tribunal that rules there is no serious and imminent danger without hearing evidence will therefore err in law – Masiak (above). If, however, an employer shows that it was, or would have been, so negligent of the employee to take the steps that he or she took, or proposed to take, that a reasonable employer might have dismissed him or her, then the employee's

523

dismissal will not be regarded as automatically unfair – S.100(3). In these circumstances, the fairness of the dismissal will be determined according to the usual test under S.98(4).

10.45 The test under S.100(2) will obviously be one of proportionality – i.e. whether the employee's response was in proportion to the danger posed. But the test does allow for some subjectivity in so far as the appropriateness of the steps taken must be gauged according to the employee's perception of the danger and his or her understanding of the situation. It would be no defence, therefore, for an employer to say that it had taken steps to remedy the situation if the employee was unaware of this. In Begum v Sunlight Services Group Ltd (discussed under 'Section 100(1)(d) – reasonable belief' above), the tribunal found that S.100(1)(e) also applied to the situation that B found herself in. The fact that there was no means of objective assessment of the temperature and that the employer did not investigate the complaint meant that it was reasonable for B to leave the premises. S.100(3) did not apply since B was not endangering anyone's life by leaving the premises and there was no active machinery that might have caused harm as a result of B leaving when she did.

According to the EAT in Oudahar v Esporta Group Ltd 2011 ICR 1406, EAT, the proper approach to any consideration of S.100(1)(e) is for the tribunal to apply a two-stage approach. First, it should consider whether the criteria set out in that provision have been met as a matter of fact. Were there circumstances of danger that the employee reasonably believed to be serious or imminent? Did he or she take or propose to take appropriate steps to protect him or herself or other persons from the danger or – following the EAT's decision in Balfour Kilpatrick Ltd v Acheson and ors 2003 IRLR 683, EAT (considered under 'Informing employer' below) – take steps to communicate these circumstances to the employer by the appropriate means? If these criteria are not satisfied, then S.100(1)(e) is not engaged. However, if the criteria are made out, the second stage is for the tribunal to consider whether the employer's sole or principal reason for dismissal was that the employee took or proposed to take appropriate steps. If so, the dismissal must be regarded as unfair.

10.46 In the Oudahar case the claimant had been dismissed after refusing to mop an area where maintenance was being carried out and wiring was exposed. The tribunal rejected his claim under S.100(1)(e) on the basis that the employer had investigated the matter and had reasonably satisfied itself that there was no risk to health and safety. In allowing the claimant's appeal and remitting the matter to be reconsidered by the tribunal, the EAT stressed that the fact that the employer had preferred the account of a managerial witness and concluded there was no risk to health and safety is irrelevant to the question of whether the reason for dismissal falls within S.100(1)(e). It serves the interests of health and safety that an employee should be protected so long as he or she acts honestly and reasonably in the circumstances covered by S.100(1)(c)–(e) ERA.

524

If employees were liable to dismissal merely because their employers disagreed with their account of the facts or opinions as to the action required, the statutory provisions would confer little protection. The tribunal should have considered whether the criteria set out in S.100(1)(e) had been made out, adopting the approved two-stage approach. Instead, it had reached a conclusion about the second stage without properly addressing the first.

Informing employer. Words were written into S.100(1)(e) by the EAT in **10.47** Balfour Kilpatrick Ltd v Acheson and ors (above), to bring S.100 into line with EU Directive No.89/391 on the introduction of measures to encourage improvements in the safety and health of workers at work, which obliges employees to 'immediately inform the employer and/or the workers with specific responsibility for the safety and health of workers of any work situation they have reasonable grounds for considering represents a serious and immediate danger to safety and health and of any shortcomings in the protection arrangements'. This was done to fill a lacuna in the scope of subsection (c), which provides that, when raising a health and safety concern, employees should go through a safety committee or representative wherever possible, rather than directly to the employer. According to the EAT, in order to ensure that S.100 was compatible with the Directive, subsection (e) should read: 'in circumstances of danger which the employee reasonably believed to be serious and imminent, he took (or proposed to take) appropriate steps to protect himself or other persons from the danger *or to communicate these circumstances by any appropriate means to the employer*' (our stress) – see 'Section 100(1)(c) – appropriate channels' above for further details.

Protected disclosures. An employee may be tempted to 'blow the whistle' on **10.48** an employer by referring a health and safety matter to an outside body, such as the Health and Safety Executive, or even a newspaper. An employee dismissed in these circumstances might be able to bring a claim under this subsection, although a tribunal would have to consider whether he or she had taken 'appropriate steps' to protect him or herself or other persons from danger. What is perhaps more likely is that the employee would bring a claim under S.103A ERA, which protects whistleblowers who are dismissed for making a 'protected disclosure'. One of the categories of disclosure covered by that provision is that which tends to show 'that the health or safety of any individual has been, is being or is likely to be endangered'. This right, which is subject to qualifications, exists entirely independently of the rights contained in S.100 and is in many ways wider than the protection conferred by that provision. More details can be found in IDS Employment Law Handbook, 'Whistleblowing at Work' (2013), Chapter 3, 'Qualifying disclosures', under 'Endangerment of health and safety'.

525

11 Dismissal for asserting a statutory right

Assertion of a statutory right

Requirement of good faith

Reason for dismissal

Under S.104 of the Employment Rights Act 1996 (ERA), an employee's **11.1** dismissal is automatically unfair if the reason or principal reason for the dismissal was that:

- the employee brought proceedings against the employer to enforce a relevant statutory right – S.104(1)(a), or

- the employee alleged that the employer had infringed a relevant statutory right – S.104(1)(b).

It is also automatically unfair to select an employee for redundancy for one of the reasons specified in S.104(1) where the reason (or principal reason) for the dismissal was redundancy but the redundancy situation applied equally to one or more other employees in the same undertaking who held positions similar to that held by the employee and who were not dismissed – S.105(1) and (7).

It is immaterial whether the employee actually had the statutory right in **11.2** question or whether the right had been infringed, but the employee's claim to the right and its infringement must have been made in good faith – S.104(2). Furthermore, it is sufficient that the employee made it reasonably clear to the employer what the right claimed to have been infringed was; it is not necessary actually to specify the right – S.104(3).

An employee may bring a claim of unfair dismissal for asserting a statutory right whatever his or her length of service – the two-year qualifying period normally required to bring an unfair dismissal claim does not apply.

In a claim brought under S.104, there are three main requirements: **11.3**

- the employee must have asserted a relevant statutory right

- the assertion must have been made in good faith, and

- the assertion must have been the reason or principal reason for the dismissal.

These requirements are considered in turn below.

527

11.4 Assertion of a statutory right

The first requirement is that the employee must have asserted a relevant statutory right, either by bringing proceedings against the employer to enforce such a right, or by alleging that the employer has infringed such a right – S.104(1).

11.5 Relevant statutory rights

Section 104 does not apply to all statutory rights but only to the 'relevant' statutory rights referred to in S.104(4). These include 'any right conferred by this Act [i.e. the ERA] for which the remedy for its infringement is by way of a complaint or reference to an employment tribunal' – S.104(4)(a). This means that when a new employment right is inserted into the ERA it automatically becomes a relevant statutory right, provided of course that the remedy for infringement of that right is by way of a complaint to an employment tribunal.

The relevant statutory rights covered by S.104(4)(a) are:

- the right to receive a written statement of employment particulars, a statement of changes to particulars or an itemised pay statement – Ss.1, 4 and 8 ERA

- protection of wages rights – Ss.13, 15, 18 and 21 ERA

- the right to a guarantee payment – S.28 ERA

- protection from detriment rights (jury service; health and safety; Sunday working; working time; trustees of occupational pension schemes; employee representatives; paid time off for study or training; protected disclosures; maternity, paternity, adoption, unpaid parental and shared parental leave; time off for dependants; time off for adoption appointments or ante-natal appointments; tax credits; flexible working; study and training; and refusing an offer to become an employee shareholder) – Ss.43M–47G ERA

- the right to time off for public duties – S.50 ERA

- the right of redundant employees to paid time off to look for work or arrange training – Ss.52 and 53 ERA

- the right to paid time off for ante-natal care – Ss.55 and 56 ERA

- the right to time off to accompany a woman to ante-natal appointments – S.57ZE ERA

- the right to paid or unpaid time off to attend adoption appointments – Ss.57ZJ, 57ZK and 57ZL

- the right to time off for dependants – S.57A ERA

- the right of pension scheme trustees to paid time off – Ss.58 and 59 ERA

528

- the right of employee representatives to paid time off – Ss.61 and 62 ERA

- the right to paid time off for a young person in Wales or Scotland for study or training – Ss.63A and 63B ERA

- the right to make a request in relation to study and training, and have it properly considered by the employer – Ss.63D and 63F ERA

- the right to remuneration on suspension on medical grounds – S.64 ERA

- the right to alternative work and remuneration for maternity suspension – Ss.67 and 68 ERA

- the right to unpaid parental leave – S.76 ERA

- the right to make a request for flexible working and have it properly considered – Ss.80F and 80G ERA

- the right to receive a written statement of reasons for dismissal – S.92 ERA

- the right not to be unfairly dismissed – S.94 ERA

- the right to a redundancy payment – S.135 ERA.

A number of additional relevant statutory rights are listed in paragraphs (b) to **11.6** (e) of S.104(4). These are:

- the right to minimum notice – S.86 ERA (this right is not caught by the catch-all provision of S.104(4)(a) because the remedy for infringement is a common law claim for damages for wrongful dismissal)

- the right not to suffer unauthorised deductions from wages in respect of union subscriptions – S.68 Trade Union and Labour Relations (Consolidation) Act 1992 (TULR(C)A)

- the right not to suffer unauthorised deductions from wages in respect of a union political fund – S.86 TULR(C)A

- the right not to be offered an inducement in relation to union membership or activities – S.145A TULR(C)A

- the right not to be offered an inducement in relation to collective bargaining – S.145B TULR(C)A

- the right not to be subjected to a detriment on grounds related to union membership or activities – S.146 TULR(C)A

- the right of union officials to paid time off for union duties – Ss.168 and 169 TULR(C)A

- the right of union learning representatives to paid time off for learning and training activities – Ss.168A and 169 TULR(C)A

- the right of union members to time off for union activities – S.170 TULR(C)A

529

- any of the rights conferred by the Working Time Regulations 1998 SI 1998/1833 (the Working Time Regulations 1998); the Merchant Shipping (Hours of Work) Regulations 2002 SI 2002/2125; the Merchant Shipping (Working Time: Inland Waterways) Regulations 2003 SI 2003/3049; the Fishing Vessels (Working Time: Sea-fishermen) Regulations 2004 SI 2004/1713; or the Crossborder Railway Services (Working Time) Regulations 2008 SI 2008/1660

- the rights conferred by the Transfer of Undertakings (Protection of Employment) Regulations 2006 SI 2006/246 (TUPE).

To establish a claim of automatic unfair dismissal for asserting a statutory right under S.104, it is crucial that the right asserted falls within one of the above lists. There are a number of employment rights that do not appear above and a claim under S.104 cannot therefore be brought in respect of them – e.g. the right to be accompanied under S.10 of the Employment Relations Act 1999. Similarly, a claim under S.104 cannot be brought in respect of any of the anti-discrimination rights contained in the Equality Act 2010 (EqA). However, employees who bring a discrimination, harassment or equal pay claim are protected from less favourable treatment (including dismissal) at the hands of their employer for bringing the claim under the statutory 'victimisation' provisions contained in the EqA – see IDS Employment Law Handbook, 'Discrimination at Work' (2012), Chapter 19, 'Victimisation'.

11.7 **Inclusion of TUPE rights.** A little-known but significant amendment to S.104(4) was the inclusion – from April 2006 – of the rights conferred by the Transfer of Undertakings (Protection of Employment) Regulations 2006 SI 2006/246 (TUPE). The rights under the previous incarnation of the Regulations, the Transfer of Undertakings (Protection of Employment) Regulations 1981 SI 1981/1794, were not included.

There are two reasons why this change is significant. First, prior to the 2006 amendment, an employee dismissed for asserting a right to the same rate of pay as he or she enjoyed prior to a transfer would need to establish both a right under TUPE *and* a relevant statutory right under the ERA. Secondly, the inclusion of TUPE rights in S.104(4) affords a degree of TUPE protection to employees who do not meet the two-year continuous service threshold in S.108(1) – see Chapter 2, 'Exclusions from right to claim', under 'Continuous service threshold'. Unlike most other forms of automatically unfair dismissal, TUPE dismissals are subject to the S.108(1) qualifying period. This is not the case for unfair dismissal claims under S.104, which can be brought from the first day of employment.

For details of the rights afforded to employees under TUPE, see IDS Employment Law Handbook, 'Transfer of Undertakings' (2011).

Asserting the right

An employee asserts a relevant statutory right in one of two ways: by bringing tribunal proceedings to enforce the right – S.104(1)(a), or by alleging that the employer has infringed the right – S.104(1)(b). As we will see below, the majority of cases are brought under the latter provision. First, however, two examples of cases brought under S.104(1)(a):

- **Budzynska v Resource Management Holdings Ltd t/a Malla Technical Recruitment Consultancy** ET Case No.6005608/99: B was employed by an employment agency to work for one of its clients, HY. In January 1999, B claimed that she was entitled to paid holidays. Dissatisfied with the response she received, B brought tribunal proceedings, which were settled through Acas. As a result of the settlement, B's basic rate of pay was increased, which meant that when national insurance contributions were taken into account the total cost of her services to the agency was 96p an hour more than it was charging HY. The agency tried to renegotiate the arrangement with HY and when this proved impossible it terminated B's contract. A tribunal found that the principal reason for B's dismissal was that she had brought a claim under the Working Time Regulations 1998 and held that her dismissal was therefore automatically unfair under S.104(1)(a)

- **Stanford v City Centre Restaurants (UK) Ltd** ET Case No.2306191/03: S was employed as a waiter by CCR Ltd at one of its restaurants in June 2003 after an informal interview. He had been employed at another of its restaurants until March that year and had brought an unfair dismissal claim against the company. When the HR director discovered this, he told S that he could only continue in his job if he dropped the claim, and further added that the claim was weak and would leave S with hefty legal bills. When S refused to withdraw the claim, he was dismissed with immediate effect. The tribunal found that the reason for dismissal was that S had brought an unfair dismissal claim against CCR Ltd.

Section 104(2) states that it is immaterial whether or not the employee has the right in question. It is therefore irrelevant whether the tribunal proceedings are destined to be successful. In M-Choice UK Ltd v Aalders EAT 0227/11 A was given six months' notice of dismissal, due to expire on the same date she would accrue one year's continuous employment (as required at the time). During her notice period she instituted tribunal proceedings (S.111 ERA allows such a claim to proceed despite the fact that it has been lodged before the effective date of termination (EDT)). However, MCUK Ltd then summarily dismissed A just less than two weeks before the original notice was due to expire. The EAT held that, in accordance with established principles, the summary dismissal brought forward the EDT, meaning that A had not accrued one year's continuous employment and therefore had no right to complain of 'ordinary' unfair dismissal. However, she could complain of automatic unfair dismissal for asserting a statutory right in relation to the summary dismissal if it could be proved that the reason for it was that she had brought an unfair dismissal claim.

As mentioned above, the majority of cases decided to date have been brought under the second limb of S.104(1) (i.e. S.104(1)(b)), which covers the situation where an employee alleges that the employer has infringed his or her relevant statutory right. The leading case is Mennell v Newell and Wright (Transport Contractors) Ltd 1997 ICR 1039, CA, where M, an HGV driver, refused to sign a draft contract that would have allowed his employer to make deductions from his wages on termination of employment in order to recoup training costs. M was told that he would be sacked if he did not sign. He persisted in his refusal and was dismissed. M claimed that he had been unfairly dismissed for asserting his statutory right to not suffer unlawful deductions from wages under S.13 ERA. A tribunal dismissed the claim on the basis that there had been no infringement of S.13, only the possibility of such an infringement in the future. The EAT overturned the tribunal's decision, holding that, in the light of S.104(2), it was sufficient that the employee had alleged in good faith that the employer had infringed a relevant statutory right; there was no requirement for the employer to have actually infringed the right in question. While this was enough to determine the appeal, the EAT went one step further, stating that if the employer 'sought by threat of dismissal to impose a variation of the contract of employment to incorporate a term which negated the employee's statutory right not to suffer a deduction of wages without his freely given consent, that is, or might be, an infringement of his statutory right at the time when the threat is made, bearing in mind the words of [S.104(2)]'.

11.10 The case subsequently came before the Court of Appeal, which agreed with the EAT that S.104 is not confined to cases where a statutory right has actually been infringed. It is sufficient if the employee has alleged that the employer has infringed a statutory right and that the making of that allegation was the reason or the principal reason for the dismissal. The allegation need not be specific, provided it has been made reasonably clear to the employer what right was claimed to have been infringed. Furthermore, the allegation need not be correct, either as to the entitlement to the right or as to its infringement, provided the claim was made in good faith. The important point is that the employee must have made an allegation of the kind protected by S.104; if he or she did not, the making of such an allegation could not have been the reason for his or her dismissal. To that extent, the Court upheld the EAT's decision. However, the Court decided that, on the facts of the case, M had not alleged an infringement by his employer of his statutory rights, since he was unable to say when, where, to whom or in what terms he had made the allegation. The most he was able to say was that he had told management that he would sign the agreement only if the clause relating to the repayment of training expenses was amended and this was not sufficient for the purposes of S.104(1)(b). The employer's appeal was allowed on that basis.

Actual or threatened infringement? The Court of Appeal's judgment in **11.11** Mennell v Newell and Wright (Transport Contractors) Ltd (above) makes it clear that an employer does not actually need to have infringed a statutory right in order for the claim to succeed. However, despite the EAT's suggestion that an employer's threat to make an unauthorised deduction from wages may amount to an actual infringement of S.13 ERA, it would seem that it is still necessary for the employee to have alleged that the employer *has actually infringed* a statutory right. Based on a strict interpretation of the wording of S.104(1)(b) – which requires the employee to have 'alleged that the employer *had* infringed a right of his which is a relevant statutory right' (our stress) – an allegation that the employer has merely proposed or threatened to infringe such a right is not sufficient.

Indeed, this was the interpretation adopted by the EAT in McPartland v Pybus EAT 170/99. There, the employer wrote to M on 7 August informing her that her pay was to be reduced from £5 to £3.50 per hour. M replied by letter on 12 August stating that she did not accept this change to her terms and conditions and that if her next salary payment were made at the lower rate this would amount to an illegal deduction from her wages. The employer made a payment of salary to M at the lower rate on 14 August and, on the same date, dismissed her by letter stating that it would not be possible to reach a satisfactory conclusion. M's claim that her dismissal was automatically unfair under S.104 was dismissed by a tribunal on the basis that the allegation she had made related to a *prospective* infringement of a statutory right. The EAT upheld the tribunal's decision, stating that: 'The key to the right under S.104 is that there had been an infringement before the allegation is made. In this case, it is quite clear that the infringement, that is, the unauthorised deduction, did not take place until 14 August. The allegation that was made in the letter of 12 August related to a prospective deduction and to an anticipatory breach of contract. That is insufficient, in our judgment, for the purpose of S.104 of the Act.'

What constitutes an allegation of infringement? The employee's case in **11.12** Mennell v Newell and Wright (Transport Contractors) Ltd (above) ultimately failed because the Court of Appeal held that the fact that he told his employer that he would only sign the agreement if it were amended was not enough to amount to an allegation that his statutory right had been infringed. This raises the question as to what exactly the employee must allege in order to comply with S.104(1)(b). Ultimately this will be a question of fact for the tribunal to decide in each case. In the following cases, the tribunal found that an employee's allegations did amount to an assertion that the employer had infringed a statutory right:

533

- **Albion Hotel (Freshwater) Ltd v Silva and anor** 2002 IRLR 200, EAT: Mr and Mrs S were employed as managers of a hotel. Under their contracts of employment they were entitled to an annual bonus calculated by reference to the 'per person average bed night cost'. The hotel did not fare well under their management and when the bonus was due the employer made no payment. At a meeting between Mr and Mrs S and two company directors, Mr and Mrs S asserted that a bonus was due to them and the directors stated that no bonus was likely to be payable on the figures they had available. Mr and Mrs S continued to demand payment of the bonus and complained that it had not been paid. They were subsequently dismissed for 'poor management'. The tribunal found that the reason for their dismissal was in fact their assertion that a substantial bonus was due to them. Accordingly, the tribunal found that the employer had dismissed them for asserting that the employer had infringed a statutory right – namely, the right not to have an unlawful deduction made from wages under S.13 ERA. The EAT upheld this aspect of the tribunal's decision

- **Hutton v Wright** ET Case No.2103491/00: H was employed as a bar worker. One Sunday, she agreed to stay past her usual finishing time of midnight after her co-worker had to leave. When H prepared to leave, her employer, W, tried to stop her by telling her that there were still customers to serve. H pointed out to W that she was entitled to go home as she was only paid until midnight and by then it was 12.20 a.m. W told H that she had to stay until he said she could go. H said that she was prepared to stay if she was paid. W refused to pay her. H left and was dismissed. Before leaving, she had told W that he could not dismiss her for asking to be paid for the hours that she had worked. H brought a claim that she had been dismissed for asserting a statutory right. The tribunal held that the principal reason for her dismissal was her refusal to stay at work without being paid and that W's failure to pay her for time worked was an unlawful deduction from wages within the meaning of S.13(1) ERA. H was dismissed for asserting a right under S.13 and the dismissal was therefore automatically unfair under S.104

- **Power and anor v CDS Superstores International Ltd** ET Case No.2104109/10: the employees worked as a plumber and plumber's assistant respectively. Their contracts of employment required them to work 40 hours per week but in practice they worked on average 54 hours per week. At short notice, their employer asked them to work over a full weekend, including the Sunday. Believing that they were legally entitled to say no to working on the Sunday because of the number of days they would then have worked without a day's rest, they told the employer as much and said they would work the Saturday but then not return to work until the Monday. They were subsequently dismissed. A tribunal held that this amounted to an automatically unfair dismissal under S.104. The employees had thought they were entitled to refuse to work on the Sunday under the Working Time Regulations and had asserted as much in good faith. It was irrelevant that they did not actually have the right in question.

In Fraser v Carter Refrigeration and Retail Services Ltd ET Case No.2202270/00, **11.13** on the other hand, the employee's complaints were not sufficient to satisfy S.104(1)(b). F worked for CRRS Ltd as a duty refrigeration engineer operating from home. He responded to customers' calls to attend their premises to service their refrigerators during normal working hours. In addition, one week in five he was on emergency call-out outside normal working hours. Following complaints by a couple of customers that he had arrived late to their call-out requests, CRRS Ltd gave F a final written warning. Similar customer complaints followed. At a meeting to discuss the complaints F explained to CRRS Ltd that the reason he had not responded to one of the calls was that he had slept through his alarm as a result of having worked 37 hours over a weekend period without an adequate break. F was subsequently dismissed. He claimed that he had been dismissed for asserting his rights under health and safety legislation and under the Working Time Regulations 1998. The tribunal held that F's comments to his managers that he was fatigued on account of lack of sleep were not sufficient to amount to an allegation that CRRS Ltd had infringed his statutory rights.

Request for information. It appears that a simple request for information **11.14** relating to a statutory right does not of itself amount to an assertion. In Angel v Pitts-Tucker and Co ET Case No.3202086/97 A wrote a memo to her employer saying that she would like to know her benefits and asking for clarification on sick pay, wage reviews and bonuses. She was dismissed. The tribunal held that her memo was 'merely a request for information' and did not amount to an allegation that a relevant statutory right had been infringed.

Ultimately, however, whether or not an employee's request amounts to an assertion of a statutory right will be a question of fact for the tribunal to decide in each case. The EAT in Albion Hotel (Freshwater) Ltd v Silva and anor (above) recognised that there is a 'somewhat fine distinction between asking for a bonus (which would not be regarded as an assertion of a breach of the statutory right) and asking persistently, which might amount to an assertion of breach of a statutory right'.

Details of allegation
11.15
Section 104(3) expressly states that it is sufficient that the employee made it reasonably clear to the employer what the right claimed to have been infringed was; it is not necessary for the employee actually to specify the right. Clearly, an employee is not required to cite the section number of the right in question, or quote the precise statutory wording. However, it must still be made reasonably clear to the employer what right the employee is relying on.

535

In Armstrong v Walter Scott Motors (London) Ltd EAT 766/02 A worked as a car salesman. He wrote a letter to his employer to complain about a term in the staff handbook which provided that he would not accrue leave entitlement during the first year of employment. A wrote: 'I find this requirement morally indefensible in this day and age. I find it astonishing and infuriating that such a requirement was ever enforced, and fail to understand how any employee could be expected to work for a full year without taking leave.' He went on to request that he be allowed to take paid leave. A was dismissed and brought a claim for unfair dismissal under S.104 ERA. The tribunal decided unanimously that A had been dismissed because he had written the letter of complaint. However, the majority of the tribunal went on to find that A had not alleged, within S.104(1)(b), that his employer had infringed a statutory right. The majority considered that A had not suggested that his employer had failed to comply with 'any statutory right, as opposed to contractual arrangement or moral obligation'. More was required to make it reasonably clear to the employer what right was infringed. On appeal, the EAT stated that, in its view, A had made it 'reasonably clear to his employer that he had a right, in common with all others, not to have to wait for a year in order to take his holiday'. The EAT noted further that A did indeed have this right under the Working Time Regulations 1998 and that the right was being infringed. The EAT concluded that A had alleged that his employer was infringing his right to paid holiday under the Regulations. It followed, in the light of the tribunal's finding that A had been dismissed because he had written his letter of complaint, that A had been unfairly dismissed under S.104 for asserting a statutory right.

11.16 However, in Jones v Cutting Edge Services Ltd EAT 204/97 the EAT took the view that asserting a statutory right required the employee to do more than simply state that he believed himself to be entitled to a particular benefit. Although there was no need to refer to a particular piece of legislation, the employee had to assert that he or she had 'a right in law' to the benefit in question – in that case, to be paid at time and a half or to have a bonus increased as a condition of working overtime. The Jones case was referred to in Elizabeth Claire Care Management Ltd v Francis 2005 IRLR 858, EAT, in which the Appeal Tribunal took a broader approach. There, the employer had not paid F her salary when it was due. F, a single mother, was therefore unable to pay for childcare and could not come in to work. She made numerous phone calls to her employer explaining the reason for her absence and complaining that she had not been paid what she was owed. Several days later, F was dismissed, allegedly for failing to follow the employer's absence reporting procedures and disobeying management instructions in relation to a separate incident. A tribunal rejected the employer's evidence as to the reasons for dismissal and held that F's dismissal was automatically unfair under S.104. On appeal, the EAT agreed, stating that 'by complaining that she had not been paid, [F] was asserting "a relevant statutory right", which was not to have deductions made from her pay'.

Nonetheless, the requirement to make it reasonably clear to the employer what right is being relied on means that an employee who claims that he or she has been dismissed for asserting a particular right must at least refer to the constituent elements of that right, even if he or she does not point to the specific legal entitlement. In Jimenez v Nelabrook Ltd EAT 614/97, for example, J repeatedly asked her employer for her correct tax code in an attempt to ascertain whether tax was being paid on her behalf. Her employer dismissed her. J claimed that she had been dismissed for asserting her statutory right to an itemised pay statement under S.8 ERA. A tribunal found that J had not sought an itemised pay statement: the principal reason for the dismissal was the fact that she had requested information about her tax code. It concluded that she had not been dismissed for asserting a statutory right. J appealed to the EAT, which held that, in the light of the Court of Appeal's judgment in Mennell v Newell and Wright (Transport Contractors) Ltd (above), the crucial question was whether J was able to identify any occasion on which she had alleged that her employer had infringed her rights under S.8. Although S.104(3) made it clear that it was not necessary for J to refer specifically to S.8, the EAT thought that at the very least it was incumbent on her to ask for the details that would have been contained in an itemised pay statement. On the tribunal's findings of fact, she had not done so and accordingly she had not asserted a statutory right. Her appeal was therefore dismissed.

Timing of allegation

11.17

In order to be able to bring a claim under S.104 the employee's assertion that the employer has infringed a relevant statutory right must be made *prior* to dismissal. In Capitol Security Services Ltd v Blake EAT 961/97 B argued that his main complaint was of a change in pay arrangements which amounted to an unauthorised reduction in pay contrary to S.13 ERA. The EAT noted that, since the proceedings referred to in S.104(1)(a) or the allegation referred to in S.104(1)(b) must be the reason for the dismissal, they or it must precede the dismissal. The very proceedings before the tribunal itself cannot therefore be relied upon, nor allegations made in initiating or prosecuting those proceedings. As the tribunal in the instant case had made no findings of fact as to whether there were any allegations relating to pay prior to dismissal, the EAT remitted the matter to the tribunal so that the necessary facts could be established.

A similar point arose in Wilcox v Select Products Ltd ET Case No.1601394/99. There W was employed as a shift worker by SP Ltd. He had worked a 12-hour shift on a number of occasions without complaint. However, one Saturday after coming off shift at 6 a.m. he was asked by his manager to work another 12-hour shift starting at 6 p.m. the same day. W refused and was dismissed. Following W's dismissal, a Citizens Advice Bureau drafted a letter for him to

537

give to his employer stating, among other things, that he was owed a week's pay in lieu of notice. W later claimed that he had been dismissed for asserting a statutory right. The tribunal held that W's refusal to work a further 12-hour shift did not amount to an allegation that a statutory right had been infringed. Since he had made no other allegation prior to his dismissal, his claim under S.104 had to fail.

11.18 Requirement of good faith

Section 104(2) provides that it is immaterial whether or not the employee actually has the relevant statutory right or whether the right has been infringed. However, the subsection goes on to state that the employee's claim to the right – and that it has been infringed – must be made in good faith. It follows that an employee's genuine but mistaken belief that he or she has the statutory right in question will suffice. This point is illustrated by Power and anor v CDS Superstores International Ltd ET Case No. 2104109/10, where the tribunal held that P and E, a plumber and a plumber's assistant, had been dismissed for asserting a statutory right under the Working Time Regulations 1998 and their dismissals were therefore automatically unfair. It was irrelevant, for the purposes of S.104(1), that they did not actually have the right in question. Their claim to the right and their belief that it had been infringed had been made in good faith and therefore, by virtue of S.104(2), they could bring claims under S.104.

Section 104(2) also covers the situation where the employee has the right in question but there has been no actual infringement by the employer. The Court of Appeal's judgment in Mennell v Newell and Wright (Transport Contractors) Ltd 1997 ICR 1039, CA, makes it clear that the employer does not actually need to have infringed a statutory right in order for the claim to succeed. It is sufficient that the employee genuinely believes that an infringement has occurred.

11.19 For example, in Philip Hodges and Co v Crush EAT 1061/95 C agreed to a reduction in salary in the face of a threat of dismissal by her employer. After C's earnings had been reduced, a law centre adviser wrote to her employer on her behalf claiming that she had suffered unlawful deductions from her wages contrary to S.13 ERA. Following discussions with her employer, during which C again asserted that what had happened was unlawful, she was dismissed. The letter of dismissal specifically referred to the fact that she had taken outside legal advice. A tribunal found that C had agreed to the variation in contract and that consequently no unauthorised deductions had taken place. However, it held that the reason for C's dismissal was that she had asserted a relevant statutory right. On the employer's appeal, the EAT upheld the tribunal's finding that the reason for the dismissal was one that fell within S.104. In the EAT's opinion, the fact that the employee had authorised the

538

reduction in her salary and that there had therefore been no unlawful deductions was irrelevant. The tribunal had found that the claim that the employer had made unlawful deductions was made in good faith and this was sufficient to bring S.104 into play.

The question of whether an employee has acted in good faith in asserting that his or her statutory right has been infringed is one of fact for the tribunal to determine in each case. In Albion Hotel (Freshwater) Ltd v Silva and anor 2002 IRLR 200, EAT, the tribunal took the view that Mr and Mrs S's allegations were 'completely exaggerated' and that they had 'little hesitation in adding to their evidence matters which are self-serving'. However, the tribunal concluded that, in making a claim for a substantial bonus, Mr and Mrs S were acting in good faith, 'however misguided they may have been'. The EAT refused to interfere with this finding. The question of whether or not the employees acted in good faith in making their claim that they were entitled to a bonus and had been denied it was one of fact for the tribunal. The tribunal had taken into account the fact that the employees may have been misguided in claiming that they were entitled to a bonus, but concluded that they had nonetheless done so in good faith. The tribunal was not required to make a finding as to whether any bonus was in fact due to the employees. It was sufficient for the tribunal to find that the employees believed in good faith that a bonus was due. It was therefore irrelevant that, given the poor trading of the hotel under their management, the employees may not in fact have been due a bonus at all.

Reason for dismissal   11.20

The final requirement under S.104 is that the assertion of the relevant statutory right must be the reason, or the principal reason, for the employee's dismissal. The burden of proof is on the employee to establish the reason for dismissal, on the balance of probabilities. Where the parties advance different reasons, it is for the tribunal to decide, as a question of fact, which reason caused (or principally caused) the dismissal. The decision of the EAT in Derbyshire v Davis and anor t/a Samuel Davis (a firm) EAT 0703/03 provides some guidance on how this works in practice. There, a tribunal found that the employee was dismissed for asserting her statutory right to itemised pay slips and to payment in accordance with her contract of employment (i.e. the right not to suffer unlawful deductions from her pay). On appeal, the employer argued that despite reciting in the decision that the burden of proving that the principal reason for the dismissal was the assertion of statutory rights lay on the employee, the tribunal had in fact approached the matter by determining whether or not it accepted the explanations put forward by the employer and, when it did not, found the case proved. The employer argued that this amounted to a reversal of the burden of proof and, as such, an error of law. The EAT held that since the only assertions or alternate reasons that the tribunal had before it other

539

than those that were put forward by the employee were those given by the employer, the tribunal had to reach a view as to their veracity. To do so was not to reverse the burden of proof.

In JP Fitzpatrick (Cable TV) Ltd v Whicker EAT 1165/97 W found it difficult to carry out her job during her basic working hours and accordingly regularly worked overtime. On one occasion she put in an application for 45 minutes' overtime, which was refused partly on the basis that she was not performing well. W complained that she was not being paid what she was owed and that she would not work unpaid overtime. This amounted to an assertion of a statutory right. She subsequently decided not to work any overtime, which meant that some of her work remained unfinished. A few days later, W's employer terminated her employment, saying that she did not fit in. Before the tribunal, W claimed that she had been dismissed for asserting a statutory right. Her employer advanced other reasons for her dismissal, including that W was inefficient and deliberately left work unfinished. The EAT upheld the tribunal's finding that W had been dismissed for asserting a statutory right. The fact that W had asserted a statutory right, coupled with her dismissal eight days later, called for an explanation from the employer. Having rejected each of the reasons put forward by the employer, the tribunal correctly inferred that the reason or principal reason for dismissal was that advanced by W. Furthermore, the EAT held that there was a sufficient causative link between the assertion of the statutory right and the dismissal. Having complained that she had not been paid for overtime worked, W resolved to operate a personal overtime ban. Her employer felt this showed a lack of cooperation on W's part, which explained the employer's comment that W did not 'fit in'. It was for this reason that she was dismissed.

11.21 Some further examples:

- **Dance v Mitie Cleaning (North) Ltd** ET Case No.2508310/04: D had been employed by MC Ltd to work at Nissan's premises at a rate of £6.33 an hour. Following a complaint by Nissan, which made it clear that the company was no longer prepared to have D working at its premises, he was moved to other work as a janitor and his pay reduced to £6.17 an hour. D successfully brought a claim for unlawful deductions from wages over the reduction, following which MC Ltd decided it could not afford to employ him at the higher rate. He was called to a meeting, dismissed and offered re-engagement at the lower rate. Before the tribunal, MC Ltd argued that there was 'some other substantial reason' for the dismissal; namely, that Nissan no longer wanted D working on its premises. However, the tribunal disagreed, finding that the real reason for dismissal was that MC Ltd did not want to pay D at the higher rate in respect of which he had asserted a statutory right. The dismissal was therefore automatically unfair under S.104

- **King v Gurso Plant and Linings Ltd** ET Case No. 1301878/12: K began working for GP and L Ltd in June 2011. His contractual hours were 40 per week but he initially worked in excess of 48 hours per week, including working on Saturdays. In August 2011, K learned that he was legally entitled to refuse to work more than 48 hours per week and thereafter limited his hours to 48 per week and refused to work on Saturdays. In the following months, K's manager became unfriendly towards him and K felt under pressure to increase his hours and to work on Saturdays. On 28 October 2011, K's manager told him that he would have to work more than 48 hours per week and work on Saturdays but K refused and later that day he was called to a meeting and told that he was being laid off. In its defence to K's claim under S.104, the company argued that it had decided not to keep K on past the end of his probationary period because of his poor attitude and aggressive behaviour at work. The tribunal identified numerous inconsistencies in its evidence, finding that K's employment had not been made subject to a probationary period and noting that, if K's behaviour was as bad as alleged, it would surely have taken action against K before 28 October 2011. The tribunal concluded that the reason for K's dismissal was that he had asserted his statutory right not to work more than 48 hours per week and the dismissal was therefore automatically unfair

- **Mills v Dhinsa Dental Ltd** ET Case No.1803846/10: M worked as a dental nurse. Her contract of employment provided that she would be paid on the 28th of each month. On 28 January, the dentist said to M that she must be happy as it was pay day. When M checked her bank account, however, her pay had not gone in. On 29 January M confronted the dentist about this and he said that he had transferred the money and gave M permission to visit a cash machine during working hours to check her balance again. Shortly after this exchange, a colleague told M that the practice manager had said that M was to go home immediately. When M next came into work on 1 February, she was told to go home as she was not required. M then received a letter dismissing her. The letter stated that the reason for M's dismissal was her conduct, focusing in particular on how she had handled the pay issue and alleging that she had been rude and threatening towards the practice manager. The letter also made reference to an incident in which M was alleged to have left an elderly patient to stand outside the surgery in the cold when the surgery should have been open. The tribunal preferred M's evidence over that of the employer, taking the view that neither the dentist nor the practice manager was a credible witness and rejecting the employer's case that M had been rude or threatening when discussing the pay issue. The tribunal considered that the dismissal letter's reference to the patient incident was an afterthought and it was therefore clear that M was dismissed for asserting her right to be paid on time.

541

11.22 Each case turns on its own facts, however. In Nicol v Nightingale Group Ltd ET Case No.2900161/98, for example, the employer succeeded in showing that the reason for dismissal was not the fact that the employee had asserted a relevant statutory right. NG Ltd believed N was helping a colleague to advance a claim for compensation for personal injury that was not entirely genuine. As a result, foreseeing a question mark over N's continued employment, payment for a training course was withheld. The agreement with regard to training fees provided that, should N leave employment, the course fees would be deducted from her final pay or would otherwise be repayable by her. N complained about the non-payment while her employer continued to investigate matters relating to her colleague's personal injury claim and she was dismissed on 26 December. N claimed that she was dismissed because she had asserted her right to receive her pay in full. A tribunal found that she was dismissed because her employer had doubts about her loyalty, not because of her assertion of a statutory right. Her claim of automatically unfair dismissal therefore failed.

Similarly, in Arendt v Lincolnshire Pallet Co Ltd ET Case No.6600482/99 a tribunal held that the employee was dismissed for poor performance, not for asserting a statutory right. On 28 June 1999, A began working as a trainee pallet repairer for a four-week trial period. The employer called A to a meeting on 16 July because his work rate had actually gone down over the three weeks of his employment, rather than going up as expected. During the meeting, A complained that he was being paid less than the national minimum wage. He said that his work rate was poor because he was working on pallets that required more attention than others. The employer investigated, decided that there was no merit in A's assertions about the pallets and dismissed him for lack of suitability. When A again raised the issue of the national minimum wage, the employer conceded that there was a shortfall in his wages and met the deficit. A's claim that he was dismissed for asserting his statutory right to be paid the national minimum wage failed. The tribunal noted that the employer had called A to a meeting because of concerns about his performance and that A had not raised the issue of pay prior to that meeting. The employer had then investigated A's explanation for his poor work rate but had not been satisfied with it. That – and not A's assertion of a right to be paid the national minimum wage – was the reason for his dismissal.

11.23 In Budzynska v Resource Management Holdings Ltd t/a Malla Technical Recruitment Consultancy ET Case No.6005608/99 the tribunal applied the 'but for' test to establish the true reason for dismissal: but for the employee's allegation of an infringement, would he or she have been dismissed? In that case B's employer argued that the principal reason for her dismissal was that it was no longer economic to employ her. However, the tribunal found that but for B's claim for paid holiday and the fact that she had thereby secured an increase in pay, she would not have been dismissed. The principal reason for her dismissal was therefore the fact that she had brought a claim alleging a breach of the Working Time Regulations 1998.

Constructive dismissal

11.24

It can be particularly difficult for a tribunal to determine whether an allegation that a statutory right has been infringed is the reason for dismissal in cases where the employee has resigned and claimed constructive dismissal. The employee must demonstrate that he or she resigned in response to the employer's repudiatory breach of contract, and that the employer's actions related to the employee's assertion of a statutory right. Two contrasting examples:

- **McMahon and anor v Millington t/a Poppy** ET Case No.2901530/99: the claimants were employed as mobile cleaners. They repeatedly raised concerns with their employer about pay statements, deductions for tax and national insurance contributions, and holiday pay. The employer promised to do something but never gave the claimants a satisfactory reply. After three months of inaction on the part of the employer, the claimants resigned and claimed constructive dismissal for a reason relating to the assertion of a statutory right. The tribunal found that their complaints amounted to the assertion of a statutory right. They were entitled to take their employer's protracted inaction as a refusal to deal with their complaints, which entitled them to resign and claim constructive dismissal. As the reason for their resignations was the assertion of a statutory right, the tribunal held that they had been automatically unfairly dismissed under S.104

- **Scott v Lowe** EAT 780/98: S resigned after her wages cheque bounced on two separate occasions. She argued that she had been constructively dismissed under S.104 for asserting that she had suffered an unlawful deduction from her wages. However, the tribunal rejected her claim, holding that the principal reason for S's resignation was her entirely legitimate concern that her employer's financial position was such that there was some doubt as to whether she would be promptly paid in full on subsequent occasions. It emphasised that S.104 does not protect an employee who suffers an unlawful deduction from wages, but only an employee who is dismissed because there has been an allegation of such an unlawful deduction. The EAT refused to intervene, holding that the tribunal's approach could not be faulted.

Multiple reasons for dismissal

11.25

It is important to note that a claim under S.104 may succeed even if there is more than one reason for the dismissal. S.104(1) expressly states that it is sufficient that the *principal* reason for dismissal is the assertion of a relevant statutory right. In Callaghan v Park Welding and Fabrication Co Ltd ET Case No.1800087/96, for example, C was recruited as a sheet-metal worker. He started work on a trial basis at an hourly rate of £4.50 but was told that his

543

hourly rate would increase by 25p a month until it reached the level of £5.50 an hour. After one month C was given a rise of 25p an hour but at the end of the second month he was refused a further increase because his employer was dissatisfied with his performance. C became disillusioned and his performance deteriorated. He left a letter on his manager's desk asking for a written statement of terms and conditions and demanding the pay rise to which he believed he was entitled. The letter stated that the refusal to award a pay increase amounted to an unlawful deduction from wages contrary to S.13 ERA. Later that afternoon, C was invited to a meeting with his manager and was dismissed. The tribunal found that the reason for the dismissal was a combination of C's written request to his employer and the employer's disappointment in C's performance. On the balance of probabilities, however, and bearing in mind that the employer had received C's letter only a matter of hours before deciding to dismiss him, the tribunal found that the contents of the letter were the principal reason for the dismissal. Accordingly, the dismissal was automatically unfair under S.104.

11.26 However, where there are mixed reasons for the dismissal, tribunals will not necessarily find that the principal reason is the one falling within S.104. Three examples:

- **Sivagurunathan v Harpalani t/a Harpers** ET Case No.3200838/00: S was employed from 14 July 1999 as a paralegal. He maintained that he was taken on with a view to a training contract so that he could qualify as a solicitor. On 24 November S wrote to his employer concerning three issues: he said he was entitled by law to 20 days' paid holiday a year; he wanted a pay increase as a matter of urgency; and he was not prepared to work for much longer without a training contract. S was dismissed and subsequently claimed that he was dismissed for asserting his rights under the Working Time Regulations 1998. The tribunal dismissed the application. It thought that S was dismissed because of financial pressures and because of his request for a training contract. The request for paid holiday had some bearing, but it was not the principal reason for dismissal by any means

- **Foxall v Cygnet Security Services Ltd** ET Case No.3101928/97: F sent a letter to his employer, setting out various demands. The tribunal recognised that one of these, which related to the right to written details of employment, concerned a statutory right under the ERA. However, the tribunal decided that because F had made many other demands that did not concern a breach of a statutory right, he was unable to prove that the principal reason for his dismissal was the demand for written particulars of employment. Accordingly, S.104 did not apply

- **Copeman v Metcalfe t/a The Three Horseshoes** ET Case No.1500634/05: C's employment transferred to M in February 2005 when M took over the pub in which she worked. C originally worked 19.5 hours a week but, soon after the takeover, M asked her to change her contracted hours. He also informed her that he would not be responsible for paying her maternity pay when she took maternity leave (she was pregnant at the time). C became very worried about the situation and gave M a medical certificate saying she was suffering from stress and should remain off work for a week. She was then told that her role was no longer required and was given £100 in lieu of notice. The tribunal held that C was dismissed for a combination of reasons – her refusal to change her hours, her sick leave so soon after M took over and her assertion that she was entitled to be paid maternity pay. However, the tribunal was not satisfied that the foremost reason was C's assertion of a statutory right, so her unfair dismissal claim under this head failed.

Manner in which complaints made   11.27

Where an employee raises his or her complaint in a vigorous or aggressive manner, the employer could argue that it was not the nature of the complaint or allegation that led to the dismissal but, rather, the manner in which the complaint was made. This is a difficult distinction to make, particularly as the allegation is so bound up with the behaviour in question, but a tribunal may sometimes accept the argument that it was really the manner of complaint that caused the dismissal. Indeed, it has been recognised that there are limits on the protection offered by S.104 ERA in this context. In Khan v Trident Safeguards Ltd EAT 0621/04, for example, Mrs Justice Cox commented that S.104 is 'intended to shield an employee from unreasonable behaviour by the employer as a consequence of the employee acting reasonably in accordance with his or her statutory rights'. It is not, however, intended to 'enable an employee to act as they see fit without fear of any possible consequences to continued employment'.

The abusive manner in which the employee raised his concerns was found to be the reason for dismissal in Hummerston v Akhter Computers Ltd ET Case No.3200086/98 where H, who worked as a computer assembler, received a salary, profit-related pay and a monthly bonus that was dependent on performance at work and attendance. H's bonus payments varied each month. In September, representatives of a client came to inspect the factory, one of whom was disabled. While they were being shown around, H made noises described by his manager as akin to monkey noises. H was given a first written warning about his behaviour and poor conduct. When H did not receive a bonus in respect of that month he raised the issue with his manager, who explained to him that he was not receiving a bonus because of his poor conduct. H exploded into a torrent of abuse against the manager, who told H to leave and take four weeks' notice. The tribunal held that withholding the bonus was an unlawful deduction – the employer had never made it clear to H that it could be withdrawn for misconduct – but that the principal reason for H's dismissal was the abusive manner in which he raised his concerns about the bonus with

545

his manager. Therefore, his dismissal was not in response to his assertion of a statutory right and was not automatically unfair.

11.28 However, if the employee simply raises his or her statutory right in a firm and assertive manner the tribunal is likely to find that the true reason for dismissal falls within S.104. Two examples:

- **Smith v Strongvalue Ltd t/a Stirk House Hotel** ET Case No.2403598/99: S's employer was generally dissatisfied with her demeanour and attitude. During the three weeks of her employment she had to work more than 48 hours a week on average. She complained about the work rota and said she was not willing to work more than 48 hours a week. She was dismissed. The tribunal held that although there was a strong likelihood (amounting almost to a certainty) that S would have been dismissed in any event within a short period, the principal reason for her dismissal was her complaint about working hours. She was unfairly dismissed for asserting a statutory right

- **Greenwood v Picnic Anywhere Ltd** ET Case No.1101660/08: G submitted a grievance in which she stated that she had spoken to her local Citizens Advice Bureau and had been informed that she was entitled to holiday and sick pay. Her employer responded that, due to the 'adversarial tone' of G's grievance, it had no choice but to dismiss her. The tribunal concluded that the reason for dismissal was not the tone of the grievance but the substance of it – G had asserted her right to paid annual leave and had been unfairly dismissed for that reason.

12 Remedies

When a tribunal finds that a complaint of unfair dismissal is well founded, it **12.1** must decide the appropriate remedy. There are three remedies for unfair dismissal. These, in the order in which tribunals should consider them, are:

- reinstatement – i.e. an order that the employee be re-employed in his or her old job with no financial loss

- re-engagement – i.e. an order that the employee be re-employed in a job comparable to that from which he or she was dismissed, or in other suitable employment

- compensation – i.e. a monetary award to the employee.

The sequence in which a tribunal must consider these remedies is strict. Thus, when an employee wishes to be re-employed but the tribunal decides not to make an order for reinstatement, it must then move on to consider re-engagement and, failing that, compensation – Ss.112(4) and 116(1) and (2) Employment Rights Act 1996 (ERA). As a result, although the EAT has recommended in the past that a claimant plead both forms of re-employment 'in the alternative' – Arab-British Chamber of Commerce v Saleh EAT 394/88 – this should not really be necessary in practice.

In Telcon Metals Ltd v Henry EAT 287/87 Mr Justice Popplewell emphasised **12.2** that employers would be wrong to think that reinstatement and re-engagement are remedies which tribunals should be slow to consider. On dismissing an employee unfairly, an employer should not imagine that it can simply pay out money to be rid of that employee. Popplewell J stressed that reinstatement and re-engagement are the primary remedies which the legislation directs tribunals to consider before awarding compensation. In reality, though, re-employment orders are very rare. According to the Employment Tribunals and EAT statistics for 2011/12 (the most recent available information on tribunal claim outcomes), of the 5,100 unfair dismissal complaints upheld following a hearing, only five (less than 0.1 per cent) resulted in an order for reinstatement or re-engagement.

The wording of Ss.112 and 116 ERA makes it clear that reinstatement, re-engagement and compensation are mutually exclusive remedies. In Oxford Health NHS Foundation Trust v Laakkonen and ors EAT 0536/12 an employment tribunal, having found that three claimants were unfairly dismissed when they were dismissed and re-employed on less favourable terms, ordered

547

that they be reinstated on their original terms. It also awarded them a basic award and, in the case of one claimant, compensation representing expenses incurred. On appeal, the EAT set aside the basic awards, noting that it is clear from S.112 ERA that an order of reinstatement/re-engagement and a monetary award are mutually exclusive. However, the EAT upheld the award of compensation in respect of expenses on the alternative basis of S.114(2) (see 'Arrears of pay and expenses' below).

12.3 In some cases it is possible for a tribunal to make what amounts to a declaration that the employee was unfairly dismissed but decline to couple this with a reinstatement or re-engagement order or an award of compensation. This might be appropriate where the employee was wholly responsible for his or her dismissal (although the dismissal was nonetheless technically unfair). Or it might occur where gross misconduct by the employee only came to light after the dismissal. In either case, a tribunal can decide that it would not be just and equitable in the circumstances to award any compensation to the employee – see Chapter 13, 'Basic awards', under 'Reductions in basic award', and Chapter 16, 'Compensatory awards: adjustments', under '"Just and equitable" reductions' and 'Contributory conduct'.

This chapter explains employment tribunals' powers to make reinstatement and re-engagement orders and also describes in outline the types of monetary award that can be made. More detailed discussion of monetary awards can be found in Chapter 13, 'Basic awards'; Chapter 14, 'Compensatory awards: types of loss'; Chapter 15, 'Compensatory awards: pension loss'; and Chapter 16, 'Compensatory awards: adjustments'. Additional awards, which are available where an employer fails to comply with a reinstatement or re-engagement order, and interim relief orders, which preserve an employee's contract pending the hearing of a claim of unfair dismissal on one of the protected grounds specified in S.128(1)(b) ERA, are considered in Chapter 17, 'Additional awards and interim relief'.

12.4 Reinstatement and re-engagement

Reinstatement under S.113 ERA is the first remedy a tribunal should consider and it is only if the tribunal decides that reinstatement is not a suitable remedy that it should go on to consider the alternative remedy of re-engagement – S.116(1) and (2). When a tribunal upholds an unfair dismissal complaint, S.112(2) provides that it must explain its powers to make reinstatement or re-engagement orders under S.113 and ask the claimant if he or she wishes such an order to be made. The remedies the claimant seeks should be stated on the claim form (ET1). However, even if the claimant made no specific request for reinstatement or re-engagement on this form, he or she will not be barred from doing so at the tribunal hearing.

Although the requirements of S.112 are mandatory, a tribunal's failure to explain its powers of reinstatement or re-engagement to the claimant will not necessarily render its decision on compensation a nullity. In Cowley v Manson Timber Ltd 1995 ICR 367, CA, the Court of Appeal held that it all depends on whether the employee has suffered prejudice or injustice as a result of the failure to comply with S.112. In that case the Court ruled that the employee had suffered no injustice – he had been represented at the hearing, his ET1 had stated that he wanted compensation only, and neither he nor his representative had suggested at the hearing that he wished to be re-employed. Nonetheless, failure by a tribunal to explain its powers to award reinstatement or re-engagement is likely to make the EAT more inclined to remit the case on the question of remedies where it cannot be shown that the claimant suffered no prejudice or injustice – Constantine v McGregor Cory Ltd 2000 ICR 938, EAT. The practicability of reinstatement or re-engagement must be considered as at the date of the remedies hearing – King v Royal Bank of Canada (Europe) Ltd 2012 IRLR 280, EAT. Thus, in that case, the EAT could not accept that no prejudice or injustice was caused by a tribunal's failure to consider a S.113 order on the basis that, at the date of a redundancy dismissal, no alternative employment was available. The case was therefore remitted to a different tribunal to reconsider the matter.

12.5 When explaining its powers in line with S.112(2), a tribunal is not obliged to use the terms 'reinstatement' and 're-engagement'. Given the informality of employment tribunal proceedings and the frequent appearance of parties without legal representation, it can often be more appropriate for a tribunal to explain its powers in lay terms. So long as the tribunal has explained both the nature of the orders available to it and the circumstances in which they may be made, and has asked the claimant whether he or she wishes the tribunal to make such an order, S.112(2) will have been complied with – Bass v Travis Perkins Trading Company Ltd EAT 0352/07.

The EAT has recognised that it is unnecessary in some situations to follow S.112 to the letter – e.g. where the claimant has settled into new employment (Richardson v Walker EAT 312/79), or has contributed 100 per cent to a dismissal that is unfair only on technical grounds (Pratt v Pickfords Removals Ltd EAT 43/86). In Afolayan v MRCS Ltd EAT 0406/10 the tribunal made no explicit reference to reinstatement, despite the claimant having raised the point. At a review hearing the tribunal rejected the claimant's suggestion that it had failed to consider the issue. It identified several factors noted in its earlier judgment that rendered re-employment inappropriate, including the fact that three years had elapsed since the dismissal, the claimant had found alternative employment, and he had substantially contributed to his own dismissal. On appeal, the EAT held that this dealt with the issue satisfactorily – although the tribunal did not explicitly set out its reasons for refusing

549

re-employment in its original decision, it was inconceivable that it would have been ordered anyway.

12.6 Generally speaking, however, if a claimant asks for reinstatement (or re-engagement) and the tribunal decides against making a re-employment order, it must give reasons for this – Plumley v AD International Ltd EAT 592/82. Reasons for rejection need not be elaborate, however. If, for example, there is substantial contributory conduct on the part of the employee, it may be sufficient to say: 'Having regard to the decision we have come to on the question of contribution, it would not be just to make a reinstatement order.'

12.7 **Continuity of employment.** Section 219 ERA provides that the Secretary of State may make regulations concerning the preservation of continuity of employment where a dismissed employee is reinstated or re-engaged by his or her employer or by a successor or associated employer. Under the Employment Protection (Continuity of Employment) Regulations 1996 SI 1996/3147 ('the 1996 Regulations'), where an employee is reinstated or re-engaged as a result of a tribunal complaint, his or her continuity of employment is deemed to be preserved and the period beginning with the date on which the dismissal takes effect and ending with the date of reinstatement or re-engagement counts in the computation of the employee's period of continuous employment – Reg 3. This is so even if the employee works for another employer during the gap in employment – Lipinski v Ebbsfleet Autospray Centre Ltd EAT 0288/12.

For a detailed discussion on continuity of employment generally, see IDS Employment Law Handbook, 'Continuity of Employment' (2012).

12.8 **Reinstatement**

The contents of a reinstatement order are prescribed by statute and tribunals have no discretion to vary the statutory requirements. A reinstatement order must require that the employer treat the complainant in all respects as if he or she had not been dismissed – S.114(1). In McBride v Scottish Police Services Authority 2013 IRLR 297, Ct Sess (Inner House), the Court of Session held that this means that the complainant must be returned in all respects to his or her contractual position with the employer. This was consistent with S.114(3), which specifies that a person reinstated must benefit from any improvement in the terms and conditions of employment that would have come into effect had he or she not been dismissed. The employment tribunal had therefore erred in ordering the claimant to be reinstated to the job she had done immediately prior to her dismissal, in which she had not been permitted to undertake the full range of her contractual duties. The Court of Appeal noted that the tribunal could have achieved its objective by making an order for re-engagement (see 'Re-engagement' below), but for the fact that the claimant had made it clear that she wanted to return to full duties.

550

A reinstatement order must specify:

- the amount payable by the employer in respect of pay and other benefits lost by the employee between the date the employment ended and the date of reinstatement

- the rights and privileges, including seniority and pension rights, which must be restored to the employee. Note that the restoration of pension rights may require the employee to fulfil certain conditions – in Whelan v Sutcliffe Catering West Ltd ET Case No.1027/88, for example, an order was made dependent on the employee refunding to the pension scheme the lump sum and pension payments received

- the date by which the reinstatement order must be complied with – S.114(2).

12.9 The amount payable to the employee must take into account any improvement in terms and conditions – e.g. a pay increase – that the employee would have received had he or she not been dismissed – S.114(3). As a quid pro quo, the tribunal is also required to take into account any sums received by the employee between dismissal and reinstatement (see 'Arrears of pay and expenses' below).

Re-engagement

12.10 If the tribunal decides not to make an order for reinstatement, then, as already mentioned, it must go on to consider re-engagement – S.116(2). This is a more flexible remedy than reinstatement and tribunals have a wide discretion as to the terms of a re-engagement order. This added flexibility means that re-engagement may be appropriate in situations where reinstatement is not. For example, in Andrew v Veolia ET Case No.2301921/10 A and his brother, who both worked for the same employer as refuse collectors, were dismissed for accepting money to collect unauthorised refuse. The employer decided to dismiss both of them but, on appeal, found that since A's brother had not directly taken part in the receipt of the money his dismissal should be replaced by a final warning and transfer to another depot. A succeeded in his unfair dismissal claim but the tribunal considered that it would not be just to reinstate him, given that his brother had not been restored to the same position, and ordered re-engagement instead.

The only real statutory restriction on the tribunal's discretion in this regard is that the re-engagement must be on terms which are, so far as is reasonably practicable, as favourable as an order for reinstatement (unless there has been contributory conduct, which is discussed below) – S.116(4). This works both ways. In Rank Xerox (UK) Ltd v Stryczek 1995 IRLR 568, EAT, for example, the EAT held that a tribunal had erred in ordering the re-engagement of an employee in a position which would have amounted to a promotion – the position included a substantially higher salary than the employee had enjoyed prior to his dismissal and also a company car. The EAT stated that it is not

551

permissible for a tribunal to order re-engagement on terms that are significantly more favourable than those which the employee would have obtained had reinstatement been ordered.

12.11 Under S.115(1), re-engagement need only be in employment comparable to that from which the employee was dismissed or other suitable employment. In contrast with a reinstatement order, re-engagement need not be with the same employer but may be with a successor – i.e. another employer who has taken over the business or with an associated employer such as another company in the same group. A somewhat unusual example of re-engagement is provided by Department of Health v Bruce and anor EAT 14/92. B was employed at the time of her dismissal by the DSS, which had been part of the Department of Health and Social Security until that department was split into the DSS and the DH. The tribunal ordered that B be re-engaged, but with the DH rather than the DSS. The EAT held that the tribunal was wrong to find that the Civil Service was one 'inalienable whole' for the purpose of determining B's employer. Nevertheless, the majority of the Appeal Tribunal (the chairman dissenting) took the view that the special relationship between the two new departments justified the order of re-engagement with the DH.

Although tribunals have considerable latitude as to the nature of the terms they order for re-engagement, they must specify terms under the following heads:

- the identity of the employer – i.e. whether re-engagement is with the same employer or with a successor or an associated employer

- the nature of the employment

- remuneration

- any arrears of pay and other benefits awarded for the period between dismissal and re-engagement

- any rights and privileges, including seniority and pension rights, to be restored to the employee

- the date by which re-engagement must take place – S.115(2).

12.12 In British Telecommunications plc v Thompson EAT 883/95 an order for the re-engagement of an employee who was suffering from a stress-related illness stated that the employer had to comply within 14 days of the date when the employee's doctor certified that he was fit for work. The EAT held that the order was invalid because there was no specified date of return.

In Pirelli General Cable Works Ltd v Murray 1979 IRLR 190, EAT, the EAT ruled that a tribunal had not discharged its statutory obligations by simply ordering re-engagement on terms to be agreed between the parties. Similarly, in Stena Houlder Ltd v Keenan EAT 543/93 the tribunal ordered re-engagement of an employee 'in employment comparable to that from which he was dismissed or other suitable employment as agreed between the parties and on terms and conditions and remuneration also to be agreed'. The EAT held that the order was invalid because it failed to specify either the nature of the employment or the rate of remuneration as required by S.115. The Appeal Tribunal could understand how the tribunal had come to make such an order since the employer had accepted at the hearing that, if re-engagement were to be ordered, suitable arrangements could be made for the re-employment of the employee. Moreover, when the order was read in conjunction with the tribunal's statement of reasons, there emerged sufficiently clear guidance as to what the nature of the re-employment would be. But the order has to be read by itself and it must be sufficiently specific as to leave no doubt as to what steps are required to comply with it.

That said, the EAT has stated that it is undesirable for a tribunal to order re- **12.13** engagement in respect of a specific job, as distinct from identifying the nature of the proposed employment. There might, however, be some circumstances where identifying a particular job is appropriate, such as where there is only one post in which a claimant could be re-engaged, but generally such an approach will not be permissible – Rank Xerox (UK) Ltd v Stryczek (above).

If the terms of a re-engagement order are silent or ambiguous on an important issue, the tribunal is entitled to review the order and fill out its terms. In Electronic Data Processing Ltd v Wright 1986 ICR 76, EAT, the tribunal had omitted to state the location at which re-engagement was to take place – because this is not one of the statutory particulars to be specified – and was unaware that the employer operated at more than one location. The EAT ruled that the tribunal could review the order and specify one particular location. (Note that the review procedure is now called 'reconsideration' – see IDS Employment Law Handbook, 'Employment Tribunal Practice and Procedure' (2014), Chapter 15, 'Reconsideration of tribunal judgments and decisions').

Finally, in Lilley Construction Ltd v Dunn 1984 IRLR 483, EAT, the Appeal **12.14** Tribunal advised tribunals not to make 'offer directions' – i.e. directions to employers to make re-engagement offers to employees. The EAT doubted whether tribunals had any jurisdiction to make such orders and also pointed to the confusion that could be caused if the employee refused an offer of re-engagement stemming from a tribunal direction of dubious validity.

Re-engagement where employee already re-employed. In Manchester College **12.15** v Hazel and anor 2014 ICR 989, CA, the Court of Appeal confirmed that an order of re-engagement is possible even where the dismissed employee has already been re-employed by the employer. There, two employees who were transferred into the College's employment under the Transfer of Undertakings (Protection of Employment) Regulations 2006 SI 2006/246 (TUPE) refused to accept a pay cut as part of a harmonisation exercise. They were therefore dismissed and re-employed on the less favourable terms. When they succeeded

553

in claims of automatically unfair dismissal the tribunal ordered that they be re-engaged at their pre-dismissal rate of pay. After the EAT dismissed the College's appeal, the College appealed to the Court of Appeal, arguing, among other things, that once the employees had signed up to the new terms, the employment relationship continued and so there was no scope for them to be re-engaged. The Court rejected this argument. The remedies available under Part X of the ERA depend on there having been a dismissal, i.e. a termination of contract. The fact that the employment relationship continued did not alter the fact that there had been a dismissal.

Although the above case involved an automatically unfair dismissal related to a TUPE transfer, there is no reason why the principle should not apply in an ordinary unfair dismissal case where the employee has been dismissed and re-employed on less favourable terms. Lord Justice Underhill observed that the College's argument was wrong in principle in a TUPE context, given that the Regulations are designed to protect terms and conditions on a transfer. However, his main reason for rejecting the appeal focused on the language of the ERA rather than on the purpose of the TUPE provisions, which suggests that the reasoning has wider application.

12.16 Costs

Note that under rule 76(3) of the Employment Tribunal Rules of Procedure (contained in Schedule 1 to the Employment Tribunals (Constitution and Rules of Procedure) Regulations 2013 SI 2013/1237), a tribunal must make a costs order against a respondent where, in an unfair dismissal case, a final hearing has been postponed or adjourned and (a) the claimant informed the respondent not less than seven days before the hearing that he or she wanted to be reinstated or re-engaged, and (b) the postponement or adjournment was caused by the respondent failing, without a special reason, to provide reasonable evidence as to the availability of the job from which the claimant was dismissed, or of comparable or suitable employment. Such orders are discussed in more detail in IDS Employment Law Handbook, 'Employment Tribunal Practice and Procedure' (2014), Chapter 20, 'Costs and penalties', under 'What orders can employment tribunal make? – order against respondent when unfair dismissal hearing postponed'.

12.17 *Arrears of pay and expenses*

As already noted, a tribunal making a re-employment order (i.e. an order for either reinstatement or re-engagement) must specify any amount payable by the employer in respect of any benefit which the employee might reasonably be expected to have received but for the dismissal – Ss.114(2)(a) and 115(2)(d). The largest part of this award will, of course, be arrears of pay between the date of dismissal and the date of re-employment. The award must be based on what the employee would actually have earned during the period between

554

dismissal and re-employment. This may not necessarily correspond with what he or she was earning before dismissal because the employee may have been employed in a seasonal business with fluctuating opportunities for overtime, commission, etc. Tribunals should investigate these matters and adjust their awards accordingly – Coakley v Hutchison's Coaches (Overtown) Ltd EAT 247/85. In Foot v Ministry of Defence ET Case No.4153/84 there was an interval of seven months between F's dismissal and his reinstatement, during which time F had been fit for three months but then unfit for four months. The tribunal therefore made a monetary award of three months' full pay (including overtime) and four months' sick pay.

Where an employee is re-engaged on different terms, salary or arrears of pay for the period between dismissal and re-engagement should be based on the salary before dismissal and not on the salary after re-engagement – Electronic Data Processing Ltd v Wright 1986 IRLR 8, EAT.

12.18 Under S.114(3), an order for reinstatement must require that the employee be treated as benefiting from any improvements in terms and conditions which he or she would have benefited from but for the dismissal from the date on which such improvements came into effect. However, the Court of Appeal confirmed in O'Laoire v Jackel International Ltd (No.2) 1991 ICR 718, CA, that this only applies to benefits from contractual improvements in the terms and conditions of employment that have arisen in the interim period.

There is no limit to the amount of back pay and benefits that can be awarded to cover an employee's monetary loss between dismissal and the tribunal's order. In particular, the ceiling of £78,335 or a year's pay (whichever is the lower) that currently applies to a compensatory award for unfair dismissal has no application in the context of such orders (see also 'Enforcement of order' below). Certain sums, however, are to be deducted from these awards. They are:

- wages in lieu of notice or ex gratia payments made by the employer

- remuneration received from another employer

- any other benefits the tribunal thinks appropriate in the circumstances – Ss.114(4) and 115(3).

12.19 Sums awarded under S.114(2) or S.115(2) cannot be reduced on the ground that the employee has failed to mitigate his or her loss – see City and Hackney Health Authority v Crisp 1990 ICR 95, EAT, where the employer had sought a reduction on the ground that the employee could have brought her claim sooner. Nor should they be reduced in the case of a procedurally unfair dismissal to reflect the fact that, had compensation been awarded instead of reinstatement, it could have been reduced under the principle set down in Polkey v AE Dayton Services Ltd 1988 ICR 142, HL, to reflect the likelihood that the claimant

555

would have been fairly dismissed had a proper procedure been followed – Arriva London Ltd v Eleftheriou 2013 ICR D9, EAT. The sums can, however, be reduced to take account of the claimant's contributory conduct – see 'Contributory conduct' below.

In obiter remarks in an earlier hearing of the O'Laoire case mentioned above (O'Laoire v Jackel International Ltd 1990 ICR 197, CA), Lord Donaldson advised that reinstatement orders should not specify a lump sum to be paid to the employee in respect of arrears of pay because, in theory at least, reinstatement could take place before the date by which it must take place under the reinstatement order. Instead, Lord Donaldson thought that the order should specify the amounts payable by reference to rates of pay or other applicable formulae so that the appropriate calculations of the amount owed to the employee could be made when the actual date of reinstatement was known. Furthermore, no financial provision should be made as to what is to happen if reinstatement takes place after the date specified in the tribunal's order as, once this date has passed, any purported reinstatement would be a breach by the employer of the terms of the reinstatement order and therefore invalid. Although Lord Donaldson's comments were concerned with reinstatement orders under what is now S.114(2), they would presumably apply equally to re-engagement orders under S.115(2).

12.20 Expenses. Where the employee incurs reasonable expenses as a result of being unfairly dismissed, they should be reimbursed. In Oxford Health NHS Foundation Trust v Laakkonen and ors EAT 0536/12 the EAT held that expenses were properly ordered by the tribunal under S.114. According to the EAT, 'but for the dismissal [the employee] would have received her full salary without incurring the specified expenses. In order to put her in the position in all respects as if she had not been dismissed... those expenses are recoverable'.

12.21 Employee preventing compliance

A re-employment order will only be made at the employee's request or with his or her agreement. It would be unusual, therefore, for an employee to prevent the order from being complied with. If, however, he or she does so unreasonably, S.117(8) states that the tribunal will take that conduct into account as a failure on the employee's part to mitigate his or her loss when making an award of compensation. In Miller v Liquidator for Matthew Primrose and Co Ltd EAT 17/77 the employee did not return to work after a tribunal had made a reinstatement order. The working atmosphere had deteriorated and the employer subsequently went into liquidation. The EAT held that the employee's refusal to comply with the reinstatement order was not unreasonable in the circumstances.

12.22 Factors to be taken into account

When considering whether to make an order for reinstatement or re-engagement, tribunals have a specific duty under S.116 to consider:

- whether the employee wants an order to be made and, in the case of re-engagement, what sort of order he or she wants – S.116(1)(a) and (3)(a). (Many employees do not wish to be re-employed with the same company and in such cases tribunals can move directly to considering compensation)

- whether it is practicable for the employer to comply. In the case of re-engagement, the test of practicability is extended to successors of the employer and to associated employers – S.116(1)(b) and (3)(b)

- whether it would be just to make either type of order where the employee's conduct caused or contributed to some extent to his or her dismissal and if so, in the case of re-engagement, on what terms – S.116(1)(c) and (3)(c).

The requirements of S.116 are mandatory to the extent that tribunals must take the factors listed therein into account when considering whether or not to grant a re-employment order – Kelvin International Services v Stephenson EAT 1057/95. However, tribunals are not limited to these considerations and they have a 'general discretion' to take into account a wide range of other factors, including the consequences for industrial relations if the order is complied with – Port of London Authority v Payne and ors 1994 ICR 555, CA. For instance, in Securicor Ltd v Smith EAT 252/87 the treatment meted out to a third party employee – who had been reinstated after his dismissal was revoked – was held to be a valid consideration for the tribunal when assessing whether reinstatement would be an appropriate remedy in S's case. And in Cowen v Rentokil Initial Facility Services (UK) Ltd t/a Initial Transport Services EAT 0473/07 the EAT considered that the refusal by the employee of a previous offer of re-engagement by the employer, and the fact that the post offered had subsequently been filled, were both potentially relevant factors for the tribunal to take into account. However, the offer and refusal in that case had taken place amidst 'without prejudice' negotiations and therefore attracted legal professional privilege. In those circumstances, the tribunal should not have been referred to the fact that an offer had been made.

12.23 The tribunal's general discretion to take into account other factors must nonetheless be exercised appropriately. In First Glasgow Ltd v Robertson EATS 0052/11 the EAT considered that the tribunal had erred in relying upon its 'judicial knowledge' that the company had been advertising vacancies for bus drivers, when this was unsubstantiated and unspecific. More importantly, in the EAT's view, it was fundamentally unfair for a tribunal to make a decision on the basis of a fact that did not form part of the evidence and/or was not raised by the parties. The tribunal ought not to have relied upon any knowledge it had about job advertisements without at least raising it with the parties before the end of the hearing.

One factor that should *not* be taken into account is the fact that no compensation would have been awarded for the unfair dismissal under the principles established in Polkey v AE Dayton Services Ltd 1988 ICR 142, HL (see Chapter 16, 'Compensatory awards: adjustments', under '"Polkey reductions"'). In Manchester College v Hazel and anor 2014 ICR 989, CA, two employees were dismissed when they refused to accept changes to their terms and conditions following a transfer to which TUPE applied. A tribunal found that they had been automatically unfairly dismissed for a TUPE-related reason and stated that it would alternatively have found them unfairly dismissed for procedural reasons under 'ordinary' unfair dismissal principles. The tribunal ordered re-engagement, as requested by the claimants. The tribunal went on to note that it would not have awarded any compensation for unfair dismissal as the claimants would have been dismissed in any event, even if the procedural defects had not occurred. Appealing against the re-engagement order, the employer argued that, if Polkey applied, it could not be just and equitable to order re-engagement. The EAT rejected that argument as misconceived. The only crossover between the 'just and equitable' discretion in relation to compensation under S.123 ERA and the factors to be taken into account under S.116 is on the question of contribution, which was not an issue here. The employer attempted to renew this argument on further appeal to the Court of Appeal but was unsuccessful.

12.24 A differently constituted EAT reached the same conclusion in respect of reinstatement a few months later in Arriva London Ltd v Eleftheriou 2013 ICR D9, EAT, but without referring to the Hazel decision. There, the claimant, E, was a bus driver who was dismissed five months after suffering an injury that prevented him working. Although E was due to undergo surgery, his manager decided that it was highly unlikely he would return to work on the predicted date. A tribunal found the dismissal unfair on the basis that the manager had failed to seek specialist medical advice, as the employer's policy required. However, it also found that there was a 60 per cent chance that E would have been dismissed in any event following the proper medical investigation. By the time of the tribunal hearing, E was fully recovered and the tribunal acceded to his request for an order for reinstatement. On appeal, the EAT rejected the employer's argument that it should not have done so, given its findings that there was a high chance that E would have been dismissed in any event. It emphasised that Polkey v AE Dayton Services Ltd (above) is concerned with compensation, not reinstatement. The EAT did not rule out the possibility that, in some cases, matters relevant to a Polkey deduction may also be relevant to the statutory criteria according to which a tribunal must decide whether or not to order reinstatement – for example, in a conduct case, the nature of the employee's conduct may be relevant to the Polkey question and to S.116(1)(c). However, there was no such crossover here and so the tribunal's failure to have regard to Polkey in its decision on reinstatement was no error of law.

558

Practicability 12.25

'Practicability' is by far the most important factor for tribunals to take into account when considering whether or not to make an order for re-employment. It is a question of fact for the tribunal, which has discretion to decide whether or not to make a re-employment order. It follows that any appeal against a decision based upon the issue of practicability will only succeed if the tribunal has taken into account the wrong considerations, ignored the right considerations (for example, ignored the issue of practicability completely), or reached a legally perverse decision. In Clancy v Cannock Chase Technical College and anor 2001 IRLR 331, EAT, the EAT reiterated that it will rarely interfere with a tribunal's findings on the issue of practicability and will do so only if the tribunal's decision is perverse in the circumstances. Where a tribunal has directed itself properly on the law and has heard evidence on the issue of practicability, a plea of perversity will be hard to get off the ground. In the words of Mr Justice Lindsay, then President of the EAT: 'Of all the subjects properly to be left as the exclusive province of an employment tribunal as the "industrial jury", few can be more obviously their territory than the issue of "practicability" within S.116(1)(b) and... S.116(3)(b).'

The EAT has stated that, when assessing practicability, tribunals should not try to analyse in too much detail the application of the word 'practicable' but should look at the circumstances of each case and take a 'broad common sense view' – Meridian Ltd v Gomersall and anor 1977 ICR 597, EAT. It should be borne in mind, however, that the test is one of 'practicability' not 'expediency'. In Qualcast (Wolverhampton) Ltd v Ross 1979 ICR 386, EAT, the Appeal Tribunal remitted the question of reinstatement to the tribunal for reconsideration, refusing to accept the tribunal's decision to decline an order for reinstatement because it had not considered it expedient to make such an order.

It is important to note that there are two stages at which a tribunal may have 12.26 to assess the question of practicability. The first arises when the tribunal considers whether to make an order for reinstatement or re-engagement at the remedies hearing, having found the employer liable for unfair dismissal. The second arises later but only if the employer refuses to comply with a re-employment order, in which case a second remedies hearing will be necessary. At this second hearing the onus is on the employer to show – on the balance of probabilities – that it was not practicable for it to comply with the order. If it fails to do so, it will have to pay an additional award of compensation of between 26 and 52 weeks' pay, on top of the ordinary compensation awards – S.117 (see Chapter 17, 'Additional awards and interim relief', under 'Additional awards'). The EAT ruled in Timex Corporation v Thomson 1981 IRLR 522, EAT, that a lesser emphasis on practicability is required at the first stage, when the tribunal has only to take into account the consideration of practicability and does not need to make a final determination on the issue.

559

This was endorsed by the Court of Appeal in Port of London Authority v Payne and ors 1994 ICR 555, CA, where it stated that at the first stage, prior to making an order, the tribunal need only make a provisional determination or assessment on the evidence before it as to whether it is practicable for the employer to reinstate or re-engage the employee. It is only at the second stage, where the employer has not complied with the order and seeks to show that it was not practicable to do so, that a tribunal must make a final determination on practicability.

According to the EAT in Rembiszewski v Atkins Ltd EAT 0402/11 – following Great Ormond Street Hospital for Children NHS Trust v Patel EAT 0085/07 – the date at which the practicability of an order for re-engagement is to be considered is when such re-engagement would take effect. In practice, this will often mean the date of the remedies hearing. However, in the present case, where further written evidence was submitted to the tribunal following the remedies hearing, the tribunal ought to have taken that evidence into account and made the assessment as at the date the last relevant submission was received, three months after the hearing.

12.27 In First Glasgow Ltd v Robertson EATS 0052/11 the EAT held that a tribunal deciding to order the reinstatement of a bus driver should not have taken into account the fact that the employer did not lead evidence or make any submissions on the issue of practicability. The EAT stressed that a respondent does not bear the onus of establishing that reinstatement is not practicable. As the EAT put it, 'there is no statutory presumption of practicability' – the issue of practicability is one which the tribunal is required to determine in the light of the circumstances of the case as a whole. The Appeal Tribunal emphasised that it is only if an employer seeks subsequently to avoid being penalised for having failed to comply with an order that it then bears the burden of showing that it was not practicable to comply.

12.28 **Effect on business.** Reinstating a dismissed employee should never necessitate redundancies or significant overstaffing. In Freemans plc v Flynn 1984 ICR 874, EAT, the EAT rejected the argument that the effect of a re-engagement order was to impose a duty on the employer to find a place for the dismissed employee irrespective of whether there were vacancies. This placed too high a duty on employers. That reasoning was followed in Cold Drawn Tubes Ltd v Middleton 1992 ICR 318, EAT, where the EAT emphasised that 'it would be contrary to the spirit of the legislation to compel redundancies, and it would be contrary to common sense and to justice to enforce overmanning', although in Highland Fish Farmers Ltd v Thorburn and anor EAT 1094/94 the EAT held that Mr Justice Tucker in the Middleton case was drawing attention to a very important consideration, but not purporting to lay down an absolute rule. (Note, also, the special provisions on employing a permanent replacement – see 'Replacements' below.)

In Port of London Authority v Payne and ors 1994 ICR 555, CA, the Court of Appeal stressed that the test is one of practicability, not possibility. In that case a tribunal rejected the employer's argument that a lack of vacancies had made it impracticable to comply with re-engagement orders. The tribunal took the view that the employer should have invited applications for voluntary severance from the existing workforce. The Court of Appeal held that the tribunal had applied too high a standard. Although tribunals should carefully scrutinise the reasons advanced by employers, due weight should be given to their commercial judgement: 'The employer cannot be expected to explore every possible avenue which ingenuity might suggest. The employer does not have to show that reinstatement or re-engagement was impossible. It is a matter of what is practicable in the circumstances of the employer's business at the relevant time.' Two further examples:

- **United States Navy v Coady** EAT 275/94: C was purportedly dismissed for redundancy. A tribunal found that no redundancy situation in fact existed; the employer had simply replaced C with someone it considered better at the job. The tribunal ordered reinstatement, despite the employer's objection that this would cause overstaffing. The EAT upheld the decision. The services of the employee were not redundant and reinstatement would simply put matters back to where they were before the dismissal. Any resulting overstaffing would be the result, not of the reinstatement, but of the way in which the employer had gone about the management of the club in which C worked and the termination of his employment. It might be inexpedient for the employer to reinstate C, but it was not impracticable

- **Carpenter v ABB Industrial Systems Ltd** ET Case No.1500/95: C, an engineer, was unfairly dismissed for redundancy. The employer failed to comply with the tribunal's order for reinstatement on the ground that it would have forced the company to make someone else redundant. However, during the course of the tribunal hearing, it emerged that the company had in fact, since the first practicability hearing, taken on a contract engineer from an agency and that this worker was still there. The tribunal held that, in the circumstances, reinstatement was certainly practicable.

In Cruickshank v London Borough of Richmond EAT 483/97 C was successful **12.29** in his unfair dismissal claim. On his ET1 he had sought reinstatement and he reiterated that wish at the remedies hearing before the tribunal. However, less than a month before the hearing on liability the employer had 'deleted' C's post. On remitting the case to the tribunal on the question of remedies, the EAT directed it to consider in particular whether the deletion of C's post was done solely to frustrate the possibility of his reinstatement. The possibility of frustrating the purpose of the legislation was also at issue in Morley and anor v Buckinghamshire and Milton Keynes Fire Authority ET Case No.3304195/13, where the employer submitted that the tribunal should not go behind its

561

commercial judgement as to the financial practicability of re-engagement. The tribunal rejected that submission. It observed that, if it were not permitted to examine and question an employer's financial judgement, it might be very difficult for an employee ever to achieve an order for reinstatement or re-engagement.

12.30 **Replacements.** Employing a permanent replacement for a dismissed employee will not of itself make re-employment impracticable. S.116(5) and (6) states that, in deciding whether to make a re-employment order, a tribunal must ignore the employment of a replacement unless the employer shows:

- that it was not practicable to arrange for the dismissed employee's work to be done without engaging a permanent replacement, or

- that before engaging a permanent replacement a reasonable period had gone by without word from the dismissed employee as to whether he or she wanted re-employment and there was no reasonable alternative to hiring a permanent replacement.

(Much the same applies to the consideration of practicability at the second stage following an employer's non-compliance with an order – S.117(7).)

In practice, this may mean that a large employer with significant resources will find it harder to rely on the S.116(6) exception than a smaller, less well-resourced employer.

12.31 **Relationship with colleagues.** The personal relationship between the employee and his or her colleagues is clearly a relevant factor that will affect the question of practicability and/or the tribunal's exercise of its discretion. Re-employment is unlikely to be on the cards if relations at work have become irretrievably soured. For example, in Intercity East Coast Ltd v McGregor EAT 473/96 the acrimonious relationship between the employee and his supervisor had been an important factor leading up to the dismissal, to which the employee had been found to have contributed by 20 per cent. The EAT held that it was 'not practicable to order two parties to reunite when war has broken out'. However, not all incidences of workplace strife will present a bar to re-employment. Two examples:

- **Baldwin v KLM Royal Dutch Airlines** ET Case No.67019/95: the tribunal ordered the reinstatement of B even though he had been dismissed for assaulting a colleague, H. The tribunal found that B was a good employee and that the assault was a one-off incident. Although H had said that he could no longer work with B, the tribunal did not think that he should be able to veto B's return to work

- **Sodje v Look Ahead Housing and Care** ET Case No.3300755/11: the tribunal found that S had contributed to her own unfair dismissal to the extent of 50 per cent but nonetheless went on to order reinstatement. S's conduct was a one-off emotional outburst and was really not the kind of misconduct that would make it unjust to order reinstatement. Although the employer maintained that there had been an irretrievable breakdown in the working relationship, S had continued to work for three months after her outburst and the tribunal could see no reason why both parties could not put this incident behind them and move on.

The threat of industrial unrest may also have some relevance. In Thamesdown **12.32** Borough Council v Turrell EAT 459/97 the EAT overturned a tribunal decision to order reinstatement in circumstances where a reorganisation that resulted in the deletion of T's job had been completed by the time of the final hearing on remedies and where there was a real threat of industrial action if T returned to work because his colleagues had lost faith in him.

In Arhin v Enfield Primary Care Trust 2010 EWCA Civ 1481, CA, the Court of Appeal accepted that a tribunal had erred in relying on the 'strained relationship' between A and her line manager as a factor against reinstatement when the line manager had left the employer and emigrated shortly before the remedies hearing. However, the Court of Appeal was satisfied that the tribunal's remaining factors against re-engagement, including the lack of a suitable job, the underlying need to economise and A's conduct in relation to an internal dispute, remained cogent and sufficient grounds on which to uphold the tribunal's conclusion. There was never a case for re-engagement despite evidence that A was well-liked and respected by a number of colleagues.

The question of personality clashes is closely bound up with the size of **12.33** employer or employment unit. In Enessy Co SA t/a The Tulchan Estate v Minoprio and anor 1978 IRLR 489, EAT, the employees were a married couple employed as cooks in a small hotel. The EAT took the obiter view that it was one thing to order reinstatement where the employee works in a factory or other substantial organisation, but it would only be in exceptional circumstances that it would be appropriate to force upon a reluctant employer the reinstatement of employees with whom he would have to work in a close relationship unless the tribunal was persuaded by powerful evidence that such an arrangement would succeed.

Trust and confidence. A breakdown of trust and confidence between employer **12.34** and employee may be sufficient to render re-employment impracticable. In Wood Group Heavy Industrial Turbines Ltd v Crossan 1998 IRLR 680, EAT, for example, the employer genuinely believed that C had been dealing drugs at work and the EAT held that this was enough to present a barrier to re-engagement. Furthermore, lack of trust on the employee's part may also make re-employment impracticable. In Nothman v London Borough of Barnet (No.2) 1980 IRLR 65, CA, the Court of Appeal held that the employee's allegations of a long-standing conspiracy by colleagues to oust her from her job made it impracticable to order reinstatement. And in Sulehria v A and B Investments ET Case No.3200160/09 the tribunal refused S's request for reinstatement or re-engagement on the basis that his conduct in refusing to allow one of the employer's senior managers to contact him throughout the course of his dispute and subsequently accusing that manager of having committed bigamy was a clear indication that trust and confidence had broken down.

One of the most common grounds on which lack of trust and confidence is asserted is that the employer genuinely believes that the employee has committed some misconduct. Two examples:

- **Baxendale v United Biscuits (UK) Ltd** ET Case No.2404439/08: B was dismissed because she had denied seeing a colleague, who gave her a lift home at the end of a night shift, damage a manager's car. UB Ltd concluded that B had committed 'conduct that violates decency and morality' (a reason set out in its disciplinary rules as amounting to gross misconduct), in that her denial was a falsehood and therefore immoral. A tribunal found that the dismissal was unfair, given that B had almost ten years' unblemished service and that, by the time of her dismissal, the person who had committed the damage had already been identified and dismissed. However, it refused to order reinstatement or re-engagement because of loss of trust. On the balance of probabilities, B did in fact see her colleague damage the manager's car and he was the manager of the shift on which B had worked

- **Hartley v Sainsbury's Supermarkets Ltd** ET Case No.1102053/09: H worked for SS Ltd as a baker. A colleague, K, accused her of having eaten one of SS Ltd's sandwiches. K did not say anything to H at the time but later told SS Ltd that she and H's supervisor had found the sandwich wrapper hidden at the bottom of the bin. H was interviewed and suspended. He denied the allegation and continued to do so at an investigatory meeting and again at the disciplinary hearing. However, SS Ltd chose to believe K and H was summarily dismissed. A tribunal found that H had been unfairly dismissed – SS Ltd had accepted K's statement as true and accurate from the outset simply on the basis that she was a team leader and had made no further enquiry of her when H credibly denied the allegation. The tribunal nonetheless found that SS Ltd's continued belief in H's dishonesty made a reinstatement or re-engagement order impracticable, even though there was insufficient evidence of any contributory conduct to warrant a reduction in H's compensation.

12.35 **Conduct during litigation.** In Oasis Community Learning v Wolff EAT 0364/12 the Appeal Tribunal acknowledged that the manner in which a dismissed employee has pursued his or her successful complaint of unfair dismissal may have so soured the relationship with colleagues that reinstatement or re-engagement is impracticable. However, the instant case – which involved a teacher who had made serious allegations against his employer while fighting his case – was not one where working relationships had been irreparably damaged. Here, it would have been practicable for him to be re-engaged at a different school, with wholly new colleagues and 'no history to live down'. In Central and North West London NHS Foundation Trust v Abimbola EAT 0542/08, on the other hand, the EAT concluded that a tribunal had been wrong to exclude from its consideration of practicability both the dishonesty of the claimant at the remedies hearing and the fact that, in the light of one proven instance of assault and three unproven allegations, the respondent could no longer be expected to trust the claimant. And in Rembiszewski v Atkins Ltd EAT 0402/11 the EAT accepted that a tribunal could consider whether an employee's application for costs against the employer, on the basis that the employer had acted vexatiously, abusively, disruptively or otherwise unreasonably in the proceedings, was couched in such terms as to display a lack of trust and confidence in the employer.

Tribunals should, however, be careful not to hold against the employee allegations made in the course of litigation and should be wary of assessing an employee's attitude solely from his or her performance during the litigation – Cruickshank v London Borough of Richmond (above). In Mills v Norwich Systems and Accounting ET Case No.29275/95 a tribunal was unconvinced by the employer's claim that the experience of contesting the unfair dismissal claim had left a legacy of bitterness which rendered reinstatement impracticable. The tribunal added that it was surprised to hear such an argument advanced by a company that employed over 140 people. However, where the employee makes specific and personal allegations, this may have such a disruptive effect that a harmonious working relationship is no longer possible. In Brar v TNT UK Ltd ET Case No.2704704/10, for example, a tribunal refused re-employment after proceedings in which B had made a number of serious allegations against his colleagues. The tribunal considered that the form in which these allegations had been made had caused considerable disquiet.

Capability and ill health. Issues of capability and ill health will also be **12.36** relevant to the question of practicability. In SMT Sales and Service Co Ltd v Irwin EAT 485/79 the EAT held that it would not be practicable for the company to re-engage a senior manager in whom it had genuinely lost confidence, whether the reasons for doing so were well founded or not. In Hemmings v Redland Bricks Ltd ET Case No.9432/96, on the other hand, the employer argued that, although the employee had satisfactory appraisals and no disciplinary record, there had in fact been serious shortcomings in her performance. No action had been taken on these shortcomings because they would have been difficult to prove. The tribunal said that in the circumstances it could not be expected to attach much weight to these alleged shortcomings and reinstatement was ordered.

In British Telecommunications plc v Thompson EAT 883/95 T was dismissed following a stress-related illness. A tribunal ordered re-engagement, to be complied with once T was fit to return to full-time employment. The EAT held that, apart from making the order invalid, the fact that the tribunal was unable to specify a date for re-engagement also betrayed the real reason why re-engagement was not in fact practicable. The EAT also expressed surprise that the tribunal had considered it appropriate for such a vulnerable employee to return to a senior post in a highly stressful business. In another case, McGarry v British Railways Board EAT 63/91, the EAT held that a tribunal was entitled to hold that reinstatement was impracticable, even though the tribunal had not heard any evidence specifically on that point. The tribunal had been given the whole history of M's employment, which showed that M had suffered from recurrent periods of unfitness for work and that it was very doubtful that he would be fit for any form of work within the company. In such circumstances it was not necessary for the tribunal to hear evidence from the employer in order to entitle it to decide that re-engagement was manifestly impracticable.

12.37 **Training.** Tribunals have been known to take an employee's training into account when deciding on practicability. In Blackhurst v St Helens and Knowsley Health Authority ET Case No.8102/85, for example, a tribunal ordered the reinstatement of a claimant who had five months of his training course as a nurse to run.

12.38 **Security checks.** The need for an employer to carry out security screening checks for a reinstated or re-engaged employee will not necessarily make a re-employment order impracticable. In Ojo v G4S Security Services (UK) Ltd ET Case No.2200328/09 the employer argued that, since it would have to submit O to a Criminal Records Bureau (CRB) check as if he were a new employee – a process that can take up to three months – it was not practicable for him to be re-engaged. However, the tribunal disagreed, finding that a company of the respondent's size could re-engage O on full pay, but either assign him no duties or assign him to duties that did not require a CRB check. (Note that the CRB was replaced by the Disclosure and Barring Service in 2012.)

12.39 **Risk to public.** The existence of a duty owed to the public will not necessarily determine the issue of practicability. Even where an employer genuinely believes that a dismissed employee could pose a risk to the public, re-employment will not automatically be impracticable. A tribunal will, however, judge each case on its merits and clearly a serious offence such as sexual assault will present a greater obstacle to practicability than, for example, petty theft. In ILEA v Gravett 1988 IRLR 497, EAT, a tribunal was justified in refusing to grant an order for the re-employment of a swimming instructor who was dismissed for indecent exposure and indecent assault.

12.40 **Company image.** Even where there is no risk to the public, an employer's public image and relations may have some relevance. In London Borough of Greenwich v Dell EAT 1166/94 a tribunal found that a caretaker employed by a local authority was unfairly dismissed on account of his political activities on behalf of the British National Party. The tribunal found that it would be impracticable to reinstate the employee in his former position on a multiracial housing estate but ordered the authority to re-engage him in a post where he would not have any contact with ethnic minorities. The EAT overturned the tribunal's decision, stating that the notion of the employee being appointed to some segregated post free of any contact with racial minorities was offensive to a local authority which advocated racial equality.

Contributory conduct

12.41

Tribunals are required by statute to consider whether it would be just to make a reinstatement or re-engagement order where the employee caused or contributed to some extent to the dismissal – S.116(1)(c) and (3)(c). Contributory conduct will also be highly relevant to the question of practicability – e.g. where the employee's misconduct has soured the working relationship. In Kelvin International Services v Stephenson EAT 1057/95 the EAT allowed an appeal against a tribunal's order of reinstatement on the ground that no consideration had been given to the question of conduct. The case concerned a dismissal for suspected theft where the mutual trust and confidence between employer and employee had broken down. The question of whether the employee's conduct had contributed to the dismissal was therefore highly material both to the issue of practicability and to the question of whether it was just to order reinstatement.

There is no reason in principle why a tribunal should not make a re-employment order even where there is a large degree of contributory conduct, provided it forms a reasonable view that the circumstances warrant it. In Automatic Cooling Engineers Ltd v Scott EAT 545/81, for example, the EAT upheld a re-engagement order (in favour of an apprentice) in a case where contribution had been assessed at 75 per cent.

However, in United Distillers Ltd v Harrower EAT 1151/96 the EAT took the **12.42** view that it could not be practicable to reinstate an employee where the conduct related to an established and admitted act of dishonesty. In United Distillers and Vintners Ltd v Brown EAT 1471/99, on the other hand, the Appeal Tribunal upheld a tribunal decision to order the reinstatement of an employee who had been found to have contributed to his dismissal by 10 per cent. However, the EAT stressed the importance of the tribunal's finding that issues of honesty were not at stake and that trust and confidence between the employee and the employer were intact. In cases where the contribution assessment was high, the EAT cautioned that it may be necessary for a tribunal to consider whether or not the employer could genuinely trust the employee again, although each case would depend on its own facts.

In the case of re-engagement, tribunals must also take contributory conduct into account when considering the terms of the order – S.116(3)(c). In British Airways plc v Valencia 2014 ICR D29, EAT, the EAT explained that the correct approach under this provision is to first consider whether re-engagement would

567

be just in light of the conduct, and only then go on to consider the effect the conduct should have on the order's terms. However, even where there has been significant contributory fault, the EAT has counselled against ordering re-engagement of a senior employee in a demoted position – Atlantic Steam Navigation Co Ltd v Murdoch EAT 234/83, although in Johnson Matthey plc v Watters EAT 0236/06 the EAT held that a tribunal had been entitled to order that an employee be re-engaged at one point lower in the grade scale than his original role, to take account of his 20 per cent contribution to the dismissal.

12.43 In practice, tribunals often take the employee's conduct into account by reducing or even eliminating an award of back pay, etc, for the period between dismissal and re-engagement. In Gray v University of Warwick ET Case No.1302304/09, for example, the tribunal found that G had been unfairly dismissed but that he had made a 20 per cent contribution to his dismissal by his own misconduct. The University opposed a reinstatement order, arguing that it had lost trust and confidence in G. However, the tribunal noted that G was no more culpable than three of his colleagues who had not been dismissed, and the only reason he had been dismissed and they had not was that G had an unrelated 'live' warning on his personnel file. Any loss of trust and confidence 'flowed from a flawed investigation and disciplinary process' and could not be relied on by the University to resist a reinstatement order. However, the sum in arrears due to G from the date of his dismissal to the date of his reinstatement order was reduced by 20 per cent to take account of his contributory conduct.

The flexibility of a re-engagement order to recognise contributory conduct can only go so far, however. In British Airways plc v Valencia (above), the tribunal found that, although V had been unfairly dismissed, his conduct contributed 80 per cent to the dismissal. It ordered that V be re-engaged as cabin crew on the same terms and conditions as he previously held but made no award for arrears of pay between dismissal and the order. The EAT overturned the order on appeal. Having concluded that reinstatement was unjust because of the high level of contributory conduct, the tribunal could not then make an order for reinstatement but call it a re-engagement order. Furthermore, in finding that a re-engagement order in those terms would be just, the tribunal had relied on the flexibility that S.116(2)(c) provides in relation to the arrears to be ordered. It had not given any consideration to whether V's conduct was such that re-engagement would not be just in the circumstances. The EAT could not see how a proper application of the statutory provisions could result in any conclusion other than that it was not just to order re-engagement for the same reason that it was not just to order reinstatement. It therefore remitted the case for the tribunal to consider compensation.

12.44 **Protected industrial action.** In the case of an unfair dismissal for participation in protected industrial action, S.239(4)(a) of the Trade Union and Labour

Relations (Consolidation) Act 1992 provides that a tribunal shall not make any order for reinstatement or re-engagement until after the conclusion of the protected industrial action.

Enforcement of order

The remedy for an employer's failure to abide by a reinstatement or re-engagement order depends on whether there has been partial compliance or complete non-compliance. If the employer reinstates or re-engages the employee but the terms of the order are not fully complied with (i.e. there has been partial compliance), S.117(1) provides that the tribunal will make an award of compensation to the employee. The amount of the award will be such as the tribunal thinks fit having regard to the loss sustained by the employee as a result of the employer's failure to comply fully with the order – S.117(2).

If there is a total failure to comply on the employer's part – i.e. the employer refuses to reinstate or re-engage the employee – the tribunal will go on to assess the employee's compensation for unfair dismissal in the normal way – S117(3)(a). (If the employee unreasonably prevented compliance, this should be taken into account as a failure by him or her to mitigate his or her losses – S.112(8).) The tribunal will also make an additional award unless the employer can show that it was not practicable to comply with the order – S.117(3)(b) and (4)(a). The question of practicability is discussed above and additional awards are dealt with in Chapter 17, 'Additional awards and interim relief', under 'Additional awards'. Note that, at this stage, it is not open to the employee to seek a further order for re-employment – Mabirizi v National Hospital for Nervous Diseases 1990 ICR 281, EAT.

It used to be the case that, where the employee was highly paid or there had **12.46** been a long delay between the date of dismissal and the date of the tribunal's hearing, the amount of arrears of pay which the employer would have to pay in pursuance of a tribunal's order for re-employment meant that it was cheaper for the employer to refuse to comply (or only partially comply) with the order. This was because the compensation that a tribunal could award on account of the employer's partial compliance or total non-compliance was subject to the same statutory limit as applied to compensatory awards. (This limit is currently £78,335 or one year's pay, whichever is the lower, but prior to 25 October 1999 was only £12,000.) In O'Laoire v Jackel International Ltd 1990 ICR 197, CA, the claimant's actual losses consequent on the dismissal exceeded £100,000, but the maximum the tribunal could award him as compensation at that time was £12,185. When the matter reached the Court of Appeal, Lord Donaldson noted that 'the present maximum level of award... can positively discourage employers from complying with an order for reinstatement, contrary to the interests of Parliament, and in addition causes injustice to higher paid employees'. This anomaly was later removed and S.124(3) ERA now provides that, in the case of partial compliance, the statutory limit may be lifted by such

569

amount as is necessary to enable the award fully to reflect the amount specified as arrears of pay and benefits in the original reinstatement or re-engagement order. Similarly, in the case of total non-compliance, the statutory limit may be exceeded by the extent necessary to enable the aggregate of the compensatory and additional awards fully to reflect the amount of arrears of pay and benefits specified in the original order – S.124(4).

Note, however, that, in cases of total non-compliance with a reinstatement order made under S.114, i.e. where an additional award is made under S.117(3)(b) as well as a compensatory award under S.117(3)(a), the statutory limit should only be exceeded to the extent of the S.114 loss (i.e. the loss incurred between dismissal and when reinstatement should have occurred) less the additional award – Selfridges Ltd v Malik 1998 ICR 268, EAT. This is because the S.114 loss is not a free-standing head of damage to be awarded whether or not reinstatement is complied with. The S.114 loss is only payable in respect of a reinstatement order which *has* been complied with. If there is total non-compliance, then the S.114 loss forms part of the compensatory award. The same principle applies to loss under S.115 where an employer totally fails to comply with a re-engagement order. This approach has since been endorsed by the EAT in Midland Mainline v Wade EAT 1382/01 and, more recently, by the Court of Appeal in Parry v National Westminster Bank plc 2005 ICR 396, CA.

12.47 It is for the tribunal to decide whether or not the employer has complied properly with the order. In Electronic Data Processing Ltd v Wright 1986 ICR 76, EAT, W was unfairly dismissed for redundancy and a tribunal made an order that she be re-engaged in a lower-paid trainee's position. W had been employed in Sheffield but the employer offered her a post in Manchester. The tribunal decided that this was not a proper offer of re-engagement. This was upheld by the EAT on the basis that the tribunal was entitled to interpret its own order. If the terms of the order had been ambiguous, it would have been open to the tribunal to give effect to its original intentions by filling out the terms of the order to stipulate that re-engagement must be in Sheffield.

The distinction between non-compliance and a failure 'fully' to comply is an important one since, as noted above, it is only in cases of total non-compliance that an additional award is payable under S.117(3)(b). In some cases, however, the line between the two may be hard to draw – for example, where the employee is re-engaged but not in the type of post ordered by the tribunal. In Artisan Press v Srawley and anor 1986 ICR 328, EAT, S and P were unfairly dismissed from their jobs as security staff. A tribunal made reinstatement orders, with which the employer purported to comply. However, S and P were in fact re-employed as cleaners with some minor security functions so that their jobs were significantly different from those they had performed before dismissal. The tribunal held that the employer had failed to comply with the reinstatement order. On appeal, the employer argued that there had only been a failure to comply 'fully' with the order and that compensation should have been awarded under what is now S.117(1) and not S.117(3). However, the EAT held that 'reinstatement' means treating the employee in all respects as if he or she has not been dismissed. If an employee is 'reinstated' in a different job on less favourable terms, then he or she has not been reinstated at all and there has been a total failure to comply with the reinstatement order. The tribunal's award was therefore correct.

The EAT went on to say that a failure to comply 'fully' with a reinstatement **12.48** order must refer to ancillary matters that may be specified in the order and not to the terms of the order itself. For example, an order will specify the date by which the employee is to be reinstated. If the employer is two weeks late in taking the employee back but does reinstate the employee properly in his or her old job with no change to terms and conditions, that would seem to be only a failure to comply fully with the order and would properly be compensated for by an award of two weeks' pay rather than an additional award (but note Lord Donaldson's later conflicting obiter remarks in the Court of Appeal in O'Laoire v Jackel International Ltd 1990 ICR 197, CA, as to the validity of purported re-employment after the deadline for compliance – see 'Arrears of pay and expenses' above).

Compensation
12.49

Despite the emphasis on re-employment orders in the ERA, in practice the only remedy awarded in the vast majority of successful unfair dismissal claims is monetary compensation. Most awards of compensation fall under two main heads:

- the basic award (see S.118(1)(a)), normally calculated in exactly the same way as a redundancy payment and intended to compensate the employee for loss of job security – see Chapter 13, 'Basic awards', for details

- the compensatory award (see S.118(1)(b)), intended to compensate the employee for financial loss suffered as the result of the unfair dismissal (subject to a current maximum of £78,335 or one year's pay, whichever is the lower). There is no formula for calculating a compensatory award other than what the tribunal considers 'just and equitable' – this test is considered in detail in Chapter 14, 'Compensatory awards: types of loss'; Chapter 15, 'Compensatory awards: pension loss'; and Chapter 16, 'Compensatory awards: adjustments'.

In addition to the basic and compensatory awards, there is a further form of compensation that may come into play in cases where re-employment has been ordered. The tribunal may order an additional award under S.117(3)(b) ERA where it has made a reinstatement or re-engagement order but the employer

571

has totally failed to comply with that order. Such an award need not be directly related to the employee's loss but may be penal. For further details, see 'Reinstatement and re-engagement – enforcement of order' above, and Chapter 17, 'Additional awards and interim relief', under 'Additional awards'.

12.50 In addition to the awards mentioned above, tribunals have the power to make interim relief orders in certain circumstances. An interim relief order is a mechanism for keeping an employee's contract alive – normally through what is, in effect, an order for suspension on full pay – pending a full tribunal hearing. These orders are only available to employees who claim to have been dismissed on one of the specified statutory grounds benefiting from special protection under S.128(1) ERA – see Chapter 17, 'Additional awards and interim relief', under 'Interim relief', for details.

Finally, it should be noted that S.126 ERA prohibits double recovery of losses under the ERA and the Equality Act 2010 in respect of the same complaint.

12.51 Taxation

As explained in Chapter 14, 'Compensatory awards: types of loss', the amount of compensation due is generally calculated net of tax, the claimant being awarded an amount based on his or her take-home pay. The practice avoids the need for both sides to account for income tax and national insurance contributions on what would otherwise be earnings. However, some types of tribunal award, including awards for future loss of earnings consequent on dismissal, are taxable in themselves under S.401 of the Income Tax (Earnings and Pensions) Act 2003 in so far as they exceed £30,000. When tax is payable on compensation under S.401, the standard practice is for tribunals to 'gross up' the award. This means increasing the amount of compensation so that, once the appropriate amount has been paid to HM Revenue and Customs, the claimant is left with the figure the tribunal originally intended to award. For example, in Somerset County Council v Chaloner EAT 0063/14 the EAT held that, in order to achieve an award that is just and equitable, it was necessary to gross up any part of the compensatory award that exceeded £30,000.

Mr Justice Langstaff, President of the EAT, confirmed the correct approach to grossing-up in Hall v Durham County Council and ors EAT 0256/14. There, the tribunal had decided on the amount that it wished to award, then calculated what tax the claimant would have to pay on such an amount and added that sum on top. On appeal, Langstaff P held that this approach was incorrect, since it would leave the claimant with less than she was entitled to. Langstaff P illustrated the problem by way of example. If a claimant were entitled to be paid £80 and the applicable tax rate were 25 per cent, then the tribunal's approach would be to add £20 (i.e. 25 per cent of £80) and so award a total of £100. When the claimant came to account for tax, however, he or she would pay 25 per cent on the total award, i.e. £25, leaving only £75. The claimant would therefore end up with £5 less than the tribunal intended to award. Instead, the tribunal ought to calculate the sum which, when taxation was applied at the appropriate rate, would yield a net sum equal to the total figure of compensation that the tribunal had awarded. Thus, in this example, if the tribunal considered that the claimant should be left with £80, it should award £106.67, which would be reduced to £80 when taxed at 25 per cent.

When it comes to the correct order of adjustments to an award of compensation **12.52** for unfair dismissal, a tribunal contemplating making a compensatory award in excess of the £30,000 should gross up the figure to allow for the incidence of tax before applying the statutory cap imposed by S.124 ERA – Hardie Grant London Ltd v Aspden 2012 ICR D6, EAT. In other words, the grossing-up cannot result in the claimant being awarded a sum in excess of the statutory cap.

13 Basic awards

Calculation of basic award

Reductions in basic award

Settlements and ex gratia payments

Order of deductions

In the majority of successful unfair dismissal claims the remedy will be an **13.1** award of monetary compensation made up – ordinarily – of a basic award and a compensatory award – S.118(1)(a) and (b) Employment Rights Act 1996 (ERA). The basic award is designed to compensate the employee for the loss of job security caused by the unfair dismissal by awarding him or her a sum almost exactly equivalent to a statutory redundancy payment. The compensatory award is intended to reflect the actual losses that the employee suffers as a consequence of being unfairly dismissed.

This chapter explains how a basic award is calculated. It also deals with the circumstances in which a tribunal may reduce or eliminate a basic award and considers how far ex gratia payments made by employers may affect liability for paying a basic award. Interest on tribunal awards is dealt with in Chapter 14, 'Compensatory awards: types of loss', under 'Interest'. Compensatory awards are dealt with in Chapter 14; Chapter 15, 'Compensatory awards: pension loss'; and Chapter 16, 'Compensatory awards: adjustments'.

Calculation of basic award
13.2

The basic award is calculated in units of a week's pay as defined in Ss.220–229 ERA – for details see IDS Employment Law Handbook, 'Wages' (2011), Chapter 10, 'A week's pay'. The total will usually depend on the employee's age and length of continuous service and the relevant amount of a week's pay. There are, however, some exceptions to this rule. The first is where the reason for the dismissal (or selection for redundancy) was a trade union reason (so that the dismissal was automatically unfair under S.152(1) or S.153 of the Trade Union and Labour Relations (Consolidation) Act 1992 (TULR(C)A)), in which case a minimum basic award applies under S.156 TULR(C)A – see IDS Employment Law Handbook, 'Trade Unions' (2013), Chapter 12, 'Unfair dismissal'. The minimum, which is currently £5,807, is usually increased in February each year.

The second exception arises if the dismissal was for one of the inadmissible reasons set out in S.120 ERA, namely:

575

- dismissal for carrying out health and safety activities or being a health and safety representative under S.100(1)(a) or (b) ERA – S.120(1)

- dismissal for being a working time representative for the purposes of the Working Time Regulations 1998 SI 1998/1833 under S.101A(d) ERA – S.120(1)

- dismissal for being a trustee of the occupational pension scheme under S.102(1) ERA – S.120(1)

- dismissal for being an employee representative for collective redundancy consultation purposes (under Chapter II of Part IV TULR(C)A) or for consultation with regard to a transfer of an undertaking (under the Transfer of Undertakings (Protection of Employment) Regulations 2006 SI 2006/246) under S.103 ERA – S.120(1)

- dismissal relating to trade union 'blacklists' under S.104F – S.120(1C).

13.3 Where S.120(1) applies (i.e. in respect of the first four types of dismissal listed above), the minimum is £5,807 (normally increased each year in February). Where S.120(1C) applies (i.e. 'blacklisting' dismissals), the minimum is £5,000. This figure is not subject to annual uprating.

These statutory minimums apply before any reduction is made under S.122 – see 'Reductions in basic award' below. If the basic award calculated normally would be higher than these figures, then the employee should be awarded the higher amount subject to the normal maximum – see 'Formula for calculating basic award' below.

13.4 A final exception to the normal rule arises where the employee has been dismissed because of redundancy but he or she is not entitled to a redundancy payment, having unreasonably refused an offer of suitable alternative employment or unreasonably walked out of such employment during a trial period. In such circumstances the basic award will be two weeks' pay – S.121.

Note that the express linking of the basic award to a week's pay *as defined in the ERA* prevents a tribunal from taking into account factors that might affect the claimant's pay over the relevant period. In Toni and Guys (St Paul's) Ltd v Georgiou 2013 ICR 1356, EAT, the EAT overturned a tribunal's decision to calculate the basic award on the basis of what the claimant's actual earnings would have been had she not been suspended and had work diverted away from her. This was an error of law, given the clear formula set out in Ss.220–229 ERA. The EAT rejected the claimant's argument that the tribunal had, in effect, found a breach of the implied term of trust and confidence but for which the claimant would have been remunerated on the basis found by the judge. However, the employer's actions in capriciously diverting away from the claimant work on which she would have earned additional commission could be considered loss of earnings for the purpose of the compensatory award as it would not be just and equitable to permit the employer to benefit from behaviour that formed part of the unfairness of the dismissal.

Formula for calculating basic award   13.5

To calculate the basic award, a statutory formula is applied. The employee's years of continuous employment are counted backwards from the effective date of termination (EDT) – S.119(1). The EDT is the date on which the employment contract ended unless the employer dismissed the employee with no notice or with inadequate notice, in which case the EDT is postponed to the date on which the statutory (not contractual) minimum notice under S.86 ERA would have expired – S.97(2) ERA (for a detailed explanation of how the EDT is established, see IDS Employment Law Handbook, 'Contracts of Employment' (2014), Chapter 14, 'Date of termination'). A maximum of 20 years' continuous employment can be counted – S.119(3).

The amount of the award is:

- 1½ weeks' pay for each year in which the employee was 41 years old or older – S.119(2)(a) ERA

- one week's pay for each year in which the employee was below the age of 41 but not younger than 22 – S.119(2)(b)

- half a week's pay for each year in which the employee was below the age of 22 – S.119(2)(c).

There is no lower age limit for a basic award and so the employee's period of **13.6** continuous employment, for calculation purposes, can include years in which the employee was under 18. Note, however, that it is illegal to employ a child below the age of 13 – see S.18 of the Children and Young Persons Act 1933.

Age discrimination. Given that the formula for calculating the basic award **13.7** relies on age-based factors, the Government reviewed the scheme prior to the coming into force of the Employment Equality (Age) Regulations 2006 SI 2006/1031 on 1 October 2006 (since subsumed into the Equality Act 2010). In its 'Coming of Age' consultation document, published in July 2005, it expressed an intention to remove the three age bands for calculating redundancy payments and basic awards. In the end, however, the Government decided to retain these bands, despite the fact that the multiplier based on age bands would appear to amount to direct discrimination and the multiplier based on length of service would seem to be indirectly discriminatory. In the context of the redundancy scheme, the Government opined that there were three groups benefiting from payments under the scheme – younger, prime age and older workers – which each represent a distinct economic category. At one end of the spectrum, younger workers tend not to be out of work for long and only experience a small fall in pay when switching jobs. Older workers, on the other

577

hand, face difficulties in finding new jobs, experience a substantial fall in pay if they do find new employment and are much more likely to become long-term unemployed. As a result, the Government felt that the practice of applying different 'multipliers' to different age bands so as to give greater financial assistance to older workers is justified. In the nearly ten years since age discrimination in employment was prohibited in domestic law, there has been (to our knowledge) no legal challenge to that assumption.

13.8 Calculation date

For the purpose of calculating the basic award, the calculation date (i.e. the date on which a week's pay is calculated) is:

- the employee's last day of work, if the notice given is less than the statutory minimum period of notice laid down in S.86 ERA

- where the notice is the same as or more than the statutory minimum, the date as determined by ascertaining the statutory minimum period applicable and calculating the latest day when the employer would have needed to give that notice in order for the employee's contract to have been terminated on the day that he or she actually left work – S.226(3) ERA.

The current ceiling on the amount of a week's pay is £475 and anything earned in excess of this is disregarded. This figure is usually adjusted upwards every February. Since a maximum of 20 years' service can count and the pay ceiling is £475, the maximum possible basic award at present is £14,250. To obtain this an employee would have to earn at least £475 per week and be able to show 20 years' service during which he or she was at least 41 years old. (Note that where the employee's wage is actually lower than the national minimum wage (NMW) under the National Minimum Wage Act 1998, then the NMW must be used to calculate a week's pay, not the employee's actual wage – Paggetti v Cobb 2002 IRLR 861, EAT).

13.9 Reductions in basic award

There are five grounds on which a tribunal may reduce a basic award:

- where the employee has unreasonably refused an offer of reinstatement – S.122(1) ERA

- where the employee's conduct before dismissal makes a reduction just and equitable – S.122(2)

- where the employee has been awarded any amount in respect of the dismissal under a designated dismissal procedures agreement – S.122(3A)

- where the employee has been dismissed for redundancy and has received a redundancy payment – S.122(4)

578

- where the employee has been unfairly dismissed for a reason relating to a trade union 'blacklist' under S.104F ERA and has received a basic award in respect of the same dismissal under S.156 TULR(C)A – S.122(5).

It is also possible that a reduction to the basic award can be made where the employee has been automatically unfairly dismissed under S.103A for making a protected disclosure but he or she acted in bad faith in making the disclosure – see IDS Employment Law Handbook, 'Whistleblowing at Work' (2013), Chapter 6, 'Dismissal'. This is because S.123(6A) states that a tribunal may reduce 'any award' in such a case by up to 25 per cent when it appears that the disclosure was not made in good faith – see IDS Employment Law Handbook, 'Whistleblowing at Work' (2013), Chapter 7, 'Enforcement and remedies', under 'Remedies in unfair dismissal claims – adjustments and reductions'. The phrase 'any award' suggests that this reduction can apply to the basic award as well as the compensatory award. However, the title of S.123 is 'Compensatory award' and its other subsections focus on reductions from that award only. Furthermore, providing for an adjustment to the basic award in S.123 would represent a departure in terms of the drafting of the ERA, since all other adjustments are set out in S.122. It is therefore unclear whether this provision does apply to the basic award and to our knowledge no case law has yet arisen to clarify the situation.

13.10 Reductions in the basic award can only be made where expressly permitted by statute – Cadbury Ltd v Doddington 1977 ICR 982, EAT. As a result, the grounds listed above are the only permissible grounds for reducing basic awards and there is no overarching requirement that it should be just and equitable to make the award in the first place – Belcher and ors v Great Bear Distribution Ltd EAT 0453/05. Unlike the compensatory award, a basic award cannot, for example, be reduced to take into account the applicant's failure to mitigate his or her loss (see Lock v Connell Estate Agents 1994 ICR 983, EAT) or be subject to a 'Polkey deduction' representing the likelihood that the employer would have fairly dismissed the employee if it followed a reasonable procedure (see Taylor and ors v John Webster, Buildings Civil Engineering 1999 ICR 561, EAT). Furthermore, the provisions allowing tribunals to adjust awards by up to 25 per cent where either party has unreasonably failed to comply with the Acas Code of Practice on Disciplinary and Grievance Procedures do not apply to basic awards – see S.124A ERA.

Since the basic award is not intended to compensate for direct financial loss, it is not open to a tribunal to reduce or eliminate it because an employee has suffered no financial loss through his or her dismissal. It is the compensatory award that is meant to make good financial loss. The basic award simply compensates for loss of job security. Two illustrations:

- **Cadbury Ltd v Doddington** 1977 ICR 982, EAT: a tribunal found D's dismissal, after a long sickness absence, procedurally unfair but awarded no

579

compensation because D would not have been fit to return to work anyway. The EAT said that this was not a ground for reducing the basic award but only for withholding a compensatory award

- **Bartlett v EDF Energy plc** ET Case No.2513943/10: a tribunal found that B was unfairly dismissed when he was required to stand down from a seconded role and return to his original job. It awarded B a basic award even though he remained in EDFE plc's employment.

13.11 Unreasonable refusal of reinstatement offer

If the tribunal finds that the employee unreasonably refused an offer of reinstatement, it must reduce the basic award by the amount that it considers just and equitable –S.122(1) ERA. This only applies to offers of reinstatement that would have had the effect of reinstating the employee in all respects as if he or she had not been dismissed. (For the avoidance of confusion, it is important to bear in mind that the issue here is an offer by the employer to reinstate the employee, not an order by the tribunal to reinstate the employee under S.114 ERA – see Chapter 12, 'Remedies', under 'Reinstatement and re-engagement', for details of such orders.)

Refusal of an offer made on different terms and conditions, even if the refusal is unreasonable, should not be grounds for reducing the basic award under this head. In contrast, refusal of an offer that entails changes to purely discretionary benefits may engage the rule. In Hedley v J and J Nichol ET Case No.2505828/09, for example, H had been given notice of dismissal for redundancy by JJN but it attempted to 'rescind' the dismissal the following day when it won new business. H refused to accept the withdrawal of the dismissal because JJN also proposed to reduce his travelling allowances. The tribunal found that the dismissal could not be withdrawn and that it was unfair but reduced the basic award by half to reflect H's refusal to accept reinstatement. It accepted JJN's evidence that the travel allowance was not a term or condition of employment but a discretionary payment. (The tribunal also found that H had thereby failed to mitigate his loss and so no compensatory award was payable. Mitigation of loss in respect of the compensatory award is discussed in Chapter 16, 'Compensatory awards: adjustments', under 'Failure to mitigate losses'.)

13.12 For S.122(1) to apply, the offer of reinstatement must be one that can be accepted as such in a legal sense, not just in layperson's terms. In McDonald v Capital Coaches Ltd EAT 140/94 M was summarily dismissed for misconduct. Soon afterwards, the employer wrote to him stating that, since his record prior to the events leading to his dismissal was very good, the company would like him to come into work 'to discuss any problems... and see if these can be resolved amicably'. M declined and brought tribunal proceedings. The tribunal found the dismissal unfair but reduced M's basic award to nil under S.122(1). The EAT held that the tribunal had erred in construing the employer's letter as an offer of reinstatement. It was no more than an invitation to have a chat about the situation surrounding M's dismissal.

In Parkes v Banham Patent Locks Ltd EAT 207/96 Mr Justice Mummery recommended that tribunals adopt the following step-by-step approach to S.122(1):

- has the employer made an offer?

- if that offer were to be accepted, would it have the effect of reinstating the employee as if he or she had not been dismissed?

- if so, did the employee refuse the offer? And if he or she did refuse the offer, did he or she act reasonably or unreasonably in doing so?

- if the employee acted unreasonably in refusing the offer, the tribunal must ask whether, and to what extent, it is just and equitable to reduce the basic award.

The EAT also confirmed that there was no reason why S.122(1) should not **13.13** apply to offers of reinstatement following a constructive dismissal.

The question of reasonableness was considered by the Court of Appeal in Wilding v British Telecommunications plc 2002 ICR 1079, CA, in the context of compensatory awards, offers of re-employment and mitigation of loss. Lord Justice Potter stated that the test of unreasonableness is an objective one based on the totality of the evidence and, in applying that test, the circumstances in which the offer was made and refused, the attitude of the employer, the way in which the former employee had been treated and all the surrounding circumstances should be taken into account. Two contrasting examples:

- **Cockram v Honda of UK Manufacturing Ltd** ET Case No.1400708/08: C was unfairly dismissed for breaching the company's smoking ban. Within three weeks he found another job in a completely different field of work on a broadly comparable wage but involving longer working hours. The new job provided a stakeholder pension, rather than the final salary pension scheme he had enjoyed with H Ltd. After the merits hearing the company's solicitor made an offer of reinstatement. C did not reply to the offer and it remained open at the date of the remedies hearing. At that hearing C stated that he was depressed about what had happened to him and that he could not go through it again. He said it made him feel physically sick even to think about it. He also said he was a loyal worker and was grateful to his new company for employing him. The tribunal held that, although the offer was made at a late stage, H Ltd had openly accepted the tribunal's decision and had sought to take appropriate steps to put the matter right. It had also apologised to C. There was no evidence that C would find it impossible to return to work for the company and as a result he was found to have

581

unreasonably refused the offer of reinstatement and his award was limited to the basic award, reduced by 25 per cent for his unreasonable refusal

- **Payne and anor v Paragon Automotive Ltd** ET Case No.1804807/09: two employees were unfairly dismissed by PA Ltd. On the day their notice expired they both accepted new contracts of employment with the company under protest, pursuing their tribunal claims. They continued working until they were subsequently dismissed again, in summer 2009, for gross misconduct. In January 2010 PA Ltd offered them reinstatement from the date of their first dismissal through to their second dismissal for gross misconduct. They refused and PA Ltd argued before the tribunal that they should not be paid a basic award as they had unreasonably refused an offer of reinstatement. (There was no compensatory award since neither claimant had suffered any loss as a result of the first dismissal.) The tribunal rejected this argument. Even putting aside the fact that the employees could not return to their jobs under the offer made to them, since the offer ceased to have effect as from the date of the second dismissals, it was not unreasonable for them to refuse the offer of reinstatement. The offer was hollow: there was no job for the employees to return to at the date the offer was made and it was hard to see why an employee should accept such an offer.

13.14 Note that an employee's refusal to accept an offer of an alternative job made *before* he or she is dismissed could in certain circumstances warrant a reduction in the basic award on the ground of the employee's conduct under S.122(2) – see 'Employee's conduct' below. This happened in Fulton v RMC Russell plc EAT 0055/03, where the EAT refused to interfere with a tribunal's finding that F's basic award should be reduced by 50 per cent under S.122(2) to reflect his conduct after he failed to apply for a different job and was subsequently dismissed.

13.15 **Employee's conduct**
A reduction on the ground of the employee's conduct must be made where 'the tribunal considers that any conduct of the complainant before the dismissal (or, where the dismissal was with notice, before the notice was given) was such that it would be just and equitable to reduce or further reduce the amount of the basic award to any extent' – S.122(2). (But note that this section does not apply where the reason for dismissal was redundancy unless the selection was for an inadmissible reason entitling the employee to a minimum basic award, in which case special provisions apply – see 'Redundancy cases' below.)

It is the conduct of the employee alone that should be considered here, not that of any other employee – Parker Foundry Ltd v Slack 1992 ICR 302, CA – or, for that matter, the employer. Furthermore, according to the case law interpreting the similar (but not identical) conditions for reducing the compensatory award, the conduct should be 'culpable or blameworthy' – Nelson v British Broadcasting

Corporation (No.2) 1980 ICR 110, CA. The EAT in Langston v Department for Business, Enterprise and Regulatory Reform EAT 0534/09 confirmed that the same criterion applies to deductions from the basic award. The meaning of 'culpable or blameworthy' is examined in detail in relation to the compensatory award in Chapter 16, 'Compensatory awards: adjustments', under 'Contributory conduct – "culpable or blameworthy conduct"'.

In Steen v ASP Packaging Ltd 2014 ICR 56, EAT, the EAT, summarising the **13.16** correct approach under S.122(2), held that it is for the tribunal to:

- identify the conduct which is said to give rise to possible contributory fault

- decide whether that conduct is culpable or blameworthy, and

- decide whether it is just and equitable to reduce the amount of the basic award to any extent.

However, the tribunal is not required to consider a reduction of its own motion – Carmelli Bakeries Ltd v Benali EAT 0616/12. In that case a tribunal found that B's dismissal, ostensibly for misconduct, was 'tainted' by complaints that he had raised about his disability and that he had therefore been victimised and unfairly dismissed. CB Ltd did not raise the question of a reduction in unfair dismissal compensation for contributory conduct before the tribunal but argued on appeal that the tribunal should have considered it of its own motion. The EAT held that in the absence of a finding that it would be just and equitable to reduce the basic award by reason of the claimant's conduct, the tribunal is not required to consider a reduction of its own motion. According to the EAT, 'the mandatory obligation on an [employment tribunal] is to reduce the basic award if but only if it has made a prior finding that by reason of the conduct of the claimant, it would be just and equitable to reduce the award. There was no such finding... in this case. Accordingly, the reduction in compensation not having been raised by the respondent, unlike the compensatory award, the [employment tribunal] was not obliged to consider of its own motion the reduction in the basic award.' The tribunal had, however, made a finding that B had committed gross misconduct and although that was not the 'operative' reason for dismissal, it had 'contributed' to it for the purpose of S.123(6). The tribunal should therefore have considered whether and to what extent it should reduce the compensatory award.

Where a tribunal decides to make a reduction, particularly if it decides to make **13.17** a 100 per cent reduction, it must give clear reasons. Referring to its earlier decision in Lemonious v Church Commissioners EAT 0253/12, the EAT also confirmed that a reduction to nil should be an unusual finding. As Mr Justice Langstaff, President of the EAT, put it in Lemonious, 'even if the conduct were wholly responsible for the dismissal, it might still not be just and equitable to reduce compensation to nil. Though there might be cases where conduct is so

583

egregious that that is the case, it calls for a spelling out by the tribunal of its reasons for taking what is undoubtedly a rare course.'

Tribunals will only be able to make a reduction under S.122(2) if they have sufficient evidence before them of the misconduct in question. In Western Leisure v Flynn and anor EAT 375/92 the circumstances were such that the employer knew that one of two employees was guilty of dishonesty and so decided to dismiss both. A tribunal held the dismissals to be unfair because the employer had failed to carry out a proper investigation. The tribunal nevertheless reduced the compensatory awards to nil on the ground that, had a proper investigation been carried out, the employees would inevitably have been dismissed. The employer appealed, arguing that the tribunal should also have declined to make any basic award. The EAT pointed out that the employees' compensatory awards had not been reduced on account of contributory conduct under S.123(6) but under the 'just and equitable' provision in S.123(1). The employer had put forward no evidence of dishonesty against either employee and the tribunal could not be expected to conduct its own investigation into whether one or other, or both, of the employees had in fact been dishonest. In contrast, in Hall v Royal Mail Group Ltd ET Case No.2390765/11 there was slight but sufficient evidence of misconduct such as to warrant a reduction. H was summarily dismissed for having referred to a black employee as a 'monkey' following an argument, although he maintained that he had used the word 'manager'. A tribunal found the dismissal unfair for procedural failings but reduced the compensatory award to nil to reflect the likelihood that H would have been fairly dismissed following a proper procedure. The tribunal went on to find that there was no persuasive evidence as to which version of facts was true and so the summary dismissal was in breach of contract. It noted that, for the same reason, it could not reduce the basic award for contributory conduct in relation to the use of the word 'monkey'. However, it was satisfied that H's conduct was nonetheless aggressive and potentially intimidating and that it was therefore sufficiently unreasonable to warrant a 60 per cent reduction in the basic award.

13.18 An employee's unacceptable conduct should not be ignored simply because it was connected with a background or underlying illness. In Sinclair v Wandsworth Council EAT 0145/07 the tribunal found that the employer's failure to apply its alcohol policy when dismissing S for being drunk at work rendered the dismissal unfair. However, the EAT held that the tribunal had erred in deciding that actions arising from S's alcoholism could not amount to contributory conduct for the purpose of S.122. If the tribunal was right on this point, then totally unacceptable conduct in the workplace could be excused by reference to underlying illness. In reaching this conclusion, the EAT referred to an earlier case, Edmund Nuttall Ltd v Butterfield 2006 ICR 77, EAT, in which another division of the EAT held that the fact that the matters causing an employee's dismissal arose as a result of his mental illness did not mean that his award for unfair dismissal could not be reduced. In the EAT's view, the same logic should apply with regard to S's alcoholism.

Conduct need not contribute to dismissal. The wording of S.122(2) makes it **13.19** clear that, unlike deductions from the compensatory award for contributory conduct under S.123(6), it is unnecessary that the employee's conduct should have caused or contributed to the dismissal. Indeed, the misconduct may only come to light after the dismissal. In Hutchinson v Arkon Group Ltd and anor ET Case No.56347/92, for example, the employer demoted H, who then resigned and brought a successful claim of unfair constructive dismissal. After H left, the employer discovered that he had, while still in the company's employ, set up a rival business. The tribunal held that this breach of trust and confidence warranted a 100 per cent reduction in the basic award.

However, the misconduct must have taken place before the dismissal (where the dismissal was summary) or before notice was given (where the dismissal was with notice) – see Belcher and ors v Great Bear Distribution Ltd EAT 0453/05. In Bell v Service Engines (Newcastle) Ltd ET Case No.3456/85 B was unfairly dismissed but committed various thefts from his employer during his notice period, for which he was convicted and fined. The tribunal decided that it was not just and equitable to make any compensatory award but it was constrained by the wording of S.122(2) to make a basic award in full.

Deductions from compensatory award for contributory conduct. One **13.20** question that has arisen in a number of cases is the extent to which tribunals are justified in treating the basic award and the compensatory award differently in respect of deductions for misconduct. In RSPCA v Cruden 1986 ICR 205, EAT, the EAT held that a tribunal is not necessarily bound to reduce the basic and compensatory awards in precisely the same proportions, pointing out that deductions for contributory conduct are a matter for the tribunal's discretion and that the wording of the two provisions is not identical. It added, however, that in light of the similarity between the provisions, it was likely to be only in exceptional circumstances that the deductions from the basic award and the compensatory award would differ. In Charles Robertson (Developments) Ltd v White and anor 1995 ICR 349, EAT, a tribunal made a 100 per cent reduction in the compensatory award on account of contributory conduct but reduced the basic award by only 50 per cent. The tribunal took the view that it would not be just and equitable to reduce the basic award to nil because the employees, in being dismissed without a fair hearing, had been deprived of an important right. The EAT upheld the decision on the basis that a discrepancy in reductions to the two awards was not wrong in principle. The two provisions are worded differently and different considerations apply to each. Similarly, in Optikinetics Ltd v Whooley 1999 ICR 984, EAT, the EAT noted that under S.122(2) a tribunal has a wide discretion in deciding whether or not it is just and equitable to reduce the basic award on the ground of conduct and can choose not to do so. By contrast, this would not be a permissible option in relation to the compensatory award where a reduction for contributory conduct is mandatory (albeit only if that conduct has contributed to or caused the dismissal). However, in the majority of cases, the reduction for conduct will be the same for both awards. If a tribunal does reduce the basic and compensatory awards by different proportions, it should give its reasons for doing so – Sterling Granada Contract Services Ltd v Hodgkinson EAT 894/95.

In Siddons and anor v Tontine Hotel EATS 0054/10 two hotel employees were dismissed for having consumed drinks at the bar without paying for them first. They had admitted the misconduct but both claimed that the barman had either refused to accept payment or had offered to pay for the drinks himself. A tribunal found that there was a fair reason for dismissal – namely, consuming drinks that the employees knew had not yet been paid for – but that the dismissals were procedurally unfair. It reduced the compensatory award to nil because it was certain that the employees would have been fairly dismissed had a proper procedure been followed. However, it only reduced the basic award by 75 per cent, taking into account the possibility that the employees' explanations were true. The EAT overturned the finding of unfairness on appeal. Although it did not then need to do so, it went on to consider the correctness of the remedy decision. It agreed with the employer that the tribunal's speculation that the claimants' explanation might have been true was irrelevant. The facts as found were that the employees had consumed drinks that they knew had not been paid for. Furthermore, the tribunal ought to have taken into account the fact that the employees had changed their stories as the disciplinary procedures progressed. In these circumstances, the reduction in the basic award should also have been 100 per cent.

13.21 One situation in which the deductions from the two awards may well differ is where the tribunal not only makes a finding of contributory conduct but also decides that it would be just and equitable under S.123(1) to reduce the compensatory award to reflect the chance that the employee would have been dismissed even if a fair procedure had been followed. (Details of these 'no difference' dismissals are discussed in Chapter 16, 'Compensatory awards: adjustments', under '"Polkey reductions"'.) In Rao v Civil Aviation Authority 1994 ICR 495, CA, the Court of Appeal pointed out that in such cases the same misconduct may result in the basic award being reduced by a greater percentage than the compensatory award. This is because, in deciding the extent to which the employee's compensatory award should be reduced for contributory conduct under S.123(6), the tribunal is entitled to take into account the amount by which the award has already been reduced on just and equitable grounds under S.123(1). The tribunal in Granchester Construction (Eastern) Ltd v Attrill EAT 0327/12 fell into error in this particular respect. Having reduced the compensatory award by 50 per cent to reflect the chance of a fair dismissal, it moderated the further deduction for contributory fault to 10 per cent and applied this same level of deduction to the basic award. On appeal, the EAT held that it was wrong to do so, for the reasons set out in Rao. Given the tribunal's findings on the extent of A's contributory conduct, it was plain that a 10 per cent deduction from the basic award was perversely low.

Redundancy cases. As already noted, a reduction for misconduct under S.122(2) **13.22** can only be made in limited circumstances in redundancy cases. These are where a minimum basic award applies under S.120(1) because the employee was selected for redundancy for one of a number of inadmissible reasons (see 'Calculation of basic award' above). In such cases, a reduction for contributory conduct may be made under S.122(2) but only to 'so much of the basic award as is payable because of S.120' – S.122(3). Equivalent provision is made for cases where the employee is entitled to a minimum basic award because he or she was unfairly selected for redundancy for trade union reasons – S.156(2) TULR(C)A.

In other words, the percentage reduction for contributory conduct may only be applied to the amount by which the minimum award of £5,807 exceeds what the normal basic award would otherwise have been. Take, for example, a case where the normal basic award would have been £2,000 but, because the selection for redundancy was for an inadmissible reason, it is raised to £5,807. If the tribunal then decides to reduce compensation by 50 per cent for contributory conduct, it can only apply this reduction to the difference between £5,807 and £2,000. The employee will receive £3,938.50 (£2,000 plus 50 per cent of £3,807) after the reduction, instead of the £2,903.50 that he or she would have received if the reduction had been applied to the full amount of the basic award.

Trade union dismissals. Where the dismissal or selection for redundancy was **13.23** for trade union reasons, the tribunal must disregard conduct leading to the dismissal that was a breach of a contractual term relating to union membership. Tribunals must also disregard a refusal to pay, or to allow deductions from pay to be made in favour of, somebody other than a union (a charity, for example) – S.155 TULR(C)A. The House of Lords confirmed in Tracey and ors v Crosville Wales Ltd 1997 ICR 862, HL, that, in this context, tribunals must ignore any industrial action in which the applicant participated. The House of Lords did, however, agree with the Court of Appeal that there were limited circumstances in which conduct could, in theory, be taken into account; namely, where there was individual blameworthy conduct additional to, or separate from, the mere act of participation in industrial action. In Transport and General Workers' Union v Howard 1992 ICR 106, EAT, the EAT emphasised that S.155 permitted a distinction to be drawn between what was done by the employee and the way in which it was done. The case was remitted to the tribunal to determine whether the confrontational conduct by the employee was sufficiently independent to be considered contributory fault justifying a reduction in the basic award.

587

13.24 Designated dismissal procedures agreements

Section 122(3A) provides that where the employee has already received a payment under a designated dismissal procedures agreement, the tribunal must reduce a basic award by an amount that it considers just and equitable having regard to that payment.

Section 110 ERA sets out the stringent requirements for such agreements which, if met, effectively displace the protection from unfair dismissal set out in S.94 ERA and substitute a collective regime for dismissal with recourse to arbitration in case of disputes. As the consent of the Secretary of State is required for a designated dismissal procedures agreement to take effect, such agreements are rare in practice.

13.25 Receipt of redundancy payment

Any redundancy payment received by an employee must be deducted from the basic award – S.122(4) ERA. In most cases this will extinguish the basic award altogether. If the amount of the basic award is lower than the redundancy payment, the excess is deductible from the compensatory award – S.123(7).

'Redundancy payment' in this context is not confined to a statutory redundancy payment but includes any payment made by the employer on the ground of redundancy. Thus it would cover corresponding payments made to civil servants and NHS employees who are excluded from the statutory redundancy scheme. It would also cover certain ex gratia payments – see 'Settlements and ex gratia payments' below. Note, however, that for S.122(4) to apply, the dismissal must in fact have been by reason of redundancy. In Boorman v Allmakes Ltd 1995 ICR 842, CA, B was dismissed and given an ex gratia payment of £5,000, which was stated to incorporate his statutory redundancy entitlement. A tribunal found that B was not in fact redundant and went on to hold that his dismissal was unfair. Despite the ex gratia payment that B had received, the tribunal made a basic award of £2,079. The Court of Appeal upheld the award on the ground that, since B's dismissal was not a result of redundancy, S.122(4) did not apply. Similarly, in Ashman v Sainsbury's Supermarkets Ltd ET Case No.2201620/08 A was dismissed during a redundancy situation not because her role was redundant but because she was unable to carry it out on capability grounds and SS Ltd decided that it would be kinder to make her redundant at the same time as her colleagues. A tribunal found the dismissal unfair but made no compensatory award since A would have been dismissed fairly in any event. It did, however, make a full basic award even though A had received a redundancy payment.

13.26 Trade union blacklists

Section 122(5) provides that where an employee has been unfairly dismissed for a reason relating to the use of a trade union 'blacklist' under S.104F ERA and receives a basic award in respect of the same dismissal under S.156

TULR(C)A, the amount of the basic award under the ERA will be reduced accordingly. S.156 TULR(C)A applies a minimum basic award in cases of dismissal on grounds related to trade union membership or activities under S.152 or S.153 TULR(C)A. There is obviously considerable overlap between these provisions and S.104F ERA, in effect giving 'blacklisted' employees two causes of action in respect of the same dismissal. Where an employee successfully claims under both Acts, S.122(5) ensures that he or she does not receive the statutory minimum basic award in respect of both claims, thereby preventing double recovery.

Settlements and ex gratia payments 13.27

Any agreement to forgo a statutory employment right is void under S.203 ERA. Thus, an attempt by an employer to settle an unfair dismissal claim will be void and the agreement will not preclude the employee from pursuing a claim even if he or she accepts the money. There are, however, a number of exceptions to this rule, of which three are relevant in the present context: (i) where the settlement is formally incorporated in a tribunal decision; (ii) where it is reached under the auspices of an Acas conciliator in accordance with S.203(2)(e); or (iii) where it satisfies the conditions for settlement agreements contained in S.203(3). These three options are discussed in Chapter 2, 'Exclusions from right to claim', under 'Settlements and contracting out'.

If an ex gratia payment does not fall within any of these exceptions, there is nothing to prevent the employee pressing ahead with an unfair dismissal claim. The ex gratia payment will then be offset against any compensatory award (since it will go towards lessening the employee's direct financial loss) and, possibly, against any additional award, if one is made, but it will not necessarily be treated as meeting any liability for a basic award.

The leading case is Chelsea Football Club and Athletic Co Ltd v Heath 1981 **13.28** ICR 323, EAT. There H was unfairly dismissed and then given a cheque for £7,500 by the employer which was described simply as 'ex gratia compensation'. The tribunal held that none of the statutory grounds for reducing a basic award (see 'Reductions in basic award' above) applied. Therefore, although £7,500 exceeded the maximum amount which it could have awarded H at that time, the tribunal proceeded to make a basic award of £1,920. On appeal, the EAT pointed out that the employer's argument was not that there should be a reduction in the basic award but rather that it should not be ordered to pay one at all because it had already paid the basic award as part of the £7,500. The EAT said that whether or not a severance payment should be treated as extinguishing liability for a basic award was a 'question of construction'. If an employer stated clearly that a severance payment was intended to meet any possible liability for basic or compensatory awards that might be made by a tribunal, then it would have no further liability (provided the payment was

589

large enough). However, when the employer simply makes a general payment – particularly one expressed as being 'ex gratia' – it will run the risk of a tribunal treating that payment as if it did not refer to unfair dismissal liability at all.

The message for employers is clear. Any severance payment to a dismissed employee should expressly be stated to cover all possible liability arising out of the employee's complaint to a tribunal. In the Chelsea FC case, the EAT did in fact set aside the tribunal award. Use of the word 'compensation' by the employer seems to have tipped the scales and the EAT accepted that the employer's intention was to compensate H for rights arising from his dismissal. In Pomphrey of Sittingbourne Ltd v Reed EAT 457/94, however, R was paid 12 weeks' salary in lieu of notice on the termination of his employment. Following the tribunal's finding of unfair dismissal, the company sought to argue that, in view of the long period that R had been off sick by the time of his dismissal, there had been no contractual obligation to make any payment in lieu of notice and, therefore, the payment should be offset against the basic award. The EAT held that, regardless of whether contractually obliged to do so, the company had made a payment that was expressly stated to be a payment in lieu of notice. It could not later change its mind and have the payment appropriated to the basic award.

13.29 In Boorman v Allmakes Ltd 1995 ICR 842, CA, the employer made an ex gratia payment that was expressed to include the employee's statutory redundancy entitlement. A tribunal found that the dismissal was not in fact on account of redundancy and made a basic award of £2,079. The Court of Appeal rejected the employer's argument that the ex gratia payment included the payment of £2,079, either as a basic award or as a redundancy payment. A payment expressed to be ex gratia and to incorporate a statutory redundancy entitlement could not be construed as incorporating a payment to which the employee would only be entitled had he or she been unfairly dismissed.

Note that if an ex gratia payment is set off against the basic award, any surplus that remains should be applied against the compensatory award (see Chelsea Football Club and Athletic Co Ltd v Heath (above)). Any remaining surplus should be carried over to be set off against an additional award, if one is made (see Darr and anor v LRC Products Ltd 1993 IRLR 257, EAT, and Chapter 17, 'Additional awards and interim relief').

13.30 Ideally, from an employer's perspective, any severance payment should be endorsed by an Acas conciliator (if Acas has been involved in promoting a settlement) or should satisfy the conditions for settlement agreements contained in S.203(3). This would prevent the employee pursuing an unfair dismissal claim later and sidestep the issue of whether the payment could be interpreted as extinguishing a basic award.

Order of deductions 13.31

By analogy with compensatory awards, it would seem that ex gratia payments should be deducted from the basic award before any other reductions (for contributory conduct or on any other ground set out under 'Reductions in basic award' above) are applied. However, an employer who has made a statutory or contractual redundancy payment is entitled to have this deducted last (i.e. after all other deductions have been made) – see Chapter 16, 'Compensatory awards: adjustments', under 'Order of adjustments'.

14 Compensatory awards: types of loss

Nature and maximum amount of award

Immediate loss

Future loss

Expenses

Loss of statutory rights

Pension loss

Interest

Drafting schedules of loss

The second (and usually the largest) element of the compensation awarded in cases of unfair dismissal is the compensatory award. Unlike the basic award, which is calculated by reference to a statutory formula that bears little relation to the employee's real financial loss, the compensatory award is intended to reflect the actual losses that the employee suffers as a consequence of being unfairly dismissed. To this end, employment tribunals are directed by statute to award 'such amount as the tribunal considers just and equitable in all the circumstances having regard to the loss sustained by the complainant in consequence of the dismissal in so far as that loss is attributable to action taken by the employer' – S.123(1) Employment Rights Act 1996 (ERA). **14.1**

When assessing what the employee has actually lost as a consequence of being unfairly dismissed, the tribunal looks at the net remuneration that the employee would have continued to receive if the dismissal had not occurred. This raises a number of questions: does the employee have to give credit for a severance payment received from the employer? Must credit be given for earnings received from a new employer? For which lost benefits will the employee be compensated? At which point in time will the employee's losses no longer be attributable to the dismissal? Before such questions can be answered, there are some general points concerning the amount and nature of the compensatory award that should be noted.

Nature and maximum amount of award **14.2**

Section 123 ERA, as set out above, requires an employment tribunal to have regard to the loss incurred by the employee as a result of the dismissal, but other factors apart from actual loss can be taken into account. The objective is to award what the tribunal considers to be a 'just and equitable' amount. It follows that the compensatory award can, in appropriate cases, be something other than a precise arithmetical computation of the employee's losses.

Certain general points, however, apply to limit the otherwise wide discretion a tribunal has to adopt a broad-brush approach to the calculation of the compensatory award. These limits are discussed below.

14.3 Unfairness must have made a difference
The fundamental limit to the compensation that a tribunal may award on a finding of unfair dismissal is that it must only cover loss that flows from the unfair dismissal. Thus, if a tribunal finds that the employee would have been dismissed in any event, and on the same day, the compensatory award will generally be nil – in such circumstances the unfairness makes no difference. An example:

- **Ros and Angel t/a Cherry Tree Day Nursery v Fanstone** EAT 0273/07: F had been summarily dismissed on the day her resignation had been due to take effect, and her employer had refused to supply her with a reference, leading her prospective new employer to withdraw a job offer. The tribunal, having found the dismissal unfair, awarded a sum of £4,000 to reflect the immediate and future loss of earnings that F would experience as a result of the dismissal. On appeal, the EAT set aside the award of compensation. The losses were not attributable to the dismissal, since F would have departed at the end of the day on which she was dismissed. Rather, the losses – at their highest – were attributable to the refusal to provide a reference, something for which a tribunal cannot award compensation.

If a tribunal finds that the unfairness merely hastened a dismissal that would have occurred at a later date, then, in addition to the basic award, it should only award compensation covering the period between when the dismissal did occur and when it considers that the dismissal would have occurred had the employer acted fairly. In King and ors v Eaton Ltd (No.2) 1998 IRLR 686, Ct Sess (Inner House), the Court of Session stated that while it may not always be appropriate to classify a case as one of 'procedural' or 'substantive' unfairness, such a distinction can assist a tribunal in reaching a hypothetical view on what might have happened had the unfairness not occurred. In cases where the employer's only failing was procedural, it may be reasonably straightforward to establish what would have happened had a fair procedure been adopted, and to award compensation accordingly. Where the failing is more substantive in nature, it may be more difficult to determine what would have happened.

14.4 It is clear from the above that a tribunal is entitled to limit the compensatory award in a case where, had a proper dismissal procedure been applied, dismissal would have occurred in any event, albeit at a later date. But whereas King and ors v Eaton Ltd (No.2) (above) suggests that this kind of reduction is confined mainly to cases of procedural failings, decisions in subsequent cases have in fact extended the capacity to limit the compensatory award in this way to cases where the unfairness is substantive rather than purely procedural. For example, in Lambe v 186K Ltd 2005 ICR 307, CA, the Court of Appeal held that a tribunal had been entitled to find on the evidence that, despite the fact that both the process of selection for redundancy and the lack of consultation were unfair, the claimant would have been dismissed in any event after a period of seven weeks' consultation. The tribunal had therefore been justified in limiting the compensation the claimant received to seven weeks of loss.

Where a tribunal considers that there is only a chance that, had there been no unfairness, the dismissal would have occurred in any event, it may reduce the compensation by a percentage that reflects its assessment of that chance. This is known as a 'Polkey reduction', after the case of Polkey v AE Dayton Services Ltd 1988 ICR 142, HL, and is addressed at length in Chapter 16, 'Compensatory awards: adjustments', under '"Polkey reductions"'.

Amount of week's pay and statutory cap **14.5**

As the tribunal is seeking to ascertain the employee's true losses, there is no upper limit placed on the amount of a week's pay, as there is with the calculation of the basic award. If the employee's net earnings were £1,000 a week, then this is the amount on which the tribunal will base its calculations. However, at the other end of the scale, the employee's weekly earnings for the purposes of the compensatory award must comply with national minimum wage legislation. If the employer is paying the employee an amount less than the national minimum wage, the tribunal is obliged to ensure that, in calculating a week's pay, it takes the national minimum wage into account – Paggetti v Cobb 2002 IRLR 861, EAT.

In theory, at least, there is no limit on the period over which losses can be assessed (but see 'Immediate loss – new employment' below on the effects of obtaining new employment and the employee's duty to mitigate his or her loss). S.124(1) ERA does, however, place a statutory limit on the size of a compensatory award, which takes effect once all the calculations, including deductions, have been made.

Until 29 July 2013, the statutory limit was simply a figure – then £74,200 – that **14.6** was subject to review every year. However, on that date, the Unfair Dismissal (Variation of the Limit of Compensatory Award) Order 2013 SI 2013/1949 amended the ERA and introduced an alternative cap of a year's salary (which applies to all dismissals on or after 29 July 2013). The Government's reasons for this change are evident from its 'Ending the Employment Relationship' consultation, which ran from 14 September to 23 November 2012: the additional cap is intended to address misperceptions among employees and employers as to the likely level of unfair dismissal tribunal awards, encourage

595

earlier resolution of disputes and provide greater certainty as to the cost of disputes.

Section 124(1ZA) ERA now states that the statutory limit shall be the *lower* of:

- a set amount (i.e. £78,335, from 6 April 2015), and

- the product of 52 multiplied by a week's pay of the employee concerned.

In other words, the upper limit on the compensatory award is now the lower of a year's salary or £78,335. In assessing a year's salary, a week's pay is calculated according to the rules set down in Ss.221–229 ERA but without applying the limit on a week's pay set out in S.227 ERA.

14.7 The introduction of the additional cap means that employees who earn less than £78,335 per year are now entitled to potentially much less compensation than previously. However, an attempt to challenge the legality of the additional cap on the ground of discrimination failed before the High Court in R (on the application of Compromise Agreements Ltd) v Secretary of State for Business, Innovation and Skills 2014 EWHC 3303 (Admin), QBD. CA Ltd, an employment law firm, applied for permission to bring judicial review proceedings of the Government's decision to impose the 12-month compensatory cap. The High Court refused the application and, upon CA Ltd's request to reconsider its refusal, upheld its original decision. The reason for the rejection was that CA Ltd failed to make its application sufficiently promptly – it had only applied to the Court in October 2013, whereas the introduction of the new cap was proposed as early as September 2012 as part of the Government's 'Ending the Employment Relationship' consultation. Nor was the Court convinced that there were compelling grounds for allowing the application to proceed. The Court specifically rejected CA Ltd's argument that the new cap was indirectly age discriminatory, as older workers were taking much longer to find new employment and were therefore more likely than younger workers to receive compensatory awards in excess of 12 months' pay. According to the Court, the evidence did not support the view that the cap would have a disproportionate impact on older employees. In the year before the 'Ending the Employment Relationship' consultation was published, only 0.25% of tribunal claimants actually obtained an award in excess of 12 months' pay. That translated to just 115 out of a total of 50,000 claimants. Furthermore, there was no strong evidence available to suggest that a disproportionate number of those people had a protected characteristic. The Court also rejected CA Ltd's argument that the Secretary of State, when proposing to introduce the new cap, failed to have due regard to the public sector equality duty under the Equality Act 2010. (Note that this case is on appeal to the Court of Appeal and judgment is expected in the course of 2015).

14.8 **Exceptions to statutory limit.** As discussed in Chapter 9, 'Automatically unfair dismissals', S.124(1A) ERA removes the statutory limit on the

596

compensatory award in certain circumstances. There is no statutory maximum on the compensatory award that can be made where the reason for the dismissal was that the employee:

- carried out or proposed to carry out activities in connection with preventing or reducing risks to health and safety at work, having been designated by the employer to do so (S.100(1)(a) ERA)

- performed or proposed to perform the functions of a health and safety representative, or member of a safety committee, either in accordance with arrangements established by statute or after being recognised as such by the employer (S.100(1)(b))

- took part, or proposed to take part, in consultation with the employer pursuant to the Health and Safety (Consultation with Employees) Regulations 1996 SI 1996/1513 or in an election of safety representatives within the meaning of those Regulations, whether as a candidate or otherwise (S.100(1)(ba))

- brought to the employer's attention, by reasonable means, circumstances connected with his or her work which he or she reasonably believed were harmful or potentially harmful to health or safety (S.100(1)(c))

- in circumstances of danger which he or she reasonably believed to be serious and imminent and which he or she could not reasonably be expected to avert, left, proposed to leave or (while the danger persisted) refused to return to his or her place of work or any dangerous part of his or her place of work (S.100(1)(d))

- in circumstances of danger took, or proposed to take, appropriate steps to protect him or herself or other persons from danger which he or she reasonably believed to be serious and imminent (S.100(1)(e))

- made a protected disclosure (S.103A), or

- was selected for redundancy and the reason for selection was one of the above reasons (S.105(3) and (6A)).

Furthermore, in limited circumstances the compensatory award can be increased by an additional award – see Chapter 17, 'Additional awards and interim relief', under 'Additional awards – additional awards and arrears of pay', for details.

Compensation, not punishment

14.9

The compensatory award is strictly limited to making good the employee's financial loss. In no sense should the tribunal seek to bring into its calculations any consideration of what would be 'just' in order to punish the employer or reflect its disapproval of the employer's employment practices. Nor should its

597

award reflect any feelings of sympathy for the employee or the tribunal's view of what a fair severance payment would be – see Lifeguard Assurance Ltd v Zadrozny and anor 1977 IRLR 56, EAT.

The principle that the purpose of the compensatory award is confined to compensating only proven financial loss and is not in any sense to be used to penalise the employer was confirmed by the EAT in Morgans v Alpha Plus Security Ltd 2005 ICR 525, EAT. In that case, the Appeal Tribunal, presided over by Mr Justice Burton, rejected the contention that invalidity benefits received by the unfairly dismissed employee did not have to be offset in full from the compensatory award. In support of this conclusion, the EAT relied upon the House of Lords' ruling in Dunnachie v Kingston upon Hull City Council 2004 ICR 1052, HL, to the effect that compensation under S.123 ERA is not recoverable in respect of non-economic losses. In the course of giving judgment, Burton J stated: 'If there is no loss, no compensation can be recovered even for the most unfair of unfair dismissals... but the basic award marks the disapproval of the tribunal.'

14.10 Manner of dismissal

Following the ruling of the National Industrial Relations Court in Norton Tool Co Ltd v Tewson 1972 ICR 501, NIRC, it was settled law for over 30 years that compensation for unfair dismissal covers economic loss alone and that a tribunal should not normally take account of the manner of dismissal (including injury to feelings) when assessing compensation under S.123 ERA unless there was cogent evidence that the manner of the dismissal had caused actual financial loss ('the Norton Tool rule').

However, uncertainty as to the Norton Tool rule arose as a result of comments made in the House of Lords by Lord Hoffmann in Johnson v Unisys Ltd 2001 ICR 480, HL. In that case, the House of Lords decided that the implied term of mutual trust and confidence did not apply to the manner of dismissal, so no damages could be recovered at common law where the manner of dismissal caused psychiatric damage and consequential loss of earnings. Part of the House of Lords' reasoning was that a common law right should not be developed which would effectively cover the same ground as the statutory right not to be unfairly dismissed. During his judgment, Lord Hoffmann suggested that 'in an appropriate case' unfair dismissal compensation could cover not just financial loss but also 'distress, humiliation, damage to reputation in the community or to family life'.

14.11 Lord Hoffmann's comments led to a spirited debate as to whether, in unfair dismissal cases, tribunals should set aside the Norton Tool rule and make awards for non-pecuniary losses in appropriate circumstances. It was not clear whether Lord Hoffmann's remarks were part of the binding ratio of his judgment or were merely obiter – i.e. incidental to his decision and reasoning.

After a fair amount of confusion, the matter was finally resolved by a further decision of the House of Lords in Dunnachie v Kingston upon Hull City Council (above). That was a case where the employee won his claim of unfair (constructive) dismissal on the basis that he had been subjected to a prolonged campaign of bullying and undermining by his erstwhile manager. A tribunal found that, in failing to deal with the matter, his employer's actions had reduced him to a 'state of overt despair', and it awarded the claimant £10,000 to reflect the injury to his feelings in addition to his financial losses on the basis that Lord Hoffmann's remarks in Johnson permitted such an award.

When the case eventually reached the House of Lords their Lordships unanimously ruled that S.123 ERA precludes the award of non-economic loss. Lord Steyn, who gave the main judgment with which the other Law Lords all agreed, explained his reasoning as follows:

- the remarks of Lord Hoffmann in Johnson v Unisys Ltd (above) were, in fact, merely obiter dicta and not essential to his decision in that case. Therefore, the fact that two other Law Lords in Johnson expressed agreement with Lord Hoffmann's decision was not to be taken as indicating their approval of his remarks concerning the Norton Tool rule

- S.123(1) ERA, which governs the position on the compensatory award, stipulates that a tribunal may award such amount as it 'considers just and equitable in all the circumstances having regard to the loss sustained by the complainant'. 'Loss', in this context, is confined to financial losses. It precludes – as the NIRC held in Norton Tool Co Ltd v Tewson (above) – the award of non-economic losses such as injury to feelings.

As Sir John Donaldson had explained in the Norton Tool case, the phrase 'just **14.12** and equitable' gives tribunals a degree of flexibility as regards the informality of their procedures, so that precise and detailed proof of every item of loss does not necessarily have to be demanded of a complainant. But it does not permit tribunals to award additional sums that do not amount to 'loss' as defined.

Unfair dismissal compensation aside, the House of Lords' decision in Johnson v Unisys Ltd (above) should be understood as definitively ruling out the prospect of a claimant recovering damages at common law for the manner of his or her dismissal: this would intrude on the statutory remedy of unfair dismissal. However, their Lordships later clarified – in Eastwood and anor v Magnox Electric plc 2004 ICR 1064, HL – that a distinction should be drawn between events leading up to the dismissal, in respect of which a common law breach of contract claim may still be brought, and the dismissal itself, for which the only remedy is an unfair dismissal claim – see IDS Employment Handbook, 'Contracts of Employment' (2014), Chapter 4, 'Implied term of mutual trust and confidence', under 'Manner of dismissal'.

599

14.13 Stigma damages

On a related point, as a result of the House of Lords' decision in Malik and anor v Bank of Credit and Commerce International SA (in compulsory liquidation) 1997 ICR 606, HL, damages for wrongful dismissal (breach of contract) may include losses resulting from difficulties that the employee experiences in the labour market in securing new employment as a result of the employer's poor reputation at the time of dismissal. In that case, the claimant employees had been 'tarnished' by the corrupt and dishonest means by which the employer had operated BCCI – that tarnish taking the form of damage to their reputations in the labour market, with resultant harm being done to their prospects of future employment even though they themselves were entirely innocent of corruption or dishonesty. The House of Lords held that the losses flowing from the damage to the employees' reputations was recoverable in a claim for breach of contract on the ground that the company had, by its conduct, breached the implied term of trust and confidence. Losses to reputation were, in Lord Nicholls' phrase, 'continuing financial losses' – as distinct from 'premature termination losses' – inasmuch as the repercussions of the damage to reputation continued to cause foreseeable financial loss after the employment relationship had ended. Such losses were recoverable in claims for breach of contract (and, presumably, unfair constructive dismissal) – subject to proof that a breach of the implied term has occurred, that the damage to reputation was actually caused by the breach, and that the employee had taken steps to mitigate his or her loss.

The issue of stigma damages was given further consideration by the Court of Appeal in Abbey National plc and anor v Chagger 2010 ICR 397, CA, a case which seems to confirm, albeit by indirect means, that stigma damages are recoverable in unfair dismissal claims. C had successfully argued that his selection for redundancy was both an unfair dismissal and an act of race discrimination. He contended that compensation should reflect his decreased chances of finding other employment after leaving AN plc due to the 'stigma' of having brought race discrimination proceedings. AN plc argued that such damages are not appropriate, since any employer refusing to recruit an employee on the basis that the employee has brought discrimination proceedings against a former employer would be committing an act of unlawful victimisation under S.2 of the Race Relations Act 1976 (since repealed and re-enacted in the Equality Act 2010). Lord Justice Elias, giving judgment for the Court, examined the decision in Malik and anor v Bank of Credit and Commerce International SA (in compulsory liquidation) (above) and concluded that, while the stigma in C's case was of a different nature, the House of Lords' reasoning applied to it just as much as it did to the stigma of a failed and disgraced former employer. The pivotal issue was whether the fact that the third party's conduct would be unlawful should change matters. In Elias LJ's view, there are a number of public policy reasons why it should not. Among them is the fact that a third party employer could lawfully refuse to recruit an employee who had brought unfair dismissal proceedings against his or her former employer – there is no equivalent to the victimisation provisions in respect of unfair dismissal. Elias LJ stated that it would be 'unsatisfactory and somewhat artificial if tribunals were obliged to discount stigma loss in the context of discrimination law but not in other contexts'.

Implicit in Elias LJ's reasoning is the notion that stigma damages are potentially **14.14** available in unfair dismissal claims (and, for that matter, all employment tribunal claims in which there is an element of future loss). However, he went on to point out that the effect of any stigma is not a separate head of damage, but rather a factor to be taken into consideration when a tribunal calculates the degree of future loss that the claimant will experience (see further under 'Future loss' below).

The EAT went one step further in Ur-Rehman v Ahmad (on behalf of Doncaster Jamia Mosque) 2013 ICR 28, EAT, when it accepted that stigma damages may be payable where the employee has been disadvantaged as a result of having brought unfair dismissal proceedings against a former employer. However, it emphasised that such a claim will only succeed where there is evidence that the employee has found it difficult to obtain or keep employment because of stigma and none had been produced in the instant case. U-R was an imam at a mosque until 16 April 2009, when he was dismissed. The reason for his dismissal was that he was not fluent in English – and the mosque had determined that it needed an English-speaking imam for its members. Following his dismissal, U-R found short-term employment from June to October and in December became employed by an educational trust. In August 2010 the trust dismissed him for gross misconduct. In May 2011 an employment tribunal heard his unfair dismissal claim against the mosque and found in his favour. At the remedies hearing, U-R argued that the tribunal should make an award for stigma damages arising out of the circumstances of his dismissal by the trust. He alleged that a member of the mosque had told his new employer that he had taken the mosque to the employment tribunal and that he was certain to 'repeat that trick' with the trust. He further claimed that the mosque had put pressure on the trust to get him to drop the proceedings. The tribunal refused to award stigma damages, finding that there was insufficient evidence before it to show that U-R had suffered such loss.

The EAT, while accepting that stigma damages are recoverable in unfair **14.15** dismissal proceedings, upheld the tribunal's decision on appeal. As the tribunal had correctly found, a claim for loss consisting of difficulty in obtaining or keeping employment due to 'stigma', particularly where the stigma consists not of taking unjustified proceedings but of bringing successful ones against a former employer, must be supported by evidence. A mere suggestion or suspicion that stigma might be at work is not sufficient. In every case, the EAT

601

continued, it is necessary to answer the question of whether, in relation to finding new employment, stigma from the former employee's previous employment had a real and substantial effect and, if it did, how great an effect. In answering that question, it is appropriate to have regard to the entire history of the former employee's search for new employment, including the number of jobs applied for, how well targeted and presented the applications had been, the number of interviews obtained, how the interviews had gone and any reasons given for rejection. While each application was relevant, it was necessary to answer the question on the basis of the job search as a whole. It was not necessary as a matter of law for the former employee to call evidence from prospective employers in relation to the effect of stigma on the particular applications that had been made to them. In the instant case, the tribunal had found that there was insufficient evidence to support U-R's claim for stigma damages. It concluded that, whatever the member of the mosque had told the trust, it had not caused the trust to dismiss him. Nor did U-R have any difficulty in finding employment following his dismissal by the mosque, as evidenced by the fact that he had first obtained short-term employment and thereafter permanent employment with the trust. The EAT could find no fault with the tribunal's conclusion on the issue of stigma damages and U-R's appeal was accordingly dismissed.

14.16 'Deemed losses' and Norton Tool rule

Although, as stated above, the House of Lords in Dunnachie v Kingston upon Hull City Council 2004 ICR 1052, HL, approved Sir John Donaldson's statement in Norton Tool Co Ltd v Tewson 1972 ICR 501, NIRC, that the compensatory award should be used only to compensate proven financial loss, one other aspect of the NIRC's ruling did not receive much attention from their Lordships. This was its decision that an employee who had been unfairly dismissed without notice, and who had taken up fresh employment during what would have been the notice period, was entitled to receive a sum equivalent to notice pay as part of his or her unfair dismissal compensation without giving credit for the monies he or she had earned from the new employment. This aspect of Norton Tool was followed by the EAT in TBA Industrial Products Ltd v Locke 1984 ICR 228, EAT, and approved, although obiter (i.e. not binding), by the Court of Appeal in Addison v Babcock FATA Ltd 1987 ICR 805, CA. In the light of Dunnachie, the question obviously arose as to whether the Norton Tool principle remained good law, and this fell to be considered by different divisions of the EAT in Morgans v Alpha Plus Security Ltd 2005 ICR 525, EAT, and Voith Turbo Ltd v Stowe 2005 ICR 543, EAT.

The issue that lay at the heart of the Morgans case was whether incapacity benefits received by the employee during the period covered by the compensatory award should be deducted from that award. The EAT, presided over by its then President Mr Justice Burton, held that the social security benefits did have to be deducted in full, reasoning that in the light of Dunnachie v Kingston upon Hull City Council (above), there was no room for the approach in Norton Tool Co Ltd v Tewson (above) whereby an employee can be 'treated' as having suffered loss if no actual loss has occurred. In reaching this conclusion, Burton J relied heavily on the similar legal reasoning he adopted in Hardy v Polk (Leeds) Ltd 2004 ICR 557, EAT, when holding that an employee who mitigated the loss caused by his summary dismissal by finding new employment during what would have been his notice period was required to offset his earnings from that new employment against the compensatory award.

However, a different view was taken by the EAT in Voith, presided over by His **14.17** Honour Judge McMullen. In that case, which concerned exactly the same issue as Hardy v Polk (above), the EAT expressed the view that the decisions of Burton J in that case and in the Morgans case flew in the face of the established 'good industrial practice' promoted by the NIRC in Norton Tool Co Ltd v Tewson (above). The EAT specifically cited Norton Tool as justification for not requiring an employee who had been paid in lieu of notice to give credit for monies earned from fresh employment during the notice period.

Neither Morgans v Alpha Plus Security Ltd (above) nor Voith Turbo Ltd v Stowe (above) progressed to the Court of Appeal, but the scope of Norton Tool Co Ltd v Tewson (above) was eventually given detailed consideration by that court in Langley and anor v Burlo 2007 ICR 390, CA. In that case B was unfairly and wrongfully dismissed from her role as a nanny at a time when she was recovering from a car accident. Due to her injuries, B would have been unable to work during her eight-week contractual notice period, and under the terms of her contract would only have been entitled to statutory sick pay. In assessing B's compensatory award, the tribunal did not take account of the eight weeks' notice period since it had already awarded eight weeks' pay in respect of the wrongful dismissal. The award for wrongful dismissal was overturned on appeal, but in her cross-appeal B contended that the principle in Norton Tool – that, since it is good industrial practice to give full pay in lieu of notice to an employee who is dismissed without notice, an employee's compensation should include a sum equivalent to the pay in lieu of notice which he or she should have had, irrespective of whether he or she has found other work during the notice period – should be extended to cases where the employee is unable to work his or her notice period due to sickness.

The EAT accepted that good industrial practice was as B had described it, but **14.18** held, by a majority, that the Norton Tool principle was no longer a legitimate basis for awarding full compensation for the notice period. The Appeal Tribunal stated that the principle had been undermined by the House of Lords' decision in Dunnachie v Kingston upon Hull City Council (above) that S.123 permits only the award of sums which reflect the loss resulting from the dismissal and that it is not legitimate to award sums which are additional to such loss.

603

When the case reached the Court of Appeal, the result was the same – B was not entitled to full pay for the extent of her notice period – but the reasoning was very different. Unlike the EAT, the Court considered that Norton Tool Co Ltd v Tewson (above) remains good law, observing that it had neither been expressly nor impliedly overruled by Dunnachie. However, the Court stated that the authority of Norton Tool is restricted to the narrow point that, since it is good industrial practice for an employer who has dismissed an employee without notice to make a full payment in lieu of notice, a tribunal in assessing compensation for dismissal should not subject this payment to any deduction for sums earned in other employment during the notice period. There are no grounds for extending the principle to cover other facets of good industrial relations practice which, if applied to the award of compensation under S.123, would result in an award greater than the loss caused to the employee as a consequence of the dismissal. As a result, B had only been entitled to statutory sick pay during her notice period.

While there was undoubtedly a degree of logic to the reasoning that Dunnachie v Kingston upon Hull City Council (above) put paid to any flexibility on the part of tribunals to treat anything other than actual financial loss as comprising 'loss' for the purposes of S.123 ERA, the Court in Langley and anor v Burlo (above) was clearly swayed by the fact that the Norton Tool principle has been applied in tribunals for over 30 years and, in the words of Lord Justice Mummery, 'has not been shown to have worked unfairly'. Therefore, until such time as the Supreme Court says otherwise, courts and tribunals should continue to apply the narrow Norton Tool principle in calculating compensation for wages in lieu of notice in unfair dismissal cases.

14.19 So the Norton Tool exception to the rule that the compensatory award should be based solely on actual loss remains valid. However, as the Burlo case makes clear, the scope of the exception will be tightly defined. This is fully apparent from the Court of Appeal's subsequent decision in Stuart Peters Ltd v Bell 2009 ICR 1556, CA, where it was held that the principle in Norton Tool Co Ltd v Tewson (above) does not apply to claims of unfair constructive dismissal. In the Stuart Peters case the claimant, B, had been unfairly constructively dismissed without being paid her six months' contractual notice pay. In awarding compensation, the tribunal relied on the Norton Tool principle and did not give credit for the earnings from three months of temporary work that the claimant had performed during the notice period. The EAT upheld this decision, but the Court of Appeal saw things differently. Lord Justice Elias, who gave the leading judgment, stressed that the Norton Tool principle is not simply designed to give full compensation during what would have been the notice period had the contract been terminated with notice. Rather, it is designed to uphold expectations that will result from the application of good industrial relations practice where the employer has chosen to terminate the contract. Its purpose is to ensure that an employer who fails to comply with good industrial relations

604

practice is not in a better position than it would have been in if it had followed the practice. Even if the employer genuinely believes that it is entitled to dismiss summarily for gross misconduct, it must take the consequences of getting this assessment wrong.

Lord Justice Elias then contrasted this situation with that of a constructive dismissal, where entirely different considerations arise. If the employee resigns in response to the employer's alleged repudiatory breach of contract, there is no general – let alone appropriate – practice of making a payment in lieu of notice. In fact, the employer will usually dispute that there has been a repudiatory breach at all – it is purporting to keep the contract alive and is willing to continue to pay the wages. Elias LJ emphasised that it is not that a different legal rule operates in such circumstances, simply that there is a difference in good practice, which leads to a different result. Even if this means that the employer avoids the application of the Norton Tool principle where it commits a breach of contract, this is simply the effect of the principle being rooted in good practice rather than 'wider considerations of justice or logic'.

Tribunals' discretion
14.20

In some cases it will be possible to assess compensation with a high degree of accuracy. For example, where the employee promptly obtains a new job that pays more than the old one, the losses will be limited to the short period of unemployment between the two jobs. In other cases – e.g. where the claimant is still unemployed when the tribunal comes to assess compensation, or where a new job pays less than the old one – the tribunal will be forced to adopt a far more speculative approach to assessing likely periods of unemployment or likely future earnings.

So far as possible, tribunals should use the facts that are at their disposal in order to reach an accurate assessment of compensation. But the fact that they will often be compelled to adopt a broad-brush approach has long been recognised by the courts. In Norton Tool Co Ltd v Tewson 1972 ICR 501, NIRC, for example, Sir John Donaldson recognised that what is now S.123(1) gives tribunals a good deal of discretion when assessing compensatory awards and said that the award was 'not to be assessed by adopting the approach of a conscientious and skilled cost accountant or actuary'.

The extent of this discretion means that an appeal against a tribunal's assessment **14.21** of compensation is unlikely to meet with much success unless it can be shown that the tribunal misdirected itself in law or made a decision that no reasonable tribunal could have made. The appeal courts may even be prepared to overlook minor errors in the tribunal's calculations – Fougère v Phoenix Motor Co Ltd 1976 ICR 495, EAT.

There are limits to the tribunals' discretion, however. In the Norton Tool case Sir John Donaldson stated that the object of the compensatory award is 'to

605

compensate, and compensate fully, but not to award a bonus' and went on to say that tribunals must exercise their discretion 'judicially and upon the basis of principle', and that they should break down a compensatory award into heads of compensation so that the parties can follow how the compensation was assessed. These heads of compensation are outlined below.

14.22 Heads of compensation

The heads of compensation normally used by tribunals are:

- immediate loss of earnings – i.e. loss between the dismissal and the hearing at which the tribunal decides on compensation

- future loss of earnings – i.e. estimated loss after the hearing

- expenses incurred as a consequence of the dismissal

- loss of statutory employment protection rights – this covers, for example, the fact that an unfairly dismissed employee will be unable to bring another unfair dismissal claim until he or she has had two years' continuous employment in a new job

- loss of pension rights.

It is the employee's duty to provide evidence of his or her losses. In the words of Mr Justice Bristow in Adda International Ltd v Curcio 1976 IRLR 425, EAT, 'the tribunal must have something to bite on, and if an applicant produces nothing for it to bite on, he will have only himself to thank'. Claimants must therefore be fully prepared to show evidence of loss under each head of damage because the tribunal will not be required to take any particular point into account on compensation unless the claimant produces evidence in support. Very often, tribunals now require claimants to provide a 'schedule of loss' to the respondent as part of the case management process leading up to a tribunal hearing – see 'Drafting schedules of loss' at the end of this chapter. Tribunals have a duty, however, to enquire into each head of compensation – Tidman v Aveling Marshall Ltd 1977 ICR 506, EAT. A tribunal should also briefly explain the manner and reasoning by which it arrived at its figures. The very discipline of setting out and explaining the heads of compensation is seen as a way of both guarding against and highlighting any errors, while also steering the tribunal towards a reasonable figure.

14.23 Before explaining the methods by which the various heads of compensation are assessed, and the circumstances in which a compensatory award may be reduced, it is worth noting the comments of His Honour Judge Hull QC in Garage Equipment Maintenance Co Ltd v Holloway EAT 582/94, where he pointed out that the kind of precise argument that goes into assessing damages at common law in personal injury claims is inappropriate in cases of unfair dismissal. Matters of compensation raise extremely difficult questions of logic and causation, but it is clear both from the wide wording of S.123(1) and from countless decided cases that tribunals are enjoined to use a very broad-brush approach. This approach may have its drawbacks: it will inevitably mean that a great many imponderables which could be investigated at length will be put to one side and a very general view taken, 'but it does have the advantage that it is relatively simple and straightforward'. Common sense and a just approach are more important than an over-adherence to strict logic.

Taxation

If the total amount of compensation awarded (together with any other termination payments) is less than £30,000, it will be exempt from tax (although when assessing loss, the tribunal will have looked at the *net* remuneration that the employee would have continued to receive if the dismissal had not occurred). Any amount above £30,000 will be taxed as a termination payment under S.401 of the Income Tax (Earnings and Pensions) Act 2003, although employment tribunals will generally 'gross up' the award to take this into account. For further discussion of the tax treatment of unfair dismissal awards, see Chapter 12, 'Remedies', under 'Compensation – taxation'.

Immediate loss

The employee's 'immediate loss' is the loss incurred between the effective date of termination of the contract of employment and the date when the tribunal assesses the loss (i.e. at the remedies hearing). Subject to what is said below about the employee obtaining new employment, immediate loss is assessed up to this date even if the final compensation hearing is subject to considerable delay because of protracted appeals on the issue of liability – Gilham and ors v Kent County Council (No.3) 1986 ICR 52, EAT.

This period covered by 'immediate loss' as defined above is also the period that is subject to the recoupment provisions under the Employment Protection (Recoupment of Benefits) Regulations 1996 SI 1996/2349. These provisions put in place a procedure whereby the employer is directed to deduct from compensation awarded to the employee any sums received by the employee of Jobseeker's Allowance, income-related Employment and Support Allowance, Income Support or Universal Credit. The employer is then obliged to pay over such sums to Jobcentre Plus (the executive agency of the Department for Work and Pensions that administers social security payments) as a way of enabling it to recoup the social security payments it has made during the relevant period. In an unfair dismissal case the recoupment provisions potentially apply to that part of the compensatory award covering lost earnings up to the conclusion of proceedings but not any award the tribunal may make for future loss. For more detail on the Recoupment Regulations, see Chapter 18, 'Recoupment'.

607

14.26　In contrast to the basic award (see Chapter 13, 'Basic awards'), for the purposes of the compensatory award, loss is assessed by reference to the net pay that the employee would have earned but for the dismissal. It is normally the salary attached to the employee's position at the time of dismissal that is relevant for these purposes. For example, in Countrywide Estate Agents and ors v Turner EAT 0208/13 the EAT held that an employment tribunal had been wrong to base the compensatory award on the employee's income in a more senior role, which he had left four months before the effective date of termination, rather than on his lower income in the more junior role he held at the time of his constructive dismissal. The EAT stressed that the tribunal is only entitled to award the losses arising in consequence of the dismissal itself. In the instant case, the employee had freely accepted the new contractual position with reduced pay and the tribunal was only entitled to compensate him for the losses arising in consequence of the dismissal itself. In other words, the loss of the more senior salary did not flow from the dismissal.

The particular circumstances of the case may warrant a departure from the general approach, however, as is evident from the EAT's decision in Toni and Guys (St Paul's) Ltd v Georgiou 2013 ICR 1356, EAT. There, G worked as a senior hair stylist on a commission-only basis at a rate of 34 per cent of her net takings. In June 2011 she was unfairly dismissed and, at the remedies hearing, she successfully argued that during June her earnings had been artificially low because the employer had suspended her, blackened her name, caused her to lose the goodwill of her clients and diverted work away from her. The tribunal therefore awarded her compensation on the basis of what she would have earned during that period (which it determined by having regard to the financial performance of the other stylists and the fact that G was far more experienced than them). On appeal, the EAT upheld the tribunal's decision. In its view, S.123(1) ERA gives the tribunal a wide discretion to compensate a claimant for the loss sustained as a result of dismissal attributable to action taken by the employer. In the instant case, the action taken by the employer, as found by the tribunal, included capriciously diverting away from G work on which she would have earned additional commission. In these circumstances, it would not be just and equitable to permit the employer to benefit from behaviour that formed a part of the unfairness of the dismissal. In order to correct that injustice, the tribunal had been entitled to compensate G for her lost earnings post-dismissal on the basis of what she would have earned but for her unfair dismissal.

14.27　The compensatory award is intended to compensate the employee only for actual loss stemming from the dismissal. Therefore, as part of the general rule that sums received in mitigation of loss should be offset against the losses claimed, the employee must give credit where he or she receives pay in lieu of notice or an ex gratia payment from the employer (see, for example, DCM Optical Clinic plc v Stark EAT 0124/04). The employee must also give credit for earnings from any new employment obtained since dismissal (subject to an exception regarding the notice period that is considered under 'New earnings, notice pay and the notice period' below).

New employment   14.28
An important point arises concerning the situation where an employee obtains new employment in the period between the date of dismissal and the date on which the tribunal assesses compensation.

The Ging rule: new earnings required to be offset. The general rule is that a   14.29
tribunal should offset the employee's new earnings against his or her losses to discover what the overall loss has been during this period – Ging v Ellward Lancs Ltd 1991 ICR 222, EAT. (Note that this case was actually decided in 1977.) So, taking the example of a dismissed employee who obtains a better-paid job after a period of unemployment, the compensation will be based on his or her old pay for the period of unemployment, less what has since been earned in excess of the old salary in the new job. (If the new job pays *less* than the old one, then the employee can be compensated for the difference between the old and the new levels of pay.)

However, this approach can produce some unacceptable results. It is not hard to imagine a situation where the employee's new salary, coupled with a delay in the tribunal proceedings, would mean that losses between dismissal and the date when the employee started the new job were cancelled out by the time of the tribunal hearing. Such a result is seen as undesirable, partly because the amount of compensation should not depend so greatly on a random factor like the timing of the tribunal hearing, and partly because the dismissed employee is penalised for obtaining new, well-paid work.

Exceptions to Ging rule. An exception to the rule in Ging was first developed   14.30
in relation to the situation where the employee is deemed to have entered new *permanent* employment before the tribunal hearing on compensation. In Courtaulds Northern Spinning Ltd v Moosa 1984 ICR 218, EAT, the hearing did not take place until more than three years after the dismissal date. For 18 months of those three years, M had worked for a new employer. He was then made redundant. In this case the respondent's liability was held to have ceased when M entered the new job because, according to the EAT, it was an equivalent permanent job. Thus, neither M's earnings in the new job nor his renewed losses when he became unemployed again before the hearing were taken into account. (It may be worth noting here, however, that the measure by which the EAT identified the new employment as being permanent was the fact that it had lasted long enough for M to have acquired new employment protection rights.)

The fact that S.123(1) ERA requires tribunals to award such sums as they consider just and equitable leaves some scope for them to use their discretion to circumvent the more undesirable aspects of the decision in Ging v Ellward

609

Lancs Ltd (above). This has been confirmed in two Scottish cases. In Lytlarch Ltd v Reid 1991 ICR 216, EAT, the Appeal Tribunal, while acknowledging the general rule in Ging, said that the rule may not necessarily apply where there is a long delay between dismissal and the compensation hearing. And in Fentiman v Fluid Engineering Products Ltd 1991 ICR 570, EAT, the Appeal Tribunal added that the Ging method of calculation will not necessarily be appropriate in circumstances where new earnings are considerably higher than the old and where a significant period of time has passed between the employee starting the new job and the date of the tribunal's assessment of compensation. In that case a period of 39 weeks in the new job was considered to be sufficiently 'permanent' to justify limiting the assessment of the claimant's compensation to the date when he started the new job. In both these cases the EAT confirmed that the Ging rule remains the general rule, but exceptions have now clearly been established.

14.31 Even so, this is a matter that could do with further clarification by the courts because we seem to be left with a rather rigid 'all or nothing' approach. If Ging does apply, new earnings will be fully offset up to the tribunal hearing. If it does not apply, assessment of losses will abruptly cease at the point when the employee obtains a new job. Note that where the employee's new job pays less than the old one, assessment of losses based on the difference between those earnings can continue over a substantial period.

An attempt to provide clarification of this difficult issue was made by the EAT in Whelan and anor v Richardson 1998 ICR 318, EAT. In that case an employee was unfairly dismissed from her job that paid her £72 per week. She found employment in another job that paid £52 per week and that lasted 18 weeks. She then got a job paying £96 per week. She was still in that job when, some 15 months after her dismissal, the tribunal held a hearing to assess her loss. The assessment was made by calculating the wages she would have received from the date of dismissal to the date she started the higher-paid job, and then deducting the money she earned during her 18 weeks' temporary employment in the lower-paid job. The EAT upheld the tribunal's calculation, stating that it had been correct to treat as the cut-off point the date that the employee secured permanent employment that was at least as well paid as the original job. The EAT laid down a series of propositions to be applied when assessing an employee's loss:

- the assessment of loss must be judged on the basis of the facts as they appear at the date of the remedies hearing

- where the employee has been unemployed during the period from the dismissal to the date of the remedies hearing, then, subject to the duty to mitigate, the employee will recover what he or she would have earned during that period had he or she not been dismissed. The tribunal should also consider for how long the loss is likely to continue

610

- where the employee has found alternative work that pays less than the job from which he or she was dismissed, the employee will be compensated in the same manner as described in the previous proposition, save that the new, lower income will be deducted from the loss of earnings

- if, at the date of the remedies hearing, the employee has found alternative permanent employment which pays at least as much as the job from which he or she was dismissed, then the tribunal should only assess the employee's loss from the date of dismissal to the date on which he or she started the new job. The dismissing employer cannot rely on the employee's increased earnings to reduce the loss sustained prior to taking the new employment.

Earnings from temporary new employment. It is for the tribunal to decide **14.32** whether employment taken by the employee following his or her dismissal is in fact temporary or permanent. The EAT in Whelan and anor v Richardson (above) added that a dismissed employee should not be discouraged from taking temporary employment because of a fear that the employer will not be liable for losses which continue after the temporary employment comes to an end.

However, in Dench v Flynn and Partners 1998 IRLR 653, CA, the Court of Appeal held that an employer's liability for the loss suffered by an unfairly dismissed employee does not necessarily cease once the employee commences new employment of a permanent nature at a salary equivalent to or higher than that which the employee previously enjoyed. The Court acknowledged that in many cases the loss consequent upon unfair dismissal will cease on such an event. But to regard the obtaining of equivalent permanent employment as always putting an end to the attribution of the loss to the unfair dismissal can in some cases lead to an award that is not just and equitable. This was particularly so where the new employment appears to be permanent when entered into but which, through no fault of the employee's, proves to be of only a short duration. The Court of Appeal ruled that, in such a case, the reason why any subsequent employment did not last will be an important consideration. If the employee simply resigned for no good reason or was dismissed for incompetence or misconduct, for example, it is likely that a tribunal would take the view that any losses that the employee had subsequently suffered were attributable to his or her own behaviour and were not in consequence of the original unfair dismissal.

Self-employment and earnings from insecure employment. It is not just **14.33** earnings from a subsequent employer that may be taken into account. Some employees, for example, become self-employed after being unfairly dismissed. In such cases their earnings will be set off against their losses in the usual way. However, an issue arises when the claimant's earnings from being self-employed are highly variable. In Islam Channel Ltd v Ridley EAT 0083/09 the claimant had not sustained an immediate loss of earnings after dismissal because she had obtained freelance work that paid her approximately £5,000 more than

611

she would have earned but for the dismissal. However, having noted that the work was inherently insecure and that, by the date of the hearing, R had begun to sustain a monthly loss, the tribunal awarded a sum for future loss without giving any credit for the £5,000 excess earned during the period of immediate loss. Upholding this decision, the EAT noted that, as a result of Dench v Flynn and Partners (above), it is clear that the obtaining of higher paid work will not always break the chain of causation. The tribunal in the instant case had exercised its discretion to award compensation that was 'just and equitable', a discretion that affords tribunals the room to adopt different approaches to the fundamentally different tasks of assessing immediate and future loss. The EAT added that, if it were wrong on that point, the tribunal's decision not to give credit for the £5,000 could be viewed as a reflection of the risk that what freelance work R still had could dry up during the period of future loss.

A dismissed employee who decides to set up his or her own business rather than find other employment will inevitably incur start-up costs in order to get the business off the ground. In Baillon v Gwent Police EAT 0354/14, a case concerning the automatically unfair constructive dismissal of a police officer who had made protected disclosures, the EAT held that the employment tribunal had erred by failing to take such costs into account when assessing B's loss of earnings. The tribunal had acknowledged that B had incurred costs of over £10,000 when he started a new woodworking business following his dismissal, but the earnings that had been offset against B's losses for the first year were just £2,000 lower than that for the second year. The EAT concluded that the tribunal's figures 'were arbitrary and had no clear rationale'.

14.34 **Higher education grants.** In Justfern Ltd v D'Ingerthorpe and ors 1994 IRLR 164, EAT, the question arose of whether a £4,000 educational grant that the employee had received following his dismissal should be taken into account in determining his loss. A tribunal declined to offset the grant on the ground that it would not be just and equitable for the employer to benefit from the employee's efforts to improve himself. The EAT held that the grant was sufficiently remote from the matter of the compensatory award to justify the tribunal's decision.

14.35 **Duty to mitigate losses.** It should be noted that the final amount of compensation that an employee receives depends to a great extent on whether he or she has taken reasonable steps to mitigate his or her loss. Accepting a lower-paid job, becoming self-employed, or even pursuing a course of study may or may not amount to reasonable mitigation of loss. This issue is considered in detail in Chapter 16, 'Compensatory awards: adjustments', under 'Failure to mitigate losses'.

Sums received in settlement of claims against other parties   14.36
In cases where there are two or more respondents, a claimant may well settle the claim against one respondent (thereby receiving a sum of money), while continuing the same claim against the other respondent(s). In the context of unfair dismissal, this commonly occurs when the claim relates to a transfer to which the Transfer of Undertakings (Protection of Employment) Regulations 2006 SI 2006/246 (TUPE) apply. If it is unclear to whom a claimant's employment has transferred, or even whether there has been a transfer at all, the claimant may wish to bring a claim against more than one respondent. In such a scenario, if he or she successfully negotiates a settlement with one of the respondents, credit must be given for the amount of that settlement agreement if he or she succeeds in the claim against one of the other parties.

In Optimum Group Services plc v Muir 2013 IRLR 339, EAT, M was dismissed by OGS plc in circumstances that he contended were connected to a TUPE transfer. He brought a claim against OGS plc and nine other companies, asserting that his employment had transferred to all or any of them. A tribunal later found that there had been no relevant transfer. However, in the meantime, M successfully negotiated a conciliated settlement with one of the nine putative transferees, BE Ltd. When the employment tribunal upheld M's unfair dismissal claim against OGS plc and calculated his loss of earnings for the purpose of compensation, it declined to take into account the £20,000 that M had received from BE Ltd. The tribunal considered that it had a discretion under S.123 ERA to award the sum it thought just and equitable. It took into account the possibility that M might in fact have been under-compensated by BE Ltd, and that OGS plc might benefit from a windfall if M had to give credit for the payment.

The EAT overturned the tribunal's decision, holding that it had to abide by the   14.37
principle that there should be no double recovery for the same loss. Since awards under S.123 are designed to be compensatory and not punitive, if a claimant's loss arising from the dismissal has already been made good to any extent, that must be taken into account. Just as any sums earned in the relevant post-dismissal period have to be deducted, so must any sum paid by one of the respondents in respect of the claim for unfair dismissal. The tribunal had no discretion in this matter. Even if it did, it could not be relevant that M took a risk in settling his claim against BE Ltd at less than what he perceived to be full value, nor that OGS plc might receive a windfall – this was merely a fact of litigation. The EAT therefore substituted a compensatory award taking into account the £20,000 already received by M.

Social security benefits   14.38
Social security benefits are another potential source of income for a dismissed employee. As we have seen above, where the employee receives Jobseeker's Allowance, income-related Employment and Support Allowance, Income

613

Support or Universal Credit after being unfairly dismissed, these benefits are not offset against the employee's immediate losses but are instead subject to the recoupment procedure – see Chapter 18, 'Recoupment'. The effect on the compensatory award of receipt of other welfare benefits is more problematic, as we shall see below.

14.39 **Incapacity benefits.** There has historically been a degree of uncertainty surrounding the question of whether employees who are in receipt of state incapacity benefits following dismissal should have these benefits deducted from the compensatory award. For many years this type of benefit was known as Invalidity Benefit and then Incapacity Benefit. It is now called Employment and Support Allowance (ESA), although the income-related element of ESA – which is governed by the recoupment procedure – is gradually being replaced by Universal Credit. In Hilton International Hotels (UK) Ltd v Faraji 1994 ICR 259, EAT, the Appeal Tribunal took the view that sums received by an employee by way of Invalidity Benefit following his or her unfair dismissal should not be offset against the compensatory award. Although this meant that an employee might receive more in compensation than he or she would have received if he or she had remained in employment, the EAT pointed out that the right to Invalidity Benefit arises as a result of the national insurance scheme and is dependent to some degree upon the amount of payments made to that scheme by the employee. Accordingly, Invalidity Benefit could properly be classified as an insurance benefit. As such, it came within the well-established common law principle that the proceeds of insurance constitute an exception to the general principle that an injured party should be awarded such sum as will place him or her in the position he or she would have been in but for the injury. This meant that the value of such benefits did not fall to be offset against the employee's loss of earnings when calculating the compensatory award.

In Puglia v C James and Sons 1996 ICR 301, EAT, by contrast, a differently constituted Appeal Tribunal took the view that the Hilton decision had been reached without the assistance of all the relevant authorities and should not be followed. In particular, the EAT referred to Sun and Sand Ltd v Fitzjohn 1979 ICR 268, EAT, in which it had been held that, unless there was a provision in the contract of employment entitling the employee to receive full wages or salary in addition to sick pay, the amount of any sickness benefit received by the employee during the period covered by the compensatory award should be deducted from the award.

14.40 However, in Rubenstein and anor v McGloughlin 1997 ICR 318, EAT, the Appeal Tribunal declined to follow either the Faraji or the Puglia decisions. It stated that there was no need for an 'all or nothing' approach. The obligation under S.123(1) ERA to award what is just and equitable in all the circumstances conferred on a tribunal a good deal of flexibility in the matter. The EAT concluded that tribunals should treat the employer and employee equally by deducting one half of the Invalidity Benefit received by an employee from his or her compensatory award.

The EAT's most recent pronouncement on the subject came in Morgans v Alpha Plus Security Ltd 2005 ICR 525, EAT. In that case the Appeal Tribunal conducted a thorough review of all the previous case law and concluded that Incapacity Benefit received by the claimant from the date of his or her unfair dismissal to the date of the remedies hearing should be deducted in full from his or her immediate losses. In so holding, the EAT reached the same conclusion as that reached in Puglia v C James and Sons (above). Mr Justice Burton supported his reasoning by citing the House of Lords' decision in Dunnachie v Kingston upon Hull City Council 2004 ICR 1052, HL, in which their Lordships had laid to rest the 'heresy' that S.123 enables a dismissed employee to recover more than his or her actual economic losses. In Burton J's view, this meant that there was no longer room for the approach taken by the NIRC in Norton Tool Co Ltd v Tewson 1972 ICR 501, NIRC, under which an employee could be treated as having suffered a loss where he or she recovers less than he or she would have received in accordance with good industrial practice.

14.41 The EAT in the Morgans case concluded that it was not possible to disregard the receipt of monies from third party sources such as the Department of Social Security (now part of the Department for Work and Pensions) following dismissal. To do so would put the claimant in a better position than he or she would have been in had he or she remained in employment, which would not accord with S.123. In the words of Burton J: 'Loss which is in fact recouped by receipt of monies from third parties is simply not a loss suffered, and in our judgment such receipts cannot be disregarded.' The EAT accordingly upheld the employment tribunal's decision to the effect that the claimant's actual economic loss should be reduced by the total amount of Incapacity Benefit received.

As explained under 'Nature and amount of award – "deemed losses" and Norton Tool rule' above, the Court of Appeal in Langley and anor v Burlo 2007 ICR 390, CA, held that the approach in Norton Tool Co Ltd v Tewson (above) still applies, but only to the narrow situation where an employee has been dismissed without notice and has found further employment during the notice period. The Court rejected the extension of the rule to other aspects of good industrial practice. It is therefore difficult to see how, in the absence of a further judgment from the Court of Appeal or Supreme Court overruling Morgans v Alpha Plus Security Ltd (above), a tribunal has any choice but to deduct in full from the compensatory award any incapacity benefits received by the employee. Subsequent decisions have confirmed that it is now considered normal practice for the full amount of Incapacity Benefit to be deducted from the pre-termination net wage for the purpose of calculating the loss of earnings element in the compensatory award – see, for example, Brien t/a Merafield

615

View Nursing Home v Crisp EAT 0056/05 and Whyte v London Borough of Lewisham EAT 0256/12.

14.42 Beginning in October 2008, Incapacity Benefit has gradually been replaced by ESA, which comes in two forms: income-related ESA and contribution-based ESA. As noted above, income-related ESA, which is itself now gradually being replaced by Universal Credit, is specifically mentioned in the Employment Protection (Recoupment of Benefits) Regulations 1996 SI 1996/2349 and is therefore subject to the recoupment procedure. By contrast, contribution-based ESA, payment of which is dependent upon the employee's national insurance contributions, is omitted from the recoupment procedure altogether. It is therefore arguable that it will be treated in the same way as Incapacity Benefit and should be deducted in full from any compensatory award. Similar reasoning will also presumably apply to those elements of Universal Credit that are not subject to the recoupment procedure.

One further point to note in relation to Incapacity Benefit is that the fact that a claimant is in receipt of such benefits does not prevent the tribunal making an award for loss of earnings. In Sheffield Forgemasters International Ltd v Fox; Telindus Ltd v Brading 2009 ICR 333, EAT, the Appeal Tribunal noted that the Social Security (Incapacity for Work) (General) Regulations 1995 SI 1995/311 provide for situations where a claimant is deemed to be incapable of work and so eligible to receive Incapacity Benefit but is nonetheless able to do some work (and earn wages). As a result, the receipt of Incapacity Benefit cannot be considered a conclusive indication that a claimant is or was unable to work during a given period. It therefore remains open to a tribunal to award loss of earnings for the same period, although credit would obviously need to be given for any sums received by way of Incapacity Benefit. (The same reasoning would appear to apply in relation to ESA and Universal Credit. This is because eligibility for these benefits is based on similar scoring criteria to those applicable during the second period of entitlement to short-term Incapacity Benefit (i.e. after the first 28 weeks) and also acknowledges the possibility that an individual may be able to do some work despite qualifying for the benefit.)

14.43 **Housing Benefit.** In Savage v Saxena 1998 ICR 357, EAT, the EAT had to consider whether or not Housing Benefit should be taken into account when assessing the compensatory award. The majority of the EAT held that the starting point in assessing compensation was S.123(1), which, as previously stated, provides that the compensatory award 'shall be such amount as the tribunal considers just and equitable in all the circumstances having regard to the loss sustained by the complainant in consequence of the dismissal in so far as that loss is attributable to action taken by the employer'. Under the common law principles governing the assessment of compensation, account must be taken of sums to which the injured party would not have been entitled had it not been for the injury. However, the majority of the EAT thought that Housing Benefit did not fall within that rule because it was not sufficiently proximate to the loss sustained in consequence of the dismissal in so far as that loss is attributable to the employer's actions. The payment of Housing Benefit results from the inability of a claimant to meet reasonable housing needs from his or her resources. It is paid in respect of the needs of the household, not the individual, and therefore differs markedly from Invalidity Benefit.

The EAT also noted that the Regulations then in force – the Housing Benefit (General) Regulations 1987 SI 1987/1971 – contained provisions whereby the authorities may recover Housing Benefit when employees are awarded unfair dismissal compensation. Accordingly, the fact that a tribunal did not take Housing Benefit into account when assessing unfair dismissal compensation would not result in double recovery for the employee, since the award would be subject to the 'claw-back' provisions. On the other hand, there was no provision under the Regulations for the authorities to take the tribunal's method of calculating the compensatory award into account, so that if the tribunal were to reduce the compensatory award by the amount of Housing Benefit received, the right to claw back Housing Benefit would still apply. That outcome would not be just and equitable, because the defaulting employer would obtain a benefit and the employee would be doubly penalised. The EAT concluded by a majority that the tribunal had erred in taking Housing Benefit into account when assessing the employee's compensation.

Similar arguments are likely to apply under the current Regulations – the **14.44** Housing Benefit Regulations 2006 SI 2006/213 – which provide that when calculating 'earnings' for the purpose of determining Housing Benefit, compensation for unfair dismissal should be included – see Reg 35(1)(g). Thus, Housing Benefit will be reduced at source where compensation is paid and ought not, therefore, be taken into account by an employment tribunal when assessing compensation for unfair dismissal.

Note that Housing Benefit is gradually being replaced by the housing costs element of Universal Credit. However, it is likely that similar considerations will apply, albeit on a somewhat different basis. In so far as Universal Credit is concerned, it seems that compensation for unfair dismissal will be treated as capital. As the capital limit for Universal Credit is £16,000 (see Reg 18 of the Universal Credit Regulations 2013 SI 2013/376) any award that is greater than that (or which pushes the total amount of capital to over that figure when added to any other savings or capital) would render the employee ineligible for Universal Credit. If the award (or total amount of capital including the award) falls between £6,000 and £16,000, Universal Credit will be reduced according to a statutory formula. Capital of less than £6,000 is disregarded for the purposes of Universal Credit.

617

14.45 Early retirement schemes

Sums that an employee receives under a scheme for early retirement or retirement on the ground of ill health will not normally be deducted from a compensatory award should the employee subsequently claim unfair dismissal. This is because such sums are the fruits of money set aside in the past in respect of past work. This forms an exception to the general rule in cases of unfair and wrongful dismissal that financial benefits which the employee would not have received but for the dismissal are deducted from damages for lost earnings. The payments here represent an entitlement over and above the pay that the employer would have provided but for the dismissal – see Smoker v London Fire and Civil Defence Authority; Wood v British Coal Corporation 1991 ICR 449, HL.

14.46 Remoteness of loss

Section 123(1) ERA states that in assessing compensation a tribunal must only consider losses that are attributable to action taken by the employer. This leaves scope for the employer to argue that, after a certain point, the employee's losses become too remote from the original dismissal for the employer to continue to remain liable (i.e. the chain of causation has been broken). For example, an unfairly dismissed employee may work in a new job for a considerable period of time before leaving or being dismissed again. When the hearing into the question of compensation for the original unfair dismissal subsequently takes place, the first employer may seek to argue that the employee's losses incurred since leaving the second job are no longer attributable to the earlier dismissal and that liability to pay compensation therefore ceases at the point when the new job was obtained. It was precisely this argument that succeeded in Courtaulds Northern Spinning Ltd v Moosa 1984 ICR 218, EAT, discussed under 'New employment' above.

It will be appreciated that Ging v Ellward Lancs Ltd 1991 ICR 222, EAT, and Courtaulds Northern Spinning Ltd v Moosa (see 'New employment' above) are to some extent mirror images of each other. It will sometimes be to the advantage of the employer if its liability to pay compensation continues right up to the tribunal hearing (thereby allowing the employee's superior new earnings to be offset, so far as possible, against his or her losses). On the other hand, in circumstances like those in the Courtaulds case – i.e. where the employee is no longer in the new employment by the time of the tribunal hearing and is therefore suffering renewed losses – the employer is likely to seek to establish that liability ceased when the employee obtained new employment. In Mabey Plant Hire Ltd v Richens, unreported 6.5.93, CA, the Court of Appeal decided that where an employee is unfairly dismissed and, before the assessment of compensation, obtains alternative employment which could have been permanent but which ends for reasons unrelated to the first employer, the chain

618

of causation between the dismissal by the first employer and the employee's full loss of earnings is broken.

The question of remoteness of loss is considered in more detail under 'Future **14.47** loss' below. It should be noted that the question of whether the respondent employer remains liable to pay compensation after the employee has obtained, and then left, new employment is also very much a question of whether the employee has mitigated his or her loss – see Chapter 16, 'Compensatory awards: adjustments', under 'Failure to mitigate losses'.

New earnings, notice pay and the notice period **14.48**
Before we consider in detail how to assess an employee's loss, there is one more preliminary matter to be considered. An employee's notice entitlement may affect those matters that fall to be offset against his or her losses. There are three situations for consideration here:

- where the employer dismisses unfairly and without giving notice or pay in lieu of notice

- where the employer dismisses unfairly and without giving notice, but does give pay in lieu of notice

- where the employee resigns without notice and successfully claims constructive dismissal.

In any of these scenarios, the employee may find other work during what would have been the notice period. From this point on, the employee actually suffers either no net loss of earnings or only a reduced loss.

No payment in lieu. Where an employer dismisses an employee without notice **14.49** and without pay in lieu of notice, the general rule is that the employee is entitled to include net pay for the statutory or contractual notice period in his or her claim for immediate loss from the dismissal – Norton Tool Co Ltd v Tewson 1972 ICR 501, NIRC. This is because good industrial practice requires employers to make payments in lieu of notice when they dismiss employees with no, or inadequate, notice.

New employment during notice period. An employee who has been dismissed **14.50** without notice is entitled to claim notice pay in full despite having found paid employment during the notice period. In the Norton Tool case the National Industrial Relations Court (the predecessor of the EAT) took the view that, had the employee, in accordance with good industrial practice, been paid his wages in lieu at the time of dismissal, he would not have had to make any repayment upon obtaining new employment while the notice period was still running. His compensation, therefore, did not fall to be reduced by any sums earned during the notice period. This was followed in TBA Industrial Products Ltd v Locke 1984 ICR 228, EAT, and approved, although obiter (i.e. not binding), by the

619

Court of Appeal in Addison v Babcock FATA Ltd 1987 ICR 805, CA. And, as explained under 'Nature and amount of award – "deemed losses" and Norton Tool rule', the Court of Appeal in Langley and anor v Burlo 2007 ICR 390, CA, expressly held that the approach in Norton Tool still applies in this narrow context.

The general rule that an employee does not have to give credit for any wages earned during the notice period when claiming notice pay seems, however, to be subject to exceptions. The employer may be able to argue that notice pay should be offset against actual earnings where, for example, the notice period is very long and the employee's prospects of re-employment are very high (see Addison v Babcock FATA Ltd (above)), or where the contract is for a fixed term with a substantial unexpired portion. In Isleworth Studios Ltd v Rickard 1988 ICR 432, EAT, the Appeal Tribunal took the view that the 'Norton principle' did not extend to the situation where an employee made substantial gains from new earnings following the summary termination of his fixed-term contract with a lengthy period left to run.

14.51 One very clear exception to the Norton principle is where there has been a constructive dismissal. In Stuart Peters Ltd v Bell 2009 ICR 1556, CA, the Court of Appeal explained that the principle exists to ensure that an employer who does not follow good industrial relations practice is not put in a more advantageous position than if it had followed such practice. There is, the Court explained, no industrial practice of making a full payment in lieu of notice where termination is triggered by the employee, since an employer will generally dispute that there has been a breach of contract and will regard the employee as simply having resigned. As a result, a tribunal calculating compensation for an unfair constructive dismissal should take full account of any sums earned during the notice period and set these off against the sum in respect of notice pay to which the employee is entitled.

14.52 **Credit for payments in lieu.** Where an employer has dismissed an employee without notice but has made a payment in lieu of notice, the employee must give credit for the notice money already paid – Addison v Babcock FATA Ltd (above). If this were not so, the employee would receive double remuneration for the statutory notice period.

The position, however, may be different in Scotland, where the authorities are somewhat confused on the matter. In Finnie v Top Hat Frozen Foods 1985 ICR 433, EAT, the Scottish EAT (which is technically not bound by decisions of the Court of Appeal) reached the conclusion that payments in lieu of notice do not fall to be offset against the award for immediate loss. But in Heggie v Uniroyal Englebert Tyres Ltd 1999 IRLR 802, Ct Sess (Inner House) – a decision of the Court of Session concerning the order in which various deductions including one for contributory fault should be made – it was implied that a payment in lieu should be taken into account when calculating immediate loss. It would, however, seem prudent for those practising in Scotland to assume that credit for payments in lieu of notice should be given by a tribunal, particularly as this accords with the principle in Dunnachie v Kingston upon Hull City Council 2004 ICR 1052, HL (a House of Lords decision that binds Scottish courts), that compensation for unfair dismissal should reflect an employee's actual loss.

Credit to be given for gross payments. As previously stated, when calculating **14.53** the compensatory award, it is the employee's net, rather than gross, loss that has to be considered. The same rule applies to payments in lieu of notice. If an employer pays an employee a payment in lieu of notice based on the employee's gross pay, the entire sum has to be offset against any award of compensation. The employee cannot argue that only the net sum falls to be deducted, and that the difference between the net and the gross sum represents a windfall which is not to be taken into account when calculating immediate loss – see MBS Ltd v Calo 1983 ICR 459, EAT, and Marshalls of Cambridge Aerospace Ltd v Warnock EAT 0250/03.

Waiver of notice. An employee can waive the right to statutory notice – S.86(3) **14.54** ERA. Waiver will mean that the employee also loses the right to receive a payment in lieu of notice because the termination of the employment contract without notice will no longer amount to a breach of contract for which damages would be due – Trotter v Forth Ports Authority 1991 IRLR 419, Ct Sess (Outer House). Where an employee who waives the notice entitlement is subsequently unfairly dismissed, he or she will be entitled to compensation for losses incurred from the date of dismissal in the normal way. However, any new earnings during the notional notice period clearly will be offset against the employee's overall losses.

Termination payments
14.55

Termination payments made by the employer – be they on an ex gratia basis or in the form of contractual redundancy payments – are an important factor in the calculation of loss. The general approach is that any ex gratia payment should be set off against the losses incurred by the employee – Horizon Holidays Ltd v Grassi 1987 ICR 851, EAT; DCM Optical Clinic plc v Stark EAT 0124/04. But, as we shall see, redundancy payments are a special case to which specific rules apply.

General guidance as to the correct approach to be adopted for taking account of severance payments (including redundancy packages) was given by the EAT in Darr and anor v LRC Products Ltd 1993 IRLR 257, EAT. In that case an employment tribunal failed to give adequate reasons for declining to make a compensatory award, stating simply that the severance payment that the employee had received on being dismissed for redundancy more than covered any compensation that the tribunal would or could have awarded. The EAT stated that the tribunal should first have assessed the employee's loss of

621

earnings over the appropriate period, then deducted the part of the severance payment which was not already apportioned to the basic award and, finally, have applied the statutory maximum to the net sum. The tribunal's reasons were insufficient to show that it had adopted the correct approach or made the necessary calculations.

14.56 **Treatment of ex gratia payments.** Outside of the specific statutory provisions dealing with redundancy payments (see 'Treatment of redundancy payments' below), the general flexibility accorded to the calculation of the compensatory award by virtue of S.123(1) ERA permits the taking into account of ex gratia payments to be approached differently according to circumstance. In Addison v Babcock FATA Ltd 1987 ICR 805, CA, the employee had been given an ex gratia payment when he was unfairly dismissed for redundancy. However, the tribunal found that he would have been dismissed in any event some 15 months later along with the rest of the workforce and that he would have received an ex gratia payment at that time. It was therefore conceded before the Court of Appeal that the ex gratia payment was demonstrably part of the employee's future loss, so that he would not be properly compensated if it were deducted from the part of the compensatory award representing immediate loss. This exception was extended in Roadchef Ltd v Hastings EAT 593/87. There, a redundancy dismissal, although procedurally unfair, was found to be inevitable because a proper consultation period would merely have delayed dismissal by four weeks. The tribunal held that an ex gratia payment that the employer had added to the redundancy payment should not be deducted from the compensatory award of four weeks' pay because there was no reason to suppose that the extra payment would not have been granted if the dismissal had been delayed by proper consultation.

Note, however, that in Rushton v Harcros Timber and Building Supplies Ltd 1993 ICR 230, EAT, the EAT explicitly declined to follow the line of authority outlined above. In that case the employee was made redundant and received a statutory redundancy payment of £4,730 and an additional ex gratia payment of £5,320. The dismissal was held to be unfair for lack of warning but the tribunal declined to award any compensation on the grounds that the basic award was extinguished by the redundancy payment and any compensatory award was more than covered by the ex gratia payment. The employee argued that he should have been awarded the four weeks' pay he would have earned if a fair amount of warning had been given and that the ex gratia payment should not have been deducted from that amount. The EAT upheld the tribunal's decision on the ground that there was no evidence to suggest that the employee would have received the same ex gratia payment following a fair dismissal. The EAT went on, however, to express the view that credit should always be given for severance payments made by the employer. It stated that the manifest purpose of the specific redundancy payment deduction provision in S.123(7) ERA – discussed under 'Treatment of redundancy payments' below – is to encourage employers who find it necessary to dismiss for redundancy to be generous in making ex gratia payments. The frequency and levels of such payments would be reduced if employers had to take into account the possibility of a tribunal award over and above the ex gratia payment, however generous that payment may be.

In Simrad Ltd v Scott 1997 IRLR 147, EAT, the question arose as to whether a **14.57** sum which the employer had lent the employee during her employment could be offset against the compensatory award. The loan was an unusual one in that it was made to the employee on the understanding that it would be repaid by her working overtime. The EAT pointed out that an ex gratia payment is usually a payment arising directly from the dismissal. It also pointed out that, in dismissing the employee, the employer had denied her the means by which it had been agreed that the loan would be repaid. The EAT therefore concluded that it would not be just and equitable to offset the loan against the employee's compensatory award.

Treatment of redundancy payments. By virtue of S.122(4)(b) ERA, the **14.58** amount paid by the employer by way of a redundancy payment serves to reduce the employer's liability for the basic award in circumstances where a dismissal is found to be unfair – see further Chapter 13, 'Basic awards', under 'Reductions in basic award – receipt of redundancy payment'. S.123(7) ERA then further provides that 'if the amount of any payment made by the employer to the employee on the ground that the dismissal was by reason of redundancy (whether in pursuance of Part XI [ERA] or otherwise) exceeds the amount of the basic award... that excess goes to reduce the amount of the compensatory award'. Thus, if the employer's redundancy scheme is more generous than the statutory redundancy scheme and the dismissal is subsequently judged by a tribunal to be unfair, the part of the redundancy payment that corresponds to a statutory redundancy payment will normally extinguish entitlement to a basic award, with the excess then serving to reduce the compensatory award.

A crucial point in respect of S.123(7) is that Parliament has specifically stipulated that any excess should be offset against the *compensatory award*, not against the claimant's *losses*. In Digital Equipment Co Ltd v Clements (No.2) 1998 ICR 258, CA, the Court of Appeal explained that this means that, unlike with ex gratia payments and factors that might reduce an employee's losses, the deduction should come after any Polkey reductions or adjustments for contributory fault (see Chapter 16, 'Compensatory awards: adjustments', under 'Offsetting enhanced redundancy payments').

Where the employer pays the employee what is described as a 'redundancy **14.59** payment' but it transpires that the payment is mislabelled because no genuine redundancy situation has arisen, it would seem that S.123(7) does not apply. As explained above, that provision defines a 'redundancy payment' as 'any payment made by the employer to the employee on the ground that the

623

dismissal was by reason of redundancy (whether in pursuance of Part XI or otherwise)'. It is noteworthy that exactly the same wording appears in S.122(4)(b), which, as previously stated, requires that the amount of a basic award be reduced by the amount of any redundancy payment already paid to the employee. In Boorman v Allmakes Ltd 1995 ICR 842, CA, the Court of Appeal, having considered the meaning of this wording, held that S.122(4)(b) only applies if the dismissal was in fact by reason of a genuine redundancy (i.e. as defined in Part XI of the ERA). Given that this wording is identical to that in S.123(7), it is highly arguable that the two provisions should be interpreted consistently, leading to the conclusion that S.123(7) also only applies to payments made in the context of genuine redundancies. If that is so, then where a payment is mislabelled as a redundancy payment, the tribunal should approach it in the same way as if it were an ex gratia termination payment – i.e. it should give credit for the payment when calculating the 'net loss' the claimant has incurred, before any deductions or adjustments are made (see 'Treatment of ex gratia payments' above). Where, however, an enhanced redundancy payment is paid in the context of a genuine redundancy, it should be left out of account when calculating the claimant's full losses. Then, once these have been ascertained and the nominal compensatory award calculated on the basis of them, the redundancy payment should be deducted from the award in accordance with S.123(7). (For details about the correct stages at which various adjustments/deductions to and from the compensatory award should be made, see Chapter 16, 'Compensatory awards: adjustments', under 'Order of adjustments'.)

14.60 Calculation of immediate loss

We have seen that immediate loss relates to the net remuneration that would have been received had the employee not been dismissed. We have also seen that credit must usually be given for any new earnings, etc. We now consider how tribunals assess exactly what an employee has lost. (Remember, there is no rigid formula or maximum amount for calculating a 'week's pay'. The only limit is the overall limit on the size of a compensatory award, currently standing at £78,335 or a year's pay (whichever is the lower) – see 'Nature and maximum amount of award' above.)

First, it should be noted that remuneration for these purposes is not limited to basic pay but can cover any regular bonuses or fringe benefits that an employee may have been receiving in the job. This is not restricted to benefits that are explicitly authorised by the contract: what counts is take-home pay, plus other contractual or non-contractual benefits that the employee would expect to receive in the period under review. Having said this, if the remuneration is disputed, the tribunal will obviously use the contract as the main means to identify the employee's entitlement – Kinzley v Minories Finance Ltd 1988 ICR 113, EAT.

624

In addition to basic pay and regular bonus payments, the following are taken **14.61**
into account when assessing immediate loss:

- overtime, whether contractual or not, where there is a reasonable expectation
  that it would have been worked – Mullet v Brush Electrical Machines Ltd
  1977 ICR 829, EAT

- tips, whether they are paid directly to the employee by customers or shared
  out among employees from a tronc, provided tax is deducted – Palmanor
  Ltd t/a Chaplins Night Club v Cedron 1978 ICR 1008, EAT

- pay increases that the employee would have received during the relevant
  period, even if the employee had no contractual right to an increase – Leske
  v Rogers of Saltcoats (ES) Ltd EAT 520/82. Compensation can be awarded
  for increases that the employee would probably have received, although
  it may be made subject to a reduction to reflect the tribunal's view of the
  likelihood of this happening – York Trailer Co Ltd v Sparkes 1973 ICR
  518, NIRC

- a backdated pay increase if it is backdated to a date before the dismissal and
  would have been awarded to the employee – Leske v Rogers of Saltcoats
  (ES) Ltd (above)

- expenses, provided these are regular, and only to the extent that they
  represent a profit or 'perk' in the hands of the employee over and above
  what is spent purely on the employer's behalf – S and U Stores Ltd v Wilkes
  1974 ICR 645, NIRC. The fact that benefits of this kind are taxed will help
  to indicate that they form part of the employee's remuneration and should
  therefore be compensated. In contrast, tax-free 'benefits' tend to suggest
  that the sums were intended merely to reimburse genuine expenses incurred
  on the employer's behalf and are therefore not remuneration. (Note that
  if an allowance for expenses is merely a device to give the employee some
  tax-free remuneration the whole contract may be illegal and unenforceable
  – see IDS Employment Law Handbook, 'Contracts of Employment' (2014),
  Chapter 7, 'Void terms and illegality', under 'Illegality'.)

Expectation of enhanced redundancy payment. A dismissed employee may **14.62**
be able to receive compensation for a thwarted expectation that he or she
would receive a more generous redundancy payment than the statutory
entitlement. In Lee v IPC Business Press Ltd 1984 ICR 306, EAT, the Appeal
Tribunal confirmed that the expectation of receiving an especially favourable
redundancy payment is something that may be lost as a result of unfair dismissal
and is something that should be compensated by the tribunal where appropriate.
(The EAT thought that this could include cases where the expectation was
based on a non-contractual agreement that was 'binding in honour' only.)

625

Note, however, that S.123(3) ERA provides that the loss of any entitlement or potential entitlement to a redundancy payment (statutory or contractual) or any expectation of such a payment should be compensated only to the extent to which it exceeds the basic award.

14.63 In MacCulloch v Imperial Chemical Industries Ltd EAT 0275/09 M had been paid an enhanced redundancy payment when she was dismissed. Having found her dismissal unfair, the tribunal held that she would have been dismissed in any event at a later date, but would have been entitled to a more generous enhanced redundancy payment. The tribunal offset the amount of the payment that M had received against her losses, and went on to deduct from M's compensatory award the amount by which her redundancy payment had exceeded the basic award. On appeal, the EAT rejected this approach. What the tribunal should have done was to include in the calculation of loss a sum that reflects the payment the claimant *would* have received, minus the amount of a basic award. Only once the losses had been calculated, and any other adjustments or deductions made, should the tribunal have deducted from the compensatory award the amount by which the redundancy payment that the employee *did* receive exceeded the basic award.

Finally, note also that special rules apply to the order of deductions under S.123. This topic is dealt with in Chapter 16, 'Compensatory awards: adjustments', under 'Order of adjustments'.

14.64 **Fringe benefits and benefits in kind**
The assessment of loss is not confined to pay received by the employee in the form of money. Fringe benefits and benefits in kind can also be counted so long as they were received on a regular basis and were not one-off payments – Mullet v Brush Electrical Machines Ltd 1977 ICR 829, EAT. Here we look at how tribunals assess the value of such benefits. Note also that any increase in benefits which the employee would have enjoyed but for the dismissal should also be taken into account – York Trailer Co Ltd v Sparkes 1973 ICR 518, NIRC.

14.65 **Loss of company car.** This is an obvious item of loss. However, there is no general rule as to how such loss to the employee should be assessed because of the wide range of terms and conditions on which employees are supplied with company cars. Business use of a car and reimbursement of associated expenses should be disregarded: it is only the loss of a car for *private* purposes that should be compensated – Texet Ltd v Greenhough EAT 410/82. Many tribunals in practice adopt a broad-brush approach and award a conventional figure of £50–150 per week for the value of the car, depending on the type of car and the basis upon which it was supplied (in particular, the level of private, as opposed to business, use). Other more detailed methods for valuing the loss of private use of a company car are:

626

- using the annual tables produced by the AA, which set out the worth and running costs of different capacities of car. AA estimates were used in the wrongful dismissal case of Shove v Downs Surgical plc 1984 ICR 532, QBD, where, after reducing the estimated running costs by the ratio of business use to private use, the judge arrived at a figure of £10,000 for the loss of a company Daimler over a 30-month period

- using the car benefit assessments prepared by HM Revenue and Customs for taxation purposes. Use of the Revenue's scales was, however, rejected in Shove v Downs Surgical plc (above) on the ground that they simply represented a valuation for tax purposes and not an assessment of the benefit to the employee. Note that the basis upon which car benefit is assessed for taxation purposes has undergone radical revision since the Shove case. Since April 2002, a new system for assessing taxable benefit has applied under which a percentage reduction to the car's list price is applied depending on the carbon dioxide emissions of the vehicle. This may make the use of the Inland Revenue scales even less helpful than previously in assessing the actual value of the loss of private use of the vehicle for compensation purposes. (The Revenue's company car and car fuel calculator is available online (at www.hmrc.gov.uk/calcs/cars.htm)

- taking account of actual car transactions carried out by the employee. In Nohar v Granitstone (Galloway) Ltd 1974 ICR 273, NIRC, N lost his company car when he was dismissed, bought himself a new car and then resold it at a loss when he found another job with a company car. The NIRC allowed the award to cover most of the loss on resale and the cost of taxing and insuring N's car while he owned it

- taking account of the cost of hiring a car. This can produce a reasonable result in circumstances like those in the Nohar case (above) where the period for assessment is relatively short. However, the employee's compensation may be assessed too highly by this method because the hire costs will include the hire company's profits.

14.66 Free fuel for private use of a company car is also a taxable benefit, the loss of which should be compensated. Since 6 April 2003, the taxable value of this benefit has been calculated using the same percentage figure as that used to calculate the taxable benefit of the car (see above) applied to an amount set each year in the Chancellor of the Exchequer's Budget. Other car-related benefits such as free maintenance, road tax and insurance are also relevant considerations. If, unusually, a private mileage allowance is payable to the employee as a benefit, the Revenue classifies this as earnings, so this would also potentially be a recoverable head of loss.

Although an employee is entitled to be compensated for the loss of a company car and fuel allowance following unfair dismissal, the tribunal will generally make deductions under this head where the employee subsequently receives these benefits from a new employer. In Commercial Motors (Wales) Ltd v Howley EAT 0636/11 H was entitled under his contract of employment to an executive car plus fuel. The tribunal awarded him £3,993.36 in respect of the loss of the executive car and £300 in respect of the loss of the fuel allowance for the duration of his contractual notice period. On appeal, the EAT reduced the compensation to take account of the fact that H had subsequently found temporary employment in respect of which he was provided with another company car with fuel allowance.

14.67 **Free or subsidised accommodation.** This benefit may be valued by estimating its worth on the open market, perhaps with the help of an estate agent or surveyor. Alternatively, it can be valued by comparing it with the cost of the employee's new accommodation. In Denyer v Cowdray Estate ET Case No.2830/89 D, a golf-course keeper, was effectively ousted from premises of which he was a service tenant when he was unfairly dismissed. Looking at the accommodation benefit that D had lost and at the value of the council accommodation that he subsequently obtained, the employment tribunal assessed D's annual loss at £1,300. (Note that much will depend here on the period of future loss determined by the tribunal – e.g. if the employee has prospects of obtaining more lucrative employment, the tribunal will limit the period for which compensation is awarded – see below.)

Where a dismissed employee remains in free or subsidised accommodation, the value of this may be offset against the losses incurred as a result of losing the job. In Gibbons v Smith ET Case No.16284/81 G's free use of a cottage cancelled out any immediate losses. However, the tribunal did make an award for future loss to cover the rent that G would have to pay once a possession order took effect. In cases where the employer obtains an order stating that the ex-employee must pay rent until a possession order takes effect, the sums paid may be recovered by the employee as part of his or her compensatory award – Jackson v Shavington Social Club and Institute Ltd ET Case No.18471/80.

14.68 **Other benefits.** The loss of free meals, free medical or life insurance, low interest loans and mortgages, profits under a profit-share scheme and private health care are all examples of other benefits that can be taken into account when assessing an employee's immediate losses. The value of these benefits can usually be assessed simply by taking the difference between the cost to the employee of the benefit before dismissal and the cost on the open market after dismissal. If the employer wishes to argue for a different basis of assessment, this must be done at the tribunal hearing as it will be too late to raise the matter on appeal – UBAF Bank Ltd v Davis 1978 IRLR 442, EAT.

Usually, the loss of the benefit of an insurance policy is compensated by damages covering the cost to the employee of securing equivalent insurance him or herself. However, in the unusual circumstances of Fox v British Airways plc

2013 ICR 1257, CA, the Court of Appeal held that the full value of a death-in-service benefit would be payable in an unfair dismissal claim brought by the estate of a deceased former employee. F died less than a month after his dismissal by BA plc. Had he died while employed, his family would have been entitled to a contractual death-in-service benefit of over £85,000. When F's father brought an unfair dismissal claim on behalf of F's estate, an employment judge ruled that, if the claim succeeded, compensation in respect of the death-in-service benefit would be limited to around £350, being the cost of replacing the insurance cover. The judge considered that the full value of the death-in-service payout was not a loss suffered by F within S.123 ERA but a loss suffered by his beneficiaries. On appeal, the EAT overturned that decision and, on further appeal, the Court of Appeal agreed with the EAT. The Court held that the loss of the chance of a death-in-service benefit being paid was to be regarded as a pecuniary loss suffered by F, for which he could have claimed in proceedings brought prior to his death. As for quantification of that loss, the Court acknowledged that, in ordinary circumstances, the appropriate measure of damage would be the cost of securing an equivalent benefit. However, on the particular and very unusual facts of the case, it was necessary to go back to first principles and seek to put F's estate in the position that F would have been in if he had not been dismissed when he was. Since he would almost certainly still have been in employment at the date of his death, his beneficiaries would have become entitled to the payment of £85,000 and, since that entitlement was to be regarded as a benefit to him, F – or his estate – could only be put in the position that he would have been in but for his dismissal if he were put in a position to enable an equivalent payment to be made. That could only be done by awarding compensation in the full amount.

14.69 Tribunals are used to making informed guesses when calculating the compensatory award and will place a value even on those benefits that are very difficult to quantify. In Casey v Texas Homecare Ltd EAT 632/87 the EAT held that a tribunal was wrong to decline to estimate the value to the employee of a share option scheme on the ground that it was too 'speculative and indefinite' a matter. Having sufficient evidence on which to rely, the EAT arrived at a figure of £1,000 after making deductions from its original figure to take account of the possibility that share prices might fall and the fact that the employee had received accelerated payment of the benefit through the compensatory award.

14.70 **Loss of national insurance contributions.** The loss of NI contributions can form part of the dismissed employee's losses. Normally an unemployed person getting Jobseeker's Allowance, Income Support or Universal Credit during the period covered by 'immediate loss' will receive NI credits. However, where the individual is unemployed as a result of being unfairly dismissed, he or she is not entitled to claim benefit during the period in respect of which the *future* element of a compensatory award applies – see further the section on 'Future loss' below, under 'Circumstances in which future losses occur – national insurance

629

contributions'. The halting of NI contributions during this period may eventually cause loss to the employee if the contributions are interrupted long enough to have an effect on his or her entitlement to benefits. In Allen v Key Markets Ltd ET Case No.10088/83 a tribunal treated a break in contributions of 52 weeks – i.e. the period covered by the award for future loss – as substantial enough to justify an extra £4.30 being added to the compensatory award for each of those 52 weeks. This would allow the employee to make his own contributions.

14.71 **Pension loss.** Loss of rights under an occupational pension scheme is considered separately in Chapter 15, 'Compensatory awards: pension loss'.

14.72 Future loss

Immediate loss can normally be assessed fairly accurately since the tribunal will have information before it on the employee's actual earnings (if any) following dismissal and on what the employee's earnings would have been in the old job. However, assessment of the employee's future loss is, by its very nature, a far more speculative exercise. There may, of course, be no future loss – e.g. where the employee has already obtained reasonably secure and equally lucrative new employment – but where this is not the case the tribunal will have to look into the future and attempt to guess how long the employee's losses will continue and how much they are likely to be.

14.73 **Question of fact.** Since tribunal findings on the question of future loss are largely a matter of informed guesswork, they will normally be difficult to challenge on appeal. In Sandown Pier Ltd v Moonan EAT 399/93 an employment tribunal held that a 50-year-old employee was likely to remain unemployed for 15 years. While making it fairly clear that it would not have reached the same conclusion, the EAT noted that the tribunal's finding was supported by some evidence – the employee lived in an area of high unemployment and had already made a number of vain attempts to find work – and held that there were therefore no grounds for overturning the decision.

There will be situations, however, where the EAT finds fault with the tribunal's approach and remits the matter of compensation, either to the same or to a fresh tribunal. In NCP Services Ltd v Topliss EAT 0147/09 the Appeal Tribunal held that a tribunal calculating future loss in a case that has been remitted by the EAT should make its decision on the basis of facts known at the date of the remitted hearing, rather than limiting itself to facts known at the time of the original hearing. This, the EAT explained, 'has the result of substituting certainty for that which was uncertain though estimated on the best available evidence' and is preferable to substituting a hypothetical situation that bears no relation to current reality.

The scope of a tribunal's powers of reassessment on remission was given fuller **14.74** consideration by the Court of Appeal in Griffin v Plymouth Hospital NHS Trust 2015 ICR 347, CA. There, Lord Justice Underhill, giving the Court's judgment, observed that where a court or tribunal is assessing compensation, it is well established that it must have regard to all the facts known to it at the date of assessment. It followed that – as the EAT had held in the Topliss case – where a tribunal has made a flawed assessment of an employee's future loss of earnings, and an appellate court or tribunal remits the case for the tribunal to make a fresh assessment, the tribunal should do so as at the date of the remitted hearing, not of the initial hearing. However, Underhill LJ continued, this situation should be distinguished from that where an appellate court is asked to admit evidence of events occurring subsequent to the primary assessment. In such cases, a valid final award has been made and the general approach is that it would be contrary to the principle of the finality of litigation for a party to reopen an assessment of future loss, simply because things turned out differently than expected. Nevertheless, Underhill LJ acknowledged that in exceptional cases the courts may exercise their discretion to allow an appeal based on subsequent events that undermine the basis on which the original award was made. As the House of Lords noted in Mulholland and anor v Mitchell 1971 AC 666, HL, fresh evidence should not be admitted when it falls within 'the field or area of uncertainty in which the trial judge's estimate has previously been made'. However, it may be admitted if subsequent events reveal that some basic assumptions, common to both sides, have clearly been falsified or if to refuse the fresh evidence would affront common sense or a sense of justice.

Having set out the correct legal approach, Underhill LJ then considered into **14.75** which category the present case fell. He noted that at first sight the case might appear to fall into the first category – i.e. where the tribunal was asked to make a fresh assessment of compensation at the remitted hearing. However, the claimant's compensatory award had been remitted to the tribunal for partial reassessment only: the EAT had specifically remitted the case for the tribunal to review its decision on 'continuing loss of earnings', meaning the rate of remuneration in the employment which the tribunal had found that the claimant was likely to obtain. However, the tribunal's finding as to the date at which she would obtain that job was unchallenged. Given this, Underhill LJ considered that to the extent that the claimant's new evidence was relevant to the task the EAT had given the tribunal to perform on remission – i.e. the assessment of her likely level of earnings in her new employment – it would have to be admitted. However, if she was asking the tribunal to admit the evidence so as to revisit its decision as to the likely date on which she would obtain new employment, the decision as to whether or not to admit it would be a matter for the tribunal's discretion, to be exercised in accordance with the guidance in Mulholland. Turning to the new evidence that the claimant wanted to adduce, Underhill LJ noted that all it established was that she had not yet obtained employment, that she was getting administrative experience at a charity, and that she was hoping to obtain an NVQ in business administration. This did not assist in determining the level of job she might in due course hope to obtain, or her likely level of pay. In Underhill LJ's view, had the claimant asked the tribunal to revisit its finding as to the likely date at which she would find employment, it would have been wrong to do so. The likely date of re-employment was an estimate, and was bound, in practice, to be inaccurate, but this was an inevitable consequence of a once-and-for-all system of assessment. It would equally have been impossible for the employer to apply to reopen the issue if the claimant had unexpectedly obtained fresh employment at her original level of remuneration after six months.

14.76 **Tribunal's duty to give its assessment of future loss.** Although an employment tribunal is entitled to take a broad-brush approach to ascertaining the extent of future loss, it is still under a duty to give full reasons for its decision. In Lancaster Fibre Technology Ltd v Walshaw EAT 1028/02 a tribunal held that 'we think we have to come to a figure which is not a mathematical figure reflecting all those difficulties and the figure that we have come to for all those losses, trying to reflect as far as we can all those difficulties, is £20,000'. The EAT noted that the tribunal failed to give any indication in its decision as to what period it was considering as appropriate for the calculation of future loss or what, if any, multiplier in respect of future loss it had in mind. The EAT therefore remitted the case to a fresh tribunal on the issue of future loss. Similarly, in Thornett v Scope 2007 ICR 236, CA, the Court of Appeal remitted the matter of future loss, holding that while there was material before the tribunal which might have justified limiting T's losses to six months, the reasons for the tribunal's decision did not emerge with sufficient clarity to permit its determination to be upheld. There was, for example, no analysis in the tribunal's decision as to how T's employment was expected to have ended after six months.

Like immediate loss, future loss is assessed by reference to the employee's net earnings in the job from which he or she was dismissed. However, these earnings will not be treated as static and account will be taken of possible future pay increases (or decreases) – York Trailer Co Ltd v Sparkes 1973 ICR 518, NIRC.

14.77 **Circumstances in which future losses occur**

There are three basic situations in which the tribunal will have to consider the question of future loss:

- where the employee has found a new job that pays as least as well as the old one by the time of the tribunal hearing on compensation. In this situation, there will usually be no future loss, so the tribunal can restrict compensation for loss of earnings to 'immediate loss' – see 'Immediate loss' above. (Note, however, the Court of Appeal's caution in Dench v Flynn and Partners 1998

IRLR 653, CA, that it will not always be just and equitable to treat the acquisition of permanent alternative employment as breaking the chain of causation for attribution of loss. In particular, if the employment ends unexpectedly after a relatively short duration, the tribunal should consider the reasons for and effect of this when assessing the appropriate award for future loss)

- where the employee has found a new job that does not pay as well as the old one. Here, there may be evidence that earnings in the new job will increase to the old level in the foreseeable future. Based, as far as possible, on such evidence, tribunals simply have to guess how long it will take the employee to catch up to the old level of earnings and make an award for the difference up to that time. However, it may be that the new earnings will never reach the old level. Despite this, tribunals usually set a limit on the continuing loss, unless the employee's prospects are particularly dim (see 'Career-long loss' below)

- where the employee has not yet found a new job. In such a case, tribunals simply have to do the best they can from their knowledge of the employee and of the local labour market to assess how long the employee is likely to be out of work and how much he or she is likely to earn when a job is eventually found.

14.78 In theory, an award for a period of future loss could cover the remainder of the employee's working life in an appropriately extreme case. In Morganite Electrical Carbon Ltd v Donne 1988 ICR 18, EAT, for example, the EAT rejected the argument that a period of 82 weeks was excessive. In practice, however, most tribunals seem to settle on a figure somewhere between 13 and 39 weeks. In any event, in most cases a period of future loss that lasts longer than a year will run up against the statutory cap on the compensatory award of the lower of a year's salary or (currently) £78,335 – see 'Nature and maximum amount of award – amount of week's pay and statutory cap' above. Career-long loss is discussed below.

14.79 **Social security benefits and recoupment.** Note that, unlike immediate loss, the future loss element of the compensatory award is *not* subject to the recoupment provisions because the employee will not be eligible to claim Jobseeker's Allowance, income-related Employment and Support Allowance or Income Support for the period covered by an award for future loss. The effect of the Jobseeker's Allowance Regulations 1996 SI 1996/207, the Employment and Support Allowance Regulations 2008 SI 2008/794 and the Income Support (General) Regulations 1987 SI 1987/1967 is that any lump sum award for future loss of earnings will be treated as 'earnings' over the period to which it applies, for the purposes of assessing a claimant's eligibility for these benefits. A tribunal need not, therefore, concern itself that the claimant may enjoy an element of double recovery during the period of future loss.

633

Note that the above benefits are gradually being replaced by Universal Credit. However, it is likely that similar considerations will apply, albeit on a somewhat different basis. In so far as Universal Credit is concerned, it seems that compensation for unfair dismissal will be treated as capital. As the capital limit for Universal Credit is £16,000 (see Reg 18 of the Universal Credit Regulations 2013 SI 2013/376) any award that is greater than that (or which pushes the total amount of capital to over that figure when added to any other savings or capital) would render the employee ineligible for Universal Credit. If the award (or total amount of capital including the award) falls between £6,000 and £16,000, Universal Credit will be reduced according to a statutory formula. Capital of less than £6,000 is disregarded for the purposes of Universal Credit.

14.80 **National insurance contributions.** As explained in the section on 'Immediate loss' above, under 'Fringe benefits and benefits in kind – loss of national insurance contributions', the loss of NI contributions can form part of the dismissed employee's losses. Normally an unemployed person getting Jobseeker's Allowance, Income Support or Universal Credit during the period covered by 'immediate loss' will receive NI credits. However, where the individual is unemployed as a result of being unfairly dismissed, he or she is not entitled to claim benefit during the period in respect of which the *future* element of a compensatory award applies. The halting of NI contributions during this period may eventually cause loss to the employee if the contributions are interrupted long enough to have an effect on his or her entitlement to benefits. In Allen v Key Markets Ltd ET Case No.10088/83 a tribunal treated a break in contributions of 52 weeks – i.e. the period covered by the award for future loss – as substantial enough to justify an extra £4.30 being added to the compensatory award for each of those 52 weeks. This would allow the employee to make his own contributions.

14.81 **Evidence and speculation**
Future loss generally presents tribunals with greater problems than immediate loss as, rather than assessing what has happened and whether the employer bears responsibility, the tribunal is attempting to predict what might happen, and will often have scant evidence to go on. If the employer seeks to contend that the employee would or might have ceased to be employed in any event had fair procedures been followed, or alternatively would not have continued in employment indefinitely, it is for the employer to adduce any relevant evidence on which it wishes to rely – Software 2000 Ltd v Andrews and ors 2007 ICR 825, EAT.

The nature of the predictive task faced by tribunals was examined by the Court of Appeal in Thornett v Scope 2007 ICR 236, CA. In that case, the tribunal had made a finding that, had she not been unfairly dismissed, the claimant would only have remained in her role for a further six months due to ongoing disagreements with her colleagues. On appeal, the EAT held that the tribunal should not have launched itself upon 'a sea of speculation' and should have accepted that it could not, on the evidence before it, 'sensibly recreate the world as it might have been'. Given the evidence about how the claimant and her colleagues could work together, the EAT considered that it was wrong to place a limitation in time as to the duration of the relationship and to reduce the losses accordingly. However, when the case reached the Court of Appeal, Lord Justice Pill stated that deciding compensation for future loss of earnings will 'almost inevitably involve a consideration of uncertainties'. There may be cases in which evidence to the contrary is so sparse that a tribunal should work on the basis that loss of earnings would have continued indefinitely but where there is evidence that this may not have been so, that evidence must be taken into account.

Applying this reasoning, Pill LJ found that there was evidence in the instant **14.82** case which, taken at its lowest, created a risk that the claimant's employment would not have continued indefinitely. Accordingly, he disagreed with the EAT's conclusion that the tribunal had erred in embarking on a speculative venture. In his Lordship's view, 'any assessment of a future loss, including one that the employment will continue indefinitely, is by way of prediction and inevitably involves a speculative element. Judges and tribunals are familiar with making predictions based on the evidence they have heard. The tribunal's statutory duty may involve making such predictions and tribunals cannot be expected, or even allowed, to opt out of that duty because their task is a difficult one and may involve speculation.'

However, it is important, observed Pill LJ, that when a tribunal reaches a conclusion as to what is likely to have happened had the employment been allowed to continue, the reasons for that conclusion and the factors relied on are sufficiently stated. In the instant case, while there was material before the tribunal that might have justified the six-month limit on future losses, the reasons for the tribunal's decision did not emerge with sufficient clarity to permit its determination to be upheld. There was, for example, no analysis in the tribunal's decision as to how the employee's employment was expected to have ended after six months: whether by disciplinary action, a breakdown of attempts to work together which would have permitted a fair dismissal, or resignation by the claimant.

The Thornett decision was followed by the EAT in Software 2000 Ltd v **14.83** Andrews and ors (above) in which Mr Justice Elias (as he then was) accepted that there will be circumstances where the nature of the evidence which the employer wishes to adduce, or on which it seeks to rely, is so unreliable that the tribunal may decide that the whole exercise of seeking to reconstruct what might have been would be so riddled with uncertainty that no sensible prediction based on that evidence could properly be made. Whether that is the position is a matter of impression and judgement for the tribunal. But in determining this,

635

the tribunal must direct itself properly by recognising that it should have regard to any material and reliable evidence that might assist it in fixing just compensation, even if there are limits to the extent to which it can confidently predict what might have been; and it must appreciate that a degree of uncertainty is an inevitable feature of the exercise.

Similar sentiments were expressed by Mr Justice Langstaff, President of the EAT, in Contract Bottling Ltd v Cave and anor 2015 ICR 146, EAT. In that case, Langstaff P (sitting alone) reviewed the relevant authorities and set out some general guidance for tribunals on determining a claimant's compensation. On the face of it, a claimant who is dismissed from a job suffers an open-ended loss of the income he or she was receiving from that job immediately prior to dismissal. In practice, however, the tribunal should moderate this position based on its assessment of the likelihood of possible future events. So the tribunal must consider a claimant's chance of obtaining alternative employment. In this regard, it must ask whether such employment is likely to be at the same rate of pay as the claimant's previous job, and how long it is likely to take the claimant to obtain such employment after dismissal. It is also necessary for the tribunal to assess whether, had the claimant not been dismissed, he or she would have remained in the same role at the same rate of pay. There are a number of circumstances that may have an impact on this question. They include ill health, retirement, expiry of a migrant worker's leave to remain and the regulatory restrictions applicable to certain industries. The individual choices of the claimant and/or employer may also play a part. The claimant might seek promotion in another company, or make lifestyle choices that would cause him or her to leave that particular employment. Or the employer might at some stage decide to restructure its business, or to terminate the claimant's employment for a good reason.

14.84 Langstaff P was keen to emphasise that assessment of compensation and the appropriate amount of any reduction will 'necessarily involve a number of imponderables'. However, this does not mean that the tribunal should not grapple with the issues 'in so far as it can'. Nobody can know for certain whether, and if so when, a claimant will succeed in finding a new job. Nor is it possible to predict precisely what salary the claimant will receive in such a role. The tribunal may legitimately assess these factors and reflect them in its award without necessarily mentioning each one individually.

14.85 **Loss of opportunity to benefit dependent on third party.** A special approach to causation and quantification applies to cases where the claimant has lost the opportunity of gaining a benefit that depends on a third party acting in a particular way. This approach derives from a negligence case – Allied Maples Group Ltd v Simmons and Simmons 1995 1 WLR 1602, CA – but the EAT held in Timothy James Consulting Ltd v Wilton 2015 IRLR 368, EAT, that a tribunal was correct to apply it in the context of a claim for unfair and discriminatory constructive dismissal. Under this special approach, the claimant is not required to prove, on the balance of probabilities, that the third party would have acted in the required way, only that there was a real and substantial chance that he or she would. This is still a question of causation, not of quantification, but if the claimant does establish that there was such a real and substantial chance, then when it comes to quantification, compensation will be assessed not at 100 per cent of the value of the benefit he or she would have obtained, but at the appropriate percentage having regard to the chances of obtaining it.

In the Wilton case the claimant, having established that she had been unfairly constructively dismissed, claimed she had lost out on the opportunity to be awarded equity in her employer's company and to then profit by several hundred thousand pounds when the company was sold. However, the tribunal found that she was unable to clear the first hurdle of establishing that there was a real and substantial chance of the company being sold, and this decision was upheld by the EAT.

Career-long loss
14.86

If a tribunal finds that a claimant has no prospect, or only limited prospects, of securing employment equivalent to that from which he or she has been unfairly dismissed, it may make an award of compensation covering the whole of the claimant's working life. Although such awards will normally run up against the statutory cap on compensation (see 'Nature and maximum amount of award – amount of week's pay and statutory cap' above), a full estimation of the appropriate compensation is still required.

The availability of such awards was confirmed by the Court of Appeal in Wardle v Crédit Agricole Corporate and Investment Bank 2011 ICR 1290, CA, although it indicated that it is likely to be a rare case where compensation is assessed over a career lifetime. An award for career-long loss will only be appropriate where the tribunal considers on the evidence before it that there is no real prospect of an employee ever obtaining an equivalent job for the rest of his or her working life. In such rare cases, the tribunal should assess what the employee would have been likely to earn over his or her career had he or she not been unlawfully treated compared with what he or she is now likely to earn. The difference should then be reduced to reflect the vicissitudes of life (for example, the possibility of the employee's fair dismissal in any event, death or early retirement) and the benefit of accelerated payment (see 'Discount for accelerated receipt' below).

In the majority of cases, however, career-long loss will not be appropriate and **14.87** the tribunal will need to assess the loss up to the point where the employee would be likely to obtain an equivalent job. In other words, if the tribunal finds that, by some point in the future, there is a more than 50 per cent chance the

637

claimant will have secured equivalent employment, it must limit compensation to that point. In the Wardle case itself, the tribunal had made a finding that there was a 70 per cent chance that the claimant, who was dismissed at the end of July 2008, would have found an equivalent job by the end of December 2011. On that basis, it applied a reduction of 70 per cent to the career-long loss from that point onwards. The Court of Appeal held that it was wrong to do so – the tribunal should have identified the point in time at which it was more likely than not (i.e. a probability of more than 50 per cent) that the claimant would have found equivalent employment. In the Court's view, that point was June 2011, and so it directed that compensation should not be awarded for any later period.

14.88 **Use of 'Ogden Tables'.** In Kingston Upon Hull City Council v Dunnachie (No.3) 2004 ICR 227, EAT, the EAT considered the extent to which tribunals are entitled to rely on the 'Ogden Tables' – which are issued by the Government Actuary's Department and which allow for an actuarial adjustment of compensation for future loss in personal injury cases – in helping to assess future loss in unfair dismissal cases. (The seventh edition of these tables was published by the Government Actuary's Department in 2011 and is available on the gov.uk website.) The EAT concluded that reliance on such tables is appropriate only where it is established that the claimant is likely to suffer a career-long future loss of earnings. The tribunal should determine whether on the balance of probabilities this is the case by comparing 'old job facts' and 'new job facts'. 'Old job facts' include personal factors (such as health, family situation and location); economic factors (such as the introduction of new technology and the possibility of lay-offs or redundancies); whether the claimant would have taken early retirement or considered a second career; and whether it is likely that the claimant's earnings in the old job would have remained stable. 'New job facts' include an assessment of whether and when the claimant is likely to obtain a new job; whether this will entail a pay cut; if so, whether the claimant will eventually obtain better paid employment; and the claimant's prospects of securing promotion or a pay rise in the new job.

In the subsequent case of Birmingham City Council v Jaddoo EAT 0448/04 the EAT reiterated the point made in the Dunnachie case that use of the Ogden Tables is only ever appropriate where a tribunal is satisfied that the loss caused by the actions of the employer is likely to be sustained by the employee across the remainder of his or her career. In Jaddoo the EAT's President, Mr Justice Burton, specifically remarked that great caution should be exercised by a tribunal in relation to a conclusion as to the existence of lifelong loss where the claimant is as young as 31 or 32, as was so in that particular case. Burton J also emphasised that whenever an assessment of career-long loss is undertaken, allowance has to be made within the tribunal's calculations for the employee's duty to take reasonable steps to mitigate his or her loss (see Chapter 16, 'Compensatory awards: adjustments', under 'Failure to mitigate losses').

The EAT also held in Kingston Upon Hull City Council v Dunnachie (No.3) **14.89** (above) that the Ogden Tables are relevant only once the tribunal has determined a figure for estimated annual future loss and an estimated period of loss lasting until retirement. It is unlikely that a tribunal will arrive at a single annual figure for estimated loss. In some cases one figure in respect of the first one or two years and then a lower figure in respect of later periods will be appropriate. Whenever it is appropriate to use the Ogden Tables, the tribunal should adopt the discount rate in force under the Damages Act 1996 (currently 2.5 per cent) to take account of accelerated receipt of compensation (see 'Discount for accelerated receipt' below). Once the tribunal has applied the Ogden Table multipliers, it is generally inappropriate for it then to apply a large percentage discount for contingencies, since such contingencies should have been taken into account at the outset in order to arrive at the multiplicand (the figure for estimated annual loss) and period of loss.

Employee's health and fitness

14.90

The health and fitness of the employee, both before and after the dismissal, are important factors in the assessment of future loss. In Fougère v Phoenix Motor Co Ltd 1976 ICR 495, EAT, the Appeal Tribunal found that a tribunal had wrongly based its assessment of F's future loss on the likely period of unemployment for an average employee in good health. F, however, was 58 and suffering from a hernia and bronchitis which, the EAT said, were highly relevant factors. On the one hand, F's unemployment was likely to be extended by his circumstances; on the other, the employer might have dismissed him fairly on the ground of incapacity in the not-too-distant future. Either way, the tribunal should have taken F's personal circumstances into account and the EAT remitted the case for it to do so.

In Curtis v James Paterson (Darlington) Ltd 1973 ICR 496, NIRC, the tribunal lowered its assessment of the claimant's future loss because his ill health would probably have led to absences and therefore lower wages even if he had not been dismissed. In contrast, the tribunal in Wilson v Glenrose (Fishmerchants) Ltd and ors EAT 444/91 found that the fact that the claimant's workmates had known about his back problem and had helped him with any heavy lifting work meant that he would have been able to hold his job until retirement age had he not been dismissed.

The task for tribunals in assessing the contribution of ill health to an employee's **14.91** losses is different in respect of immediate and future loss. In Seafield Holdings Ltd (t/a Seafield Logistics) v Drewett 2006 ICR 1413, EAT, the claimant had suffered from a long-standing medical condition that was exacerbated by conduct on the part of her employer that led her to resign and claim unfair constructive dismissal. Following her dismissal, the claimant's condition left her unable to work. In awarding compensation, the tribunal adopted a 'but for' approach, concluding that, but for the actions of the employer, the claimant

639

would have been able to return to work. Allowing the employer's appeal in part, the EAT was satisfied that a 'but for' approach was appropriate for determining the employee's loss between the date of dismissal and the tribunal hearing (i.e. her immediate losses). However, it concluded that such an approach is wholly unsuitable for the task of determining future loss. Instead, tribunals should make an estimate of the chance that, had the employer not acted in the way it did, the employee's illness would still have prevented him or her from working.

In Devine v Designer Flowers Wholesale Florist Sundries Ltd 1993 IRLR 517, EAT, the Appeal Tribunal reminded itself that an employee can only recover losses that are attributable to action taken by the employer. In that case, the employee's dismissal caused her to suffer anxiety and depression, which rendered her unfit for work. The EAT stated that the fact that the employee's incapacity was caused by the unfair dismissal did not necessarily mean that she was entitled to compensation for the whole period of incapacity. It was for the tribunal to decide how far an employee's losses are attributable to action taken by the employer and to arrive at a sum that is just and equitable. The tribunal may want to consider, for example, whether the illness would have manifested itself in any event. It is also important to ascertain the extent to which the illness was actually caused by the dismissal, as opposed to the manner in which the dismissal was carried out. (As discussed under 'Nature and maximum amount of award – manner of dismissal' above, the House of Lords reconfirmed in Dunnachie v Kingston upon Hull City Council 2004 ICR 1052, HL, that non-economic loss – e.g. for manner of dismissal – is not recoverable under S.123(1).)

14.92 In Dignity Funerals Ltd v Bruce 2005 IRLR 189, Ct Sess (Inner House), the Court of Session agreed with the Scottish EAT that the tribunal had erred in failing to give any satisfactory reason for its decision to make no compensatory award for the period between dismissal and the date of the tribunal hearing. The claimant, who had been dismissed for gross misconduct, was diagnosed with reactive depression, a condition from which he had also suffered for five years before dismissal. The Court of Session noted, referring to Devine v Designer Flowers Wholesale Florist Sundries Ltd (above), that the tribunal should have decided 'whether the depression in the period after the dismissal was caused to any material extent by the dismissal itself; whether, if so, it had continued to be so caused for all or part of the period up to the hearing; and, if it was still caused at the date of the hearing, for how long it would continue to be so caused'. In the absence of any proper basis of findings of fact, however, the EAT should not have substituted its own figure for the compensatory award, but rather should have remitted the issue to the tribunal for consideration.

The question of how a claimant's losses should be assessed if he or she suffers both from a psychiatric illness caused by the dismissal and a separate physical illness arose in R and M Gaskarth v Mooney and anor EAT 0196/12. An employment tribunal found that M and her husband were unfairly dismissed when their contracts – under which they had been employed as live-in pub managers – were terminated with immediate effect and they, along with their four children, were required to leave the premises. The loss of her job and home caused M to develop depression, rendering her unfit for work. Independently from the depression, M also began to suffer from severe abdominal pain caused by hydronephrosis and gallstones. At the date of the remedies hearing over a year later M was still unable to work. She was awaiting surgery for her physical conditions but she continued to suffer from depression. The tribunal concluded that M's inability to work 'was attributable in no small part to the respondent's opportunistic and unscrupulous actions' and awarded her full loss of earnings to the date of the remedies hearing and six months beyond.

The EAT upheld the tribunal's award upon appeal. It noted that the medical **14.93** evidence before the tribunal did not set out the extent to which M's psychiatric symptoms on the one hand and her physical symptoms on the other had caused her absence from work at any particular time. Although 'in a perfect world' or in a case involving 'greater stakes' it might have done so, the EAT held that the evidence supported the tribunal's conclusions that M's depressive condition was caused by the dismissal and that M's absence from work was 'in no small part' attributable to that condition. There was no evidence that M's depression had improved such that she would have been fit for work had it not been for her physical complaints. Although the tribunal had failed to ask whether M's unfitness for work was 'to any material extent' caused by her dismissal – the test established by the Court of Session in Dignity Funerals Ltd v Bruce (above) – its finding that M's unfitness for work was 'in no small part' so attributable was if anything a more stringent application of that test. Therefore the tribunal could not be criticised for failing to apply the correct test.

Supervening illness. Two fairly recent decisions at EAT level have considered **14.94** the impact of an employee's supervening illness on the compensatory award. In the first – Wood v Mitchell SA Ltd EAT 0018/10 – the EAT cautioned against treating the date the employee becomes unfit for work due to supervening illness as the 'cut-off point' for the employee's compensation. In that case, W, a driver employed by MSA Ltd, was diagnosed with hepatitis C in mid-2006 and by November was signed off sick for two weeks, becoming entitled to statutory sick pay (SSP). MSA Ltd, concerned about W's ability to work, dismissed him on the ground of incapability with effect from 15 December. An employment tribunal upheld W's complaint of unfair dismissal on the basis that the employer had not made sufficient enquiries about his illness before deciding to dismiss him. In considering the appropriate level of compensation, the tribunal found that – had W not been dismissed – he would have continued to receive SSP from 15 December and resumed work with MSA Ltd on 1 February 2007. It therefore awarded loss of SSP for that period. It also accepted that W had made reasonable

641

attempts to mitigate his loss between January and March 2007 and awarded loss of earnings accordingly. However, it limited his compensatory award to 31 March 2007. This was because around that date W had become incapacitated due to mental ill health. In the tribunal's view, this supervening illness – completely unrelated to his employment – had stopped his losses being attributable to the dismissal. W appealed against this aspect of the tribunal's decision.

The EAT overturned the decision, holding that the tribunal had erred in only awarding W losses up to the point when he became unfit to work because of his psychiatric illness. In order to assess the losses consequent upon the dismissal, the EAT considered that a tribunal would have to estimate what the employee would have earned or received but for the unfair dismissal, including – by virtue of S.123(2)(b) ERA – any benefits he or she might reasonably have expected. The first step in making this estimate was to consider how long the employment would have continued had dismissal not occurred. This required taking into account an employee's contractual and statutory rights which are of benefit even if he or she becomes ill, including sick pay and the right to notice. Moreover, if an employee goes on sick leave, an employer is expected to investigate whether a return to work is feasible before being able to dismiss fairly on the ground of incapability. It followed that the date at which any ill health supervenes will not generally be a cut-off point when assessing compensation arising from unfair dismissal, even though the illness is not attributable to the employer's action. Rather, the tribunal should seek to gauge how long the employment would have continued from that date; what pay and benefits would have accrued during that time; and whether the employee would have returned to work. In the instant case, the tribunal had failed to follow this approach. The EAT emphasised that it was not completely discounting the possibility of an employee bringing a supervening illness on him or herself to such an extent that it would be just and equitable to treat the illness as a cut-off point for compensation purposes. However, this would be an unusual occurrence and would certainly not apply to psychiatric illnesses. Accordingly, W's appeal was allowed and his case was remitted to the tribunal.

14.95 In the second case, Avia Technique Ltd v Kalia EAT 0382/12, a differently constituted Appeal Tribunal confirmed that an employment tribunal had not erred in failing to identify a cut-off point for the award of compensation when the employee became seriously ill after the termination of her employment. K was unfairly dismissed by AT Ltd. She found short-term lower paid employment, but then became ill and was paid SSP by her new employer. The tribunal made a compensatory award of 40 weeks from dismissal, assessed on the basis of the difference between K's old and new pay rates. AT Ltd appealed, arguing that for the majority of that 40-week period K was incapable of any work for a reason wholly unconnected with her employment with AT Ltd and she should not receive compensation for that period. In support of this argument, AT Ltd cited Devine v Designer Flowers Wholesale Florist Sundries Ltd (above) in which the EAT stated that where an employee becomes ill after dismissal, this may be considered an intervening act, after which the employee's losses are no longer attributable to the dismissal. The EAT in the instant case was not persuaded by that argument: rather than follow the reasoning in Devine, it preferred the approach adopted in Wood v Mitchell SA Ltd (above). In its view, the correct approach for the tribunal was to assess the loss flowing from a dismissal using common sense, experience and a sense of justice. This required the tribunal to ask: for what period would the employee have remained in employment but for the dismissal? The ascertainment of such a period, the EAT continued, must be taken to subsume the possibility that during that period the employee may, by reason of some accident, injury or illness, become incapable of work or of reduced capacity. The appropriate question then becomes: what would have happened in relation to such illness or injury but for the dismissal? If the employment would have continued and wages and salary would have continued to have been paid during that period of illness or injury then such a loss can be said to be attributable to the dismissal. Accordingly, the tribunal had not erred in failing to adopt a cut-off point when K became incapable of work. However, the EAT accepted AT Ltd's alternative argument that, if K was entitled to compensation for 40 weeks from dismissal, the tribunal had erred in treating her as suffering the continuing loss of her full previous wages. Rather, any compensation should have been limited to the difference between what she did receive from her subsequent employer and what payment she would have received, while sick, from AT Ltd. As, on the facts of the case, the entitlement was the same – i.e. SSP – she had not suffered any loss. Consequently, the tribunal's award was set aside.

In the light of these decisions, it should not be assumed that the losses of an employee who becomes unfit for work following an unfair dismissal will thereby be curtailed on the basis that they are no longer attributable to the dismissal. This line of argument would only be open to an employer if there are 'unusual circumstances' surrounding the illness, a limited exception on which the EAT in Wood v Mitchell SA Ltd (above) gave little guidance. Provided the employee has mitigated his or her losses up to the date of the illness, he or she will generally be entitled to be compensated for loss of any benefits he or she would have received had it not been for the dismissal. This will entail a tribunal having to decide how long an employer would have kept the employee in employment following consultation and a medical investigation.

14.96 (On the vexed question of whether incapacity benefits received by an employee during the period covered by the compensatory award should be offset, see the discussion under 'Immediate loss – social security benefits' above.)

14.97 **Constructive dismissal.** The issue of how ill health affects future loss can prove particularly troublesome in cases of constructive dismissal. In GAB

643

Robins (UK) Ltd v Triggs 2008 ICR 529, CA, the claimant had been bullied and overworked by her manager, leading to anxiety, depression and a lengthy sickness absence. She had exhausted her entitlement to full sick pay when she resigned and claimed unfair constructive dismissal. Having found her dismissal unfair, the employment tribunal determined that it was appropriate to award a sum in respect of future loss of earnings, even though the claimant had been signed off work at the time of her dismissal and her entitlement to sick pay had run out by the time her resignation took effect. The employer appealed unsuccessfully to the EAT, which agreed with the tribunal that the employer's repudiatory conduct had to be considered as part of a cumulative sequence of events that led to the employee's acceptance of the fundamental breach of her employment contract. As such, the ill health and subsequent reduced earning capacity that the claimant suffered as a result of that conduct had to be treated as a consequence of her dismissal, giving rise to compensation under S.123 ERA. On further appeal, the Court of Appeal expressed a degree of 'instinctive sympathy' with the approach of the employment tribunal and the EAT, but held that it offended the principle that loss must flow from the dismissal. While the employer's repudiatory conduct is an essential condition of constructive dismissal, it is not that conduct, but rather the employee's acceptance of the breach, which effects the dismissal. Damage – in the instant case, the claimant's anxiety and depression – caused by the repudiatory conduct is damage in respect of which an employee has already accrued a cause of action at common law, and does not fall within the remit of S.123.

In light of the GAB Robbins decision, claimants wishing to recover damages for future loss caused by repudiatory conduct that led to a constructive dismissal must pursue a claim for damages for breach of contract (or possibly negligence) in the county court or High Court. Such a claim has the advantage that losses will not be subject to the statutory cap (see 'Nature and maximum amount of award – amount of week's pay and statutory cap' above), and is subject to a substantially longer time limit – three years in a personal injury claim as opposed to three months in an unfair dismissal claim.

14.98 Assessing future loss: other considerations

An employment tribunal will usually have regard to a number of factors when trying to predict how long the claimant's losses will continue. As Lord Justice Underhill observed in Griffin v Plymouth Hospital NHS Trust 2014 IRLR 962, CA, the tribunal's task in assessing the appropriate amount of compensation is 'bound to be to a considerable extent an exercise in speculation, based on [the tribunal's] assessment of the claimant herself – that is, her attitude and abilities – and of the local job market'. Below, we consider some of the main factors that an employment tribunal will take into account when making its assessment of future loss.

Local labour market. The tribunal will be expected to use its industrial **14.99** knowledge and understanding of the local labour market. In Welburn v Luxihomes Ltd ET Case No.6633/95 the tribunal noted that the employee lived in a holiday resort and that most of the work in the area was seasonal. It assessed her future loss for a period of 45 weeks until the next holiday season began. In times of high unemployment and recession, awards for future loss are likely to be greatest as tribunals take a less optimistic view of the time it will take for an employee to obtain equivalent new employment.

Personal circumstances of employee. The employee's personal circumstances **14.100** must be taken into account. In Haslam v Manchetts Cleaning Supplies Ltd ET Case No.33984/95, for example, the tribunal found that the employee might have difficulty in obtaining a new job because she lived in a country area without a car. And in Malcolm v Balmstore Ltd t/a Thompson's Bakery ET Case No.35476/94 the employee was a young Afro-Caribbean with no formal qualifications and poor communication skills, although he had worked with adequate skill and confidence at a specialist West Indian bakery until his dismissal. The tribunal thought it likely that he would have great difficulty finding other employment. In Gerbaldi v Jones t/a Milton Business Products ET Case No.14248/95 a tribunal found that the employer's failure to give a dismissed employee a reference despite her excellent work record would hamper her attempts to find a job. It assessed her period of future loss at 52 weeks.

Clearly, the employee's age, experience and level of qualification are all important factors. An apprentice dismissed before his or her period of training has been completed will have higher losses as a result of the early termination of the apprenticeship – see FC Shepherd and Co Ltd v Jerrom 1986 ICR 802, CA. It is also an unfortunate fact that older people are particularly likely to experience difficulties obtaining equivalent new employment, despite the prohibition on age discrimination in the Equality Act 2010. Tribunals may therefore take the view that older employees will be unlikely to find another appropriate job and, so far as the statutory maximum allows, award compensation up to normal retiring age. (Compensation may even be awarded beyond normal retiring age if the evidence shows that the employee would have stayed on past that age – Barrel Plating and Phosphating Co Ltd v Danks 1976 ICR 503, EAT.) Two examples:

- **Kerley v New Forest Bakeries Ltd (in liquidation) and ors** ET Case No.7405/83: K was a 59-year-old baker with no experience in any other trade. The tribunal thought that his prospects of obtaining employment before retirement were 'virtually nil' and went straight to the maximum figure for his compensatory award

- **Machan v New Longmoor Club** ET Case No.10876/87: M was a 53-year-old cleaner. The tribunal thought that the average age of office cleaners was well over 50 and that there was a 60 per cent staff turnover in the trade,

645

so that jobs were continuously available for which age was no barrier. It awarded nothing for future loss because M should be able to obtain a job comparable to her previous one almost immediately.

14.101 These cases show that the employee's age, while certainly a relevant factor, will not be sufficient on its own to justify awarding loss until the employee's retirement date. The tribunal must always consider the employee's age in the context of his or her chances of obtaining another job. In West Hertfordshire Hospitals NHS Trust v Evans EAT 0398/09 the EAT held that the tribunal had fallen into error by not examining the employee's claim for career-long loss in the appropriate way. E was unfairly dismissed from her role as health care assistant with the Trust and subsequently received incapacity benefits. At the remedies hearing, she claimed loss of earnings until retirement on the basis of her age and medical incapacity. The tribunal agreed, noting that she was 58 years and four months old at the date of the hearing and that 'her age would be a disadvantage to her in looking for further work'. On that basis, it awarded her loss of earnings until she attained the age of 60. The EAT overturned the tribunal's decision, holding that the tribunal had failed to make any findings as to E's medical ability to work after her dismissal or as to the availability of suitable work for her in her local area. The matter was remitted to a different tribunal for reconsideration.

In Griffin v Plymouth Hospital NHS Trust (above) the employee was unfairly dismissed from her job as a specialist clinical technician in bone densitometry at a hospital in Plymouth. The tribunal found that, given what had happened, she would not be able to return to work at the hospital and, since it was not reasonable to expect her to leave the Plymouth area and the Trust was the only employer in that area with a need for her specialist skills, she would not be able to find other employment as a clinical technician. However, it decided that she would in due course be able to take a management role and that she would gradually return to her previous level of earnings over a period of 12 years. The Court of Appeal upheld the decision on appeal, holding that the tribunal had been entitled to find that her attitude and abilities justified a conclusion that she would eventually regain her previous level of earnings. The tribunal had considered extensive evidence about the kinds of work available to her. Moreover, while expressing 'every sympathy' with the claimant in suffering from lupus (which had led her to resign and successfully claim unfair constructive dismissal and disability discrimination), the Court did not think that the tribunal was obliged to take the view that the disease prevented her, as someone with ability and determination, from ever again undertaking a job involving some degree of responsibility.

14.102 In Rachabattuni Ram v JD Wetherspoon plc EAT 0080/11 the employment tribunal identified the employee's immigration status as a personal circumstance limiting compensation. R, an Indian national, had a work permit that allowed him to work for JDW plc for a period of five years. He was dismissed in the fifth year of his employment (i.e. before his permit expired) and a tribunal found that dismissal was unfair. However, it awarded no compensation beyond the five-year period of R's leave to remain, believing that R could no longer lawfully work for JDW plc after that time and so any further loss would not be attributable to the dismissal. The EAT overturned that decision. It noted that, were it not for the dismissal, R would still have been employed at the time when his work permit expired and there was no reason to suppose that he would not then have applied for indefinite leave to remain. This was in fact what he had done. Thus, the crucial question was what effect that application had on his right to remain in employment. The tribunal had decided that R's right to work would not have been extended by the application. The EAT held that that was a misinterpretation of the relevant law. Having regard to the Court of Appeal's decision in Hounslow London Borough Council v Klusova 2008 ICR 396, CA, and the relevant immigration rules, it should have been clear that R's application for indefinite leave to remain would automatically extend his right to remain and work for JDW plc pending determination. Accordingly, the tribunal erred in limiting compensation to the period of the original work permit.

Although the EAT in the Rachabattuni Ram case disagreed with the tribunal's interpretation of the applicable law, it did not object in principle to the idea that the expiry of an individual's leave to work might limit compensation for unfair dismissal. Thus, in a case where there is no automatic extension of the right to remain and work, a cap on compensation might well be appropriate. In Kings Castle Church v Okukusie EAT 0472/11, for example, O, a Nigerian national, worked for the church as a pastor. The job did not require a work permit and he had leave to remain in the United Kingdom until October 2009. In January 2010, the Border Agency rejected his application for indefinite leave to remain, but told him that he could stay pending determination of any appeal against its decision. O was dismissed shortly after in circumstances that an employment tribunal later found to be unfair. As part of his compensation, the tribunal awarded him six months' loss of earnings from the date of dismissal. On appeal, the EAT set aside the award, holding that no compensation was due for future loss in respect of a period when the individual would not have been permitted to continue in employment. Here, the tribunal had been put on notice in January 2010 that there were questions about O's immigration status and, although it had correctly proceeded on the basis that he could remain and work while any appeal was pending, it had failed to enquire whether O had in fact appealed and, if so, whether the appeal had been determined. That enquiry would have revealed that O had no leave to remain in the country after 10 May 2010. Accordingly, the EAT substituted an award for loss of earnings calculated up to the last day O was permitted to work.

647

14.103 **Self-employment, retraining and study.** Some employees become self-employed after being dismissed. Where this happens, the tribunal will take account of earnings from self-employment and – subject to the employee showing that self-employment was a reasonable way of mitigating losses – compensation can be awarded in order to make up any difference between the employee's new and old earnings. In Praxis Real Estate Management Ltd v Nichols EAT 0502/12 N was unfairly dismissed from his role as property asset manager. Finding it difficult to obtain alternative employment in the same field, he decided to start his own property investment business. At the remedies hearing, the tribunal rejected the employer's submission that N's decision to become self-employed was not a reasonable attempt to mitigate his loss, particularly given his lack of experience in property investment. Given the specialist nature of N's job, the geographical location and the reason for his dismissal (i.e. capability), the tribunal found that it was not an unreasonable risk for him to start a business. Furthermore, there was evidence to suggest that his efforts were beginning to bring a return. By the time of the hearing, he was close to securing deals that would generate fees of approximately £23,170. The tribunal found that he would build the business to the point where he would not suffer continuing loss over a total period of 18 months. On appeal, the tribunal's assessment of N's compensation for future loss was upheld by the EAT.

If the new earnings from self-employment are already higher than those from the old job by the time the tribunal comes to calculate compensation, the excess will be deducted from the immediate loss in the normal way. However, it will not always be safe to assume that there will be no award for future loss. In Islam Channel Ltd v Ridley EAT 0083/09 the claimant, R, found freelance work as a television journalist after being dismissed. In the 49 weeks between the date of dismissal and the remedies hearing, she had earned roughly £5,000 more from the freelance work than she would have earned had she remained employed. However, all of this 'profit' came from the first 30 weeks of that period: for the last 19 weeks, the frequency of freelance work had dropped off and R was earning around £500 a month less than in her previous job. After finding that R had been unfairly dismissed, the tribunal declined to award any immediate loss of earnings as R had not incurred any loss during the relevant period. Turning to future loss, the tribunal noted that the new freelance work was inherently insecure and proceeded to award R £6,149, representing one year's future loss (a period which it described as 'modest') at just over £512 a month. Furthermore, it decided that the claimant need not give credit for the £5,000 'profit' earned during the period of immediate loss.

14.104 Before the EAT, the employer argued that credit had to be given for the £5,000. To do otherwise, it contended, would be to land R with a windfall and unfairly punish the employer. The Appeal Tribunal noted that, as a result of the Court of Appeal's decision in Dench v Flynn and Partners 1998 IRLR 653, CA, the

648

obtaining of new work does not act as an 'automatic guillotine' to sever the causal link between the dismissal and any future losses the claimant may experience. It was therefore open to the tribunal, in assessing what would be 'just and equitable' compensation, to treat losses sustained after the first 30 weeks of the freelance work as flowing from the dismissal. On the question of whether credit should be given for the 'profit' earned during the period of immediate loss, the EAT stated that, as an alternative to treating immediate and future losses as one and deducting any sums earned in mitigation, it is open to a tribunal in seeking to settle on just and equitable compensation to draw a line between past and future losses. In addition, the EAT stated that, if it were wrong that a tribunal has the discretion to separate past and future losses, there was an alternative way in which the tribunal could have assessed compensation which would have led to substantially the same result. Given its finding that R's new job was inherently insecure, the tribunal could have required R to give credit for the £5,000 excess she had earned prior to the remedies hearing, but increased her award for future loss based on an assessment of the risk of losing the new job. Had the tribunal assessed that risk at 20 per cent and increased R's compensation accordingly, it would have reached approximately the same overall figure. The EAT acknowledged that this was an exercise conducted after the event but stated that it supported the conclusion that the tribunal's award was just and equitable.

Four further cases where compensation was awarded to employees who became **14.105** self-employed after dismissal:

- **Oliver v Panayi t/a Criss Hair Dressers** ET Case No.7637/78: a dismissed hairdresser established her own salon. A tribunal awarded a year's net loss of previous earnings to allow for the build-up of the business to the point where she would be as well off as in her previous employment

- **Sparkes v ET Barwick Mills Ltd** ET Case No.41388/76: a dismissed employee decided to set up on his own as a commission agent. A tribunal awarded two years' interest on the capital borrowed to set up the business as part of compensation for future loss. Since he had previously had a company car, it also awarded the employee the down-payment on a car he thought necessary for his new business

- **Glen Henderson Ltd v Nisbet** EAT 34/90: N was unfairly dismissed for redundancy. She then went on a five-week business enterprise course with a view to becoming self-employed. Thereafter she was self-employed. A tribunal awarded her compensation for the time she was on the course and one year's future loss on the basis of her self-employed earnings. This decision was upheld by the EAT

- **Pacific Direct Ltd v Riaz** EAT 0072/02: R was unfairly dismissed following her failure to accept a new commission structure. She then set up her own business, working from home. By October 2001, when the tribunal hearing took place, R had generated £10,300 from the start of the year. However, due to a fire at her flat during the summer, she had been unable to generate any income in June, July or August, although she had been pursuing her business since then and was actively seeking other work. The tribunal found that she was entitled to recover loss of earnings on a basis of an income of £30,000 from January 2001 for a period of 15 months, from which the £10,300 already earned would be deducted. The employer's appeal on the basis that the fire at R's flat should have broken the chain of causation was dismissed. In the EAT's view, the tribunal had taken this setback into account but did not regard it as terminating the loss consequent upon the dismissal that was attributable to the employer's action. It was a permissible approach to decide that R had reasonably mitigated her loss but would not achieve the same earnings level as before until April 2002.

14.106 In the Nisbet case (above), the EAT considered that the claimant's five-week course was merely part of her mitigation of loss through her decision to become self-employed. But employees who embark upon a training course following dismissal may well be considered to have voluntarily removed themselves from the job market, with the result that the employer is no longer liable for their losses. In Holroyd v Gravure Cylinders Ltd 1984 IRLR 259, EAT, for example, the employee decided to take a 12-month postgraduate university course after his dismissal. A tribunal refused to extend his compensation past the date on which he began the course. On appeal to the EAT, Lord McDonald said that it had been correct to do so. The employee had decided to take himself out of the labour market for 12 months and so should not be compensated for that period. Any suggestion of continuing future loss after the end of the course was 'so remote as to be incapable... of calculation'.

Similarly, in Simrad Ltd v Scott 1997 IRLR 147, EAT, the Appeal Tribunal instructed a tribunal to ignore all losses directly arising from the employee's decision to retrain as a nurse. However, the EAT made it clear in Khanum v IBC Vehicles Ltd EAT 685/98 that the Simrad case did not create a rule of law that embarking upon a course of further education necessarily breaks the chain of causation. The EAT also said that the fact that it may have been reasonable for an employee to go to college did not determine the issue either way. The issue for the tribunal is whether the decision to undertake the course is a direct result of the dismissal. Given that the tribunal had found that the claimant in the instant case had no choice but to attend university, the EAT said that the loss she suffered in doing so must be a direct result of her dismissal. (Note that both this case and the Simrad case are discussed in more detail under 'Remoteness of loss' below.)

14.107 **Mitigation.** The amount awarded for future loss is greatly affected by the question of what steps it is reasonable to expect the employee to take to mitigate his or her losses. For instance, if the dismissed employee has accepted a much lower-paid job than the previous one, the tribunal is unlikely to award the full difference in pay for either immediate or future loss unless the employee can show that, in the circumstances, it was reasonable to accept such a low-paid job. We consider this question in more detail in Chapter 16, 'Compensatory awards: adjustments', under 'Failure to mitigate losses'.

Discount for accelerated receipt

14.108

As any award for future years is payable by the employer up front in a single lump sum, a discount rate is usually applied (unless the award is fairly small) to take into account the benefit to the employee of receiving the money early, on the assumption that it can then be invested to yield growth. The Court of Appeal confirmed in Bentwood Bros (Manchester) Ltd v Shepherd 2003 ICR 1000, CA, that tribunals should not ignore the fact that the employee has the benefit of receiving immediately money he or she would otherwise have had to wait for and should therefore apply a discount for accelerated receipt. However, in that particular case, the tribunal applied a single deduction of 5 per cent of the total compensation designed to compensate two and a half years' future earnings and ten years' pension payments. The Court of Appeal held that, in doing this, the tribunal had failed to recognise that the conventional investment rate of 5 per cent, referred to in textbooks such as *Harvey on Industrial Relations and Employment Law*, was intended to be an annual rate. The Court also held that 5 per cent was arguably on the high side, given that until recently 4.5 per cent was the statutory discount rate applicable in personal injury cases and that this had since been reduced to 2.5 per cent. The question of the appropriate rate to apply as a discount for accelerated receipt was therefore remitted to the tribunal for reconsideration. The tribunal subsequently concluded that 3 per cent was the appropriate discount for accelerated receipt.

In Benchmark Dental Laboratories Group Ltd v Perfitt EAT 0304/04 the EAT considered two matters of general interest with regard to discount from the compensatory award for accelerated receipt. The first concerned the appropriate discount rate. The EAT pointed out that the rate prescribed for use in personal injury cases is set by the Lord Chancellor pursuant to S.1 of the Damages Act 1996. The Damages (Personal Injuries) Order 2001 SI 2001/2301 currently prescribes 2.5 per cent as the assumed rate of return on investment of awards of personal injury damages. Although employment tribunals are not bound by this discount, the EAT observed that it is good practice for them to adopt it.

The second issue concerned the application of that rate to the particular circumstances of the case. The employment tribunal found that the employee had been unfairly dismissed and subjected to disability discrimination. It further found that, at the age of 57, the period of the employee's loss would be likely to continue until his retirement age, i.e. for eight years. It calculated his actual financial loss as being £121,864 and then applied a 2.5 per cent discount for accelerated payment to that entire sum, resulting in an award of £118,818. On

14.109

651

appeal, the EAT ruled that the tribunal had erred by applying the 2.5 per cent discount to the entire period of loss. That was because receipt of the entire sum was not accelerated to the same extent equally across the whole period: the benefit to the employee of early receipt was far greater in respect of that part of the award for lost earnings at the end of the period. Taking a broad-brush approach, the EAT held that one appropriate way of calculating the discount for accelerated receipt in the instant case was to apply a total discount of 10 per cent to half the award, since it was the second half of the award in respect of which early receipt was most accelerated. This would represent a discount of 2.5 per cent multiplied by half the number of years covered by the compensation award (in this case, four). If greater sophistication were required, the parties should refer the tribunal to appropriate compensation tables, such as the Ogden Tables (see below). But the EAT made it clear that in the absence of a more sophisticated approach, a tribunal would not err in law by applying a discount for accelerated receipt on the basis of the broad considerations set out above.

Note that where a multiplier and multiplicand are being used (e.g. where the Ogden Tables are being relied upon to assess career-long loss of earnings), the formula may already incorporate a discount for accelerated receipt. However, as has previously been explained, the EAT in Kingston Upon Hull City Council v Dunnachie (No.3) 2004 ICR 227, EAT, emphasised that the use of the Ogden Tables in unfair dismissal cases will be rare – see 'Career-long loss' above. Turning to consider how tribunals should use the Ogden Tables whenever they are appropriate, the EAT pointed out that the tables were of use only once the tribunal had determined a figure for estimated annual loss (i.e. the multiplicand). In the EAT's view, it was unlikely that a tribunal would arrive at a single annual figure for estimated loss. In some cases one figure in respect of the first one or two years and then a lower figure in respect of later periods would be appropriate. However, where an employee was close to retirement a tribunal could adopt a single multiplicand and then apply the Ogden Tables and a discount for (i) contingencies and (ii) accelerated receipt. So far as the latter is concerned, a tribunal should adopt the prevailing rate of return specified under the Damages Act 1996 (currently 2.5 per cent). Once a tribunal had applied a multiplier from a relevant Ogden Table, it was inappropriate for it then to apply a large percentage discount for generalised contingencies since, if there were contingencies justifying something in the order of a 50 per cent discount, it was likely that the assessment that the employee was likely to sustain career-long loss would have been unjustified in the first place.

14.110 **'Decelerated' payment.** In Melia v Magna Kansei Ltd 2006 ICR 410, CA, the issue arose as to whether an employee could recover as part of the compensatory award the obverse of accelerated receipt; namely, any loss that flowed from being denied the opportunity to invest compensation prior to the conclusion of the tribunal proceedings. The question of whether tribunals are able to make such an award is discussed under 'Interest' below.

652

Remoteness of loss

14.111

Section 123(1) ERA expressly states that the loss suffered by the employee must be attributable to action taken by the employer. We have seen in the case of Courtaulds Northern Spinning Ltd v Moosa 1984 ICR 218, EAT (see the section on 'Immediate loss' above, under 'New employment – exceptions to the Ging rule'), how an employer may successfully argue that the employee's losses are no longer attributable to the employer's action. That case concerned an employee who worked in new employment for 18 months but was then dismissed again before the tribunal hearing of the original claim. The EAT held that the original employer's liability ceased when the employee entered the new employment.

In Mabey Plant Hire Ltd v Richens, unreported 6.5.93, CA, an employee got a new job for which he was overqualified, at a lower rate of pay. He was dismissed from that job a few months later on account of a clash of personalities and a failure to comply with company rules. The Court of Appeal held that the new employment could have been permanent and that it came to an end for reasons unrelated to any action taken by the original employer. The chain of causation was therefore broken and any future loss was restricted to the difference between the employee's original salary and the salary he would have continued to earn with the second employer but for the second dismissal.

In other cases, however, a tribunal may conclude that the employee's loss after a second dismissal is still attributable to the first dismissal – for example, where the period of new employment is short. In Dundee Plant Co Ltd v Riddler EAT 377/88 the employee found a new job but gave it up after three months when it proved unsuitable (reasonably, said the tribunal). The EAT upheld the tribunal's finding that the employer's liability did not terminate when the employee found the new job. And in Witham Weld v Hedley EAT 176/95 the employee gained new employment immediately after her dismissal but it proved to be unsuitable and she left after four weeks. The EAT stated that 'a reasonable but unsuccessful attempt to mitigate does not cut the chain between the wrongdoing and loss which on ordinary principles of causation flowed from it'.

14.112

The Court of Appeal came to a similar conclusion in Dench v Flynn and Partners 1998 IRLR 653, CA, overturning a tribunal decision that the claimant was not entitled to compensation after she had taken up new employment, even though the new job had been terminated after only two months. The Court took the view that, contrary to the EAT's approach in Whelan and anor v Richardson 1998 ICR 318, EAT, there is no hard-and-fast rule as to whether permanent alternative employment breaks the chain of causation for loss. The tribunal's only duty is to award what is just and equitable in the circumstances and the tribunal must consider the effect of the unfair dismissal and the effect of the termination of any subsequent employment.

14.113   The issue of causation may also arise where the employee is unable to find new employment because of some factor in his or her background that makes him or her unemployable. In Carr Gomm Scotland Ltd v Sneddon EATS 0010/13, for example, the employee, a care worker, was unable to find new employment due to an adverse entry on his enhanced disclosure form. The EAT held that the tribunal had erred in awarding compensation for future loss without giving proper consideration to the extent to which it was this entry, rather than the dismissal, that caused his future loss. Although the adverse entry related to the incident for which the employee had been unfairly dismissed, it was the local authority and not the employer that was responsible for making the entry. Therefore any loss suffered by him did not necessarily result from his dismissal. The case was remitted to the tribunal to reconsider compensation.

In determining whether loss was attributable to the dismissal, an employment tribunal is not limited by the strict rules of causation that apply in civil cases. This was made clear by the Court of Session in Leonard and ors v Strathclyde Buses Ltd 1998 IRLR 693, Ct Sess (Inner House), where the employees were forced to sell their shares in SB Ltd back to the company when they were dismissed. SB Ltd was soon after taken over by another company, which paid significantly more for the shares than SB Ltd had done. The employees claimed as part of their compensation the enhanced value which they would have received for their shares but for their dismissals, and the tribunal upheld that claim. Overturning that decision on appeal, the EAT stated that it was not enough for the employees to establish that, but for their dismissals, they would have received more for their shares. The increase in value of the shares had occurred as a result of the intervention of a third party and was not, therefore, attributable to the conduct of the employer. On further appeal to the Court of Session, however, the tribunal's decision was restored. The Court cautioned against introducing into the assessment of compensation for unfair dismissal principles of foreseeability or remoteness, at least in the technical sense in which those concepts apply in other legal contexts such as tort and contract. In the instant case, the increased value of the shares was a benefit that the employees would have enjoyed had they continued in employment to the date of the takeover. It followed that the tribunal's decision to compensate the employees for the loss of share value was one that fell within the limits of a proper exercise of its discretion.

14.114   There is obviously a very close connection here between the issue of remoteness and the question of whether an employee has taken reasonable steps to mitigate his or her losses. In cases like Holroyd v Gravure Cylinders Ltd 1984 IRLR 259, EAT (see 'Assessing future loss: other considerations – self-employment, retraining and study' above) and Dundee Plant Co Ltd v Riddler (above) the question of whether the employees' actions in undertaking a training course on the one hand, and leaving a new job on the other, were reasonable mitigation of loss is almost identical to the question of whether their ongoing losses were

654

still attributable to the actions of the employers. In other words, if the employee's attempts to mitigate loss are considered reasonable, the chain of causation is unlikely to be broken and the losses sustained by the employee will still be attributable to the original dismissal. But if the employee's actions following dismissal are considered to be unreasonable, they may well constitute a novus actus interveniens – or 'intervening act' – following which the employee's losses can no longer be said to be attributable to the dismissal by the employer.

Notwithstanding their similarity, however, issues of remoteness and mitigation need to be kept separate. In Wilson v Glenrose (Fishmerchants) Ltd and ors EAT 444/91 an employee who had poor prospects of obtaining new employment chose to claim sickness benefits for two years before becoming 'unemployed'. The EAT held that the tribunal was wrong to award no future loss on the ground that causation between the employee's dismissal and his current unemployment had been broken by his claiming sickness benefit. It should first have considered whether claiming for that period was, in the circumstances, a reasonable action in mitigation of loss.

Change of career. A radical approach to the question of how far an employee's **14.115** losses are attributable to actions of the employer – and the relationship between this question and that of mitigation – was adopted by the EAT in Simrad Ltd v Scott 1997 IRLR 147, EAT. In that case the employee was dismissed from her job as an electronics technician and decided to retrain as a nurse. The tribunal found that it was reasonable in the circumstances for her to seek to change careers in this way and assessed her future loss for a period of 15 months. On appeal, the EAT stated that the approach a tribunal should adopt consists of three stages. First, the tribunal must quantify the losses claimed. Secondly, it must consider the extent to which any or all of those losses are attributable to action taken by the employer. Thirdly, the tribunal must consider whether, in all the circumstances, it is just and equitable to make the relevant award. It is largely at this third stage that the question of mitigation arises since, while the facts relating to mitigation will frequently bear upon the question of causative link, it is essentially an equitable plea to be judged in the context of reasonableness.

Having set out this approach, the EAT formed the opinion that the tribunal had erred by missing out the second stage and merely asking itself whether the employee acted reasonably in deciding on a career change. The EAT stated that, if an element of loss fails the 'attribution test' at stage two, it cannot be awarded on just and equitable grounds at stage three. The EAT went on to hold that the employee's decision to embark upon a nursing career was not sufficiently linked to the original dismissal. Although it would not have happened but for the dismissal, her decision to become a nurse was too remote 'both in time and content' to be properly attributable to the employer's conduct. Accordingly, all

655

losses directly arising from the decision to become a nurse had to be ignored for compensation purposes.

14.116 The Simrad case was cited with approval in Jones v Lingfield Leisure plc EAT 712/97, a case involving a fitness trainer employed at a leisure centre who also ran a number of additional classes on a self-employed basis. Because she was employed at the centre, she did not have to pay the fee that other self-employed instructors paid. She was unfairly dismissed and claimed as part of her compensation the loss of the self-employed earnings. The EAT upheld a tribunal ruling that these losses were too remote. In the EAT's view, the compensatory award is not meant to compensate an employee for losses arising out of the discontinuance by the employee of a business that she was carrying out while employed by the employer. The EAT was prepared to accept, however, that the fact that the claimant had not paid any fee to the centre for her classes might constitute a lost fringe benefit for which she could claim. (The decision was subsequently upheld by the Court of Appeal – see 'Loss of private income' below.)

However, in Khanum v IBC Vehicles Ltd EAT 685/98 the EAT sought to temper the significance of the decision in Simrad Ltd v Scott (above), emphasising that the outcome in that case had turned very much on its own facts and that it did not create a rule of law to the effect that embarking upon a course of further education necessarily breaks the chain of causation. The claimant, an apprentice robotics technician qualified in electronics to ONC and HNC level, had told her employer that she was interested in taking a degree course. The claimant's subsequent dismissal for attending a university open day was found to be unfair. At the remedies hearing, the tribunal learned that the employee had been diagnosed as suffering from depression shortly before her dismissal. After the dismissal, she had made several unsuccessful job applications. Her former employer dominated the local automobile industry and there was evidence (which the tribunal accepted) that she had been 'blacklisted'. Ten months after dismissal, the employee started a degree course in computer systems engineering. The tribunal decided that it was sensible and laudable for her to take the course, but that her decision to do so 'inevitably' broke the chain of causation between her dismissal and her financial loss.

14.117 On appeal, the EAT overturned the tribunal's conclusions in view of the fact that the employee had had no choice but to attend university. The EAT identified three special factors governing her case. The first was that she had completed an apprenticeship for a specialist job in the car industry. The second was that her employer's dominant position in that industry could prevent the employee from pursuing her chosen career and there was evidence that it had blacklisted her. And the third was that she was unfairly and unlawfully dismissed. Taking those factors together, it was reasonably foreseeable that the employee would or might have had to retrain in a different career as a result of her dismissal. The EAT further noted that the tribunal had not considered whether it would

656

have been 'just and reasonable' to award compensation to the claimant. In view of the tribunal's findings as to the difficulties she experienced in obtaining employment and her state of health, it was clear that the tribunal had not directed itself properly on the third stage identified in the Simrad case (i.e. whether it was just and equitable to make the award).

In assessing the period for which to award compensation for future loss, the tribunal will also take account of other contingencies that may intervene to break the link between the dismissal and the employee's ongoing losses – e.g. where the evidence shows that the employee would shortly have left the old job of his or her own accord or where the employee would have been dismissed fairly at a later date. For instance, in James W Cook and Co (Wivenhoe) Ltd v Tipper and ors 1990 ICR 716, CA, the claimant was one of a number of employees unfairly dismissed shortly before the shipyard where they worked was closed. The Court of Appeal limited the employees' compensation to losses up to the date when the shipyard closed, at which point they would have been dismissed in any case.

In Garage Equipment Maintenance Co Ltd v Holloway EAT 582/94 the employee gained new employment in October 1992 at a slighter lower salary, which was subsequently reduced by £8,000 in April 1993. In the assessment of his future loss, the tribunal awarded him the difference between the salary in his former job and that in his new job, taking into account the £8,000 reduction. On appeal, the original employer argued that the reduction in salary that the employee suffered in his new job was not the result of its actions and that the tribunal had in effect made it compensate him for something for which it, as former employer, bore no responsibility. The EAT rejected the appeal, holding that the tribunal was entitled to take a broad-brush approach and that there had been no error of law.

Loss of private income. It will be a question of fact for a tribunal whether or not loss of the ability to generate private income associated with the lost employment will be recoverable as part of the award for future loss. In Jones v Lingfield Leisure plc 1999 EWCA Civ 1456, CA, a duty manager at a leisure club was allowed to give classes as an instructor and fitness trainer at the premises, which generated a substantial private income. Following her dismissal, an employment tribunal concluded that it was only empowered to compensate the employee for her loss as an employee and therefore any loss which she might have suffered as a result of losing her ability to work on her own account at her ex-employer's premises was not a matter within its jurisdiction. That finding was upheld by the EAT and the Court of Appeal. However, the Court of Appeal noted that it was not excluding the possibility that there could be situations where the opportunity to earn other money in a self-employed capacity, using the employer's facilities, could fall within S.123 ERA for the purposes of quantifying future loss. **14.118**

657

In Schlesinger v Swindon and Marlborough NHS Trust EAT 0072/04 the claimant was a consultant gynaecologist working under a part-time contract that allowed him to work within the private sector as well. He therefore also worked at a private hospital. He was suspended following his arrest and subsequently dismissed. A tribunal decided that his dismissal was unfair and awarded compensation of £12,918. The employee appealed in relation to the tribunal's refusal to make an award in respect of loss of private income. In light of S.123, there were two tests to be considered, namely: (i) whether the loss was attributable to the employer's action, and (ii) if so, whether the amount claimed was just and equitable in all the circumstances. The EAT held that there were no grounds for interfering with the tribunal's decision. While it was accepted that the contract allowed the employee to take on private work, it had been a matter for the particular specialist as to whether he did or did not take on that work. In the instant case, there was not a sufficient contractual link to allow the employee to claim loss of private income.

14.119 Tax rebates

Where an employee is dismissed and then unemployed for a time, he or she may become entitled to a tax rebate. The general rule is that such matters are not to be taken into account by a tribunal when assessing the compensatory award because consideration of detailed tax calculations would introduce unnecessary complications into a system that is supposed to be simple and informal – Adda International Ltd v Curcio 1976 ICR 407, EAT. However, in MBS Ltd v Calo 1983 ICR 459, EAT, the Appeal Tribunal, while endorsing the above principle, suggested that it might be proper for tax rebates to be offset against the employee's losses where high earners were involved and the sums in question could be substantial.

Interestingly, the employees in Lucas and ors v Laurence Scott Electromotors Ltd 1983 ICR 309, EAT, managed to recover compensation for loss of a tax rebate. There the employees were dismissed in March 1981 in circumstances that meant that they would have been fairly dismissed in July 1981. The employees remained unemployed for the whole of the financial year starting from April 1981. Had the employees been dismissed in July rather than in March, they would have been entitled to a rebate when they ceased working for the rest of that financial year. The tribunal's decision that this loss was attributable to the employer's action was upheld on appeal by the EAT.

14.120 Expenses

Section 123(2)(a) ERA expressly states that assessment of an employee's loss shall be taken to include any expenses reasonably incurred by the complainant in consequence of the dismissal. These may include:

658

- sums reasonably spent in looking for a new job – e.g. telephone calls, postage and the cost of attending interviews

- removal expenses if the employee has to move out of tied accommodation or move to a different area in order to secure another job.

Home removal costs. In Daykin v IHW Engineering Ltd ET Case No.01838/83 **14.121** the claimant had to sell his house and move into a council flat while looking for work. The tribunal awarded him removal expenses and also solicitors' conveyancing charges and estate agents' commission on the sale of the house. The employee had satisfied the tribunal that the sale of the house was a direct consequence of his dismissal.

School fees. In Derrick v DeVilbiss Co Ltd ET Case No.15631/83 the claimant **14.122** found a new job in another area after his dismissal. He had settled his daughter in a private school and was anxious to leave her there until she took her GCE – now GCSE – exams. He decided to move and leave his daughter as a boarder and claimed £1,800 for extra school fees and expenses. The tribunal thought it was an inevitable result of his dismissal that the claimant would either incur extra travelling expenses through long-distance commuting to his new job or extra school fees. It therefore awarded the £1,800 in full.

Business set-up costs. Expenses incurred by ex-employees in setting themselves **14.123** up in business on their own account may also be awarded if the tribunal considers that this is a reasonable way of mitigating the loss arising from dismissal. In Gardiner-Hill v Roland Berger Technics Ltd 1982 IRLR 498, EAT, the Appeal Tribunal considered a claim by an ex-managing director for £500 worth of expenses in setting up a consultancy service to be reasonable.

Legal costs. The legal fees involved in bringing an unfair dismissal claim cannot **14.124** be included in a compensatory award – Nohar v Granitstone (Galloway) Ltd 1974 ICR 273, NIRC. This is because the award of legal costs and expenses to parties at tribunal hearings is governed strictly by the Employment Tribunals (Constitution and Rules of Procedure) Regulations 2013 SI 2013/1237, which provide that costs can be awarded only in limited circumstances – see IDS Employment Law Handbook, 'Employment Tribunal Practice and Procedure' (2014), Chapter 20, 'Costs and penalties', for more detail on the power of employment tribunals to award costs.

This prohibition does not extend to other costs reasonably incurred in bringing an unfair dismissal claim, however. In Bailes v First Bristol Ltd ET Case No.1401728/12, for example, the claimant, a bus driver, was dismissed after testing positive for cocaine. He denied ever having taken cocaine and argued that the positive result came about because of his having handled contaminated bank notes in the course of his work. The claimant commissioned his own test, which proved that he had not taken cocaine within the last 90 days. A tribunal upheld his unfair dismissal claim and awarded him a total of £83,910, which

659

included £388 for the cost of the drugs test report he had commissioned (less the cost of the actual test itself, which had been commissioned while he was suspended prior to dismissal and could not therefore be said to have been sustained in consequence of the dismissal).

14.125 Loss of statutory rights

An employee who has been unfairly dismissed will – unless reinstated or re-engaged – lose a number of statutory employment protection rights that are dependent on the employee having remained in employment for a qualifying period. Most notably, the employee will lose the right not to be unfairly dismissed until he or she has worked long enough for a new employer – i.e. for two years – to qualify for the right again. It is commonplace for tribunals to award a nominal sum to reflect the loss of these rights – see, for example, SH Muffett Ltd v Head 1987 ICR 1, EAT. In that decision the EAT also decided to increase substantially the nominal sum awardable from £20 (at which it had stood since being set by the National Industrial Relations Court in Norton Tool Co Ltd v Tewson 1972 ICR 501, NIRC) to £100, on the basis that the pound had undergone considerable devaluation in the interim. The EAT further suggested that the figure of £100 should be reviewed within three to four years. In fact, however, the figure awarded by tribunals has remained fairly static since that time and appears largely unrelated to inflation and the retail prices index.

Loss of rights to statutory notice can also be compensated. This may be a serious loss for a long-serving employee who has, for example, worked for 12 years and become entitled to the statutory maximum of 12 weeks' notice, since it will take him or her 12 years with a new employer to recover his or her position. In Daley v AE Dorsett (Almar Dolls) Ltd 1982 ICR 1, EAT, it was held that in such a case it would be reasonable to award net pay for half the statutory notice period to compensate for loss of an intangible benefit. Thus, an employee with 12 years' service should get six weeks' net pay. In Annansingh v AW Lawson and Co Ltd EAT 733/85, for example, a tribunal awarded an employee just £20 for loss of statutory rights, although he had been continuously employed for 24 years. The EAT held that the minimum figure the tribunal should have awarded under this head was six weeks' pay – i.e. half the employee's statutory notice entitlement.

14.126 That said, the Daley decision was qualified in SH Muffett Ltd v Head (above), where the EAT added that only in exceptional cases should the tribunal award pay for half of the statutory notice period; less would usually be more appropriate. In Arthur Guinness Son and Co (GB) Ltd v Green 1989 ICR 241, EAT, for example, the EAT reduced the award of ten weeks' pay a tribunal had made to an employee with 28 years' service to a mere four weeks.

It is now fairly common practice for tribunals to award between £250 and £450 as a global sum for both loss of protection from unfair dismissal and loss of the accrued right to statutory notice.

Note that an employee may receive no award for loss of statutory rights if the tribunal is satisfied that he or she would shortly have been fairly dismissed from his or her employment anyway – Puglia v C James and Sons 1996 ICR 301, EAT. However, in Tyson v Concurrent Systems Inc Ltd EAT 0028/03 the EAT held that a tribunal cannot simply neglect to deal with a claim for compensation for loss of statutory rights and it therefore awarded £200 under this head of loss.

14.127

Pension loss

14.128

One of the most significant losses that an employee is likely to sustain as a result of being unfairly dismissed is that of pension rights, particularly where the employee was a member of a final salary (defined benefits) occupational pension scheme. For many years, such losses tended to be calculated in a rough-and-ready way, since the statutory cap on the compensatory award frequently got in the way of tribunals awarding anything like the full losses involved. However, following the raising of the cap from £12,000 to £50,000 in October 1999 and the subsequent annual inflation indexing of that figure so that it currently stands (as from 6 April 2015) at £78,335 or a year's pay (whichever is the lower), the scope for awarding substantial sums by way of pension loss has increased significantly. As a consequence, the approach that tribunals adopt to the calculation of such loss has become more sophisticated.

Pension loss is discussed in detail in Chapter 15, 'Compensatory awards: pension loss'. One point that should be mentioned here, however, is that it is not open to a tribunal to separate the issue of causation in respect of pension loss from causation in respect of the employee's other losses. In Aegon UK Corporate Services Ltd v Roberts 2010 ICR 596, CA, the claimant, R, had been a member of a final salary pension scheme before she was unfairly dismissed. Soon after dismissal, she found another job with JR Ltd that paid her more than she had previously earned. However, the new job came with a defined contribution pension scheme that was much less valuable and, by the time the tribunal came to assess compensation, R had lost the new job. With regard to causation, the tribunal decided that, so far as remuneration was concerned, the new job broke the chain of causation so that R's loss of earnings beyond the termination of that job could not be attributed to A Ltd. However, with regard to pension loss, the tribunal took the view that such loss could continue even though the claimant obtained permanent employment paying an equivalent or higher salary. It considered that R's final salary pension was a 'unique type of benefit' which she did not obtain on joining JR Ltd and which she would be unlikely to obtain in any other employment. The tribunal therefore decided

661

that the pension loss should not be 'thrown in' with other benefits and treated as part of the total remuneration package, and awarded R over £37,000.

14.129 The EAT agreed with the tribunal that a break in the chain of causation does not have to apply for all purposes and in respect of each benefit. It further took the view that the tribunal was entitled to treat pension benefits as a 'very significant factor', the loss of which could not be quantified in purely monetary terms. The case progressed to the Court of Appeal, which held that a pension does not have any special status in the calculation of future loss, but is simply part of the overall remuneration package and must be assessed in monetary terms. A tribunal does not have leeway to apply different principles of causation to different aspects of the remuneration package. Thus, having found that there was no shortfall in remuneration because, even taking account of the pension loss, the overall package with JR Ltd was more favourable than it had been with A Ltd, the tribunal was not entitled to award R pension loss.

14.130 **Interest**

Following the enactment of the Employment Tribunals (Interest) Order 1990 SI 1990/479 ('the Interest Order 1990'), interest accrues automatically on compensation awarded by employment tribunals. It used to be that interest only began to accrue when the tribunal's monetary award remained unpaid for 42 days after promulgation of the award. (The tribunal promulgates an award when the documentary confirmation of that part of its decision is recorded as having been sent to the parties.) However, in respect of claims presented to the tribunal on or after 29 July 2013, interest on any award begins to accrue *on the day after the date of promulgation* – Employment Tribunals (Interest) Order (Amendment) Order 2013 SI 2013/1671. This is subject to the condition that if payment of the full amount of the award is made within 14 days of the promulgation date, no interest shall be payable – Article 3(4) Interest Order 1990.

Interest still accrues from the same date even if the tribunal's decision is subject to review but, if the result of the review is to vary the amount payable, interest accrues on the amount as varied.

14.131 With regard to appeals to the EAT, much will depend on whether the appeal process was commenced before or after promulgation of the award by the tribunal. If the appeal is brought against a tribunal decision that already contained a promulgated award, then interest will begin to accrue the day after that original decision was promulgated. But if the appeal is against a tribunal decision that did not contain an order for payment of compensation, then interest will only begin to accrue the day after the appellate court promulgates an order for compensation (if this ever happens). The same principle operates where further appeals are pursued. Again, where an appeal results in the amount of compensation being varied, any interest will accrue on the amount as varied.

The remittal of a case for a fresh tribunal hearing may affect the accrual of interest in one of three ways:

- where the original tribunal's decision on compensation was not promulgated to the parties, any interest will only begin to accrue the day after the new tribunal has promulgated the award

- where the original tribunal's decision on compensation was promulgated and the case is remitted to a new tribunal on a question which does not affect the assessment of compensation, interest still accrues from the day after the original award was promulgated

- where the original tribunal's decision on compensation was promulgated, but the amount of compensation is eventually altered on a remit, interest will accrue on the new, varied amount of compensation, but from the day after the original award was promulgated.

Computation of interest   14.132

Interest is based on any part of the compensation that remains unpaid the day after the relevant promulgation (for which see above), subject to the condition that no interest accrues if full payment is made within 14 days. Any interest payable will be simple interest accruing from day to day – Article 3(1) Interest Order 1990. Article 4 of that Order stipulates that the rate of interest is that specified in S.17 of the Judgments Act 1838. The rate at the time of writing (which has remained unchanged since 1 April 1993) is 8 per cent. Should the rate alter, the relevant rate is the rate specified by S.17 of the 1838 Act as at the date of promulgation of the tribunal's decision.

Certain sums are to be disregarded when determining the amount of the monetary award upon which interest will accrue. These are:

- any award by the tribunal of costs or expenses

- any part of the monetary award which is subject to recoupment (see Chapter 18, 'Recoupment')

- any part of the award which the payer – i.e. the employer – is required, under statutory provision, to deduct and pay over to the tax authorities in respect of tax or National Insurance contributions.

Pre-judgment interest   14.133

In High Court proceedings, the Court is empowered under the Supreme Court Act 1981 to award not only post-judgment interest but also interest backdated to such date as it concludes is appropriate. This can be as far back as the date when the debt accrued. Employment tribunals have no such express power in

663

unfair dismissal cases. However, in Melia v Magna Kansei Ltd 2006 ICR 410, CA, the question arose whether an employee could, in fact, recover such a sum as a head of loss under the compensatory award on the basis of what is 'just and equitable'. In that case, the tribunal had made a deduction of 2.5 per cent on account of accelerated receipt of the award covering pension loss and loss of future earnings. The claimant argued that if it was just and equitable to make such a deduction, it should surely be just and equitable to include as a head of loss the obverse; namely, 'a premium for decelerated or delayed payment'. On appeal, the EAT could find no case authority prohibiting such an award and reasoned that 'in a case where, as here, a deduction of 2.5 per cent per annum is made from a calculation in order to make an allowance for accelerated payment, so there ought to be an increase or premium of 2.5 per cent per annum in respect of what one might loosely call "decelerated" or "delayed" payment; if the one is doable within the ordinary concept of common law damages or, here, of just and equitable compensation, so should the latter'.

The EAT went on to observe that the rate of the premium should be the same as that applied for accelerated receipt. The current standard rate in personal injury cases is 2.5 per cent – the rate that the tribunal applied in the instant case – and it is that rate which another division of the EAT recommended tribunals to adopt in Benchmark Dental Laboratories Group Ltd v Perfitt EAT 0304/04 – see 'Future loss – discount for accelerated receipt' above. The EAT acknowledged that this was considerably less than the annual rate of interest on judgment debts, but given that an award for 'decelerated receipt' would, in the EAT's view, only be applicable in a case where a corresponding deduction for accelerated receipt has been made, 'it is simple fairness to apply the same rate both ways'.

14.134 When the case reached the Court of Appeal, Lord Justice Chadwick (giving the leading judgment) agreed with the EAT that there was an 'obvious unfairness' in discounting the money that the claimant would have received in the future from his employment to recognise the fact that he was getting it earlier but in failing to reflect the money that he should have had in relation to past years to recognise the fact that he had not received it when he should have done. More importantly, Chadwick LJ rejected the employer's submission that the EAT had not been entitled to give credit for the latter as part of its assessment of the claimant's compensatory award. A tribunal's task under S.123(1) is to assess the compensatory award in such amount as it considers just and equitable in all the circumstances, having regard to the loss sustained by the claimant in consequence of the dismissal. In a case where the loss sustained includes a loss of past earnings as well as of future earnings, it is just and equitable to treat the two losses in a consistent way. Thus, if loss of future earnings is to be discounted to reflect the early receipt of that money, so loss of past earnings should be increased to reflect the late receipt of that money. According to Chadwick LJ, such an increase does not constitute an award of interest on the amount of the compensatory award. Rather, in deciding what the amount of the compensatory award should be, the tribunal takes into account the fact that full compensation requires a recognition that money which is paid later than it should have been gives rise to a loss. In that context, interest is a measure of the loss of the use of the money that the recipient should have had earlier. The employer's appeal was therefore dismissed.

The Court of Appeal therefore approved an uplift in compensation to reflect late payment of loss of earnings. But in doing so Chadwick LJ observed that it may be necessary, in future cases, to consider whether such an approach should be adopted in cases where the tribunal is not also awarding compensation for future loss. However, at the time of writing, we are not aware of any cases that deal directly with this point. Furthermore, it appears that awards for decelerated receipt remain rare. In Francois v Castle Rock Properties Ltd (t/a Electric Ballroom) EAT 0260/10, for example, the EAT observed that it is not the routine practice of tribunals to make any form of award for decelerated receipt.

Drafting schedules of loss   14.135

A schedule of loss is a claimant's statement of the loss he or she has suffered as a result of the employer's actions. The employment tribunal will usually order the claimant to produce such a schedule at an early stage in proceedings as part of its general power to make case management orders. Both parties and the tribunal are then clear as to what the claimant is seeking, which may encourage settlement. The schedule usually sets out the claimant's losses at the time of drafting, which may, of course, increase by the time of the hearing if the claimant has not found a new job. It should therefore be updated just prior to the hearing.

In an unfair dismissal claim, the claimant will need to set out details of the basic and compensatory awards. As explained in Chapter 13, 'Basic awards', the former is calculated according to the claimant's age, length of service and week's pay (currently capped at £475). It is the compensatory award, however, that will form the bulk of the drafting work. Ideally, the individual elements of immediate loss – loss of earnings, benefits, pension contributions, etc – should be set out first. A sum for loss of statutory rights can be included at this stage (see 'Loss of statutory rights' above). The schedule should then set out any pay the employee received in lieu of notice and any sums received from the employer by way of a redundancy, severance or ex gratia payment. A claimant will also need to provide details of the extent to which he or she has mitigated losses by finding new employment or claiming state benefits. Note, however, that if the employee was dismissed without notice, no credit need be given for sums earned during what would have been the notice period. If the claim is likely to involve an award of future loss that will see a reduction for accelerated payment, the schedule should include a percentage premium on the award for immediate loss

665

to take account of decelerated payment. This percentage should be the same as the discount for accelerated payment.

14.136 When considering future losses, a general rule of thumb is that, barring exceptional circumstances, the tribunal is unlikely to make an award that continues for more than two years at most. More usual is a period of six months to a year (from the date of the hearing). The claimant can be expected to be put to proof in verifying the nature and scale of any losses, so claims for future loss should be realistic. The typical way to express future loss of earnings is by assessing the weekly loss and multiplying that by the number of weeks for which the loss is expected to continue. The schedule should also include any anticipated future loss relating to benefits and pensions. As with immediate loss, any sums in mitigation should be included – these will be the sums that the claimant expects to receive from other employment or incapacity benefits. To take account of the fact that the claimant will receive the award for future loss all at once, rather than spread out over a number of years, the sum claimed for future loss should be reduced by the same percentage by which the sum claimed for immediate loss was increased.

Once the total losses have been set out in the schedule of loss, it is necessary to consider any deductions or adjustments that should be made. The types of adjustment and deduction that can be made in an unfair dismissal claim, along with the order in which they should be made, are explored in detail in Chapter 16, 'Compensatory awards: adjustments'. Claimants often dispute, or do not own up to, the applicability of deductions and adjustments that may be unfavourable to their case. However, if it is obvious that such an adjustment will be made, it is better to include it in the schedule and increase its overall credibility with the tribunal. Note that, where the claimant has received a redundancy payment (contractual or statutory), the final deduction should be the extent to which the payment exceeds the amount of the basic award.

14.137 Unless the claim is one of those to which the statutory cap of, currently, £78,335 or a year's pay (whichever is the lower) does not apply (see 'Nature and maximum amount of award – amount of week's pay and statutory cap' above), the total amount claimed should not exceed the cap. It would, however, seem prudent to list the full extent of the losses and then apply the cap, as this is likely to make the tribunal's task in calculating compensation somewhat easier.

If the unfair dismissal claim is accompanied by a complaint of discrimination (e.g. based on the allegation that a dismissal was both unfair and discriminatory on, say, the ground of race), then the claimant will want to consider any additional financial loss, injury to feelings, personal injury, aggravated damages (in particularly serious cases of discrimination) and interest. Such sums should be clearly marked and kept separate from the compensation for unfair dismissal, since there is no guarantee that the tribunal will uphold both complaints. For more details on these elements of compensation, see IDS Employment Law

Handbook, 'Discrimination at Work' (2012), Chapter 36, 'Compensation: heads of damage'.

From the employer's point of view, it is good practice to prepare a counter- **14.138** schedule, particularly where the basis for calculation or the heads of loss are disputed. This will help narrow the issues in dispute and may encourage settlement. It is also the ideal place for a respondent to raise the issue of any deductions or adjustments that it thinks should be made to compensation. The employer should also ask the claimant to provide evidence of his or her attempts to mitigate loss. Remember, it is for the claimant to prove his or her loss but for the respondent to prove the claimant's failure to mitigate that loss.

As a general rule, the more accurate the claimant's schedule of loss, the fewer holes the employer will be able to pick in it, so that while the schedule should put the claimant's losses at their highest, it should not be fanciful. If wholly unrealistic, it may come back to haunt the claimant at a later stage. In particular, it may result in a loss of credibility, which may weaken the claimant's case in a general sense so far as the tribunal is concerned.

15 Compensatory awards: pension loss

Principles of loss

Tribunal guidelines

Types of pension

'Simplified loss' approach

'Substantial loss' approach

Where an employee who is a member of an occupational pension scheme is **15.1** unfairly dismissed, the loss of his or her pension rights can form one of the most important elements of the compensatory award. Sometimes the benefits of belonging to a pension scheme will form a significant part of the remuneration package and losses under this head will therefore be substantial. It often used to be the case (before the statutory limit on compensatory awards was substantially increased from £12,000 to £50,000 in October 1999) that it was obvious, even before the tribunal had finished its calculations, that the employee's total losses had exceeded the statutory limit. In such cases tribunals would frequently dispense with the need for complex actuarial calculations of pension loss. However, after the increase of the statutory cap in October 1999, and the subsequent annual inflation indexing of that figure, the scope for awarding significant sums by way of pension loss increased substantially. As a consequence, tribunals had to adopt a more sophisticated approach to the assessment of pension loss involving far more precise calculations of the monetary value of the pension rights that the employee had lost. Given, too, that this century has seen the closure of the vast majority of private sector final salary (defined benefit) pension schemes to new members – meaning that an employee who belonged to such a scheme prior to dismissal would be unlikely to obtain an equivalent pension in any future employment – claimants became more likely to seek compensation for a sustained period of pension loss.

However, this effect was mitigated by the introduction of an additional statutory cap on compensation with effect from 29 July 2013. Before that, the limit was simply a figure which was subject to review every year. In July 2013 the Employment Rights Act 1996 was amended with the effect that the upper limit on compensation became *the lower of* a year's salary or the relevant statutory figure (since 6 April 2015, £78,335) – S.124(1) and (1ZA) ERA. As such compensation includes pension loss, those who earn less than £78,335 per year are entitled to potentially much less compensation than would have

669

been the case before July 2013, and may not recover any pension loss at all depending on the circumstances. Note, however, that the statutory cap does *not* apply to certain unfair dismissal claims – see S.124(1A) ERA and Chapter 14, 'Compensatory awards: types of loss', in the section 'Nature and maximum amount of award', under 'Amount of week's pay and statutory cap – exceptions to statutory limit'. Nor does it apply to discrimination claims, where pension loss (and compensation generally) is otherwise assessed according to the same principles as apply to unfair dismissal – see IDS Employment Law Handbook, 'Discrimination at Work' (2012), Chapter 36, 'Compensation: heads of damage', under 'Pension loss'. Thus, where a claimant falls within an exception, or successfully claims both unfair dismissal and discrimination, he or she is likely to recover full pension loss and the way in which this is assessed is more likely to be critical.

15.2 Principles of loss

While the process for calculating pension loss can be very different to that for calculating loss of earnings, the fundamental principles are the same: the tribunal should award such amount as it considers just and equitable in all the circumstances, having regard to the loss sustained by the complainant in consequence of the dismissal in so far as that loss is attributable to action taken by the employer – S.123 Employment Rights Act 1996 (ERA) (see Chapter 14, 'Compensatory awards: types of loss'). The fact that an employment tribunal, rather than a civil court, is tasked with calculating the loss should not be overlooked. The discretion and flexibility afforded to tribunals by the 'just and equitable' formula in S.123 is substantial, and means that tribunals can adopt a relatively broad-brush approach to calculating pension loss that might not be acceptable in, for example, a High Court personal injury claim. Successful appeals are therefore rare. An award may be overturned only where there is a misdirection as to legal principle or perversity in a tribunal's decision – see, for example, Aegon UK Corporate Services Ltd v Roberts 2010 ICR 596, CA (discussed under 'Relationship with loss of earnings' below).

In Somerset County Council v Chaloner EAT 0063/14 the EAT explained that there are three stages to the assessment of compensation under S.123. First, the tribunal has to undertake a factual quantification of the losses claimed. Secondly, it has to assess the extent to which any or all of those losses are attributable to the dismissal or action taken by the employer: that is, to see whether there is a direct and natural link between the losses claimed and the employer's conduct in dismissing. Thirdly, in all the circumstances, taking into account its conclusions reached on the first and second questions, the tribunal must ask what award would be just and equitable. These principles are as applicable to determining an appropriate award in respect of pensions loss as they are to determining compensation generally.

Relationship with loss of earnings 15.3

For practical reasons, pension loss is generally dealt with by tribunals as a separate head of loss, distinct from immediate and future loss of earnings. However, in reality, a pension is merely part of an employee's remuneration package – Aegon UK Corporate Services Ltd v Roberts 2010 ICR 596, CA. In that case the tribunal found that the claimant was unlikely ever again to enjoy membership of a final salary pension scheme. However, it also found that, even taking into account her pension loss, the remuneration package she received in the new job was more favourable than that which she had enjoyed with the respondent. The tribunal considered that, upon the claimant gaining new employment, the chain of causation had been broken in respect of the loss of earnings, but it nevertheless awarded a sum to reflect the loss of a final salary pension. Although the EAT endorsed this approach, Lord Justice Elias in the Court of Appeal stated that pensions do not enjoy any special status in the calculation of loss, are essentially part of the remuneration package (albeit in a deferred form), and must be assessed according to the same principles as loss of earnings. The tribunal had erred in applying a different standard of causation to pension loss, and the EAT had been wrong to class a final salary pension as an 'unquantifiable benefit' that justified different treatment: tribunals must translate pension loss into monetary terms, no matter how difficult and speculative the exercise, otherwise assessing loss would be impossible.

Although the Aegon decision makes it clear that a tribunal cannot apply different standards of causation to pension loss and loss of earnings, a tribunal is not bound to find that both types of loss will end at the same time. In Bentwood Bros (Manchester) Ltd v Shepherd 2003 ICR 1000, CA, the tribunal awarded compensation for loss of earnings for a period of two and a half years, but went on to award compensation for pension loss for a period of ten years. Although the Court of Appeal was surprised by the finding that the claimant would never again gain pensionable employment, that finding was supported by evidence and was therefore neither perverse nor an error of law.

Burden of proof 15.4

In an unfair dismissal case, the burden of proving loss lies firmly on the employee, so if he or she claims loss of pension rights as an element of compensation it is up to him or her to prove what that loss is – Copson and anor v Eversure Accessories Ltd 1974 ICR 636, NIRC. In that case the National Industrial Relations Court (the predecessor to the EAT) said that tribunals should help claimants in appropriate cases: if it is apparent that there is a pension scheme and that its details are relevant, the tribunal should tell the employee that he or she is entitled to apply for an order requiring the employer to disclose those details. In Tidman v Aveling Marshall Ltd 1977 ICR 506, EAT, the EAT went further and said that it is the duty of the tribunal to enquire into possible heads of compensation and to raise the issue of pension rights:

while proof of loss still rests with the claimant, tribunals should be generous with unrepresented claimants.

Tribunals and appellate courts may be less sympathetic to claimants who are legally represented or who ought to understand their pension scheme, however. For example, in Cawthorn and Sinclair Ltd v Hedger 1974 ICR 146, NIRC, the NIRC thought that the assessment by a tribunal of H's pension loss was ungenerous but refused to change it. As Sir Hugh Griffiths said: 'The burden of proving a loss lies upon the employee. He had made scant attempt to discharge it in this case.' H had been the Chief Accountant and could have been expected to be familiar with the company pension scheme.

15.5 Tribunal guidelines

Although no *statutory* guidance is given as to how the calculation of pension loss is to be made, tribunals may refer to guidelines prepared by a committee of employment judges in consultation with the Government Actuary's Department, first issued in 1990. The revised third edition, entitled 'Compensation for loss of pension rights: Employment Tribunals', was published in 2003. This booklet – referred to as the 'tribunal guidelines' throughout this chapter – has proved highly valuable for tribunals and representatives alike and is available online from The Stationery Office and the Government website. The tribunal guidelines offer two alternative methods to assessing pension loss. They suggest that the one likely to be appropriate in the majority of cases is what is termed, in the guidelines, the 'simplified approach'. This method, which is retained from previous editions of the guidelines but was formerly called the 'contributions method', is discussed under '"Simplified loss" approach' below. The third edition of the tribunal guidelines also introduced a new method – the 'substantial loss approach' – which is akin to the method for assessing pension loss in cases of personal injury. This is likely to be relevant in more complex cases requiring actuarial input where there is potential career-long loss, and is discussed under '"Substantial loss" approach' below.

The page on the Government website hosting the tribunal guidelines warns that they are 'now out of date and have been withdrawn', presumably on the basis of Lord Justice Underhill's comments in Griffin v Plymouth Hospital NHS Trust 2015 ICR 347, CA. In that case (discussed under '"Substantial loss" approach' below) Underhill LJ called for an updated version of the tribunal guidelines, observing that while the guidelines were extremely valuable, there had been a number of important changes in pension law and practice since the current edition was published in 2003, and the extent to which its recommendations on particular points remained valid would need to be considered increasingly carefully. However, the President of Employment Tribunals (England and Wales), Judge Doyle, confirmed at a meeting of the Employment Tribunal National User Group on 13 March 2015 that the judicial

672

position is that the 2003 tribunal guidelines may still be used. According to the President, it is for the parties to consider how best to put their case on pensions loss: in many cases, the existing tribunal guidelines will be adequate to the calculation; in other cases, tribunals will require actuarial evidence and legal submissions to assist them in an appropriate calculation. Nevertheless, the two Presidents in England and Wales and in Scotland (Judge Doyle and Judge Simon) have set up a working group to develop proposals for wider consultation later in 2015 to amend and update the tribunal guidelines. It is possible that this will result in Presidential Guidance on the calculation of pensions loss rather than the publication of a new edition of the existing guidelines. (See National employment tribunal national user group minutes, March 2015, available on www.gov.uk.)

Although the original tribunal guidelines received the general approval of the **15.6** EAT in Benson v Dairy Crest Ltd EAT 192/89 and the method of assessing pension loss has been gratefully adopted by tribunals, it should be stressed that they remain only guidelines and, as such, have no statutory force. In Bingham v Hobourn Engineering Ltd 1992 IRLR 298, EAT, the Appeal Tribunal held that the tribunal did not commit an error of law when it failed to follow exactly the scheme recommended in the then extant guidelines. Mr Justice Knox said the booklet was a 'valuable guide', but added that the factors in each case should be evaluated to see what adjustment should be made or whether, in the circumstances, the guidelines were a safe guide at all. The Court of Appeal has since reiterated that 'it should not be assumed that [using the tribunal guidelines] will be the correct approach in every case' – Griffin v Plymouth Hospital NHS Trust (above).

Indeed, in Port of Tilbury (London) Ltd v Birch and ors 2005 IRLR 92, EAT, the EAT ruled that a tribunal had erred in preferring, without detailed explanation, the simplified approach recommended in the tribunal guidelines to the alternative approaches advocated by the legal representatives of the parties in that case. The EAT observed: 'The point about the [tribunal guidelines] is that [they] may assist an employment tribunal when there is little forthcoming from the parties as to how to approach what is recognised to be a difficult area, that is to say assessing a proper compensation of loss of pension rights... [W]here the parties or one of the parties puts forward credible evidence and submissions on that matter, it seems to us that the first duty of the tribunal is to consider that evidence and those submissions in order to ascertain whether a fair and equitable assessment of the loss of pension rights can be worked out on that basis. If it cannot, the employment tribunal must adequately explain why not. To say... that it rejects the parties' submissions entirely on the basis that it is not one suggested in the booklet is in our view an error of law.'

Despite the fact that a tribunal is not bound to use the tribunal guidelines, if it **15.7** considers it appropriate to do so then the appellate courts are entitled to have

673

regard to the wording of the guidelines in determining whether the tribunal erred in choosing the simplified approach over the substantial approach, or vice versa – Sibbit v Governing Body of St Cuthbert's Catholic Primary School EAT 0070/10. Thus, in Griffin v Plymouth Hospitals NHS Trust (above), the Court of Appeal rejected a submission that a tribunal's decision to adopt the simplified approach was a matter for its discretion. The only conclusion open to the tribunal, in the circumstances of the case and in the light of its other findings, was that it should follow the substantial loss approach. (For further discussion, see '"Substantial loss" approach' below.)

In Greenhoff v Barnsley Metropolitan Borough Council 2006 ICR 1514, EAT, a tribunal's award of pension loss was overturned on the basis that it had failed to explain why it had adopted the approach it did in preference to either of the approaches set out in the tribunal guidelines. The EAT suggested that tribunals could avoid many of the problems that arise in such cases by:

- identifying all possible benefits that the employee could obtain under the pension scheme

- setting out the terms of the pension scheme relevant to each benefit

- considering in respect of each such possible benefit, first, the advantages and disadvantages of applying the 'simplified loss approach' or the 'substantial loss approach' (see '"Simplified loss" approach' and '"Substantial loss" approach' below) and also any other approach that might be considered appropriate by the tribunal or the parties

- explaining why it adopted a particular approach and rejected any other possible approach; and

- setting out its conclusions and explaining the compensation arrived at in respect of each head of claim so that the parties and the EAT can then ascertain if it has made an error.

15.8 The EAT held that a tribunal had failed to follow this approach in Tan v Solihull Community Housing Ltd EAT 0050/14 because it had not given sufficient reasons for reducing its award for pension loss by 85 per cent. It had merely accepted the employer's suggestion that a 15 per cent chance of continued employment was 'realistic', without analysing the factors relied on by the employer and contested by the claimant. And in Lund v St Edmund's School, Canterbury 2013 ICR D26, EAT, the EAT overturned a tribunal's award relating to pension loss because it had simply assumed that since L had asked for his loss to be calculated by reference to the employer's contributions towards his pension, no alternative methodology of calculating it needed to be considered.

Types of pension

15.9

Before we consider the different types of pension loss that may occur when an employee is dismissed, it is helpful to look at the various types of pension available. Very generally, an occupational pension scheme is a scheme dependent on contributions by the employer and (usually) the employee that provides for a pension on retirement at a level over and above that provided by the state scheme.

State scheme

15.10

The state scheme is made up of the following components:

- basic state pension – a flat-rate pension (i.e. independent of earnings levels) payable to all who attain the state pension age provided that certain contribution requirements have been met

- SERPS – the state earnings-related pension scheme (also known as the additional state pension), which varies according to an employee's earnings between the lower and upper earnings limit on which he or she paid full national insurance contributions between April 1978 and March 2002

- S2P – the state second pension brought in to replace SERPS from April 2002 to April 2016. The main reason for the change was to provide a more generous pension provision for people earning less than the lower earnings limit.

These components are being replaced with a new single state pension scheme for those who reach state pension age on or after 6 April 2016.

It is possible for employers to *contract out* of the additional state pension any employees who are members of an occupational pension scheme that satisfies certain criteria. It is also possible for individual employees to opt out of the additional state pension and/or their employers' schemes and to operate their own personal pension scheme. Some employers make contributions to personal schemes. The tribunal guidelines recommend the assumption that there is no loss of basic state pension on dismissal. The onus is then on the employee to prove otherwise. However, if a dismissed employee who is not in a contracted-out occupational or personal pension scheme is dismissed, he or she may lose the second state pension element for the period of unemployment and this is an area of potential loss that should be covered.

Types of occupational scheme

15.11

There are two basic types of occupational pension scheme: 'final salary' schemes and 'money purchase' schemes. These are also called 'defined benefit' schemes and 'defined contribution' schemes respectively – names that more clearly indicate their nature.

675

15.12 **Final salary schemes.** Under defined benefit schemes, the pension benefits received on retirement are based on a proportion of pensionable pay as at retirement multiplied by the number of years of pensionable service. Typically, benefits are calculated at 1/60th or 1/80th of final salary for each year of pensionable service. Thus, if an employee retires on a salary of £30,000 pa after 25 years' pensionable service and the scheme is based on 1/60th of final salary, he or she will receive an annual pension of 25/60 x £30,000 = £12,500.

The employer's contributions to a final salary scheme are not fixed: the employer simply undertakes to put into the scheme whatever is necessary to provide the scheme's members with the final predefined benefits. The employer's contributions are not earmarked for the benefit of any individual employee and individual pensions will not necessarily be directly related to the employee's and the employer's contributions. Typically, an employer's contributions to a 'good' occupational pension scheme – i.e. one that provides a level of benefit significantly better than SERPS or S2P – will, if it is a contributory scheme, be 20 per cent of the total payroll of scheme members. The employees' contributions, if any, are usually around 5 per cent of salary.

15.13 Final salary schemes come in different shapes and sizes. The essential point, however, is that they are based on predefined rules relating to the employee's earnings and years of pensionable service and not to contributions to the pension fund (whether from employee or employer). Final salary schemes are becoming increasingly rare due to the cost to the employer and the difficulties in budgeting accurately as to the employer's liability for such an open-ended commitment. As a result, over recent years, many employers have diluted the fraction of final salary payable or have closed their final salary schemes to new members. In some cases, employers have even closed the final salary scheme to existing members and have opted to offer money purchase schemes instead.

Although non-funded schemes (such as some that exist in the public sector) may seem different to normal final salary schemes because they lack a fund, the tribunal guidelines assert that membership of such a scheme should be treated in the same way as a normal final salary scheme, since the level of employer contributions is usually pegged as though it were funded. Deferred pensions from such schemes, though, do seem to be more generous.

15.14 Additional Voluntary Contributions (AVCs) allow an employee to top up his or her occupational pension, normally on a money purchase basis (irrespective of whether the scheme itself is final salary) and losses arising under this head should therefore be treated in the same way as money purchase schemes. As AVCs are usually only made by the employee, they have little impact on future pension loss, but as they are not transferable (unlike free-standing AVCs), the tribunal guidelines state that there may be a loss in the form of charges for setting up a replacement scheme. Some public sector schemes allow members to buy *extra years* and, in such cases, working out final salary loss will need to take those extra years into account.

Money purchase schemes. Defined contributions schemes are quite different **15.15** to final salary schemes. The contributions by either employer or employee, or both, are at predetermined rates and are earmarked for the individual employee. The ultimate benefits depend on the value of the fund built up during the employee's membership of the scheme. The amount of the pension will vary in accordance with factors such as the success of the scheme's investment policy and interest rates current at retiring age. So, if an employee has been in a scheme for 25 years, it is necessary to look at the total contributions by employer and employee, calculate the present value of those contributions, and then work out what annuity this sum will purchase.

It is comparatively easy to calculate an employee's loss arising from premature exclusion from a money purchase scheme. What has been contributed already remains invested for the benefit of the employee and what he or she loses is simply the prospective value of further contributions that would have been made by the employer. This is subject to any penalty for early leaving, but such penalty will be quantifiable under the rules of the scheme.

As final salary schemes have closed their doors to new entrants, money purchase **15.16** schemes – which are generally much cheaper to run for employers – have naturally become more prevalent. Two legislative moves have also contributed to an increasing proportion of the workforce being covered by money purchase schemes. First, the Welfare Reform and Pensions Act 1999 made it compulsory for all employers (unless there are fewer than five employees or there is already a suitable pension scheme in place) to offer their employees, as a minimum, access to a *stakeholder scheme* providing money purchase benefits. The 1999 Act does not place any obligation on an employer to make contributions to such a scheme. However, the reforms introduced by the Pensions Act 2008 go further, providing for the automatic enrolment of staff into contributory workplace pension schemes – see 'Auto-enrolment' below. As part of these reforms, the Government has established the National Employment Savings Trust, a defined contribution scheme.

Other pension options. The employer and the employee can agree for both or **15.17** either of them to make contributions to a private pension policy with a pension provider (often an individual life insurance company) of the employee's choice. This allows the employee to control the investment decisions in respect of the pension fund. In appropriate cases, such a personal pension plan vehicle can be used to contract out of SERPS and S2P. Clearly, the use of such schemes may be unwieldy for a large organisation wanting to make pension provision for its entire workforce – arrangements of this type will more commonly arise in cases involving small employers.

15.18 **Life assurance cover.** Life assurance benefits are commonly provided by pension schemes and the tribunal guidelines advise that this head of loss could be compensated by awarding an amount equal to the cost to the employee of replicating the cover on the open market.

15.19 ### Auto-enrolment

The Pensions Act 2008 represents the biggest change to occupational pension provision in a generation. It provides for the automatic enrolment of 'jobholders' (a wide category that includes employees, workers and agency workers) into a workplace pension scheme. Furthermore, the Act also requires that employers make contributions of at least 3 per cent of 'qualifying earnings', as defined by S.13 of the Pensions Act 2008.

These measures are being brought into force in stages under the Employers' Duties (Implementation) Regulations 2010 SI 2010/4. Very large employers – i.e. those with 120,000 or more members in their PAYE schemes – were covered from 1 October 2012, while employers with 50,000 or more PAYE members were covered from 1 November 2012. The scheme is being gradually extended to smaller employers, with all employers due to be covered by April 2017. The full list of dates is available from the Pensions Regulator's website.

15.20 Although many of the jobholders covered by the 2008 Act will be workers or agency workers, rather than employees, and therefore unable to claim unfair dismissal, it is likely that a large number of employees will gain pension rights for the first time as a result of the reforms. The likely effect of this will be to make pension loss a more common element of compensation for unfair dismissal, since the vast majority of dismissed employees will be losing out on pension contributions. At the same time, however, the reforms will make it easier for respondents to resist submissions that the claimant will never again find pensionable employment.

15.21 ## 'Simplified loss' approach

The 'simplified loss' approach set out in the tribunal guidelines takes the tribunal through three stages, requiring separate calculations under three distinct heads of pension loss, as follows:

- loss of enhancement of accrued pension rights – i.e. rights that had already accrued at the date of dismissal

- loss of pension rights which would have accrued during the period between the date of dismissal and the date of the tribunal hearing

- loss of future pension rights that would have accrued between the hearing date and the date of retirement.

678

Each of these three calculations is discussed below, under 'Calculating loss of enhancement of accrued rights', 'Calculating loss between dismissal and remedies hearing', and 'Calculating loss of future pension rights'.

When to use simplified loss approach 15.22

As noted above under 'Tribunal guidelines', the tribunal guidelines suggest that the simplified approach will be suitable to use in the majority of cases. The attraction of this approach is that it does not require tribunals to embark on an assessment of whole career loss, which can be a difficult task given the uncertainties of employment in modern economic conditions. However, if the circumstances of the case indicate that it is appropriate to use the substantial loss approach, then a tribunal will be liable to err if it uses the simplified loss approach instead. So a tribunal considering which approach to use will need to consider whether factors are present that indicate that the substantial loss approach would be appropriate – see '"Substantial loss" approach – when to use substantial loss approach' below. In particular, where there is a clearly quantifiable continuing loss – because, for example, the claimant will not find new employment before retiring, or because he or she has found or will find new employment and the new pension provision, if any, is quantifiable – the simplified approach is not appropriate.

Coker v Wandsworth Borough Council EAT 0421/13 is an example of a case in which a tribunal was justified in adopting the simplified loss approach. C was unfairly constructively dismissed while she was on sick leave. An employment tribunal found that had she not been unfairly dismissed she would have remained off sick until her entitlement to sick pay ran out and then resigned. As this meant that her employment would have ended within a year, and there was no question of career-long loss, it used the simplified loss approach to calculate her pension award. The EAT upheld this aspect of its decision. Given the tribunal's finding that C would have resigned in the near future, there was no substantial loss of pension rights and therefore the substantial loss approach was inapplicable.

Calculating loss of enhancement of accrued rights 15.23

As a result of dismissal, the employee may have lost the benefit of further enhancement of the rights that have already accrued under the pension scheme. If the scheme is a *money purchase scheme*, calculation of loss in this respect does not present a particular problem because the sums invested on behalf of the employee up to dismissal remain invested and will hopefully continue to increase in value. There may be a penalty for leaving the scheme early but this will be easily quantifiable.

Things are much more complicated if the scheme is a *final salary scheme*. To explain what the employee stands to lose, it is first necessary to explain the concept of a *deferred pension*. This is what a member of a final salary scheme

679

becomes entitled to if he or she leaves the scheme early – e.g. where the employee is dismissed before reaching retirement age. A deferred pension is a pension payable in the future on what would have been the employee's retirement date but calculated with reference to the employee's earnings and service at the date of dismissal. So, if the scheme is based on 1/60th of final salary for each year, and the employee has ten years' pensionable service, the entitlement will be to 10/60ths of the employee's earnings at the date of dismissal. If those earnings were £30,000, this will mean a basic deferred pension of £5,000 a year.

15.24 The problem that arises is that the simplified approach uses the employee's salary at the date employment terminated as the 'final' salary. In fact, the employee *might* have remained with the employer and retired with a substantially higher final salary, significantly more years of service and, consequently, a much more valuable pension. In this sense the employee stands to lose a considerable amount. Suppose the same employee had worked for another ten years and then retired normally on a salary of £45,000. His or her pension would have been 20/60ths x £45,000 = £15,000, £7,500 of which would relate to the first ten years of service. So, by enforced early leaving the employee has lost £2,500 a year between retirement and death – the difference between £7,500 and £5,000 – even on the assumption that he or she moves into a new job with identical salary, pension scheme and salary progression.

In order to provide a measure of protection to employees in these circumstances, the Pension Schemes Act 1993 requires that the deferred pension be revalued in line with increases to the cost of living index up to retirement age (when the deferred pension becomes payable) subject to a maximum increase of 5 per cent per annum over the accumulation period. (Note that the annual rate of increase after retirement age will depend on the rules of the scheme.) However, as the tribunal guidelines point out, the modest protection against inflation provided by the 1993 Act does not necessarily prevent loss of enhancement of accrued pension rights in the way outlined above because the employee's salary may have increased at a faster rate than 5 per cent (and at a faster rate than inflation). In other words, loss relating to the accrued rights could still occur and the compensatory award must reflect this.

15.25 Under Part IV of the Pension Schemes Act 1993, an individual can require his or her ex-employer to transfer the value of his or her accrued pension either to a comparable scheme operated by the new employer or to a personal pension scheme, where compatible. The tribunal guidelines remark, however, that there is a common fallacy that an employee who requests such a transfer suffers no financial loss. In fact, in most cases in the private sector (though not necessarily in the public sector), the transfer value will be assessed on the basis of the value of the deferred pension alone, which means, of course, that loss of accrued rights will still need to be compensated.

680

Many imponderables arise when assessing loss of accrued rights. For example, the employee might have received a wage rise and a better pension through being promoted. On the other hand, the company might have gone into liquidation or the employee might have been fairly dismissed or resigned from the job at a later date. Once again, the tribunal is asked to look to the future and to attempt to estimate how far and for how long losses incurred by the employee are attributable to the unfair dismissal. Helpfully, in view of these exigencies, the tribunal guidelines provide a revised and simplified actuarial method for conducting the initial valuation of losses relating to accrued rights. Once losses have been calculated using this method, the tribunal can make deductions to take account of the various contingencies that may have caused the employee to withdraw from the scheme for a reason other than unfair dismissal.

15.26 The guidelines recommend two ways of dealing with the loss of enhancement of accrued rights, depending on the circumstances. These are:

- awarding no compensation at all

- using the simplified actuarial method.

15.27 **No compensation.** There are certain categories of case in which it is thought right not to make any award of compensation in respect of accrued pension rights, although there may well be compensation payable in respect of loss between dismissal and the tribunal hearing and future loss. These are where:

- the employee is within five years of normal retiring age (the previous guidelines limited this exception to private sector schemes but the current version makes no such distinction)

- the tribunal finds that employment would have ended in any event within a year. For example, in Coker v Wandsworth Borough Council EAT 0421/13 the EAT upheld a tribunal's decision not to make an award for loss of enhancement of accrued pension rights on the basis of its finding that the employee would in any event have resigned once her sick pay ran out within the year.

(There is a potential third category which is absent from the revised guidelines – i.e. inflation-proofed public sector schemes that are not subject to the 5 per cent formula.)

15.28 The first of the above categories assumes that little or no loss of enhancement will occur in so short a space of time. However, this is based on the assumption that the statutory indexation of 5 per cent is reasonable. Where price increases run at substantially more than 5 per cent, this assumption may need to be reviewed. Additionally, earnings often rise faster than prices, so inflation-proofing based solely on price increases may not correspond to anticipated increases in salary.

681

15.29 **Actuarial method.** The tribunal guidelines contain a simplified actuarial method, produced by the Government Actuary's Department, to assess the losses relating to accrued rights that are incurred by employees with more than five years to go until retirement. The method consists of a table of multipliers based on the employee's age, normal retirement age under the scheme, sex, and whether the scheme is a public or private sector one (see Appendix 4 to the guidelines). The appropriate multiplier is applied to the deferred pension to which the employee is entitled. The resulting figure represents the initial assessment of the employee's losses for loss of enhancement of accrued rights from which any appropriate deductions should then be made.

Taking the example of a male private sector employee who was 51 years old when dismissed, whose normal retirement age would have been 60, and who is entitled to a deferred pension of £6,000: the appropriate multiplier from the table will be 1.99. Therefore, the initial assessment of losses relating to the employee's accrued rights will be just under £12,000. This is not the end of the matter, however. The table assumes that the employee would not have left the employment for any reason other than death or disability. Employees do, of course, frequently leave their employment for other reasons. It is to take account of possibilities such as this that the tribunal may subsequently reduce the figure – see 'Deductions for "withdrawal factor"' below.

15.30 The Government Actuary's Department table makes various assumptions (which take into account both inflation and taxation considerations). If these assumptions are inappropriate, then adjustments will have to be made to the method used. These assumptions are that:

- private sector pensions are based on a defined amount of pension (usually 1/60th of final salary), of which part can be taken as a lump sum. Public sector schemes have a lump sum payable in addition to the pension – equal to three years of pension payments at the initial rate

- there is a widow(er)'s pension at 50 per cent of the employee's rate

- the maximum possible amount is taken as a lump sum

- post-retirement, pensions increase annually in line with the Retail Prices Index (up to 5 per cent in the private sector)

- contracting-out is ignored.

15.31 **Deductions for 'withdrawal factor'.** The tribunal guidelines expressly state that the table of multipliers assumes that the employee would not have left his or her employment before retirement for any reason other than death or disability. As mentioned previously, there may be a number of factors in a particular case which make this assumption incorrect. As we have seen, a tribunal is likely to make deductions from the figure that is produced by the actuarial calculation to take account of any of the multitude of reasons which might have caused the employee to leave the employment at a later date even if he or she had not been unfairly dismissed. The Government Actuary's Department used to provide a table of age-based reduction factors to take account of the likelihood of withdrawal before normal retiring age. However, the tribunal guidelines conclude that it is inappropriate to set a percentage 'withdrawal factor' calculation by reference to a table, and that this percentage is best left to the discretion of the tribunal which has had the benefit of hearing the case and seeing the parties. (It should be noted that the appropriate reduction is not the same as the likelihood that the employee would have left employment anyway: if he or she had stayed for a few more years, the accrued pension would still have been enhanced.)

The matters which an employment tribunal may take into account when assessing the likelihood of early withdrawal include the age, work record, status and health of the claimant and the strength of the former employer's business. For example, in Hearne v Manpower Ltd ET Case No.27327/82 – a case which dates from the period when the Government Actuary's Department provided tables of withdrawal factors – the employer argued for a withdrawal factor of 50 per cent, on the basis of very high turnover and mobility of labour in its particular industry. The tribunal accepted that a high withdrawal factor would be justified for many employees, but not for the claimant. The evidence showed he was a 'stayer', who had voluntarily changed his job only once, and so the tribunal used a withdrawal factor of 20 per cent.

15.32 Another case dating from that period is TBA Industrial Products Ltd v Locke 1984 ICR 228, EAT, where a tribunal applied a high withdrawal factor of 70 per cent because it thought there was a high degree of probability that L would have been fairly dismissed in any event, either for redundancy or because of his unsatisfactory work performance. It then further reduced L's overall compensatory award by an additional 70 per cent to reflect L's conduct contributing to his dismissal. L argued on appeal that this meant that he was being penalised twice over for his poor work performance. The EAT, however, said that the tribunal had been quite correct because it had taken L's performance into account for two distinct purposes – assessing the present value of L's future pension rights and reducing his compensation because of his contribution to his own dismissal.

Note that the guidelines stress that no calculation of the value of accrued rights is necessary if the tribunal is adopting the 'substantial loss' approach to assessing future loss (as this head of loss is already built into the actuarial calculation). This approach is discussed in detail later in this chapter under '"Substantial loss" approach'.

15.33 **Calculating loss between dismissal and remedies hearing**

If the pension is a *money purchase scheme*, assessing the loss between the dismissal and the hearing is simply a matter of calculating the value of the additional contributions which the employer would have made to the employee's pension during this time. An early leaver may also be required to pay a penalty and this loss, which is easily quantifiable, should be factored in.

The position in relation to assessing losses arising from early departure from a *final salary scheme* is more complex because the employer's contributions towards an individual's pension are not predetermined. What the employee has actually lost is the prospective right to a pension based on his or her final salary on retirement. The loss is therefore the difference between the deferred pension (inclusive of cost of living rises and other benefits) to which the employee is entitled and the pension and other benefits which would have been received had the dismissal not taken place.

15.34 In terms of assessing the value of the loss of final salary pension rights between dismissal and the remedies hearing, the tribunal guidelines recognise that the actual loss is the difference between the actual deferred pension received and the slightly higher one for which the employee would have qualified had he or she remained employed for that extra period. However, for the sake of simplicity (and in the interests of what the authors of the guidelines believe is most just and equitable to both parties), the guidelines advocate looking not at the additional contingent benefits that would have accrued but rather at the contributions that the employer would have made to the pension fund during this period. The guidelines therefore recommend basing compensation for the period between the dismissal and the remedies hearing on the notional contributions that the employer would have made towards the employee's pension had the employee still been in employment. The weekly loss figure is then simply multiplied by the number of weeks between the dismissal and the hearing.

As the guidelines recognise, this is not a technically correct approach because, where the scheme in question is final salary, the employer does not in fact make a specific contribution to each individual employee's pension; instead, it makes a contribution to the general pension fund that represents a percentage of the total pensionable wage bill. The actual percentage payable under the scheme is normally shown in the scheme's actuarial report. The proportion of this percentage that is attributable to the individual employee usually increases with age. While in a simple case it might be considered unnecessary to try to allow for this, not to do so can make a difference of as much as 25 per cent to the multiplicand. Accordingly, in more complex cases or in those in which age is an issue, tribunals should apply the factors in Tables 1 and 2 of Appendix 7 to the guidelines in order to make the appropriate adjustment.

15.35 Tribunals should always be sensitive to arguments in a particular case that, owing to the nature of the scheme in question or the claimant's personal

684

circumstances, losses are more or less substantial during this period than the broad-brush method discussed above allows for. In Forshaw v Forshaw Ltd EAT 0462/03 the EAT allowed an appeal on the basis that the tribunal had failed to consider the claimant's argument that he had lost 'notional contributions' to a small self-administrated pension scheme (effectively a hybrid scheme in which benefits were calculated on a money purchase basis) even though no actual contributions had been made to the scheme during the period in question.

The following points should also be noted:

- pensionable pay may not be the same as actual pay. Pensionable pay may be restricted to basic pay and may exclude fluctuating payments such as bonuses, commission and overtime. It will be up to the employer to produce evidence to challenge the assumption that gross pay is equivalent to pensionable pay

- the percentage contributed by the employer may not be known. In this case a standard figure of 20 per cent of payroll (15 per cent from the employer and 5 per cent from the employee) should be assumed, according to the tribunal guidelines

- the percentage currently contributed by the employer may be anomalous – e.g. because of a 'contributions holiday'. The guidelines recommend that calculations take no account of such anomalies

- pension provision is not part of pay for the purposes of the Recoupment Regulations and this element of compensation is not therefore subject to recoupment of social security benefits (see Chapter 18, 'Recoupment').

15.36 Finally, and importantly, the guidelines stress that, as with the calculation of the value of accrued rights, calculating loss between dismissal and the remedies hearing is not necessary if the tribunal is adopting the 'substantial loss' approach to assessing future loss (as this head of loss is already built into the actuarial calculation). This approach is discussed in detail later in this chapter under '"Substantial loss" approach'.

Calculating loss of future pension rights

15.37 The employee's loss on dismissal may include loss of benefits that would have accrued under the employer's pension scheme if he or she had continued to be in the same employment beyond the date of the hearing. Where the period of loss of future earnings is unlikely to exceed two years, the tribunal guidelines recommend using employer's contributions (or notional contributions in the case of final salary schemes) as the basis for calculating compensation for loss of future pension rights (i.e. the same basis as for calculating losses from dismissal to the date of the remedies hearing set out above). Where pension loss beyond two years is being claimed, the substantial loss formula rather than the simplified approach should normally be adopted – Orthet Ltd v Vince-Cain 2005 ICR 374, EAT.

The guidelines also advise that the simplified approach should only be used in circumstances where the tribunal decides that, when the claimant finds employment, it will be either with a comparable pension scheme or at a higher salary to offset the absence of such a scheme. In Lund v St Edmund's School, Canterbury 2013 ICR D26, EAT, the EAT overturned a tribunal's award relating to pension loss in part because the tribunal had failed to make any finding as to the chances of L, who was about five years from retirement, obtaining *pensionable* alternative employment following his dismissal. The EAT observed that this was a critical component in determining what methodology should be used to assess his pension loss.

15.38 Where the lost pension is a money purchase scheme, the guidelines state that the future loss during the relevant period (i.e. from the date of the tribunal hearing until the estimated date when the claimant will enter new employment with equivalent pension provision) is calculated by aggregating the contributions that the employer would have made during this period (bearing in mind that they are tax-free). A discount for accelerated receipt should then be made.

Where the lost pension was a final salary scheme, the same approach should be adopted using the notional contributions approach (the same as set out under 'Calculating loss between dismissal and remedies hearing' above). Again, a deduction for accelerated receipt must be made. Any contributions holiday or other anomaly should be ignored and, as before, account should be taken of the difference in contributions applicable for older claimants.

15.39 Where there is no pension scheme or the employee was in a scheme which was not contracted out, losses may still arise as a result of S2P not accruing. A chart to calculate the value of this loss, using a simple formula, is set out in Appendix 3 to the tribunal guidelines.

The simplified approach does not deal specifically with the situation where the employee has *already* found a new job. In these circumstances, there are two possibilities:

- there is a pension scheme in the new job. In this case, the tribunal will have to evaluate this new scheme against the old one. A simple method will be to compare the employer's contributions under the new scheme with the employer's contributions under the old scheme and to treat the difference as the loss (or profit)

- there is no pension scheme in the new job. In this case, any continuing loss of earnings will have to be increased by the continuing loss of the previous employer's pension contributions.

If earnings in the new job are higher than in the old, this may compensate for **15.40** the loss of pension rights. This was the case in Aegon UK Corporate Services Ltd v Roberts 2010 ICR 596, CA, where the Court rejected the notion that the loss of a final salary pension was an 'unquantifiable' benefit that could not be covered by the increase in the employee's earnings (see 'Principles of loss – relationship with loss of earnings' above). If, however, the new earnings are lower, the tribunal may be able to estimate when they will rise to a sufficiently high level to compensate for the absence of a pension scheme. The same logic applies to the situation where the employee elects to become self-employed after being dismissed (and such action is found to be reasonable mitigation of his or her loss).

Finally, two further points should be made about future loss generally. First, such loss may include the lost opportunity of joining a pension scheme where the employee is dismissed from a job that is covered by a scheme that has a qualifying period or age and the employee has not yet qualified. Entitlement will probably depend upon whether or not the employee is considered a 'stayer'. In Samuels v Clifford Chance EAT 559/90 employees did not qualify for the occupational pension scheme until they had completed five years' service at the firm. S was unfairly dismissed after two and a half years' service and the tribunal therefore had to assess the likelihood that she would, but for her dismissal, have remained with the firm for the further two and a half years necessary to qualify. The tribunal looked at S's curriculum vitae, which showed that she had never in fact stayed with one employer for as long as five years. It also heard her own testimony as to her intentions prior to her dismissal. The tribunal came to the conclusion that there was no guarantee that she would have stayed in CC's employ for five years and declined to make any award in respect of loss of pension rights. On appeal, the EAT upheld the tribunal's decision. (It should be noted, however, that substantial qualifying periods in respect of membership of occupational pension schemes are, these days, unusual.)

Secondly, tribunals tend to restrict awards for future loss to a period of months **15.41** rather than years (and this is in line with the guidelines' recommendation of a fixed period of up to two years in most cases). But this is not always so. In Hearne v Manpower Ltd ET Case No.27327/82, for example, H was unfairly dismissed at the age of 43. He rapidly found a job in the same industry but with no occupational pension scheme. It was agreed that his pension loss was £563 a year. The employer argued that only two years' loss should be awarded because of the high labour turnover in the industry and the chance that H would soon find another job with a pension scheme. H argued that he was a natural 'stayer' who would not change jobs at his age and that the award should therefore be of 22 years' loss – i.e. to retiring age. The tribunal agreed that H was unlikely to move and that he had no foreseeable prospects of a pension scheme. It thought, however, that compensating him up to retiring age

687

was pushing matters too far because of imponderables and it settled for a ten-year multiplier to apply to his annual loss.

It is important to note that the above calculations for future loss should not be applied if the 'substantial loss' approach is being adopted (as this head of loss is already built into the actuarial calculation). The appropriate method if such circumstances apply is set out below.

15.42 'Substantial loss' approach

If the circumstances indicate that the tribunal should be endeavouring to calculate pension loss for the whole of the claimant's remaining career, then the substantial loss approach should be used. This is especially useful in calculating loss from defined benefit schemes. Broadly, it uses actuarial tables to find the value of the pension rights the claimant could have accrued to retirement had he or she remained in employment, and then deducts the value of the pension actually accrued as at the date of dismissal, and the value of any pension he or she is expected to build up to retirement age in any new employment. This approach is discussed in more detail under 'Calculation of long-term loss', '"Withdrawal factor" deductions' and 'Other considerations' below.

15.43 Ogden tables and multipliers

The tribunal guidelines note that the Ogden tables, which are prepared by the Government Actuary's Department for use in personal injury cases, are also occasionally used by tribunals for assessing future loss of earnings – see Chapter 14, 'Compensatory awards: types of loss', under 'Future loss – career-long loss'. In Kingston Upon Hull City Council v Dunnachie (No.3) 2004 ICR 227, EAT, the EAT approved the use of the Ogden tables in circumstances where career-long loss of earnings was being assessed. However, it stated: 'Nothing that we have said in the course of this judgment (or indeed that was addressed to us in argument) impinges on the question of the applicability of the use of Ogden Tables in relation to pension loss, where different questions may arise.' The issue was therefore left open until the EAT in Evans v Barclays Bank plc EAT 0137/09 held that a tribunal had not erred by using the Ogden tables in preference to the guidelines when assessing the career-long loss a claimant had experienced upon being dismissed from a role that carried with it a final salary pension scheme.

However, while the Ogden tables *may* be used by a tribunal in determining the degree of pension loss (in the sense that it is not necessarily an error of law for a tribunal to use them), it is submitted that the more appropriate tables for a tribunal to use would be the tables of multipliers for pension loss set out in the appendices to the tribunal guidelines. Like the Ogden tables, these are prepared by the Government Actuary's Department. However, unlike the Ogden tables, they have been expressly designed by the Actuary for the purpose of assessing long-term or complex pension loss.

When to use substantial loss approach

15.44

Generally speaking, the tribunal guidelines advocate that the use of the substantial loss approach be restricted to those cases where the claimant was a long-standing employee, in a stable job, whose age means he or she would be unlikely to be looking to move. However, it is important to note that these are not essential requirements, but rather factors that increase the likelihood that the employee would, but for the dismissal, *still have been an active member of his or her pension scheme at retirement* – Griffin v Plymouth Hospital NHS Trust 2015 ICR 347, CA. Depending on the circumstances, it may be suitable to use the substantial loss approach even where the claimant was relatively young at the time of dismissal. In the Griffin case, Lord Justice Underhill noted that circumstances which increase this likelihood tend to justify the use of the substantial loss approach because this method starts with an assumption of 'whole-career loss', which may then be discounted. By contrast, in a case where the employee would probably have changed jobs, and thus have left the scheme, before retirement, it is more appropriate simply to award lost contributions up to that date, in line with the simplified approach.

More specifically, the circumstances that would suggest use of the substantial loss approach (because they involve quantifiable ongoing losses) include findings by the tribunal as follows:

- permanent new employment by the date of the remedies hearing, but little chance of moving on to better paid employment in the future

- no permanent new employment, and, on the balance of probabilities, no new employment likely before state pension age (usually severe disability cases)

- no permanent new employment, but likely to find alternative employment in time, which involves valuing loss to retirement and beyond before applying a reduction for the percentage chance that the claimant would not have remained in the original career until retirement (Ministry of Defence v Cannock and ors 1994 ICR 918, EAT).

An example of a case in which the substantial loss approach was clearly appropriate is Sibbit v Governing Body of St Cuthbert's Catholic Primary School EAT 0070/10. In that case the claimant, a teacher, was dismissed after 23 years' service about a year before she had been intending to retire. The EAT overturned a tribunal's decision to use the simplified loss approach to assessing her pension loss. While the EAT recognised that tribunals have been reluctant to embark on an assessment of whole career loss, in this case the two matters which would discourage such an assessment were absent. There was no

15.45

689

uncertainty as to S's employment, as she was to work for a further year and then retire, and nor was there any uncertainty as to economic conditions, as she was a public sector teacher. The facts that her employment was of a stable nature, she had been employed for a considerable time, she was unlikely to be affected by the economic cycle and was unlikely to be looking for 'new pastures' all pointed firmly in favour of using the substantial approach. Furthermore, there was a quantifiable continuing loss: instead of receiving 24/80ths of her final salary, S would forever receive 23/80ths. It was plain what the loss was and the tribunal had chosen a method which would not remedy that loss, so its decision had to be set aside.

While the claimant in the above case was close to retirement, it does not follow that the substantial loss approach will only be appropriate for older employees. In Griffin v Plymouth Hospital NHS Trust (above) the Court of Appeal held that a tribunal had erred in not applying the substantial loss approach to assess the pension loss of a claimant who would have been likely, on the evidence, to have stayed in her employment until retirement, even though she was only 34 at the time her employment ended. Her role as a clinical technician in bone densitometry was highly specialised; the principal (and possibly only) market for her skills was in the NHS; and she suffered from a medical condition that made her cautious about embarking on major change. Lord Justice Underhill noted that the tribunal's reasons for rejecting the substantial loss approach at the first hearing appeared to have turned entirely on its interpretation of the reference in the tribunal guidelines to whether the claimant had been in the employment 'for a considerable time'. The tribunal had said that that factor did not apply, even though G had been employed for ten years, as she was still a long way from retirement. However, in Underhill LJ's view, this approach failed to engage with the thrust of the relevant paragraph – namely, whether G was likely to stay the course up to retirement date. The tribunal had not identified or addressed that question at all, and G's age alone could not be treated as determining it. Underhill LJ drew support for his conclusions from the decision of the EAT in Network Rail Infrastructure Ltd v Booth EAT 0071/06. In that case the claimant was a 36-year-old engineer who had worked for her employer for 14 years, and was a member of a final salary scheme. The tribunal applied the substantial loss approach to assess her pension loss, and the EAT upheld that decision, endorsing submissions that as the employee was employed in a very specialist industry in which there was effectively only one employer, and as she had spent all her working life in that industry, there was every expectation that she would have remained there, but for her dismissal.

15.46 Similarly, in Hall v Durham County Council and ors EAT 0256/14 H was a teacher who had the benefit of a final salary pension scheme. A tribunal found that she would never return to teaching, but that had she not been unfairly dismissed, she would have continued teaching for the rest of her career. The EAT upheld the tribunal's decision to adopt the substantial loss approach to assessing H's pension loss. H had been employed for ten years as a teacher; her employment in the field of teaching would be considered stable and the tribunal had considered it so; and, in the tribunal's view, she would have been unlikely ever to be looking for new pastures. The tribunal had been 'unarguably entitled' to apply the substantial loss approach, even though H had only been in her late thirties when she was dismissed.

Calculation of long-term loss   15.47

To calculate the loss figure, the following equation is used:

- loss of pension rights = A minus B minus C

where

A = value of prospective final salary rights up to normal retirement age in former employment (had the dismissal not occurred). The relevant period of service is from commencement of employment through to normal retirement age.

B = value of accrued final salary pension rights to date of dismissal. The relevant period of service is up to the date of dismissal only.

C = value of prospective final salary rights to normal retirement age in new employment. The relevant period of service is from commencement in the new job until normal retirement age in the new job.

Note that C will have no value if the claimant is unlikely to find pensionable employment again or has joined a money purchase or stakeholder scheme. Loss of employer contributions is already factored into the equation but will need to be taken into account when assessing loss of earnings in order to work out whether or not there is a continuing loss of earnings. Also, note that, in the interests of simplicity, guaranteed minimum pension or top-up pension rights are ignored.

For both A and B, the annual amount of pension is worked out on the basis of **15.48** pensionable earnings in the year up to dismissal (or according to the rules of the scheme in question). In each case, the annual pension must be worked out using the scheme rules.

Once the annual amounts have been established, these are then multiplied by the appropriate multiplier corresponding to the claimant's age set out in Tables 1–4 of Appendix 5 to the guidelines (for A and C) and Tables 1–4 of Appendix 6 (for B). In the case of A and B the relevant age is as at the date of dismissal. In the case of C the relevant age is as at the date of commencing the new job.

As observed under 'Tribunal guidelines' above, tribunals do not have to follow **15.49** the tribunal guidelines uncritically where it might be appropriate to adjust them in the circumstances of an individual case. The case of Hall v Durham County

691

Council and ors EAT 0256/14 provides a good example of the kind of adjustment to the substantial loss approach that might be made on the facts of a particular case. In that case H was a teacher who had the benefit of a final salary pension scheme. She was unfairly dismissed, and the tribunal found that she would not work again as a teacher given the significant psychiatric symptoms her dismissal had caused her. In the tribunal's view, had she not been unfairly dismissed, she would have continued in her profession to retirement at age 65, and would certainly have been promoted to head teacher. It decided to adopt the substantial loss approach to assessing her pension loss. However, rather than adopting H's pensionable earnings in the year up to dismissal as the starting point for its assessment of pension loss, it based its assessment on what she would be earning assuming that she would have been promoted to head teacher at the date of retirement. The employer sought to challenge this approach, arguing that the tribunal guidelines required tribunals to base their assessment on salary at the date of dismissal, and that factors such as inflation and future career progression are accounted for in the mathematical factors to be applied. However, the EAT observed that if a tribunal knows for certain what the position will be on retirement, it would be artificial not to take this into account. If the tribunal found that H would be a head teacher at the date of retirement, and would have been so for the requisite time under the pension scheme, then her pension under a final salary pension scheme would be based on those last year's earnings. Those promoted earnings would necessarily be greater than the unpromoted wages she would have been receiving at the date of dismissal. If the employer succeeded in challenging the tribunal's assessment that H had a 100 per cent chance of becoming a head teacher, the promoted earnings could be discounted to reflect the correct percentage chance of her promotion. The EAT concluded that the tribunal's method of calculation could not be said to be in error.

15.50 **Assessing the retirement age.** It should be noted that while normal retirement ages continue to be used for occupational pension schemes, the statutory 'default retirement age' has been abolished since October 2011. While employers may still operate a compulsory retirement age if they can objectively justify doing so under the Equality Act 2010, in many cases no particular 'normal' age for retirement will apply. If so, tribunals attempting to assess career-length loss may need to identify a suitable notional retirement date based on the specific circumstances of each case. For more on the effect of the abolition of the default retirement age in the context of unfair dismissal law, see Chapter 8, 'Some other substantial reason', under 'Retirement dismissals'.

15.51 **'Withdrawal factor' deductions**
When a figure has been arrived at using this formula, the tribunal should assess and then deduct the amount of any 'withdrawal factors'. The guidelines offer no useful tables in this regard and the decision as to what deduction to make is at the tribunal's discretion, taking into account factors such as the age, work

record, status and health of the claimant and the strength of the former employer's business. The guidelines state that the Government Actuary's Department is opposed to the use of a blanket percentage chance or withdrawal factor as there may be specific facts which allow the tribunal to adopt a more sophisticated approach to the withdrawal factor. If, for example, the percentage chance of losing the old job was higher than that in the new job, this should be reflected by using different percentage reduction figures for A and B (which relate to the old job) and C (which relates to the new job).

In Somerset County Council v Chaloner EAT 0063/14 the EAT took the view that a tribunal's decision to apply a 60 per cent withdrawal factor to a claimant's pension loss award was probably sustainable (though for other reasons it ultimately overturned the decision on remedy as a whole). In reaching this factor, the tribunal had had regard to the claimant's employment history (she had previously held a variety of positions in her career, many of which had been part time) and the employer's financial situation (it was undergoing significant cuts and its involvement in the conference centre where the claimant had been employed was under review). Taking into account, on the other hand, the fact that the claimant had relocated to Somerset to take up what she had considered to be a long-term role with the employer, the tribunal considered that a withdrawal factor of 60 per cent was just and equitable.

Other considerations
15.52

If the claimant was obliged to contribute to the scheme in his or her former employment, the fact that he or she is relieved of this financial burden should be taken into account by deducting any employee contributions from net earnings before applying the appropriate multiplier. As a corollary to this, if the claimant is joining a contributory scheme, this financial outlay should be accommodated by ensuring that this value is included in C. If the claimant's new employment allows for the accrual of S2P, the value of this (see Table 3.2 in Appendix 3 to the guidelines) should be deducted from the resultant value of A minus B.

The guidelines recommend (though not strictly within the substantial loss approach) that where the lost pension is a money purchase scheme and the new job pays less and has no equivalent pension scheme, the employer's contributions should be added to the continuing loss of earnings before applying the relevant multiplier from the Ogden tables. Note, however, that this approach using the Ogden tables is only applicable if there is long-term loss. If not, then the simplified approach should be used.

Finally, the guidelines emphasise that the substantial loss approach automatically **15.53** builds in compensation for loss of enhancement of accrued rights, loss of pension rights from dismissal to the remedies hearing and future pension loss, so these do not need to be calculated separately as they do for the simplified approach set out above.

693

16 Compensatory awards: adjustments

Payments received by employee

Failure to mitigate losses

'Just and equitable' reductions

'Polkey reductions'

Adjustments for breach of Acas Code of Practice

Adjustments for failure to provide written particulars

Contributory conduct

Reductions for lack of good faith in whistleblowing cases

Offsetting enhanced redundancy payments

Application of statutory cap

Order of adjustments

The first task of an employment tribunal, when assessing the compensatory **16.1** award, is to calculate the actual loss sustained by the employee. In calculating such loss, credit has to be given for any sums already paid by the employer to the employee in respect of the dismissal in the form of an ex gratia payment or payment in lieu of notice. This ensures that the employee is not awarded a head of compensation in respect of which he or she has already been compensated ('double recovery') – see Chapter 14, 'Compensatory awards: types of loss', under 'Immediate loss'.

A different rule applies in the case of enhanced redundancy payments. As explained under 'Payments received by employee' below, any payment made by the employer on account of redundancy in excess of the statutory payment falls to be taken into account in calculating the compensatory award, but only after all other relevant deductions have been made.

Once the total loss has been calculated, the tribunal will turn its attention to **16.2** considering whether to make any other appropriate adjustment or deduction. In this regard, there are various circumstances in which the amount of the compensatory award is liable to be reduced (or increased) according to specific statutory provisions. Briefly, these circumstances are:

695

- where the employee fails to take reasonable steps to mitigate his or her losses – S.123(4) Employment Rights Act 1996 (ERA)

- where the tribunal considers it 'just and equitable' to award a lesser amount than would otherwise be appropriate (which embraces so-called 'Polkey reductions', which apply where the employee would have been dismissed in any event had the procedural failings which rendered the dismissal unfair not occurred) – S.123(1) ERA

- where the employee has caused or contributed to his or her dismissal – i.e. is guilty of 'contributory conduct' – S.123(6) ERA

- where the employee was unfairly dismissed for making a protected disclosure but he or she did not make the disclosure in good faith – S.123(6A) ERA

- where the employer or employee has failed to comply with the provisions of the Acas Code of Practice on Disciplinary and Grievance Procedures – S.207A Trade Union and Labour Relations (Consolidation) Act 1992

- where the employer has failed to provide full and accurate written particulars of employment and the employment tribunal makes a finding to this effect in the course of proceedings for unfair dismissal – S.38 Employment Act 2002.

(A further head under which an employee's compensation can effectively be reduced is that of 'recoupment' of social security benefits (i.e. Jobseeker's Allowance, income-related Employment and Support Allowance, Universal Credit and Income Support). Recoupment is explained in Chapter 18, 'Recoupment'. Other benefits that are not subject to recoupment – such as Housing Benefit – may fall to be deducted as a payment received by the employee. These are dealt with in Chapter 14, 'Compensatory awards: types of loss', under 'Immediate loss – social security benefits'.)

16.3 Each of the six types of statutory adjustment/deduction listed above is discussed in detail in the following sections of this chapter. However, an important general point needs to be made first.

16.4 **Importance of order in which adjustments/deductions are made.** Where more than one adjustment or deduction has to be made from the total compensatory award, the order in which those adjustments/deductions are made can have a crucial effect on the resulting compensation figure. This is particularly so where one of the relevant adjustments or deductions is in the nature of a percentage increase or decrease as opposed to a specific sum. If the point at which that percentage is applied occurs before other deductions or adjustments have been made, the effect of that deduction will be greater than if it is applied after other specific monetary deductions have been made. To illustrate this point, let us assume that a tribunal assesses an employee's total loss at £20,000 but orders two deductions from that sum to be made, namely: (i) a 25 per cent deduction on account of the employee's contribution towards dismissal; and (ii) a deduction of an ex gratia payment of £4,000 paid by the employer. If the contribution deduction is applied first, followed by the ex gratia payment deduction, the resulting award would be £11,000 (i.e. £20,000 – 25 per cent = £15,000 – £4,000 = £11,000). If the reverse order for the deductions is applied, the resulting figure would be £12,000 (i.e. £20,000 – £4,000 = £16,000 – 25 per cent = £12,000).

It is similarly the case that the stage at which any adjustment for breach of the Acas Code of Practice on Disciplinary and Grievance Procedures is made can have a significant impact on 'quantum' – i.e. the amount of compensation awarded. Since the adjustment can be up to plus or minus 25 per cent of the total compensatory award, the order in which this adjustment is made – especially if made in conjunction with other deductions or adjustments – is of considerable significance.

16.5 The exact order in which adjustments should be made to the compensatory award is considered under 'Order of adjustments' below. Suffice it to say here that the order in which the various deductions and adjustments are discussed in this chapter reflects the order in which they have to be made (if applicable) when calculating the compensatory award.

Payments received by employee **16.6**

In Chapter 14, 'Compensatory awards: types of loss', under 'Immediate loss – termination payments', we saw that when an employment tribunal calculates the degree of loss experienced by a dismissed employee it should give credit for any sums received by way of an ex gratia payment. Similarly, the tribunal should give credit for any sums paid out by way of incapacity benefits (see Chapter 14, 'Compensatory awards: types of loss', under 'Immediate loss – social security benefits'). Much of the case law in this area has described such sums as being offset against, or deducted from, the *compensatory award*, but in our view such terminology is not entirely accurate. Rather, these sums are offset against a claimant's *losses* to determine the 'net loss' – the starting point for the compensatory award, prior to any adjustments or deductions.

However, a different approach must be taken in respect of enhanced redundancy payments in so far as the payments exceed the amount of the basic award. These are not covered by the general principles governing the computation of an employee's losses, but instead by a specific provision – S.123(7) ERA, which is discussed under 'Offsetting enhanced redundancy payments' below.

16.7 Note that certain social security benefits – Jobseeker's Allowance, income-related Employment and Support Allowance, Income Support and Universal Credit – should not be factored into the calculation of loss, and nor should they be deducted by the tribunal. Instead, they are subject to the recoupment procedure outlined in Chapter 18, 'Recoupment'.

697

16.8 Failure to mitigate losses

Claims for damages at common law are subject to the rule that claimants must take reasonable steps to mitigate their losses. This rule is given statutory force in its application to the compensatory award in unfair dismissal cases by S.123(4) ERA, which provides that: 'In ascertaining the loss [sustained by the claimant] the tribunal shall apply the same rule concerning the duty of a person to mitigate his loss as applies to damages recoverable under the common law of England and Wales or (as the case may be) Scotland.' The test is simply whether the employee's conduct – e.g. in taking or refusing a particular source of income – is reasonable on the facts of each case – Yetton v Eastwoods Froy Ltd 1966 3 All ER 353, QBD.

16.9 General principles

The duty to mitigate in accordance with S.123(4) ERA does not arise unless and until the employee has actually been dismissed. A refusal to agree to a transfer during the currency of employment would not, therefore, constitute a failure to mitigate loss unless the offer of the transferred employment remained on the table after the employee had been dismissed – see McAndrew v Prestwick Circuits Ltd 1988 IRLR 514, EAT.

16.10 Correct approach to making deductions for failure to mitigate.

When calculating the compensatory award, the calculation should initially be based on the assumption that the employee has taken all reasonable steps to reduce his or her loss. If the employee in fact failed to take such steps – e.g. by turning down suitable new employment – the compensatory award should be reduced so as to cover only those losses that would have been incurred even if the employee had taken the appropriate steps. A useful approach to this matter was suggested by Sir John Donaldson in Archbold Freightage Ltd v Wilson 1974 IRLR 10, NIRC: the dismissed employee's duty to mitigate his or her loss will be fulfilled if he or she can be said to have acted as a reasonable person would do if he or she had no hope of seeking compensation from his or her previous employer.

In Savage v Saxena 1998 ICR 357, EAT, the EAT recommended a three-step approach to determining whether an employee has failed to mitigate his or her losses:

- identify what steps should have been taken by the claimant to mitigate his or her loss

- find the date upon which such steps would have produced an alternative income

- thereafter reduce the amount of compensation by the amount of income which would have been earned.

698

This approach is easy to follow in a case where an employee has not found new **16.11** employment by the date of the remedies hearing. However, step two above will need to be adjusted if, by the date of the hearing, the employee has secured an alternative income but at a lower rate than that which he or she enjoyed under the old job. In such a case, as the EAT makes clear in Glasgow City Council v Rayton EAT 0005/07, it will be necessary for the tribunal to establish the date on which the employee would have secured the same or better-paid employment.

Where an employee is found by an employment tribunal to have failed to mitigate his or her losses, it should not simply reduce the whole compensatory award by a percentage. Instead, it should attempt to estimate from the available evidence exactly when the employee should have got a suitable job. The tribunal should then take into account the earnings that it thinks would have been earned from that point onwards and reduce the compensation accordingly – Peara v Enderlin Ltd 1979 ICR 804, EAT. In Ladbroke Racing Ltd v Connolly EAT 160/83 the EAT added that the tribunal should estimate the amount of earnings the employee would have received had appropriate steps been taken and, if the employee would still have earned less than in the original job, further compensation can be awarded for the partial loss incurred thereafter.

Tribunals must be careful not to impose arbitrary cut-off dates in this regard, **16.12** up to which full loss of earnings is awarded and then nothing else for ongoing loss. In Mears v Lloyd Green and Co EAT 0707/02 the claimant succeeded in her appeal against a tribunal decision to impose a three-month cut-off period for full loss of earnings based on its findings that the claimant had been unwise in mentioning to employment agencies her pending tribunal proceedings against the respondent, as that was an irrelevant factor to take into account. A similar conclusion was reached by the EAT in Glasgow City Council v Rayton (above), where the tribunal, having decided that the employee had failed to mitigate, appeared to use the date of the remedies hearing as a cut-off date. Saying that the claimant was not entitled to be compensated for loss of earnings from that date was not the same thing as identifying when a proper mitigatory course of action would have made a difference to the employee's earning position. In so holding, the EAT rejected the contention that it was permissible for the tribunal to apply the remedies hearing date as a cut-off pursuant to its broad discretion to award 'just and equitable' compensation under S.123(1) ERA in the absence of clear reasons why that date was relevant to the issue of mitigation.

Focus must be on individual's particular circumstances. Whether an **16.13** employee has done enough to fulfil the duty to mitigate depends on the circumstances of each case and is to be judged subjectively – Johnson v Hobart Manufacturing Co Ltd EAT 210/89. For instance, an employer cannot argue that a younger or fitter employee would have found new work sooner: the question is whether the employee in question has taken reasonable steps to minimise his or her losses – Fougère v Phoenix Motor Co Ltd 1976 ICR 495,

699

EAT. But it is not the case that the tribunal should simply accept the subjective view of the claimant: while this certainly has to be taken into account, the tribunal's task is to consider all the circumstances in deciding whether the claimant has acted unreasonably in failing to find fresh employment or some alternative means of mitigating the losses as a result of having been unfairly dismissed – Beijing Ton Ren Tang (UK) Ltd v Wang EAT 0024/09.

In Tandem Bars Ltd v Pilloni EAT 0050/12 the EAT stressed that, rather than concentrating on what the employee actually did to find work, the tribunal's focus should be on the steps that were reasonable for him or her to take in the circumstances. In that case the tribunal had accepted that P made reasonable attempts to mitigate his loss when his efforts to find new work as a waiter by going round restaurants and asking whether they had work for him proved unsuccessful. This was consistent with his previous practice of obtaining work. The EAT overturned the decision on appeal, holding that the tribunal had failed to assess whether the steps taken by P were such as would have been taken by a reasonable employee. This issue was remitted to the tribunal for reconsideration, but the EAT noted that the steps that might usually be expected of a person in P's situation, such as making written job applications and invoking the assistance of the Jobcentre in finding a job, had not been taken by him.

16.14 Where suitable alternative employment is available, an employee's failure to apply for it will not be looked upon favourably. In Kelly v University of Southampton EAT 0139/10 K failed to apply for either of two vacant posts within the University's School of Biological Sciences, where she had worked as a lecturer until her unfair dismissal. She submitted that there was every chance she would not have been appointed to either post, given that the school received 30 to 60 applications for each advertised post and that she had been in dispute with the university about her refusal to carry out some teaching duties. The tribunal rejected this argument, finding that it was 'extremely' likely that she would have been appointed: she was qualified for both posts, had worked for the university for four years in a similar role and had lost that post in circumstances that 'hardly reflected adversely on her at all'. Accordingly, she had failed to mitigate her loss by not applying. The EAT refused to interfere with the tribunal's decision on appeal.

In determining whether the employee has sufficiently mitigated his or her loss, much will depend on variables such as local levels of unemployment, whether the employee's skills are readily transferable to other available employment, and the personal characteristics of the employee. For example, older employees, pregnant employees and people in poor health are particularly likely to have problems obtaining new employment. In Bennett v Tippins EAT 361/89 the claimant was unfairly dismissed from her job as a waitress on account of her pregnancy. The employer argued that her compensation should be reduced because she had failed to get another job despite the great shortage of bar and restaurant staff in her area. The EAT, however, stated that T's pregnancy made the general availability of jobs irrelevant since employers are reluctant to take on staff who are pregnant.

It has been recognised by the EAT that the issues that need to be taken on board **16.15** by a tribunal when determining whether and to what extent an employee has failed to mitigate his or her loss are tricky and that mitigation 'is a notoriously difficult area for a tribunal to have to deal with' – per Mr Justice Elias (as he then was) in Patel v Clemence Hoar Cummings EAT 0605/07. In that case the EAT upheld a tribunal's decision that an unfairly dismissed accountant should have found equivalent paid employment within 12 months. The tribunal had properly taken into account such factors as the employee's failure to consider jobs outside accountancy and his failure to maximise self-employed earnings following his dismissal.

It may not be reasonable to expect an employee to take the first job that comes along, especially one with lower pay than the employee might reasonably expect to receive. In particular, a skilled or highly educated employee does not necessarily have to lower his or her sights immediately as regards the kind of job he or she is prepared to apply for in seeking new employment – Orthet Ltd v Vince-Cain 2005 ICR 374, EAT. On the other hand, undue delay in accepting something in the vain hope of a better offer may result in compensation being reduced. It should always be borne in mind that employees can, of course, claim any partial loss arising from acceptance of suitable, though less well-paid, employment, as discussed under 'Correct approach to making deductions for failure to mitigate' above.

The effect of the dismissal on the individual employee may well be a relevant **16.16** matter in determining whether there has been a failure to mitigate. In Beijing Ton Ren Tang (UK) Ltd v Wang (above) the EAT held that an employment tribunal had correctly found that it would not have been reasonable to expect the claimant to have got herself straight back into the job market given her circumstances. She had been recruited in China to carry out a particular job for 12 months and had expected to return to China after that; she had been greatly shocked by her sudden dismissal, spoke no English, felt isolated, and did not know the country outside London. On these facts, the EAT ruled that the tribunal had been entitled to find that the employee had not failed to mitigate her loss even though she had not sought new employment for the 17-week period from the date of her dismissal until the date she would, in any event, have returned to China.

The reason for the dismissal may also have an impact on an employee's ability to mitigate his or her loss. In Bailes v First Bristol Ltd ET Case No.1401728/12, for example, the claimant, a bus driver, was dismissed after testing positive for cocaine. He denied ever having taken cocaine and argued that the positive result came about as a result of his having handled contaminated bank notes in the course of his work. The claimant then commissioned his own test, which proved that he had not taken cocaine within the last 90 days. A tribunal upheld his unfair dismissal claim and awarded him a total of £83,910. The claimant had struggled to find work after his dismissal but the tribunal rejected the employer's argument that he had failed to mitigate his loss. It concluded that the claimant's dismissal for testing positive for cocaine in a work-related drug test had created significant disadvantages for him in finding alternative work.

16.17 A similar view might well be taken in circumstances where a claimant has, say, been traumatically dismissed on discriminatory grounds and feels unable to contemplate returning to a work environment for a substantial period. Furthermore, it may be that the very fact that the employee has been discriminatorily dismissed has an impact on the length of time he or she will be on the labour market. This was recognised by the Court of Appeal in Abbey National plc and anor v Chagger 2010 ICR 397, CA. Since the employee will not be looking for new employment at a time of his or her own choosing, his or her prospects may be adversely affected and he or she may have been stigmatised by bringing tribunal proceedings, which also have an adverse effect on the chances of obtaining new employment. In consequence of factors such as these, the discriminatory dismissal may well alter the employee's subsequent career path and thus significantly delay the point at which it can reasonably be said that the employee should have found an alternative income.

16.18 **Burden of proof.** The onus of showing a failure to mitigate lies on the employer as the party who is alleging that the employee has failed to mitigate his or her losses – Fyfe v Scientific Furnishings Ltd 1989 ICR 648, EAT. It follows that tribunals are under no duty to consider the question of mitigation unless the employer raises it and adduces some evidence of failure to mitigate.

16.19 **Sufficiency of tribunal's reasons.** A tribunal will be expected to give clear reasons for its decision regarding mitigation. The failure to do so may well make the decision vulnerable on appeal. In C and A Pumps Ltd v Thompson EAT 0218/06, for example, an employment tribunal was found to have erred in law when it awarded the employee full loss for six months despite evidence that he could and should have found alternative employment within four to six weeks. The tribunal had failed to set out its reasons on this matter sufficiently. The EAT speculated that the tribunal might have had in mind that the employee had been suffering from stress and that it had been reasonable for him not to start looking for work during the first six months after he was dismissed. But the tribunal had not spelled out either the condition from which the employee was suffering or its effect on his ability to find new employment. Furthermore, the tribunal had also awarded the employee 26 weeks' partial loss at £150 a week without any explanation of the basis on which these figures were arrived at. They appeared to derive from the tribunal's general awareness about the type of alternative employment that might have been available, but it was wholly unclear what that was and why a person with the employee's qualifications and experience should only have taken a job at a level that entailed an ongoing loss of £150. The EAT concluded that the tribunal had given inadequate consideration to the issue of mitigation in its decision and remitted the case to the same tribunal for reconsideration.

The EAT in NSM Music Ltd v McArdle EAT 0516/09 similarly found the tribunal's reasons deficient. The tribunal had compensated M for the time it took him to train and qualify as a teacher. The EAT accepted that it was open to a tribunal to find that a career change was a reasonable attempt by the employee to mitigate his or her loss. However, in the instant case, the tribunal had failed to make sufficient findings of fact on which to base this conclusion. It had made no findings of fact as to how much M had looked for other employment, as to the level of employment in his particular area or as to how long it would take him to find a job at or about the same level. The case was therefore remitted to the same tribunal for reconsideration.

Failure to utilise internal appeal against dismissal

16.20

There has been some controversy over the question of whether the failure to pursue internal appeal procedures following dismissal can constitute a failure to mitigate loss. In Hoover Ltd v Forde 1980 ICR 239, EAT, the EAT held that it could, but the opposite view was taken by the EAT in Scotland in William Muir (Bond 9) Ltd v Lamb 1985 IRLR 95, EAT. Both these decisions were considered in Lock v Connell Estate Agents 1994 ICR 983, EAT, where the EAT took the view that the William Muir decision was to be preferred. In the opinion of His Honour Judge Hull, the suggestion that an employee may be under a duty to mitigate his or her loss by appealing to the employer was a strange one. 'The employer has made up his mind to dismiss the applicant, presumably after taking proper thought and carrying out the procedural duties of fairness as well as considering the merits. If the decision was a careful and responsible one, then the prospect of it being reversed on appeal must be remote. The prospect may be even more remote in the unlikely event that the decision has been an irresponsible and hasty one; in that event, what possible confidence can the employee have in the integrity of the employer?' HHJ Hull also pointed out that to place employees under an obligation to mitigate in this way could cause extreme inconvenience for tribunals assessing compensation, since they may be drawn into hearing extensive evidence from both sides on the likelihood that the appeal would have been successful. Therefore, a failure to invoke internal procedures before dismissal will not amount to a failure to mitigate by the employee.

Note, however, that as from 6 April 2009 employment tribunals have been entitled under S.207A of the Trade Union and Labour Relations (Consolidation) Act 1992 to penalise employees (as well as employers) for failure to comply

703

with any provision of the Acas Code of Practice on Disciplinary and Grievance Procedures that is relevant to certain specified claims (which include unfair dismissal) – see 'Adjustments for breach of Acas Code of Practice' below. Para 26 of the Code specifically states that: 'Where an employee feels that disciplinary action taken against them is wrong or unjust they should appeal against that decision.' It is therefore possible that tribunals may, in certain circumstances, conclude that an employee's failure to utilise an internal appeal against dismissal justifies making a reduction in the compensatory award of up to 25 per cent under S.207A. In Baker v Birmingham Metropolitan College ET Case No.1301355/11, for example, the tribunal did exactly that: it reduced the employee's compensatory award by 20 per cent on account of his unreasonable refusal to appeal against his dismissal. According to the tribunal, this meant that a chance for the parties to come together and resolve their differences, and for the employer to right any mistakes it had made, had been lost. The tribunal considered that a reduction towards the top of the range was therefore appropriate.

16.21 Refusal of offer of re-employment or settlement

An unreasonable refusal of an offer of re-employment may amount to a failure to mitigate. It should be borne in mind, however, that the duty to mitigate only arises after dismissal, so refusing offers made before employment was terminated cannot amount to a failure to mitigate – Savoia v Chiltern Herb Farms Ltd 1981 IRLR 65, EAT. A refusal is more likely to be reasonable if the employee has been badly treated by the employer – Fyfe v Scientific Furnishings Ltd 1989 ICR 648, EAT. And an employee's refusal to accept an offer of reinstatement in the old job is less likely to be reasonable than a refusal to accept an offer of re-engagement in a different job, but everything is subject to the reasonableness test. Some examples:

- **Comeau v Hart and anor** ET Case No.32364/86: a dismissal was held to be unfair because the employer had taken too much account of the conduct of the employee's husband when dismissing her. The employer had later recanted and indicated that she could be reinstated in her old job. Her rejection of this offer was held to be unreasonable: she should have recognised that immediate dismissal was an understandable reaction to her husband's threatening behaviour and she should have avoided further loss by resuming employment

- **Cocking v Moulinex Swan Holdings Ltd** EAT 1233/94: about three weeks after his dismissal for redundancy, C was offered re-engagement. He declined because he had committed himself to setting up a business with someone else. The EAT upheld the tribunal's decision that the refusal was unreasonable. The offer was of suitable alternative employment with an employer with whom there had been no falling-out and C's commitment to

704

the proposed business venture was not such as to prevent him withdrawing from it in order to mitigate his loss

- **F and G Cleaners Ltd v Saddington and ors** 2012 IRLR 892, EAT: S and O argued that, following a retendering exercise, their contracts of employment had transferred to FGC Ltd under the Transfer of Undertakings (Protection of Employment) Regulations 2006 SI 2006/246 ('TUPE'). FGC Ltd denied that TUPE applied but offered S and O alternative work on a self-employed basis, which they refused. An employment tribunal found that a transfer had taken place, that FGC Ltd's offers of self-employment amounted to a proposed change in working conditions to their material detriment entitling them to treat themselves as dismissed and that their dismissals were automatically unfair. When it came to the question of compensation, the tribunal rejected FGC Ltd's argument that, in refusing the alternative work, S and O had unreasonably failed to mitigate their loss. The tribunal took into account that, before the transfer, S and O were in PAYE employment, had a Monday-to-Friday working week and were entitled to holiday pay. Furthermore, O received expenses. Under FGC Ltd's proposed terms, they would have been self-employed on a lower daily rate of pay, subject to a one-month trial period, and with no guaranteed five-day week, holiday pay or expenses. Given this, the tribunal found that S and O did not act unreasonably in rejecting the less advantageous terms. On appeal, the EAT approved that decision but added that, in any event, the duty to mitigate did not arise as the offers of self-employment had been made before the date of dismissal.

In Wilding v British Telecommunications plc 2002 ICR 1079, CA (a **16.22** discrimination case, where the same duty to mitigate applies), W was offered re-employment with BT on a part-time basis shortly after BT had lodged an appeal against a tribunal finding that W had been discriminated against on the ground of disability. W rejected the offer of re-employment and set out a number of grounds for so doing, including the fact that he viewed BT's appeal against the decision on liability as inconsistent with its offer of re-employment; the manner of his dismissal; the injury to feelings he had suffered; and the way in which his appeal against dismissal had been conducted. An employment tribunal concluded that W had acted unreasonably in refusing BT's offer and had therefore failed to mitigate his loss. The EAT agreed, as did the Court of Appeal, which rejected the notion that the test for mitigation is a purely objective one. In the Court's view, it also requires the tribunal to look at all the circumstances of the case, including the subjective reasons that the complainant has given for turning down the offer. It followed that where the claimant has given a full explanation as to why he or she turned down the offer, the ultimate question for the tribunal was whether he or she acted unreasonably in doing so. The answer to this should be determined after taking into account the history and all the circumstances of the case, including the claimant's state of mind,

705

and bearing in mind that the burden of proof and the standard of reasonableness to be applied is not too high.

It should be remembered that the issue of reasonableness is directed at the employee's actions, not those of the employer. The EAT observed in Debique v Ministry of Defence EAT 0075/11 – another discrimination case – that the question is 'not whether it was reasonable for the employer to make the offer in question, but whether it was unreasonable for the employee to refuse it'. In that case, which concerned compensation for sex and race discrimination, the EAT upheld an employment tribunal's decision that D, a soldier, had been unreasonable to refuse an offer of redeployment. The dispute had arisen over the MoD's failure to accommodate D's childcare commitments. Once D had commenced tribunal proceedings, the MoD offered her an alternative role that would be compatible with her childcare arrangements. The posting would have been for five years and the senior officer who outlined the offer stated that it came with a guarantee of non-deployment, i.e. that D would not be sent into active service during that time. In assessing whether D was reasonable to reject the offer on the basis of her doubts over that guarantee, the tribunal took into account that, as a matter of strict military law, there could be no absolute guarantee of non-deployment. However, it accepted that it was highly unlikely that D would in fact be deployed during the five-year posting and was satisfied that the offer – and the explanation of the steps that had been taken to ensure that it was secure – should have given D sufficient assurances about her future. The EAT held that that was a permissible finding of fact. It therefore rejected D's appeal against the tribunal's decision to reduce compensation.

16.23 Although a refusal to accept redeployment or a transfer before the dismissal cannot amount to a failure to mitigate, continuing to reject such offers after the dismissal has been executed may do so. This may be the case even if the employer's attempts to force this change on the employee were the very reason the dismissal was unfair in the first place – Pearson v Leeds Polytechnic Students' Union EAT 182/84.

Even where the employer's conduct has justified the employee resigning and claiming unfair constructive dismissal, inflexibility on the part of an employee, or a refusal to listen to the employer's attempts to explain, may amount to a failure to mitigate. In Coote v McAlpine Humberoak Ltd ET Case No.20948/83, for example, a manager resigned after being questioned about thefts in a way that made him believe he was no longer trusted. Although this amounted to unfair dismissal, his refusal to meet or hear any explanation from management was a failure to mitigate and no compensatory award was made.

16.24 In another case – Plewinski v McDermott Engineering London EAT 465/88 – an offshore oil worker elected to resign and become self-employed after a unilateral cut in his overtime was imposed. He later became unemployed. Despite a finding of unfair constructive dismissal, this course of action was held to amount to an unreasonable failure to mitigate. Although becoming self-employed can be a good mitigation of loss (see 'Becoming self-employed' below), here a long-serving employee had given up a good salary and pension at a time when the oil industry was depressed and prospects were poor. The employee should have reconsidered his position and accepted the modified terms and no compensation for future loss was therefore awarded.

However, in other cases the employer's actions leading to the constructive dismissal have been found to justify an employee's subsequent refusal to return to his or her job. In Touchstone Productions Ltd v Patrick EAT 1216/95, for example, it was held to be wholly unrealistic to expect an employee who had been physically assaulted by one of his managers to accept an offer of re-engagement. And in Bloxwich Fencing Ltd v Banks EAT 0469/09 an employee was held not to have failed to mitigate his loss when he refused an offer of re-engagement made almost immediately after he was laid off without pay in fundamental breach of contract. The employer had sought to deliberately use the lay-off provisions to take advantage of the economic conditions.

16.25 Similarly, in Symonds t/a Symonds Solicitors v Redmond-Ord 2014 ICR D6, EAT, the EAT held that where the employer refused to allow the employee to return to her job after a sabbatical, in fundamental breach of contract, she acted reasonably in not wanting to return once her job became available again. R-O, who worked for S as a secretary, took a period of unpaid leave, which was due to end in February 2010. On 15 February S informed R-O that he had taken on another secretary in her absence and that her job would only become available again in July 2010. R-O raised a formal grievance and, when S failed to deal with it, resigned in April and claimed unfair constructive dismissal. The employment tribunal, upholding her claim, rejected S's argument that R-O had failed to mitigate her loss by not returning to work in July 2010. On appeal, the EAT could find no fault with this decision. Given that S had committed serious breaches of contract by failing to allow R-O to return to work and failing to deal with her grievance, it was reasonable for R-O to decide that she wished to work for someone else rather than return to work for S.

Note that, where a tribunal has ordered the reinstatement or re-engagement of an employee (see Chapter 12, 'Remedies', under 'Reinstatement and re-engagement – employee preventing compliance'), the employee will be taken to have failed to mitigate his or her loss if he or she unreasonably prevents the order from being complied with – S.117(8) ERA.

16.26 **Refusal of offer of settlement.** The question of whether a claimant's refusal of an employer's settlement offer may amount to a failure to mitigate came before the EAT in Konczak v BAE Systems (Operations) Ltd EAT 0498/11. An employment tribunal had awarded K approximately £45,000 in compensation for, among other things, unfair dismissal. This incorporated loss of earnings up to 11 July 2008. The tribunal found that on that date the employer made a

707

reasonable offer of settlement in the sum of £75,000, which K ought to have accepted. By refusing that offer, the tribunal considered that she had failed to mitigate her loss so that no loss of earnings claim persisted beyond that date. The EAT overturned the tribunal's decision. It noted that K had put in a counter-offer of £85,000, which was not accepted by the employer. Further negotiations between the parties culminated in an offer of £200,000 during the week prior to the remedies hearing. Against the background of a schedule of loss totalling £489,927, it was, in the EAT's view, 'legally impermissible' for the employment tribunal to find that refusal of the offer of £75,000 was so unreasonable as to terminate the loss otherwise flowing from the employer's act of dismissal.

This decision leaves open the possibility that a claimant may behave so unreasonably in refusing a settlement offer that he or she will have failed to mitigate his or her loss. Nevertheless, in most cases this possibility is likely to be more theoretical than real, given that settlement negotiations will almost always be 'without prejudice', meaning that they are inadmissible in evidence. The 'without prejudice' rule, which generally applies when there is a genuine attempt to resolve a dispute, is intended to encourage parties to settle without putting their case in jeopardy in the event that they cannot reach agreement. In the above case, the claimant was held to have waived the without prejudice privilege because she chose to disclose a note of a meeting which expressly referred to the £75,000 settlement offer. For more information on the 'without prejudice' rule, see IDS Employment Law Handbook, 'Employment Tribunal Practice and Procedure' (2014), Chapter 13, 'Evidence', under 'Evidence of settlement negotiations – "without prejudice" negotiations'.

16.27 Seeking new employment

Remaining unemployed unnecessarily or taking low-paid employment when higher-paid work is available will clearly amount to a failure to mitigate and a tribunal will cut the employee's compensation accordingly. However, the kind of work a dismissed employee should seek varies greatly between individuals and from area to area. High levels of unemployment can play their part in the determination of what constitutes reasonable mitigation. For instance, difficulties in obtaining suitable employment might justify the acceptance of lower-paid employment than would otherwise have been reasonable. One London teacher was unfairly dismissed when school populations were declining and there were job shortages in the South-East. The only offer came from Wales, at a lower salary and minus London weighting. The tribunal found it reasonable for her to accept this and awarded her a full year's net difference between the two salaries – Collen v Lewis and anor ET Case No.33173/83.

Conversely, high unemployment can also work to reduce compensation where a dismissed employee unrealistically refuses lower-paid employment. Breach of the mitigation rule in this way is particularly likely if the employee has already made fruitless attempts to get better-paid work over a reasonable period. It has even been suggested that the value of having a job during times of high unemployment may make a job refusal unreasonable even where the money offered is less than state benefits – Daley v AE Dorsett (Almar Dolls) Ltd 1982 ICR 1, EAT.

16.28 Simply signing on at a Jobcentre (now rebranded Jobcentre Plus) was held to be insufficient mitigation of loss in Burns v George Boyd (Engineering) Ltd EAT 458/84. At the very least, regular visits to the Jobcentre seem to be required – Bristol Garage (Brighton) Ltd v Lowen 1979 IRLR 86, EAT. In practice, tribunals are likely to expect more than this and claimants would be well advised to keep copies and records of job applications and interviews in order to rebut any charges that they have failed to take reasonable steps to mitigate their losses.

16.29 **Abandoning new employment.** The duty to mitigate will not be allowed to operate oppressively. For instance, it may be reasonable for an employee to give up a new job which proves unsuitable – e.g. because it involves too high a degree of responsibility, or too much travelling for that particular employee – see Dundee Plant Co Ltd v Riddler EAT 377/88, where an employee gave up a new job after three months because of the unacceptable amount of travelling involved.

16.30 **Registering as sick or disabled.** It may be reasonable mitigation of loss for an employee to register as sick or disabled, but this should not be regarded as all that has to be done in mitigation unless the circumstances warrant it – Plessey Military Communications Ltd v Brough EAT 518/84.

16.31 **Accepting part-time employment.** In Ahunanya v Scottish and Southern Energy plc EAT 0540/08 the EAT upheld an employment tribunal's decision that an employee who had been dismissed from a full-time job failed to mitigate his loss from the point at which he accepted part-time employment. There was evidence to show that the employee had applied for only one other job in addition to the part-time job vacancy and that part-time employment now suited his personal circumstances. The tribunal was therefore entitled, said the EAT, to award the employee his full loss (uprated to the national minimum wage hourly rate in view of the employer's failure to pay this) until the date the employee began working in the part-time job, but then not to award any further loss on the ground that the employee had failed to mitigate from that date onwards.

In Bailes v First Bristol Ltd ET Case No.1401728/12, on the other hand, the claimant had mitigated his loss by accepting part-time employment as this was the only employment available to him at the time. He had been unfairly dismissed for failing a drugs test and this fact made it very difficult for him to obtain alternative work. He had applied for or enquired about a large number of jobs and had attended a job fair, registered with online agencies and made

709

his CV searchable online but had been unsuccessful in finding full-time work. Even after he had started his part-time job he continued his search, looking for either part-time work to complement his current job or full-time work to replace it.

16.32 Part-time work was also at issue in Somerset County Council v Chaloner EAT 0063/14 where C, who was in her 50s, took up a job with the Council in November 2009. However, she was made redundant just over a year later and, a few weeks after that, she accepted an alternative part-time role. An employment tribunal upheld C's complaint that she was unfairly dismissed by the Council, but ruled that C's claim for loss of earnings (in terms of basic pay) was limited to the date at which she took up the part-time position because she had failed to mitigate her losses by not attempting to seek further work once she had obtained a part-time position. However, the tribunal did award C continuing pension loss. Following an appeal by both sides, the EAT set aside the decision on remedy and remitted the case to a fresh tribunal. In the EAT's view, it was hard to see a consistent basis for the two aspects of the decision. As regards C's alleged failure to mitigate, the tribunal had failed to adopt the approach – laid down by the EAT in Gardiner-Hill v Roland Berger Technics Ltd 1982 IRLR 498, EAT and Savage v Saxena 1998 ICR 357, EAT (see 'General principles – correct approach to making deductions for failure to mitigate' above) – of assessing what steps should have been taken by C; identifying the date on which such steps would have produced alternative income; and then reducing the compensation by the amount of that alternative income. Similarly, in respect of the decision on continuing pension loss, the tribunal should have assessed what income (including pension benefits) would have been earned had C taken adequate steps to mitigate.

16.33 **Temporary employment.** In some circumstances, it is possible that the chain of causation between an unfair dismissal and the losses flowing from that dismissal is not broken by the acceptance of temporary new employment. This may be so whether the new employment in question was always intended to be temporary or just worked out that way. In Dench v Flynn and Partners 1998 IRLR 653, CA, the Court of Appeal rejected the contention that the loss flowing from an unfair dismissal automatically comes to an end once permanent employment has been obtained, even where that employment is terminated shortly thereafter. Lord Justice Beldam, with whose judgment the two other judges agreed, said that it was wrong to conclude in every case that the taking of new employment necessarily broke the chain of causation.

In Cowen v Rentokil Initial Facility Services (UK) Ltd t/a Initial Transport Services EAT 0473/07 the EAT relied on Beldam LJ's comments in the Dench case to overturn a tribunal's decision that an employee's losses ended when he accepted new employment that turned out to be temporary. The tribunal had incorrectly assumed that the obtaining of permanent employment at an equivalent or higher level of salary necessarily broke the chain of causation. In that case, the new employment was very different from the employee's former job and it came to an end because he was unable to satisfy the new employer that he was the right man for the job. Moreover, it was obvious when the job was taken up that it might only last for the probationary period, and that was in fact what happened. In those circumstances, the EAT felt justified in concluding that the chain of causation had not been broken and that compensation should be calculated as including a period of loss subsequent to the termination of the employee's new job.

In the Cowen case, Mr Justice Elias (as he then was) made it clear that the **16.34** EAT's decision should not be interpreted as suggesting that where a new job is of relatively short duration, that will inevitably mean that causation is not broken. It all depends on the circumstances of the case. The reason why an employee loses the second job may have a bearing on the question. So, for example, if the reason for the employee's dismissal from the alternative job was culpable misconduct on his or her part, that might well break the chain of causation. Elias J cautioned tribunals, however, not to become embroiled in satellite litigation as to the precise circumstances in which the second dismissal took place.

Clearly, the length of time that an employee remains in the new employment may also be an important factor. For example, an employee who was dismissed 18 months after starting new employment was not, according to the EAT in Courtaulds Northern Spinning Ltd v Moosa 1984 ICR 218, EAT, entitled to claim ongoing loss against the first employer following the termination of his second job. By contrast, in Commercial Motors (Wales) Ltd v Howley EAT 0636/11 the EAT upheld a tribunal's decision that the claimant's short-term two-month consultancy work for another company did not affect his ongoing losses arising from his unfair dismissal.

Higher-paid employment. Where an employee successfully mitigates his or **16.35** her loss by finding new employment at a salary or wage that is higher than that enjoyed in the old job, the question arises as to what effect this has on his or her compensation. In particular, does the higher payment have to be offset against the employee's losses for the purpose of the compensatory award? This issue is dealt with in detail in Chapter 14, 'Compensatory awards: types of loss', under 'Immediate loss – new employment'.

Becoming self-employed
16.36

Becoming self-employed instead of seeking new employment can amount to reasonable mitigation of loss, especially where the individual is older or is in a specialised trade where employment openings are few and far between. In such cases profits may not be immediately forthcoming so that losses from dismissal will tend to be heavier than where an employee simply seeks and obtains work

711

with another employer. In Gardiner-Hill v Roland Berger Technics Ltd 1982 IRLR 498, EAT, a managing director spent 80 per cent of his time between dismissal and the tribunal hearing trying to set up his own company. The employer argued that this had prevented him from looking for salaried work and so the 'lost earnings' element of his compensatory award should be reduced accordingly. Reversing the tribunal's decision, the EAT held that the employee's duty is to take such steps as are reasonable in the circumstances. This case concerned a 55-year-old managing director with 16 years' experience in a specialist business. In seeking to market his expertise and experience in his own business he had acted prudently.

The employee's move into self-employment was also held to amount to sufficient mitigation of loss in Praxis Real Estate Management Ltd v Nichols EAT 0502/12. N was unfairly dismissed from his role as property asset manager. Finding it difficult to obtain alternative employment in the same field, he decided to start his own property investment business. At the remedies hearing, the employer argued that N's decision to become self-employed was not a reasonable attempt to mitigate his loss, particularly given his lack of experience in property investment. The tribunal disagreed. Given the specialist nature of N's job, the geographical location and the reason for his dismissal (i.e. capability), the tribunal found that it was not an unreasonable risk for him to start a business. There were limited job opportunities in property asset management in the North of England and the reference that N would have been given by the employer made it unlikely that he would have obtained one of the few jobs available. Furthermore, there was some prospect of crossover between the two types of business – in terms of skills and possible clients – and N was working alongside his father's property business, which meant that he was able to utilise his father's contacts, experience and resources. There was also evidence to suggest that his efforts were beginning to bring a return. By the time of the hearing, he was close to securing deals that would generate fees of approximately £23,170. The tribunal found that he would build the business to the point where he would not suffer continuing loss over a total period of 18 months. The EAT approved the tribunal's decision on appeal.

16.37 An employee may also be able to claim expenses incurred in setting up a business. In United Freight Distribution Ltd v McDougall EAT 218/94 an employee decided to set up his own business following his dismissal. The tribunal found this to be a reasonable course of action and it also reimbursed him the £550 legal fees that he had incurred in selling his house and another £2,500 that he had borrowed from his father. The EAT upheld the award of £550, stating that the tribunal had clearly considered the legal fees to be a reasonable expense incurred in the setting up of the business. In respect of the £2,500 loan, however, the tribunal had failed to establish what the employee had spent the money on and the EAT remitted the case for the tribunal to consider the matter further.

712

Opting for retraining or further education

16.38

Some employees decide to go on a training or re-education course after being dismissed to aid their eventual search for employment. Taking oneself off the employment market in this way may well amount to a failure to mitigate, although in some cases the tribunal may decide that an employee acted reasonably in seeking retraining. In Layte v Tavern Wholesaling Ltd ET Case No.56291/95, for example, a former office manager made efforts to gain alternative employment following her dismissal, then decided to take a two-year course in business and finance studies. A tribunal found that, having regard to the level of remuneration in her previous job and the state of the employment market generally in her area, this was a reasonable course for her to take.

The EAT emphasised in Hibiscus Housing Association Ltd v McIntosh EAT 0534/08 that it is certainly not the law that an employee who seeks higher or further education after having been unfairly dismissed thereby fails to mitigate his or her loss. But nor is it the case that, even if there is no failure to mitigate, once the employee embarks upon the course, he or she is entitled to pursue it to the very end at the employer's expense. On the facts of the particular case, the EAT upheld an employment tribunal's decision that it was not unreasonable for the employee to take up a part-time university course alongside obtaining part-time employment in the circumstances, especially given that her former employer had declined to offer a satisfactory job reference.

In Sealey v Avon Aluminium Co Ltd EAT 516/78 the claimant was compensated **16.39** for the loss of 52 weeks' pay, although for 29 of these he was back at college. His compensation was reduced only by so much of the maintenance element of his grant as was attributable to 29 weeks out of the 52. Similarly, in Glen Henderson Ltd v Nisbet EAT 34/90 the employee followed the advice of her Jobcentre and embarked on a five-week business enterprise course with a view to becoming self-employed. The tribunal found this behaviour reasonable and awarded her compensation for loss of earnings while she was on the course and also one year's future loss on the basis of her self-employed earnings. The EAT upheld the tribunal's decision.

Note that where a tribunal finds that an employee has failed to mitigate his or her loss it should not necessarily treat that failure as bringing the period of compensation to an end. Thus, where an employee's decision to embark upon a course is held to be unreasonable, the tribunal should judge when the employee ought to have obtained fresh employment at a similar level – Mullarkey v Up the Creek Ltd EAT 263/95. In practice, however, tribunals often treat the date the course started as the cut-off point, presumably because the course is considered to be an intervening act, after which the employee's losses are too remote to be attributable to the unfair dismissal.

713

16.40 The Mullarkey case demonstrates the confusion that often exists between questions of mitigation and remoteness of loss. The tribunal in that case found the employee's decision to embark on a full-time course to be a reasonable act of mitigation. It nevertheless decided to award her no compensation from the date her course started because any losses suffered from that date onwards were a result of her own actions and were not caused by the dismissal. The EAT held this to be wrong. If the employee's actions were reasonable mitigation, then they could not have broken the chain of causation. But for the unfair dismissal, the employee would not have embarked on the course and would still have been in salaried employment with the employer.

This is to be contrasted with the decision in Simrad Ltd v Scott 1997 IRLR 147, EAT, where the EAT, in spite of a tribunal finding that the employee acted reasonably in retraining as a nurse, held that her losses from the date she started her course were too remote to be attributable to the actions of the employer. In our view, the Mullarkey approach is to be preferred on this point. Only if the employee's decision was unreasonable could it plausibly be considered to be an intervening act that relieves the employer of any further liability for the employee's losses.

16.41 In Tchoula v ICTS (UK) Ltd 2000 ICR 1191, EAT, a tribunal found that T, a security guard who had been victimised on the ground of race, had mitigated his loss by retraining in the IT sector. The EAT sympathised with ICTS's argument on appeal that it should not be responsible for funding T's change of career. However, the question for the EAT was whether the employment tribunal's finding that T had mitigated his loss was perverse. The EAT did not think that it was. It was open to the tribunal to find that it was reasonable for T to retrain in the IT sector and that it was reasonably foreseeable that such a course would be necessary as a result of T's unlawful dismissal. The tribunal was entitled to accept T's evidence that he did not pursue work in the security field as he would have needed a clean record to do so and because of his dismissal by ICTS he did not have such a record.

In Khanum v IBC Vehicles Ltd EAT 685/98 the EAT held that an employment tribunal should have allowed the claimant to recover losses incurred after embarking on her course of study as she had not failed to mitigate her loss. The claimant's former employer had dominated the local automobile industry in which she had worked and there was evidence that she had been 'blacklisted'. In the light of this, it had been reasonable for the claimant to enrol for a degree course. In so concluding, the EAT distinguished the decision in Simrad Ltd v Scott (above) and rejected the employer's contention that the decision in that case established a general rule of law that, for the purposes of compensation, the chain of causation is necessarily broken where an employee goes on to further education after being dismissed. Similarly, in Orthet Ltd v Vince-Cain 2005 ICR 374, EAT, the EAT upheld a tribunal's conclusion that the claimant's

714

decision to undertake a four-year undergraduate course in dietetics, when her efforts to find another suitably senior position in retail management failed, amounted to reasonable mitigation. The employee had childcare responsibilities which meant that she required reasonable flexibility in her working hours, which would not have been accommodated had she set her sights lower at a store management position (rather than a more senior position) in retail. It was therefore reasonable for her to seek to maintain that flexibility in any new work which she found. The EAT approved the tribunal's award based on loss of earnings for nine months in each of the four years of the course, giving credit for work during vacations.

Mitigation during the notice period 16.42

In Norton Tool Co Ltd v Tewson 1972 ICR 501, NIRC, the National Industrial Relations Court held that an employee is entitled to unfair dismissal compensation covering the period from the date of his or her dismissal to the date when notice – had it been properly given – would have expired, even though the employee has entered fresh employment during that period. The NIRC reasoned that it was 'just and equitable' (within the meaning of what is now S.123(1) ERA) to treat the employee as having suffered a loss in so far as he had received less than he should have done had the employer acted in accordance with 'good industrial practice' by giving notice or making a payment in lieu.

Highly cogent arguments presented in subsequent decisions called into question the validity of the so-called Norton Tool principle. In particular, it was argued – and in some cases accepted – that the principle offended the cardinal rule that the compensatory award should be based only on the employee's actual losses. However, the validity of the principle seemed to be settled when it was approved by the Court of Appeal in Addison v Babcock FATA Ltd 1987 ICR 805, CA. In that case the Court refused to extend the Norton Tool principle to the situation in which the employee has received a full payment in lieu of notice from the employer and subsequently seeks to recover compensation in respect of exactly the same notice period as part of an unfair dismissal compensatory award. The Court held that a notice payment is not an independent right to which an employee is entitled in addition to, and apart from, any compensation from the ex-employer for lost earnings during the period of notice. Accordingly, the employee had to give credit for the notice payment by offsetting it against such part of a compensatory award as covers the notional notice period. It logically followed that the Norton Tool principle should not be extended to allow an employee to reap the benefit of a double payment in respect of the same period of loss – namely, a payment in lieu of notice on the one hand, and a compensatory award covering lost earnings during the notice period on the other. Subject to this, however, the Court of Appeal did approve the Norton Tool principle as being correct so long as it remains confined to its proper ambit – i.e. earnings

715

from new employment during the notice period. Any such earnings did not fall to be deducted from the compensatory award.

16.43 The position thus seemed to be settled until the House of Lords handed down its seminal decision in Dunnachie v Kingston Upon Hull City Council 2004 ICR 1052, HL. There, it was held that the general provision governing the calculation of the compensatory award – S.123(1) ERA – permits only the award of sums in unfair dismissal cases that reflect the actual loss resulting from the dismissal. This meant that it is not legitimate to award sums that are additional to such loss, such as injury to feelings caused by the dismissal. As a result of this decision, many commentators considered that the Norton Tool principle could not survive. In the event, however, it appears to have done precisely that. For in Langley and anor v Burlo 2007 ICR 390, CA, the Court of Appeal took the view that the Dunnachie decision should not be regarded as authority for the proposition that Norton Tool was no longer good law, since the issue of whether the principle remained valid had not arisen for specific consideration in that case. In the Court of Appeal's view, the Norton Tool principle survived 'and should be applied by tribunals unless and until there is another decision which is directly in point'.

Even so, the Court of Appeal in Burlo made it clear that the Norton Tool principle has a narrow compass. In particular, it could not be applied in a way that resulted in an award of compensation greater than the loss caused to the employee as a consequence of the dismissal. It followed that a claimant was not entitled to receive, as part of her compensatory award, full pay for her notice period in circumstances where she would not have been able to work during her notice as a result of a physical injury and her contract expressly provided that she would be paid only statutory sick pay in periods of incapacity for work. Even if it were true that good industrial practice requires that an employee who is summarily dismissed while unfit for work through sickness should receive pay in lieu of notice at the normal rate of pay, that precept could not be prayed in aid in the assessment of the claimant's compensation. If the claimant had not been dismissed she would have received statutory sick pay during her period of absence. Therefore statutory sick pay was the correct measure of her weekly loss during the notice period and the compensatory award had to be calculated on that basis.

16.44 It follows from this that the Norton Tool principle has a limited scope: it applies where an employee has been deprived of his or her full contractual notice, remains fit and able to work and secures new employment during the notional notice period. In such a case, the employee's new earnings during that period do not have to be set off against his or her losses when calculating the compensatory award. Furthermore, in a case where the employer makes a payment in lieu of notice and the employee secures new employment during the notice period, although the employee will not be entitled to receive

716

compensation for unfair dismissal for lost earnings in respect of the notice period, his or her earnings from the new employment during that period will be ignored. In other words, the employee will not have to give credit for those earnings by offsetting them against the losses on which compensation for unfair dismissal is awarded.

For a more detailed discussion of the application of the Norton Tool principle in assessing loss upon which the compensatory award is based, see Chapter 14, 'Compensatory awards: types of loss', under 'Nature and maximum amount of award – "deemed losses" and Norton Tool rule'. And for further discussion of the specific effect the Norton Tool principle has on the treatment of new earnings during notice periods for compensatory award purposes, see Chapter 14, 'Compensatory awards: types of loss', under 'Immediate loss – new earnings, notice pay and the notice period'.

Application in constructive dismissal cases. In Stuart Peters Ltd v Bell 2009 **16.45** ICR 1556, CA, the Court of Appeal, while approving the workings of the Norton Tool principle as described above, held that it did not apply to constructive dismissal cases. In Lord Justice Elias's judgment, there is no industrial relations practice of making a full payment in lieu of notice where termination is triggered by the employee. As a result, an employee who succeeds in a claim of unfair constructive dismissal is entitled to compensation in respect of the entire notice period. However, account must be taken of earnings received from any new employment during that period by off-setting these against the losses which form the basis for the assessment of the compensatory award.

'Just and equitable' reductions   16.46

As explained in the introduction to Chapter 14, 'Compensatory awards: types of loss', S.123(1) ERA provides that the compensatory award shall be 'such amount as the tribunal considers just and equitable in all the circumstances having regard to the loss sustained by the complainant in consequence of the dismissal'. Under this subsection the employment tribunal can effectively reduce the compensatory award (but not the basic award) to reflect general considerations of fairness.

The cases where tribunals may decide that it is just and equitable to reduce compensation under this head can be divided roughly into two types:

- cases where, by the time of the tribunal hearing, the employer can show that the employee is guilty of misconduct that would have merited dismissal, even if the employer did not know about that misconduct at the time of the dismissal

- cases where the dismissal has been rendered unfair solely because of procedural failings in the dismissal procedure, but the tribunal is satisfied

717

that the employee could nevertheless have been fairly dismissed at a later date or if the employer had followed a proper procedure.

16.47 The second type of reduction is commonly known as a 'Polkey reduction' (or deduction) after the case in which the House of Lords confirmed that such a reduction was possible – Polkey v AE Dayton Services Ltd 1988 ICR 142, HL. In practice, it is now by far the most common basis on which reductions in the compensatory award are made by tribunals. However, as previously stated, a Polkey reduction is merely a sub-category of the reductions tribunals may make when calculating the amount that it is 'just and equitable' to award employees who have been unfairly dismissed after having regard to their actual losses. But in view of the considerable amount of case law and judicial guidance that so-called Polkey reductions have attracted, we discuss these reductions in a separate section below. First, however, we look at the other common form of 'just and equitable' reduction – see 'Misconduct not known to employer at date of dismissal' below.

Note that one factor that *cannot* be taken into account under the 'just and equitable' formula is the employer's ability to pay. In Tao Herbs and Acupuncture Ltd v Jin EAT 1477/09 the employer argued that the compensation a tribunal had awarded against it for unfair dismissal was too substantial, since it would force the business into liquidation. The EAT held that that argument had no reasonable prospect of success. It noted that while 'there are places in the employment protection canon where ability to pay is a feature... in the assessment of damages for a statutory tort, the possibility that the employer will be in difficulty paying an award is not a relevant consideration'.

16.48 Misconduct not known to employer at date of dismissal
What happens if an employer dismisses an employee on grounds that are held by a tribunal to be inadequate (and thus unfair) but subsequently discovers that the employee was guilty of misconduct that would have formed the basis for a fair dismissal had the employer known about it at the time? Clearly, such misconduct cannot be said to have 'caused or contributed' to the dismissal so as to justify a reduction in the compensatory award for contributory fault under S.123(6) ERA, since the conduct in question was not in the mind of the employer at the time of dismissal. However, although the unfairness of the dismissal will be unaltered by misconduct that comes to light after the dismissal, the tribunal is entitled to take it into account in accordance with the general statutory provision governing the calculation of the compensatory award – S.123(1) ERA. The inclusion of the words 'such amount as is just and equitable' in that provision implicitly allows a tribunal to take into account a factor such as the employee's wrongdoing in order to limit or reduce the amount of the compensatory award that would otherwise have been awarded.

718

A leading example of this principle being applied is the House of Lords' decision in W Devis and Sons Ltd v Atkins 1977 ICR 662, HL. In that case, the employee was the manager of an abattoir who was dismissed because the employer was not satisfied with his methods of making purchases. Several weeks later, the employer received information suggesting that the employee had been dishonestly dealing in live animals. A tribunal ruled the employee's dismissal to be unfair but decided, in the light of the subsequently discovered information, that it was not just and equitable to make any award. The House of Lords, upholding the tribunal's decision, said it was clear, on the basis of the information that subsequently came to light, that the employee could have been fairly dismissed if the employer had known about his conduct. The fact that the employee had not suffered any injustice meant that, applying what is now S.123(1), it was not just and equitable that he should receive any award.

In Atkinson v Community Gateway Association 2015 ICR 1, EAT, the Appeal Tribunal took the view that the same principle applied in cases of unfair constructive dismissal. On the main issue that came before the EAT in that case, it held that a tribunal had erred in law by deciding that an unfair constructive dismissal claim could not succeed because the claimant was himself in repudiatory breach of contract. The EAT explained that an employee is not prevented from claiming constructive dismissal by the fact that he or she is in breach of contract at the time of the employer's breach. However, if the tribunal finds the dismissal unfair, the employee's breach can then be taken into account at the remedy stage to reduce compensation. In the EAT's view, such a breach could reduce compensation by up to 100 per cent if it could or would have resulted in a fair dismissal had the employer been aware of it.

Limits on power to make 'just and equitable' reductions. There are, however, **16.49** limits on the tribunal's power to reduce the compensatory award under S.123(1) on account of misconduct not known to the employer at the time dismissal takes place. First and foremost, it is well established that S.123(1) applies only to pre-termination conduct that does not come to light until after the dismissal: post-termination conduct cannot be taken into account as a basis for a reduction – Soros and anor v Davison and anor 1994 ICR 590, EAT. In Soros, an employment tribunal found that the employees had been unfairly dismissed at a hearing on liability. Following that hearing, but prior to the hearing on remedy, the employees sold information about their former employer to a national newspaper. The employer applied for a stay on the remedy hearing until a High Court action for breach of confidentiality had been heard. The tribunal refused the application on the ground that the alleged breaches of duty were not relevant to the issue of remedies for unfair dismissal because they occurred after the employees had been dismissed. The EAT agreed, stating that the calculation of the compensatory award for unfair dismissal under S.123(1) is only concerned with events that occur during the currency of the contract of employment.

In Mullinger v Department for Work and Pensions EAT 0515/05 the EAT relied on the Soros case as authority for ruling that misconduct on the part of the employee occurring after his or her employment had ended could not form the basis for a reduction in the compensatory payment awardable for unfair dismissal. In that case, in support of the argument that it would be 'just and equitable' to reduce compensation under S.123(1), counsel for the employer posited some extreme hypothetical examples, such as where an employee faced with a letter of dismissal becomes so incensed that he or she assaults or even kills the messenger who delivers the letter. Perhaps a more realistic scenario might be where a dismissed employee re-enters the former employer's premises and sabotages the computer system. Even when faced with examples of this kind, the EAT was unimpressed with the submission that S.123(1) allows the employee's actions to be taken into account when calculating the compensatory award. Mr Justice Langstaff stated: 'We would merely observe that if it is the case that there is some financial consequence to an employer of some action taken by a former employee after his employment has ceased then there are remedies in law which an employer may be able to take advantage of. It does not seem to us to be at all unjust to leave the employer to those remedies. It does seem to us to strain the language of the statute, to be inconsistent with Soros, and to establish a principle with uncertain boundaries if we were to accede to [counsel for the employer's] submission.' (Note that, although the Mullinger case was appealed further – Mullinger v Department for Work and Pensions 2007 EWCA Civ 1334, CA – the Court of Appeal was not called upon to consider the particular observations of Langstaff J above, whose judgment on other aspects was upheld.)

16.50 In Cumbria County Council and anor v Bates EAT 0398/11, however, the EAT found a way around the restriction imposed by Soros and anor v Davison and anor (above). The case concerned B, who was unfairly dismissed from his teaching job. After the tribunal's liability hearing, but before any assessment of remedy, B was convicted of common assault on a former pupil and sentenced to six weeks' imprisonment. The employer argued that B's conviction was relevant to the question of remedy, potentially acting as a cut-off for his compensation for loss of earnings and reducing his pension claim. However, the tribunal considered itself bound by Soros: as the conviction for common assault related to matters occurring some 14 months after B's dismissal, the conviction was not relevant to the determination of what amount was just and equitable to award him by way of compensation. The tribunal made a compensatory award in excess of £69,000 (subject to the then statutory cap of £66,200) based on its assessment that, had he not been unfairly dismissed, B would have remained employed until the age of 65.

Before the EAT, the employer argued that the tribunal had misunderstood the basis on which it sought a reduction of B's compensatory award. It was not arguing that B's compensation should be reduced because of post-dismissal misconduct, but that a Polkey reduction should be made to reflect the fact that he would have been dismissed at some point before his retirement following the conviction. The EAT agreed, holding that the tribunal had erred and that the principles set out in Thornett v Scope 2007 ICR 236, CA, and Software 2000 Ltd v Andrews and ors 2007 ICR 825, EAT, applied. These require the tribunal, when awarding future loss, to make an assessment of how long the employee would have remained employed but for the dismissal. Since B's conviction and imprisonment may have substantially reduced his pension loss, the EAT held that the tribunal was plainly entitled to take it into account. Accordingly, Soros and anor v Davison and anor (above) did not prevent the tribunal taking B's conviction into account. (Note that Polkey reductions are discussed in detail under '"Polkey reductions"' below.)

A second limitation on the ability of tribunals to take into account misconduct **16.51** unknown to the employer at the time of dismissal is that, although tribunals are entitled to take a view as to what is just and equitable to award in all the circumstances, they must do so after 'having regard to the loss sustained by the complainant'. In effect, this ensures that considerations of justice and equity do not extend so far as empowering tribunals to award compensation simply on a 'feels fair' basis, with no regard to the actual financial losses sustained by the employee as a result of having been unfairly dismissed. The interplay between 'justice and equity' on the one hand, and 'having regard to the loss sustained' on the other, was clearly explained by Mr Justice Tudor Evans in Soros and anor v Davison and anor (above) when commenting on the principle established by the House of Lords in W Devis and Sons Ltd v Atkins (above). He observed: 'In our opinion, the House of Lords in [the Devis case] held that when assessing compensation for unfair dismissal, a tribunal should have regard to the loss sustained in consequence of the dismissal but should then ask itself whether it is just and equitable that the employee should be compensated, fully or at all, for that loss, bearing in mind the circumstances [of the particular case].'

The constraint to have regard to the actual losses of the complainant is illustrated by the EAT's decision in Abbey Motors (Hemel Hempstead) Ltd v Carta EAT 403/95. There, the employee deliberately misled the tribunal when he told it that he had not been able to find work during the 18 months following his dismissal. The employer produced evidence that he had earned £2,000 since that date. The tribunal decided to reduce C's compensatory award by double the amount of his post-dismissal earnings (although this still resulted in his receiving the maximum compensatory award applicable at that time). The employer appealed, arguing that the award should have been reduced to nothing to reflect the employee's behaviour. The EAT, however, in upholding the tribunal's decision, held that the tribunal was entitled to take account of the veracity of witnesses in respect of calculating the loss actually sustained and to adjust the amount of the award where, as in this case, the employee had tried to mislead the tribunal. But a nil award would not have been appropriate

721

because it is clear from S.123(1) that a tribunal is not entitled to assess compensation without any regard to the actual loss sustained by the employee in consequence of the dismissal.

16.52 A possible further limitation on tribunals' power to make a reduction under S.123(1) applies in respect of misconduct that could have been relied on and was known to the employer at the time of dismissal but which formed no part of the employer's decision to dismiss. It would seem from the Court of Appeal's decision in Devonshire v Trico-Folberth Ltd 1989 ICR 747, CA, that it is not just and equitable for a tribunal to take account of such misconduct as a basis for reducing the compensatory award. In that case the employee was dismissed on account of her absence record. She appealed against this decision and the appeal panel decided that she should not be dismissed for her attendance record but that her employment should be terminated on medical grounds. A tribunal found that the dismissal on medical grounds was unfair but that if the employee had been dismissed on the original ground the dismissal would have been fair. It awarded compensation of £9,057. The employer appealed, claiming that it was not just and equitable to make the compensatory award as the dismissal would have been fair if it had given a different reason for it. Both the EAT and the Court of Appeal rejected the employer's contention. The employer had specifically chosen not to rely on the employee's attendance as a reason for dismissal and therefore could not rely on it when attempting to reduce her compensatory award.

The distinguishing factor for the Court of Appeal seems to have been that, factually speaking, the case was not one of subsequently discovered misconduct (as was the case in W Devis and Sons Ltd v Atkins (above)): rather, the employer had made a conscious decision not to dismiss on the ground of attendance. Nevertheless, the decision is hard to reconcile with the actual reasoning in Devis. If compensation can be reduced on the basis of facts coming to light after the dismissal that would have justified the dismissal, the same logic would seem to apply where circumstances existed at the time of the dismissal which, if the employer had relied on them, would have made for a fair dismissal. This seems to have been the view taken by the EAT in McNee v Charles Tennant and Co Ltd EAT 338/90. In that case the employee was also originally dismissed for poor attendance, but this reason was changed to medical reasons on internal appeal. The EAT upheld a tribunal's decision not to make a compensatory award on the ground that the employee could have been dismissed fairly on several previous occasions for his absence record.

16.53 **Considerations of fairness remain paramount**
Even in a case of misconduct occurring prior to dismissal but only coming to the employer's attention after dismissal, tribunals must be careful not to leap to the conclusion that it is invariably just and equitable to reduce the compensatory award in the light of the misconduct. In Panama v London Borough of Hackney

722

2003 IRLR 278, CA, the Court of Appeal enjoined tribunals always to have regard to the consideration of overall fairness in such cases, which it described as being 'paramount'.

In the Panama case, the employment tribunal was held to have erred in finding that an unfairly dismissed employee was not entitled to compensation because evidence of fraudulent conduct that came to the employer's attention shortly after the dismissal meant that the employee would have been fairly dismissed in any event. Although the tribunal was asking itself a hypothetical question as to what would have happened if the employer had known of the allegations of fraud, it still had to approach the issue on the basis of whether a later dismissal would have been fair or unfair, bearing in mind the statutory test for establishing the reasonableness of the decision to dismiss set out in S.98(4) ERA and the well-known guidelines in British Home Stores Ltd v Burchell 1980 ICR 303, EAT (see the introduction to Chapter 6, 'Conduct'). In the particular case, a dismissal on the ground of fraud would not have been fair because the employer had failed to carry out a reasonable investigation into the allegations of fraud and therefore did not have reasonable grounds for its belief that the employee was guilty of dishonesty. There was therefore no basis for making any deduction from the claimant's compensatory award on the ground that 'it was just and equitable' to do so.

'Polkey reductions'

16.54

The other main type of cases in which employment tribunals often make 'just and equitable' reductions under S.123(1) ERA is where the unfairly dismissed employee could have been dismissed fairly at a later date or if a proper procedure had been followed. Ever since the House of Lords' landmark decision in Polkey v AE Dayton Services Ltd 1988 ICR 142, HL, 'procedural unfairness' cases – in which the dismissal is held to be unfair purely on procedural grounds but compensation is reduced to reflect the likelihood that the employee would still have been dismissed in any event had a proper procedure been followed – represent by far the most common type of reduction made by employment tribunals.

The 'Polkey principle'

16.55

The House of Lords' decision in Polkey v AE Dayton Services Ltd (above) ended what had become known as the 'no difference rule'. That rule provided that where there was a proven procedural irregularity in an otherwise fair dismissal – e.g. failure to warn or consult before a redundancy, or failure to allow the employee to state his or her case before a misconduct dismissal – but it could be shown that carrying out the proper procedure would have made 'no difference', then the dismissal would be fair. The House of Lords overturned this rule in all cases, except those where it would be 'utterly useless' or 'futile'

723

to carry out the required procedure. This meant that the reasonableness of the employer's action in dispensing with normal procedural requirements remained highly relevant to the question of whether the dismissal was fair, but the question of whether such a procedure would have made any difference was no longer a relevant consideration. The practical upshot was undoubtedly an increase in the number of findings of unfair dismissal.

However, although the House of Lords held that it should not be open to an employer to argue that 'no difference' dismissals should be regarded as fair, it was prepared to accept that the 'no difference rule' should live on as regards compensation. The basic principle stems from the earlier decision of the House of Lords in W Devis and Sons Ltd v Atkins 1977 ICR 662, HL (discussed under '"Just and equitable" reductions – misconduct not known to employer at date of dismissal' above). In that case Viscount Dilhorne asserted that 'it cannot be just and equitable that a sum should be awarded in compensation when in fact the employee has suffered no injustice by being dismissed'. This approach was taken up in the Polkey case, where the House of Lords ruled that the question of whether the employee ultimately suffered any injustice – i.e. whether the procedural irregularities really made any difference – was to be taken into account when assessing compensation.

16.56 **Current status of rule in Polkey.** In the autumn of 2004, the legislative landscape against which compensation for unfair dismissal operates profoundly changed with the introduction of statutory disciplinary and dismissal procedures (DDPs). The effect was to render dismissals automatically unfair in cases where employers failed to comply with certain basic procedures, and to impose virtually automatic uplifts to the resulting compensation of between 10 and 50 per cent. However, the statutory provisions further provided that so long as an employer complied with the relevant statutory DDPs, any failure to follow due procedure over and above what the DDPs required would not render the dismissal unfair provided that the employer could show that it would have decided to dismiss the employee in any event, regardless of the breach of procedure. The effect of this provision was to enact a limited reversal of the rule in Polkey by reinstating the 'no difference' rule that the Polkey case overturned.

As it turned out, these statutory provisions were short-lived. Following widespread criticism about their complexity and the fact that they had served to make internal dispute mechanisms within the workplace far too formal, they were repealed with effect from 6 April 2009. From that date, the law reverted back pretty much to how it was before the advent of the DDPs. The one significant change was the introduction of a statutory provision – S.207A of the Trade Union and Labour Relations Act 1992 – allowing for the compensatory award to be increased or reduced by up to 25 per cent for any failure by the employer or the employee to comply with the Acas Code of Practice on

Disciplinary and Grievance Procedures. This adjustment is discussed in detail under 'Adjustments for breach of Acas Code of Practice' below. Suffice it to say here that the principle in Polkey flourishes now as strongly as it did before the advent of the statutory DDPs.

Types of case to which Polkey principle applies   16.57

In Polkey v AE Dayton Services Ltd (above) the reason for dismissal was never in dispute, as both sides accepted that the real reason was redundancy. The issue was simply whether the complete lack of prior warning and consultation had rendered the dismissal unfair. But it is reasonably clear from the House of Lords' decision that their Lordships did not intend their ruling to be limited to any specific reason for dismissal. Whether an employer dismisses for redundancy, misconduct, incapability or for another permissible reason, it will not be able to elude a finding of unfair dismissal by pleading that a failure of procedure made no difference to the outcome of the dismissal process. But in all such cases, tribunals will be entitled, when assessing the compensatory award payable in respect of the unfair dismissal, to consider whether a reduction should be made on the ground that the lack of a fair procedure made no practical difference to the decision to dismiss.

Accepting that the Polkey principle potentially applies to all types of case irrespective of the reason for dismissal, its precise scope has nevertheless been called into question on certain other bases.

Cases where reason for dismissal in dispute. In Gover and ors v Propertycare   16.58
Ltd 2006 ICR 1073, CA, it was contended that it was not open to apply the Polkey principle to a case where the reason for dismissal was found by an employment tribunal to be different from that on which the employer relied when dismissing. In Gover, two employees resigned and claimed unfair constructive dismissal following the unilateral imposition by their employer of detrimental changes to their commission terms. A tribunal found that the dismissal was unfair in view of the complete lack of consultation about the change to the employees' terms and conditions. However, the tribunal went on to find that, even if there had been proper consultation as a result of which the employer made its proposed change of commission terms far more reasonable, the employees would have remained intransigent and would still have refused those terms. In those circumstances, the tribunal applied a Polkey reduction by limiting the period of the compensatory award to four months – the period of time it would have taken, in the tribunal's view, for the employer to conduct proper consultation. The employees appealed, contending that the tribunal's speculation about what would have happened during consultation and the reaction of the employer at the end of this process fundamentally altered the reason for the dismissal. They claimed that it was not open to the tribunal to apply a Polkey reduction based on that degree of speculation and on a set of

725

hypothetical circumstances that bore no relation to the actual dismissal which had taken place.

The Court of Appeal ultimately rejected this argument on the basis that it had not properly been raised in the notice of appeal. Lord Justice Buxton did, however, set out a detailed obiter (i.e. non-binding) view rejecting the employees' contention that the Polkey principle is limited to the same or similar facts as occurred in Polkey itself. In particular, Buxton LJ emphasised that Polkey is not restricted to cases where the employer has a valid reason for dismissal but has acted unfairly in its mode of reliance on that reason and the hypothesised future and fair dismissal would have been for that same reason. He observed that the Polkey principle was merely an example of the general application of the requirements of S.123(1) ERA in awarding what is just and equitable having regard to the loss sustained by the complainant. In any event, on the particular facts of the instant case, his Lordship pointed out that the real dismissal and the hypothesised dismissal (i.e. the one based on what would have occurred had there been proper consultation) both entailed a refusal by the employees to accept changes to their terms. The reason for dismissal was therefore basically the same.

16.59 The facts of the Gover case are similar, in many ways, to those in Henderson and ors v Mite Olscot Ltd EATS 0030/07, where the employees were dismissed ostensibly for redundancy, having refused to agree to changes in their terms and conditions. An employment tribunal ruled that their dismissals were unfair on the basis that the real explanation for the decision to dismiss was not redundancy but that the employees delayed in accepting the changes to their terms and conditions. However, it declined to award a compensatory award because, as it transpired that the employer had ceased to trade on the same day as the dismissals, it was clear that the employees would have been dismissed in any event, so they had not suffered any loss. In the alternative, the tribunal reasoned that the employees were authors of their misfortune because the closure of the employer's business would not have occurred had they not dug their heels in about agreeing to changes to their pay terms. In those circumstances, it was not 'just and equitable' within the meaning of S.123(1) ERA to award compensation for loss.

On appeal to the EAT, the employees contended that the tribunal had erred by making a Polkey reduction in view of the fact that the employer's asserted reason for dismissal – redundancy – was found not to have been the real reason. The Appeal Tribunal, however, held that both planks of the tribunal's reasoning in declining to make a compensatory award had been correct. This was not a case where any issue of a Polkey reduction arose given that the closure of the business had coincided with the date of the dismissals and it had been shown that the dismissals would have occurred by reason of the closure in any event. As a result, the employees had sustained no loss on the basis of which they

726

should have been compensated, and therefore there was no compensatory award from which to make any reduction. Additionally, the EAT ruled that the tribunal's alternative reasoning – that it was just and equitable not to make any compensatory award – was one that was reasonably open to it in the circumstances. In so holding, the EAT implicitly rejected the employee's contention that a Polkey reduction can never be made where it transpires that the real reason for dismissal is different from that relied upon by the employer when dismissing.

In O'Donoghue v Redcar and Cleveland Borough Council 2001 IRLR 615, **16.60** CA, the Court of Appeal held that where an employee had been found to have been unfairly dismissed on sex discriminatory grounds, the employment tribunal had been entitled to deploy Polkey-type reasoning to limit the period of loss. On the evidence, the tribunal concluded that the employee would have been dismissed in any event within six months by reason of her antagonistic and intransigent attitude.

Cases where observance of proper procedure would have delayed dismissal. **16.61** Even before Polkey v AE Dayton Services Ltd (above), an unfairly dismissed employee's compensation was sometimes limited to the period between dismissal and the time the employment would have been fairly terminated in any case (see, for example, Young's of Gosport Ltd v Kendell 1977 ICR 907, EAT). The most typical examples of this today are cases of redundancy dismissals that are unfair owing to lack of consultation but where a proper consultation would merely have delayed a fair dismissal. In such cases it will not be appropriate for the tribunal to award nil compensation because loss has clearly been sustained during the notional consultation period. In Mining Supplies (Longwall) Ltd v Baker 1988 ICR 676, EAT, for example, B was found to have been unfairly dismissed for redundancy as there had not been appropriate consultation with him on his selection. The tribunal awarded him six weeks' pay for his compensatory award as it decided that this was how much time the necessary consultations would have taken, after which he would inevitably have been selected for redundancy anyway. The EAT upheld the decision to award compensation but reduced the amount. There was no principle that if the tribunal found that consultation would make no difference, no compensatory award should be made. However, each case depended on its own facts. In this case two weeks' pay was a reasonable amount to award for the time consultation would have taken.

However, the EAT took a different approach in Elkouil v Coney Island Ltd 2002 IRLR 174, EAT. In that case, a tribunal found that redundancy consultation should have begun ten weeks before dismissal. It further found that, as consultation would have prolonged E's employment by two weeks, E should be awarded a compensatory award equal to two weeks' pay. The EAT overturned this because if consultation had commenced when it should have, E would have

727

had the benefit of looking for a new job ten weeks earlier than he actually did. This should have been reflected in a compensatory award of ten weeks.

16.62 In Walker and ors v Dysch Rosen Shoes Ltd and anor EAT 341/90 W was dismissed for a reason connected with the imminent transfer of the business in which he worked. The tribunal found that even if the dismissal was for an 'economic, technical or organisational reason' (and thus not automatically unfair under the Transfer of Undertakings (Protection of Employment) Regulations 2006 SI 2006/246), it was still unfair in this case owing to procedural failings. The tribunal then reduced the compensatory award by 90 per cent on the ground that W's dismissal was inevitable because the new employer was clearly determined to dismiss him. The EAT said that the tribunal was wrong on this point: in assessing compensation, it should have gone on to consider whether W would have been dismissed fairly by his new employer (following proper procedures, etc). The EAT held that full compensation should be awarded for the period in which proper consultation would have taken place. The likelihood of a (fair) dismissal being inevitable (because consultation would have made no difference) was to be taken into account from this point on.

The same logic may apply in other types of case where a fair procedure would have delayed an otherwise inevitable dismissal. For example, Slaughter v C Brewer and Sons Ltd 1990 ICR 730, EAT, concerned an ill-health dismissal. Although the EAT remitted the case to a tribunal to hear further evidence on compensation, it canvassed the possibility that 'a dismissal may be unfair on procedural grounds yet it may be quite apparent from the medical evidence that an applicant was, at the date of dismissal, quite incapable of carrying out her or his proper function. In another case there may have been insufficient medical evidence, hence unfairness, but the subsequent investigation would have shown that the dismissal was inevitable. In such a case a possible view might be that such an investigation would have taken some days or weeks and that compensation should cover that period.'

16.63 It should be pointed out, however, that there is a difference between the nature of the procedural requirements in a redundancy case and those in, say, a case of dismissal for incapability. In the former, a reasonable consultation period will usually be between two and four weeks, so it will be quite reasonable to award full compensation for that period even if the dismissal was inevitable. In cases of incapability, however, an employer's failure to allow the employee an opportunity to improve before dismissing may represent a very considerable period by which a proper procedure would have delayed the dismissal. In such cases the tribunal may be more likely to seek to reduce the compensation by the relevant percentage figure from the outset – see the pre-Polkey case of Winterhalter Gastronom Ltd v Webb 1973 ICR 245, NIRC.

In the misconduct case of Stonehouse Coaches Ltd v Smith 2014 ICR D14, EAT, the EAT refused to interfere with a tribunal's decision that a fair procedure would have delayed the employee's dismissal by four weeks. S, a bus driver, was dismissed after allegedly swearing at a female passenger in front of schoolchildren. After the dismissal, but before his unfair dismissal claim was heard, the employer received statements from two passengers alleging that S had committed an earlier act of misconduct. The tribunal found S's dismissal procedurally unfair but that, had a fair procedure been followed, he would have been dismissed after four weeks. The employer appealed, arguing that the tribunal should have considered the passengers' evidence when addressing the question of compensation. The EAT disagreed. Mr Justice Langstaff, sitting alone in the EAT, noted that Polkey involves an assessment of the chance of future dismissal. In his view, 'there is always likely to be a time gap between an actual decision to dismiss, reached unfairly by unfair procedure, and a decision which would or might have been reached following a fair procedure. That gap is a period of time during which the employee would remain in employment and for which the employee is entitled to be compensated.' In the instant case, the tribunal had assessed that period to be four weeks. The passengers' evidence only came to light long after the four-week period had passed, meaning that it could have made no difference to the assessment of the date of S's likely dismissal in the event of a fair procedure. Nor could it be argued that the evidence would have escalated the charge against S from misconduct to gross misconduct, such that he could properly have been dismissed summarily. The EAT did accept the possibility that, in another case, if later-discovered material suggested that there were additional reasons for dismissal, that might affect a tribunal's decision on how likely it was that there would have been a fair dismissal. However, such evidence could have no effect in a case such as the present one where the tribunal had already found dismissal to be 100 per cent certain and the only question was how long a fair procedure would have taken.

16.64 Note that when applying the Polkey principle, a tribunal should consider not only how long a fair procedure might have taken but also whether there was a real chance that the claimant might have remained in employment if a fair procedure had been followed. In Venkatesan v Surabi Ltd and anor EAT 0193/14, for example, the EAT held that the tribunal had erred by focusing purely on how long a fair procedure would have taken. What it should have done was consider whether there was a chance that, had such a procedure been followed, V could have shown that he had the right to remain and work in the UK and therefore would not have been dismissed. This issue is discussed further under 'Amount of reduction – no "all or nothing" approach' below.

16.65 **Cases of 'substantive' as opposed to 'procedural' unfairness.** It has been suggested in several cases that the Polkey principle applies only to cases where the unfairness of the dismissal derives from procedural failings rather than substantive injustice. The basic reasoning underlying this view is that it is only

729

appropriate to speculate about what would have happened or might have happened in the context of procedural failings, since only in such cases is it feasible to construct the world as it might have been by positing what the fate of the employee would have been if the procedural failures had not occurred. In contrast, it is far more difficult and, so the argument goes, neither just nor equitable to speculate about what would or might have been the position where an employee has been dismissed in circumstances that are substantively unfair – for example, because of the employer's lack of a reasonably held and genuine belief in the employee's misconduct or, in a redundancy case, because of the inherent unfairness of the redundancy selection.

It is clear that the courts have struggled with the proposition that Polkey only applies to procedural unfair dismissals, but, after some doubt, they seem to have come down decisively in favour of rejecting it. Initially, the argument did hold sway. In Steel Stockholders (Birmingham) Ltd v Kirkwood 1993 IRLR 515, EAT, for example, the EAT expressly stated that the Polkey principle did not apply where the decision to dismiss was substantively unfair. On the facts of the case before it, the Appeal Tribunal held that no reduction should be made since the reason the employee's redundancy dismissal was unfair was that the employer had adopted an artificially narrow pool for selection, thereby denying the employee the right to be compared with all the other employees who were involved in the employer's reorganisation. This was no mere procedural irregularity: rather, the employer's failure impugned the very basis for the dismissal itself and thus caused it to be substantively unfair. Accordingly, there were no grounds for assessing what might have happened had the employer adopted an appropriate pool for selection.

16.66 The chief problem with this approach, as subsequent cases have made clear, is that the distinction between what is 'procedural' and what is 'substantive' can be very difficult to draw. In O'Dea v ISC Chemicals Ltd 1996 ICR 222, CA, the Court of Appeal described the decision in Steel Stockholders as 'controversial' and held the procedural/substantive distinction made in that case to be unwarranted. In O'Dea the tribunal had found the employee to have been dismissed for redundancy and not, as the employee claimed, by reason of his trade union activities. It went on to find that the employee's dismissal was unfair because of a serious breach of procedure and reduced his compensatory award by 80 per cent to reflect the fact that he had only a one-in-five chance of being retained by the employer even if a fair procedure had been adopted. Upholding that decision when it reached the Court of Appeal, Lord Justice Peter Gibson observed: 'I do not regard it as helpful to characterise the defect as procedural or substantive nor in my view should the [employment] tribunal be expected to do so, though in fact in the present case the [employment] tribunal did repeatedly describe the defect as procedural. The fact of the matter is that the applicant lost only a one-in-five chance of being retained, and I can see no arguable case that he should have been compensated on the same footing as if he was bound to have been retained but for his trade union activities.'

However, although the decision in Steel Stockholders (Birmingham) Ltd v Kirkwood (above) should no longer be considered good law, there are a number of cases that warn against an overzealous use of Polkey reductions. For example, in Chloride Ltd v Cain and anor EAT 564/94 a tribunal found that there had been a complete lack of consultation by the employer, no objective selection criteria and no consideration of possible alternative employment. The EAT rejected the employer's argument that the tribunal, in assessing compensation, should have reduced the award to reflect the chance that the employees would have been fairly dismissed if a proper procedure had been adopted. While the EAT accepted that the Steel Stockholders decision was wrong, it shared that decision's antipathy 'towards an employer who has used unfair criteria seeking to maintain subsequently that a different and fair basis of selection would or might have led to the same result'. The EAT stated that the tribunal was entitled to decide that the employer had used unfair criteria in selecting an employee for redundancy and that the overall justice and equity of the case was not much affected by the fact that other criteria might have been adopted. And in Eclipse Blinds Ltd v Bill EAT 818/92 the EAT stressed that the task of the tribunal was to take into account all the circumstances rather than to isolate one factor, such as whether consultation would have made any difference.

In King and ors v Eaton Ltd (No.2) 1998 IRLR 686, Ct Sess (Inner House), the **16.67** Court of Session held that, in considering the question of what would have happened had the unfairness not occurred ('the hypothetical question', to use the phrase used by the EAT in Fisher v California Cake and Cookie Ltd 1997 IRLR 212, EAT), making a distinction between the 'merely' procedural and the more genuinely substantive will often be of some practical use. If there has been a merely procedural lapse or omission, it may be relatively straightforward to envisage what the course of events might have been if procedures had stayed on track. If, on the other hand, what went wrong was more fundamental, and seems to have gone 'to the heart of the matter', it may well be difficult to envisage what would have happened in the hypothetical situation of the unfairness not having occurred. In that case, the tribunal cannot be expected to 'embark on a sea of speculation'.

It might be thought that the observations made by the Court of Session above offer a commonsense approach towards the issue of making Polkey reductions. The approach advocates the avoidance of too formulaic an application of the procedural/substantive distinction, while making it clear that in the case of seriously flawed dismissal procedures a tribunal cannot be expected to speculate about what might have happened had the employer acted totally differently. Even so, in subsequent decisions the Court of Appeal has downplayed the relevance of the distinction between procedural and substantive unfairness, as the case below illustrates.

16.68 In O'Donoghue v Redcar and Cleveland Borough Council 2001 IRLR 615, CA, a claimant unsuccessfully contended before the Court of Appeal that it was not open to a tribunal – in the light of the King decision – to make a finding on the inevitability of her dismissal, since her dismissal had been found to be substantively unfair. The tribunal in that case had found that the claimant had been both unfairly dismissed and victimised, but that she would have been fairly dismissed in any event within six months because of her unacceptable attitude towards colleagues and the complaints that had arisen as a result of her behaviour. Accordingly, it limited her compensation to the period of six months during which her employment would have continued. The Court of Appeal rejected the employee's appeal, stating that: 'If the facts are such that an [employment] tribunal, while finding that an employee/applicant has been dismissed unfairly (whether substantively or procedurally), concludes that, but for the dismissal, the applicant would have been bound soon thereafter to be dismissed (fairly) by reason of some course of conduct or characteristic attitude which the employer reasonably regards as unacceptable but which the employee cannot or will not moderate, then it is just and equitable that compensation for the unfair dismissal should be awarded on that basis. We do not read Polkey or King v Eaton Ltd as precluding such an analysis.'

Taking their cue from this, more recent decisions of the appellate courts have moved away from a detailed discussion of the procedural/substantive issue and have shifted the focus onto whether tribunals come under an absolute duty to consider making a Polkey reduction whenever there is evidence to suggest that the employee might have been fairly dismissed, either when the unfair dismissal actually occurred or at some later date – see Gover v Propertycare Ltd 2006 ICR 1073, CA; Thornett v Scope 2007 ICR 236, CA; Software 2000 Ltd v Andrews and ors 2007 ICR 825, EAT; and Contract Bottling Ltd v Cave and anor 2015 ICR 146, EAT. While all these cases recognise the wisdom of the remarks made by Lord Prosser in King and ors v Eaton Ltd (No.2) (above), it is clear that the courts are increasingly reluctant to support the view that there is a clear dividing line between procedural and substantive unfairness, still less that such a line should be used to determine when it is and is not appropriate to make a Polkey reduction. This issue, along with the cases mentioned above, is further discussed under 'Tribunals' duty to consider making Polkey reduction' below.

16.69 Finally, it is interesting to note, with reference back to King and ors v Eaton Ltd (No.2) (above), that the appellate courts will interfere with a Polkey percentage assessment by a tribunal on the ground that the unfairness of the dismissal was so unjust as to preclude any speculation about whether the employee could and would have been fairly dismissed at some later date. In Davidson v Industrial

732

and Marine Engineering Services Ltd EAT 0071/03 the EAT quashed a tribunal's decision to make a 60 per cent Polkey reduction on the basis that the process adopted by the employer was so fundamentally flawed that it was impossible to assess the percentage chance of the claimant still being dismissed had a fair procedure been followed. A similar conclusion was reached by the EAT in Scotland in Manzie v Optos plc EATS 0029/04, where the EAT quashed a finding of a 50 per cent Polkey reduction on the ground that it could not conceive how it could be said that dismissal could have been considered likely. The EAT ruled that the way in which the employee had been treated by the employer 'offends practically every aspect of fairness that can be imagined'.

Cases of automatically unfair dismissal. In Audere Medical Services Ltd v **16.70** Sanderson EAT 0409/12 an employment tribunal found that S, a hospital technician, was automatically unfairly dismissed for making a protected disclosure under the whistleblowing provisions of the ERA. The tribunal awarded £20,779.12 in compensation. The employer argued that this figure should be reduced under Polkey because there was a chance that, had he not been dismissed for making the disclosure, S would eventually have been dismissed for his alleged misconduct at the hospital. The tribunal accepted that, prior to S's disclosure, the employer had legitimate concerns about his conduct. However, it refused to reduce S's compensation, taking the view that it would be illogical and inappropriate to make a Polkey reduction, or a reduction for contributory fault, given its finding of automatic unfair dismissal. As the main reason that S was dismissed was that he had made a protected disclosure, the tribunal could not see how any Polkey or contributory fault argument could be mounted. On appeal, the EAT observed that it had been shown no case law authority regarding the making of such reductions in cases of automatically unfair dismissal. However, it held that as a matter of principle there was no reason why a Polkey reduction or a reduction for contributory fault could not be made in such cases, provided the circumstances warranted it. The employment tribunal had therefore erred in not taking into account the possibility that contributory conduct and Polkey reductions might have been appropriate on the facts of the case. In this regard, the EAT highlighted the tribunal's finding that the employer had reasonable grounds for considering that some of S's pre-dismissal actions amounted to misconduct. The EAT therefore remitted the case to the tribunal to decide whether or not any reduction was appropriate.

Polkey reductions and redundancy. Although, as we have seen, the Polkey **16.71** principle potentially covers all types of dismissal, it features particularly prominently in redundancy cases. Indeed, the EAT has held that an employment tribunal will be regarded as having erred in law if it fails to consider whether it is just and equitable to award full compensation in a case where the employer has failed to consult before a redundancy – Hepworth Refractories Ltd v Lingard EAT 555/90.

733

But the fact that redundancy dismissal was inevitable even if adequate consultation had taken place does not automatically mean that the dismissal is the cut-off point for compensation. In Stroud Rugby Football Club v Monkman EAT 0143/13 the tribunal found that it was likely that, if the employer had consulted, an arrangement whereby the dismissed employee would have remained working for the employer on a casual basis, for less money, would have been agreed. The EAT held that the tribunal was entitled to take this into account and award compensation on the basis of what the employee would have earned under such an arrangement. The compensation properly reflected the fact that what the employee had lost was the opportunity to discuss ways in which she might have continued to earn some remuneration from the employer.

16.72 Where, in a redundancy case, the tribunal finds that a proper procedure might have led to an offer of alternative employment, it should identify the job that would have been offered and base its assessment of the employee's losses on the wages that would have been earned in that alternative job. Take the example of an employee who earned £400 per week before being made redundant without sufficient consultation. If the tribunal subsequently finds that proper consultation would have given the employee a 50 per cent chance of securing alternative employment with the employer in a post paying £300 per week, then the employee's losses for the purpose of calculating the compensatory award should be assessed at £150 per week (50 per cent of £300 per week) – see Red Bank Manufacturing Co Ltd v Meadows 1992 ICR 204, EAT. Two examples:

- **Thompson Wholesale Foods v Norris** EAT 800/92: the claimant was dismissed for redundancy but the tribunal found that his dismissal was unfair for lack of consultation and that, had the consultation been carried out, there was a chance that the employee would have accepted alternative employment in a job with lower pay. The employment tribunal awarded N compensation for a period of one year from the date of his dismissal, calculated at the rate of his pre-dismissal earnings. The EAT held that this was wrong: the tribunal should have assessed the chance that the outcome would have been different if a fair procedure had been followed and should also have determined the rate of pay that the employee would have been likely to receive in any new position

- **Howells School v Gerrard** EAT 0079/12: the tribunal had found procedural shortcomings in the claimant's redundancy dismissal and moved on to the assessment of remedies. Considering the possible outcome if a fair procedure had been followed, it found that it was 'likely' that the claimant, who worked as a yard manager at an equestrian centre, would have remained as an employee and decided upon a 20 per cent Polkey reduction to reflect the chance of dismissal. It then asked what would have been her salary if she had been kept on. However, instead of answering that question, the tribunal proceeded to make a compensatory award based on her pre-dismissal earnings. The EAT held that the tribunal had fallen into error in doing so. The evidence showed that, due to the financial constraints suffered by the employer's business, it was likely that the claimant's salary would have been reduced. In fact, by the time of the tribunal hearing, there remained only one employee at the equestrian centre and that employee earned only £7,200. Consequently, the most that the claimant could have hoped to have earned during the two-year period which the tribunal, in its discretion, had assessed as the appropriate compensatory period was £14,400.

The timing and availability of suitable alternative employment arose for **16.73** consideration in King v Royal Bank of Canada (Europe) Ltd 2012 IRLR 280, EAT. In that case the employee was made redundant without any prior warning. An employment tribunal upheld her claim of unfair dismissal and awarded her a basic award plus two months' pay, representing the period it believed the employer should have taken to carry out a fair dismissal. The EAT allowed the appeal against the finding on compensation. It noted that where an employer has dismissed an employee without consultation, a tribunal must take account of the chance that suitable alternative employment might have arisen at any point during the period of consultation that should have taken place. In the instant case, the tribunal had found that proper consultation would have taken two months. It followed that the tribunal should not have restricted itself to considering a single list of vacancies produced by the employer shortly after the employee's dismissal. The employer should have put before the tribunal evidence of vacancies to cover the whole period during which it should have consulted the employee about her redundancy. It was not satisfactory to adduce a list that was no more than a 'snapshot' when subsequent suitable vacancies may have arisen during the two-month period.

Note, however, that while the initial burden of adducing evidence on alternative employment is on the employer, it is for the employee to show what job, or kind of job, he or she believes was available and to provide supporting evidence that such employment would have been accepted. This was made clear by the EAT in Virgin Media Ltd v Seddington and anor EAT 0539/08, which is discussed in more detail under 'Tribunals' duty to consider making Polkey reduction – burden of proof' below.

Tribunals' duty to consider making Polkey reduction   16.74

One question of considerable practical importance is: in what circumstances does an employment tribunal have to consider whether to make a Polkey reduction? In King and ors v Eaton Ltd (No.2) 1998 IRLR 686, Ct Sess (Inner House), Lord Prosser (giving the lead judgment of the Court of Session) observed: '[T]he matter will be one of impression and judgement, so that a tribunal will have to decide whether the unfair departure from what should have happened was of a kind which makes it possible to say, with more or less

735

confidence, that the failure makes no difference, or whether the failure was such that one cannot sensibly reconstruct the world as it might have been.'

This statement has been expressly approved in many cases since. But at the same time as making the statement, Lord Prosser also accepted that a useful distinction might be drawn between procedural and substantive unfairness and suggested that, in cases where dismissals are unfair owing to substantive unfairness, it might sometimes be a step too far for them to speculate about what could or would have been the case if the employee had not been fairly dismissed by the employer. We have already seen, however, that this distinction no longer finds judicial support – see 'Types of case to which Polkey principle applies – cases of "substantive" as opposed to "procedural" unfairness' above. Instead, the Court of Appeal and the EAT have suggested that, regardless of the type of case or nature of the unfairness, employment tribunals will be expected to consider making a Polkey reduction whenever there is evidence to support the view that the employee might have been dismissed if the employer had acted fairly. In reaching its conclusion, the tribunal needs to consider both whether the employer *could* have dismissed fairly and whether it *would* have done so. Furthermore, the enquiry is directed at what the particular employer would have done, not what a hypothetical fair employer would have done – Hill v Governing Body of Great Tey Primary School 2013 ICR 691, EAT.

16.75 **Degree of speculation expected of tribunals.** In Gover and ors v Propertycare Ltd 2006 ICR 1073, CA, Lord Justice Buxton expressly approved the way in which His Honour Judge McMullen at EAT level had formulated the basis for considering whether or not a Polkey reduction should be made. In that case, the employment tribunal found that the compensatory award for employees who had been unfairly dismissed for refusing to agree to changes in their terms and conditions should be limited to four months' losses. That was the period of time the tribunal said it would have taken to conduct proper consultation about the proposed changes, at the end of which the employees would have been fairly dismissed, as it was likely, in the tribunal's view, that the employer would have offered more reasonable terms but the employees would have continued to reject them. On appeal, upholding the tribunal's Polkey reduction, HHJ McMullen observed: 'The tribunal [was] doing what it [was] engaged to do: to draw upon its industrial experience of circumstances such as this and to construct, from evidence not from speculation, a framework which is a working hypothesis about what would have occurred had the [employer] behaved differently and fairly... The criticism advanced by [counsel] is that in seeking to construct the hypothesis the tribunal had so many pieces of the jigsaw missing that the only correct approach was to disallow any kind of Polkey reduction. We do not accept that proposition because the findings, based upon a careful analysis of the material which it had before it, and drawing upon its experience, do indicate that it was satisfied that there was material sufficient to make a judgement.'

736

The Court of Appeal's approval of HHJ McMullen's formulation suggests that tribunals may be required to hypothesise about 'what ifs' and 'maybes' in their deliberations as to remedy to a far greater extent than was previously understood. This impression has been reinforced by subsequent decisions of the Court of Appeal and the EAT, as discussed below.

In Thornett v Scope 2007 ICR 236, CA, the employee was dismissed when she **16.76** refused to relocate after being suspended from work for bullying and harassing a colleague. An employment tribunal held that her dismissal was unfair, but limited the compensatory award to six months' loss on the basis that if the employer had encouraged the parties in the dispute to try to work together this would have been bound to have resulted in failure after six months. On appeal, the EAT held that the tribunal had erred by launching itself upon 'a sea of speculation' and should have accepted that it could not, on the evidence before it, 'sensibly recreate the world as it might have been'. Given the evidence about how the parties could work together, it was wrong to place a limitation in time as to the duration of the relationship and to reduce the losses accordingly.

However, on further appeal, the Court of Appeal overturned the EAT's judgment and reinstated the decision of the employment tribunal. It held that a tribunal's task when assessing compensation for future loss of earnings will almost inevitably involve a consideration of uncertainties. Any assessment of future loss is by way of prediction and therefore involves a speculative element. A tribunal's statutory duty may involve making such predictions and tribunals cannot be expected, or even allowed, to opt out of that duty merely because their task is a difficult one and may involve speculation. Although there may be cases in which evidence to the contrary is so sparse that a tribunal should approach the question on the basis that loss of earnings would have continued indefinitely, whenever there is any evidence at all that it may not have been the case this must be taken into account. Applying this reasoning to the facts of the particular case, the tribunal had been entitled to limit the unfairly dismissed employee's compensation to a period of six months on the ground that her employment would in any event have ended within six months of her dismissal.

In Software 2000 Ltd v Andrews and ors 2007 ICR 825, EAT, Mr Justice Elias, **16.77** the then President of the EAT, reviewed all the authorities on the application of Polkey, including Gover and ors v Propertycare Ltd (above) and Thornett v Scope (above), and summarised the principles to be extracted from them. These included:

- in assessing compensation for unfair dismissal, the employment tribunal must assess the loss flowing from that dismissal, which will normally involve an assessment of how long the employee would have been employed but for the dismissal

737

- if the employer contends that the employee would or might have ceased to have been employed in any event had fair procedures been adopted, the tribunal must have regard to all relevant evidence, including any evidence from the employee (for example, to the effect that he or she intended to retire in the near future)

- there will be circumstances where the nature of the evidence for this purpose is so unreliable that the tribunal may reasonably take the view that the exercise of seeking to reconstruct what might have been is so riddled with uncertainty that no sensible prediction based on the evidence can properly be made. Whether that is the position is a matter of impression and judgement for the tribunal

- however, the tribunal must recognise that it should have regard to any material and reliable evidence that might assist it in fixing just and equitable compensation, even if there are limits to the extent to which it can confidently predict what might have been; and it must appreciate that a degree of uncertainty is an inevitable feature of the exercise. The mere fact that an element of speculation is involved is not a reason for refusing to have regard to the evidence

- a finding that an employee would have continued in employment indefinitely on the same terms should only be made where the evidence to the contrary (i.e. that employment might have been terminated earlier) is so scant that it can effectively be ignored.

16.78 These principles have been consistently applied by the EAT in later cases, including Butler v GR Carr (Essex) Ltd EAT 0128/07; Wilson UK Ltd v Turton and anor EAT 0348/08; Allied Distillers Ltd v Handley and ors EATS 0020/08; Cumbria County Council and anor v Bates EAT 0398/11; and London Borough of Hillingdon v Gormanley and ors EAT 0169/14. Of particular note is Elias J's observation that tribunals must have regard to any material and reliable evidence that might assist it in fixing just and equitable compensation even if there are limits to the extent to which it can confidently predict what might have been. In other words, it is not just the evidence adduced by the employer that will be used to determine the Polkey question. At another point in his judgment, Elias J made it clear just how limited the scope is for tribunals to evade the task of making a Polkey reduction on the ground that determining what could or would have happened is just too speculative: 'The question is not whether the tribunal can predict with confidence all that would have occurred; rather it is whether it can make any assessment with sufficient confidence about what is likely to have happened, using its common sense, experience and sense of justice. It may not be able to complete the jigsaw but may have sufficient pieces for some conclusions to be drawn as to how the picture would have developed. For example, there may be insufficient evidence, or it may be too unreliable, to enable a tribunal to say with any precision whether an employee would, on the balance of probabilities, have been dismissed, and yet sufficient evidence for the tribunal to conclude that on any view there must have been some realistic chance that he would have been. Some assessment must be made of that risk when calculating the compensation even though it will be a difficult and to some extent speculative exercise.'

The practical impact of Elias J's guidance is apparent from the outcome of the employer's appeal in the Software 2000 case itself. The employment tribunal had found that the claimants had been unfairly dismissed because the criteria that had been used to select them for redundancy were too subjective and had been improperly applied. The employer submitted that, even if the selection exercise had been properly conducted, the claimants would still have been dismissed. However, the tribunal declined to make a Polkey reduction on the ground that the selection procedure was so flawed that it was impossible to say what the outcome would have been. On appeal, applying its own guidance to the facts as found, the EAT ruled that the tribunal had erred in law. In particular, it had ignored valid evidence that to some extent would have helped it to decide whether the employees would – absent the procedural failings – have been dismissed in any event. For example, two of the claimants, P and T, had received the lowest scores (44 and 48 respectively) out of a total pool of 22 employees. The 'break mark' had been set at 60, and the next lowest scored employee had been given a score of 59. The employer had conceded that T had been scored too low on one of the more acceptable criteria it had used in the redundancy exercise. But even accepting that, T would still have fallen well short of the break mark. The EAT accepted that this was plainly evidence (among other examples) that the tribunal should have considered, and it was erroneous to have simply ignored that evidence or treated it as being too unreliable.

16.79 Further guidance on the assessment of a claimant's compensation and the impact of Polkey was recently given by the EAT in Contract Bottling Ltd v Cave and anor 2015 ICR 146, EAT. In that case, Mr Justice Langstaff, President of the EAT (sitting alone), reviewed the relevant authorities and set out some general guidance for tribunals on determining a claimant's compensation. He began with a reminder that a Polkey reduction is merely one part of what is in fact a complex assessment. On the face of it, a claimant who is dismissed from a job suffers an open-ended loss of the income he or she was receiving from that job immediately prior to dismissal. In practice, however, the tribunal should moderate this position based on its assessment of the likelihood of possible future events. So, the tribunal must consider a claimant's chance of obtaining alternative employment. It is also necessary for the tribunal to assess whether, had the claimant not been dismissed, he or she would have remained in the same role at the same rate of pay. The individual choices of the claimant and/or employer may also play a part. The claimant might seek promotion in another company or make lifestyle choices that would cause him or her to leave that particular employment. Or the employer might at some stage decide to

739

restructure its business, or to terminate the claimant's employment for a good reason. This last point indicates the possibility of a fair dismissal at some time in the future and it is only here that the prospect of a Polkey reduction arises.

Langstaff P was keen to emphasise that assessment of compensation and the appropriate amount of any Polkey reduction will 'necessarily involve a number of imponderables'. However, this does not mean that the tribunal should not grapple with the issues 'in so far as it can'. In assessing the chance that a fair dismissal would have occurred, the tribunal should seek to identify the probability of a future event occurring, rather than of a past event having happened. The tribunal must consider not just whether a fair dismissal might have taken place, but also *when* it is likely to have done so. The use of percentages for such an assessment has the advantage of transparency. When adopting a particular percentage, the tribunal should 'spell out, as best it can' what factors have influenced it. However, a party will have no grounds to challenge the tribunal's decision unless the percentage the tribunal has adopted is 'manifestly' inappropriate or its decision 'simply unreasoned'.

16.80 Applying the above principles to the facts of the instant case, Langstaff P held that the tribunal's judgment was inadequately reasoned. All but one of the factors cited by the tribunal in support of its decision to make a 20 per cent Polkey reduction 'had no obvious relevance to an assessment of future chance'; rather, they appeared to be an assessment of past probability. At the request of both parties, Langstaff P agreed to substitute his own decision and held that a Polkey reduction of 33 per cent would be appropriate. To reach that figure, he analysed the facts as found by the tribunal, noting that some redundancies from among the administrative staff (which included the claimants, C and M) were inevitable and that four out of ten such staff had in fact lost their jobs. On a purely mathematical basis, this could suggest that a reduction of 40 per cent – representing a four-in-ten chance of dismissal – would be appropriate. However, it was necessary to adjust that figure to reflect the specific circumstances of C and M.

In this regard, Langstaff P considered that the introduction of a new financial software package meant less accounts work, which may have made C – and particularly M – more vulnerable to redundancy than the other administrative staff. However, there was evidence that C – and possibly also M – had offered to accept a lower salary in return for remaining in employment and, had a fair process been followed, the employer might have accepted this offer and saved their jobs. There was also a possibility that one of the claimants could have been retained in place of W, who had recently been hired to act as a Finance Director when no such position had previously existed, and whose daily rate was more expensive than either M or C's salary. Furthermore, as between C and M, it was possible to argue that M had a greater chance of dismissal than C, since C's salary was partly funded by a third party, and it was M's role that

740

was particularly affected by the introduction of the financial software package. However, M's salary was lower than C's, so her dismissal would not have produced as great a saving. On balance, Langstaff P therefore considered that each claimant should suffer the same reduction.

One of the points emphasised in the Cave case was that tribunals should not **16.81** shy away from considering whether or not to make a Polkey reduction on the ground that the exercise would be too speculative. Below, we consider some cases where the EAT held that the employment tribunal had done exactly that:

- **Secor Consulting Ltd v Meffen** EAT 0180/05: M, a highly paid employee responsible for securing lucrative accounts for S Ltd's consultancy business, was dismissed for redundancy after his failure to find sufficient new business to justify his salary. An employment tribunal found his dismissal unfair for lack of consultation. S Ltd contended that if proper dismissal procedures had been applied, M would either have been dismissed or would have accepted alternative employment at a lower salary. The tribunal accepted that it was a distinct possibility that M might have been offered (and accepted) continued employment at a lower salary, but it declined to make a Polkey reduction on this basis since it had 'no means of deciding at what level to place a hypothetical alternative salary'. On appeal, the EAT (by a majority) held that the tribunal had erred. Whether or not M would have accepted alternative employment or agreed to do the same job at a lower salary were matters that had been specifically raised by S Ltd. Moreover, it had adduced evidence as to what alternative employment options existed and the salaries applicable to those options. In these circumstances, the tribunal had an obligation, difficult though it was, to consider on the evidence before it what the percentage chance was that M would have accepted an alternative job offer and at what level of salary. The case was remitted to enable this exercise to be undertaken

- **CEX Ltd v Lewis** EAT 0013/07: an employment tribunal found that L had been unfairly dismissed after being made redundant following a flawed procedure that involved no consultation. C Ltd had also failed to follow the statutory dismissal procedures applicable at that time. The tribunal awarded a 10 per cent uplift in compensation due to the failure to observe the statutory procedures, but declined to make a Polkey reduction on the ground that, even if a proper consultation had occurred, there was a 100 per cent chance that L would have retained his job. On appeal, the EAT referred to the guidance given in Software 2000 Ltd v Andrews and ors (above), and in particular the point made in that case that a finding that an employee would have continued in employment indefinitely on the same terms should only be made where the evidence to the contrary (i.e. that employment might have been terminated earlier) is so scant that it can effectively be ignored. In this case there was evidence before the tribunal that L would still have been

741

dismissed if proper consultation had taken place and the tribunal had not found that evidence to be so unreliable or of so little substance that it could be ignored. Therefore, it had erred in law in finding that there was a 100 per cent certainty that L would have been retained

- **Wilson UK Ltd v Turton and anor** EAT 0348/08: T and L were unfairly dismissed by reason of redundancy owing to the complete lack of a proper procedure in selecting them from among a pool of five employees. The employment tribunal decided not to make any Polkey reduction because it reasoned that, in view of the fundamental flaws in the procedure and the fact that any one of the five employees could have performed the work of the others, it could not be certain that both T and L would inevitably have been selected for redundancy if a fair procedure had been followed. On appeal, the EAT held that the tribunal had erred. That the failure to consult was a fundamental defect did not preclude consideration of any assessment of the outcome if proper consultation had taken place. The tribunal's reasoning revealed that it was looking for 'certainty' of outcome rather than 'possibility'. Citing the guidance given by Elias J in Software 2000 Ltd v Andrews and ors (above), the EAT observed that certainty is not what is required when dealing with the possibilities inherent in a Polkey reduction. There were two important factors upon which such a reduction could, and indeed should, have been based in this case: (i) the tribunal had found that there was a genuine redundancy situation (making it inevitable that two of the five employees within the pool would have been dismissed had a proper procedure been followed), and (ii) both T and L had formed part of the pool. These factors were sufficient to trigger a Polkey reduction of some kind and the case was therefore remitted to enable the tribunal to reconsider its decision on this point.

16.82 In Ventrac Sheet Metals Ltd v Fairley EATS 0064/10 F was one of two trainees employed by VSM Ltd, a company that manufactured and installed air conditioning systems. F worked mainly on the installation side of the business, whereas the other trainee, M, worked primarily on the manufacturing side. Following a significant downturn in installation work, VSM Ltd decided that redundancies were necessary, including among its trainees. Following a management meeting, F was told that there was no more work for him and that he was dismissed with immediate effect. An employment tribunal upheld his claim for unfair dismissal, finding that there had been a complete absence of consultation on the company's part when deciding to make F redundant. In particular, no appraisals, scoring or matrices were used, which meant that there was no basis for it to speculate whether, if a proper procedure had been adopted, F would still have been dismissed. In calculating the compensatory award, the tribunal reminded itself that a Polkey reduction is considered within the context of S.123(1), which was a provision 'founded on justice and equity'. It continued: '[It] would be quite unjust to seek to construct a hypothesis which the respondent

742

company itself never envisaged in order to reduce the compensatory award. There was no evidence that the company had adopted even the most elementary of measures to determine objectively which of the two employees... should be selected for redundancy and there is no basis for the tribunal to consider or speculate whether if a proper procedure had been adopted it would have made no difference.' Accordingly, the tribunal declined to make a Polkey reduction.

The EAT overturned the tribunal's decision on appeal, holding that the tribunal had given no consideration to the guidance in Software 2000 Ltd v Andrews and ors (above). In the instant case, there was a pool of two trainees, one of whom was to be dismissed as redundant. On the tribunal's findings, there was little to choose between F and M – i.e. they did the same type of work and were similarly qualified. According to the EAT, these factual findings presented the tribunal with a proper evidential basis on which to reach a working hypothesis for Polkey purposes. The tribunal had refused to do so on two grounds, neither of which the EAT held to be sustainable on appeal. The first was that the tribunal appeared to suggest that the employer was to be deprived of the possibility of a Polkey reduction because the procedural failings were heinous. However, punishment is not a relevant aspect of assessing compensation under S.123. The second was that the tribunal would have had to construct a hypothesis that the employer had not itself envisaged. That was not the correct legal test. On the facts of the case, it was clear that one of the two trainees was bound to be dismissed. As there was plainly a chance of F being dismissed, the tribunal should have made a Polkey reduction. The EAT proceeded to assess that chance itself and decided that there was a 35 per cent chance that F would have been dismissed if VSM Ltd had followed a fair redundancy procedure.

16.83 It should not go unnoticed that the great majority of cases mentioned above concern unfair redundancy dismissals. In Swanston New Golf Club Ltd v Gallagher EATS 0033/13 the EAT suggested that the speculative exercise undertaken by a tribunal for the purposes of Polkey may be less onerous in that type of case than in those where the employee was unfairly dismissed for a reason other than redundancy, where it may be more difficult to predict with some confidence what might have happened if a fair procedure had been carried out. It considered that the facts of the instant case fell into the latter category. G, who worked as head green keeper at a golf club, was granted a few hours off work to deal with a personal matter. The employer thought that he was attending to his ill wife but G informed his manager the following day that he had gone to help his son, who was involved in an altercation. A year later, the employer discovered that G, accompanied by a friend who had an intimidating appearance, had gone to another golf club and confronted the person who had been involved in the altercation with his son. G was suspended and, following an investigation into the incident, dismissed for gross misconduct on account of two charges: lying about the reason for requesting time off work and intimidatory conduct. In deciding upon dismissal as the appropriate sanction,

743

the employer also took into account previous incidents at work where G's conduct had given cause for concern. The employment tribunal found that G's dismissal was unfair as the employer had not been able to demonstrate that it was in possession of evidence that would provide reasonable grounds to conclude that G was guilty of gross misconduct in relation to the alleged dishonesty or the alleged intimidation. The tribunal also found that no reduction should be made to G's compensatory award for the chance that the employer might have dismissed him fairly. In its view, there had been both procedural and substantive defects. There was considerable information that was not put to G during the disciplinary process and a fair procedure would have allowed G's explanations to be fully taken into account. Because of this, the tribunal considered it 'too speculative' to suggest that dismissal would have taken place had a fair procedure been followed.

On appeal, the EAT refused to interfere with the tribunal's decision on Polkey. It noted that the guidance in Software 2000 Ltd v Andrews and ors (above) made it clear that, while a tribunal should consider the possibility of a Polkey reduction, there will be cases where it is too speculative for any tribunal to make even a percentage assessment of a chance of a fair dismissal. In the instant case, the tribunal had found that G's misconduct dismissal had been handled unfairly and that material that was used in the disciplinary process had not been given to him. It further found that other matters had been used to bolster the case against him – matters which had not been formally investigated. In those circumstances, it was difficult to assess what the chances of dismissal would have been if a fair procedure had been followed. In particular, it would be necessary to speculate about what would have happened at a hearing in which the bolstering material was absent and the other material was notified to G timeously. The EAT accepted that this was a more difficult exercise than in a case where the unfair dismissal was due, for example, to unfair selection for redundancy and the evidence showed that the employees were made redundant shortly after the event. According to the EAT, it may be that unfair dismissals concerned with misconduct or capability will involve more speculation than some other cases.

16.84 **Is tribunal under duty to consider Polkey of its own motion?** In Boulton and Paul Ltd v Arnold 1994 IRLR 532, EAT, the EAT held that the tribunal, having found that the employer had adopted redundancy selection criteria that were intrinsically unfair and different from those that had been agreed upon, was not under any obligation to consider of its own motion whether the compensatory award should have been reduced to reflect the possibility that the employee might in any event have been dismissed under a fair procedure. However, the opposite conclusion was reached in Fisher v California Cake and Cookie Ltd 1997 IRLR 212, EAT, where it was held that in addressing the hypothetical question as to whether adopting a fair procedure would have achieved the same result, a tribunal must conduct its own investigation into the matter and reach its own conclusion. In the EAT's view, where the tribunal determines that there is any evidence at all to support the contention that dismissal might have occurred in any event, it is necessary for it to go on to address the question of whether the dismissal would or would not have occurred as a matter of probability expressed in percentage terms. In many cases, the failure to address this question will render the tribunal's approach flawed.

We would suggest that the approach adopted in the Fisher case sits more easily with the flurry of recent cases on Polkey reductions – see Gover and ors v Propertycare Ltd, Thornett v Scope, Software 2000 Ltd v Andrews and ors and Contract Bottling Ltd v Cave and anor (all discussed under 'Degree of speculation expected of tribunals' above) – which emphasise that if there is any evidence at all that the employee would have been dismissed in any event, a tribunal cannot shirk its obligation to consider making a Polkey reduction simply by saying that the exercise is too speculative. Clearly, the upshot of any Polkey consideration will depend on the actual evidence before the tribunal and, in this regard, an employer who wishes to argue that the employee might have been dismissed in any event should present the tribunal with some evidence to that effect. But essentially the duty falls on to the tribunal to construct a 'working hypothesis' (to use HHJ McMullen's phrase in Gover and ors v Propertycare Ltd (above)) as to what could or would have occurred. If the tribunal fails to do this off its own bat it is likely to be regarded as having made an error of law.

Burden of proof. In Britool Ltd v Roberts and ors 1993 IRLR 481, EAT, the **16.85** EAT stated that the burden of proving that an employee would have been dismissed in any event was on the employer. While it is for the employee to show what loss he or she has suffered as a result of the dismissal, this burden is not a heavy one since the fact that there has been an unfair dismissal in itself creates a prima facie loss. Accordingly, so long as the employee can put forward an arguable case that he or she would have been retained were it not for the unfair procedure, the evidential burden shifts to the employer to show that the dismissal might have occurred even if a correct procedure had been followed. Thus, on the facts of the case, the EAT held that the tribunal had not erred in declining to make a Polkey reduction. Although the dismissed employee had performed very badly in the employer's selection procedure, that procedure had been found to be unfair and the employer had not adduced any evidence that a fair procedure would equally have led to the employee's dismissal.

In Virgin Media Ltd v Seddington and anor EAT 0539/08 the question arose whether a tribunal had erred in declining to make a Polkey reduction following a finding of unfair redundancy. It was clear from the evidence that the employees were unquestionably redundant and so would inevitably have lost their jobs even if a fair procedure had been applied. In those circumstances, the EAT held that the relevant consideration was whether, if the employer had acted fairly,

745

the employees would have been offered and accepted alternative employment and, if so, on what terms. When undertaking a Polkey exercise in this form, the Appeal Tribunal observed that the burden does not necessarily fall entirely on the employer to adduce evidence about what would have happened. The employer may well have the initial burden of showing that there was no suitable employment that the employee could or would have accepted and for providing appropriate evidential support for that assertion. But once the employer raises a prima facie case to this effect, the burden shifts onto the employee to show what actual or type of job he or she believes was available and to provide supporting evidence that such employment would have been accepted.

16.86 On the facts of the particular case, the EAT conceded that it was not easy to judge whether the burden had shifted on to the employees. A list of available jobs had been put before the tribunal and it would have been easy for the claimants to flesh out the vague generalities made about these in their witness statements by identifying particular jobs on the list which they would or might have accepted. But it was also arguable that the employer had not itself done enough to put the issue into play. The case was therefore remitted to the tribunal to determine whether a Polkey reduction issue arose and, if appropriate, to determine the level of reduction.

The EAT in Seddington also made the more general point that reliance on the burden of proof in borderline cases was inherently unsatisfactory. Mr Justice Underhill, then President of the EAT, observed: 'In the field of compensation in particular, there may often be uncertainty as to precisely who has to prove what, and in what degree of detail, before the burden shifts to the other party. Parties would be well advised to make clear well in advance of any hearing what their case is on any point of importance, irrespective of the burden of proof, and be prepared to adduce appropriate evidence (and if necessary seek appropriate disclosure). It is not right that tribunals should have to consider the [Polkey] issue on the basis of inadequate evidence – or, in extreme cases, decline to decide it at all – because the parties have failed to anticipate it or because each has thought that the burden was on the other.'

16.87 **Requirement to provide adequate reasons.** In Whitehead v Robertson Partnership EAT 0331/01 the EAT stressed the importance of employment tribunals adequately explaining their reasons for making a Polkey reduction. In the EAT's view, it was incumbent upon the tribunal to demonstrate its analysis of the hypothetical question by explaining its conclusions on the following:

- what potentially fair reason for dismissal, if any, might emerge as a result of a proper investigation and disciplinary process?

- depending on the principal reason for any future hypothetical dismissal, would dismissal for that reason be fair or unfair?

- even if a potentially fair dismissal was available, would the employer in fact have dismissed the employee as opposed to imposing some lesser penalty, and if so, would that have ensured the employee's continued employment?

The need for tribunals to articulate the evidential and factual bases for their conclusions is apparent from the EAT's decision in Photo Corporation (UK) Ltd v Truelove EAT 0054/04. In that case T, a loyal and hardworking employee of 15 years' standing, became involved with an ex-colleague. When the ex-colleague began working for a competitor, T was immediately suspended from work due to confidentiality concerns. She resigned and claimed unfair constructive dismissal. A tribunal awarded her a compensatory award and chose not to make a Polkey reduction. On appeal, the EAT remitted the question of a Polkey reduction to the tribunal on the basis that the tribunal should have considered the inevitability of T's dismissal. The tribunal, reconsidering the issue, 'guestimated' that there was a 66 per cent chance that T would have retained her employment had a fair procedure been followed, and reduced her compensatory award accordingly.

When the matter returned to the EAT on further appeal, the Appeal Tribunal **16.88** accepted that the tribunal had been right to come up with a hypothetical answer, but noted that the answer should be one that was reasoned and based on the facts. The tribunal had given no clue as to why it had reached the 66 per cent figure. The question that the tribunal should have asked itself was: if proper and full consultation had taken place, would a solution have been reached to resolve the employer's concerns about leakage of confidential information that would have allowed T to remain in her post or an alternative post? The EAT concluded that the tribunal was bound to decide that, following a three-week consultation period (as the tribunal had decided would have been appropriate), there was a 100 per cent chance that T would have been dismissed. The EAT therefore substituted this finding in place of the tribunal's and accordingly reduced T's compensatory award to nil.

Amount of reduction **16.89**

In any case where the employer has dismissed for a substantively fair reason but has failed to follow a fair procedure, the compensatory award (but not the basic award) may be reduced – potentially to nil – so long as it can be shown that a fair procedure would have resulted in a dismissal anyway. The logic for a nil award (or to express it differently, a 100 per cent reduction) is that any procedural failure that served to render the dismissal unfair made absolutely no difference: the outcome would have been exactly the same even if a fair procedure had been adopted. The phrase 'exactly the same' in this context means that the employee would have been fairly dismissed on the same date as he or she was unfairly dismissed.

So, for example, in Cormack v Saltire Vehicles Ltd EAT 209/90 a car mechanic was dismissed for misconduct after he left one vehicle in a dangerous condition and failed to carry out an MOT test properly on another. He was refused an internal appeal, despite having a contractual right to one. The employment tribunal found his dismissal unfair as a result of this breach of procedure, but held that it was not just and equitable to make a compensatory award as the employer had, in all other respects, acted reasonably, and a fuller appeal procedure would ultimately have made no difference at all. The EAT upheld this decision on appeal.

16.90 The obverse finding – that had a proper procedure been carried out there was a 100 per cent likelihood of the employee not only retaining his or her employment but doing so on exactly the same terms and conditions – will lead the tribunal to conclude that it is not just and equitable to reduce the compensatory award at all. However, a finding that a claimant's employment would have continued indefinitely should be reached only where evidence that it might have been terminated earlier is so scant that it can be effectively ignored – Software 2000 Ltd v Andrews and ors 2007 ICR 825, EAT.

16.91 **No 'all or nothing' approach.** In Polkey v AE Dayton Services Ltd 1988 ICR 142, HL, Lord Bridge was at pains to point out that there is no need for an 'all or nothing' approach when making an appropriate reduction. He cited with approval the case of Sillifant v Powell Duffryn Timber Ltd 1983 IRLR 91, EAT, in which Mr Justice Browne-Wilkinson pointed out that 'if the... tribunal thinks there is a doubt whether or not the employee would have been dismissed, this element can be reflected by reducing the normal amount of compensation by a percentage representing the chance that the employee would still have lost his employment'. Thus it would be quite reasonable to make a 20 per cent award if, for example, there is only a one in five chance that a fair procedure would have made any difference to the outcome.

In Hamer v Kaltz Ltd EAT 0502/13 the EAT expressed itself in similar terms. Referring to the House of Lords' decision in Polkey, it reiterated that the exercise under S.123(1) – i.e. the assessment of what would have occurred but for the dismissal – was not an 'all or nothing' one but one where the tribunal was required to take into account chances or prospects. It might express its view in percentage terms or by alighting upon a date, taking into account the chances on either side by which the employment might have ended. This meant that it remained open to the tribunal to conclude that the employment would still have ended on the same date as the unfair dismissal, but if it did so, it was making the strong finding that there was no chance that the employment would continue. With this in mind, the EAT considered the tribunal's conclusions on the Polkey issue in the instant case and held that it was impossible to understand, from the tribunal's reasons, how it had concluded that it was inevitable that the employer, if it had acted fairly, would have dismissed the claimant on the very

748

same day. Looking at the facts, there was at least a chance that she would not have been dismissed. Given this, the EAT substituted its own assessment of the appropriate reduction under Polkey – 40 per cent.

Note that the question of a Polkey deduction requires the tribunal to consider **16.92** both whether the employer *could* have dismissed fairly and whether it *would* have done so. Furthermore, the enquiry is directed at what the particular employer before the tribunal would have done, not what a hypothetical fair employer would have done. These points were emphasised by the EAT in Hill v Governing Body of Great Tey Primary School 2013 ICR 691, EAT. There, the EAT allowed an appeal against the tribunal's assessment of compensation because the tribunal appeared to have based its decision on a consideration of whether, if the employer had followed a fair procedure, a tribunal would have concluded that the resulting decision to dismiss was fair. This was not the proper test.

The following cases illustrate the correct approach:

- **Akram v Rieter Automotive Carpets Ltd** EAT 1319/95: A was made redundant and refused an offer of alternative employment. A tribunal found that the dismissal was procedurally unfair but awarded no compensation on the ground that a proper procedure would have made no difference. The EAT held that the decision not to make an award was inconsistent with the tribunal's finding that, if a proper procedure had been adopted, there was a chance that A would have accepted the alternative job offer. The case was therefore remitted for the tribunal to calculate the compensatory award on the basis of the percentage chance of A accepting the alternative work

- **Wolesley Centers Ltd v Simmons** 1994 ICR 503, EAT: S's dismissal for redundancy was unfair because there had been no consultation or warning and no attempt to find alternative employment. In assessing compensation, the tribunal chose not to make a Polkey reduction because it took the view that 'on a balance of probabilities' the employee would not have been dismissed had a proper procedure been followed. The EAT held that the tribunal had fallen into the error of adopting an 'all or nothing' approach. In cases where it is reasonably clear that the employee would not have been dismissed following a fair procedure, there is no need for a percentage assessment of the chance of a different outcome. But it was clear from the tribunal's reference to the 'balance of probabilities', and its acknowledgement that the recession would have made it difficult for the employer to find the employee an alternative position, that the tribunal considered the issue in this case to be far from clear-cut. Accordingly, it should have assessed the chance that the employee would have been retained had the employer behaved fairly

- **Venkatesan v Surabi Ltd and anor** EAT 0193/14: V was working for S Ltd on a visa that gave him the right to remain and work in the UK. Following

749

the visa's expiry in December 2011, V applied for an extension, which was initially refused. He appealed and was finally given discretionary leave to remain for 12 months in February 2013, by which time he had already been dismissed. An employment tribunal found that the dismissal was unfair but applied a 100 per cent reduction to the compensatory award on the basis that S Ltd would have dismissed V fairly within one month (which he had already been paid for) because by then it would have concluded – wrongly – that he did not have the right to work in the UK. Allowing V's appeal, the EAT noted that if S Ltd had properly investigated the position, it would have found that it could continue to employ V on the same terms as before, until his appeal to the Immigration and Asylum Tribunal had been determined. The tribunal had therefore erred by focusing purely on how long a fair procedure would have taken. What it should have done was consider whether there was a chance that, had such a procedure been followed, V could have shown that he had the right to remain and work in the UK. The issue of compensation was remitted to a different tribunal to be considered afresh.

16.93 **Is 'percentage approach' to reductions always appropriate?** An employment tribunal's assessment of whether a proper procedure would have made any difference is usually made on a percentage basis. So if, for example, a tribunal assesses in an unfair redundancy case that there was a 20 per cent likelihood that the employee would not have been selected for redundancy had a proper consultation process taken place, the tribunal should award full compensation for the period over which consultation should notionally have occurred. It should then apply an 80 per cent reduction to the compensation for losses beyond this point. The following case confirms this approach, while also demonstrating the high level of speculation often required of tribunals in such cases:

- **Walker and ors v Dysch Rosen Shoes Ltd and anor** EAT 341/90: W was dismissed for a reason connected with the imminent transfer of the undertaking in which he worked. The tribunal held that even if the dismissal was for an 'economic, technical or organisational reason' (and thus not automatically unfair under the Transfer of Undertakings (Protection of Employment) Regulations 2006 SI 2006/246), it was still unfair in this case owing to procedural failings. The tribunal then reduced the compensatory award by 90 per cent on the ground that W's dismissal was inevitable because the new employer was clearly determined to dismiss him. The EAT said that the tribunal was wrong on this point: in assessing compensation, it should have gone on to consider whether W would have been dismissed fairly by his new employer (following proper procedures, etc). The EAT held that full compensation should be awarded for the period in which proper consultation would have taken place. The likelihood of a (fair) dismissal

750

being inevitable (because consultation would have made no difference) was to be taken into account from this point on.

Making a percentage reduction is not, however, the correct method of proceeding where a tribunal categorically finds that the employee would have been dismissed in any event at the end of the period during which fair procedures were applied. In such a case the compensatory award will properly be confined to compensating the employee for the losses he or she has sustained during the time it would have taken for a fair procedure to be completed. A percentage reduction is not appropriate because there is an absolute cut-off date representing the date when the employee would have been dismissed – fairly – in any event. Up until that date, he or she would be entitled to recover full losses since these are directly attributable to the unfair dismissal. But from that date forwards, he or she suffers no further loss at all. This approach was approved by the Court of Appeal in O'Donoghue v Redcar and Cleveland Borough Council 2001 IRLR 615, CA.

However, as Akram v Rieter Automotive Carpets Ltd and Wolesley Centers Ltd **16.94** v Simmons (discussed above) demonstrate, this straightforward 'limiting the loss period' approach is not feasible where the tribunal is far less certain as to whether employment would have continued had the employee not been unfairly dismissed. In such circumstances it will still be appropriate for a tribunal to apply a percentage approach to its assessment of likelihood. So, for example, in an incapability dismissal context, a tribunal might conclude there was a 75 per cent chance that the employee's performance would not have sufficiently improved over, say, a three-month review period. In other words, after three months there was only a 25 per cent chance of the employee avoiding a fair dismissal. In those circumstances, assuming the employee's net salary was £2,000 a month and that he or she was entitled to one month's notice, the correct calculation of the compensatory award would be:

- 3 x £2,000 (i.e. salary over the notional performance review period) plus

- 1 x £2,000 (i.e. salary during the notional notice period) plus

- 25 per cent x £2,000 (i.e. £500) x as many months/years as the tribunal feels is just and equitable to reflect the employee's ongoing loss.

It is the last-mentioned head of loss that reflects the Polkey reduction.

Reduction applies to all heads of compensatory award. In Hope v Jordan **16.95** Engineering Ltd EAT 0545/07 the question arose whether the Polkey reduction applied to all heads of loss comprising the compensatory award, including, for example, compensation for loss of statutory rights or long notice. In that particular case, the tribunal had applied a 100 per cent reduction to an employee's compensatory award on the basis that, even if a fair redundancy procedure had been applied, she would have been dismissed in any event. The

751

EAT ruled that this reduction covered all heads of the compensatory award. Giving the Appeal Tribunal's judgment, His Honour Judge Peter Clark remarked: 'It seems to us that there is no warrant in Polkey v AE Dayton Services Ltd... for the proposition that any head of [the] compensatory award escapes the Polkey deduction. Once a tribunal finds that it is a 100 per cent Polkey deduction case, there is no purpose in carrying out an assessment of loss under the compensatory award.'

Driving home this point, HHJ Clark, when turning to the uplift of between 10 and 50 per cent that should notionally have been applied to the compensatory award in order to penalise the employer for breaching the statutory dismissal and disciplinary procedures that then applied, observed: 'If there is no compensatory award as here, no uplift falls to be applied... That makes sense to us. 10–50 per cent of 0 still equals 0.' Notwithstanding the repeal of the statutory procedures, these comments may have continuing validity in view of the power under S.207A TULR(C)A for tribunals to adjust the compensatory award upwards or downwards in respect of flagrant breaches of the Acas Code of Practice on Disciplinary and Grievance Procedures. For further details, see 'Adjustments for breach of Acas Code of Practice' below.

16.96 **Relationship with contributory conduct**
The legal basis for making Polkey reductions under S.123(1) ERA and reductions on account of employees' contributory conduct under S.123(6) ERA are very different (the latter are discussed in detail under 'Contributory conduct' below). In particular, the evidence that is germane to whether or not an employee has 'caused or contributed' to his or her dismissal may not be the same as that relevant to assessing what is 'just and equitable' to award the complainant having regard to the loss sustained in consequence of the unfair dismissal. However, an unwary tribunal can easily fall into the trap of blurring the line between the two different types of reduction.

In some cases, an employment tribunal may have good grounds for making both types of reduction. For example, it might find that there was a 50 per cent chance that the employee would have been dismissed even if a fair procedure had been followed and also that the employee was 20 per cent to blame for the dismissal in the first place. In Rao v Civil Aviation Authority 1994 ICR 495, CA, the Court of Appeal rejected the contention that the making of both deductions would amount to a double penalty for the employee. The Court held that the proper approach in these circumstances is first to assess the loss sustained by the employee in accordance with S.123(1), which will include the percentage deduction to reflect the chance that he or she would have been dismissed in any event, and then to make the deduction for contributory fault.

16.97 However, in deciding the extent of the employee's contributory conduct and the amount by which it would be just and equitable to reduce the award for that

752

reason under S.123(6), the Court in Rao made it clear that the tribunal should bear in mind that there has already been a deduction under S.123(1). Comments to similar effect were made by the EAT in Granchester Construction (Eastern) Ltd v Attrill EAT 0327/12. Hearing an appeal against an employment tribunal's remedies decision, Mr Justice Langstaff referred to the Court of Appeal's decision in Rao before noting that it may be 'appropriate to moderate what would otherwise be the degree of contributory fault that would reduce an award because there have been matters of conduct taken into account in assessing the chances of a fair dismissal'. Were this not so, he continued, 'it might be in effect double-counting to impose upon the claimant a further reduction by way of contributory conduct'. It was therefore not wrong, as a matter of principle, for the tribunal, having already applied a 50 per cent Polkey reduction to the compensatory award to reflect the chance of a fair dismissal, to set a further reduction for contributory conduct at 10 per cent only in order to 'avoid the injustice of an excessive and disproportionate reduction'. This was despite the fact that the tribunal had thought the employee guilty of 'significant contributory fault'.

Adjustments for breach of Acas Code of Practice

16.98

As mentioned in the section '"Polkey reductions"' above, the legislative landscape changed in the autumn of 2004 with the introduction of mandatory statutory dispute resolution procedures. Provisions contained in the Employment Act 2002 made it obligatory to comply with certain statutory dismissal and disciplinary procedures (DDPs), and a failure to comply with these would have a significant impact on the amount of compensation awarded following a finding of unfair dismissal. In particular, tribunals were obliged, in appropriate circumstances, to increase the compensatory award by at least 10 per cent and up to a maximum of 50 per cent where a DDP had not been completed and the failure was attributable to the employer.

The way in which these statutory procedures worked in practice attracted a high level of criticism and following a Government-commissioned review, they were repealed (with effect from 6 April 2009) and replaced by a much less prescriptive regime aimed at encouraging dispute resolution in the workplace. This regime centres on the Acas Code of Practice on Disciplinary and Grievance Procedures ('the Code'), as explained below. The latest version of the Code, issued under S.199 of the Trade Union and Labour Relations (Consolidation) Act 1992 (TULR(C)A), came into effect on 11 March 2015.

Relevance of Code

16.99

Although the Acas Code has been in existence since 1977, its provisions were substantially revised to coincide with the legislative changes introduced in

2009. Crucially, for present purposes, the potential for adjusting the compensatory award to penalise serious breaches of the Code was introduced – see 'Increase or reduction in compensatory award' below. Details of the contents of the Code – and when it applies – are given in Chapter 3, 'Unfairness', under 'Fairness of internal procedure – Acas Code of Practice'.

In accordance with S.207 TULR(C)A, the revised Code is admissible in any employment tribunal proceedings and the tribunal is obliged to take into account any relevant provision of the Code when determining those proceedings. A breach of the Code does not in itself give rise to legal proceedings, but a failure by either party to abide by its provisions will be taken into account by a tribunal as evidence when determining a relevant claim.

16.100 Accompanying the Code (which is 12 pages long) is an 87-page non-statutory guide, 'Discipline and grievances at work' ('the Acas Guide'). This provides more detailed advice and guidance, much of which was taken from the 2004 version of the Code. It is designed to complement the Code and contains a number of sample disciplinary and grievance procedures. However, tribunals are not obliged to take this Guide into account when reaching a decision. Both Code and Guide are available on the Acas website.

16.101 **Impact of Code on unfair dismissal claims.** With specific regard to unfair dismissal, the Code impacts on claims in relation to both liability and remedy. The employer's compliance with the Code is a factor to be taken into account when determining the reasonableness of the dismissal in accordance with the statutory test of reasonableness under S.98(4) ERA. If the dismissal is found to be unfair, compliance by both employer and employee is then taken into account when determining whether there should be an adjustment to any compensatory award made under S.207A TULR(C)A.

With regard to the provisions of the Code dealing with grievances (as opposed to disciplinary procedures), these do not impose liability on the employer because no claim specifically arises from an employer's failure to follow a fair procedure in and of itself. However, a breach of these provisions may be relevant to both parties in relation to the adjustment of any award made by a tribunal in respect of a successful claim brought by the employee. This is because an alleged failure to deal adequately with a grievance could be evidence of, for example, discrimination. Equally, a failure to deal adequately with a grievance may amount to a breach of contract leading to a constructive dismissal claim.

16.102 **Is tribunal under duty to consider Code of its own motion?** There is no obligation on an employment tribunal to consider whether an uplift should be made for non-compliance with the Code where the issue has not been put before it – Pipecoil Technology Ltd v Heathcote EAT 0432/11. However, where the tribunal decides (as it is entitled to do) to deal with the matter of its own motion, it must give both parties an opportunity to make submissions on it.

This was established by the EAT in *Tandem Bars Ltd v Pilloni* EAT 0050/12 where a tribunal was held to have erred in applying the maximum uplift of 25 per cent without giving the employer any opportunity to make submissions on the matter.

Increase or reduction in compensatory award

16.103

Section 207A(2) TULR(C)A provides that: 'If, in any proceedings to which this section applies, it appears to the employment tribunal that – (a) the claim to which the proceedings relate concerns a matter to which a relevant Code of Practice applies, (b) the employer has failed to comply with that Code in relation to that matter, and (c) the failure was unreasonable, the employment tribunal may, if it considers it just and equitable in all the circumstances to do so, increase any award it makes to the employee by no more than 25 per cent.'

An identical provision in respect of any failure to comply by an employee is set out in S.207A(3). This reflects the fact that the Code is aimed at encouraging compliance by both employers and employees, so an employee's failure to follow the Code in respect of disciplinary action commenced by the employer or in respect of a grievance raised by him or her is as likely to lead to a compensation adjustment as a failure by the employer to follow the correct procedures.

The all-important list of proceedings (or 'jurisdictions') to which S.207A(2) **16.104** and (3) applies is set out in Schedule A2 TULR(C)A – S.207A(1). Unfair dismissal is included in the list, as are, inter alia, unlawful detriment, discrimination, unauthorised deductions from wages, redundancy payments, breach of the Working Time Regulations 1998 and breach of contract claims arising on or outstanding at the date of termination of employment. S.207A(6) empowers the Secretary of State to add or subtract jurisdictions to or from the list.

Section 207A(4) makes it clear that the reference in S.207A(2) and (3) to 'a relevant Code of Practice' is to any Code which 'relates exclusively or primarily to procedure for the resolution of disputes'. The relevant Code for unfair dismissal purposes is the revised Acas Code of Practice on Disciplinary and Grievance Procedures.

Adjustment only applies to compensatory award. By virtue of S.124A ERA, **16.105** it is clear that any adjustment made in accordance with S.207A applies to the compensatory award only. In other words, the adjustment – whether taking the form of an uplift in favour of the employee or a reduction in favour of the employer – does not apply to the basic award, protective award or any other type of compensation awardable by a tribunal.

Impact of interim payment. Where the compensatory award has been reduced **16.106** as a result of an interim payment having been made by the employer prior to

755

the remedies hearing, and that payment has been accepted by the employee, any uplift under S.207A will only be applied to the amount of compensation that remains outstanding. This was confirmed by the EAT in Tim Arrow and Sons (A firm) v Onley EAT 0527/08. However, that case was distinguished in University of the Arts London v Rule EAT 0245/10, where the Appeal Tribunal held that it did not apply where an employer unilaterally paid a sum of money into the claimant's bank account to satisfy a tribunal's oral judgment at a remedies hearing. Even if the award was not made until it was set out in a written judgment, the EAT considered that Onley would still not apply because the money was not paid as an interim payment in respect of a hearing that was yet to take place, and nor had the employee accepted it as such.

Both cases were decided under the now-repealed statutory dismissal and disciplinary procedures, but the principles derived from them would appear to apply equally in respect of payments made to discharge liability for an uplift awarded for non-compliance with the Acas Code.

16.107 **Unreasonable failure to comply.** The potential for adjustment to the compensatory award under S.207A only applies if the employer's or employee's failure to comply with the provisions of the Code is 'unreasonable'. As Her Honour Judge Eady observed in Kuehne and Nagel Ltd v Cosgrove EAT 0165/13, this means that an employment tribunal may only consider adjusting the compensatory award once it has made an express finding that a failure to follow the Code was unreasonable – adjustment does not automatically follow from a breach of the Code. While the comment was made in the context of an employer's failure to comply, there is no reason to suppose that the principle would not apply equally to a failure to comply by an employee.

It follows from the wording of S.207A and the decision in Cosgrove that there may be circumstances in which a failure to follow the Code may be reasonable. That said, it seems likely that, in unfair dismissal cases at least, adjustments will be fairly common. This is because, as mentioned above, a failure to follow the Code is relevant to the question of liability as well as remedy and may render the dismissal procedurally unfair under S.98(4) ERA on the ground that the employer has not acted reasonably in all the circumstances. It is difficult to envisage a situation in which a tribunal could find that an employer has acted unreasonably in failing to comply with the Code when deciding on liability but then go on to hold that that failure was reasonable when it comes to deciding whether there should be an uplift in compensation. And if it does, can it really be said that the dismissal was unfair in the first place?

16.108 From an employer's perspective, it is worth emphasising that an employer's failure to follow its own internal procedures will not necessarily lead to a finding of a breach of the Acas Code, warranting an uplift in unfair dismissal compensation. This was made clear by the EAT in Coker v Wandsworth Borough Council EAT 0421/13, where it refused to interfere with a tribunal's decision not to make any uplift for unreasonable failure to comply with the Acas Code. Although the tribunal's findings of fact were that the Council had failed to act in accordance with its own procedures, it was entitled to conclude, on the evidence, that the Council had not breached the Acas Code: a number of meetings had been arranged, some of the delays in the handling of the grievance process had been caused by the claimant herself and some investigatory meetings had taken place.

Tribunal's discretion: 'just and equitable'. Where there has been an **16.109** unreasonable failure to comply with the Code, the tribunal may increase or reduce the award if it 'considers it just and equitable in all the circumstances to do so'. As yet, there has been very little case law at appellate level providing guidance on how to determine the amount of adjustment, if any. Thankfully, the terminology is very similar to that used under the old statutory dispute resolution procedures, so case law decided under that regime would appear to remain relevant to adjustments under S.207A. Some of these cases are discussed below.

In Lawless v Print Plus EAT 0333/09 Mr Justice Underhill, then President of the EAT, pointed out that although the phrase 'just and equitable in all the circumstances' connoted a broad discretion, the relevant circumstances were confined to those which were related in some way to the failure to comply with the statutory procedures. We would suggest that similar reasoning applies, mutatis mutandis, to breaches of the Acas Code.

So, for example, the uplift ought not be used by a tribunal to mark its disapproval **16.110** of the employer's conduct in respect of unrelated matters – see Aptuit (Edinburgh) Ltd v Kennedy EAT 0057/06. The EAT adopted similar reasoning in Drewett v Penfold EAT 0395/09 when holding that an employment tribunal had erred in limiting an uplift to 20 per cent solely because the employer (a sole trader) had been going through a distressing family situation after the loss of his wife. The tribunal made it clear that, but for that consideration, it would have awarded a higher percentage uplift. The EAT ruled that the factor relied upon by the tribunal was irrelevant because (a) it was a circumstance outwith the employer's role as an employer and the employment relationship generally; and (b) it was not a circumstance surrounding, related to or causally resulting in the failure to complete the statutory procedure. The EAT substituted a finding of 50 per cent uplift (the maximum awardable for breach of the statutory procedures).

In Lawless v Print Plus (above) Underhill J acknowledged that the relevant circumstances to be taken into account by tribunals when considering uplifts would vary from case to case but should always include the following:

- whether the procedures were applied to some extent or were ignored altogether

757

- whether the failure to comply with the procedures was deliberate or inadvertent, and

- whether there were circumstances that mitigated the blameworthiness of the failure to comply.

16.111 Furthermore, the size and resources of the employer were capable of amounting to a relevant factor in the tribunal's consideration of whether an uplift was appropriate and, if so, how much. Relevance would depend on whether that factor aggravated or mitigated the culpability and/or seriousness of the employer's failure. But it should not be thought that failures by small businesses were always to be regarded as venial.

16.112 **Level of uplift.** Under the now-repealed statutory DDPs, tribunals had a discretion to award uplifts in favour of employees of up to 50 per cent. Save where there were exceptional circumstances, the minimum uplift was 10 per cent. This contrasts with the current position in respect of breaches of the Acas Code where the maximum limit is 25 per cent (with no minimum). The general view is that, given the much-reduced ceiling, the EAT and higher courts are likely to be even less willing to interfere in the amount of an uplift awarded by tribunals than they were under the old procedures. One situation in which it may be appropriate to set aside a tribunal's assessment of the level of uplift is where the tribunal failed to give reasons to explain why it alighted on one particular percentage as opposed to another. In Allma Construction Ltd v Laing EATS 0041/11, for example, the tribunal decided to award the maximum 25 per cent uplift pursuant to S.207A. However, it did so after simply stating that the Acas Code applied, that the employer had clearly failed to comply with it and that it was reasonable to award an uplift of 25 per cent. The EAT held that this was not sufficient: clear reasons for the uplift needed to be given by the tribunal.

In McKindless Group v McLaughlin 2008 IRLR 678, EAT, Lady Smith set out what was quite a prescriptive approach to how tribunals should approach uplifts in the context of the DDPs. She made it clear that the discretion accorded to tribunals to go beyond the minimum 10 per cent should only be exercised by reference to particular facts or circumstances surrounding the failure to complete the statutory procedure that made it just and equitable that the employer should be penalised further. There was no room for exercising the discretion where there was no evidence from which the tribunal could make findings of fact as to the circumstances surrounding the dismissal and how and why it was that the failure to complete the statutory procedure occurred. The mere failure to carry out any stage of the three-stage statutory procedure would not necessarily point to an uplift beyond the minimum. It would depend on the circumstances of the failure, including the level of culpability concerned. Furthermore, the employer was not, in Lady Smith's view, obliged to explain the failure. This meant that the evidential burden was firmly on the employee

758

to place material before the tribunal in support of any argument that the uplift should be greater than 10 per cent.

On the facts of the McKindless case, the employment tribunal had awarded an **16.113** employee a 50 per cent uplift in his compensatory award on account of the employer's complete failure to carry out the DDP. The tribunal was persuaded to award the maximum uplift because the employer had conceded only at a late stage that the employee's dismissal was automatically unfair owing to its failure to comply with the statutory procedure. Had the employer conceded earlier, it was possible that the case would have settled. On appeal, the EAT held that this was an entirely irrelevant consideration. As the tribunal had not given any additional reason for awarding the 50 per cent uplift, the EAT allowed the employer's appeal and substituted an uplift of 10 per cent.

It is clear from both the McKindless case and other EAT decisions that one important factor in determining the level of an uplift is the degree of culpability on the part of the defaulting party. In Virgin Media Ltd v Seddington and anor EAT 0539/08 the EAT overturned a 40 per cent uplift awarded partly on the basis that, in awarding this, the tribunal had not expressly considered the issue of culpability at all. The obverse happened in Lawless v Print Plus (discussed above). There, the EAT held that where there had been wholesale failure to comply with the statutory procedures, aggravated by the employer's deliberate and intemperate refusal to permit an appeal (which was the third stage of the three-stage statutory DDPs), the starting point for the tribunal's consideration of the appropriate uplift should have been at or close to the top of the scale (i.e. 50 per cent). Although the small scale of the employer's business and the haste with which the decision to dismiss had been taken were both relevant factors, the tribunal had given too much weight to them when awarding an uplift of only 10 per cent given the degree of culpability on the employer's part. The EAT accordingly substituted a 40 per cent uplift.

In other cases, where it is clear that tribunals have specifically addressed the **16.114** matter of culpability, the EAT has been content to uphold the levels of uplift awarded. For example, in Metrobus Ltd v Cook EAT 0490/06 the Appeal Tribunal upheld an uplift of 40 per cent for a 'blatant' breach of the statutory procedures, accepting the tribunal's view that the provision was 'more penal than compensatory in nature'. A similar approach was taken by another division of the EAT in CEX Ltd v Lewis EAT 0013/07, when it held that the reason for the employer's failure to complete a statutory disciplinary procedure was ignorance rather than deliberate disregard, and this entitled a tribunal to limit the uplift to the 10 per cent minimum adjustment under the statutory procedures.

A further matter that might influence the level of uplift is the size of the total compensation awarded. In Abbey National plc and anor v Chagger 2010 ICR 397, CA, an employment tribunal awarded almost £2.8 million to a claimant

759

found to have been both unfairly dismissed and discriminated against on the ground of his racial origins. The tribunal awarded an uplift of only 2 per cent, utilising a specific provision in the Employment Act 2002 to award less than the normal minimum of 10 per cent for non-compliance with the statutory procedures if there were 'exceptional circumstances' for doing so. In this particular case the tribunal had calculated that a 10 per cent uplift would have resulted in the employer being penalised to the extent of almost £300,000 in respect of its procedural failings. In the tribunal's view, the size of the award made the circumstances of this case exceptional. On appeal, both the EAT and the Court of Appeal upheld the tribunal's decision on this point. Lord Justice Elias, giving the judgment of the Court of Appeal, observed that 'we do not think Parliament would have intended the sums awarded to be wholly disproportionate to the nature of the breach'.

16.115 Although the Chagger case was concerned with a specific statutory provision governing the now defunct statutory procedures, it arguably established the broader principle that a tribunal can take into account the overall level of compensation when considering what adjustment to make. In fact, Lord Justice Elias later went further in Wardle v Crédit Agricole Corporate and Investment Bank 2011 ICR 1290, CA, where the Court of Appeal disapproved a tribunal's decision to award a 50 per cent uplift. In Elias LJ's view, the maximum uplift should be 'very exceptional indeed' and should apply only in the most serious cases. The tribunal should have had regard to the size of the award in determining the uplift and its failure to do so was an error of law. Thus, it seems that not only is a tribunal entitled to take into account the size of the award when setting the level of uplift (if any) it deems to be just and equitable, it is obliged to do so.

16.116 Adjustments for failure to provide written particulars

Section 38 of the Employment Act 2002 states that tribunals must award compensation to an employee where, upon a successful claim being made under any of the tribunal jurisdictions listed in Schedule 5, it becomes evident that the employer was in breach of its duty to provide full and accurate written particulars under S.1 ERA – S.38(1)–(3) EA 2002. The duty is discussed in detail in IDS Employment Law Handbook, 'Contracts of Employment' (2014), Chapter 6, 'Written particulars'.

The list of jurisdictions set out in Schedule 5 is fairly extensive and includes unfair dismissal. But it is important to note that S.38 does not give employees a free-standing right to claim compensation for failure to provide full and accurate written particulars. The right to compensation is dependent upon a successful claim being brought by the employee under one of the jurisdictions listed in Schedule 5 (whether or not the tribunal would otherwise have awarded compensation). However, an award under S.38 is not dependent on a claim having been brought under S.11 ERA for a breach by the employer of the duty imposed by S.1 ERA. It is sufficient that the tribunal make a finding at the hearing that the employer was in breach of S.1 at the time the main proceedings were begun – S.38(2)(b) and (3)(b) EA 2002.

Amount of award. The tribunal must award the 'minimum amount' of two **16.117** weeks' pay and may, if it considers it just and equitable in the circumstances, award the 'higher amount' of four weeks' pay – S.38(2), (3) and (4) EA 2002. The tribunal does not have to make any award under S.38 if there are exceptional circumstances which would make an award or increase unjust or inequitable – S.38(5) EA 2002.

An award made under S.38 is on top of any award the tribunal may already have made in respect of the main claim, but is not dependent on the making of any such award. The tribunal can still make an award for failure to give written particulars where it has found in favour of the employee in the main claim but has not awarded compensation – S.38(2).

A 'week's pay' is calculated in accordance with Ss.220–229 ERA and is limited **16.118** to the maximum under S.227 (currently £475) – S.38(6) EA 2002. The date of calculation is either the date on which the main proceedings were commenced or, if the employee was no longer employed at that date, the effective date of termination of employment – S.38(7) EA 2002. For details of how to calculate a week's pay for these purposes, see IDS Employment Law Handbook, 'Wages' (2011), Chapter 10, 'A week's pay'.

In an unfair dismissal claim, any S.38 increase is applied to the compensatory award before the application of the statutory maximum (currently £78,335 or a year's pay, whichever is the lower) – S.124A ERA. For more detail on the order in which deductions and increases are made to compensatory awards, see 'Order of adjustments' below.

Contributory conduct 16.119

Section 123(6) ERA states that: 'Where the tribunal finds that the dismissal was to any extent caused or contributed to by any action of the complainant, it shall reduce the amount of the compensatory award by such proportion as it considers just and equitable having regard to that finding.' This ground for making a reduction is commonly referred to as 'contributory conduct' or 'contributory fault' – the latter being the term used extensively in the context of damages for tort, where plaintiffs are similarly liable to have their damages awards reduced on account of actions of their own that contributed to the injury or wrong suffered.

761

16.120 **Differences between compensatory and basic award reductions.** Under the ERA, there is an equivalent provision for reduction of the basic award contained in S.122(2). However, the actual statutory language used in respect of that particular reduction differs from that used in S.123(6) regarding reductions in the compensatory award. In the light of this difference of wording, the EAT held in Optikinetics Ltd v Whooley 1999 ICR 984, EAT, that S.122(2) gives tribunals a wide discretion whether or not to reduce the basic award on the ground of *any* kind of conduct on the employee's part that occurred prior to the dismissal and that this discretion allowed a tribunal to choose, in an appropriate case, to make no reduction at all. This contrasts with the position under S.123(6) where, to justify any reduction at all on account of an employee's conduct, the conduct in question must be shown to have caused or contributed to the employee's dismissal. In that sense, the capacity to make reductions to the compensatory award is more restrictive than in respect of the basic award.

This point is illustrated by the EAT's decision in Nixon v Ross Coates Solicitors and anor EAT 0108/10. N was employed by RCS at its Ipswich office. She was in a relationship with one of the firm's solicitors. However, at the staff Christmas party on 22 December 2007 she ended up publicly kissing the IT manager and they spent the night together in a room charged to the firm's account. Following the party N took annual leave and then sick leave in January 2008, during which she informed the firm's managing director (MD) that she was eight weeks' pregnant but did not want this disclosed until she had crossed the 12-week threshold. However, the HR manager, O, found out and started gossiping about who the father might be. N was very upset and submitted a grievance about O's behaviour and about the fact that RCS was refusing to allow her to relocate to its nearby Kesgrave office in the meantime. The MD, however, told her that she had to return to work at Ipswich and that any formal complaint about O would be dealt with in accordance with the firm's complaints procedure. N did not return to work and complained, among other things, of unfair constructive dismissal. The tribunal upheld her unfair dismissal complaint and listed a date for a remedies hearing to determine the appropriate compensation. However, it indicated that it would reduce her basic award – under S.122(2) ERA – and compensatory award – under S.123(6) ERA – by 90 per cent because of what it termed her foolish conduct at the Christmas party.

16.121 The EAT upheld the tribunal's finding of unfair constructive dismissal on appeal, holding that RCS's failure to deal with N's grievance and its insistence that she return to an atmosphere that she found intolerable constituted a breach of the implied term of trust and confidence. Turning to remedy, the EAT noted that S.122(2) allowed 'any conduct of the complainant before the dismissal' to be taken into account when assessing the basic award. This would include N's conduct at the Christmas party. However, for the purposes of S.123(6) and the compensatory award, only conduct that 'caused or contributed' to the dismissal could be counted. The tribunal in the instant case had found the reason for N's constructive dismissal to be RCS's failure to deal with her grievance in a suitable manner, not N's conduct at the party. Although not completely ruling out the possibility of there being a connection between this conduct and her constructive dismissal, the EAT considered that the tribunal had wrongly let its own views about N's conduct affect its judgment in this regard. It accordingly set aside the tribunal's decision on compensation.

Once the employee's conduct has been shown to have caused or contributed to the dismissal for the purpose of S.123(6), however, a tribunal has no option but to make such a reduction, since the relevant provision stipulates that the tribunal '*shall* reduce the amount of the compensatory award' (our stress). Its discretion lies only in the amount of the reduction, which must be 'such proportion as it considers just and equitable' having regard to the finding that the employee caused or contributed to his or her dismissal. These aspects of S.123(6) are discussed in more detail under 'General principles' below. In contrast, far greater latitude is given to tribunals as to whether or not to make reductions in the basic award even where contributory conduct is found to have occurred. This means that, while the percentage deduction for conduct will usually be the same for both the basic and the compensatory award, this will not always be the case. In Montracon Ltd v Hardcastle EAT 0307/12, for example, the EAT held that different percentage assessments in respect of the basic and compensatory elements of the award were appropriate on the facts of the case, although it did not agree with the figures decided upon by the tribunal. H was summarily dismissed after causing £2,500 worth of damage when the trailer he was driving collided with a low bridge. A majority of the tribunal found that he was unfairly dismissed, but that he had contributed to his dismissal to the extent of 60 per cent – i.e. he forgot the height of the trailer – and that his compensatory award should be reduced accordingly under S.123(6). However, it declined to make any reduction of the basic award under S.122(2) on the ground that H had 20 years' unblemished service with the employer. On appeal, the EAT accepted that different percentage assessments to reflect the employee's conduct may be appropriate under each section. However, given the majority's finding as to the level of H's culpability, the EAT thought that no reasonable tribunal, properly directing itself, could have concluded that a nil reduction was appropriate for the basic award. Instead, the EAT considered that, balancing H's conduct against his long unblemished service, it was just and equitable to impose a reduction of 30 per cent in respect of that award. The EAT adjusted H's compensation accordingly.

16.122 For further discussion of the principles governing reductions from the basic award on grounds of contributory conduct under S.122(2) ERA, and for a detailed discussion of the case law on whether and to what extent it is permissible to make different levels of contributory conduct reductions to the basic and compensatory awards, see Chapter 13, 'Basic awards', under 'Reductions in basic award – employee's conduct'.

16.123   **When is reduction for contributory conduct appropriate?** In Nelson v BBC (No.2) 1980 ICR 110, CA, the Court of Appeal said that three factors must be satisfied if the tribunal is to find contributory conduct:

- the relevant action must be culpable or blameworthy

- it must have actually caused or contributed to the dismissal

- it must be just and equitable to reduce the award by the proportion specified.

Provided these three factors are satisfied, the fact that the dismissal was automatically, as opposed to ordinarily, unfair is of no relevance – Audere Medical Services Ltd v Sanderson EAT 0409/12 (discussed in detail in the section '"Polkey reductions"' above, under 'Types of case to which Polkey principle applies – cases of automatically unfair dismissal'.)

16.124   Each of the factors listed in the Nelson case is discussed in detail under separate headings later in this section. The first two factors focus on the nature of the conduct that is said to have caused or contributed to the unfairly dismissed employee's dismissal. The third factor in effect deals with quantum: by how much should the tribunal reduce the compensatory award once it has found that such a reduction is appropriate? However, before turning to these matters it is appropriate to examine the general principles that apply to reductions made under S.123(6) ERA.

16.125   **General principles**

Before discussing in detail the kind of conduct capable of giving rise to a reduction of the compensatory award on the ground of the employee's contributory conduct/fault, we first set out some of the general principles that apply to the making of such a reduction.

16.126   **Duty on tribunals to consider contributory conduct.** What is clear from the case authorities is that S.123(6) ERA imposes an absolute duty on employment tribunals to consider the issue of contributory fault in any case where it was possible that there was blameworthy conduct on the part of the employee. This is so regardless of whether the issue was raised by the parties – Swallow Security Services Ltd v Millicent EAT 0297/08. Whether or not this duty is triggered will depend on the findings of fact made by the tribunal and, in particular, whether those findings reveal proven conduct attributable to the employee that potentially caused his or her dismissal or contributed in any way to it. On the facts of the Swallow case, the EAT ruled that the employment tribunal had erred when it failed to consider the issue of contributory fault given its findings that the employee had knowingly taken holiday leave in excess of her entitlement and extended the period of unauthorised absence by reporting sick. Although her dismissal nominally for redundancy was found to be a sham and therefore unfair, the EAT ruled that the employee's conduct in taking excess holiday leave and then going off sick was potentially

764

'blameworthy' or 'culpable', and that, as such, the tribunal should have considered whether that conduct contributed to the dismissal and therefore justified a reduction in the employee's compensatory award under S.123(6).

A similar conclusion was reached by another division of the EAT in Callow (t/a Callow Building Services) v Anthony EAT 0136/11. There, A was dismissed after submitting falsified timesheets. At the internal appeal against his dismissal, the employer accepted that A had made a mistake because he was suffering from stress at the time. Nevertheless, it confirmed the original decision to dismiss. The tribunal found that the decision to dismiss fell outside the band of reasonable responses in the circumstances and upheld A's unfair dismissal claim. However, the EAT allowed the employer's appeal against the amount of A's compensation on the ground that the tribunal failed to consider whether A's 'mistake' in compiling the timesheets was blameworthy and therefore justified an assessment of contribution. According to the EAT, the tribunal's findings of fact 'cried out' for a consideration of whether, and to what extent, A's actions contributed to his dismissal. The case was remitted to a different tribunal for reconsideration.

In Sodexho Defence Services Ltd v Steele EAT 0378/08 the EAT went on to **16.127** observe that whether it is appropriate for the tribunal to consider the issue of contributory conduct at the liability or remedies hearing (if held separately) was a matter of judgement for the particular tribunal. That said, it was crucial that by the time the issue of remedy is being considered, the parties are aware of the findings of fact made by the tribunal because these will be needed in order to address matters that are relevant to whether the employee caused or contributed to his or her dismissal.

Distinction between findings relating to fairness and contributory conduct. **16.128** As long ago as 1984, the EAT was cautioning tribunals to mark a clear distinction between considerations relevant to an investigation of fairness of dismissal on the one hand, and those relevant to an investigation of contributory fault on the other – see Iggesund Converters Ltd v Lewis 1984 ICR 544, EAT. The latter requires clear findings of fact as to what (if any) blameworthy conduct on the employee's part the employer knew about at the time of dismissal. The question of fairness, on the other hand, entails the tribunal considering whether, in all the circumstances, the employer's decision to dismiss fell within the band of reasonable responses.

The need to draw a sharp distinction between these matters was similarly emphasised by the Court of Appeal in London Ambulance Service NHS Trust v Small 2009 IRLR 563, CA. In that case an ambulance paramedic was dismissed following a complaint from the daughter of a patient on whom the employee had attended during an emergency home call-out. In particular, the employee was accused of making an inappropriate remark and failing to administer pain relief. The employment tribunal ruled that the dismissal was unfair as it fell outside the band of reasonable responses but that the employee had contributed to the extent of 10 per cent towards his dismissal. This low level of contribution was based on the tribunal's specific finding that the inappropriate remark was made with the best of intentions and the failure to give pain relief constituted an honest if mistaken belief as to the correctness of administering it. The EAT rejected the employer's appeal against the finding of unfair dismissal and the employer appealed to the Court of Appeal.

16.129 Before the Court of Appeal the employer contended that the employment tribunal had wrongly substituted its own view of the reasonableness of the decision to dismiss for that of the employer. In so doing, it had allowed itself to be influenced by its findings on the contributory fault issue. Lord Justice Mummery, giving the judgment of the Court, agreed. He accepted that the tribunal had been bound to make findings of fact about the employee's conduct for the purpose of deciding the extent to which his conduct contributed to his dismissal. But that was a different issue from whether the employer had unfairly dismissed the employee for misconduct. Contributory fault only arose for decision if it was established that the dismissal was unfair. The contributory fault decision was one for the tribunal to make on the evidence that it heard, and was not one for the employer to make. This made it different from the actual decision to dismiss, which was a decision for the employer to make. It was not the role of the tribunal to conduct a rehearing of the facts that formed the basis for the decision to dismiss, still less to substitute its decision for that of the employer. In this case, the tribunal had failed to keep the issues and relevant facts pertaining to the two distinct issues separate.

16.130 **Conduct of employer or other employees irrelevant.** Only the blameworthy conduct of the employee is relevant when considering whether compensation should be reduced under S.123(6) ERA, not that of the employer or other employees. In Parker Foundry Ltd v Slack 1992 ICR 302, CA, the claimant's dismissal for fighting at work was held to be unfair on procedural grounds but his compensation was then reduced by 50 per cent for contributory fault. The claimant appealed against this reduction, saying that the tribunal should have taken account of the fact that the other employee involved in the fight had merely been suspended from work. The EAT rejected this argument: although the consistency of treatment of the two was relevant to the fairness of the dismissal, it was not a matter for the tribunal to consider when assessing contributory fault. The tribunal had found that both employees were 50 per cent to blame for the fight so it was entitled to find that the claimant, by his conduct, had contributed to his dismissal to that extent. The Court of Appeal subsequently upheld this decision.

Similarly, in Salmon v Ribble Motor Services Ltd EAT 51/91 an employment tribunal found an employee's dismissal for organising a union meeting during working hours, which resulted in an unofficial stoppage, to be unfair on procedural grounds but held that by his involvement in the meeting he had contributed to his dismissal by 60 per cent. The EAT held that the fact that two other employees who had been equally responsible for calling the meeting had not been dismissed gave no grounds for overturning the tribunal's finding on contribution.

More recently, in Sandwell and anor v Westwood EAT 0032/09, an employment **16.131** tribunal's disinclination to make a reduction for contributory fault solely because of the employer's own inept conduct was held on appeal to be misconceived. The tribunal had stated that, but for the employer's ineptitude, it would have made a finding that the claimant had contributed to her dismissal to the tune of 20 per cent. The EAT ruled that the tribunal had erred by regarding the employer's conduct as being a relevant consideration to the decision not to make a reduction on account of contributory fault. Also, when intimating that it would have made a reduction but for the employer's conduct, the tribunal had erred by not sufficiently identifying the conduct of the employee it had in mind as the basis for making the putative reduction, and by failing to explain the rationale for setting the reduction at 20 per cent. The case was remitted to the tribunal to allow it to rectify these errors.

In Live Nation (Venues) Ltd and ors v Hussain EAT 0234/08 an employment tribunal gave two reasons for refusing to make a contributory fault reduction. The first was that, in its estimation, there was no blameworthy conduct on the part of the claimant that had caused or contributed to his dismissal. The second was that, in any event, the employer's own conduct in dismissing the claimant – about which the tribunal was highly critical – meant that it was not just and equitable to make a reduction in any case. On appeal, the EAT accepted that the second of these reasons amounted to an error of law because the conduct of the employer was immaterial. The focus should have been exclusively on the conduct of the employee. However, the tribunal's error did not affect its principal conclusion that there was no blameworthy conduct so as to trigger a finding of contributory fault.

By contrast, an employment tribunal's finding on contributory fault was **16.132** overturned on appeal in CK Heating Ltd v Doro EATS 0029/11. There, the tribunal determined at the end of the hearing that, owing to the claimant's refusal to obey a management instruction to sweep the yard, it was appropriate to reduce his compensation for unfair dismissal by 30 per cent. However, when the tribunal issued its written reasons, it stated that 'insufficient attention' had been paid to the possibility that the instruction to sweep the yard was part of a course of conduct which represented a fundamental breach of contract by the employer and recalled its decision. The tribunal subsequently concluded that the employer was in breach of contract, and declined to apply a reduction for contributory fault. Overturning that decision on appeal and applying a 30 per cent reduction to both the basic and compensatory awards, the EAT stressed

767

that there is nothing in S.122(2) or S.123(6) which would entitle a tribunal to look beyond the claimant's conduct when considering whether a reduction is just and equitable. Given the finding that the claimant had refused an instruction which he believed to be legitimate, and that this refusal directly led to his dismissal, there was no option but to reduce compensation.

16.133 **Employee's actions post-dismissal irrelevant.** By definition, deductions can only be made under S.123(6) in respect of actions by the employee that took place *prior* to the dismissal and of which the employer had knowledge when the decision to dismiss was taken. This is because the employee's conduct must be shown to have actually caused or contributed to the employer's decision to dismiss. In Nawaz v John Haggas Ltd EAT 838/83 the employee's compensation for unfair dismissal was reduced by 20 per cent because of his failure to make any representations about his dismissal before presenting his tribunal application. The EAT said this was an error of law because conduct after dismissal cannot be contributory conduct within the meaning of S.123(6): the tribunal was confusing contributory conduct and mitigation of loss – as to which see under 'Failure to mitigate losses' above.

The proposition that post-dismissal conduct cannot constitute a basis for making a reduction on the ground of contributory fault was affirmed in Mullinger v Department for Work and Pensions EAT 0515/05. In that case, an employee was found to have been unfairly dismissed but the tribunal made a reduction of 75 per cent for contributory conduct based on two separate considerations: (i) the employee's misuse of office computer equipment while still in employment; and (ii) his intransigence in refusing to return official documents after his employment had been terminated. In setting the level of contribution, the tribunal acknowledged that the second of these considerations was not a factor in the employee's dismissal. Nevertheless, the tribunal felt that it was a factor 'that must be taken into account in considering what is, in all the material circumstances, just and equitable'. On appeal, the EAT ruled that the tribunal had erred in law by taking account of misconduct that the employee perpetrated after his dismissal. Such conduct had no bearing on the issue of contribution and the case was therefore remitted to a fresh tribunal to decide the extent (if any) of the employee's contribution based solely on the misconduct that had been perpetrated prior to dismissal. The Court of Appeal subsequently upheld the EAT's decision to remit on this basis – Mullinger v Department for Work and Pensions 2007 EWCA Civ 1334, CA.

16.134 The more problematic issue arising in the Mullinger case was whether post-dismissal misconduct can ever legitimately lead to a reduction in the overall compensatory award on some other statutory basis. The employer's contention was that, even if post-dismissal conduct could not properly form the basis for a finding of contributory fault under S.123(6), there was no reason why, in the exercise of its discretion to award 'such amount as is just and equitable' under

S.123(1) ERA, a tribunal should not take account of such conduct for this purpose. For reasons fully elaborated under '"Just and equitable" reductions – misconduct not known to employer at date of dismissal' above, the EAT rejected this interpretation of S.123(1). In its view, there was no scope for adjusting compensation on account of an employee's misconduct if this occurs after the date of dismissal. This was in contrast to misconduct occurring before that of dismissal but which is only discovered by the employer after that date. The EAT made it clear that conduct of the latter kind can be taken into account in considering what is just and equitable to award by way of a compensatory award. (The EAT's observations on S.123(1) were, in effect, obiter, and were not considered by the Court of Appeal when the case was unsuccessfully appealed by the employer.)

That is not to say, however, that a tribunal is altogether precluded from considering a reduction of the employee's compensatory award by reason of his or her post-dismissal conduct. In Cumbria County Council and anor v Bates EAT 0398/11 the EAT held that the employee's post-dismissal conduct can impact upon the assessment of how long he or she would have remained employed but for the dismissal. On this basis, post-dismissal conduct that is relevant to the question of what loss is attributable to the dismissal may be taken into account (see further Chapter 14, 'Compensatory awards: types of loss').

Is finding of contributory conduct bar to reinstatement? Section 116(1) and **16.135** (3) ERA specifically states that, in determining whether to order the reinstatement or re-engagement of an unfairly dismissed employee, an employment tribunal should have regard to three specific factors. One of these is whether it would be just to order reinstatement/re-engagement where the employee has caused or contributed to some extent to his or her dismissal. The EAT has made it clear that the test of whether conduct amounts to contributory fault for the purposes of S.116(1) and (3) is exactly the same as that for determining whether a reduction in the compensatory award should be made under S.123(6) – see Boots Company plc v Lees-Collier 1986 ICR 728, EAT.

Clearly, the fact that there is contributory fault does not present an absolute bar to the capacity of a tribunal to order re-employment: if this were the case, S.116(1) and (3) would have said so. But contributory fault is patently a factor that must to be taken into account when a tribunal exercises its discretion over re-employment orders – the implication being that where an employee has caused or contributed to the dismissal, this may well make re-employment less likely. The extent of any contribution will properly be a relevant consideration in this regard. In Thornton v British Telecommunications plc ET Case No.1700376/08, for example, an employment tribunal ordered the employee to be reinstated despite it finding that he had made a 15 per cent contribution to his dismissal. That level of contribution – which was made because of the employee's attitude towards time-keeping rules that he found to be irksome – did not, in the tribunal's view, preclude an order for reinstatement. By way of contrast, in Pathak v Next Directory Ltd ET Case No.1902284/08 a tribunal declined to order reinstatement in respect of an employee found to have contributed 50 per cent towards her dismissal. The tribunal felt in this case that such a level of contribution made reinstatement inappropriate.

16.136 'Culpable or blameworthy conduct'

As stated at the beginning of this secton, for conduct to be the basis for a finding of contributory fault under S.123(6) ERA, it has to have the characteristic of culpability or blameworthiness. This was firmly established by the Court of Appeal in Nelson v BBC (No.2) 1980 ICR 110, CA, where Lord Justice Brandon explained that, in view of the wording of what is now S.123(6), it could never be just and equitable to reduce a successful complainant's compensation unless the conduct on his or her part was culpable or blameworthy. Put another way, if a person is blameless, it can neither be just nor equitable to reduce his or her compensation on the ground that he or she caused or contributed to the dismissal.

Conduct by the employee capable of causing or contributing to dismissal is not limited to actions that amount to breaches of contract or that are illegal in nature. In the Nelson case the Court said that it could also include conduct that was 'perverse or foolish', 'bloody-minded' or merely 'unreasonable in all the circumstances'. Whether the conduct is unreasonable will depend on the facts. The most typical forms of blameworthy conduct are 'misconduct' in the conventional sense – e.g. disloyalty, dishonesty, taking a holiday without permission or acting in competition with the employer. But S.123(6) can cover wider forms of conduct where, for example, the employee manages to aggravate a situation or precipitate the dismissal. Some examples of less obvious forms of 'blameworthy conduct':

- refusing to reveal the names of fellow employees involved in misconduct – Simpson v British Steel Corporation EAT 594/83

- walking out of a meeting that had been set up to resolve the employee's difficulties regarding her terms and conditions of employment – Wall v Brookside Metal Co Ltd EAT 579/89

- responding aggressively when the employer issued a final warning – Daykin v IHW Engineering Ltd ET Case No.01838/83

- breaking a restraining order which led to the employee being sent to prison and therefore being unable to perform his work – Prior v City Plumbing Supplies Ltd EAT 0535/11.

16.137 There are, of course, limits to how far tribunals will view conduct as 'blameworthy'. In Glenrose (Fish Merchants) Ltd v Chapman and ors EAT

770

467/91, for example, the EAT upheld a tribunal's decision that a number of employees who had refused to work overtime in protest at what they understood to be a unilateral variation of contract imposed by their employer had not, in the circumstances, contributed to their dismissals, even though they were effectively acting in breach of contract. And in Doyle-Davidson v Ormerods Ltd ET Case No.48770/94 an employee was dismissed for refusing to sign a new contract with less favourable terms, for writing to the employer in aggressive language and for being provocative in the way she completed her time sheets. A tribunal refused to accept that she had been guilty of contributory conduct and accordingly it made no reduction in her compensation. The employee was entitled to express her reservations about the proposed changes and the language in her letter was not unreasonable. Nor was it unreasonable for her to make a point about her working hours when completing time sheets.

Knowledge that conduct is wrong. The fact that an employee did not know **16.138** that what he or she was doing was wrong will not necessarily prevent a finding of contributory conduct. In Allen v Hammett 1982 ICR 227, EAT, the claimant employee, acting entirely on the advice of his solicitor, refused to return a cheque that had been paid to him in error by his employer. This refusal eventually led to his dismissal, which was judged to be unfair by the tribunal. However, his compensation was reduced by 60 per cent for contributory conduct. Before the EAT, the employee argued that because he had acted in good faith upon his solicitor's advice, his conduct could not be regarded as culpable or blameworthy under the Nelson test. The EAT, however, while sympathetic to the employee's position, stated that it was a general principle of law that a person is held responsible for the actions of his or her agents. The tribunal had been entitled to make the reduction it had. The employee's remedy lay in legal action against his solicitor for negligence.

Tribunals will usually be alive to the particular circumstances in which misconduct on an employee's part occurs, especially if mitigating circumstances explain the conduct in question despite the fact that the employee knows he or she has done wrong. In Peled-Hada and anor v Windsor Great Perk Ltd ET Case No.2700087/08, for example, two employees claimed they were too ill to come into work, although this was untrue. This was one of a number of incidents that led directly to their dismissals. They were found to have been unfairly dismissed but the tribunal let them off the hook so far as a finding of contributory conduct was concerned. It recognised that they had been working under great stress – employees and suppliers had not been paid owing to the employer's financial difficulties and court bailiffs had entered the premises on more than one occasion. In these circumstances, although the tribunal made it clear that it was not condoning the employees' actions, it concluded that their conduct had not reached the required threshold to trigger a reduction in their compensation award.

16.139 Even if the employee does not know that his or her conduct is wrong, there may nonetheless be a reduction for contributory fault if he or she ought to have known. This will depend on the circumstances of the case. In Department for Work and Pensions v Coulson EAT 0572/12 C was dismissed for having accessed, without authority, personal records held by the DWP relating to members of her family. A tribunal found that the dismissal was unfair because the DWP did not properly take into account mitigating circumstances, including her ill health. When it came to consider contributory fault, the tribunal found that, despite having worked for the DWP for 20 years, C did not appreciate that her actions constituted a serious breach of the data security policy. On that basis, her conduct was not 'culpable and blameworthy' so as to entail a reduction in compensation. On appeal by the DWP, the EAT held that the tribunal had erred. During the disciplinary proceedings leading up to dismissal, C had accepted that she did know that she was in the wrong and so the DWP was entitled to proceed on that basis. It was not until the tribunal made its own findings of fact that C's ignorance was established. The EAT went on to state that it was sceptical of the viewpoint that an employee working for this length of time in these surroundings, who was not mentally ill such as to be unable to perform her job (although she plainly had medical problems), could not be 'culpable and blameworthy'. It noted that the lay members in particular had emphasised that the fact that an employee, who has had appropriate training and time on the job, is able to show subjectively that he or she did not know that what he or she was doing was against the employer's policies is rarely, if ever, likely to render misconduct neither culpable nor blameworthy.

16.140 **Employee's failure to explain his/her actions.** An employee's failure to give the employer an explanation for his or her conduct can contribute to a dismissal. In Kwik Save Stores Ltd v Clerkin EAT 295/95 a tribunal accepted the claimant's contention that his dismissal for allegedly falsifying the clocking-off cards of employees was unfair because he had in fact only been carrying out what he had thought to be standard company procedure. However, the tribunal found that his failure to raise this defence to his actions at the disciplinary hearing contributed to his dismissal by 40 per cent. And in Blair v British Steel plc ET Case No.9271/95 the employee was dismissed for playing football while off sick. The tribunal found that the dismissal was unfair for lack of investigation into the incident. But it reduced the compensatory award by 80 per cent because the employee, although represented by skilled advisers at his disciplinary hearings, had omitted to draw the employer's attention to the full circumstances of his absence, the potentially therapeutic nature of playing football, or the need for a medical opinion.

16.141 **Refusal to participate in disciplinary process.** In Vassoo v Gambro Healthcare UK Ltd and ors ET Case No.2300615/07 an employment tribunal declined to make a contributory fault reduction in respect of the employee's refusal to participate in the disciplinary process prior to dismissal. The tribunal found that this failure could not be said to be 'blameworthy'. Employees are entitled to say that they do not wish to ask or answer questions in the context of a disciplinary hearing. The tribunal observed that although such action may make it more likely that disciplinary allegations will be upheld, it cannot be said to amount to blameworthy conduct justifying a reduction in the compensation awarded. Similar reasoning applies in respect of a failure by an employee to utilise internal appeals – see 'Failure to utilise internal appeal' below.

Conduct during disciplinary process. Whereas there is – according to the **16.142** employment tribunal in Vassoo v Gambro Healthcare UK Ltd (see above) – no room for a finding of contributory fault where an employee refuses to cooperate with a disciplinary procedure, there appears to be more leeway to find contributory fault in respect of the manner in which an employee conducts him or herself during a disciplinary process. That said, the case law suggests that the scope for such a finding remains limited – see British Steel Corporation v Williams EAT 776/82 and Sidhu v Superdrug Stores plc EAT 0244/06. In the latter case, an employment tribunal made a 90 per cent reduction in the employee's compensatory award because he could have done far more to assist himself during the course of two disciplinary hearings by probing the evidence submitted by the employer to support the allegation of gross misconduct and by attempting to call witnesses at the disciplinary hearing. On appeal, the EAT cautioned that a finding of contributory conduct in such a case was only appropriate if the tribunal is sure that the employee has caused or contributed to his or her dismissal by some aspect of his or her conduct during the disciplinary process. Although the EAT did not say so expressly, the implication is that such conduct will be rare.

The outcome in the Sidhu case can be contrasted with that in Bell v Governing Body of Grampian Primary School EAT 0142/07, where the EAT upheld an employment tribunal's decision that the employee's sarcastic and aggressive behaviour during the disciplinary process justified a reduction in the compensatory award for contributory fault. In that case, it was specifically found by the tribunal that the employee's conduct had been in the mind of the employer when deciding to dismiss, and that, had the employee behaved more acceptably, the chances were that a lesser disciplinary penalty would have been imposed.

In Nelson v Clapham t/a Clapham's Solicitors EATS 0037/11 the claimant was **16.143** dismissed when the employer found a print-out of a personal e-mail criticising the employer on the office printer. During the disciplinary procedure, the claimant denied that she had left the print-out lying around, refused to apologise for its content, and accused the employer of having taken it out of her handbag. Upholding the decision of an employment tribunal to reduce her basic and compensatory awards by 80 per cent, the EAT stated: 'We see no reason why, if an employee engages in culpable conduct at the disciplinary hearing – such as

773

by being dishonest or casting ill-founded aspersions of dishonesty on her employer – that conduct cannot be taken into account when considering reduction of the basic and compensatory awards. There is nothing in the wording of the relevant statutory provisions – where the terms "any conduct" and "any action" are wide and general – to suggest that such conduct should be excluded from consideration.'

Similarly, in Perkin v St George's Healthcare NHS Trust 2006 ICR 617, CA, the Court of Appeal appeared to uphold an employment tribunal's finding of a 100 per cent contribution based on the manner in which the employee had behaved during a disciplinary inquiry. However, despite a lengthily reasoned principal judgment from Lord Justice Wall, the Court undertook very little analysis of S.123(6) and in particular of how the conduct – which was based on the employee's personality and accusatory management style – had actually caused or contributed to the employee's dismissal within the meaning of S.123(6). (In contrast, Wall LJ's reasoning in upholding the tribunal's alternative finding of a 100 per cent 'Polkey reduction' from the employee's compensatory award was far more extensive – see '"Polkey reductions"' above. The employment tribunal had observed that the manner in which the employee had conducted himself during the disciplinary hearing was illustrative of the difficulties the employer had faced when dealing with the employee throughout his employment. In the Court of Appeal's view, the tribunal was entitled to conclude that it would have been impossible for the employee to remain a member of the employer's senior executive team and that, had a proper disciplinary process been undertaken, it would have ended with the same result.)

16.144 **Failure to utilise internal appeal.** An employee's failure to make use of an internal appeals procedure to reverse a decision to dismiss cannot normally be considered under S.123(6) ERA because it is not conduct that can in any way be said to have contributed to the dismissal. Only if the dismissal did not occur until after the appeal can such conduct be taken into account – see Hoover Ltd v Forde 1980 ICR 239, EAT.

16.145 **Unreasonable refusal to accept suitable alternative employment.** An employee's refusal to accept an offer of re-engagement from the employer made after the dismissal will not justify a reduction in compensation for contributory conduct under S.123(6), but may be considered in the context of mitigation – see 'Failure to mitigate losses – refusal of offer of re-employment or settlement' above. Note, however, that by virtue of S.122(1) ERA, the unreasonable refusal of an offer of re-engagement can specifically serve to reduce a basic award (see Chapter 13, 'Basic awards', under 'Reductions in basic award – unreasonable refusal of reinstatement offer').

16.146 **Ill-health and capability dismissals.** The issue of contributory fault typically arises in cases where misconduct was the reason for dismissal. In cases of dismissal for incapability or ill health the 'conduct' in question is likely to be

774

beyond the employee's control, so the element of blameworthiness or culpability is lacking. In Slaughter v C Brewer and Sons Ltd 1990 ICR 730, EAT, the EAT affirmed that, for this reason, dismissals on the ground of ill health will rarely give rise to a finding of contributory conduct. Much the same applies to capability dismissals. In Kraft Foods Ltd v Fox 1978 ICR 311, EAT, the EAT stated that if an employee is incompetent or incapable and cannot measure up to the job, it is wrong to say that this can be a factor contributing to the dismissal. 'The whole point about contribution,' the EAT continued, 'is that it is something by way of conduct on the part of the employee over which he has control.' In Frith Accountants Ltd v Law 2014 ICR 805, EAT, the EAT similarly emphasised that mere poor performance was unlikely to be sufficiently culpable or blameworthy to constitute contributory conduct. This was particularly true where, as in the present case, the employer had not considered formal capability proceedings to be warranted.

In some cases where an employee is judged to have been unfairly dismissed on the ground of capability owing to the lack of an adequate performance review procedure, the tribunal will proceed to limit the compensatory award in accordance with its discretion under S.123(1) ERA to award 'such amount as [it] considers just and equitable having regard to the loss sustained by the complainant'. The basis for limiting the award in this way is often that the tribunal is satisfied that the adoption of a fair procedure would, at best, only have delayed the inevitable, in that the employee would have been dismissed in any event. In Plumley v AD International Ltd EAT 592/82 the EAT held that, where compensation is limited because an employee's performance is unlikely to improve, it should not be further reduced for contributing to his or her own dismissal.

16.147 One possible circumstance in which contribution in the context of an ill-health or capability dismissal might be appropriate is where the employee has blatantly and persistently refused to obtain medical reports, undergo a medical examination or ignored medical advice. In Hague v Clean Factory and Office Services Ltd ET Case No.5942/95, for example, the claimant ignored his GP's advice to stay off work on account of a viral infection. The infection affected his ability to do his job properly. A client complained about the employee's work, by which time he had been forced to take sick leave. He was held to have been unfairly dismissed but was found to have contributed to his dismissal by not taking his GP's advice.

The Hague case can be contrasted with that of Claymore Graphics Ltd v Simpson EAT 450/99, in which the employee became sick with stress and depression. His doctor predicted he would recover fully in 4–6 weeks. While he was unwell, the employee went into the office outside working hours, smoked in a no-smoking area, and left a colleague an abusive note, for which he was summarily dismissed in absentia as he was too ill to attend the hearing. A

775

tribunal found the dismissal unfair because it was clear that the employee's conduct might well have had its origins in his mental state, and even if it did not, he was not well enough to answer the disciplinary charges. The tribunal ruled that any reasonable employer would have waited 4–6 weeks until the employee had recovered before deciding whether disciplinary action was appropriate. On appeal, the EAT upheld the tribunal's decision on the basis that the employee's misconduct could well have been attributable to stress and depression and that it could be 'involuntary in the sense of attributable to a problematic mental state'. This was all the more reason for not classifying it as contributory conduct.

16.148 Cases of genuine incapability should be distinguished from those in which the incapability was the employee's own fault, in the sense that he or she was lazy, negligent or idle, or did not try to improve. In reality, such cases are more akin to misconduct than genuine incapability and the degree of contribution may be considerable. For example, in Chauhan and anor v Man Truck and Bus UK Ltd EAT 931/94 the tribunal accepted that the employee's dismissal raised issues of incapability in that he was not really up to the job. Nevertheless, the tribunal assessed contribution at 75 per cent on account of his lack of initiative and failure to make a proper effort.

16.149 **Mental illness and alcoholism.** The fact that an employee's conduct or capability is explicable by a mental illness or mental condition is unlikely, without more, to constitute a sound basis for making a finding of contributory conduct. A person's mental state is not, on the whole, culpable or blameworthy conduct over which that person has any control. However, where a mental condition leads to pre-planned misconduct, the position may well be different.

In Edmund Nuttall Ltd v Butterfield 2006 ICR 77, EAT, the employee's duties entailed extensive travel by car. On his way home from a business trip, he committed two offences of indecent exposure and one of dangerous driving. The following day, he was admitted to hospital after having suffered a nervous breakdown. The employee was subsequently convicted in the criminal courts and sentenced to a three-year Community Rehabilitation Order with a condition of medical treatment. He was also disqualified from driving for two years. It transpired that he had been exposing himself to females over an 18-month period. At a later date, the employer found out about the employee's conviction and this led to his eventual dismissal for gross misconduct. He brought claims of disability discrimination and unfair dismissal, both of which were upheld by an employment tribunal. In respect of compensation for unfair dismissal, the tribunal held that the employee had not been guilty of culpable conduct and accordingly there was no basis for making a reduction for contributory fault under S.123(6) ERA. On appeal, the EAT overturned the tribunal's decision on this point. Although the Appeal Tribunal upheld the finding of unfair dismissal, it concluded that the employment tribunal's decision that the employee was not guilty of culpable or blameworthy conduct was perverse. In the EAT's view, while it was entirely proper that the degree of culpability was reflected in the tribunal's findings as to the employee's mental state, the fact that he had committed pre-planned offences of a criminal nature and then concealed the true position (including his convictions) from the employer was plainly culpable conduct that merited a reduction in the compensatory award under S.123(6). The case was remitted to a different tribunal to consider what the extent of that reduction should be.

A similar conclusion was reached by the EAT in Sinclair v Wandsworth Council **16.150** EAT 0145/07, albeit in a rather different context. In that case the employee (who admitted that he was an alcoholic) was dismissed when he was found to be under the influence of alcohol at work in breach of the employer's alcohol policy. His dismissal was held to be unfair because he had not been given sufficient details of the policy and, in particular, the steps he was expected to take to avoid disciplinary action in respect of his condition. In awarding compensation, although the tribunal did find contributory fault to the extent of 25 per cent on grounds unrelated to the employee's alcoholism, it specifically refused to increase the percentage reduction further on account of the employee's breach of the alcohol policy. It took the view that alcoholism was an illness and so could not be categorised as culpable or blameworthy conduct. On appeal, the EAT overturned the tribunal's decision on this point, ruling that it was not the case that unacceptable conduct can be excused by reference to a background or underlying illness. The fact was that the employer had been faced with such conduct in the workplace. The case was remitted to the same tribunal to decide whether and by how much to increase the finding of contributory fault beyond 25 per cent.

Personality clashes. In Bell v Governing Body of Grampian Primary School **16.151** EAT 0142/07 a school teacher was found to have been unfairly dismissed owing to the employer's failure to comply with the then applicable statutory dismissal procedures. The employment tribunal went on to make a 75 per cent reduction in the employee's compensatory award on account of the blame it laid at the employee's door for his dismissal. The contributory conduct in question took several forms, including making 'silly' comments to the head teacher when he queried remarks the employee had made about a parent who had complained about the employee; the aggressive manner in which the employee had conducted himself during the disciplinary process; 'trying to be clever' in the retorts he gave to questions during the disciplinary process; and soliciting other teachers to bring a grievance against the head teacher.

On appeal, the EAT emphasised that when making a reduction under S.123(6) ERA, the tribunal must be satisfied that there is actual culpable or blameworthy conduct on the part of the employee, which must go beyond an issue of personality, disposition or a tendency towards unhelpfulness. That said, in the

777

instant case, the Appeal Tribunal concluded that this was not a case in which the employment tribunal had found simple instances of non-participation in the disciplinary process or unhelpfulness. On the facts, it had been entitled to find that the employee's conduct had operated on the mind of the employer and had been part of the background that had induced the disciplinary panel to uphold the allegations made against him and to choose to deal with the matter by way of dismissal.

16.152 **Conduct protected by statute.** A finding of contributory fault would be wholly inappropriate where the conduct in question was statutorily protected behaviour – e.g. where the employee had not disclosed a 'spent' criminal conviction – Property Guards Ltd v Taylor and anor 1982 IRLR 175, EAT.

16.153 **Industrial pressure to dismiss.** Employment tribunals are specifically prohibited from taking account of industrial pressure to dismiss an employee when deciding on the fairness of a dismissal – S.107 ERA. Industrial pressure in this context comprises calling, organising, procuring or financing a strike or other industrial action, or threatening to do so. Nor can such industrial pressure be taken into account when assessing the compensatory award – S.123(5). In other words, employers cannot plead for a reduction in compensation because they faced industrial action if they did not dismiss the employee. However, under the contributory conduct provision of S.123(6), the compensation for any unfair dismissal may be reduced if the employee in some way brought about both the industrial pressure and the subsequent unfair dismissal.

In Colwyn Borough Council v Dutton 1980 IRLR 420, EAT, for example, the employee was a dustcart driver whose colleagues refused to go out with him following several careless driving incidents. Although industrial pressure was the reason for his dismissal, the EAT said that the employee's careless driving was a factor and his compensation should be reduced accordingly. And in Sulemanji v Toughened Glass Ltd and anor 1979 ICR 799, EAT, an employee's uncooperative attitude towards resolving a dispute with other workers was found to be contributory conduct justifying a 100 per cent reduction.

16.154 **Industrial action.** Special provisions apply to dismissals for participating in official industrial action – see IDS Employment Law Handbook, 'Industrial Action' (2010), Chapter 8, 'Industrial action dismissals'. Basically, under S.238 of the Trade Union and Labour Relations (Consolidation) Act 1992 (TULR(C)A) an employee who is dismissed while participating in official industrial action cannot bring a claim of unfair dismissal unless at least one other employee who was also taking part in the action was either not dismissed or was (in contrast to the claimant) re-engaged within three months. In Courtaulds Northern Spinning Ltd v Moosa 1984 ICR 218, EAT, the EAT held that the policy behind these special provisions was that an employment tribunal should be prevented from going into the rights or wrongs of an

778

industrial dispute. It followed, said the EAT, that an employee's participation in industrial action could not constitute contributory conduct.

The Moosa case was approved by the House of Lords in Tracey and ors v Crosville Wales Ltd 1997 ICR 862, HL, where their Lordships held that it was impossible to allocate blame for industrial action to any individual employee, particularly in cases where the collective blame for the industrial action is shared by employees who have been re-engaged. This conclusion merely reflected the fact that any reduction in compensation should be just and equitable. The House of Lords agreed with the comments of Lord Justice Waite in the Court of Appeal on the limited circumstances in which conduct could in theory be taken into account; namely, where there was individual blameworthy conduct additional to, or separate from, the mere act of participation in industrial action. According to the Court of Appeal, the question that tribunals must ask themselves is: 'Have these applicants been responsible, in addition to mere participation in the relevant industrial action, for any conduct of their own contributing to the dismissal which was sufficiently blameworthy to make it just and equitable to reduce their compensation?' The Court said, for example, that if the leaders of the industrial action were dismissed, their particular activities as leaders could properly be examined and the tribunal would be entitled to make a deduction for contributory fault if it found that the conduct had been overhasty or inflammatory.

16.155 The House of Lords' decision has the virtue of clarifying the point that normally an individual who has demonstrated that he or she has been unfairly dismissed when participating in industrial action – not an easy task in itself due to the procedural rules that apply in such cases – should not have his or her compensation for that dismissal reduced on the ground that he or she contributed to the dismissal by participating in industrial action. But the acknowledged exception to this rule where the employee's conduct is 'individual blameworthy conduct additional to or separate from the mere act of participation in industrial action' raises the obvious question as to what type of conduct can be taken into account.

Transport and General Workers' Union v Howard 1992 ICR 106, EAT, is one example of a case in which confrontational conduct of the employee during industrial action was held to be sufficiently independent (rather than collective) to be considered contributory fault, justifying a reduction. Similarly, in Gosling v Ford Motor Co Ltd EAT 221/90 a tribunal's decision to reduce the employee's compensation by 75 per cent for contributory fault was upheld by the EAT. In that case the employee had substantially contributed to his own dismissal by his unjustifiable conduct in inciting industrial action (regardless of the merits of the industrial action) and by his refusal to sign an undertaking that he would not be involved in any unconstitutional action. A similar conclusion was reached in Crowther v British Railways Board EAT 1118/95, where the EAT

779

decided that the employee's behaviour in inciting industrial action outside the normal procedures for the industry could amount to conduct justifying a reduction in his compensation.

16.156 The decisions above – particularly Gosling and Crowther – raise the possibility that the person who incites industrial action will be more likely to have his or her compensation reduced than a mere participant in the action. While from one perspective this certainly has a degree of logic about it, from another it potentially undermines the right to undertake lawful industrial action. The organisers of industrial action are the people most likely to be victimised by employers. Surely, if UK law is to genuinely protect the right to organise (and participate in) lawful industrial action, they should not therefore be unduly penalised under S.123(6). We would argue that, as long as an individual is acting within the scope of normal procedures for calling industrial action and is not offending against the criminal law, the exception to the general rule acknowledged by the House of Lords should not be invoked. It is submitted that, in interpreting this exception, the realities of the situation – particularly the often heated nature of industrial disputes – should be borne in mind.

16.157 **Union membership, activities and use of union services.** Specific provisions apply where the reason for dismissal or selection for redundancy is shown to have been a trade union reason. In considering whether to reduce the compensatory award on the ground of an employee's conduct, a tribunal must completely disregard conduct leading to the dismissal that comprises a breach (or proposed breach) of an arrangement or contractual term requiring the employee (a) to be or become a member of a union or cease to be a member; (b) to take part or not take part in union activities; or (c) not to make use of the services of a union – S.155(2) TULR(C)A.

Tribunals must also disregard a refusal to pay, or to allow deductions from pay to be made in favour of, somebody other than a union (e.g. a charity) – S.155(4) TULR(C)A. A similar disregard applies where the conduct in question comprises: (a) the refusal by the employee of an offer by the employer the main purpose of which is to induce the employee not to be or seek to become a member of a trade union, make use of its services or participate in its activities; or (b) the refusal by the employee of an offer that has the intended result that the employee's terms and conditions will not (or will no longer be) determined by collective agreement negotiated by the union – S.155(2A) TULR(C)A.

16.158 **Causal link between conduct and dismissal**
In order for a deduction to be made under S.123(6) ERA, a causal link between the employee's conduct and the dismissal must be shown. This means that the conduct must have taken place before the dismissal; the employer must have been aware of the conduct; and the employer must then have dismissed the employee at least partly in consequence of that conduct. An employment

780

tribunal cannot simply point to some misbehaviour by the employee and reduce compensation on that count. In Hutchinson v Enfield Rolling Mills Ltd 1981 IRLR 318, EAT, the employee was seen at a demonstration in Brighton while absent from work through ill health. A tribunal found that he had been unfairly dismissed but assessed his contribution at 100 per cent because of his generally obstreperous attitude. On appeal, the EAT held that, while the employee's attendance at the demonstration was capable of constituting contributory conduct, his attitude had no bearing on the dismissal and so the tribunal had erred in reducing the award for contributory fault.

In Smith and anor v McPhee and anor EAT 338/89 conduct that at first glance seemed clearly to have contributed to the dismissal was held not to have done so when the real reason for dismissal became apparent. M, a hotel barmaid, had filled a lemonade bottle with caustic soda for her own use but accidentally left it on the bar overnight. The next morning the employer herself used the bottle to clean a sink and then put it back on the bar. Later on another barmaid mistook it for lemonade with the result that an unfortunate customer suffered severe burns to his mouth. M was promptly dismissed for leaving the item on the bar. The tribunal came to the conclusion that M had not in reality been dismissed on account of her own conduct but in order to divert attention away from the employer's own careless behaviour and thus protect the reputation of the hotel. The EAT upheld the tribunal's decision that, since the real reason for M's dismissal was not her conduct but the need for a scapegoat, the dismissal was unfair and her conduct, though reprehensible, had not in fact contributed to that dismissal.

The need to focus solely on matters that led to the employee's dismissal was **16.159** also stressed by the EAT in Nejjary v Aramark Ltd EAT 0054/12. In that case, N, who worked for A Ltd as a hospitality manager, was dismissed following three specific work incidents. However, upon hearing N's appeal against his dismissal, A Ltd upheld the decision to dismiss for gross misconduct based on only one of the incidents: N's failure to check the booking sheet for an event, leading to a customer complaint, which brought the company into disrepute. The tribunal rejected N's claim for unfair dismissal but found that, if it had concluded otherwise, it would have reduced his compensation by 100 per cent on the basis of his contributory conduct. The EAT overturned the tribunal's decision on appeal. Given that A Ltd had based its decision to dismiss entirely on a single act of misconduct, it had not been open to the tribunal to bring into the equation matters – such as N's work record – that A Ltd did not have in mind when dismissing. The tribunal should have considered only whether the specific reason for which N was dismissed – namely, the single failure to check the booking sheet – was sufficient for his dismissal to fall within the range of reasonable responses. The tribunal had clearly recorded that no reasonable employer would have dismissed N for that single act, and the EAT accordingly substituted a finding of unfair dismissal. Similarly, the EAT continued, the tribunal should have confined itself to matters 'causally connected or related' to the dismissal in finding contributory conduct under S.123(6). However, when referring to N's conduct in this regard, the tribunal had also been referring to the additional matters (specifically N's previous record) that it had erroneously relied upon as justifying his dismissal under S.98(4). N's previous record could not have causally contributed to his dismissal because it had not played any part in A Ltd's decision. The case was therefore remitted for determination of remedy.

16.160 **Conduct contributing to but not sole reason for dismissal.** When considering the issue of contributory fault, tribunals are entitled to rely on a broad view of the employee's conduct, including behaviour which, although not relating to the main reason for dismissal, nonetheless played a material part in the dismissal. In Robert Whiting Designs Ltd v Lamb 1978 ICR 89, EAT, the employee was dismissed for lack of competence but the EAT found that his improper bonus claims were factors contributing to his dismissal. And in Arthur v Pronto Services (UK) Ltd ET Case No.5175/95 the employee, an accident-prone driver, crashed a company vehicle through his own negligence. When his employer threatened to deduct the repair cost from his pay, he counter-threatened to bring a claim of unlawful deduction from his wages and was promptly dismissed. A tribunal found that the reason for the employee's dismissal was that he had asserted a statutory right and that the dismissal was therefore automatically unfair under S.104 ERA. However, it found that he had contributed to his dismissal by his negligent driving.

Similarly, in BSW Ltd v Brown EAT 0835/04 B was the principal shareholder of the company as well as its employee. He was dismissed after it was discovered that he had committed the company to a lease for premises without authority. An employment tribunal, in ruling that B had been unfairly dismissed, found that the real reason for dismissal was that the company's chairman had already resolved to dismiss B and that the issue of the lease merely provided a cover under which to carry out the dismissal. However, the tribunal reduced B's compensatory award by 50 per cent on account of his conduct concerning the lease. On appeal, the EAT upheld the tribunal's decision. The lease issue had been a factor in the company's mind to the extent that it was the primary ground advanced by the employer as explaining the dismissal. This was so even though the real reason was camouflaged and overtaken by the legitimate reason concerning the employee's conduct over the lease.

16.161 In Carmelli Bakeries Ltd v Benali EAT 0616/12 B, a pastry chef, was dismissed after knowingly using non-kosher jam in a product at a kosher bakery. A tribunal upheld his unfair dismissal claim, a decision which was also upheld on appeal by the EAT. However, the Appeal Tribunal went on to hold that the tribunal had erred in failing to consider contributory fault pursuant to S.123(6) in assessing compensation. On a fair reading of the tribunal's judgment,

782

B's misconduct in relation to the jam incident was not the 'operative reason for dismissal'. Rather, the reason the sanction of dismissal was applied without any proper investigation or fair hearing was that B, who had made a number of disability-related requests and complaints, was regarded as a 'problem employee'. Nevertheless, the tribunal found that B's misconduct had still contributed to his dismissal. The tribunal had therefore erred in failing to consider whether, and if so to what extent, it was just and equitable to reduce the compensatory award. B's case was remitted to the tribunal for reconsideration of his compensation.

Failure to establish potentially fair reason for dismissal. The fact that an **16.162** employer has failed to establish a potentially fair reason for dismissal within the terms of S.98(1)(b) and (2) ERA does not preclude a finding of contributory conduct. In Chauhan and anor v Man Truck and Bus UK Ltd EAT 931/94 the tribunal rejected the employer's claim that an employee had been dismissed for 'some other substantial reason' and found that it had failed to establish that the dismissal came under any of the permissible reasons listed in S.98(2) ERA. It nevertheless ruled that the employee's poor performance had contributed to the dismissal by 75 per cent, a finding upheld on appeal by the EAT.

Constructive dismissal. It used to be considered highly unlikely that a tribunal **16.163** could legitimately make a finding of contributory conduct in a constructive dismissal case. This was because it was felt that if the tribunal were to find contributory conduct it would be difficult to conclude that the employer's conduct was sufficiently serious to constitute the fundamental breach of contract required to give rise to a constructive dismissal. In Holroyd v Gravure Cylinders Ltd 1984 IRLR 259, EAT, Lord McDonald went so far as to say that it would only be in 'exceptional' cases that a finding of contributory conduct would accompany one of constructive dismissal. However, that statement has been modified in subsequent cases.

In Morrison v Amalgamated Transport and General Workers' Union 1989 IRLR 361, NICA, the employee was suspended without pay and resigned. The suspension was held to be in fundamental breach of contract and M succeeded in her claim of unfair constructive dismissal. However, the tribunal reduced her compensation by 40 per cent because she had by her conduct 'provoked and precipitated' the employer's unlawful reaction. The employee appealed against the reduction, citing the Holroyd case to the effect that the tribunal had failed to identify any exceptional circumstances justifying a finding of contributory conduct in a constructive dismissal case. The Northern Ireland Court of Appeal, however, stated that Lord McDonald's dictum should not be taken as a statement of legal principle. It was simply an observation that contributory conduct will be comparatively rare where the employee has been constructively dismissed. The Court went on to point out that, since it was open to a tribunal

783

to declare a constructive dismissal fair, there could be no inconsistency in its finding that the employee contributed to the dismissal in the first place.

16.164 If contribution is to apply, there must be a connection between the employee's conduct and the fundamental breach. In British Rail Staff Association (Newcastle Central Branch) v Robson EAT 4/89 R, a club stewardess, overheard a meeting of the club committee at which she thought she was being unfairly criticised. She complained to the committee about what she had heard but nothing was done to put matters right. The tribunal found that the failure of the committee to clear up the matter had destroyed the necessary degree of confidence and trust between the parties, and that R had been unfairly constructively dismissed. However, the tribunal reduced her award by one third to reflect the fact that the chain of events had been started by R's improper behaviour in listening in upon the private deliberations of the committee. The EAT upheld the employee's appeal against the finding of contributory conduct. It stated that however blameworthy R's eavesdropping might have been, it had in no way caused or compounded that behaviour of her employer which entitled her to treat herself as being constructively dismissed. It therefore ruled that the tribunal had been wrong in law to make any reduction.

By way of contrast, in Polentarutti v Autokraft Ltd 1991 ICR 757, EAT, a sufficient causal connection was found between the constructive dismissal and the contributory conduct of the employee. In that case P had, in the course of an afternoon's work, machined 24 hub-caps, of which 23 were found to be defective. Subsequently the employer refused to pay P for some overtime work and he resigned and brought a claim for unfair constructive dismissal. An employment tribunal upheld P's claim but reduced his award by two thirds because he had contributed to his dismissal. On appeal, P argued that there was an insufficient connection between his shoddy workmanship and A Ltd's repudiatory breach of contract. The EAT accepted that the employer's breach was not caused solely by P's poor workmanship but stated that a tribunal does not require a direct causal link in order to make a reduction. All that is required is that the action of the employee to some extent contributed to the dismissal. In the present case, said the EAT, there was ample evidence upon which the tribunal could find a sufficient link to justify its finding of contributory conduct.

16.165 Constructive dismissal cases often entail the build-up of separate incidents that culminate in a 'final straw' in response to which the employee resigns and claims constructive dismissal. In such cases the employee's own conduct may be found to have contributed to the dismissal, and, in order to assess the level of the contribution, the tribunal should look broadly at the conduct over the whole period and not just at the culminating incidents – Garner v Grange Furnishing Ltd 1977 IRLR 206, EAT.

784

Amount of reduction – 'just and equitable' proportion   16.166

Once the element of contributory fault has been established, the amount of any reduction is a matter of fact and degree for the tribunal's discretion. In this regard, it is useful to provide a reminder of the wording of S.123(6) ERA, which is: 'Where the tribunal finds that the dismissal was to any extent caused or contributed to by any action of the complainant, it shall reduce the amount of the compensatory award *by such proportion as it considers just and equitable* having regard to that finding' (our stress). It is important to note that the just and equitable consideration in the context of contributory conduct applies only to the proportion (i.e. the percentage amount) by which the tribunal reduces the award. It does not apply to whether or not to make a reduction in the first place, or entitle the tribunal to take into account matters other than conduct that is causative or contributory to the dismissal – see Parker Foundry Ltd v Slack 1992 ICR 302, CA, per Lord Justice Balcombe. Where a tribunal has found, on the evidence, that an employee has to some extent caused or contributed to his or her dismissal, it 'shall' (i.e. must) reduce the award. The only discretion left to it is by how much.

Any reduction decided on by the employment tribunal must be applied to the compensatory award as a whole. In Riverside Industrial Equipment Ltd v Audsley EAT 0105/13 the tribunal decided that a 50 per cent reduction was appropriate in respect of the employee's contributory conduct but failed to apply it to three elements of the compensatory award: notice pay, loss of statutory rights and the recoupment of training costs. The EAT held that this was an error of law. An employment tribunal is not entitled to reduce some elements of the compensatory award, but not others.

It should also be noted that in cases where there are no grounds for making a   16.167
reduction on account of contributory fault under S.123(6) – e.g. because the 'culpability' element is lacking in, say, a capability dismissal – the compensatory award, but not the basic award, may still be reduced under S.123(1) ERA on the basis that it is just and equitable to do so. One example would be where a dismissal was unfair on procedural grounds in circumstances in which the evidence showed that the employee was indeed incapable of performing the job. Another would be where an employer only discovers the fact that an employee has committed an act of misconduct after he or she has been dismissed even though that act occurred before the date of dismissal. Although neither scenario would provide the basis for a finding of contributory fault, a tribunal would be entitled to take into account the justice and equity of the situation when assessing the overall compensatory award under S.123(1). This point is discussed further under '"Just and equitable" reductions' above.

Guidance on the amount of reduction. In Hollier v Plysu Ltd 1983 IRLR   16.168
260, EAT, the EAT suggested that the contribution should be assessed broadly and should generally fall within the following categories: wholly to blame

785

(100 per cent); largely to blame (75 per cent); employer and employee equally to blame (50 per cent); slightly to blame (25 per cent).

Although this suggestion provides useful guidance, tribunals retain their discretion and findings of 90 per cent or 10 per cent are occasionally made. This is despite the obiter remarks of Lord MacDonald in Yorke v Brown EAT 262/84 to the effect that the assessment of an employee's contribution as low as 10 per cent is almost de minimis and that tribunals should in general apportion responsibility for the dismissal on a broader basis or not at all. In Alexander v Ellwood Glass Ltd ET Case No.28122/95 the employee was dismissed after informing the employer that he needed six weeks' unpaid leave to look after his wife following an operation. A tribunal found that no reasonable employer would have dismissed in those circumstances. Nevertheless, it went on to hold that the employee must have known that his wife was going to need looking after and that his failure to plan or discuss the time off with the employer at an earlier stage contributed to the dismissal by 10 per cent.

16.169 Since the assessment of contribution is a matter of discretion for the tribunal, few appeals succeed on this point. The EAT will only interfere if the tribunal has erred in law or made a perverse decision. In Foster v Somerset County Council 2004 EWCA Civ 222, CA, the Court of Appeal (applying Hollier v Plysu Ltd (above)) held that the EAT's decision to reduce a 100 per cent reduction for contributory fault to 90 per cent, in circumstances where it did not find the tribunal's decision on contribution to be perverse, was an error of law. And in LA Recruitment and Management Services Ltd v MacKinnon EAT 0020/04 the EAT, while confirming that a tribunal's decision regarding the degree of contribution will rarely be interfered with on appeal, observed that such interference may be more appropriate where the gap between what the claimant seeks by way of compensation and what the tribunal actually awards is very substantial.

The following are examples of where the EAT has felt justified in interfering with the amount of contribution determined by tribunals:

- **Coalter v Walter Craven Ltd** 1980 IRLR 262, EAT: a funeral receptionist was unfairly dismissed after failing to notice when two bodies were mixed up and placed in the wrong coffins. The tribunal assessed her contributory conduct at 50 per cent but the EAT reduced it to 25 per cent, pointing out that it was her first mistake and that she had been given no clear written instructions as to her duties

- **Cornelius v London Borough of Hackney** EAT 1061/94: an in-house auditor was unfairly dismissed for disclosing confidential information concerning internal corruption to the councillor chairing the investigating committee and to union representatives. The tribunal found him to be 50 per cent responsible for his dismissal on the basis that he should have passed the documents to management. The EAT found the tribunal's decision perverse and held that C had not contributed to his dismissal at all. It was his duty to uncover corruption and he had not acted out of any improper motive

- **Nairne v Highland and Islands Fire Brigade** 1989 IRLR 366, Ct Sess (Inner House): a high-ranking fire officer who needed to drive as part of his job was dismissed following a second disqualification for a drink-driving offence. The EAT increased the contribution from 25 per cent to 75 per cent. This decision was upheld by the Court of Session

- **Allma Construction Ltd v Laing** EATS 0041/11: the EAT overturned a tribunal's decision that the employee's contributory conduct should be reflected in a 5 per cent reduction to his compensatory award. The tribunal had misunderstood the facts and had failed to appreciate that the employee's conduct involved knowingly breaching an important health and safety rule, which had put the employer at risk of being found to be in breach of its statutory obligations. In these circumstances, a reduction for contribution of only 5 per cent was so low as to be perverse.

Nil awards (100 per cent contribution). As already noted, the power of **16.170** tribunals to reduce compensation extends to finding a 100 per cent 'contribution'. The ability to reduce compensation to this degree was first recognised by the National Industrial Relations Court (the precursor of the EAT) in Maris v Rotherham Corporation 1974 IRLR 147, NIRC. Following that decision, the EAT in England and Scotland were for a time divided on the extent to which 100 per cent deductions were, in practice, permissible, but the divergence came to an end in 1977 with the House of Lords' decision in W Devis and Sons Ltd v Atkins 1977 ICR 662, HL. In that case their Lordships unanimously held that there was no inconsistency in finding that an employee was unfairly dismissed and that he or she had contributed 100 per cent to this dismissal, so reducing the compensatory award to nil.

While it has been clear since the Devis case that 100 per cent deductions are possible, they are rare and there is ample case authority that both recognises this and encourages the situation to remain so. In Moreland v David Newton (t/a Aden Castings) EAT 435/92, for example, the EAT said that a reduction of 100 per cent is unusual and a tribunal must fully justify such a course of action by reference to facts and reasons in its decision. Similarly, in Lemonious v Church Commissioners EAT 0253/12 the EAT held that a tribunal should have set out its reasoning as to why it was just and equitable to reduce the claimant's award to nil. In that case, an employee was dismissed after 37 years' service for sending e-mails in the names of other employees, and denying that he had done so. The tribunal found that the employer had made a number of procedural errors that rendered his dismissal unfair, but reduced both his basic award and compensatory award to nil. The EAT commented that it was not obvious why the tribunal felt it was just and equitable to do so, given that the employer had

787

not dealt fairly with a long-serving employee and had classed the offending e-mails as 'relatively mild'.

16.171 The most likely situation in which a 100 per cent reduction will be ordered is where the tribunal considers that the employee's misconduct was such that dismissal was wholly justified but nonetheless feels compelled to find the dismissal unfair because of procedural flaws in the dismissal procedure. Even then, a finding of 100 per cent contribution will not automatically follow, since the question of the appropriate level of contribution remains, as we have seen, one for the tribunal's discretion. Three examples:

- **Smith v Lodge Bros (Funerals) Ltd** EAT 92/88: S was dismissed for being absent from work without informing his employer. A tribunal found his dismissal unfair because he had been dismissed by letter and given no opportunity to state his case but it went on to reduce his compensation by 100 per cent. On appeal, S argued that it was legally impossible to reduce compensation by 100 per cent when the employer had been guilty of a major procedural defect. The EAT rejected this argument. It said that the tribunal had expressly found that S's conduct had caused the dismissal while the employer's conduct, although wrong, had not caused the dismissal in any shape or form

- **Ardyne Scaffolding Ltd v Rennie** EAT 688/93: R was dismissed after returning to work drunk following a Christmas lunch. A tribunal found that the employer had handled the dismissal unfairly but reduced the compensatory award by 75 per cent on account of the employee's conduct. The EAT rejected the employer's argument that, since R's conduct was the sole occasion for the dismissal, the tribunal should have made a much higher assessment of the employee's contribution

- **Palmer v Clark and Symonds Ltd** EAT 388/98: P worked as a receptionist for a car repair company and her job was to obtain insurance excess charges direct from customers. While P was on holiday, her employer carried out an investigation. Eight customers had paid P cash but there was no record of their payments in the company's books. P was arrested on return from holiday and never returned to work. The tribunal found unfair dismissal but awarded compensation subject to 100 per cent contribution. P's appeal on the basis that the tribunal had failed to consider what outcome might have followed from a fair procedure was rejected by the EAT because, in any event, the result would have remained the same and P would still have been subject to the 100 per cent reduction.

Although it can be gleaned from the above cases that the EAT will rarely interfere with a tribunal's decision regarding the amount of contribution, a finding of 100 per cent contributory fault has to be firmly based on logic that is consistent with the tribunal's findings of fact. If such findings accept some

788

measure of fault on both sides regarding the cause of the dismissal, or if the dismissal is contributed to by a mixture of blameworthy and non-blameworthy conduct on the part of the employee, it is difficult to see how a 100 per cent reduction could, in principle, be justified.

16.172 This point is illustrated by the EAT's decision in Langston v Department for Business, Enterprise and Regulatory Reform EAT 0534/09. In that case, the complainant was a senior employee with specialist knowledge of nuclear and explosion issues. His post attracted a high level of security clearance. However, while attending a conference abroad, his colleagues became concerned about his unusual behaviour, which included unfounded allegations that his room had been broken into and that money and personal effects had been stolen. He was later diagnosed by the employer's medical adviser as having suffered an 'acute transient psychotic disorder', which occurred in parallel with the employee being highly stressed as the result of the demands of his job. The medical adviser reported that a repeat episode could not be ruled out in the future. As a result, the employee's security clearance was revoked. For a while, the employer sought to find suitable alternative employment, but these efforts were overtaken by the need to make redundancies and the employee was eventually made redundant.

An employment tribunal found that the employee had been unfairly dismissed because the real reason for his dismissal was not redundancy but the decision to delete his post, which itself was linked to the removal of his personal security clearance. His dismissal for 'some other substantial reason' was held to be automatically unfair because the employer failed to carry out the statutory dismissal procedures applicable at the time. However, the tribunal went on to make a finding of 100 per cent contribution against the employee on account of his 'bizarre and misjudged' conduct at the conference, which, in the tribunal's view, had destroyed the employer's trust and confidence in him. The EAT allowed the employee's appeal on the ground that the tribunal had failed to consider whether the conduct relied on as the basis for the contributory fault finding was within the control of the employee and was 'culpable or blameworthy', as it was required to be – see 'Culpable or blameworthy conduct' above. Had the tribunal properly addressed that matter, then in the context of the facts as found it could not have properly concluded that a 100 per cent reduction, or anything anywhere near it, was appropriate. The EAT therefore remitted the case to a new tribunal to consider afresh the extent to which (if any) the employee's conduct had contributed to his dismissal.

16.173 In effect, the Langston case illustrates the proposition that, for a 100 per cent contribution finding to be permissible, the employee's conduct must be found to be the sole reason for the dismissal. This proposition is confirmed by the obiter remarks of Mr Justice Elias (as he then was) in Kelly-Madden v Manor Surgery 2007 ICR 203, EAT. This is not the same thing as saying that just

789

because there is fault on the employer's part means that a 100 per cent finding is impossible. If that were the case, no such finding would be permissible in any case where the employer has been guilty of procedural errors that led to a finding that the dismissal was unfair. Reflecting on what he had said in the Kelly-Madden case, Elias J clarified the role that procedural fault on the part of the employer might have in this context in Ingram v Bristol Street Parts EAT 0601/06. He observed that sometimes procedural failings by the employer will be causally relevant to the dismissal itself, in which case a finding of 100 per cent contribution would not be justified. But if the employee's blameworthy conduct was found to be the sole factor resulting in the dismissal, then a 100 per cent finding could be justifiable.

However, a finding that an employee's conduct is the sole cause of his or her dismissal will not inevitably result in a nil compensatory award. In Lemonious v Church Commissioners (above) the EAT said that even where a tribunal finds no reason for dismissal other than the employee's conduct, it might still have to modify the percentage reduction in light of what is just and equitable.

16.174 **The 'Polkey effect'.** Under '"Polkey reductions"' above, we discuss the effects of the House of Lords' decision in Polkey v AE Dayton Services Ltd 1988 ICR 142, HL, on the calculation of compensation. That case established that, based on the wording of what is now S.123(1) ERA, tribunals are entitled to reduce the amount of the compensatory award in circumstances where dismissal is found to be unfair by reason of procedural failures by the employer. The amount of any such reduction depends on an assessment by the tribunal of the likelihood that, had the procedural irregularities not occurred, the employee would have still been dismissed. Where a reduction is made on this basis, there may also be an element of contributory fault in respect of which a separate and additional reduction is made. The precise relationship between Ss.123(1) and 123(6) is considered under '"Polkey reductions"' above.

16.175 **Tribunal's duty to provide sufficient reasons**

It should be noted that although the wording of S.123(6) is mandatory – an employment tribunal 'shall reduce the amount of the compensatory award' – the tribunal is nonetheless obliged to give its reasons for making (or not making) a reduction – Nairne v Highland and Islands Fire Brigade 1989 IRLR 366, Ct Sess (Inner House). In South West Trains v Miles EAT 0039/03 the EAT held that a tribunal considering contribution ought, if it is going to find no contribution at all, to make a clear finding with proper reasons that the employee was neither blameworthy nor culpable. Extending that theme, in Mars UK Ltd t/a Masterfoods v Parker EAT 0412/05 the EAT doubted that there would be many cases where it would be sufficient for a tribunal simply to declare that an employee did not contribute to his or her dismissal without explaining why: only if it is obvious from the remainder of its full reasoned decision why there was no contributory fault would such a minimalist approach be permissible.

On the other hand, if the tribunal does find contributory fault, it must be satisfied that the employee did actually commit the acts that contributed to the dismissal and should explain why this is so. In London Borough of Lewisham v James EAT 0581/03 the EAT stated that 'it is quite plain that S.123(6) is not satisfied by reference to a finding simply that an employer had reasonable belief in the conduct. The conduct which is to form the basis of a deduction for contributory fault, whatever it is, must be established, proved and identified by the tribunal.'

16.176 In Cornwall County Council and anor v McCabe EAT 147/97 M, a teacher, was dismissed following allegations by two female pupils that he had fondled them. A tribunal found the dismissal to be unfair due to a woefully inadequate investigation, but nonetheless reduced M's award by 20 per cent for contributory conduct. The EAT set aside the deduction: there was nothing in the tribunal's decision to show what misconduct M had actually committed. A 'no smoke without fire' approach was not acceptable.

Allowing relevant evidence to be given
16.177

Tribunals must be careful not to exclude evidence that may be relevant to showing that the employee contributed to his or her dismissal simply because of the overwhelming case that the employee was unfairly dismissed. In PJ and ME Egan t/a Dell Care Home v Owen EAT 0035/08 it was obvious on the face of the employer's own admissions that it had completely failed to conduct a sufficient investigation into allegations of misconduct against the employee. For that reason, the employment tribunal found that the employee had been unfairly dismissed. The tribunal proceeded to refuse to hear three witnesses whom the employer wished to call for the purpose of proving the truth behind at least some of the allegations that had caused the employee to be dismissed. On appeal, the EAT ruled that this was an error of law. Although the evidence that the employer wished to call was not material to the question of fairness of the dismissal, it was relevant both to considerations of contribution under S.123(6) and the amount of the compensatory award under S.123(1), and therefore should not have been excluded.

Separation of findings relevant to unfairness and contribution. As we have **16.178** seen, tribunals are expected to keep separate findings relevant to the question of the fairness of dismissal from those relevant to the question of contributory fault and other aspects of compensation – see the discussion of London Ambulance Service NHS Trust v Small 2009 IRLR 563, CA, under 'General principles – distinction between findings relating to fairness and contributory conduct' above. In that case Lord Justice Mummery advised that, as a general rule, it would be good practice for tribunals to keep their findings on these

791

matters separate. Although some facts may be relevant to more than one issue, the legal elements of the different issues and the role of the tribunal in adjudicating them are not necessarily the same. Making separate and sequential findings of fact on discrete issues might therefore help to avoid errors of law, even if this leads to a degree of duplication.

Since the decision in Small, the Court of Appeal has had a further opportunity to consider the way in which tribunals should approach evidence relevant to the fairness of dismissal on the one hand, and evidence relevant to contributory fault on the other. In Salford Royal NHS Foundation Trust v Roldan 2010 ICR 1457, CA, Lord Justice Elias, giving the only reasoned judgment of the Court of Appeal, accepted that Mummery LJ in Small had said it would be helpful, when looking at questions of fairness, contributory fault and 'Polkey reductions', etc, for tribunals to set out separately their relevant findings of fact with respect to each issue. But Elias LJ considered that Mummery LJ had not been laying down any fixed rule about this and that, in any event, his observations did not amount to a requirement that witnesses should give their evidence on these matters in a 'compartmentalised' way. In particular, it was not appropriate in the normal run of things for witnesses to give evidence first on liability and then separately to give similar (if not identical) evidence dealing with the question of contributory fault. This was especially true where the tribunal has made it clear in advance of the hearing that the parties will be expected to adduce evidence as to liability and remedy at the same hearing. But even where there is a split hearing on issues of liability and remedy, it was not the case that tribunals are required to hear all witnesses twice: such a notion would only add to the length and cost of hearings without having any obvious benefit. Elias LJ observed that it was important that the parties clarify with the tribunal precisely what issues the tribunal wishes to have determined at which stage. If there is any doubt about when a party needs to adduce evidence on a particular point, that matter ought to be raised with the tribunal.

16.179 The outcome in the Roldan case was that the Court of Appeal reinstated the employment tribunal's decision that the employee had been unfairly dismissed but that there should be no reduction made to her compensation on account of contributory fault. The case concerned S, an experienced registered nurse, who was accused by a relatively inexperienced nurse of mistreating a vulnerable patient by, among other things, throwing wet wipes at his face and making an abusive 'V' sign gesture. The employment tribunal found her dismissal to be unfair, principally for lack of a sufficient investigation. At the subsequent remedies hearing, the tribunal refused to allow the nurse who had witnessed the alleged incidents to be recalled to give evidence relevant to the issue of contributory fault. On appeal, the EAT overturned the tribunal's decision on liability and also concluded that the tribunal had erred in shutting out evidence pertaining to contributory conduct. Citing the Court of Appeal's decision in London Ambulance Service NHS Trust v Small (above), the EAT held that the tribunal should have allowed the junior nurse to be recalled to provide further evidence pertaining to the question of whether S's conduct had contributed to her dismissal. However, on further appeal, the Court of Appeal overturned the EAT's decision on both the liability and the contributory fault issues for the reasons discussed above.

Reductions for lack of good faith in whistleblowing cases

16.180

A package of changes to the whistleblowing provisions in the ERA, introduced by the Enterprise and Regulatory Reform Act 2013, included a new ground on which compensation can be reduced. This applies where a claimant has successfully claimed automatically unfair dismissal contrary to S.103A ERA, which applies to dismissals for making a protected disclosure (so called 'whistleblowing' dismissals). S.123(6A) ERA, which was brought into force on 25 June 2013, provides that 'where the reason (or principal reason) for the dismissal is that the complainant made a protected disclosure, and it appears to the tribunal that the disclosure was not made in good faith, the tribunal may, if it considers it just and equitable in all the circumstances to do so, reduce any award it makes to the complainant by no more than 25 per cent'.

The introduction of this provision coincided with the insertion of a public interest test into the whistleblowing provisions and the removal of the requirement in Ss.43C and 43E–43H that certain types of disclosure had to be made in good faith to qualify for statutory protection. In essence, the question of good faith has been moved from the liability stage of a claim to the remedy stage, and the consequences for an employee making a disclosure in bad faith have been made much less severe: rather than losing out on any possibility of claiming automatically unfair dismissal, he or she will, at worst, lose a quarter of the compensation to be awarded.

Although the new ground for reduction has been placed in S.123 ERA, which **16.181** is titled 'Compensatory award', it is not altogether clear that the power to reduce the award by up to 25 per cent is limited to the compensatory award. As outlined above, S.123(6A) states that a tribunal may reduce any award. In contrast, S.123(6), which allows a tribunal to make a reduction for the employee's contributory conduct, specifically refers to the compensatory award (and a separate provision for reducing the basic award for contributory conduct is found in S.122(2)). Given this difference, a possible construction of S.123(6A) is that it allows a tribunal to reduce the basic award and/or the compensatory award by up to 25 per cent where it appears that a disclosure was not made in good faith. If that is the case, then it represents a departure in terms of the drafting of the ERA: to date, all adjustments to the basic award have been set out in S.122 (see Chapter 13, 'Basic awards', under 'Reductions in basic award').

793

These issues are discussed in more detail in IDS Employment Law Handbook, 'Whistleblowing at Work' (2013), Chapter 7, 'Enforcement and remedies', under 'Remedies in unfair dismissal claims – adjustments and reductions'.

16.182 Offsetting enhanced redundancy payments

Section 123(7) ERA makes special provision in respect of the setting off of redundancy payments. It provides that if the amount of any redundancy payment – whether statutory or otherwise – made by the employer exceeds the amount of the basic award, 'that excess goes to reduce the amount of the *compensatory award*' (our stress). Thus, if the employer's redundancy scheme is more generous than the statutory scheme and the dismissal is subsequently judged by a tribunal to be unfair, the part of the redundancy payment that corresponds to the statutory entitlement will normally extinguish entitlement to a basic award (see Chapter 13, 'Basic awards', under 'Reductions in basic award – receipt of redundancy payment'), with the excess then serving to reduce the compensatory award.

In Digital Equipment Co Ltd v Clements (No.2) 1997 ICR 237, EAT, the employee had received a contractual redundancy payment that exceeded his statutory entitlement by £20,685. The EAT held that an excess redundancy payment should be treated no differently from any other payment made upon termination of employment. Accordingly, the EAT deducted the £20,685 from the assessment of the employee's losses before applying a 50 per cent Polkey reduction. However, when the case reached the Court of Appeal – reported at Digital Equipment Co Ltd v Clements (No.2) 1998 ICR 258, CA – the Court held that this was wrong. Enhanced redundancy payments must be subtracted from the compensatory award after the percentage deduction. In its view, 'Parliament has drawn a clear distinction in the treatment of the excess of redundancy payments... and the other elements which go to make up the loss'.

16.183 The distinction is that S.123(7) specifically provides that excess redundancy payments should be deducted from the compensatory award itself, rather than being treated as part of the calculation of the employee's losses which go to make up the amount of the compensatory award. The correct approach, therefore, is first to assess the employee's loss, making any proportional reductions to ensure that the compensation is just and equitable, and then to deduct from the resulting compensatory award the excess redundancy payment. This method, said the Court, accords with the clear intention of S.123(7) that employers should receive full credit for redundancy payments that are larger than required by statute.

It is important to note that S.123(7) only applies to redundancy payments, whether statutory or contractual. Thus, if there is no genuine redundancy

794

situation, a payment labelled as a redundancy payment would fall to be offset against the claimant's losses in the same way as an ex gratia termination payment – see Chapter 14, 'Compensatory awards: types of loss', under 'Immediate loss – termination payments'.

Provided a redundancy payment is genuine, a tribunal should effectively take **16.184** no account of it until it has calculated the measure of loss and applied any other deductions and adjustments. In MacCulloch v Imperial Chemical Industries Ltd EAT 0275/09 a tribunal fell into error by offsetting an enhanced redundancy payment against the claimant's losses, and then deducting the amount of the payment that exceeded the basic award from the claimant's compensatory award. The EAT explained that, in circumstances such as the instant case where a tribunal determines that, but for the dismissal, the claimant would have received a larger enhanced redundancy payment at a later date, the correct approach is to include in the calculation of loss a sum that reflects the payment the claimant would have received, minus the amount of a basic award to which the claimant would have been entitled at the later date. Only once the losses have been calculated, and any other adjustments or deductions made, should the tribunal deduct from the compensatory award the amount by which the redundancy payment that the employee *did* receive exceeds the basic award.

Application of statutory cap   16.185

All relevant adjustments and deductions have to be made *before* the application of the statutory cap on compensation. In most cases of unfair dismissal a statutory ceiling is placed on the amount of the compensatory award (currently £78,335 (as from 6 April 2015) or a year's pay, whichever is the lower), although there are a few exceptions where no such ceiling is imposed – see Chapter 14, 'Compensatory awards: types of loss', in the section 'Nature and maximum amount of award, under 'Amount of week's pay and statutory cap – exceptions to statutory limit'. Whenever the statutory cap does apply, it is only if the total figure for the compensatory award exceeds the prevailing maximum once all relevant adjustments and deductions have been made that the tribunal should reduce the level of its award to the prevailing maximum – see Walter Braund (London) Ltd v Murray 1991 ICR 327, EAT. So, for example, if the employee's losses amount to £100,000 and the tribunal assesses his or her contribution towards the dismissal at 20 per cent, a 20 per cent reduction should be applied to the £100,000 to leave £80,000. If the employee's salary is higher than this, then the appropriate limit would be £78,335. Since the loss exceeds the statutory maximum, the compensatory award would then be reduced to the prevailing statutory maximum. It would be wrong first to apply the statutory maximum of (currently) £78,335 and then reduce it by 20 per cent to arrive at a figure of £62,668.

795

16.186 ## Order of adjustments

Having considered the different types of deduction that can be made from the compensatory award, it is important to be aware of the order in which adjustments and deductions – if applicable – should be made. Sometimes a tribunal, in assessing the compensatory award, may have to make a deduction of an ex gratia payment made by the employer as well making a percentage deduction for contributory conduct under S.123(6) ERA and/or a reduction to reflect what is 'just and equitable' under S.123(1) ERA. Where this happens, the question arises as to which deduction should be made first.

To take a simple example: a tribunal assesses the employee's losses, before any deductions, at £10,000. It also finds that the employer made an ex gratia payment of £2,000 that must be offset against those losses and that the employee contributed 50 per cent to the dismissal. If the tribunal first deducts the £2,000 ex gratia payment, then applies the 50 per cent deduction for contributory fault to the remaining £8,000, the employee will come away with £4,000. If, however, the tribunal does the calculation the other way round, applying the 50 per cent deduction first to arrive at a figure of £5,000 and then offsetting the £2,000 payment, the employee will end up with the lesser sum of £3,000. Clearly, therefore, the order in which the calculation is done can make a considerable difference to the amount of the final compensatory award.

16.187 **General principles.** Faced with a number of conflicting EAT decisions on the matter, the then President of the EAT, Mr Justice Morison, decided to lay down some guidelines for tribunals to follow in Digital Equipment Co Ltd v Clements (No.2) 1997 ICR 237, EAT. He held that the correct approach is first to offset any contractual or ex gratia termination payments (including a payment in lieu of notice) in order to arrive at the employee's 'net loss', then to make any proportionate reduction necessary to reflect contributory fault or, in a case of a procedurally unfair dismissal, the chance that the employee would have been dismissed in any event (see '"Polkey reductions"' above). The EAT stated that it was important to bear in mind the difference between a proportionate reduction of an award and a deduction or set-off. A deduction in the latter sense takes place as part of the calculation of the award itself, which then falls to be proportionately reduced to reflect contributory conduct or a Polkey reduction. A deduction for failure to mitigate should be made before any percentage reduction.

Considerable support for this approach has since come from the Court of Appeal in Ministry of Defence v Wheeler and ors 1998 ICR 242, CA, where a similar view was taken as to the order of deductions. Furthermore, in Heggie v Uniroyal Englebert Tyres Ltd 1999 IRLR 802, Ct Sess (Inner House), the Inner House of the Court of Session confirmed that any payment in lieu of notice should be deducted before any proportionate deduction for contributory conduct on the employee's part.

796

Where a tribunal has to make both a Polkey reduction and a reduction for **16.188** contributory conduct, it will make no difference to the final amount which percentage is applied first. However, in Rao v Civil Aviation Authority 1994 ICR 495, CA, the Court of Appeal held that an employment tribunal should first make the Polkey reduction under S.123(1). The size of that reduction may well have a significant bearing on what further reduction falls to be made for contributory conduct under S.123(6).

Enhanced redundancy payments. It is crucial to note, however, that different **16.189** considerations apply to the setting-off of redundancy payments. As explained under 'Offsetting enhanced redundancy payments' above, S.123(7) ERA specifically provides that, if the amount of any redundancy payment made by the employer exceeds the amount of the basic award, 'that excess goes to reduce the amount of the compensatory award'. In Digital Equipment Co Ltd v Clements (No.2) (above), the employee had received a contractual redundancy payment that exceeded his statutory entitlement by £20,685. The EAT held that an excess redundancy payment should be treated no differently from any other payment made upon termination of employment. Accordingly, following the guidelines set out above, the EAT deducted the £20,685 from the assessment of the employee's losses before applying a 50 per cent Polkey reduction. However, when the case reached the Court of Appeal – Digital Equipment Co Ltd v Clements (No.2) 1998 ICR 258, CA – the Court held that this was wrong. Enhanced redundancy payments must be subtracted from the compensatory award *after* the percentage deduction. In its view, 'Parliament has drawn a clear distinction in the treatment of the excess of redundancy payments… and the other elements which go to make up the loss'.

The distinction is that S.123(7) specifically provides that excess redundancy payments should be deducted from the compensatory award itself, rather than be treated as part of the calculation of the employee's losses which go to make up the amount of the compensatory award. The correct approach, therefore, is first to assess the employee's loss, making any proportional reductions to ensure that the compensation is just and equitable, and then to deduct from the resulting compensatory award the excess redundancy payment. This method, said the Court, accords with the clear intention of S.123(7) that employers should receive full credit for redundancy payments which are larger than required by statute.

Section 207A TULR(C)A and S.38 EA 2002 adjustments. The question **16.190** arises whether any adjustment to the compensatory award pursuant to the statutory provision for making adjustments of up to 25 per cent in respect of breaches of the Acas Code of Practice on Disciplinary and Grievance Procedures – S.207A TULR(C)A – has to be made before or after any reduction on account of: (i) payment by the employer to the employee of an ex gratia payment or payment in lieu of notice; (ii) failure to mitigate; (iii) a 'just and equitable'

797

reduction in accordance with S.123(1) ERA (including a Polkey reduction to reflect the chance that dismissal would have occurred even if the proper procedure had been followed); (iv) contributory fault; (v) payment of an enhanced redundancy payment in excess of the amount of the basic award; and (vi) adjustment made under S.38 EA 2002 in respect of a failure to provide full and accurate written particulars of employment.

In respect of the reductions mentioned in (i), (ii) and (iii), any percentage adjustment for breach of the Acas Code should be made *after* any such reduction has first been made in accordance with the EAT's guidance set out in Digital Equipment Co Ltd v Clements (No.2) (above).

16.191 In respect of (iv) and (v), S.124A ERA stipulates that: 'Where an award of compensation for unfair dismissal falls to be reduced or increased – (a) under S.207A of the TULR(C)A 1992... or (b) increased under S.38 of the [EA 2002]... the adjustment... shall be applied *immediately before* any reduction under S.123(6) or (7)' (our stress). This means that any reduction on account of contributory fault or payment of an enhanced redundancy payment must be made immediately after the adjustment for breach of the Acas Code or the increase of up to four weeks' pay for a failure to provide written particulars of employment is applied.

Regarding (vi), S.207A(5) TULR(C)A provides that: 'Where an award falls to be adjusted under [S.207A for breach of the Acas Code] and under S.38 EA 2002, the adjustment under [S.207A] shall be made *before* the adjustment under [S.38]' (our stress). In other words, the appropriate adjustment for breach of the Acas Code is made before any adjustment in respect of the employer's failure to provide accurate written particulars.

16.192 **Reductions under S.123(6A).** As outlined under 'Reductions for lack of good faith in whistleblowing cases' above, S.123(6A) permits a tribunal to reduce any award it makes to an employee dismissed contrary to S.103A ERA by up to 25 per cent where it appears to the tribunal that the protected disclosure which led to the dismissal was not made in good faith.

Frustratingly, there is no provision in the ERA specifying when this particular reduction should be made. In accordance with the guidance set out by the EAT in Digital Equipment Co Ltd v Clements (No.2) (above), it is clear that it must be made after any reductions made in respect of an ex-gratia payment or because of a failure to mitigate, and any 'just and equitable' reduction under S.123(1) ERA. It would also appear to follow from the Court of Appeal's decision in that case that the reduction should be made before the off-setting of any enhanced redundancy payment under S.123(7).

16.193 However, existing case law does not provide the answer to whether a S.123(6A) reduction should precede or follow adjustments made under S.207A TULR(C)A and S.38 EA 2002 (see 'Section 207A TULR(C)A and S.38 EA

2002 adjustments' immediately above). We would argue that, since contributory fault and a lack of good faith are conceptually very similar, it would make little sense for one to precede the TULR(C)A and EA 2002 adjustments and the other to follow them, and that the S.123(6A) reduction should therefore come after the TULR(C)A and EA 2002 adjustments. That leaves the question of whether a good faith reduction should be made before or after a reduction for contributory fault: this will only be of importance in the rare situation where a tribunal settles on a different percentage reduction under each head. It may be that the Parliamentary draftsman or woman has left a clue as to the correct order by his or her choice of numbering for the subsection – 6A – which falls between contributory fault and the off-setting of redundancy payments. Nevertheless, it seems inevitable that it will now fall to the EAT or appellate courts to provide a definitive answer as to the correct order of reductions in a S.123(6A) case.

Statutory ceiling on compensatory award. If the statutory cap on the **16.194** compensatory award (currently £78,335 (as from 6 April 2015) or a year's salary, whichever is the lower) applies, the cap must be applied after *all* deductions and other adjustments have been made. The circumstances in which the cap does and does not apply are discussed in Chapter 14, 'Compensatory awards: types of loss', in the section 'Nature and maximum amount of award', under 'Amount of week's pay and statutory cap – exceptions to statutory limit'.

Summary of principles   **16.195**

The correct order for deductions as discussed above is summarised below. The summary reflects the Court of Appeal's comments in Digital Equipment Co Ltd v Clements (No.2) (above), but duly modified to include, at the appropriate point, adjustments that fall to be made under S.207A TULR(C)A in respect of breaches of the Acas Code of Practice.

To calculate the compensatory award, it is first necessary to ascertain the employee's total loss in consequence of the dismissal, in so far as that loss is attributable to the employer's actions – S.123(1) ERA (see Chapter 14, 'Compensatory award: types of loss'). Deductions and adjustments (if applicable) should then be made strictly in the following order:

- deduction of any payment already made by the employer as compensation for the dismissal (e.g. an ex gratia payment or payment in lieu of notice) but not any enhanced redundancy payment

- deduction of sums earned by way of mitigation, or to reflect the employee's failure to take reasonable steps in mitigation – S.123(4) ERA

- 'just and equitable' reductions based on S.123(1) ERA, including reductions in accordance with the principle in Polkey v AE Dayton Services Ltd 1988 ICR 142, HL

799

- increase or reduction (adjustment) of up to 25 per cent where the employer or employee failed to comply with a material provision of the Acas Code of Practice on Disciplinary and Grievance Procedures – S.207A TULR(C)A

- adjustment of up to four weeks' pay in respect of the employer's failure to provide full and accurate written particulars – S.38 EA 2002

- percentage reduction for the employee's contributory fault – S.123(6) ERA

- deduction of any enhanced redundancy payment to the extent that it exceeds the basic award (liability for the basic award will also have been set off by the statutory redundancy payment under S.122(4)) – S.123(7) ERA

- application of the statutory cap (currently £78,335 (as from 6 April 2015) or a year's salary, whichever is the lower) – S.124 ERA.

Finally, although there is no judicial guidance on the matter, we would argue that any percentage reduction under S.123(6A) in a whistleblowing claim where there has been a lack of good faith on the part of the employee should apply immediately after any reduction for contributory fault.

16.196 Taxation

As explained in Chapter 14, 'Compensatory awards: types of loss', the amount of compensation due is generally calculated net of tax, the claimant being awarded an amount based on his or her take-home pay. The practice avoids the need for both sides to account for income tax and national insurance contributions on what would otherwise be earnings. However, some types of tribunal award, including awards for future loss of earnings consequent on dismissal, are taxable in themselves under S.401 of the Income Tax (Earnings and Pensions) Act 2003 in so far as they exceed £30,000. When this happens, the standard practice is for tribunals to 'gross up' the award. This means increasing the amount of compensation so that, once the appropriate amount has been paid to HM Revenue and Customs, the claimant is left with the figure the tribunal originally intended to award. For example, in Somerset County Council v Chaloner EAT 0063/14 the EAT held that, in order to achieve an award that is just and equitable, it was necessary to gross up any part of the compensatory award that exceeded £30,000.

In the context of the correct order for adjustments to the claimant's unfair dismissal compensation, the EAT made it clear in Hardie Grant London Ltd v Aspden 2012 ICR D6, EAT, that where a tribunal was contemplating making a compensatory award in excess of the £30,000 tax-free figure, the grossing-up of the figure to allow for the incidence of tax should take place before applying the statutory cap imposed by S.124 ERA.

17 Additional awards and interim relief

Additional awards

Interim relief

In most cases in which an employee succeeds in an unfair dismissal complaint **17.1**
before an employment tribunal, his or her remedy will be an award of financial
compensation. In the great majority of cases this will consist of a basic award
and a compensatory award, as discussed in the four preceding chapters. However,
as explained in Chapter 12, 'Remedies', the tribunal must first consider whether
it is appropriate to grant reinstatement or re-engagement of the employee. In the
rare cases that an order for reinstatement/re-engagement is made, the tribunal
has the power to make an additional award under S.117(3)(b) of the Employment
Rights Act 1996 (ERA) where the employer totally fails to comply (and has been
unable to show the tribunal that it was impracticable to do so).

Note that 'special awards' – which used to be available under S.118(2) and (3)
ERA where the dismissal was for one of a number of automatically unfair
reasons (e.g. health and safety, working time) and the employee had asked for
reinstatement or re-engagement – were repealed by the Employment Relations
Act 1999 (ERelA). As a corollary, the amount that can be awarded by a tribunal
by way of an additional award under S.117(3)(b) ERA was significantly
increased from between 13–26 weeks' pay to between 26–52 weeks' pay (see
'Additional awards' below for more details). Prior to the amendments made by
the ERelA, additional awards did not apply to trade union dismissals under
S.152 or S.153 of the Trade Union and Labour Relations (Consolidation) Act
1992 (TULR(C)A), although employees could claim a 'special award' under
S.157 of that Act. However, the ERelA repealed S.157 and extended additional
awards to cover trade union dismissals.

This chapter explains the circumstances in which an additional award may be **17.2**
made and also considers the special remedy of interim relief, which may be
available in certain cases between the date of dismissal and the date of the
tribunal's full hearing of the unfair dismissal complaint.

Additional awards
17.3

If an order for reinstatement or re-engagement has been made by a tribunal
but the employer has not complied with it at all, the tribunal *must* make an
additional award on top of the normal basic and compensatory awards unless

801

the employer satisfies the tribunal that it was not practicable to comply with the order – S.117(4)(a) ERA. The question of practicability is discussed in Chapter 12, 'Remedies', under 'Reinstatement and re-engagement – practicability'. It is worth reiterating here that an additional award is only available where the employer has *totally* failed to comply with the tribunal's order to re-employ – i.e. has refused to reinstate or re-engage the employee. It is not available where the employer has taken the employee back but has only partially complied with the terms of the order. For the compensation available in cases of partial compliance – and a discussion of the distinction between partial and total non-compliance – see Chapter 12, 'Remedies', under 'Reinstatement and re-engagement – enforcement of order'.

17.4 Size of award

Under S.117(3)(b) ERA, tribunals have considerable discretion as to how much to grant by way of additional award but the award must be of an amount *not less than 26 weeks' pay and not more than 52 weeks' pay*. These limits were introduced by the ERelA and replaced the previous two-tier system under which an additional award of between 13 and 26 weeks' pay was available for non-compliance with a re-employment order in an ordinary unfair dismissal case and a higher additional award of between 26 and 52 weeks' pay was applicable where the dismissal amounted to an act of unlawful sex, race or disability discrimination.

A week's pay is calculated in accordance with Ss.220–229 ERA – for details see IDS Employment Law Handbook, 'Wages' (2011), Chapter 10, 'A week's pay'. A week's pay in this context is subject to a current maximum of £475 (a figure which is normally increased each year). Thus, the minimum possible additional award is currently £12,350, while the maximum is £24,700.

17.5 The calculation date (i.e. the date on which the employee's pay is ascertained) is the date the employer's notice was given (not the date on which it expired): if no notice was given, it is the effective date of termination of the contract – S.226(2) ERA.

The EAT has pointed out that tribunals have a wide discretion in fixing an additional award within the statutory limits, although it has said that 'some sort of proper assessment and balancing must take place' – Morganite Electrical Carbon Ltd v Donne 1988 ICR 18, EAT. A tribunal that simply announced a maximum additional award without any explanation had misapplied the law by not carrying out any sort of reasoned exercise to determine what the figure should be. The EAT in that case also held that a tribunal may not, in an effort to ensure compliance, simply decree in advance that it will make the maximum additional award if the employer fails to comply with a re-employment order. The way in which the tribunal exercises its discretion should properly take into account the true purpose of an additional award. In the words of Judge Knox

802

in Mabirizi v National Hospital for Nervous Diseases 1990 ICR 281, EAT, 'the compensation is not intended to be a precisely calculated substitute for financial loss but rather a general solatium to be arrived at by fixing the appropriate point on the scale which Parliament has fixed'.

The loss sustained by the employee will be an important factor to take into **17.6** account when assessing how much to award. S.117(2) expressly states that the amount of compensation shall be such as the tribunal thinks fit, having regard to the loss sustained by the employee in consequence of the failure to comply. Another factor that is commonly taken into account by tribunals is the conduct of the employer in refusing to comply with the re-employment order. These are two rather different considerations: the latter views the award as a penalty on an unmeritorious employer; the former concentrates on compensation to the employee.

Below are some examples of cases in which an additional award was made. (However, it should be noted that all of these cases bar one pre-date the changes made by the ERelA and were therefore decided when the two-tier system for additional awards outlined above was still in place, so that the maximum additional award that could be made in a normal unfair dismissal case was 26 weeks' pay):

- **Bowden v Crest Nicholson Operations Ltd** ET Case No.1100186/03: B was employed as regional managing director until his dismissal. The employer admitted that the dismissal was unfair but opposed B's application for re-engagement, maintaining that it was not practicable to re-employ him. Bearing in mind B's conciliatory attitude and his willingness to work with others constructively, the tribunal rejected this argument, holding that, taking into account both the operation of the company and also that of associated employers, it was practicable to place B in comparable or other suitable employment. It found that the employer failed to comply with the order without good reason and awarded the maximum additional award of 52 weeks' pay

- **Goodall v University of Lincolnshire and Humberside** ET Case No.1801296/98: on Monday morning G, a caretaker, reported a substantial amount of damage to the premises after it had been used for a Christmas party on the previous Friday night. However, the duty caretaker on the night in question had stated that there was no damage at the end of the night. A tribunal found G's subsequent dismissal unfair and ordered reinstatement but the university refused to agree. A number of staff did not accept that the tribunal's decision was correct: they believed that if G was exonerated, they must be being blamed; and other members of the caretaking staff said they could no longer work with him. The tribunal decided that there had been a wilful refusal to reinstate for no other reason than a desire to uphold the original decision. However, it accepted that the employer's concerns

803

were genuine, albeit misconceived. For that reason, it awarded 22 weeks' additional award, rather than the maximum 26 weeks

- **Travers v Chief Constable, Dorset Constabulary** ET Case No.3103759/98: T was dismissed for being under the influence of alcohol at work. It was submitted that she had a drink problem and was taking steps to deal with it. The tribunal found the dismissal to be unfair. No reasonable employer would have dismissed without endeavouring to assist the employee. The Chief Constable was ordered to reinstate T but refused, claiming there had been a breach of trust and confidence. The tribunal rejected that contention – the Constabulary had failed to offer T any help not because of any breach of trust but because it did not want her back in her old job. This was a blatant case of failure to take an award of reinstatement seriously. The tribunal awarded the maximum additional award

- **Motherwell Railway Club v McQueen and anor** 1989 ICR 418, EAT: when making additional awards of 20 weeks' pay to M and his wife, the tribunal took into account the fact that, unknown to the employer, M had been certified unfit for work. On appeal, the EAT rejected the employer's argument that no additional award should have been made since M's health made reinstatement impossible. It pointed out that it was because the employer made no attempt to comply with the reinstatement order that the facts about M's illness did not come to light. Since the employer had done nothing to show that reinstatement was not practicable at the time, the tribunal was bound to make an award. It was correct to penalise the employer by more than the minimum, but less than the maximum

- **Initial Textile Services v Ritchie** EAT 358/89: R was unfairly dismissed (a fact conceded by ITS). The tribunal found no significant contribution on her part and made a reinstatement order, against which ITS appealed unsuccessfully. It refused to reinstate R and the tribunal made a maximum award of 26 weeks' pay. ITS argued before the EAT that the tribunal should have made a minimum award of only 13 weeks' pay because it had lost confidence in R as an employee and R had already been fully compensated by her compensatory award. The EAT, however, thought that more than the minimum was called for: the employer had conceded unfairness, reinstatement was practicable, and there had been no contribution by the employee. But the tribunal had not taken all the circumstances into account – in particular, that R had been fully compensated – and the EAT therefore reduced the additional award to one of 20 weeks' pay.

17.7 As these cases demonstrate, a wilful refusal to re-employ an employee is likely to attract an award towards the top end of the scale. However, a tribunal is entitled, when deciding the appropriate level of additional award, to take into account the employer's genuinely felt objection to reinstatement/re-engagement, irrespective of its earlier finding on the question of practicability. In Mabirizi v

804

National Hospital for Nervous Diseases (above), the hospital failed to produce evidence at the remedies hearing to the effect that reinstatement would be impracticable and the tribunal ordered that M should be reinstated. The hospital failed to comply with the order. However, when fixing the additional award payable to M, the tribunal took account of evidence given by the hospital that it had lost trust and confidence in M as it had concerns that, while off sick, M had been working elsewhere. Therefore its failure to reinstate her had not been mere wilful refusal. The employee appealed unsuccessfully to the EAT. As put rather colourfully by Judge Knox: 'The Act... expressly contemplates that an employer should be able both to try to persuade the industrial tribunal... that reinstatement would be impracticable and to try to persuade the industrial tribunal after the event of non-compliance... that it was not practicable to comply with the order. One process looks forward, the other looks back and although it may be that a cherry that is rejected at the first bite will be likely to be regarded as indigestible at the second, there is in our view no doubt at all that two bites are allowed.'

Deductions from additional awards. In Mabirizi v National Hospital for **17.8** Nervous Diseases (above) the EAT also confirmed that a tribunal is entitled to take into account any failure on the claimant's part to mitigate his or her loss when considering the additional award. However, this should not be used as a factor resulting in a quantifiable reduction in the sum to which the employee would otherwise be entitled. This is because additional awards are not subject to deduction in the same way as compensatory awards. For example, an additional award cannot be reduced to take account of the employee's contributory conduct. It will, of course, be fairly rare for a tribunal to order re-engagement in the first place where there is any significant degree of contributory conduct, but the tribunals did so in Ayub v Vauxhall Motors Ltd 1978 IRLR 428, ET, and Gordon v Greater Glasgow Health Board SCOET S/1920/84, both cases in which the employee was held to have contributed by 50 per cent to the dismissal. Since re-engagement was practicable but refused by the employers in both cases, the tribunals were obliged to make additional awards: in each case they made 19-week awards – about halfway between 13 and 26 weeks (the limits then applicable) – to reflect the employee's responsibility for the dismissal.

An ex gratia payment by the employer may, however, be set off against the additional award. In Darr and anor v LRC Products Ltd 1993 IRLR 257, EAT, a tribunal declined to make any basic, compensatory or additional award on the ground that the employer had made a severance payment that more than covered any compensation the tribunal would have awarded. The EAT remitted the case because the tribunal had failed to give adequate reasons as to how it had come to that conclusion. Nevertheless, the EAT said that there was no reason in law why a severance payment should not be offset against the additional award. The matter would turn on whether, as a matter of construction,

805

the payment was offered and accepted on the understanding that it was in satisfaction of any compensation, including any additional award, that might be awarded as a result of the dismissal.

17.9   **Additional awards and arrears of pay.** As explained in Chapter 12, 'Remedies', under 'Reinstatement or re-engagement – arrears of pay and expenses', in making a reinstatement or re-engagement order a tribunal will usually make an award of back pay and other benefits that the employee, but for the dismissal, would have received in the period from dismissal to the date the order is complied with. If the order is not complied with, the employee receives compensation in the normal way – i.e. a basic and a compensatory award, and, if the employer fails to establish that it was not practicable to comply, an additional award. Since the compensatory award is subject to a statutory cap (currently £78,335 or a year's pay, whichever is the lower), it used to be the case (before the cap was increased substantially from £12,000 to £50,000 in October 1999) that, if the employee was highly paid or a long period of time had elapsed between the dismissal and the tribunal hearing, it could be financially advantageous for the employer not to comply with the tribunal's order. That is, the arrears of pay that the employer would have to pay in complying with the order would amount to more than the combined amount of any compensatory and additional awards that the tribunal could make for non-compliance. This loophole was closed by the Trade Union Reform and Employment Rights Act 1993 and S.124(4) ERA provides that the statutory limit on the compensatory award may be exceeded to the extent necessary to enable the aggregate of the compensatory and additional awards fully to reflect the amount of arrears of pay and benefits specified in the original order.

Note, however, that, where an additional award is made under S.117(3)(b) and a compensatory award under S.117(3)(a), the statutory limit should only be exceeded to the extent of the loss incurred between dismissal and when re-employment should have occurred *less* the additional award – Selfridges Ltd v Malik 1998 ICR 268, EAT. This is because back pay, etc, is not a free-standing head of damage to be awarded whether or not re-employment is complied with. It is only payable in respect of a re-employment order which *has* been complied with. If there is total non-compliance with the order, then loss forms part of the compensatory award. See Chapter 12, 'Remedies', under 'Reinstatement and re-engagement – enforcement of order' for more details.

17.10   Interim relief

Interim relief is a remedy available to employees who claim to have been dismissed for one of a number of inadmissible reasons (see 'Availability of interim relief' below). It is an emergency interlocutory procedure designed, in appropriate cases, to ensure the preservation of the status quo pending the hearing of the unfair dismissal complaint. It is only available in specified categories of cases deemed by statute to be deserving of such protection and should be sought promptly by the claimant, who must apply for interim relief no later than seven days after dismissal.

If the employee complies with the tightly defined application procedure and satisfies a tribunal at a special hearing that he or she is likely to succeed at a full hearing in showing that the dismissal was for one of the relevant inadmissible reasons, then interim relief prevents the dismissal from taking full effect before the full hearing. This is because the tribunal may make a reinstatement or re-engagement order pending the full hearing or, alternatively, a continuation of contract order, which will have the effect of keeping the employee suspended on full pay until the full tribunal hearing.

Availability of interim relief   17.11

Under S.128(1) ERA, an employee alleging unfair dismissal can claim interim relief if the reason (or principal reason) for the dismissal was that he or she:

- carried out (or proposed to carry out) any designated health and safety activities (S.100(1)(a))

- performed (or proposed to perform) any functions as a health and safety representative or as a member of a safety committee (S.100(1)(b))

- performed (or proposed to perform) any functions or activities as a working time representative or as a candidate for such a role (S.101A(1)(d))

- performed (or proposed to perform) any functions as a trustee of a relevant occupational pension scheme (S.102(1))

- performed (or proposed to perform) any functions or activities as an employee representative (or candidate for such a role) for the purposes of consultation on collective redundancies (under Chapter II of Part IV TULR(C)A) or a proposed transfer of an undertaking (under Regs 9, 13 and 15 of the Transfer of Undertakings (Protection of Employment) Regulations 2006 SI 2006/246) (S.103 ERA)

- made a protected disclosure under the Public Interest Disclosure Act 1998 (S.103A ERA)

- was dismissed for a reason connected with the statutory trade union recognition procedures contained in Schedule A1 to the TULR(C)A (para 161(2) of Schedule A1)

- was selected for dismissal for a reason relating to a trade union blacklist prohibited under the Employment Relations Act 1999 (Blacklists) Regulations 2010 SI 2010/493 (S.104F(1) ERA).

In addition, S.12(5) ERelA provides that interim relief may be sought where the reason (or principal reason) for the dismissal was that the worker exercised (or

807

sought to exercise) the right under S.10 of that Act to be accompanied at a disciplinary or grievance hearing, or accompanied or sought to accompany another worker (whether of the same employer or not) to such a hearing. Similarly, under Reg 18(5) of the Employee Study and Training (Procedural Requirements) Regulations 2010 SI 2010/155 interim relief may be available where the reason (or principal reason) for the dismissal was that the person exercised (or sought to exercise) the right under Reg 16 to be accompanied at a meeting to consider a request to enter into study or training, or accompanied or sought to accompany an employee to such a meeting. In either case, the provisions of Ss.128–132 ERA will apply.

17.12 Interim relief is also available under the TULR(C)A in respect of trade union dismissal cases. Under S.161(1) TULR(C)A, an employee alleging unfair dismissal on any of the grounds set out in S.152 TULR(C)A can claim interim relief. S.152(1) provides that the dismissal of an employee will be automatically unfair if the reason for it (or, if more than one, the principal reason) was that the employee:

- was, or proposed to become, a member of an independent trade union

- had taken part, or proposed to take part, in the activities of an independent trade union at an appropriate time

- had made use of, or proposed to make use of, trade union services at an appropriate time

- had failed to accept an offer made by the employer of inducements relating to trade union membership or activities or to collective bargaining; or

- was not a member of any trade union, or of a particular trade union, or of one of a number of particular trade unions, or had refused, or proposed to refuse, to become or remain a member.

Interim relief in trade union cases is fully discussed in IDS Employment Law Handbook, 'Trade Unions' (2013), Chapter 12, 'Unfair dismissal', under 'Tribunal proceedings and remedies – interim relief'.

17.13 Note that interim relief is not available in cases of selection for redundancy for any of the inadmissible reasons listed above. This means that where there is a genuine redundancy situation, claimants will be hard pushed to persuade a tribunal that they were in fact dismissed for the inadmissible reason – and are therefore entitled to interim relief – and not by reason of redundancy. For example, in McConnell and anor v Bombardier Aerospace/Short Brothers plc (No.2) 2009 IRLR 201, NICA, the Northern Ireland Court of Appeal held that a tribunal had been entitled to find that it had no jurisdiction to hear the claimants' application for interim relief. Although the claimants maintained that they were dismissed because of their trade union and health and safety representative activities, the tribunal correctly found that the reason (or principal reason) for their dismissals was redundancy. Accordingly, interim relief was not available.

Application procedure

An application for interim relief should state that the dismissal was unfair for one of the inadmissible reasons and state what the alleged reason was. Time is of the essence because the employee must present an application for interim relief, together with the claim form (ET1) claiming unfair dismissal for one of the inadmissible reasons, by the end of the *seven* days immediately following the effective date of termination – S.161(2) TULR(C)A; S.128(2) ERA. If an employee is dismissed on a Monday, the application must therefore be presented by the following Monday. Tribunals have no jurisdiction to extend this time limit for any reason. (Note that the obligation on employees under S.18A of the Employment Tribunals Act 1996 to contact Acas and be offered 'early conciliation' before being allowed to submit a tribunal claim does not apply where the employee is also making an application for interim relief under S.128 ERA or S.161 TULR(C)A – Reg 3(1)(d) Employment Tribunals (Early Conciliation: Exemptions and Rules of Procedure) Regulations 2014 SI 2014/254. (For full details of the early conciliation scheme, see IDS Employment Law Handbook, 'Employment Tribunal Practice and Procedure' (2014), Chapter 3, 'Conciliation, settlements and ADR', under 'Early conciliation'.)

Tribunals do, however, have discretion to allow subsequent amendment of a timeous application. In Barley and ors v Amey Roadstone Corporation Ltd 1977 ICR 546, EAT, for example, the applications were in time and they referred to interim relief and unfair dismissal but they did not in terms claim that the claimants had been dismissed for trade union reasons or state what those reasons were. The EAT held that the applications were not nullities and that they could be corrected outside the seven-day time limit.

Certificate required in cases of trade union membership/activities. When an employee is claiming to have been dismissed because of actual or proposed union membership or participation in union activities, he or she must also produce (within the seven-day time limit) a certificate from an authorised union official – S.161(3) TULR(C)A. (No certificate is required if the employee is claiming that the dismissal was because of actual or proposed non-membership of a union. Nor is there any analogous provision requiring any sort of certificate under S.128 ERA, S.12(5) ERelA or Reg 18(5) of the Employee Study and Training (Procedural Requirements) Regulations 2010 SI 2010/155).

Section 161(3) TULR(C)A sets out precise requirements for the official's certificate. It must:

- be in writing and be signed by an authorised official of the independent union of which the employee was a member or which he or she was proposing to join

- state that at the date of dismissal the employee was or proposed to become a member of the union

- state that there appear to be reasonable grounds for supposing that the reason (or principal reason) for the employee's dismissal was one alleged in the unfair dismissal complaint – i.e. a reason related to trade union activities or membership under S.152.

17.16 For further details, see IDS Employment Law Handbook, 'Trade Unions' (2013), Chapter 12, 'Unfair dismissal', under 'Tribunal proceedings and remedies – interim relief'.

17.17 Prompt determination of application

Once a valid and timeous application for interim relief has been made, the tribunal is required to determine the issue as soon as is practicable – S.128(3) ERA/S.162(1) TULR(C)A. It must give the employer at least seven days' notice of the hearing, together with a copy of the application and, where relevant, of any accompanying certificate – S.128(4)/S.162(2). The tribunal is not allowed to postpone a hearing of an application for interim relief unless special circumstances justify such a course of action – S.128(5)/S.162(4).

17.18 Likelihood of success

Once the employee has successfully surmounted the procedural hurdles to making an application for interim relief, the employment tribunal must go on to decide whether it is likely that he or she will succeed at a full hearing of the unfair dismissal complaint – S.129(1) ERA/S.163(1) TULR(C)A. The statutory test is not whether the claim is ultimately likely to succeed, but whether 'it appears to the tribunal' that this is likely – a point emphasised by the EAT in London City Airport Ltd v Chacko 2013 IRLR 610, EAT. The Appeal Tribunal stated that this requires the tribunal to carry out an 'expeditious summary assessment' as to how the matter appears on the material available, doing the best it can with the untested evidence advanced by each party. This, it observed, necessarily involves a far less detailed scrutiny of the parties' cases than will ultimately be undertaken at the full hearing.

It is worth pointing out that the statutory test does not require the tribunal to make any findings of fact. Rather, as the tribunal reminded itself in Ryb v Nomura International plc ET Case No.3202174/09, it must make a decision as to the likelihood of the claimant's success at a full hearing of the unfair dismissal complaint based on the material before it, which will usually consist of the parties' pleadings, the witness statements and any other relevant documentary evidence. As the tribunal put it, the basic task and function is to make 'a broad

810

assessment on the material available to try to give the tribunal a feel and to make a prediction about what is likely to happen at the eventual hearing before a full tribunal'. This was so regardless of the volume or complexity of the material before it. Accordingly, in Raja v Secretary of State for Justice EAT 0364/09 the EAT held that the employment judge had erred in holding that interim relief applications were not suitable in cases involving complicated, long-running disputes and should be restricted to simple factual conflicts. In so finding, the judge had added an additional criterion for which there was no statutory or judicial authority. Once the claimant has complied with the procedural requirements, he or she is entitled as a right to have the application heard by a tribunal. That said, where there were hundreds of pages of documentation before the tribunal, the EAT suggested that it was advisable for the tribunal to ask the parties to direct its attention to the parts relevant to the interim relief application.

When considering the 'likelihood' of the claimant succeeding at tribunal, the **17.19** correct test to be applied is whether he or she has a 'pretty good chance of success' at the full hearing – Taplin v C Shippam Ltd 1978 ICR 1068, EAT. In that case, the EAT expressly ruled out alternative tests such as a 'real possibility' or 'reasonable prospect' of success, or a 51 per cent or better chance of success. According to the EAT, the burden of proof in an interim relief application was intended to be greater than that at the full hearing, where the tribunal need only be satisfied on the 'balance of probabilities' that the claimant has made out his or her case – i.e. the '51 per cent or better' test. This approach was endorsed by the EAT in Dandpat v University of Bath and anor EAT 0408/09 and, more recently, in London City Airport Ltd v Chacko (above).

Three cases where there was a 'pretty good chance' of success and interim relief was granted:

- **Holden v Allpay Ltd** ET Case No.1311950/13: H, the company's finance director, wrote to A Ltd on 15 February 2013 objecting to a proposed restructure that would remove him from the main board and, in his view, diminish his contractual rights. On 20 March 2013 he was suspended to enable A Ltd to investigate an unspecified complaint. The investigation included asking employees if they were aware of any incidents where H had acted inappropriately. He was subsequently dismissed and lodged a claim for interim relief. An employment tribunal considered that A Ltd had a clear duty to allow H to carry out his statutory function and that H owed duties not just to the board but also to the wider public. The letter to the board therefore clearly amounted to a protected disclosure. A Ltd's conduct in failing to particularise the allegations against H, removing him as a director and dismissing him for alleged misconduct when the main thrust of the complaints against him were unspecified matters of capability smacked of an authoritarian managing director wanting to get his own way and being

811

reluctant to accept a challenge from H regarding his ability and statutory duties. There was a 'pretty good chance' that H would establish that he was dismissed for making a protected disclosure and the tribunal ordered that his contract be continued

- **Saini v BAA Airports Ltd** ET Case No.2702662/12: S began working for BAA Ltd as a security officer in 1994. He became a shop steward for Unite the Union in 2006 and was summarily dismissed without a disciplinary hearing in 2012 – for insubordination, among other things. S's application for interim relief was upheld. The tribunal observed that most if not all of the matters relied on by BAA Ltd to dismiss S concerned the performance of his duties as a shop steward. It concluded that there was a good chance that the tribunal hearing the claim would find that S was dismissed because he was a difficult shop steward. There was a 'pretty good chance' – something nearer to certainty than mere probability – that S would establish that he had taken part in union activities at an appropriate time (as required under S.152(1)(b) TULR(C)A)

- **Daniels v E Ivor Hughes Educational Foundation** ET Case No.3317706/06: D began working for the employer – a private school – as a teacher in September 2005. He raised issues about the behaviour of certain pupils, including bullying and threats of violence, with the head teacher and referred a particularly serious incident to the police. At around the same time the employer decided that there were matters about D's behaviour that needed investigating. After an investigation he was called to a disciplinary hearing and dismissed. He claimed he was dismissed for making protected disclosures and made an application for interim relief. The tribunal acceded to his application, finding that the employer had made no mention of any concerns about D's behaviour before he made the protected disclosures. Given the timing of the disciplinary hearing and dismissal, the tribunal believed that there was a 'pretty good chance' of D's claim being upheld.

17.20 Two cases where the 'pretty good chance' test was not satisfied:

- **Knight and anor v CC and RJ Emerson Ltd** ET Case No.1901155/98: a tribunal held that there were many reasons to suggest that the employer wanted to get rid of K because of his union membership: the coincidence of the build-up of the dispute between them and the date K joined the union was a powerful argument to suggest that it may have been the reason for dismissal. However, the employer's stated reason for dismissal was that K had falsified travelling expenses. K said that he had made a genuine mistake but the tribunal found that he had been caught out in a conscious fiddle. Although the dismissal was likely to be found unfair, and there was a significant chance that the reason for the dismissal would be held to be K's union membership, the test in Taplin v C Shippam Ltd (above) had not been satisfied and the application for interim relief was therefore dismissed

- **Pickles v Peter Reed (Textiles) Ltd** ET Case No.1116/96: P was asked early in 1995 to become a shop steward, in place of the previous steward who had retired. He refused and no steward was appointed or elected. However, P acted as 'quasi' steward, distributing ballot papers and union literature as and when required. Later in 1995 the employer decided one redundancy was necessary and selected P on the basis of his disciplinary record. The tribunal dismissed P's application for interim relief as he had failed to persuade it that he had 'a pretty good chance' of succeeding in his claim that he was dismissed by reason of his union activities.

In trade union cases an employer's hostility to unions has often been treated as a persuasive factor in applications for interim relief. In Lorenz v Excelsior Packers ET Case No.25037/84, for example, the employer refused to recognise the TGWU even though 40 out of 46 workers were members. There was also evidence that union members had been threatened with dismissal if they took part in union activities and that the employer refused to allow Acas onto its premises. This background helped the tribunal to conclude that the claimant was likely to succeed in his claim that he was dismissed because of union membership.

Similarly, if the employer advances an implausible alternative reason for dismissal, the tribunal may find that it is likely to be a cover-up for a true, inadmissible reason. In Griffin and anor v Unipack Ltd ET Case No.15506/77, for example, the claimants were dismissed for leaving the premises to make a phone call to a union official and the employer argued that this was a straightforward dismissal for misconduct. The tribunal thought that this was spurious since leaving the premises for a few minutes fell far short of warranting instant dismissal. Since there was also evidence of the employer's hostility towards unions, interim relief was granted. And in O'Brien v Thames Water Utilities Ltd ET Case No.23918/95 a shop steward was dismissed for gross misconduct after a three-month period of surveillance and monitoring by the employer had produced eight charges of misconduct against him. The tribunal noted that there was no warrant in the employer's disciplinary code for the kind of monitoring and accumulation of charges that had occurred. The employer had clearly identified the employee as a troublemaker on account of his trade union activities and had 'banked up' a number of charges over a period of time so as to justify his dismissal. Interim relief was granted. **17.21**

Tribunal powers

17.22

Where a tribunal is satisfied that interim relief should be granted, it must explain its powers to the parties and, in particular, must ask the employer whether it is willing to reinstate or re-engage the employee pending a full hearing or a settlement – S.129(1), (2) and (3) ERA/S.163(1) and (2) TULR(C)A. If the employer is willing to reinstate (i.e. to treat the employee in all respects as if he or she had not been dismissed), the tribunal must make a reinstatement order – S.129(5)/S.163(4).

Additional considerations apply to re-engagement. If the employer is willing to re-engage the employee in another job on terms and conditions not less favourable than those that would have applied but for the dismissal, the following steps apply:

- the tribunal must ask the employee if he or she is willing to accept re-engagement on those terms and conditions. If the employee is willing, the tribunal must make an order to that effect – S.129(6) and (7)/S.163(5)(a)

- if the employee is unwilling and the tribunal considers that the refusal is reasonable, then it must make a continuation of contract order (see 'Continuation of contract' below) – S.129(8)(a)/S.163(5)(b)

- if the tribunal considers that the employee's refusal is unreasonable, however, then it will make no order at all – i.e. the employee will derive no benefit from the interim relief proceedings – S.129(8)(b)/S.163(5)(b).

17.23 If the employer is not willing to re-employ the employee, as is often the case in practice, then the tribunal must make a continuation of contract order – S.129(9)(b)/S.163(6).

17.24 Continuation of contract

A continuation of contract order (CCO) *must* be made if the employer refuses to re-employ or if the employee reasonably refuses an offer of re-engagement – S.129(8)(a) and 9(b) ERA/S.163(5)(b) and (6) TULR(C)A. An unreasonable refusal on the employee's part will result in no order at all – S.129(8)(b)/S.163(5)(b). It is not clear what the appropriate test for reasonableness is in this context, although it is likely to be an objective test – i.e. would a reasonable employee have refused in similar circumstances? A CCO must also be made if the employer fails to attend the interim relief hearing (and the employee is successful at the hearing) – S.129(9)(a)/S.163(6).

In effect a CCO is an order for suspension on full pay, together with any other benefits (such as pension rights) derived from the employment – S.130(1) ERA/S.164(1) TULR(C)A. The order will include back pay from the date of dismissal and must specify an amount, corresponding to what the employee could reasonably have been expected to earn, to be paid in respect of each normal pay period – S.130(2)/S.164(2). Back pay must be paid within such time as may be specified in the order – S.130(3)(b)/S.164(3)(b). Future amounts must be paid on the normal pay day within each pay period – S.130(3)(a)/S.164(3)(a). It appears that the tribunal has power to specify the method of payment, in order to ensure that payment takes place on the normal pay day. In Blitz v Vectone Group Holding Ltd EAT 0306/09 the EAT held that the employer, who repeatedly failed to pay B's monthly salary on time by providing him with cheques that took time to clear, should be ordered to make any future

814

payments by bank transfer. It therefore invited the parties to agree a suitable form of wording to amend the employment judge's order.

Payments made by the employer to the employee – e.g. pay in lieu of notice – **17.25** go towards discharging a CCO – S.130(5) and (6)/S.164(5) and (6). Similarly, pay received from *another* employer will be offset under those provisions. In Williams v G and R Cadwallader Ltd ET Case No.09465/87 the employee got a new job at comparable pay within two weeks of dismissal. The tribunal limited the CCO award to two weeks' pay because of the new earnings: the employee could not expect to be earning under the original contract if he was in fact working for somebody else.

A CCO continues in force *until the determination or settlement of the complaint* – S.130(1)/S.164(1). This will include any appeal from the tribunal's decision. In Zucker v Astrid Jewels Ltd 1978 ICR 1088, EAT, Z succeeded at an interim relief hearing and the tribunal made a CCO. However, she lost her case at the full tribunal hearing and the CCO appeared to have lapsed from the date the decision was announced. Z appealed to the EAT, which allowed the appeal and remitted the case for a rehearing by a fresh tribunal. It was understood that Z had by that time obtained new employment. The EAT said that the CCO should not have lapsed when it did – because Z's complaint had not been finally determined – but should have continued until the date when she found other employment and been revoked with effect from that date.

Any payments made under a CCO are *not* recoverable in the event of the **17.26** employee losing his or her unfair dismissal claim at the full hearing. Nor can a CCO be stayed in anticipation of the employee losing the claim. In Initial Textile Services v Rendell EAT 383/91 R submitted a claim to a tribunal alleging that he had been unfairly dismissed for his involvement in trade union activities. Owing to a listing error, the interim relief hearing did not take place until more than four months after the date the claim was lodged. At that hearing the tribunal was satisfied that it was likely that R would establish that he had been dismissed for his involvement in trade union activities and made a CCO for £217 per week and awarded £3,605 back pay. Anxious to avoid payment of such a large sum, the employer appealed against the tribunal's decision on the ground of perversity. However, since the appeal might not be heard for several months, it lodged an interlocutory (i.e. interim) appeal asking the EAT to stay the CCO pending the hearing of the full appeal on the ground that the money due for payment under the order would be irrecoverable in the event of R losing his claim.

The EAT dismissed this application, having failed to identify any error made by the tribunal that would definitely result in a successful appeal. The EAT also doubted whether it had the power to stay an interim relief order pending appeal because it would not be clear until the appeal was heard whether there would be a valid ground for allowing that appeal. Finally, the statutory provisions

815

were clearly intended to be stringent provisions designed to protect 'the work of shop stewards in the trade union movement'. Turning to those provisions, the EAT noted that once a tribunal has concluded that an employee is likely to establish that he or she was dismissed for a S.152 TULR(C)A reason, the employer has the opportunity to re-employ the employee. In the event of that not happening, the tribunal is obliged to make an order under S.164, including back pay and wages, until the matter is finally settled. The EAT was bound by these provisions and could find no reason to stay the CCO. Accordingly, the appeal was dismissed but with a recommendation that the unfair dismissal claim should take place as a matter of extreme urgency and be heard by a differently constituted tribunal.

17.27 **Transfer of undertakings.** In Dowling v ME Ilic Haulage and anor 2004 ICR 1176, EAT, the EAT held that, in the event of a relevant transfer of undertaking for the purposes of the Transfer of Undertakings (Protection of Employment) Regulations 2006 SI 2006/246 (TUPE), liability for a CCO does not pass from the transferor to the transferee employer. This case is discussed in detail in IDS Employment Law Handbook, 'Transfer of Undertakings' (2011), Chapter 3, 'What transfers?', under 'Rights and liabilities that do not transfer – continuation orders'. But, in short, the EAT essentially reached this conclusion on the basis that, upon dismissal, the employee's contract of employment comes to an end and is replaced with a statutory and unilateral 'contract' between the parties, in that the employee receives pay but has no corresponding obligation to provide services. According to Mr Justice Burton, then President of the EAT, an individual who is the subject of a CCO is an ex-employee and there is no subsisting employment contract to which TUPE can apply, so as to transfer the rights and liabilities under it to the new employer.

With respect, this interpretation seems fraught with difficulties and does not appear to accord with the purpose of the interim relief provisions. A CCO clearly envisages a continuation of the employment relationship and the effect of any such order is generally understood to be that the individual remains the employer's employee, albeit that he or she is suspended on full pay. It is strongly arguable, therefore, that TUPE does operate in these circumstances. However, until we have authority to this effect, Dowling remains the only case specifically on the point.

17.28 That said, some support for the view that TUPE does apply to transfer liability for a CCO from the transferor to the transferee can be gleaned from the EAT's decision in Langton v Secretary of State for Health 2014 ICR D2, EAT, which, although not a TUPE case, suggests that a tribunal's power to make a CCO should not be defeated by a transfer of liabilities under an employment contract. L was employed by an NHS Trust and was dismissed on 31 March, the same day that the Trust was dissolved under the Health and Social Care Act 2012. On 4 April she lodged a claim of automatically unfair dismissal under S.103A ERA, asserting that she had been dismissed for having made a protected disclosure. She named the Trust as respondent and sought interim relief under S.128 ERA. Before the tribunal dealt with the question of interim relief, it accepted an application from the Secretary of State for Health to be substituted for the Trust as the respondent to the claim. The Secretary of State adopted the Trust's stated reasons for dismissal and sought to defend the S.103A claim. The tribunal decided that, in these circumstances, it could not make a CCO, given that the employer – the Trust – no longer existed. On appeal, the EAT rejected this analysis of the law. It held that the Secretary of State had stepped into the shoes of the Trust for the purpose of litigation, having regard to the fact that, under S.70 of the National Health Service Act 2006, the Secretary of State was statutorily required to ensure that all of the Trust's civil liabilities were dealt with. This included any potential liability for an order under Ss.128–130 ERA. Referring to Dowling v ME Ilic Haulage and anor (above), the EAT noted that the effect of a CCO would not be to create a new contract of employment, but simply to preserve L's right to pay and other benefits and to deal, if necessary, with the question of continuity of employment. It would not, therefore, be a case of ordering the Secretary of State to enter into a contract of employment with L.

In our opinion, this analysis would also apply, by very close analogy, to a situation where the transfer of liabilities has been effected by TUPE. His Honour Judge Peter Clark summed up his reasoning in clear terms: 'There is nothing in my view in Ss.128–130 ERA that prevents the tribunal making a continuation order against a party who has chosen to substitute himself for the original respondent but is not the employer as defined in S.230(4) ERA.' Apart, perhaps, from the reference to 'choosing' to stand in the previous employer's shoes, this neatly describes the position of a transferee under TUPE.

Change of circumstances   17.29

If either party considers that there has been a relevant change of circumstances since the making of an interim relief order, that party may apply to the tribunal for revocation or variation of the order – S.131(1) ERA/S.165(1) TULR(C)A. This would typically happen if the employee has found new employment or has decided to leave the job market by, for example, starting a full-time course of further education.

An application to revoke or vary a CCO can be made to any tribunal, not necessarily the tribunal which originally made the order. In British Coal Corporation v McGinty 1987 ICR 912, EAT, a tribunal made a CCO after interim relief proceedings. The substantive unfair dismissal hearing began several weeks later before a different tribunal. The hearing was protracted and, after it had been in progress for some months, the employer applied for the CCO to be revoked. The second tribunal thought that it lacked jurisdiction to entertain the application and that this could only be done by the tribunal which made the original CCO. The EAT ruled that this was wrong and that such an

817

application could be heard by any tribunal having jurisdiction to hear cases from the locality. The EAT also made the point that it is undesirable that a tribunal which had made (or refused to make) an interim relief order should conduct the full hearing of the unfair dismissal claim. This is because the tribunal could well be thought to have come to a provisional view of the merits of the case – i.e. to have prejudged the issue before the full hearing.

17.30 Failure to comply

If the employer fails to comply with the terms of an order for reinstatement or re-engagement pending the full hearing, the tribunal will, on the application of the employee, make a CCO and also order the employer to pay such amount of compensation as it considers just and equitable, having regard to the infringement of the employee's right to be re-employed in pursuance of the order and to any loss suffered by the employee in consequence of the non-compliance – S.132(1) and (2) ERA/S.166(1) TULR(C)A.

The employee can also make an application to the tribunal if the employer has failed to comply with a CCO – S.132(4)/S.166(3). If the non-compliance consists of a failure to pay the amount ordered, the tribunal will determine the amount outstanding and order the employer to pay it – S.132(5)(a)/S.166(4). This amount will be in addition to any compensation for unfair dismissal that the employee may receive at the full hearing – S.132(5)(b)/S.166(4). If the non-compliance is in regard to any other aspect of the order, the tribunal will award the employee such compensation as it considers just and equitable in all the circumstances having regard to any loss suffered by the employee in consequence of the non-compliance – S.132(6)/S.166(5).

18 Recoupment

Types of loss

Scope of Recoupment Regulations

Monetary awards

Protective awards

Challenging recoupment

An employee who has been dismissed may well need to draw social security **18.1** benefits in order to alleviate the financial hardship that the dismissal will cause. A subsequent finding by an employment tribunal that the dismissal was unfair may lead to an award of compensation that is aimed at removing that hardship altogether. This raises two issues. How is an employment tribunal, in fixing the level of compensation, to allow for the fact that the dismissed employee has been in receipt of social security payments? And how is Jobcentre Plus (the executive agency of the Department for Work and Pensions that administers such payments) to treat that employee's past and potential claims for such benefits?

Types of loss   18.2

The interaction between the compensation awarded by an employment tribunal and social security benefits varies depending on both the type of benefit in question and, in so far as the compensatory award for unfair dismissal is concerned, whether the award is intended to compensate for immediate or future loss.

Immediate loss   18.3
So far as loss incurred *before* the hearing is concerned, the position is governed by the Employment Protection (Recoupment of Benefits) Regulations 1996 SI 1996/2349, which are the focus of this chapter. The procedure is as follows:

- the tribunal assesses the employee's loss without regard to Jobseeker's Allowance (JSA), income-related Employment and Support Allowance (ESA), Income Support or Universal Credit

- Jobcentre Plus recoups from the employer the amount of JSA, income-related ESA, Income Support or Universal Credit paid to the employee over the relevant period

819

- the employer deducts the amount paid to Jobcentre Plus from the amount due to the employee under the tribunal award before paying the remainder to the employee.

The employee receives what he or she is due, with no double recovery, but the employer takes full responsibility for the loss inflicted on the employee and receives no subsidy from the social security system.

18.4 The Recoupment Regulations do not cover other social security benefits, such as contributory Employment and Support Allowance, Personal Independence Payments and Housing Benefit, and there has been widespread confusion and inconsistency in the way such benefits are treated by tribunals. The current consensus appears to be that credit for most individual social security benefits must be given by the employee and the amount received should therefore be deducted in full from any award of compensation. However, Housing Benefit is treated differently and will not be taken into account by a tribunal when determining the level of any award but may be clawed back by the authorities where a tribunal award would otherwise result in double recovery for the employee – for further discussion on this topic, see Chapter 14, 'Compensatory awards: types of loss', under 'Immediate loss – social security benefits'.

18.5 Universal Credit. Universal Credit is a new form of social security benefit, the framework for which was established by the Welfare Reform Act 2012. Its operation is governed by the Universal Credit Regulations 2013 SI 2013/376, supplemented by various other sets of regulations. It is being phased in gradually across the UK – having been introduced for new claimants in a few 'pathfinder' areas in April 2013, a nationwide rollout began in February 2015 and is due to be completed by the end of 2017 for all claimants. Universal Credit is intended to replace the following benefits with a single monthly payment and is payable jointly for couples:

- Child Tax Credit
- Housing Benefit
- income-related Employment and Support Allowance
- income-based Jobseeker's Allowance
- Income Support
- parts of the Social Fund
- Working Tax Credit.

Since some of the benefits being replaced by Universal Credit are covered by the Recoupment Regulations while others are not, consideration will have to be given to how the recoupable amount should be calculated where a claimant is in receipt of Universal Credit (see 'Monetary awards – computing recoupable amount' below).

Future loss   18.6

In relation to awards made in respect of future loss – i.e. losses that the claimant is projected to sustain subsequent to the conclusion of tribunal proceedings – the position is relatively straightforward. By virtue of the Jobseeker's Allowance Regulations 1996 SI 1996/207, the Employment and Support Allowance Regulations 2008 SI 2008/794 and 2013 SI 2013/379, and the Income Support (General) Regulations 1987 SI 1987/1967, a compensatory award for unfair dismissal will be treated as 'earnings' over the period to which it applies for the purpose of assessing a claimant's eligibility for JSA, income-related ESA or Income Support under the Jobseeker's Act 1995, the Welfare Reform Act 2007 and the Social Security Act 1986 respectively. There will therefore be no element of double recovery if a tribunal awards compensation for loss of future earnings and the tribunal is not required to consider JSA, income-related ESA or IS when calculating such loss.

The position is different for Universal Credit as there is no equivalent provision in the Universal Credit Regulations providing for compensatory awards for future loss to be treated as 'earnings'. Instead, since such awards are made as one lump sum, they will be treated as capital. As the capital limit for Universal Credit is £16,000 (see Reg 18 of the 2013 Regulations) any award that is greater than that (or which pushes the employee's total capital to over that figure when added to any other savings or capital) would render the employee ineligible for Universal Credit. If the award (or total capital including the award) falls between £6,000 and £16,000, Universal Credit will be reduced according to a statutory formula which is based on the assumption that the capital itself will yield income at a certain level. Capital of less than £6,000 is disregarded for the purposes of Universal Credit.

On the calculation of future loss generally, see Chapter 14, 'Compensatory awards: types of loss'.

Scope of Recoupment Regulations   18.7

The Employment Protection (Recoupment of Benefits) Regulations 1996 SI 1996/2349 ('the Recoupment Regulations') apply to two categories of award:

- monetary awards – Reg 3(1)(a) and the Schedule to the Regulations
- protective awards – Reg 3(1)(b) – (see 'Protective awards' below).

The types of tribunal award that are categorised as 'monetary awards' are set out in the Schedule to the Regulations. They are:

- guarantee payments

821

- awards made under a collective agreement for guaranteed remuneration in a case where there is an exemption order excluding the right to statutory guarantee payments

- payments of remuneration for a period of suspension on medical or maternity grounds

- payments accompanying orders for reinstatement or re-engagement in unfair dismissal cases (see Chapter 12, 'Remedies', under 'Reinstatement and re-engagement')

- compensatory awards covering immediate loss in unfair dismissal cases (see Chapter 14, 'Compensatory awards: types of loss', under 'Immediate loss')

- additional awards of compensation in unfair dismissal cases where a reinstatement or re-engagement order has not been complied with (see Chapter 17, 'Additional awards and interim relief')

- payments made in respect of interim relief orders and orders for continuation of contract (see Chapter 17, 'Additional awards and interim relief')

- payments ordered on an employer's default in paying a protective award.

18.8 **Redundancy and discrimination claims.** The Recoupment Regulations do not apply to statutory redundancy payments as these are calculated by reference to past service and are not intended to cover the same period as social security payments. Nor do the Regulations cover compensation for discrimination, even when the discrimination complained of takes the form of a dismissal and the tribunal's award is similar to a compensatory award in an unfair dismissal case. In such cases tribunals will prevent double recovery by deducting from the award of compensation an amount corresponding to the amount of social security benefit already paid.

18.9 **Settlement of claims.** The Recoupment Regulations only apply to monetary awards actually made by tribunals. They do not apply to settlements arrived at by the parties. This may act as an incentive to both employees and employers to settle claims, since any payment under the settlement will not be subject to recoupment of social security benefits received. This incentive will be strongest in cases where the employee was on low wages because recoupment may have the effect of removing most, if not all, of the award. Take the case of an employee who receives £2,000 by way of JSA between dismissal and the date set for the tribunal hearing, but who would have earned £4,000 in that period if he or she had stayed in employment. Success before the tribunal would mean £4,000 being awarded for loss of earnings so far, but £2,000 of this would be subject to recoupment, leaving the employee with only £2,000 compensation for immediate loss. If there was no significant element of future loss, this might make an offer of settlement from the employer of £3,000 very attractive to the

822

employee because there would be no recoupment, and he or she would therefore be £1,000 better off. The employer in turn would save £1,000 by settling the case in advance because there is no obligation to pay any sum to Jobcentre Plus.

Monetary awards

For the purposes of the Recoupment Regulations, a 'monetary award' is any award set out in the Schedule to the Regulations – Reg 3(1)(a) (see the list under 'Scope of Recoupment Regulations' above). The process for recoupment of benefits from monetary awards requires both the tribunal and Jobcentre Plus to take certain specified actions.

Duties of employment tribunal and Secretary of Tribunals 18.11

In any case in which it makes a monetary award, a tribunal must first assess the total amount of the award without taking any account of JSA, income-related ESA, Income Support or Universal Credit – Reg 4(1). It must then calculate – and set out in its decision – the following particulars:

- the total monetary award
- the amount of the 'prescribed element'
- the period to which the 'prescribed element' relates
- the amount, if any, by which the total monetary award exceeds the 'prescribed element' – Reg 4(3).

The prescribed element. The Schedule to the Recoupment Regulations sets 18.12 out, in respect of each type of award to which the Regulations apply, the 'prescribed element' of the award that is subject to recoupment of JSA, income-related ESA, Income Support or Universal Credit. In every instance, the prescribed element is that part of the monetary award covering the employee's losses up to the conclusion of the tribunal proceedings. Thus, in an unfair dismissal case the prescribed element will be that part of the award that covers lost earnings up to the conclusion of proceedings (i.e. immediate loss) but not any award the tribunal may make for future loss. In the case of guarantee payments or suspension pay, the prescribed element will be the entire award.

The 'conclusion of tribunal proceedings' is the date on which the tribunal announces its decision on compensation or, if the decision is not given orally, the date on which its written decision is sent to the parties – Reg 2(3). If there is more than one tribunal hearing – e.g. because of intervening appeals – the conclusion of proceedings is the date of the final hearing – Reg 2(5). In Tipton v West Midlands Co-operative Society Ltd EAT 859/86 a tribunal found the claimant's dismissal unfair and made a reinstatement order in September 1982, the dismissal having taken effect in February 1982. After appeals to the EAT, the Court of Appeal and the House of Lords the case returned to the tribunal,

823

which made an award of compensation (instead of reinstatement) in October 1986. This was subject to a further appeal to the EAT, heard in September 1987, which resulted in a further remit to the tribunal with instructions to settle the amount of the prescribed element. Tribunal proceedings were not concluded until the final hearing on remit, so the period covered by the prescribed element was over five years.

18.13 *Effect where there has been failure to mitigate.* If a compensatory award is subject to a cut-off point before the date of the final hearing on account of the employee's failure to mitigate, then recoupment can only apply to the period covered by the compensatory award. In Homan v A1 Bacon Co Ltd 1996 ICR 721, EAT, the period between the date of the claimant's dismissal and the date of the tribunal's decision was just over ten months. However, the tribunal ruled that the claimant had failed to mitigate her loss during that period and therefore limited her compensatory award to six months. For the purposes of recoupment, however, the tribunal defined the period of the prescribed element as equating to the period between the dismissal and the tribunal's decision (i.e. ten months). On appeal, the EAT held that this was wrong. The prescribed element deals only with the element in the compensatory award attributable to actual financial loss, which means that the only period to which it can apply is the period in respect of which compensation is actually awarded. Accordingly, the period of the prescribed element in the instant case was six rather than ten months.

Similarly, in Bramley v Tesco Ltd EAT 776/77 a tribunal awarded only four weeks' pay as compensation and the EAT held that the Department of Employment could recoup only four weeks' JSA.

18.14 *Effect of contributory fault or application of statutory cap.* If the amount of the compensatory award is reduced either because of the employee's contributory fault or because it exceeds the prevailing statutory limit, the prescribed element must be reduced proportionately – Reg 4(2). In Mason v Wimpey Waste Management Ltd and anor 1982 IRLR 454, EAT, a tribunal assessed the claimant's monetary loss at £7,712, of which £5,918 was referable to the period from the date of dismissal to the conclusion of tribunal proceedings. The statutory maximum for a compensatory award was then £5,200, so the tribunal took this to be the prescribed element since the whole sum clearly referred to the period between dismissal and the final tribunal hearing. The EAT held that it should have reduced £5,918 – the 'original' prescribed element – by the same proportion as the reduction from £7,712 to £5,200 for the total compensatory award, which would have produced a revised figure for the prescribed element of £3,991. This was beneficial to the claimant, since it is only the prescribed element that is subject to recoupment.

18.15 **Application of recoupment where no relevant benefits claimed or received.** A tribunal's duties in respect of recoupment of monetary awards do not apply if it is satisfied that the claimant has neither received nor claimed JSA,

824

income-related ESA, Income Support or Universal Credit in respect of the relevant period – Reg 4(8).

Where a claimant has claimed, but not received, JSA, income-related ESA, Income Support or Universal Credit in respect of the relevant period, the tribunal's duties under Reg 4 do apply. However, none of the monetary award will in practice be recoupable, due to the way in which the recoupable amount is calculated under Reg 8(2) – see 'Computing recoupable amount' below. This was confirmed by the EAT in Sim v Moss Kaye Pembertons Ltd EAT 0274/03. There the tribunal had no evidence before it as to whether the claimant had received any benefits, so it set out the relevant particulars in its judgment. On appeal, the claimant clarified that she had not been in receipt of benefits, and the EAT consequently held that the details relating to recoupment were 'of no practical effect' since there was 'nothing to be recouped by the relevant department of state' and the compensatory award was therefore payable in full by the employer to the claimant.

Communication of oral or written decision. Under Rule 61 of the Employment **18.16** Tribunal Rules of Procedure 2013 (contained in the Schedule to the Employment Tribunals (Constitution and Rules of Procedure) Regulations 2013 SI 2013/1237), a tribunal may announce its decision orally at a hearing or reserve it to be sent to the parties as soon as practicable in writing. Where a decision is announced orally, a written record must nevertheless be provided to the parties as soon as practicable.

As noted above, Reg 4(3) requires the tribunal to 'set out in any decision which includes a monetary award' certain specified particulars. The Regulations do not spell out whether the particulars identified in Reg 4(3) must be included in an oral announcement or only in the written record of the decision. However, Reg 4(4) stipulates that where a tribunal at the hearing announces to the parties its decision to make a monetary award, it must at the same time inform the parties of the amount of any prescribed element included in that award and explain the effect of the recoupment procedure applicable under Regs 7 and 8.

In Kwakye-Manu v City of Hackney Health Authority EAT 329/95 the EAT **18.17** suggested that there is no need for the tribunal to explain the effect of the Recoupment Regulations in a written decision, taking the view that the duty under Reg 4(4) is confined to an oral explanation at the time of the hearing and the purpose of that explanation is simply to alert the parties to the fact that recoupment applies. This approach is understandable given the context of the appeal – a challenge by the claimant against the level of compensation she was awarded in respect of her unfair dismissal – but it appears to ignore the requirement in Reg 4(7) that *any* decision mentioned in Reg 4(3) 'shall contain a statement explaining the effect of Regulations 7 and 8... in relation to the prescribed element'. Indeed, in Turner Coulston v Janko EAT 1394/99, where

825

an employer had mistakenly believed it was required to pay the entirety of the prescribed element to the Benefits Agency (the agency that dealt with recoupment before this responsibility passed to Jobcentre Plus), the EAT commented that this confusion had most likely arisen because the notification of recoupment form produced by the tribunal did not include 'as it should' an explanation of the relevant Regulations. The EAT's comments in the Janko case were *obiter* but – in light of the apparently clear requirement for a written explanation under Reg 4(7) – we suggest that they reflect the correct approach. In practice, tribunals do now appear to be appending an explanation of the effect of the Regulations to their judgments in cases where recoupment applies.

Once the tribunal has made an oral announcement of its decision under Reg 4(4), it must notify Jobcentre Plus 'forthwith' that it has decided to make a monetary award that includes a prescribed element and provide to Jobcentre Plus the particulars set out in Reg 4(3) – Reg 4(5). In addition, once a written record of the decision containing the particulars set out in Reg 4(3) has been sent to the parties, the Secretary of the Tribunals must send a copy of that decision to Jobcentre Plus as soon as reasonably practicable – Reg 4(6).

18.18 Recoupment procedure

Under Reg 7(2), the prescribed element of a monetary award is treated as stayed and an employer should not pay it to the employee until Jobcentre Plus has served a recoupment notice, or given written notification that it does not intend to serve a notice. (If the employer does make the payment, it will still be liable to pay the recoupable amount to Jobcentre Plus – Reg 8(9).)

Jobcentre Plus should serve the notice or notification on the employer within 21 days of the tribunal's announcement of its decision or within nine days of the written decision being sent to the parties, whichever is the later, or as soon as practicable thereafter – Reg 8(5) and (6). If the tribunal's decision is reserved, the 21-day period runs from the date it is sent to the parties – Reg 8(6)(b). A copy of the recoupment notice must also be sent to the employee and, if requested, to the Secretary of the Tribunals – Reg 8(4).

18.19 A recoupment notice operates as an instruction to the employer to pay the 'recoupable amount' to Jobcentre Plus from out of the prescribed element of the monetary award (the recoupable amount being computed in accordance with Reg 8(2) – see 'Computing recoupable amount' below) – Reg 8(8). Payment to Jobcentre Plus completely discharges the employer's obligations to the employee to pay the amount equivalent to the recoupable amount by way of the monetary award – Reg 8(10). However, such payment does not affect the employer's obligation to pay any balance of the monetary award to the employee – Reg 8(8).

Although in theory this procedure is straightforward, in practice much depends on the efficiency of Jobcentre Plus. A survey conducted by the Employment

Law Committee of the Law Society in 2008 highlighted various difficulties experienced by solicitors representing both employers and employees in this regard. These included tribunals failing to write to Jobcentre Plus and local offices of Jobcentre Plus being unaware of what recoupment notices were or how the system should operate. This prompted consultation between the Department of Work and Pensions and the employment tribunals, and the establishment in 2009 of a centralised address for correspondence regarding recoupment cases. However, the success of this system is questionable, as the following case demonstrates:

- **Whyte v London Borough of Lewisham** EAT 0256/12: the tribunal notified Jobcentre Plus of the monetary award but Jobcentre Plus failed to send the employer the notice required under Reg 7(2). Instead, it wrote to the claimant stating that it did not intend to reclaim any benefits. When the employer contacted Jobcentre Plus to make enquiries it was told that Jobcentre Plus could not talk about the matter without the claimant's consent. The EAT noted that the letter to the claimant did not lift the stay on payment by the employer and that it was 'absurd' for Jobcentre Plus to insist on the claimant's consent before talking to the employer. All that was required was for Jobcentre Plus to comply with its clear duty under Reg 7(2).

Computing recoupable amount   18.20

Regulation 8(2) sets out the method for calculating how much of an individual's benefit payments should be recouped from the prescribed element of a monetary award.

For JSA, income-related ESA and Income Support, the position is quite simple – the recoupable amount is the lesser of:

- the amount of the prescribed element (less any tax or social security contributions which fall to be deducted by the employer), and

- the amount of JSA, income-related ESA or Income Support paid to the employee during the period to which the prescribed element relates – Reg 8(2)(a) and (b)(i).

For Universal Credit, the position is somewhat more complex. Reg 8(2)(a) and **18.21** (b)(ii) provide that the recoupable amount shall be the lesser of:

- the amount of the prescribed element (less any tax or social security contributions which fall to be deducted by the employer); and

- 'in the case of an employee entitled to an award of universal credit for any period ("the UC period") which coincides with any part of the period to which the prescribed element is attributable, any amount paid by way of or on account of universal credit for the UC period that would not have been paid

827

if the person's earned income for that period was the same as immediately before the period to which the prescribed element is attributable'.

'Earned income' for these purposes has the meaning given in Reg 52 of the Universal Credit Regulations – Reg 8(12) Recoupment Regulations. That is, remuneration or profit derived from any of the following: employment under a contract of service or in an office; a trade, profession or vocation; or any other paid work.

18.22 Following amendments to the Income Tax (Pay As You Earn) Regulations 2003 SI 2003/2682 in 2012, employers are required to make reports on their payroll to HMRC in real time. One of the reasons real-time reporting was introduced was to enable the amount of Universal Credit an individual receives to be adjusted according to his or her monthly income. In theory, therefore, an individual who already receives Universal Credit should see his or her Universal Credit payments increase if he or she is dismissed from employment, in order to make up for the loss of income he or she would otherwise suffer, and an individual who has not previously been eligible to receive Universal Credit may become eligible for it due to his or her lack of income post-dismissal. It is this post-dismissal increase in Universal Credit payments at which Reg 8(2)(b)(ii) appears to be targeted. However, it remains to be seen exactly how the calculation will operate in practice. In particular, the fact that some of the benefits that Universal Credit is replacing are not otherwise recoupable under the Regulations and that – unlike other benefits – Universal Credit payments are made jointly for couples, could give rise to complications.

18.23 ## Protective awards

A protective award is an award of pay made to employees affected by their employer's failure to consult properly over collective redundancies, as required under S.188 of the Trade Union and Labour Relations (Consolidation) Act 1992 (TULR(C)A) – see IDS Employment Law Handbook, 'Redundancy' (2011), Chapter 12, 'Collective redundancies'. The procedure for the recoupment of protective awards differs slightly from that applicable to monetary awards.

(Note that where an employee brings a claim under S.192 TULR(C)A to enforce a protective award, an award made by the tribunal in those enforcement proceedings is treated as a monetary award and the applicable procedure for recoupment shall be that which applies to monetary awards – Reg 3(2) and the Schedule to the Recoupment Regulations (see 'Monetary awards' above). However, Reg 9 provides that in relation to the application of the Regulations to an award in S.192 enforcement proceedings, the tribunal or Jobcentre Plus, as applicable, may take into account anything already done under or in consequence of the Regulations in relation to the original protective award.)

Duties of employment tribunal and Secretary of Tribunals

When a tribunal makes a protective award, whether orally or in a reserved written decision, the Secretary of the Tribunals must 'forthwith' give Jobcentre Plus the particulars specified in Reg 5(1). These are:

- the date of the hearing where the decision was announced orally, or the date the decision was sent to the parties

- the location of the tribunal

- the name and address of the employer

- the description of the employees concerned

- the dates of the protected period – for the purposes of the Regulations, the 'protected period' has the same meaning as in S.189(4) TULR(C)A, i.e. a period of such length as the tribunal considers just and equitable in all the circumstances, having regard to the seriousness of the employer's default, although it must not exceed 90 days. It begins with the earlier of the date of the award and the date on which the first of the dismissals to which the complaint relates takes effect.

If announcing an oral decision at the hearing, the tribunal must explain orally both what the employer is required to do under Reg 6 (see 'Duties of employer' below) and the effect of Regs 7 and 8 (see 'Recoupment procedure' and 'Computing recoupable amount' below) in relation to payment of the protective award. This information must also be included in the written record of the tribunal's oral decision or, if the tribunal does not announce its decision orally, in its written decision – Reg 5(2).

Duties of employer

Under Reg 6(1), the employer must inform Jobcentre Plus in writing of:

- the name, address and national insurance number of each employee to whom the award relates

- the date (or proposed date) of termination of employment for each such employee.

The employer must provide this information within ten days of the date on which the tribunal announces its decision orally or, if the tribunal makes no such announcement, within ten days of the date on which the written decision is sent to the parties. If it is not reasonably practicable for an employer to comply within these time limits, it must do so as soon as reasonably practicable thereafter – Reg 6(2) and (3).

18.26 Recoupment procedure

Under Reg 7(2), the payment of the protective award is treated as stayed and an employer should not make any such payment until Jobcentre Plus has served a recoupment notice, or given a written notification that it does not intend to serve a recoupment notice. Jobcentre Plus must serve a recoupment notice or notification on the employer within 21 days of receipt of the required information from the employer, or as soon as practicable thereafter – Reg 8(5) and (7).

However, the delay in payment by the employer does not prevent an employee from complaining to a tribunal under S.192 TULR(C)A that the employer has failed to pay remuneration due under a protective award – Reg 7(3).

18.27 Computing recoupable amount

Regulation 8(3) sets out the method for calculating how much of an individual's benefit payments should be recouped from a protective award.

For recipients of JSA, income-related ESA or Income Support, the recoupable amount shall be the lesser of:

- the amount (less any tax or social security contributions which fall to be deducted by the employer) accrued due to the employee in respect of so much of the protected period as falls before the date on which the employer provides Jobcentre Plus with the information required under Reg 6 (see 'Duties of employer' above); or

- the amount paid by way of or on account of JSA, income-related ESA or Income Support during that period – Reg 8(3)(a) and (b)(i).

18.28 For individuals who are entitled to an award of Universal Credit for any period (the 'UC period') that coincides with any part of the protected period falling before the employer has complied with its Reg 6 obligations (see 'Duties of employer' above), the recoupable amount shall be the lesser of:

- the amount (less any tax or social security contributions which fall to be deducted by the employer) accrued due to the employee in respect of so much of the protected period as falls before the date on which the employer complies with its Reg 6 obligations, or

- any amount paid by way of or on account of Universal Credit for the UC period that would not have been paid if the person's earned income for that period was the same as immediately before the protected period – Reg 8(3)(a) and (b)(ii).

'Earned income' for these purposes has the meaning given in Reg 52 of the Universal Credit Regulations – Reg 8(12) Recoupment Regulations. That is, remuneration or profit derived from any of the following: employment under a contract of service or in an office; a trade, profession or vocation; or any other paid work.

Challenging recoupment

18.29

An employee who has received a copy of a recoupment notice in respect of a monetary award or a protective award and who disagrees with the amount specified in it may notify Jobcentre Plus in writing that he or she disagrees with its assessment – Reg 10(1) Recoupment Regulations. This should be done within 21 days, subject to possible extension by Jobcentre Plus for 'special reasons'. The Regulations do not define what will amount to 'special reasons' and we are not aware of any reported cases on the matter.

Where such a notice is served on Jobcentre Plus, its officials will make a decision as to the amount of JSA, income-related ESA, Income Support or Universal Credit actually paid in respect of the relevant period. Reg 10(2) provides that, for monetary awards, the relevant period is the period to which the 'prescribed element' is attributable, whereas for protective awards it is any part of the protected period that falls before the date on which the employer complies with its obligations under Reg 6 (see 'Duties of employer' above). Jobcentre Plus is entitled to revise any decision made pursuant to Reg 10(2), either of its own motion or on application by a party to the tribunal proceedings – Reg 10(2A). An employee is entitled to appeal to the First-tier Tribunal against any decision made by Jobcentre Plus under Reg 10(2) or (2A) – Reg 10(2B).

If, as a result of the employee's complaint under Reg 10(1), it turns out that **18.30** Jobcentre Plus has recovered too much from the employer, Jobcentre Plus is required to pay the difference to the employee – Reg 10(3).

In circumstances where Jobcentre Plus has recovered money from the employer by way of recoupment of benefits but the original tribunal decision is subsequently varied following a rehearing or varied or set aside on appeal, Jobcentre Plus must repay the employer or, as the case may be, pay the employee such amount as it considers should properly be paid having regard to the decision on rehearing or appeal – Reg 10(4).

19 Written reasons for dismissal

Entitlement

Employer's obligation

Grounds for complaint

Remedies

By virtue of S.92 of the Employment Rights Act 1996 (ERA) a dismissed **19.1** employee with two years' continuous employment is entitled, on request, to a written statement from his or her employer giving particulars of the reasons for dismissal. If an employer unreasonably fails to provide a written statement within 14 days of a request being made, or if the reasons given are inadequate or untrue, the employee concerned may seek redress from an employment tribunal under S.93. If a written statement is provided in accordance with S.92, the employee in question may rely on it as evidence in a claim of unfair dismissal or in any other legal proceedings – S.92(5).

Entitlement **19.2**

An employee's right under S.92 arises in any of the following circumstances:

- where an employer gives notice of dismissal – S.92(1)(a)

- where an employer dismisses without notice – S.92(1)(b), or

- where the employee is employed under a limited-term contract and the contract terminates by virtue of the limiting event without being renewed under the same contract – S.92(1)(c). (A 'limited-term' contract is explained in Chapter 1, 'Dismissal', under 'Non-renewal of limited-term contracts'.)

The right cannot apply to cases of constructive dismissal, since it is the employee who takes the initiative in such cases by terminating the contract.

There may be circumstances where the employee claims to have been dismissed **19.3** but the employer denies this – see, for example, Hogg v Dover College 1990 ICR 39, EAT (discussed in Chapter 1, 'Dismissal', under 'Express dismissal – ambiguous conduct'). Where an employer seeks to avoid liability under S.92 by denying that there has been a dismissal within the terms of that section, the tribunal must first decide whether or not a dismissal has taken place – Brown v Stuart Scott and Co 1981 ICR 166, EAT. The test is objective: whether there was in fact a dismissal, not whether the employer subjectively believed that there was – Broomsgrove v Eagle Alexander Ltd 1981 IRLR 127, EAT. It is up to the employee to show that a relevant dismissal has occurred. But even if the employee is successful in showing this, the employer's genuine and reasonable belief that there has been no dismissal may render a failure to supply written reasons reasonable, meaning that the employer can escape liability – see 'Grounds for complaint – unreasonable failure' below.

19.4 Qualifying employees

Members of the armed forces, share fishermen and women, and police officers do not qualify for the right to request written reasons for dismissal – Ss.192, 199, 200 ERA. Furthermore, as a general rule, S.92 does not assist employees who have less than two years' continuous service on the effective date of termination (EDT) of the employment contract – S.92(3). The EDT for these purposes is the date on which notice expires or, where the contract is terminated without notice, the date on which the termination takes effect – S.92(6)(a) and (b). In relation to an employee who is employed under a limited-term contract which terminates by virtue of the limiting event without being renewed under the same contract, the EDT is the date on which the termination takes effect – S.92(6)(c).

Usually, therefore, an employee's period of continuous service ends when the employment contract ends. However, S.92(7) provides for an artificial postponement of the EDT where the employer terminates the contract of employment without notice or with less than the statutory minimum notice. In such a case the EDT for the purposes of calculating continuous service will be the date on which the statutory minimum notice would have expired had it been given. (For a detailed discussion of how to calculate the EDT, see IDS Employment Law Handbook, 'Contracts of Employment' (2014), Chapter 14, 'Date of termination'.)

19.5 There are two exceptions to the continuous employment rule in S.92(3), which are contained in S.92(4) and (4A). These provide that an employee who is dismissed while pregnant or during ordinary or additional maternity leave (S.92(4)) or during ordinary or additional adoption leave (S.92(4A)) is entitled to receive written reasons irrespective of his or her length of service and without having to make a request. (This does not apply to paternity or parental leave, or to any other automatically unfair reasons for dismissal.) However, where, in the opinion of a Minister of the Crown, disclosure of the information would be contrary to the interests of national security there is no obligation on an employer to provide written reasons in accordance with S.92(4) – S.202 ERA. This exemption does not appear to extend to S.94(4A), which we assume must be an oversight on the part of the Parliamentary draftsman.

19.6 Request

Section 92(2) stipulates that, subject to S.92(4) and (4A), an employer is under no obligation to provide a written statement unless a request has been made by the employee. S.92(4) and (4A) provides that, where an employee is dismissed while pregnant or during ordinary or additional maternity or adoption leave, he or she is entitled to receive written reasons without having to make a request.

An employee's request for written reasons may be made either orally or in writing at any time after dismissal, or within the notice period if the employer dismisses with notice. Guidance as to what constitutes a request for written reasons was provided by the EAT in HT Greenwood Ltd t/a Greenwood Savings and Loans v Miller EAT 499/87. In that case an employee's solicitors wrote to their client's former employer requesting a number of documents, including a 'statutory letter dismissing her and giving her reason for dismissal'. The EAT stated that the letter was arguably too vague to constitute a S.92 request, finding that the provision envisages that a request will be 'a separate and specific statement or at any rate a clearly defined sentence'.

19.7 Other than in pregnancy or maternity/adoption leave cases under S.92(4) and (4A), if an employer provides an employee with written reasons for dismissal without having received a specific request from the employee, a tribunal is not empowered to consider whether the reasons provided are inadequate or untrue for the purposes of a S.93 claim – Catherine Haigh Harlequin Hair Design v Seed 1990 IRLR 175, EAT. An employee in these circumstances would have to make a formal request for written reasons, despite the fact that they had already been supplied, in order to be able to argue before an employment tribunal that they were inadequate or untrue.

Employer's obligation

19.8

Once a request has been made the employer is obliged to provide a written statement giving particulars of the reasons for dismissal within 14 days. Written reasons must be sent or given either directly to the employee in question or to his or her authorised agent. The employer should not simply send written reasons to the tribunal, despite the fact that the tribunal will pass them on to the employee.

There has been some debate as to whether an employer fulfils its obligations simply by putting a written statement of reasons into the post. In Kennedy v JGS Bell 'Jim's Inn' EAT 103/78 the EAT suggested that the posting of a written statement was sufficient to comply with what is now S.92. The EAT added, however, that a prudent employer would send written reasons by recorded delivery and that any employer who failed to do so would run the risk of having its evidence on that point rejected. In Keen v Dymo Ltd 1977 IRLR 118, ET, an employment tribunal held that there was a breach where the written reasons had been sent by second class post within the time limit but arrived one day late: they had to arrive with the employee before the end of the 14th day in order to comply. Certainly, an employer would be well advised to take steps to

835

ensure that a statement of written reasons actually reaches the employee in question within the 14-day time limit.

19.9   In practice, of course, an employer should not wait for a dismissed employee to request written reasons for dismissal before providing them. Giving an employee a written explanation for any disciplinary action was described as a core principle of reasonable behaviour in the 2004 version of the Acas Code of Practice on Disciplinary and Grievance Procedures, although the current 2015 version does not put it quite so strongly. Para 18 of the 2015 Code states that after a disciplinary meeting the employer should decide whether or not disciplinary or any other action is justified and inform the employee accordingly in writing. Para 22 goes on to provide that following a decision to dismiss, the employee should be informed as soon as possible of the reasons for the dismissal. Furthermore, the Acas Guide, 'Discipline and Grievances at Work', which supplements the Code but has no statutory standing, still states that it is good practice to give written reasons for all dismissals. A failure to comply with the Code (where it applies) is relevant to the question of liability for unfair dismissal (see Chapter 3, 'Unfairness', under 'Fairness of internal procedure – Acas Code of Practice') and compensation (see Chapter 16, 'Compensatory awards: adjustments', under 'Adjustments for breach of Acas Code of Practice').

19.10   Grounds for complaint

Section 93(1) specifies two grounds on which a dismissed employee can make a complaint to a tribunal. The first is that his or her employer has unreasonably failed to provide a written statement of reasons for dismissal within 14 days of the employee's request. The second is that the particulars given by the employer in purported compliance with its obligations are inadequate or untrue.

The two grounds for complaint are separate, although an employee is entitled to claim in the alternative – Arlett v AMK (Property Management) Ltd EAT 475/81. The distinction between the two grounds is important. If an employee can show that written reasons were given but that they were inadequate or untrue, he or she is entitled to compensation regardless of whether or not the employer has acted reasonably in failing to provide adequate or true reasons.

19.11   Unreasonable failure
There are two questions to be considered under this head: (i) was there a failure to provide written reasons? and (ii) if so, was that failure unreasonable?

19.12   **Was there a failure?** Prior to amendments made by the Trade Union Reform and Employment Rights Act 1993, an employer would only be in breach of what is now S.93 by refusing to provide written reasons. Although a refusal could be either explicit or by conduct, it certainly had to include some element of deliberate or intentional withholding of the reasons for dismissal. A mere

836

failure to provide written reasons within the 14-day time limit did not automatically amount to a refusal. Under the current provisions, however, a refusal is not required. An employer is potentially in breach of S.93 if it simply fails to provide written reasons for whatever reason. The current provision seems to be fairly straightforward. It will usually be clear whether or not an employer has failed to provide written reasons within the time limit.

Was failure unreasonable? Once an employee has shown that his or her **19.13** employer has failed to provide written reasons, the next hurdle is to prove that the failure was unreasonable. Whether or not the employee succeeds will depend on the facts of the individual case. In Daynecourt Insurance Brokers Ltd v Iles 1978 IRLR 335, EAT, the EAT stated that the test of reasonableness was objective and that tribunals should have regard to 'the behaviour to be expected of the reasonable employer' in reaching their decision. In that case, an employee under police investigation for theft requested written reasons for dismissal from his employer. The employer ignored the request in reliance on a general direction from the police not to answer correspondence or deal with any matter related to the investigation. The tribunal decided that a reasonable employer would have sought the advice of the police on this specific matter and that, accordingly, the refusal to provide written reasons was unreasonable. The EAT upheld the tribunal's decision.

The fact that an employee knows perfectly well why he or she has been dismissed will not of itself render an employer's failure to provide written reasons reasonable. This is because one purpose of S.92 is to enable employees to have some documentation to produce to third parties – McBrearty v Thomson t/a Highfield Mini-Market EAT 653/90. However, an employee's knowledge of the reasons for dismissal may be relevant if exceptional circumstances exist, although it is difficult to predict when this will be the case. In Petch v DHSS EAT 851/86 the EAT held that an employer's refusal to provide written reasons was reasonable where the employee knew the reasons for dismissal and where the provision of written reasons would have prejudiced the employee's retirement arrangements.

Finally, as mentioned under 'Entitlement' above, a failure to supply written **19.14** reasons can, in some circumstances, be justified by an employer's mistaken belief that no dismissal in fact took place . In Broomsgrove v Eagle Alexander Ltd 1981 IRLR 127, EAT, the EAT held that an objective test must be applied: did the employer genuinely and reasonably believe that no dismissal had occurred? However, in Brown v Stuart Scott and Co 1981 ICR 166, EAT, a different division of the EAT suggested that an employer's conscientious belief that there had been no dismissal would suffice. The apparent discrepancy may be explained by the fact that in the latter case the employee was claiming that the employer did not honestly believe that there had been a dismissal. Given that the statute refers to an 'unreasonable' failure, we would submit that the proper test is the objective one propounded by the EAT in Broomsgrove.

19.15 Inadequate reasons

Section 92 requires an employer to give 'particulars of the reasons for... dismissal'. This raises the question of how much detail will be considered adequate to comply with the duty. In Earl v Valleythorn Ltd EAT 376/81 the EAT said that an employer was not required to give 'full particulars of each act relied upon as constituting conduct giving rise to the dismissal' and held that it had been sufficient for the employer to state that the employee had been dismissed for 'dishonesty'. Furthermore, in Walls v City Bakeries EAT 759/86 the EAT held that an employer's reference to 'grounds of gross industrial misconduct concerning the incidents that took place on Saturday 26th October, 1985' had been sufficiently specific and that there had been no need for the employer to state that the employee had been dismissed for 'attempted theft'.

Nevertheless, it is generally accepted that employers are obliged to do more than simply indicate which of the 'potentially fair' reasons for dismissal listed in S.98 ERA is applicable. It is clear that S.92 intends employers to be clear about the underlying reasons for dismissal rather than simply to use the technical label given to such reasons.

19.16 There has been some debate as to whether an employer may answer an employee's request for written reasons by referring to existing documents. In Gilham and ors v Kent County Council (No.1) 1985 ICR 227, CA, the Court of Appeal held that a letter which referred to two earlier documents, copies of which were enclosed, contained adequate particulars of the reasons for dismissal. The Court distinguished the EAT's earlier decision in Horsley Smith and Sherry Ltd v Dutton 1977 ICR 594, EAT, that a letter which simply referred to an interview and letter prior to dismissal was inadequate on the ground that in that case, the employer had not given any written reasons to the employee. Accordingly, if an employer wishes to explain the reasons for a dismissal by reference to another document, the employer should provide a copy of that document together with the written statement.

If a tribunal finds a reference to an earlier document to be inadequate, it is nevertheless possible for it to hold that the employer's failure to provide written reasons was reasonable in the circumstances. In Marchant v Earley Town Council 1979 ICR 891, EAT, for example, the EAT held that an employer's refusal to provide written reasons was not unreasonable where the employer's sole reason for refusal was the belief that the information had already been supplied in writing.

19.17 Untrue reasons

It is often difficult for an employee to prove that the reasons given for dismissal are untrue. To do so, he or she must point to inconsistent conduct or statements by the employer, or show that the facts surrounding the dismissal are such that the employer could not genuinely have believed in the reason put forward.

838

In practice, if an employee believes that the reasons for dismissal put forward by his or her employer are untrue, he or she is more likely to bring an unfair dismissal or discrimination claim either in addition to, or instead of, a claim under S.93.

The written reasons given by the employer have to be 'true' in the sense that they must be the reasons which the employer actually relied on in dismissing the employee. It is clear that an employee is not entitled under S.93 to complain that the employer was mistaken in believing these reasons to be true in fact or that these reasons did not justify dismissal. That issue is the sole preserve of unfair dismissal claims. In Harvard Securities plc v Younghusband 1990 IRLR 17, EAT, the employer stated that the reason for dismissing an employee was that he had improperly divulged to a third party confidential information relating to the business of the company. The employee argued that this was an 'untrue' reason because the information could not properly be regarded as confidential. The EAT rejected this argument, adding that the aim of what is now S.92 is to require employers to state truthfully from the outset the reason on which they relied. Whether or not they were justified in dismissing the employee for that reason was irrelevant. A similar conclusion was reached in Lynes v Devon County Council EAT 618/96 where the EAT held that the truth to be established under S.93 was not the truth of the complaints relied upon by the employer but the truth that those complaints were really the reasons that the employer had in mind when dismissing.

Remedies

19.18

Where a complaint under S.93 is well founded the tribunal has two remedies at its disposal. First, it may make a declaration as to what it finds were the employer's reasons for dismissing the employee. Secondly, it must order that the employer pay the employee a sum equal to two weeks' pay. The tribunal has no discretion in the latter instance either to refuse to make an award or over how much to award. A week's pay is calculated by reference to Ss.220–229 ERA (see IDS Employment Law Handbook, 'Wages' (2011), Chapter 10, 'A week's pay'). There is no maximum limit on a week's pay for this purpose.

Time limits

19.19

A complaint that an employer has not complied with S.92 must be brought within three months of the effective date of termination (EDT) unless it is not reasonably practicable for the complaint to be brought within that time – Ss.93(3) and 111(2) ERA. The time limit may also be extended to allow for early conciliation or cross-border mediation – Ss.207A and 207B ERA. It should be noted that the EDT for this purpose will be the actual date of dismissal and will not be artificially postponed by virtue of S.92(7). (For a detailed discussion of how to calculate the EDT, see IDS Employment Law Handbook, 'Contracts of Employment' (2014), Chapter 14, 'Date of termination'.)

Case list

(Note that employment tribunal cases are not included in this list.)

A

A v B 2003 IRLR 405, EAT	6.230, 6.242, 6.247, 6.262
AAH Pharmaceuticals v Carmichael EAT 0325/03	6.91
ABC News Intercontinental Inc v Gizbert EAT 0160/06	10.26
AEI Cables Ltd v McLay 1980 IRLR 84, Ct Sess (Inner House)	6.188
AJ Dunning and Sons (Shopfitters) Ltd v Jacomb 1973 ICR 448, NIRC	4.5, 4.57, 6.69
Abbey Motors (Hemel Hempstead) Ltd v Carta EAT 403/95	16.51
Abbey National plc and anor v Chagger 2010 ICR 397, CA	14.13, 16.17, 16.114
Abbycars (West Horndon) Ltd v Ford EAT 0472/07	1.46
Abernethy v Mott, Hay and Anderson 1974 ICR 323, CA	3.4, 3.10, 4.3, 9.38
Abiaefo v Enfield Community Care NHS Trust EAT 152/96	8.82
Adama v Partnerships in Care Ltd EAT 0047/14	3.30
Adamson v B and L Cleaning Services Ltd 1995 IRLR 193, EAT	6.109
Adda International Ltd v Curcio 1976 ICR 407, EAT; 1976 IRLR 425, EAT	14.119, 14.22
Addison v Babcock FATA Ltd 1987 ICR 805, CA	14.16, 14.50, 14.52, 14.56, 16.42
Adegbola v Marks and Spencer plc 2013 EWCA Civ 1808, CA	6.296
Adeshina v St George's University Hospitals NHS Foundation Trust and ors EAT 0293/14	6.315
Aegon UK Corporate Services Ltd v Roberts 2010 ICR 596, CA	14.128, 15.2, 15.3, 15.40
Afolayan v MRCS Ltd EAT 0406/10	12.5
Ahunanya v Scottish and Southern Energy plc EAT 0540/08	16.31
Airbus UK Ltd v Webb 2008 ICR 561, CA	4.66, 6.297, 6.298
Airbus UK Ltd v Wilson EAT 0061/06	5.36, 5.39
Aitken v Weatherford UK Ltd 2005 1 SC 360, Ct Sess (Inner House)	6.78
Akintola v Capita Symonds Ltd 2010 EWCA Civ 405, CA	10.38
Akram v Rieter Automotive Carpets Ltd EAT 1319/95	16.92, 16.94
Albion Hotel (Freshwater) Ltd v Silva and anor 2002 IRLR 200, EAT	11.12, 11.14, 11.19
Alboni v Ind Coope Retail Ltd 1998 IRLR 131, CA	3.49
Alidair Ltd v Taylor 1978 ICR 445, CA	3.5, 4.18, 4.21, 4.23, 4.40, 4.58
Ali v Joseph Dawson Ltd EAT 43/89	6.30
Ali v Sovereign Buses (London) Ltd EAT 0274/06	6.258
Allen v Hammett 1982 ICR 227, EAT	16.138
Allied Distillers Ltd v Handley and ors EATS 0020/08	16.78
Allied Maples Group Ltd v Simmons and Simmons 1995 1 WLR 1602, CA	14.85
Allma Construction Ltd v Bonner EATS 0060/09	2.45
Allma Construction Ltd v Laing EATS 0041/11	16.112, 16.169
Amazon.co.uk Ltd v Hurdus EAT 0377/10	3.90
Anderson v Chesterfield High School EAT 0206/14	8.31
Anderson v Safety Kleen UK Ltd EAT 306/90	4.16
Anglian Home Improvements Ltd v Kelly 2005 ICR 242, CA	6.187
Angus Council v Edgley EAT 289/99	5.114
Annansingh v AW Lawson and Co Ltd EAT 733/85	14.125

841

843

850

853

M

856

862

W

Index

883

895